READING & WRITING ABOUT LITERATURE

FICTION, POETRY, DRAMA, AND THE ESSAY

READING & WRITING ABOUT LITERATURE

FICTION, POETRY, DRAMA, AND THE ESSAY

EDWARD PROFFITT

Manhattan College

HARCOURT BRACE JOVANOVICH, PUBLISHERS

San Diego   New York   Chicago   Austin   Washington, D.C.
London   Sydney   Tokyo   Toronto

To Tom, Mark, Chris, and Terence
—students dear in memory
and continuing friendship

PREFACE

This book provides an introduction to writing and an introduction to the four major genres of literature—fiction, poetry, drama, and the essay. Section I centers on the principles and process of writing—of both the paragraph and the essay—using Robert Frost's "The Road Not Taken" and John Coover's "A Sudden Story" as reference points. In the course of Section I, the student, while focusing on writing, also encounters literary analysis and is introduced to what writing on literary works entails.

Section II is devoted to prose fiction: its definition (Chapter 1), the delineation of the central idea of theme (Chapter 2), and a consideration of the elements of which fiction is composed (Chapters 3–7). Each chapter introduction from Chapters 2 through 7 is followed by from five to nine very short stories, themselves followed by study questions and writing assignments. Because of their length, the stories give maximum flexibility while allowing for thorough coverage. Chapter 8 of Section II entails a summing up by way of Stephen Crane's "An Episode of War," which is treated fully. The aim here is to help students consolidate the understanding they have gained from the previous chapters. Sample essays are to be found in both Chapters 1 and 8; each of the other chapters contains a detailed discussion of writing on the element(s) at hand.

Section III, on poetry, proceeds in much the same way as Section II. Again, sample essays are found in the first and last chapters, and the other chapters all contain detailed discussions of writing on imagery, metaphor, rhythm, or whatever. Each chapter from 1 through 7 concludes with six or more selected poems accompanied by study questions and writing assignments. After a summing up and a sample essay, Chapter 8 concludes with a wide selection of poems by three major American poets: Emily Dickinson, Robert Frost, and William Carlos Williams. The relatively large number of poems in the book by each of these poets should help students understand the difference a context makes in reading any single poem as well as lend depth to their study of poetry. Finally, Section III ends with an anthology of poems, many that are widely taught but also some that will perhaps be new to the instructor.

The final two parts of the book, Sections IV and V, are arranged differently, both because their subject matter suggests a different arrangement and because many of the elements taken up here have been covered in depth in Sections II and III (cross-referenced when needed). Section IV, on drama, begins with a substantial introduction to drama—its types and elements—that ends with a discussion of writing on drama and two sample essays on Susan Glaspell's "Trifles," which is reprinted in the introduction. Here, the connections between stories, poems, and plays are established; simultaneously, attention is also paid to what distinguishes the drama from the other genres. After the introduction, there are gathered five classic plays with study questions and writing assignments: *Oedipus Rex, Hamlet, The Importance of Being Earnest, A Doll's House,* and *The Glass Menagerie.*

Like Section IV, Section V, on the essay, begins with a lengthy introduction to the essay—its definition and elements. The essay, of course, offers a unique opportunity for writing in that, as I say in the text, an essay can be both written *on,* like stories and poems, and written *after.* That is, one can model an essay of one's own after the structure, the style, or some other feature of an essay by someone else and learn a great deal in the process. The two sample essays that end the introduction demonstrate the point—one being on and one after E. M. Forster's "My Wood." A number of the writing assignments that follow the essays gathered in Section V ask the student to imitate this, that, or the other aspect of the essay at hand—most often something having to do with structure and coherence. These assignments are highly specific in what they call for. Indeed, all of the study questions and writing assignments in Section V have been kept highly directed and focused on matters mainly of a formal nature in order to help students come to a greater understanding of the form closest to their immediate concerns. To be sure, throughout the book I have by and large kept away from general questions of a philosophical cast and kept to language, structure, and the other elements of a piece. But in Section V, I have done so with particular rigor. My focus here may seem somewhat narrow, therefore, but it is sharp and, I believe, on target.

Throughout, then, the purpose of this book is dual. One aim is to help students toward a greater understanding, and therefore enjoyment, of literature. The other aim, no less important, is to instruct students in the writing process. The discussions of the four literary genres and the study questions asked in each section, on the one hand, and, on the other, the discussions of writing, the sample essays, and the writing assignments embody these two aims, offering practice in literary analysis and, simultaneously, in the use of the various types and structures of expository prose. Students will find help with terminology in the Glossary at the end of the book, which covers all literary and writing terms used in the book. The Alternate Groupings by Element, Theme, and Mode, also in the back of the book, should help students see some of the many connections that can be made between various works and serve as a spur to discussion and writing alike. The Appendix, "A Brief Guide to the Use and Documentation of Sources and Related Matters," offers advice on quoting, paraphrasing, summarizing, and documenting sources; it adheres to the style adopted by the Modern Language Association (MLA) in 1984.

The value of writing on literary works is self-evident. Not only does a story, poem, play, or essay supply content—something to write about—but, because all are made out of words, they all can teach exactly those things that all writers must learn. To come to understand the concept of diction through poetry, for instance, is as valuable for writing prose as it is for understanding poetry. So my experience as a teacher has taught me, at any rate. It has also taught me that we who have the opportunity of introducing students to the excitement of learning through reading and writing are fortunate indeed. My hope is that my own love of these endeavors as transmitted in this book will prove contagious.

ACKNOWLEDGMENTS

I owe thanks to George Freije for his many insights about teaching poems to freshmen and about teaching writing; to Mary Ann O'Donnell for her advice on documentation; and to Marie Duchon for her invaluable help with regard to permissions. My thanks also to John Pahl, Northwestern Michigan College, for his review of the manuscript. As always, I am in debt to my wife, Nancy, for reading and proofing manuscripts, galleys, and page proof; and to the many students whose insights inform this book and some of whose poems are to be found herein. Finally, I wish to express thanks to the many wonderful people at Harcourt Brace Jovanovich: Stuart Miller, my always cheerful editor; Eleanor Garner, permissions editor and confidant; Catherine Fauver, copy editor extraordinary; Kay Faust, who designed the striking cover; and Kenneth Fine, who shepherded the book through the production process.

Edward Proffitt

CONTENTS

SECTION II

FICTION

Chapter 4   Characterization   98

Stories for Study and Writing Assignments   104

Chapter 5   Narration and Point of View   121

Stories for Study and Writing Assignments   128

Chapter 6   Mood, Irony, and Style   150

Stories for Study and Writing Assignments   157

Chapter 7   Setting and Symbolism   179

Stories for Study and Writing Assignments   186

Chapter 8   Pulling It All Together

SECTION III

POETRY

Chapter 1   What Poetry Is (and Isn't)

Poems for Study and Writing Assignments

Chapter 2   Voice, Tone, and Diction

Anthology   442

S E C T I O N   I V

——————— ❖ ———————

DRAMA

Plays for Study and Writing Assignments 563

S E C T I O N V

THE ESSAY

Essays for Study and Writing Assignments 896

READING AND WRITING

"How can I know what I think till I see what I say," says a character in an E. M. Forster novel. Exactly so. In large part we write in order to know, especially to know ourselves. Of course, we write as well to let others know what we think; and as writers we must never forget the audience we are addressing. Still, the most wonderful potential of writing is that it can show us ourselves.

For the purposes of writing, however, you might wonder why you should read works of literature. After all, your English class excepted, you are unlikely ever to be called upon to write a story or a lyric poem, a play or even the type of essay represented in this book (though you might choose to write one or another for your own purposes). One answer is that reading anything worth reading can enlarge the reader's capacity for handling language. But reading literary works specifically has an edge: because our greatest writers have written stories, poems, plays, or essays—all of which entail the full use of the resources of language—reading literature is one of the best ways of coming to understand the possibilities of sentence structure, for instance, or the possible effects of diction on tone, or the nature of style, or the kinds and uses of metaphor. Moreover, most people find reading the various kinds of literature to be fun. So reading literary works in connection with writing combines instruction with pleasure.

As a subject to write about, literature offers further advantages. As we shall see momentarily, even the shortest work of literature provides an abundance of materials to write on; and all literary works give us something concrete to hold on to—characters, images, scenes, structures, or whatever. In other words, while any given piece of literature stimulates ideas and thus gives the reader something to write about, it also limits what can be said and so helps to organize the ideas it stimulates.

READING LITERATURE

Before we move to a more detailed discussion of literature and the writing process, a few general comments on reading literature might prove helpful. These summary comments will be fleshed out as this book unfolds. First, then, be aware that literature asks that you be active as you read: to bring to your reading your experience of the world and also to open yourself to new experience as you actively construct in your mind scenes, images, actions, and so forth. There is no single definition of literature that is fully adequate, but the following is on target: literature is a type of writing that engages the reader in constructing its meaning. So as you read, bring to bear what you know about life and about people and the ways they behave; try to participate even when you come to works that seem alien, expressing values and understandings different from yours. Literature asks that you participate, not that you believe. It is the reverse of propaganda, which seeks to close the mind to everything except the values its originators would have us accept. By asking us actively to participate in its unfolding designs, literature aims to expand our understanding of others and deepen our knowledge of ourselves.

Unlike propaganda, that is, literature asks us to ask questions all along the line and then actively to pursue answers. If the questions are appropriate and the texts significant, there will be answers, answers interesting enough to write on. But again, activity is the key. Don't sit back passively as you read, aimlessly drifting from word to word. Keep asking "why": why this type of narrator, why that kind of rhyme scheme, why this sort of action, why that kind of sentence structure. Also, be alert to implications. Implication is the writer's way of involving the reader, of creating an effect *in* the reader rather than just conveying information. But the reader must be ready to draw the appropriate inferences and to relate them to the context at large. Much of this book is aimed at helping you do just that.

At this point, let's take two short works of literature—a poem and a story—and see what questions each brings up and what answers each suggests either directly or by way of implication. The answers should lead us to the heart of the poem and the story, and thus to an understanding of each—understanding being the result of questioning in the first place.

THE ROAD NOT TAKEN

— Robert Frost —

Two roads diverged in a yellow wood,
And sorry I could not travel both
And be one traveler, long I stood
And looked down one as far as I could
To where it bent in the undergrowth;   5

Then took the other, as just as fair,
And having perhaps the better claim,
Because it was grassy and wanted wear;
Though as for that the passing there
Had worn them really about the same,   10

And both that morning equally lay
In leaves no step had trodden black.
Oh, I kept the first for another day!
Yet knowing how way leads on to way,
I doubted if I should ever come back.   15

I shall be telling this with a sigh
Somewhere ages and ages hence:
Two roads diverged in a wood, and I—
I took the one less traveled by,
And that has made all the difference.   20

[1916—U.S.A.]

As most readers would immediately infer, both the traveling of the speaker here and the choice with which he is presented are symbolic: traveling signifies life's journey, and so the choice of roads that the speaker must make suggests the choices we all must make on our journey through life—a choice of a career, for instance, or of a marriage partner. But many readers, reading idly, come to the line "I took the one less traveled by" (line 19) and quickly conclude that the poem concerns individualism and praises individualistic choice, as though Frost were a propagandist on the side of the angels. The active reader moves more slowly and more carefully, pausing over the title, for instance, and wondering why its focus is not on the road taken. And why does the speaker say that he took the road he did because it "wanted wear" when he goes on immediately to state in four full lines (9–12) that there really was no difference at all between the two roads? Further, why should the speaker keep thinking about the other road (that he does is implied by the poem's title and by line 13), and why is the last stanza so ambiguous? (Will the "sigh" be of pleasure or regret? Will "the difference" be for the better or the worse?) Finally, given what he says in lines 9–12, why does the speaker go on to say, "I took the one less traveled by"?

Of course, he says no such thing. Look at the last stanza of the poem and observe its tense. What the speaker actually says is that sometime in the future he *will* say, "I took the one less traveled by." In other words, in years to come he will forget the truth of the matter and will rationalize his choice thus. Now that we have read carefully and observed the tense used in the last stanza, we should be able to answer the questions posed in the preceding paragraph. Having nothing to do with some easy idea of "individualism," "The Road Not Taken" explores in its complexity a subject that touches us all—the difficulty of choosing and the psychology of choice: how hard choices are, especially when, as is usually the case, there is no clear-cut basis for choice; how we cannot but wonder what would have been had we chosen the other way; how every choice limits future possibilities in ways we can never know beforehand (thus the ambiguity of the last stanza); and how we rationalize our choices after the fact, imposing reasons for our having chosen this or that when, really, rationality did not come into play at all when the choice was made.

Reading in this way, the active reader finds a much more interesting poem—one that rings true emotionally and psychologically—than does the reader who does not ask the appropriate questions. The poem itself, note, directs the questions that should be asked of it; and once they are asked, answers—whether arrived at directly or by inference—are not difficult to come by. Each question and answer opens the poem out a little more, until at last it is truly ours. Reading actively, we come to understand the poem's truth on our pulses; by being both intellectually and emotionally engaged, we come to see that its truth touches our own lives and the difficulties we face on our journey.

A SUDDEN STORY

— Robert Coover —

Once upon a time, suddenly, while it still could, the story began. For the hero, setting forth, there was of course nothing sudden about it, neither about the setting forth, which he'd spent his entire lifetime anticipating, nor about any conceivable endings, which seemed, like the horizon, to be always somewhere else. For the dragon, however, who was stupid, everything was sudden. He was suddenly hungry and then he was suddenly eating something. Always, it was like the first time. Then, all of a sudden, he'd remember having eaten something like that before: a certain familiar sourness . . . And, just as suddenly, he'd forget. The hero, coming suddenly upon the dragon (he'd been trekking for years through enchanted forests, endless deserts, cities carbonized by dragon-breath, for him suddenly was not exactly the word), found himself envying, as he drew his sword (a possible ending had just loomed up before him, as though the horizon had, with the desperate illusion of suddenness, tipped), the dragon's tenseless freedom. Freedom? the dragon might have asked, had he not been so stupid, chewing over meanwhile the sudden familiar sourness (a memory . . . ?) on his breath. From what? (Forgotten.)

[1986—U.S.A.]

The first sentence sets up a fairy-tale atmosphere, appropriate in that the story concerns a hero in quest of a dragon. But why the phrase "while it still could," which seems to indicate some kind of distinction? Might there be a contrast implied here between two meanings of the word "story": "event" or "happening" (as in "news story") and "tale" (that is, a piece of literature)? With respect to suddenness and time, another distinction seems to be implied, one between the dragon and the hero. What is the point of this distinction? Further, how, if at all, are the two pairs of distinctions (event versus tale, dragon versus hero) related? Finally, what does "tenseless freedom" mean, and is there any special meaning implied by the hero's being devoured at the end of the story? One should also question one's own feelings—what the tale makes you feel and why.

Reading the story over again, I am struck most by the contrast drawn between the hero and the dragon, which widens into a contrast between human and animal existence. The dragon lives in a world in which everything happens suddenly. With no memory to speak of, it exists in the eternal present, free of the tyranny of time (thus, "tenseless freedom"). It is not free as to action, however; because everything is sudden in its world, it acts without volition. In contrast, the hero, though weighed down with thoughts of past and future, acts with volition because he lives *in* time, the consciousness of his temporal existence making deliberate choice possible. Yet, while ironically envying the dragon's "tenseless freedom," the hero is consumed, in a sense, by that freedom, as we all are consumed at the last by the ever on-rushing present.

Running parallel to the contrast between dragon and hero is the distinction hinted at in the first sentence of this miniature between "story" as event and "story" as tale. Events are always stuck in time and occur always and only in the present: so the story of the hero could happen only at a certain time (thus, "while it still could"). Tales, on the other hand, can range through time: the present story, for example, was written recently, but through the imagination it takes us back to a world of heroes and dragons. The telling of tales—a uniquely human act—is, thus, a way of being human, a way of exercising our human ability of "looking before and after," as Shakespeare put it. Tales further reflect our humanity by concerning our struggles in time and with time. Beginning "Once upon a time," the present story is a good example. It is about time, finally, or how our sense of past, present, and future is what distinguishes us from the rest of the animal world and makes us human.

As to feeling, I found the story intriguing at first and somewhat sad (because of the implications of the hero's death). Having read the story several times, I now feel less a sense of sadness than of triumph, for, though the dragon wins the day, the story contains the dragon. Through literature, that is, the human spirit overcomes and endures.

READING FOR WRITING

Reading literature requires alertness, the willingness to ask questions, and the ability to draw inferences. But at first, read a work for pleasure, for its effect. Let it sink in. Then read it again, this time jotting down any ideas it stimulates in you and any questions it brings to mind, and noting whatever feelings it evokes. Mull over your jotted ideas and questions, seeking answers to the latter, and test the aptness of your feelings and responses. If the work in question is short enough, you might even wish to read it a third time to carry out this testing and checking. Finally, taking everything into account, try to articulate the meaning of the work. Write down a few sentences about its possible meaning and indicate what in the work has led you to this conclusion, what details support your interpretation, what aspects of the way the work is put together lend further credence.

Moving step by step, the activities just described—activities often categorized as "prewriting"—are aimed at preparing you for writing. By following through on them as you read story, poem, play, or essay, you should arrive at a conscious awareness of your feelings, some tested ideas that you could use in your writing, and perhaps even a sense of the direction in which your thoughts and feelings might take you as you write. In questioning "The Road Not Taken" and "A Sudden Story," in seeking answers that could be supported by each of the two texts, and in moving toward a sense of the overall meaning of the poem and then the story, I followed the same procedure. Look back a few pages and quickly review that material. I think you will agree that in both cases I am left with a good deal to write on. If you follow the steps outlined in the last paragraph as you move on in this book to read stories, poems, and so forth, you should find yourself in the same position. You might also find yourself more confident once the writing stage begins and therefore more capable of writing with fluency, precision, and verve.

FROM READING TO WRITING

Yes, literature provides a good deal to write about. The pressing question, therefore, is not what to write about but what and how to choose from the many topics that present themselves. In deciding, first look to yourself. What do you want to write? What most moves you or stimulates in you anger or delight? Good writing demands personal commitment. Then, what you choose must be feasible with regard to the projected length of what you are going to write: that is, just as your idea cannot be so narrow that you are left nothing to write, it must not be so broad as to require you to write a book (unless you are writing a book). For instance, "Coover's 'A Sudden Story' is laid in medieval times" is far too narrow; "The beast of time and the human hero" is too broad and unfocused. Though the phrase might serve as a title, it needs to be limited to, say, "Coover shows in 'A Sudden Story' how our humanity rests on memory and the awareness of time." So stated, the idea could generate either a paragraph or a paper. The difference between the two is not so much a matter of thesis as of the amount of material brought to bear for support and the depth of the discussion generally.

Topic/Opinion/Thesis

But let's pause over the word "thesis." You might be wondering, "What exactly is a thesis? Is it the same thing as the topic of a paper? Or is it just an opinion?" No, a thesis is neither a topic nor merely an opinion, and the distinctions are important. As to the first, a topic is the general area from which a thesis is drawn. Consider the following examples of topics:

The Speaker of Frost's "The Road Not Taken"
Man and Beast in Coover's "A Sudden Story"
Memory and Time in "A Sudden Story"
Choice in "The Road Not Taken"

I've deliberately cast these phrases in the form of titles because each could be a title. In fact, titles often indicate topic areas, stimulating in the reader thereby the question, "What about it?" Having a topic in mind, the writer needs to ask the same question. "Choice in 'The Road Not Taken' "—what about it? One answer might be: "In 'The Road Not Taken,' Frost presents us with a choice that is not really a choice at all in that the poem's speaker has no basis upon which to choose the path he will take." Here is a possible thesis, stated in a complete sentence (if you don't have at least one complete sentence—that is, a complete statement of an idea— then you don't have a thesis) and in such a way as to suggest how the essay to follow might proceed—from a consideration of what the speaker actually says about the road chosen, say, to a discussion of his problems stemming from the likeness of the two roads to a conclusion arguing that the line "I took the one less traveled by" is only a rationalization that serves to underscore the speaker's difficulty as expressed throughout the poem. The whole projected paper, notice, flows from the thesis statement, broad enough to leave something to say yet narrow enough to keep what is said specific and directed toward a specific end.

So a thesis is not a topic. Nor is it an opinion, at least not a "mere" opinion, though the two might superficially resemble each other. "Oranges are the best fruit there is" is not a thesis but a mere opinion, as unarguable as it is uninteresting. In contrast, "Oranges may cure cancer" is a thesis, for conceivably it could be argued by way of facts and an appeal to authority (that is, by way of statements of experts in a given field). But if you wish to think of a thesis as an opinion, think of it as a *kind* of opinion (as opposed to a mere opinion) that can be supported by facts and informed judgments.

In sum, in deciding what to write, let your feelings guide you to a topic. Then decide what it is *about* the topic you have to say. Write down your answer in at least one complete sentence. Then judge what you have written: Is your statement still too broad, or is it now too narrow to be of any help to you and your reader? If either is the case, ask "what about it?" of your topic again and come up with another answer. Once you are satisfied that your statement is both one you feel committed to and one that will serve as a springboard for the work to come, you are ready to write. Before we get to the writing stage, however, there are a few more considerations—which you should have in mind as you begin to write—that need attention. The first, which many rhetoricians regard as being of primary importance, is the nature of your audience.

Considering Your Audience

Though what I said in the opening paragraph about writing as a tool of self-discovery is true, it is also true that one usually writes for other people as well as for oneself. Because many of the decisions one has to make when writing depend (or should depend) on the makeup of one's audience, it is important to judge that audience at the outset and to keep it in mind throughout the writing process. To take an analogy, suppose you have to give a speech on some technical matter to a high school audience that knows nothing about your subject. You would realize, no doubt, that you had to simplify your presentation and define all terms. If you didn't, you would run the risk of putting your audience to sleep or of being booed off the stage. But if you were giving the speech to a group of experts in the field, you could rely on their knowing your terms and being able to deal with the subject in its complexity. For this audience you would not want to define most terms—if you did, your listeners might think you condescending—and you would want to treat your subject as fully as possible. In each case, your audience would be your measuring rod.

The same is true of writing in general: the audience must be assessed and kept in mind. But how is the student's audience to be judged? To some extent, that depends on the type of course in question, but what I am now going to say about writing done for an English class applies to most other courses as well. You should think of your audience as consisting of your instructor and fellow students. It is, then, a knowledgeable audience, one familiar with your topic area and with literary analysis in general but not with your specific approach to a text or with the arguments you will bring to bear in backing up your ideas. In other words, you can assume that your audience knows about the technical aspects of fiction, poetry, et cetera and has read the work that you intend to discuss—at least if it has been assigned. You need not define literary terms, therefore, or summarize a plot, say, or a line of argument just for the purpose of filling your reader in. Rather, use your limited space to exemplify and argue your thesis. That is where your focus should be. By keeping your audience in view, you should find that the problem of deciding what need not be said and what absolutely must be said is greatly reduced. As a result, the writing process you go through should be greatly facilitated.

Expository Prose

We shall return to the writing process shortly and consider the stages of composing expository prose—the kind of prose you are reading now and the kind college students are normally called on to write. Before we move on, though, we should take a look at what exposition (or expository prose) is, both its functions and its types. As to function, exposition is prose designed to "expose," that is, to set forth facts, ideas, and informed opinions in an orderly fashion so as to come to a fuller understanding oneself of some aspect of a topic and to communicate that understanding to the intended audience. "In an orderly fashion" is the key phrase here. Because exposition has ready understanding as its primary goal, its greatest asset is clarity, and clarity demands that facts, ideas, and informed opinions be set forth point by point, with each point clearly related to the next and with some plan of movement from point to point clearly followed. Perhaps that seems forbidding. But take heart: the more one writes, the less difficult writing becomes, just as the more time one puts in practicing a sport, the less difficult the sport becomes and the greater one's facility. One must know the ground rules to begin with, of course, as well as the purposes of and ways of handling whatever equipment the sport entails. The same is true of writing. To continue the analogy, this whole chapter is aimed at acquainting you with the ground rules of exposition. As to equipment, we have the types of exposition, each type being a different piece of equipment that you need to learn how to handle. Again, expository prose is prose designed to set forth facts, ideas, and informed opinions. Accordingly, there are three fundamental types of exposition, any of which a college student might encounter on assignments: informational, analytic, persuasive.

Informational. As the name implies, informational prose delivers information. If, for instance, you became interested in Robert Frost, you might do some research on his life and write up what you find. Or you might write an essay on his growth as a poet, detailing the differences between his earliest poems and the poems that later made him famous. In both cases you would primarily be presenting information. Informational prose places two demands on the writer: first, it must be factual; second, like all expository prose, it must proceed in an orderly fashion. It requires that some way of organizing be chosen, according to the nature of the material, and followed through.

Analytic. From the Greek meaning "to break up," analysis entails first the breaking up of a subject into its component parts and then a detailed discussion part by part. For instance, if asked to write on Coover's "A Sudden Story," I might select the contrast of the dragon and the hero for analysis. My thesis would be that, representing animal existence, the dragon lives in a timeless world and therefore a world without volition; in sharp contrast, the world of the hero, who represents humanity and the human condition, is defined by time, his every act informed by an awareness of past and future. Having stated my thesis, I would move on to examine the story closely, focusing first on what it reveals about the dragon; then, taking the story's hero as representative of humanity, I would make the contrast implied in the story and move to conclude by discussing what that contrast reveals about being human. Note that I have broken the story into its parts, analyzed each in relation to the others, and organized my analysis so as to build to my most important point. Analysis always proceeds in a way of this sort. Analytic prose, it should be pointed out, can incorporate informational prose. If you were writing on a poem of Frost's, for example, you might have reason to discuss some aspect of his biography. But analytic prose is different in purpose from straight informational prose. Its purpose is not to set forth fact but to use fact to uncover and clarify meaning. For this reason, analytic prose is more complex than informational. Of the three broad types of exposition, it is analytic prose that you will most often be called on to write in college. This is so because the ability to analyze in general is one of the main marks of an educated mind.

Persuasive.   Analytic prose overlaps with persuasive in that when writing an analysis, one wishes the reader to accept one's ideas, and when trying to persuade a reader, one must be able to analyze the reasons for the position the reader is asked to accept. And both analytic and persuasive prose can incorporate information. Yet persuasive prose is a category unto itself, for it is not so much ideas as judgments, feelings, and opinions (informed, it is to be hoped) that the writer of such prose hopes to sway the reader to adopt. For instance, should your thesis be that "The Road Not Taken" is a great poem, one that vividly pictures the ambiguity of the modern situation, or, conversely, that it succeeds only in losing the reader in its own ambiguity, then you would be engaged in persuasion. You would be writing criticism in the purest sense of the word. Book reviews are of this order. Aimed at convincing the reader of a book's merit or lack thereof, a typical review proceeds to analyze why the reviewer has concluded that the book is or is not worth reading. Analysis comes into play, but the goal, finally, is persuasion. Indeed, the difference between all three types of exposition can be summed up in terms of goal: setting forth of factual material (informational); interpreting facts and delving into ideas (analytic); defending judgments aroused by ideas.

WRITING THE COLLEGE ESSAY

Whatever one writes, in whatever kind of format, it is useful to divide the work into stages and to proceed step by step. To exemplify, I will use my own experience of writing and tell you what I do. After I have done all the preparations I am going to do, thought out all that I can think out beforehand, finished, in other words, the prewriting stage, I wind up with a stack of notes, one note per slip of paper. Sitting down to my typewriter, I look through these notes carefully, dividing them into categories and setting aside anything that might be of use for the beginning and for the end. With some plan of organization in mind, I begin to write. Generally, my notes—which ease me into writing by giving me things to write about—help me to organize my thoughts and to stay on target more or less. But I do not restrain myself too much as I write my first draft. I let things flow as much as they will. Then, however, I become a critic; I look with the critic's eye at what I have written and usually feel a moment of despair. It passes as I get down to the real work of writing, which is rewriting. I pinpoint what does not move easily, where more support is necessary, where I have digressed from my topic or included material that is redundant. Next, I do a second draft, rearranging sentences or even whole paragraphs and providing transitions when necessary, adding any supports that now seem needed, and deleting what seems digressive or repetitive. I am usually left with a draft that can be checked for grammar, spelling, and the nuances of style. After checking and correcting, I am ready to type the final draft. Such is my writing process, which proceeds in steps because the brain cannot do everything at once. Note that what is crucial in the whole process is the matter of organization. Comprehensible organization is of primary importance if communication is to take place. So we shall go into the business of organization in some detail.

When you sit down to write, you probably have a number of things to say. How can they be brought together into an organized whole? That is *the* difficulty faced by every writer, and there are no rules to go by. But there are guidelines that can help you organize your thoughts and remarks, guidelines perhaps best exemplified by the one-paragraph essay (a form often required, incidentally, on examinations). The one-paragraph essay—hereafter called the discrete paragraph— is a model in its organization of the multiparagraph essay. To master the structure of the discrete paragraph, therefore, is to go far toward mastering the structure of the essay proper.

The Discrete Paragraph

Like the larger essay, the discrete paragraph has a beginning, a middle, and an end. The thesis statement—usually a sentence, though sometimes two or even three sentences—normally comes at the beginning. A thesis statement is necessary so that your reader will know what you are talking about, and so that you will too. When the writing of my own students goes astray, it usually does so because there is no thesis statement provided to guide them as writers and me as the reader. So their work rambles on, making unrelated points and not conveying anything in particular. Getting a clear thesis statement and keeping to it is half the battle when it comes to writing. What follows the thesis statement—the middle—is a series of sentences designed to support that statement: to lend it credence, to develop its implications, to expand upon its meaning, to fill in the details. And the last sentence or two—the end—serves to conclude, ideally lending the paragraph a sense of wholeness and completion. The following is a model of the shape and movement of the discrete paragraph.

The Problem of Choice

Thesis

In "The Road Not Taken," Robert Frost dramatizes the difficulty we most often have when it comes to making an important choice. One source of that difficulty is

Support

expressed at the beginning of the poem through its speaker's stated regret at having had to make a choice at all ("sorry I could not travel both"): we would eat our cake and have it too. But we must make

Support

choices. So we look for a basis upon which to choose. The basis Frost's speaker points to for his choice is that the road he chose some time ago "was grassy and wanted wear." Yet immediately he goes on to tell us that in fact the two roads were exactly the same, equally "worn" and equally covered in leaves "no step had trodden black." Thus, making the choice doubly difficult, there was no rational basis upon which to make it. No doubt, this is a prime reason for the speaker's ambivalence, expressed by the poem's title and by his desire to keep the other road "for another day." In the last

Support

stanza of the poem, the speaker moves from the past into the distant future and suggests that then he <u>will</u> say that his reason for choosing the road he did was that it was "the one less traveled by." But we know that this will be merely a rationalization for a choice made reluctantly and without any real basis. The

Support   emotional ambiguity of the last stanza also
suggests the reluctance of the speaker as
well as his uneasiness with the choice
made: Will the "sigh" be one of
satisfaction, we must ask, or of regret?
Will "the difference" be for the better or
for the worse? We never know beforehand
what the outcome of a choice will be, just
as more often than not we have no real basis
for making it in the first place. "The Road

Ending   Not Taken," then, concerns the difficulty
that human choice entails: our reluctance
to choose; our mixed feelings once we have
chosen; and our tendency to rationalize our
choices at some later date. We must make
choices, of course; but choosing is
difficult for us, both because of the
unknowns in the outer world and especially
because of the conflicts within.

Note that except for the first, each support can be divided into major support and minor support, the minor support serving to back up the major support, which in turn demonstrates, clarifies, or argues the general thesis. For instance, the second major support—that the speaker was and remains ambivalent about his choice of roads (his ambivalence being part of his difficulty)—is itself supported by textual evidence leading up to the statement about ambivalence, the evidence showing contradiction in what we are told. Observe, too, how the ending refers back to the thesis statement while taking that statement a bit further and generalizing it. This kind of an ending is typical not only of the discrete paragraph but of the essay as well.

But what is most important to grasp about the sample paragraph is how the support material proceeds. The main writing problem posed by the discrete paragraph and the essay alike is that of arrangement of supports, whether sentences in a paragraph or the paragraphs themselves. What should come first, what second, what third, and so on? To decide, the writer must think into the subject at hand and see what kind of a plan it suggests. Then the writer must consciously follow through. It would not be possible here to specify all of the many ways material can be organized, nor would it probably be desirable in any case. The most common ways should be mastered first, and those are:

Chronology.   Whenever something occurs in time, it can be written about in chronological sequence. Following the chronological sequence of "The Road Not Taken," for instance, the sample paragraph proceeds chronologically, from the past to the future. The markers of this movement—called *transitions*—are, simply: "some time ago" and "from the past into the distant future." Chronological arrangement is not difficult once its possibility is recognized. All one must do is follow the sequence of events as given, making sure the sequence is clear. Because most pieces of literature themselves move chronologically, chronological arrangement is usually possible when a literary work is under discussion.

Spatial Sequence.   Whenever something exists in space or can be thought of in terms of space, spatial sequence can come into play: left to right or right to left, upward or downward, inward or outward, far to near or near to far, and so forth. For instance, Frost's speaker suggests a spatial sequence when he says that he "looked down one [road] as far as [he] could / To where it bent in the undergrowth." Here we have a sequence moving from near to far, which is probably how items would have been arranged had he described anything along the way. At least, barring some special effect, they would not have been presented randomly. In expository prose, the same is true: one must proceed according to some plan of order, spatial sequence being one possible plan. As with chronological arrangement, a spatial sequence must be clear to you when writing no less than to your reader when reading.

Comparison and Contrast.   Comparison and contrast is a prime way of understanding: in everyday life we frequently come to grasp something by seeing how it is like and how unlike something else. No less is true when we write. For the writer, comparison and contrast is a tool of analysis that also suggests ways in which a paragraph, paper, report, or whatever can be organized.

Technically, comparison emphasizes similarity and contrast emphasizes difference. The distinction, however, is not really helpful, for comparison involves contrast and contrast involves comparison. This is so because what makes a comparison meaningful is that the like things being compared actually have some significant difference, and what makes a contrast striking is that the unlike things being contrasted actually share some fundamental likeness. One could compare Frost's speaker and Coover's hero, for instance. Both are symbolic travelers representative of the human lot, and both take us into uniquely human situations entailing time. But what makes the comparison significant once likeness has been established is that Coover's hero is described as having acted with a single mind in his pursuit of the dragon, whereas Frost's speaker equivocates and finds it difficult to accept fully his own action in the past (his choice of a road). The difference, perhaps, reflects a peculiarly modern quandary: free to choose as we will, without being hampered by tradition and traditional roles, we find the bases of choice to be elusive and so are rarely single-minded in choosing or acting. Conversely, one could contrast the two works in terms of theme or point. "A Sudden Story" concerns how human freedom results only from our existence in time, with memory being the cornerstone of volition. In contrast, "The Road Not Taken" suggests how our choices in time (the past) condition and limit our freedom thereafter (the future). Yet Coover's hero envies the dragon's "tenseless freedom" no less than Frost's speaker regrets having had to choose. This would be the point of the contrast: to show that, however different otherwise, both story and poem give voice to our deep ambivalence about time, an ambivalence that is very much an aspect of being human.

As to organization, comparisons and contrasts can be arranged in several ways. What is important is to choose a way that will work for you and then to follow through. For instance, a comparison or a contrast could proceed point by point: A/B, A/B, A/B; or either could move in blocks: all of A and then all of B, with the comparison/contrast drawn in the B block. Both examples discussed in the preceding paragraph could be organized in either of these ways: hero/speaker, hero/speaker, hero/speaker, or everything about Coover's hero first followed by everything about Frost's speaker in comparison/contrast with Coover's hero—and then, whichever the mode of organization, the crucial point of difference or similarity and its meaning. Or you may find that some combination of these two types of arrangement is best on a given assignment, or that another type of arrangement entirely will serve you best. (One could group material according to topics, for instance, and proceed topic by topic; or one could discuss A in and of itself and—making sure to provide a bridge—B in and of itself, and then move to the comparison/contrast in a C section.) Make your judgment according to the effect you desire and the length of the paper you have to write. If you wish your pace to be quick, use the point-by-point type of arrangement; if you wish the pace to be more leisurely, use the block type. If you are writing a long paper, it might be best to move point by point, each paragraph perhaps concerning one point of comparison or contrast (a block organization in a longer paper runs the risk that readers will forget what is said in the paragraphs that constitute the A block by the time they get to those that constitute block B); if the paper you are doing is short, however, then blocking might be ideal. Whatever the case, what should come before what is a final decision that must be made. That is, let's say that you have decided to move point by point: A/B, A/B, A/B. But which A/B to put first, which second, which third? And how should the points be demarked? Here you should consider enumeration and especially order of climax.

Enumeration.   In enumerating, the writer usually lists in the thesis statement the points to be made in the paragraph or paper to follow, or at least suggests that a certain number of points will be taken up, and then goes on to develop them one by one. For example, one might state the thesis of a piece involving the implications of the use of tense in "The Road Not Taken" as follows: "While speaking in the present tense, the speaker of 'The Road Not Taken' takes the reader back to the past in the poem's first three stanzas and then into the far future in the last stanza. This movement in time, from the past to the future through the medium of the present, suggests the nature of human awareness and of human thought." The three degrees of time referred to would then be enumerated in the hypothetical paragraph or paper accordingly, the structure of paragraph or paper being laid out by the thesis as stated. You as writer would first consider why the poet cast the first three stanzas into the past tense (couldn't they have been written just as well in the present tense?); then, following the thesis as stated, you would move on to consider the shift to the future tense in the last stanza and why the speaker projects himself not just into the future but into the far future; finally, you would analyze the possible significance of the poem's being spoken in the present.

In arranging the parts in an enumerative structure, of course, you must have a reason for placing the first item first, the second second, and so forth. With respect to "The Road Not Taken," as we have just seen, you could simply follow the poem's movement from the past to the future, with the present acting as a way of drawing to an end. However, you might feel that the introduction of the future tense is of special significance, in which case you might restate the thesis (putting reference to the future last) and arrange the parts according to your sense of climax, with discussion of the future coming last. Whatever the decision, the principle is the same: the parts must be recognized, delineated, and ordered according to some viable plan.

Order of Climax.   I have saved order of climax—that is, building to the most important item—for last because of its special importance. Climactic arrangement is of particular importance because it has application to all the other ways of organizing. Should you be enumerating, for example, or comparing and contrasting, order of climax could help you decide what to take up first, what second, and—most important—what last. And spatial as well as chronological sequence, though having their own sequential logic, often move climactically (from a cause in the past, say, to its result subsequently). If your material suggests no other kind of arrangement, order of climax is always a possibility: decide what is more important and what less, and then arrange your parts from the least important to the most. But even if you are working with some other pattern, order of climax should not be wholly out of mind. If for no other reason than to avoid the sense of anticlimax, order of climax should be checked when it comes to arranging supports in a paragraph and then the paragraphs themselves into a essay.

Writing Assignment: A Paragraph

Write a discrete paragraph of your own, perhaps using as a model the one that appears a few pages back. Take your thesis from some topic area related to "The Road Not Taken" and/or "A Sudden Story" that interests you. State your thesis clearly so that you understand it; then gather your support materials, arrange them in some sensible way (remember to consider order of climax especially), and conclude. Try to make the paragraph coherent: that is, as you move from support to support, try to leave no gaps. The reader should always know the relationship of supports to each other as well as to the overriding thesis. Follow this diagram:

Title

Thesis statement _____ .
Major support _____ .
   Minor support(s)   _____ .
     (if any)

Major support _____ .
   Minor support(s)   _____ .
     (if any)
Major support _____ .
   Minor support(s)   _____ .
     (if any)
Ending _____ .

The Essay

Like the discrete paragraph, the full essay (of any length) has a beginning, a middle, and an end. And, again, the beginning usually entails a statement of the thesis, the middle involves support and demonstration, and the end serves to tie things together in one way or another. As we look at each in turn, keep in mind this brief outline of the functions of beginning, middle, and end. For the shape each of these takes depends on its function.

The Beginning.   The beginning of an essay is special—and especially difficult to write. The problem the beginning poses is how to present or lead to the thesis statement. Simply to state the thesis in the first sentence would usually seem too abrupt. Most often, it is better to lead readers gently from wherever they are mentally to where one wants them to be. For this reason, a particularly useful kind of beginning is the "funnel," which very naturally leads the reader to the thesis statement. Also, of the many ways to begin, the funnel beginning is the one way that will *always* work.

The funnel can narrow down to the thesis statement in various ways. You may lead to your thesis by way of analogy, for instance, or by a striking comparison that touches on some aspect of your thesis and so can lead to its explicit statement. For a thesis that is likely to be new to your reader, a way to set up a funnel beginning is to start with some aspect of the thesis that you know is familiar to your projected audience and then to move to the full statement of the thesis in question. Contrast, too, is often a good way to move, perhaps from something that you consider wrong to a statement of what you are going to argue is right (your thesis), or from a negative to a positive way of viewing something, or whatever. And many essays begin with a movement from the general to the particular: from a generalization related to the thesis to the specific thesis itself. In every case, the funnel beginning draws the reader naturally and smoothly to the thesis statement. The funnel beginning also allows the writer to move smoothly into the body (that is, the middle paragraphs) of an essay because the thesis comes at the end of the funnel and so immediately before the first support paragraph. It thus provides a jumping-off point for the essay as a whole.

A sample should help clarify. Notice that the writer begins with material related to the thesis but not with the thesis itself; moving from the general to the particular, the paragraph builds down to the particular thesis stated at the end. Observe, too, how the paragraph lays out the terms of inquiry that would inform the essay that it (the paragraph) would head.

```
     Time can often weigh us down:  the load
of the past, which each of us carries in
memory, can bend us and even cause us to
buckle; the burden of the future, which we
cannot help but project ourselves into, can
be equally irksome and difficult to bear.
It is no wonder that now and again we all
feel time as oppressive and wish for a mode
of existence out of time.  Yet it is only by
living in time--with the past and the future
informing all of our thoughts in the
present--that we can choose consciously and
act with volition; therefore, it is only
because we live in time that we are human.
Contrasting animal existence and human,
Robert Coover comes to exactly this
conclusion in his story "A Sudden Story."
```

Now the paper to follow should not be so hard to write: subsequent paragraphs or clusters of paragraphs would concern the hero's momentary envy of the dragon's "tenseless freedom" and the meaning of such freedom—the nature of animal existence as imagined in the story—and the contrasting nature of human existence. Well thought out, note, a thesis paragraph will usually lay out the paper to come, which is why much of the work of writing lies in writing a strong beginning, whenever it is written.

As that last phrase suggests, however, there is no rule that the beginning must be written first. To be sure, there are certain advantages in writing it up front: a good beginning, as we have seen, can guide the writer through the middle paragraphs; and because it leads to a clear statement of thesis, a funnel beginning can help the writer stay on track. Nevertheless, as long as you have a fairly clear thesis in mind, you may find that it is best to write the middle first, or even the end, and then to work up the beginning. People work in different ways, and even a person who customarily starts with the beginning may need to proceed in some other way on a given writing project. A well-constructed beginning makes what follows seem natural to the reader and satisfying. But because the reader does not know when the beginning was written, the writer need not be concerned about the matter. What is important is that the beginning as finally written be well constructed. Then it will accomplish its task: to engage the reader, to inform the reader as to what the writer is going to do, and to make the reader wish to read on.

Middle Paragraphs.   Middle paragraphs contain the meat of an essay. Here is where the thesis is exemplified, argued, demonstrated, or whatever. With the exception of paragraphs whose purpose is only to provide transition, each middle paragraph comes from and is somehow or other related to the thesis. That is, each develops some central idea (one per paragraph) that backs up, demonstrates, exemplifies, or otherwise expands on the thesis statement of the essay. The central idea of each middle paragraph is usually stated in a single sentence (though sometimes two or even three sentences are needed), which, though it may be found anywhere in the paragraph, is most commonly found at its beginning. The sentence containing the central idea of a paragraph is often called the "topic sentence."

Like the discrete paragraph, each middle paragraph must be organized internally according to an appropriate plan (the ways of organizing discussed previously all apply to middle paragraphs). In addition, like individual sentences in a paragraph, the individual middle paragraphs in a paper must be arranged into some comprehensible sequence. Just as one must decide what to put first, what second, and so on within a single paragraph, one must do so with the middle paragraphs in the essay as a whole. Should you be writing on the plot of a story, for instance, chronology might serve, or a spatial sequence if your concern is the setting of a story; if your thesis entails comparison and contrast, then that may be your governing strategy; or perhaps enumeration is what is called for because your thesis involves a list of steps. And, of course, order of climax is always to be considered, now with respect to the arrangement of paragraphs and their movement one to the next.

Having a suitable design in the first place and then following through on it will provide a coherent foundation for whatever paper you write. But transitional links between middle paragraphs are often needed, just as they are within paragraphs. Whenever a particular progression or relationship is not clear—even when the overall structure of the paper is apparent—some phrase, sentence, or even a whole paragraph (in longer papers) serving only the purposes of transition must be supplied to make the relationship clear and the movement fluid. When you read the sample essay that begins on page 21, note how the paragraphs are linked by phrases transitional in design and how, in large part because of these transitions, the paragraphs move easily one to the next.

The Ending.   Like beginning, ending demands some type of stratagem. Now, what can be done to tie things up and create a sense of completion? A summary is one possibility. The summary has the advantage of pulling ideas together and of reminding readers of the main points made in an essay, some of which the reader may have lost sight of. Especially when writing a long paper, consider the summary as a possible way of ending. A full summary, however, is not generally as well suited to the short essay, for readers can be counted on to retain the points of an argument through five or six paragraphs. But a brief summary—like that stated in the next to last sentence of the sample discrete paragraph (p. 13)—in combination with, say, a concluding statement—like the statement made in the last sentence of the sample paragraph—can serve the needs of any kind of paper. Or one might end with an analogy, which can serve both to summarize (indirectly) and to widen the scope of an essay. Another way of ending, suitable to the long and short paper alike, is to restate the thesis in such a way that it now applies not only to one's specific topic but also to a wider range of things or number of people. This movement from the particular to the general is called the "reverse funnel." Or one might ask a question about some central point made in the middle and end by answering it. This is the general pattern of the sample ending that follows, which also makes reference to the governing thesis stated in the sample beginning (p. 18) as it (the ending) fans out to generalization (the reverse funnel).

```
        But why is the hero so perfunctorily
    gobbled up by the dragon at the end of the
    story?  The dragon, living only in the
    present, comes to represent the present.
    The hero, who carries past and future with
    him at all times, is, in a sense, at war
    with the simple present, which, however
    enticing, we cannot enter and remain human.
    It is because we live in time through memory
    and projection that we are human.  It is
    this that separates us from all else that we
    see in creation.  Ironically, however, time
    always catches us up:  like Coover's hero,
    each of us is at the last consumed by the present,
    the eternal present of nonbeing, of death.
```

Two things in particular should be noted about this paragraph. First, the sentence "It is because we live in time through memory and projection that we are human" refers back to the thesis statement at the end of the sample beginning. Such a referring back helps give an essay a sense of roundness and thus of closure. Second, proceeding from question to answer, the sample ending attains final resolution through a generalized statement. Opening out to suggest wider applicability, this way of ending—the reverse funnel—achieves the effect of climax and thereby gives the paragraph and consequently the essay it would end the feel of closure, the sense of an ending.

Sample Essay.   Let us now draw the whole thing together, beginning, middle, and end. An expansion of the discrete paragraph found on pages 12–13, the sample essay that follows sums up in its structure the various points about organization and coherence made so far. Observe where the thesis statement comes and how it is led to; note how the middle paragraphs are related to it and to each other, as well as how they are internally organized and arranged; mark how the last paragraph moves from the particular to a conclusion general in scope (the reverse funnel). Then try your hand at a like essay of your own.

The Problem of Choice

Funnel
beginning

Well over a hundred years ago, the British philosopher John Stuart Mill defined "modern" in connection with the freedom of choice: "human beings are no longer born to their place in life," Mill observed, "but are free to employ their faculties . . . to achieve the lot which may appear to them most desireable" (143). Our lives are no longer mapped out by tradition; we are free to choose what college to attend, whom we shall marry, what occupation to pursue. But upon what grounds can we make our choices? That's the difficulty. Our precious freedom most often leaves us in a quandary; so left, we are usually reluctant to choose and then ambivalent about having chosen. In "The Road Not Taken," Robert

Thesis

Frost dramatizes our difficulty by way of a speaker who is representative of human beings loosed from tradition but not comfortable with this relatively new freedom of ours.

Transition

Topic
sentence

Before we turn to Frost's speaker, however, it should be noted that the situation he describes is symbolic, as most readers probably understand intuitively.

Support

Traveling down a road generally signifies life's journey, and a fork in the road

signifies an important choice to be made as
to the subsequent direction of one's life.
This age-old symbolism is so common in our
culture as to need no further comment. It
should be remarked, though, that Frost uses
these symbols with great skill: his
treatment of them makes them seem fresh and
newly meaningful.

Transition

Topic sentences

But to return to the poem's speaker, he
expresses one reason for his difficulty in
choosing his road at the beginning of the
poem when he says, "sorry I could not travel
both." That is, he didn't wish to make a
choice at all. (His regret at having to
choose, incidentally, is implied as well by
the poem's title.) Confronted with an

Support

important choice, most of us feel the same;
we would eat our cake and have it too. When
asked what she might like to be, a child I
know replied, "A policewoman, a reporter, a
ballet dancer, and a doctor." Along the
line, of course, she will narrow her list
down, finally, to one occupation, but
probably with a certain sense of narrowness
and of lost possibilities. To some extent,
we all regret not being able to take all of
the roads before us. At any rate, the

Support

speaker's difficulty in choosing, as that
difficulty stems from his wishing not to
limit his possibilities, is internal, an

Transition

aspect of the psychology of the chooser
rather than inherent in the things he must
choose between.

Topic sentence

But this second potential source of

difficulty, a source external to the self,
is suggested as well as the poem moves on.

Support

Though the speaker says that one of the two
roads "was grassy and wanted wear," he
immediately refutes himself by saying that
in fact the two roads were exactly the same,
equally worn and equally covered "In leaves
no step had trodden black." So, really,
there was no rational basis for a choice of
road. This kind of difficulty is inherent
externally in the things that must be chosen
between. The speaker's reaction to this

Support

external difficulty, however, takes us again
to the inner sphere, and once again we see
that the speaker's thought and feeling are
marked by reluctance and ambivalence––
expressed now by the speaker's desire to
keep the other road "for another day." With
so little basis upon which to choose, what
else could one feel? He feels what many of
us feel, having little more basis for our
choices than he had for his.

Transition

This lack of basis along with the
feelings the lack produces helps explain the
last stanza of Frost's poem. Here, the

Support

speaker takes us from the past (stanzas 1–3)
to the distant future ("ages and ages
hence"), suggesting thereby how for us the
past remains present and always conditions
the future. Sometime way in the future, he
tells us, he will say that his reason for
choosing the road he did was that it was
"the one less traveled by," the one that
"was grassy and wanted wear." But we know

Support

that this will be a rationalization for a choice made regretfully and without any real basis. Yet who among us would say, "I chose my college, my career, my wife or husband by the flip of a coin"? Psychologically, we need to feel that we have chosen, even if—no, especially if—chance has been what in fact has directed us. And when enough time has gone by, we do start to remember reasons for choices that had no rational basis in fact. Frost's speaker underscores this

Topic sentence

process by his projection into the future of his future distortion of the past.

"The Road Not Taken," then, concerns the difficulty that choice entails for us: our reluctance to choose, our mixed feelings once we have chosen, and our tendency to rationalize our choices at some later date. We must choose, but making choices is difficult both because of the imponderables of the external world and especially—as "The Road Not Taken" brings home—because of the conflicts within. The irony of it is that, unlike most people who have ever lived on this earth, we have the luxury of choice but often find that luxury burdensome. Freedom of choice, it seems, brings its own

Reverse funnel ending

set of problems and its own psychological dilemmas.

Writing Assignment: An Essay

Using the essay you have just read as a model for structure, write a full essay of your own. If you wish, take the discrete paragraph you wrote for the earlier writing assignment and develop it into an essay, as was done with respect to the sample essay we have just looked at. Or get a new topic and thesis entirely if you would rather start afresh. I suggest that you read the next section before writing, or at least before rewriting. It should help to clarify the nature of and need for transitional material.

WRITING TO REWRITING

Writing is difficult, so don't think that there is something wrong with you if you have difficulty doing it. Everyone does. What helps is to understand that, because the mind can't do everything at once, writing must proceed in stages, as I suggested when discussing the writing process: first a few jottings; then some thought about how to structure ideas; then a rough draft; then, usually, extensive revision; and finally proofreading and final typing. We will now turn to revision, or rewriting, which many writers consider to be the crucial stage of the writing process.

Revision, too, entails a number of steps. First of all, check what you have written, paragraph by paragraph, against your thesis statement. Should you find that you have wandered away from the point, either bring the suspect passage into line or cut it out. You may even find that most of a paper does not go with the thesis as stated. One solution here would be to change the thesis. Because writing is a dynamic process, one never truly knows what one has to say until it is said. It is not surprising, therefore, that writers sometimes discover somewhere along the way that they actually have something other to say than what they initially thought they were going to say. Second, check the arrangement of your paragraphs to make sure that they move easily one to the next. You might find that some paragraphs should be repositioned. So reposition, making sure to change any transitional words or phrases as necessary. Third, check each paragraph internally for unity and coherence (see below), and check that you have provided whatever transitions are necessary between paragraphs. Finally, every time you look over what you have written, keep an eye out for what can be polished—a better word here, a more felicitous expression there—and polish as you go along.

Unity and Coherence

The main business of rewriting is to make sure that everything is to the point and follows as logically and gracefully as possible. These are the marks of readable prose. Prose that does not show unity and coherence is like the rambling of one of those radio talk-show callers who go on and on aimlessly. They are painful to listen to. Readers, too, want the writer to make a point and to stick to it (this is what "unity" means), as well as to relate all secondary ideas to it and to each other (coherence). Unity and coherence, therefore, should be checked and rechecked as you go through the process of rewriting.

Unity and coherence can be gained in a number of ways. Simple deletion, for instance, is a ready way of improving unity. If some sentence seems irrelevant, drop it. However, you may want to keep some of the information expressed in the sentence. Here, subordination will solve the problem: put the information in a subordinate clause or a phrase of some sort and combine the phrase or clause with a sentence with which it makes sense. Subordination is a technique of coherence as well as of unity. When sentences do not follow readily, the problem can often be solved by subordinating one idea to another, thereby expressing the relationship of ideas grammatically. Coherence can be gained as well by overt explanation of how a support relates to the thesis or to another support if the relationship is not clear. And, as we have seen, coherence is gained by the use of transitions, the sole purpose of which is to spell out the kind of relationship that exists between sentences and paragraphs when that relationship is not self-evident. An example should underscore the difference between writing that seems aimless because it lacks unity and coherence and writing that, because it is unified and coherent, stays to a point and makes it. Compare the sets of paragraphs that follow to see how the first set has been made readable by deletion, subordination, and the introduction of transitions when called for. The subject matter here is Cynthia Ozick's "The Shawl," a story that we shall look at in some detail in the first chapter of Section II of this book.

1

Cynthia Ozick is a very fine writer. Her story "The Shawl" is laid in Nazi Germany. Six million Jews were killed by Germans. My grandfather took part in World War II. He told me how horrible the death camps were where Jews were systematically slaughtered. They were forced into the camps. It must be a terrible thing to be deprived of liberty and put into a stinking hole. Many people went mad in the death camps.

Rosa is a good woman, unselfish and caring. She reasons with herself whether or not to give her baby away. Magda is a poor, pathetic creature who is slowly starving to death. Rosa decides not to give her away because of the danger. She is rational. Her physical condition is bad. She goes mad. We see her sucking the shawl at the end of the story.

2

Deletion and subordination

Cynthia Ozick depicts in her story "The Shawl" the time when six million Jews were

Subordination
Deletion

[Polishing]

killed by the Nazis. Forced into death
camps, they were systematically
slaughtered. It must surely be terrible to
be deprived of liberty and placed in a
stinking hole. No wonder many people went
mad in these so-called "camps."

Subordination

Transition
between
paragraphs

Transition

Subordination

Subordination

Transitions

Subordination

A good woman, unselfish and caring,
Rosa is an example of how systematic
dehumanization can drive a person mad. At
first, she is clearly sane, evidenced by her
reasoning with herself whether or not to
give away Magda, a poor, pathetic creature
who is slowly starving to death. That Rosa
decides not to give away her baby because of
the danger demonstrates her sanity despite
her physical condition. But over the course
of the story she goes mad. At the end, when
we leave her sucking Magda's shawl, we
realize fully the effects on the mind that
dehumanization can have.

The first set of paragraphs lacks both unity and coherence from the first sentence on. In the revision, the first sentence has been deleted because, although it may be true, it really has nothing to do with the business at hand. The second sentence is not strictly true and it relates to nothing around it as stated. In fact, none of the first four sentences shows anything like a clear relationship; the reader is left to decipher what possible connections there could be. Few readers would even try. Read the first four sentences again quickly. When I do, I'm tempted to add, "and how's your grandmother?" Everything seems to come from left field. To be sure, except for the first, each sentence relates to World War II. But how do they relate to each other? That's the question. And the answer is that as stated they don't. Look now at the first revised paragraph. To gain unity, the first and fourth sentences have been dropped, and the second and third sentences have been combined by subordination for the sake of coherence, as have the fifth and sixth. The last two sentences have been retained but polished. Because similar problems mark the second paragraph of the original and similar solutions are found in its revised counterpart, you should be able to spot both problems and solutions yourself. Notice, though, the transition supplied between the two revised paragraphs and how it makes the relationship clear and meaningful. This is the sort of thing that rewriting entails.

Almost any piece of writing can be made to be unified and coherent. But the writer must spot the changes needed to effect unity and coherence and then go about making them.

Proofreading and Titling

After you have gone through all the steps outlined thus far in this section and have revised accordingly, you should have a final draft in hand. You are close to the end. What's left is careful proofreading. Because, once more, the mind cannot do everything at once, proofreading should also be done in steps. As I always suggest to my own students (and this is my own practice), read your final draft checking for subject-verb agreement only. Then read it again checking only for pronoun reference and agreement. These are potential problem spots of our language, and therefore they require careful attention. Next, read your paper for spelling, punctuation, and other matters of mechanics, preferably aloud so that you can also check the sound of your prose. Watch especially for errors that you know you are prone to make.

After you have finished with these steps, give your paper a title. To be sure, you may have had a tentative title in mind from the beginning. But it is best to wait until the last to make a final decision about the title, for one cannot be sure of what one has to say until it is said. A good title, note, usually points to the thesis without stating it. (As I will discuss in Section V, "The Essay," however, occasionally a title may serve as a thesis statement.) For example, the title of the sample essay, "The Problem of Choice," ties in directly with the thesis of the essay, but, naming the topic area, the title is much more general than the specific thesis the essay pursues. And by being more general, the title also anticipates the essay's conclusion and so furthers the sense of roundness that an essay should ultimately impart. Remember that a title—the first thing a reader sees—is a tool for focusing the reader's attention and drawing the reader into the writer's discourse. The title is also what the reader is most likely to remember. A good title, then, can help the writer achieve several important aims. Having decided on a title, you are now ready for the final typing, after which you should check your work one last time for typographical errors.

We come back to where we began. As you read the stories, poems, plays, and essays in this book, read with an eye toward writing. The reading should help stimulate ideas; the writing will help concretize those ideas and thus help you better understand both the work under consideration and yourself in relationship to it. Reading and writing alike should bring both the world and the self into play. "Into play"—the phrase leads me to two final points. First, whatever the genre (lyric poetry, tragic drama, and so forth), whatever the content, and whatever the feeling evoked in the reader (melancholy and sadness no less than joy), literature delights in itself as literature—delights in the play of words and verbal structures—and asks that the reader join in that delight. Second, writing, too, can be wonderful fun if approached as a way of engaging the world and exploring the self. Certainly, the play of the mind is full of delight when the mind allows itself room to play.

SECTION II

FICTION

CHAPTER

✳ 1 ✳

WHAT FICTION IS

THE REALM OF FICTION

We all respond to fiction. How many of us did not like to be read stories by our parents or teachers when we were children? How many of us do not go to the movies from time to time or watch television, the fare of which is primarily fiction? And we devise our own fictions every night when we dream. Probably because of the structure of the brain itself, fiction continues to have power both to move us and to expand our understanding. But what is fiction?

Because dreams are fictions, we can move to an answer by way of dreams. Think of a dream you've had that seemed of some particular significance when you awoke. Of what was the dream composed? Surely it entailed some people in some locale doing something, as well as an "author" (you as dreamer) and feelings of some sort. Although both people and locale were most likely drawn from the external or "real" world, the dream created its own world. When you awoke, you might have wondered about the meaning of the dream and even tried to interpret it in light of its details and the way it made you feel. Your dream, then, became a text and you its reader. If you went further and told your dream to someone else, then you became a narrator with respect to the material of the dream.

Like dreams, formal works of fiction present characters located somewhere, engaged in something; formal works of fiction, too, involve feelings—the feelings of characters within the fiction and the feelings aroused in the reader. Also, although the people and locales in formal fiction may be drawn from the external world, every piece of fiction creates its own world. And in no formal fiction of any complexity does anyone simply tell us the meaning. We must interpret meaning for ourselves, just as we must interpret our own dreams. Fictions of whatever sort are dramatic rather than discursive: that is, they speak through action, mood, symbol rather than by logical proposition. In the words of Flannery O'Connor, a fine contemporary writer, "The fiction writer doesn't state, he shows, renders." Finally, our interpretations of formal fictions, as of dreams, are always in some sense incomplete: an interpretation is like a map, always simpler than the region it is meant to guide the traveler through.

In sum, just as a dream is a means of communication from one part of the self to another, formal fiction is a means of communication from one self to another. Indeed, fiction is one of the chief devices by which human beings communicate in *concrete terms* their understandings of the world, the self, and the human situation.

Fact and Fiction

"Why bother with fiction, which means 'untrue,' doesn't it?" This double question, which might be nagging at you, is indirectly answered by what has been said in the preceding paragraphs. The direct answer lies in what we go to fiction for. Granted, every piece of fiction is a story that to some extent is made up and so is untrue in the limited sense that it is not restricted to the merely factual. This is not to say that fictions do not contain facts, but only that we read fiction for something other than fact. The truth of fiction is not the truth of history or of science, but the more personal truth of human feeling and disposition, communicated best when that substantial part of ourselves that understands primarily through the senses and the emotions is touched. In other words, for a recounting of fact we go to history books, biographies, science texts, and so forth. We go to fiction for exactly what history and science cannot deliver: an intimate sense of the inner lives of people, their deepest feelings, their conflicts and confusions, their most secret joys and fears—all of which can only be imagined and which can be communicated only through concrete depictions of characters and their thoughts and actions. We go to fiction to understand life not in the abstract, but in the flesh. The beauty of fiction is that because it is fictional it can be constructed to reveal what can be revealed in no other way. Through its various elements, fiction reveals our inner lives. Such is fiction's realm, its concern and its truth.

Fiction and the Written Word

Because fiction is made out of words, let us consider it briefly within the world of other things made of words, such as news reports and human interest stories. Think of the typical news story first. Reporters, we are told, ask five questions: who? what? when? where? and why?—that is, who did what at what time, in what place, and for what reason? So a brief report of a fatal accident might read:

> On Saturday morning Harold Taylor, 52, of 57 Acre Lane, Sloatsburg, New York, was fatally injured when his car went out of control at the corner of Broadway and Main. Evidently Mr. Taylor, who was proceeding west on Main, hit a patch of ice as he tried to make it through the intersection on a yellow light. According to Alice Miller, who witnessed the incident, before Mr. Taylor could regain control, his car was struck by a dump truck, which skidded through the intersection as it attempted to slow for the red light. The driver of the truck was treated for minor injuries at Mercy Hospital and released. Coincidentally, Mr. Taylor's wife had died of a heart attack the morning before.

There are the facts, analogous to some of the facts of fiction—characters, an occurrence or situation, a setting. But the facts never tell all.

Newspapers, of course, also contain human interest stories, in which the reporter tries to fill in what is missing from the straight report: the backgrounds of the people involved, their states of mind if such can be determined, their feelings about what has occurred. Here we are moving closer to fiction. The reporter, however, is still strictly held to what can be thought of as fact: to circumstantial evidence as reported by eyewitnesses, to whatever is unearthed by field investigation, to what the people involved say of their motivation. That is, even in a human interest story, nothing not a matter of fact or of well-grounded supposition can be included.

In contrast, fiction is not limited to circumstantial fact, and so it can take us into occurrences, situations, and minds to a degree that no news report or human interest story could. While fiction portrays particular characters and events, it also goes beyond the particular to a concern with the general, with revealing something about the nature of human beings and human life. But the fiction writer doesn't tell us anything directly except a story, which is designed to probe into human life via dramatic presentation of incident and character. This combination of the particular and the general, with the general *embodied* in the particular, is the hallmark not only of fiction but of every kind of literature, and is the source of its impact. Because literature is fashioned to have the effect of immediate experience, it involves the reader personally.

Thus, like the other types of literature, fiction is double in nature: it asks us to focus on the particular (on details of plot, for instance, or character) yet to feel in the particular something of general consequence. That is, it asks us to see, through its unique happenings and characters, something generally true of human beings and the human condition. Every literary artist—the poet, for instance, no less than the writer of prose fiction—has the same aim: to embody in words some significant perception of human life. What distinguishes the various types of literature is not the end striven for but the means used to attain that end. In one genre (or type of literature)—lyric poetry, for instance—figures of speech, rhythms, and patterns of sound are prominent means; in another genre—tragic drama, say—visual symbols, soliloquies, and physical movement are prominent. (To be sure, though each genre is distinct with respect to its combination of elements, there is an overlapping of elements between the genres, as we shall see as we move along.) The specific tools of the writer of prose fiction are: plot, characterization, narration, mood, style, setting, and symbol. In some combination or other (every piece of fiction does not necessarily contain all of the elements just enumerated), these constitute the means of fiction. The more fully we understand these means, the more readily we can move to interpretation and grasp what a given story is about—its theme.

UNDERSTANDING FICTION

Part of coming to terms with a story, then, is looking to see how it is constructed, or how the elements it is made of are used. Somewhere along the line, active readers ask of stories questions like those that follow.

Of plot: What happens in the story? How are its incidents linked? What is the significance of what happens?

Of character: What kind of people does the story present? How are they drawn? What makes them do what they do? Is there anything to be learned from them?

Of narrators and narration: Who tells the story? Is the narrator one of its characters? Can the narrator be trusted? What is the narrator's (or narrative) point of view? Does the narrator somehow shed light on the story's meaning?

Of mood: What does the story make me feel? Why this mood (for instance, comic, grim, nostalgic, tragic)? How does the story's mood help establish its meaning? Does irony, which always entails a sense of discrepancy, play a role in establishing mood?

Of style: What kinds of sentence structure does the author use? What kinds of vocabulary? Is the story's language figurative or mainly literal? What is the effect of the story's style? Why?

Of setting: Where does the story take place? Is its setting merely backdrop or does it have some particular significance? If the latter, what?

Of symbol: Is there anything in the story—an object, perhaps, or a descriptive detail— that could have meaning beyond its literal function in the story? In the context of the story, what special significance might this object, detail, or whatever have?

Of theme: What is the general, or overall, meaning of the story that the elements in combination serve to establish?

As I suggested earlier, read a story first for pleasure, for its effect. Let it sink in. Then question how the story is made, for the meaning of a story depends immediately on how that story is put together. Students often ask about the "intention" of an author. The answer is that we can never know the author's intention directly; so we speak of the "implied intention," implied by how a story is constructed. Because no author has to write a story in a set way, the choices made by an author allow us to infer intention and arrive at meaning. But first we must observe what choices were made, or, again, actively consider the elements from which a story is molded.

As you read and especially reread Cynthia Ozick's "The Shawl," determine the elements from which it is constructed and then consider their functions by asking of each of its elements the questions just outlined. Also, go through the reading process discussed in Section I of this book (pp. 2–6) and summarized here with respect to fiction specifically.

1. As you read, write down any ideas and/or questions the story stirs in you.
2. Note whatever feelings it evokes from you.
3. Mull over all this, seeking answers to your questions and testing the aptness of your ideas and feelings.
4. Finally, taking everything into account, try to articulate the meaning of the story overall. Write down a few sentences about its possible meaning, perhaps noting as well some details in the story that have led you to your tentative conclusion about its meaning.

Then follow me as I go through this process myself, a process that leads to the full-fledged paper on "The Shawl" that ends this chapter. Having gone through these steps yourself, you too should wind up with both a firm grasp of the story and something precise to write about.

THE SHAWL

—————————— ❊ CYNTHIA OZICK ❊ ——————————

Stella, cold, cold, the coldness of hell. How they walked on the roads together, Rosa with Magda curled up between sore breasts, Magda wound up in the shawl. Sometimes Stella carried Magda. But she was jealous of Magda. A thin girl of fourteen, too small, with thin breasts of her own, Stella wanted to be wrapped in a shawl, hidden away, asleep, rocked by the march, a baby, a round infant in arms. Magda took Rosa's nipple, and Rosa never stopped walking, a walking cradle. There was not enough milk; sometimes Magda sucked air; then she screamed. Stella was ravenous. Her knees were tumors on sticks, her elbows chicken bones.

Rosa did not feel hunger; she felt light, not like someone walking but like someone in a faint, in trance, arrested in a fit, someone who is already a floating angel, alert and seeing everything, but in the air, not there, not touching the road. As if teetering on the tips of her fingernails. She looked into Magda's face through a gap in the shawl: a squirrel in a nest, safe, no one could reach her inside the little house of the shawl's windings. The face, very round, a pocket mirror of a face: but it was not Rosa's bleak complexion, dark like cholera, it was another kind of face altogether, eyes blue as air, smooth feathers of hair nearly as yellow as the Star sewn into Rosa's coat. You could think she was one of *their* babies.

Rosa, floating, dreamed of giving Magda away in one of the villages. She could leave the line for a minute and push Magda into the hands of any woman on the side of the road. But if she moved out of line they might shoot. And even if she fled the line for half a second and pushed the shawl-bundle at a stranger, would the woman take it? She might be surprised, or afraid; she might drop the shawl, and Magda would fall out and strike her head and die. The little round head. Such a good child, she gave up screaming, and sucked now only for the taste of the drying nipple itself. The neat grip of the tiny gums. One mite of a tooth tip sticking up in the bottom gum, how shining, an elfin tombstone of white marble, gleaming there. Without complaining, Magda relinquished Rosa's teats, first the left, then the right; both were cracked, not a sniff of milk. The duct crevice extinct, a dead volcano, blind eye, chill hole, so Magda took the corner of the shawl and milked it instead. She sucked and sucked, flooding the threads with wetness. The shawl's good flavor, milk of linen.

It was a magic shawl, it could nourish an infant for three days and three nights. Magda did not die, she stayed alive, although very quiet. A peculiar smell, of cinnamon and almonds, lifted out of her mouth. She held her eyes open every moment, forgetting how to blink or nap, and Rosa and sometimes Stella studied their blueness. On the road they raised one burden of a leg after another and studied Magda's face. "Aryan,"

Stella said, in a voice grown as thin as a string; and Rosa thought how Stella gazed at Magda like a young cannibal. And the time that Stella said "Aryan," it sounded to Rosa as if Stella had really said "Let us devour her."

But Magda lived to walk. She lived that long, but she did not walk very well, partly because she was only fifteen months old, and partly because the spindles of her legs could not hold up her fat belly. It was fat with air, full and round. Rosa gave almost all her food to Magda, Stella gave nothing; Stella was ravenous, a growing child herself, but not growing much. Stella did not menstruate. Rosa did not menstruate. Rosa was ravenous, but also not; she learned from Magda how to drink the taste of a finger in one's mouth. They were in a place without pity, all pity was annihilated in Rosa, she looked at Stella's bones without pity. She was sure that Stella was waiting for Magda to die so she could put her teeth into the little thighs.

Rosa knew Magda was going to die very soon; she should have been dead already, but she had been buried away deep inside the magic shawl, mistaken there for the shivering mound of Rosa's breasts; Rosa clung to the shawl as if it covered only herself. No one took it away from her. Magda was mute. She never cried. Rosa hid her in the barracks, under the shawl, but she knew that one day someone would inform; or one day someone, not even Stella, would steal Magda to eat her. When Magda began to walk Rosa knew that Magda was going to die very soon, something would happen. She was afraid to fall asleep; she slept with the weight of her thigh on Magda's body; she was afraid she would smother Magda under her thigh. The weight of Rosa was becoming less and less; Rosa and Stella were slowly turning into air.

Magda was quiet, but her eyes were horribly alive, like blue tigers. She watched. Sometimes she laughed—it seemed a laugh, but how could it be? Magda had never seen anyone laugh. Still, Magda laughed at her shawl when the wind blew its corners, the bad wind with pieces of black in it, that made Stella's and Rosa's eyes tear. Magda's eyes were always clear and tearless. She watched like a tiger. She guarded her shawl. No one could touch it; only Rosa could touch it. Stella was not allowed. The shawl was Magda's own baby, her pet, her little sister. She tangled herself up in it and sucked on one of the corners when she wanted to be very still.

Then Stella took the shawl away and made Magda die.

Afterward Stella said: "I was cold."

And afterward she was always cold, always. The cold went into her heart: Rosa saw that Stella's heart was cold. Magda flopped onward with her little pencil legs scribbling this way and that, in search of the shawl; the pencils faltered at the barracks opening, where the light began. Rosa saw and pursued. But already Magda was in the square outside the barracks, in the jolly light. It was the roll-call arena. Every morning Rosa had to conceal Magda under the shawl against a wall of the barracks and go out and stand in the arena with Stella and hundreds of others, sometimes for hours, and Magda, deserted, was quiet under the shawl, sucking on her corner. Every day Magda was silent, and so she did not die. Rosa saw that today Magda was going to die, and at the same time a fearful joy ran in Rosa's two palms, her fingers were on fire, she was astonished, febrile: Magda, in the sunlight, swaying on her pencil legs, was howling. Ever since the drying up of Rosa's nipples, ever since

Magda's last scream on the road, Magda had been devoid of any syllable; Magda was a mute. Rosa believed that something had gone wrong with her vocal cords, with her windpipe, with the cave of her larynx; Magda was defective, without a voice; perhaps she was deaf; there might be something amiss with her intelligence; Magda was dumb. Even the laugh that came when the ash-stippled wind made a clown out of Magda's shawl was only the air-blown showing of her teeth. Even when the lice, head lice and body lice, crazed her so that she became as wild as one of the big rats that plundered the barracks at daybreak looking for carrion, she rubbed and scratched and kicked and bit and rolled without a whimper. But now Magda's mouth was spilling a long viscous rope of clamor.

"Maaaa—"

It was the first noise Magda had ever sent out from her throat since the drying up of Rosa's nipples.

"Maaaa . . . aaa!"

Again! Magda was wavering in the perilous sunlight of the arena, scribbling on such pitiful little bent shins. Rosa saw. She saw that Magda was grieving for the loss of her shawl, she saw that Magda was going to die. A tide of commands hammered in Rosa's nipples: Fetch, get, bring! But she did not know which to go after first, Magda or the shawl. If she jumped out into the arena to snatch Magda up, the howling would not stop, because Magda would still not have the shawl; but if she ran back into the barracks to find the shawl, and if she found it, and if she came after Magda holding it and shaking it, then she would get Magda back, Magda would put the shawl in her mouth and turn dumb again.

Rosa entered the dark. It was easy to discover the shawl. Stella was heaped under it, asleep in her thin bones. Rosa tore the shawl free and flew—she could fly, she was only air—into the arena. The sunheat murmured of another life, of butterflies in summer. The light was placid, mellow. On the other side of the steel fence, far away, there were green meadows speckled with dandelions and deep-colored violets; beyond them, even farther, innocent tiger lilies, tall, lifting their orange bonnets. In the barracks they spoke of "flowers," of "rain": excrement, thick turd-braids, and the slow stinking maroon waterfall that slunk down from the upper bunks, the stink mixed with a bitter fatty floating smoke that greased Rosa's skin. She stood for an instant at the margin of the arena. Sometimes the electricity inside the fence would seem to hum; even Stella said it was only an imagining, but Rosa heard real sounds in the wire: grainy sad voices. The farther she was from the fence, the more clearly the voices crowded at her. The lamenting voices strummed so convincingly, so passionately, it was impossible to suspect them of being phantoms. The voices told her to hold up the shawl, high; the voices told her to shake it, to whip with it, to unfurl it like a flag. Rosa lifted, shook, whipped, unfurled. Far off, very far, Magda leaned across her air-fed belly, reaching out with the rods of her arms. She was high up, elevated, riding someone's shoulder. But the shoulder that carried Magda was not coming toward Rosa and the shawl, it was drifting away, the speck of Magda was moving more and more into the smoky distance. Above the shoulder a helmet glinted. The light tapped the helmet and sparkled it into a goblet. Below the helmet a black body like a domino and a pair of black boots hurled themselves in the direction of the electrified fence. The electric voices began to chatter wildly. "Maamaa, maaamaaa," they all hummed together. How far Magda was from Rosa now, across the whole square, past a dozen barracks, all the way on the other side! She was no bigger than a moth.

All at once Magda was swimming through the air. The whole of Magda traveled through loftiness. She looked like a butterfly touching a silver vine. And the moment Magda's feathered round head and her pencil legs and balloonish belly and zigzag arms splashed against the fence, the steel voices went mad in their growling, urging Rosa to run and run to the spot where Magda had fallen from her flight against the electrified fence; but of course Rosa did not obey them. She only stood, because if she ran they would shoot, and if she tried to pick up the sticks of Magda's body they would shoot, and if she let the wolf's screech ascending now through the ladder of her skeleton break out, they would shoot; so she took Magda's shawl and filled her own mouth with it, stuffed it in and stuffed it in, until she was swallowing up the wolf's screech and tasting the cinnamon and almond depth of Magda's saliva; and Rosa drank Magda's shawl until it dried.

[1980—U.S.A.]

First reading: What a story! I'm left with a host of feelings: pity, tenderness (for Rosa), outrage (for her guards), anxiety and fear (the fear of helplessness), and a sense of vertigo, my mind in a whirl from the rapidity of events.

Second reading: Having read the story a second time, I see that characterization and plot are prominent elements in it, and, because of my questions, that setting, narration, and style figure in as well. That is, all go into the making of how I feel and what I am made to see. The questions I've jotted down are these:

1. Where is the story set and why is the setting not spelled out?
2. Why the title "The Shawl"?
3. Why is the shawl called "magic"? To whom is it so? Why is the title not "The Magic Shawl"?
4. Why the deadpan narration? (Note that the narrator makes no direct comment nor expresses indignity or horror. And the description is understated, with most of the dreadful details—such as the state of the barracks—played down.)
5. Why the odd coupling of highly poetic imagery (for example, "She looked like a butterfly touching a silver vine") and savagery?

As to ideas, in general "The Shawl" makes me think of "what man has made of man" (Wordsworth). But the story is specific, making me engage myself fully with the plight of individuals. Focusing on Rosa, I am led to think about personal heroism and human endurance. I also see that Ozick touches on the fate of the individual in a world in which individuals do not count.

In looking over "The Shawl" again, I find that my initial feelings still hold: I respond in the same way, though the sense of helplessness seems even stronger to me now than on first reading. My initial ideas seem on the mark as well, but I feel that I haven't yet found adequate expression for my perception of the story overall. My statements are all too general and miss the power of this wrenching tale. By answering my questions I can perhaps come closer to an adequate statement.

1. *Where is the story set and why is the setting not spelled out?*

The reference to "the Star sewn into Rosa's coat" and the use of the word "Aryan"—details that might be overlooked on first reading—locate the story in Nazi Europe. That its location is not fully clarified, however, suggests that the story is not concerned with one historical moment only, but with a perpetual human possibility: that, alas, the Nazi atrocity is not the only such aberration perpetuated by humankind, but one of many. Also, the setting's not being specified adds to the sense of dislocation underscored by the march, seemingly from and to nowhere, described at the beginning of the story.

2. *Why the title?*

The title is apt because the shawl is a focal point and, indeed, the cause of the story's central action (a matter of plot). More, it helps us to feel Stella's need and Rosa's concern and deterioration (both matters of characterization). There's something wonderfully, horribly ironic about the title, too. What is a shawl?—something one wraps oneself in for protection. But it is exactly this—protection—that Ozick's characters lack. They are totally and horribly exposed, unprotected and helpless.

3. *Why "magic"? To whom? Why not "The Magic Shawl"?*

That the shawl offers any protection in this environment, as it seems to with respect to Magda, could almost make us believe in magic. But the title as it stands tells us otherwise. The shawl has the magic only of a security blanket. That it is believed to be magical by Rosa and Stella, however, tells us a great deal. Because of it we understand what has happened to Stella—her reversion to infancy, betokened as well by her fierce feelings of sibling rivalry. A belief in magic is a mark of early childhood. It is also a mark of mental degeneration. From the moment she begins to think of the shawl as magical, Rosa's deterioration is marked. That deterioration is complete, of course, at the end of the story, when Rosa herself becomes like her infant. What other response is possible? For here is true helplessness, its meaning laid bare. Nothing except magic could alter the situation.

4. *Why the deadpan narration?*

How many times has one been overwhelmed by pictures of the Holocaust or detailed descriptions of its horrors? And that's it—one is "overwhelmed." One can hardly grasp the larger picture because of the horrific details. By using a dispassionate narrator, who tells the story through Rosa's eyes yet uses descriptive detail sparingly and characteristically understates (both are aspects of the story's style), Ozick gains tremendous force. The disparity between statement and fact lends tension and irony, and gives all the more weight, finally, to the plight of the story's characters. At least, nothing else that I've read about imprisonment in a concentration camp has quite the impact of "The Shawl."

5. *Why the coupling of poetic imagery and savagery?*

The very beauty of some of Ozick's images underscores by way of contrast the hideous brutality inflicted on her characters. More, because we are seeing through Rosa's eyes as we read, the poetic quality of much of Ozick's imagery serves to portray Rosa as a gentle being yet also to reinforce our growing awareness of her deterioration. In context, the imagery in question has a surreal quality (dreamlike, wild, crazed) about it, a quality that makes the world of the story seem mad. And indeed it is. Rosa's madness at the end is a token of the madness of her world. In such a world it is insane not to be insane. No wonder the sense of vertigo at the end of the story. It's as though we were falling helplessly, with no prop or stay, nothing for support and nothing to protect us.

My answers help me clarify to myself how "The Shawl" gains its effect. Narration, style, setting, and plot all move toward the same end. The functions of the first three I've already suggested. Plot is the story's driving force, leading to Rosa's disintegration incident by incident. But character is its focal element: the story concerns Rosa primarily and what happens in her. Now, perhaps, I am in a position to express the story's meaning more adequately. Something I observe in my answers is the recurrence of the word "helpless" and the feeling of powerlessness. So noticing, I realize that what the story communicates most to me is the full import of what it is to be without even a modicum of control over one's own life. In a world in which power rather than pity is the ruling force, how truly terrible it is to be at the mercy of the whims of others. From the sense of dislocation at its beginning to the vertigo toward its end, Ozick's story details with extraordinary concreteness the effect of powerlessness on the human spirit.

WRITING ON FICTION

Having gone through a fairly rigorous process of reading—but no less delightful and perhaps more so for its rigor—I now feel that I have ideas and insights enough as well as support material to start writing. And, believing that I have something to say, I wish to share my understanding. Problems of paragraph structure and general organization remain to be solved during the writing stage, but my prewriting activities have given me something to say and the confidence to say it. It is primarily for this reason—the gaining of confidence—that many consider the prewriting stage the most important of the three stages of writing. In any event, in the sample essay that follows, the focus is on the meaning of "The Shawl" (that is, on its theme) as its meaning emerges from its dominant element—characterization. Read the essay in light of the preceding section of this chapter, "Understanding Fiction," focusing on how the essay develops out of the conclusions reached there. Study its structure as well and the way textual evidence is used. The essay should serve as an example of what writing on a story's overall meaning entails. (Writing on the individual elements of fiction will be considered as we take them up element by element.) The essay should prepare you, therefore, for the consideration of theme in the chapter that follows.

The Meaning of Powerlessness

Funnel beginning

For human beings to maintain a sense of integrity and, indeed, even keep our sanity, we need some degree of personal freedom. Stripped of autonomy entirely, we wither emotionally. The self literally ceases to be itself because it can have no effect in the external world. Forced into a condition like that of childhood, we tend to revert to childish modes of thought and feeling. This

Thesis

terrible effect of powerlessness on the human mind and spirit can be seen dramatically in Cynthia Ozick's "The Shawl" through the deterioration of Rosa, its central character.

Topic sentence

When we first meet Rosa, on the march, she has become physically decrepit, but her mind is still intact. Despite the

Support

dislocating effect of the march itself and the foul treatment received on it, she is still capable of logical thought and rational choice. Thus, she conceives a plan to give Magda away to someone at the side of the road; thinking the plan through, however, she realizes its impossibility and so rejects it. Here we have the operation of a rational mind. How different from this

Transition

Rosa is the Rosa we leave at the end of the story. Her deterioration proceeds subtly but inevitably.

The first mark of that deterioration occurs soon after the incident just outlined.

Support	Suddenly we are told that "It was a magic shawl," and this idea is pursued.
Support	Because Ozick's narrator makes us see through Rosa's eyes, we know that it is Rosa who has started to believe in magic. That
Support	the shawl is not magical, of course, is suggested by the story's title: the shawl is merely a shawl. Even more, the fact that
Support	it doesn't finally protect Magda but instead is the cause of her being discovered evidences its lack of magic properties. But
Support	that Rosa should come to feel the shawl to be magical quietly reveals her deterioration, or the start thereof.
Topic sentence	Resorting to a childish belief in magic, she is slowly receding into the confines of her own mind.
Topic sentence	Rosa's way of seeing as communicated by some of the story's images, especially at the end, is further indication that she is receding into herself. In the context of
Support	the prison camp as described, images like "jolly light," "a clown out of Magda's shawl," "light tapped the helmet and sparkled it into a goblet," and, most pointedly, "a butterfly touching a silver vine" suggest a mind projecting itself onto the world in order thus to change reality.
Support	There is a surreal quality to these images in context, a quality that imparts a growing sense of madness.
Topic sentences	And Rosa does go mad. At the end of the story her deterioration is complete:

Support

Support

she has herself become an infant sucking on
and trying to devour Magda's blanket. With
no choice possible as to external action,
she retreats into herself entirely. But
nothing I can say could communicate the
final stage of her deterioration as well as
the last lines of the story itself:

> so she took Magda's shawl and
> filled her own mouth with it,
> stuffed it in and stuffed it in,
> until she was swallowing up the
> wolf's screech and tasting the
> cinnamon and almond depth of
> Magda's saliva; and Rosa drank
> Magda's shawl until it dried.

Reverse
funnel
ending

Rosa's steady deterioration to this
point, portrayed subtly and in depth,
communicates vividly the effects of
powerlessness on the mind and spirit. Every
human being needs a sense of control,
however minimal, over his or her own life.
Robbed of this sense, the mind and spirit
wither. Stripped of autonomy, what can the
self do but, like Rosa, fall into fantasy
and then madness? How truly terrible
powerlessness is, but especially in a world
in which power and not pity is the dominant
force.

Again, this essay concerns the meaning or theme of Ozick's story. Because theme
is the end to which the elements are the means, a consideration of theme must go
along with a consideration of fiction itself. Therefore, the next chapter will be given
over to a discussion of theme and related matters.

CHAPTER

2

THEME

WHAT'S THE BIG IDEA?

When we speak of theme, we are referring to a story's general significance, which can be thought of as attitude, insight, or point. It is valid to think of theme in terms of the author's attitude as communicated by the story as a whole. Or we could conceive of theme as the general insight of an author into people or ideas established, again, by all the particulars of a story. Or we might think of theme simply as the point, the meaning in general terms that gives a story focus. If we are careful not to limit the meaning of the word "idea" too much, we might even say that theme is the big idea, the perception that unifies all the details in a story and accounts for why a story is structured as it is. Much of the pleasure of reading fiction lies in our pursuit of the general or big idea—that is, in our effort to arrive at the richest possible interpretation.

One important caution: never jump to interpretation. Themes, which must be inferred from the gathering particulars of stories, take shape gradually. Postpone the consideration of overall meaning until you have lived with a story long enough to master its construction, that is, to understand the elements that go into its making. Remember that theme is not an element of fiction but an end that accounts for all the means employed. To get to that end ourselves, we must first take up and examine the means that lead to it.

Bear in mind, however, that the theme is not the story. Even though you may feel that you have formulated a theme as fully and clearly as possible, the story cannot be put aside and forgotten as if it were a container from which you have poured out the meaning. The truths of fiction cannot be separated from their embodiment, just as the truths of human experience cannot be separated from that experience. Even the best formulation of a theme on the reader's part is never complete; the story retains its integrity. Think of a map: a map is a guide to a region but no substitute for traveling in it. Missing are the specific features of the region the map defines generally—the rocks and crags, paths and bypaths, springs and rivulets, not to mention sounds, odors, the variety of coloration: in a word, all that makes the place unique. So, too, theme or its articulation is no substitute for the experience of a story itself.

Still, articulating a story's theme is an essential step to understanding. I don't mean to suggest, however, that themes should be stated like philosophical postulates or that the theme of every story must be or can be formulated in a declarative statement. Many a story resolves itself only into a question or a hint at some direction of thought to be taken up by the reader. The question or direction is the theme. And in a great many stories the revelation that comes from insight into a character is the theme. Indeed, probing of human motivation and of the uncertain relation between what people feel, think, and believe is fundamental to first-rate fiction, which digs under the surface and attempts to uncover what goes on deep inside people. Its themes, therefore, are complex and worked out with subtlety; so they often cannot be stated simply.

Perhaps an example will help tie together the various points we have considered so far. Recall the news report we looked at earlier. Though it has no theme, the report contains ample material for a story. It is especially the last sentence of the report that catches my eye: "Coincidentally, Mr. Taylor's wife had died of a heart attack the morning before." In the news report, this is merely a matter of coincidence, but the fact of the wife's death could be of particular importance from the fiction writer's point of view. Conceivably, Mr. Taylor had had little sleep the night before his accident because he had to inform relatives, make the necessary arrangements, and so on. His shock and grief probably kept him awake in any case and greatly affected his judgment. Conceivably, too, he was distracted for just a moment as he headed into the intersection by the female witness, who may have reminded him of his dead wife. Possibly that, as much as icy conditions, made him lose control of his car. Reading the news report alone, we would have to settle for an explanation of the accident as having resulted from bad judgment, ice, and a skidding truck; a jury would have to come to such a conclusion. But deep down we know better. We know, for instance, that people often have accidents when they are emotionally disturbed. Someone writing a work of fiction based on incidents such as those in the report would look beneath the circumstantial evidence and explore the state of Mr. Taylor's mind just before the accident. Perhaps there was what psychologists call a "death wish" lurking under the surface, the accident's having been no accident at all, strictly speaking. There, then, could be our theme, nowhere stated in our hypothetical story but everywhere felt once the details (factual or imagined) chosen by the writer are seen clearly.

Theme Versus Moral

From all that has been said, it should be clear that a theme is different from a "moral" or a "message." But so many beginning students still look for "the moral," or at least speak in terms of "the moral of the story," that the distinction needs clarification. What "moral" or "message" means in this context, I suppose, is a statement about how people should behave. That is an important concern, but not directly a concern of fiction, at least over the past few hundred years. The fiction writer does not seek to tell us how to behave according to some abstract code of behaviour but rather to shed light on how we do behave. By so doing, fiction can show us ourselves, which seems to me to be more than enough.

There was a time, however, when fiction was aimed at specific moral instruction. In fact, from ancient days right on down to sometime in the eighteenth century, cautionary tales, fables, parables, and the like flourished, and they are still widely retold. Consider, for instance, the following version of Aesop's fable "The Ant and the Grasshopper."

> There once was an ant who was, like all ants, a paragon of industry. All summer long he worked from morning to night stocking his stores with food and fuel for the winter. Many a time his neighbor, the grasshopper, would deride his efforts, but the ant was undaunted. All he said was, "Wait until winter," and went about his work as the grasshopper, frivolous as ever, hopped hither and yon, paying no heed to the ant's warning. Summer faded into fall, and the ant worked on as the grasshopper chirped his songs and played the day away. Then came the first snowfall. Warm and cozy at his hearth, the ant heard a knock at the door. There was the grasshopper, shivering in the cold and starving. "Please, oh please, let me in," he said. "Not on your life," replied the ready ant, "you who frittered the summer and fall away and gave no heed to my warning." The ant slammed the door and went back to the fireside. The grasshopper hopped sadly away, realizing too late his folly. He died that very night.
>
> Moral: Work hard and save for a rainy (or snowy) day.

Like Aesop's other fables, and many cautionary tales, fables, and parables by others, "The Ant and the Grasshopper" still has a certain charm. But its moral, or what I call "moral tag," seems merely conventional and not very instructive at that. Because of the nature of the modern world, with its megacities and massive bureaucratic governments (not to mention credit cards), our realities are far too intricate to be caught in moral tags like this. Our fiction reflects our world by being structured to embody themes in their complexity instead of designed to communicate simple messages.

To be sure, modern fiction (especially short fiction) has its roots in older forms of literature, like the fable. The two tales by James Thurber placed first among the stories that follow suggest the relationship. But, the ancestry acknowledged, what is notable is the difference between Thurber's fables and those like Aesop's. Look at the "moral" of "The Owl Who Was God": "You can fool too many of the people too much of the time." This is substantially different in character from any conventional moral or tag. If anything, Thurber is poking fun at conventional moral tags and (this is his theme) suggesting how irrelevant they are to the complexities of modern life. (The title of the book from which the story is taken suggests as much: *Fables for Our Time.*) Thurber's theme, then, is of much greater complexity than his bogus moral, and the same is true of modern themes in general. No piece of fiction of substance resolves itself into a moral, so no moral tag will do as a statement of theme. One must phrase things more subtly, more in line with the character of what is being articulated as well as with the realities of our lives.

Articulating Fiction's Themes

Details come first. Before even thinking of interpretation, clarify the details of a story to yourself—its plot, its setting, the characteristics of the people it presents, and so on. Remember that the best interpretation accounts for the details and suggests how they are related. Also, look at titles: a title will often point to the heart of a story. Finally, as you read, keep an eye out for anything that is repeated or elaborated upon. Repetition and elaboration are likely to signal significance. Once you have come to see a story clearly, the question then is how to articulate its meaning. Here is a list of suggestions aimed at summarizing how one goes about discovering and expressing a theme.

SUMMARY SUGGESTIONS: UNDERSTANDING THEME

1. Though no statement of the theme of a work of fiction will exhaust its meaning, some statements are both richer and fuller than others. Stretching yourself, perhaps, try to express your understanding in language that does justice to that understanding as well as to the story's complexity.

2. Always check your statement of theme against the particulars of a story. What you say must not be at odds with any important detail. More, test that your statement accounts for major details: that is, your statement should implicitly make clear why an author chose, for instance, to develop one character instead of another or to emphasize setting instead of narration.

3. Be careful to distinguish between a theme and a moral. Because the themes of most stories are complex, they require more than a brief sentence to express. In fact, the themes of most stories cannot be stated adequately in one sentence alone.

4. In stating a theme, don't summarize a plot or refer to specific characters in your statement. Theme, don't forget, is the generalized meaning of a story.

5. On the other hand, fiction by its nature should keep us from blanket generalizations, for it confronts us at every turn with particulars—specific locales, a few detailed characters, definite events. Consequently, we can generalize only so far. In stating a theme, then, be a little guarded. For example, the theme of the hypothetical fiction that we constructed from the incidents in the news report should not be stated: "If the facts are known, accidents result from a death wish." A statement like the following is both more accurate and more meaningful: "Often, the causes of an accident are not exactly what they appear to be. Some accidents, at least, may result from inner turmoil as much as from external conditions. At certain points in their lives, people may even have a death wish, though they might not know that they do."

WRITING ON THEME

In some ways, writing on theme is easier than writing on any other aspect of fiction. To be sure, to articulate a theme fully, without reducing a story to some trite observation, is difficult. One must understand a story and how it is constructed first; then one must find the right words to capture its subtlety and account for its details. But once you come to the point of adequate articulation, you are home free: you have in hand both a thesis for your paper and materials to support your thesis.

That is, your articulation of a story's theme can be your thesis, as is the case with respect to my thesis in the sample essay on Ozick's "The Shawl" (pp. 34–37). Your job is now clear: you must show why you interpret the story as you do, or why you feel its theme to be what you say it is (your thesis). State the theme as you see it and then move on step by step to back up your statement. Your support materials, of course, are immediately available for you in the story you are writing on. You will, naturally, have to decide which materials to select and what order to present them in. To establish the validity of your thesis, be sure to account for and include the major facts of the story. The title, too, is often of particular significance. In writing a longer paper, you would probably want to include minor details as well. Keep your statement of theme (your thesis) in mind at all times, and be sure that everything you write is related to it.

Turn back to the sample essay on "The Shawl" as an example of what writing on theme entails. The theme there proposed for the story is the "terrible effect of powerlessness on the human mind and spirit." Rosa is singled out as the character whose experience embodies this theme, and so Rosa's experience as related in the story becomes the focal point of the essay as it proceeds. Detail by detail, the essay builds support for the statement of theme (the writer's thesis). By the end, the reader feels that, although the story may concern other matters as well or its theme may be stated in some other way, the writer has touched something significant in it. The reader now understands the story a little better. This is the task of analysis— to shed light, to increase understanding. If your articulation of theme is adequate and your marshaling of support material cogent, you will achieve your goal: to broaden your own understanding and that of your reader.

To be sure, you may wish to write on or be asked to write on something other than a story's theme—on a character, perhaps, or on a story's mood. Even so, you must still be concerned with theme, now as it relates to your topic. A paragraph might be devoted to a statement of theme followed by a discussion of how that theme relates to, sheds light on, or emerges from character, mood, or whatever it is you are writing on. For instance, if you were writing a paper on Stella's regression to infancy and how that regression is communicated, you might bring up its cause: her utter helplessness and dependency. Stella, no less than Rosa, embodies the story's theme, so in writing on her it would be a good idea to discuss how she contributes to the development of the theme overall or, conversely, what the theme of the story leads us to understand about her.

Or you could use a statement of theme for your conclusion, leaving your reader with a sense of the wider significance of your topic. That is, having gone into some aspect of a story in detail, you could move at the end to a discussion of the story's general meaning: to how what you have considered both relates to and helps establish the story's theme. To take Stella again, one could write a paper on her regression by discussing first what we know about human regression generally and then by applying that knowledge to an examination of Stella herself and the stages of her fall back to infancy. "But what is the cause of Stella's slide into infantile desires and feelings?" your conclusion could begin. Then you would specify helplessness because of her situation, and that would take you to a statement of theme, which could bring the paper to a satisfying close.

In sum, theme may be written on directly or used for support or for concluding. Whatever you write on, however, you probably will need to relate it to a story's theme. For theme is the end for which the elements are means; because means cannot be understood without an understanding of the end they serve, the elements of a story cannot be fully grasped in isolation from the theme that together they create. When you write on fiction, the full articulation of theme must come first.

STORIES FOR STUDY AND WRITING ASSIGNMENTS

THE OWL WHO WAS GOD

❋ JAMES THURBER ❋

Once upon a starless midnight there was an owl who sat on the branch of an oak tree. Two ground moles tried to slip quietly by, unnoticed. "You!" said the owl. "Who?" they quavered, in fear and astonishment, for they could not believe it was possible for anyone to see them in that thick darkness. "You two!" said the owl. The moles hurried away and told the other creatures of the field and forest that the owl was the greatest and wisest of all animals because he could see in the dark and because he could answer any question. "I'll see about that," said a secretary bird, and he called on the owl one night when it was again very dark. "How many claws am I holding up?" said the secretary bird. "Two," said the owl, and that was right. "Can you give me another expression for 'that is to say' or 'namely'?" asked the secretary bird. "To wit," said the owl. "Why does a lover call on his love?" asked the secretary bird. "To woo," said the owl.

The secretary bird hastened back to the other creatures and reported that the owl was indeed the greatest and wisest animal in the world because he could see in the dark and because he could answer any question. "Can he see in the daytime, too?" All the other creatures laughed loudly at this silly question, and they set upon the red fox and his friends and drove them out of the region. Then they sent a messenger to the owl and asked him to be their leader.

When the owl appeared among the animals it was high noon and the sun was shining brightly. He walked very slowly, which gave him an appearance of great dignity, and he peered about him with large, staring eyes, which gave him an air of tremendous importance. "He's God!" screamed a Plymouth Rock hen. And the others took up the cry "He's God!" So they followed him wherever he went and when he began to bump into things they began to bump into things, too. Finally he came to a concrete highway and he started up the middle of it and all the other creatures followed him. Presently a hawk, who was acting as outrider, observed a truck coming toward them at fifty miles an hour, and he reported to the secretary bird and the secretary bird reported to the owl. "There's danger ahead," said the secretary bird. "To wit?" said the owl. The secretary bird told him. "Aren't you afraid?" he asked. "Who?" said the owl calmly, for he could not see the truck. "He's God!" cried all the creatures again, and they were still crying "He's God!" when the truck hit them and ran them down. Some of the animals were merely injured, but most of them, including the owl, were killed.

Moral: You can fool too many of the people too much of the time.

[1939—U.S.A.]

Questions

1. Thurber backs up his "moral" by his depiction of the behavior of his chosen animals. Why are they so readily taken in?
2. The appended "moral" here seems quite different from that of a traditional fable (like Aesop's "The Fox and the Grapes" or "The Ant and the Grasshopper"). In what ways do they differ? What does the difference say about our world? Formulate the story's theme in terms of this difference.
3. Published in 1939, on the eve of World War II, the story could be seen to have political significance. How so?

Writing Assignments

1. In a paragraph, compare and contrast Thurber's story with a traditional fable. What are their similarities? How do they differ? What theme does the difference suggest?
2. In a paragraph or two, discuss the owl as fascist dictator (Mussolini, for example). How is the owl described so as to make us think of such a leader? What is the point of the allusion?
3. Write an informational paragraph on the political situation of Europe in the 1930s. (You might have to do some research here.) Then, in a separate paragraph, relate your information to "The Owl Who Was God."

THE UNICORN IN THE GARDEN

✳ JAMES THURBER ✳

Once upon a sunny morning a man who sat in a breakfast nook looked up from his scrambled eggs to see a white unicorn with a golden horn quietly cropping roses in the garden. The man went up to the bedroom where his wife was still asleep and woke her. "There's a unicorn in the garden," he said. "Eating roses." She opened one unfriendly eye and looked at him. "The unicorn is a mythical beast," she said, and turned her back on him. The man walked slowly downstairs and out into the garden. The unicorn was still there; he was now browsing among the tulips. "Here, unicorn," said the man, and he pulled up a lily and gave it to him. The unicorn ate it gravely. With a high heart, because there was a unicorn in his garden, the man went upstairs and roused his wife again. "The unicorn ate a lily," he said. His wife sat up in bed and looked at him coldly. "You are a booby," she said, "and I am going to have you put in the booby hatch." The man, who had never liked the words "booby" and "booby hatch," and who liked them even less on a shining morning when there was a unicorn in the garden, thought for a moment. "We'll see about that," he said. He walked over to the door. "He has a golden horn in the middle of his forehead," he told her. Then he went back to the garden to watch the unicorn, but the unicorn had gone away. The man sat down among the roses and went to sleep.

As soon as the husband had gone out of the house, the wife got up and dressed as fast as she could. She was very excited and there was a gloat in her eye. She telephoned the police and she telephoned a psychiatrist; she told them to hurry to her house and bring a strait jacket. When the police and the psychiatrist arrived, they sat down in chairs and looked at her with great interest. "My husband," she said, "saw a unicorn this morning." The police looked at the psychiatrist and the psychiatrist looked at the police. "He told me it ate a lily," she said. The psychiatrist looked at the police and the police looked at the psychiatrist. "He told me it had a golden horn in the middle of its forehead," she said. At a solemn signal from the psychiatrist, the police leaped from their chairs and seized the wife. They had a hard time subduing her, for she put up a terrific struggle, but they finally subdued her. Just as they got her into the strait jacket, her husband came back into the house. "Did you tell your wife you saw a unicorn?" asked the psychiatrist. "Of course not," said the husband. "The unicorn is a mythical beast." "That's all I wanted to know," said the psychiatrist. "Take her away. I'm sorry, sir, but your wife is as crazy as a jay bird." So they took her away, cursing and screaming, and shut her up in an institution. The husband lived happily ever after.

Moral: Don't count your boobies until they are hatched.

[1939—U.S.A.]

Questions

1. Contrast the husband and wife.
2. How does Thurber keep us from sympathizing with the wife, whose mood at the end of the story is certainly different from the mood induced in the reader?
3. Why are the characters not named?
4. The "moral" appended here is clearly bogus. What, then, is the story's theme? What general point does it comically make regarding the sexes and especially marriage?

Writing Assignments

1. Write a paragraph in which you contrast Thurber's husband and wife. How do they differ? How does this difference make their conflict seem inevitable? How does Thurber turn all of this to comedy?
2. In a paragraph, state and discuss the theme of "The Unicorn in the Garden." Is it dated, or does the story still have something to say about the tensions of marriage? Defend your judgment.

THE DOCTOR'S HEROISM

❖ VILLIERS DE L'ISLE-ADAM ❖

Translated by Roger B. Goodman

To kill in order to cure!
—Official Motto of the Broussais Hospital

The extraordinary case of Doctor Hallidonhill is soon to be tried in London. The facts in the matter are these:

On the 20th of last May, the two great waiting rooms of the illustrious specialist were thronged with patients, holding their tickets in their hands.

At the entrance stood the cashier, wearing a long black frock coat; he took the indispensible fee of two guineas from each patient, tested the gold with a sharp tap of the hammer, and cried automatically, "All right."

In his glassed-in office, around which were ranged great tropical shrubs, each growing in a huge Japanese pot, sat the stiff little Doctor Hallidonhill. Beside him, at a little round table, his secretary kept writing out brief prescriptions. At the swinging doors, covered with red velvet studded with gold-headed nails, stood a giant valet whose duty it was to carry the feeble consumptives to the lobby whence they were lowered in a luxurious elevator as soon as the official signal, "Next!" had been given.

The patients entered with dim and glassy eyes, stripped to the waist, with their clothes thrown over their arms. As soon as they entered they received the application of the plessimeter and the tube on back and chest.

"Tick! tick! plaff! Breathe now! . . . Plaff . . . Good . . ."

Then followed a prescription dictated in a second or two; then the well-known "Next!"

Every morning for three years, between nine o'clock and noon, this procession of sufferers filed past.

On this particular day, May 20th, just at the stroke of nine, a sort of long skeleton, with wild, wandering eyes, cavernous cheeks, and nude torso that looked like a parchment-covered cage lifted occasionally by a racking cough—in short a being so wasted that it seemed impossible for him to live—came in with a blue-fox skin mantle thrown over his arm, and tried to keep himself from falling by catching at the long leaves of the shrubs.

"Tick, tick, plaff! Oh, the devil! Can't do anything for you!" grumbled Doctor Hallidonhill. "What do you think I am—a coroner? In less than a week you will spit up the last cell of this left lung—the right is already riddled like a sieve! Next!"

The valet was just about to carry out the client, when the eminent therapeutist suddenly slapped himself on the forehead, and brusquely asked, with a dubious smile:

"Are you rich?"

"I'm a millionaire—much more than a millionaire," sobbed the unhappy being whom Hallidonhill thus peremptorily had dismissed from the world of the living.

"Very well, then. Go at once to Victoria Station. Take the eleven-o'clock express for Dover! Then the steamer for Calais. Then take the train from Calais to Marseilles—secure a sleeping car with steam in it! And then to Nice. There try to live on watercress for six months—nothing but watercress—no bread, no fruit, no wine, nor meats of any kind. One teaspoonful of iodized rainwater every two days. And watercress, watercress, watercress—pounded and brayed in its own juice . . . that is your only chance—and still, let me tell you this: this supposed cure I know of only through hearsay; it is being dinned into my ears all the time; I don't believe in it the least bit. I suggest it only because yours seems to be a hopeless case, yet I think it is worse than absurd. Still, anything is possible. . . . Next!"

The consumptive Croesus was carefully deposited in the cushioned car of the elevator; and the regular procession commenced through the office.

Six months later, the 3rd of November, just at the stroke of nine o'clock, a sort of giant, with a terrifying yet jovial voice whose tones shook every pane of glass in the doctor's office and set all the leaves of all the tropical plants a-tremble, a great chubby-cheeked colossus, clothed in rich furs—burst like a human bombshell through the sorrowful ranks of Doctor Hallidonhill's clients, and rushed, without ticket, into the sanctum of the Prince of Science, who had just come to sit down before his desk. He seized him round the body, and, bathing the wan and worn cheeks of the doctor in tears, kissed him noisily again and again. Then he set him down in his green armchair in an almost suffocated state.

"Two million francs—if you want," shouted the giant. "Or three million. I owe my breath to you—the sun, resistless passions, life—everything. Ask me for anything—anything at all."

"Who is this madman? Put him out of here," feebly protested the doctor, after a moment's prostration.

"Oh, no you don't," growled the giant, with a glance at the valet that made him recoil as from a blow. "The fact is," he continued, "I understand now, that even you, you my savior, cannot recognize me. I am the watercress man, the hopeless skeleton, the helpless patient. Nice. Watercress, watercress, watercress! Well, I've done my six months of watercress diet—look at your work now! See here—listen to that!"

And he began to drum upon his chest with two huge fists solid enough to shatter the skull of an ox.

"What!" cried the doctor, leaping to his feet, "you are—my gracious, are you the dying man whom I . . ."

"Yes, yes, a thousand times yes!" yelled the giant. "I am the very man. The moment I landed yesterday evening I ordered a bronze statue of you; and I will secure you a monument in Westminster when you die."

Then dropping himself upon an immense sofa, whose springs creaked and groaned beneath his weight, he continued with a sigh of delight, and a beatific smile:

"Ah, what a good thing life is!"

The doctor said something in a whisper, and the secretary and the valet left the room. Once alone with his resuscitated patient, Hallidonhill, stiff, wan and glacial as ever, stared at the giant's face in silence for a minute or two. Then, suddenly:

"Allow me, if you please, to take that fly off your forehead!"

And rushing forward as he spoke, the doctor pulled a short "Bulldog revolver" from his pocket, and quick as a flash fired into the left temple of the visitor.

The giant fell with his skull shattered, scattering his grateful brains over the carpet of the room. His hands thrashed automatically for a few moments.

In ten cuts of the doctor's scissors, through cloak, garments, and underwear, the dead man's breast was laid bare. The grave surgeon cut open the chest lengthwise, with a single stroke of his broad scalpel.

When, about a quarter of an hour later, a policeman entered the office to request Doctor Hallidonhill to go with him, he found him sitting calmly at his bloody desk, examining with a strong magnifying glass, an enormous pair of lungs that lay spread out before him. The Genius of Science was trying to find, from the case of the deceased, some satisfactory explanation of the more than miraculous action of water-cress.

"Constable," he said as he rose to his feet, "I felt it necessary to kill that man, as an immediate autopsy of his case might, I thought, reveal to me a secret of the gravest importance, regarding the now degenerating vitality of the human species. That is why I did not hesitate, let me confess, *to sacrifice my conscience to my duty.*"

Needless to add that the illustrious doctor was almost immediately released upon a nominal bond, his liberty being of far more importance than his detention. This strange case, as I have said, is shortly to come up before the British Assizes.

We believe that this sublime crime will not bring its hero to the gallows; for the English, as well as ourselves, are fully able to comprehend *that the exclusive love of the Humanity of the Future without any regard for the individual of the Present is, in our own time, the one sole motive that ought to justify the acquittal under any circumstances, of the magnanimous Extremists of Science.*

[1890—France]

Questions

1. Though written by a Frenchman, the story is laid in England. Why?
2. Doctor Hallidonhill's motivation is not narrowly selfish, for he stands to gain much from his living client. Is his motivation truly humanitarian, however? Are duty and conscience really at odds? Does the way in which the doctor is depicted help sway us toward an answer?
3. The theme of the story entails the values of science and scientists. Does it expose some flaw in scientific valuation?
4. Does the attitude of the narrator in the final paragraph coincide with that implied by the story as a whole? Why or why not?

Writing Assignments

1. Modern medicine is scientific. But does that mean that it is good medicine? Could humanity and science be at odds? Taking the present story as example, write a paragraph on how modern scientific medicine does not always meet the needs of individual patients.
2. Discuss the theme of this story as it relates to contemporary science generally. In its quest for knowledge, has our science possibly forgotten the purpose of rational inquiry? Give examples both from the story and from the contemporary world of how this might be so.

ON THE ROAD

 ❉ LANGSTON HUGHES ❉

He was not interested in the snow. When he got off the freight, one early evening during the depression, Sargeant never even noticed the snow. But he must have felt it seeping down his neck, cold, wet, sopping in his shoes. But if you had asked him, he wouldn't have known it was snowing. Sargeant didn't see the snow, not even under the bright lights of the main street, falling white and flaky against the night. He was too hungry, too sleepy, too tired.

The Reverend Mr. Dorset, however, saw the snow when he switched on his porch light, opened the front door of his parsonage, and found standing there before him a big black man with snow on his face, a human piece of night with snow on his face—obviously unemployed.

Said the Reverend Mr. Dorset before Sargeant even realized he'd opened his mouth: "I'm sorry. No! Go right on down this street four blocks and turn to your left, walk up seven and you'll see the Relief Shelter. I'm sorry. No!" He shut the door.

Sargeant wanted to tell the holy man that he had already been to the Relief Shelter, been to hundreds of relief shelters during the depression years, the beds were always gone and supper was over, the place was full, and they drew the color line anyhow. But the minister said, "No," and shut the door. Evidently he didn't want to hear about it. And he *had* a door to shut.

The big black man turned away. And even yet he didn't see the snow, walking right into it. Maybe he sensed it, cold, wet, sticking to his jaws, wet on his black hands, sopping in his shoes. He stopped and stood on the sidewalk hunched over—hungry, sleepy, cold—looking up and down. Then he looked right where he was—in front of a church. Of course! A church! Sure, right next to a parsonage, certainly a church.

It had *two* doors.

Broad white steps in the night all snowy white. Two high arched doors with slender stone pillars on either side. And way up, a round lacy window with a stone crucifix in the middle and Christ on the crucifix in stone. All this was pale in the street lights, solid and stony pale in the snow.

Sargeant blinked. When he looked up, the snow fell into his eyes. For the first time that night he *saw* the snow. He shook his head. He shook the snow from his coat sleeves, felt hungry, felt lost, felt not lost, felt cold. He walked up the steps of the church. He knocked at the door. No answer. He tried the handle. Locked. He put his shoulder against the door and his long black body slanted like a ramrod. He pushed. With loud rhythmic grunts, like the grunts in a chain-gang song, he pushed against the door.

"I'm tired . . . Huh! . . . Hongry . . . Uh! . . . I'm sleepy . . . Huh! I'm cold . . . I got to sleep somewheres," Sargeant said. "This here is a church, ain't it? Well, uh!"

He pushed against the door.

Suddenly, with an undue cracking and screaking, the door began to give way to the tall black Negro who pushed ferociously against it.

By now two or three white people had stopped in the street, and Sargeant was vaguely aware of some of them yelling at him concerning the door. Three or four more came running, yelling at him.

"Hey!"

"Uh-huh," answered the big tall Negro, "I know it's a white folks' church, but I got to sleep somewhere." He gave another lunge at the door. "Huh!"

And the door broke open.

But just when the door gave way, two white cops arrived in a car, ran up the steps with their clubs, and grabbed Sargeant. But Sargeant for once had no intention of being pulled or pushed away from the door.

Sargeant grabbed, but not for anything so weak as a broken door. He grabbed for one of the tall stone pillars beside the door, grabbed at it and caught it. And held it. The cops pulled and Sargeant pulled. Most of the people in the street got behind the cops and helped them pull.

"A big black unemployed Negro holding onto our church!" thought the people. "The idea!"

The cops began to beat Sargeant over the head, and nobody protested. But he held on.

And then the church fell down.

Gradually, the big stone front of the church fell down, the walls and the rafters, the crucifix and the Christ. Then the whole thing fell down, covering the cops and the people with bricks and stones and debris. The whole church fell down in the snow.

Sargeant got out from under the church and went walking on up the street with the stone pillar on his shoulder. He was under the impression that he had buried the parsonage and the Reverend Mr. Dorset who said, "No!" So he laughed, and threw the pillar six blocks up the street and went on.

Sargeant thought he was alone, but listening to the *crunch, crunch, crunch* on the snow of his own footsteps, he heard other footsteps, too, doubling his own. He looked around, and there was Christ walking along beside him, the same Christ that had been on the cross on the church—still stone with a rough stone surface, walking along beside him just like he was broken off the cross when the church fell down.

"Well, I'll be dogged," said Sargeant. "This here's the first time I ever seed you off the cross."

"Yes," said Christ, crunching his feet in the snow. "You had to pull the church down to get me off the cross."

"You glad?" said Sargeant.

"I sure am," said Christ.

They both laughed.

"I'm a hell of a fellow, ain't I?" said Sargeant. "Done pulled the church down!"

"You did a good job," said Christ. "They have kept me nailed on a cross for nearly two thousand years."

"Whee-ee-e!" said Sargeant. "I know you are glad to get off."

"I sure am," said Christ.

They walked on in the snow. Sargeant looked at the man of stone.

"And you have been up there two thousand years?"

"I sure have," Christ said.

"Well, if I had a little cash," said Sargeant, "I'd show you around a bit."

"I been around," said Christ.

"Yeah, but that was a long time ago."

"All the same," said Christ, "I've been around."

They walked on in the snow until they came to the railroad yards. Sargeant was tired, sweating and tired.

"Where you goin'?" Sargeant said, stopping by the tracks. He looked at Christ. Sargeant said, "I'm just a bum on the road. How about you? Where you goin'?"

"God knows," Christ said, "but I'm leavin' here."

They saw the red and green lights of the railroad yard half veiled by the snow that fell out of the night. Away down the track they saw a fire in a hobo jungle.

"I can go there and sleep," Sargeant said.

"You can?"

"Sure," said Sargeant. "That place ain't got no doors."

Outside the town, along the tracks, there were barren trees and bushes below the embankment, snow-gray in the dark. And down among the trees and bushes there were makeshift houses made out of boxes and tin and old pieces of wood and canvas. You couldn't see them in the dark, but you knew they were there if you'd ever been on the road, if you had ever lived with the homeless and hungry in a depression.

"I'm side-tracking," Sargeant said. "I'm tired."

"I'm gonna make it on to Kansas City," said Christ.

"O.K.," Sargeant said. "So long!"

He went down into the hobo jungle and found himself a place to sleep. He never did see Christ no more. About 6:00 A.M. a freight came by. Sargeant scrambled out of the jungle with a dozen or so more hobos and ran along the track, grabbing at the freight. It was dawn, early dawn, cold and gray.

"Wonder where Christ is by now?" Sargeant thought. "He musta gone on way on down the road. He didn't sleep in this jungle."

Sargeant grabbed the train and started to pull himself up into a moving coal car, over the edge of a wheeling coal car. But strangely enough, the car was full of cops. The nearest cop rapped Sargeant soundly across the knuckles with his night stick. Wham! Rapped his big black hands for clinging to the top of the car. Wham! but Sargeant did not turn loose. He clung on and tried to pull himself into the car. He hollered at the top of his voice, "Damn it, lemme in this car!"

"Shut up," barked the cop. "You crazy coon!" He rapped Sargeant across the knuckles and punched him in the stomach. "You ain't out in no jungle now. This ain't no train. You in jail."

Wham! across his bare black fingers clinging to the bars of his cell. Wham! between the steel bars low down against his shins.

Suddenly Sargeant realized that he really was in jail. He wasn't on no train. The blood of the night before had dried on his face, his head hurt terribly, and a cop outside in the corridor was hitting him across the knuckles for holding onto the door, yelling and shaking the cell door.

"They musta took me to jail for breaking down the door last night," Sargeant thought, "that church door."

Sargeant went over and sat on a wooden bench against the cold stone wall. He was emptier than ever. His clothes were wet, clammy cold wet, and shoes sloppy with snow water. It was just about dawn. There he was, locked up behind a cell door, nursing his bruised fingers.

The bruised fingers were his, but not the *door.*

Not the *club,* but the fingers.

"You wait," mumbled Sargeant, black against the jail wall. "I'm gonna break down this door, too."

"Shut up—or I'll paste you one," said the cop.

"I'm gonna break down this door," yelled Sargeant as he stood up in his cell.

Then he must have been talking to himself because he said, "I wonder where Christ's gone? I wonder if he's gone to Kansas City?"

[1935—U.S.A.]

Questions

1. What does Hughes's title make you think of? In what way does it apply to Christ?
2. What biblical hero does Sargeant become in his fantasy? Who, then, must the townspeople be? What comment does Sargeant's fantasy make on the town and its people?
3. What is the significance of what happens to Christ in Sargeant's fantasy? Why does Christ intend to leave town?
4. Sargeant's question as to "where Christ's gone" summarizes in brief the thematic content of "On the Road." How so? How would you articulate its theme?

Writing Assignments

1. Do some research into the social conditions of blacks in this country in the 1930s. Then write an informational paragraph aimed at providing background for and thereby shedding light on Hughes's story.
2. Read Judges 16 in the Old Testament. Then write a paragraph addressing question 2 above. Point out specifically how Hughes draws the parallel between Sargeant and the biblical hero in question. Go on to discuss the significance of the whole biblical account to what Hughes is saying about the town in his story and generally about American life in his day.

SWADDLING CLOTHES

—❋ YUKIO MISHIMA ❋—

Translated by Ivan Morris

He was always busy, Toshiko's husband. Even tonight he had to dash off to an appointment, leaving her to go home alone by taxi. But what else could a woman expect when she married an actor—an attractive one? No doubt she had been foolish to hope that he would spend the evening with her. And yet he must have known how she dreaded going back to their house, unhomely with its Western-style furniture and with the bloodstains still showing on the floor.

Toshiko had been oversensitive since girlhood: that was her nature. As the result of constant worrying she never put on weight, and now, an adult woman, she looked more like a transparent picture than a creature of flesh and blood. Her delicacy of spirit was evident to her most casual acquaintance.

Earlier that evening, when she had joined her husband at a night club, she had been shocked to find him entertaining friends with an account of "the incident." Sitting there in his American-style suit, puffing at a cigarette, he had seemed to her almost a stranger.

"It's a fantastic story," he was saying, gesturing flamboyantly as if in an attempt to outweigh the attractions of the dance band. "Here this new nurse for our baby arrives from the employment agency, and the very first thing I notice about her is her stomach. It's enormous—as if she had a pillow stuck under her kimono! No wonder, I thought, for I soon saw that she could eat more than the rest of us put together. She polished off the contents of our rice bin like that. . . ." He snapped his fingers. " 'Gastric dilation'—that's how she explained her girth and her appetite. Well, the day before yesterday we heard groans and moans coming from the nursery. We rushed in and found her squatting on the floor, holding her stomach in her two hands, and moaning like a cow. Next to her our baby lay in his cot, scared out of his wits and crying at the top of his lungs. A pretty scene, I can tell you!"

"So the cat was out of the bag?" suggested one of their friends, a film actor like Toshiko's husband.

"Indeed it was! And it gave me the shock of my life. You see, I'd completely swallowed that story about 'gastric dilation.' Well, I didn't waste any time. I rescued our good rug from the floor and spread a blanket for her to lie on. The whole time the girl was yelling like a stuck pig. By the time the doctor from the maternity clinic arrived, the baby had already been born. But our sitting room was a pretty shambles!"

"Oh, that I'm sure of!" said another of their friends, and the whole company burst into laughter.

Toshiko was dumbfounded to hear her husband discussing the horrifying happening as though it were no more than an amusing incident which they chanced to have witnessed. She shut her eyes for a moment and all at once she saw the newborn baby lying before her: on the parquet floor the infant lay, and his frail body was wrapped in bloodstained newspapers.

Toshiko was sure that the doctor had done the whole thing out of spite. As if to emphasize his scorn for this mother who had given birth to a bastard under such sordid conditions, he had told his assistant to wrap the baby in some loose newspapers, rather than proper swaddling. This callous treatment of the newborn child had offended Toshiko. Overcoming her disgust at the entire scene, she had fetched a brand-new piece of flannel from her cupboard and, having swaddled the baby in it, had laid him carefully in an armchair.

This all had taken place in the evening after her husband had left the house. Toshiko had told him nothing of it, fearing that he would think her oversoft, oversentimental; yet the scene had engraved itself deeply in her mind. Tonight she sat silently thinking back on it, while the jazz orchestra brayed and her husband chatted cheerfully with his friends. She knew that she would never forget the sight of the baby, wrapped in stained newspapers and lying on the floor—it was a scene fit for a butchershop. Toshiko, whose own life had been spent in solid comfort, poignantly felt the wretchedness of the illegitimate baby.

I am the only person to have witnessed its shame, the thought occurred to her. The mother never saw her child lying there in its newspaper wrappings, and the baby itself of course didn't know. I alone shall have to preserve that terrible scene in my memory. When the baby grows up and wants to find out about his birth, there will be no one to tell him, so long as I preserve silence. How strange that I should have this feeling of guilt! After all, it was I who took him up from the floor, swathed him properly in flannel, and laid him down to sleep in the armchair.

They left the night club and Toshiko stepped into the taxi that her husband had called for her. "Take this lady to Ushigomé," he told the driver and shut the door from the outside. Toshiko gazed through the window at her husband's smiling face and noticed his strong, white teeth. Then she leaned back in the seat, oppressed by the knowledge that their life together was in some way too easy, too painless. It would have been difficult for her to put her thoughts into words. Through the rear window of the taxi she took a last look at her husband. He was striding along the street toward his Nash car, and soon the back of his rather garish tweed coat had blended with the figures of the passers-by.

The taxi drove off, passed down a street dotted with bars and then by a theatre, in front of which the throngs of people jostled each other on the pavement. Although the performance had only just ended, the lights had already been turned out and in the half dark outside it was depressingly obvious that the cherry blossoms decorating the front of the theatre were merely scraps of white paper.

Even if that baby should grow up in ignorance of the secret of his birth, he can never become a respectable citizen, reflected Toshiko, pursuing the same train of thoughts. Those soiled newspaper swaddling clothes will be the symbol of his entire life. But why should I keep worrying about him so much? Is it because I feel uneasy about the future of my own child? Say twenty years from now, when our boy will have grown up into a fine, carefully educated young man, one day by a quirk of fate he meets that other boy, who then will also have turned twenty. And say that the other boy, who has been sinned against, savagely stabs him with a knife. . . .

It was a warm, overcast April night, but thoughts of the future made Toshiko feel cold and miserable. She shivered on the back seat of the car.

No, when the time comes I shall take my son's place, she told herself suddenly. Twenty years from now I shall be forty-three. I shall go to that young man and tell him straight out about everything—about his newspaper swaddling clothes, and about how I went and wrapped him in flannel.

The taxi ran along the dark wide road that was bordered by the park and by the Imperial Palace moat. In the distance Toshiko noticed the pinpricks of light which came from the block of tall office buildings.

Twenty years from now that wretched child will be in utter misery. He will be living a desolate, hopeless, poverty-stricken existence—a lonely rat. What else could happen to a baby who has had such a birth? He'll be wandering through the streets by himself, cursing his father, loathing his mother.

No doubt Toshiko derived a certain satisfaction from her somber thoughts: she tortured herself with them without cease. The taxi approached Hanzomon and drove past the compound of the British Embassy. At that point the famous rows of cherry trees were spread out before Toshiko in all their purity. On the spur of the moment she decided to go and view the blossoms by herself in the dark night. It was a strange decision for a timid and unadventurous young woman, but then she was in a strange state of mind and she dreaded the return home. That evening all sorts of unsettling fancies had burst open in her mind.

She crossed the wide street—a slim, solitary figure in the darkness. As a rule when she walked in the traffic Toshiko used to cling fearfully to her companion, but tonight she darted alone between the cars and a moment later had reached the long narrow park that borders the Palace moat. Chidorigafuchi, it is called—the Abyss of the Thousand Birds.

Tonight the whole park had become a grove of blossoming cherry trees. Under the calm cloudy sky the blossoms formed a mass of solid whiteness. The paper lanterns that hung from wires between the trees had been put out; in their place electric light bulbs, red, yellow, and green, shone dully beneath the blossoms. It was well past ten o'clock and most of the flower-viewers had gone home. As the occasional passers-by strolled through the park, they would automatically kick aside the empty bottles or crush the waste paper beneath their feet.

Newspapers, thought Toshiko, her mind going back once again to those happenings. Bloodstained newspapers. If a man were ever to hear of that piteous birth and know that it was he who had lain there, it would ruin his entire life. To think that I, a perfect stranger, should from now on have to keep such a secret—the secret of a man's whole existence. . . .

Lost in these thoughts, Toshiko walked on through the park. Most of the people still remaining there were quiet couples; no one paid her any attention. She noticed two people sitting on a stone bench beside the moat, not looking at the blossoms, but gazing silently at the water. Pitch black it was, and swathed in heavy shadows. Beyond the moat the somber forest of the Imperial Palace blocked her view. The trees reached up, to form a solid dark mass against the night sky. Toshiko walked slowly along the path beneath the blossoms hanging heavily overhead.

On a stone bench, slightly apart from the others, she noticed a pale object—not, as she had at first imagined, a pile of cherry blossoms, nor a garment forgotten by one of the visitors to the park. Only when she came closer did she see that it was a human form lying on the bench. Was it, she wondered, one of those miserable drunks often to be seen sleeping in public places? Obviously not, for the body had been systematically covered with newspapers, and it was the whiteness of those papers that had attracted Toshiko's attention. Standing by the bench, she gazed down at the sleeping figure.

It was a man in a brown jersey who lay there, curled up on layers of newspapers, other newspapers covering him. No doubt this had become his normal night residence now that spring had arrived. Toshiko gazed down at the man's dirty, unkempt hair, which in places had become hopelessly matted. As she observed the sleeping figure wrapped in its newspapers, she was inevitably reminded of the baby who had lain on the floor in its wretched swaddling clothes. The shoulder of the man's jersey rose and fell in the darkness in time with his heavy breathing.

It seemed to Toshiko that all her fears and premonitions had suddenly taken concrete form. In the darkness the man's pale forehead stood out, and it was a young forehead, though carved with the wrinkles of long poverty and hardship. His khaki trousers had been slightly pulled up; on his sockless feet he wore a pair of battered gym shoes. She could not see his face and suddenly had an overmastering desire to get one glimpse of it.

She walked to the head of the bench and looked down. The man's head was half buried in his arms, but Toshiko could see that he was surprisingly young. She noticed the thick eyebrows and the fine bridge of his nose. His slightly open mouth was alive with youth.

But Toshiko had approached too close. In the silent night the newspaper bedding rustled, and abruptly the man opened his eyes. Seeing the young woman standing directly beside him, he raised himself with a jerk, and his eyes lit up. A second later a powerful hand reached out and seized Toshiko by her slender wrist.

She did not feel in the least afraid and made no effort to free herself. In a flash the thought had struck her, Ah, so the twenty years have already gone by! The forest of the Imperial Palace was pitch dark and utterly silent.

[1966—Japan]

Questions

1. What is the import of the many references to the West: for example, "Western-style furniture," "his American-style suit," "block of tall office buildings," "the British Embassy"? In what way is the fact that Toshiko's husband is a "film actor" significant?
2. What does Toshiko's finding the incident with the baby a "horrifying happening" but her husband's finding it "no more than an amusing incident" reveal about each? What does the implied difference in their feelings about their furniture reveal? What values or ways of seeing, then, does each represent? Toward which would the story sway us?
3. Why is Toshiko so moved and upset by the baby's being wrapped in newspaper? What is the origin of her guilt? Why should her "somber thoughts" give her "a certain satisfaction"?
4. With its cherry trees and proximity to the "Palace moat" and "somber forest of the Imperial Palace," what does the park represent to Toshiko? Why does she come here? Might she have some unconscious motive?
5. The end of "Swaddling Clothes" could be read as realistic or as surrealistic. How so? In either case, it is also symbolic, as is the story as a whole. What symbolic statement does "Swaddling Clothes" make? What is its general theme?

Writing Assignments

1. Write a discrete paragraph in which you contrast Toshiko and her husband. Establish the contrast with reference to the story's details (see the first and second questions above); then conclude with a consideration of what each represents in the world of Mishima's story and how the contrast points to the story's theme.
2. To a greater or lesser extent, we are all culture-bound. In a short analytic essay, consider how we humans define ourselves in accordance with the culture each of us is born into. As you conclude, suggest to what extent we are free agents and to what we are tied to the definitions, biases, and so forth of our cultural backgrounds.
3. And what of you in this regard? Write a paragraph about your own cultural background and how it has shaped the person you are.

JUST LATHER, THAT'S ALL

 HERNANDO TELLEZ

Translated by Angel Flores

He said nothing when he entered. I was passing the best of my razors back and forth on a strop. When I recognized him I started to tremble. But he didn't notice. Hoping to conceal my emotion, I continued sharpening the razor. I tested it on the meat of my thumb, and then held it up to the light. At that moment he took off the bullet-studded belt that his gun holster dangled from. He hung it up on a wall hook and placed his military cap over it. Then he turned to me, loosening the knot of his tie, and said, "It's hot as hell. Give me a shave." He sat in the chair.

I estimated he had a four-day beard. The four days taken up by the latest expedition in search of our troops. His face seemed reddened, burned by the sun. Carefully, I began to prepare the soap. I cut off a few slices, dropped them into the cup, mixed in a bit of warm water, and began to stir with the brush. Immediately the foam began to rise. "The other boys in the group should have this much beard, too." I continued stirring the lather.

"But we did all right, you know. We got the main ones. We brought back some dead, and we've got some others still alive. But pretty soon they'll all be dead."

"How many did you catch?" I asked.

"Fourteen. We had to go pretty deep into the woods to find them. But we'll get even. Not one of them comes out of this alive, not one."

He leaned back on the chair when he saw me with the lather-covered brush in my hand. I still had to put the sheet on him. No doubt about it, I was upset. I took a sheet out of a drawer and knotted it around my customer's neck. He wouldn't stop talking. He probably thought I was in sympathy with his party.

"The town must have learned a lesson from what we did the other day," he said.

"Yes," I replied, securing the knot at the base of his dark, sweaty neck.

"That was a fine show, eh?"

"Very good," I answered, turning back for the brush. The man closed his eyes with a gesture of fatigue and sat waiting for the cool caress of the soap. I had never had him so close to me. The day he ordered the whole town to file into the patio of the school to see the four rebels hanging there, I came face to face with him for an instant. But the sight of the mutilated bodies kept me from noticing the face of the man who had directed it all, the face I was now about to take into my hands. It was not an unpleasant face, certainly. And the beard, which made him seem a bit older than he was, didn't suit him badly at all. His name was Torres. Captain Torres. A man of imagination, because who else would have thought of hanging the naked rebels and then holding target practice on certain parts of their bodies? I began to apply the first layer of soap. With his eyes closed, he continued. "Without any effort I could go straight to sleep," he said, "but there's plenty to do this afternoon." I stopped the lathering and asked with a feigned lack of interest: "A firing squad?" "Something like that, but a little slower." I got on with the job of lathering his beard. My hands started trembling again. The man could not possibly realize it, and this was in my favor. But I would have preferred that he hadn't come. It was likely that many of our faction had seen him enter. And an enemy under one's roof imposes certain conditions. I would be obliged to shave that beard like any other one, carefully, gently, like that of any customer, taking pains to see that no single pore emitted a drop of blood. Being careful to see that the little tufts of hair did not lead the blade astray. Seeing that his skin ended up clean, soft, and healthy, so that passing the back of my hand over it I couldn't feel a hair. Yes, I was secretly a rebel, but I was also a conscientious barber, and proud of the preciseness of my profession. And this four-days' growth of beard was a fitting challenge.

I took the razor, opened up the two protective arms, exposed the blade and began the job, from one of the sideburns downward. The razor responded beautifully. His beard was inflexible and hard, not too long, but thick. Bit by bit the skin emerged. The razor rasped along, making its customary sound as fluffs of lather mixed with bits of hair gathered along the blade. I paused a moment to clean it, then took up the strop again to sharpen the razor, because I'm a barber who does things properly. The man, who had kept his eyes closed, opened them now, removed one of his hands from under the sheet, felt the spot on his face where the soap had been cleared off, and said, "Come to the school today at six o'clock." "The same thing as the other day?" I asked horrified. "It could be better," he replied. "What do you plan to do?" "I don't know yet. But we'll amuse ourselves." Once more he leaned back and closed his eyes. I approached him with the razor poised. "Do you plan to punish them all?" I ventured timidly. "All." The soap was drying on his face. I had to hurry. In the mirror I looked toward the street. It was the same as ever: the grocery store with two or three customers in it. Then I glanced at the clock: two-twenty in the afternoon. The razor continued on its downward stroke. Now from the other sideburn down. A thick, blue beard. He should have let it grow like some poets or priests do. It would suit him well. A lot of people wouldn't recognize him. Much to his benefit, I thought, as I attempted to cover the neck area smoothly. There, for sure, the razor had to be handled masterfully, since the hair, although softer, grew into little swirls. A curly beard. One of the tiny pores could be opened up and issue forth its pearl of blood. A good barber such as I prides himself on never allowing this to happen to a client. And this was a first-class client. How many of us had he ordered shot? How many of us had he ordered mutilated? It was better not to think about it. Torres did not know that I was his enemy. He did not know it nor did the rest. It was a secret shared by very few, precisely so that I could inform the revolutionaries of what Torres was doing in the town and of what he was planning each time he undertook a rebel-hunting excursion. So it was going to be very difficult to explain that I had him right in my hands and let him go peacefully—alive and shaved.

The beard was now almost completely gone. He seemed younger, less burdened by years than when he had arrived. I suppose this always happens with men who visit barber shops. Under the stroke of my razor Torres was being rejuvenated—rejuvenated because I am a good barber, the best in the town, if I may say so. A little more lather here, under his chin, on his Adam's apple, on this big vein. How hot it is getting! Torres must be sweating as much as I. But he is not afraid. He is a calm man, who is not even thinking about what he is going to do with the prisoners this afternoon. On the other hand I, with this razor in my hands, stroking and restroking this skin, trying to keep blood from oozing from these pores, can't even think clearly. Damn him for coming, because I'm a revolutionary and not a murderer. And how easy it would be to kill him. And he deserves it. Does he? No! What the devil! No one deserves to have someone else make the sacrifice of becoming a murderer. What do you gain by it? Nothing. Others come along and still others, and the first ones kill the second ones and they the next ones and it goes on like this until everything is a sea of blood. I could cut this throat just so, zip! zip! I wouldn't give him time to complain and since he has his eyes closed he wouldn't see the glistening knife blade or my glistening eyes. But I'm trembling like a real murderer. Out of his neck a gush of blood would spout onto the sheet, on the chair, on my hands, on the floor. I would have to close the door. And the blood would keep inching along the floor, warm, ineradicable, uncontainable, until it reached the street, like a little scarlet stream. I'm sure that one solid stroke, one deep incision, would prevent any pain. He wouldn't suffer. But what would I do with the body? Where would I hide it? I would have to flee, leaving all I have behind, and take refuge far away, far, far away. But they would follow until they found me. "Captain Torres' murderer. He slit his throat while he was shaving him—a coward." And then on the other side. "The avenger of us all. A name to remember. (And here they would mention my name.) He was the town barber. No one knew he was defending our cause."

And what of all this? Murderer or hero? My destiny depends on the edge of this blade. I can turn my hand a bit more, press a little harder on the razor, and sink it in. The skin would give way like silk, like rubber, like the strop. There is nothing more tender than human skin and the blood is always there, ready to pour forth. A blade like this doesn't fail. It is my best. But I don't want to be a murderer, no sir. You come to me for a shave. And I perform my work honorably. . . . I don't want blood on my hands. Just lather, that's all. You are an executioner and I am only a barber. Each person has his own place in the scheme of things. That's right. His own place.

Now his chin had been stroked clean and smooth. The man sat up and looked into the mirror. He rubbed his hands over his skin and felt it fresh, like new.

"Thanks," he said. He went to the hanger for his belt, pistol and cap. I must have been very pale; my shirt felt soaked. Torres finished adjusting the buckle, straightened his pistol in the holster and after automatically smoothing down his hair, he put on the cap. From his pants pocket he took out several coins to pay me for my services. And he began to head toward the door. In the doorway he paused for a moment, and turning to me he said:

"They told me that you'd kill me. I came to find out. But killing isn't easy. You can take my word for it." And he headed on down the street.

[1950—Colombia]

Questions

1. Is it meaningful that we are not told where (that is, in what country) the story takes place or what the political issues are and what has caused the revolution? How so?
2. The conflict and drama here are entirely internal. What obligations are at odds within the barber?
3. Though true, the facts that the barber would lose his cover if he killed his customer and that nothing much would be accomplished anyway because another would only come to

take the place of Captain Torres are rationalizations. What are the barber's true reasons for not murdering the Captain?

4. The last sentence of the story suggests that the Captain thinks the barber to be a coward. Is he?

5. What does the barber come to realize during the course of "Just Lather, That's All"? What, finally, is the theme of the story?

Writing Assignments

1. In a paragraph, argue that the barber is wrong and that he should kill Captain Torres. Why should he? Specify possible benefits that could come to the revolutionaries from the killing. In not killing the Captain, is the barber selfish? In another paragraph, argue that he is and that in choosing private integrity he sacrifices public good.

2. But can public good ever really result from the sacrifice of individual integrity? In a short essay, argue the opposite case: that the barber is right, not only with respect to himself but, indeed, with respect to the revolutionary cause he has served.

3. Which of the two views just proposed seems better to describe the attitude conveyed by "Just Lather, That's All"? Write an essay in which you consider both views and defend your choice with specifics drawn from the story.

CHAPTER

✳ **3** ✳

PLOT AND SITUATION

PLOT AS CAUSAL SEQUENCE

Plot entails action. It also entails causality, or a sense of what it is that brought about an action and, thus, what the meaning of that action is. As E. M. Forster observes, the sentence "The queen died; then the king died" does not exhibit a plot; the sentence "The queen died; therefore, the king died" does (86). Plot, then, is a structural element, always pointing to the springs of action, to the relationship of cause and effect. So instead of "plot," people sometimes speak of "the *course* of events" or "the story *line*" of a work of fiction. Both the word "course" and the word "line" suggest that a plot is more than a simple description of events. It is, rather, the construction of events into a coherent sequence, with the sequence shedding light on the events that compose it.

But you know all this already. The last time you told someone about a movie you had seen, you probably summarized its plot: this happened and so that happened and then the other thing happened because this and that happened. And if something happened in the movie that was not causally related to the action overall, violating your sense of its inner logic, you probably criticized the movie for "not holding together." You also know that a plot does not have to proceed chronologically, which alone suggests that it is different from a simple narrative report. Many works of fiction, like many movies, begin in the middle of things (critics say *"in medias res"*) or even at the end, and many show earlier events in flashbacks, in which, for example, we are taken back to scenes from a character's childhood to help explain his or her actions in the present. Once again, it is the establishing of the relationship of cause and effect that turns what otherwise would be a simple narrative report of events into a plot.

MEANS AND ENDS

Because it is the easiest element to summarize, plot—the sequenced events or occurrences in a story—is what beginning students inevitably speak of when asked what a story is about: "This story is about a man who does such and such, and as a result so and so happens, and therefore it turns out that he shouldn't have done such and such in the first place." But no story is *about* its plot. Plot can point to theme (what a story *is* about) in many ways, but the plot itself is not the meaning. It is not an end in itself but a means. Granted, some modes of fiction depend heavily on plot: mysteries, for example, and often comedies gain their effects by the twists and turns of an intricately plotted story line. Even here, however, plot is a means to an end—specifically, to the creation of suspense or the provocation of laughter. However elaborate the plot, then, it functions as a means and must be taken as such.

But plots don't have to be elaborate to function. Though first-rate fiction can be intricately plotted, suspenseful, and charged with physical action, many fine stories have none of these traits. Some have plots—and their plots are important—that are relatively slender, straightforward, and quiet. Other stories have so little plot, if any, that there is no point in speaking of their plot at all. In this kind of fiction nothing much happens in terms of external action: there are no events, no occurrences, no happenings of any consequence, and so no plot. In such stories we attend, rather, to internal states of feeling or to the nuances of personality. "Just Lather, That's All" (Chapter 2) is of this sort. The drama here is purely internal. We find the central character (or protagonist) in a situation and attend not to what he does but to what he feels as a result of the situation he is in. A situation can serve as well as a plot to anchor a story in the world and to lead to character revelation, for instance, or to mood.

PLOT AND THE OTHER ELEMENTS OF FICTION

Each a means rather than an end, all the elements that compose a story work together toward the embodiment of some significant perception of human life. (Remember, incidentally, that in a given work some elements will be more prominent than others, and some might not figure in at all.) And always, the elements that are present are interlinked, one helping to establish another. How plot goes into the making of mood, for example, can be seen in Thurber's "The Night the Bed Fell" (pp. 88–91). Here the sequence of actions—the plot—is humorous; the mood of the story, therefore, is comic. Plot in this case creates mood, which shapes our attitude toward the material of the story and so moves us toward an understanding of theme. To give another example, plot is usually an agent of characterization. Just as what a person does in real life reveals something about that person, so what a character does in a story shows us something important about that character. Here again plot leads us toward theme, for character is usually a prime element in establishing theme and in many stories what is revealed about character *is* the theme.

CONFLICT AND HAPPY ENDINGS

In one way or another, the plots of most works of fiction involve conflict: between characters and the world (natural or social), between one character and another, or between opposing sides within a single character. Conflict in first-rate fiction, whether established by plot or situation, is usually subtle and complex; as in life, there are no simple rights and wrongs, judgments are hard to come by, and resolutions are seldom clear-cut. And because resolutions are seldom clear-cut, few stories worth the reader's effort have happy endings. "And they lived happily ever after," most fairy tales tell us. But no one's life is altogether happy and no one lives *ever* after; even if our lives were conflict free, which seems all but impossible to imagine, we would still have to face growing old and dying. In good fiction—whether plotted or situational—such realities are never out of mind; thus, we are most often left to ponder an ironic or indeterminate end, one that smacks of the realities of life rather than the wishes of fairy tales.

As we have seen previously, worthwhile fiction involves us actively as readers in probing the complexity of human beings and human life. Though perhaps satisfying on a certain level, fiction that casts opposing forces in simple terms of right and wrong, and whose plot builds to a happy ending with the triumph of right, leaves little to think about. There is nothing like irony, or inconclusiveness, or the sting of a tragic end, to spur the mind into action of its own, to involve us immediately, that is, and to lead us to probe more deeply into the nature of things. Marked by subtle conflict and plots (or situations) that do not necessarily resolve themselves, at least in any simplistic way, fiction can do just that.

SUMMARY SUGGESTIONS: UNDERSTANDING PLOT AND SITUATION

1. When you are reading a story, put aside the question of what will happen next and ask instead why what is happening is happening. It is the why and not the what that will lead you to comprehension.

2. Decide whether a given story presents a plot or a situation. If the latter, then there is nothing more to be concerned with along the lines of plot, though, like plot, a situation must be considered in relation to a story's other elements.

3. If the story contains a plot, clarify to yourself how the plot moves by determining the causal relationship between events. Then judge whether or not the relationship between events within the world of the story is consistent in light of the type of world created by the story. This world may be very different from your own, but still you can judge as to whether its causal relationships make sense. If they don't, either you have missed something in the story or its plot is inept or dishonest, contrived by the writer merely to produce an effect. You must be the judge as to which is the case.

4. Look to see how the plot (or situation if the story has no plot) functions with respect to the other elements from which the story is constructed. Does the plot (or situation) help to create mood? Is plot an agent of characterization? Does it produce irony? What other functions does it serve? By considering how the plot functions, you will be moving toward theme.

WRITING ON PLOT AND SITUATION

Good writing on plot (or situation) always involves far more than summarizing, but at times a summary may be useful or even essential. For instance, take a movie review or the review of a novel. Though reviews do not confine themselves to mere summaries of plots, most contain summaries somewhere along the line, usually toward the beginning. Similarly, an essay on a story might easily call for a plot summary as support material. Should a summary help to support your argument, you have good reason to incorporate it.

Further, following the plot can often help structure an essay even though the plot is not summarized anywhere in the essay. The sample essay in Chapter 1 is structured in this way (by reference to the plot of "The Shawl"). By following the movement of Ozick's plot, the essay gains coherence as well as a certain forward momentum. When writing on a story, you can often gain coherence in this way: by following the movement of the story itself as you move from point to point.

Plot can also be the central focus of paragraph or essay. For instance, you could write an analysis of a plot (in which case you would probably want to summarize it at the start). Plot analysis involves the consideration of the inner logic of a story: not just what happens first and then what happens next, but the causal relationship of events—*why* one event leads to another, the *meaning* of their interaction. For example, in analyzing the plot of "The Shawl," the writer would want to discuss *how* the stealing of the shawl gives rise to Magda's death and *how,* therefore, Magda's death results from Stella's sibling rivalry. Another kind of paper focusing centrally on plot would be one that examines how plot functions with respect to one or more of the other elements in a given piece of fiction. In either kind of paper, of course, what is finally important is the function of plot in the fiction as a whole. For instance, as we have noted, a plot might help create a story's mood, which, because it shapes our attitude, moves us toward theme. In arriving at a statement of the theme of the story, you would surely want to think out the relation between its plot and its mood. In writing a paper on the story thereafter, you might bring up the relationship between the story's plot and mood in order to argue whatever you have to say about its theme. Or a story's situation might give rise to irony, which in turn points toward theme. Such is the case in Chekhov's "The Lottery Ticket," found right after this introduction. One of many things that could be written on the story is an analysis of its situation and resultant irony. Such a paper could conclude with a statement of theme as it springs from the irony of the story overall.

There is much, then, that can be done with plot (or situation) when one comes to writing on fiction. Plot can be summarized to serve as support or used to structure an essay. It can also be made the subject of an essay, analyzed either in and of itself or in its relationship to the other elements of a story. In any case, the purpose is always to shed light in one way or another on the full meaning of the story. Whatever you choose to do, remember that a simple summary, standing alone, will not satisfy your reader. Your reader will want to learn more than the plot; your reader will want to see how plot (or situation) functions in the story in relation to the theme.

STORIES FOR STUDY AND WRITING ASSIGNMENTS

THE LOTTERY TICKET

ANTON CHEKHOV

Translated by Constance Garnett

Ivan Dmitritch, a middle-class man who lived with his family on an income of twelve hundred a year and was very well satisfied with his lot, sat down on the sofa after supper and began reading the newspaper.

"I forgot to look at the newspaper today," his wife said to him as she cleared the table. "Look and see whether the list of drawings is there."

"Yes, it is," said Ivan Dmitritch; "but hasn't your ticket lapsed?"

"No; I took the interest on Tuesday."

"What is the number?"

"Series 9,499, number 26."

"All right . . . we will look . . . 9,499 and 26."

Ivan Dmitritch had no faith in lottery luck, and would not, as a rule, have consented to look at the lists of winning numbers, but now, as he had nothing else to do and as the newspaper was before his eyes, he passed his finger downwards along the column of numbers. And immediately, as though in mockery of his scepticism, no further than the second line from the top, his eye was caught by the figure 9,499! Unable to believe his eyes, he hurriedly dropped the paper on his knees without looking to see the number of the ticket, and, just as though some one had given him a douche of cold water, he felt an agreeable chill in the pit of the stomach; tingling and terrible and sweet!

"Masha, 9,499 is there!" he said in a hollow voice.

His wife looked at his astonished and panic-stricken face, and realized that he was not joking.

"9,499?" she asked, turning pale and dropping the folded tablecloth on the table.

"Yes, yes . . . it really is there!"

"And the number of the ticket?"

"Oh, yes! There's the number of the ticket too. But stay . . . wait! No, I say! Anyway, the number of our series is there! Anyway, you understand. . . ."

Looking at his wife, Ivan Dmitritch gave a broad, senseless smile, like a baby when a bright object is shown it. His wife smiled too; it was as pleasant to her as to him that he only mentioned the series, and did not try to find out the number of the winning ticket. To torment and tantalize oneself with hopes of possible fortune is so sweet, so thrilling!

"It is our series," said Ivan Dmitritch, after a long silence. "So there is a probability that we have won. It's only a probability, but there it is!"

"Well, now look!"

"Wait a little. We have plenty of time to be disappointed. It's on the second line from the top, so the prize is seventy-five thousand. That's not money, but power, capital! And in a minute I shall look at the list, and there—26! Eh? I say, what if we really have won?"

The husband and wife began laughing and staring at one another in silence. The possibility of winning bewildered them; they could not have said, could not have dreamed, what they both needed that seventy-five thousand for, what they would buy, where they would go. They thought only of the figures 9,499 and 75,000 and pictured them in their imagination, while somehow they could not think of the happiness itself which was so possible.

Ivan Dmitritch, holding the paper in his hand, walked several times from corner to corner, and only when he had recovered from the first impression began dreaming a little.

"And if we have won," he said—"why, it will be a new life, it will be a transformation! The ticket is yours, but if it were mine I should, first of all, of course, spend twenty-five thousand on real property in the shape of an estate; ten thousand on immediate expenses, new furnishing . . . travelling . . . paying debts, and so on. . . . The other forty thousand I would put in the bank and get interest on it."

"Yes, an estate, that would be nice," said his wife, sitting down and dropping her hands in her lap.

"Somewhere in the Tula or Oryol provinces. . . . In the first place we shouldn't need a summer villa, and besides, it would always bring in an income."

And pictures came crowding on his imagination, each more gracious and poetical than the last. And in all these pictures he saw himself well-fed, serene, healthy, felt warm, even hot! Here, after eating a summer soup, cold as ice, he lay on his back on the burning sand close to a stream or in the garden under a lime-tree . . . It is hot . . . His little boy and girl are crawling about near him, digging in the sand or catching ladybirds in the grass. He dozes sweetly, thinking of nothing, and feeling all over that he need not go to the office today, tomorrow, or the day after. Or, tired of lying still, he goes to the hayfield, or to the forest for mushrooms, or watches the peasants catching fish with a net. When the sun sets he takes a towel and soap and saunters to the bathing shed, where he undresses at his leisure, slowly rubs his bare chest with his hands, and goes into the water. And in the water, near the opaque soapy circles, little fish flit to and fro and green water-weeds nod their heads. After bathing there is tea with cream and milk rolls. . . . In the evening a walk or *vint* with the neighbors.

"Yes, it would be nice to buy an estate," said his wife, also dreaming, and from her face it was evident that she was enchanted by her thoughts.

Ivan Dmitritch pictured to himself autumn with its rains, its cold evenings, and its St. Martin's summer. At that season he would have to take longer walks about the garden and beside the river, so as to get thoroughly chilled, and then drink a big glass of vodka and eat a salted mushroom or a soused cucumber, and then—

drink another. . . . The children would come running from the kitchen-garden, bringing a carrot and a radish smelling of fresh earth . . . And then, he would lie stretched full length on the sofa, and in leisurely fashion turn over the pages of some illustrated magazine, or, covering his face with it and unbuttoning his waistcoat, give himself up to slumber.

The St. Martin's summer is followed by cloudy, gloomy weather. It rains day and night, the bare trees weep, the wind is damp and cold. The dogs, the horses, the fowls—all are wet, depressed, downcast. There is nowhere to walk; one can't go out for days together; one has to pace up and down the room, looking despondently at the grey window. It is dreary!

Ivan Dmitritch stopped and looked at his wife.

"I should go abroad, you know, Masha," he said.

And he began thinking how nice it would be in late autumn to go abroad somewhere to the South of France . . . to Italy . . . to India!

"I should certainly go abroad too," his wife said. "But look at the number of the ticket!"

"Wait, wait! . . ."

He walked about the room and went on thinking. It occurred to him: what if his wife really did go abroad? It is pleasant to travel alone, or in the society of light, careless women who live in the present, and not such as think and talk all the journey about nothing but their children, sigh, and tremble with dismay over every farthing. Ivan Dmitritch imagined his wife in the train with a multitude of parcels, baskets, and bags; she would be sighing over something, complaining that the train made her head ache, that she had spent so much money . . . At the stations he would continually be having to run for boiling water, bread and butter . . . She wouldn't have dinner because of its being too dear. . . .

"She would begrudge me every farthing," he thought, with a glance at his wife. "The lottery ticket is hers, not mine! Besides, what is the use of her going abroad? What does she want there? She would shut herself up in the hotel, and not let me out of her sight . . . I know!"

And for the first time in his life his mind dwelt on the fact that his wife had grown elderly and plain, and that she was saturated through and through with the smell of cooking, while he was still young, fresh, and healthy, and might well have got married again.

"Of course, all that is silly nonsense," he thought; "but . . . why should she go abroad? What would she make of it? And yet she would go, of course . . . I can fancy. . . . In reality it is all one to her, whether it is Naples or Klin. She would only be in my way. I should be dependent upon her. I can fancy how, like a regular woman, she will lock the money up as soon as she gets it. . . . She will look after her relations and grudge me every farthing."

Ivan Dmitritch thought of her relations. All those wretched brothers and sisters and aunts and uncles would come crawling about as soon as they heard of the winning ticket, would begin whining like beggars, and fawning upon them with oily, hypocritical smiles. Wretched, detestable people! If they were given anything, they would ask for more; while if they were refused, they would swear at them, slander them, and wish them every kind of misfortune.

Ivan Dmitritch remembered his own relations, and their faces, at which he had looked impartially in the past, struck him now as repulsive and hateful.

"They are such reptiles!" he thought.

And his wife's face, too, struck him as repulsive and hateful. Anger surged up in his heart against her, and he thought malignantly:

"She knows nothing about money, and so she is stingy. If she won it she would give me a hundred roubles, and put the rest away under lock and key."

And he looked at his wife, not with a smile now, but with hatred. She glanced at him too, and also with hatred and anger. She had her own daydreams, her own plans, her own reflections; she understood perfectly well what her husband's dreams were. She knew who would be the first to try to grab her winnings.

"It's very nice making daydreams at other people's expense!" is what her eyes expressed. "No, don't you dare!"

Her husband understood her look, hatred began stirring again in his breast, and in order to annoy his wife he glanced quickly, to spite her at the fourth page on the newspaper and read out triumphantly:

"Series 9,499, number 46! Not 26!"

Hatred and hope both disappeared at once, and it began immediately to seem to Ivan Dmitritch and his wife that their rooms were dark and small and low-pitched, that the supper they had been eating was not doing them good, but lying heavy on their stomachs, that the evenings were long and wearisome. . . .

"What the devil's the meaning of it?" said Ivan Dmitritch, beginning to be ill-humored. "Wherever one steps there are bits of paper under one's feet, crumbs, husks. The rooms are never swept! One is simply forced to go out. Damnation take my soul entirely! I shall go and hang myself on the first aspen-tree!"

[1886—Russia]

Questions

1. Does Chekhov's story present us with a plot or a situation?
2. The story is narrated from Ivan's point of view. Why didn't Chekhov simply have Ivan tell of the incident in the first person?
3. By the end of the story we know that Ivan is thoroughly discontented with his lot. Why, then, are we told at the beginning that he is "very well satisfied"? What do we call this kind of discrepancy?
4. Is it plausible that Ivan should come to feel what he does "for the first time in his life"?
5. The drama of this story is internal, the drama of developing self-knowledge. The knowledge that Ivan and his wife gain will surely prevent them from continuing as though nothing had happened. What are the likely consequences of their new self-knowledge? What might be Chekhov's theme with respect to self-knowledge?

Writing Assignments

1. Write a paragraph in which you describe Ivan as you imagine him just before the story takes place. What did he think of his life? Did he think much at all? Given that it takes only a trivial circumstance to raise up in him a wealth of discontent, what must he really have felt without allowing his feelings to surface? What conclusion can be drawn from all this?
2. (a) In a paragraph, explain how the situation of "The Lottery Ticket" contributes to both mood and characterization.
   (b) In a separate paragraph, state your response to the story and explain why you respond as you do. Be specific.
3. We tend to believe that knowledge is an absolute good—always desirable. Write an essay on how "The Lottery Ticket" calls this assumption into question.

A STRING OF BEADS

SOMERSET MAUGHAM

"What a bit of luck that I'm placed next to you," said Laura, as we sat down to dinner.

"For me," I replied politely.

"That remains to be seen. I particularly wanted to have the chance of talking to you. I've got a story to tell you."

At this my heart sank a little.

"I'd sooner you talked about yourself," I answered. "Or even about me."

"Oh, but I must tell you the story. I think you'll be able to use it."

"If you must, you must. But let's look at the menu first."

"Don't you want me to?" she said, somewhat aggrieved. "I thought you'd be pleased."

"I am. You might have written a play and wanted to read me that."

"It happened to some friends of mine. It's perfectly true."

"That's no recommendation. A true story is never quite so true as an invented one."

"What does that mean?"

"Nothing very much," I admitted. "But I thought it sounded well."

"I wish you'd let me get on with it."

"I'm all attention. I'm not going to eat the soup. It's fattening."

She gave me a pinched look and then glanced at the menu. She uttered a little sigh.

"Oh, well, if you're going to deny yourself I suppose I must too. Heaven knows, I can't afford to take liberties with my figure."

"And yet is there any soup more heavenly than the sort of soup in which you put a great dollop of cream?"

"Borsht," she sighed. "It's the only soup I really like."

"Never mind. Tell me your story and we'll forget about food till the fish comes."

"Well, I was actually there when it happened. I was dining with the Livingstones. Do you know the Livingstones?"

"No, I don't think I do."

"Well, you can ask them and they'll confirm every word I say. They'd asked their governess to come in to dinner because some woman had thrown them over at the last moment—you know how inconsiderate people are—and they would have been thirteen at table. Their governess was a Miss Robinson, quite a nice girl, young, you know, twenty or twenty-one, and rather pretty. Personally I would never engage a governess who was young and pretty. One never knows."

"But one hopes for the best."

Laura paid no attention to my remark.

"The chances are that she'll be thinking of young men instead of attending to her duties and then, just when she's got used to your ways, she'll want to go and get married. But Miss Robinson had excellent references, and I must allow that she was a very nice, respectable person. I believe in point of fact she was a clergyman's daughter.

"There was a man at dinner whom I don't suppose you've ever heard of, but who's quite a celebrity in his way. He's a Count Borselli and he knows more about precious stones than anyone in the world. He was sitting next to Mary Lyngate, who rather fancies herself on her pearls, and in the course of conversation she asked him what he thought of the string she was wearing. He said it was very pretty. She was rather piqued at this and told him it was valued at eight thousand pounds.

" 'Yes, it's worth that,' " he said.

"Miss Robinson was sitting opposite to him. She was looking rather nice that evening. Of course I recognized her dress, it was one of Sophie's old ones; but if you hadn't known Miss Robinson was the governess you would never have suspected it.

" 'That's a very beautiful necklace that young lady has on,' said Borselli.

" 'Oh, but that's Mrs. Livingstone's governess,' said Mary Lyngate.

" 'I can't help that,' he said. 'She's wearing one of the finest strings of pearls for its size that I've ever seen in my life. It must be worth fifty thousand pounds.'

" 'Nonsense.'

" 'I give you my word it is.'

"Mary Lyngate leant over. She has rather a shrill voice.

" 'Miss Robinson, do you know what Count Borselli says?' she exclaimed. 'He says that string of pearls you're wearing is worth fifty thousand pounds.'

"Just at that moment there was a sort of pause in the conversation so that everybody heard. We all turned and looked at Miss Robinson. She flushed a little and laughed.

" 'Well, I made a very good bargain,' she said, 'because I paid fifteen shillings for it.'

" 'You certainly did.'

"We all laughed. It was of course absurd. We've all heard of wives palming off on their husbands as false a string of pearls that was real and expensive. That story is as old as the hills."

"Thank you," I said, thinking of a little narrative of my own.

"But it was too ridiculous to suppose that a governess would remain a governess if she owned a string of pearls worth fifty thousand pounds. It was obvious that the Count had made a bloomer. Then an extraordinary thing happened. The long arm of coincidence came in."

"It shouldn't," I retorted. "It's had too much exercise. Haven't you seen that charming book called *A Dictionary of English Usage?*"

"I wish you wouldn't interrupt just when I'm really getting to the exciting point."

But I had to do so again, for just then a young grilled salmon was insinuated round my left elbow.

"Mrs. Livingstone is giving us a heavenly dinner," I said.

"Is salmon fattening?" asked Laura.

"Very," I answered as I took a large helping.

"Bunk," she said.

"Go on," I begged her. "The long arm of coincidence was about to make a gesture."

"Well, at that very moment the butler bent over Miss Robinson and whispered something in her ear. I thought she turned a trifle pale. It's such a mistake not to wear rouge; you never know what tricks nature will play on you. She certainly looked startled. She leant forwards.

" 'Mrs. Livingstone, Dawson says there are two men in the hall who want to speak to me at once.'

" 'Well, you'd better go,' said Sophie Livingstone.

"Miss Robinson got up and left the room. Of course the same thought flashed through all our minds, but I said it first.

" 'I hope they haven't come to arrest her,' I said to Sophie. 'It would be too dreadful for you, my dear.'

" 'Are you sure it was a real necklace, Borselli?' she asked.

" 'Oh, quite.'

" 'She could hardly have had the nerve to wear it tonight if it were stolen,' I said.

"Sophie Livingstone turned as pale as death under her makeup, and I saw she was wondering if everything was all right in her jewel case. I only had on a little chain of diamonds, but instinctively I put my hand up to my neck to feel if it was still there.

" 'Don't talk nonsense,' said Mr. Livingstone. 'How on earth would Miss Robinson have had the chance of sneaking a valuable string of pearls?'

" 'She may be a receiver,' I said.

" 'Oh, but she had such wonderful references,' said Sophie.

" 'They always do,' I said."

I was positively forced to interrupt Laura once more.

"You don't seem to have been determined to take a very bright view of the case," I remarked.

"Of course I knew nothing against Miss Robinson, and I had every reason to think her a very nice girl, but it would have been rather thrilling to find out that she was a notorious thief and a well-known member of a gang of international crooks."

"Just like a film. I'm dreadfully afraid that it's only in films that exciting things like that happen."

"Well, we waited in breathless suspense. There was not a sound. I expected to hear a scuffle in the hall or at least a smothered shriek. I thought the silence very ominous. Then the door opened and Miss Robinson walked in. I noticed at once that the necklace was gone. I could see that she was pale and excited. She came back to the table, sat down and with a smile threw on it . . ."

"On what?"

"On the table, you fool. A string of pearls.

" 'There's my necklace,' she said.

"Count Borselli leant forwards.

" 'Oh, but those are false,' he said.

" 'I told you they were,' she laughed.

" 'That's not the same string that you had on a few moments ago,' he said.

"She shook her head and smiled mysteriously. We were all intrigued. I don't know that Sophie Livingstone was so very much pleased at her governess making herself the centre of interest like that and I thought there was a suspicion of tartness in her manner when she suggested that Miss Robinson had better explain. Well, Miss Robinson said that when she went into the hall she found two men who said they'd come from Jarrot's Stores. She'd bought her string there, as she said, for fifteen shillings, and she'd taken it back because the clasp was loose and had only fetched it that afternoon. The men said they had given her the wrong string. Someone had left a string of real pearls to be re-strung and the assistant had made a mistake. Of course I can't understand how anyone could be so stupid as to take a really valuable string to Jarrot's, they aren't used to dealing with that sort of thing, and they wouldn't know real pearls from false; but you know what fools some women are. Anyhow, it was the string Miss Robinson was wearing, and it was valued at fifty thousand pounds. She naturally gave it back to them—she couldn't do anything else, I suppose, though it must have been a wrench—and they returned her own string to her; then they said that although of course they were under no obligation— you know the silly, pompous way men talk when they're trying to be businesslike— they were instructed, as a solatium or whatever you call it, to offer her a cheque for three hundred pounds. Miss Robinson actually showed it to us. She was as pleased as Punch."

"Well, it was a piece of luck, wasn't it?"

"You'd have thought so. As it turned out it was the ruin of her."

"Oh, how was that?"

"Well, when the time came for her to go on her holiday she told Sophie Livingstone that she'd made up her mind to go to Deauville for a month and blow the whole three hundred pounds. Of course Sophie tried to dissuade her, and begged her to put the money in the savings bank, but she wouldn't hear of it. She said she'd never had such a chance before and would never have it again and she meant for at least four weeks to live like a duchess. Sophie couldn't really do anything and so she gave way. She sold Miss Robinson a lot of clothes that she didn't want; she'd been wearing them all through the season and was sick to death of them; she says she gave them to her, but I don't suppose she quite did that—I dare say she sold them very cheap—and Miss Robinson started off, entirely alone, for Deauville. What do you think happened then?"

"I haven't a notion," I replied. "I hope she had the time of her life."

"Well, a week before she was due to come back she wrote to Sophie and said that she'd changed her plans and had entered another profession, and hoped that Mrs. Livingstone would forgive her if she didn't return. Of course poor Sophie was furious. What had actually happened was that Miss Robinson had picked up a rich Argentine in Deauville and had gone off to Paris with him. She's been in Paris ever since. I've seen her myself at Florence's, with bracelets right up to her elbow and ropes of pearls round her neck. Of course I cut her dead. They say she has a house in the Bois de Boulogne and I know she has a Rolls. She threw over the Argentine in a few months and then got hold of a Greek; I don't know who she's with now, but the long and short of it is that she's far and away the smartest cocotte in Paris."

"When you say she was ruined you use the word in a purely technical sense, I conclude," said I.

"I don't know what you mean by that," said Laura. "But don't you think you could make a story out of it?"

"Unfortunately I've already written a story about a pearl necklace. One can't go on writing stories about pearl necklaces."

"I've got half a mind to write it myself. Only, of course, I should change the end."

"Oh, how would you end it?"

"Well, I should have had her engaged to a bank clerk who had been badly knocked about in the war, with only one leg, say, or half his face shot away; and they'd be dreadfully poor and there would be no prospect of their marriage for years, and he would be putting all his savings into buying a little house in the suburbs, and they'd have arranged to marry when he had saved the last installment. And then she takes him the three hundred pounds and they can hardly believe it, they're so happy, and he cries on her shoulder. He just cries like a child. And they get the little house in the suburbs and they marry, and they have his old mother to live with them, and he goes to the bank every day, and if she's careful not to have babies she can still go out as a daily governess, and he's often ill—with his wound, you know—and she nurses him, and it's all very pathetic and sweet and lovely."

"It sounds rather dull to me," I ventured.
"Yes, but moral," said Laura.

[1936—Great Britain]

Questions

1. Maugham's story presents us with both a situation—the circumstance in which Laura tells her story—and a plot. Summarize both.
2. What is Laura's dinner companion (the writer) getting at with the question, "When you say she was ruined you use the word in a purely technical sense, I conclude"? What might "technical sense" mean here?
3. Compare and contrast the story's two narrators—Laura, who tells the pearl story, and the writer to whom she tells her story and who, presumably, is telling us the story of Laura's telling of the pearl story. Which of the two do you prefer? Why?
4. Why didn't Maugham just tell the pearl story? Why the framework of a dinner conversation?
5. In light of its somewhat elaborate framework, what is the story as a whole about? In answering this question, consider the personality differences between Laura and her dinner companion and their differing views as to the function of storytelling. Toward which view would the story sway us?

Writing Assignments

1. Write an essay that is based on the comparison called for in question 3 above and moves to a consideration of which of the two characters the story would sway the reader to prefer.
2. In a paragraph, explain how the situation of the story shifts the focus away from Laura's plotty tale and onto Laura herself, and what the purpose of this shift is.
3. Write an essay arguing that "A String of Beads" is about two types of fiction and hence two types of reader.

AFTER THE FAIR

❋ DYLAN THOMAS ❋

The fair was over, the lights in the cocoanut stalls were put out, and the wooden horses stood still in the darkness, waiting for the music and the hum of the machines that would set them trotting forward. One by one, in every booth, the naphtha jets were turned down and the canvases pulled over the little gambling tables. The crowd went home, and there were lights in the windows of the caravans.

Nobody had noticed the girl. In her black clothes she stood against the side of the roundabouts, hearing the last feet tread upon the sawdust and the last voices die into the distance. Then, all alone on the deserted ground, surrounded by the shapes of wooden horses and cheap fairy boats, she looked for a place to sleep. Now here and now there, she raised the canvas that shrouded the cocoanut stalls and peered into the warm darkness. She was frightened to step inside, and as a mouse scampered across the littered shavings on the floor, or as the canvas creaked and a rush of wind set it dancing, she ran away and hid again near the roundabouts. Once she stepped on the boards; the bells round a horse's throat jingled and were still; she did not dare breathe until all was quiet again and the darkness had forgotten the noise of the bells. Then here and there she went peeping for a bed, into each gondola, under each tent. But there was nowhere, nowhere in all the fair for her to sleep. One place was too silent, and in another was the noise of mice. There was straw in the corner of the Astrologer's tent, but it moved as she touched it; she knelt by its side and put out her hand; she felt a baby's hand upon her own.

Now there was nowhere; so slowly she turned towards the caravans, and reaching them where they stood on the outskirts of the field, found all but two to be unlit. She stood, clutching her empty bag, and wondering which caravan she should disturb. At last she decided to knock upon the window of the little, shabby one near her and standing on tiptoe, she looked in. The fattest man she had ever seen was sitting in front of the stove, toasting a piece of bread. She tapped three times on the glass, then hid in the shadows. She heard him come to the top of the steps and call out Who? Who? but she dared not answer. Who? Who? he called again; she laughed at his voice which was as thin as he was fat. He heard her laughter and turned to where the darkness concealed her. First you tap, he said. Then you hide, then, by jingo, you laugh. She stepped into the circle of light, knowing she need no longer hide herself. A girl, he said, Come in and wipe your feet. He did not wait but retreated into his caravan, and she could do nothing but follow him up the steps and into the crowded room. He was seated again, and toasting the same piece of bread. Have you come in? he said, for his back was towards her. Shall I close the door? she asked, and closed it before he replied.

She sat on the bed and watched him toasting the bread until it burnt. I can toast better than you, she said. I don't doubt it, said the Fat Man. She watched him put down the charred toast upon a plate by his side, take another round of bread and hold that, too, in front of the stove. It burnt very quickly. Let me toast it for you, she said. Ungraciously he handed her the fork and the loaf. Cut it, he said, Toast it, and eat it, by jingo. She sat on the chair. See the dent you've made on my bed, said the Fat Man. Who are you to come in and dent my bed? My name is Annie, she told him. Soon all the bread was toasted and buttered, so she put it in the centre of the table and arranged two chairs. I'll have mine on the bed, said the Fat Man. You'll have it here.

When they had finished their supper, he pushed back his chair and stared at her across the table. I am the Fat Man, he said. My home is Treorchy; the Fortune Teller next door is Aberdare. I am nothing to do with the fair—I am Cardiff, she said. There's a town, agreed the Fat Man. He asked her why she had come away. Money, said Annie. I have one and three, said the Fat Man. I have nothing, said Annie.

Then he told her about the fair and the places he had been to and the people he had met. He told her his age and his weight and the names of his brothers and what he would call his son. He showed her a picture of Boston Harbour and the photograph of his mother who lifted weights. He told her how summer looked in Ireland. I've always been a fat man, he said. And now I'm *the* Fat Man; there's nobody to touch me for fatness. He told her of a heat wave in Sicily and of the Mediterranean Sea and of the wonders of the South stars. She told him of the baby in the Astrologer's tent.

That's the stars again, by jingo; looking at the stars doesn't do anybody any good.

The baby'll die, said Annie. He opened the door and walked out into the darkness. She looked about her but did not move, wondering if he had gone to fetch a policeman. It would never do to be caught by the policeman again. She stared through the open door into the inhospitable night and drew her chair closer to the stove. Better to be caught in the warmth, she said. But she trembled at the sound of the Fat Man approaching, and pressed her hands upon her thin breast, as he climbed up the steps like a walking mountain. She could see him smile in the darkness. See what the stars have done, he said, and brought in the Astrologer's baby in his arms.

After she had nursed it against her and it had cried on the bosom of her dress, she told him how she had feared his going. What should I be doing with a policeman? She told him that the policeman wanted her. What have you done for a policeman to be wanting you? She did not answer but took the child nearer again to her wasted breast. If it was money, I could have given you one and three, he said. Then he understood her and begged her pardon. I'm not quick, he told her. I'm just fat; sometimes I think I'm almost too fat. She was feeding the child; he saw her thinness. You must eat, Cardiff, he said.

Then the child began to cry. From a little wail its crying rose into a tempest of despair. The girl rocked it to and fro on her lap, but nothing soothed it. All the woe of a child's world flooded its tiny voice. Stop it, stop it, said the Fat Man, and the tears increased. Annie smothered it in kisses, but its wild cry broke on her lips like water upon rocks. We must do something, she said. Sing it a lullabee. She sang, but the child did not like her singing.

There's only one thing, said Annie, we must take it on the roundabouts. With the child's arm around her neck, she stumbled down the steps and ran towards the deserted fair, the Fat Man panting behind her. She found her way through the tents and stalls into the centre of the ground where the wooden horses stood waiting, and clambered up on to a saddle. Start the engine, she called out. In the distance the Fat Man could be heard cranking up the antique machine that drove the horses all the day into a wooden gallop. She heard the sudden spasmodic humming of the engine; the boards rattled under the horses' feet. She saw the Fat Man clamber up by her side, pull the central lever and climb on to the saddle of the smallest horse of all. As the roundabout started, slowly at first and slowly gaining speed, the child at the girl's breast stopped crying, clutched its hands together, and crowed with joy. The night wind tore through its hair, the music jangled in its ears. Round and round the wooden horses sped, drowning the cries of the wind with the beating of their wooden hooves.

And so the men from the caravans found them, the Fat Man and the girl in black with a baby in her arms, racing round and round on their mechanical steeds to the ever-increasing music of the organ.

[1939—Great Britain]

Questions

1. Summarize the plot of this highly poetic story. What is the primary incident that the plot turns on? In what ways does this incident set into motion what follows?
2. The protagonists of "After the Fair" are outsiders, misfits. Yet at the end of the story, we come to feel their humanity by seeing the common ground we share with this "family" of derelicts. How does the plot contribute to this effect?
3. What, then, is the theme of this story, and how does the plot help to establish it?

Writing Assignments

1. In a paragraph, describe the effect of the image with which we are left at the end of the story. In the same or in a second paragraph, relate this effect to the story's theme.
2. Though relatively slight, the plot of "After the Fair" is crucial. Write an essay showing how the events form a chain leading to the story's conclusion and thus serve as an agent of theme.

BOOK OF HARLEM

❋ ZORA NEALE HURSTON ❋

1. A pestilence visiteth the land of Hokum, and the people cry out.   4. Toothsome, a son of Georgia returns from Babylon, and stirreth up the Hamites.   10. Mandolin heareth him and resolveth to see Babylon.   11. He convinceth his father and departs for Babylon.   21. A red-cap toteth his bag, and uttereth blasphemy against Mandolin.   26. He lodgeth with Toothsome, and trieth to make the females of Harlem, but is scorned by them.   28. One frail biddeth him sit upon a tack.   29. He taketh council with Toothsome and is comforted.   33. He goeth to an hall of dancing, and meeting a damsel there, shaketh vehemently with her.   42. He discloseth himself to her and she telleth him what to read.   49. He becometh Panic.   50. The Book of Harlem.

1. And in those days when King Volstead sat upon the throne in Hokum, then came a mighty drought upon the land, many cried out in agony thereof.

2. Then did the throat parch and the tongue was thrust into the cheek of many voters.

3. And men grew restless and went up and down in the land saying, "We are verily the dry-bones of which the prophet Ezekiel prophesied."

4. Then returned one called Toothsome unto his town of Standard Bottom, which is in the province of Georgia. And he was of the tribe of Ham.

5. And his raiment was very glad, for he had sojourned in the city of Babylon, which is ruled by the tribe of Tammany. And his garments putteth out the street lamps, and the vaseline upon his head, yea verily the slickness thereof did outshine the sun at noonday.

6. And the maidens looked upon him and were glad, but the men gnasheth together their bridgework at sight of him. But they drew near unto him and listened to his accounts of the doings of Babylon, for they all yearned unto that city.

7. And the mouth of Toothsome flapped loudly and fluently in the marketplace, and the envy of his hearers increased an hundredfold.

8. Then stood one youth before him, and his name was called Mandolin. And he questioned Toothsome eagerly, asking "how come" and "wherefore" many times.

9. And Toothsome answered him according to his wit. Moreover he said unto the youth, "Come thou also to the city as unto the ant, and consider her ways and be wise."

10. And the heart of Mandolin was inflamed, and he stood before his father and said, "I beseech thee now, papa, to give unto me now my portion that I may go hence to great Babylon and see life."

11. But his father's heart yearned towards him, and he said, "Nay, my son, for Babylon is full of wickedness, and thou art but a youth."

12. But Mandolin answered him saying, "I crave to gaze upon its sins. What do you think I go to see, a prayer-meeting?"

13. But his father strove with him and said, "Why dost thou crave Babylon when Gussie Smith, the daughter of our neighbor, will make thee a good wife? Tarry now and take her to wife, for verily she is a mighty biscuit-cooker before the Lord."

14. Then snorted Mandolin with scorn and he said, "What care I for biscuit-cookers when there be Shebas of high voltage on every street in Harlem? For verily man liveth not by bread alone, but by every drop of banana oil that drippeth from the tongue of the lovely."

15. Then strove they together all night. But at daybreak did Mandolin touch the old man upon the hip, yea verily upon the pocket-bearing joint, and triumphed.

16. So the father gave him his blessing, and he departed out of Standard Bottom on his journey to Babylon.

17. And he carried with him of dreams forty-and-four thousands, and of wishes ten thousands, and of hopes ten thousands.

18. But of tears or sorrows carried he none out of all that land. Neither bore he any fears away with him.

19. And journeyed he many days upon the caravan of steel, and came at last unto the city of Babylon, and got him down within the place.

20. Then rushed there many upon him who wore scarlet caps upon the head, saying "Porter? Shall I tote thy bags for thee?"

21. And he marvelled greatly within himself, saying, "How charitably are the Babylons, seeing they permit no stranger to tote his own bag! With what great kindness am I met!"

22. And he suffered one to prevail and tote his bag for him. Moreover he questioned him concerning the way to Harlem which is a city of Ham in Babylonia.

23. And when he of the scarlet cap had conducted Mandolin unto a bus, then did Mandolin shake hands with him and thank him greatly for his kindness, and stepped upon the chariot as it rolled away, and took his way unto Harlem.

24. Then did the bag-toter blaspheme greatly, saying, "Oh, the cock-eyed son of a wood louse! Oh, the hawg! Oh, the sea-buzzard! Oh, the splay-footed son of a doodle bug and cockroach! What does he take me for? The mule's daddy! The clod-hopper! If only I might lay my hands upon him, verily would I smite him, yea, until he smelt like onions!"

25. But Mandolin journeyed on to Harlem, knowing none of these things.

26. And when he had come unto the place, he lodged himself with Toothsome, and was glad.

27. And each evening stood he before the Lafayette theatre and ahemmed at the knees that passed, but none took notice of him.

28. Moreover one frail of exceeding sassiness bade him go to and cook an radish, and seat himself upon a tack, which being interpreted is slander.

29. Then went he unto his roommate and saith, "How now doth the damsel think me? Have I not a smiling countenance, and coin in my jeans? My heart is heavy for I have sojourned in Harlem for many weeks, but as yet I have spoken to no female."

30. Then spoke Toothsome, and answered him saying, "Seek not swell Shebas in mail-order britches. Go thou into the marketplace and get thee Oxford bags and jacket thyself likewise. Procure thee shoes and socks. Yea, anoint thy head with oil until it runneth over so that thou dare not hurl thyself into bed unless thou wear Weed chains upon the head, lest thou skid out again."

31. "Moreover lubricate thy tongue with banana oil, for from the oily lips proceedeth the breath of love."

32. And Mandolin hastened to do all that his counsellor bade him.

33. Then hied him to the hall of dancing where many leaped with the cymbal, and shook with the drums.

34. And his belly was moved, for he saw young men seize upon damsels and they stood upon the floor and "messed around" meanly. Moreover many "bumped" them vehemently. Yea, there were those among them who shook with many shakings.

35. And when he saw all these things, Mandolin yearned within his heart to do likewise, but as yet he had spoken to no maiden.

36. But one damsel of scarlet lips smiled broadly upon him, and encouraged him with her eyes, and the water of his knees turned to bone, and he drew nigh unto her.

37. And his mouth flew open and he said, "See now how the others do dance with the cymbal and harp, yea, even the saxophone? Come thou and let us do likewise."

38. And he drew her and they stood upon the floor. Now this maiden was a mighty dancer before the Lord; yea, of the mightiest of all the tribe of Ham. And the shakings

of the others was as one stricken with paralysis beside a bowl of gelatine. And the heart of the youth leaped for joy.

39. And he was emboldened, and his mouth flew open and the banana oil did drip from his lips, yea even down to the floor, and the maiden was moved.

40. And he said, "Thou sure art propaganda! Yea, verily thou shakest a wicked ankle."

41. And she being pleased, answered him, "Thou art some sheik thyself. I do shoot a little pizen to de ankle if I do say so myself. Where has thou been all my life that I have not seen thee?"

42. Then did his mouth fly open, and he told her everything of Standard Bottom, Georgia, and of Babylon, and of all those things which touched him.

43. And her heart yearned towards him, and she resolved to take him unto herself and to make him wise.

44. And she said unto him, "Go thou and buy the books and writings of certain scribes and Pharisees which I shall name unto you, and thou shalt learn everything of good and of evil. Yea, thou shalt know as much as the Chief of the Niggerati, who is called Carl Van Vechten."

45. And Mandolin diligently sought all these books and writings that he was bidden, and read them.

46. Then was he sought for all feasts, and stomps, and shakings, and none was complete without him. Both on 139th street and on Lenox avenue was he sought, and his fame was great.

47. And his name became Panic, for they asked one of the other, "Is he not a riot in all that he doeth?"

48. Then did he devise poetry, and played it upon the piano, saying:

> *Skirt by skirt on every flirt*
> *They're getting higher and higher*
> *Day by day in every way*
> *There's more to admire*
> *Sock by sock and knee by knee*
> *The more they show, the more we see*
> *The skirts run up, the socks run down*
> *Jingling bells run round and round*
> *Oh week by week, and day by day*
> *Let's hope that things keep on this way*
> *Let's kneel right down and pray.*

49. And the women all sought him, and damsels and the matrons and the grandmothers and all those who wear the skirt, and with them his name was continually Panic.

50. Of his doings and success after that, is it not written in The Book of Harlem?

[1927—U.S.A.]

Questions

1. Look up in an encyclopedia the following: Volstead Act, Tammany Hall, Carl Van Vechten, Harlem Renaissance. Be ready in class to discuss how a knowledge of these references sheds light on Hurston's story.

2. What is the effect of Hurston's combination of a biblical structure and biblical language with a mundane, everyday plot?
3. That plot is the central element of the present story is highlighted by the Bible-like summary of plot at the beginning. In what way does the theme of "Book of Harlem" make the emphasis on plot inevitable?

Writing Assignments

1. Write an essay on the story's humor and how it functions. That is, after establishing in what ways the story is funny, relate its comic mood to its theme.
2. Write a paragraph or more suggesting how the story's plot and its general high-spiritedness reflect the mood of Harlem in the 1920s. You will probably have to do some research before you begin writing. Start by looking up the references cited in question 1 above if you have not already done so.

THE NIGHT THE BED FELL

❊ JAMES THURBER ❊

I suppose that the high-water mark of my youth in Columbus, Ohio, was the night the bed fell on my father. It makes a better recitation (unless, as some friends of mine have said, one has heard it five or six times) than it does a piece of writing, for it is almost necessary to throw furniture around, shake doors, and bark like a dog, to lend the proper atmosphere and verisimilitude to what is admittedly a somewhat incredible tale. Still, it did take place.

It happened, then, that my father had decided to sleep in the attic one night, to be away where he could think. My mother opposed the notion strongly because, she said, the old wooden bed up there was unsafe: it was wobbly and the heavy headboard would crash down on father's head in case the bed fell, and kill him. There was no dissuading him, however, and at a quarter past ten he closed the attic door behind him and went up the narrow twisting stairs. We later heard ominous creakings as he crawled into bed. Grandfather, who usually slept in the attic bed when he was with us, had disappeared some days before. (On these occasions he was usually gone six or eight days and returned growling and out of temper, with the news that the federal Union was run by a passel of blockheads and that the Army of the Potomac didn't have any more chance than a fiddler's bitch.)

We had visiting us at this time a nervous first cousin of mine named Briggs Beall, who believed that he was likely to cease breathing when he was asleep. It was his feeling that if he were not awakened every hour during the night, he might die of suffocation. He had been accustomed to setting an alarm clock to ring at intervals until morning, but I persuaded him to abandon this. He slept in my room and I told him that I was such a light sleeper that if anybody quit breathing in the same room with me, I would wake instantly. He tested me the first night—which I had suspected he would—by holding his breath after my regular breathing had convinced him I was asleep. I was not asleep, however, and called to him. This seemed to allay his fears a little, but he took the precaution of putting a glass of spirits of camphor on a little table at the head of his bed. In case I didn't arouse him until he was almost gone, he said, he would sniff the camphor, a powerful reviver. Briggs was not the only member of his family who had his crotchets. Old Aunt Melissa Beall (who could whistle like a man, with two fingers in her mouth) suffered under the premonition that she was destined to die on South High Street, because she had been born on South High Street and married on South High Street. Then there was Aunt Sarah Shoaf, who never went to bed at night without the fear that a burglar was going to get in and blow chloroform under her door through a tube. To avert this calamity—for she was in greater dread of anesthetics than of losing her household goods—she always piled her money, silverware, and other valuables in a neat stack just outside her bedroom, with a note reading: "This is all I have. Please take it and do not use your chloroform, as this is all I have." Aunt Gracie Shoaf also had a burglar phobia, but she met it with more fortitude. She was confident that burglars had been getting into her house every night for forty years. The fact that she never missed anything was to her no proof to the contrary. She always claimed that she scared them off before they could take anything, by throwing shoes down the hallway. When she went to bed she piled, where she could get at them handily, all the shoes there were about her house. Five minutes after she had turned off the light, she would sit up in bed and say "Hark!" Her husband, who had learned to ignore the whole situation as long ago as 1903, would either be sound asleep or pretend to be sound asleep. In either case he would not respond to her tugging and pulling, so that presently she would arise, tiptoe to the door, open it slightly and heave a shoe down the hall in one direction and its mate down the hall in the other direction. Some nights she threw them all, some nights only a couple of pair.

But I am straying from the remarkable incidents that took place during the night that the bed fell on father. By midnight we were all in bed. The layout of the rooms and the disposition of their occupants is important to an understanding of what later occurred. In the front room upstairs (just under father's attic bedroom) were my mother and my brother Herman, who sometimes sang in his sleep, usually "Marching Through Georgia" or "Onward, Christian Soldiers." Briggs Beall and myself were in a room adjoining this one. My brother Roy was in a room across the hall from ours. Our bull terrier, Rex, slept in the hall.

My bed was an army cot, one of those affairs which are made wide enough to sleep on comfortably only by putting up, flat with the middle section, the two sides which ordinarily hang down like the sideboards of a drop-leaf table. When these sides are up, it is perilous to roll too far toward the edge, for then the cot is likely to tip completely over, bringing the whole bed down on top of one with a tremendous banging crash. This, in fact, is precisely what happened, about two o'clock in the morning. (It was my mother who, in recalling the scene later, first referred to it as "the night the bed fell on your father.")

Always a deep sleeper, slow to arouse (I had lied to Briggs), I was at first unconscious of what had happened when the iron cot rolled me onto the floor and toppled over on me. It left me still warmly bundled up and unhurt, for the bed rested above me like a canopy. Hence I did not wake up, only reached the edge of consciousness and went back. The racket, however, instantly awakened my mother, in the next room, who came to the immediate conclusion that her worst dread was realized: the big wooden bed upstairs had fallen on father. She therefore screamed, "Let's go to your poor father!" It was this shout, rather than the noise of my cot falling, that awakened my brother Herman, in the same room with her. He thought that mother had become, for no apparent reason, hysterical. "You're all right, mamma!" he shouted, trying to calm her. They exchanged shout for shout perhaps ten seconds: "Let's go to your poor father!" and "You're all right!" That woke up Briggs. By this time I was conscious of what was going on, in a vague way, but did not yet realize that I was under my bed instead of on it. Briggs, awakening in the midst of loud shouts of fear and apprehension, came to the quick conclusion that he was suffocating and that we were all trying to "bring him out." With a low moan, he grasped the glass of camphor at the head of his bed and instead of sniffing it poured it over himself. The room reeked of camphor. "Ugf, ahfg!" choked Briggs, like a drowning man, for he had almost succeeded in stopping his breath under the deluge of pungent spirits. He leaped out of bed and groped toward the open window, but he came up against one that was closed. With his hand, he beat out the glass, and I could hear it crash and tinkle in the alleyway below. It was at this juncture that I, in trying to get up, had the uncanny sensation of feeling my bed above me! Foggy with sleep, I now suspected, in my turn, that the whole uproar was being made in a frantic endeavor to extricate me from what must be an unheard-of and perilous situation. "Get me out of this!" I bawled. "Get me out!" I think I had the nightmarish belief that I was entombed in a mine. "Gugh!" gasped Briggs, floundering in his camphor.

By this time my mother, still shouting, pursued by Herman, still shouting, was trying to open the door to the attic, in order to go up and get my father's body out of the wreckage. The door was stuck, however, and wouldn't yield. Her frantic pulls on it only added to the general banging and confusion. Roy and the dog were now up, the one shouting questions, the other barking.

Father, farthest away and soundest sleeper of all, had by this time been awakened by the battering on the attic door. He decided that the house was on fire. "I'm coming, I'm coming!" he wailed in a slow, sleepy voice—it took him many minutes to regain full consciousness. My mother, still believing he was caught under the bed, detected in his "I'm coming!" the mournful, resigned note of one who is preparing to meet his Maker. "He's dying!" she shouted.

"I'm all right!" Briggs yelled, to reassure her. "I'm all right!" He still believed that it was his own closeness to death that was worrying mother. I found at last the light switch in my room, unlocked the door, and Briggs and I joined the others at the attic door. The dog, who never did like Briggs, jumped for him—assuming that he was the culprit in whatever was going on—and Roy had to throw Rex and hold him. We could hear father crawling out of bed upstairs. Roy pulled the attic door open, with a mighty jerk, and father came down the stairs, sleepy and irritable but safe and sound. My mother began to weep when she saw him. Rex began to howl. "What in the name of God is going on here?" asked father.

The situation was finally put together like a gigantic jigsaw puzzle. Father caught a cold from prowling around in his bare feet but there were no other bad results. "I'm glad," said mother, who always looked on the bright side of things, "that your grandfather wasn't here."

[1933—U.S.A.]

Questions

1. Are Thurber's characters at all realistic? What is it about them that helps make the story comic? Why did Thurber include Aunt Beall and the Shoaf aunts, who have nothing to do with the action of the story?
2. How does Thurber, even while creating suspense, keep the reader from fearing the worst, thus freeing the reader to laugh?
3. How does Thurber make us believe in the story, however improbable and outrageous his characters and their actions may be? Consider in this regard the time when the story takes place and its narrator's tone in general.
4. How does the story's plot contribute to its comic mood?
5. Thematically, the story conveys a sense of what might be called "jumping to delusions." What light does it shed in this regard on human behavior generally? What attitude would Thurber have us take toward our quirkiness? What kind of laughter, then, does the story evoke—derisive, affectionate, appalled, liberating?

Writing Assignments

1. The intricacy of cause and effect is a prime source of this story's humor. Write a paragraph detailing this intricacy and pointing out how it gives rise to laughter.
2. Under the right circumstances, most of us can act in a ludicrous way. Narrate an incident in your life that could be seen as farcical. Try to make the incident seem as funny to the reader as it does to you.
3. Write a brief review of Thurber's story for a reader who has not read it. Does the story succeed or fail in your judgment? Explain why you judge it as you do.

A CONVERSATION WITH MY FATHER

❉ GRACE PALEY ❉

My father is eighty-six years old and in bed. His heart, that bloody motor, is equally old and will not do certain jobs any more. It still floods his head with brainy light. But it won't let his legs carry the weight of his body around the house. Despite my metaphors, this muscle failure is not due to his old heart, he says, but to a potassium shortage. Sitting on one pillow, leaning on three, he offers last-minute advice and makes a request.

"I would like you to write a simple story just once more," he says, "the kind de Maupassant wrote, or Chekhov, the kind you used to write. Just recognizable people and then write down what happened to them next."

I say, "Yes, why not? That's possible." I want to please him, though I don't remember writing that way. I *would* like to try to tell such a story, if he means the kind that begins: "There was a woman . . ." followed by plot, the absolute line between two points which I've always despised. Not for literary reasons, but because it takes all hope away. Everyone, real or invented, deserves the open destiny of life.

Finally I thought of a story that had been happening for a couple of years right across the street. I wrote it down, then read it aloud. "Pa," I said, "how about this? Do you mean something like this?"

> Once in my time there was a woman and she had a son. They lived nicely, in a small apartment in Manhattan. This boy at about fifteen became a junkie, which is not unusual in our neighborhood. In order to maintain her close friendship with him, she became a junkie too. She said it was part of the youth culture, with which she felt very much at home. After a while, for a number of reasons, the boy gave it all up and left the city and his mother in disgust. Hopeless and alone, she grieved. We all visit her.

"O.K., Pa, that's it," I said, "an unadorned and miserable tale."

"But that's not what I mean," my father said. "You misunderstood me on purpose. You know there's a lot more to it. You know that. You left everything out. Turgenev wouldn't do that. Chekhov wouldn't do that. There are in fact Russian writers you never heard of, you don't have an inkling of, as good as anyone, who can write a plain ordinary story, who would not leave out what you have left out. I object not to facts but to people sitting in trees talking senselessly, voices from who knows where . . ."

"Forget that one, Pa, what have I left out now? In this one?"

"Her looks, for instance."

"Oh. Quite handsome, I think. Yes."

"Her hair?"

"Dark, with heavy braids, as though she were a girl or a foreigner."

"What were her parents like, her stock? That she became such a person. It's interesting, you know."

"From out of town. Professional people. The first to be divorced in their county. How's that? Enough?" I asked.

"With you, it's all a joke," he said. "What about the boy's father? Why didn't you mention him? Who was he? Or was the boy born out of wedlock?"

"Yes," I said. "He was born out of wedlock."

"For Godsakes, doesn't anyone in your stories get married? Doesn't anyone have the time to run down to City Hall before they jump into bed?"

"No," I said. "In real life, yes. But in my stories, no."

"Why do you answer me like that?"

"Oh, Pa, this is a simple story about a smart woman who came to N.Y.C. full of interest love trust excitement very up to date, and about her son, what a hard time she had in this world. Married or not, it's of small consequence."

"It is of great consequence," he said.

"O.K.," I said.

"O.K. O.K. yourself," he said, "but listen. I believe you that she's good-looking but I don't think she was so smart."

"That's true," I said. "Actually that's the trouble with stories. People start out fantastic. You think they're extraordinary, but it turns out as the work goes along, they're just average with a good education. Sometimes the other way around, the person's a kind of dumb innocent, but he outwits you and you can't even think of an ending good enough."

"What do you do then?" he asked. He had been a doctor for a couple of decades and then an artist for a couple of decades and he's still interested in details, craft, technique.

"Well, you just have to let the story lie around till some agreement can be reached between you and the stubborn hero."

"Aren't you talking silly, now?" he asked. "Start again," he said. "It so happens I'm not going out this evening. Tell the story again. See what you can do this time."

"O.K.," I said. "But it's not a five-minute job." Second attempt:

Once, across the street from us, there was a fine handsome woman, our neighbor. She had a son whom she loved because she'd known him since birth (in helpless chubby infancy, and in the wrestling, hugging ages, seven to ten, as well as earlier and later). This boy, when he fell into the fist of adolescence, became a junkie. He was not a hopeless one. He was in fact hopeful, an ideologue and successful converter. With his busy brilliance, he wrote persuasive articles for his high-school newspaper. Seeking a wider audience, using important connections, he drummed into Lower Manhattan news-stand distribution a periodical called *Oh! Golden Horse!*

In order to keep him from feeling guilty (because guilt is the stony heart of nine tenths of all clinically diagnosed cancers in America today, she said), and because she had always believed in giving bad habits room at home where one could keep an eye on them, she too became a junkie. Her kitchen was famous for a while—a center for intellectual addicts who knew what they were doing. A few felt artistic like Coleridge and others were scientific and revolutionary like Leary. Although she was often high herself, certain good mothering reflexes remained, and she saw to it that there was lots of orange juice around and honey and milk and vitamin pills. However, she never cooked anything but chili, and that no more than once a week. She explained, when we talked to her, seriously, with neighborly concern, that it was her part in the youth culture and she would rather be with the young, it was an honor, than with her own generation.

One week, while nodding through an Antonioni film, this boy was severely jabbed by the elbow of a stern and proselytizing girl, sitting beside him. She offered immediate apricots and nuts for his sugar level, spoke to him sharply, and took him home.

She had heard of him and his work and she herself published, edited, and wrote a competitive journal called *Man Does Live By Bread Alone*. In the organic heat of her continuous presence he could not help but become interested once more in his muscles, his arteries, and nerve connections. In fact he began to love them, treasure them, praise them with funny little songs in *Man Does Live* . . .

> the fingers of my flesh transcend
> my transcendental soul
> the tightness in my shoulders end
> my teeth have made me whole

To the mouth of his head (glory of will and determination) he brought hard apples, nuts, wheat germ, and soy-bean oil. He said to his old friends, From now on, I guess I'll keep my wits about me. I'm going on the natch. He said he was about to begin a spiritual deep-breathing journey. How about you too, Mom? he asked kindly.

His conversion was so radiant, splendid, that neighborhood kids his age began to say that he had never been a real addict at all, only a journalist along for the smell of the story. The mother tried several times to give up what had become without her son and his friends a lonely habit. This effort only brought it to supportable levels. The boy and his girl took their electronic mimeograph and moved to the bushy edge of another borough. They were very strict. They said they would not see her again until she had been off drugs for sixty days.

At home alone in the evening, weeping, the mother read and reread the seven issues of *Oh! Golden Horse!* They seemed to her as truthful as ever. We often crossed the street to visit and console. But if we mentioned any of our children who were at college or in the hospital or dropouts at home, she would cry out, My baby! My baby! and burst into terrible, face-scarring, time-consuming tears. The End.

First my father was silent, then he said, "Number One: You have a nice sense of humor. Number Two: I see you can't tell a plain story. So don't waste time." Then he said sadly, "Number Three: I suppose that means she was alone, she was left like that, his mother. Alone. Probably sick?"

I said, "Yes."

"Poor woman. Poor girl, to be born in a time of fools, to live among fools. The end. The end. You were right to put that down. The end."

I didn't want to argue, but I had to say, "Well, it is not necessarily the end, Pa."

"Yes," he said, "what a tragedy. The end of a person."

"No, Pa," I begged him. "It doesn't have to be. She's only about forty. She could be a hundred different things in this world as time goes on. A teacher or a social worker. An ex-junkie! Sometimes it's better than having a master's in education."

"Jokes," he said. "As a writer that's your main trouble. You don't want to recognize it. Tragedy! Plain tragedy! Historical tragedy! No hope. The end."

"Oh, Pa," I said. "She could change."

"In your own life, too, you have to look it in the face." He took a couple of nitroglycerin. "Turn to five," he said, pointing to the dial on the oxygen tank. He inserted the tubes into his nostrils and breathed deep. He closed his eyes and said, "No."

I had promised the family to always let him have the last word when arguing, but in this case I had a different responsibility. That woman lives across the street. She's my knowledge and my invention. I'm sorry for her. I'm not going to leave her there in that house crying. (Actually neither would Life, which unlike me has no pity.)

Therefore: She did change. Of course her son never came home again. But right now, she's the receptionist in a storefront community clinic in the East Village. Most of the customers are young people, some old friends. The head doctor has said to her, "If we only had three people in this clinic with your experiences . . ."

"The doctor said that?" My father took the oxygen tubes out of his nostrils and said, "Jokes. Jokes again."

"No, Pa, it could really happen that way, it's a funny world nowadays."

"No," he said. "Truth first. She will slide back. A person must have character. She does not."

"No, Pa," I said. "That's it. She's got a job. Forget it. She's in that storefront working."

"How long will it be?" he asked. "Tragedy! You too. When will you look it in the face?"

[1972—U.S.A.]

Questions

1. Why does the father dislike his daughter's stories? What does he feel she leaves out? In what way does what she leaves out amount to an avoidance, at least in his eyes, not just in her fiction but in her life?
2. How does the narrator define "plot" and why does she dislike it? Father and daughter seem to agree on the relation of plot to life. How so?
3. The father believes that stories should concern "recognizable people," which he does not find in his daughter's stories. Why might the daughter dislike character as well as plot?
4. Does the second version of the daughter's story have a greater sense of plot than the first? Does the second version have a plot according to the daughter's definition of the word?
5. In what way, if any, is the father's final judgment of his daughter (see the story's last sentence) not a judgment of Grace Paley herself as author?

Writing Assignments

1. In a short essay compare and contrast the two versions of the story told by Paley's narrator. Conclude by considering whether their likenesses or their differences are more significant in terms of the story as a whole.
2. Write a paper pinpointing the differences between the narrator's story (in both versions)

and the "conversation" in which she is one of the characters. What theme do these differences suggest?

3. Read Grace Paley's "Wants" (pp. 112–14). Then write a paragraph or short paper on it from the point of view of the father in "Conversation with My Father." What would be his criteria of judgment? Does "Wants" fulfill those criteria? Would the story satisfy him finally?

CONTINUITY OF PARKS

❋ JULIO CORTÁZAR ❋

Translated by Paul Blackburn

He had begun to read the novel a few days before. He had put it down because of some urgent business conferences, opened it again on his way back to the estate by train; he permitted himself a slowly growing interest in the plot, in the characterizations. That afternoon, after writing a letter giving his power of attorney and discussing a matter of joint ownership with the manager of his estate, he returned to the book in the tranquillity of his study which looked out upon the park with its oaks. Sprawled in his favorite armchair, its back toward the door—even the possibility of an intrusion would have irritated him, had he thought of it—he let his left hand caress repeatedly the green velvet upholstery and set to reading the final chapters. He remembered effortlessly the names and his mental images of the characters; the novel spread its glamour over him almost at once. He tasted the almost perverse pleasure of disengaging himself line by line from the things around him, and at the same time feeling his head rest comfortably on the green velvet of the chair with its high back, sensing that the cigarettes rested within reach of his hand, that beyond the great windows the air of afternoon danced under the oak trees in the park. Word by word, licked up by the sordid dilemma of the hero and heroine, letting himself be absorbed to the point where the images settled down and took on color and movement, he was witness to the final encounter in the mountain cabin. The woman arrived first, apprehensive; now the lover came in, his face cut by the backlash of a branch. Admirably, she stanched the blood with her kisses, but he rebuffed her caresses, he had not come to perform again the ceremonies of a secret passion, protected by a world of dry leaves and furtive paths through the forest. The dagger warmed itself against his chest, and underneath liberty pounded, hidden close. A lustful, panting dialogue raced down the pages like a rivulet of snakes, and one felt it had all been decided from eternity. Even to those caresses which writhed about the lover's body, as though wishing to keep him there, to dissuade him from it; they sketched abominably the frame of that other body it was necessary to destroy. Nothing had been forgotten: alibis, unforeseen hazards, possible mistakes. From this hour on, each instant had its use minutely assigned. The cold-blooded, twice-gone-over re-examination of the details was barely broken off so that a hand could caress a cheek. It was beginning to get dark.

Not looking at one another now, rigidly fixed upon the task which awaited them, they separated at the cabin door. She was to follow the trail that led north. On the path leading in the opposite direction, he turned for a moment to watch her running, her hair loosened and flying. He ran in turn, crouching among the trees and hedges until, in the yellowish fog of dusk, he could distinguish the avenue of trees which led up to the house. The dogs were not supposed to bark, they did not bark. The estate manager would not be there at this hour, and he was not there. He went up the three porch steps and entered. The woman's words reached him over the thudding of blood in his ears: first a blue chamber, then a hall, then a carpeted stairway. At the top, two doors. No one in the first room, no one in the second. The door of the salon, and then, the knife in hand, the light from the great windows, the high back of an armchair covered in green velvet, the head of the man in the chair reading a novel.

[1963—Argentina]

Questions

1. Summarize what we know of the plot of the novel being read in the story. Now summarize the plot of the story.
2. Are we to believe that what the man reads about in the novel actually happens to him, or is it that he is totally absorbed in the novel imaginatively?
3. How is your own relation to Cortázar's story like or unlike the relation between the reader and the novel in the story?
4. In what way or ways might "Continuity of Parks" be about the relation between language and reality?

Writing Assignments

1. Write a paragraph or two explaining how the plot of the novel being read in the story and the plot of the story itself coincide and what this coincidence suggests about the relation of language and reality.
2. In a short essay, compare the reader of the novel in "Continuity of Parks" and yourself as reader of the story, and consider the theme of the story in light of this comparison.

✳ 4 ✳

CHARACTERIZATION

FICTION'S PEOPLE

Almost anything in a story can serve to establish and delineate its characters—to dramatize their motivations, their emotions, their natures. As we have seen, for example, plot can be an agent of characterization: we see who people are by observing what they do. In turn, like the other elements of fiction, characterization helps lead to theme, and in some stories what is revealed about characters is the theme. People are interested in people. In fact, most of us are more interested in people than in anything else. Whatever it is that makes human beings tick is theme enough.

This does not mean, however, that we must recognize ourselves in every character we encounter. Fiction does not ask us to identify in that way with its people. If it did, then no one could be moved by more than a handful of stories; most would leave us cold. It asks instead for imaginative participation in the circumstances and lives of people often of vastly different backgrounds, values, potentials, and understanding from ourselves. If a character does strike home, fine; but many will not. Certainly, fiction contains a good number of unsavory characters, with whom we would not want to identify in any way. Still, such characters can be fascinating. One of the beauties of fiction is that it offers us a world of people to observe. By observing closely, we can come to participate in their imagined lives and thereby come to new insights.

In real life we can never truly get inside another person's skin. Our insights into people's behavior must be fragmentary, incomplete at best. Fictional characters, just because they are fictional, offer us a unique opportunity to penetrate into human complexity. We can look at a character from every side, ponder the details that go into the making of that character, then come back and look at the character again. Fiction allows us to hold life in crystal, so to speak, and see into the mystery of human personality. By so doing, it can lead to a heightened compassion for all kinds of people—all human, all caught with us in this mortal condition, but different from us with respect to the particulars of their lives.

MODES OF CHARACTERIZATION

But how do we come to an understanding of a character in a story? How can the intangibles of personality be captured in words? One way is for the narrator simply to tell everything an author wants us to know about a character: "Miss Jones was a vain young woman, always primping and fussing, little concerned with the feelings of others." And narrators sometimes do tell us things of this sort. The experienced reader, however, understands that narrators are not always to be trusted (we'll return to this matter in the next chapter). Of greater immediate importance, telling does not involve us: we want to be shown. We want to observe for ourselves the qualities that make up a character. Even if I am told that Miss Jones is vain, I want to see her vanity concretely: I want to look into her wardrobe, catch her in front of a mirror, watch how she interacts with others. From all this I can then infer her vanity with conviction.

Inference of this sort is the key to understanding literary characters as it is to understanding people in everyday life. Only the most naive of us simply takes people at their own word. For some will be dishonest, and even those who are totally honest can be self-deceived. In determining people's character, we know that we must be somewhat wary and base our judgment on observation of what they do and how they respond to the situations we find them in. Similarly, plot or situation in fiction can expose some aspect of a character, so our judgment of characters is usually based at least in part on the interplay of plot/situation and the inner lives of characters. We also infer much about people from their appearance and possessions. The same is true of the appearance and possessions of literary characters: both become symbolic, telling us something about the intangible qualities of personality as revealed by their tangible manifestations. Setting, too—the time and place in which we find characters—can suggest something about them. Also important is how they speak—not just what they say, but how they say it. Though what people say is important, it must be weighed against our perception of them generally, for we know that we cannot necessarily believe everything we are told. On the other hand, how people speak can be immediately revealing. An author might have a character speak in short, incomplete sentences to convey the character's excitement; a character who speaks in long, complex sentences, in contrast, will convey something quite different.

Most important, in coming to conclusions about people, we watch how they interact; we compare one person with another and listen to what they say to and about each other. Of course, we generally heed only those who have proved themselves to be reliable. As we read a story we must be sure to determine each character's reliability—truthfulness, knowledge, and so forth. Then, if a character whom we have judged to be reliable says something about another, we know that what is said is prime information. Even if limited in scope, what is said about one character by others can show us different sides of that character. In some stories, though, we learn everything about the characters from interaction alone; we are told nothing directly. One story in the last chapter—Somerset Maugham's "A String of Beads"—

is an excellent example. What we learn about the male speaker engaged in a dialogue with a rather garrulous female as well as what we learn about her comes almost entirely from comparing the two as they interact. Our assessments, note, are based on inference, but valid inference, derived from the textual facts available.

TYPES OF CHARACTER

Many stories do not present us with highly developed characters, and even those that do usually treat only a few characters in any depth. Accordingly, in analyzing fiction we can divide characters into two broad categories: flat and round. **Round characters** are the sort we have been speaking of, characters treated in some depth, constructed by the reader by way of inference from plot, situation, setting, style, character contrast, and so on. As we watch them acting and responding, hear them speaking and interacting, and observe them undergoing internal change, we come to know them well. In contrast, we know **flat characters** only by a few prevailing characteristics, which most often remain constant over the course of a work. This is not to say that flat characters are unrealistic. In a sense, they are probably more true to life than round ones in that most people we come in contact with every day are flat to us, seen in one limited role only. And we seldom if ever see into another human being as thoroughly as we can a round character in fiction. As readers we tend to prefer round characters, but we should realize that fiction couldn't do without flat characters as well. It is a matter of both space and focus. There simply is not enough space even in the longest novel to develop every character fully, and even if there were, to do so would not be desirable because then there would be no focus. We can focus on only so much at a time, after all. In some stories, too, character is not really significant. These stories have their focus elsewhere, so it would be erroneous for the reader to look for developed characters. We as readers must determine the kind of characters we are presented with and adapt ourselves accordingly.

Finally, a word should be said about a particular type of flat character: the **stock** or **type character**—the mad scientist, the absent-minded professor, the strong but silent lawman. Even flatter than the usual flat character, stock characters are easily recognizable because the stereotypes they are based on are widespread in the culture. Stock characters are the stuff of propaganda on the one hand and of second-rate fiction on the other. However, we also find them in certain types of the best fiction, though in the hands of a topflight writer stock characters have a way of becoming particularized and memorable. Such characters are especially suitable to comedy and satire, for the less we see into a character the more likely we are to laugh at that character. That is why Dickens is full of stock characters. To be sure, there are many wonderfully round characters in Dickens (Nicholas Nickleby and his friend Smike, David Copperfield, and even old Scrooge, perhaps) as well as many memorable flat characters (Bob Cratchit and Tiny Tim). But it is the parade of stock characters, each lovingly particularized by some trait or manner, that one associates most with Dickens—the cousins, the uncles, the aunts; the beggars and street people; the fops;

and all manner of lost souls. All are stock characters, yet all are made to come to life if only for an instant.

CHARACTER AND THEME

Fictional characters of any sort result from the human desire both to individualize and to typify. Thus, even the roundest of characters typifies one or another human possibility, and even a purely stock character, if handled by a competent writer, will have marks of individuality. We are back again to the business of the particular and the general. Particularization gives a story life; generalization gives it meaning. Therefore, while appearing as individuals, characters in fiction tend to raise general questions. Conversely, because ideas in fiction are seen in connection with people, we're made to feel concretely what otherwise would be impersonal abstraction.

For example, take Cynthia Ozick's "The Shawl" once more. The story concerns powerlessness, as we have seen. But powerlessness is only an idea. In "The Shawl" it is made to live by way of Magda, Stella, and especially Rosa, as round a character as is possible in three pages or so. In coming to see what happens to Rosa as she deteriorates, we see what powerlessness means in the flesh. Because the theme of the story concerns the effect of powerlessness on the human spirit, the story necessarily centers on character. There are stories, however, whose themes are more philosophical (as opposed to psychological). In stories of this sort, character and characterization are often secondary, while some other element (symbolism, for example) becomes controlling. The themes of those stories that focus on the human psyche or soul might be thought of as "internal," whereas the themes of stories whose focus is elsewhere might be thought of as "external." In any case, no story can do without some degree of characterization, and in many stories character is a prime element.

SUMMARY SUGGESTIONS: UNDERSTANDING CHARACTERS

1. As you read a story determine the prime elements that go into its making. By determining what elements are prime and what are secondary, one can start to perceive where the focus of a story lies and so begin to think about theme. And if character is prime, then character or character revelation may be theme.

2. Evaluate the types of character used in a story—round, flat, stock. If all the characters seem flat or stock, then character revelation is probably not the point. Your attention should be elsewhere.

3. If a character starts to seem round, however, or seems important for some other reason, then attend to the matters of characterization that we have discussed. What elements help to establish or reveal character (such as plot, setting) and how? How is the character like or unlike other characters in the story? What do we learn from other characters about the character in question? What can be inferred from these and other of the story's details about the character?

4. You might also check for character consistency. Ask questions like "Are a character's actions and motives consistent with what we know about the character? Does the character undergo any change? If so, how?"

5. Finally, determine the trustworthiness of characters. If they prove trustworthy, you may take their judgments as evidence. If they are untrustworthy, there is a reason, and that reason is significant and should be taken into account.

WRITING ON CHARACTERS

Almost any character in fiction might be made the subject of an interesting paper. This is especially true of those stories in which the revelation of character is thematically central. Here you might explore, for example, how plot or situation helps us to understand a character; what the setting suggests; what the character's manner of speech reveals; what we learn from what other characters say and from character interaction; and so forth. In the case of a story focused on character, your thesis would probably be a statement of your assessment of the character central to the story; your support would be a step-by-step consideration of what in the story validates the judgment that is your thesis.

Even minor characters, flat or stock, may be worth looking at. Consider, for instance, Stella in Ozick's "The Shawl." One could easily write an essay on her. To do so, one could make a statement about her regression to infantile behavior, exemplify it, and then suggest why she regresses. Her stealing of the shawl—a matter of plot— certainly marks this regression, which is also displayed in various ways by her interactions with both Magda and Rosa. What has caused her regression, of course, is her circumstance; here the setting—in both place and time—comes into play. When you are writing on any kind of character in any kind of story, remember that you must support your thesis with the particulars of the story itself if your paper is to be convincing.

Another possible focus for a paper on characters is consistency or the lack of it. If a character seems inconsistent, you have an immediate thesis: in such and such a story so and so is inconsistent. Now, how so and why? Your first task is to analyze and demonstrate the inconsistency; your second is to draw a conclusion as to why. If you can discern no valid reason, then perhaps the writer is inept or manipulative. Such would be your conclusion. Remember, however, that sometimes character inconsistency can be well motivated (we all can act "out of character" when given the right circumstance). If this is the case, then the inconsistency is crucial information, telling us even more than we knew before about the character at hand. And remember that, like real people, characters in fiction can change. Indeed, to detail how and why a character grows or perhaps deteriorates is a fine thing to do. If you perceive change, then you have a ready-made thesis and support material that should be immediately apparent.

Even when you write on something other than character, you may find it useful to discuss character somewhere along the way. For example, if you were writing on the meaning of a story's setting, you would probably get into characterization because, at least in part, the setting would probably be an agent of characterization.

Still, you would be writing on setting and not characterization. The latter would be secondary in this case, support rather than thesis.

A final word. When reading about and writing on characters, bring everything you know about people, including yourself, to bear. You already have a wide experience of life. Don't leave it at the door when it comes to reading and writing. You know much about people—how we act or respond in one or another circumstance; how we can fool others and ourselves; how we relate to one another and how we don't. Carry all this with you when it comes to dealing with fiction's people. In turn, let your reading and then your writing broaden your experience. There is much to be learned from fiction, especially about people and their interactions.

STORIES FOR STUDY AND WRITING ASSIGNMENTS

CHAOS, DISORDER AND THE LATE SHOW

❋ WARREN MILLER ❋

I am a certified public accountant and a rational man. More exactly, and putting things in their proper order, I am a rational man first and an accountant second. I insist on order; I like the symbols of order—a blunt, hardy plus sign or a forthright minus delights me. I make lists, I am always punctual, I wear a hat. Maltz believes this has caused my hairline to recede. Maltz is one of my associates at the office. He married too young and he regrets it.

In fact, there is no scientific foundation for his view that wearing a hat causes the hairline to recede. Such things are largely a matter of heredity, although my father has a luxuriant head of hair. But what of my grandfathers? I have no doubt that one of them accounts for my high forehead. Talent, I believe I have read somewhere, often skips a generation or jumps from uncle to nephew. Studies have been made. Naturally there are exceptions. But it provides one with the beginning of an explanation. The notion of having been an adopted child is a fancy I have never indulged. I have never doubted that my parents are my true parents. But I sometimes suspect they think I am not their true son.

Let me say just this about my father: He is a high-school history teacher, and every summer for twenty-five years he has had a three-month vacation. Not once has he ever put this time to any real use. He could have been a counselor at a camp, taught the summer session, clerked at a department store or . . . any number of things. I recall that he spent one entire summer lying on the sofa, reading. Some years he goes to the beach. Once he went to Mexico. His income is, to be sure, adequate, but I am certain that one major illness would wipe out his savings. I have tried to speak to him about preplanning; he listens, but he does not seem to hear.

My mother—I think this one example will suffice—my mother believes that Leslie Howard, who was a Hollywood actor killed in the war, is still alive. My father merely smiles when she speaks of Leslie Howard—I believe he actually enjoys it— but I have brought home almanacs and circled references in *Harper's* and other magazines attesting to the fact that Leslie Howard is, in fact and in truth, dead. Definitive proof.

Not that I care; not that I care very deeply. It is a harmless-enough delusion; but it is sloppy. I believe that the world tends naturally to chaos and that we all have to make our daily—even hourly—contribution toward order. My parents, in my opinion, are unwilling to shoulder their share of this responsibility.

I have, once or twice, discussed the matter with Maltz, whose wife has proved to be unreliable in some ways and who has a sympathy in matters of this kind.

Maltz agrees that my father is mistaken in his indulgent attitude; on the other hand, he believes it would, perhaps, be better psychologically if I ignored my mother's pitiful little delusion—as he called it.

But it is like a pebble in my shoe or loose hair under my shirt collar. Chaos and disorder in the world, in the natural scheme of things, is bad enough; one does not want to put up with it at home too. The subways are dirty and unreliable; the crosstown buses are not properly spaced; clerks in stores never know where their stock is.

The extent of the breakdown is incredible. Every year at this time I rent an empty store on upper Broadway and help people with their income-tax returns. These people keep no records! They have no receipts! They lose their canceled checks! They guess! The year just past is, to them, a fast-fading and already incomplete collection of snapshots. It was full of medical and business expenses and deductions for entertaining, yet they remember nothing. Believe me, the chaos of subways and crosstown buses and our traffic problems is as nothing compared to the disorder in the heads of *people*. Every year I am struck with this anew.

This extra-time work continues for three months and becomes more intense as deadline time draws near. It is amazing how many people wait until the last possible moment. Often I am there until nearly midnight.

At the beginning of March I hire Maltz and pay him by the head. He is not as fast as I would like, but he is reliable and, because of his wife and her extravagances, he needs the money. "It would embarrass me," he says, "if I had to tell you how much she spends every week on magazines alone." Poor guy.

I live with my parents. The store I rent is near their apartment, a matter of three blocks, walking distance. It is a neighborhood of small shops and large supermarkets which once were movie houses; their marquees now advertise turkeys and hams. Maltz occasionally will walk me to my door.

That night, the night of the incident, it was snowing. It had been snowing all day. No one had cleaned his sidewalk, and it made walking treacherous. I almost slipped twice.

"Isn't there a city ordinance about people cleaning their sidewalks? Isn't it mandatory?" I asked.

Maltz said, "There is such an ordinance, Norman, but it is more honored in the breach than in the practice."

The sadness of his marriage has given Maltz a kind of wisdom. The next time he slipped I took his arm, and I thought, Here is a man who might one day be my friend. The loneliness of the mismated is a terrible thing to see. It touches me. I believe I understand it. At the door of my building I said good night and I watched for a moment as Maltz proceeded reluctantly toward home.

The elevator was out of order again. When a breakdown occurs, tenants must use the freight elevator at the rear of the lobby. I had to ring for it three times and wait more than five minutes; then I had to ride up with two open garbage cans. It was not very pleasant. The elevator man said, "How's business, Mr Whitehead?"

"Very good, thank you, Oscar," I said.

"I'll be in to see you real soon, Mr. Whitehead."

I nodded. I knew he'd wait, as he did last year, until the last possible moment. I tried to shrug it off. It's no good trying to carry the next man's share on your own shoulders, I told myself. Forget it, I thought.

Because I had come up in the freight elevator, I therefore entered our apartment by way of the kitchen. I took off my rubbers and carried them in with me, my briefcase in the other hand. As a result the door slammed shut, since I had no free hand to close it slowly.

"Is it you?" my mother called.

She was at the kitchen table having her midnight cup of tea; she said it calmed her and made sleeping easier to have tea before bed. I have tried to explain to her that tea has a higher percentage of caffeine than coffee, but she continues to drink it.

She was smiling.

"What is it?" I said.

"Mr. Know-it-all, come here and I would like to show you something."

She had a newspaper on the table. I did not move. "What is it?" I asked.

"Come here and I will show you, Norman," she said, still smiling.

At this point my father shouted something unintelligible from their bedroom. "What did you say, dear? What?"

"Bette Davis on the late show. *Dark Victory!*"

My mother put her hand to her heart. "I remember the day I saw it," she said. "At the Rivoli, with Millie Brandon." She sat there, staring at nothing; she had forgotten all about me.

"What was it you wanted, Mother?" I said.

"Twenty-five cents if you got there before noon, would you believe it," she said.

I looked at the newspaper. I was astonished to see that she had brought such a newspaper into the house. There it was, beside her teacup, one of those weekly papers that always has headlines such as: MOTHER POISONS HER FIVE BABIES or TAB HUNTER SAYS "I AM LONELY." The inside pages, I have been told, are devoted to racing news.

"Mr. Know-it-all," she said and began to smile again.

"What are you doing with *that* paper, Mother?"

"Millie called me this afternoon and I ran out and bought it. Look!" she cried, and with an all-too-typical dramatic flourish she unfolded it and showed me the front page. The headline read: LESLIE HOWARD STILL ALIVE.

"So much for your almanacs and your definitive proof," she said. "Now what have you got to say, my dear?"

"Two minutes, dear," my father called in on her. "Commercial on now."

"Coming," she called back.

"Mother," I said, "you know very well what kind of paper this is."

"Why should they pick this subject?" she said, tapping the headline with her fingernail. "Why should they pick this particular subject right out of the blue? I would like to ask you that."

"Did you read the article itself, Mother? Is there one iota of hard fact in it?"

"There are facts, and there are facts, my dear boy."

I was very patient with her. "Mother," I said, "he is dead. It is well known that he is dead. He went down at sea in a transport plane . . ."

"First of all, Mr. Smart One, it was not a transport. It was a Spitfire. He always flew Spitfires. He and David Niven."

"Well, then, Mother, just tell me this," I said. "If he's alive, where is he? Where is he?"

"It's starting, dear," my father called.

"The loveliest man who ever walked this earth," she said.

"I have never had the pleasure of seeing him, Mother."

"Steel-rimmed glasses. A pipe. Tweed jackets."

"Well, where is he, Mother?"

"So gentle. Gentle, yet dashing. If everybody was like Leslie Howard, wouldn't this be one beautiful world. Oh, what a beautiful world it would be!"

"Under no circumstances would I trust that particular newspaper," I said.

"This newspaper, my dear boy, is like every other newspaper. It is sometimes right."

I put my rubbers under the sink.

"The year you were born I saw him in *Intermezzo,* Ingrid Bergman's first American movie. Produced by Selznick, who was then still married, I believe, to Louis B. Mayer's daughter Irene." She sipped her tea and looked at the headline. She said, "These days they don't even name boys Leslie anymore. *Girls* are now named Leslie. Before the war people had such lovely names. Leslie, Cary, Myrna, Fay, Claudette. What has happened?"

She looked at me as if it were all my fault. "I don't know what's happened, Mother," I said, perhaps a little testily.

"It's your world, my dear; therefore you should know," she said. "Nowadays they even name them after the days of the week."

"I have named no one after any day of the week, Mother," I said, but she was not listening.

"You could always find a parking place. People were polite. Self-service was unheard of. Frozen food was something to be avoided at all costs."

"I can put no confidence at all in that particular newspaper," I said. "Absolutely none."

"Then I am sorry for you and I pity you," she said in a manner that I thought entirely uncalled for.

"Why? Why should you be sorry for me and pity me?" I asked.

I waited for her to answer, but she went back to sipping her tea and reading the headline.

"I have a good job," I said, "and I am doing the work I like."

"Nevertheless, Norman, I feel sorry for you."

I had not even taken off my overcoat, and I was forced to put up with an attack of this nature! I was struck by the unfairness of it. I said, "You *know* what a silly newspaper that is, Mother. What is the matter with you? You know he is dead. I know you know it. Everybody knows that he is dead."

She banged down her cup. "He is not!" she said. "He is not dead! He is not!"

"What's going on in there?" my father called.

"He is alive!"

"Then where is he?" I demanded, and I raised my voice, too; I admit that I raised my voice. "Where is he?"

"Oh," she said as if she were completely disgusted with me. "Oh, Mr. Born Too Late, I'll tell you where he is," she said, getting up from her chair, the newspaper in her hand. And she began to hit me on the head with it. She hit me on the head with it. Every time she mentioned a name she hit me. "I'll tell you where he is, I'll tell you where he is. He is with Carole Lombard and Glenn Miller and Will Rogers and Franklin . . ."

I ran out of the room. Why argue? She has a harmless delusion. From now on I will try to ignore her when she gets on this particular subject. Maltz may be right about this. I hung up my coat. Fortunately it is only when I stand at my closet door that I can hear the sound of their television set, which often goes on until three in the morning. Once I shut that door, however, my room is perfectly silent.

[1963—U.S.A.]

Questions

1. Does this story present us with a plot or a situation? Why is the one or the other appropriate to its content?
2. Contrast Norman with his mother and father. What type of character is each (round, flat, stock)? What do we learn about Norman by these contrasts? Of the three, whom do you sympathize with and why?
3. What can we tell about Norman from his general reaction to things, from his manner of dress, from his "perfectly silent" room? Is Norman truly a rational man?
4. *Dark Victory,* a movie of much emotional turmoil, which Norman has never seen, hovers in the background of this story. What does reference to it serve to do here?
5. Would the world according to Norman (that is, the world as he would like it to be) be better or worse than it is now? How so?

Writing Assignments

1. In a few paragraphs compare and contrast Norman with his mother and father. Be specific, providing examples to support what you say about each character.
2. Write an essay on how Norman is characterized. What elements of the story go into his making and help to condition the reader's response to him? In light of the response the story directs us toward, what might be its theme?

MISS BRILL

❊ KATHERINE MANSFIELD ❊

Although it was so brilliantly fine—the blue sky powdered with gold and great spots of light like white wine splashed over the Jardins Publiques—Miss Brill was glad that she had decided on her fur. The air was motionless, but when you opened your mouth there was just a faint chill, like a chill from a glass of iced water before you sip, and now and again a leaf came drifting—from nowhere, from the sky. Miss Brill put up her hand and touched her fur. Dear little thing! It was nice to feel it again. She had taken it out of its box that afternoon, shaken out the moth-powder, given it a good brush, and rubbed the life back into the dim little eyes. "What has been happening to me?" said the sad little eyes. Oh, how sweet it was to see them snap at her again from the red eiderdown! . . . But the nose, which was of some black composition, wasn't at all firm. It must have had a knock, somehow. Never mind—a little dab of black sealing-wax when the time came—when it was absolutely necessary. . . . Little rogue! Yes, she really felt like that about it. Little rogue biting its tail just by her left ear. She could have taken it off and laid it on her lap and stroked it. She felt a tingling in her hands and arms, but that came from walking, she supposed. And when she breathed, something light and sad—no, not sad, exactly— something gentle seemed to move in her bosom.

There were a number of people out this afternoon, far more than last Sunday. And the band sounded louder and gayer. That was because the Season had begun. For although the band played all the year round on Sundays, out of season it was never the same. It was like some one playing with only the family to listen; it didn't care how it played if there weren't any strangers present. Wasn't the conductor wearing a new coat, too? She was sure it was new. He scraped with his foot and flapped his arms like a rooster about to crow, and the bandsmen sitting in the green rotunda blew out their cheeks and glared at the music. Now there came a little "flutey" bit—very pretty!—a little chain of bright drops. She was sure it would be repeated. It was; she lifted her head and smiled.

Only two people shared her "special" seat: a fine old man in a velvet coat, his hands clasped over a huge carved walking-stick, and a big old woman, sitting upright, with a roll of knitting on her embroidered apron. They did not speak. This was disappointing, for Miss Brill always looked forward to the conversation. She had become really quite expert, she thought, at listening as though she didn't listen, at sitting in other people's lives just for a minute while they talked round her.

She glanced, sideways, at the old couple. Perhaps they would go soon. Last Sunday, too, hadn't been as interesting as usual. An Englishman and his wife, he wearing a dreadful Panama hat and she button boots. And she'd gone on the whole time about how she ought to wear spectacles; she knew she needed them, but that it was no good getting any; they'd be sure to break and they'd never keep on. And he'd been so patient. He'd suggested everything—gold rims, the kind that curved round your ears, little pads inside the bridge. No, nothing would please her. "They'll always be sliding down my nose!" Miss Brill had wanted to shake her.

The old people sat on the bench, still as statues. Never mind, there was always the crowd to watch. To and fro, in front of the flower-beds and the band rotunda, the couples and groups paraded, stopped to talk, to greet, to buy a handful of flowers from the old beggar who had his tray fixed to the railings. Little children ran among them, swooping and laughing; little boys with big white silk bows under their chins, little girls, little French dolls, dressed up in velvet and lace. And sometimes a tiny staggerer came suddenly rocking into the open from under the trees, stopped, stared, as suddenly sat down "flop," until its small high-stepping mother, like a young hen, rushed scolding to its rescue. Other people sat on the benches and green chairs, but they were nearly always the same, Sunday after Sunday, and— Miss Brill had often noticed—there was something funny about nearly all of them. They were odd, silent, nearly all old, and from the way they stared they looked as though they'd just come from dark little rooms or even—even cupboards!

Behind the rotunda the slender trees with yellow leaves down drooping, and through them just a line of sea, and beyond the blue sky with gold-veined clouds.

Tum-tum-tum tiddle-um! tiddle-um! tum tiddley-um tum ta! blew the band.

Two young girls in red came by and two young soldiers in blue met them, and they laughed and paired and went off arm-in-arm. Two peasant women with funny straw hats passed, gravely, leading beautiful smoke-coloured donkeys. A cold, pale nun hurried by. A beautiful woman came along and dropped her bunch of violets, and a little boy ran after to hand them to her, and she took them and threw them away as if they'd been poisoned. Dear me! Miss Brill didn't know whether to admire that or not! And now an ermine toque and a gentleman in grey met just in front of her. He was tall, stiff, dignified, and she was wearing the ermine toque she'd bought when her hair was yellow. Now everything, her hair, her face, even her eyes, was the same colour as the shabby ermine, and her hand, in its cleaned glove, lifted to dab her lips, was a tiny yellowish paw. Oh, she was so pleased to see him—delighted! She rather thought they were going to meet that afternoon. She described where she'd been—everywhere, here, there, along by the sea. The day was so charming— didn't he agree? And wouldn't he, perhaps? . . . But he shook his head, lighted a cigarette, slowly breathed a great deep puff into her face, and even while she was still talking and laughing, flicked the match away and walked on. The ermine toque was alone; she smiled more brightly than ever. But even the band seemed to know what she was feeling and played more softly, played tenderly, and the drum beat, "The Brute! The Brute!" over and over. What would she do? What was going to happen now? But as Miss Brill wondered, the ermine toque turned, raised her hand as though she'd seen some one else, much nicer, just over there, and pattered away. And the band changed again and played more quickly, more gaily than ever, and the old couple on Miss Brill's seat got up and marched away, and such a funny old man with long whiskers hobbled along in time to the music and was nearly knocked over by four girls walking abreast.

Oh, how fascinating it was! How she enjoyed it! How she loved sitting here, watching it all! It was like a play. It was exactly like a play. Who could believe the sky at the back wasn't painted? But it wasn't till a little brown dog trotted on solemn and then slowly trotted off, like a little "theatre" dog, a little dog that had been drugged, that Miss Brill discovered what it was that made it so exciting. They were all on the stage. They weren't only the audience, not only looking on; they were acting. Even she had a part and came every Sunday. No doubt somebody would have noticed if she hadn't been there; she was part of the performance after all. How strange she'd never thought of it like that before! And yet it explained why she made such a point of starting from home at just the same time each week—so as not to be late for the performance—and it also explained why she had quite a queer, shy feeling at telling her English pupils how she spent her Sunday afternoons. No wonder! Miss Brill nearly laughed out loud. She was on the stage. She thought of the old invalid gentleman to whom she read the newspaper four afternoons a week while he slept in the garden. She had got quite used to the frail head on the cotton pillow, the hollowed eyes, the open mouth and the high pinched nose. If he'd been dead she mightn't have noticed for weeks; she wouldn't have minded. But suddenly he knew he was having the paper read to him by an actress! "An actress!" The old head lifted; two points of light quivered in the old eyes. "An actress—are ye?" And Miss Brill smoothed the newspaper as though it were the manuscript of her part and said gently: "Yes, I have been an actress for a long time."

The band had been having a rest. Now they started again. And what they played was warm, sunny, yet there was just a faint chill—a something, what was it?—not sadness—no, not sadness—a something that made you want to sing. The tune lifted, lifted, the light shone; and it seemed to Miss Brill that in another moment all of them, all the whole company, would begin singing. The young ones, the laughing ones who were moving together, they would begin, and the men's voices, very resolute and brave, would join them. And then she too, she too, and the others on the benches—they would come in with a kind of accompaniment—something low, that scarcely rose or fell, something so beautiful—moving. . . . And Miss Brill's eyes filled with tears and she looked smiling at all the other members of the company. Yes, we understand, we understand, she thought—though what they understood she didn't know.

Just at that moment a boy and a girl came and sat down where the old couple had been. They were beautifully dressed; they were in love. The hero and heroine, of course, just arrived from his father's yacht. And still soundlessly singing, still with that trembling smile, Miss Brill prepared to listen.

"No, not now," said the girl. "Not here, I can't."

"But why? Because of that stupid old thing at the end there?" asked the boy. "Why does she come here at all—who wants her? Why doesn't she keep her silly old mug at home?"

"It's her fu-fur which is so funny," giggled the girl. "It's exactly like a fried whiting."

"Ah, be off with you!" said the boy in an angry whisper. Then: "Tell me, ma petite chère—"

"No, not here," said the girl. "Not *yet.*"

On her way home she usually bought a slice of honey-cake at the baker's. It was her Sunday treat. Sometimes there was an almond in her slice, sometimes not. It made a great difference. If there was an almond it was like carrying home a tiny present—a surprise—something that might very well not have been there. She hurried on the almond Sundays and struck the match for the kettle in quite a dashing way.

But to-day she passed the baker's by, climbed the stairs, went into the little dark room—her room like a cupboard—and sat down on the red eiderdown. She sat there for a long time. The box that the fur came out of was on the bed. She unclasped the necklet quickly; quickly, without looking, laid it inside. But when she put the lid on she thought she heard something crying.

[1922—Great Britain]

Questions

1. Is Miss Brill a round, flat, or stock character? Does the conclusion of the story round her out in any way?
2. In what season is "Miss Brill" set? Does this particular setting tell us anything about Miss Brill herself?
3. "All the world's a stage," wrote Shakespeare, and Miss Brill would agree. Pinpoint some of the many references in the story to the theatre. Why would Miss Brill wish to see the world as a stage and all the men and women, herself included, as players?
4. The story skillfully suggests that until its end Miss Brill has a distorted view of things. In what way does she mentally alter what she sees? Comment on her shifting reception of the music she hears and on her feeling that "in another moment all of them, all the whole company, would begin singing."
5. Miss Brill changes during the course of her story. How does her fur piece as described at the beginning and the end help to reinforce the reader's sense of that change?
6. With the introduction of the "hero and heroine," the story suddenly takes a different direction. How so? What is its mood before and what after the appearance of the young man and woman?

Writing Assignments

1. (a) Write a paragraph showing two or three ways by which Miss Brill is characterized. What does each reveal about her?
   (b) What is your response to the story? In a separate paragraph, state your response and defend it.
2. In a paragraph or short paper, compare and contrast Norman ("Chaos, Disorder and the Late Show") with Miss Brill. Or write a dialogue between the two aimed at showing their differences yet also their fundamental similarity.
3. Write an essay on the change in Miss Brill that takes place in the story. How does she change? What in the story signals the change and symbolizes it? How is our perception of her altered? How does the change in Miss Brill lead to the story's theme?

WANTS

-*- GRACE PALEY -*-

I saw my ex-husband in the street. I was sitting on the steps of the new library.

Hello, my life, I said. We had once been married for twenty-seven years, so I felt justified.

He said, What? What life? No life of mine.

I said, O.K. I don't argue when there's real disagreement. I got up and went into the library to see how much I owed them.

The librarian said $32 even and you've owed it for eighteen years. I didn't deny anything. Because I don't understand how time passes. I have had those books. I have often thought of them. The library is only two blocks away.

My ex-husband followed me to the Books Returned desk. He interrupted the librarian, who had more to tell. In many ways, he said, as I look back, I attribute the dissolution of our marriage to the fact that you never invited the Bertrams to dinner.

That's possible, I said. But really, if you remember: first, my father was sick that Friday, then the children were born, then I had those Tuesday-night meetings, then the war began. Then we didn't seem to know them any more. But you're right. I should have had them to dinner.

I gave the librarian a check for $32. Immediately she trusted me, put my past behind her, wiped the record clean, which is just what most other municipal and/ or state bureaucracies will *not* do.

I checked out the two Edith Wharton books I had just returned because I'd read them so long ago and they are more apropos now than ever. They were *The House of Mirth* and *The Children,* which is about how life in the United States in New York changed in twenty-seven years fifty years ago.

A nice thing I do remember is breakfast, my ex-husband said. I was surprised. All we ever had was coffee. Then I remembered there was a hole in the back of the kitchen closet which opened into the apartment next door. There, they always ate sugar-cured smoked bacon. It gave us a very grand feeling about breakfast, but we never got stuffed and sluggish.

That was when we were poor, I said.

When were we ever rich? he asked.

Oh, as time went on, as our responsibilities increased, we didn't go in need. You took adequate financial care, I reminded him. The children went to camp four weeks a year and in decent ponchos with sleeping bags and boots, just like everyone else. They looked very nice. Our place was warm in winter, and we had nice red pillows and things.

I wanted a sailboat, he said. But you didn't want anything.

Don't be bitter, I said. It's never too late.

No, he said with a great deal of bitterness. I may get a sailboat. As a matter of fact I have money down on an eighteen-foot two-rigger. I'm doing well this year and can look forward to better. But as for you, it's too late. You'll always want nothing.

He had had a habit throughout the twenty-seven years of making a narrow remark which, like a plumber's snake, could work its way through the ear down the throat, halfway to my heart. He would then disappear, leaving me choking with equipment. What I mean is, I sat down on the library steps and he went away.

I looked through *The House of Mirth,* but lost interest. I felt extremely accused. Now, it's true, I'm short of requests and absolute requirements. But I do want *something.*

I want, for instance, to be a different person. I want to be the woman who brings these two books back in two weeks. I want to be the effective citizen who changes the school system and addresses the Board of Estimate on the troubles of this dear urban center.

I *had* promised my children to end the war before they grew up.

I wanted to have been married forever to one person, my ex-husband or my present one. Either has enough character for a whole life, which as it turns out is really not such a long time. You couldn't exhaust either man's qualities or get under the rock of his reasons in one short life.

Just this morning I looked out the window to watch the street for a while and saw that the little sycamores the city had dreamily planted a couple of years before the kids were born had come that day to the prime of their lives.

Well! I decided to bring those two books back to the library. Which proves that when a person or an event comes along to jolt or appraise me I *can* take some appropriate action, although I am better known for my hospitable remarks.

[1971—U.S.A.]

Questions

1. What does Paley's narrator want? What does her ex-husband want? In what ways do their wants differ?
2. How else do the two differ? Why did they get divorced?
3. What kind of person is Paley's narrator? What in the story helps to characterize her?
4. What is the point of this story? In addressing this question, consider the title, "Wants."

Writing Assignments

1. Write a paragraph addressed to question 3 above. Give examples of how we learn about Paley's narrator.
2. In a paragraph or more, analyze the wants of Paley's narrator as contrasted with those of her ex-husband. What do their differing wants tell us about each of them? In what way does the difference in what each wants help to explain their divorce?
3. At one point or another in life, many people desire to change. Consider Paley's narrator in this regard. Write a short essay describing what kind of a person she is and what kind of a person she would like to be. Is there any evidence in the story that she is changing? Will she become the person she can imagine being?

THE TEST

❊ ANGELICA GIBBS ❊

On the afternoon Marian took her second driver's test, Mrs. Ericson went with her. "It's probably better to have someone a little older with you," Mrs. Ericson said as Marian slipped into the driver's seat beside her. "Perhaps the last time your Cousin Bill made you nervous, talking too much on the way."

"Yes, Ma'am," Marian said in her soft unaccented voice. "They probably do like it better if a white person shows up with you."

"Oh, I don't think it's *that*," Mrs. Ericson began, and subsided after a glance at the girl's set profile. Marian drove the car slowly through the shady suburban streets. It was one of the first hot days in June, and when they reached the boulevard they found it crowded with cars headed for the beaches.

"Do you want me to drive?" Mrs. Ericson asked. "I'll be glad to if you're feeling jumpy." Marian shook her head. Mrs. Ericson watched her dark, competent hands and wondered for the thousandth time how the house had ever managed to get along without her, or how she had lived through those earlier years when her household had been presided over by a series of slatternly white girls who had considered housework demeaning and the care of children an added insult. "You drive beautifully, Marian," she said. "Now, don't think of the last time. Anybody would slide on a steep hill on a wet day like that."

"It takes four mistakes to flunk you," Marian said. "I don't remember doing all the things the inspector marked down on my blank."

"People say that they only want you to slip them a little something," Mrs. Ericson said doubtfully.

"No," Marian said. "That would only make it worse, Mrs. Ericson, I know."

The car turned right, at a traffic signal, into a side road and slid up to the curb at the rear of a short line of parked cars. The inspectors had not arrived yet.

"You have the papers," Mrs. Ericson asked. Marian took them out of her bag: her learner's permit, the car registration, and her birth certificate. They settled down to the dreary business of waiting.

"It will be marvellous to have someone dependable to drive the children to school every day," Mrs. Ericson said.

Marian looked up from the list of driving requirements she had been studying. "It'll make things simpler at the house, won't it?" she said.

"Oh, Marian," Mrs. Ericson exclaimed, "if I could only pay you half of what you're worth!"

"Now, Mrs. Ericson," Marian said firmly. They looked at each other and smiled with affection.

Two cars with official insignia on their doors stopped across the street. The inspectors leaped out, very brisk and military in their neat uniforms. Marian's hands tightened on the wheel. "There's the one who flunked me last time," she whispered, pointing to a stocky, self-important man who had begun to shout directions at the driver at the head of the line. "Oh, Mrs. Ericson."

"Now, Marian," Mrs. Ericson said. They smiled at each other again, rather weakly.

The inspector who finally reached their car was not the stocky one but a genial, middle-aged man who grinned broadly as he thumbed over their papers. Mrs. Ericson started to get out of the car. "Don't you want to come along?" the inspector asked. "Mandy and I don't mind company."

Mrs. Ericson was bewildered for a moment. "No," she said, and stepped to the curb. "I might make Marian self-conscious. She's a fine driver, Inspector."

"Sure thing," the inspector said, winking at Mrs. Ericson. He slid into the seat beside Marian. "Turn right at the corner, Mandy-Lou."

From the curb, Mrs. Ericson watched the car move smoothly up the street.

The inspector made notations in a small black book. "Age?" he inquired presently, as they drove along.

"Twenty-seven."

He looked at Marian out of the corner of his eye. "Old enough to have quite a flock of pickaninnies, eh?"

Marian did not answer.

"Left at this corner," the inspector said, "and park between that truck and the green Buick."

The two cars were very close together, but Marian squeezed in between them without too much maneuvering. "Driven before, Mandy-Lou?" the inspector asked.

"Yes, sir. I had a license for three years in Pennsylvania."

"Why do you want to drive a car?"

"My employer needs me to take her children to and from school."

"Sure you don't really want to sneak out nights to meet some young blood?" the inspector asked. He laughed as Marian shook her head.

"Let's see you take a left at the corner and then turn around in the middle of the next block," the inspector said. He began to whistle "Swanee River." "Make you homesick?" he asked.

Marian put out her hand, swung around neatly in the street, and headed back in the direction from which they had come. "No," she said. "I was born in Scranton, Pennsylvania."

The inspector feigned astonishment. "You-all ain't Southern?" he said. "Well, dog my cats if I didn't think you-all came from down yondah."

"No, sir," Marian said.

"Turn onto Main Street and let's see how you-all does in heavier traffic."

They followed a line of cars along Main Street for several blocks until they came in sight of a concrete bridge which arched high over the railroad tracks.

"Read that sign at the end of the bridge," the inspector said.

" 'Proceed with caution. Dangerous in slippery weather,' " Marian said.

"You-all sho can read fine," the inspector exclaimed. "Where d'you learn to do that, Mandy?"

"I got my college degree last year," Marian said. Her voice was not quite steady.

As the car crept up the slope of the bridge the inspector burst out laughing. He laughed so hard he could scarcely give his next direction. "Stop here," he said, wiping his eyes, "then start'er up again. Mandy got her degree, did she? Dog my cats!"

Marian pulled up beside the curb. She put the car in neutral, pulled on the emergency, waited a moment, and then put the car into gear again. Her face was set. As she released the brake her foot slipped off the clutch pedal and the engine stalled.

"Now, Mistress Mandy," the inspector said, "remember your degree."

"*Damn* you!" Marian cried. She started the car with a jerk.

The inspector lost his joviality in an instant. "Return to the starting place, please," he said, and made four very black crosses at random in the squares on Marian's application blank.

Mrs. Ericson was waiting at the curb where they had left her. As Marian stopped the car, the inspector jumped out and brushed past her, his face purple. "What happened?" Mrs. Ericson asked, looking after him with alarm.

Marian stared down at the wheel and her lip trembled.

"Oh, Marian, *again?*" Mrs. Ericson said.

Marian nodded. "In a sort of different way," she said, and slid over to the right-hand side of the car.

[1940—U.S.A.]

Questions

1. What character type is Mrs. Ericson? Marian? The driving inspector? Characterize each of the three. In what way is the inspector's character type appropriate to the villain he is?
2. Why is Marian, a woman with a college degree, a maid? Why is her reaction to the inspector so long in coming and so relatively mild? Why is his final response to her so vindictive? Before answering, consider the social context of this realistic piece in light of its date of publication.
3. Mood, as will be discussed later in the book, is the feeling a story raises in a reader. What is the mood of "The Test"? In what way is its mood, established especially by character and plot, related to its theme?
4. Why the title? Why "the" instead of "a"? What are the wider implications of the story in light of its title?

Writing Assignments

1. An ill-tempered villain may be easier to cope with than a jocular one. Develop this idea in a paragraph, using Gibbs's driving inspector as a case in point. First characterize him; then consider why the particular way he vents his bigotry is particularly insidious.
2. With respect to the bigotry it depicts, is "The Test" still relevant today? Have things changed for blacks since the story was written, or are blacks still second-class citizens? Using what evidence you have, write an essay arguing one side or the other of this matter. Along the way, take note of the arguments on the opposite side.

MY FIRST GOOSE

❊ ISAAC BABEL ❊

Translated by Walter Morison

Savitsky, Commander of the VI Division, rose when he saw me, and I wondered at the beauty of his giant's body. He rose, the purple of his riding breeches and the crimson of his little tilted cap and the decorations stuck on his chest cleaving the hut as a standard cleaves the sky. A smell of scent and the sickly sweet freshness of soap emanated from him. His long legs were like girls sheathed to the neck in shining riding boots.

He smiled at me, struck his riding whip on the table, and drew toward him an order that the Chief of Staff had just finished dictating. It was an order for Ivan Chesnokov to advance on Chugunov-Dobryvodka with the regiment entrusted to him, to make contact with the enemy and destroy the same.

"For which destruction," the Commander began to write, smearing the whole sheet, "I make this same Chesnokov entirely responsible, up to and including the supreme penalty, and will if necessary strike him down on the spot; which you, Chesnokov, who have been working with me at the front for some months now, cannot doubt."

The Commander signed the order with a flourish, tossed it to his orderlies and turned upon me gray eyes that danced with merriment.

I handed him a paper with my appointment to the Staff of the Division.

"Put it down in the Order of the Day," said the Commander. "Put him down for every satisfaction save the front one. Can you read and write?"

"Yes, I can read and write," I replied, envying the flower and iron of that youthfulness. "I graduated in law from St. Petersburg University."

"Oh, are you one of those grinds?" he laughed. "Specs on your nose, too! What a nasty little object! They've sent you along without making any enquiries; and this is a hot place for specs. Think you'll get on with us?"

"I'll get on all right," I answered, and went off to the village with the quartermaster to find a billet for the night.

The quartermaster carried my trunk on his shoulder. Before us stretched the village street. The dying sun, round and yellow as a pumpkin, was giving up its roseate ghost to the skies.

We went up to a hut painted over with garlands. The quartermaster stopped, and said suddenly, with a guilty smile:

"Nuisance with specs. Can't do anything to stop it, either. Not a life for the brainy type here. But you go and mess up a lady, and a good lady too, and you'll have the boys patting you on the back."

He hesitated, my little trunk on his shoulder; then he came quite close to me, only to dart away again despairingly and run to the nearest yard. Cossacks were sitting there, shaving one another.

"Here, you soldiers," said the quartermaster, setting my little trunk down on the ground. "Comrade Savitsky's orders are that you're to take this chap in your billets, so no nonsense about it, because the chap's been through a lot in the learning line."

The quartermaster, purple in the face, left us without looking back. I raised my hand to my cap and saluted the Cossacks. A lad with long straight flaxen hair and the handsome face of the Ryazan Cossacks went over to my little trunk and tossed it out at the gate. Then he turned his back on me and with remarkable skill emitted a series of shameful noises.

"To your guns—number double-zero!" an older Cossack shouted at him, and burst out laughing. "Running fire!"

His guileless art exhausted, the lad made off. Then, crawling over the ground, I began to gather together the manuscripts and tattered garments that had fallen out of the trunk. I gathered them up and carried them to the other end of the yard. Near the hut, on a brick stove, stood a cauldron in which pork was cooking. The steam that rose from it was like the far-off smoke of home in the village, and it mingled hunger with desperate loneliness in my head. Then I covered my little broken trunk with hay, turning it into a pillow, and lay down on the ground to read in *Pravda* Lenin's speech at the Second Congress of the Comintern. The sun fell upon me from behind the toothed hillocks, the Cossacks trod on my feet, the lad made fun of me untiringly, the beloved lines came toward me along a thorny path and could not reach me. Then I put aside the paper and went out to the landlady, who was spinning on the porch.

"Landlady," I said, "I've got to eat."

The old woman raised to me the diffused whites of her purblind eyes and lowered them again.

"Comrade," she said, after a pause, "what with all this going on, I want to go and hang myself."

"Christ!" I muttered, and pushed the old woman in the chest with my fist. "You don't suppose I'm going to go into explanations with you, do you?"

And turning around I saw somebody's sword lying within reach. A severe-looking goose was waddling about the yard, inoffensively preening its feathers. I overtook it and pressed it to the ground. Its head cracked beneath my boot, cracked and emptied itself. The white neck lay stretched out in the dung, the wings twitched.

"Christ!" I said, digging into the goose with my sword. "Go and cook it for me, landlady."

Her blind eyes and glasses glistening, the old woman picked up the slaughtered bird, wrapped it in her apron, and started to bear it off toward the kitchen.

"Comrade," she said to me, after a while, "I want to go and hang myself." And she closed the door behind her.

The Cossacks in the yard were already sitting around their cauldron. They sat motionless, stiff as heathen priests at a sacrifice, and had not looked at the goose.

"The lad's all right," one of them said, winking and scooping up the cabbage soup with his spoon.

The Cossacks commenced their supper with all the elegance and restraint of peasants who respect one another. And I wiped the sword with sand, went out at the gate, and came in again, depressed. Already the moon hung above the yard like a cheap earring.

"Hey, you," suddenly said Surovkov, an older Cossack. "Sit down and feed with us till your goose is done."

He produced a spare spoon from his boot and handed it to me. We supped up the cabbage soup they had made, and ate the pork.

"What's in the newspaper?" asked the flaxen-haired lad, making room for me.

"Lenin writes in the paper," I said, pulling out *Pravda*. "Lenin writes that there's a shortage of everything."

And loudly, like a triumphant man hard of hearing, I read Lenin's speech out to the Cossacks.

Evening wrapped about me the quickening moisture of its twilight sheets; evening laid a mother's hand upon my burning forehead. I read on and rejoiced, spying out exultingly the secret curve of Lenin's straight line.

"Truth tickles everyone's nostrils," said Surovkov, when I had come to the end. "The question is, how's it to be pulled from the heap. But he goes and strikes at it straight off like a hen pecking at a grain!"

This remark about Lenin was made by Surovkov, platoon commander of the Staff Squadron; after which we lay down to sleep in the hayloft. We slept, all six of us, beneath a wooden roof that let in the stars, warming one another, our legs intermingled. I dreamed: and in my dreams saw women. But my heart, stained with bloodshed, grated and brimmed over.

[1926—U.S.S.R.]

Questions

1. From the clues given in the story, describe the narrator's physical appearance.
2. Just as we sometimes think of other people in broad terms, as though they were stock characters, so the characters in "My First Goose" view the narrator. What kind of stock character do they see him as? Point to specifics that support your answer.
3. Describe the personality of the narrator. How do we come to see him as clearly as we do (consider such things as plot, character contrast, the narrator's personal effects, his style of speech, and so forth)?
4. "The lad's all right," says one Cossack after the narrator has brutally killed the goose and tormented the old woman. Why? In what way is the Cossack's reason related to something said earlier: "Not a life for the brainy type here. But you go and mess up a lady, and a good lady too, and you'll have the boys patting you on the back"?
5. The narrator needs to be, and indeed wants to be, accepted by his fellow soldiers. At what price to himself does he gain their acceptance? What in the story indicates that the change in the narrator brought about by his circumstances is for the worse?
6. What does the title suggest?

Writing Assignments

1. Write a paragraph describing the protagonist both physically and emotionally. What does his physical appearance tell us about him? In what way does the kind of person he is give rise to his admiration of Savitsky and the Cossacks?
2. Write a short essay on the theme of the present story as its theme relates to character revelation and change. How does its narrator change? The tale ends on a note of profound regret. What does this tell us about the change in the narrator and his own attitude toward that change? Generally, how does experience sometimes alter people for the worse?

✳ **5** ✳

NARRATION AND POINT OF VIEW

THE NARRATOR

Every story must somehow get told. The teller is "the narrator" and what the narrator says is called "the narration." What is most important to grasp about narrators from the start is that they should not be confused with authors. The writer of a piece of fiction stands outside of it, constructing its plot, shaping its characters, *and* manipulating its narrator to achieve the end desired. Authors are like puppeteers, invisibly pulling the strings of characters and narrators alike to produce the show as a whole. The writer's attitude is expressed through the story overall rather than through one or another of its components. As to narration, there are many ways in which stories can be told, and each affects meaning in its own way. Narration, therefore, is intimately related to theme: how we come to understand a piece of fiction depends in large measure on the way in which its narrator presents things. What the reader must understand about narration is that what we are told is not always meant to be taken at face value. Like real people, narrators can vary in reliability from complete trustworthiness to utter blindness. They may even be made to lie. Consequently, what is said (that is, the narration) must be questioned and evaluated according to our judgment of who says it (that is, the narrator). The discussion that follows should help clarify the nature of narrators and their points of view.

Before we move on, however, we should establish what is meant by "narrative point of view." A **narrative point of view** is simply the perspective (or sometimes perspectives) devised by the author through which a story's characters, actions, setting, and so forth are presented to the reader. In this regard we might think of a narrator as a camera. Looking through a camera's eyepiece, one can, if the lens is clear, see a scene as though looking at it directly. However, the image seen through the camera's eye can be distorted because of poor focus or altered in various ways by different kinds of filters. Some narrators, too, seem all but invisible, like a clear lens. Most, however, filter what they present to one degree or another, and some are out of focus, distorting entirely what they report. Narrative point of view, thus, is dependent on the kind of narrator chosen by an author.

MODES OF NARRATION

It is possible to write a story without a narrator by confining it to dialogue between the characters—the mode of Dorothy Parker's "You Were Perfectly Fine" (pp. 128–30). Turn to the story for a second and just look at it. You'll notice that even here there is a bit of narration (the first paragraph, for instance). But because what is narrated amounts to something like "stage directions," we can say that, like most plays, the story has no narrator. The advantage of this technique is that it lends the story a sense of immediacy, for it entails no mediating consciousness between reader and characters. Nevertheless, there are few stories composed entirely of dialogue. The reason is that dialogue is all talk and no action. Whereas in a play we can see actors doing things while they talk, in a story we must be told what characters are doing, which means there must be a narrator.

How, then, can a story be told? Almost always, fiction is written either from the perspective of a character in the story telling it in the first person (I) or from the perspective of someone not involved in the story telling it in the third person (he, she, it, they). Whichever the case, there is always a narrative voice to be heard, and consequently a tone of voice, which can be intimate, austere, kindly, urbane, harsh, and so forth, just like the tones of voice that we project every day when talking to others. Because first-person narrators are to be thought of as people, it is only natural that what they say should be heard as utterance exhibiting tone of voice. But third-person narrators, though not to be thought of as people, also betray various tones of voice. The point is that stories should be heard as spoken by a narrator, and therefore, in one way or another, all exhibit tone. With this in mind, let's now take up each narrative perspective in turn.

First-Person Narration

First-person narrators are always characters in the stories they narrate and are always meant to be thought of as people. They might be protagonists, minor characters, or merely bystanders, but they are characters and must be treated accordingly. In other words, we must remember to question first-person narrators and to judge what they say according to our gradually developing awareness of who they are. Sometimes we can accept what they say; sometimes we can't. There are, consequently, two types of first-person narration.

First-Person Credible.   "You don't know about me without you have read a book by the name of *The Adventures of Tom Sawyer*. That book was made by Mr. Mark Twain, and he told the truth, mainly"—so begins *The Adventures of Huckleberry Finn,* by Mark Twain. This is an example of first-person narration. But can we believe the narrator? That is the prime question that the first-person narrative point of view demands the reader ask. Having observed the narrator and compared his or her judgments with our own, we determine whether the narrator is credible. If so, we accept the narrator as a guide in forming our own attitudes and interpretation. Somerset Maugham's description of this kind of narrator is apt:

> There is one point I want to make about these stories. The reader will notice that many of my stories are written in the first person singular. That is a literary convention which is as old as the hills. It was used by Petronius Arbiter in the *Satyricon* and by many of the story-tellers in *The Thousand and One Nights*. Its object is of course to achieve credibility, for when someone tells you what he states happened to himself you are more likely to believe that he is telling the truth than when he tells you what happened to somebody else. It has besides the merit from the story-teller's point of view that he need only tell you what he knows for a fact and can leave to your imagination what he doesn't or couldn't know. Some of the older novelists who wrote in the first person were in this respect very careless. They would narrate long conversations that they couldn't possibly have heard and incidents which in the nature of things they couldn't possibly have witnessed. Thus they lost the great advantage of verisimilitude which writing in the first person singular offers. But the *I* who writes is just as much a character in the story as the other persons with whom it is concerned. He may be the hero or he may be an onlooker or a confidant. But he is a character. The writer who uses this device is writing fiction and if he makes the *I* of his story a little quicker on the uptake, a little more level-headed, a little shrewder, a little braver, a little more ingenious, a little wittier, a little wiser than he, the writer, really is, the reader must show indulgence. He must remember that the author is not drawing a faithful portrait of himself, but creating a character for the particular purposes of his story. (Maugham 2:7)

Maugham's own "The Ant and the Grasshopper" (pp. 159–62) is a perfect example: its narrator proves to be credible, and because he does, he becomes an agent directing us in our judgments of the other characters in the story and ultimately guiding us toward its theme.

First-Person Unreliable. Some narrators, however, are not to be trusted. If in our judgment a narrator is naive (a child as narrator, for instance) or biased, then the point of the story becomes something other than the narrator's point. But we must recognize the narrator to be unreliable. Unreliable narration can be tricky for the reader because we are ever inclined to believe narrators. Take William Carlos Williams's "The Buffalos" (pp. 137–40), a story that is usually missed by students because they take the narrator at his word. But here the narrator is unreliable. If we attend closely, we start to realize not only that the narrator contradicts himself (a sure sign of unreliability) but that, though he protests his love for the woman he discusses, he knows very little about her. Because we, through him, learn almost nothing about her, we can conclude that this terribly biased narrator is rather juvenile; he is in love with love and not with a particular person. Once we see this, the story suddenly turns around 180 degrees. Its point is the opposite of its narrator's, the revelation of whose character becomes the story's theme. Potentially, unreliable narration can have great impact. It also allows for all kinds of irony. We'll take up irony when we consider mood and style, but in anticipation you might look at Chekhov's "At Sea" (pp. 134–36) with an eye to the fact that we know more than its naive narrator. Chekhov's story is another example of unreliable narration, its young narrator proving blind to the meaning of what he relates; therein lies the irony.

Third-Person Narration

A story narrated in the third person is one in which the narrator is not a character in the story and, indeed, is not to be thought of as a person at all. Third-person narrators can be used by authors in several ways; that is, several narrative points of view are possible.

Third-Person Omniscient. Omniscient means all-knowing. An omniscient narrator can tell us what characters are thinking, show us scenes that only the characters are party to, make judgments about characters and events, and even tell us how to respond. By convention, omniscient narrators are to be trusted implicitly because they are all-knowing. Any attitude that such a narrator expresses, whether directly or indirectly (for example, by choice of adjectives and adverbs), is prime information meant to be accepted. Some omniscient narrators, to be sure, give us much less information than others, and some even tell us things that might be misleading. For instance, think of mysteries, whose narrators try to throw us off the track. Actually, though, we are given all the information we need to solve the mystery. We just miss (as we are meant to miss) the clues. All the information we need, however much or little, is what all omniscient narrators provide. The omniscient point of view is so common that you are probably familiar with it already, but if you are not, look at the first paragraph of H. H. Munro's "Sredni Vashtar" (pp. 140–41) for a typical example.

Third-Person Subjective. Also called "limited omniscient narration," third-person subjective narration is omniscient, but only with respect to certain characters rather than to all. The main function of subjective narrators is to voice characters' feelings and states of mind. Usually, the subjective narrator conveys the view of a major character; but this kind of narrator can tell a story from the vantage point of a minor character or even of one and then of another character in turn. Chekhov's "The Lottery Ticket" (pp. 72–75) provides an example. Here the narrator tells the story almost entirely through the outlook of a disgruntled husband. At a critical moment in the story, however, we get a passage narrated from the wife's position. This changes everything. If you are wondering why a writer would choose third-person subjective rather than first-person narration, there are at least two answers. First, the author might wish to shift perspectives, as does Chekhov. Or the character through whose eyes events are seen may not be able to render an account (think of Rosa in "The Shawl"), perhaps because the character is inarticulate, confused, or otherwise unable to relate a story. In all such cases, third-person subjective narration is ideal.

Third-Person Objective. Omniscient and third-person subjective narrators show us things through lenses tinted to one degree or another. The objective narrator is impartial, recording scenes and characters through, or so it seems, a clear lens.

That is, objective narrators express no attitudes, whether their own or those of characters, and do not predispose the reader toward any attitude. They tell their stories from the outside, as it were, noting external details but not telling us anything about what characters are thinking or feeling and not swaying us in any way as to our judgments of characters. Mikhail Zoshchenko's "A Confession" (pp. 148–49) is a good example. Here we are introduced to two characters without being told much of anything about either. We must judge entirely for ourselves. This type of story demands maximum attention on the reader's part; it offers as reward maximum involvement.

NARRATOR, AUTHOR, AND STORY

It is important to realize that often the meaning of a story depends on our judgment of the type of narrator *the author devised* to tell it. Again, narrators should not be confused with authors. The writer's attitude is expressed through the story as a whole, not through just one of its components. A story narrated by a child, for instance, is not to be taken as a story written by that child. The adult author has chosen such a narrator for the purpose at hand, and that purpose is what must be attended to. In other words, the attitude of the narrator does not necessarily coincide with the attitude expressed by a story as a whole. Especially in stories with first-person or third-person subjective narration, the distinction is often crucial. If you remember to keep questioning narrators until you are sure of the kind of narrator a story is spoken by, you will not fall into the trap of confusing the point of a story with that of its narrator if the two diverge.

SUMMARY SUGGESTIONS: UNDERSTANDING NARRATION

1. Separate in your mind author and narrator. Remember that the point of a story might be quite different from any point the narrator makes.

2. Determine as quickly as possible what kind of narrator you are dealing with. You can distinguish between first-person and third-person narration almost immediately. The finer distinctions—especially between credible and unreliable narration—will have to be tested as you continue reading.

3. If you think that you have an unreliable narrator, keep questioning what the narrator says. Does the narrator make statements that contradict each other? Does the narrator say something that you know not to be true? What do other characters have to say about the narrator? All these are considerations that aid in judging narrators.

4. If you think you have a third-person subjective narrator, remember that this type of narrator expresses the outlook of one or another character. Therefore, what this narrator says must be questioned no less than what any other character says.

5. Finally, relate a story's narration to its theme. Because the mode of narration the author has chosen helps to shape the reader's responses, it is closely connected to the theme. This is true even of stories with unreliable narrators, though here the relationship between theme and narrator will probably be ironic.

WRITING ON NARRATORS AND NARRATION

Narrators and narration can be great fun to write on. The first-person credible narrator, for instance, is usually likable, so writing about such a narrator can hold the same pleasure as talking about a friend. Or take the unreliable narrator. The recognition that a narrator is limited or completely unreliable may change the meaning of a story entirely. To treat such a narrator, then, is not only to get at the meaning of a story but to do so with subtlety, which offers the delight of exercising and displaying one's mental agility. Third-person subjective narration is equally interesting, especially if the perspective shifts between characters. Whatever one's focus, narration of any type is so basic to what fiction is that to write on it is to be at the very heart of both fiction's means and its purpose.

The easiest and often most interesting narrator to write about is the first-person narrator. Is the narrator credible or not? How does the author persuade us of this? What kind of a person is the narrator? Why did the author choose to have this type of person narrate the story? How does the narrator shape our attitudes toward other characters? In what way does the narrator help us to understand the point of the story overall? As you think about a story, these are some of the questions to ask of its narrator. Your answers will provide any number of topics on which you could write an engaging paper. Take Maugham's story "The Ant and the Grasshopper" (pp. 159–62), in which the narrative point of view is pivotal. We see George, the story's protagonist, through the narrator's eyes and so see him quite differently from the way he sees himself. What Maugham accomplishes by having us see George as we do could be the basis of a fine paper on the story. Here one would want to discuss the character of the narrator and then move to consider how we are swayed to laugh at George because of our acceptance of the narrator's credibility.

If a story's narrator is unreliable, as exemplified by Williams's "The Buffalos" (pp. 137–40), this unreliability is also rich in possibilities for writing. How do we come to judge the narrator as unreliable? What difference does the judgment make in our reading of the story? What is the narrator like? Why did the author choose unreliable narration? Given that the narrator is unreliable, what, then, is the point of the story? To answer questions of this sort is to be well on the way to an interesting piece of writing. For example, your perception that the narrator of "The Buffalos" is a rampant sexist, among other things, might lead you to reject his explanations entirely, a judgment that would affect your interpretation of the story. A paper explaining how you arrived at such a judgment and therefore how you interpret the story could be compelling.

The possibilities are less obvious for writing on third-person narration. Nevertheless, third-person narration offers a number of topics if we look for them. For instance, the shifting of perspective of a third-person subjective narrator if a shift occurs in a story can be a rewarding topic. The narration of Chekhov's "The Lottery Ticket" (pp. 72–75) is a case in point. By shifting from the husband's to the wife's perspective, the narrator reveals a conflict that affects our understanding of the story. To take a further example, in my treatment of "The Shawl" (pp. 34–37), I point to narration when imputing to Rosa a belief in magic. Recognizing the story's narrator to be third-person subjective, I realized that it is Rosa's attitude the narrator expresses. For obvious reasons—Rosa has gone mad by the end of the story and is probably soon to die—Rosa could not narrate her story herself. Still, we see through her eyes from beginning to end because of the type of narration used. Once more, narration proves instrumental to meaning.

In considering a story narrated from the third-person objective point of view, one could write a stimulating paper focused on the effect of the contrast between the impersonal tone of the narrator and the highly personal struggles of the characters. Zoshchenko's "A Confession" (pp. 148–49) could be explored in this way. Indeed, the tone of any narrator, if the specific tone can be related to the story's meaning, can be a good subject for writing. We saw as much when discussing "The Shawl" in Chapter 1. The omniscient point of view provides many other possible topics. Why, for instance, since the omniscient narrator knows all, are we told only certain things and not others? Often, too, we may be given information that appears to have no real bearing on the story. Why? A paper could address what the reasons for the narrator's giving us such information might be. Another interesting topic is how omniscient narration leads the reader to adopt a particular attitude, whether toward a character, an event, or some other element or aspect of a story. In this regard, "Sredni Vashtar" (pp. 140–43) might be intriguing to write on: specifically, how the reader is moved by the narrator to accept the boy's outlook could be an excellent topic. One final thing to be aware of with respect to the narrative points of view we have just considered (objective and omniscient) is that, no matter what aspect of a story you may be writing on, anything said from these points of view can be used as reliable evidence to support your argument.

Whatever you do when it comes to writing on stories, do not forget that how a story gets told and by whom is usually crucial to interpreting it. Therefore, narration is always a consideration and always a possible source of support as well as of thesis.

STORIES FOR STUDY AND WRITING ASSIGNMENTS

YOU WERE PERFECTLY FINE

❖ DOROTHY PARKER ❖

The pale young man eased himself carefully into the low chair, and rolled his head to the side, so that the cool chintz comforted his cheek and temple.

"Oh, dear," he said. "Oh, dear, oh, dear, oh, dear. Oh."

The clear-eyed girl, sitting light and erect on the couch, smiled brightly at him.

"Not feeling so well today?" she said.

"Oh, I'm great," he said. "Corking, I am. Know what time I got up? Four o'clock this afternoon, sharp. I kept trying to make it, and every time I took my head off the pillow, it would roll under the bed. This isn't my head I've got on now. I think this is something that used to belong to Walt Whitman. Oh, dear, oh, dear, oh, dear."

"Do you think maybe a drink would make you feel better?" she said.

"The hair of the mastiff that bit me?" he said. "Oh, no, thank you. Please never speak of anything like that again. I'm through. I'm all, all through. Look at that hand, steady as a humming-bird. Tell me, was I very terrible last night?"

"Oh, goodness," she said, "everybody was feeling pretty high. You were all right."

"Yeah," he said. "I must have been dandy. Is everybody sore at me?"

"Good heavens, no," she said. "Everyone thought you were terribly funny. Of course, Jim Pierson was a little stuffy, there for a minute at dinner. But people sort of held him back in his chair, and got him calmed down. I don't think anybody at the other tables noticed it at all. Hardly anybody."

"He was going to sock me?" he said. "Oh, Lord. What did I do to him?"

"Why, you didn't do a thing," she said. "You were perfectly fine. But you know how silly Jim gets, when he thinks anybody is making too much fuss over Elinor."

"Was I making a pass at Elinor?" he said. "Did I do that?"

"Of course you didn't," she said. "You were only fooling, that's all. She thought you were awfully amusing. She was having a marvelous time. She only got a little tiny bit annoyed just once, when you poured the clam-juice down her back."

"My God," he said. "Clam-juice down that back. And every vertebra a little Cabot. Dear God. What'll I ever do?"

"Oh, she'll be all right," she said. "Just send her some flowers, or something. Don't worry about it. It isn't anything."

"No, I won't worry," he said. "I haven't got a care in the world. I'm sitting pretty. Oh, dear, oh, dear. Did I do any other fascinating tricks at dinner?"

"You were fine," she said. "Don't be so foolish about it. Everybody was crazy about you. The maître d'hôtel was a little worried because you wouldn't stop singing, but he really didn't mind. All he said was, he was afraid they'd close the place again, if there was so much noise. But he didn't care a bit, himself. I think he loved seeing you have such a good time. Oh, you were just singing away, there, for about an hour. It wasn't so terribly loud, at all."

"So I sang," he said. "That must have been a treat. I sang."

"Don't you remember?" she said. "You just sang one song after another. Everybody in the place was listening. They loved it. Only you kept insisting that you wanted to sing some song about some kind of fusiliers or other, and everybody kept shushing you, and you'd keep trying to start it again. You were wonderful. We were all trying to make you stop singing for a minute, and eat something, but you wouldn't hear of it. My, you were funny."

"Didn't I eat any dinner?" he said.

"Oh, not a thing," she said. "Every time the waiter would offer you something, you'd give it right back to him, because you said that he was your long-lost brother, changed in the cradle by a gypsy band, and that anything you had was his. You had him simply roaring at you."

"I bet I did," he said. "I bet I was comical. Society's Pet, I must have been. And what happened then, after my overwhelming success with the waiter?"

"Why, nothing much," she said. "You took a sort of dislike to some old man with white hair, sitting across the room, because you didn't like his necktie and you wanted to tell him about it. But we got you out, before he got really mad."

"Oh, we got out," he said. "Did I walk?"

"Walk? Of course you did," she said. "You were absolutely all right. There was that nasty stretch of ice on the sidewalk, and you did sit down awfully hard, you poor dear. But good heavens, that might have happened to anybody."

"Oh, surely," he said. "Mrs. Hoover or anybody. So I fell down on the sidewalk. That would explain what's the matter with my— Yes. I see. And then what, if you don't mind?"

"Ah, now, Peter!" she said. "You can't sit there and say you don't remember what happened after that! I did think that maybe you were just a little tight at dinner— oh, you were perfectly all right, and all that, but I did know you were feeling pretty gay. But you were so serious, from the time you fell down—I never knew you to be that way. Don't you know, how you told me I had never seen your real self before? Oh, Peter, I just couldn't bear it, if you didn't remember that lovely long ride we took together in the taxi! Please, you do remember that, don't you? I think it would simply kill me, if you didn't."

"Oh, yes," he said. "Riding in the taxi. Oh, yes, sure. Pretty long ride, hmm?"

"Round and round and round the park," she said. "Oh, and the trees were shining so in the moonlight. And you said you never knew before that you really had a soul."

"Yes," he said. "I said that. That was me."

"You said such lovely, lovely things," she said. "And I'd never known, all this time, how you had been feeling about me, and I'd never dared to let you see how I felt about you. And then last night—oh, Peter dear, I think that taxi ride was the most important thing that ever happened to us in our lives."

"Yes," he said. "I guess it must have been."

"And we're going to be so happy," she said. "Oh, I just want to tell everybody! But I don't know—I think maybe it would be sweeter to keep it all to ourselves."

"I think it would be," he said.

"Isn't it lovely?" she said.

"Yes," he said. "Great."

"Lovely!" she said.

"Look here," he said, "do you mind if I have a drink? I mean, just medicinally, you know. I'm off the stuff for life, so help me. But I think I feel a collapse coming on."

"Oh, I think it would do you good," she said. "You poor boy, it's a shame you feel so awful. I'll go make you a highball."

"Honestly," he said, "I don't see how you could ever want to speak to me again, after I made such a fool of myself, last night. I think I'd better go join a monastery in Tibet."

"You crazy idiot!" she said. "As if I could ever let you go away now! Stop talking like that. You were perfectly fine."

She jumped up from the couch, kissed him quickly on the forehead, and ran out of the room.

The pale young man looked after her and shook his head long and slowly, then dropped it in his damp and trembling hands.

"Oh, dear," he said. "Oh, dear, oh, dear, oh, dear."

[1929—U.S.A.]

Questions

1. What kind of characters—flat, round, or stock—do we find engaged in dialogue here? In what way might Parker's female be thought of as stock?
2. What is the female up to in this story? Why does Peter want a drink toward the end?
3. Though slight, the story dramatizes a theme of some social significance, at least with respect to the time in which it was written. What is that theme?
4. What are the limitations of a dialogue format that you can detect from this story?
5. Some stories seem relevant though written hundreds and even thousands of years ago. Others, even of relatively recent origin, do not. Has "You Were Perfectly Fine" aged well, or does it now seem a period piece? Why do some works endure and others become dated?

Writing Assignments

1. In a paragraph or two, write a critique of this story in which you judge its merits as story along with its relevance to a contemporary audience. Is it simply dated, or does it still have something to say about the relationship of men and women in our culture?
2. Write an essay in which you suggest why some works endure and others become dated. Use other stories you have read as examples, as well as "You Were Perfectly Fine."

PERSONAL LETTER

──────── ❊ WILLIAM MARCH ❊ ────────

Hamburg, Germany,
December 17th, 1932

DEAR MR. TYLER:

I wrote you a long, official letter last week and forwarded same via the S.S. *Manhattan.* That letter, which should be in your hands by the time you receive this, contained information you wanted regarding berthing facilities, pilotage in and out, tug hire, stevedoring costs, etc., etc. If I failed to cover any point that you had in mind, or if any part of my report is not detailed enough, please let me know, and I'll remedy the situation promptly.

As you will remember, you also asked me to drop a line under private cover regarding my personal impression of this country, and that is what I would like to do in this letter. I have thought a good deal about the best way to accomplish this, and have come to the conclusion that the easiest way to do it is to simply recount a little incident which happened the other night in a cafe.

First, let me say again that the agents you have in mind for representing us here are very efficient and have co-operated with me at all times. Herr Voelker, director of the agency, has been especially helpful. He is an intelligent and highly educated man. A few nights ago, he asked me to have dinner with him and attend the opera later, which I did. After that, he suggested we take in a beer cafe that he knew of, and so we went there, too. This place was pretty well filled up when we arrived, mostly with men in storm trooper uniforms. I won't explain who they are, as I covered that point in my first letter under the heading of Political Situation and Future Outlook, to which I refer you.

Well, Herr Voelker and I went to the basement bar and ordered our drinks, talking together all the time. We were speaking in English and discussing business matters and things in general, and at first I didn't notice that a group of these storm troopers had closed around us, shutting us off from the others at the bar.

To make a long story short, the leader of the group touched me on the shoulder and told me that I was in Germany now, and that while I was in Germany I would speak German or nothing at all. Most of these North Germans speak English very well indeed, since they have eight years of it in school, and so, naturally, this fellow spoke English, too.

I twisted around and looked these boys over, but they only held their backs stiffer, threw out their chests and frowned, just like something out of the opera I'd just seen. I still couldn't believe I'd heard correctly, and so I said, "Were you speaking to me?" And this leader answered in a voice which trembled with anger, "I repeat for the last time. When you are in Germany, you are to speak German. If you cannot speak German, you are to remain silent. Is that clear? We will endure no further insults from foreigners."

By that time I was sure it was some sort of a gag which Herr Voelker and his boys had cooked up for me. You know the sort of thing I mean, don't you? Like the time at the Traffic Association dinner when they played that joke on Oscar Wilcoxon. If you remember now, a girl with a baby in her arms burst into the dining-room just before the speeches began. She asked if there was a man present named Oscar Wilcoxon, and when the master of ceremonies said that there was, she demanded that he marry her, like he had promised to do, and give a name to his child.

Everybody was in on the stunt except Oscar himself, and it got a lot of laughs. Oscar kept trying to explain that somebody else must have been using his name illegally, because he'd never seen the young lady before in his life; but this girl had been carefully coached in her part, and the more Oscar tried to explain matters, the worse things got. I kept thinking to myself at the time that if anybody pulled a trick like that on me, I'd fall right in with the gag and say yes, I was the father of the baby all right, but I couldn't be sure about the mother because it was always so dark in the alley back of the pickle works where we met.

Well, when the storm trooper said what he did about not speaking English in Germany, I wanted to laugh, it struck me as comical, but I didn't. I'd already decided to play it their way and pretend to take the whole thing seriously. So I kept a straight face and said, "You gentlemen would like others to believe that you are real Germans, but you are not real Germans at all. If a real German heard what you have just said, he'd cover his face with shame."

I waited a moment and then added, "If you were real Germans, like you pretend to be, you'd realize that since I'm not a German, but an American, that I'm not as bright as you are. You'd know that Americans haven't got your culture, and that we haven't had your natural advantages. Americans think slowly," I said. "They don't master languages the way you do." Then I sighed and turned back to Herr Voelker, as if the subject was ended, as far as I was concerned.

The storm troopers seemed nonplused at my attitude, and they went into a huddle at one end of the bar. My German isn't the best in the world, but I could understand most of what they said without any trouble. The gist of it was that I was right, and that they were wrong; that even though I was a foreigner, I had the true philosophy. Well, I let them talk it over for a while, and then suddenly I wheeled around and gave them the other barrel. "A true German doesn't expect the same perfection from inferior people that he expects from himself," I said. "I thought that was something everybody knew by this time."

I said all this in a quick, stern voice, Mr. Tyler, and the troopers straightened up and stood at attention while I gave them a thorough dressing down. At the end of my speech, I said, "So you see? If you were true Germans, and believed in your mission, you wouldn't humiliate me before my friends. Oh, no, you wouldn't do that at all! Instead, you'd come to me as a teacher and say, 'Let me instruct you in our beautiful language! Let me explain to you our wonderful way of life!' " I waited a moment and then said sadly, "No. No, you are not true Germans. You only pretend to be. And now go away please before I lose the last of my illusions."

I nudged Herr Voelker with my elbow and winked behind my hand, but he only raised his eyes and stared at me over the edge of his glass. By that time there were tears in the eyes of the leader of the troopers. He wanted to buy me a drink, to prove that everything was all right, but I thought I'd keep the thing going a little longer, and played hard to butter up. Finally, I did let him buy me a drink, and then I bought him one in return. I thought, then, that the joke would break, and the laughter and the explanations come, but that didn't happen, and I began to feel a little uneasy.

Not long afterwards, Herr Voelker and I got up to leave. When we were outside, Herr Voelker said he was sorry such an unpleasant incident had occurred, and that he would have prevented it if he had been able to do so. He said he thought I had acted with rare presence of mind in being frank and aboveboard with the storm troopers, instead of trying to lie my way out of the situation. I was so astonished that I stood still on the pavement and said, "Did you think I meant what I said? An intelligent, educated man like yourself? Did you really believe I was in earnest?"

And, before God, Mr. Tyler, Herr Voelker drew himself up haughtily and said, "Why shouldn't I think you meant it? Every point you made was logical and entirely true."

Mr. Tyler, I've often read in books about an icy hand which clutched at somebody-or-other's heart. I never before took the words seriously, thinking it was just a phrase that writers used, but now I know that it's a true expression. That's exactly the way I felt as I walked along with Herr Voelker until we reached the taxi rank on the corner, and I got into a cab alone, and went back to my hotel.

Now, maybe there isn't anything important in the incident, but I think there is. There's something going on beneath the surface here as sure as you're a foot high. I don't quite know what it is so far, but I do know that it's something horrible.

This turned out to be a long letter, didn't it? I suppose you'll be receiving it during the Christmas holidays, so let me take this opportunity of wishing you a happy Christmas and a prosperous New Year. People here celebrate Christmas in a big way. They gather together in groups, sing songs about the Christ child, and weep over the loved ones who are far away. It is the season of love, goodwill, and the renewal of old affections, or so Herr Voelker tells me. He invited me, as a special compliment, to spend the day in the bosom of his own family, so I could see first hand what a German Christmas is really like; but I expressed my regrets, and said that business obligations made it necessary for me to be in Paris on that day. To tell you the truth, Mr. Tyler, everybody here frightens me a little—they are all so full of sentiment and fury.

With best regards, and again wishing you the compliments of the season, I remain,

Sincerely yours,

ROBERT B. MCINTOSH.

[1945—U.S.A.]

Questions

1. What kind of a person is Mr. McIntosh? How does what he says serve to characterize him? How are we to judge the narrative point of view here?

2. Because we have witnessed the outcome of the historical event that McIntosh is witnessing at the outset, we know more than he. What is the effect of this disparity?

3. In what way does this story reach beyond its particular historical situation to express a pattern that has often repeated itself in human history?

4. How is Herr Voelker characterized toward the beginning of the story? In what way is the story's second climax (about Herr Voelker) more significant than its first (about the storm troopers)? Why doesn't McIntosh accept Voelker's Christmas invitation? With respect to Herr Voelker, what is the point of the story?

5. In the story's second paragraph, the letter writer states the method he has chosen for his report. What method is it? How is the method central to fiction generally?

Writing Assignments

1. Write a paragraph on the disparity referred to in question 2 above and the effect of this disparity. In what way does the disparity heighten the story's impact?

2. In a paragraph, analyze the means by which McIntosh is characterized. Consider his values as well as his personal traits and how, indeed, his values shape those traits.

3. Write a letter about some contemporary movement or trend like McIntosh's letter on the rise of Nazi Germany. Proceed in the same manner, that is, by way of example. Your example, like McIntosh's, should embody your attitude toward your subject.

AT SEA

A Sailor's Story

 ❖ ANTON CHEKHOV ❖

Translated by Ann Dunnigan

Only the dimming lights of the receding harbor were visible in an ink-black sky. We could feel the heavy storm clouds overhead about to burst into rain, and it was suffocating, in spite of the wind and cold.

Crowded together in the crew's quarters we, the sailors, were casting lots. Loud, drunken laughter filled the air. One of our comrades was playfully crowing like a cock. A slight shiver ran through me from the back of my heels, as if cold small shot were pouring down my naked body from a hole in the back of my head. I was shivering both from the cold and certain other causes, which I wish to describe.

In my opinion, man is, as a rule, foul; and the sailor can sometimes be the foulest of all the creatures of the earth—fouler than the lowest beast, which has, at least, the excuse of obeying his instincts. It is possible that I may be mistaken, since I do not know life, but it appears to me that a sailor has more occasion than anyone else to despise and curse himself. A man who at any moment may fall headlong from a mast to be forever hidden beneath a wave, a man who may drown, God alone knows when, has need of nothing, and one on dry land feels pity for him. We sailors drink a lot of vodka and are dissolute because we do not know what one needs virtue for at sea. However, I shall continue.

We were casting lots. There were twenty-two of us who, having stood watch, were now at liberty. Out of this number only two were to have the luck of enjoying a rare spectacle. On this particular night the honeymoon cabin was occupied, but the wall of the cabin had only two holes at our disposal. One of them I myself had made with a fine saw, after boring through with a corkscrew; the other had been cut out with a knife by one of my comrades. We had worked at it for more than a week.

"You got one hole!"

"Who?"

They pointed to me. "Who got the other?"

"Your father."

My father, a humpbacked old sailor with a face like a baked apple, came up to me and clapped me on the back. "Today, my boy, we're lucky!" he said. "Do you hear, boy? Luck came to us both at the same time. That means something." Impatiently he asked the time; it was only eleven o'clock.

I went up on deck, lit my pipe and gazed out to sea. It was dark, but it can be assumed that my eyes reflected what was taking place in my soul, as I made out images on the background of the night, visualizing what was so lacking in my own still young but already ruined life. . . .

At midnight I walked past the saloon and glanced in at the door. The bridegroom, a young pastor with a handsome blond head, sat at a table holding the Gospels in his hands. He was explaining something to a tall, gaunt Englishwoman. The bride, a very beautiful, shapely young woman, sat at her husband's side with her light blue eyes fixed on him. A tall, plump, elderly Englishman, a banker, with a repulsive red face, paced up and down the saloon. He was the husband of the middle-aged lady to whom the pastor was talking.

"Pastors have a habit of talking for hours," I thought. "He won't finish before morning." At one o'clock my father came to me, pulled me by the sleeve and said: "It's time. They've left the saloon."

In the twinkling of an eye I flew down the companionway and approached the familiar wall. Between this wall and the side of the ship there was a space where soot, water, and rats collected. I soon heard the heavy tread of the old man, my father. He cursed as he stumbled over a mat-sack and some kerosene cans. I felt for the hole in the wall and pulled out the square piece of wood I had so painstakingly sawed. I was looking at a thin, transparent muslin through which penetrated a soft, rosy light. Together with the light, my burning face was caressed by a delightful, sultry fragrance; this, no doubt, was the smell of an aristocratic bedroom. In order to see the room it was necessary to draw aside the muslin with two fingers, which I hastened to do. I saw bronze, velvet, lace, all bathed in a pink glow. About ten feet from my face stood the bed.

"Let me have your place," said my father, impatiently pushing me aside. "I can see better here." I did not answer him. "Your eyes are better than mine, boy, and it makes no difference to you if you look from far or near."

"Be quiet," I said, "they might hear us."

The bride sat on the side of the bed, dangling her little feet in a foot muff. She was staring at the floor. Before her stood her husband, the young pastor. He was telling her something, what I do not know; the noise of the steamer made it impossible for me to hear. He spoke passionately, with gestures, his eyes flashing. She listened and shook her head in refusal.

"The devil!" my father muttered. "A rat bit me!"

I pressed my chest to the wall, as if fearing my heart would jump out. My head was burning.

The bride and groom talked at great length. At last he sank to his knees and held out his arms, imploring her. She shook her head in refusal. He leaped to his feet, crossed the cabin, and from the expression on his face and the movements of his arms I surmised that he was threatening her. The young wife rose and went slowly towards the wall where I was standing. She stopped near the opening and stood motionless in thought. I devoured her face with my eyes. It seemed to me that she was suffering, struggling with herself, not knowing what to do; but at the same time her features expressed anger. I did not understand it.

We continued to stand there face to face for above five minutes, then she moved slowly away and, pausing in the middle of the cabin, nodded to the pastor—a sign of consent, undoubtedly. He smiled happily, kissed her hand and went out.

Within three minutes the door opened and the pastor reentered followed by the tall, plump Englishman whom I mentioned above. The Englishman went over to the bed and asked the beautiful woman a question. Pale, not looking at him, she nodded her head affirmatively. The banker then took out of his pocket a packet of some sort—evidently bank notes—and handed it to the pastor, who examined it, counted it, bowed and went out. The elderly Englishman locked the door after him.

I sprang away from the wall as if I had been stung. I was frightened. It seemed to me the wind was tearing our ship to pieces, that we were going down. My father, that drunken, debauched old man, took me by the arm and said: "Let's go away from here! You shouldn't see that. You're still a boy."

He was hardly able to stand. I carried him up the steep winding stairs. Above an autumn rain had begun to fall.

[1884—Russia]

Questions

1. What do we as well as the two sailors believe to be happening in the cabin as the new bride argues with her husband? Why do we assume what we do?
2. What does the story say about the relation of convention and reality?
3. Characterize the narrator. What kind of narrator is he? Is he really base? If not, why does he think of himself as such? Why are we inclined to accept what he tells us?

4. What other elements of fiction does Chekhov work with here? Comment especially on the plot and setting (the crawl space as opposed to the bridal cabin).
5. What is the overall effect of the story? In what way does the story demonstrate dramatically that we are all bound by conventional views?

Writing Assignments

1. In a paragraph or two, analyze the story with regard to its narrative point of view. What clues are we given well before the end as to the type of narrator we are dealing with? What might keep us from picking up on these clues until a second reading?
2. Convention is a powerful force, as Chekhov's story brings home. Write an essay on some incident, perhaps from your own life, that illustrates how we tend to see things through the prism of convention and how seeing thus restricts our understanding of reality.

THE BUFFALOS

 WILLIAM CARLOS WILLIAMS

Once I had a beautiful friend whom I loved and who loved me. It was not easy for us to see each other, every moment that we could spend together having to be stolen. So that it was only at great cost of trouble and invention that we succeeded in our small enterprises. Even then, it was sometimes months together before we could meet at all.

Thus our moments were very precious and for a long time we enjoyed them to the full. What did we do? Is it necessary to say, for who would believe it, either way? We were happy together and we were young enough to have illusions so that the time passed pleasantly uphill and downhill as it does under such circumstances.

But the lady, whom I shall call Francie, had one defect—or habit, rather, which at first amused me. She was a great talker for woman's rights.

All this happened in those days when Mrs. Pankhurst in England and the others here would be parading the streets with banners demanding equal rights with men. Votes for Women was their slogan which they put forward on every occasion.

This might be well enough for the run of those who with seamed faces and angry looks talked from platforms and even upon street corners but it was nothing for the lovely woman with whom I rushed so eagerly to spend my hardly won minutes.

Often such matters did not come into our talk but we would sway as one person in thought and word during an entire afternoon.

But at other times, whether it was the moon or what we had eaten that day or how we had slept the night before or what, things would at once on my arrival start to run away. And the invariable twist which the conversation would take would be toward politics and woman's rights.

I objected. It wasted our time. But this only inflamed the spirit of the lady to such a point that I found I was getting nowhere. Of course it was important, she objected, for women to have the vote. What did I mean?

I meant, I tried to explain, that the important thing for us to do when we were together was to enjoy each other and not to run off on something which concerned us not at all.

No, she almost snorted, it does not concern us. It does not concern you, you mean. You have the vote, what do you care? But we who are the mothers of the nation are not supposed to have the brains for it. No, we haven't the brains of a street cleaner.

But that isn't it, I tried to say. I acknowledge that you women are perhaps far more suited to rule than we men are but why bother about such a trifle. I would gladly give you my vote, I said, if I could. But you, my dear, are beautiful, do you not understand?

Rot, she retorted. You are trying to treat me like a child. If you haven't the manhood to treasure the vote, your prerogative as a citizen of the United States, I must say I thought more of you. President Roosevelt . . .

Oh, my God, I couldn't help crying.

Yes, Roosevelt, she repeated. And I must explain that the lady always pronounced the former president's name as though it had an a in the middle. Roosavelt is for us and with his help, I tell you, it will go through. But you are a Democrat, she ended haughtily.

Don't imagine that she was fooling when she said these things. Not on your life. And that is what gave me my first idea. I could have pretended to be won over or I might perhaps have diverted the flood of conversation with a gift or a loving gesture of some startling sort. But one day when Francie was in the middle of one of her suffragist tirades I noted how beautiful she was in the heat of her excitement and I resolved then and there that I was luckier than I thought.

I took it as my pleasure from that time forward for almost a month to be greatly interested in what she had to say, raising objection after objection to torment her. Meanwhile I drank in the fiery looks of her scornful eyes, the lovely curl of her lips. I watched the glow mount in her cheeks. All her features would brighten, take a form and a fire that was delectable to me. I had found a way to enjoy this bad habit from which I could not break her.

Occasionally at the very height of her railing at me I would quietly take her in my arms. And if she did not grow at once furiously angry she would say no more and the time for my departure would rush upon us like a storm.

But the woman was really obsessed with this idea. I grew tired of my pastime of inciting her to display her plumage, so to speak. It really was too much. What in the world could she mean? Was it a form of shyness, of dull wit? an attempt to upset my too tranquil pleasure in her till it became something more biting? Was she not really trying to defend herself, to break down my guard—to have me take her—more seriously than I desired? I thought of all the reasons but decided finally that I didn't give a damn for them anyway. Beautiful as she was—and often a passionate mistress—I was growing bored.

So one day when she had started again on her favorite theme I halted her rather abruptly. Let me tell you a story, I said.

She made no reply but sat up a little straighter, her full lips pressed firmly together, and looked me square in the eye.

I have been down in the meadows on an inspection trip today, I told her, and while I was there one of the foremen of our ditching gang pointed out a hut to me. It is his own but he has rented it to three men who live there the year round, except in the cold of winter, when they board in Jersey City, he told me.

There are three of them, young fellows who earn their living there in that desolate spot, can you imagine how? In the late fall they begin to gather the down from the dry cattails which they pack into bags and sell as stuffing for cheap furniture. Later they trap muskrats. There are many of these rodents still in the swamps, and do you know what a muskrat skin brings? A dollar and a half for a good one sometimes. And in the spring and summer they pick blueberries.

But what has this to do with me? Francie asked.

Do you not see? answered I. The men earn their living that way, they are independent, self-supporting. The three work together; when two are out the third prepares the meals. They even have a few dollars over sometimes for small pleasures. Then the three go off together, to Jersey City, to Hoboken or wherever it might be.

Yes, I suppose they go to a saloon and get drunk.

Oh, I suppose so, but at least they manage it very well together and have done so for several years.

Now this gave me an idea, I continued. What is it that causes all the trouble in this world? Property, of course. It is what we own, the thing that gives us our importance—as it seems—the thing that has been largely the monopoly of the male down through the centuries, the thing finally that has governed the vote. And the thing for which we go to war, the thing for which we fight, even to quarrels between lovers.

And my idea is this. Let the men get rid of their property. If the women want the vote, give it to them, give them all the votes there are to be had, give them the votes the men have had also. And at the same time give them all the property of the world. They are the ones who biologically need it most, they are the ones economically, reasonably who should have it. You have convinced me by your suffragist arguments that you are right.

Francie looked at me hard but said nothing, perhaps she already sensed my waning affections.

And then, I said, we should have a society something like this: The women, possessing all the land, all the means for acquiring industrial wealth, would live in cities scattered over the country, walled cities defended by whatever weapons or armaments happened to be the fashion and from which all men should be excluded.

Meanwhile the men would gather in herds about the woods and plains, like the buffalo who used to be seen from the train windows on the great plains in the middle of the last century. Divided into tribes the men would spend their time hunting, fishing and fighting as men used to do—with fists, with stones, clubs as they may desire—and no doubt they would be far happier than now.

Then once a year, at the proper times certain women of the cities would send out chosen emissaries, eunuchs perhaps, to trade with the tribes—then in the pink of condition, trained, hardened by their rigorous life out of doors—and those most able, most vigorous, most desirable would be admitted for the breeding.

At this Francie jumped to her feet, fire in her eyes and turning her back on me left the room. I quietly took up my hat, took out a cigarette and lit it and jumping into my roadster before the door turned quietly down the driveway and went my way. Perhaps as I went I saw a curtain slightly rustled in a window of the second floor, perhaps it was only my vanity that made me believe this.

[1932—U.S.A.]

Questions

1. "You are trying to treat me like a child," Francie is reported to have said to Williams's narrator. What evidence is there in the story that she was right?
2. What was the narrator's attitude toward Francie when he visited her? What do we learn of her through him? Did he truly love her, as he says he did?
3. What else can we say about the narrator here? Does he contradict himself anywhere? Is he serious in his discourse on the separation of men into herds? What do you make of his last sentence? What kind of narrator is he?
4. What does the title imply? What is the point of the story (as opposed to the point of its narrator)?

Writing Assignments

1. In a paragraph, argue that the narrator is right or that he is wrong in his judgments of Francie. Use evidence from the story for support, and explain what attitude the story sways the reader to take.
2. Write an essay describing the narrator of "The Buffalos." Define his mentality in some detail, support your judgment point by point, and draw a conclusion as to the story's theme from what you say about its narrator.
3. Write a diary entry on the last visit of the narrator of "The Buffalos" from Francie's outlook (it is her diary). Try to be true to whatever you learn about her in the story (for instance, if you think she is refined, then don't have her rant and rave). What might she think about the man and the end of their relationship?

SREDNI VASHTAR

❖ H. H. MUNRO ❖

Conradin was ten years old, and the doctor had pronounced his professional opinion that the boy would not live another five years. The doctor was silky and effete, and counted for little, but his opinion was endorsed by Mrs. de Ropp, who counted for nearly everything. Mrs. de Ropp was Conradin's cousin and guardian, and in his eyes she represented those three-fifths of the world that are necessary and disagreeable and real; the other two-fifths, in perpetual antagonism to the foregoing, were summed up in himself and his imagination. One of these days Conradin supposed he would succumb to the mastering pressure of wearisome necessary things—such as illnesses and coddling restrictions and drawn-out dullness. Without his imagination, which was rampant under the spur of loneliness, he would have succumbed long ago.

Mrs. de Ropp would never, in her honestest moments, have confessed to herself that she disliked Conradin, though she might have been dimly aware that thwarting him "for his good" was a duty which she did not find particularly irksome. Conradin hated her with a desperate sincerity which he was perfectly able to mask. Such few pleasures as he could contrive for himself gained an added relish from the likelihood that they would be displeasing to his guardian, and from the realm of his imagination she was locked out—an unclean thing, which should find no entrance.

In the dull, cheerless garden, overlooked by so many windows that were ready to open with a message not to do this or that, or a reminder that medicines were due, he found little attraction. The few fruit-trees that it contained were set jealously apart from his plucking, as though they were rare specimens of their kind blooming in an arid waste; it would probably have been difficult to find a market-gardener who would have offered ten shillings for their entire yearly produce. In a forgotten corner, however, almost hidden behind a dismal shrubbery, was a disused tool-shed of respectable proportions, and within its walls Conradin found a haven, something that took on the varying aspects of a playroom and a cathedral. He had peopled it with a legion of familiar phantoms, evoked partly from fragments of history and partly from his own brain, but it also boasted two inmates of flesh and blood. In one corner lived a ragged-plumaged Houdan hen, on which the boy lavished an affection that had scarcely another outlet. Further back in the gloom stood a large hutch, divided into two compartments, one of which was fronted with close iron bars. This was the abode of a large polecat-ferret, which a friendly butcher-boy had once smuggled, cage and all, into its present quarters, in exchange for a long-secreted hoard of small silver. Conradin was dreadfully afraid of the lithe, sharp-fanged beast, but it was his most treasured possession. Its very presence in the tool-shed was a secret and fearful joy, to be kept scrupulously from the knowledge of the Woman, as he privately dubbed his cousin. And one day, out of Heaven knows what material, he spun the beast a wonderful name, and from that moment it grew into a god and a religion. The Woman indulged in religion once a week at a church near by, and took Conradin with her, but to him the church service was an alien rite in the House of Rimmon. Every Thursday, in the dim and musty silence of the tool-shed, he worshipped with mystic and elaborate ceremonial before the wooden hutch where dwelt Sredni Vashtar, the great ferret. Red flowers in their season and scarlet berries in the winter-time were offered at his shrine, for he was a god who laid some special stress on the fierce impatient side of things, as opposed to the Woman's religion, which, as far as Conradin could observe, went to great lengths in the contrary direction. And on great festivals powdered nutmeg was strewn in front of his hutch, an important feature of the offering being that the nutmeg had to be stolen. These festivals were of irregular occurrence, and were chiefly appointed to celebrate some passing event. On one occasion, when Mrs. de Ropp suffered from acute toothache for three days, Conradin kept up the festival during the entire three days, and almost succeeded in persuading himself that Sredni Vashtar was personally responsible for the toothache. If the malady had lasted for another day the supply of nutmeg would have given out.

The Houdan hen was never drawn into the cult of Sredni Vashtar. Conradin had long ago settled that she was an Anabaptist. He did not pretend to have the remotest knowledge as to what an Anabaptist was, but he privately hoped that it was dashing and not very respectable. Mrs. de Ropp was the ground plan on which he based and detested all respectability.

After a while Conradin's absorption in the tool-shed began to attract the notice of his guardian. "It is not good for him to be pottering down there in all weathers." She promptly decided, and at breakfast one morning she announced that the Houdan hen had been sold and taken away overnight. With her short-sighted eyes she peered at Conradin, waiting for an outbreak of rage and sorrow, which she was ready to rebuke with a flow of excellent precepts and reasoning. But Conradin said nothing: there was nothing to be said. Something perhaps in his white set face gave her a momentary qualm, for at tea that afternoon there was toast on the table, a delicacy which she usually banned on the ground that it was bad for him; also because the making of it "gave trouble," a deadly offence in the middle-class feminine eye.

"I thought you liked toast," she exclaimed, with an injured air, observing that he did not touch it.

"Sometimes," said Conradin.

In the shed that evening there was an innovation in the worship of the hutch-god. Conradin had been wont to chant his praises, tonight he asked a boon.

"Do one thing for me, Sredni Vashtar."

The thing was not specified. As Sredni Vashtar was a god he must be supposed to know. And choking back a sob as he looked at that other empty corner, Conradin went back to the world he so hated.

And every night, in the welcome darkness of his bedroom, and every evening in the dusk of the tool-shed, Conradin's bitter litany went up: "Do one thing for me, Sredni Vashtar."

Mrs. de Ropp noticed that the visits to the shed did not cease, and one day she made a further journey of inspection.

"What are you keeping in that locked hutch?" she asked. "I believe it's guinea-pigs. I'll have them all cleared away."

Conradin shut his lips tight, but the Woman ransacked his bedroom till she found the carefully hidden key, and forthwith marched down to the shed to complete her discovery. It was a cold afternoon, and Conradin had been bidden to keep to the house. From the furthest window of the dining-room the door of the shed could just be seen beyond the corner of the shrubbery, and there Conradin stationed himself. He saw the Woman enter, and then he imagined her opening the door of the sacred hutch and peering down with her short-sighted eyes into the thick straw bed where his god lay hidden. Perhaps she would prod at the straw in her clumsy impatience. And Conradin fervently breathed his prayer for the last time. But he knew as he prayed that he did not believe. He knew that the Woman would come out presently with that pursed smile he loathed so well on her face, and that in an hour or two the gardener would carry away his wonderful god, a god no longer, but a simple brown ferret in a hutch. And he knew that the Woman would triumph always as she triumphed now, and that he would grow ever more sickly under her pestering and domineering and superior wisdom, till one day nothing would matter much more with him, and the doctor would be proved right. And in the sting and misery of his defeat, he began to chant loudly and defiantly the hymn of his threatened idol:

> Sredni Vashtar went forth,
> His thoughts were red thoughts and his teeth were white.
> His enemies called for peace, but he brought them death.
> Sredni Vashtar the Beautiful.

And then of a sudden he stopped his chanting and drew closer to the windowpane. The door of the shed still stood ajar as it had been left, and the minutes were slipping by. They were long minutes, but they slipped by nevertheless. He watched the starlings running and flying in little parties across the lawn; he counted them over and over again, with one eye always on that swinging door. A sour-faced maid came in to lay the table for tea, and still Conradin stood and waited and watched. Hope had crept by inches into his heart, and now a look of triumph began to blaze in his eyes that had only known the wistful patience of defeat. Under his breath, with a furtive exultation, he began once again the paean of victory and devastation. And presently his eyes were rewarded: out through that doorway came a long, low, yellow-and-brown beast, with eyes a-blink at the waning daylight, and dark wet stains around the fur of jaws and throat. Conradin dropped on his knees. The great polecat-ferret made its way down to a small brook at the foot of the garden, drank for a moment, then crossed a little plank bridge and was lost to sight in the bushes. Such was the passing of Sredni Vashtar.

"Tea is ready," said the sour-faced maid; "where is the mistress?"

"She went down to the shed some time ago," said Conradin.

And while the maid went to summon her mistress to tea, Conradin fished a toasting-fork out of the sideboard drawer and proceeded to toast himself a piece of bread. And during the toasting of it and the buttering of it with much butter and the slow enjoyment of eating it, Conradin listened to the noises and silences which fell in quick spasms beyond the dining-room door. The loud foolish screaming of the maid, the answering chorus of wondering ejaculations from the kitchen region, the scuttering footsteps and hurried embassies for outside help, and then, after a lull, the scared sobbings and the shuffling tread of those who bore a heavy burden into the house.

"Whoever will break it to the poor child? I couldn't for the life of me!" exclaimed a shrill voice. And while they debated the matter among themselves, Conradin made himself another piece of toast.

[1927—Great Britain]

Questions

1. What is the narrative point of view of this story? Does the narrator sway the reader in judging Mrs. de Ropp and Conradin?
2. What contrasting values do Mrs. de Ropp and Conradin have and perhaps even represent? Which values would the story move us to affirm? What is the theme of the story?
3. Is there anything symbolic about Mrs. de Ropp's shortsightedness? What is ironic about the last paragraph?
4. Some critics have found Munro to be sentimental and superficial. Judge this story in that regard, pointing to specifics.
5. Whatever your answer to the preceding question, "Sredni Vashtar" certainly shows the power that plot can have. How so?

Writing Assignments

1. Write a paragraph in which you contrast the values of Mrs. de Ropp and Conradin. Consider which of the two characters and value systems the story would sway us to accept, and state the theme of the story in light of that consideration.
2. In a short essay, contrast "Sredni Vashtar" and "A Confession" (pp. 148–49) as to their narration. In doing so, be sure to discuss exactly how Munro's narrator moves the reader toward one outlook and away from another.
3. Write a short review of "Sredni Vashtar" in which you judge the worth of the story with respect to how it is put together, its effect on the reader, and what it says. Whatever your judgment, support it with evidence from the story. Assume an audience familiar with the story.

SIX YEARS AFTER

❊ KATHERINE MANSFIELD ❊

It was not the afternoon to be on deck—on the contrary. It was exactly the afternoon when there is no snugger place than a warm cabin, a warm bunk. Tucked up with a rug, a hot-water bottle and a piping hot cup of tea she would not have minded the weather in the least. But he—hated cabins, hated to be inside anywhere more than was absolutely necessary. He had a passion for keeping, as he called it, above board, especially when he was travelling. And it wasn't surprising, considering the enormous amount of time he spent cooped up in the office. So, when he rushed away from her as soon as they got on board and came back five minutes later to say he had secured two deck chairs on the lee side and the steward was undoing the rugs, her voice through the high sealskin collar murmured "Good"; and because he was looking at her, she smiled with bright eyes and blinked quickly, as if to say, "Yes, perfectly all right—absolutely," and she meant it.

"Then we'd better—" said he, and he tucked her hand inside his arm and began to rush her off to where the two chairs stood. But she just had time to breathe, "Not so fast, Daddy, please," when he remembered too and slowed down.

Strange! They had been married twenty-eight years, and it was still an effort to him, each time, to adapt his pace to hers.

"Not cold, are you?" he asked, glancing sideways at her. Her little nose, geranium pink above the dark fur, was answer enough. But she thrust her free hand into the velvet pocket of her jacket and murmured gaily, "I shall be glad of my rug."

He pressed her tighter to his side—a quick, nervous pressure. He knew, of course, that she ought to be down in the cabin; he knew that it was no afternoon for her to be sitting on deck, in this cold and raw mist, lee side or no lee side, rugs or no rugs, and he realized how she must be hating it. But he had come to believe that it really was easier for her to make these sacrifices than it was for him. Take their present case, for instance. If he had gone down to the cabin with her, he would have been miserable the whole time, and he couldn't have helped showing it. At any rate, she would have found him out. Whereas, having made up her mind to fall in with his ideas, he would have betted anybody she would even go so far as to enjoy the experience. Not because she was without personality of her own. Good Lord! She was absolutely brimming with it. But because . . . but here his thoughts always stopped. Here they always felt the need of a cigar, as it were. And, looking at the cigar-tip, his fine blue eyes narrowed. It was a law of marriage, he supposed. . . . All the same, he always felt guilty when he asked these sacrifices of her. That was what the quick pressure meant. His being said to her being: "You do understand, don't you?" and there was an answering tremor of her fingers. "I *understand.*"

Certainly, the steward—good little chap—had done all in his power to make them comfortable. He had put up their chairs in whatever warmth there was and out of the smell. She did hope he would be tipped adequately. It was on occasions like these (and her life seemed to be full of such occasions) that she wished it was the woman who controlled the purse.

"Thank you, steward. That will do beautifully."

"Why are stewards so often delicate-looking?" she wondered, as her feet were tucked under. "This poor little chap looks as though he'd got a chest, and yet one would have thought . . . the sea air. . . ."

The button of the pigskin purse was undone. The tray was tilted. She saw sixpences, shillings, half-crowns.

"I should give him five shillings," she decided, "and tell him to buy himself a good nourishing—"

He was given a shilling, and he touched his cap and seemed genuinely grateful.

Well, it might have been worse. It might have been sixpence. It might, indeed. For at that moment Father turned towards her and said, half-apologetically, stuffing the purse back, "I gave him a shilling. I think it was worth it, don't you?"

"Oh, quite! Every bit!" said she.

It is extraordinary how peaceful it feels on a little steamer once the bustle of leaving port is over. In a quarter of an hour one might have been at sea for days. There is something almost touching, childish, in the way people submit themselves to the new conditions. They go to bed in the early afternoon, they shut their eyes and "it's night" like little children who turn the table upside down and cover themselves with the table-cloth. And those who remain on deck—they seem to be always the same, those few hardened men travellers—pause, light their pipes, stamp softly, gaze out to sea, and their voices are subdued as they walk up and down. The long-legged little girl chases after the red-cheeked boy, but soon both are captured; and the old sailor, swinging an unlighted lantern, passes and disappears. . . .

He lay back, the rug up to his chin and she saw he was breathing deeply. Sea air! If anyone believed in sea air, it was he. He had the strongest faith in its tonic qualities. But the great thing was, according to him, to fill the lungs with it the moment you came on board. Otherwise, the sheer strength of it was enough to give you a chill. . . .

She gave a small chuckle, and he turned to her quickly. "What is it?"

"It's your cap," she said. "I never can get used to you in a cap. You look such a thorough burglar."

"Well, what the deuce am I to wear?" He shot up one grey eyebrow and wrinkled his nose. "It's a very good cap, too. Very fine specimen of its kind. It's got a very rich white satin lining." He paused. He declaimed, as he had hundreds of times before at this stage, "Rich and rare were the gems she wore."

But she was thinking he really was childishly proud of the white satin lining. He would like to have taken off his cap and made her feel it. "Feel the quality!" How often had she rubbed between finger and thumb his coat, his shirt cuff, tie, sock, linen handkerchief, while he said that.

She slipped down more deeply into her chair.

And the little steamer pressed on, pitching gently, over the grey, unbroken, gently-moving water, that was veiled with slanting rain.

Far out, as though idly, listlessly, gulls were flying. Now they settled on the waves, now they beat up into the rainy air, and shone against the pale sky like the lights within the pearl. They looked cold and lonely. How lonely it will be when we have passed by, she thought. There will be nothing but the waves and those birds and rain falling.

She gazed through the rust-spotted railing along which big drops trembled, until suddenly she shut her lips. It was as if a warning voice inside her had said, "Don't look!"

"No, I won't," she decided. "It's too depressing, much too depressing."

But immediately, she opened her eyes and looked again. Lonely birds, water lifting, white pale sky—how were they changed?

And it seemed to her there was a presence far out there, between the sky and the water; someone very desolate and longing watched them pass and cried as if to stop them—but cried to her alone.

"Mother!"

"Don't leave me," sounded the cry. "Don't forget me! You are forgetting me, you know you are!" And it was as though from her own breast there came the sound of childish weeping.

"My son—my precious child—it isn't true!"

Sh! How was it possible that she was sitting there on that quiet steamer beside Father and at the same time she was hushing and holding a little slender boy—so pale—who had just waked out of a dreadful dream?

"I dreamed I was in a wood—somewhere far away from everybody,—and I was lying down and a great blackberry vine grew over me. And I called and called to you—and you wouldn't come—you wouldn't come—so I had to lie there for ever."

What a terrible dream! He had always had terrible dreams. How often, years ago, when he was small, she had made some excuse and escaped from their friends in the dining-room or the drawing-room to come to the foot of the stairs and listen. "Mother!" And when he was asleep, his dream had journeyed with her back into the circle of lamplight; it had taken its place there like a ghost. And now—

Far more often—at all times—in all places—like now, for instance—she never settled down, she was never off her guard for a moment but she heard him. He wanted her. "I am coming as fast as I can! As fast as I can!" But the dark stairs have no ending, and the worst dream of all—the one that is always the same—goes for ever and ever uncomforted.

This is anguish! How is it to be borne? Still, it is not the idea of her suffering which is unbearable—it is his. Can one do nothing for the dead? And for a long time the answer had been—Nothing!

. . . But softly without a sound the dark curtain has rolled down. There is no more to come. That is the end of the play. But it can't end like that—so suddenly. There must be more. No, it's cold, it's still. There is nothing to be gained by waiting.

But—did he go back again? Or, when the war was over, did he come home for good? Surely, he will marry—later on—not for several years. Surely, one day I shall remember his wedding and my first grandchild—a beautiful dark-haired boy born in the early morning—a lovely morning—spring!

"Oh, Mother, it's not fair to me to put these ideas into my head! Stop, Mother, stop! When I think of all I have missed, I can't bear it."

"I can't bear it!" She sits up breathing the words and tosses the dark rug away. It is colder than ever, and now the dusk is falling, falling like ash upon the pallid water.

And the little steamer, growing determined, throbbed on, pressed on, as if at the end of the journey there waited. . . .

[1923—Great Britain]

Questions

1. We see through the eyes of both characters in "Six Years After." Where do we see through the husband's eyes? Where through the wife's?
2. Contrast the husband and wife of Mansfield's delicate story. What character type is each: stock, flat, or round? Similarly, contrast the story's beginning and concluding paragraphs. What do the former serve to do with respect to the latter?
3. The wife's "toss[ing] the dark rug away" at the end of the story could be taken as symbolic. What could it mean?

Writing Assignments

1. Write a paragraph examining the type of narration found in "Six Years After." Evaluate the effectiveness of Mansfield's treatment of narration as it helps the reader to understand the characters.
2. In a paragraph or more contrast the states of mind of the story's two main characters. In light of this contrast, what might be the theme of the story?
3. Is it really possible to make ethical judgments when it comes to the different ways people respond to death? Write a paper on the subject using "Six Years After" for examples, as well as anything in your own experience that has relevance.

A CONFESSION

MIKHAIL ZOSHCHENKO

Translated by John W. Strahan and Rosalind Zoglin

During the final week of Lent, Fekla threw caution to the winds, spent a goodly portion of her savings on a twenty-kopeck candle, and placed it before one of the saints.

With the utmost care and deliberation, Fekla arranged the candle close by the image. When she'd adjusted it, she stepped back a bit and, admiring her handiwork, set about her prayers, requesting various absolutions and graces as recompense for her expenditure of twenty kopecks.

Fekla prayed at length, mumbling her petitions under her breath; and then, having pressed her brow to the dirty stone floor, went to confession with much sighing and groaning.

Confession was administered at the altar behind a screen.

Fekla took her place in line behind a very old woman and fussily began crossing herself and muttering. They didn't detain a person long behind the screen.

The confessors would go in and, after a moment, with a sigh and a hushed cough, they'd return and make their obeisances before the saints.

"The priest's hurrying things along," thought Fekla. "What's the rush? He's not going to a fire."

Fekla went behind the screen, bowed low before the priest, and kissed his hand.

"What is your name?" the priest asked, giving his blessing.

"They call me Fekla."

"Now then, tell me, Fekla," said the priest, "what are your transgressions? Wherein have you sinned? Have you given vain utterance to evil thoughts? Haven't you been coming before your God rather rarely?"

"Indeed, Father, I am a sinner," said Fekla, bowing.

"God will pardon," said the priest, covering Fekla with his stole. "You *do* however believe in God? You don't harbor any doubts?"

"I most certainly do believe in God," said Fekla. "My son, though, just take him for example . . . he gives out with his opinions and, if I dare say a word or two, does do some criticizing . . . But I believe."

"That's good, Mother," said the priest. "Don't be an easy prey to temptation. By the way, tell me, what does your boy say? In what way does he criticize?"

"Oh, he's a faultfinder," said Fekla. " 'It's all fiddle-faddle—their faith,' he says. 'No,' he says, 'there is no God. Even if you explored the entire sky and the clouds . . .' "

"There is a God," the priest said severely. "Don't fall for that . . . And do you remember anything else that your son said?"

"Yes—he's been saying many of the same kind of things—various things."

"The same kind of various things!" the priest said angrily. "And whence came all that surrounds us? Whence the planets, stars, moon, if there is no God? Your son didn't by any chance say where all that surrounds us came from, did he? It couldn't by any chance be just plain chemistry."

"He didn't say."

"Maybe it *is* just chemistry," said the priest, pondering. "It is of course possible, my little Mother, that if there isn't a God, that the whole answer lies in . . . chemistry . . ."

Fekla looked at the priest in terror. But he placed his stole on her head and began muttering the words of a prayer.

"Well, be off now, my good woman, be off," the priest said dismally. Don't detain the faithful."

Fekla, rather frightened, looked once again at the priest and left, sighing and coughing meekly. Then she went up to her saint, examined the candle, straightened the burnt wick, and left the church.

[1923—U.S.S.R.]

Questions

1. Do we learn anything about the narrator here? Does the narrator predispose us in any way as to our reception of the story's characters? What kind of narration, then, do we have in "A Confession"?
2. What kind of character is Fekla (flat, round, stock)? And the priest? Whose story is it, finally?
3. Why might the priest have been "hurrying things along"? Comment on the ironic nature of the title.
4. Given the story's date of publication as well as its country of origin (what was happening in the U.S.S.R. in 1923?), what large theme does it touch on despite its limited compass?

Writing Assignments

1. In a paragraph or more, discuss the conflicts felt by the priest and their cause.
2. In a paragraph, classify the type of narration that "A Confession" exhibits and discuss the effect of the disparity between the impersonal tone of the narration and the inner turmoil and terror we witness in Zoshchenko's characters.

CHAPTER
✳ 6 ✳

MOOD, IRONY, AND STYLE

INTERPRETING MOOD

Applied to fiction, **mood** means what it means in our everyday conversation when we speak of feeling happy, gloomy, angry, and so forth. Described by such adjectives as "lighthearted," "nostalgic," "humorous," "sad," or "tragic," mood, then, is the emotional state that a story produces in the reader. Every story creates a mood of some sort, and some stories arouse several different moods. Of course, no one tells us how we should feel as we read a story, just as no one tells us what kind of a narrator we have, or what is ironic, or what symbols a story contains and what they mean. These things we must judge for ourselves. As to mood specifically, in order to interpret the mood of a story, what is most important is for you to be aware of your own feelings. Does a story make you feel sad, or happy, or nostalgic, or angry? Although one can respond inappropriately to a story just as one can to an event in real life, the chances are good that what you feel as you read is what you should feel. If you are aware of your own feelings, that is, you will most likely be in touch with the mood of the given story. And if you are aware of its mood, you will be close to its theme, for mood and theme are intimately linked. To feel that one story is comic and another tragic is in each case to infer attitude; and attitude, as we have discussed, is often equivalent to theme.

Notice that I said "your own feelings." Here we must make another crucial distinction, like the one between author and narrator. When reading, you must clearly distinguish between the moods of characters within a story—including its narrator—and the mood or moods created in you by the story overall. Quickly look back at Thurber's "The Unicorn in the Garden" in this regard (pp. 50–51). To us, the wife's being carted off to the "booby hatch" is funny; Thurber has characterized her in such a way as to curtail any sympathy we might have. We are glad to see her dragged off protesting all the way, though we realize that *she* does not feel happy about the turn of events. A character in a story, then, might feel sad, yet the story itself be comic; so *we* don't feel sad. The story overall makes us laugh; so its mood is humorous, however sad a particular character might feel. To be sure, in many stories the mood of one character or another does coincide with that of the story. Stories of this sort are so constructed as to make us sympathize with these characters and thus to assume their moods ourselves. But that is not true of all pieces of fiction. If you always make the distinction between the moods of characters and the mood of the story overall, you will be prepared to deal with stories in which the two diverge; stories in which the two coincide will take care of themselves.

One more point about mood should be stressed: mood is created entirely by other elements. When analyzing the mood of a story, therefore, one must look at the other elements that go into its making in order to demonstrate its mood. We have seen that characterization can be an agent of mood; so can setting. For example, the setting of the typical horror story (lightning, thunder, rain, an old castle, a wolf howling) very much creates mood. In analyzing the mood of such a story, then, one would need to consider setting. Plot, too, especially if it builds suspense or takes an ironic turn, can give rise to mood. Style is also important in establishing mood, as we will see shortly. In sum, you must take into account all the elements found in a story when focusing on its mood and how that mood is aroused in you, the reader.

INCONGRUITY: LIFE AND FICTION

I have mentioned irony already several times in passing, for, though irony is not a mood as such, the recognition of irony always establishes mood. Spanning both the tragic and the comic, the satiric and the pathetic, **irony** inevitably involves a sense of discrepancy. Rationality aside, human existence is a mass of incongruities. We know that appearances can deceive, that language can be used to conceal as well as reveal, that expectations and realizations can and often do diverge. The very texture of human life seems in good measure to be ironic. It is no wonder, then, that irony should be prevalent in literature, for literary irony simply reflects and acts as a comment upon the ironies of everyday existence. The doubleness of irony allows an author to capture concisely the complexity of human awareness in the face of life's contradictions, incongruities, discrepancies. Most important, irony in a text immediately governs our understanding. But we must be able to spot irony when irony is present. To do so it is useful to know the three primary types of irony: verbal, circumstantial, and dramatic.

Verbal Irony

The simplest type of irony, this type entails saying the opposite of what is meant. The discrepancy lies between what has been said and what is known to be true. So you might say, "What a beautiful day," when it's really rotten out; or "Boy, are you smart," when what is meant is "stupid." (The latter, with its mocking tone, is an example of **sarcasm,** which is a subtype of verbal irony.) But how is such irony recognized? The answer is *by the context.* Take "What a beautiful day," meaning "unutterably horrible." The speaker would signal an ironic intent by facial expression, gesture, and tone of voice (perhaps by giving the word "beautiful" a special twist); but our recognition of an ironic possibility in the first place comes from our knowledge that it is not a beautiful day. Unless we had reason to think the speaker mad, we would grasp the ironic nature of the statement because it would be at odds with the facts. In fiction, context is all. We must weigh every statement of every character (including the narrator) against the known facts as established in a story. If there is a discrepancy, then the character is either lying or being ironic. The function of verbal irony in fiction is the same as its function in ordinary discourse: whenever it is found, verbal irony is a rhetorical device that helps drive home a point with concision and with force.

Circumstantial Irony

The discrepancy of this type of irony (also called "situational irony") lies in the difference between what seems (or is expected) to be and what actually is; or between what is expected (or intended) to happen and what does happen. It is ironic, for instance, that the pastor in Chekhov's "At Sea" (pp. 134–36) turns out to be entirely different from what he seems and what we expect; it is equally ironic that Tom, in Maugham's "The Ant and the Grasshopper" (pp. 159–62), should unexpectedly, and through no effort of his own, wind up rich. Guy de Maupassant's "The Venus of Braniza" (pp. 163–65) provides another example of circumstantial irony. In this story a man finds himself trapped by his own beliefs. Unwittingly, he has helped to create that very trap by teaching some of those beliefs to his wife. He is thus "hoisted by his own petard" (that is, blown up by his own bomb).

Dramatic Irony

Here the discrepancy lies between what is believed by a character (or characters) and what the reader knows to be true. A character might be blind to something, or believe something about another character, or even about himself or herself, that isn't true. The reader, however, knows better and so is in a position to assess the character's judgments and beliefs. In Maugham's "The Ant and the Grasshopper" (pp. 159–62), for instance, we come to know a good deal more about George than George himself knows. He believes that he is suffering because of his brother, Tom; we know that he suffers because of his own bad character as well as his childish notion of fairness. A sense of irony results from the divergence of understanding, his and ours, and in this case enables us to laugh at George at the end. Irony here very much helps to create a comic mood.

The hallmark of irony, whatever the type, is a sense of discrepancy or incongruity, a sense to which you should try to be alert and responsive. For irony always helps to shape the reader's attitude without intervening explanation (and thus helps the writer to dramatize and to gain compression). That is, to say that the mood of a story entails tragic irony, or sardonic irony, or comic irony, is to suggest the attitude we are to take toward the material at hand. Irony can make us laugh, or move us to tears, or instill horror or wonder or both. It touches us because we recognize in it some deep truth.

STYLE: THE MEDIUM AND THE MESSAGE

In everyday life we convey meaning as much by the various tones we project when speaking as by the meanings of our words and sentences. The same is true of fiction. Consider the following passage from Virginia Woolf's *Mrs. Dalloway:*

> Sir William Bradshaw stopped at the door to look at a picture. He looked in the corner for the engraver's name. His wife looked too. Sir William Bradshaw was so interested in art.

Was he, really? No, for the tone of the passage is mockingly ironic. Note the childish sentence pattern, as banal as judging a work of art by the name in the corner. Note the repetition of the name "Sir William Bradshaw" and how the repetition lends an air of pomposity. Note especially the single word "so," which serves to undercut the literal sense of the last sentence entirely. Much can be inferred from this passage: that Sir William's interest is in money and not art; that his wife shares that interest; that both are probably snobs. All of this we sense from the tone of voice of the narrator, and that tone is created by the author's style in the passage.

Style, then, is instrumental in establishing meaning. To borrow Marshall McLuhan's phrase, we might say that "the medium is the message." Certainly, how something is said greatly affects what is said. "I believe you are in error," for instance, is not the same statement as "You're wrong," and both are quite different from "You're full of it." A matter of style, the difference in the choice of words here is responsible for the radically different tones. **Style** refers to the words used (diction) and the sentence patterns they form (syntax), as well as to the effect gained by the choice of words and sentence patterns.

Diction means the selection of words, or the kind of words selected, in a given passage. It can be abstract or concrete ("a meal" versus "a juicy steak"); literal or metaphorical ("the surface of the sea" versus "the breast of the sea"); denotative or connotative ("domicile" versus "home"). Is the language of a given passage flat or lyrical? Is the author's use of adjectives and adverbs copious or spare? Is the vocabulary primarily that of standard English, or is it marked by slang or perhaps by technical jargon? Even the sounds of words should be considered: some passages gain their effect by purposefully chosen patterns of sound, harsh and grating or liquid and soothing.

Syntax covers that aspect of verbal style having to do with how words and phrases are put together into sentences. Certainly, a story written in long, involved sentences will have an effect quite different from a story written in short, simple sentences, just as a story whose vocabulary tends to be literal and denotative will have a different effect from a story whose vocabulary is predominantly metaphorical and connotative. Sentences can be loose or periodic, with the main information coming either at the head or at the end; simple or complex, marked by much coordination or by much subordination; recurrent in pattern, with one type of pattern repeating, or varied. And all the choices an author makes as to syntax go into the making of the rhythm of a passage or a story overall, prose rhythm being a subtle contributor to how fiction affects us.

Particular stylistic choices tend to be characteristic of particular writers. One writer is characteristically metaphorical and prefers complex sentences; another writes story after story in which syntax is simple and diction is slangy. Hemingway's style, for instance, is generally simple and Faulkner's is complex; and the two styles have vastly different effects on the reader, effects closely related to meaning. This does not mean, however, that the style of a story is uniform. The writer adjusts style to particular characters and circumstances. Therefore, we can often tell as much about characters from the ways in which they speak as we can about real people. Character contrast, too, is facilitated by an author's fashioning of different manners of speech for characters of different backgrounds and capacities.

Writers must make many choices about language in order to maintain control over their stories. In our turn, we as readers need to develop sensitivity to the intricate relationship between style and meaning, the medium and the message. To know an author well is to understand that author's characteristic choices; to grasp a particular story well is to understand how all aspects of its style contribute to its meaning. The more one reads, of course, the more precisely one can make determinations of this sort.

SUMMARY SUGGESTIONS: UNDERSTANDING MOOD, IRONY, AND STYLE

1. As you read, be aware of what you are feeling. What you feel has probably been engineered by the writer, so your feeling is a guide to meaning.

2. Be sure to distinguish the mood of a story overall from the mood or moods of individual characters. The two do not necessarily coincide.

3. Look for discrepancies between what is said and what is meant, or between what is expected and what happens, or between what a character believes and what you as the reader know to be true. Such discrepancies generally signal an ironic intent.

4. Hear the voices as you read and try to catch their various tones. Don't forget how much our tones of voice condition the meaning of what we say to each other. No less is true of the written language.

5. Determine the main stylistic features of the text at hand—long or short sentences, figurative or literal language, recurring patterns of verbal constructions. Though style will work its ends whether we know why or not, some attention to the language used in a story is always rewarding.

6. Most of all, take the crucial step from mood, tone, and style to meaning. That is, relate these qualities of a story to what you think it is about. Or perhaps I should put this the other way round: test what you think the theme of a story is

against your perception of its mood, tone, and style overall. If the two judgments fit, the story is yours.

WRITING ON MOOD, IRONY, AND STYLE

Though mood, irony, and style are intimately linked, the best way to proceed in our discussion of writing on these topics is to take each up in turn. So, mood first. Should you choose or be asked to write about the mood of a story, you will be writing about what it makes you feel and why (not, note, what you feel *about* it, which is a different matter). As usual, the *why* will be the substance of what you write. That is, you must explain what it is about the story that creates in you the mood you feel when reading it. To support your thesis you will need to consider characterization, descriptive details, plot, and the like—whatever contributes to the mood. How does this or that character affect the way you feel? Does the plot take a surprising turn, thereby affecting you in some special way? Or perhaps the kind of language used touches you and makes you feel joyous, or angry, or reflective. Certainly you would also want to consider the theme of the story in so far as mood helps to establish the theme. Finally, you should always consider irony when writing on mood, for irony when present is instrumental in creating mood.

But if a story is ironic to the core, as is Chekhov's "At Sea" (pp. 134–36), then irony itself can be taken as the basis of a paper. In writing on "At Sea," you might argue that the story is thematically or structurally ironic (your thesis); demonstrate how this is so by considering what discrepancy the theme itself involves and how this discrepancy is enacted in the story; and consider how the story entraps the reader in its irony in order to drive home its point.

Another way of dealing with irony is to classify the type of irony a given story exhibits and then to discuss the story in terms of that classification. Circumstantial and dramatic irony are especially well suited to use in this way. To suggest that a story is built on circumstantial or dramatic irony is to have a thesis immediately. What is left to do is to demonstrate how the story establishes the one or the other and how its type of irony goes into the making of its mood and theme. Maugham's "Appointment in Samarra" (pp. 162–63) would be an excellent story to treat in this way. Exemplifying both circumstantial and dramatic irony, the story creates a sense of divergence between what the servant believes and what the reader knows will happen (here would be your thesis); it does so by plot especially, which is structured so that the story's ironic revelation comes in its last sentence (support); the discrepancy produces a chill in the reader (mood, which points to the story's fatalistic theme) and allows the reader both to judge the servant's expectations and to see his circumstance as representative of how, finally, we are all trapped by fate (theme). For a paper, this outline would have to be expanded. But by classifying the type of irony found in Maugham's story, you have a thesis that could easily lead to a paper and that clearly directs what must be done.

One of the most interesting things to do with style is to compare authors as to style. Another is to consider several stories by the same author in order to define the author's characteristic style. To be sure, the general style of an author is perhaps the most challenging topic one can write on. For though omnipresent, style is elusive, and the stylistic habits of an author must be clearly distinguished from styles created for characters, including narrators. Nevertheless, fine pieces of writing have been done on Hemingway's terseness, Woolf's liquid rhythms, Faulkner's figurative language, and so forth. In pieces of this sort, the writer first specifies some general stylistic trait or traits of the author (thesis) and then exemplifies in detail from at least several works by that author (support). What is difficult about writing on style is not so much how to proceed as what evidence to use. If you are adventuresome and decide to write on style, you will need to take into account all that has been said about style in this chapter. Diction, imagery, figurative language, rhythm, and so forth—these will be your concerns.

Style in fiction, though a complex subject, is one of the most rewarding you can choose. Tackle it and do the best you can. With time and practice in analyzing style, you should find that your understanding of language and what it can do has deepened and, very possibly, that your own writing has improved. It is necessary to examine many types of style and to see the language used well in various ways before one can ever use it truly well oneself. But if you pursue the subject, then you will perhaps develop a style of your own.

STORIES FOR STUDY AND WRITING ASSIGNMENTS

THE BLUE BOUQUET

OCTAVIO PAZ

Translated by Eliot Weinberger

I woke covered with sweat. Hot steam rose from the newly sprayed, red-brick pavement. A gray-winged butterfly, dazzled, circled the yellow light. I jumped from my hammock and crossed the room barefoot, careful not to step on some scorpion leaving his hideout for a bit of fresh air. I went to the little window and inhaled the country air. One could hear the breathing of the night, feminine, enormous. I returned to the center of the room, emptied water from a jar into a pewter basin, and wet my towel. I rubbed my chest and legs with the soaked cloth, dried myself a little, and, making sure that no bugs were hidden in the folds of my clothes, got dressed. I ran down the green stairway. At the door of the boardinghouse I bumped into the owner, a one-eyed taciturn fellow. Sitting on a wicker stool, he smoked, his eye half closed. In a hoarse voice, he asked:

"Where are you going?"

"To take a walk. It's too hot."

"Hmmm—everything's closed. And no streetlights around here. You'd better stay put."

I shrugged my shoulders, muttered "back soon" and plunged into the darkness. At first I couldn't see anything. I fumbled along the cobblestone street. I lit a cigarette. Suddenly the moon appeared from behind a black cloud, lighting a white wall that was crumbled in places. I stopped, blinded by such whiteness. Wind whistled slightly. I breathed the air of the tamarinds. The night hummed, full of leaves and insects. Crickets bivouacked in the tall grass. I raised my head: up there the stars too had set up camp. I thought that the universe was a vast system of signs, a conversation between giant beings. My actions, the cricket's saw, the star's blink, were nothing but pauses and syllables, scattered phrases from that dialogue. What word could it be, of which I saw only a syllable? Who speaks the word? To whom is it spoken? I threw my cigarette down on the sidewalk. Falling, it drew a shining curve, shooting out brief sparks like a tiny comet.

I walked a long time, slowly. I felt free, secure between the lips that were at that moment speaking me with such happiness. The night was a garden of eyes. As I crossed the street, I heard someone come out of a doorway. I turned around, but could not distinguish anything. I hurried on. A few moments later I heard the dull shuffle of sandals on the hot stone. I didn't want to turn around, although I felt the shadow getting closer with every step. I tried to run. I couldn't. Suddenly I stopped short. Before I could defend myself, I felt the point of a knife in my back, and a sweet voice:

"Don't move, mister, or I'll stick it in."

Without turning, I asked:

"What do you want?"

"Your eyes, mister," answered the soft, almost painful voice.

"My eyes? What do you want with my eyes? Look, I've got some money. Not much, but it's something. I'll give you everything I have if you let me go. Don't kill me."

"Don't be afraid, mister. I won't kill you. I'm only going to take your eyes."

"But why do you want my eyes?" I asked again.

"My girlfriend has this whim. She wants a bouquet of blue eyes. And around here they're hard to find."

"My eyes won't help you. They're brown, not blue."

"Don't try to fool me, mister. I know very well that yours are blue."

"Don't take the eyes of a fellow man. I'll give you something else."

"Don't play saint with me," he said harshly. "Turn around."

I turned. He was small and fragile. His palm sombrero covered half his face. In his right hand he held a country machete that shone in the moonlight.

"Let me see your face."

I struck a match and put it close to my face. The brightness made me squint. He opened my eyelids with a firm hand. He couldn't see very well. Standing on tiptoe, he stared at me intensely. The flame burned my fingers. I dropped it. A silent moment passed.

"Are you convinced now? They're not blue."

"Pretty clever, aren't you?" he answered. "Let's see. Light another one."

I struck another match, and put it near my eyes. Grabbing my sleeve, he ordered:

"Kneel down."

I knelt. With one hand he grabbed me by the hair, pulling my head back. He bent over me, curious and tense, while his machete slowly dropped until it grazed my eyelids. I closed my eyes.

"Keep them open," he ordered.

I opened my eyes. The flame burned my lashes. All of the sudden, he let me go.

"All right, they're not blue. Beat it."

He vanished. I leaned against the wall, my head in my hands. I pulled myself together. Stumbling, falling, trying to get up again. I ran for an hour through the deserted town. When I got to the plaza, I saw the owner of the boardinghouse, still sitting in front of the door. I went in without saying a word. The next day I left town.

[1969—Mexico]

Questions

1. The first paragraph of this story sets a somewhat foreboding mood. How?
2. Shortly before the central incident, the narrator says, "I thought that the universe was a vast system of signs." Is that view borne out as the story proceeds?

3. In his momentary happiness the narrator declares, "The night was a garden of eyes." In light of what happens, what is ironic here?
4. Why is the beginning of the sixth paragraph ("I walked a long time") ironic with respect to what follows? Who, finally, "speaks the word," a purposeful God or blind chance?
5. What is the mood of this story overall? How is it established?

Writing Assignments

1. (a) Write a paragraph in answer to question 5 above. In doing so, consider how plot and irony are agents of mood.
   (b) In discussing the story's mood, you were stating what the story makes you feel. Now, in a separate paragraph, discuss what you feel *about* the story. That is, what is your response, and what in "The Blue Bouquet" accounts for that response?
2. In a paragraph or more, discuss the discrepancy between the narrator's mood upon setting out and the terror that follows. How does this ironic contrast heighten the mood of the story overall? What theme does the contrast help to establish?
3. In a short paper, establish the theme of Paz's story and, using examples, discuss how this somewhat abstract theme is made concrete.

THE ANT AND THE GRASSHOPPER

 SOMERSET MAUGHAM

When I was a very small boy I was made to learn by heart certain of the fables of La Fontaine, and the moral of each was carefully explained to me. Among those I learnt was *The Ant and The Grasshopper,* which is devised to bring home to the young the useful lesson that in an imperfect world industry is rewarded and giddiness punished. In this admirable fable (I apologize for telling something which everyone is politely, but inexactly, supposed to know) the ant spends a laborious summer gathering its winter store, while the grasshopper sits on a blade of grass singing to the sun. Winter comes and the ant is comfortably provided for, but the grasshopper has an empty larder: he goes to the ant and begs for a little food. Then the ant gives him her classic answer:

"What were you doing in the summer time?"

"Saving your presence, I sang, I sang all day, all night."

"You sang. Why, then go and dance."

I do not ascribe it to perversity on my part, but rather to the inconsequence of childhood, which is deficient in moral sense, that I could never quite reconcile myself to the lesson. My sympathies were with the grasshopper and for some time I never saw an ant without putting my foot on it. In this summary (and as I have discovered since, entirely human) fashion I sought to express my disapproval of prudence and common sense.

I could not help thinking of this fable when the other day I saw George Ramsay lunching by himself in a restaurant. I never saw anyone wear an expression of such deep gloom. He was staring into space. He looked as though the burden of the whole world sat on his shoulders. I was sorry for him: I suspected at once that his unfortunate brother had been causing trouble again. I went up to him and held out my hand.

"How are you?" I asked.

"I'm not in hilarious spirits," he answered.

"Is it Tom again?"

He sighed.

"Yes, it's Tom again."

"Why don't you chuck him? You've done everything in the world for him. You must know by now that he's quite hopeless."

I suppose every family has a black sheep. Tom had been a sore trial to his for twenty years. He had begun life decently enough: he went into business, married, and had two children. The Ramsays were perfectly respectable people and there was every reason to suppose that Tom Ramsay would have a useful and honourable career. But one day, without warning, he announced that he didn't like work and that he wasn't suited for marriage. He wanted to enjoy himself. He would listen to no expostulations. He left his wife and his office. He had a little money and he spent two happy years in the various capitals of Europe. Rumours of his doings reached his relations from time to time and they were profoundly shocked. He certainly had a very good time. They shook their heads and asked what would happen when his money was spent. They soon found out: he borrowed. He was charming and unscrupulous. I have never met anyone to whom it was more difficult to refuse a loan. He made a steady income from his friends and he made friends easily. But he always said that the money you spent on necessities was boring; the money that was amusing to spend was the money you spent on luxuries. For this he depended on his brother George. He did not waste his charm on him. George was a serious man and insensible to such enticements. George was respectable. Once or twice he fell to Tom's promises of amendment and gave him considerable sums in order that he might make a fresh start. On these Tom bought a motor-car and some very nice jewellery. But when circumstances forced George to realize that his brother would never settle down and he washed his hands of him, Tom, without a qualm, began to blackmail him. It was not very nice for a respectable lawyer to find his brother shaking cocktails behind the bar of his favourite restaurant or to see him waiting on the box-seat of a taxi outside his club. Tom said that to serve in a bar or to drive a taxi was a perfectly decent occupation, but if George could oblige him with a couple of hundred pounds he didn't mind for the honour of the family giving it up. George paid.

Once Tom nearly went to prison. George was terribly upset. He went into the whole discreditable affair. Really Tom had gone too far. He had been wild, thoughtless, and selfish, but he had never before done anything dishonest, by which George meant illegal; and if he were prosecuted he would assuredly be convicted. But you cannot allow your only brother to go to gaol. The man Tom had cheated, a man called Cronshaw, was vindictive. He was determined to take the matter into court; he said Tom was a scoundrel and should be punished. It cost George an infinite deal of trouble and five hundred pounds to settle the affair. I have never seen him in such a rage as when he heard that Tom and Cronshaw had gone off together to Monte Carlo the moment they cashed the cheque. They spent a happy month there.

For twenty years Tom raced and gambled, philandered with the prettiest girls, danced, ate in the most expensive restaurants, and dressed beautifully. He always looked as if he had just stepped out of a bandbox. Though he was forty-six you would never have taken him for more than thirty-five. He was a most amusing companion and though you knew he was perfectly worthless you could not but enjoy his society. He had high spirits, an unfailing gaiety, and incredible charm. I never grudged the contributions he regularly levied on me for the necessities of his existence. I never lent him fifty pounds without feeling that I was in his debt. Tom Ramsay knew everyone and everyone knew Tom Ramsay. You could not approve of him, but you could not help liking him.

Poor George, only a year older than his scapegrace brother, looked sixty. He had never taken more than a fortnight's holiday in the year for a quarter of a century. He was in his office every morning at nine-thirty and never left it till six. He was honest, industrious, and worthy. He had a good wife, to whom he had never been unfaithful even in thought, and four daughters to whom he was the best of fathers. He made a point of saving a third of his income and his plan was to retire at fifty-five to a little house in the country where he proposed to cultivate his garden and play golf. His life was blameless. He was glad that he was growing old because Tom was growing old too. He rubbed his hands and said:

"It was all very well when Tom was young and good-looking, but he's only a year younger than I am. In four years he'll be fifty. He won't find life so easy then. I shall have thirty thousand pounds by the time I'm fifty. For twenty-five years I've said that Tom would end in the gutter. And we shall see how he likes that. We shall see if it really pays best to work or be idle."

Poor George! I sympathized with him. I wondered now as I sat down beside him what infamous thing Tom had done. George was evidently very much upset.

"Do you know what's happened now?" he asked me.

I was prepared for the worst. I wondered if Tom had got into the hands of the police at last. George could hardly bring himself to speak.

"You're not going to deny that all my life I've been hardworking, decent, respectable, and straightforward. After a life of industry and thrift I can look forward to retiring on a small income in gilt-edged securities. I've always done my duty in that state of life in which it has pleased Providence to place me."

"True."

"And you can't deny that Tom has been an idle, worthless, dissolute, and dishonourable rogue. If there were any justice he'd be in the workhouse."

"True."

George grew red in the face.

"A few weeks ago he became engaged to a woman old enough to be his mother. And now she's died and left him everything she had. Half a million pounds, a yacht, a house in London, and a house in the country."

George Ramsay beat his clenched fist on the table.

"It's not fair, I tell you, it's not fair. Damn it, it's not fair."

I could not help it. I burst into a shout of laughter as I looked at George's wrathful face, I rolled in my chair, I very nearly fell on the floor. George never forgave me. But Tom often asks me to excellent dinners in his charming house in Mayfair, and if he occasionally borrows a trifle from me, that is merely from force of habit. It is never more than a sovereign.

[1924—Great Britain]

Questions

1. Characterize the narrator of this story. Are we to accept his judgments or are we to side with George?
2. Characterize George and Tom, the fabled ant and grasshopper come to life. Which of the two is preferable as a human being and why?
3. In what way is the story ironic when read in light of the fable for which it is named? What does "The Ant and the Grasshopper" suggest about fables? What is its theme?
4. In what ways do plot, narration, and characterization all go into the making here of a comic mood?
5. Whose mood are we to share at the end, George's or the narrator's? Why?

Writing Assignments

1. Write a paper in which you first contrast George and Tom, and then contrast both with the narrator. Discuss how each contributes to the comic mood of the story.
2. In a paragraph or short paper, classify the type of irony Maugham incorporates, and then explain how irony helps to shape mood and to establish theme.

APPOINTMENT IN SAMARRA

❖ SOMERSET MAUGHAM ❖

There was a merchant in Bagdad who sent his servant to market to buy provisions, and in a little while the servant came back, white and trembling, and said, "Master, just now when I was in the market-place I was jostled by a woman in the crowd and when I turned I saw it was Death that jostled me. She looked at me and made a threatening gesture; now, lend me your horse, and I will ride away from this city and avoid my fate. I will go to Samarra and there Death will not find me." The merchant lent him his horse, and the servant mounted it, and he dug his spurs in its flanks and as fast as the horse could gallop he went. Then the merchant went down to the market-place and he saw Death standing in the crowd and he came to Death and said, "Why did you make a threatening gesture to my servant when you saw him this morning?" "That was not a threatening gesture," Death said. "It was only a start of surprise. I was astonished to see him in Bagdad, for I had an appointment with him tonight in Samarra."

[1933—Great Britain]

Questions

1. What is ironic here? What kind of irony marks Maugham's story?
2. The theme of this miniature has something to do with fate. What?
3. What is the mood of this piece? How is its mood related to its view of human existence?

Writing Assignments

1. Write a paragraph in which you first classify the type of irony that this story exhibits and then discuss the story in terms of that classification. In other words, use Maugham's tale to exemplify the type of irony it embodies.
2. In a paragraph, describe and account for the mood of this miniature. You might conclude by suggesting how mood here is theme.

THE VENUS OF BRANIZA

❋ GUY DE MAUPASSANT ❋

Translated by M. Walter Dunne

Some years ago there lived in Braniza a celebrated Talmudist, renowned no less on account of his beautiful wife, than for his wisdom, his learning, and his fear of God. The Venus of Braniza deserved that name thoroughly; she deserved it for herself, on account of her singular beauty, and even more as the wife of a man deeply versed in the Talmud, for the wives of the Jewish philosophers are, as a rule, ugly or possess some bodily defect.

The Talmud explains this in the following manner: It is well known that marriages are made in heaven, and at the birth of a boy a divine voice calls out the name of his future wife, and *vice versâ*. But just as a good father tries to get rid of his good wares out of doors, and only uses the damaged stuff at home for his children, so God bestows on the Talmudists those women whom other men would not care to have.

Well, God made an exception in the case of our Talmudist, and had bestowed a Venus on him, perhaps only in order to confirm the rule by means of this exception, and to make it appear less hard. This philosopher's wife was a woman who would have done honor to any king's throne, or to a pedestal in any sculpture gallery. Tall, and with a wonderfully voluptuous figure, she carried a strikingly beautiful head, surmounted by thick, black plaits, on her proud shoulders. Two large, dark eyes languished and glowed beneath long lashes, and her beautiful hands looked as if they were carved out of ivory.

This glorious woman, who seemed to have been designed by nature to rule, to see slaves at her feet, to provide occupation for the painter's brush, the sculptor's chisel, and the poet's pen, lived the life of a rare and beautiful flower shut up in a hothouse. She would sit the whole day long wrapped up in her costly furs looking down dreamily into the street.

She had no children; her husband, the philosopher, studied and prayed and studied again from early morning until late at night; his mistress was "the Veiled Beauty," as the Talmudists call the Kabbalah. She paid no attention to her house, for she was rich, and everything went of its own accord like a clock which has only to be wound up once a week; nobody came to see her, and she never went out of the house; she sat and dreamed and brooded and—yawned.

One day when a terrible storm of thunder and lightning had spent its fury over the town, and all windows had been opened in order to let the Messias in, the Jewish Venus was sitting as usual in her comfortable easy-chair, shivering in spite of her furs, and thinking. Suddenly she fixed her glowing eyes on her husband who was sitting before the Talmud, swaying his body backward and forward, and said suddenly:

"Just tell me, when will Messias, the son of David, come?"

"He will come," the philosopher replied, "when all the Jews have become either altogether virtuous or altogether vicious, says the Talmud."

"Do you believe that all the Jews will ever become virtuous?" the Venus continued.

"How am I to believe that?"

"So Messias will come when all the Jews have become vicious?"

The philosopher shrugged his shoulders, and lost himself again in the labyrinth of the Talmud, out of which, so it is said, only one man returned in perfect sanity. The beautiful woman at the window again looked dreamily out into the heavy rain, while her white fingers played unconsciously with the dark furs of her splendid robe.

One day the Jewish philosopher had gone to a neighboring town, where an important question of ritual was to be decided. Thanks to his learning, the question was settled sooner than he had expected, and instead of returning the next morning, as he had intended, he came back the same evening with a friend who was no less learned than himself. He got out of the carriage at his friend's house and went home on foot. He was not a little surprised when he saw his windows brilliantly illuminated, and found an officer's servant comfortably smoking his pipe in front of his house.

"What are you doing here?" he asked in a friendly manner, but with some curiosity, nevertheless.

"I am on guard, lest the husband of the beautiful Jewess should come home unexpectedly."

"Indeed? Well, mind and keep a good lookout."

Saying this, the philosopher pretended to go away, but went into the house through the garden entrance at the back. When he got into the first room, he found a table laid for two, which had evidently only been left a short time previously. His wife was sitting as usual at her bedroom window wrapped in her furs, but her cheeks were suspiciously red, and her dark eyes had not their usual languishing look, but now rested on her husband with a gaze which expressed at the same time satisfaction and mockery. At that moment his foot struck against an object on the floor, which gave out a strange sound. He picked it up and examined it in the light. It was a pair of spurs.

"Who has been here with you?" asked the Talmudist.

The Jewish Venus shrugged her shoulders contemptuously, but did not reply.

"Shall I tell you? The Captain of Hussars has been with you."

"And why should he not have been here with me?" she said, smoothing the fur on her jacket with her white hand.

"Woman! are you out of your mind?"

"I am in full possession of my senses," she replied, and a knowing smile hovered round her red voluptuous lips. "But must I not also do my part, in order that Messias may come and redeem us poor Jews?"

[1884—France]

Questions

1. What type of character is Maupassant working with in his "Venus"? Why is this type appropriate given the mood of the story?
2. What is the mood? What is the relation of mood to ironic effect?
3. What, exactly, is ironic here? What type of irony is exemplified?
4. The philosopher's mood at the end is clearly not the mood of the story overall. Elaborate.

Writing Assignments

1. In a paragraph or two, classify the type of irony found in "The Venus of Braniza," establish the defining characteristics of the class, and apply those characteristics point by point to Maupassant's tale.
2. In a short paper, analyze the mood of this story. Having stated what the mood is, point as specifically as possible to the elements (for instance, characterization) that establish it.

THE ECLIPSE

AUGUSTO MONTERROSO

Translated by Wilfrido H. Corral

When Brother Bartolome Arrazola felt lost he accepted that nothing could save him anymore. The powerful Guatemalan jungle had trapped him inexorably and definitively. Before his topographical ignorance he sat quietly awaiting death. He wanted to die there, hopelessly and alone, with his thoughts fixed on far-away Spain, particularly on the Los Abrojos convent where Charles the Fifth had once condescended to lessen his prominence and tell him that he trusted the religious zeal of his redemptive work.

Upon awakening he found himself surrounded by a group of indifferent natives who were getting ready to sacrifice him in front of an altar, an altar that to Bartolome seemed to be the place in which he would finally rest from his fears, his destiny, from himself.

Three years in the land had given him a fair knowledge of the native tongues. He tried something. He said a few words which were understood.

He then had an idea he considered worthy of his talent, universal culture and steep knowledge of Aristotle. He remembered that a total eclipse of the sun was expected on that day and in his innermost thoughts he decided to use that knowledge to deceive his oppressors and save his life.

"If you kill me"—he told them, "I can darken the sun in its heights."

The natives looked at him fixedly and Bartolome caught the incredulity in their eyes. He saw that a small counsel was set up and waited confidently, not without some disdain.

Two hours later Brother Bartolome Arrazola's heart spilled its fiery blood on the sacrificial stone (brilliant under the opaque light of an eclipsed sun), while one of the natives recited without raising his voice, unhurriedly, one by one, the infinite dates in which there would be solar and lunar eclipses, that the astronomers of the Mayan community had foreseen and written on their codices without Aristotle's valuable help.

[1952—Mexico]

Questions

1. What type of irony marks Monterroso's story?
2. If we take Brother Bartolome as a representative of European civilization, what does the story suggest about the West's historical attitude toward non-Western cultures?
3. What is the mood of the story overall?

Writing Assignments

1. In a paragraph, address question 2 above. Be sure to state the story's theme somewhere in your paragraph.
2. In a paragraph, define what is ironic about what happens in "The Eclipse." Consider the discrepancy between the reader's knowledge and Brother Bartolome's, and how this discrepancy shapes our feelings as we follow Bartolome to his end.

THE USE OF FORCE

❊ WILLIAM CARLOS WILLIAMS ❊

They were new patients to me, all I had was the name, Olson. Please come down as soon as you can, my daughter is very sick.

When I arrived I was met by the mother, a big startled looking woman, very clean and apologetic who merely said, Is this the doctor? and let me in. In the back, she added. You must excuse us, doctor, we have her in the kitchen where it is warm. It is very damp here sometimes.

The child was fully dressed and sitting on her father's lap near the kitchen table. He tried to get up, but I motioned for him not to bother, took off my overcoat and started to look things over. I could see that they were all very nervous, eyeing me up and down distrustfully. As often, in such cases, they weren't telling me more than they had to, it was up to me to tell them; that's why they were spending three dollars on me.

The child was fairly eating me up with her cold, steady eyes, and no expression to her face whatever. She did not move and seemed, inwardly, quiet; an unusually attractive little thing, and as strong as a heifer in appearance. But her face was flushed, she was breathing rapidly, and I realized that she had a high fever. She had magnificent blonde hair, in profusion. One of those picture children often reproduced in advertising leaflets and the photogravure sections of the Sunday papers.

She's had a fever for three days, began the father and we don't know what it comes from. My wife has given her things, you know, like people do, but it don't do no good. And there's been a lot of sickness around. So we tho't you'd better look her over and tell us what is the matter.

As doctors often do I took a trial shot at it as a point of departure. Has she had a sore throat?

Both parents answered me together, No . . . No, she says her throat don't hurt her.

Does your throat hurt you? added the mother to the child. But the little girl's expression didn't change nor did she move her eyes from my face.

Have you looked?

I tried to, said the mother, but I couldn't see.

As it happens we had been having a number of cases of diphtheria in the school to which this child went during that month and we were all, quite apparently, thinking of that, though no one had as yet spoken of the thing.

Well, I said, suppose we take a look at the throat first. I smiled in my best professional manner and asking for the child's first name I said, come on, Mathilda, open your mouth and let's take a look at your throat.

Nothing doing.

Aw, come on, I coaxed, just open your mouth wide and let me take a look. Look, I said opening both hands wide, I haven't anything in my hands. Just open up and let me see.

Such a nice man, put in the mother. Look how kind he is to you. Come on, do what he tells you to. He won't hurt you.

At that I ground my teeth in disgust. If only they wouldn't use the word "hurt" I might be able to get somewhere. But I did not allow myself to be hurried or disturbed but speaking quietly and slowly I approached the child again.

As I moved my chair a little nearer suddenly with one catlike movement both her hands clawed instinctively for my eyes and she almost reached them too. In fact she knocked my glasses flying and they fell, though unbroken, several feet away from me on the kitchen floor.

Both the mother and father almost turned themselves inside out in embarrassment and apology. You bad girl, said the mother, taking her and shaking her by one arm. Look what you've done. The nice man . . .

For heaven's sake, I broke in. Don't call me a nice man to her. I'm here to look at her throat on the chance that she might have diphtheria and possibly die of it. But that's nothing to her. Look here, I said to the child, we're going to look at your throat. You're old enough to understand what I'm saying. Will you open it now by yourself or shall we have to open it for you?

Not a move. Even her expression hadn't changed. Her breaths however were coming faster and faster. Then the battle began. I had to do it. I had to have a throat culture for her own protection. But first I told the parents that it was entirely up to them. I explained the danger but said that I would not insist on a throat examination so long as they would take the responsibility.

If you don't do what the doctor says you'll have to go to the hospital, the mother admonished her severely.

Oh yeah? I had to smile to myself. After all, I had already fallen in love with the savage brat, the parents were contemptible to me. In the ensuing struggle they grew more and more abject, crushed, exhausted while she surely rose to magnificent heights of insane fury of effort bred of her terror of me.

The father tried his best, and he was a big man but the fact that she was his daughter, his shame at her behavior and his dread of hurting her made him release her just at the critical moment several times when I had almost achieved success, till I wanted to kill him. But his dread also that she might have diphtheria made him tell me to go on, go on though he himself was almost fainting, while the mother moved back and forth behind us raising and lowering her hands in an agony of apprehension.

Put her in front of you on your lap, I ordered, and hold both her wrists.

But as soon as he did the child let out a scream. Don't you're hurting me. Let go of my hands. Let them go I tell you. Then she shrieked terrifyingly, hysterically. Stop it! Stop it! You're killing me!

Do you think she can stand it, doctor! said the mother.

You get out, said the husband to his wife. Do you want her to die of diphtheria?

Come on now, hold her, I said.

Then I grasped the child's head with my left hand and tried to get the wooden tongue depressor between her teeth. She fought, with clenched teeth, desperately! But now I also had grown furious—at a child. I tried to hold myself down but I couldn't. I know how to expose a throat for inspection. And I did my best. When finally I got the wooden spatula behind the last teeth and just the point of it into the mouth cavity, she opened up for an instant but before I could see anything she came down again and gripping the wooden blade between her molars she reduced it to splinters before I could get it out again.

Aren't you ashamed, the mother yelled at her. Aren't you ashamed to act like that in front of the doctor?

Get me a smooth-handled spoon of some sort, I told the mother. We're going through with this. The child's mouth was already bleeding. Her tongue was cut and she was screaming in wild hysterical shrieks. Perhaps I should have desisted and come back in an hour or more. No doubt it would have been better. But I have seen at least two children lying dead in bed of neglect in such cases, and feeling that I must get a diagnosis now or never I went at it again. But the worst of it was that I too had got beyond reason. I could have torn the child apart in my own fury and enjoyed it. It was a pleasure to attack her. My face was burning with it.

The damned little brat must be protected against her own idiocy, one says to one's self at such times. Others must be protected against her. It is social necessity. And all these things are true. But a blind fury, a feeling of adult shame, bred of a longing for muscular release are the operatives. One goes on to the end.

In a final unreasoning assault I overpowered the child's neck and jaws. I forced the heavy silver spoon back of her teeth and down her throat till she gagged. And there it was—both tonsils covered with membrane. She had fought valiantly to keep me from knowing her secret. She had been hiding that sore throat for three days at least and lying to her parents in order to escape just such an outcome as this.

Now truly she *was* furious. She had been on the defensive before but now she attacked. Tried to get off her father's lap and fly at me while tears of defeat blinded her eyes.

[1938—U.S.A.]

Questions

1. Focusing on the conflict between the doctor and the parents as well as between the doctor and the girl, summarize the plot of "The Use of Force."
2. What kind of narration do we have here? Characterize the narrator as thoroughly as you can. Consider in particular his self-knowledge and his motivation.

3. What does the style of the story reveal about its narrator?
4. The doctor talks of the need to protect others from the girl and her from herself. "And all these things are true," he adds. However, this statement would be mere rationalization if he chose to probe no further. How so?
5. The title of this story points directly to its theme. What does the story dramatize about the use of force?
6. Had the girl turned out not to have diphtheria, the story would be ironic. But Williams was careful to keep out any major irony. Why? But do you find any irony in passing?

Writing Assignments

1. Write a short essay on how "The Use of Force" compels us to keep the doctor's act and his motives distinct.
2. How would the story be different if the girl turned out not to have diphtheria? Write a paragraph answering this question.
3. At two crucial points toward the end of his story, Williams could have made it ironic: he could have had the doctor be blind to his own motives, and he could have had the girl show no sign of diphtheria. In both cases Williams chose against irony. Write an essay in which you analyze the importance of these choices to Williams's theme. In order to do this, note, you must first verbalize the story's theme with care and precision.

AN INNOCENT AT RINKSIDE

 WILLIAM FAULKNER ✳

The vacant ice looked tired though it shouldn't have. They told him it had been put down only a few minutes ago following a basketball game and after the hockey match it would be taken up again to make room for something else. But it looked out expectant but resigned, like the mirror simulating ice in the Christmas store window, not before the miniature fir trees and reindeer and cosy lamplit cottage were arranged upon it, but after they had been dismantled and cleared away.

Then it was filled with motion, speed. To the innocent, who had never seen it before, it seemed discorded and inconsequent, bizarre and paradoxical like the frantic darting of the weightless bugs which run on the surface of stagnant pools. Then it would break, coalesce through a kind of kaleidoscopic whirl like a child's toy, into a pattern, a design almost beautiful, as if an inspired choreographer had drilled a willing and patient and hard-working troupe of dancers—a pattern, design which was trying to tell him something, say something to him urgent and important and true in that second before, already bulging with the motion and the speed, it began to disintegrate and dissolve.

Then he learned to find the puck and follow it. Then the individual players would emerge. They would not emerge like the sweating bare-handed behemoths from the troglodyte mass of football, but instead as fluid and fast and effortless as rapier thrusts of lightning—Richard with something of the passionate glittering fatal alien quality of snakes, Geoffrion like an agile ruthless precocious boy who maybe couldn't do anything else but then he didn't need to; and others—the veteran Laprade, still with the know-how and the grace. But he had time too now, or rather time had him, and what remained was no longer expendable that recklessly, heedlessly, successfully; not enough of it left now to buy fresh passion and fresh triumph with.

Excitement: men in rapid, hard, close physical conflict, not just with bare hands, but armed with the knife blades of skates and the hard, fast, deft sticks which break bones when used right. He had noticed how many women were among the spectators, and for just a moment he thought that perhaps this was why—that here actual male blood could flow, not from the crude impact of a heavier fist but from the rapid and delicate stroke of weapons, which, like the European rapier or the frontier pistol, reduced mere size and brawn to its proper perspective to the passion and the will. But only for a moment because he, the innocent, didn't like that idea either. It was the excitement of speed and grace, with the puck for catalyst, to give it reason, meaning.

He watched it—the figure-darted glare of ice, the concentric tiers rising in sections stipulated by the hand-lettered names of the individual fan-club idols, vanishing upward into the pall of tobacco smoke trapped by the roof—the roof which stopped and trapped all that intent and tense watching, and concentrated it downward upon the glare of ice frantic and frenetic with motion; until the byproduct of the speed and the motion—their violence—had no chance to exhaust itself upward into space and so leave on the ice only the swift glittering changing pattern. And he thought how perhaps something is happening to sport in America (assuming that by definition sport is something you do yourself, in solitude or not, because it is fun), and that something is the roof we are putting over it and them. Skating, basketball, tennis, track meets and even steeplechasing have moved indoors; football and baseball function beneath covers of arc lights and in time will be rain and coldproofed too. There still remain the proper working of a fly over trout water or the taking of a rise of birds in front of a dog or the right placing of a bullet in a deer or even a bigger animal which will hurt you if you don't. But not for long: in time that will be indoors too beneath lights and the trapped pall of spectator tobacco, the concentric sections bearing the name and device of the lion or the fish as well as that of the Richard or Geoffrion of the scoped rifle or four-ounce rod.

But (to repeat) not for long, because the innocent did not quite believe that either. We—Americans—like to watch, we like the adrenalic discharge of vicarious excitement or triumph or success. But we like to do also: the discharge of the personal excitement of the triumph and the fear to be had from actually setting the horse at the stone wall or pointing the overcanvased sloop or finding by actual test if you can line up two sights and one buffalo in time. There must have been little boys in that throng too, frantic with the slow excruciating passage of time, panting for the hour when they would be Richard or Geoffrion or Laprade—the same little

Negro boys whom the innocent has seen shadowboxing in front of a photograph of Joe Louis in his own Mississippi town, the same little Norwegian boys he watched staring up the snowless slope of the Holmenkollen jump one July day in the hills above Oslo.

Only he (the innocent) did wonder just what a professional hockey-match, whose purpose is to make a decent and reasonable profit for its owners, had to do with our National Anthem. What are we afraid of? Is it our national character of which we are so in doubt, so fearful that it might not hold up in the clutch, that we not only dare not open a professional athletic contest or a beauty-pageant or a real-estate auction, but we must even use a Chamber of Commerce race for Miss Sewage Disposal or a wildcat land-sale, to remind us that liberty gained without honor and sacrifice and held without constant vigilance and undiminished honor and complete willingness to sacrifice again at need, was not worth having to begin with? Or, by blaring or chanting it at ourselves every time ten or twelve or eighteen or twenty-two young men engage formally for the possession of a puck or a ball, or just one young woman walks across a lighted platform in a bathing-suit, do we hope to so dull and eviscerate the words and tune with repetition, that when we do hear it we will not be disturbed from that dream-like state in which "honor" is a break and "truth" an angle?

[1955—U.S.A.]

Questions

1. What kind of narrator tells us of the innocent here? Characterize the innocent. Whom do we know more about by the end of this piece, the boy or the narrator?
2. Is this piece a story or an essay with fictional trappings? Defend your judgment.
3. Compare and contrast "An Innocent at Rinkside" and Hemingway's "A Clean, Well-Lighted Place" (which follows) as to sentence length and complexity. What are the differing effects of each style?
4. Jot down a few of Faulkner's many metaphors and analyze their effect in context.

Writing Assignments

1. Consider question 2 above and write a paragraph stating and defending your judgment.
2. Assuming a reader not familiar with the story, write a review of "An Innocent at Rinkside." Try to persuade your reader of the rightness of your assessment by backing it up with evidence from the story itself.
3. Whether a story or not, "An Innocent at Rinkside" displays Faulkner's unique way of putting words together. In a paragraph, analyze the attributes of Faulkner's style as seen here. Then weigh its merits and judge its effectiveness.

A CLEAN, WELL-LIGHTED PLACE

❖ ERNEST HEMINGWAY ❖

It was late and every one had left the café except an old man who sat in the shadow the leaves of the tree made against the electric light. In the day time the street was dusty, but at night the dew settled the dust and the old man liked to sit late because he was deaf and now at night it was quiet and he felt the difference. The two waiters inside the café knew that the old man was a little drunk, and while he was a good client they knew that if he became too drunk he would leave without paying, so they kept watch on him.

"Last week he tried to commit suicide," one waiter said.

"Why?"

"He was in despair."

"What about?"

"Nothing."

"How do you know it was nothing?"

"He has plenty of money."

They sat together at a table that was close against the wall near the door of the café and looked at the terrace where the tables were all empty except where the old man sat in the shadow of the leaves of the tree that moved slightly in the wind. A girl and a soldier went by in the street. The street light shone on the brass number on his collar. The girl wore no head covering and hurried beside him.

"The guard will pick him up," one waiter said.

"What does it matter if he gets what he's after?"

"He had better get off the street now. The guard will get him. They went by five minutes ago."

The old man sitting in the shadow rapped on his saucer with his glass. The younger waiter went over to him.

"What do you want?"

The old man looked at him. "Another brandy," he said.

"You'll be drunk," the waiter said. The old man looked at him. The waiter went away.

"He'll stay all night," he said to his colleague. "I'm sleepy now. I never get into bed before three o'clock. He should have killed himself last week."

The waiter took the brandy bottle and another saucer from the counter inside the café and marched out to the old man's table. He put down the saucer and poured the glass full of brandy.

"You should have killed yourself last week," he said to the deaf man. The old man motioned with his finger. "A little more," he said. The waiter poured on into the glass so that the brandy slopped over and ran down the stem into the top saucer of the pile. "Thank you," the old man said. The waiter took the bottle back inside the café. He sat down at the table with his colleague again.

"He's drunk now," he said.

"He's drunk every night."

"What did he want to kill himself for?"

"How should I know."

"How did he do it?"

"He hung himself with a rope."

"Who cut him down?"

"His niece."

"Why did they do it?"

"Fear for his soul."

"How much money has he got?"

"He's got plenty."

"He must be eighty years old."

"Anyway I should say he was eighty."

"I wish he would go home. I never get to bed before three o'clock. What kind of hour is that to go to bed?"

"He stays up because he likes it."

"He's lonely. I'm not lonely. I have a wife waiting in bed for me."

"He had a wife once too."

"A wife would be no good to him now."

"You can't tell. He might be better with a wife."

"His niece looks after him."

"I know. You said she cut him down."

"I wouldn't want to be that old. An old man is a nasty thing."

"Not always. This old man is clean. He drinks without spilling. Even now, drunk. Look at him."

"I don't want to look at him. I wish he would go home. He has no regard for those who must work."

The old man looked from his glass across the square, then over at the waiters.

"Another brandy," he said, pointing to his glass. The waiter who was in a hurry came over.

"Finished," he said, speaking with that omission of syntax stupid people employ when talking to drunk people or foreigners. "No more tonight. Close now."

"Another," said the old man.

"No. Finished." The waiter wiped the edge of the table with a towel and shook his head.

The old man stood up, slowly counted the saucers, took a leather coin purse from his pocket and paid for the drinks, leaving half a peseta tip.

The waiter watched him go down the street, a very old man walking unsteadily but with dignity.

"Why didn't you let him stay and drink?" the unhurried waiter asked. They were putting up the shutters. "It is not half-past two."

"I want to go home to bed."

"What is an hour?"

"More to me than to him."

"An hour is the same."

"You talk like an old man yourself. He can buy a bottle and drink at home."

"It's not the same."

"No, it is not," agreed the waiter with a wife. He did not wish to be unjust. He was only in a hurry.

"And you? You have no fear of going home before your usual hour?"

"Are you trying to insult me?"

"No, hombre, only to make a joke."

"No," the waiter who was in a hurry said, rising from pulling down the metal shutters. "I have confidence. I am all confidence."

"You have youth, confidence, and a job," the older waiter said. "You have everything."

"And what do you lack?"

"Everything but work."

"You have everything I have."

"No. I have never had confidence and I am not young."

"Come on. Stop talking nonsense and lock up."

"I am of those who like to stay late at the café," the older waiter said. "With all those who do not want to go to bed. With all those who need a light for the night."

"I want to go home and into bed."

"We are of two different kinds," the older waiter said. He was now dressed to go home. "It is not only a question of youth and confidence although those things are very beautiful. Each night I am reluctant to close up because there may be some one who needs the café."

"Hombre, there are bodegas open all night long."

"You do not understand. This is a clean and pleasant café. It is well lighted. The light is very good and also, now, there are shadows of the leaves."

"Good night," said the younger waiter.

"Good night," the other said. Turning off the electric light he continued the conversation with himself. It is the light of course but it is necessary that the place be clean and pleasant. You do not want music. Certainly you do not want music. Nor can you stand before a bar with dignity although that is all that is provided for these hours. What did he fear? It was not fear or dread. It was nothing that he knew too well. It was all a nothing and a man was nothing too. It was only that and light was all it needed and a certain cleanness and order. Some lived in it and never felt it but he knew it all was nada y pues nada y nada y pues nada. Our nada who art in nada, nada be thy name thy kingdom nada thy will be nada in nada as it is in nada. Give us this nada our daily nada and nada us our nada as we nada our nadas and nada us not into nada but deliver us from nada; pues nada. Hail nothing full of nothing, nothing is with thee. He smiled and stood before a bar with a shining steam pressure coffee machine.

"What's yours?" asked the barman.

"Nada."

"Otro loco mas," said the barman and turned away.

"A little cup," said the waiter.

The barman poured it for him.

"The light is very bright and pleasant but the bar is unpolished," the waiter said.

The barman looked at him but did not answer. It was too late at night for conversation.

"You want another copita?" the barman asked.

"No, thank you," said the waiter and went out. He disliked bars and bodegas. A clean, well-lighted café was a very different thing. Now, without thinking further, he would go home to his room. He would lie in the bed and finally, with daylight, he would go to sleep. After all, he said to himself, it is probably only insomnia. Many must have it.

[1933—U.S.A.]

Questions

1. Contrast the two waiters, whose characterization emphasizes their differences. With which of the two do you sympathize? Why?
2. Why does the older waiter sympathize with the old man? Why does the younger waiter not understand him?
3. In light of the story as it unfolds, the use of the word "nothing" (or "nada") is ironic. How so?
4. Light, primarily, and cleanliness and order, secondarily, are symbolic here. What do they symbolize?
5. Why is the older waiter's final thought a rationalization only? What is intimated as the true cause of his sleeplessness? What theme does this story explore?
6. Analyze Hemingway's style. Take into account sentence length and structure; repetition of sentence patterns and the rhythm that results; diction; and the use of adjectives and adverbs. How is the story's style appropriate to its theme? Compare the effects of Hemingway's style and Faulkner's ("An Innocent at Rinkside"), and Hemingway's and Woolf's ("A Haunted House," which follows).

Writing Assignments

1. Determine the main features of Hemingway's style as seen in the present story. Then write a short dialogue or paragraph in this style. Try to be aware of the stylistic choices you are making as you make them.
2. In a paragraph or two, compare and contrast Hemingway's style and that of William Carlos Williams as seen in "The Use of Force" (pp. 167–69). There are many similarities, yet the overall effect is quite different. Define the similarities and try to account for the difference in effect.
3. In a paragraph or more, discuss the relationship of Hemingway's style to his theme in "A Clean, Well-Lighted Place." Establish what his theme is and identify the special qualities of Hemingway's style that seem in accord with his theme.
4. In a short essay, contrast Hemingway's story and Faulkner's "An Innocent at Rinkside" as to style. Establish the main features of the style of each author and analyze the difference between the two styles and their effects.

A HAUNTED HOUSE

————————— ❊ VIRGINIA WOOLF ❊ —————————

Whatever hour you woke there was a door shutting. From room to room they went, hand in hand, lifting here, opening there, making sure—a ghostly couple.

"Here we left it," she said. And he added, "Oh, but here too!" "It's upstairs," she murmured. "And in the garden," he whispered. "Quietly," they said, "or we shall wake them."

But it wasn't that you woke us. Oh, no. "They're looking for it; they're drawing the curtain," one might say, and so read on a page or two. "Now they've found it," one would be certain, stopping the pencil on the margin. And then, tired of reading, one might rise and see for oneself, the house all empty, the doors standing open, only the wood pigeons bubbling with content and the hum of the threshing machine sounding from the farm. "What did I come in here for? What did I want to find?" My hands were empty. "Perhaps it's upstairs then?" The apples were in the loft. And so down again, the garden still as ever, only the book had slipped into the grass.

But they had found it in the drawing-room. Not that one could ever see them. The window panes reflected apples, reflected roses; all the leaves were green in the glass. If they moved in the drawing-room, the apple only turned its yellow side. Yet, the moment after, if the door was opened, spread about the floor, hung upon the walls, pendant from the ceiling—what? My hands were empty. The shadow of a thrush crossed the carpet; from the deepest wells of silence the wood pigeon drew its bubble of sound. "Safe, safe, safe," the pulse of the house beat softly. "The treasure buried; the room . . ." the pulse stopped short. Oh, was that the buried treasure?

A moment later the light had faded. Out in the garden then? But the trees spun darkness for a wandering beam of sun. So fine, so rare, coolly sunk beneath the surface the beam I sought always burnt behind the glass. Death was the glass; death was between us; coming to the woman first, hundreds of years ago, leaving the house, sealing all the windows; the rooms were darkened. He left it, left her, went North, went East, saw the stars turned in the Southern sky; sought the house, found it dropped beneath the Downs. "Safe, safe, safe," the pulse of the house beat gladly. "The Treasure yours."

The wind roars up the avenue. Trees stoop and bend this way and that. Moonbeams splash and spill wildly in the rain. But the beam of the lamp falls straight from the window. The candle burns stiff and still. Wandering through the house, opening the windows, whispering not to wake us, the ghostly couple seek their joy.

"Here we slept," she says. And he adds, "Kisses without number." "Waking in the morning—" "Silver between the trees—" "Upstairs—" "In the garden—" "When summer came—" "In winter snowtime—" The doors go shutting far in the distance, gently knocking like the pulse of a heart.

Nearer they come; cease at the doorway. The wind falls, the rain slides silver down the glass. Our eyes darken; we hear no steps beside us; we see no lady spread her ghostly cloak. His hands shield the lantern. "Look," he breathes. "Sound asleep. Love upon their lips."

Stooping, holding their silver lamp above us, long they look and deeply. Long they pause. The wind drives straightly; the flame stoops slightly. Wild beams of moonlight cross both floor and wall, and, meeting, stain the faces bent; the faces pondering; the faces that search the sleepers and seek their hidden joy.

"Safe, safe, safe," the heart of the house beats proudly. "Long years—" he sighs. "Again you found me." "Here," she murmurs, "sleeping; in the garden reading; laughing, rolling apples in the loft. Here we left our treasure—" Stooping, their light lifts the lids upon my eyes. "Safe! safe! safe!" the pulse of the house beats wildly. Waking, I cry "Oh, is this *your* buried treasure? The light in the heart."

[1921—Great Britain]

Questions

1. Read aloud a passage from each of the last three stories. In general, how do they differ tonally and rhythmically? In what ways are the special qualities of each appropriate to each?
2. This first-person monologue concerns all older houses (thus "a" rather than "the" in the title) with new occupants. How so?
3. Describe the narrator's mood, which here coincides with that of the story. How does Woolf's style contribute to the mood overall?

Writing Assignments

1. Woolf's narrator engages in a daydream. Write a paragraph on how the style of the story helps to create the mood and feel of daydreaming.
2. In an essay, compare and contrast the styles of Faulkner, Hemingway, and Woolf. Because Woolf's style is similar in one way or another to both Faulkner's and Hemingway's, hers might be the best to focus on in getting at the likenesses and differences.

CHAPTER
✳ 7 ✳

SETTING AND SYMBOLISM

OF TIME AND PLACE

The word **setting** refers to all of a story's details that go into the making in our minds of a specific physical locale, whether real or imagined, and a specific cultural environment. Every story has a setting of some sort, though, to be sure, in many stories setting is not of great importance; it is present only as backdrop, mentioned only in passing and only because people do not exist except in specific times and places. But in many other stories setting is essential to the meaning. For example, should we fail to realize that Graham Greene's "I Spy" (pp. 191–93) is set during wartime (World War I), we would have no hope of grasping the story.

This doesn't mean that a setting has to be especially emphasized to function in a story. If anything, the setting of "I Spy" is underplayed; yet it is primarily its wartime setting that activates the story's plot. Setting, then, can inform and drive a plot. It can also be an agent of mood. Times and places often have special atmospheric qualities about them. By exploiting these qualities, or by evoking the feelings people generally associate with distinct times and places, writers can create and guide mood overall. A story set in Italy during the Renaissance will certainly be quite different in mood from a story set in Antarctica at present. Or take horror and ghost stories, with their howling storms and haunted houses. Setting is usually a key agent of mood in fictions of this type. Setting may even contribute directly to our perception of theme: for instance, the place in Hemingway's "A Clean, Well-Lighted Place" (pp. 173–76) is central with respect to the theme of the story.

Especially, setting can contribute to characterization. As I suggested when speaking of characterization, one can usually tell much about a person from that person's home region, as one can from a person's cultural background (both matters of location in place and time). Moreover, people express themselves through their personal effects, their homes, their modes of dress. We judge one person tasteful and another a boor, one well adjusted and another neurotic, on the basis of their possessions, their habitual ways of dressing, the condition of where they live. In fiction, these various aspects of setting reveal no less than they do in life. The historical context in many stories can also help to reveal something of the inner lives of

179

characters, as can the geographical locale (the sea, a desert, and so on). Setting can inform us, as well, about what has shaped a character and determined the character's way of seeing. For example, the Dublin of Joyce's "Eveline" (pp. 194–97) becomes of special importance in our understanding of the story's protagonist and her psychological disability.

That a setting may manifest psychological traits of characters further suggests that setting can provide a writer with a rich source of symbols, and so it can. In a story depicting a fugitive riding across a wide, deserted plain, for example, description of the plain would probably be a token of the loneliness of the fugitive. That is, the story's setting would become symbolic, conveying meaning over and above its relevance as literal backdrop. Psychological traits and emotional states are intangible. How can they be depicted dramatically without the incursion of direct comment? This is a question that every writer faces with respect to the inner lives of characters. Of course, a narrator can simply describe the traits and states of characters. But undramatic, lengthy description is a bore; and the shorter a story is, the less room there is for protracted description. How much better to make details serve double duty, as they are made to serve in Sean O'Faolain's "The Trout" (pp. 199–202). Here, a tunnel of trees and a pool with a trout in it function literally, but they also objectify the inner state of the story's young protagonist. By functioning symbolically as well as literally, the setting helps to create the general revelation the story entails.

THE LITERARY IMPULSE

I have just defined, in effect, what I conceive to be the fundamental literary impulse: to make every detail in a work take its place in a chain of details each of which finally contributes to some general revelation. No word is wasted; no detail that does not further a story's progress toward meaning can be allowed in. Given this impulse toward unity, writers naturally tend to choose details that serve multiple functions—not only to set the scene but also to establish character; not only to further plot but also to enhance mood. The symbol is our case in point.

From one vantage point, everything in human life is symbolic: every gesture and facial expression carries special significance; every word stands in for whatever the word denotes; every image we conjure up represents some aspect of the self. From this outlook, every story, too, is a symbol—the embodiment of an idea or the concrete expression of a general insight. But this view is too broad to be of much help when it comes to dealing with specific symbols. For the purposes of literary analysis, we usually restrict the word **symbol** to anything that in its context suggests meaning over and above or other than its literal significance. Dreams are full of symbols in this sense. You dream that you're walking down a street when suddenly a steamroller heads right at you; you try to escape, but the more you run, the closer the steamroller gets. Though a literal agent of the action of the dream, the steamroller is also symbolic, embodying a wealth of meaning from the felt experience of the dreamer. That many pages would probably be required to spell out that meaning in full points to why writers use symbols. The beauty of the symbol is its compactness. Like irony, symbolism allows for compression (much said in few words) as well as for dramatic presentation. That is, the symbol is a means of expressing attitudes, feelings, and ideas concretely through objects, actions, situations, or whatever. The "dust" mentioned in "Eveline," for example, is literal dust, an aspect of the story's setting and an atmospheric detail. Yet during the course of the story it comes to mean more. Indeed, by the end of "Eveline" one feels that its meaning can almost be summed up by the one word "dust." Because of the context, this descriptive detail becomes a symbol, helping to embody and reinforce the story's theme.

Again, the symbol is a means of expressing attitudes, feelings, ideas through objects, actions, situations, or whatever. We have just seen that an object—dust— can become a symbol. A familiar example of the object-as-symbol is the hats worn in classical Hollywood Westerns. The hats are literal hats, but they also signify by way of their colors (white or black) the moral qualities of their wearers, good or bad. Names, too, can be symbolic. In life, names tell us little except perhaps for nationality. And when a name does seem to have a symbolic ring to it, we're struck by a sense of irony because we don't expect names to be symbolic: I've heard of a judge named "Fix," a welfare supervisor named "Overcash," and a sewer commissioner named "Drainoff." Pseudonyms are a different matter. Chosen by their bearers, many are pointedly symbolic: "Lenin," meaning "man of iron"; "Stalin," meaning "man of steel"; the first names of a good number of Hollywood actors ("Rip," "Rock," and so forth), suggesting virility. We sometimes find names like these in fiction: Dickens's "M'Choakumchild," for a brutal Scottish teacher; Galsworthy's "Forsyte," for a practical lawyer; "Darth Vader," evocative in associations and sound alike. All are literal names of characters, yet all carry meaning over and above their literal significance as names.

Titles of stories may be symbolic as well, which is yet another reason why it is good to pay attention to titles. Hemingway's title "A Clean, Well-Lighted Place," for instance, poignantly captures the human yearning for order and stability to which the story as a whole gives voice. Finally, as we have noted, situations and actions may have symbolic weight. For example, the situation in Graham Greene's "I Spy" seems particularly meaningful: the boy's spying on his father proves an ironic prelude to the father's being arrested as a spy. Here, too, there is symbolic action—the boy's smoking of a cigarette. This action signifies the boy's movement to adulthood, which is what the story is about. Or take the girl's refusal to open her mouth in Williams's "The Use of Force" (pp. 167–69). Aside from being a token of her fierce independence, her refusal suggests the unconscious mechanism of denial and repression that the doctor who must open her mouth fights off in himself.

But how does one recognize symbols in the first place and interpret them once recognized? Here are some guidelines, first for recognition and then for interpretation.

Recognizing Symbols

Broadly speaking, symbols can be divided into two types: conventional and created. **Conventional symbols** are a matter of general knowledge. The flag, the cross, and "mom and apple pie" are examples of conventional cultural symbols in the West, "mom and apple pie" being further restricted to American culture. In fiction as in life, conventional symbols are apparent because we've grown up with them. If one is attuned to one's culture, conventional symbols by and large take care of themselves. (Older literature, however, and literature of other cultures usually require some groundwork in order for one to recognize specific conventional symbols.) Created symbols, on the other hand, are more or less unique to their contexts. It is the created symbol that requires special attention to spot and interpret.

Anything that becomes symbolic by virtue of its context alone is a **created symbol.** Most dream symbols are of this sort. What draws our attention to the possibility that an object, an action, a situation is symbolic is the context. With respect to fiction, this means that a story *itself* must signal that one or another of its details is symbolic. It can do so by way of repetition, elaboration, and placement. For example, both repetition and placement suggest that dust in "Eveline" is symbolic as well as literal: Joyce tells of the dustiness of Eveline's home four times, once in the first paragraph (beginnings and endings are of special importance). Why? Or why should an author elaborate on a detail if it is nothing more than part of the descriptive background? The answer in both cases is that the element is not merely descriptive. Repetition, elaboration, and placement usually indicate that more is going on. Therefore, if something is repeated, elaborated, or placed in a significant spot, we have reason to think that it might be symbolic.

Sometimes, too, the question "If not symbolic, what?" will lead to immediate recognition of symbolic intent. When I remember a dream, the main reason I have for taking its various features as symbols is that they don't make a great deal of sense taken literally. There are stories like this. For example, Nigel Dennis's "The Pukey" (pp. 186–89) is a story that does not present much on a literal level at all. In that we know that there is no such thing as a pukey, we must conclude that the story is either crazy or thoroughly symbolic.

Finally, some details will show themselves to be symbolic if we ask the question "Why this rather than that?" In "Eveline," for instance, the city of Buenos Aires is mentioned twice as the place to which Eveline's sailor would take her. Why Buenos Aires rather than Paris, or Madrid, or New York? The story suggests an answer. Therefore, Joyce's chosen city is not only a literal place but also symbolic, conveying meaning different from its meaning as literal referent.

Interpreting Symbols

Conventional symbols in fiction are understood according to their cultural associations. For instance, in Katherine Anne Porter's story "The Grave" (pp. 202–06), a silver dove and a gold ring figure prominently. Both are conventional symbols, the dove of peace, the ring of unity and completion. And both have these meanings within the story. Once we recognize dove and ring to be symbols, we still have to come to an understanding of their functions in the fictional context; but by bringing to the story a general awareness of our culture's conventional symbolism, we have already access to the primary symbolic meanings of both dove and ring and, as a consequence, at least partial access to the story as it unfolds.

Whereas we find the meaning of a conventional symbol in our culture, we must think our way into the meaning of a created symbol. That is, we must construct the symbolic meaning by carefully considering both the attributes of the thing (or place, person, action) itself and its associations in the particular story. In Sean O'Faolain's "The Trout" (pp. 199–202), for instance, there is a dark walk of trees forming a tunnel. This passageway is frightening to Julia, the story's protagonist, who is on the verge of adolescence. In the context of the story, the dark walkway suggests—both by virtue of what it is literally (a passageway) and by virtue of the associations of apprehensiveness or even fear that it evokes—the passage that is adolescence and all its attendant fears. Symbolic meanings must differ from literal meanings, of course, or there could be no symbols in the first place. Still, they are usually closely related.

Conventional or created, every symbol must be taken in context. Even conventional symbols must be seen in the given context for their functions to be understood. And created symbols have only their specific contexts to lead us to see them as symbols and to guide and validate interpretation. We considered a while back that the girl's refusal to open her mouth in "The Use of Force" (pp. 167–69) could be taken as symbolic of denial and repression generally, which is something over and above its literal meaning in the story. But we have to add *"in this context."* For the suggestion makes sense only in light of the fact that the story itself brings to consciousness the usually unconscious mechanism of denial and repression, which its protagonist fights off in himself. In other words, we are not just conjuring up meaning out of nowhere. We take our cue from the context, and in turn we must relate everything we have to say about symbols to the context.

Before concluding, we should note that most stories are literal by and large. What symbols they contain are reinforcing—that is, they don't control our understanding of a story but rather serve to buttress its literal meaning. The symbols in "Eveline" are of this sort. One can miss them entirely yet still grasp the import of the story. It is best, therefore, not to become a symbol hunter, looking for symbolic significance in every detail. To do so would be to distort the average story. Remember, a story itself must somehow give indication as to whether a detail has symbolic weight.

In some stories, however, symbols carry or control so much of the meaning that the stories cannot be understood unless we grasp their symbolic structure. Porter's "The Grave" and Alice Walker's "The Flowers" (pp. 198–99) are both of this type, though they are quite different in effect. "The Grave" is like a dream: it has a literal level, but its literal aspect seems somewhat inconsequential. Like a dream, the story is centrally symbolic and cannot be comprehended without an understanding of its symbols in relationship to one another. Even then, the story refuses to be neatly translated. Its symbols are multidimensional, dense and rich in emotional resonance. As the novelist Henry James said of symbols of this sort, they "cast long shadows." "The Flowers" is also centrally symbolic, having virtually no literal level. In contrast to "The Grave," however, the symbolic elements of "The Flowers" resolve themselves into neat equivalents (this equals that). The reason for this difference is that "The Flowers" is an **allegory,** that is, a work in which characters and events enact the ideas they stand for.

Stories in which symbols are essential to the meaning are easy enough to spot: they quickly give rise to the question "If not symbolic, what?" If a story does not force this question, then whatever symbols it contains are most likely reinforcing and not controlling. They enrich, they deepen, but they do not direct. To be sure, we are not always conscious of symbols and their reverberations as we encounter them in daily life or in fiction. To become fully responsive readers, though, we need to be sensitive to the symbols writers use and the possible meanings of those symbols in context.

SUMMARY SUGGESTIONS: UNDERSTANDING SETTING AND SYMBOL

1. When considering the setting of a story, ask if the story could be set in another time or place. If it could, then setting is of little consequence, nothing more than a backdrop. If it could not, then setting is probably one of the elements in the story that go into the making of the story's meaning. Just as narration is (usually) a controlling element, directing us toward attitude and theme, so setting may control, governing mood, for instance, and thereby helping to establish theme. We must make that determination as we read. If setting is only backdrop, it can be pushed to the back of the mind. If it is more, it must be attended to.

2. Remember that setting is often a means of characterization, suggesting various qualities of the characters. Therefore, though setting may sometimes be pushed to the back of the mind, it should not be pushed out entirely. Even in stories in which setting is little more than backdrop, it frequently tells us something about characters. Therefore, it should always be considered at least briefly with respect to characterization.

3. Remember, too, that certain aspects of a setting may be symbolic. It is usually rewarding to consider this possibility if a certain detail of a setting calls attention to itself.

4. As to symbols, almost anything in a story can be symbolic—a setting, an object, an action, a situation. What makes something symbolic, remember, is that it conveys meaning different from (though related to) its literal meaning. Don't forget, too, that the meaning you feel a symbol to have must be tested as to relevance against the general context. And the context must itself suggest that a detail is more than literal. Context is all.

5. Don't be a symbol hunter. However, do try to be open to symbolic possibilities as they present themselves. Be alert to such matters of structure as repetition, elaboration, and placement, all of which can signal special significance. Writers gain emphasis by way of structure. We, in our turn, must learn to respond appropriately to the clues given. The writer's job is to create a story that contains its own meaning; our job as readers is to live through that meaning and make it our own.

WRITING ON SYMBOLS AND SYMBOLISM

Once one has grasped a few symbols in a text, or perhaps seen that its very structure is symbolic, the question is how to use these insights. What can be done with symbols and symbolism when it comes to writing? Our consideration earlier of the interpretation of symbols gives us a clue. Both reinforcing symbols and controlling symbols can provide material for writing, though in somewhat different ways.

The analysis of a single reinforcing symbol could give rise to an interesting paragraph or short essay. Such a paper might examine how a given detail in a story is established as a symbol and how its meaning—which you would want to specify—relates to that of the story overall. The image of dust in "Eveline" would be ideal for this kind of exploration. Here you could point to the repetition of the image as the means by which it is established as a symbol, suggest its possible symbolic meanings by detailing its associations, and demonstrate the relevance of these meanings to the story at large, especially to the life of its protagonist as we leave her.

Or take two prominent images at the end of "Eveline," both related to setting—the "seas," in which Eveline fears she will drown, and the "iron railing" that she grips "in frenzy." Why these details, one must ask, and why did Joyce place them conspicuously at the end of the story? The answer to the second question is that they are symbols, established as such in part by placement; the answer to the first involves their meaning in context—and this would be the subject of your paper. The two symbolic images sum up the meaning of the story as a whole. Here would be a good thesis. You could proceed to argue it by suggesting what each image means in and of itself and then by relating these meanings to other of the story's symbolic images and other of its elements (especially the characterization of Eveline). By so doing, you would wind up with an interpretation of the symbols in question derived from their associations and relevance in context and, in turn, a deeper understanding of the story overall.

When writing about a story whose symbols are controlling, you are working near the heart of the story, engaged directly with the story's meaning. All the meaning of "The Grave," for instance, is housed in its images of dove, ring, and rabbit. Although you could discuss other things about the story—characterization, say, in which case reference to the story's individual symbols could be used as support—to get at its theme you would ultimately have to tackle its symbolism head on. You would need to name its controlling symbols and discuss how they are established; analyze their conventional meanings and then carry over those meanings to the story, examining their relevance in the context the author provides; and relate the story's symbolism to its theme.

Writing on symbolism, note, requires a measure of deftness and flexibility on the part of the writer. For symbols are usually multidimensional. Thus, you must be prepared to interpret a symbol in different lights. Porter's dove, for instance, means different things to her two characters. To explicate its meaning fully, therefore, one would have to discuss what those different meanings are and how they are related to the dove as conventional symbol rather than forcing a single meaning to prevail.

Symbolism is especially challenging to write on. But it can also be especially rewarding. Stories in which symbolism is prominent require time for thought, a maximum of intellectual agility, and a stretching of one's verbal capacities to articulate the meaning of their symbolism. Yet it is by taking up challenges like this that we grow. If you give yourself over to the task, writing on symbolism will help you become more subtle in your thought and more expressive in your writing generally.

STORIES FOR STUDY AND WRITING ASSIGNMENTS

THE PUKEY

❖ NIGEL DENNIS ❖

Mr. Troy's refusal to have a pukey in the house had caused enormous trouble in the family. "Pukeys are nasty, degenerate things," he said: "they make filthy messes all over the floor, they corrupt the young, they interrupt homework and sap the nation, and we have nowhere to put one." His wife would answer: "Well, well, we are getting distinguished, aren't we? It seems we're the Duke of Devonshire. Let me tell you that Blanche and Mabel both have pukeys in their drawing-rooms, and far from being corrupted, they are happier." Young Miss Troy appealed to her father's sense of status, saying: "Everywhere I go, Father, it's always: 'What did your pukey do last night?' I have to admit we haven't got one." "Oh, all right," said Mr. Troy, after a couple of years, "I'll let the pukey-man come and give a demonstration."

A few days later, the man arrived with the pukey and put its box against the wall opposite the fireplace. When Mrs. Troy asked: "Won't it catch the draught there?" the pukey-man only laughed and said: "The point about a pukey, madam, is that it's bred to be insensible." "But it is *alive,* isn't it?" asked Mrs. Troy quickly, "because we'd never pay for something dead. And if it's alive, won't the dog resent it?" "Both dog and budgie will be unconscious of it, madam," said the pukey-man, "a pukey speaks only to a human brain." "Well, cut the brainy cackle and open the box," said Mr. Troy roughly.

Let us admit at once that the first impression the pukey made on Mr. Troy was a good one. Even lying stupefied on the carpet, its eyes had a wondering gaze that fell hardly short of sweetness. "It's not just going to flop down like that all the time, is it?" asked Mr. Troy, to hide the fact that he liked it so far. "Give it a minute, my dear sir!" begged the pukey-man, "it's hardly got its bearings." "Pay him no attention!" exclaimed Mrs. Troy, "he's been picking on pukeys for years." "Oh, what shall we *call* it?" said Miss Troy.

She had hardly spoken when the pukey shuddered from snout to stern and let its muzzle fall right open, showing six rows of vivid pink gums and bubbles of sparkling saliva: "No teeth; that's curious!" muttered Mr. Troy. Then, with no warning, it vomited all over the carpet—a perfectly-filthy, greenish-yellow mess—causing Mrs. Troy to cry spontaneously: "Oh, the filthy little beast!" and Miss Troy to say: "Oh, Mum, don't *fuss!*" and Mr. Troy to say: "I told you it would foul everything up. Take the little brute away!" "An ounce of patience, if you please," asked the pukey-man, "or how can it grow on you?" "I'm sure that's true—and I don't mean I don't like it," said Mrs. Troy, rallying. "Isn't it actually *good* for the carpet?" Miss Troy asked the pukey-man, "I know the Vicar said, reasonably used, it was." "That is perfectly correct, Miss Troy," said the pukey-man, "it's not the vomit but the abuse of it." "Now, there's a remark I always like to hear," said Mr. Troy.

At that moment the pukey, which had been staring at its own emission in a rather vague, contented way, changed its expression entirely. A sort of pathetic anguish came over its whole face: it held its snout sideways and looked at Miss Troy in a pleading, tender way. "Oh, *look!*" cried Mrs. Troy, "it's trying to say it didn't mean bad." They were all wrenched by the pukey's fawning expression, and when it slobbered and grovelled and brownish tears dripped from the corners of its eyes, Mrs. Troy could have hugged it. "Damned sentimental, hypocritical brute!" said Mr. Troy, "I still reserve my judgement." But he was the first to jump in his seat when the pukey, suddenly throwing-up on to the carpet a clot of gritty mucus, followed this up with a string of shrieks and groans. Everyone was deafened except Miss Troy, who sensed at once that the pukey was illustrating the dilemma of girls of her own age in search of happiness. "Why, bless my soul!" said Mrs. Troy soon, "it's trying to have *sex,* that's what it is"—and sure enough, the pukey was now twisting its hind-parts in the most indecent way and rubbing its flanks in its own vomit. "I'll not have that in *my* house," said Mrs. Troy, pursing her lips, "it's just plain filth, and showing-off." "My dear madam, it never actually *gets* there," said the pukey-man: "nothing ever really *happens.*" "Oh, Mother, you and Father make everything seem obscene!" said Miss Troy, "even love." "Well, as long as it only suggests but can't actually do it, I don't mind," said Mrs. Troy, watching the pukey with a new curiosity. "My mind is still unmade up," said Mr. Troy.

Worn out, it seemed, by sexual frustration, the pukey lay still for a moment. Then, suddenly fixing its eye on Mrs. Troy, it gave her such a glare of horrible malignancy that she reached for her husband's arm. Next minute, there was a dreadful spectacle: throwing itself into a spasm of rage, the pukey began tearing and biting at its own body, like a thing bent on suicide. "Stop it! Stop it! Put the lid on!" screamed Mrs. Troy, "it's cruel, and drawing blood." "Frankly, you'll have to adjust to that, madam," said the pukey-man, "because it fights more than anything else." "Oh, then, that's decisive for me," said Mr. Troy, "because I love to see a good scrap." "It *is* the men who like that best," agreed the pukey-man, as the pukey went through the motions of winding its entrails round the throat of an enemy and jumping on his face. "I don't *mind* its fighting," Mrs. Troy said grudgingly, "but I'll put its lid on if it overdoes it. I like *beautiful* things best." The words, alas, were hardly out of her mouth when the pukey, sighting backwards over its spine like a mounted cowboy firing at his pursuers, shot her full in the face with an outrageous report. "Now, no grumbling, Mother!" screamed poor Miss Troy, knowing her mother's readiness to take affront. "But it's *not* nice!" protested Mrs. Troy, fanning herself with an evening paper. "Oh, Mother, can't you see it *means* nothing?" cried Miss Troy, "it's not like *us,* with our standards." "Standards or no," said Mrs. Troy, "I never saw Mabel's pukey do that to *her.*" "Ah, but this is an improved model, madam," said the pukey-man.

"Am I correct in supposing," asked Mr. Troy, "that nothing substantial ever comes out of its rear end anyway?" "That is correct, sir," answered the pukey-man, "all secretion and excretion are purely visual and oral. The vent is hot air at most:

hence, no sand-box." "Yet it has a belly on it," said Mr. Troy, "I know because I can see one." "You can see a belly, sir," answered the pukey-man, "but you can't see any guts, can you?" They all laughed at this, because it was so true.

After throwing-up another couple of times ("Mercy, what a messy little perisher it is!" said kind Mrs. Troy), the pukey became inordinately grave and a whole rash of wettish pimples spread over its face. "Well, you are in luck!" said the pukey-man, jumping up as if genuinely interested, "it never does this more than once a week at most. Can you guess what it is?" They all racked their brains, guessing everything from sewage farming to guitar-playing, and still couldn't imagine; until Miss Troy, who was the quickest of the family, screamed: "*I* know! It's *thinking!*" "*Mes compliments,* young lady," said the pukey-man, bowing.

They all watched the pukey thinking because it was so unexpected; but none of them really liked it. "When it vomits, it only makes me laugh," said Mr. Troy, "but when it thinks, *I* feel like vomiting." "I just feel nervous and embarrassed, like it was something you'd seen and shouldn't," said Mrs. Troy, and even Miss Troy for once agreed with her mother, saying, "You feel it's only doing it as a change from being sick, but it's the same really." "Don't judge it too hardly," said the pukey-man, "surely the wonder is that with no brains it can think at all." "Has it really no brains?" asked Mr. Troy, curious. "No, sir," said the pukey-man: "that's *why* its thinking makes you sick." "Funny sort of animal, I must say," said Mr. Troy, "thinks without brains, bites without teeth, throws-up with no guts, and screws without sex." "Oh, *please* stop it thinking!" begged Mrs. Troy. "I had an experience once that smelt like that." At which words, the pukey's pimples disappeared completely and, lying prone with its paws out, it gave Mrs. Troy a smug, complacent look, showing all its gums in a pleading whimpering. "Oh, the little angel! It wants to be congratulated for having thought!" cried Mrs. Troy: "then we *will*—yes! we *will,* you smelly little darling—you little, stinking, clever, mother's thing!" "I find that touching, too," said Mr. Troy, "no wonder there's so much nicker in pukeys." "It's for love and culture, too, Dad," Miss Troy reminded. "Thank you, Miss Troy," said the pukey-man, "we breeders tell ourselves that too."

During the next hour the pukey did all manner of things—such as marching like the Coldstream Guards, dancing and balancing on one paw like Pavlova, folding its arms like a Member of Parliament, singing the national anthem, plucking away at its parts mysteriously, fighting like mad, and making such vulgar explosive noises at both ends that the Troys were all left speechless with wonder. What charmed them as much as anything was feeling that the pukey made no distinction about what it did: whether it was fawning or screeching, or thinking or puking, it made it all like the same, because it loved each thing equally and looked at you always so proudly for it. "I can only say you breeders must be jolly highly-skilled," summed-up Mr. Troy, "to root out all the natural organs and still poison the air." "It's more a sixth sense than a skill," said the pukey-man modestly, "and one which your wife, I may say, seems to have instinctively." This was the first compliment Mrs. Troy had had since she gave birth to Miss Troy, and to cover her natural embarrassment she said sharply, "Well, put its lid on again now and take it away. We'll come and fill out the Never-never forms tomorrow."

With the pukey gone, it wasn't like the same home. The walls seemed to have been sprayed with a dribble the colour of maple-syrup, and dead flies kept dropping from the ceiling. The state of the carpet was beyond description, although the last thing the pukey had done before the lid closed was puff a sort of scented detergent powder over the stinking mess it had made. But the Troys were much too impressed to worry about the room: they could only think of buying the pukey and doing this every night. "It baffles me," said Mr. Troy, as they went to bed: "it's not human, it's not mechanical, it's not like any animal I've ever known." "What it leaves on the carpet is human through-and-through," said Mrs. Troy, and they all laughed at this because it was so true.

[1957—Great Britain]

Questions

1. "The Pukey" demonstrates the nature and process of thinking in analogies. What is the pukey analogous to? In answering, consider the cultural context as well as the fictional context.
2. Test your initial guess about what the pukey is analogous to against the gathering details of the story as it unfolds. Everything we are told about the pukey must apply as well to what the pukey stands in for. If anything isn't accounted for, then either your initial guess is wrong or you haven't felt out the analogy fully.
3. Now, what is the point of the analogy? Why didn't Dennis just come right out with what he had to say?

Writing Assignments

1. (a) Write a paragraph in which you explain what the pukey stands in for. Show how at least three attributes of this imaginary creature satirize what it represents.
   (b) What is your response to this story? In a separate paragraph state your response and analyze your reasons for responding thus.
2. What is the point of Dennis's analogy? In an essay, consider what Dennis achieves by way of the pukey, focusing especially on how the story is a satire.

OBERFEST

 JAMES STEVENSON

Through scenery of surpassing loveliness, we descend into the tranquil valley, and make our way to the ancient, fortified town of Oberfest. The origin of the old town is veiled in the poetic darkness of tradition. For many centuries, it has ruled itself, and coined its own monies. As one enters the square, the Town Hall is admirably brought before the eye. It is the very embodiment of grandeur and sublimity: a colossal, many-towered, complex structure, aspiring toward heaven, with countless gables and spires, turrets, and gilded cupolas. One is compelled to venerate the simple townsfolk whose stern virtue and zeal have

enabled them to oppose the incursions of those who would conquer, yet have made of their town a repository of all that is grand in antiquity, and ceaselessly striven to beautify and adorn, to elevate and refine. . . . Rising above the sunlit pinnacles of the Hall loom mountains of extraordinary steepness, and awesome, savage magnificence. In winter, it is said, fearful avalanches roll down from these heights.

*—"A Traveller in Europe," by G. Brown, F.B.S.,
with Numerous Wood Engravings by the Best Artists, 1871.*

On a morning in early spring, 1873, the people of Oberfest left their houses and took refuge in the town hall. No one knows why, precisely. A number of rumors had raced through the town during recent weeks, and there was a profound uneasiness among the people. Idle talk and gossip were passed on and converted to news; predictions became certainties. On this particular morning, fear turned into terror, and people rushed through the narrow streets, carrying their most precious possessions, pulling their children, and dashed into the great hall. The first to arrive occupied the largest rooms; the others found space in smaller rooms, in hallways, on stairs, in the towers. The doors were nailed shut, and men took turns watching out the windows. Two days passed. Order was maintained. The unruly, the sick, and the unstable were consigned to the cellars; the cellar stairs were guarded. When no disaster came, the fear grew worse, because the people began to suspect that the danger was already within the hall, locked inside. No one spoke to anybody else; people watched each other, looking for signs. It was the children who rang the great bell in the first bell tower—a small band of bored children, unable to bear the silence and having run through all the halls, slid down all the bannisters, climbed all the turrets. They found the bell rope and swung on it—set the bell clanging. This was the traditional signal of alarm, and in a moment the elders were dashing in panic to all the other bell towers and ringing the bells. For nearly an hour, the valley reverberated with the wild clangor—and then, a thousand feet above, the snow began to crack, and the avalanche began; a massive cataract of ice and snow thundered down and buried the town, silencing the bells. There is no trace of Oberfest today, not even a spire, because the snow is so deep; and, in the shadow of the mountains, it is very cold.

[1971—U.S.A.]

Questions

1. How is what happens in this story a direct result of its Alpine setting, or a result of the effect this setting has on the story's characters?
2. We're told in the epigraph, "One is compelled to venerate the simple townsfolk whose stern virtue and zeal have enabled them to oppose the incursions of those who would conquer." What is ironic about this statement when read in connection with the story that follows? What is the prime irony upon which "Oberfest" turns?
3. "The danger was already within the hall, locked inside." In light of this statement, what is the story's theme?
4. Compare the lengthy epigraph and the story. What is the difference in focus and point between the two? Why is one a piece of exposition and the other a story? Comment on their stylistic differences.

Writing Assignments

1. In a paragraph, address question 2 above. Remember that irony entails discrepancy. What is the discrepancy implied here?
2. Focusing on the differences between the epigraph and the story proper, discuss in a paragraph or short paper what makes one a piece of exposition and the other a piece of fiction.
3. In "Oberfest," the setting instigates the plot and together both lead to the theme. In a short paper, argue that the statement just made accurately describes the story. Consider, too, how irony shapes the mood and therefore, along with setting and plot, contributes to manifesting the story's theme.

I SPY

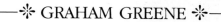
✳ GRAHAM GREENE ✳

Charlie Stowe waited until he heard his mother snore before he got out of bed. Even then he moved with caution and tiptoed to the window. The front of the house was irregular, so that it was possible to see a light burning in his mother's room. But now all the windows were dark. A searchlight passed across the sky, lighting the banks of cloud and probing the dark deep spaces between, seeking enemy airships. The wind blew from the sea, and Charlie Stowe could hear behind his mother's snores the beating of the waves. A draught through the cracks in the window-frame stirred his nightshirt. Charlie Stowe was frightened.

But the thought of the tobacconist's shop which his father kept down a dozen wooden stairs drew him on. He was twelve years old, and already boys at the County School mocked him because he had never smoked a cigarette. The packets were piled twelve deep below, Gold Flake and Players, De Reszke, Abdulla, Woodbines, and the little shop lay under a thin haze of stale smoke which would completely disguise his crime. That it was a crime to steal some of his father's stock Charlie Stowe had no doubt, but he did not love his father; his father was unreal to him, a wraith, pale, thin, and indefinite, who noticed him only spasmodically and left even punishment to his mother. For his mother he felt a passionate demonstrative love; her large boisterous presence and her noisy charity filled the world for him; from her speech he judged her the friend of everyone, from the rector's wife to the "dear Queen," except the "Huns," the monsters who lurked in Zeppelins in the clouds. But his father's affection and dislike were as indefinite as his movements. Tonight he had said he would be in Norwich, and yet you never knew. Charlie Stowe had no sense of safety as he crept down the wooden stairs. When they creaked he clenched his fingers on the collar of his nightshirt.

At the bottom of the stairs he came out quite suddenly into the little shop. It was too dark to see his way, and he did not dare touch the switch. For half a minute he sat in despair on the bottom step with his chin cupped in his hands. Then the regular movement of the searchlight was reflected through an upper window and the boy had time to fix in memory the pile of cigarettes, the counter, and the small hole under it. The footsteps of a policeman on the pavement made him grab the first packet to his hand and dive for the hole. A light shone along the floor and a hand tried the door, then the footsteps passed on, and Charlie cowered in the darkness.

At last he got his courage back by telling himself in his curiously adult way that if he were caught now there was nothing to be done about it, and he might as well have his smoke. He put a cigarette in his mouth and then remembered that he had no matches. For a while he dared not move. Three times the searchlight lit the shop, while he muttered taunts and encouragements. "May as well be hung for a sheep," "Cowardy, cowardy custard," grown-up and childish exhortations oddly mixed.

But as he moved he heard footfalls in the street, the sound of several men walking rapidly. Charlie Stowe was old enough to feel surprise that anybody was about. The footsteps came nearer, stopped; a key was turned in the shop door, a voice said, "Let him in," and then he heard his father, "If you wouldn't mind being quiet, gentlemen. I don't want to wake up the family." There was a note unfamiliar to Charlie in the undecided voice. A torch flashed and the electric globe burst into blue light. The boy held his breath; he wondered whether his father would hear his heart beating, and he clutched his nightshirt tightly and prayed, "O God, don't let me be caught." Through a crack in the counter he could see his father where he stood, one hand held to his high stiff collar, between two men in bowler hats and belted mackintoshes. They were strangers.

"Have a cigarette," his father said in a voice dry as a biscuit. One of the men shook his head. "It wouldn't do, not when we are on duty. Thank you all the same." He spoke gently, but without kindness; Charlie Stowe thought his father must be ill.

"Mind if I put a few in my pocket?" Mr. Stowe asked, and when the man nodded he lifted a pile of Gold Flake and Players from a shelf and caressed the packets with the tips of his fingers.

"Well," he said, "there's nothing to be done about it, and I may as well have my smokes." For a moment Charlie Stowe feared discovery, his father stared round the shop so thoroughly; he might have been seeing it for the first time. "It's a good little business," he said, "for those that like it. The wife will sell out, I suppose. Else the neighbours'll be wrecking it. Well, you want to be off. A stitch in time. I'll get my coat."

"One of us'll come with you, if you don't mind," said the stranger gently.

"You needn't trouble. It's on the peg here. There, I'm all ready."

The other man said in an embarrassed way: "Don't you want to speak to your wife?" The thin voice was decided. "Not me. Never do today what you can put off till tomorrow. She'll have her chance later, won't she?"

"Yes, yes," one of the strangers said and he became very cheerful and encouraging. "Don't you worry too much. While there's life . . ." And suddenly his father tried to laugh.

When the door had closed Charlie Stowe tiptoed upstairs and got into bed. He wondered why his father had left the house again so late at night and who the strangers were. Surprise and awe kept him for a little while awake. It was as if a familiar photograph had stepped from the frame to reproach him with neglect. He remembered how his father had held tight to his collar and fortified himself with proverbs, and he thought for the first time that, while his mother was boisterous and kindly, his father was very like himself, doing things in the dark which frightened him. It would have pleased him to go down to his father and tell him that he loved him, but he could hear through the window the quick steps going away. He was alone in the house with his mother, and he fell asleep.

[1930—Great Britain]

Questions

1. In what period of time is this story set? What details tell us of its time frame? Why is the temporal setting significant?
2. What kind of a narrator tells this story? Why this kind?
3. What is ironic about the story's title?
4. The boy's smoking is symbolic. What kind of a symbol is this act? What does it signify?
5. A mystery of sorts, "I Spy" leaves us to figure out what the boy is still too young to understand: why and by whom the father is taken away. How do you answer these questions?
6. In terms of general theme, this story is akin to a number of others in this book: for example, "My First Goose," "The Trout," "An Episode of War," and "The Grave." How so? What is its theme in full? In answering, consider the story's mood.

Writing Assignments

1. The wartime setting of "I Spy" is crucial. Write a paragraph on when the story is set, how we come to recognize its time frame, and how our knowledge of its setting in time allows us to grasp the gravity of what we witness along with the boy.
2. In a paragraph, enumerate the passing symbols found in "I Spy" and suggest the meaning of each. Consider, for example, the boy's smoking and the "belted mackintoshes" worn by the strangers. What kind of symbols are these? How are they significant to our understanding of the story as it proceeds?
3. Write an essay comparing and contrasting "I Spy" with any of the stories referred to in question 6 above. Consider both similarity of theme and the differences in the ways theme is treated. Note especially irony and mood as you weigh "I Spy" against the other story you choose.
4. What were you blind to when young but now understand? How did coming to that understanding help move you from a childish mentality to a more adult awareness of things? Write a short essay detailing your experience and the difference between your perception when you were a child and your perception now.

EVELINE

❖ JAMES JOYCE ❖

She sat at the window watching the evening invade the avenue. Her head was leaned against the window curtains and in her nostrils was the odour of dusty cretonne. She was tired.

Few people passed. The man out of the last house passed on his way home; she heard his footsteps clacking along the concrete pavement and afterwards crunching on the cinder path before the new red houses. One time there used to be a field there in which they used to play every evening with other people's children. Then a man from Belfast bought the field and built houses in it—not like their little brown houses but bright brick houses with shining roofs. The children of the avenue used to play together in that field—the Devines, the Waters, the Dunns, little Keogh the cripple, she and her brothers and sisters. Ernest, however, never played: he was too grown up. Her father used often to hunt them in out of the field with his blackthorn stick; but usually little Keogh used to keep *nix* and call out when he saw her father coming. Still they seemed to have been rather happy then. Her father was not so bad then; and besides, her mother was alive. That was a long time ago; she and her brothers and sisters were all grown up; her mother was dead. Tizzie Dunn was dead, too, and the Waters had gone back to England. Everything changes. Now she was going to go away like the others, to leave her home.

Home! She looked round the room, reviewing all its familiar objects which she had dusted once a week for so many years, wondering where on earth all the dust came from. Perhaps she would never see again those familiar objects from which she had never dreamed of being divided. And yet during all those years she had never found out the name of the priest whose yellowing photograph hung on the wall above the broken harmonium beside the coloured print of the promises made to Blessed Margaret Mary Alacoque. He had been a school friend of her father. Whenever he showed the photograph to a visitor her father used to pass it with a casual word:

"He is in Melbourne now."

She had consented to go away, to leave her home. Was that wise? She tried to weigh each side of the question. In her home anyway she had shelter and food; she had those whom she had known all her life about her. Of course she had to work hard, both in the house and at business. What would they say of her in the Stores when they found out that she had run away with a fellow? Say she was a fool, perhaps; and her place would be filled up by advertisement. Miss Gavan would be glad. She had always had an edge on her, especially whenever there were people listening.

"Miss Hill, don't you see these ladies are waiting?"

"Look lively, Miss Hill, please."

She would not cry many tears at leaving the Stores.

But in her new home, in a distant unknown country, it would not be like that. Then she would be married—she, Eveline. People would treat her with respect then. She would not be treated as her mother had been. Even now, though she was over nineteen, she sometimes felt herself in danger of her father's violence. She knew it was that that had given her the palpitations. When they were growing up he had never gone for her, like he used to go for Harry and Ernest, because she was a girl; but latterly he had begun to threaten her and say what he would do to her only for her dead mother's sake. And now she had nobody to protect her. Ernest was dead and Harry, who was in the church decorating business, was nearly always down somewhere in the country. Besides, the invariable squabble for money on Saturday nights had begun to weary her unspeakably. She always gave her entire wages—seven—shillings—and Harry always sent up what he could but the trouble was to get any money from her father. He said she used to squander the money, that she had no head, that he wasn't going to give her his hard-earned money to throw about the streets, and much more, for he was usually fairly bad on Saturday night. In the end he would give her the money and ask her had she any intention of buying Sunday's dinner. Then she had to rush out as quickly as she could and do her marketing, holding her black leather purse tightly in her hand as she elbowed her way through the crowds and returning home late under her load of provisions. She had hard work to keep the house together and to see that the two young children who had been left to her charge went to school regularly and got their meals regularly. It was hard work—a hard life—but now that she was about to leave it she did not find it a wholly undesirable life.

She was about to explore another life with Frank. Frank was very kind, manly, open-hearted. She was to go away with him by the night-boat to be his wife and to live with him in Buenos Ayres where he had a home waiting for her. How well she remembered the first time she had seen him; he was lodging in a house on the main road where she used to visit. It seemed a few weeks ago. He was standing at the gate, his peaked cap pushed back on his head and his hair tumbled forward over a face of bronze. Then they had come to know each other. He used to meet her outside the Stores every evening and see her home. He took her to see *The Bohemian Girl* and she felt elated as she sat in an unaccustomed part of the theatre with him. He was awfully fond of music and sang a little. People knew that they were courting and, when he sang about the lass that loves a sailor, she always felt pleasantly confused. He used to call her Poppens out of fun. First of all it had been an excitement for her to have a fellow and then she had begun to like him. He had tales of distant countries. He had started as a deck boy at a pound a month on a ship of the Allan Line going out to Canada. He told her the names of the ships he had been on and the names of the different services. He had sailed through the Straits of Magellan and he told her stories of the terrible Patagonians. He had fallen on his feet in Buenos Ayres, he said, and had come over to the old country just for a holiday. Of course, her father had found out the affair and had forbidden her to have anything to say to him.

"I know these sailor chaps," he said.

One day he had quarrelled with Frank and after that she had to meet her lover secretly.

The evening deepened in the avenue. The white of the two letters in her lap grew indistinct. One was to Harry; the other was to her father. Ernest had been her favourite but she liked Harry too. Her father was becoming old lately, she noticed; he would miss her. Sometimes he could be very nice. Not long before, when she had been laid up for a day, he had read her out a ghost story and made toast for her at the fire. Another day, when their mother was alive, they had all gone for a picnic to the Hill of Howth. She remembered her father putting on her mother's bonnet to make the children laugh.

Her time was running out but she continued to sit by the window, leaning her head against the window curtain, inhaling the odour of dusty cretonne. Down far in the avenue she could hear a street organ playing. She knew the air. Strange that it should come that very night to remind her of the promise to her mother, her promise to keep the home together as long as she could. She remembered the last night of her mother's illness; she was again in the close dark room at the other side of the hall and outside she heard a melancholy air of Italy. The organ-player had been ordered to go away and given sixpence. She remembered her father strutting back into the sickroom saying:

"Damned Italians! coming over here!"

As she mused the pitiful vision of her mother's life laid its spell on the very quick of her being—that life of commonplace sacrifices closing in final craziness. She trembled as she heard again her mother's voice saying constantly with foolish insistence:

"Derevaun Seraun! Derevaun Seraun!"

She stood up in a sudden impulse of terror. Escape! She must escape! Frank would save her. He would give her life, perhaps love, too. But she wanted to live. Why should she be unhappy? She had a right to happiness. Frank would take her in his arms, fold her in his arms. He would save her.

She stood among the swaying crowd in the station at the North Wall. He held her hand and she knew that he was speaking to her, saying something about the passage over and over again. The station was full of soldiers with brown baggages. Through the wide doors of the sheds she caught a glimpse of the black mass of the boat, lying in beside the quay wall, with illumined portholes. She answered nothing. She felt her cheek pale and cold and, out of a maze of distress, she prayed to God to direct her, to show her what was her duty. The boat blew a long mournful whistle into the mist. If she went, tomorrow she would be on the sea with Frank, steaming towards Buenos Ayres. Their passage had been booked. Could she still draw back after all he had done for her? Her distress awoke a nausea in her body and she kept moving her lips in silent fervent prayer.

A bell clanged upon her heart. She felt him seize her hand:

"Come!"

All the seas of the world tumbled about her heart. He was drawing her into them: he would drown her. She gripped with both hands at the iron railing.

"Come!"

No! No! No! It was impossible. Her hands clutched the iron in frenzy. Amid the seas she sent a cry of anguish.

"Eveline! Evvy!"

He rushed beyond the barrier and called to her to follow. He was shouted at to go on but he still called to her. She set her white face to him, passive, like a helpless animal. Her eyes gave him no sign of love or farewell or recognition.

[1905—Ireland]

Questions

1. Characterize Eveline. What does the description of her house and neighborhood tell us about her?
2. The two primary reinforcing symbols in this text are "dust" and "Buenos Ayres." What meaning do these symbols carry in connection with each other?
3. Do any other details in the story have symbolic overtones? Which ones? What meanings other than the literal do they suggest?
4. Consider the end of the story carefully. What is suggested by Eveline's clutching the iron railing? Why doesn't she go with Frank? What symbolic meaning could Joyce's water imagery have?
5. *Dubliners,* the book in which "Eveline" appears, ends with a long story called "The Dead." What light might this information shed on "Eveline"?

Writing Assignments

1. Write a paragraph or two on the symbolism of the closing images of "Eveline"—specifically, "All the seas of the world" and "She gripped with both hands at the iron railing." Discuss how the water imagery embodies Eveline's fear and her reasons for not going, and how the image of her gripping the railing concretizes her state of mind and being as we leave her.
2. Write a letter from Eveline to Frank explaining why she could not leave. Try to make the tone and diction of the letter appropriate to Eveline as you come to understand her in the story; try as well to keep the letter in line with what we know about her psychology. Don't, for instance, have her engage in extensive self-analysis. If possible, imply her deeper reasons by way of a few significant details that symbolically suggest her true reasons for not going.
3. Anything that Joyce wrote has prompted a wealth of critical interpretation. Do some research (read at least three interpretations of "Eveline"), and then write a research paper on the story. Don't just summarize what other critics have said. Rather, get a thesis of your own and use your research to support that thesis. Of course, quote and cite appropriately.

THE FLOWERS

❊ ALICE WALKER ❊

It seemed to Myop as she skipped lightly from hen house to pigpen to smoke-house that the days had never been as beautiful as these. The air held a keenness that made her nose twitch. The harvesting of the corn and cotton, peanuts and squash, made each day a golden surprise that caused excited little tremors to run up her jaws.

Myop carried a short, knobby stick. She struck out at random at chickens she liked, and worked out the beat of a song on the fence around the pigpen. She felt light and good in the warm sun. She was ten, and nothing existed for her but her song, the stick clutched in her dark brown hand, and the tat-de-ta-ta-ta of accompaniment.

Turning her back on the rusty boards of her family's sharecropper cabin, Myop walked along the fence till it ran into the stream made by the spring. Around the spring, where the family got drinking water, silver ferns and wildflowers grew. Along the shallow banks pigs rooted. Myop watched the tiny white bubbles disrupt the thin black scale of soil and the water that silently rose and slid away down the stream.

She had explored the woods behind the house many times. Often, in late autumn, her mother took her to gather nuts among the fallen leaves. Today she made her own path, bouncing this way and that way, vaguely keeping an eye out for snakes. She found, in addition to various common but pretty ferns and leaves, an armful of strange blue flowers with velvety ridges and a sweetsuds bush full of the brown, fragrant buds.

By twelve o'clock, her arms laden with sprigs of her findings, she was a mile or more from home. She had often been as far before, but the strangeness of the land made it not as pleasant as her usual haunts. It seemed gloomy in the little cove in which she found herself. The air was damp, the silence close and deep.

Myop began to circle back to the house, back to the peacefulness of the morning. It was then she stepped smack into his eyes. Her heel became lodged in the broken ridge between brow and nose, and she reached down quickly, unafraid, to free herself. It was only when she saw his naked grin that she gave a little yelp of surprise.

He had been a tall man. From feet to neck covered a long space. His head lay beside him. When she pushed back the leaves and layers of earth and debris Myop saw that he'd had large white teeth, all of them cracked or broken, long fingers, and very big bones. All his clothes had rotted away except some threads of blue denim from his overalls. The buckles of the overalls had turned green.

Myop gazed around the spot with interest. Very near where she'd stepped into the head was a wild pink rose. As she picked it to add to her bundle she noticed a raised mound, a ring, around the rose's root. It was the rotted remains of a noose, a bit of shredding plowline, now blending benignly into the soil. Around an overhanging limb of a great spreading oak clung another piece. Frayed, rotted, bleached, and frazzled—barely there—but spinning restlessly in the breeze. Myop laid down her flowers.

And the summer was over.

[1967—U.S.A.]

Questions

1. The plot of "The Flowers" turns on a shocking past event. What is it?
2. What is the function of the mood of the first five paragraphs with respect to the rest of the story?
3. What can we infer about Myop's world from her lack of terror? Does her lack of terror seem plausible? Why or why not?
4. If we don't take Myop's lack of terror literally, what could be made of it? Might the story be an allegory? Comment on Myop's name and her laying down of her flowers in this regard.

Writing Assignments

1. Write an essay explaining how Myop's lack of terror is pivotal in interpreting "The Flowers." Consider how the implausibility of her response suggests that we should look at the story as something other than a realistic accounting of an incident in the life of one little girl.
2. A rewarding comparison could be made between Walker's story and Lewis Allan's lyric "Strange Fruit," made famous by Billie Holiday. Read Allan's poem (p. 294) and write a short essay comparing the two works. In particular, what do both reveal about black consciousness with respect to black history in America?

THE TROUT

✳ SEAN O'FAOLAIN ✳

One of the first places Julia always ran to when they arrived in G— was The Dark Walk. It is a laurel walk, very cold; almost gone wild, a lofty midnight tunnel of smooth, sinewy branches. Underfoot the tough brown leaves are never dry enough to crackle: there is always a suggestion of damp and cool trickle.

She raced right into it. For the first few yards she always had the memory of the sun behind her, then she felt the dusk closing swiftly down on her so that she screamed with pleasure and raced on to reach the light at the far end; and it was always just a little too long in coming so that she emerged gasping, clasping her hands, laughing, drinking in the sun. When she was filled with the heat and glare she would turn and consider the ordeal again.

This year she had the extra joy of showing it to her small brother, and of terrifying him as well as herself. And for him the fear lasted longer because his legs were so short and she had gone out at the far end while he was still screaming and racing.

When they had done this many times they came back to the house to tell everybody that they had done it. He boasted. She mocked. They squabbled.

"Cry babby!"

"You were afraid yourself, so there!"

"I won't take you anymore."

"You're a big pig."

"I hate you."

Tears were threatening so somebody said, "Did you see the well?" She opened her eyes at that and held up her long lovely neck suspiciously and decided to be incredulous. She was twelve and at that age little girls are beginning to suspect most stories: they have already found out too many, from Santa Claus to the Stork. How could there be a well! In The Dark Walk? That she had visited year after year? Haughtily she said, "Nonsense."

But she went back, pretending to be going somewhere else, and she found a hole scooped in the rock at the side of the walk, choked with damp leaves, so shrouded by ferns that she only uncovered it after much searching. At the back of this little cavern there was about a quart of water. In the water she suddenly perceived a panting trout. She rushed for Stephen and dragged him to see, and they were both so excited that they were no longer afraid of the darkness as they hunched down and peered in at the fish panting in his tiny prison, his silver stomach going up and down like an engine.

Nobody knew how the trout got there. Even old Martin in the kitchen-garden laughed and refused to believe that it was there, or pretended not to believe, until she forced him to come down and see. Kneeling and pushing back his tattered old cap he peered in.

"Be cripes, you're right. How the divil in hell did that fella get there?"

She stared at him suspiciously.

"You knew?" she accused; but he said, "The divil a know"; and reached down to lift it out. Convinced she hauled him back. If she had found it then it was her trout.

Her mother suggested that a bird had carried the spawn. Her father thought that in the winter a small streamlet might have carried it down there as a baby, and it had been safe until the summer came and the water began to dry up. She said, "I see," and went back to look again and consider the matter in private. Her brother remained behind, wanting to hear the whole story of the trout, not really interested in the actual trout but much interested in the story which his mummy began to make up for him on the lines of, "So one day Daddy Trout and Mammy trout . . ." When he retailed it to her she said, "Pooh."

It troubled her that the trout was always in the same position; he had no room to turn; all the time the silver belly went up and down; otherwise he was motionless. She wondered what he ate and in between visits to Joey Pony, and the boat and a bathe to get cool, she thought of his hunger. She brought him down bits of dough; once she brought him a worm. He ignored the food. He just went on panting.

Hunched over him she thought how, all the winter, while she was at school he had been in there. All the winter, in The Dark Walk, all day, all night, floating around alone. She drew the leaf of her hat down around her ears and chin and stared. She was still thinking of it as she lay in bed.

It was late June, the longest days of the year. The sun had sat still for a week, burning up the world. Although it was after ten o'clock it was still bright and still hot. She lay on her back under a single sheet, with her long legs spread, trying to keep cool. She could see the D of the moon through the fir-tree—they slept on the ground floor. Before they went to bed her mummy had told Stephen the story of the trout again, and she, in her bed, had resolutely presented her back to them and read her book. But she kept one ear cocked.

"And so, in the end, this naughty fish who would not stay at home got bigger and bigger and bigger, and the water got smaller and smaller . . ."

Passionately she had whirled and cried, "Mummy, don't make it a horrible old moral story!" Her mummy had brought in a Fairy Godmother, then, who sent lots of rain, and filled the well, and a stream poured out and the trout floated away down to the river below. Staring at the moon she knew that there are no such things as Fairy Godmothers and that the trout, down in The Dark Walk, was panting like an engine. She heard somebody unwind a fishing-reel. Would the beasts fish him out!

She sat up. Stephen was a hot lump of sleep, lazy thing. The Dark Walk would be full of little scraps of moon. She leaped up and looked out the window, and somehow it was not so lightsome now that she saw the dim mountains far away and the black firs against the breathing land and heard a dog say, bark-bark. Quietly she lifted the ewer of water, and climbed out the window and scuttled along the cool but cruel gravel down to the maw of the tunnel. Her pyjamas were very short so that when she splashed water it wet her ankles. She peered into the tunnel. Something alive rustled inside there. She raced in, and up and down she raced, and flurried, and cried aloud, "Oh, Gosh, I can't find it," and then at last she did. Kneeling down in the damp she put her hand into the slimy hole. When the body lashed they were both mad with fright. But she gripped him and shoved him into the ewer and raced, with her teeth ground, out to the other end of the tunnel and down the steep paths to the river's edge.

All the time she could feel him lashing his tail against the side of the ewer. She was afraid he would jump right out. The gravel cut into her soles until she came to the cool ooze of the river's bank where the moon-mice on the water crept into her feet. She poured out watching until he plopped. For a second he was visible in the water. She hoped he was not dizzy. Then all she saw was the glimmer of the moon in the silent-flowing river, the dark firs, the dim mountains, and the radiant pointed face laughing down at her out of the empty sky.

She scuttled up the hill, in the window, plonked down the ewer and flew through the air like a bird into bed. The dog said bark-bark. She heard the fishing-reel whirring. She hugged herself and giggled. Like a river of joy her holiday spread before her.

In the morning Stephen rushed to her, shouting that "he" was gone, and asking "where" and "how." Lifting her nose in the air she said superciliously, "Fairy God-mother, I suppose?" and strolled away patting the palms of her hands.

[1945—Ireland]

Questions

1. Though there is a literal level here, it doesn't amount to much. This story exists primarily at the symbolic level. What, then, are its major symbols? (To answer, consider prominence, placement, and repetition.)
2. Think into these symbolic images. What do they suggest by virtue of what they are in themselves? How does what they suggest function in the literary context?
3. Characterize Julia. What stage in life is she going through? What do the story's symbols reveal about her?
4. Two great sources of pleasure to be derived from literature are recognition of the known and confrontation with the unknown. Which of these does the pleasure one feels in reading "The Trout" spring from? Elaborate.

Writing Assignments

1. (a) In a paragraph, address question 3 above. Be sure to discuss how we come to understand what we do about Julia (that is, what serves to characterize her in the story).
   (b) In a separate paragraph, discuss your response to the story—what that response is and why you so respond.
2. Write a short paper on the symbolism of "The Trout." Isolate the main symbols, think into them (see question 2 above), and determine their significance in context. In your paper, state what the story's symbols are, suggest how they are recognized to be symbols, and analyze their meaning in relation to Julia and the moment in life she is going through.

THE GRAVE

❖ KATHERINE ANNE PORTER ❖

The grandfather, dead for more than thirty years, had been twice disturbed in his long repose by the constancy and possessiveness of his widow. She removed his bones first to Louisiana and then to Texas as if she had set out to find her own burial place, knowing well she would never return to the places she had left. In Texas she set up a small cemetery in a corner of her first farm, and as the family connection grew, and oddments of relations came over from Kentucky to settle, it contained at last about twenty graves. After the grandmother's death, part of her land was to be sold for the benefit of certain of her children, and the cemetery happened to lie in the part set aside for sale. It was necessary to take up the bodies and bury them again in the family plot in the big new public cemetery, where the grandmother had been buried. At last her husband was to lie beside her for eternity, as she had planned.

The family cemetery had been a pleasant small neglected garden of tangled rose bushes and ragged cedar trees and cypress, the simple flat stones rising out of uncropped sweet-smelling wild grass. The graves were lying open and empty one burning day when Miranda and her brother Paul, who often went together to hunt rabbits and doves, propped their twenty-two Winchester rifles carefully against the rail fence, climbed over and explored among the graves. She was nine years old and he was twelve.

They peered into the pits all shaped alike with such purposeful accuracy, and looking at each other with pleased adventurous eyes, they said in solemn tones: "These were graves!" trying by words to shape a special, suitable emotion in their minds, but they felt nothing except an agreeable thrill of wonder: they were seeing a new sight, doing something they had not done before. In them both there was also a small disappointment at the entire commonplaceness of the actual spectacle. Even if it had once contained a coffin for years upon years, when the coffin was gone a grave was just a hole in the ground. Miranda leaped into the pit that had held her grandfather's bones. Scratching around aimlessly and pleasurably as any young animal, she scooped up a lump of earth and weighed it in her palm. It had a pleasantly sweet, corrupt smell, being mixed with cedar needles and small leaves, and as the crumbs fell apart, she saw a silver dove no larger than a hazel nut, with spread wings and a neat fan-shaped tail. The breast had a deep round hollow in it. Turning it up to the fierce sunlight, she saw that the inside of the hollow was cut in little whorls. She scrambled out, over the pile of loose earth that had fallen back into one end of the grave, calling to Paul that she had found something, he must guess what . . . His head appeared smiling over the rim of another grave. He waved a closed hand at her. "I've got something too!" They ran to compare treasures, making a game of it, so many guesses each, all wrong, and a final showdown with opened palms. Paul had found a thin wide gold ring carved with intricate flowers and leaves. Miranda was smitten at sight of the ring and wished to have it. Paul seemed more impressed by the dove. They made a trade, with some little bickering. After he had got the dove in his hand, Paul said, "Don't you know what this is? This is a screw head for a *coffin*! . . . I'll bet nobody else in the world has one like this!"

Miranda glanced at it without covetousness. She had the gold ring on her thumb; it fitted perfectly. "Maybe we ought to go now," she said, "maybe one of the niggers'll see us and tell somebody." They knew the land had been sold, the cemetery was no longer theirs, and they felt like trespassers. They climbed back over the fence, slung their rifles loosely under their arms—they had been shooting at targets with various kinds of firearms since they were seven years old—and set out to look for the rabbits and doves or whatever small game might happen along. On these expeditions Miranda always followed at Paul's heels along the path, obeying instructions about handling her gun when going through fences; learning how to stand it up properly so it would not slip and fire unexpectedly; how to wait her time for a shot and not just bang away in the air without looking, spoiling shots for Paul, who really could hit things if given a chance. Now and then, in her excitement at seeing birds whizz up suddenly before her face, or a rabbit leap across her very toes, she lost her head, and almost without sighting she flung her rifle up and pulled the trigger. She hardly ever hit any sort of mark. She had no proper sense of hunting at all. Her brother would be often completely disgusted with her. "You don't care whether you get your bird or not," he said. "That's no way to hunt." Miranda could not understand his indignation. She had seen him smash his hat and yell with fury when he had missed his aim. "What I like about shooting," said Miranda, with exasperating inconsequence, "is pulling the trigger and hearing the noise."

"Then, by golly," said Paul, "whyn't you go back to the range and shoot at bulls-eyes?"

"I'd just as soon," said Miranda, "only like this, we walk around more."

"Well, you just stay behind and stop spoiling my shots," said Paul, who, when he made a kill, wanted to be certain he had made it. Miranda, who alone brought down a bird once in twenty rounds, always claimed as her own any game they got when they fired at the same moment. It was tiresome and unfair and her brother was sick of it.

"Now, the first dove we see, or the first rabbit, is mine," he told her. "And the next will be yours. Remember that and don't get smarty."

"What about snakes?" asked Miranda idly. "Can I have the first snake?"

Waving her thumb gently and watching her gold ring glitter, Miranda lost interest in shooting. She was wearing her summer roughing outfit: dark blue overalls, a light blue shirt, a hired-man's straw hat, and thick brown sandals. Her brother had the same outfit except his was a sober hickory-nut color. Ordinarily Miranda preferred her overalls to any other dress, though it was making rather a scandal in the countryside, for the year was 1903, and in the back country the law of female decorum had teeth in it. Her father had been criticized for letting his girls dress like boys and go careering around astride barebacked horses. Big sister Maria, the really independent and fearless one, in spite of her rather affected ways, rode at a dead run with only a rope knotted around her horse's nose. It was said the motherless family was running down, with the Grandmother no longer there to hold it together. It was known that she had discriminated against her son Harry in her will, and that he was in straits about money. Some of his old neighbors reflected with vicious satisfaction that now he would probably not be so stiffnecked, nor have any more high-stepping horses either. Miranda knew this, though she could not say how. She had met along the road old women of the kind who smoked corn-cob pipes, who had treated her grandmother with most sincere respect. They slanted their gummy old eyes sideways at the granddaughter and said, "Ain't you ashamed of yoself, Missy? It's against the Scriptures to dress like that. Whut yo Pappy thinkin about?" Miranda, with her powerful social sense, which was like a fine set of antennae radiating from every pore of her skin, would feel ashamed because she knew well it was rude and ill-bred to shock anybody, even bad-tempered old crones, though she had faith in her father's judgment and was perfectly comfortable in the clothes. Her father had said, "They're just what you need, and they'll save your dresses for school . . ." This sounded quite simple and natural to her. She had been brought up in rigorous economy. Wastefulness was vulgar. It was also a sin. These were truths; she had heard them repeated many times and never once disputed.

Now the ring, shining with the serene purity of fine gold on her rather grubby thumb, turned her feelings against her overalls and sockless feet, toes sticking through the thick brown leather straps. She wanted to go back to the farmhouse, take a good cold bath, dust herself with plenty of Maria's violet talcum powder—provided Maria was not present to object, of course—put on the thinnest, most becoming dress she owned, with a big sash, and sit in a wicker chair under the trees . . . These things were not all she wanted, of course; she had vague stirrings of desire for luxury and a grand way of living which could not take precise form in her imagination but were founded on family legend of past wealth and leisure. These immediate comforts were what she could have, and she wanted them at once. She lagged rather far behind Paul, and once she thought of just turning back without a word and going home. She stopped, thinking that Paul would never do that to her, and so she would have to tell him. When a rabbit leaped, she let Paul have it without dispute. He killed it with one shot.

When she came up with him, he was already kneeling, examining the wound, the rabbit trailing from his hands. "Right through the head," he said complacently, as if he had aimed for it. He took out his sharp, competent bowie knife and started to skin the body. He did it very cleanly and quickly. Uncle Jimbilly knew how to prepare the skins so that Miranda always had fur coats for her dolls, for though she never cared much for her dolls she liked seeing them in fur coats. The children knelt facing each other over the dead animal. Miranda watched admiringly while her brother stripped the skin away as if he were taking off a glove. The flayed flesh emerged dark scarlet, sleek, firm; Miranda with thumb and finger felt the long fine muscles with the silvery flat strips binding them to the joints. Brother lifted the oddly bloated belly. "Look," he said, in a low amazed voice. "It was going to have young ones."

Very carefully he slit the thin flesh from the center ribs to the flanks, and a scarlet bag appeared. He slit again and pulled the bag open, and there lay a bundle of tiny rabbits, each wrapped in a thin scarlet veil. The brother pulled these off and there they were, dark gray, their sleek wet down lying in minute even ripples, like a baby's head just washed, their unbelievably small delicate ears folded close, their little blind faces almost featureless.

Miranda said, "Oh, I want to *see,*" under her breath. She looked and looked— excited but not frightened, for she was accustomed to the sight of animals killed in hunting—filled with pity and astonishment and a kind of shocked delight in the wonderful little creatures for their own sakes, they were so pretty. She touched one of them ever so carefully, "Ah, there's blood running over them," she said and began to tremble without knowing why. Yet she wanted most deeply to see and to know. Having seen, she felt at once as if she had known all along. The very memory of her former ignorance faded, she had always known just this. No one had ever told her anything outright, she had been rather unobservant of the animal life around her because she was so accustomed to animals. They seemed simply disorderly and unaccountably rude in their habits, but altogether natural and not very interesting. Her brother had spoken as if he had known about everything all along. He may have seen all this before. He had never said a word to her, but she knew now a part at least of what he knew. She understood a little of the secret formless intuitions in her own mind and body, which had been clearing up, taking form, so gradually and so steadily she had not realized that she was learning what she had to know. Paul said cautiously, as if he were talking about something forbidden: "They were just about ready to be born." His voice dropped on the last word. "I know," said Miranda, "like kittens. I know, like babies." She was quietly and terribly agitated, standing again with her rifle under her arm, looking down at the bloody heap. "I don't want the skin," she said, "I won't have it." Paul buried the young rabbits again in their mother's body, wrapped the skin around her, carried her to a clump of sage bushes, and hid her away. He came out again at once and said to Miranda, with an eager friendliness, a confidential tone quite unusual in him, as if he were taking her into an important secret on equal terms: "Listen now. Now you listen to me, and don't ever forget. Don't you ever tell a living soul that you saw this. Don't tell a soul. Don't tell Dad because I'll get into trouble. He'll say I'm leading you into things you ought not to do. He's always saying that. So now don't you go and forget and blab out sometime the way you're always doing . . . Now, that's a secret. Don't you tell."

Miranda never told, she did not even wish to tell anybody. She thought about the whole worrisome affair with confused unhappiness for a few days. Then it sank quietly into her mind and was heaped over by accumulated thousands of impressions, for nearly twenty years. One day she was picking her path among the puddles and crushed refuse of a market street in a strange city of a strange country, when without warning, plain and clear in its true colors as if she looked through a frame upon a scene that had not stirred nor changed since the moment it happened, the episode of that far-off day leaped from its burial place before her mind's eye. She was so reasonlessly horrified she halted suddenly staring, the scene before her eyes dimmed by the vision back of them. An Indian vendor had held up before her a tray of dyed sugar sweets, in the shapes of all kinds of small creatures: birds, baby chicks, baby rabbits, lambs, baby pigs. They were in gay colors and smelled of vanilla, maybe. . . . It was a very hot day and the smell in the market, with its piles of raw flesh and wilting flowers, was like the mingled sweetness and corruption she had smelled that other day in the empty cemetery at home: the day she had remembered always until now vaguely as the time she and her brother had found treasure in the opened graves. Instantly upon this thought the dreadful vision faded, and she saw clearly her brother, whose childhood face she had forgotten, standing again in the blazing sunshine, again twelve years old, a pleased sober smile in his eyes, turning the silver dove over and over in his hands.

[1934—U.S.A.]

Questions

1. What do dove, ring, and rabbits symbolize in our culture?
2. Describe the specific ring that Paul finds. Why does Miranda want the ring? What does it mean to her and reveal about her? What of the rabbit with its young in this regard?
3. Why the title, with its definite article? Dove, ring, and rabbits, as well as the children and

Miranda's memory of that day they killed the rabbit ("the episode of that far-off day leaped from its burial place before her mind's eye"), are all associated with graves. What is the symbolic significance of these linked associations? Why, incidentally, the word "leaped" in the passage just quoted?

4. How does the story's final scene derive from and bring to a climax its opening scene in the graveyard and its central scene with the rabbits?
5. What does the story say, finally, about the relationship of childhood and maturity, of past and present, and most especially of life and death?
6. Porter's symbolism accomplishes what Paul and Miranda cannot in mere words—"to shape a special, suitable emotion in their minds." Explain.

Writing Assignments

1. In a short paper, compare and contrast "The Grave" and "The Trout" (the story before this) with respect to symbolism. What kinds of symbol does each contain (conventional or created)? Is the symbolism of each reinforcing or controlling? How do their symbols announce themselves and how are their symbols related to their themes?
2. Consider the three prime symbols of this story—dove, ring, and rabbit. Write a paper on these symbols as used by Porter. Classify them and discuss what they symbolize in our culture at large. How does what they symbolize carry over to "The Grave" and how does Porter adapt their symbolic meanings to the specific purposes of her story? In answering the latter part of this question, consider the facts that both dove and ring are found in a grave and that the rabbit becomes a kind of grave with respect to her young.
3. Write a research paper on "The Grave." First find out what its critics have to say. Then write an analysis of the story using your research to support *your* interpretation. That is, your interpretation should be your own, though you will want to refer to what others have had to say to support your argument as you go.

CHAPTER
✳ 8 ✳

PULLING IT ALL TOGETHER

Having studied the elements from which fiction is made, you should now be in a position to read a story in its wholeness—that is, with all of its elements in mind. Of course, all the possible elements will not necessarily be significant or even present in any given story. Your job as reader is to identify the elements of a story that are prominent and to see how they function and interact. Do exactly this as you read the story that follows, noting the elements that are prominent in it and determining their relationship and their significance. Then read the sample essay to see how a story should be read and written on: that is, in its entirety.

AN EPISODE OF WAR

✳ STEPHEN CRANE ✳

The lieutenant's rubber blanket lay on the ground, and upon it he had poured the company's supply of coffee. Corporals and other representatives of the grimy and hot-throated men who lined the breastwork had come for each squad's portion.

The lieutenant was frowning and serious at this task of division. His lips pursed as he drew with his sword various crevices in the heap until brown squares of coffee, astoundingly equal in size, appeared on the blanket. He was on the verge of a great triumph in mathematics and the corporals were thronging forward, each to reap a little square, when suddenly the lieutenant cried out and looked quickly at a man near him as if he suspected it was a case of personal assault. The others cried out also when they saw blood upon the lieutenant's sleeve.

He had winced like a man stung, swayed dangerously, and then straightened. The sound of his hoarse breathing was plainly audible. He looked sadly, mystically, over the breastwork at the green face of a wood where now were many little puffs of white smoke. During this moment, the men about him gazed statue-like and silent, astonished and awed by this catastrophe which had happened when catastrophes were not expected—when they had leisure to observe it.

As the lieutenant stared at the wood, they too swung their heads so that for another moment all hands, still silent, contemplated the distant forest as if their minds were fixed upon the mystery of a bullet's journey.

The officer had, of course, been compelled to take his sword at once into his left hand. He did not hold it by the hilt. He gripped it at the middle of the blade, awkwardly. Turning his eyes from the hostile wood, he looked at the sword as he held it there, and seemed puzzled as to what to do with it, where to put it. In short this weapon had of a sudden become a strange thing to him. He looked at it in a kind of stupefaction, as if he had been miraculously endowed with a trident, a sceptre, or a spade.

Finally, he tried to sheath it. To sheath a sword held by the left hand, at the middle of the blade, in a scabbard hung at the left hip, is a feat worthy of a sawdust ring. This wounded officer engaged in a desperate struggle with the sword and the wobbling scabbard, and during the time of it, he breathed like a wrestler.

But at this instant the men, the spectators, awoke from their stone-like poses and crowded forward sympathetically. The orderly-sergeant took the sword and tenderly placed it in the scabbard. At the time, he leaned nervously backward, and did not allow even his finger to brush the body of the lieutenant. A wound gives strange dignity to him who bears it. Well men shy from this new and terrible majesty. It is as if the wounded man's hand is upon the curtain which hangs before the revelations of all existence, the meaning of ants, potentates, wars, cities, sunshine, snow, a feather dropped from a bird's wing, and the power of it sheds radiance upon a bloody form, and makes the other men understand sometimes that they are little. His comrades look at him with large eyes thoughtfully. Moreover, they fear vaguely that the weight of a finger upon him might send him headlong, precipitate the tragedy, hurl him at once into the dim grey unknown. And so the orderly-sergeant while sheathing the sword leaned nervously backward.

There were others who proffered assistance. One timidly presented his shoulder and asked the lieutenant if he cared to lean upon it, but the latter waved them away mournfully. He wore the look of one who knows he is the victim of a terrible disease and understands his helplessness. He again stared over the breastwork at the forest, and then turning went slowly rearward. He held his right wrist tenderly in his left hand, as if the wounded arm was made of very brittle glass.

And the men in silence stared at the wood, then at the departing lieutenant— then at the wood, then at the lieutenant.

As the wounded officer passed from the line of battle, he was enabled to see many things which as a participant in the fight were unknown to him. He saw a general on a black horse gazing over the lines of blue infantry at the green woods which veiled his problems. An aide galloped furiously, dragged his horse suddenly to a halt, saluted, and presented a paper. It was, for a wonder, precisely like an historical painting.

To the rear of the general and his staff, a group, composed of a bugler, two or three orderlies, and the bearer of the corps standard, all upon maniacal horses, were working like slaves to hold their ground, preserve their respectful interval, while the shells bloomed in the air about them, and caused their chargers to make furious quivering leaps.

A battery, a tumultuous and shining mass, was swirling toward the right. The wild thud of hoofs, the cries of the riders shouting blame and praise, menace and encouragement, and, last, the roar of the wheels, the slant of the glistening guns, brought the lieutenant to an intent pause. The battery swept in curves that stirred the heart; it made halts as dramatic as the crash of a wave on the rocks, and when it fled onward, this aggregation of wheels, levers, motors, had a beautiful unity, as if it were a missile. The sound of it was a war-chorus that reached into the depths of man's emotion.

The lieutenant, still holding his arm as if it were of glass, stood watching this battery until all detail of it was lost, save the figures of the riders, which rose and fell and waved lashes over the black mass.

Later he turned his eyes toward the battle where the shooting sometimes crackled like bush-fires, sometimes sputtered with exasperating irregularity, and sometimes reverberated like the thunder. He saw the smoke rolling upward and saw crowds of men who ran and cheered, or stood and blazed away at the inscrutable distance.

He came upon some stragglers and they told him how to find the field hospital. They described its exact location. In fact these men, no longer having part in the battle, knew more of it than others. They told the performance of every corps, every division, the opinion of every general. The lieutenant, carrying his wounded arm rearward, looked upon them with wonder.

At the roadside a brigade was making coffee and buzzing with talk like a girls' boarding-school. Several officers came out to him and inquired concerning things of which he knew nothing. One, seeing his arm, began to scold. "Why, man, that's no way to do. You want to fix that thing." He appropriated the lieutenant and the lieutenant's wound. He cut the sleeve and laid bare the arm, every nerve of which softly fluttered under his touch. He bound his handkerchief over the wound, scolding away in the meantime. His tone allowed one to think that he was in the habit of being wounded every day. The lieutenant hung his head, feeling, in this presence, that he did not know how to be correctly wounded.

The low white tents of the hospital were grouped around an old school-house. There was here a singular commotion. In the foreground two ambulances interlocked wheels in the deep mud. The drivers were tossing the blame of it back and forth, gesticulating and berating, while from the ambulances, both crammed with wounded, there came an occasional groan. An interminable crowd of bandaged men were coming and going. Great numbers sat under the trees nursing heads or arms or legs. There was a dispute of some kind raging on the steps of the school-house. Sitting with his back against a tree a man with a face as grey as a new army blanket was serenely smoking a corn-cob pipe. The lieutenant wished to rush forward and inform him that he was dying.

A busy surgeon was passing near the lieutenant. "Good morning," he said with a friendly smile. Then he caught sight of the lieutenant's arm and his face at once changed. "Well, let's have a look at it." He seemed possessed suddenly of a great contempt for the lieutenant. This wound evidently placed the latter on a very low social plane. The doctor cried out impatiently. What mutton-head had tied it up that way anyhow. The lieutenant answered: "Oh, a man."

When the wound was disclosed the doctor fingered it disdainfully. "Humph," he said. "You come along with me and I'll tend to you." His voice contained the same scorn as if he were saying: "You will have to go to jail."

The lieutenant had been very meek but now his face flushed, and he looked into the doctor's eyes. "I guess I won't have it amputated," he said.

"Nonsense, man! nonsense! nonsense!" cried the doctor. "Come along, now. I won't amputate it. Come along. Don't be a baby."

"Let go of me," said the lieutenant, holding back wrathfully. His glance fixed upon the door of the old school-house, as sinister to him as the portals of death.

And this is the story of how the lieutenant lost his arm. When he reached home his sisters, his mother, his wife, sobbed for a long time at the sight of the flat sleeve. "Oh, well," he said, standing shamefaced amid these tears, "I don't suppose it matters so much as all that."

[1899—U.S.A.]

A Matter of Perspective

Funnel beginning

Thesis

Is human life significant, played out on a scale of titanic proportions? Or are we of no more importance from a universal perspective than ants are to us? In "An Episode of War," Stephen Crane answers in the negative, driving home our unimportance with especial force by the way the story is constructed.

Transition

A story in which perspective is crucial, "An Episode of War," or its meaning, could be summed up by the phrase "they are little." Like "well men" who

Support (by contrast)

"shy" away from the wounded, most of us turn away from this belittling truth. But some,

Topic sentence

removed from others for whatever reason and put at a distance, face head on our smallness and insignificance, or "the meaning of ants, [and] potentates" (the

Support

juxtaposition says it all). They lift a corner of the veil (I am picking up on Crane's image) and see for a moment "the inscrutable distance" and in consequence learn that things "don't . . . matter . . . so much as all that."

Transition and topic sentence

Support

The central character of "An Episode of War" is such a man. Because of his special situation, which separates him from the other soldiers, the unnamed lieutenant-- unnamed, perhaps, to suggest how unimportant we are from the universal perspective-- cannot turn away. Having attained, because

Support

of his situation, a wide view of the battle, he cannot help but see the absurd smallness of its participants. A result of his

Transition

distanced view, his perspective carries with it a sense of cosmic irony, of the universe mocking us and playing with us as boys play with ants.

Topic sentence

This perspective is embodied and dramatized by the story as much by elements not present as by those that are. A story with no plot to speak of, "An Episode of

Support

War" also contains little by way of characterization: the very absence of these most intimately human of the elements of fiction (most human because they entail our actions in the world and our selves) suggests how insignificant humanity is in the face of the inscrutable distance (absence here is presence). Those elements

Support

that do function in the story serve the same end. Its narration, for instance, and its

style are cool and distancing. Both
narration and style help to keep the reader
at a remove from the story's characters and
situation and so enable the reader to see
things from what I have called the
"universal perspective" (that is, the
perspective of the universe, or our
perspective when we see ourselves against
the backdrop of the universe).

Topic sentence

Setting is another functional element
in "An Episode of War"; indeed, it is the
most prominent element (note the unusually
large amount of descriptive detail in the
story). Why this should be so, or what the
function of the setting is, is clear enough

Support

in the story: it is largely by way of
setting--innately the most external and thus
detached of the elements--that Crane gains
his universal perspective. He paints his
people on a huge canvas (I am again picking
up on Crane's image) depicting an immense
natural backdrop. But from such a
perspective, how tiny they are! How
unimportant they seem! In this regard, we

Support

could say that the setting is symbolic, but
if so, it is symbolic not of any meaning but
of the absence of meaning, or of
inscrutability alone. So it might be better
to say that the setting is not symbolic, and
by failing to be symbolic, it paradoxically
symbolizes the blankness of the landscape
(nature, the universe) and so the
meaninglessness of human life.

Topic sentence

Finally, mood is an important element

Support

Support

Summary
ending

in the story as it unfolds. In fact, its
theme might best be thought of in terms of
its mood--a kind of painful, pitying
wonder. Established especially by irony--
the cosmic irony that results from the
lieutenant's distanced perspective and the
irony evident in the discrepancy between the
human desire for meaning and the impassivity
of the universe--the mood of the story
leaves one feeling that, though things
"don't . . . matter . . . so much as all
that" from the universal perspective, they
do matter from a human perspective; and
being human, we cannot help but wonder at
the state of things and pity our fellow
beings, however insignificant they might be
when seen against the inscrutable distance.

In sum, "An Episode of War" dramatizes
the human situation as Crane saw it both by
the elements that are prominent in it and by
several that are absent. Its theme entails
the double perspective of man and universe,
and the pity and wonder we often feel when
we realize our own insignificance.

SECTION III

POETRY

CHAPTER
✳ 1 ✳

WHAT POETRY IS (AND ISN'T)

POETRY AND FICTION

Stories and poems are alike in a number of ways: for instance, both present us with people located in settings (usually) and caught in some revealing circumstance; then, too, just as we should distinguish between authors and narrators, we should distinguish (normally) between poets and the speakers who speak their poems. Poetry and fiction differ, of course, in some of the elements that go into the making of each, but they are enough alike for me to suggest that you bring over to your study of poetry most of what you have learned from studying fiction. Indeed, you may even wish to think of poems as highly condensed stories that, because of their concision, call for a high degree of inference and attention to detail. Let's take a well-known poem and see how far we can go by thinking of it as a story. As you read the poem, ask the kind of question that we asked of stories in the fiction portion of this text: Who is speaking? What is the setting? Is there a plot or a situation? What does the one or the other reveal? Are there any symbols? What is the theme?

STOPPING BY WOODS ON A SNOWY EVENING
— Robert Frost —

Whose woods these are I think I know.
His house is in the village though;
He will not see me stopping here
To watch his woods fill up with snow.

My little horse must think it queer
To stop without a farmhouse near
Between the woods and frozen lake
The darkest evening of the year.

5

He gives his harness bells a shake
To ask if there is some mistake.   10
The only other sound's the sweep
Of easy wind and downy flake.

The woods are lovely, dark, and deep,
But I have promises to keep,
And miles to go before I sleep,   15
And miles to go before I sleep.

[1923—U.S.A.]

We have here a succinct story concerning a man who, out late on a winter's night, is on his way somewhere when the beauty of the natural scene catches him up and causes him to pause and look. Why he is out so late at this time of year we are not told. Is he a traveler who used bad judgment in timing his return home? Is he a country doctor of yore going out to see a dying patient? The poem is mute. It does tell us, however, that the speaker is from the general area (thus, he even thinks he knows the owner of the woods) and probably from "the village" he refers to (note his use of the definite article). Further, if we look closely, the poem tells us a good deal about the mentality of this late-night sojourner. For one thing, he is a practical man, one not given to such impracticalities (that is, from his normal perspective) as stopping by woods on a snowy evening. Thus, he would not wish anyone to see him (the implication of the first two lines) doing what he is doing. Thus, too, his projection onto his horse: surely it is not the horse but the speaker who *thinks* "it queer / To stop." Also, listen to the tonal quality of the voice speaking lines 1–10, every line coming to a pause at its end. There is a matter-of-factness in the tone of voice here that bespeaks a practical man, a man who usually forgoes aesthetic considerations.

But why, then, has he stopped? The answer, I think, lies in lines 11 and 12. With one line merging into the next, the tone of the speaker's voice suddenly takes on a sense of mystery and wonder. For the first time in his life, perhaps, he has felt a sense of aesthetic awe in contemplating the natural scene. Perhaps, too, he feels a desire to be at one with this setting, to leave behind the complex human world and to die into nature (a sense of death emanating from the images of the "frozen lake" and "The darkest evening of the year"). Certainly, should he indeed go into the woods, lie down, and watch them as they fill up with snow, he would die. A fleeting desire to be one with nature (and thus to die) is suggested as well by the hushed, almost reverential line "The woods are lovely, dark, and deep." The attraction here to the darkness and deepness of the scene is the attraction of the self to the non-self, the attraction of dissolution. In sum, the speaker, who seems tired and weighed down with human burdens, momentarily experiences a wish to "cease upon the midnight with no pain" (Keats). *But* he has "promises to keep"— not obligations imposed on him, but obligations he has committed himself to and wishes to fulfill. Tired from his journey, no doubt, he feels a momentary desire to be at the end of all journeys; his literal miles are burdensome. But with miles (metaphorical) to go before the final sleep of death, he withdraws from the peaceful scene and returns to the human world of promises and obligations.

So, the poem can be read as a story about a character (its speaker) who finds himself in a situation that arouses in him feelings of which he had formerly been unaware, feelings of aesthetic awe as well as a partial desire for cessation. How utterly human! Are we not all open to such feelings, both positive and negative? In "Stopping by Woods," Frost gives voice to a complex of feelings that mark our nature and drives them home through the drama of the poem.

To be sure, the poem is different from a story. Thus, I could not speak of it without mentioning the effect on tone of its division into lines. Still, to think of a poem as a highly condensed story is a way of entering the poem, a way that will carry you far toward full participation. And participation, as we shall see shortly, is the key to understanding poetry.

THE REALM OF POETRY

Many students approach poetry with apprehension, if not downright dread. They assume that poems are "hard to understand" and wonder why people should write so cryptically instead of just saying what they mean. The apprehension of such students, I think, results from a misconception: poetry is not what they think it to be. Nor is it a number of other things with which it has been associated. Before we move on, then, we should dispel the various misconceptions that people have about poems and poetry.

What Poems and Poetry Aren't

1. Poems are not cryptic messages or puzzles to be solved.
2. Poetry is not a complicated way of saying things. In fact, poetry isn't a way of *saying* things at all.
3. Nor are poems pretty, flowery expressions of sentimental feelings. Poems are not greeting cards (and vice versa).
4. Poetry is not something that rhymes and has meter.
5. Poems are not necessarily or usually "smooth flowing."
6. Poetry is not abstract.

But if poetry isn't any of the above, what is it? The contrasting list that follows should provide answers in part; these answers will be fleshed out as we move along.

What Poems and Poetry Are

1. Poetry should be viewed in terms of experience. Poems are not cryptic messages, but things to be lived through by the reader. That is, a great poem read by an engaged reader has the force of immediate experience, touching the reader physically and emotionally as well as intellectually.

2. Therefore, poetry is not simply a way of "saying" things. It is, rather, a way of using words to maximize the involvement of the reader and to communicate through that involvement.

3. As you will see, poetry is not limited in subject matter to anything, much less to matters "flowery." Poetry concerns everything: beauty and love, of course, but also war, death, misery, God, the nature of things, and whatever else you can think of. Thus, although some poems are pretty, most are not. Most deal with the hard realities of life in appropriate language and imagery. (Yet all take a certain delight in themselves as poems, communicating that delight to the active reader.)

4. Widely different in subject matter, poems are also widely different in construction. To be sure, for reasons we shall consider in later chapters, many poems rhyme, many are in meter, and many both rhyme and are in meter. But rhyme and meter *do not define* poetry. They are possible tools only, as is evidenced by the fact that many poems are neither rhymed nor in meter.

5. Everything works to one end in a poem. Therefore, few poems "flow smoothly." They move, rather, according to what they mean, and they mean, in part, according to how they move. The way a poem moves, that is, depends on what its speaker is saying. And if a speaker is addressing the carnage of battle, say, or the agony of personal loss, or the terror of God, it would hardly be appropriate for the words of the poem to glide smoothly along.

6. Poetry is the most concrete way of writing, the most sensory (producing and evoking sensations) and sensorially vivid way of using words. And that takes us back to the beginning of this list: poetry is itself a type of experience, as sensory as any nonverbal experience; poems are things made of words designed to involve the reader as fully as possible, the body no less than the mind.

In a word, the realm of poetry is the realm of concretion. For poetry involves the reader through sensation: literal sensation with respect to movement, sound patterns, rhythms, tone, and forms—all of which can be either seen, heard, or felt kinesthetically; and, with respect to imagery and figures of speech, sensation realized in the imagination. The poet Wallace Stevens had much the same understanding in mind when he wrote: "The poet, the musician, both have explicit meanings but they express them in the forms these take and not in explanation" (Item 18). That is, if a poem rhymes, its rhyming has something to do with the meaning; the tone of a poem and the way it moves always are intimately related to what it means; so, too, its look and shape, or the kind of visual form it takes. The best short definition of poetry I know is: poetry is a kind of writing in which an emotionally significant correlation is forged between meaning and form in all of its aspects. In other words, a poem communicates through what it literally is—through its formal elements rather than through explanation. By attending carefully to what a poem is, therefore, we can come to full understanding and appreciation.

The mark of an active reader, close attention of this sort is necessary to reading a poem. Because of its high degree of concentration (poetry is the most concentrated of all genres), poetry requires the active participation of its readers in the making of meaning; in turn, poetry allows for a wide range of creative responses and thus can help to bring out and hone our creative abilities. As Barbara H. Smith puts the matter: "It is partly by virtue of the . . . indeterminacy . . . of 'meaning' in poetry . . . that poems acquire value for us. For they thereby become the occasion for the exercise of the reader's own imaginative powers" (144). Read aright, poems stimulate the mind into activity, activity that not only makes sense of the poem at hand but that helps sharpen the mind's creative abilities generally. But to gain such a significant benefit, you must be willing to open yourself up and respond, to think and to feel with your whole self, to engage yourself fully as you read.

To do so, you must bring to the poems you read:

1. The willingness and good grace to look up anything in a poem that you don't know, whether the meaning of a word, the name of a place, a historical fact, or whatever.

2. A knowledge of the elements of poetry as you gain that knowledge in subsequent chapters.

3. And your own experience of life—of people in various aspects, of the country and the city, of the tastes and smells of things, of sorrow, of joy, of all that it means to be a human creature.

By bringing a willingness to learn, a developing knowledge of the elements of poetry, and your own experience to your reading of poems, you should be well on your way toward having the kind of experience that reading a great poem can be. "Nothing ever becomes real till it is experienced," Keats held. But Keats knew that reading a poem actively can be as much an experience as any activity in the outer world. Therefore, a poem can make something as real to us and significant as any other kind of experience. Perhaps a poem will bring home the point.

MY SON, MY EXECUTIONER
— Donald Hall —

My son, my executioner,
    I take you in my arms,
Quiet and small and just astir,
    And whom my body warms.

Sweet death, small son, our instrument   5
    Of immortality,
Your cries and hungers document
    Our bodily decay.

We twenty-five and twenty-two,
    Who seemed to live forever,   10
Observe enduring life in you
    And start to die together.

[1955—U.S.A.]

I have deliberately chosen a poem that should cause no one trouble as to its paraphrasable statement: biologically, our children are our replacements, and so, though we gain a kind of immortality through them, their birth announces our death. But how different the poem is from its paraphrase! As I read the poem, I feel physically the tension between parent and child established from the first with the syntactically taut phrase "My son, my executioner." The tautness continues with "Sweet death, small son, our instrument / Of immortality." Positioned between "death" and "immortality," the son paradoxically means both. The inherent tension of the paradox and the syntax here is reinforced by something that happens in the sound of the first two stanzas: *arms/warms* and *immortality/decay* are not real rhymes. In a context of rhyme, these off-rhymes set me a little on edge, make me feel a little tense simply because of the way they sound. Yet—and this I feel in my muscles— the poem moves in a rather stately way, slow and graceful. The grace of its forward motion (and perhaps, too, the full rhymes of its third stanza) lends to this little lyric a sense of something like a calm acceptance of life and the life cycle. Altogether, syntax, sound, and rhythm (some aspects of the poem's form) communicate through sensation the ambivalent feelings that people have about the biological relation between themselves and their children.

A good deal more could be said about "My Son, My Executioner," but I believe I have said enough to back up my point. Overall, the poem makes a statement, but it makes that statement real by way of concretions, which the reader experiences directly: its taut syntax, its dissonant off-rhymes, its forward motion. Again, the realm of poetry is the realm of concretion, where words are things having weight and texture, where communication takes place by way of the body no less than the mind.

UNDERSTANDING POETRY

A good part of coming to terms with a poem, then, is looking to see how it is constructed: how it sounds, how it moves, how its sentences fall (that is, whether its lines and sentences coincide or its sentences spill over into two or more lines), how rhyme and/or meter come into play (if they do), how imagery and figuration are used and to what effect, and so forth. Somewhere along the line, active readers question all the formal attributes of a poem and try to relate what happens formally to the meaning, or (and this is a better way of putting it) try to arrive at the poem's meaning through its form. For it is its formal attributes that we experience. But because what happens in poems formally needs special attention to understand fully, we will have to put off tackling poems in their entirety until the end of our study. In the meantime, just try to grasp each element of poetry as we go into it and then bring your growing knowledge to bear when reading poems in subsequent chapters.

Getting Started

There are questions of a nonformal nature, however, that you can and should ask of poems from the outset, essential questions that active readers ask automatically of every poem they read:

1. What does the poem's title reveal, if anything?

2. Who speaks the poem? Why? What can be said about the speaker? That is, what do we learn in the poem about its speaker?

3. What is the setting if there is one? Is the setting significant (as it is in Frost's "Stopping By Woods") or just a necessary backdrop? If the former, how is it significant?

4. What other characters, if any, are found in the poem? What are they like? How do they function?

5. What situation, if any, does the poem present? Is the poem's speaker in the situation, or does the speaker only narrate what other characters (other than the speaker) are doing, thinking, feeling?

6. How does the poem move generally? Is its movement steady, choppy, rough, smooth? Why?

7. What tone of voice does the speaker project? Why?

8. What implications seem clear in the poem? What can be clearly inferred?

Most of these questions, you may have observed, probe the story aspects of poems. As I suggested earlier, this is a good place to begin. Asking these questions of poems and then looking for answers will take you far toward understanding. You have seen as much already, in fact, when we looked at "Stopping By Woods on a Snowy Evening." Except for my mentioning that each of its lines comes to a pause at the line break except for line 11, which doesn't, everything I say about the poem is in answer to one or another of the above questions. But let's take another poem at this point and see how far our eight questions will take us toward understanding.

MARIN—AM

— Gary Snyder —

sun breaks over the eucalyptus
grove below the wet pasture,
water's about hot,
I sit in the open window
& roll a smoke.   5

distant dogs bark, a pair of
cawing crows; the twang
of a pygmy nuthatch high in a pine—
from behind the cypress windrow
the mare moves up, grazing.   10

a soft continuous roar
comes out of the far valley

of the six-lane highway—thousands
and thousands of cars
driving men to work.   15

[1968—U.S.A.]

The title sets the poem in both place and time: it is morning in Marin County, California, a county adjacent to San Francisco (here is the type of thing you should look up if you don't know). Both time and locale are more specifically located in the first stanza: "pasture," therefore a farm; "sun breaks" and "wet pasture" (the dew is still on the grass), therefore it is fairly early in the morning. In this setting we find a speaker, probably male ("roll a smoke" seems a masculine thing to do), who has just gotten up and who lounges around waiting for his coffee water to heat up. Sitting "in the open window," he hears pleasant rural sounds and watches the peaceful landscape before him. He is also aware, however, of the "soft continuous roar" in the far distance of commuters rushing to work over one of California's famous "six-lane highway[s]." His unexpected phrase "cars / driving men to work" takes us into the speaker and shows us something of his values: he sees such men as slaves driven by forces out of their control; he, in contrast, feels free because his life is self-determined. In free verse (that is, its lines are not in meter), the poem in its very movement embodies this sense of freedom. It seems to move from some inner necessity, as opposed to an imperative external to itself. And this, I would say, is the poem's theme: the contrast between the speaker, whose values are rooted in the land, and the speeding commuters embodies an attitude that it is far better to be self-directed than to be directed by time clocks, schedules, and the like, far better to act from inner necessity than from external constraints.

Of course, like life itself, the poem gives us only sense details; it does not openly profess a meaning at all. But by questioning the poem's story elements (speaker, setting, situation), by imaginatively hearing and seeing what is described, and by inferring what can be readily inferred, we can construct a meaning that is satisfactory and satisfying, even if not complete with respect to what is taken into account. As you continue on in this book, you should be able to become more and more subtle in your treatment of poems, bringing to your readings a greater and greater understanding of poetic construction. But there is already much that you can do in interpreting poems if you remember to ask the questions I have outlined.

WRITING ON POETRY AT THE OUTSET

What I have just said applies to writing on poems as well. Don't worry about meter or metaphor or stanzaic form or whatever for now; don't be intimidated by your having to write about a poem. Just think of the poem as a kind of story and move on from there. And remember that you don't have to say everything to say something. The sample essay that follows should show you how best to treat a poem at present. As you add to your knowledge of poetry, you will find more to say, but still, what is said in the essay is basic and not to be overlooked by even the most sophisticated reader of the poem in question.

HOW ANNANDALE WENT OUT

— E. A. Robinson —

"They called it Annandale—and I was there
To flourish, to find words, and to attend:
Liar, physician, hypocrite, and friend,
I watched him; and the sight was not so fair
As one or two that I have seen elsewhere: 5
An apparatus not for me to mend—
A wreck, with hell between him and the end,
Remained of Annandale; and I was there.

"I knew the ruin as I knew the man;
So put the two together, if you can,   10
Remembering the worst you know of me.
Now view yourself as I was, on the spot—
With a slight kind of engine. Do you see?
Like this . . . You wouldn't hang me? I thought not."

[1910—U.S.A.]

A Moral Dilemma

Funnel
beginning   Death can come gently in old age,
carrying a soul away in peaceful sleep. Or
it can be long and drawn out, causing agony
to the person dying and misery to all
around. When it comes in this second way,
what can we do, only watch and wait? The
speaker of E. A. Robinson's "How Annandale
Thesis   Went Out" found something else to do,
something, however, that gnaws on his
conscience and will not let him rest.

Topic
sentence   What do we learn about this speaker,
whom we find in an act of confession to an
unidentified listener? For one thing, he is
Support   a doctor and was Annandale's "physician."
Support   For another, he was Annandale's "friend."
His relationship to his patient, then, was

Support

not simply professional; it was personal as
well and so fraught with personal feeling.
We also learn that the speaker is a good
man: thus, he can afford to say to his
listener, "Remembering the worst you know of
me"; and he is a man of conscience: his
self—accusation as to his being a "Liar" and
a "hypocrite" (no doubt because he did not
tell Annandale the truth about his condition
and prospects) reveals that he (the speaker)
is a man of moral fiber who deviates from
truth and right at the expense of guilt.

Support

And guilt is the dominant feeling that the
speaker projects. He is confessing because
he feels an urgent need of absolution.
Unsure of the morality of what he has done,
he needs confirmation that it was right.

Transition

But what has he done? Clearly, he put
his friend Annandale out of his agony "With
a slight kind of engine" (a hypodermic
needle). The poem, then, touches on the
question of euthanasia. It is not about
euthanasia, however. Rather, it is about

Topic
sentence

the moral dilemma that mercy killing
presents us with. On the one hand, it does

Support

not seem moral to let hopeless suffering
continue until the bitter end; on the other,
our Judeo—Christian inheritance as well as
the Hippocratic oath taken by doctors
teaches the value of life whatever the
circumstance and strictly prohibits the
taking of life for whatever reason. It is

Transition

no wonder that the speaker should feel
guilty.

And yet, was he wrong? Annandale had

Topic
sentences

Support

become an "it," an "apparatus" not able to
be mended, "A wreck, with hell between him
and the end," a "ruin." How could anyone
stand by and watch a friend suffer so? This
is the other side of the dilemma that the
poem dramatizes. On which side does
morality lie? The poem does not give an
answer (and its inability to answer is part
of its point). The dilemma remains a
dilemma. Thus, though the listener agrees
with the speaker that he should not be
hanged for his act of compassion, his guilt
will probably not be assuaged, for he is
caught in a moral tangle that probably
cannot be resolved.

Reverse
funnel
ending

Though written toward the beginning of
this century, "How Annandale Went Out" is
strikingly contemporary in the questions it
implies and its theme overall. With our
marvelous high-tech devices, we can prolong
a life for years—sometimes agonizing years
—beyond its natural span. But should we?
Or should someone pull the plug? Who?
Under what circumstances? When? "How
Annandale Went Out" raises these very
questions and, though it may not offer any
final answers, suggests the quandary that mercy
killing seems to entail whatever side—pro or
con—we are inclined to take.

POEMS FOR STUDY AND WRITING ASSIGNMENTS

THE JEWEL STAIRS' GRIEVANCE

— [Translated from the Chinese by] Ezra Pound —

The jewelled steps are already quite white with dew,
It is so late that the dew soaks my gauze stockings,
And I let down the crystal curtain
And watch the moon through clear autumn.

[1915—U.S.A.]

Questions

1. Characterize the speaker of the poem. What do its details—for instance, "jewelled steps" and "crystal curtain"—suggest about the speaker's background and class?
2. Is the speaker male or female? How can we tell?
3. Why has the speaker come to this place and stayed, evidently, for some time?
4. Overall, what story does the poem quietly tell? What is the "grievance" referred to in its title?
5. What, generally, is the feeling conveyed by the last line? How does its sound contribute to our understanding of the feeling?

Writing Assignments

1. Write a paragraph on what it feels like to be mistreated in a love relationship. Relate what you say to the poem at hand.
2. In a paragraph, summarize the implied story of the poem at hand and point to its universality.

THE FARMER'S BRIDE

— Charlotte Mew —

Three Summers since I chose a maid,
  Too young maybe—but more's to do
At harvest-time than bide and woo.
  When us was wed she turned afraid
Of love and me and all things human;
Like the shut of a winter's day
Her smile went out and 'twadn't a woman—
  More like a little frightened fay.
    One night, in the Fall, she runned away.

5

"Out 'mong the sheep, her be," they said,   10
'Should properly have been abed;
But sure enough she wadn't there
Lying awake with her wide brown stare.
So over seven-acre field and up-along across the down
We chased her, flying like a hare   15
Before our lanterns. To Church-Town
        All in a shiver and a scare
We caught her, fetched her home at last
        And turned the key upon her, fast.

She does the work about the house   20
As well as most, but like a mouse:
        Happy enough to chat and play
        With birds and rabbits and such as they,
        So long as men-folk keep away.
"Not near, not near!" her eyes beseech   25

When one of us comes within reach.
        The women say that beasts in stall
        Look round like children at her call.
        I've hardly heard her speak at all.

Shy as a leveret, swift as he,   30
Straight and slight as a young larch tree,
Sweet as the first wild violets, she,
To her wild self. But what to me?

The short days shorten and the oaks are brown,
        The blue smoke rises to the low grey sky,   35
One leaf in the still air falls slowly down,
        A magpie's spotted feathers lie
On the black earth spread white with rime,
The berries redden up to Christmas-time.
        What's Christmas-time without there be   40
        Some other in the house than we!

        She sleeps up in the attic there
        Alone, poor maid. 'Tis but a stair
Betwixt us. Oh! my God! the down,
        The soft young down of her, the brown,   45
The brown of her—her eyes, her hair, her hair!

                          [1953—Great Britain]

THE FARMER'S BRIDE   **30.** *leveret:* a hare in its first year.

Questions

1. Who speaks this poem?
2. What do we learn about the speaker's bride? What lines convey what we need to know about her?
3. Summarize the story the poem tells.
4. The last stanza is full of pathos. Why? What general theme does the poem suggest?

Writing Assignments

1. Write a monologue—like "The Jewel Stairs' Grievance" and "The Farmer's Bride"—in which your speaker reveals (without simply naming) some feeling in response to the situation that can be inferred from your presentation.
2. Like every other poem, "The Farmer's Bride" asks us to project ourselves by way of the imagination into the situation of its speaker. Write a short paper on how such projection can lead us to a wider understanding of and a heightened sympathy for people unlike ourselves in most ways. What is the value of sympathy of this sort?

A SLUMBER DID MY SPIRIT SEAL
— William Wordsworth —

A slumber did my spirit seal;
  I had no human fears:
She seemed a thing that could not feel
  The touch of earthly years.

No motion has she now, no force;   5
  She neither hears nor sees;
Rolled round in earth's diurnal course,
  With rocks, and stones, and trees.

[1800—Great Britain]

Questions

1. What are "human fears"? Why might the speaker have been insulated from such fears before the death of the poem's "she"?
2. Who might this "she" have been? What might have been the relationship between her and the speaker?
3. Summarize the story line of the poem. In doing so, pay close attention to Wordsworth's handling of tense.
4. Comment on the pile of negatives ("No," "no," "neither . . . nor") in the second stanza. What does the sound of its first line suggest?
5. How does the word "diurnal" strike you? What feeling(s) does the last line of the poem suggest?

Writing Assignments

1. Let us say that you have lost someone very dear to you. What were your feelings (if you actually have lost someone), or what do you imagine your feelings would be? Write a paragraph or short paper on personal loss, relating what you say to Wordsworth's lyric poem.
2. The last two lines of the poem have been read in diverse ways, communicating to some a sense of the grotesque inertness of the beloved and thus the impossibility of consolation in a purely natural framework, and to others a sense of a calm acceptance of death as simply part of nature's cycle. How do you take the lines? Write a short paper examining your response, what it is and how it both derives from and sheds light on Wordsworth's short yet profound lyric.

UNITED 555

— Richard Eberhart —

St. Paul never saw a sight like this.
Seven miles up, fifty five below outside,
Wide open flat top of cloud vista to the far horizon,
As the sun descends reddening the upworld spectacle.

St. Paul never got off the ground, and, for that matter,   5
Christ was nailed to a Cross a few feet above the earth.
Here I sit seven miles up feeling nothing,
No visceral reaction, dollar martini, endless vista.

I must say it could not be more beautiful.
O think of Akhnaton, who never got off the ground either.   10
Raciest to think of the baboons in East Africa at Treetops,
Who could not imagine to come to such a pass as this.

Christ and Paul never knew what height is,
They never polluted the atmosphere.
I am Twentieth Century Man riding high,   15
Going into the sunset, Seven Up, feeling no pain.

[1976—U.S.A.]

Questions

1. What is the situation of this poem?
2. The poem is a meditation stemming from the speaker's situation. What is the focus of the meditation? Toward what conclusion does the meditation lead the poem's speaker?

UNITED 555.   **10.** *Akhnaton:* Egyptian pharaoh (c. 1375–1358 B.C.) who held that there was one god—the sun—and who gave rise to a cult of nature worship.

3. Despite its short compass, much of human history—both biological and cultural—is spanned in "United 555." Why?
4. Though making no direct statement, the poem implies a clear attitude about the modern world as opposed to the older worlds touched on in the speaker's internal soliloquy. What is the point of contrast? What is the speaker's attitude, finally, about the modern world? What is the poem's theme?

Writing Assignments

1. Is there something about the modern world that you react to negatively? If so, write a paragraph about your feelings and relate them, if possible, to the view of our world presented in Eberhart's poem.
2. Write a paragraph or short essay in which you discuss the contrasts in "United 555" and their meaning.

REUBEN BRIGHT

— E. A. Robinson —

Because he was a butcher and thereby
Did earn an honest living (and did right),
I would not have you think that Reuben Bright
Was any more a brute than you or I;
For when they told him that his wife must die,   5
He stared at them, and shook with grief and fright,
And cried like a great baby half that night,
And made the women cry to see him cry.

And after she was dead, and he had paid
The singers and the sexton and the rest,   10
He packed a lot of things that she had made
Most mournfully away in an old chest
Of hers, and put some chopped-up cedar boughs
In with them, and tore down the slaughter-house.

[1897—U.S.A.]

Questions

1. Who is the speaker here? Does it really matter in this case?
2. What is the speaker at pains to communicate in the first four lines of the poem? Why?
3. Characterize Reuben Bright. What does the phrase "a great baby" tell us about him and what he felt when he was told that there was no hope?
4. Describe the action of the poem. In what way does its story line help provide a sense of structure?

5. How do the last six lines move? How is this movement apt given what Reuben was feeling? How does this movement help to embody and communicate what Reuben felt?
6. What contrasts inform the last four lines? How do these contrasts lend a sense of pathos?
7. Why did Reuben *tear* down (note the violence of the word "tore") "the slaughter-house"? In a poem titled "The Ruined Cottage," Wordsworth speaks of "the impotence of grief." In what way does the phrase help to explain Reuben's final action?

Writing Assignments

1. In a paragraph, describe the story of this poem and discuss how its story helps create the pathos of its ending.
2. In a paper, discuss point by point what we learn about Reuben and how. In what way is the revelation of character the point here?

THE ONION
— John Fandel —

The medium white onion
in the wooden bowl
(shaped by a craftsman)
on the kitchen counter
has sprouted three slender shoots   5
primevally green as April.

What do you think you're doing,
I say to it,
making an oasis
while waiting to be pared.   10

And I say to my soul,
Observe it, look at it.

I say,
Observe.

[1977—U.S.A.]

Questions

1. This poem presents us with a rather slight story, but a story nevertheless. Recount it.
2. Why does the speaker see the onion as an "oasis"? In what ways is the reference to an oasis apt here?
3. Onion, "craftsman," and poet are analogous. How so?

4. How might the speaker change, as he seems to wish to, should he take his advice to "observe"—that is, to see and understand? What lesson does the onion teach?
5. In what way does the shape of this poem reflect its meaning?

Writing Assignments

1. Sometimes, little things can teach great truths. Write a paragraph in which you discuss this aspect of "The Onion" and, if you can, relate a similar experience of your own as evidence for the truth of the poem.
2. Answer the questions above to your own satisfaction and then write an interpretation of "The Onion," taking into account as many aspects of the poem as you can coherently. You may also wish to discuss your response to and judgment of the poem.

CHAPTER

✳ **2** ✳

VOICE, TONE, AND DICTION

THE PEOPLE IN POETRY

Listeners

Some speaking and some not, some central and some peripheral, the people in poetry fall into three categories: speakers, listeners, and players. Of these, the listener is the easiest to define. The **listener** (if there is one) is a fictional character inside a poem to whom it is fictively spoken. We have already witnessed such a character in "How Annandale Went Out" (p. 224), in which we are made aware of a listener by the speaker's reference to "you." This is a typical way by which poets indicate that speakers are to be heard (that is, by the reader) as speaking to someone other than themselves in soliloquy or to the reader directly. Another common way by which the presence of a listener is indicated is the suggestion of one in a title: for example, Andrew Marvell's title "To His Coy Mistress" (pp. 256–57) indicates that the poem is to be heard as spoken to a young woman. We rarely learn much about listeners, but they do serve at least two functions: they help provide a certain aura of realism, and their presence often heightens the sense of drama. That is certainly the case in "How Annandale Went Out," in which the imagined presence of a listener is instrumental in leading us to feel the poem as a tormented confession.

Players

By **players** I mean characters in poems—other than their speakers—who are described to some degree (little or great) and who either speak directly themselves (as would be the case in a dialogue) or are paraphrased or quoted by the speaker. Like secondary characters in stories, players usually require some degree of attention on our part—sometimes only a little, sometimes a good deal more. The "men" in Snyder's "cars / driving men to work" ("Marin—AM," pp. 222–23) could be considered players as we are using the word. To be sure, we learn little about them; if they were in a piece of fiction, they would be called stock characters. Nevertheless, their role in the poem is significant in that its theme is established through them. An example of a fuller character who is a player is the Duchess of Browning's "My Last Duchess." As you read the poem, try to see what emerges about her despite the Duke's biased perspective and how our understanding of her conditions our understanding of the Duke and thus of the poem as a whole.

MY LAST DUCHESS
— Robert Browning —

FERRARA

That's my last duchess painted on the wall,
Looking as if she were alive. I call
That piece a wonder, now: Frà Pandolf's hands
Worked busily a day, and there she stands.
Will't please you sit and look at her? I said   5
"Frà Pandolf" by design, for never read
Strangers like you that pictured countenance,
The depth and passion of its earnest glance,
But to myself they turned (since none puts by
The curtain I have drawn for you, but I)   10
And seemed as they would ask me, if they durst,
How such a glance came there; so, not the first
Are you to turn and ask thus. Sir, 'twas not
Her husband's presence only, called that spot
Of joy into the Duchess' cheek: perhaps   15
Frà Pandolf chanced to say "Her mantle laps
"Over my lady's wrist too much," or "Paint
"Must never hope to reproduce the faint
"Half-flush that dies along her throat": such stuff
Was courtesy, she thought, and cause enough   20
For calling up that spot of joy. She had
A heart—how shall I say?—too soon made glad,
Too easily impressed; she liked whate'er
She looked on, and her looks went everywhere.
Sir, 'twas all one! My favor at her breast,   25
The dropping of the daylight in the West,
The bough of cherries some officious fool
Broke in the orchard for her, the white mule
She rode with round the terrace—all and each

MY LAST DUCHESS.   The poem is spoken by Alfonso II d'Este, Duke of Ferrara, Italy. Alfonso's first wife, whom he married when she was fourteen, died in 1561 under suspicious circumstances.

Would draw from her alike the approving speech,   30
Or blush, at least. She thanked men—good! but thanked
Somehow—I know not how—as if she ranked
My gift of a nine-hundred-years-old name
With anybody's gift. Who'd stoop to blame
This sort of trifling? Even had you skill   35
In speech—which I have not—to make your will
Quite clear to such an one, and say, "Just this
"Or that in you disgusts me; here you miss,
"Or there exceed the mark"—and if she let
Herself be lessoned so, nor plainly set   40
Her wits to yours, forsooth, and made excuse,
—E'en then would be some stooping; and I choose
Never to stoop. Oh sir, she smiled, no doubt,
Whene'er I passed her; but who passed without
Much the same smile? This grew; I gave commands;   45
Then all smiles stopped together. There she stands
As if alive. Will't please you rise? We'll meet
The company below, then. I repeat,
The Count your master's known munificence
Is ample warrant that no just pretense   50
Of mine for dowry will be disallowed;
Though his fair daughter's self, as I avowed
At starting, is my object. Nay, we'll go
Together down, sir. Notice Neptune, though,
Taming a sea-horse, thought a rarity,   55
Which Claus of Innsbruck cast in bronze for me!

[1842—Great Britain]

Here we find a speaker (the Duke), a listener (the envoy of the Count), and an important player (the Duchess). Why the Duke is speaking to the envoy is made clear at the end of the poem (starting at line 49): the Duke is hoping to marry the Count's daughter. But how are we to respond to the Duke? In large measure, the answer lies in our understanding of the Duchess. Look carefully at what we learn about her: a mere girl, she was naturally delighted by a compliment or a gift (like the "bough of cherries"); her spirits were high, as befits an adolescent, and her heart was full of gladness; all in all, she was a charming creature, vivacious and outgoing. Are we given one sound reason for the Duke's disdain and his final decision to have her put out of the way ("I gave commands; / Then all smiles stopped together")? No, we are not. By understanding the Duchess, then, we come to see the Duke for what he is: an unbridled egomaniac who is so caught up in himself and so blindly confident of his own rightness that he unhesitatingly reveals what he does about his treatment of his last wife to, of all people, the envoy of his next wife (or so he hopes). He is a man who loves possessions, objects, and to whom people are objects no different from statues. He must possess or destroy. The poem as a whole is a character study of such a man, a study of egomania and of insane self-righteousness.

Speakers

From "My Last Duchess" we can see that listeners and players can be as important in shaping our understanding as speakers. Also, notice that **speakers,** like fictional narrators, can speak in the first or third person and can be unreliable (which is the case with the Duke). Finally, note that character revelation can be a possible end (theme) of a poem just as it can be of a story. An important difference between poetry and fiction, however, is that poems are *always* to be heard as *spoken*—either by speakers to themselves in soliloquy ("Stopping By Woods on a Snowy Evening," "Marin—AM"), or to imagined listeners ("My Son, My Executioner," "How Annandale Went Out," "My Last Duchess"), or directly to the reader ("Methought I Saw," p. 238), or sometimes by two or more speakers conversing with each other ("Reason," pp. 239–40). Like the drama, poetry is language framed to be heard. Therefore, poems should be read aloud whenever possible, or at least sounded out in the imagination.

The key concept here is that of **voice:** a poem should be taken as an utterance, not just seen on the page but heard. Heard well, poems carry all the nuances of actual speech. Also, the dimension of hearing is an aspect of a poem's concreteness: what we actually hear is concrete by definition. So listen as you read; hear the voice(s) of each poem, especially that of the speaker.

A Character as Speaker.   Speakers can be divided into three types: a character (or sometimes characters), a persona, and the poet. "My Last Duchess" is a good example of a poem in which a character is the speaker, as are "How Annandale Went Out" (p. 224) and "The Ruined Maid" (pp. 248–49—a dialogue, this poem presents us with two characters speaking). One thing to note about poems in which characters are speakers is that we usually refer to such speakers by name, if a name is given, or by some attribute like occupation, if no name is given, when discussing or writing about them: we would refer to the speaker of "My Last Duchess" as *the Duke* and to the speaker of "How Annandale Went Out" as *the doctor* (though one can also say *the speaker* if need be). One thing more about poems in which a character is the speaker: you must look for clues at the outset to make the determination that the speaker is a character. The quotation marks around the whole of "How Annandale Went Out," for instance, and the specification "Ferrara" at the beginning of "My Last Duchess" indicate that each poem is spoken by a character and not by the poet nor even by a persona.

A Persona as Speaker.   Derived from the Latin meaning "mask," a **persona** is a kind of speaker—usually referred to as "the speaker"—that falls between the other two kinds (character and poet). That is, a persona is not a character on the one hand nor clearly the poet on the other. Consider "Marin—AM" (pp. 222–23) in this regard. Is the speaker to be taken as a character or the poet himself? We have no way of knowing. Therefore, we must take him as a persona. "Stopping By Woods on a Snowy Evening" (pp. 216–17) and "My Son, My Executioner" (p. 220) present us with opposite cases: the first could be seen as spoken by a character (a local doctor, for instance) and the second by the poet himself addressing his actual infant son. But we have no grounds, really, for either assumption. The speaker of "Stopping By Woods" is not specifically identified (neither as character nor poet) and that of "My Son . . ." need not indeed be the poet (one does not have to have a son in reality to write a poem in which the speaker has a son). Poets often imagine themselves in situations and write poems that are not in fact autobiographical in the narrow sense that whatever is said in the poem actually happened to them. So, if a poem is spoken neither by a clear-cut character nor by the poet in direct address, think of its speaker as a persona and refer to the speaker simply as "the speaker."

The Poet as Speaker.   Finally, there is the poet as speaker, in which case we refer to the speaker as "the poet" or "Milton," "Dickinson," "Wordsworth," or whomever. Take as an example the following poem by the blind poet John Milton about a dream concerning his deceased second wife.

METHOUGHT I SAW
— John Milton —

Methought I saw my late espousèd saint
   Brought to me like Alcestis from the grave,
   Whom Jove's great son to her glad husband gave,
   Rescued from Death by force, though pale and faint.
Mine, as whom washed from spot of child-bed taint   5
   Purification in the Old Law did save,
   And such, as yet once more I trust to have
   Full sight of her in heaven without restraint,
Came vested all in white, pure as her mind.
   Her face was veiled; yet to my fancied sight   10
   Love, sweetness, goodness, in her person shined
So clear as in no face with more delight.
   But O, as to embrace me she inclined,
   I waked, she fled, and day brought back my night.

[c. 1658—Great Britain]

METHOUGHT I SAW.   **1.** *saint:* Milton's "saint" (which means "a soul in heaven") is his second wife, who died in 1658, less than two years after her marriage (thus, "Late espousèd"). In that Milton had become blind in 1651, he probably had never seen his second wife. **2.** *Alcestis:* Admetus's wife, brought back from the dead by Hercules ("Jove's great son") in Euripides' play *Alcestis.* **5–6.** *Mine . . . save:* Milton's wife died in childbirth and was purified according to the rituals prescribed by Hebrew law.

Addressed, it seems, to the reader, the poem is clearly personal, autobiographical in reference and feeling (especially the pain communicated in the last line, the pain of the blind poet waking to darkness). It would be foolish, thus, to think of the poem as spoken by anyone other than the poet himself. If there is no way of telling whether a poem is autobiographical, take the speaker as a persona; if, however, a poem clearly concerns the life lived as opposed to imagined by its author, then you have every reason to hear the poet speaking in his or her own voice directly to you.

TONE OF VOICE

Whether a poem is spoken by a character, a persona, or the poet, listen carefully to its voice(s) and try to determine its **tone(s).** Just as our tones of voice and the attitudes they reveal are crucial to meaning when we speak to each other, so the tones of voice in poems and the attitudes they reveal are fundamental to how poems mean. Should you say with a sneer in your voice, "Oh boy, ain't you smart," your tone—created in part by your use of the word "ain't"—would indicate an ironic intent and your statement would be taken to mean the opposite of what it means literally. Conversely, you might say with great deference, "Please, sir, let me have the job," in which case your attitude would be understood as respectful. In poetry, tone works in the same way: the kind of words chosen and the way they move and sound communicate a speaker's intent and attitude. In "Stopping By Woods on a Snowy Evening," for instance, the matter-of-fact tone, created in part by the poem's simple vocabulary and in part by the management of the poem's lines, goes far in revealing the speaker's general attitude, his normal way of viewing things. Or take "My Last Duchess," a poem of shifting tones. When the Duke speaks of his art works, his tone is that of a confident man full of a sense of self-importance; but when he speaks of the Duchess, he falters (human relationships are not his forte) as his tone becomes vindictive and self-righteous; and when, at the end of the poem, he speaks to the envoy ("Nay, we'll go / Together down, sir"—lines 53–54), his tone is deliberately ingratiating.

Whatever the tone and however it is created, tone in poetry is always meaningful. Take the following poem, in which five separate tones of voice are to be heard. Created especially by diction (we will return to this matter shortly), the tones here reveal much about each of the poem's four speakers and what each is feeling.

REASON
— Josephine Miles —

Said, Pull her up a bit will you, Mac, I want to unload there.
Said, Pull her up my rear end, first come first serve.

REASON.   " 'Reason' is a favorite one of my poems because I like the idea of speech . . . as the material from which poetry is made."—Miles's note.

Said, Give her the gun, Bud, he needs a taste of his own bumper.
Then the usher came out and got into the act:

Said, Pull her up, pull her up a bit, we need this space, sir.   5
Said, For God's sake, is this still a free country or what?
You go back and take care of Gary Cooper's horse
And leave me handle my own car.

Saw them unloading the lame old lady,
Ducked out under the wheel and gave her an elbow,   10
Said, All you needed to do was just explain;
Reason, Reason is my middle name.

[1955—U.S.A.]

The first speaker, a truck or taxi driver (suggested by the words "unload" and especially "Mac"), is more or less polite in tone, a sense of politeness resulting from his adding "a bit." In contrast, the second speaker, the owner of the car in the way of the first speaker, is hostile: "Pull her up my rear end" is hardly a friendly thing to say. The third speaker, probably a passerby, is obviously indignant at the second speaker's refusal to move, for indignity is the tone of "Give her the gun, Bud, he needs a taste of his own bumper." Then the usher enters, with a tone as deferential as possible (created by his "a bit" and "sir"). With his talk of a "free country" and "Gary Cooper's horse," the second speaker (the owner of the offending car) remains hostile as he addresses the usher. Then, however, his tone becomes conciliatory and even concerned (the fifth tone to be heard) as he realizes why the taxi driver wished him to pull up: the unloading of "the lame old lady." Suddenly, the second speaker becomes all reason and light. The poem's last line, however, is meant ironically, not by the speaker but by the poet pulling the strings: that this utterly unreasonable man believes himself to be reason itself smacks of the kind of irony that life faces us with constantly.

There, then—four separate voices and five distinct tones, each of which reflects how the individual speaker feels at the moment of utterance and how, therefore, we should take each. But what the poem serves best to demonstrate has to do with the matter of hearing itself. "Reason" could not be truly understood if not heard. The hearing of it is what makes it a delight. So, again, hear as you read. If you do, poems will prove much less difficult than you perhaps have thought them to be.

DICTION AND TONE

Of all of the things that help to create tone, diction is the most important. **Diction** refers to the selection of words or the kind of words selected in a given passage or work, kind being determined by the history of a word and its current usage. Diction, note, is a consideration of equal importance in studying all the genres— stories, poems, plays, and essays alike—and what can be said about diction with regard to one is true of all. Therefore, what I had to say about diction when we were looking at fiction is equally true of poetry: "diction can be abstract or concrete ('a meal' versus 'a juicy steak'); literal or metaphorical ('the surface of the sea' versus 'the breast of the sea'); denotative or connotative ('domicile' versus 'home')." There are many other categories of diction as well: for instance, diction can be Latinate or Saxon, depending on which wordstock the writer draws on (Latin and Saxon being the two diverse languages that formed English as we know it); technical or common (jargon as opposed to colloquial English); formal or informal; elevated or plain; archaic or slangy; mature or childish; flowery or gutsy; general or specific; and so on. One example, perhaps, will suffice to demonstrate the difference in *tone* that diction can effect: "excrement" is Latin and formal; "dodo" is informal and childish. The two terms point to the same thing, but because of their histories and current usage (that is, their diction), they are quite different in tone and so quite different in effect.

The above list of possible categories of diction contains many pairs that overlap: for instance, our Latin vocabulary tends to be formal and the base of many technical words; our Saxon vocabulary tends to be informal and the base of our common, everyday words. But the pair abstract/concrete should be kept distinct from both the pair denotative/connotative and the pair general/specific. For, while it is true that many abstract words are denotative and specific (most scientific terms, for in-stance—like *polymyositis,* a specific muscle disorder), many others are highly connota-tive and general (*love, communism, home*); conversely, though concrete words tend to be connotative and specific (*tiger, sour balls, stretch*), many are general and as denotative as connotative (*bird* as opposed to *robin, tree* as opposed to *oak* or *maple, street* as opposed to *Forty-second Street*). Be aware, too, that though the vocabulary of poetry tends to be concrete, poets use abstract words as well, and often to great effect (for instance, "diurnal" in Wordsworth's "A Slumber Did My Spirit Seal," p. 229). Therefore, no valid statement can be made about the diction of poetry in general. Each poem must be weighed individually as to its diction and resulting tone. And doing so is part of the fun of coming to terms with a poem.

The Effect of Diction on Tone

With this in mind, look back to Milton's sonnet "Methought I Saw" (p. 238), especially its last two lines. Like the twelve lines that precede it, line 13 is highly Latinate ("embrace" and "inclined" both derive from Latin), formal, and, as a result, elevated in tone. In contrast, the last line—consisting entirely of monosyllables—is Saxon, colloquial, and down-to-earth. Lines 1–13 take us into the sublime heaven of Milton's dream; line 14 brings us to the poet's waking reality with a sense of tremendous pain, the pain of a blind man waking to the dark of day. More than anything else, it is the dictional contrast that causes the change in tone and drives home the poet's pain and longing. A full understanding of the poem, therefore, requires that its diction and dictional contrast be observed and their effects experi-enced.

Dictional contrast is also important in the following poem, the delight of which lies especially in the poet's management of diction.

ONE PERFECT ROSE
— Dorothy Parker —

A single flow'r he sent me, since we met.
    All tenderly his messenger he chose;
Deep-hearted, pure, with scented dew still wet—
    One perfect rose.

I knew the language of the floweret;   5
    "My fragile leaves," it said, "his heart enclose."
Love long has taken for his amulet
    One perfect rose.

Why is it no one has sent me yet
    One perfect limousine, do you suppose?   10
Ah no, it's just my luck to get
    One perfect rose.

[1926—U.S.A.]

    The first two stanzas could be called "flowery." This is greeting-card verse, dripping with sentiment and sentimentality. But the sentiment is utterly destroyed by the third stanza, in which the diction of "limousine" plays a key role. "Limousine" just isn't the *kind* of word one associates with love poems. Its use, thus, undercuts everything said in the first two stanzas and thereby comically brings into question the worth of "romantic" love, the question of its value being the poem's theme. To be sure, the paraphrasable meaning of the last stanza also helps to establish this theme, but the shift in diction and the resulting shift in tone (from sentimental to ironic) are what make us sit up and take notice.

    The effect of diction on tone is quite different in the next poem. As you read it, see if you can pick out and name the types of diction marked in it and their effect(s).

DOLOR
— Theodore Roethke —

I have known the inexorable sadness of pencils,
Neat in their boxes, dolor of pad and paper-weight,
All the misery of manilla folders and mucilage,
Desolation in immaculate public places,
Lonely reception room, lavatory, switchboard,   5

DOLOR. *Dolor* means "sadness," with perhaps a pun on "dollar."

The unalterable pathos of basin and pitcher,
Ritual of multigraph, paper-clip, comma,
Endless duplication of lives and objects.
And I have seen dust from the walls of institutions,
Finer than flour, alive, more dangerous than silica,   10
Sift, almost invisible, through long afternoons of tedium,
Dropping a fine film on nails and delicate eyebrows,
Glazing the pale hair, the duplicate gray standard faces.

[1948—U.S.A.]

In part abstract, formal, Latinate (for instance, "inexorable," "mucilage," "Desolation") and in part concrete, colloquial, Saxon (for instance, "pencils," "boxes," "paperweight"), the poem is mixed in diction. The effect of this dictional mix is to raise the mundane lives of human beings who work in offices and "institutions" to the level of tragedy while simultaneously suggesting the terrible reduction of human dignity that the modern workplace entails. The poem's formal vocabulary creates an elevated tone of high seriousness (suggesting tragedy) against which its colloquial vocabulary sounds especially mundane and tame (suggesting diminishment). But from either perspective, "Dolor" communicates equally an emotion it names: "pathos," a tragic pathos of lives confined, routinized, and wasted. This theme is embodied and imparted here primarily through diction.

The last poem we will look at is one in which tone (or attitude) is of primary importance in determining theme, tone here established almost solely by diction. Question particularly, as you read, the diction and tone of the last two lines.

TO A FRIEND WHOSE WORK HAS COME TO TRIUMPH
— Anne Sexton —

Consider Icarus, pasting those sticky wings on,
testing that strange little tug at his shoulder blade,
and think of that first flawless moment over the lawn
of the labyrinth. Think of the difference it made!
There below are the trees, as awkward as camels;   5
and here are the shocked starlings pumping past
and think of innocent Icarus who is doing quite well:
larger than a sail, over the fog and the blast
of the plushy ocean, he goes. Admire his wings!

TO A FRIEND.   Compare this poem with Yeats's "To a Friend Whose Work Has Come to Nothing" (p. 522).   **1.** *Icarus:* A figure in Greek mythology. Icarus is the son of Daedalus, who fashioned two pairs of wings out of feathers and wax. Daedalus warned his son not to fly too high (too close to the sun); but Icarus failed to heed the warning, so his wings melted and he plunged into the sea.   **4.** *labyrinth:* Daedalus also engineered the great labyrinth of Crete. Ironically, both he and his son were subsequently imprisoned in it, the only way out being up (thus the invention of the wings).

Feel the fire at his neck and see how casually   10
he glances up and is caught, wonderously tunneling
into that hot eye. Who cares that he fell back to the sea?
See him acclaiming the sun and come plunging down
while his sensible daddy goes straight into town.

[1962—U.S.A.]

This poem is marked throughout by dictional shifts that help establish a distinction between the mundane and the miraculous: "sticky" and "pumping past" as against "first flawless moment," or "doing quite well" as against "Admire his wings!" But the contrast is especially prominent in the poem's last two lines. "See him acclaiming the sun and come plunging down" has a grandeur to it, a sense of elevation, and a tone of wonder; "while his sensible daddy goes straight into town," on the other hand, is rhythmically boring and dictionally vapid. "Acclaiming" and "plunging" could describe a hero, but not "sensible daddy." Because of the diction and tone of the lines, we can say with certainty that the speaker thinks "acclaiming the sun" is more than worth the price of "plunging down," while going "straight into town" is of no consequence at all: that is, the grand attempt, even if it ends in failure, is more of a triumph than the safe course, even if it succeeds. "Who cares that he fell back to the sea?" all but states this theme. But what most conveys the attitude of the speaker is the tonal contrast suggested by the contrasting diction of the poem's last two lines.

SUMMARY SUGGESTIONS: UNDERSTANDING VOICE, TONE, AND DICTION

1. Determine what people a poem presents you with. There will always be a speaker, but is there also a listener? Are there any players of importance? Determine the relationship of speaker and listener (if there is one) and look to see how players function—especially what they tell us about the speaker.

2. As to speakers, determine as soon as possible whether the speaker of a given poem is a character, a persona, or the poet. This determination often makes all the difference between understanding a poem and being baffled by it. Surely, for instance, to take a speaker like the Duke ("My Last Duchess") as the poet would be to misconstrue the tone of the poem and so miss the meaning entirely.

3. Take each poem as an utterance and hear as you read. If possible, read poems aloud; if not, at least sound them out in your head.

4. Be alert to the tones of voice that can and must be heard in poems. Tone, remember, expresses attitude, and attitude can be the theme. Really to hear the tone(s) of a poem, then, and to be able to describe its tone or perhaps contrasting tones can be the best way of getting at and articulating its theme.

5. Always pay close attention to the words of a poem, not just to their dictionary meanings but equally to their dictional qualities. Are they colloquial or formal, concrete or abstract, literal or metaphorical, and so forth? These questions need to be asked

and answered of every poem, for diction is instrumental in creating tone, and tone, once more, is central in our understanding of the meaning.

WRITING ON THE PEOPLE IN POETRY

Writing about the people in poetry is in many ways similar to writing about the people in fiction. Consequently, you may wish quickly to review what we have considered about the latter in Section II (pp. 102–03). There are, of course, significant differences as well. Poetry demands more inference on the part of the reader than does prose fiction, and the types of people in poetry are fewer than those found in fiction, reducible to three types of speaker (a character, a persona, the poet), to listeners, and to players.

Of these, the speaker who is a character—like the Duke in "My Last Duchess" (pp. 235–36)—is always appealing to write on. Since the point of such a poem is most often character revelation, the object of a critical paper would be the delineation of the nature of the speaker by way of details from the text. For instance, the thesis of an essay on "My Last Duchess" could be that the Duke is an egomaniac who can tolerate nothing and no one not under his complete control. To support this thesis, you would simply need to outline the implied story of his relationship with his last Duchess, suggesting that she was in no way at fault and thus that his growing detestation reveals *his* mania. You could also, of course, bring other aspects of the poem to bear as support. The way the Duke speaks—fluid on matters of art, faltering on human relationships—tells us much, as does his interest in a possible dowry (however much he protests otherwise) and his pride in the statue of Neptune "Taming a sea-horse" (which seems symbolic of the Duke and his Duchess). In sum, because the object of the poem is character revelation (its theme), the object of your paper would be to show what is revealed and how.

In so showing, note, you would have to be selective. Most poems contain much more direct or implied information than could be used in any one paper. You must pick and choose according to your needs and what you are trying to accomplish, as I did earlier when treating "My Last Duchess." In that treatment, I did not even mention the business of the dowry or the statue of Neptune because, however revealing, these details were not immediately relevant to my purpose. Note, too, that when dealing with speakers of any type—character, persona, poet—certain questions are helpful in coming to understand what evidence one might muster in talking about a speaker: What is the setting (in both place and time) in which we find the speaker? What situation is he or she in? (Both setting and situation are covered in the next chapter.) What has happened in the past as revealed in the poem that might help support one's analysis? What does the speaker say about others that is revealing? Is there a listener? What role does the listener, if there is one, play in revealing the speaker? What does the speaker say about himself or herself? What kind of words (a matter of diction) does the speaker use? What is the speaker's tone? Can we believe the speaker? By answering these questions before you begin to write, you should be well on your way to a significant paper on the speaker of your chosen poem, whether character, persona, or poet.

Writing on a persona can be much like writing on a speaker who is a character, depending on the amount of information we are given. Some poems, to be sure, give so little information that there really isn't much to be said in particular about their speakers. What, for instance, do we learn about the persona who speaks "My Son, My Executioner" (p. 220)? Well, he is probably twenty-five, he is the father of a new-born son, and he feels his mortality intensely for the first time in his life because of the infant. All we can conclude from this information is that the speaker of the poem is generic, its voice less that of an individual than of collective humanity. But this conclusion itself could be a thesis: with its generic speaker, "My Son, My Executioner" is aimed at reflecting feelings about parenthood that are universal. One's support here could come from the insights of psychology, for instance, and/or from personal experience, and/or from other literary works that touch on the same kind of feelings.

Many other poems spoken by personae (the plural of persona), however, contain more than enough information to write directly on their speakers. For example, consider "Stopping By Woods on a Snowy Evening" (pp. 216–17) and "To a Friend Whose Work Has Come to Triumph" (pp. 243–44). In different ways, each provides solid material for a paper on its speaker. We learn a good deal about the speaker of the Frost poem: he wouldn't want anyone to see him stopping; indeed, he thinks it strange himself; his normal frame of mind is matter-of-fact and businesslike; he is weary from his journey; he has probably never felt before what he feels during the course of the poem, as the shift in tone toward the end suggests; and so forth. All this information could be used in analyzing the speaker and demonstrating that the poem's theme concerns the complexity of human feelings underlying the roles we play and the masks we put on for others and for ourselves. Writing on "To a Friend Whose Work Has Come to Triumph" might seem more difficult because we are given so little information about its speaker overtly. We know that she is addressing herself to a friend who has suffered a grand failure and is trying to console the friend with a story she has taken from Greek mythology. She is probably, therefore, fairly well educated and possibly warm and loving. More we cannot say until we consider the poem's last two lines. Because the diction and resulting tone of these lines are attributable to its speaker, whatever can be said about these lines is evidence for an analysis of the speaker. And a good deal can be said. A paper on the persona speaking the poem, thus, could take off from its closure and concern her mentality and values as implied there: admiring the daring Icarus rather than his "sensible daddy," she is a romantic in the full meaning of the word. That could be your thesis; you would support it by textual evidence (the diction and tone of the last lines, for instance) and by bringing a viable definition of "romantic" to bear on the poem and its speaker. Thereby, both the poem's speaker and its theme would be illuminated.

When the speaker is clearly the poet, one thing you can do is to research the biography of the poet and use what you find to help support some thesis having to do with the poet-speaker. For instance, if you did not know that Milton was blind, research would reveal the fact, which, brought to your reading of "Methought I Saw" (p. 238), would clarify the poem and be prime evidence for what you might say about its speaker—his situation, his concerns, his feelings. But the poet-speaker need not be treated any differently from the other two types of speaker. Though we can almost always (though not always) trust the poet as to what is said in a poem of a personal nature, what we learn about the poet is no different from what we learn about characters or personae. After all, characters and personae are also people, or at least are meant to be thought of as such. And we must pay attention to matters like diction and tone just as much in a poem spoken by the poet as in a poem spoken by a character or persona. In other words, if you write a paper about a speaker who can be identified as the poet, you can treat the speaker just as you would a character, the only difference being that your textual evidence will probably be biographically true instead of imagined.

Because the function of listeners is to listen, we usually learn almost nothing about them. All we learn about the listener in "My Last Duchess" (pp. 235–36) is that he is an envoy of a Count whose daughter the Duke wishes to marry; all we learn about the listener in "How Annandale Went Out" (p. 224) is that he agrees that the speaker should not be hanged. Therefore, nothing much could be written about either as a separate character. Nevertheless, listeners have important functions and can provide material for writing. Why *this* listener? How does the indicated presence of the specified listener change the poem? What does the listener help reveal about the speaker? These are some of the questions to ask of listeners, questions whose answers can provide excellent support for a paper on a speaker or the basis of a thesis for a paper on the function of the listener. For example, that the Duke is speaking to the envoy of the Count whose daughter he (the Duke) hopes to marry is so outrageous—because of what the Duke reveals—that we can only stand amazed at the egomania of the man. The identity of the listener, then, would be the crowning piece of support in a paper on the egomaniacal nature of the Duke. Or you could write a paper on irony in "My Last Duchess," given its particular listener, in which case your thesis would be that the function of the envoy is to provide ironic commentary on the Duke and his prospects. Or you could argue that the function of the listener in "How Annandale Went Out" is to make the poem's perspective on euthanasia clear despite the emotional turmoil experienced by the doctor who speaks the poem. Whatever the case, listeners are often instrumental in poems and so should not be overlooked when it comes to writing.

Finally, there are players—characters other than the speaker who play a crucial role in our understanding of the speaker and the poem as a whole. Players can be just as compelling as speakers to write on and always offer prime support for whatever is said about speakers. We saw this earlier when we looked at "My Last Duchess": I focused on the Duchess and thereby came to an understanding of the Duke. Any paper on the Duke would have to use as evidence what could be justly inferred about the Duchess. But you could also write a paper on the Duchess alone, your thesis being, say, that she was not the creature the Duke would have us believe. In this case, anything said about the Duke would be support. When reading and then writing about players, ask: How is the player described? Can I trust the speaker doing the describing? If the player speaks directly or is quoted, what is his or her diction and tone? What do they tell? How does the player interact with the speaker and other players? How does the player act generally? What does the player say, think, feel? Answering these questions can lead to a greater understanding of the poem at hand as well as to a thesis adequate for a paper of some dimension.

POEMS FOR STUDY AND WRITING ASSIGNMENTS

MY LAST DUCHESS
— Robert Browning —

Writing Assignment

Suppose that the envoy of "My Last Duchess" (pp. 235–36) is to write a report about his interview, assessing the personality of the Duke and his eligibility to marry the Count's daughter. What might the envoy write? Write the report yourself, expressing the envoy's reasoning and conclusions.

THE RUINED MAID
— Thomas Hardy —

"O'Melia, my dear, this does everything crown!
Who could have supposed I should meet you in Town?
And whence such fair garments, such prosperi-ty?"
"O didn't you know I'd been ruined?" said she.

"You left us in tatters, without shoes or socks,   5
Tired of digging potatoes, and spudding up docks;
And now you've gay bracelets and bright feathers three!"
"Yes: that's how we dress when we're ruined," said she.

"At home in the barton° you said 'thee' and 'thou,'   *farm*
And 'thik oon,' and 'theäs oon,' and 't'other'; but now   10
Your talking quite fits 'ee for high compa-ny!"
"Some polish is gained with one's ruin," said she.

"Your hands were like paws then, your face blue and bleak
But now I'm bewitched by your delicate cheek,
And your little gloves fit as on any la-dy!"   15
"We never do work when we're ruined," said she.

"You used to call home-life a hag-ridden dream,
And you'd sigh, and you'd sock; but at present you seem

THE RUINED MAID. *Ruined:* in the Victorian sense. **6.** *spudding up docks:* digging up weedy herbs.

To know not of megrims° or melancho-ly!"   *low spirits*
"True. One's pretty lively when ruined," said she.   20

"I wish I had feathers, a fine sweeping gown,
And a delicate face, and could strut about Town!"
"My dear—a raw country girl, such as you be,
Cannot quite expect that. You ain't ruined," said she.

[c. 1886—Great Britain]

Questions

1. By what means are the two voices of this poem distinguished? For instance, how does the diction of each speaker differ and what does the difference tell about each?
2. Describe Melia's tone. How does it differ from her friend's?
3. What is ironic about Melia's final statement?
4. What does the irony of the poem imply about Victorian morality in general? What is the poem's theme?

Writing Assignments

1. Though it contains no direct reference to Victorian social mores, "The Ruined Maid" makes a satirical statement about Victorian morality. Write a dialogue of your own in which something (your school's administration, for instance) is criticized without being overtly mentioned.
2. In a paragraph, write a critique of this poem. Is it successful as to its satiric intent? Is it successful technically (for example, in its management of diction and tone)? Defend your judgments with textual evidence.
3. Write a short paper comparing and contrasting the poem's two speakers. Consider what in the poem leads us to see each as we do. Also, consider how the poem's theme emerges out of the comparison of Melia and her country friend.

NAMING OF PARTS
— Henry Reed —

Today we have naming of parts. Yesterday,
We had daily cleaning. And tomorrow morning,
We shall have what to do after firing. But today,
Today we have naming of parts. Japonica
Glistens like coral in all of the neighboring gardens,   5
   And today we have naming of parts.

This is the lower sling swivel. And this
Is the upper sling swivel, whose use you will see,
When you are given your slings. And this is the piling swivel,

Which in your case you have not got. The branches   10
Hold in the gardens their silent, eloquent gestures,
    Which in our case we have not got.

This is the safety-catch, which is always released
With an easy flick of the thumb. And please do not let me
See anyone using his finger. You can do it quite easy   15
If you have any strength in your thumb. The blossoms
Are fragile and motionless, never letting anyone see
    Any of them using their finger.

And this you can see is the bolt. The purpose of this
Is to open the breech, as you see. We can slide it   20
Rapidly backwards and forwards: we call this
Easing the spring. And rapidly backwards and forwards
The early bees are assaulting and fumbling the flowers:
    They call it easing the Spring.

They call it easing the Spring: it is perfectly easy   25
If you have any strength in your thumb: like the bolt,
And the breech, and the cocking-piece, and the point of balance,
Which in our case we have not got; and the almond-blossom
Silent in all of the gardens and the bees going backwards and forwards,
    For today we have naming of parts.   30

[1946—U.S.A.]

Questions

1. There are two contrasting voices in this poem, one that of a drill instructor and one that of a green recruit being instructed in the names of the parts of a rifle. Where does the first voice stop and the second begin in each stanza?
2. What indicates where one voice stops and the other begins? What, for example, is different about the diction and tone of each voice?
3. Are there any other differences helping us to distinguish the two?
4. Where do you imagine the instructor and the recruit(s) to be? What is the relevance of the poem's setting?
5. What point does the poem make by means of the contrast of instructor and recruit?

Writing Assignments

1. Write a short paper on the differences between the two voices of "Naming of Parts"—how they are established, what they sound like, and what the point of the contrast is.
2. Write an essay contrasting the instructor and the recruit as to mentality, sensitivity, beliefs, and values. Toward which of the two would the poem sway us? How do you know?

SOLILOQUY OF THE SPANISH CLOISTER
— Robert Browning —

1

Gr-r-r—there go, my heart's abhorrence!
   Water your damned flower-pots, do!
If hate killed men, Brother Lawrence,
   God's blood, would not mine kill you!
What? your myrtle-bush wants trimming?   5
   Oh, that rose has prior claims—
Needs its leaden vase filled brimming?
   Hell dry you up with its flames!

2

At the meal we sit together:
   Salve tibi! I must hear   10
Wise talk of the kind of weather,
   Sort of season, time of year:
Not a plenteous cork-crop: scarcely
   Dare we hope oak-galls, I doubt:
What's the Latin name for "parsley"?   15
   What's the Greek name for Swine's Snout?

3

Whew! We'll have our platter burnished,
   Laid with care on our own shelf!
With a fire-new spoon we're furnished,
   And a goblet for ourself,   20
Rinsed like something sacrificial
   Ere 'tis fit to touch our chaps°—   *jaws*
Marked with L for our initial!
   (He-he! There his lily snaps!)

4

Saint, forsooth! While brown Dolores   25
   Squats outside the Convent bank
With Sanchicha, telling stories,
   Steeping tresses in the tank,

SOLILOQUY OF THE SPANISH CLOISTER.   No date is given, but we might imagine a medieval setting.   **10.** *Salve tibi:* "Hail to thee." The words in italics that follow are Brother Lawrence's.   **14.** *oak-galls:* abnormal growths on oak leaves used for tanning.

Blue-black, lustrous, thick like horsehairs,
  —Can't I see his dead eye glow,   30
Bright as 'twere a Barbary corsair's?
  (That is, if he'd let it show!)

5

When he finishes refection,°   *dinner*
  Knife and fork he never lays
Cross-wise, to my recollection,   35
  As do I, in Jesu's praise.
I the Trinity illustrate,
  Drinking watered orange-pulp—
In three sips the Arian frustrate;
  While he drains his at one gulp.   40

6

Oh, those melons? If he's able
  We're to have a feast! so nice!
One goes to the Abbot's table,
  All of us get each a slice.
How go on your flowers? None double?   45
  Not one fruit-sort can you spy?
Strange! And I, too, at such trouble,
  Keep them close-nipped on the sly!

7

There's a great text in Galatians,
  Once you trip on it, entails   50
Twenty-nine distinct damnations,
  One sure, if another fails:
If I trip him just a-dying,
  Sure of heaven as sure can be,
Spin him round and send him flying   55
  Off to hell, a Manichee?

8

Or, my scrofulous° French novel   *evil*
  On grey paper with blunt type!

---

31. *Barbary corsair:* The Barbary Coast was the haven for pirates, known for lechery.   **39.** *Arian:* a Christian heresy that denied the doctrine of the trinity.   **49.** *Galatians:* In Galatians 15–23, St. Paul enumerates various "works of the flesh" that can lead to damnation. Our speaker, perhaps overreading, has found "twenty-nine" possibilities.   **56.** *Manichee:* a reference to the Manichean heresy, which involved the concept that evil is a self-contained force outside of the domain of God.

Simply glance at it, you grovel
    Hand and foot in Belial's gripe: 60
If I double down its pages
    At the woeful sixteenth print,
When he gathers his greengages,
    Ope a sieve and slip it in't?

9

Or, there's Satan! one might venture   65
    Pledge one's soul to him, yet leave
Such a flaw in the indenture
    As he'd miss till, past retrieve,
Blasted lay that rose-acacia
    We're so proud of! *Hy, Zy, Hine* . . .   70
'St, there's vespers! *Plena gratiâ*
    Ave, Virgo! Gr-r-r—you swine!

[1842—Great Britain]

Questions

1. Where is the unnamed monk who speaks this soliloquy? Where is Brother Lawrence? Draw a sketch of the monastery grounds and locate the two men.
2. Why does the speaker hate Brother Lawrence? What are his reasons? Is Brother Lawrence truly hateable?
3. Comment on any dictional effects in the poem that seem to stand out. What do they reveal about the speaker?
4. What is the speaker's tone overall? How does his tone affect you?
5. Characterize the speaker and support your conclusions about him from the poem. Is he trustworthy? Is he evil? Is he a warm, loving man who has been foully wronged by Brother Lawrence? Is he a half-crazed lunatic who should be locked up?

Writing Assignments

1. (a) Write a paragraph describing the tone of the poem's speaker and how that tone is established.
   (b) In a separate paragraph, discuss your response to "Soliloquy of the Spanish Cloister" and why you so respond.
2. Write a paper in answer to question 5 above. Begin by stating your conclusion as to the kind of person the speaker is. Then support that statement (your thesis) by a commentary

---

60. *Belial:* one of the chief devils.   **69–70.** Knowing that he can't touch Lawrence, the speaker is willing to sell his soul (though he believes himself clever enough to outwit Satan at the last) to have Lawrence's prize "rose-acacia" blasted. *Hy, Zy, Hine:* an invocation to the Devil or the grunts of a madman.   **71–72.** *Plena gratiâ / Ave, Virgo:* the speaker reverses the opening words of the *"Ave Maria"* ("Hail Mary, full of grace").

on the poem stanza by stanza, using something from each stanza as textual evidence for your characterization of the speaker.

THE UNKNOWN CITIZEN
— W. H. Auden —

(to JS/07/M/378
This Marble Monument
Is Erected by the State)

He was found by the Bureau of Statistics to be
One against whom there was no official complaint,
And all the reports on his conduct agree
That, in the modern sense of an old-fashioned word, he was a saint,
For in everything he did he served the Greater Community.   5
Except for the War till the day he retired
He worked in a factory and never got fired,
But satisfied his employers, Fudge Motors Inc.
Yet he wasn't a scab or odd in his views,
For his Union reports that he paid his dues,   10
(Our report on his Union shows it was sound)
And our Social Psychology workers found
That he was popular with his mates and liked a drink.
The Press are convinced that he bought a paper every day
And that his reactions to advertisements were normal in every way. 15
Policies taken out in his name prove that he was fully insured,
And his Health-card shows he was once in hospital but left it cured.
Both Producers Research and High-Grade Living declare
He was fully sensible to the advantages of the Instalment Plan
And had everything necessary to the Modern Man,   20
A phonograph, a radio, a car and a frigidaire.
Our researchers into Public Opinion are content
That he held the proper opinions for the time of year;
When there was peace, he was for peace; when there was war, he went.
He was married and added five children to the population,   25
Which our Eugenist says was the right number for a parent of his generation,
And our teachers report that he never interfered with their education.
Was he free? Was he happy? The question is absurd:
Had anything been wrong, we should certainly have heard.

[1939—Great Britain]

Questions

1. Who speaks this poem? Whom or what does he speak for? On what occasion and to whom might it be spoken?
2. What kind of diction does the poem exhibit overall? What is the effect of the many unusually long lines here? What tone emerges from the combination of diction and line length?
3. What attitude is suggested by the speaker's tone?
4. What is ironic about the title? What attitude does the poem (as opposed to its speaker) suggest? What is its theme?

Writing Assignments

1. Write a paragraph or more on how "The Unknown Citizen" communicates to the reader the opposite of what its imagined speaker intends. Consider both diction and irony in this regard.
2. In a paragraph, discuss the tone of the poem—what the tone is overall, how it is created, and how it affects the reader.
3. What is it to be a citizen? Formulate a thesis and write a paper on the subject, using "The Unknown Citizen" to provide either support or contrast.

HIGH WINDOWS

— Philip Larkin —

When I see a couple of kids
And guess he's fucking her and she's
Taking pills or wearing a diaphragm,
I know this is paradise

Everyone old has dreamed of all their lives—   5
Bonds and gestures pushed to one side
Like an outdated combine harvester,
And everyone young going down the long slide

To happiness, endlessly. I wonder if
Anyone looked at me, forty years back,   10
And thought, *That'll be the life;*
No God any more, or sweating in the dark

About hell and that, or having to hide
What you think of the priest. He
And his lot will all go down the long slide   15
Like free bloody birds. And immediately

Rather than words comes the thought of high windows:
The sun-comprehending glass,
And beyond it, the deep blue air, that shows
Nothing, and is nowhere, and is endless.   20

[1974—Great Britain]

Questions

1. How does the diction of the first stanza affect you? What is its tone? What attitude does this tone reveal?
2. Contrast the tone of the first four stanzas and that of stanza five. What does the difference in tone tell us about the values and regrets of the speaker?
3. What is the meaning of "sun-comprehending"? What other word is it a pun on? In what way is the other word relevant in this context?
4. In a number of ways, including diction and tone, "High Windows" expresses an attitude about the modern world. What attitude does it express? How so?

Writing Assignments

1. Write a paragraph on the last two lines of the poem. What about the modern world does the "air," paradoxically, make concrete?
2. In a paper, discuss the modern world as you see it. What values, if any, are characteristic of our time? What seems confusing? Is this a good time in which to be alive? If you agree with the position suggested in "High Windows," use it as support; if you disagree, then argue against the view it gives voice to.
3. In a paragraph or short paper, contrast the diction and tone of the first and last stanzas of "High Windows." What attitudes on the part of the speaker does the tone of each convey? What, then, is the poem's theme?

TO HIS COY MISTRESS
— Andrew Marvell —

Had we but world enough, and time,
This coyness, lady, were no crime.
We would sit down, and think which way
To walk, and pass our long love's day.
Thou by the Indian Ganges' side   5
Shouldst rubies find; I by the tide
Of Humber would complain. I would
Love you ten years before the flood,
And you should, if you please, refuse
Till the conversion of the Jews.   10

TO HIS COY MISTRESS.   **7.** *Humber:* the Humber is a river in England, half a world away from the Ganges.   **10.** *the conversion of the Jews:* according to tradition, at the end of time.

My vegetable love should grow
Vaster than empires and more slow;
An hundred years should go to praise
Thine eyes, and on thy forehead gaze;
Two hundred to adore each breast,   15
But thirty thousand to the rest;
An age at least to every part,
And the last age should show your heart.
For, lady, you deserve this state,
Nor would I love at lower rate.   20
    But at my back I always hear
Time's wingèd chariot hurrying near;
And yonder all before us lie
Deserts of vast eternity.
Thy beauty shall no more be found,   25
Nor, in thy marble vault, shall sound
My echoing song; then worms shall try
That long-preserved virginity,
And your quaint honor turn to dust,
And into ashes all my lust: 30
The grave's a fine and private place,
But none, I think, do there embrace.
    Now therefore, while the youthful hue
Sits on thy skin like morning dew,
And while thy willing soul transpires   35
At every pore with instant fires,
Now let us sport us while we may,
And now, like amorous birds of prey,
Rather at once our time devour
Than languish in his slow-chapped power.   40
Let us roll all our strength and all
Our sweetness up into one ball,
And tear our pleasures with rough strife
Through the iron gates of life:
Thus, though we cannot make our sun   45
Stand still, yet we will make him run.

[1681—Great Britain]

11. *vegetable:* steadily growing.   **40.** *slow-chapped:* slow-jawed, time here envisioned as a monstrous mouth.   **42.** *one ball:* like the ball of the sun, our measurer of time.   **43–44.** *tear . . . gates:* as birds or prisoners, perhaps, might tear at things through the bars of their cages or cells? The reference is enigmatic. Another suggestion offered is that the "gates" are metaphorical equivalents of the labia, and that generally the reference is to the entry to the female citadel, specifically to the hymen (for the mistress is a virgin).

Questions

1. "To His Coy Mistress" is a poem of shifting tones. How so? Contrast the three sections of the poem as to tone and the effects of the tone of each.
2. How are these differences created? Consider diction and pace in this regard.
3. Characterize the speaker. What kind of a man is he? What personality traits can be ascribed to him? What are his beliefs?
4. The poem rises above its situation (an attempted seduction) to a vision of human life in the universe as we know it. What is that vision? What is the poem's theme?

Writing Assignments

1. How might the mistress respond to the speaker here? Write a reply from the young woman answering the speaker's arguments point by point. Before you do, you must decide whether or not she has been won over by his reasoning.
2. In a paragraph or more, discuss the contrasting tones of the poem. Establish what the tone of each section is and suggest how the tone of each is created. Consider as well the attitude that the speaker's tones convey, or the relationship between his various tones and the meaning overall.
3. Write a paper arguing for or against the speaker's view of things, the vision of life that the poem as a whole embodies. What is this vision? What makes it compelling or objectionable in your eyes?

SETTING, SITUATION, AND IMAGERY

CONCRETION AGAIN

There are two modes of thought and, correspondingly, two types of language or language use: the analytic and the symbolic, the abstract and the concrete. Poetry tends toward the latter in each case, toward symbolic thought and concrete language. As we have seen, the realm of poetry is the realm of concretion. A poet would always choose *a thick steak, marbled and sizzling,* over *a nutrious meal, pickled beets* over *vegetables,* or *a chocolate sundae with gobs of whipped cream* over *edibles.* That is, the diction of poetry is by and large concrete, appealing to our senses and sensory selves. Poetry is concrete in many other ways as well: in its sense of voice, in its tones, in the way it moves, and so forth. There are even poems that are visually concrete in the way they look, their words and lines organized so as to create a picture. Here are two such poems, the first by a college freshman and the second by a religious poet of the seventeenth century. Notice how the shape lends excitement to the voice of the first and mirrors the diminishment and enlargement spoken of in the second.

THE ANNOUNCER
— Paul Bicotti —

It's
3 and 2.
Here's the pitch.
Wham, out to deep left.
He's got it on the bounce.
And there's the throw,
Here's the play
At the plate.
Holy cow,
I

Think
He's gonna
Score.

EASTER WINGS
— George Herbert —

Lord, who createdst man in wealth and store,°   *abundance*
    Though foolishly he lost the same,
        Decaying   more   and   more
            Till   he   became
                Most poor: 5
                With   thee
            O   let   me   rise
      as   larks,   harmoniously,
    And   sing   this   day   thy   victories:
Then   shall   the   fall   further   the   flight   in   me.   10

My   tender   age   in   sorrow   did   begin;
    And   still   with   sicknesses   and   shame
        Thou   didst   so   punish   sin,
            That   I   became
                Most thin.   15
                With   thee
           Let   me   combine,
    And   feel   this   day   thy   victory;
    For,   if   I   imp   my   wing   on   thine,
Affliction   shall   advance   the   flight   in   me.   20

[1633—Great Britain]

The problems we have with poetry, I think, stem not from the density of poems but from our tendency to jump ahead of ourselves, looking first for ideas instead of focusing on feeling (in both senses of the word), seeking abstract meanings instead of grounding ourselves in whatever aspects of form are dominant in a poem and finding meaning there. As William Carlos Williams puts it in his poem "A Sort of a Song" (p. 436), "No ideas / but in things." A poem means through what it is, its form, its concreteness. When reading a poem, therefore, do not let your thoughts wander into the higher reaches of abstraction; always relate what you are thinking to something concrete in the poem, something that you can either literally or imaginatively hear, taste, touch, smell, see, or feel kinesthetically. Hear people speaking and their various tones, feel rhythms, and, in the mind's eye, see settings, situations,

EASTER WINGS.   **18.** *this day:* Easter.   **19.** *imp:* a term from falconry: extra feathers were "imped" (grafted) onto the wings of a hawk to improve its speed and power.

and images. Then you should be in a position to think seriously and exactly about meaning.

PLACES AND TIMES

Whether actual (a real time, a real place), imagined, or mythical, **settings** function in poems just as they do in stories. In both, a setting can be merely a backdrop (and sometimes no setting at all is suggested), or it can be important for reasons of characterization and for its symbolic implications (we will discuss this last possibility in the next chapter). The difference between poetry and fiction with respect to setting is that in fiction setting is usually specified and described in some detail, whereas in poetry it is usually only hinted at, leaving us to infer (as always) the period of time or the kind of place the poem entails. "My Last Duchess" (pp. 235–36) is an exception, for in it both time and place are specified exactly: Italy during the Renaissance, in a gallery of the palace of the Duke of Ferrara. Browning's "Soliloquy of the Spanish Cloister" (pp. 251–53), on the other hand, is fairly typical. To be sure, the title tells of the poem's setting in general (both time and place), but we must infer from what the speaker says where in particular he and Brother Lawrence are located. We can do so from the line "He-he! There his lily snaps!" Brother Lawrence must be tending flowers in a flower bed outside the monastery, and the speaker, perhaps concealed behind a bush or a tree, must be at some distance watching the object of his detestation. Other poems give us even less to go on, though setting is nevertheless important in them. Look quickly at Auden's "The Unknown Citizen" (p. 254), for instance. Where is the speaker of this eulogy, and what historical era are we to imagine? The answer to the second question is clearly our own (implied by "Fudge Motors" and other of the poem's details). As to the first, given the subject matter of the poem and especially its title and epigraph, I would locate the speaker in a graveyard, dedicating the tomb of the unknown citizen. To see the poem as spoken in such a setting is to find another layer of concretion, which acts as a commentary on the kind of state that the poem concerns.

In the following poem, setting and its details play a key role. As you read the poem, visualize, taste, and smell (in your imagination) every item of food that the speaker mentions. Thereby, try to enter the speaker's being and feel what she feels.

THE HEALTH-FOOD DINER
— Maya Angelou —

No sprouted wheat and soya shoots
And Brussels in a cake,
Carrot straw and spinach raw,
(Today, I need a steak).

Not thick brown rice and rice pilau
Or mushrooms creamed on toast,

5

Turnips mashed and parsnips hashed,
(I'm dreaming of a roast).

Health-food folks around the world
Are thinned by anxious zeal,   10
They look for help in seafood kelp
(I count on breaded veal).

No Smoking signs, raw mustard greens,
Zucchini by the ton,
Uncooked kale and bodies frail   15
Are sure to make me run

                    to

Loins of pork and chicken thighs
And standing rib, so prime,
Pork chops brown and fresh ground round   20
(I crave them all the time).

Irish stews and boiled corned beef
and hot dogs by the scores,
or any place that saves a space
For smoking carnivores.   25

[1983—U.S.A.]

Clearly, the speaker here is in the wrong place. But the better we imagine that place and the food served there, the better we can feel with the speaker and understand her desires. The poem's setting (in a health-food restaurant) provides a foil against which those desires stand out with clarity and marvelous humor. Whatever one's convictions, surely, "The Health-Food Diner" is amusing. And, finally, the point of the poem is its humor, which here springs from the interaction of setting and character.

Marvell's "The Garden" is another poem that demonstrates the importance setting can have and how it can communicate ideas and feelings in a poetic manner—that is, directly, through concretions. Read the poem with an eye toward the concretion of its setting and see if you can't come thereby to a perception of its meaning.

THE GARDEN
— Andrew Marvell —

How vainly men themselves amaze
To win the palm, the oak, or bays,

THE GARDEN.   **1.** *amaze:* perplex, drive mad.   **2.** *the palm, the oak, or bays:* symbolic crowns for athletic, civic, and poetic merit, respectively.

And their uncessant labors see
Crowned from some single herb or tree,
Whose short and narrow vergèd shade   5
Does prudently their toils upbraid;
While all flowers and all trees do close
To weave the garlands of repose.

Fair quiet, have I found thee here,
And innocence, thy sister dear!   10
Mistaken long, I sought you then
In busy companies of men;
Your sacred plants, if here below,
Only among the plants will grow.
Society is all but rude,   15
To this delicious solitude.

No white nor red was ever seen
So am'rous as this lovely green.
Fond lovers, cruel as their flame,
Cut in these trees their mistress' name;   20
Little, alas, they know or heed
How far these beauties hers exceed!
Fair trees! wheres' e'er your barks I wound,
No name shall but your own be found.

When we have run our passion's heat,   25
Love hither makes his best retreat.
The gods that mortal beauty chase,
Still in a tree did end their race:
Apollo hunted Daphne so,
Only that she might laurel grow;   30
And Pan did after Syrinx speed,
Not as a nymph, but for a reed.

What wond'rous life in this I lead!
Ripe apples drop about my head;
The luscious clusters of the vine   35
Upon my mouth do crush their wine;
The nectarine and curious peach
Into my hands themselves do reach;
Stumbling on melons as I pass,
Ensnared with flowers, I fall on grass.   40

17. *white nor red:* of a woman's face.   **28.** *Still:* always.   **29, 31.** *Daphne* and *Syrinx:* nymphs in Greek mythology who, fleeing Apollo and Pan, respectively, were turned by Zeus into a laurel and a reed.

Meanwhile the mind from pleasure less
Withdraws into its happiness;
The mind, that ocean where each kind
Does straight its own resemblance find,
Yet it creates, transcending these,   45
Far other worlds and other seas,
Annihilating all that's made
To a green thought in a green shade.

Here at the fountain's sliding foot,
Or at some fruit tree's mossy root,   50
Casting the body's vest aside,
My soul into the boughs does glide;
There like a bird it sits and sings,
Then whets, then combs its silver wings;
And till prepared for longer flight,   55
Waves in its plumes the various light.

Such was that happy garden-state,
While man there walked without a mate;
After a place so pure and sweet,
What other help could yet be meet!   60
But 'twas beyond a mortal's share
To wander solitary there;
Two paradises 'twere, in one,
To live in paradise alone.

How well the skillful gard'ner drew   65
Of flowers and herbs this dial new,
Where, from above, the milder sun
Does through a fragrant zodiac run;
And as it works, th' industrious bee
Computes its time as well as we.   70
How could such sweet and wholesome hours
Be reckoned but with herbs and flowers?

[1681—Great Britain]

We should see Marvell's garden at first as a place, one containing apple trees and melons, a fountain, and one of those sundials whose face is composed of flowers carefully chosen for color contrast. Yet this garden is also reminiscent of that mythological garden of Christian tradition—Eden, the earthly paradise. Like Eden, the garden in the present poem is an innocent place where all human needs are met without labor: the "clusters" of grapes "crush their wine" into the speaker's mouth of their own accord (lines 35–36); the nectarines and peaches put themselves into his hand (lines 37–38). Like Eden, too, Marvell's garden witnesses a fall as the speaker trips "on melons" ("melon" comes from the Greek *mēlopepōn,* meaning "apple"); but here he falls only "on grass" (line 40), for ultimately the garden paradise of this poem is not a place, as such—whether real or mythological—but a state of mind. The theme of the poem, that is, concerns the potential of the mind to be its own paradise. The mind, which contains all things (lines 43–44) and is even able to conceive of "other worlds" (line 46), can create what it does not find in the busy, bewildering world of men: quiet, innocence, solitude—all caught in the phrase "a green thought in a green shade" (line 48). The setting of "The Garden," then, is in part a backdrop against which we can envision the speaker, in part a paradise of his imagination, but most a concretion that embodies and gives shape to the wordless inner world of his concerns and hopes, which of themselves are shapeless.

CIRCUMSTANTIAL EVIDENCE

There are long narrative poems with narrators and plots just like those found in stories. But lyric poems (our primary concern) are too short to allow for anything like plot development. Instead of plots, therefore, lyric poems present us with **situations** (usually one per poem, but sometimes more). That is, most short poems take off from some circumstance (which we usually must infer) and take us into the inner world of the speaker by focusing on his or her reaction to that circumstance, which, therefore, can be prime evidence when it comes to interpreting a poem. When we were looking into stories of this sort, I suggested that situational stories concern the inner lives of characters rather than their lives in the external world of action. The same is true of lyric poems. Indeed, everything in a short poem points to the inner life of its speaker, as we have just seen when discussing setting. It is the world of felt experience that poetry draws on and embodies, and that world is made manifest in part by the circumstances or situations that we find the people of poetry in and that we in part define them against.

Think back to some of the poems we have looked at already, now with an eye to situation. "Stopping By Woods on a Snowy Evening" (pp. 216–17) presents us with the situation specified by its title: stopping by woods. This is what draws the speaker out and lets us share for a moment his inner being. The situation of "Naming of Parts" (pp. 249–50) entails class instruction in the parts of the rifle, a situation that pits two opposite mentalities against each other and lets us see into each. "To His Coy Mistress" (pp. 256–57) centers on an attempted seduction, its situation forming a base for the speaker's expressing and our understanding his world view; and "My Last Duchess" (pp. 235–36) presents two situations, one past (that of the Duke and the Duchess) and one present (that of the Duke and the envoy)—and both serve to reveal the Duke. In all these cases, the situation(s) in which we find the speaker helps us to understand the complex self he is. The same is true of the poems we have discussed so far in this chapter. "Easter Wings" presents us with a man praying to God, fervently hoping for his salvation: the mentality of the speaker is thus concretized (that is, by the situation we find him in). However different, "The Health-Food Diner" also presents us with a situation that brings out something about the inner life of its speaker. Note, incidentally, that a situation does not have to be elaborate to function. It can be nothing more than someone's sitting in a restaurant or praying to God or looking at a garden (the situation of "The Garden"). Whatever serves to bring out the inner being of a speaker is situation enough.

Let's look at a poem now with respect to its situation alone. The situation of this poem and the feeling that its situation evokes are so universal that you should have no problem understanding the poem's emotion as you participate in what the speaker says.

[A NARROW FELLOW IN THE GRASS]
— Emily Dickinson —

A narrow Fellow in the Grass
Occasionally rides—
You may have met Him—did you not
His notice sudden is—

The Grass divides as with a Comb—   5
A spotted shaft is seen—
And then it closes at your feet
And opens further on—

He likes a Boggy Acre
A Floor too cool for Corn—   10
Yet when a Boy, and Barefoot—
I more than once at Noon
Have passed, I thought, a Whip lash
Unbraiding in the Sun
When stooping to secure it   15
It wrinkled, and was gone—

Several of Nature's People
I know, and they know me—
I feel for them a transport
Of cordiality—   20

But never met this Fellow
Attended, or alone
Without a tighter breathing
And Zero at the Bone—

[c. 1866—U.S.A.]

Who has not also felt "Zero at the Bone" when coming on a snake in the grass (the poem's situation)? We all know the feeling, but it took a poet to find the right words for it. My point, however, is that the poem's situation is central, giving rise to the expression of feeling that we can imaginatively participate in and therefore feel firsthand. But to feel it firsthand, we must use our imaginations. Situations, like settings, are concretions only to the extent that we allow the imagination to work and visualize a poem's situation along with its setting (if there is one).

THE CONCRETION OF IMAGERY

As we have seen and shall continue to see, there are many types of concretion found in poetry. **Imagery** is one of the most important, images being verbal concretions (words that call up remembered sensations) used to convey states of mind, ideas, and feelings through sense impression. When you visualize a setting or imagine its sounds and smells, or when you see a speaker in a given situation, you are responding to one aspect of a poem's imagery. Setting and situation, that is, fall under the broader category of imagery, at least to the extent that they are a means of conveying thoughts and feelings concretely. Perhaps the following poem and its revision, both done by a freshman student, will help establish the nature of imagery concretely and therefore solidly.

STAR TREK

— Maria Migoya —

Streaking through the universe
at speeds of warp factor five,
the fearless crew of the Enterprise
discover strange new things
and battle with Klingons and Romulans too.
But then the hour is up
and it's time to return to reality.

"Streaking" is a good word, active and visually vivid; "fearless," however, is colorless, "things" is vague, and "return to reality" is too abstract to return us to Earth with a thud, as we should be returned for the contrast of the poem and the feeling it embodies to come across with full force. Compare the original with the revision, which ends with an image that has the impact desired.

Streaking through the universe
at speeds of warp factor five,
the intergalactic crew of the Enterprise
discover strange new worlds,
beaming down to battle Klingons and Romulans
or, with phasers set on stun,
to meet with pointed-eared Vulcans

or the Asterix of Sram.
But then the hour is up
and it's time to do the dishes.

"It's time to do the dishes"—I can feel my hands in the greasy water; I can feel the tedium of the job like a heavy weight and, generalizing, the tedium of ordinary life as compared to the excitement of the imagination (a word derived from "image"). That is what an image, as opposed to an abstract statement, can accomplish: both images and statements communicate ideas, but only the image does so in a way that fully engages the reader, body as well as mind. As you read the next poem, try to respond to its imagery physically: that is, feel in your imagination the winter's blast and then the warm spring rain on your cheek, the comfort of your own bed, and the softness of your lover's arms.

WESTERN WIND
— Anonymous —

Western wind, when will thou blow,
   The small rain down can rain?
Christ, if my love were in my arms
   And I in my bed again!

[15th cen.—Great Britain]

Picture a man a long way from home (the poem's situation) in freezing weather (the immediate setting) longing for spring and his return to the arms of his love and to his own bed (a projected setting). Can't you feel intensely the longing of the speaker as well as his pain? The voice rings true, and, by working through the senses, the imagery communicates a depth of feeling as only imagery can. And that, of course, is the point.

Imagery can also communicate ideas, ideas as complex as any stated in abstract language. The next poem, delightful because of the playfulness of its imagery, is a poem of ideas, though it communciates feeling as well.

[RATIONALISTS]
— Wallace Stevens —

Rationalists, wearing square hats,
Think, in square rooms,
Looking at the floor,

WESTERN WIND.   *Western wind:* a wind both of autumn and of spring.
[RATIONALISTS].   **1.** *square hats:* such as the hats worn by academics at graduation exercises.

Looking at the ceiling.
They confine themselves   5
To right-angled triangles.
If they tried rhomboids,
Cones, waving lines, ellipses—
As, for example, the ellipse of the half-moon—
Rationalists would wear sombreros.   10

[1923—U.S.A.]

At the beginning of this chapter I distinguished between two modes of thought—analytic and symbolic—and two corresponding types of language—abstract and concrete. That is what Stevens is doing here, though in a way more memorable (we tend to remember images and to forget abstractions) because concrete. One can see the "square hats," the "square rooms," the "right-angled triangles" of the world of Stevens's rationalists and feel the tedium, according to Stevens, of this straight-line world (tedium being the feeling of lines 3–4). How different is the world of "Cones, waving lines, ellipses," the sensual world of the man of imagination. Much is said by way of the poem's mathemetical imagery; but the single image of the "sombreros" as opposed to academic "square hats" caps the poem and brings its meaning home. The summary image of a number of rationalistic academics in sombreros is funny, and meaningful by being funny: that we can hardly imagine the two together is the poem's point, made by visual images rather than by discursive statement.

One final poem here, one that concerns poetry itself and suggests the centrality in poetry of concretion and imagery.

ARS POETICA
— Archibald MacLeish —

A poem should be palpable and mute
As a globed fruit,

Dumb
As old medallions to the thumb,

Silent as the sleeve-worn stone   5
Of casement ledges where the moss has grown—

A poem should be wordless
As the flight of birds.

A poem should be motionless in time
As the moon climbs,   10

ARS POETICA.   The title means "the art of poetry."

Leaving, as the moon releases
Twig by twig the night-entangled trees,

Leaving, as the moon behind the winter leaves,
Memory by memory the mind—

A poem should be motionless in time   15
As the moon climbs.

A poem should be equal to:
Not true.

For all the history of grief
An empty doorway and a maple leaf.   20

For love
The leaning grasses and two lights above the sea—

A poem should not mean
But be.

[1926—U.S.A.]

What is said in this poem is not strictly true, for, after all, poems are made of words, they move in time, and they mean things. Many poems also contain abstractions, as, in fact, does "Ars Poetica" itself (for instance, "A poem should be wordless" is purely abstract). Nevertheless, through its paradoxes the poem gives voice to a truth about poetry (though not the whole truth). Poems mean primarily by what they are, how they are constructed—they mean by their being, and so the being comes first. And poems are "palpable" and do tend to be "mute," communicating by way of imagery as opposed to direct statement. This is what the poet is saying as he finds for every abstraction an appropriate image, thus concretizing his thought by giving it a physical dimension. The poem's theme, at heart, is that poetry communciates through the senses, or that in poetry ideas and feelings are made real by imagery. Such, of course, has been the argument of this chapter all along.

SUMMARY SUGGESTIONS: UNDERSTANDING SETTING, SITUATION, AND IMAGERY

1. Try to visualize a poem's setting (whether in time or space) if a setting is indicated. Where is the speaker? At what time of day or in what era of history is he or she speaking? What details contribute to an understanding of the physical or temporal locale? These are the questions to ask about setting, though do not forget that some poems will not yield answers because no setting is indicated in them.

2. If a poem has a setting indicated, establish what it is, imagine it in as much detail as the poem allows, and then take the step to meaning. Why *this* setting? What does it tell about the speaker? How is it related to other elements in the poem and possibly to its theme? Sometimes the setting will be only a backdrop;

more often, however, it will be significant in one way or another. In what way is for you to decide.

3. Like a setting, a situation should be visualized if a poem presents a situation, and most do. Of situations, ask questions like: What is happening in a poem? What is the speaker's circumstance? What can be imagined to have happened before the poem begins that might have given rise to the present situation? How might its situation be taken as evidence in interpreting the poem?

4. This last question moves us toward meaning, which is always the ultimate step that must be taken. What does the speaker's circumstance reveal about him or her? How does it contribute to an understanding of the theme? These are the final and most important questions to be asked. Your answers should be tied in with everything else you perceive about a poem as you work your way toward a full interpretation.

5. What are the major images of a poem? How are they related? How do they affect you? What do they make you feel emotionally by making you feel physically? How do your associations and feelings (in both senses) with regard to the poem's imagery bear on its possible meaning? What intangible states of mind and feeling do the images convey? This is the progression of questions that should be asked of poetic imagery. Because imagery is at the heart of what a poem is, to answer these questions is to be on one's way to full comprehension.

WRITING ON IMAGERY

Because imagery is central to poetry, writing on imagery can be especially rewarding. Even a single image can provide interesting material for writing. An analysis of a single image and its relation to other aspects of a poem, for instance, could prove to be excellent support in a paper on some topic other than imagery. A discussion of one or more images could provide vital support in a consideration of a poem's mood, say, for mood in poetry is in part created by imagery. We saw this in discussing Stevens's poem about rationalists (pp. 268–69), a poem in which a comic mood results from the incongruous image of academics wearing not the traditional mortarboards but sombreros. Then, too, in discussing a poem's theme, you will almost always need to refer to one or more of its images, for theme in poetry is always expressed either partially or fully by way of imagery.

A single image can also be taken as the basis of a whole paper. In this regard, consider the following poem, composed of just one image.

IN A STATION OF THE METRO
— Ezra Pound —

The apparition of these faces in the crowd;
Petals on a wet, black bough.

[1916—U.S.A.]

Writing on the poem, you could begin by suggesting its setting and situation: the speaker is underground in the Paris subway (the Metro) looking at the faces of people in the crowd on the platform. Your thesis could be, simply, that a single image can comprise a whole poem, as is the case here, where both setting and situation serve to lead us to the poem's heart—its second line and, backdrop aside, its single image. Moving on, you would want to discuss each of the poem's two lines as to their implications, overtones, feelings, or whatever. You might note, for instance, that while the word "apparition" in the first line means "appearance" as well as "a sudden or unusual sight," it also connotes something of a spiritual nature, insubstantial and dreamlike. And this is in part the feeling of the two lines taken together. "But what," you might ask, "is unusual about seeing a crowd of people in the subway?" Your answer would be that it is not the seeing of the crowd that is unusual but the seeing of the individuals who compose it and the speaker's way of seeing them. That way of seeing is at the core of the poem and is what the second line gives shape to. "Petals on a wet, black bough"—suddenly, each face, standing out against the dimness of the platform, seems unique and precious to the speaker. Seeing the members of the crowd as unique individuals, he sees each as a spiritual being and almost unspeakably beautiful. Here is the sort of thing that you could say about the poem's core image, which embodies and radiates the love we sometimes feel for our fellow humans. That I have almost written a paper myself on the poem and its one image (and left much unsaid, at that) proves the point: if sufficiently complex, a single image in a poem can generate an entire paper.

Usually, however, it is a poem's main images (three or four, perhaps) and their relationship that form the basis for a paper having to do with imagery. Indeed, a poem can be interpreted with respect to its imagery alone. A discussion of the garden imagery and all its implications in Marvell's "The Garden" (pp. 262–64), for instance, could lead to a fairly full interpretation of the poem as well as to a substantial paper. But how would one proceed in writing such a paper? Because it is all but impossible to talk of imagery without a specific poem to refer to, let's take another poem here and see how its images and their cumulative effect could be a focus of a paper on its imagery.

SONNET 73

— William Shakespeare —

That time of year thou mayst in me behold
When yellow leaves, or none, or few, do hang
Upon those boughs which shake against the cold,
Bare ruined choirs, where late the sweet birds sang.
In me thou see'st the twilight of such day   5
As after sunset fadeth in the west;

SONNET 73.   All Shakespeare's sonnets are from a sequence of sonnets (1–154).

Which by and by black night doth take away,
Death's second self that seals up all in rest.
In me thou see'st the glowing of such fire,
That on the ashes of his youth doth lie,   10
As the deathbed whereon it must expire,
Consumed with that which it was nourished by.
This thou perceiv'st, which makes thy love more strong,
To love that well which thou must leave ere long.

[1609—Great Britain]

The poem consists of three four-line units (called "quatrains") and a concluding two-line "couplet." In the couplet, we discover that the poem has a listener and a slight situation: one person is telling another what it feels like to grow old. But what is to our immediate purpose is what happens in the three quatrains, each of which contains a central image related to the images of the other two quatrains, with the first quatrain containing a notable subsidiary image as well. A paper on the poem could proceed straightforwardly: a statement of thesis—for instance, that the poem is basically composed of three related images—then a paragraph per quatrain discussing the main image of each (with perhaps a separate paragraph given over to the secondary image in line 4), and finally a conclusion, perhaps embracing the poem's last two lines.

Of the first quatrain you would want to note that the "time of year" spoken of is autumn, in fact, late autumn. This is the first primary image, one that helps paint the setting. We are to imagine a tree with yellow leaves on one bough, none on another, and just a few on a third. The image speaks of fall and decay. We are also to feel the coldness of the season, reminding us of the winter to come. Suddenly, another image is introduced, but one that seems in perfect accord with the autumnal setting: we are to image a ruined chapel, its "choirs" (where services would be sung by a chorus) "ruined," echoing only with the whistle of the wind. The "boughs" are like such choirs because they are skeletal and because their singers (the birds) have departed. Summing up, you could say that the imagery of the first quatrain captures and communicates a sense of chill and decay. By extending that imagery, one also feels a sense of foreboding, for winter (death) is just around the corner.

You might begin your next paragraph by observing that the primary image of the second quatrain is also an image of setting: having been told of a season, we are now told of a time of day. It is twilight, and what light there is left is fading "in the west" as night approaches. Again there is a sense of chill, as one thinks of a late autumn evening; and again the specter of death hovers close, for since ancient times night has been thought of as the brother or "second self" of death. You would want to take account of these matters in treating the second quatrain. You would also want to stress that the imagery of the second quatrain and the feeling imparted by its imagery parallel and reinforce the imagery and feeling of the first.

The primary image of the third quatrain—yet another image of setting—is that of a dying fire feeding on and so consuming itself. The effect of this image taken together with the other images we have looked at could be the focus of your last middle or supporting paragraph. Picture yourself sitting by a dying fire on a late autumn evening, with the outline of a ruined chapel barely visible; no birds are to be heard, only the icy voice of the cold north wind. What do you feel? I feel cold, I feel vulnerable, I feel exposed. This is how it feels to grow old; this is what the poem communicates vividly and with immediacy. And here could be the final point of your paper: that because Shakespeare's imagery, like imagery in general, conveys thought and feeling not as information but as experience, the poem touches us physically and thence emotionally, its words working as much through the body as the mind.

You could move to a conclusion by taking off from this last point and suggesting that it is because we have been made to feel (in both senses) that the speaker can take the surprising turn he does in the couplet. We might have expected him to say: you see that I am growing old, so you should love me all the more because I won't be around much longer. Instead, the whole thing is turned on the listener/reader: love well now because of *your own* impending death, which you see in me (that is, in the speaker). The couplet can take this turn because we have been made to feel intensely the encroachment of age and death through the poem's pattern of imagery. We feel our own involvement in what the speaker is saying because the poem's imagery touches us with the force of experience. Treating the couplet in this way—that is, by relating its impact to that of the rest of the poem—could provide an excellent conclusion for an excellent paper on imagery.

As I said earlier, a poem can be interpreted in terms of its imagery alone. We have just seen how. You have perhaps also come to understand how rewarding it can be to focus on a poem's images and to see how they relate to each other. Addressing imagery can lead as well to meaningful discoveries about the relationship of poems written by the same poet. Many poets use images recurrently in their poems: bird imagery is found extensively in one, highway and motorcycle imagery in another, water and ship imagery in a third. Should you read a number of poems by the same poet (in Chapter 8, Emily Dickinson, Robert Frost, and William Carlos Williams are represented by a large selection of poems each, allowing for this kind of a study), you might find it valuable to investigate recurrent imagery in that poet. Such imagery is rich in possibilities for writing. What you might do, for instance, is to establish what image or images recur and to suggest how this knowledge illuminates the poems and perhaps also the aims and characteristic thought of the poet. (Incidentally, there is significant recurrent imagery in all three poets just mentioned.)

But whatever you write on, be aware that imagery is central to poetry and so should never be out of mind. You can always find support in one or another of a poem's images, and most poems cannot be understood in the first place if their images are neglected. So you should always consider a poem's images as you go about constructing its possible meaning and gathering your ideas for whatever paper is at hand.

POEMS FOR STUDY AND WRITING ASSIGNMENTS

CLEAN CURTAINS
— Carl Sandburg —

New neighbors came to the corner house at Congress and Green streets.

The look of their clean white curtains was the same as the rim of a nun's bonnet.

One way was an oyster pail factory, one way they made candy, one way paper boxes, strawboard cartons.

The warehouse trucks shook the dust of the ways loose and the wheels whirled dust—there was dust of hoof and wagon wheel and rubber tire—dust of police and fire wagons—dust of the winds that circled at midnights and noon listening to no prayers.

"O mother, I know the heart of you," I sang passing the rim of a nun's bonnet—O white curtains—and people clean as the prayers of Jesus here in the faded ramshackle at Congress and Green.

Dust and the thundering trucks won—the barrages of the street wheels and the lawless wind took their ways—was it five weeks or six the little mother, the new neighbors, battled and then took away the white prayers in the windows?

[1918—U.S.A.]

Questions

1. Describe the setting of this poem. What feeling does its setting convey?
2. What situation does the speaker tell us of? How does this situation give rise to the poem's central image?
3. The poem's dominant emotion is pathos. How so? Why?
4. What human desire does the image of the curtains—called "white prayers" at the end of the poem—give voice to? What is the poem's theme?

Writing Assignments

1. Write a description of something in such a way (for instance, by the use of images) that, without any direct statement, some particular feeling and perhaps some idea emerge from the description alone.
2. In a short paper, discuss the image of the "white curtains" as it relates to the poem's theme. Why are the curtains called "white prayers," and why the association of the curtains with a "nun's bonnet" and "the prayers of Jesus"? What does it mean that the dust wins out? What longing does the imagery express and, at the end, what painful understanding?

A DAY BEGINS
— Denise Levertov —

A headless squirrel, some blood
oozing from the unevenly
chewed-off neck

lies in rainsweet grass
near the woodshed door.   5
Down the driveway

the first irises
have opened since dawn,
ethereal, their mauve

almost a transparent gray,   10
their dark veins
bruise-blue.

[1965—U.S.A.]

Questions

1. What is the setting here? How is the setting important with respect to meaning as the poem proceeds?
2. What are the poem's two main images (both of which are aspects of the setting)? What feelings does each evoke?
3. In what ways are the images contrasting? What is the import of the contrast?
4. Yet "bruise-blue" suggests similarity as well. How so? To what end?
5. What do the two main images together say about nature and our human awareness of nature? What of the poem's title in this regard?

Writing Assignments

1. Write a paragraph about the contrasting images of "A Day Begins." What are the poem's central images? How are they contrasting? What is the point of the contrast?
2. In several paragraphs or a paper, discuss the nature of poetic imagery—that is, what images are and what they do in poems. Use "A Day Begins" as your source of examples throughout.

UPON JULIA'S CLOTHES
— Robert Herrick —

Whenas in silks my Julia goes,
Then, then, methinks, how sweetly flows
That liquefaction of her clothes.

Next, when I cast mine eyes, and see

That brave vibration, each way free,
O, how that glittering taketh me!

[1648—Great Britain]

Questions

1. What situation does the poem ask us to imagine?
2. In part, the speaker here is describing Julia's clothes and bearing. But the poem's imagery also intimates things about her that cannot be seen. What? (In answering, consider the word "brave," which in the Renaissance meant "boastful" or "challenging.")
3. How does the context bring out the underlying concreteness of "liquefaction" and thereby make it an image?
4. As well as suggesting the physical look and personality of Julia, this short poem communicates the feeling of its speaker. How so? What does he feel? What does the word "glittering" tell about his feeling?

Writing Assignments

1. In a paragraph, describe the personality of Julia and tell, trait by trait, how you arrived at your conclusions about her.
2. In a paragraph, describe what the speaker feels and tell how you came to understand what he is feeling.

DISILLUSIONMENT OF TEN O'CLOCK
— Wallace Stevens —

The houses are haunted
By white night-gowns.
None are green,
Or purple with green rings,
Or green with yellow rings,   5
Or yellow with blue rings.
None of them are strange,
With socks of lace
And beaded ceintures.
People are not going   10
To dream of baboons and periwinkles.
Only, here and there, an old sailor,
Drunk and asleep in his boots,
Catches tigers
In red weather.   15

[1923—U.S.A.]

DISILLUSIONMENT OF TEN O'CLOCK. **9.** *ceintures:* belts, strings, girdles.

Questions

1. What is the setting here with respect to both time and place? Why this setting?
2. What will the people haunting the "houses" dream of, do you suppose? What kind of people are they? In what ways are they in contrast with the "old sailor"?
3. What is contrasting in the imagery of the poem? How is the contrast related to the "disillusion-ment" of the poem's title?
4. In light of the poem's imagery, what is its theme?

Writing Assignments

1. In a paragraph, answer either question 2 or 3 above. Whichever you choose, be sure to state the attitude the poem embodies about the people referred to in its first two lines.
2. In a paragraph or more, discuss the poem's imagery, focusing on the feelings, attitudes, and ideas it concretizes and conveys.

THE DEATH OF THE BALL TURRET GUNNER
— Randall Jarrell —

From my mother's sleep I fell into the State,
And I hunched in its belly till my wet fur froze.
Six miles from earth, loosed from its dream of life,
I woke to black flak and the nightmare fighters.
When I died they washed me out of the turret with a hose.

[1945—U.S.A.]

Questions

1. The setting here provides the central image. What is it?
2. In his note, Jarrell states that the gunner "looked like the foetus in the womb." What phrase in the poem brings this image of a foetus to mind? If we keep this image in mind, the poem seems especially ironic. How so?
3. The gunner, a boy of probably nineteen or twenty, "woke" to conscious life because of the "black flak and the nightmare fighters." What is ironic here? What other ironies does the poem express?
4. In light of the poem's many ironies, as well as its image of the "foetus in the womb," the image of the last line might also be taken as ironic (as well as horrific). In what way is what is described like an abortion? How is this ironic? How does this extension of the foetus image act as a commentary on "the State"?

THE DEATH OF THE BALL TURRET GUNNER. *Ball Turret:* "A ball turret was a plexiglass sphere set into the belly of a B-17 or B-24, and inhabited by two .50 caliber machine-guns and one man, a short small man. When this gunner tracked with his machine guns a fighter attacking his bomber from below, he revolved with the turret; hunched upside-down in his little sphere, he looked like the foetus in the womb. The fighters which attacked him were armed with cannon firing explosive shells. The hose was a steam hose."—Jarrell's note.

5. The poem in its way (that is, poetically) makes a strong statement against war. How so? How does its imagery, which includes both its setting and its situation, communicate strong antiwar feelings?

Writing Assignments

1. (a) Write a paragraph on the poem's main ironies. What is ironic? How does irony help shape the reader's response?
   (b) In a separate paragraph, state your response to "The Death of the Ball Turret Gunner" and detail your reasons for so responding. Remember that your reasoning is more important to your reader than your statement of response alone.
2. In a short paper, discuss the poem's imagery and the irony that its images in context establish. Discuss as well the effect of the poem's images both as to their ironic character and otherwise.
3. Write a critique of "The Death of the Ball Turret Gunner." Does the poem communicate something specific and significant through its imagery (if so, what?), or is the poem disjointed, so that its images do not really hook up? Are its images vivid and moving, or are they opaque and only confusing? Quote from the poem at all points in arguing your case.

COME IN

— Robert Frost —

As I came to the edge of the woods,
Thrush music—hark!
Now if it was dusk outside,
Inside it was dark.

Too dark in the woods for a bird   5
By sleight of wing
To better its perch for the night,
Though it still could sing..

The last of the light of the sun
That had died in the west   10
Still lived for one song more
In a thrush's breast.

Far in the pillared dark
Thrush music went—
Almost like a call to come in   15
To the dark and lament.

But no, I was out for stars:
I would not come in.

I meant not even if asked,
And I hadn't been.   20

[1942—U.S.A.]

Questions

1. What are the poem's setting and situation?
2. What are the two dominant visual images that the setting entails? What associations do these images usually carry? In context, what opposite perspectives or states of mind do they suggest?
3. What other (nonvisual) image is important in the poem? How so? Why this particular kind of image?
4. What does the image "pillared dark" bring to mind? How are its associations relevant? In what way is the diction of the phrase, along with that of the second line of stanza one, contrasting with the diction of the last stanza?
5. What is the tone of the first four stanzas? In what way is the tone of the fifth stanza contrasting? What does the shift in tone suggest? State the poem's theme in terms of this tonal contrast.

Writing Assignments

1. Write a paragraph on the dominant images of "Come In." First name them, and then discuss the opposing meanings they suggest.
2. "Come In" concerns contrasting perspectives, one entertained but rejected in favor of another. In a paper, discuss these perspectives especially with regard to how they are established (through diction, tone, and imagery in particular). Point out, too, exactly what the speaker rejects and what he turns toward, and what his act of rejection suggests about external reality and the perceiving mind.
3. Reread "Stopping By Woods on a Snowy Evening" (pp. 216–17), a poem whose situation and accompanying imagery are recurrent in Frost. Now write an essay on "Stopping By Woods" and "Come In" together, pointing to the similarity of their imagery and showing how a knowledge of each sheds light on the other.

❋ 4 ❋

FIGURATION, METAPHOR, AND SYMBOL

FIGURATIVE LANGUAGE AND FIGURES OF SPEECH

All language is intended to be and is taken to be either literal or figurative, though sometimes the two get mixed up. For instance, is a sheriff coming back with his hounds from a manhunt speaking literally or figuratively when he says, "My dogs are tired"? Is he referring to his hounds or his feet? If the former, then the statement is literal; if the latter, it is figurative. Literal language, that is, is language meant to be taken at face value; figurative language, in contrast, would be absurd if so taken. Rather, it is language designed to give shape to ("figuration" means "the act of giving shape to") ideas and feelings that themselves are formless. So, about to begin a new semester, you might say, "This term I'm going to get on the stick." Clearly, you would not be speaking literally; you would be using a figurative phrase to give shape to formless feelings and intentions in a succinct way.

Such is the prime function of figurative language wherever found: to give shape to complex feelings, ideas, intentions in a succinct way. And figurative language abounds everywhere, in prose and speech as well as in poetry, the difference between poetry and other ways of using language simply being that in poetry the figurative aspects of language are concentrated and thus brought to our attention. Figures of speech crop up even when one intends to be purely literal. Take the definition of "literal language" above as "language meant to be taken at face value." Helping to define the meaning of "literal," "at face value" is itself figurative *in this context*.

Usually, note, it is context alone that determines whether something is literal or figurative. If, for example, you found some old coins, you might wonder whether they would be taken by a coin dealer at face value or whether they might be worth more or less than face value. In this context, "at face value" is not figurative. Nor does figuration come into play when a child says, before dinner, "My hands are clean." When a criminal says the same thing to the police, however, the phrase becomes figurative.

Or consider the following lines, entitled "Second Fig" (meaning "figure"—"First Fig" is to be found in Chapter 6, pp. 357–58), by Edna St. Vincent Millay:

Safe upon the solid rock the ugly houses stand:
Come and see my shining palace built upon the sand.

[1922—U.S.A.]

There is an easy commerce here between the literal and the figurative in that the literal becomes figurative before our eyes. The first line at first seems entirely literal, for houses can be and often are built on rock. In contrast, the second line is purely figurative, making use of the common phrase "built upon sand" to express a set of values totally different from those of the "solid rock" people. And in context now with the second line, the first becomes figurative in retrospect, embodying values opposite to those of the speaker.

Understatement and Exaggeration

Figurative language can be classified into a large number of **figures of speech,** as they are called. You are probably familiar with a good number, though you may not know all of their names. For instance, **understatement** and **exaggeration** (or **hyperbole**) are two figures found frequently in speech and literature alike. When we wish to stress something, we often either understate or exaggerate: "He won the race by a nose"; "She won the race by a mile." Because neither statement is intended to be taken as literally true, both are figurative, or figures of speech.

Synesthesia

Synesthesia is another common figure, this entailing a deliberate sensory confusion whereby one type of sensation is spoken of in terms of another. "A loud tie" or "a dry wine" are both examples of synesthesia, for a tie (which we can see or touch) cannot be loud literally ("loud" referring to hearing), nor can a wine literally be dry (a word that refers to the sense of touch). The following lines from Keats's "Ode to a Nightingale" show how vivid synesthesia can be. Imagining the qualities of a vintage wine, Keats writes:

Tasting of Flora and the country green,
    Dance, and Provencal song, and sunburnt mirth!
O for a beaker full of the warm South.

Oxymoron

A third common figure is **oxymoron,** which involves the linkage of two words ordinarily used as opposites. An oxymoron, then, is a kind of paradox, or a statement that seems self-contradictory but proves to have valid meaning. "Guest host" is an oxymoron, as is "heavy lightness" in the descriptive sentence "The horse jumped with a heavy lightness." Some also take "military intelligence" to be oxymoronic.

Metonymy and Synecdoche

Two related figures that are of particular importance are **metonymy** and **synecdoche.** Metonymy refers to the calling of something by the name of something else with which it is associated: "skirt" for a girl, "jock" for a male athlete, "Tex" for someone from Texas. Synecdoche refers to the calling of something by the name of one of its own parts or attributes: "wheels" for a car, "bow-wow" for a dog, "Smiley" for a car salesman. The following poem, which contains three oxymorons, is built on a synecdoche. See if you can pick out the oxymorons and determine the synecdoche in question.

DELIGHT IN DISORDER
— Robert Herrick —

A sweet disorder in the dress
Kindles in clothes a wantonness.
A lawn about the shoulders thrown
Into a fine distractiön;
An erring lace, which here and there   5
Enthralls the crimson stomacher;
A cuff neglectful, and thereby
Ribbons to flow confusedly;
A winning wave, deserving note,
In the tempestuous petticoat;   10
A careless shoestring, in whose tie
I see a wild civility;
Do more bewitch me than when art
Is too precise in every part.

[1648—Great Britain]

"Sweet disorder," "fine distractiön," and "wild civility" are the oxymorons, with which the poet gives expression to a desire for a balance of opposite qualities in female dress and what female dress is here a synecdoche of—"art," the category of things under which clothing falls. In other words, in speaking of female dress, the poet is giving shape to certain abstract qualities that he looks for in art generally and strives to attain, perhaps, in his own poems.

DELIGHT IN DISORDER.   **3.** *lawn:* a piece of fine, sheer linen or cotton.   **4.** *distractiön:* pronounced as having four syllables, like other "-ion" words of the time. But in the present context, the elongation is itself something of a distraction.   **6.** *stomacher:* an ornamental garment worn under the open (and often laced) front of a bodice.

Personification

The final figure we will look at in this section is one that you probably do know by name: **personification,** a figure of speech in which human qualities, motives, or capacities are attributed to an abstraction, an inanimate object, an animal, or whatever. When we speak of "the long arm of the law," for instance, or of "blind justice," we are making use of personification. In the next poem, the abstraction "love" is personified as Cupid, the ancient god of love, and is given attributes that the speaker sees in herself and in the cruel male she loves. The personification here works to make the nature of the relationship and the speaker's feelings about it palpable and, thus, immediate.

LOVE ARMED

— Aphra Behn —

Love in Fantastic Triumph sat,
Whilst Bleeding Hearts around him flowed,
For whom Fresh pains he did Create,
And strange Tyrannic power he showed;
From thy Bright Eyes he took his fire,   5
Which round about, in sport he hurled;
But 'twas from mine he took desire,
Enough to undo the Amorous World.

From me he took his sighs and tears,
From thee his Pride and Cruelty;   10
From me his Languishments and Fears,
And every Killing Dart from thee;
Thus thou and I, the God° have armed,   *Cupid, god of love*
And set him up a Deity;
But my poor Heart alone is harmed,   15
Whilst thine the Victor is, and free.

[1665—Great Britain]

EXPLICIT METAPHOR AND SIMILE

In that figuration entails giving shape to ideas and feelings, figures of speech necessarily incorporate images. This is true of all of the figures we have looked at thus far and of all we shall discuss hereafter. Indeed, because figures entail images, some critics include figurative language in the general category of imagery. Be that as it may, metaphors of whatever sort almost always involve images. "My love is like a red, red rose," wrote Robert Burns, defining his "love" with the image of a "red rose." This example suggests what metaphor is all about: primarily, metaphor or metaphor making is a way of defining—usually of the abstract or unknown (to the reader) *in terms of* the concrete and the known. For instance, "Deserts of vast eternity," the analogy at the heart of Marvell's poem "To His Coy Mistress" (pp. 256–57), is a metaphor that defines the abstract notion of "eternity" in terms of the concrete reality of "deserts." The word being defined—for example, "eternity"—is called the **tenor;** the word that is doing the defining—for example, "deserts"—is called the **vehicle.** The vehicle of any metaphor carries a weight of meaning over to the tenor, the passive term being defined. In fact, the word "metaphor" comes from a Greek word meaning "to transfer" or "to carry over." An **explicit metaphor** is one in which both tenor and vehicle are expressed overtly, as is the case with "Deserts of vast eternity." A **simile** is an explicit metaphor made logical by the introduction of "as" or "like" or sometimes the suffix "-y" (as in the phrase "a piggy little boy").

Analogy Versus Identity

One thing to be aware of about metaphors is that analogy is not identity. That is, to say "This tree is an oak" is simply to identify the genus and species of a particular organism. The statement, therefore, is literal. In contrast, the statement "This man is an ox" is metaphorical, involving not an identity but an analogy. Similarly, the sentence, "The houses on this block all look like one another" expresses an identity, and thus is not figurative, whereas the sentence "The houses on this block all look like diversely colored sheets drying on a line" states an analogy in the form of a simile and so is figurative. In other words, metaphors entail likeness between *unlike* things: deserts and eternity, for instance, but not deserts and sandy places. It is the unlikeness between terms that makes a statement figurative in the first place, and the perception of similarity in unlikeness that makes it metaphorical. Not all analogies, therefore, are metaphorical. Many, while not stating an identity, are nevertheless literal—for instance, "American men and Arab men are alike in what they look for in a wife." An analogy becomes a metaphor only when the terms (the things likened) are essentially different. When the terms are extremely dissimilar, the metaphor is called a **metaphysical conceit.** The speaker's observation in T. S. Eliot's "The Love Song of J. Alfred Prufrock" that "the evening is spread out against the sky / Like a patient etherized upon a table" is a well-known example.

Simile Exemplified

Eliot's simile suggests that, though the simile may be thought of as a somewhat watered-down type of explicit metaphor, a simile can, like any other type of metaphor, arrest us and make us see. The following poem, as graceful as the bat it describes, further demonstrates the point.

MIND

— Richard Wilbur —

Mind in the purest play is like some bat
That beats about in caverns all alone,
Contriving by a kind of senseless wit
Not to conclude against a wall of stone.

It has no need to falter or explore;   5
Darkly it knows what obstacles are there,
And so may weave and flitter, dip and soar
In perfect courses through the blackest air.

And has this simile a like perfection?
The mind is like a bat. Precisely. Save   10
That in the very happiest intellection
A graceful error may correct the cave.

[1956—U.S.A.]

Quietly reflective, the poem is structured on the one simile "The mind is like a bat," an appropriate analogy because most people think of the mind as existing in some dark place, like a cave, and because the motions of the mind are no less mysterious than those of a bat. The poet develops the analogy and demonstrates its validity in the first two stanzas; then, in the middle of the last stanza, the poem takes a turn in another direction. The human mind may be like a bat in many ways, but, unlike a bat, the mind can learn from error and thereby change the world around. The simile leads to an anti-simile, we might say, which here imparts a sense of discovery. Wilbur's poem demonstrates that the simile, like the other types of metaphor, can be a tool of thinking and a way of understanding.

Explicit Metaphor Exemplified

Like similes, explicit metaphors contain both tenor and vehicle:

Deserts of vast eternity

You are my sunshine

All the world's a stage

mother nature

Each of these examples presents an equation, an equation in which the tenor is defined by certain properties of the vehicle. Read the next poem, which contains two explicit metaphors, with this kind of equation in mind. Identify both tenors and both vehicles, and try to feel what is being said about the tenors by way of the vehicles.

FIRE AND ICE
— Robert Frost —

Some say the world will end in fire,
Some say in ice.
From what I've tasted of desire
I hold with those who favor fire.
But if it had to perish twice,   5
I think I know enough of hate
To say that for destruction ice
Is also great
And would suffice.

[1923—U.S.A.]

In the first two lines, "fire" and "ice" are literal; they become metaphorical, however, as soon as they are associated with "desire" and "hate." "Fire" and "ice," that is, become vehicles, with "desire" and "hate" the tenors. Now, why this association? What is being said by way of these metaphors? Think, for a moment, of hot and cold as we use these states to express various feelings: one might be "hot with lust," for instance, or "burning with desire"; conversely, when we dislike people, we give them "a chilly reception" or "the cold shoulder." In other words, "fire" and "ice" are well matched with "desire" and "hate" and give apt form to these formless feelings. Further, the poem's two metaphors in context with the literal meaning of the first two lines suggest something of larger significance than personal feelings: that if the world should come to an end, the most likely cause would be us and our collective passions and hatreds—the desires of nations for each other's wealth, for example, or the propagation of hatred by one group against another. Not literal fire and ice, then, but metaphorical will probably do us in. Frost's metaphors make us turn to ourselves for answers.

One more poem, one that touches on the same subject matter as the last poem but from a different angle, should serve to round out our discussion of explicit metaphor.

THE PURSE-SEINE
— Robinson Jeffers —

Our sardine fishermen work at night in the dark of the moon; daylight or moonlight
They could not tell where to spread the net, unable to see the phosphorescence
   of the shoals of fish.
They work northward from Monterey, coasting Santa Cruz; off New Year's Point
   or off Pigeon Point

THE PURSE-SEINE. A purse-seine is a fish net shaped like a bag. **2.** *unable to see:* [if] unable to see.
3. places in California.

The look-out man will see some lakes of milk-color light on the sea's night-
purple; he points, and the helmsman
Turns the dark prow, the motorboat circles the gleaming shoal and drifts out
her seine-net. They close the circle   5
And purse the bottom of the net, then with great labor haul it in.

I cannot tell you
How beautiful the scene is, and a little terrible, then, when the crowded fish
Know they are caught, and wildly beat from one wall to the other of their
closing destiny the phosphorescent
Water to a pool of flame, each beautiful slender body sheeted with flame, like
a live rocket   10
A comet's tail wake of clear yellow flame; while outside the narrowing
Floats and cordage of the net great sea-lions come up to watch, sighing in the
dark; the vast walls of night
Stand erect to the stars.

Lately I was looking from a night mountain-top
On a wide city, the colored splendor, galaxies of light: how could I help but
recall the seine-net   15
Gathering the luminous fish? I cannot tell you how beautiful the city appeared,
and a little terrible.
I thought, We have geared the machines and locked all together into interdepen-
dence; we have built the great cities; now
There is no escape. We have gathered vast populations incapable of free survival,
insulated
From the strong earth, each person in himself helpless, on all dependent. The
circle is closed, and the net
Is being hauled in. They hardly feel the cords drawing, yet they shine already.
The inevitable mass-disasters   20
Will not come in our time nor in our children's, but we and our children
Must watch the net draw narrower, government take all powers—or revolution,
and the new government
Take more than all, add to kept bodies kept souls—or anarchy, the mass-
disasters.

These things are Progress;
Do you marvel our verse is troubled or frowning, while it keeps its reason? Or
it lets go, lets the mood flow   25
In the manner of the recent young men into mere hysteria, splintered gleams,
crackled laughter. But they are quite wrong.
There is no reason for amazement: surely one always knew that cultures decay,
and life's end is death.

[1937—U.S.A.]

There are several metaphors in passing here—for instance, "like a live rocket /
A comet's tail wake of clear yellow flame" (lines 10–11)—but the prime metaphor,

on which the poem is built, is the analogy between sardine fishing and the fate of industrial culture. There are three parts to this metaphor: the sardines equal the people in the city, the net equals the city, and the luminescence equals the city lights. Just as the luminescence of the fish is the cause of their being netted, so the city lights (a synecdoche standing for modern technology) will be the cause of our end. Drawing ever more people into it, the city is thus a kind of net holding crowds of human beings and leading to their destruction. For the masses in the cities are "dependent" (line 19) and therefore "helpless" (line 19), like the sardines in the net. When the fuel runs out or when one of any number of things goes wrong with the great machine of our culture, we will be caught in our cities unable to survive because unable to do without the complex support system on which we depend for everything, including our daily bread. Here, as in "Fire and Ice," metaphor makes the point. It is by way of metaphor (explicit in both cases) that Frost and Jeffers show us their conceptions.

IMPLICIT AND EXTENDED METAPHOR

Implicit metaphor is a kind of metaphor in which either the vehicle or the tenor, or both, is not openly expressed but rather is immediately implied. For example, we say that we "spend time": time (tenor), therefore, is money (implicit vehicle). We also "feed computers," which come in "generations" and "spit out" information: an analogy between computers (tenor) and living creatures (implicit vehicle) lurks here. Similarly, if one's words (tenor) are "sharp" or "biting," they must be teeth (implicit vehicle).

"In political life," a political commentator wrote recently, "pygmies abound— giants are rare." Here we have the case of an expressed vehicle (pygmies/giants) and an implicit tenor (politicians). Of the same order are most proverbs. Should you have more help than you need, you might say, "Too many cooks spoil the broth." The statement would be literal if you are a cook in a kitchen full of cooks making broth. As soon as the context changes, however, the statement becomes metaphorical, the tenors for the vehicles "cooks" and "broth" being implicit in the new context. Or if you say that you feel "wounded," your feelings (implicit tenor) are like your limbs or torso (implicit vehicle), and whatever has offended you (implicit tenor) is like a knife or a bullet (implicit vehicle).

Implicit Metaphor: How Established

Implicit metaphors are established in various ways. For instance, some word— verb, adjective, noun—is used in such a way that it cannot be taken literally and so must be part of a metaphor not overtly expressed. To take an example, when the king says to a character named Hotspur, in Shakespeare's *Henry IV, Part I,* "You tread upon my patience," he is using an implicit metaphor rich with overtones. Because one cannot literally tread on patience, "patience" must be a tenor. But what could be the vehicle? What could one literally tread on in connection with a king? Surely, the answer is his robe. It would not be wise to tread on a king's robe; it would be just as foolhardy, the king's analogy suggests, to try his patience.

The king, then, is saying that Hotspur had better back off, as well as suggesting that he (the king) is a very patient man, one indeed clothed in patience.

Another way in which implicit metaphors are constructed is juxtaposition. The poem that follows illustrates how this happens. The vehicle is "bonsai tree." What is the tenor and what are we to carry over from vehicle to tenor here?

A WORK OF ARTIFICE
— Marge Piercy —

The bonsai tree
in the attractive pot
could have grown eighty feet tall
on the side of a mountain
till split by lightning.   5
But a gardener
carefully pruned it.
It is nine inches high.
Every day as he
whittles back the branches   10
the gardener croons,
It is your nature
to be small and cozy,
domestic and weak;
how lucky, little tree,   15
to have a pot to grow in.
With living creatures
one must begin very early
to dwarf their growth:
the bound feet,   20
the crippled brain,
the hair in curlers,
the hands you
love to touch.

[1973—U.S.A.]

In its first sixteen lines, the poem seems to make a literal statement about bonsai trees, how they come about and are maintained. In the closing five lines, however, the bonsai tree becomes a vehicle defining what the speaker conceives to be the condition of women in our world at large. "Bound feet" refers to the Oriental practice of binding the feet of infant girls so as to keep their feet small and thus unable to carry them far. The "curlers" and the "hands you / love to touch" refer to women in Western culture (the latter image being from an advertisement). And the phrase "the crippled brain" capsulizes all that the speaker thinks the culture of males has done to females generally. Having come to understand that "bonsai tree" is a vehicle in a metaphor the implicit tenor of which is the condition of females in a male-dominated world, we should consequently come to see that the metaphor is inherent all along. "Attractive," perhaps "nine inches" (why "nine" as opposed to eight or ten?), "cozy" (like a nest), "domestic," and "lucky . . . to have a pot" (that is, a home) all imply female concerns as defined by male culture and suggest how that culture keeps women from growing "eighty feet tall." In sum, through its implicit metaphor, established by simple juxtaposition, the poem expresses the view of its speaker that males (like the gardener) dwarf women by stunting their emotional and intellectual growth.

As I have just suggested, implicit metaphor is constructed in "A Work of Artifice" by juxtaposition. This way of metaphor making is especially prominent in poetry. What happens in both the last and the following poem happens frequently in poems: because of the introduction of something that cannot be taken literally, or the juxtaposition of something metaphorical and something that at first seems to be literal, what has seemed to be literal suddenly becomes involved in metaphor.

IT BIDS PRETTY FAIR

— Robert Frost —

The play seems out for an almost infinite run.
Don't mind a little thing like the actors fighting.
The only thing I worry about is the sun.
We'll be all right if nothing goes wrong with the lighting.

[1947—U.S.A.]

Except for hyperbole ("almost infinite"), lines 1 and 2 seem purely literal on first reading: they seem to concern the bright prospects of a new play despite the squabbles of its actors. The third line, however, does not fit well: since modern theaters use electric lighting, what does the "sun" have to do with the run of a play? With the third line, we should start to realize that Frost is not speaking of a play at all; he is speaking, rather, of the future of the human race. The play and its actors are vehicles in a metaphor the implicit tenor of which is human life and human beings. "All the world's a stage / And all the men and women merely players," Shakespeare wrote. Frost echoes the figure in his forecast of our probable future. People may fight, but the prospects of the human race are "pretty fair" (thus, "almost infinite run") as long as the sun holds out—that is the prose sense of the poem, possibly meant by Frost as an answer to the pessimism of his earlier poem "Fire and Ice." At any rate, my point is how implicit metaphors are established and how recognized. Often, they are established simply by juxtaposition. They are often recognized simply by the fact that we cannot maintain a literal reading because to do so would be to descend into nonsense. We therefore try to see if a metaphorical reading will work, and when it does, the poem yields its meaning readily, as we have just seen with regard to "It Bids Pretty Fair."

Metaphorical Extension

These last two poems—"A Work of Artifice" and "It Bids Pretty Fair"—not only contain implicit metaphors but proceed by **metaphorical extension** as well. An **extended metaphor** is a metaphor that is sustained through a number of lines, often from the beginning to the end of a poem. In the latter case, the poem is built on an extended metaphor, or structured by way of metaphorical extension. Think back to "A Work of Artifice" and what was said about it. We saw that the poem as a whole turns on one metaphor: thus, that metaphor is extended in it. We saw, too, that once the metaphor is understood, many words and phrases in the poem that seemed literal suddenly become metaphorical, involved in the larger metaphor that the poem is built on. This is common in poems that contain extended metaphors: the diction of the poem is wound up in its central metaphor, and in consequence many words and phrases that seem literal at first sight, and would be literal in a context lacking that metaphor, become implicit metaphors helping further to extend the prime metaphor central to the poem's meaning.

But it is not only poems that contain and are structured on extended metaphors. Indeed, as we will see a little later, everything said in this chapter about metaphor applies to prose fiction and expository prose as much as to poetry. Taking extended metaphor as a case in point, read the following prose passage from Charles Dickens's novel *Hard Times,* pick out its three related metaphors (all explicit), and see if you can determine the extended metaphor—here implicit—that the passage is built on. (The first word, "it," refers to the town in which the novel is set, Coketown, a town caught up in the industrial revolution.)

> It was a town of red brick, or of brick that would have been red if the smoke and ashes had allowed it; but as matters stood it was a town of unnatural red and black like the painted face of a savage. It was a town of machinery and tall chimneys, out of which interminable serpents of smoke trailed themselves for ever and ever, and never got uncoiled. It had a black canal in it, and a river that ran purple with ill-smelling dye, and vast piles of buildings full of windows where there was a rattling and a trembling all day long, and where the piston of the steam engine worked monotonously up and down, like the head of an elephant in a state of melancholy madness. It contained several large streets all very like one another, and many small streets still more like one another, inhabited by people equally like one another. . . .
>
> [1855—Great Britain]

The three explicit metaphors of this passage are "town of unnatural red and black like the painted face of a savage"; "serpents of smoke trailed . . . and never got uncoiled"; and "the piston of the steam engine worked monotonously up and down, like the head of an elephant in a state of melancholy madness." "Savage," "serpents," "elephant"—all three are animate beings reduced in context to things. So it is that the industrial world drains away life in its mechanical systems. Also, however, all three are images of the wild and of the jungle. The primary implication of the passage, thus, is that the cities of the industrial world are jungles (the implicit metaphor extended by the three explicit metaphors) and that industrialization has returned us to a state of savagery.

Now, pick out the prime metaphor (stated explicitly) in the following speech from Shakespeare's *As You Like It* and underline all the words that carry out its extension.

All the world's a stage
And all the men and women merely players:
They have their exits and their entrances;
And one man in his time plays many parts,
His acts being seven ages. At first the infant,   5
Mewling and puking in the nurse's arms.
Then the whining school-boy, with his satchel
And shining morning face, creeping like snail
Unwillingly to school. And then the lover,
Sighing like furnace, with a woeful ballad   10
Made to his mistress' eyebrow. Then a soldier,
Full of strange oaths, and bearded like the pard,
Jealous in honor, sudden and quick in quarrel,
Seeking the bubble reputation
Even in the cannon's mouth. And then the justice,   15
In fair round belly with good capon lined,
With eyes severe and beard of formal cut,
Full of wise saws and modern instances;
And so he plays his part. The sixth age shifts
Into the lean and slipper'd pantaloon,   20
With spectacles on nose and pouch on side,
His youthful hose, well saved, a world too wide
For his shrunk shank; and his big manly voice,
Turning again toward childish treble, pipes
And whistles in his sound. Last scene of all,   25
That ends this strange eventful history,
Is second childishness and mere oblivion,
Sans teeth, sans eyes, sans taste, sans every thing.

[c. 1599—Great Britain]

The prime metaphor is established in the first two lines: "the world's a stage," so we are all "players" donning costumes and playing roles. The words that accomplish the extension are "exits" and "entrances" (line 3), "parts" (line 4), "acts" (line 5),

---

from AS YOU LIKE IT.   The speech is from act 2, scene 7.   **27.** *mere:* entire, complete.   **28.** *sans:* without.

"plays his part" (line 19), "Last scene" (line 25), and "history" (line 26—"history" as in "history play"). How did you do? I should think fairly well, for once the prime metaphor of a poem built on metaphorical extension is grasped, the words and phrases that carry out the extension usually call attention to themselves.

In reading the next poem, try to answer the following questions: What is the implicit tenor for the vehicle "strange fruit"? How do we come to recognize what the tenor is? What is gained by the tenor's being kept implicit? What words in stanzas one and three serve to extend the prime metaphor? What is accomplished by stanza two?

STRANGE FRUIT

— Lewis Allan —

(as sung by Billie Holiday)

Southern trees bear a strange fruit
Blood on the leaves and blood at the root
Black fruit swinging in the Southern breeze
Strange fruit, hanging from the poplar trees.

Pastoral scene of the gallant South   5
The bulging eyes, the twisted mouth
Smell of magnolias, sweet and fresh
Then the sudden smell of putrid flesh.

Here is a fruit for the crows to pluck
For the rain to gather, for the wind to suck   10
For the sun to rot, for the tree to drop
Here is a strange and bitter crop.

[1941—U.S.A.]

In that the "strange fruit" is a lynched black man, the words that accomplish extension are "swinging," "hanging," "pluck," "gather," "suck," "rot," and "crop"— all words that are literal when used in connection with fruit but metaphorical when carried over to the lynched human being. "Blood," which clearly does not apply to fruit, should lead us to identify these words as vehicles, as should the phrases "bulging eyes," "twisted mouth," and "putrid flesh" of stanza two. What is gained by suppression of the tenor is the power of sudden recognition on the reader's part. Such power results as well from the bitterly ironic juxtapositions of "Pastoral scene" with "bulging eyes" and "Smell of magnolias" with "smell of putrid flesh." These juxtapositions underscore the disparity between convention (the myth of the South) and the terrible reality it hides. More literal than the imagery of stanzas one and three, that of stanza two both helps in the identification of the poem's tenor and serves to make the prime metaphor all the more poignant when it is picked up in stanza three. Indeed, "poignant" may be the best word to describe the effect of the poem overall. With its vivid imagery and haunting extended metaphor, the poem is deeply affecting.

Let's turn to one more poem now, a poem in which a metaphor established explicitly in the first line is extended in various ways as the poem moves on. Try to see where the metaphor is extended and how. I shall not comment on this poem except to say that here again is exemplified the power that metaphor can have. I should note, however, that the speaker's father was a baker's assistant and a man who, because of his heavy regional accent, felt looked down on and held down as to his place in the world. The rest is up to you.

MARKED WITH D.

— Tony Harrison —

When the chilled dough of his flesh went in an oven
not unlike those he fuelled all his life,
I thought of his cataracts ablaze with Heaven
and radiant with the sight of his dead wife,
light streaming from his mouth to shape her name,   5
"not Florence and not Flo but always Florrie."
I thought how his cold tongue burst into flame
but only literally, which makes me sorry,
sorry for his sake there's no Heaven to reach.
I get it all from Earth my daily bread   10
but he hungered for release from mortal speech
that kept him down, the tongue that weighed like lead.

The baker's man that no-one will see rise
and England made to feel like some dull oaf
is smoke, enough to sting one person's eyes   15
and ash (not unlike flour) for one small loaf.

[1975—Great Britain]

THE SYMBOL

Symbols can be thought of in several ways. For one, the symbol has been described as a complex type of implicit metaphor, whose vehicle is expressed and whose tenor not only is not expressed but is *not* immediately implied. The vehicle (the symbol) stands alone in its context, and the tenor is understood by reference to some broader context—other works by the same writer, for instance, or the writer's culture at large. Second, the symbol has been thought of as a synecdoche or metonymy of sufficient complexity to be something more than a simple name (like "Goldilocks" or "Little Red Riding Hood"). Viewed thus, the symbol is something that comes to stand for the general class of which it is a part or with which it is associated. Certain movie stars, for example, have come to represent cultural concepts of womanhood and female sexuality or manhood and virility (Marilyn Monroe, for instance, and John Wayne). Or consider the long-stemmed red rose, which has long been a symbol of romantic love because it has long been associated with this amorphous concept. Third, the symbol can be defined as we defined it in the fiction section of this book: a symbol is anything in a text that conveys meaning different from (though usually related to) its literal meaning. For instance, the fork in the road in Frost's "The Road Not Taken" (p. 3) is a symbol, as we saw when considering the poem, for it suggests in context the choices that must be made on life's journey—something different from what a fork in the road literally is.

All these ways of viewing the symbol are workable, it seems to me, so take your pick. Or better yet, be flexible and choose the definition that seems best to fit the circumstance. What is important is not which definition you use but whether or not the definition facilitates understanding. As to understanding, do not forget what you already know about symbols from having studied symbolism in connection with prose fiction. Because symbols function in a like manner wherever they are found, everything said previously about symbols in fiction applies equally to poetry. Therefore, you may wish to look back and refresh yourself as to what was said earlier (Chapter 7 of Section II, pp. 181–84). It is especially important that you remember what was said about how symbols are established and how recognized. I will reiterate just one point here: context is all. The same image, say, can mean very different things depending on the context: water imagery, for instance, can symbolize death, destruction, and oblivion, or life and sexuality, or rebirth, rejuvenation, and purification. What determines the meaning of a symbol is always its context, literary and/or cultural.

With this in mind, let's look first at a poem that provides its own context for the interpretation of a symbolic action that occurs at the end (that is, the symbol is "created" as defined in Section II).

THE YOUNG HOUSEWIFE
— William Carlos Williams —

At ten A.M. the young housewife
moves about in negligee behind
the wooden walls of her husband's house.
I pass solitary in my car.

Then again she comes to the curb   5
to call the ice-man, fish-man, and stands
shy, uncorseted, tucking in
stray ends of hair, and I compare her
to a fallen leaf.

The noiseless wheels of my car   10
rush with a crackling sound over
dried leaves as I bow and pass smiling.

[1925—U.S.A.]

It is fall (an aspect of the poem's setting) when the speaker, bowing his head and smiling, drives by the young housewife (such is the poem's situation). Because of the season and the woman's disheveledness, the speaker sees her as "a fallen leaf." So far the poem seems to lack tension and direction. Except for the interesting phrase "her husband's house"—the very recognition that this female is out of bounds suggests sexual interest on the speaker's part—the first eleven lines seem rather idle, offering little more than a snapshot of an urban or suburban scene. But because of the speaker's comparison ("I compare her / to a fallen leaf"), the last line makes the poem explode into meaning through its implications of the speaker's masked aggressiveness and desire to possess the young woman, about whom he has had sexual fantasies (look again at stanza one, which in view of the poem's last line is more telling than it might seem at first). Such is what the image of riding over the leaves symbolizes, the image being the vehicle and the speaker's sexual desires and fantasies the tenor. The image is symbolic because as vehicle it stands alone in its context. For the tenor we must look elsewhere—though not very far in this case, only back to the comparison of the woman to a fallen leaf.

Less immediately accessible than Williams's poem, though no less powerful, the next poem symbolizes through a series of metaphorical images six different emotional responses to a given circumstance. As you read the poem, watch for the symbolic possibilities of its imagery.

HARLEM

— Langston Hughes —

What happens to a dream deferred?

Does it dry up
like a raisin in the sun?
Or fester like a sore—
And then run?   5
Does it stink like rotten meat?
Or crust and sugar over—
like a syrupy sweet?

Maybe it just sags
like a heavy load.   10

Or does it explode?

[1951—U.S.A.]

The setting here is Harlem, New York's black enclave. A possible situation is suggested if we read the poem in connection with the title of the book it is from, *Lenox Avenue Mural.* I imagine a man with a painter's eye watching people as they pass down the avenue. Their faces and perhaps posture give rise to his series of questions about "a dream deferred"—the American Dream of betterment so long denied to black Americans. The first image—"a raisin in the sun"—is, like all the other images in the poem save one, a vehicle in a simile the tenor of which is "dream." By way of association, one might also see in the image a withered old black face. But most of all, the image is symbolic, conveying an emotional response and a state of being: one response to a "dream deferred" is to wither up emotionally and to become a hard nub of a self (note that the line is "like a raisin in the sun" and not "a grape in the sun"). That is, like all the poem's other images, "a raisin in the sun" carries meaning different from, though related to, its literal meaning and also, in this case, its simple metaphorical meaning. Another response is to "fester" inside, and a third is simply for the self to die (a state symbolized by "rotten meat"). Or one can become an Uncle Tom, with glazed eyes and "syrupy" accents. All the images thus far are of things gone bad—drying up, festering, stinking, and crusting over. This sense of decay helps further to convey the inner state of people denied and denied again: their sense of being decays along with their dream.

The ninth and tenth lines present us with a somewhat different image, one that suggests not decay but endurance. We can see through the image, perhaps, a face and a posture sagging under years of deprivation, the dream having become only a burden. More significant, however, is the feel of the image, or the feeling it embodies: again, the image is symbolic, communicating an inner state and an emotional response (endurance). To wither and decay or to endure—these are the alternatives metaphorically and symbolically posed thus far. But with its last line, the poem takes a sharp change in direction, as the tone ascends from that of melancholy reflection to the pitch of rage. Rage is the final response enumerated; what had been internalized now erupts outward in an explosion of anger and frustration. We are left with this ominous possibility, expressed in an implicit metaphor (if "it" can "explode," it must be a time bomb) that is in turn symbolic, like the poem's other images. Unlike those other images, however, the final image of an explosion symbolizes a state of being that is active rather than passive, rageful rather than self-loathing.

Hughes's poem reminds me of Blake, whose *Songs of Innocence and of Experience* also concern the dichotomy between passivity and activity, and especially repression and the destruction by society of body and soul. In the next and last poem in this section, London—the capital of the first great industrial power—comes to symbolize these effects of industrial culture as Blake saw it. London here is a cultural symbol in that we must look beyond Blake's poem to industrial culture at large to grasp the full import of what Blake is saying.

LONDON
— William Blake —

I wander thro' each charter'd street,
Near where the charter'd Thames does flow,
And mark in every face I meet
Marks of weakness, marks of woe.

In every cry of every man,   5
In every Infant's cry of fear,
In every voice, in every ban,
The mind-forg'd manacles I hear.

How the Chimney-sweeper's cry
Every blackning Church appalls;   10
And the hapless Soldier's sigh
Runs in blood down Palace walls.

But most thro' midnight streets I hear
How the youthful Harlot's curse
Blasts the new-born Infant's tear,   15
And blights with plagues the Marriage hearse.

[1794—Great Britain]

Marked by a pounding beat, the beat of factories and foundries (brought to mind also by "-forg'd" in line 8), the poem opens with a line that contains an especially interesting word—"charter'd," which is repeated in the second line. What is a charter and what does "to charter" mean? A charter can be a decree of establishment (for instance, a business charter) along with a set of rules of operation, a legal document specifying conditions, or a decree of restraint; as a verb, "charter" means to hire someone for pay. The word, then, carries associations having to do with modern business, restrictions and restraints of various kinds, and economics and economic servitude. All these associations come into play in the poem, the second two (restrictions and restraints) immediately with "ban" (line 7) and especially "mind-forg'd manacles" (line 8). With a slightly surrealistic feel (created by the disembodied faces of the synecdoche "every face I meet"—line 3), the first two stanzas create a setting (the streets of London) and through that setting a sense of things gone wrong, of people constrained by laws and by economics and by their own internalization of their culture's values (the "manacles" are "mind-forg'd") to the point that their faces betray only "weakness" and "woe." The third stanza becomes fully surreal, imparting thus the feeling of the world gone mad, as the speaker singles out two groups—chimney sweeps (almost always children) and soldiers (also usually young)—whose plight symbolizes that of all of the people in the poem, all of whom passively accept the mandates of their culture (of "Church" and "Palace"). In that the part here stands for the whole, these various symbols could be thought of as complex synecdoches.

In any case, the last stanza is the crown of the poem, the image of the "Harlot" being its most memorable symbol. Moving from daytime to "midnight" streets, the speaker holds out a vision of sick sexuality (always in Blake a symbol of societal sickness), its dark outlet and its tragic consequence. The husband, who has perhaps

LONDON.   **7.** *ban:* a law or public notice commanding or forbidding some action.   **16.** *plagues:* venereal disease.

internalized the virgin/whore dichotomy long an aspect of Western culture, seeks gratification from a harlot, contracts some form of venereal disease, and passes it on to his wife, who consequently gives birth to a blind child (the effect of gonorrhea on a fetus, and the implication of line 15) or even a dead child (the effect of syphilis). Thus, the marriage bed becomes a "Marriage hearse." But again, it is the image of the harlot that stands at the center of the stanza and perhaps of the poem as a whole. Herself a manifestation of her culture's sickness, she becomes a symbol of the modern industrial world, whose focus is on business and whose social contract is economic. That is, the harlot symbolizes the fabric of modern social life, which involves at every turn buying and selling—even of love. Tying in with the word "charter'd" of stanza one, the image of the harlot, or its symbolic thrust, summarizes everything the poem concerns.

But there is one image, finally, that towers over the poem and supersedes even that of the harlot: London itself. This image could be thought of as a complex synecdoche, the one city coming to stand for the culture of which it is a part, the culture depicted by every detail in the poem. By this logic, the poor harlot (sympathetically called "youthful," like the sweepers and soldiers of stanza 3 and the "Infant" of line 15) is merely a victim; London is the harlot and all that she represents. By way of this final and overriding symbol, Blake indicts the whole of industrial culture and its works. London is more than the name of a city or an image of an urban setting: over and above these things, it is a symbol of all the forces that lead to the bitter lives of its people, who inhabit it in woe and misery. Of course, we must go out of the poem to understand what those forces are, or bring to the poem a knowledge of the modern industrial world and its money-centeredness. As I have said, sometimes a poem establishes the necessary context and sometimes it does not. When not, we must look elsewhere, in the case of "London" to the culture that has been in place from Blake's day right on down to our own.

SUMMARY SUGGESTIONS: UNDERSTANDING FIGURATION, METAPHOR, AND SYMBOL

1. Remember to distinguish between the figurative and the literal. To do so, simply ask, "Is this word or phrase or statement impossible to take literally?" If the answer is "yes," then it must be figurative.

2. To make the judgment, of course, you must take context into account. Don't forget that something that is figurative in one context can be wholly literal in another. The context should always be your guide in deciding whether or not something is literal or figurative.

3. If something seems figurative, try to identify the type of figure it is—hyperbole, synecdoche, and so forth. Recognizing the type of figure you are dealing with should prove of great aid in your coming to understand it.

4. This is especially true of metaphors of whatever sort. Having recognized the possibility that a phrase is metaphorical, you have a clear road as to what to do: you must identify the vehicle and the tenor—either or both of which can be explicit

or implicit—and then, taking the context into account, transfer what seems relevant from the vehicle to the tenor.

5. Do the same should you recognize that a poet is working with an extended metaphor, only now you will have a series of related vehicles to identify and find the relevance of. And remember that when a poem is structured on an extended metaphor, as is often the case, your understanding of the poem will depend entirely on your grasp of its prime metaphor in extension.

6. Similarly, to grasp poems that are centrally symbolic, poems in which symbols carry the meaning, you must come to understand these symbols. Here, again, context is crucial: the context of the poem being read and often the larger context of the poet's body of work and of the culture in which that work was written. Once you realize that you are reading a symbolic poem, identify its specific symbols and do your best to think out what they mean in context. If the context of the one poem seems insufficient, then bring to bear whatever you know about the poet's other poems and the culture in which the poet worked or works.

USING METAPHORS

I noted a while back that everything said about metaphor in this chapter applies to prose as much as to poetry. I demonstrated with a passage from Dickens (p. 292). Now let's see how metaphor can serve the expository writer generally and, specifically, what you might do and should avoid doing as to this valuable tool in your own writing.

As in poetry, metaphor in prose can be explicit or implicit, and discrete or extended. Just a moment ago, for instance, I used an implicit discrete metaphor when I said, "Having recognized the possibility that a phrase is metaphorical, you have a clear road as to what to do." Recognition clears the way and points the direction; so your interpreting (tenor) of the poem at hand should be easy and pleasurable, like driving down a "clear road" (vehicle) when you know exactly what to do to get to your destination. The reason I used the metaphor—discrete because it is not picked up and extended—is that it provides the most succinct way of saying what I had to say. Succinctness is one of several things that metaphor helps the writer accomplish. Another is definition. For instance, I say in Section I, after likening learning to write and learning a sport: "this whole chapter is aimed at acquainting you with the ground rules of exposition. As to equipment, we have the types of exposition." This sports metaphor ("ground rules" and "equipment" being vehicles) is aimed at an audience that probably knows more about sports than about writing, which, in any case, is conceptual rather than perceptual. The metaphor helps to make the discussion concrete, and thus more vivid and memorable than it would be otherwise, while helping as well to define the concept in question *in terms of* something the projected audience already knows and so can relate to. Used judiciously, metaphors can help your writing be succinct and concrete and can help you define vividly and with effect.

Metaphor can also help in structuring a piece of prose and giving it forward momentum. I am thinking now of extended metaphor, which is found in prose almost as frequently as it is in poetry. At the beginning of this book there are several instances of metaphorical extension. I will use for my example here the passage that stems from the writing-and-sports metaphor discussed in the last paragraph.

> . . . the more one writes, the less difficult writing becomes, just as the more time one puts in practicing a sport, the less difficult the sport becomes and the greater one's facility. One must know the ground rules to begin with, of course, as well as the purposes of and ways of handling whatever equipment the sport entails. The same is true of writing. To continue the analogy, this whole chapter is aimed at acquainting you with the ground rules of exposition. As to equipment, we have the types of exposition, each type being a different piece of equipment that you need to learn how to handle. [A discussion of the types of exposition follows (p. 9).]

The extension here gives the passage a sense of order and movement, as it leads directly to the next part of the chapter. It also lends, I think, a certain lightness and playfulness (the play of the mind) that make the passage livelier than it would be without the extension. These, too, are qualities that metaphor can effect.

Explicit or implicit, discrete or extended, metaphor can be a great aid to writing well. However, it can also backfire if not thought through carefully. There are many ways, that is, in which metaphors can go wrong and therefore many things that you should be alert to when using metaphor. For one thing, expunge any trite metaphors—called **dead metaphors**—that creep into your writing: "clear as crystal," "white as a sheet," "ran like the wind." Used so often as no longer to have any real effect, these figures are dead and can only deaden your prose. Also, avoid metaphors that seem strained or overclever: "like a boiling lobster, the sky turned from black to red." Not only is this metaphor strained, but it brings up feelings and associations that are not relevant to a simple description of the changing colors of a sky and that work against the desired mood. Then, be on the lookout for **mixed metaphor**—that is, the piling up of unrelated metaphors in close proximity that do not go well together: "Now is the time to take a firm stand in the public eye"; "Afraid that she would never reach the top of the heap, Elsa dived into her studies, determined not to give up before the race even began." When visualized, these metaphors are ludicrous in context with each other. Because metaphors have a way of linking up, one must watch what happens between them. The result of not doing so is often nonsense.

The same is true of extended metaphors, which can easily become mixed. When extending a metaphor, make sure that you stay to the same area for all vehicles. The following goes wrong because the area from which the third vehicle is drawn is different from that of the first two vehicles: "Their struggle for power was like a championship fight between two heavyweights, and when the governor lowered his guard, the senator scored the deciding goal." For the extension to work, the last clause should be "the senator delivered the knockout punch."

Finally, be alert to the little quirks of language and, because of odd linkages, avoid using metaphor at all in certain contexts: for example, "Consumers beware! The water company is trying to bleed us dry!"; "Mrs. Johnson married an old flame, who managed to burn down her house on their wedding night." These sentences, both from newspapers, do not contain mixed metaphors as such; but a literal statement in context with a figurative statement can sometimes be ludicrous—as are the linkages of "water" and "bleed," "flame" and "burn." Both sentences would have been far better if the metaphor in each had been restated in literal language. I can't resist quoting two more like sentences, which further exemplify the need for caution when using figurative language: "It is indeed an honor to sit beside the giants upon whose shoulders we stand"; " 'As a student,' " Professor Marsh said, 'Maynard was in a class by himself.' "

In sum, there is a logic to metaphor that must be respected. When constructing and/or extending a metaphor, the writer must think out all the implications of every vehicle and make sure that there are no aberrant implications that would serve only to make the metaphor(s) ineffectual or even nonsensical; the writer must also check that discrete metaphors do not clash, making nonsense when taken together, that there are no odd linkages between metaphors and other words in a passage, and, when extending, that all vehicles are drawn from the same area. Again, there are many possible pitfalls for the unwary with regard to metaphor. But nothing can pack as much power as the right metaphor in the right place. And this is what metaphor can most help the writer accomplish: powerful expression, which the reader will remember.

WRITING ON FIGURATIVE LANGUAGE

Figurative language is so pervasive in poetry that it is all but impossible to write on a poem without referring to its figuration. In writing a paper on the Duke in "My Last Duchess" (pp. 235–36), for instance, you would probably want to mention that the image of "Neptune . . . / Taming a sea-horse" is a symbol in context, summing up at the last the Duke's possessiveness and brutality. In this case, you would be addressing one of the poem's figures in passing. A more extensive treatment of a poem's synecdoches, metaphors, symbols, or whatever is always possible and, indeed, frequently necessary; for the way into a great many poems is through their figuration.

For example, take the following poem, which yields meaning only once the nature of its figuration is understood.

THE DOLLS
— W. B. Yeats —

A doll in the doll-maker's house
Looks at the cradle and bawls:
"That is an insult to us."
But the oldest of all the dolls,
Who had seen, being kept for show,   5
Generations of his sort,
Out-screams the whole shelf: "Although

There's not a man can report
Evil of this place,
The man and the woman bring   10
Hither, to our disgrace,
A noisy and filthy thing."
Hearing him groan and stretch
The doll-maker's wife is aware
Her husband has heard the wretch,   15
And crouched by the arm of his chair,
She murmurs into his ear,
Head upon shoulder leant:
"My dear, my dear, O dear,
It was an accident."   20

[1914—Ireland]

"Doll" and "baby—these are the main figures of the poem, and each is a synecdoche (a part that stands for the whole). The doll, which is also personified, belongs to the class of human creations, or art; the baby belongs to the class of life. Thus, the poem is a kind of debate between art, which is potentially perfectable, and life, which is always "an accident." The abstractions are given form and set against each other to make the drama of the poem. But my point has to do with writing. To write on the poem, one would have to write on its figures, which here would provide more than enough material for a whole paper.

The same is true of any figure of much complexity. For example, you could take Marvell's metaphor "Deserts of vast eternity" ("To His Coy Mistress," pp. 256–57) and argue that it lies at the heart of the poem, giving rise to many subsidiary figures involving time as the poem moves on. If you did, your paper would arise from and be focused on just the one metaphor and its function in the poem as a whole. A single metaphorical image, if it is recurrent in a poet's work, can also be fit for the subject of a longer paper. In what contexts does the figure recur? What ideas and feelings (tenors) is the image (vehicle) associated with? What does the recurrence show about the poet's characteristic way of seeing things? By answering such questions, you could be on the way to an interesting essay. Finally, a single figure can be used in comparing and contrasting poets or whole eras. Consider, for example, the following comparison between three poets and two eras. We will start with a minor poet named John Denham, who wrote of the Thames river:

O could I flow like thee, and make thy stream
My great example as it is my theme!
Though deep, yet clear; though gentle, yet not dull;
Strong without rage, without o'erflowing, full.

[1655—Great Britain]

Compare this with Wordsworth's definition of poetry as "an overflow of powerful feeling" ("overflow" is the operative term) and Blake's dictum, "The cistern contains; the fountain overflows." These three examples all contain water imagery used metaphorically, but how different are the implications of "overflow" and "overflows" from Denham's "without o'erflowing." Anticipating the eighteenth century, Denham values balance and restraint; Wordsworth and Blake, romantic poets both, value much the opposite. The comparison of their water metaphors, then, reveals a good deal about the difference in valuation between the eras in question as well as the similarity of outlooks between Wordsworth and Blake. There is surely more than enough material here for a splendid paper in comparison and contrast.

But what is usually most rewarding to write on with respect to figurative language is the use of metaphors and symbols in a poem as a whole. The relationship of discrete metaphors in a poem, for instance, can be an excellent topic. Poets are particularly sensitive to metaphor and the linkages that figurative language often sets up. Therefore, even though the metaphors of a poem may be discrete, they are usually related in one way or another. Thus, one thing to do with a poem is to analyze its various metaphors and to show how they are related. In fact, we did as much when we discussed Shakespeare's sonnet that begins "That time of year thou mayst in me behold" (pp. 272–73). Here the images of fall, evening, and dying fire are discrete, yet together they paint a scene that becomes a vehicle expressing the speaker's feeling of what it is to grow old. An analysis of the relationship of the poem's metaphorical images—that relationship being what makes the poem what it is—could form the basis of a thorough-going interpretation.

When a poem is structured on a metaphor—that is, built by way of metaphorical extension—your paper is laid out. Think back, for example, to my discussion of "A Work of Artifice" (p. 290). In analyzing the poem, I suggested what its prime metaphor is and how it is established and then read the poem in light of that metaphor, pointing out how it is extended and thereby finding surprising implications of words that at first seemed literal. By analyzing the one metaphor and its extension, I also arrived at a fairly full interpretation of the poem's meaning. To discuss fully the prime metaphor in extension of a poem structured on an extended metaphor is at the same time to account for its diction and to lay bare its meaning overall. That is why I said, "Your paper is laid out." When writing on an extended metaphor, all you need do is to attend to the metaphor as it is extended step by step. Meaning should all but take care of itself.

Because the meaning of a poem built on metaphorical extension lies in the metaphor extended, you are working at the heart of the poem when writing on its figuration. So, too, when it comes to writing on poems that are centrally symbolic, poems in which one or more symbols carry the meaning. Blake's "London" (pp. 298–99) is such a poem, its primary symbols being the harlot and London itself. Any paper on the poem would have to deal with these symbols. But in a thorough analysis of it, they would be central, points of reference against which everything else said about the poem would be gauged. In writing about the symbolism of "London," you would need to establish the symbolic meaning of the harlot—that the buying and selling of love that she is literally engaged in comes to symbolize the economic social contract of the modern world—and then consider other of the poem's details with this symbolism in mind. You could remark, for instance, that both chimney sweeper and soldier are products of the tyranny of modern economics. You certainly would want to discuss the word "charter'd" in this regard, and you might even suggest that the words "mark" of the third line and "Marks . . . marks" of the fourth may be puns on German currency. It would be possible to argue as well that modern marriage, as brought up in the poem's last line, is another example of an economic as opposed to a human relationship. In any case, you can see how much there is to say here, and we haven't even mentioned the poem's title yet. That could be saved for a last paragraph or paragraph cluster, in which you could discuss the facts that London was the first industrial capital and the banker to the world. Your point would be that London, associated with the harlot, is the perfect symbol for the kind of social contract that came with the modern world and that Blake found as dehumanizing as the buying and selling of love.

Of course, writing on symbolism or any other kind of figuration requires that one be deft and flexible. For categories overlap—the categories of imagery and metaphor, for instance—and many figures are subtle and elusive, requiring tact and verbal skill to describe in other words. Yet there is no better way—none at all—to improve one's ability to use language than by working with figuration. Thus, I encourage you to master the material in this chapter and to apply what you have learned in your writing on poems and your writing in general. If you give yourself over to the task, your thinking should become more agile and your writing more expressive.

POEMS FOR STUDY AND WRITING ASSIGNMENTS

VERY LIKE A WHALE
— Ogden Nash —

One thing that literature would be greatly the better for
Would be a more restricted employment by authors of simile and metaphor.
Authors of all races, be they Greeks, Roman, Teutons or Celts,
Can't seem just to say that anything is the thing it is but have to go out of their
    way to say that it is like something else.
What does it mean when we are told   5
That the Assyrian came down like a wolf on the fold?
In the first place, George Gordon Byron had had enough experience
To know that it probably wasn't just one Assyrian, it was a lot of Assyrians.
However, as too many arguments are apt to induce apoplexy and thus hinder
    longevity,
We'll let it pass as one Assyrian for the sake of brevity.   10
Now then, this particular Assyrian, the one whose cohorts were gleaming in
    purple and gold,
Just what does the poet mean when he says he came down like a wolf on the
    fold?
In heaven and earth more than is dreamed of in our philosophy there are a
    great many things,
But I don't imagine that among them there is a wolf with purple and gold
    cohorts or purple and gold anythings.
No, no, Lord Byron, before I'll believe that this Assyrian was actually like a wolf
    I must have some kind of proof;   15
Did he run on all fours and did he have a hairy tail and a big red mouth and
    big white teeth and did he say Woof woof woof?
Frankly I think it very unlikely, and all you were entitled to say, at the very
    most,
Was that the Assyrian cohorts came down like a lot of Assyrian cohorts about
    to destroy the Hebrew host.
But that wasn't fancy enough for Lord Byron, oh dear me no, he had to invent
    a lot of figures of speech and then interpolate them,
With the result that whenever you mention Old Testament soldiers to people
    they say Oh yes, they're the ones that a lot of wolves dressed up in gold and
    purple ate them.   20

VERY LIKE A WHALE. The title is from *Hamlet* (III,ii): pretending madness, Hamlet likens the shape of a cloud to a whale. "Very like a whale," says Polonius, trying to humor the prince. **6.** *wolf on the fold:* Nash alludes to Byron's "The Destruction of Sennacherib." **13.** *many things:* an allusion to Hamlet's "There are more things in heaven and earth, Horatio, / Than are dreamt of in your philosophy" (I,v).

That's the kind of thing that's being done all the time by poets, from Homer to
    Tennyson;
They're always comparing ladies to lilies and veal to venison.
How about the man who wrote,
Her little feet stole in and out like mice beneath her petticoat?
Wouldn't anybody but a poet think twice   25
Before stating that his girl's feet were mice?
Then they always say things like that after a winter storm
The snow is a white blanket. Oh it is, is it, all right then, you sleep under a six-
    inch blanket of snow and I'll sleep under a half-inch blanket of unpoetical
    blanket material and we'll see which one keeps warm,
And after that maybe you'll begin to comprehend dimly
What I mean by too much metaphor and simile.   30

[1941—U.S.A.]

Questions

1. What might the very long lines of this poem suggest about the mentality of its speaker? What else in the poem suggests the same? What does his tone reveal about him?
2. The speaker here confuses the literal and the figurative. How so?
3. The speaker is confused as to the nature of analogy. How so? What does he confuse analogy with?
4. Whom does the poem satirize? What is its point?

Writing Assignments

1. In a paragraph or more, discuss the speaker's confusions with respect to figurative language and analogy. How does he misunderstand both and how does his misunderstanding lead to his misreadings?
2. In a short paper, describe the speaker's mentality and point out what it is in the poem that leads us to see him as we do. Discuss, as well, the satirical nature of the poem and what it is about its speaker that is satirized.

METAPHORS
— Sylvia Plath —

I'm a riddle in nine syllables,
An elephant, a ponderous house,
A melon strolling on two tendrils.
O red fruit, ivory, fine timbers!
This loaf's big with its yeasty rising.   5
Money's new-minted in this fat purse.
I'm a means, a stage, a cow in calf.

I've eaten a bag of green apples,
Boarded the train there's no getting off.

[1960—U.S.A.]

Questions

1. The speaker is a female. How do we know? How is our recognizing this fact important to our understanding of the poem?
2. Why "nine syllables" (line 1) instead of seven or eight, and why is the poem in nine lines? In what way is "stage" (line 7) a pun? What does "I've eaten a bag of green apples" suggest that is relevant in this context?
3. Is this poem built on metaphorical extension, or are its metaphors discrete? Elaborate.
4. How are the poem's metaphors related? What are they all meant to embody?
5. Overall, what does the poem say to you? What is its effect? Why, do you think, did the poet write in riddles?

Writing Assignments

1. On a sheet of paper, write down each of the poem's metaphors and next to each note what you find its relevance to the poem to be. Now write a short paper on how Plath's metaphors capture different aspects of the state her speaker is in and of her state of mind and feelings.
2. How does it feel to be you? Find a series of metaphors for your own life or present stage in life. If well chosen, your metaphors should impart a sense of who you are.
3. If you do the second assignment above, you might follow it up by writing a short paper explaining your metaphors and how together they embody something of the person you are.

FOUR STUDENT POEMS

The poems that follow—all written by freshman students—exhibit metaphorical extension. Read them with an eye to writing on the extension in one or another as well as writing a like poem yourself.

COLLEGE

— Marie Mastronardi —

Soldiers in a four-year war
Battling through long nights and tense days . . .
Casualties sustained, but the rest go on,
Fighting for their medals and discharge papers.

POETRY
— John Krieg —

A brooding, tempestuous poem—
The hurricane—
Will leave in its wake
Stormy emotions and shaken beliefs.

FISH
— Mario Parenti —

Criminals are like fish
Getting caught and hauled in.
Some are thrown in the cooler,
But the big ones usually get away.

ICE
— Tracy Degnan —

The human race is like ice:
    The normal are cubes;
    The deranged are crushed;
    And the extraordinary are dry.

    The cubes solidify in their molds;
    The crushed disintegrate from the weight of the world;
    And the dry sublime away.

Writing Assignments

1. (a) Pick any one of these poems and write a paragraph paraphrasing the meaning of its metaphor.
   (b) In a separate paragraph, discuss your response to your chosen poem and the reasons why your respond thus.
2. Pick one of the poems and write anything from a paragraph to a full essay analyzing the poem's prime metaphor and its extension.
3. Write a short poem built on metaphorical extension like the student poems here. Be sure to stay to the same general area for all your vehicles and to check that the extension works as to sense.
4. Write a paragraph or more analyzing your own poem written in answer to the last assignment. What is the prime metaphor of your poem? How is it established? What kind of metaphor

is it—explicit, implicit, a simile? What words accomplish the extension? What is the meaning of the metaphor in extension (that is, the meaning of the poem)?

[I TASTE A LIQUOR NEVER BREWED]
— Emily Dickinson —

I taste a liquor never brewed—
From Tankards scooped in Pearl—
Not all the Frankfort Berries
Yield such an Alcohol!

Inebriate of Air—am I—   5
And Debauchee of Dew—
Reeling—thro endless summer days—
From inns of Molten Blue—

When "Landlords" turn the drunken Bee
Out of the Foxglove's door—   10
When Butterflies—renounce their "dram"—
I shall but drink the more!

Till Seraphs swing their snowy Hats—
And Saints—to windows run—
To see the little Tippler   15
From Manzanilla come!

[c. 1860—U.S.A.]

Questions

1. "I Taste a Liquor" exhibits a number of different types of figures of speech. What type of figure is "Molten Blue"? What type is "inns of Molten Blue"?
2. What other figures does Dickinson use?
3. What is the prime metaphor on which the poem is built? How is the metaphor established?
4. What words and phrases serve to extend the metaphor?
5. All in all, what is the feeling imparted by "I Taste a Liquor"? How do its images and especially its central (extended) metaphor embody that feeling?

Writing Assignments

1. In a paragraph or more, discuss the prime metaphor of the poem at hand—what it is, how it is established, and how it is extended.

[I TASTE A LIQUOR NEVER BREWED].   **3.** *Frankfort Berries:* grapes used to make Rhine wine.   **16.** *Manzanilla:* a sherry wine from a region in Spain of the same name.

2. Write a paper addressed to question 5 above. After a thesis paragraph in which you perhaps discuss the relation in poems of feeling and such formal elements as diction and imagery, describe the mood of the poem—mood being, remember, the feeling a work arouses in the reader—and relate its mood to the character of its imagery and figuration.

THE ROOFWALKER
— Adrienne Rich —

—for Denise Levertov

Over the half-finished houses
night comes. The builders
stand on the roof. It is
quiet after the hammers,
the pulleys hang slack.   5
Giants, the roofwalkers,
on a listing deck, the wave
of darkness about to break
on their heads. The sky
is a torn sail where figures   10
pass magnified, shadows
on a burning deck.

I feel like them up there:
exposed, larger than life,
and due to break my neck.   15

Was it worth while to lay—
with infinite exertion—
a roof I can't live under?
—All those blueprints,
closings of gaps,   20
measurings, calculations?
A life I didn't choose
chose me: even
my tools are the wrong ones
for what I have to do.   25
I'm naked, ignorant,
a naked man fleeing
across the roofs
who could with a shade of difference
be sitting in the lamplight   30
against the cream wallpaper

reading—not with indifference—
about a naked man
fleeing across the roofs.

[1961—U.S.A.]

Questions

1. The first verse paragraph contains an extended metaphor. What is it? What feeling does it impart?
2. What is the prime metaphor extended in the poem as a whole? How is this metaphor established?
3. The extension of the poem's prime metaphor is carried out in lines 16–25. What words accomplish the extension? What does the metaphor tell us about what the speaker is feeling and her feelings about herself?
4. What is the effect and the meaning of the poem's final metaphor (see lines 27–34)? How is it related to the prime metaphor?
5. What theme is conveyed by the poem's prime metaphor in extension?

Writing Assignments

1. Have you ever felt that you were prepared for the wrong life? If so, then you should have ready access to the emotions of Rich's poem. Write an essay on your predicament and feelings about it, relating your experience whenever possible to that of the speaker of "The Roofwalker."
2. Write an analysis of "The Roofwalker" focusing on its prime metaphor and the extension of that metaphor. Discuss what the analogy is step by step and the meaning of the metaphor as extended, or what the speaker is saying through it about herself. Conclude with a consideration of the "naked man" metaphor—how it relates to the rest of the poem and what its effect is.

THE SICK ROSE
— William Blake —

O Rose, thou art sick.
The invisible worm
That flies in the night
In the howling storm

Has found out thy bed   5
Of crimson joy,
And his dark secret love
Does thy life destroy.

[1794—Great Britain]

Questions

1. Why would we think "The Sick Rose" to be symbolic? What are its symbols?
2. Why "crimson"? What does the word tell us about the "Rose"?
3. Reread "London" (pp. 298–99) and then "The Sick Rose." What similarities are there between the two poems? How does the context provided by "London" help in interpreting "The Sick Rose"?
4. What does the red rose generally symbolize in our culture? How does a knowledge of this symbolism help in understanding Blake's poem?
5. What associations do "worm" and "storm" carry? What could they symbolize?
6. Like "London," "The Sick Rose" makes a statement through its vivid symbolism about the illness of society (Blake's if not also ours). How so? What is the statement the poem makes?

Writing Assignments

1. In a paragraph or more, compare "London" (pp. 298–99) and "The Sick Rose." Your point in doing so, note, will be to show how context (in this case, the context of the poet's work) can help us to recognize and interpret specific symbols in specific poems.
2. Write a paragraph on the general cultural associations of the red rose and how a knowledge of these associations helps us to understand Blake's "Rose."
3. Do some research in secondary works about Blake (specifically, about "The Sick Rose"). Then, using your research to bolster your own insights, write a paper interpreting the symbolism of "The Sick Rose"—what its symbols are and what, taken together, they mean.

From Blake's Notebook (opposite page)

Questions

1. Compare the first three stanzas here with those of the final version of "London" (pp. 298–99). What has been altered? Why did Blake rewrite as he did?
2. Why the changes in the last stanza of "from every" to "thro wintry" to "midnight streets" and especially of "midnight harlot" to "youthful"? How does this last change affect what we feel about the harlot?
3. Perhaps picking up on the implicit metaphor suggested by "Blasts" of the next to last line, Blake settled on "blights with plagues" in the final version of the poem. What implicit metaphor does "blights" extend in connection with "Blasts"? What light does this metaphor shed on "The Sick Rose" (p. 313) and vice versa?
4. Does a knowledge of the changes a poet made before arriving at the final version of a poem make it more readily understood? Why or why not?

Writing Assignments

1. Write a paragraph on Blake's change of "midnight harlot" to "youthful." Why this change? What feeling does the final version convey that is not conveyed by the original? To what end? You might also briefly discuss how the feeling toward the harlot in "London" as revised is in accord with that toward the "Rose" in "The Sick Rose."
2. Write an essay comparing and contrasting the manuscript version of "London" with the finished poem (pp. 298–99). Be sure to discuss not only what was changed and how, but also why. That is, focus on the reason for each change you bring up.

from BLAKE'S NOTEBOOK

London

I wander thro each dirty street
Near where the dirty Thames does flow
   mark
And ~~see~~ in every face I meet
Marks of weakness marks of woe

In every cry of every man
   every infants cry of fear
In ~~every voice of every child~~
In every voice in every ban
     mind   d manacles I hear
The ~~german~~ forg— links I hear
        ed

How
~~But most~~ the chimney sweepers cry

~~Blackens oer the churches walls~~   Every blackning
                    church appalls

And the hapless soldiers sign
Runs in blood down palace walls

    But most the midnight harlots curse
    From every dismal street I hear
    Weaves around the marriage hearse
    And blasts the new born infants tear

      thro wintry
    But most ~~from every~~ streets I hear
    How the midnight harlots curse
    Blasts the new born infants tear
    And ~~hangs~~ with plagues the marriage hearse
      smites
    But most the shrieks of youth
                 I hear
    But most thro midnight &c
    How the youthful

RHYTHM, METER, AND SCANSION

THE RHYTHMS OF ENGLISH

Rhythm refers to the movement of words when they are put together. Since they always move in one way or another—fast, slow, easily, with difficulty, and so forth—all uses of any language are rhythmical. The rhythms of English specifically—which entail pace (rapidity or slowness), pause, stress and slack (what syllables are accented and what not), and inflection (the degree of stress)—are evident in each of the various manifestations of our language. The spoken language, for instance, is wonderfully rhythmic as it trips or plods along, as it moves haltingly from pause to awkward pause or as it rushes on nonstop, with every word stressed in the excitement of the moment. Prose fiction, too, has its rhythms, as you may recall my having said when we took up the subject of style in fiction, and they contribute subtly to the way in which fiction affects us. Even expository prose is rhythmic; indeed, the best exposition shows a keen sense of the rhythms of the language, its forward-moving energy, for instance, or its potential grace. Poetry, therefore, is in no way unique with respect to rhythm. But, like its images and metaphors, the rhythms of poetry are more concentrated than those of the other ways of using language; they are also more exact and so easier to analyze (they are easier to analyze, too, because there are well-established tools with which to think about poetic rhythms). Because the rhythms of poetry are more concentrated and exact than those of prose, they also count for more when it comes to interpretation. Of course, everything counts in poetry—not just the meanings of words but their sounds, the way they fall in and into lines, their metaphorical interactions, as well as the rhythms they form. Somehow or other, every aspect of a poem is related to its meaning overall. In the present chapter we shall look at rhythm in this light: that is, we shall see how rhythms are established in English poetry and, once established, how they contribute to meaning in various ways.

Stress

Of the qualities that go into the making of English rhythms enumerated above—pace, pause, stress and slack, and inflection—you are probably familiar with both pace and pause, and slack (the absence of stress) and inflection (the degree of stress) are easy enough to understand once one grasps what stress is. But, like many of my own students, you may not understand what stress is. So we must take up the subject at the start of our study, for stress is of special importance to the rhythms of our language.

A good definition of **stress** is: the relative force with which the sound of a syllable is spoken. That's good as long as we know what "force" means. What it does *not* mean is pitch or volume. When we stress normally as we speak, or stress a word or syllable for special emphasis, we don't necessarily raise our pitch or increase our volume. What we do is to release air more forcefully when saying the word or syllable than when saying other words and syllables. To see this for yourself, say "ba" ten times with no stress at all; do the same thing again, only now push hard on your diaphragm on every other "ba." You will need to stand to do this and to hold your middle tight. What you should see is that stress and inflection (the degree of stress) depends on the force with which we release air as we speak due to the relative tension or relaxation of the diaphragm.

Because stress is such an important aspect of the rhythms of English and one of the defining attributes of English meter, it is essential that you understand its meaning and function. Its meaning, I trust, is clear from what has just been said (in sum, stress, or accent, is the force given to a syllable or word to distinguish it from other syllables or words). As to function, in English there are three types of stress: metrical, lexical, and rhetorical. We will take up metrical stress when we turn to the subject of meter. **Lexical stress** is the stress placed on certain syllables (the other syllables are slack) of polysyllabic words as indicated in the dictionary. Because English is an accentual language—that is, a language in which words of more than one syllable come with set pronunciations as to which syllables are stressed and which are not (for example, the first syllable of *syl'·la·ble* is stressed and the second two syllables are slack)—lexical stress is a central feature of our mother tongue. **Rhetorical stress** refers to the stress or the degree of stress thrown on certain words or syllables for emphasis: for example, meaning to distinguish between places, one might say, "Ĭ săid ín thĕ bŏx aňd nŏt ón ĭt" (′ indicates stress and ˘ indicates slack, or no stress). It is rhetorical stress, along with rhetorical pause (we often pause, as well as stress, for emphasis), that the poet strives most to get into the written language. Many of the techniques we will be studying are aimed at getting these crucial dimensions of the spoken language into flat black and white on a page.

Line Division

Of all such techniques, poetry's division into lines, which is the one thing all poems have in common, is the most evident and fundamental. In large measure, line division is what makes poetic rhythms exact. Further, the rhythms of poetry are largely dependent on line division and the ways in which lines are divided.

Certainly, meter depends on line division, part of the definition of meter having to do with lines (as we will see when we get to meter, meter in part entails the number of syllables *per line*). And, as we will see shortly, line division is crucial to free verse as well.

One thing that deliberate division into lines allows is a choice of long lines or short or some mixture of the two. In that the rhythm and rhythmic effect of lines of different lengths vary, the choice helps the poet to fix the rhythm desired. Division also allows for **caesura**—a pause within a line—and the effects that caesuras can have on rhythm. A mid-line caesura, for instance, can create a sense of grace and balance, with each half line balanced against the other. In contrast, a caesura coming after the first word of a line, say, could momentarily disrupt the rhythmic flow and thereby create a sense of tension. But the most important thing that line division allows is what happens at the end of the line. What happens at the end of a line— which can happen, obviously, only because of division into lines in the first place— is usually of particular importance with respect to rhythm.

Now, what can happen? Basically, the voice can either come to a pause because the sense and/or grammar calls for a pause—in which case the line is called **end-stopped**—or the voice can carry over into the next line—in which case the line is called **enjambed.** By constructing a great many end-stopped lines, a poet can slow the pace of a poem, and the pace (a matter of rhythm) can in turn affect voice and tone. Remember back, for instance, to "Stopping By Woods on a Snowy Evening" (pp. 216–17). When discussing the poem, I observed that its first ten lines are all end-stopped and suggested that their being end-stopped lends a matter-of-fact tone to the speaker's voice. Conversely, by enjambing easily a poet can speed up the pace and make the lines move easily one to the next, as happens in Browning's "My Last Duchess" (pp. 235–36). Often, however, lines enjamb awkwardly because of the kind of sense unit divided (for example, splitting a compound verb is always awkward). Awkward enjambment creates a haltingness in the rhythm and a sense of tension in the voice. For instance, consider the following lines from the first poem of John Berryman's *The Dream Songs* (found in the Anthology, on pp. 445–46):

> I don't see how Henry, pried
> open for all the world to see, survived.

Contrast these lines as to effect with the following relining:

> I don't see how Henry,
> Pried open for all the world to see,
> Survived.

Because of the way the first enjambs, it is graceless and stuttering, as awkward with respect to the way it moves as Henry feels showing his grief about his father's death (the poem's situation) to others. The second is much more graceful but much less effective.

Whether a poem's lines end-stop or enjamb, and enjamb gracefully or awkwardly, the principle is this: a poet can work with the line or against it. Because our tendency is to pause at the end of a line, the poet is working with the line when a natural pause falls at its end and against the line in one way or another when it enjambs. In either case, what happens at the end of the line is always to be noted, for the way in which lines break greatly affects rhythm and thence tone and meaning.

FREE VERSE

Perhaps the easiest way to see the effects of line division—how division can establish rhetorical stress and pause, for instance, and affect movement in various ways—is through free verse. Actually, we have considered a number of free-verse poems already, from "Marin—AM" (pp. 222–23) to "The Young Housewife" (p. 296). **Free verse** is unmetered poetry. Free verse can be rhymed (though it usually isn't), but it cannot have a recurrent beat, or pattern of slack and stressed syllables (which would make it metrical). Like metrical poems, poems in free verse are divided into lines, but lines that are of no fixed length—they can be expanded or contracted at the poet's will. The line itself is the main tool with which the poet writing free verse sculpts rhythms.

For instance, let's see what happens when we take the following quotation, from the Declaration of Independence, and break it into lines in different ways: "We hold these truths to be self-evident, that all men are created equal."

> We hold these truths
> to be self-evident,
> that all men
> are created equal.
>
> We hold these
> truths to be
> self-evident,
> that all men are
> created equal.
>
> We hold
> these truths to be
> self-evident,
> that all men are created
> equal.

In the first version, all I have done is to divide the quotation into its natural sense units, thus enforcing a pause at the end of each line. In other words, I work with the line here. In contrast, I work against the line in different ways in the second two versions. What you should look for is the difference between each of the three versions as to pace, pause, stress, inflection, and consequently rhythm. The difference springs solely from the difference in the ways the original quotation has been broken into lines. Again, the line is the medium of free verse, the free-verse poet's primary tool with which to create a sense of the living voice speaking.

Here, now, are two poems in free verse. Determine where their authors work with and where against the line, and try consciously to feel the shifting rhythms that result from the varied line treatment in each.

TO A POOR OLD WOMAN
— William Carlos Williams —

munching a plum on
the street a paper bag
of them in her hand

They taste good to her
They taste good   5
to her. They taste
good to her

You can see it by
the way she gives herself
to the one half   10
sucked out in her hand

Comforted
a solace of ripe plums
seeming to fill the air
They taste good to her   15

[1935—U.S.A.]

WHEN IN ROME
— Mari Evans —

Mattie dear
the box is full
take
whatever you like
to eat   5
        (an egg
        or soup
            . . . there ain't no meat.)
there's endive there
and   10

cottage cheese
       (whew! if I had some
          black-eyed peas . . .)
there's sardines
on the shelves   15
and such
but
don't
get my anchovies
they cost   20
too much!
       (me get the
       anchovies indeed!
       what she think, she got—
       a bird to feed?)   25
there's plenty in there
to fill you up.
       (yes'm. just the
       sight's
       enough!   30

       Hope I lives till I get
       home
       I'm tired of eatin'
       what they eats in Rome . . .)

[1970—U.S.A.]

Set on a street somewhere, the Williams poem is a celebration of the simple pleasures of life. Because of its mismatch of line divisions and sense units, however, the first stanza is rhythmically clumsy, as clumsy, perhaps, as the old woman walking down the street with her bag of plums. The second stanza, with its shift of stress from "her" to "good" to "taste" (note how line division affects emphasis), communicates the pleasure the woman has in the plums. But there's still a bit of roughness in the movement of the stanza, as there is also in the third stanza. This roughness serves to keep us from forgetting the realities that circumscribe all pleasure. Nevertheless, in the fourth stanza, we are allowed momentarily the comfort of simple pleasure, as the poet works with the line and thereby creates a feeling of relaxation as well as of closure. The easy rhythm of the last stanza, especially when it is heard against the choppiness of the first, itself lends a sense of solace. Like plums, poems can also give simple pleasure, at least to those who can taste them.

"When in Rome" presents us with a comic situation in which the mistress of the house speaks to her maid, whose replies are thought rather than spoken, about what she might have to eat. The charm of the poem, I think, lies in its rhythms and the rhythmic differences between the two voices. Up until line 17, the mistress seems distracted, her thoughts being elsewhere, for she hesitates with every phrase. "Take / whatever you like / to eat," for example, suggests, if we pause at the end of each line, that the speaker's mind is not where her mouth is. Of course, she doesn't really care about what she's saying, not, that is, until line 17. Here, an earnestness enters the voice, as the mistress emphasizes what the maid should not eat and the cost of the anchovies. Again created by the way the lines break, the rhythm now is deliberate and emphatic, with heavy stress now falling on "but," "don't," the "an-" of "anchovies," "cost," and "too much." The maid's voice, in contrast, is rhythmically emphatic throughout, which suggests that she is paying attention. The maid, who is quite ironic (the poem's rhymes are all ironic in effect), is alert, no doubt, because it is her meal in question. At any rate, where stress falls and where pauses come in each case affect the way what is said moves, and the way the words of each speaker move is what determines our sense of rhythm and, consequently, our understanding of what each is feeling. This is what rhythm is all about: through rhythm we communicate not merely information but the fine nuances of feeling that underlie every act of human communication.

METER AND METRICS

Meter is the regular recurrence of some rhythmic configuration or pulse. Consider the words *although* and *today*. We pronounce both in a set way, as we do all polysyllabic words. These two we pronounce with a stress or accent on the second syllable of each and no stress (or slack) on the first:

$$\breve{a}lth\acute{o}ugh \quad t\breve{o}d\acute{a}y$$

Each word constitutes a little rhythmic unit or pulse. Should we choose words so as to create a pulsating pattern of slack and stress or stress and slack, we would have a meter:

$$T\breve{o}n\acute{i}ght,/ \; t\breve{o}n\acute{i}ght,/ \; w\breve{o}n't \; b\acute{e}/ \; j\breve{u}st \; \acute{a}n/\breve{y} \; n\acute{i}ght.$$

Note how the rhythmic configuration ˘ ′ recurs. When a pulse recurs in this way, we speak of the unit of recurrence as a **foot** or **beat.** The above line, for instance, has five feet or beats. A poet writing metrically chooses words so that they will form the desired pattern of recurrence.

Though meter always involves rhythmic recurrence, different languages have given rise to different types of meter. Poets writing in English have experimented with most, but the type characteristic of English verse from Chaucer to the present is **accentual-syllabic.** In English poetry generally, the sense of rhythmic recurrence springs from the number of syllables per line *and* the number of stresses, a set number of stressed syllables alternating with a set number of slack syllables. In other words, rhythmic recurrence, or meter, is tied to the repetition of a set number of feet or beats per line. For example, consider the last stanza of "Stopping By Woods" again:

> The woods/ are love/ly, dark,/ and deep,
> But I/ have prom/ises/ to keep,
> And miles/ to go/ before/ I sleep,
> And miles/ to go/ before/ I sleep.

Each line contains eight syllables, four stressed and four slack, with unstressed and stressed syllables alternating to form a pulsating pattern of four beats per line.

If a given rhythmic configuration recurs in a piece of writing, the piece has a meter, describable with respect to the kind of beat that recurs and the number of recurrences of that beat per line (a beat normally consists of one stressed syllable— the beat itself—and one or two unstressed syllables). The basic beats and patterns of recurrence of English metrics are:

Beats	Recurrences
iamb/iambic: although, today	*tri*meter: three, the root meaning of *tri-*
trochee/trochaic: mother, father	*tetr*ameter: four, the root meaning of *tetr-*
anapest/anapestic: in the heat/of the night (because of the nature of English, no single word exemplifies the anapest well)	*pent*ameter: five, the root meaning of *pent-*
	*hex*ameter: six, the root meaning of *hex-*
dactyl/dactylic: family, elephant	

You may have observed that the iamb and the anapest are somewhat alike, as are the trochee and the dactyl. Iambic and anapestic meters are often called "rising," for the beat of each comes at the end of the foot; conversely, trochaic and dactylic meters are called "falling." These terms can be useful in describing some metrical effects. For example, the last line of Wallace Stevens's "Sunday Morning" begins with a falling feeling and ends on a rising note:

> Downward to darkness on extended wings.

We could analyze this mixed line as containing two dactyls followed by two iambs, or a dactyl and a trochee followed by an anapest and an iamb. In either case, falling yields to rising, and the shift is very much in keeping with what is being expressed: that we all go down to death (falling), but that we can do so with grace and purpose (rising). The difference in effect between rising and falling meters depends on context, of course. But there is a difference, and poets exploit that difference for their purposes.

Aside from the beats and patterns of recurrence just named, there are a number of other beats and patterns possible. But in practice, these other possible beats are almost never recurrent in English verse, and we rarely find lines shorter than two beats or longer than six. Two other feet, however, should be noted:

spondee/spondaic: hátrack, footbáll   *pyrrhic:* in the/ begin/ning Gód

The spondaic foot contains two stressed syllables; the pyrric, two unstressed syllables. Though not recurrent, both are frequent deviants in a metrical context.

    These, then, are the terms used for naming and interpreting what happens metrically in a piece of metrical verse. When analyzing a poem in meter, we first **scan** the poem—that is, determine which syllables receive stress and which do not, as well as what type of beat recurs and how many recurrences there are per line. We name the meter accordingly: for instance, the stanza from "Stopping By Woods" scanned on page 323 is in iambic tetrameter. Finally, we take the step from meter to rhythm and then from rhythm to meaning by determining the rhythmic feel produced by the meter and then the significance of that particular rhythm to the poem as a whole.

    Following are two exercises in metrics that should help you remember the types and effects of beats and meters. I scan the first; perhaps you can try scanning the second.

METRICAL FEET
— Samuel Taylor Coleridge —

Tróchee/ trips from/ long to/ shórt.
From long/ to long/ in sól/emn sórt
Slow Spón/dee stalks;/ strong foot!/ yet ill/ áble
Éver to/ come up with/ Dáctyl tri/syllable.
Íam/bics márch/ from short/ to long;
With a leáp/ and a bóund/ the swift An/apests thróng.

[1802—Great Britain]

TERRIBLE DACTYL, SON OF RODAN
— Edward Proffitt —

As I was walking on iambic feet
At dusk, as is my wont, along a street
Of fine poetic structures, old but meet,
Terrible Dactyl came beating around,

METRICAL FEET. **1.** *long to short:* other words for stress and slack.

Clumsily pounding with hideous sound.   5
I mustered my forces and gave the sign
To an army of anapests manning the line.
But no use! All was in deepening disarray
Till I remembered the Japanese way.
Grabbing at once for any old haiku,   10
I shortened the line
And pelted out petals—
Numberless petals
Brushed with the russet color
Of the sinking sun.   15
The monster was undone.
I then returned to where I had begun.

[1977—U.S.A.]

BLANK VERSE

Beginning students sometimes confuse *blank verse* and *free verse* because of the similarity of the terms. They should be kept separate and distinguished from each other. As we have seen, free verse is poetry that is nonmetrical. **Blank verse,** on the other hand, *is* metrical: it is verse that consists of lines in iambic pentameter meter that are unrhymed (hence, "blank"). To take an example, here is a delightful poem by a freshman student:

ODE TO RAY BAREE'S PIZZA
— Ricardo Valdivia —

There is a little shop that stands alone
Whose pies are known and loved throughout this town:
A crusty pie, like home-baked bread, and cheese
one finger thick; on top, a pond of sauce.
Served hot and eaten fast, it burns your lips;
But pain like this is sheer delight, as each
Delicious morsel sizzles on the tongue.

TERRIBLE DACTYL.   **10.** *haiku:* a nonmetrical Japanese form consisting of three lines of 5–7–5 syllables each and usually concerning the more delicate aspects of nature. With respect to metrics, the haiku might help the speaker rid himself of the persistent dactylic beat in his head and thus defeat Terrible Dactyl because the haiku is nonmetrical. Metaphorically, the haiku is an apt weapon because it is a Japanese form and Terrible Dactyl (which echoes "pterodactyl") is cast in the role of one of those seemingly infinite Japanese movie monsters, like Rodan.

Note especially how "natural" these lines sound and how naturally they move. The blank verse line is close to the essence of the rhythmic norm of our language. That is why, I think, it has appealed to as many poets as it has.

It is important to know what blank verse is particularly because it is the rhythmic medium of many of the greatest poems in the language, poems by the likes of Shakespeare, Milton, Wordsworth, Browning, and Stevens. All wrote rhymed verse and verse in other meters, and Stevens wrote free verse as well. But for their most ambitious work, all turned to blank verse. The reason why, I believe, is that blank verse is a supple medium, allowing for a wide range of rhythmic effects. For instance, in the hands of Shakespeare, whose blank-verse plays are marked by common diction and straightforward syntax, the unrhymed iambic pentameter line has the effect of vigorous speech. The blank verse of Milton, whose diction and syntax are Latinate, has the effect of prophetic pronouncement. Wordsworth lies somewhere in between the two. The effect of the blank verse of his most compelling work, *The Prelude,* is that of a mind in the act of articulating its deepest motions and emotions to itself.

Or take Robert Frost's "Mending Wall," a poem in blank verse having all the vigor and nuance of language at its best. In reading the poem, try to maintain the iambic beat whenever possible, but let the feet deviate where they will. Hear the speaker speaking and try to catch his subtle tones. He is a complex mentality, a man who might not love walls (both literal and symbolic), yet who repairs the damage done to them by hunters (line 6) and who lets his neighbor know when mending time has come (line 12). As well as through what he says, this complexity is expressed rhythmically through the emphases and nuances established by the poem's meter.

MENDING WALL
— Robert Frost —

Something there is that doesn't love a wall,
That sends the frozen-ground-swell under it
And spills the upper boulders in the sun,
And makes gaps even two can pass abreast.
The work of hunters is another thing: 5
I have come after them and made repair
Where they have left not one stone on a stone,
But they would have the rabbit out of hiding,
To please the yelping dogs. The gaps I mean,
No one has seen them made or heard them made,   10
But at spring mending-time we find them there.
I let my neighbor know beyond the hill;
And on a day we meet to walk the line
And set the wall between us once again.
We keep the wall between us as we go.   15

To each the boulders that have fallen to each.
And some are loaves and some so nearly balls
We have to use a spell to make them balance:
"Stay where you are until our backs are turned!"
We wear our fingers rough with handling them.   20
Oh, just another kind of outdoor game,
One on a side. It comes to little more:
There where it is we do not need the wall:
He is all pine and I am apple orchard.
My apple trees will never get across   25
And eat the cones under his pines, I tell him.
He only says, "Good fences make good neighbors."
Spring is the mischief in me, and I wonder
If I could put a notion in his head:
"Why do they make good neighbors? Isn't it   30
Where there are cows? But here there are no cows.
Before I built a wall I'd ask to know
What I was walling in or walling out,
And to whom I was like to give offense.
Something there is that doesn't love a wall,   35
That wants it down." I could say "Elves" to him,
But it's not elves exactly, and I'd rather
He said it for himself. I see him there
Bringing a stone grasped firmly by the top
In each hand, like an old-stone savage armed.   40
He moves in darkness as it seems to me,
Not of woods only and the shade of trees.
He will not go behind his father's saying,
And he likes having thought of it so well
He says again, "Good fences make good neighbors."   45

[1914—U.S.A.]

THE FUNCTIONS OF METER

Meter is a device with which poets create rhythms of all sorts, from the slow
and ponderous to the fast and bouncy, from the lively rhythms of speech to the
elevated rhythms of prophesy, from rhythms with a rising feeling to those that mimic
falling. Like free verse, metered verse is divided into lines. Its lines, however, are
usually regular as to the number of syllables in each. But the way lines break and
what happens at the end of a line are no less significant in metered than in free
verse. In these regards the two are alike. They differ as to pliability and exactitude.
Choosing metered over free verse, the poet gives up what can be gained rhythmically

by the ability to contract or expand the line at will (there are some metrical poems, however, of variable line length); but the poet gains other advantages—like the possible effect on pace of the metrical foot chosen (the iamb, for instance, is slower than the anapest)—and potentially a level of exactitude not possible even in free verse.

Meaningful Deviation

How so? For one thing, because a metrical pattern provides a norm, it allows for syncopation, or meaningful deviation from the norm. When we name the meter of a given poem in metered verse, we are naming the norm. Every line does not necessarily adhere to the norm, however. Poets deviate from their own metrical norms for many reasons: momentarily to change the pace, for instance, or to effect a pause not suggested in some other way. But perhaps the most important reason is that deviation increases inflection and thus suggests emphasis. For instance, consider the opening lines of Frost's "Mending Wall," which I shall scan:

> Something there is that doesn't love a wall,
> That sends the frozen-ground-swell under it
> And spills the upper boulders in the sun,
> And makes gaps even two can pass abreast.
> The work of hunters is another thing:
> I have come after them and made repair
> Where they have left not one stone on a stone,

Because we always favor the lexical stress (see p. 317) when lexical stress and **metrical stress** (the stress words generally receive in metered verse because of the metrical norm) do not coincide, we know that the poem's first word is deviant, for iambic pentameter is here the norm and "Something" is a trochee. But why this deviation, we must ask here and always? The special emphasis that "Something" draws to itself because it is deviant serves to underscore the speaker's uncertainty about his present line of thought. He has a half intuition, perhaps, but only that. So he can say no more than "Something." The first foot of the sixth line is also deviant. A shifting of the stress from "have" to "I" suggests itself because "I" is a word we normally stress. When a word we normally stress comes in an unstressed position in a metrical line, note, it should usually be stressed, and thus the foot will be deviant. The deviation here underscores the fact that it is the speaker who tends the wall, however much he might question its necessity. The deviation, then, serves to alert us to the full complexity of what is explored in the poem; by so doing, the meter becomes an integral part of the meaning.

Special Effects

As well as a means of gaining strategic emphasis, meter can be used to create a host of what we might call special effects, such as the effects to be felt in lines 4 and 7 of "Mending Wall." The stressing of three contiguous syllables here (the second foot of line 4 and the fourth foot of line 7 are spondees) creates a muffled pounding sound, like the sound of boulders spilling onto the ground. Or take the last two lines of Anne Sexton's poem "To a Friend Whose Work Has Come to Triumph" (pp. 243–44):

> See him acclaiming the sun and come plunging down
> while his sensible daddy goes straight into town.

The falling rhythm of the first of these two lines echoes the falling of the son, whereas the rising rhythm of the last line mirrors the flying of "daddy." The last line also demonstrates the effect meter can have on tone, or how meter together with diction can create the tone desired. Given the diction of the line, its regular anapestic beat—fast and bouncy—makes the line sound like a children's rhyme. The meter as well as the diction mocks "sensible daddy." Such special effects, which are probably limitless, are to be found in most poems. Each such effect, of course, must be taken in context and related to the context for its meaning to be understood.

Rhetorical Stress

Yet another important function of meter has to do with rhetorical stress and monosyllabic words not normally stressed. Rhetorical stress, remember, is the stress thrown by the voice for special emphasis. It can be suggested, as we have seen, by metrical deviation. It can also be suggested by the metrical pattern itself. The principle is this: once a beat has been established, it should be adhered to as one reads on unless there is a reason to deviate from the established norm—because the lexical stress of a polysyllabic word would have to be violated for the metrical pattern to be maintained or because some word we normally stress is in an unstressed position. By trying to adhere to the norm, we allow for the possibility of rhetorical stress on words that normally would be passed over without a second thought. A powerful instance of how a metrical pattern maintained can suggest rhetorical stress is to be found in Sidney's sonnet on sleep.

ASTROPHEL AND STELLA
— Sir Philip Sidney —

No. 39

> Come sleep! Oh sleep, the certain knot of peace,
> The baiting place of wit, the balm of woe,
> The poor man's wealth, the prisoner's release,

ASTROPHEL AND STELLA. **2.** *baiting place:* feeding or resting place, and perhaps also the place (or time) where the barb of "wit" is baited.

The indifferent judge between the high and low;
With shield of proof shield me from out the prease   5
Of those fierce darts Despair at me doth throw;
Oh make in me those civil wars to cease;
I will good tribute pay, if thou do so.
Take thou of me smooth pillows, sweetest bed,
A chamber deaf to noise and blind to light,   10
A rosy garland and a weary head;
And if these things, as being thine by right,
Move not thy heavy grace, thou shalt in me,
Livelier than elsewhere, Stella's image see.

[1591—Great Britain]

In a nonmetrical context, the poem's fifth line would almost certainly be read:

With shield of proof shield me from out the prease.

The metrical context of Sidney's poem, however, points to another possible reading, one we would probably not even think of if the line were not metrical. By our maintaining of the beat, the line comes out:

With shield/ of proof/ shield me/ from out/ the prease.

That's it! With the stress on "me," the line comes alive. Sleep, the speaker says in the preceding lines, comes to everyone else. Then he screams out in his desperation, "Why not to *me?*" In the rhetorical stress suggested by the poem's meter, there can be heard all the frustration and sense of isolation that the insomniac feels while struggling for sleep late at night. It is by focusing our attention thus and asking us to choose one reading over another, while giving us guidelines in doing so, that meter creates exact rhythms and so brings out exact meanings.

So meter can be a terribly useful tool, one with which the poet can reproduce in the written language the nuances and gradations of the language as spoken. That is, with meter a poet can create rhythms as precise as those of speech, for meter can indicate each of the elements of rhythm: pace, pause, stress and slack, and inflection. Pace is affected by the choice of beat and line length in the first place as well as by deviations (deviation tends to slow); pause, too, is affected by deviation (the more radical the deviation, the more we tend to pause); slack and stress, of course, are what meter indicates primarily; and inflection can be suggested by deviation from the norm or, conversely, by adherence to it. In sum, meter, along with line division, indicates in various ways the movement of voice of a poem in meter—

5. *of proof:* of proven strength; *prease:* crowd.   **14.** *Stella:* the speaker's beloved, who is the cause of his sleeplessness.

where the speaker rushes on or slows up, pauses to gather strength, stutters, throws special emphasis, and so forth. But to pin down these effects, one needs to scan a poem. We will conclude this survey of meter and metrics with a discussion of the principles of scansion.

SCANSION: DO'S AND DON'TS

Scanning, again, means determining what syllables are stressed and what are not, dividing a poem's lines into feet, and seeing thereby what the metrical norm is and thus where deviations from the norm occur. In beginning to scan a poem, first look at its polysyllabic words, for you know how these are pronounced: just pronounce them the way you always do and scan them accordingly. For instance, an iambic beat is established in the line that follows by its opening and closing polysyllabic words, which *must* be stressed as they are in my scansion:

Remem/ber eve/rything/ you heard/ today.

But never force an accent. If the metrical stress and the lexical do not coincide, don't forget, the lexical takes precedence and a deviation is marked. In this regard, recall the first line of "Mending Wall":

Something/ there is/ that does/n't love/ a wall.

Though four of the five beats here are iambs, the word "Something" must be pronounced and scanned "Something" and not "Something." Therefore, given its context, it is deviant. As to monosyllabic words, pronounce them normally and see how they fit in with the polysyllabic words you have scanned already.

By this point, you should have a pretty good idea of what the basic beat of the poem you are scanning is. Now, try to maintain that beat as much as is possible. If you can, then this is the normal beat of the poem; all you have to do now is to count up the number of beats per line and name the poem's meter accordingly. If you cannot maintain the beat you have struck on, try some other beat. Since there are only four basic beats, you should be able to determine the norm of the poem by a process of elimination if nothing else. Because any single foot or even line of a poem can be deviant, of course, one must take more than one line into account when determining a poem's basic beat and pattern of recurrence.

Once you have determined what the meter of a poem is to your satisfaction, read all of its lines with that pattern in mind, though don't force the pattern where it does not fit. Also, do not read mechanically: daDee daDee daDee. And allow your own sense of the poem to come through. Though all skilled readers will agree on what the metrical norm of a given poem is, no two people are likely to scan it in exactly the same way. There is room, that is, for interpretative emphasis. But however you finally decide a poem should be scanned, keep in mind the following principle when you look over your scansion: there should be a reason for the scansion point by point. The reason for scanning polysyllabic words in a set way, for instance, is simply that that is the way they are pronounced. We try to maintain a beat and to weigh each line against the norm because we are working with a piece of writing in meter. Yet a beat should never be maintained rigidly; deviation must be allowed for, a major reason for a poet's establishing a metrical norm in the first place being to make deviation possible. And should your understanding call for a shift in stress, your reason for scanning as you do would be interpretative emphasis. Whatever the case may be, it is the reasoning that counts. We must also reason as to the choices that meter presents us with. Metrical verse keeps asking us to choose—between, for example, the normal stressing of monosyllabic words and their metrical stressing if the two diverge; in choosing, we must justify what we choose on the grounds of meaning. This last step—the relating of form to content—is always the most important.

At this point, let's carry a poem through the process of scansion fully, which means that we must observe what the poem's meter is and what it does—especially, what kind of rhythm it creates—and relate what it does to meaning.

MY PAPA'S WALTZ
— Theodore Roethke —

The whis/key on/ your breath
Could make/ a small/ boy diz/zy;
But I/ hung on/ like death:
Such waltz/ing was/ not eas/y.

We romped/ until/ the pans   5
Slid from/ the kitch/en shelf;
My moth/er's coun/tenance
Could not/ unfrown/ itself.

The hand/ that held/ my wrist
Was bat/tered on/ one knuck/le;   10
At eve/ry step/ you missed
My right/ ear scraped/ a buck/le.

You beat/ time on/ my head
With a palm/ caked hard /by dirt,
Then waltzed/ me off/ to bed   15
Still cling/ing to/ your shirt.

[1948—U.S.A.]

The basic beat here is the iamb; the meter, iambic trimeter. In other words, there are three iambic beats or feet per line, so each line rhythmically is something like the waltz's three-quarter time. How have I arrived at this conclusion? Well, I looked over the whole poem first and found five lines that are fairly set as to scansion because of their polysyllabic words (lines 5, 7, 8, 11, and 16); I also found three monosyllabic lines (9, 12, and 15—monosyllabic except for "buckle" in line 12) that fall very naturally into an iambic trimeter pattern. I then tried to read the poem as a whole with this meter in mind, and it worked. Of course, I allowed for deviation. Four lines here end with an extra unstressed syllable each (lines 2, 4, 10, and 12); one begins with a trochee (line 6—"Slid" is a word we would naturally stress, and there is nothing gained by stressing "from") and one with an anapest (line 14—I find no reason here to stress "with" or "a"); and one line (13) does not fall entirely into the pattern, at least not with ease, so I let my ear and my sense of the meaning of the line be my guides, which led me to hear "time on" as a spondee mimicking the beating of time on the speaker's head. Don't forget, incidentally, that stresses are not all inflected to the same degree. So when I scan the first line, for instance, as I do ("Thĕ whís/kĕy ón/ yŏur bréath"), I don't mean to suggest that "on" receives anything but the lightest of stress, much lighter than that on the first syllable of "whiskey" or on "breath."

Now, what can we say about the rhythm of the poem, or the rhythmic effect of its meter? To my ear, the poem's meter, with its regular and pronounced beat and syncopated deviations, creates a dancing rhythm. I am made to hear the dance remembered by the speaker as it is described. And hearing the dance and feeling it in my muscles, I feel happy. In other words, the poem's rhythm communicates the momentary charm and high spirits of the experience remembered. There is another note to be detected in the way the poem moves, however, a grim note of something like mania or frenzy. Though the poem depicts a joyful memory, that is, there is an undercurrent of violence to be felt as well, an undercurrent that stems from the insistence of the poem's unusually heavy beat. The image of the mother's face tells us why this should be so. Although the situation of the poem was ostensibly happy, the mother could not smile because her face wore a permanent frown caused by the father's drinking and his mercurial nature—loving one minute, violent and destructive the next. It is this most of all that the poem's rhythm, created by its meter and the way the meter is handled, captures and conveys. Such, of course, is intimated as well by the poem's depiction of the boy hanging on "like death," of the "pans" crashing down, of the boy's ear scraping "a buckle," and of "time" being beaten on his "head." As we shall discuss in a later chapter, the poet strives always to make form and content one. So they are here: the meter of "My Papa's Waltz" creates a subtle, complex rhythm that, along with the poem's imagery especially, captures the ambivalence of the speaker in remembering his loving but violent father. In fact, content and form here are indivisible, which is why the poem is as moving as it is.

SUMMARY SUGGESTIONS: UNDERSTANDING RHYTHM AND METER

1. The rhythms of English entail pace, pause, stress and slack, and inflection. These attributes of language determine how words move, and how words move determines what kind of rhythmic effect they will have. Does a poem or a passage

seem stuttering? or strained? or even and melodious? or perhaps erratic? Make this kind of judgment as you read and try to relate the rhythm you perceive to content.

2. When determining the rhythm of a poem or passage, remember that line division—the one thing that all poems have in common—greatly affects movement and thus rhythm. Remember that how lines are divided is of special importance in poetry and should always be taken into account.

3. That is, when reading a poem and listening for its rhythm, consider the qualities of its lines and how they are divided. Are they long or short or some mixture of the two? What is the effect of their length? What seems to be their pace? Why? Are the lines mainly end-stopped or enjambed? If enjambed, do they enjamb awkwardly or easily? What kind of rhythm results from the way they are divided? And again, why? These are some of the questions to ask of lines and their division.

4. When a poem is in free verse, its rhythm will depend almost entirely on line treatment. When a poem is metrical, meter is also a consideration. What meter is the poem in? What kind of movement does its meter help to effect? What deviations are to be found? What is their effect? What kind of rhythm overall does the meter help create? Why? All of these questions—the last in particular—need to be asked of a poem that is metrical.

5. That is, one must determine the function of a poem's meter. To this end, scanning a poem in meter is useful. We scan in order to determine the norm, which allows us to see where deviations occur; we scan in order better to understand the rhythmic structure of a poem and what its unique rhythm conveys.

6. In sum, whatever kind of poem you are reading, analyze what goes into the making of its rhythm in order to see clearly what its rhythm is, and then take the step to meaning. If your analysis is good, then this step should be easy and natural. For, once the rhythm of a poem is understood, its relevance and meaning in the poem usually seem self-evident.

WRITING ON RHYTHM

Whether a poem is in free verse or meter, when you are about to write on its rhythm or some aspect thereof, first *read the poem aloud* as naturally as you can, and listen to yourself as you read. Better yet, tape yourself reading and then listen critically to how you just read the poem. If you are not satisfied with your performance, tape yourself again and again until you are satisfied. Each time you listen, determine how your voice is moving with regard to pace, pause, stress, slack, and inflection. Then write down a description of how you feel the poem moves, or its rhythm overall. There are now two things left to do: establish how the rhythm is created and what its relevance is to the poem under consideration.

As to the first task, if a poem is in free verse, study its lines and how they break. Are the lines short or long, or does the poem contain a mixture of the two, perhaps creating contrasting rhythms thus? What is the general effect of the way the lines are treated? Are there any special effects? If line length varies, how does the rhythm change with the changing line lengths? How do its lines break? Which end-stop, which enjamb? How do they enjamb? How does the way the lines break affect their movement? How are basic sense units broken up? To what effect? By addressing these questions, you will be able to establish how the rhythm of your poem is created and therefore to back up your statements once you get to writing about what happens in it rhythmically.

If the poem you are working with is in meter, all considerations regarding the line are equally pertinent, except (usually) for variability of length. But now questions involving meter must also be answered. What is the basic beat? How many beats are there per line? What, then, is the poem's meter, or metrical norm? What is the effect of this meter? What deviant beats are there in the poem? Where? Why? What general rhythmic feel do line treatment and meter acting together produce? Are there any special rhythmic effects? Is the rhythm more or less the same throughout the poem, or are there points of rhythmic contrast? Where? To what purpose? To address yourself to these questions, you will have to scan the poem—that is, to mark each syllable with a sign of slack (˘) or of stress (′) and then to group and divide syllables into beats or feet. You might also underline all deviant feet. Your scansion should be included with your essay for easy reference. If done well, the scansion will provide support for what you say about the poem's meter and its rhythmic effect.

Finally, having determined the rhythm of the poem—whether in free verse or meter—and how that rhythm is created, you must focus on its significance. How does the rhythm establish, reinforce, echo, or whatever, the poem's meaning by, for instance, the way it affects tone, or what it intimates about the nature of the speaker, or its underscoring of some facet of the poem? An answer to questions of this sort will provide you with a thesis. When you write on the rhythm of a poem, that is, your thesis will necessarily involve the relationship in the poem between its rhythm and content. Why else would one write on rhythm except to get at its significance? Your support will entail a description of the poem's rhythm and rhythmic effect(s) as well as a consideration of how the poem's particular rhythm is created. The latter consideration will get you into a discussion of line treatment and division, meter (if the poem is metrical), and the like. In other words, what you must do in the prewriting stage to arrive at your specific thesis becomes crucial support for it in the writing stage.

Like any other element of poetry, rhythm can be taken as the topic of a paper or used as support. As to support, a paper on the Duke in Browning's "My Last Duchess" (pp. 235–36), for example, would benefit from the inclusion of a paragraph on the poem's rhythm and its effects on voice. This is so because, as much as anything else, the poem's rhythm is an agent of characterization. In writing a paper on the Duke, therefore, you would want to observe that the poem moves along with a strong forward motion, created in part by the poem's even beat and in part by its many lines that enjamb swiftly and easily. For instance, listen to the Duke's opening lines:

> That's my last duchess painted on the wall,
> Looking as if she were alive. I call

> That piece a wonder, now: Frà Pandolf's hands
> Worked busily a day, and there she stands.
> Will't please you sit and look at her? I said
> "Frà Pandolf" by design, for never read
> Strangers like you . . .

The all but perfectly regular iambic beat and the way the lines that do so enjamb—easily and naturally—together create a firmness in the voice: this speaker, we can conclude, is self-assured and confident of his place and importance. But, though most of the poem continues in the same manner, there are moments in it when the Duke falters. For instance, he says, "She had / A heart—how shall I say?—too soon made glad" (lines 21–22), and later (lines 31–33),

> She thanked men—good! but thanked
> Somehow—I know not how—as if she ranked
> My gift . . .

There is a faltering in the voice in both cases, a faltering suggested by the uneasy enjambments "She had / A heart" and "thanked / Somehow" and reinforced by the parenthetical comments that follow. From this faltering we can conclude that the Duke, though a man possessed of a high degree of self-confidence when in control, cannot brook self-assertion in others, for such assertion means the loss of control, which undermines his self-confidence. The poem's rhythm—fluid for the most part but faltering at certain key points—goes far in painting the Duke's mentality.

This last paragraph demonstrates how rhythm can be used for support and also what writing on rhythm is about, whether rhythm is used as support or taken as the topic of a paper. Let's turn now to this second possibility. We will begin with two premises: that you have to write a paper on the rhythm of the following poem and that your thesis is, "The rhythm and rhythmic effects of Williams's 'The Dance' beautifully capture the kind of movement that the painting is said to depict."

THE DANCE
— William Carlos Williams —

> In Breughel's great picture, The Kermess,
> the dancers go round, they go round and
> around, the squeal and the blare and the
> tweedle of bagpipes, a bugle and fiddles
> tipping their bellies (round as the thick-   5
> sided glasses whose wash they impound)
> their hips and their bellies off balance

THE DANCE.   **1.** *Breughel:* Flemish painter (1520–1569).

to turn them. Kicking and rolling about
the Fair Grounds, swinging their butts, those
shanks must be sound to bear up under such   10
rollicking measures, prance as they dance
in Breughel's great picture, The Kermess.

[1944—U.S.A.]

The painting by Breughel here described is one of vigorous, almost violent motion given rise to by joyous emotion. In the ways it moves, the poem captures in words what the painting captures in paint. In writing on the poem, you would first need to look at its meter, which is hard to label. Is the basic beat anapestic or dactylic? Are the lines trimeters or tetrameters? The answer to the second question is both, five of the lines containing four beats each (lines 4, 5, 8, 10, and 11) and the other seven containing three beats each. As to the basic beat, the poem keeps shifting between anapests and dactyls, with a number of iambs and trochees thrown in for good measure. In other words, there is no single name that we can put on the meter here. But it is the poem's very variability, you would want to observe, that gives it its rhythmic effect. The rhythm produced by this metrical variability seems to pull us in different directions at the same time, just as the people in the painting are pulled in the round; and like them, we too might feel a little dizzy, our dizziness resulting from the poem's diverse beats and the rhythm they create.

You would also need to discuss how the poem's lines break and the effect of the way they break. For instance, you might observe of line one, which is end-stopped, that its being end-stopped both allows the poem to come full circle by allowing the first line to be repeated exactly as the last (the poem's structure is metaphorical, suggesting an analogy with the round of the dance) and creates a moment of stillness that heightens the sense of motion as the dance begins and acts as an invitation to the dance (the pause is a kind of upbeat). Of the other end-stopped line in the poem (line 6), you could note that its being end-stopped creates a special effect: the pause at the end of the sixth line subtly echoes the sense of the line in that the end-stopping impounds (arrests, confines) movement just as the "glasses . . . impound" the "wash" (of paint) that they are depicted as containing. All the other lines of the poem enjamb, and—this you would want to stress—they do so roughly, in a way that is reminiscent of Breughel's rough brush strokes as well as the roughness of the dance as both painted and described. That is, the rhythmic effect of the way most of the poem's lines break, like that of its variable meter, is vigorous, almost violent motion—like the motion captured in the painting.

The thesis we began with—that the rhythm of "The Dance" embodies the kind of movement that Breughel's painting depicts—has been, I think, fairly fully argued and demonstrated. But one thing remains, which could form the nucleus of your conclusion. Williams's poem, like Breughel's painting, is joyous. And the poem is so primarily because of its rhythm. This is not the rhythm of grave events nor of heroes dying in battle nor of betrayal in love. This is the rhythm of the dance, its measures swinging and rollicking. This is the rhythm of affirmation, of life force, of joy. That would be a good note on which to conclude.

POEMS FOR STUDY AND WRITING ASSIGNMENTS

FOR JANE MYERS
— Louise Glück —

Sap rises from the sodden ditch
and glues two green ears to the dead
birch twig. Perilous beauty—
and already Jane is digging out
her colored tennis shoes,   5
one mauve, one yellow, like large crocuses.

And by the laundromat
the Bartletts in their tidy yard—

as though it were not
wearying, wearying   10

to hear in the bushes
the mild harping of the breeze,
the daffodils flocking and honking—
Look how the bluet falls apart, mud
pockets the seed.   15
Months, years, then the dull blade of the wind.
It is spring! We are going to die!

And now April raises up her plaque of flowers
and the heart
expands to admit its adversary.   20

[1975—U.S.A.]

Questions

1. Some of the lines in this poem enjamb easily and some do not. Which enjambments are fluid and which graceless? How does the kind of sense unit that is split contribute to fluidity or gracelessness?
2. Contrast lines 1–3 and lines 4–6 as to rhythm. What is the rhythmic feel of each set of lines? How is the rhythm of each created (consider enjambment and pause especially)? What does the difference in rhythm tell about the difference between the speaker and Jane?
3. Contrast lines 7–8 and lines 9–10 as to rhythm. How is the rhythm of each pair of lines created? What does the difference in rhythm tell us about the difference between the speaker and the Bartletts? The way line 9 breaks throws emphasis on "not." Why?

4. What other words in the poem receive special emphasis because of where the line breaks? Why?
5. Lines 15 and 19 are radically shortened. What is the rhythmic effect of this shortening? Why this effect?
6. Overall, what is the relationship between the poem's rhythm and its emotional content? How does the rhythm help to define the speaker and her feelings about spring, which provides the poem's setting and situation both?

Writing Assignments

1. In a paragraph or more, discuss the difference in rhythm between lines 1–3 and lines 4–6. What is the difference? How is it established? What does it tell us about the speaker in contrast with Jane?
2. Write a critique of "For Jane Myers." Is it a memorable poem or just so-so? What do you base your conclusion on? In judging the poem, be sure to discuss its rhythm and the relationship between its rhythm and its emotional content.
3. "April is the cruelest month, breeding / Lilacs out of the dead land," T. S. Eliot wrote in *The Waste Land*. Glück's speaker would agree. Write a paper analyzing the speaker in this regard. What does she feel? How does she differ from Jane and the Bartletts? How does the way the line is treated—where it breaks, how it breaks, what is emphasized because of the break—contribute to the contrasts and to our understanding of the speaker? In analyzing the speaker, keep your focus on rhythm—on what its effects are, on how it is created, and on its relation to content.

TEARS, IDLE TEARS
— Alfred, Lord Tennyson —

Tears, idle tears, I know not what they mean,
Tears from the depth of some divine despair
Rise in the heart, and gather to the eyes,
In looking on the happy autumn-fields,
And thinking of the days that are no more.   5

Fresh as the first beam glittering on a sail,
That brings our friends up from the underworld,
Sad as the last which reddens over one
That sinks with all we love below the verge;
So sad, so fresh, the days that are no more.   10

Ah, sad and strange as in dark summer dawns
The earliest pipe of half-awakened birds
To dying ears, when unto dying eyes

TEARS, IDLE TEARS.   **7.** *from the underworld*: from below the horizon.

The casement slowly grows a glimmering square;
So sad, so strange, the days that are no more.   15

    Dear as remembered kisses after death,
And sweet as those by hopeless fancy feigned
On lips that are for others; deep as love,
Deep as first love, and wild with all regret;
O Death in Life, the days that are no more!   20

[1847—Great Britain]

Questions

1. Scan the first stanza of the poem. What is its metrical norm? What is its meter?
2. What are some of the many deviant beats here? What is their effect on the poem overall, or on its rhythm? In what way is this effect at one with content?
3. Where might one choose to deviate from the metrical norm for interpretive emphasis? To what effect?
4. Every line in the poem is end-stopped. Why? What is the effect of end-stopping on the poem's rhythm?
5. How would you describe the poem's rhythm in general? How does the way it moves reflect mood? In that mood here *is* content, the poem's rhythm is its meaning. Elaborate.

Writing Assignments

1. Write a paragraph or more on the effect of metrical deviation along with insistent end-stopping on the rhythm of "Tears, Idle Tears." What is the effect and what does the resultant rhythm communicate?
2. In an essay, address question 5 above. Take the statement "the poem's rhythm is its meaning" as your thesis. Go on to argue that this is so because the poem is a mood piece and rhythm can create mood. How so? What is the rhythm here? How is it created? How does it help establish mood? It would be valuable to include a scansion of the poem showing its deviant beats especially.

SHORTSTOP

— Terence Paré —

Oquendo's error's ageless, the very same
Mistake I made eleven years ago
In Little League—a grounder lit across
The infield, blinked through an invisible gap
In my glove, sped far away into left field.   5
They scored a run, and I was charged an error
And amazed, as this young man, a Met,

Must be at his marvelous mistake,
The difficulty of the simple thing,
The ease of costly error: the passed ball,   10
The wild pitch, the heartless phrase, the dropped fly,
The love let die, errors we make as children
As easily as adults. Oquendo's now
Recovered, replaced his cap, and spit. He's bent
And tense, his eyes on home, ready, waiting   15
To redeem himself by some spectacularly
Graceful play. I watch from the stands. The score
Is close, the inning late, the pitcher's in
His stretch. And for all the craft of this green
And diamond world, the error makes the game.   20

[1985—U.S.A.]

Questions

1. Scan the poem and underline all deviations from what you determine its meter to be.
2. What is the underlying meter here? What kind of verse do we call this? What is the effect of the poem's metrical deviations?
3. Many lines here enjamb. How do they do so? What is the effect of the poem's enjambments?
4. What metaphor is offhandedly suggested here entailing Oquendo's error and the ordinary errors of day-to-day life? What attitude would the poem have us take toward error? What is its theme?
5. How does "Shortstop" sound to you? What kind of voice is created by its overriding rhythm and rhythmic feel? In what way is this voice appropriate to the poem's content?

Writing Assignments

1. (a) In a paragraph, describe the rhythm of "Shortstop" and the kind of voice the rhythm helps to create.
   (b) In a separate paragraph, state your response to "Shortstop" and suggest what it is about the poem that evokes this response.
2. Write a paragraph or more on how the rhythm of "Shortstop" is created. Consider meter, metrical deviation, line length, and enjambment especially. Conclude by suggesting how the rhythm of the poem is one with its content.
3. In a paper, contrast "Shortstop" and Tennyson's "Tears, Idle Tears" (pp. 339–40). Both are in the same kind of verse. What is it? Both also have many deviant beats. Yet the effect of deviation in the two poems is quite different. How does the effect differ? What causes the difference? How do the poems differ as to what happens at the ends of their lines? How does what happens affect rhythm? How do the poems differ in rhythm generally and rhythmic effect? These are some of the questions to answer as you proceed in contrasting the two poems at hand.

WHERE THE BEE SUCKS
— William Shakespeare —

Where the bee sucks, there suck I:
In a cowslip's bell I lie;
There I couch when owls do cry.
On the bat's back I do fly
After summer merrily.   5
Merrily, merrily shall I live now
Under the blossom that hangs on the bough.

[1623—Great Britain]

Questions

1. Scan line 5 of this lyric poem. With your scansion of line 5 in mind, scan lines 1 through 4. Then scan lines 6 and 7.
2. What is the beat of lines 1–5? How many times does it recur? What, then, is the meter? What is the meter of lines 6 and 7?
3. This lyric is sung by a character named Ariel in Shakespeare's *The Tempest*. Ariel, who has been in bondage to the magician Prospero, has been promised his freedom. The song is Ariel's response to that promise. In what ways does the poem's rhythm, created mainly by meter, reflect a prisoner's feelings about being free? In answering, consider the rhetorical stresses established by the meter on "Where" and "there" (line 1), "In" (line 2), "There" (line 3), and "On" (line 4). These are not words that are normally stressed. Why are they here?
4. If we take the meter of lines 1–5 as the norm, then lines 6 and 7 are deviant, though their beat is related to that of lines 1–5. How so? What is the effect on rhythm of the meter of lines 6 and 7?
5. Compare lines 1–5 with lines 6 and 7 as to rhythm. How does each set of lines move? How does the way they move differ? What is the rhythmic effect of each set of lines? What is the emotional significance of rhythm here?

Writing Assignments

1. In a paragraph, discuss how the meter of the present poem establishes rhetorical stress; then consider the added dimension of meaning that rhetorical stress in "Where the Bee Sucks" brings about.
2. Do a bit of research and read, if not the whole of *The Tempest,* at least the scene in which "Where the Bee Sucks" is found (act 5, scene 1). Now write a paper focused on the rhythm of the poem (what it is, how it is created) and how the rhythm is one with the meaning (what Ariel is feeling) as determined from other aspects of the song itself (other than rhythm) and from the larger context of the song (that is, Shakespeare's play).

NEITHER OUT FAR NOR IN DEEP
— Robert Frost —

The people along the sand
All turn and look one way.
They turn their back on the land.
They look at the sea all day.

As long as it takes to pass   5
A ship keeps raising its hull;
The wetter ground like glass
Reflects a standing gull.

The land may vary more;
But wherever the truth may be—   10
The water comes ashore,
And the people look at the sea.

They cannot look out far.
They cannot look in deep.
But when was that ever a bar   15
To any watch they keep?

[1936—U.S.A.]

Questions

1. Scan the poem, underlining all deviant beats. What is the meter here? What is the effect of the poem's deviant feet?
2. In some metrical poems, the beat is light; in others, it is heavy and insistent. Which is true of Frost's poem? To what effect?
3. Rhythm here creates tone. How so? Consider the length of the line chosen, the meter and the lightness or heaviness of the beat, what happens at the end of each of the poem's lines, and the kind of deviant feet allowed into it. Take all this into account in determining the tone of the poem.
4. Tone reveals attitude. What, then, is the speaker's attitude toward the "people along the sand"? Are they heroic in striving for what they cannot attain, or are they foolish boobs for the same reason? What does the poem's rhythm suggest?

Writing Assignments

1. Write a short paper on the tone of "Neither Out Far nor In Deep." You might begin with a paraphrase of what the poem seems to mean at first glance. But does it mean this after

all? Move on to consider its tone—what it is and how it is established (consider rhythm especially)—and what meaning the tone suggests.

2. Line length, meter, the qualities of the beat, what happens at the ends of lines, deviant beats—all go into the making of rhythm here, which in turn creates tone, which reveals attitude, which here is theme. Determine what the theme is (that is, what the speaker's attitude toward the "people" is) and then write an essay on this theme—what it is and how we come to understand what it is. What else in the poem, aside from rhythm and tone, intimates the speaker's attitude? Discuss rhythm and tone as well, of course. What is the speaker's tone? What rhythmic qualities of the poem suggest his tone? What makes for those qualities? Include a scansion with your paper.

PITCHER
— Robert Francis —

His art is eccentricity, his aim
How not to hit the mark he seems to aim at,

His passion how to avoid the obvious,
His technique how to vary the avoidance.

The others throw to be comprehended. He   5
Throws to be a moment misunderstood.

Yet not too much. Not errant, arrant, wild,
But every seeming aberration willed.

Not to, yet still, still to communicate
Making the batter understand too late.   10

[1960—U.S.A.]

Questions

1. Scan the poem and underscore all deviations. What are the basic beat and meter here?
2. What beats in your judgment might be read as deviant for interpretative emphasis? Justify your decisions.
3. Lines 6, 9, and 10 begin with metrical inversions (trochees, in this case). Why? How do the inversions affect inflection and to what end?
4. Why are there so many metrical deviations here? How do the poem's deviant feet help dramatize what it is about? How are form and content one with respect to these varied, unexpected, and calculated deviations?

Writing Assignments

1. In a paragraph or short paper, discuss how Francis gains emphasis by way of deviation from the metrical norm established by the first line of the poem. Determine what is emphasized thus and explain why.

2. Write an essay addressed to question 4 above. Your object will be to demonstrate the union of form and content. To this end, probe and discuss the analogy between pitcher and poet (as well as poem) that is inherent in the poem and what, finally, it concerns.

YOU, ANDREW MARVELL
— Archibald MacLeish —

And here face down beneath the sun
And here upon earth's noonward height
To feel the always coming on
The always rising of the night

To feel creep up the curving east   5
The earthy chill of dusk and slow
Upon those under lands the vast
And ever climbing shadow grow

And strange at Ecbatan the trees
Take leaf by leaf the evening strange   10
The flooding dark about their knees
The mountains over Persia change

And now at Kermanshah the gate
Dark empty and the withered grass
And through the twilight now the late   15
Few travelers in the westward pass

And Baghdad darken and the bridge
Across the silent river gone
And through Arabia the edge
Of evening widen and steal on   20

And deepen on Palmyra's street
The wheel rut in the ruined stone
And Lebanon fade out and Crete
High through the clouds and overblown

And over Sicily the air   25
Still flashing with the landward gulls
And loom and slowly disappear
The sails above the shadowy hulls

YOU, ANDREW MARVELL.   **9.** *Ecbatan:* Following the westward course of the sun, the speaker's thoughts move through time and space from Ecbatan, the capital of ancient Persia, to Kermanshah, Baghdad, and so on.

And Spain go under and the shore
Of Africa the gilded sand   30
And evening vanish and no more
The low pale light across that land

Nor now the long light on the sea
And here face downward in the sun
To feel how swift how secretly   35
The shadow of the night comes on . . . .

[1930—U.S.A.]

Questions

1. What are the setting and situation of this poem?
2. Why the title "You, Andrew Marvell"? How does Marvell's "To His Coy Mistress" (pp. 256–57) elucidate MacLeish's poem?
3. Scan the first few stanzas. What is the meter?
4. The meter here is perfectly regular. There are no deviant feet. Why should this be so? What does the poem's regularity intimate?
5. Describe the rhythm produced by the poem's meter. What does the rhythm, along with the progressively western-moving images, convey as to theme?

Writing Assignments

1. In a short paper, discuss the meaning of this poem in light of its title and its imagery, or the progression thereof. Be sure to discuss as well how the poem's rhythm contributes to its meaning as determined by such other factors as its title and imagery.
2. Write an essay on the conjunction of the poem's rhythm and its sense. How does the poem move? What creates this type of movement? How does how the poem moves (that is, its rhythm) convey the sense of inevitability that MacLeish's theme entails?

CHAPTER

✳ **6** ✳

PATTERNS OF SOUND

SOUND AND SENSE

There is an old Yiddish story about a man who puzzles over why noodles are called *noodles*. After much internal debate, he throws up his hands and says, "Ehh, they're called noodles because they look like noodles." True, the word "noodle" is noodle-ey, ending, as it does, with a little curl of sound. In fact, however, there is no historical basis for the belief that the sounds of words are linked to their meanings. Individual words are merely arbitrary signs, and when we find linkages of sound and sense, they are merely accidental. **Onomatopoetic words**—words whose sounds ostensibly do imitate the sounds of what they name (*buzz, splash, cock-a-doodle-doo*)—might seem an exception; yet other languages have completely different words for the same auditory phenomena. And in any case, for every word that somehow sounds like what it means, there are fifty that do not.

Language, it would seem, consists of sterile signs only—sterile because not expressive, not expressive because arbitrary. Whatever the history of words, however, we use them not singly but in *patterns* of our own design. That is, though the sounds of individual words have nothing necessarily to do with their sense, they can be made expressive—or a union of sound and sense can be forged—by selection and patterning. All writers achieve certain effects thus. But the poet strives to reach the ideal of total union of sense and all aspects of a poem's form, including sound. By deliberate selection and patterning, poets mold from the arbitrary givens of language a unity of form and content, sound and sense, achieving thereby a language potent and dense with meaning.

The following passage from Alexander Pope's "An Essay on Criticism"—a *tour de force* with respect to the relating of sound and sense through patterning—suggests the ideal, with each sound pattern reflecting each idea, idea by idea. To be sure, few poems reach this degree of correspondence of sound and sense. Still, all entail a relationship between the two, if not point by point, then overall. As you read the passage from Pope, at any rate, pay attention to the meter and now the sound as well. What patterns of sound can you find? What repeated consonants and vowels in the slow-moving lines? What in the fast? I am sure that you will feel the effects

347

of Pope's lines just by reading them. But by answering questions like these, you will be able to see in full how the effects are gained.

from AN ESSAY ON CRITICISM
— Alexander Pope —

'Tis not enough no harshness gives offense,
The sound must seem an echo to the sense.
Soft is the strain when Zephyr gently blows,
And the smooth stream in smoother numbers flows;
But when loud surges lash the sounding shore,   5
The hoarse, rough verse should like the torrent roar.
When Ajax strives some rock's vast weight to throw,
The line too labors, and the words move slow;
Not so when swift Camilla scours the plain,
Flies o'er the unbending corn, and skims along the main.   10

[1711—Great Britain]

This passage is a perpetual delight because of the close connection of sound and sense in it. In lines 3–4, for instance, Pope says that verse concerning a soft breeze or a "smooth stream" should itself move gently and slowly and that its sound should be smooth. With its concentration of nasals (*m*'s and *n*'s) and of the long ō͞o sound, the passage achieves the smoothness that it concerns; because of the metrically inverted "Sóft ís," the spondee "smóoth stréam," and the long ō͞o and ō sounds, it also attains the proper pace for what is being described. In contrast, lines 5–6 are loud and hoarse, imitating the surging waves they describe. The effect is achieved in part by meter (the triple stressing of "whén lóud súrgĕs" and "hóarse, róugh vérse" tends to raise the volume) and in part by patterned sound— the scratchy *g* of "surges" together with the harsh *sh* sound of "lash" (the majority of English words containing "-sh," incidentally, are violent in character) and especially the hissing *s* of "hoarse" and "verse" combine to give a raspy quality to the sound at this point. The sense of strain and laboriousness of lines 7–8, which reflect the straining of Ajax lifting a mighty rock, is achieved by triple stressing again ("róck's vást wéight," "líne tŏo lábŏrs," and "wórds móve slów") along with the juxtaposition of letters that are hard to say together. The triple stressing slows the pace and makes the verse laborious; and the phrases just quoted parenthetically are hard to say because the mouth must re-form between each word to utter the new configuration. Being hard to say, the words slow us down and so seem laborious. Just the opposite effect is to be felt in the last two lines of the passage. Here, the three slack syllables coming together in "Flies ŏ'er thĕ ŭn-" speed up the pace, as do the elisions of *s* with *o* in "Flies o'er" and *s* with *a* in "skims along." By virtue of its meter and its sounds, the last two lines move as swiftly as Camilla ever could.

The sound of a poem, then, is somehow or another a dimension of its meaning.

Again, the relation of sound and sense in most poems is not as obvious as it is in this passage by Pope. But there almost always is a relationship that needs some degree of attention. What should alert you to consider the sound as you read is the patterned repetition and concentration of consonants and/or vowels, sounds that are alike, sounds that are hard to say, and so forth. Whenever a pattern is discernible, something is going on in the poem's sound. Your job as reader is to determine what and then to feel out why.

SYNTACTICAL PATTERNS

English is a syntactical language: our words mean what they mean in sentences primarily by virtue of positioning. "Dog bites man," therefore, means one thing, and "man bites dog" means quite another. Also a matter of syntax are the different sentence patterns found in English. For instance, one could say, "I earn my money before I spend it" or "Before I spend my money, I earn it." Then, too, we often gain emphasis by syntactical inversion: "My money, I earn." In other words, though there are characteristic syntactical patterns in English, there are also alternative possibilities that can be used for special purposes.

Because **syntax** affects rhythm (the way words move) and sound generally, a poet's choice of one syntactical pattern over another is often of particular significance. For instance, consider the following passage from *Paradise Lost,* by John Milton, a master of syntax as a medium of verbal drama.

> Others apart sat on a hill retired,
> In thoughts more elevate, and reasoned high
> Of providence, foreknowledge, will, and fate,
> Fixed fate, free will, foreknowledge absolute,
> And found no end, in wandering mazes lost.

> [Book 2, lines 557–561]

Here Milton describes a band of fallen angels engaging in the intricate theological disputes of his own day. With much wit, Milton makes a syntactical maze of his words—which move tediously and sound laborious—and thereby dramatically suggests the mazy tediousness of the labyrinthine dispute.

Milton achieves marvelous effects with syntax through its effects on rhythm and sound. So do many other poets. Gerard Manley Hopkins, for instance, found in syntax a way of capturing on paper his dark night of the soul. Take the following passage, from a late sonnet by the poet. Note especially the syntax of the third line and the effect of syntax here on rhythm and sound.

> I wake and feel the fell of dark, not day.
> What hours, O what black hours we have spent
> This night! what sights, you, heart, saw; ways you went!
> And more must in yet longer light's delay.

Hopkins could have written, "what sights you saw, my heart, what ways you went." But that sounds too calm for a speaker waking from a terrible nightmare. Hopkins wrote "what sights, you, heart, saw; ways you went" because he wanted the rhythmical awkwardness and sense of strain of this alternative syntactical pattern. The pattern lends tumult to the voice and has the sound of desperation, the desperation one feels when waking in the middle of the night from a fearful dream.

Much the opposite is the effect of the passage from John Denham's *Cooper's Hill* that we looked at earlier in connection with metaphor (pp. 304–05).

> O could I flow like thee, and make thy stream
> My great example, as it is my theme!
> Though deep, yet clear; though gentle, yet not dull;
> Strong without rage, without o'erflowing, full.

The sense of balance and grace in these lines is the result of their syntax. Note especially their syntactical parallelism: for example, the parallelism between "Though deep, yet clear" and "though gentle, yet not dull." Syntax here serves to make the lines move gracefully and lends to them the sound of balance, which is the ideal they hold out.

There are many other syntactical patterns possible, perhaps as many as there are poets. In any event, the point is that syntax can create special effects in poetry and is always allied with rhythm and sound generally. Therefore, the syntactical patterns of a poem should be considered when you are focusing on its rhythms or sound. Especially when the syntax of a line or passage seems odd, ask why. Why did the poet put things this way? What is the effect of the syntax in question on rhythm and sound? How does that effect tie in with other aspects of the poem? Questions like these will get you deeper into the one poem and help you to see more fully that the meaning of poetry is expressed through all its dimensions—the denotations and connotations of words, the forms they build and the rhythms they create, and their syntax and sound.

PATTERNED CONSONANTS AND VOWELS

When patterned, consonants and vowels are also a dimension of a poem's meaning, or of the way it means. English consonants fall roughly into ten categories: the fricatives *f* and *v,* and the affricative *j;* the nasals *m* and *n;* the sibilants *s* and *z;* the plosives *b* and *p,* and the related dentals *d* and *t;* the gutturals *g* (as in "god"), *k, q,* and *x;* the aspirate *h;* the glides and rolls *r* (as in "rough"), *w,* and *y;* and the liquids *l* and *r* (as in "tiger"). There are also consonantal sounds, produced by the combining of certain consonants, called blends and digraphs: for example, *ng, sh, sp, cl, th, str, ch.* Our vowel sounds, of which there are at least sixteen in standard English (plus diphthongs such as *ai* as in "day" and *ou* as in "how"), can be long or short (for example, "say" versus "sat") and differ in frequency or pitch, as the following chart of selected vowel sounds arranged in descending order as to pitch demonstrates:

ē (see)
  ā (say)
    ī (sigh) ĭ (sit)
      ĕ (set)
       ă (sat) ŭ (suds)
        ô (saw)
         ŏ (sot) o͝o (shook)
          ō (shone)
           o͞o (shoe)

(There is a physical basis, incidentally, for one's perception of a descent of pitch here. In fact, the wavelengths of high-frequency vowels, which are formed in the front of the mouth, are shorter and more intense than those of low-frequency vowels, which come from the back of the mouth and the throat.)

These, then, are our basic consonant and vowel sounds, which, because they involve the mouth and tongue in different motions, have different feelings (physical and thence emotional) about them. The nasals (*m* and *n*) are easier to say and softer in feel than the gutturals (*g, k, q,* and *x*); the aspirate *h* is quieter than the affricative *j;* the liquids (*l, r*) are more fluid than the plosives (*b, p*), which are more explosive. As for vowels, the long vowels take more time to say than the short vowels (this quantitative difference can strongly affect rhythm), and the high-pitched vowels are brighter or more piercing than the duller or more placid low-pitched vowels.

The sounds of individual words, as I have said, do not as a rule reflect their sense. But carefully chosen words in combination can form patterns that reflect meaning in that they exploit the different innate qualities of the sounds of consonants and vowels. For instance, a concentration of low and/or long vowels will have a different effect from a concentration of high and/or short vowels: in this regard, compare "No motion has she now, no force" with "Hail to thee, blithe Spirit" and "Variety is the spice of life." Similarly, a line with a marked recurrence of aspirates and liquids will be quite different in sound and movement from a line marked by a recurrence of affricatives and dentals: "Home is where the heart is" as opposed to "Judge not lest ye be judged." The first is hushed and even in movement, its one sharp sound (the *t* of "heart") softened by elision with the vowel that follows; the second is loud and abrupt, not an exhalation of sentimental feeling but a stern command. The pattern of each is deliberate and meaningful, which is why such phrases stick in the mind: though arbitrary individually, their words are expressive in the patterns they form.

There are so many conceivable patterns of vowels and vowels, consonants and consonants, and consonants and vowels that it would not be possible to name them all. There are, however, five general terms that can be useful in studying sound and its relation to meaning in poetry: assonance, vowel gradation, consonance, alliteration, and medial sounds.

Assonance

Assonance is the repetition of similar vowel sounds in a sequence of words: "Thou still unravished br*i*de of qu*i*etness, / Thou foster ch*i*ld of s*i*lence and slow t*i*me" (John Keats); "near the w*i*nter r*i*ver w*i*th s*i*lt like s*i*lver" (William Stafford). Such repetition can have a number of different effects. If the vowels of a passage are mostly long, they tend to slow the pace; if they are mostly short, they tend to quicken it. If the vowels are mainly low-pitched, they tend to deepen or darken the sound, making it mellow or mournful; if they are mainly high-pitched, they tend to brighten the sound or to give it a sharp edge. If the patterned vowels are short and high-pitched, they can quicken and lighten; if they are long and low-pitched, they can slow and cast a pall. For example, consider the following passage from James Joyce's *A Portrait of the Artist as a Young Man* (the phenomena we have been discussing can be found in prose just as well as in poetry). Note the concentration of high-pitched vowels ($\bar{a}, \bar{e}, \bar{\imath}$) along with a pattern of glides (w), aspirates (h), and liquids (l and r).

> He was alone. He was unheeded, happy and near to the wild heart of life. He was alone and young and willful and wildhearted, alone amid a waste of wild air and brackish waters and the seaharvest of shells and tangle and veiled grey sunlight and gayclad lightclad figures, of children and girls and voices childish and girlish in the air. . . .

The passage is as lighthearted and joyous in its sound as it is in its meaning otherwise. But the sound, of course, is part of that meaning, helping to shape our feelings at each turn.

Vowel Gradation

Equally marked in effect is **vowel gradation,** the step-by-step shifting of vowels from high to low or low to high. The first line of the old blues song "St. Louis Blues" offers a striking example of purposeful gradation: "I hate to see that evenin' sun go down." Look at the line's main vowels: $\bar{\imath}, \bar{a}, \bar{e}, \breve{u}, \bar{o}, \ddot{a}/\overline{oo}$ (for the dipthong *ou* in "down"). There is here a clearly gradated movement from high-pitched to low-pitched vowels, a movement reflected in the song's melody line and reflective of the sinking the line describes. A less strictly stepwise gradation, but a gradation still, can be found in these lines by Alexander Pope:

> So when thick clouds inwrap the mountain's head,
> O'er heav'ns expanse like one black ceiling spread;
> Sudden the Thund'rer, with a flashing ray,
> Bursts thro' the darkness, and lets down the day.
> The hills shine out, the rocks in prospect rise,
> And streams, and vales, and forests strike the eyes,
> The smiling scene wide opens to the sight,
> And all th'unmeasur'd aether flames with light.

There is a deliberate pattern here of lower-pitched vowels (in the first four lines) moving to higher-pitched vowels (in the second four lines). Part of the meaning, this pattern helps convey a sense of the storm's passing and of darkness giving way to light.

Consonance

Consonance is the repetition of a sequence of consonants with a change in the intervening vowels—for example, *tick/tock, life/loaf, breed/bread*. The primary effect of consonance is dissonance, for words in consonantal relationship are so close that their internal differences tend to grate. Consonance, that is, stresses dissimilarity in similarity (in this regard, consonance is the opposite of rhyme). Wilfred Owen, the foremost poet of the First World War, used consonance to give voice to his disgust.

ARMS AND THE BOY
— Wilfred Owen —

Let the boy try along this bayonet-blade
How cold steel is, and keen with hunger of blood;
Blue with all malice, like a madman's flash;
And thinly drawn with famishing for flesh.

Lend him to stroke these blind, blunt bullet-heads   5
Which long to nuzzle in the hearts of lads,
Or give him cartridges of fine zinc teeth,
Sharp with the sharpness of grief and death.

For his teeth seem for laughing round an apple.
There lurk no claws behind his fingers supple;   10
And god will grow no talons at his heels,
Nor antlers through the thickness of his curls.

[1920—Great Britain]

Like rhyme, consonance draws attention. This is why "Arms and the Boy" is so dissonant. At the very points where we might expect the resolution of rhyme—at the crucial end-line positions—we find the opposite of rhyme, stress falling on difference rather than similarity. The effect of "blade/blood," "flash/flesh," "heads/lads," and so on is like the effect in a piece of music of a strongly dissonant chord coming just when we expect a return to the tonic (a harmonious chord that provides resolution). Both set the teeth on edge. This is the effect, too, of internal consonance ("blind, blunt bullet"); the poem's concentration of plosives (*b, p*), dentals (*d, t*), and gutturals and affricatives ("*cartridges of fine zinc*"); and its insistent lack of assonance (there is a minimum of vowel repetition here—for example, look at the

ARMS AND THE BOY.   Owen alludes to the first line of Vergil's *Aeneid:* "I sing of arms and the man."

main vowel sounds of line 4: "And th*i*nly dr*a*wn with *fa*mishing for *fl*esh"). Everything works together to produce a voice that is bitter and bitterly ironic in tone.

Alliteration

Alliteration, or the repetition of consonants at the beginning of words or of internal syllables, can have a number of effects as to rhythm and sound. For instance, in that alliterated words call attention, alliteration tends to draw stress and thus to slow the pace, as happens in the last two lines of Marvell's "To His Coy Mistress": "Thus, though we cannot make our *s*un / *S*tand *s*till, yet we will make him run." It is the alliteration that causes "stand" to be stressed and thus the alliteration that slows the pace in accordance with what is being said. Depending on the consonants alliterated, alliteration can also make for a mellow sound, for instance, or a harsh, grating sound. John Keats, speaking of the mellowness of autumn, captures a sense of that mellowness by way of alliteration: "Seaso*n* of *m*ists a*n*d *m*ellow fruitful*n*ess, / Close boso*m*-frie*n*d of the *m*aturing su*n*" ("To Autumn"). The concentration of nasals (*m* and *n*) lends to the sound of these lines a quiet warmth that reflects the season invoked. Conversely, the following line from Alfred, Lord Tennyson's *In Memoriam,* a long poem comprised of short lyrics in which Tennyson expresses his grief over the death of his dearest friend, strikes in its harsh alliterations the sound of anger and disgust: "on the *b*al*d s*tree*t b*reak*s* the *b*lan*k d*ay." Here the concentration of plosives and dentals (*b, d,* and *t*), gutturals (*k*), and sibilants (*s*) along with the *b* alliteration makes for a sound that rings with a sense of despair.

Medial Sounds

The same line from Tennyson's *In Memoriam* also exemplifies the importance to rhythm and sound of what happens *between* words when they are formed in the mouth. Read the line aloud and notice what happens in your mouth and neck: "On the bald street breaks the blank day." The line is hard to say, for its **medial sounds** (in this case, all consonants) cannot be elided; to speak the words, one must pause after each and reshape the mouth: "On the bal*d s*tree*t b*reaks the blan*k d*ay." Contrast Tennyson's straining pattern of sound with Keats's "Season of mists and mellow fruitfulness." Because of the nature of its medial consonants and vowels, Keats's line melts in the mouth, its sound being as smooth as it is warm.

Nothing of what we have been considering, of course, operates in isolation. Assonance, vowel gradation, consonance, alliteration, medial sounds—all work in consort and achieve their effects always in a specific context only. For this reason, we cannot say that assonance, for example, or alliteration will have such and such an effect in general. The effect depends on the individual context and what else is happening in that context. A concentration of high-pitched vowels in a context of nasals and liquids and much elision, for instance, will have a strikingly different sound and rhythmic effect from a concentration of high-pitched vowels in a context of gutturals and plosives and minimal elision. The point is that what happens in a poem depends, finally, on everything that happens in it. A poem depends for its final effect on the interaction of all its elements.

Let's take a poem now by way of example and see how its various patterns work together to produce a certain kind of sound—and thence tone—that communicates complex feelings exactly.

from COMMANDER LOWELL
— Robert Lowell —

Having a naval officer
for my Father was nothing to shout
about to the summer colony at "Matt."
He wasn't at all "serious,"
when he showed up on the golf course,   5
wearing a blue serge jacket and numbly cut
white ducks he'd bought
at a Pearl Harbor commissariat . . .
and took four shots with his putter to sink his putt.
"Bob," they said, "golf's a game you really ought to know how to play,   10
if you play at all."
They wrote him off as "naval,"
naturally supposed his sport was sailing.
Poor Father, his training was engineering!
Cheerful and cowed   15
among the seadogs at the Sunday yacht club,
he was never one of the crowd.

"Anchors aweigh," Daddy boomed in his bathtub,
"Anchors aweigh,"
when Lever Brothers offered to pay   20
him double what the Navy paid.
I nagged for his dress sword with gold braid,
and cringed because Mother, new
caps on all her teeth, was born anew
at forty. With seamanlike celerity,   25
Father left the Navy,
and deeded Mother his property.

He was soon fired. Year after year,
he still hummed "Anchors aweigh" in the tub—

COMMANDER LOWELL.   **3.** *"Matt":* Mattapoisett, Massachusetts—a summer resort.

whenever he left a job,   30
he bought a smarter car.

[1959—U.S.A.]

Lowell's syntax and enjambments tend to be somewhat awkward overall, and at points both are terribly so: for example, "Mother, new / caps on all her teeth, was born anew." Both the syntactical pattern here and the way the first quoted line breaks are clumsy, and the line break also produces an unpleasant shock because of the stress thrown on the unexpected "caps." The poem's rhymes are for the most part concealed and so operate below consciousness, at least on first reading; nevertheless, they create a context in which the effect of consonance and off-rhyme (which we will take up shortly)—that is, dissonance—is heightened. Syntax, line breaks, enjambment, consonance, and off-rhyme all help to create a tone of disquiet, as does the concentration (also unobtrusive) of sibilants, dentals, plosives, and low-pitched vowels along with alliteration: for instance, "ducks he'd bought" and "Daddy boomed in his bathtub." What is remarkable about the passage is that it is so highly crafted, yet its craft is almost entirely concealed. The latter accounts for the colloquial, intimately confessional tone of these lines; the former accounts for the singular feeling of unease that the passage imparts. Because of the way the passage sounds and moves, it communicates a sense of reticence and ambivalence: the poet would not speak against his father and mother, but their specters produce in him ambivalent feelings because of his sense of shortcomings—theirs and perhaps his in relation to them. Everything I have mentioned works together to concretize and convey the poet's ambivalence and unease, the gray feelings of a troubled adult recalling his troubled childhood.

RHYME AND REASON

Words **rhyme** when they end in the same vowel and consonant sounds but are otherwise different: *rhyme/chime, vowel/towel, otherwise/not my size.* In a way, then, rhyme is like metaphor: both entail the seeing of similarity in difference. By the same token, rhyme is the opposite of consonance, which emphasizes the difference between words that are similar. But why, one might wonder, would a poet choose to incur the limitations that rhyming imposes when poetry does not have to rhyme to be poetry? After all, many of the greatest poems in the language don't rhyme. On the other hand, many do. Why? There are reasons. Aurally concrete (for rhyme is something we actually hear), rhyming is another tool the poet can use for shaping movement and fashioning sound for the purpose at hand. The possible effects of and thus reasons for rhyming are too diverse for us to go into them all. A few examples, however, should be enough to suggest the diversity of possible effect and why a poet might choose to use rhyme in a given poem.

1. Along with meter, rhyme is what defines stanzaic patterns and fixed forms (like the sonnet), which have many possible uses. Because the next chapter will be devoted to this matter, we will not go into it here. Let me point out, however, that

yet another reason for line division is that it makes **end-rhymes** (rhymes at the end of lines) possible and thus stanzas and fixed forms.

2. In part, rhyming is also a game. Frost compared it to the net in tennis: it is an obstacle, and one of the delights of reading rhymed poetry is watching how this obstacle is skillfully overcome and turned to advantage. In other words, rhyme and rhyming can be just plain fun. This is especially true in comic and satiric poetry, which almost always rhymes. Why? Because rhyme can carry a punch—just what comic and satiric poets need for their humorous purposes. Listen to the next poem and try to hear how its sound (rhyme) delivers the punch.

A REASONABLE AFFLICTION
— Matthew Prior —

On his deathbed poor Lubin lies;
   His spouse is in despair:
With frequent sobs, and mutual cries,
   They both express their care.

"A different cause," says parson Sly,   5
   "The same effect may give:
Poor Lubin fears that he shall die;
   His wife, that he may live."

[1709—Great Britain]

To see that it is indeed the rhyme that delivers the punch and makes the poem comic, read the second stanza again, only substituting "His wife, that he may not" for the original last line. The rhyme makes all the difference.

3. Prior's poem also suggests that rhyme can heighten the sense of climax and create a sense of resolution. Climax is very much the effect of the rhyme at the end of Langston Hughes's "Harlem" (p. 297), for example: "Maybe it just sags / like a heavy load. / *Or does it explode?*" Similarly, Blake's ironic rhyming of "joy" and "destroy," the only rhyme in "The Sick Rose" (p. 313), brings us up short, underscoring by its effect on rhythm the bitter irony at the heart of the poem. As to resolution, read the poem that follows with an ear to the effect of rhyme—its anticipation and then its fulfillment—on pace, pause, and your sense of closure.

FIRST FIG
— Edna St. Vincent Millay —

My candle burns at both ends;
   It will not last the night;

FIRST FIG.   Fig means "figure," as in figurative language. For "Second Fig," see p. 282.

But ah, my foes, and oh, my friends—
It gives a lovely light!

[1922—U.S.A.]

4. Along with exemplifying the effect of rhyme on rhythm, the Millay poem suggests something of the lyric qualities of rhyme, qualities that offer yet another dimension of possible effect. How many popular songs do not rhyme? Nor are there many purely lyric poems that do not, for one of the potentialities of rhyme is that it can impart a lyric or melodious quality to the voice. The next poem is a good example of the potential lyricism of rhyme. Having read it, compare it with the altered version that follows after—altered only as to rhyme. I think you will see immediately that it is rhyme that makes the original lyrical.

ALBA

— Ezra Pound —

When the nightingale to his mate
Sings day-long and night late
My love and I keep state
In bower,
In flower,   5
'Till the watchman on the tower
Cry:
                    "Up! Thou rascal, Rise,
                    I see the white
                              Light   10
                    And the night
                              Flies."

[1915—U.S.A.]

When the nightingale to his spouse
Sings day-long and all night
My love and I remain
In garden,
In petals,
'Till the watchman on the tower
Cry:

ALBA.   A song sung at dawn by one lover to another warning that they must flee.

"Up! Thou rascal, Up,
I see the pale
        Rays
And the night
        Goes."

5. Finally, deliberate deviation from the expectations that rhyme sets up can have its own effects, especially if instead of rhyme at the end of a line we get **off-rhyme.** *Frown/down* rhyme; *soon/noon* rhyme; but, though not far from rhyming, *down* and *noon* do not rhyme. Their very closeness accentuates their difference, and so, as with consonance, we feel dissimilarity, or difference in likeness. Particularly when we find dissimilarity where we expect similarity—at the end of a line—the effect of off-rhyme, like that of consonance, is dissonance. Perfectly in accord with meaning, the dissonance created by off-rhyme in the following poem is marked.

NOT WAVING BUT DROWNING
— Stevie Smith —

Nobody heard him, the dead man,
But still he lay moaning:
I was much further out than you thought
And not waving but drowning.

Poor chap, he always loved larking   5
And now he's dead
It must have been too cold for him his heart gave way,
They said.

Oh, no no no, it was too cold always
(Still the dead one lay moaning)   10
I was much too far out all my life
And not waving but drowning.

[1957—Great Britain]

In context with the rhyme *dead/said,* the off-rhyme *moaning/drowning* seems doubly disquieting. In effect, its sound is like the screech of chalk on a blackboard. And that effect is part of the poem's power and very much in accord with what it concerns and conveys.

We have seen previously and will see again that a poet can work either with or against a given element—lines, meter, rhyme, and so on. Whichever the case—with or against—there must be a reason why, and it is the reader's task to determine that reason. The reason Ms. Smith works against rhyme here, for instance, is clearly that the resulting dissonance of sound reflects the dissonance of feeling. In other words, form (sound) is a function of content, a way of giving expression to what can be expressed in no other way.

SUMMARY SUGGESTIONS: UNDERSTANDING PATTERNED SOUND

1. When reading poetry, look for patterns—syntactical patterns, patterns of consonants and vowels, patterns of rhyme and off-rhyme. Establish what patterns a poet is working with first. Then try to relate the patterns you have discerned to meaning.

2. Ordinary syntax in a poem probably does not carry any special significance. But should a syntactical pattern call attention to itself—by noticeable repetition, say—or should the syntax of a line or passage seem odd, ask why. Why did the poet put things this way? What is the effect of the syntactical pattern? How does it sound? What is its meaning, then, and how does it tie in with other aspects of the poem?

3. Question as well a poem's consonants and vowels. Do they form any patterns, like assonance or alliteration? Why? Why, for instance, a concentration of high-pitched vowels? What is the effect in context? How do the poem's consonant and vowel sounds help to reinforce or even create meaning? These are some of the questions that you should ask of a poem's sound. The last, of course, is the key question always to be worked toward.

4. If a poem rhymes, feel out the effect of rhyme on pace and pause. Do you pause with the chime, for instance, or does the anticipation of closure speed the pace? Or perhaps rhyme is used for either comic or lyrical purposes. How so? Don't forget, too, that rhyme can be used to create forms of various kinds. If the poem you are reading is in a stanzaic form, look at the end-rhymes, determine the form, and then try to relate it to the content.

5. And always allow for meaningful deviation, like off-rhyme in a rhyming context. Having observed what the deviation is—for instance, an off-rhyme coming where we might have expected a rhyme—determine the effect of the deviation and relate that effect to the poem's other elements and the meaning that together the poem's elements make.

WRITING ON SOUND

Writing on a poem's sound is much like writing on its rhythm. To write on either requires careful listening first, then a consideration of effect, and finally the drawing of conclusions as to the relationship of form (rhythm or sound) and content.

When attending to a poem's sound, first listen to the poem, and as you do, scrutinize it for any patterns of sound it contains: concentrations of consonants and vowels, alliteration, rhyme if the poem rhymes, and so forth. What kinds of consonants and/or vowels repeat: dentals and plosives along with high-pitched vowels, perhaps, or nasals and liquids along with low-pitched vowels? Are there any syntactical patterns that command attention? Does consonance or off-rhyme come into play? What kind of medial consonants and vowels does the poem have?

Having determined the prominent features of your poem's sound, you should turn next to their effect. A concentration of dentals and plosives along with high-pitched vowels, for example, could seem (depending on the context) sharp and jarring; a concentration of nasals and liquids along with low-pitched vowels could seem sad and melancholy. Consonance and off-rhyme, as we have seen, can sound dissonant. Conversely, alliteration along with rhyme can be lyrical in effect. Rhyme can also affect tone in various ways, ranging in effect from the warmth of lilting laughter to the cold blast of bitter irony. Equally marked in effect, medial consonants and vowels can make a passage sound with anger, say, or with gaiety, or whatever. The possible effects of the possible patterns of sound are infinite. The patterns of any single poem, however, are specific in effect and highly directed. It is the specific effect of one or another pattern in a given poem that you must come to see and articulate.

And finally you must move to consider what this or that effect is directed at: that is, you must relate the sound of a poem to its sense. How do the poem's sound overall and the particular patterns of sound found in it establish, reinforce, echo, or whatever, the meaning of the poem? How does its sound affect tone, for instance? What does the sound reveal about the poem's speaker? In what way is the emotional effect of the poem's various sound patterns relevant to its import generally? Answering questions such as these will provide you with a thesis: your thesis, that is, will concern the nature of the relationship of sound and sense in the poem at hand. Your support will entail a description of the poem's sound and its effects along with a consideration of how these effects are created. In analyzing a poem's sounds and their effects, remember your aim at every point: to demonstrate the relationship in the poem between sound and sense—in other words, to convince your reader of the validity of your thesis.

To be sure, like rhythm, or like any other element of poetry, for that matter, sound can be used as support. If, for instance, you were writing on the psychological makeup of the maid in Mari Evans's "When in Rome" (pp. 320–21), you would do well to point out how the poem's rhymes—all of which occur in the maid's parenthetical comments—lend a cutting quality to her tone and thereby suggest an ironic intent. Or, say, you were writing on the nature of grief as depicted in the seventh poem of Tennyson's *In Memoriam* (pp. 387–88). You would surely wish to comment on the sound of the poem and how its sound embodies a sense of grief. Your point would be that the sound of the line creates a voice marked by anger, disgust, and despair—all aspects of grief here communicated by the effect of sound on tone.

But what is most interesting to do with sound is to take it as a topic and to address head on the relationship of sound and sense in a poem as a whole. To do this well, note, requires a certain degree of delicacy and much deftness. For the relationship of sound and sense is usually subtle and is never easily verbalized. Still, the poetry of a poem lies always in the relationship of its form and content, the relationship of sound and sense being an important instance. To come to see how sound and sense are related in a poem, therefore, is in large part to see what makes it a poem. Focusing on sound, let's explore one last poem now, the discussion of which should serve as an example of what writing on a poem's sound entails.

SLOW, SLOW, FRESH FOUNT
— Ben Jonson —

Slow, slow, fresh fount, keep time with my salt tears;
    Yet slower yet, oh faintly, gentle springs;
List to the heavy part the music bears,
    Woe weeps out her division when she sings.
       Droop herbs and flowers,   5
       Fall grief in showers;
       Our beauties are not ours;
         Oh, I could still,
Like melting snow upon some craggy hill,
    Drop, drop, drop, drop,   10
Since nature's pride is now a withered daffodil.

[1600—Great Britain]

In terms of content, the poem is clearly a lyric lament. It is so, too, with respect to the way it moves and sounds. In other words, form and content are one. Notice, for instance, the many *o*'s in the poem and especially the many long *ō* sounds. These sounds produce something like an undercurrent of wailing. The poem's assonance, thus, serves to reinforce its sense of sorrow. So do its many other low-pitched vowels and diphthongs (for instance, *ōō, ŏ, ä/ōō*): taken together, these sounds serve to darken and to create a feeling of gloom. Such is the kind of thing you would want to say about the poem's vowel sounds and patterns.

It would be good as well to note somewhere along the way that the lyricism of the poem results in large measure from its assonance, its heavy alliteration, and its rhyme. Rhyme also heightens—congruent with the poem's mood of grief—the dissonant effect of off-rhyme ("tears"/"bears") and helps to create a sense of something missing by way of the poem's missing a rhyme for "drop" to complete the expected pattern. In that the poem concerns loss, absence here is itself a presence. The pattern of the poem's consonants should be looked at, too, in connection with its mood. Though the poem is lyrical, observe that, along with two gutturals (*k*), there are fully fourteen plosives (*b* and *p*) and twenty-eight dentals (*d* and *t*). These are the harsher sounds of the language, sounds that in concentration are fit for expressing anger or despair. The plosives and dentals also, perhaps, are onomatopoetic, echoing the sound of the falling drops of water.

Finally, in detailing a poem's sounds and their effects, you should consider the way the poem moves and how its movement affects its tone and sound generally.

SLOW, SLOW, FRESH FOUNT.   This song, from Jonson's play *Cynthia's Revels,* is sung by the Greek demi-deity Echo, who wasted away to an echo because of her love for Narcissus. Narcissus fell in love with his own reflection in a pool of water and, according to one version of the myth, was changed into the flower that bears his name. The daffodil (line 11) is a variety of narcissus.   **4.** *division:* a section or part of a song.

In this regard, it is noteworthy that every one of Jonson's lines is end-stopped, that the poem contains an unusually large number of spondees, and that there are a great many internal pauses (caesuras). Consequently, the poem moves slowly, all the more so because of the nature of its medial vowels and consonants—for example, "Slow, slow, fresh fount," "salt tears," "List to," "Drop, drop, drop, drop." These, like many other phrases in the poem, cannot be said rapidly when read aloud; they enforce a slowness to the movement and thereby lend a heaviness to the tone. And that heaviness is right for the mood of the speaker, whose grief is expressed through every aspect of the poem's sound.

This would be your final and overriding point: that every aspect of the poem's sound gives expression to its mood (of grief). The poem gives voice to sorrow not only through its paraphrasable content but also—and this is always more immediate and dramatic—through its form, shaped by the patterns of its words in combination, and the immediate emotional effect that the form has. If you demonstrate the like when you analyze the sound of a poem—or any other aspect of its form—you will write a truly noteworthy paper, one that will teach you much and that in turn should teach your audience something worthwhile.

POEMS FOR STUDY AND WRITING ASSIGNMENTS

MUSÉE DES BEAUX ARTS
— W. H. Auden —

About suffering they were never wrong,
The Old Masters: how well they understood
Its human position; how it takes place
While someone else is eating or opening a window or just walking dully along;
How, when the aged are reverently, passionately waiting   5
For the miraculous birth, there always must be
Children who did not specially want it to happen, skating
On a pond at the edge of the wood:
They never forgot
That even the dreadful martyrdom must run its course   10
Anyhow in a corner, some untidy spot
Where the dogs go on with their doggy life and the torturer's horse
Scratches its innocent behind on a tree.

In Brueghel's *Icarus,* for instance: how everything turns away
Quite leisurely from the disaster; the ploughman may   15
Have heard the splash, the forsaken cry,
But for him it was not an important failure; the sun shone
As it had to on the white legs disappearing into the green
Water; and the expensive delicate ship that must have seen
Something amazing, a boy falling out of the sky,   20
Had somewhere to get to and sailed calmly on.

[1938—Great Britain]

Questions

1. Using letters (*a, b, c,* and so on), denote the poem's rhyme scheme. What lines do not rhyme? Why? What does the context of rhyme serve to do as to the unrhymed lines—most notably, the last?
2. What does the poem's syntax serve to do? What is the effect of Auden's unusually long lines? How do both affect rhyme, or our perception of it?
3. Analyze the vowels of the poem. What kind of vowels are concentrated here? To what effect?

MUSÉE DES BEAUX ARTS. **2.** *Old Masters:* the great painters of the Renaissance. **14.** *Brueghel:* Flemish painter (1520–1569). *Icarus:* a painting by Brueghel of Icarus falling from the sky. See the note to Sexton's "To a Friend Whose Work . . ." (p. 243).

4. Analyze the consonants of the poem. What kind of consonants are concentrated here? To what effect?
5. There is no obvious alliteration or assonance in "Musée des Beaux Arts." Why? What is the effect of these absences?
6. In what way is the sound of the poem at one with its content?

Writing Assignments

1. Go to the library and find a picture of Brueghel's *Icarus.* Now write a paragraph or more pointing out the accuracy of Auden's description and the validity of Auden's interpretation.
2. Or is his interpretation valid? Might it be a twentieth-century imposition on a work that in its day was viewed in quite a different way? Do some research on the subject and write an essay summarizing the results of that research.
3. Write a paper addressed to question 6 above. To do so you will have to establish the poem's meaning, answer all the questions that precede, and then relate the poem's content generally to its form specifically.

KUBLA KHAN
— Samuel Taylor Coleridge —

In Xanadu did Kubla Khan
A stately pleasure dome decree:
Where Alph, the sacred river, ran
Through caverns measureless to man
  Down to a sunless sea.   5
So twice five miles of fertile ground
With walls and towers were girdled round:
And there were gardens bright with sinuous rills,
Where blossomed many an incense-bearing tree;
And here were forests ancient as the hills,   10
Enfolding sunny spots of greenery.

But oh! that deep romantic chasm which slanted
Down the green hill athwart a cedarn cover!
A savage place! as holy and enchanted
As e'er beneath a waning moon was haunted   15
By woman wailing for her demon lover!
And from this chasm, with ceaseless turmoil seething,
As if this earth in fast thick pants were breathing,
A mighty fountain momently was forced:
Amid whose swift half-intermitted burst   20

KUBLA KHAN.   The first ruler of the Mongol dynasty in 13th-century China. But the poem's incidents, topography, and place-names are all fictitious, as its subtitle suggests: "A Vision in a Dream."

Huge fragments vaulted like rebounding hail,
Or chaffy grain beneath the thresher's flail:
And 'mid these dancing rocks at once and ever
It flung up momently the sacred river.
Five miles meandering with a mazy motion   25
Through wood and dale the sacred river ran,
Then reached the caverns measureless to man,
And sank in tumult to a lifeless ocean:
And 'mid this tumult Kubla heard from far
Ancestral voices prophesying war!   30
    The shadow of the dome of pleasure
      Floated midway on the waves;
    Where was heard the mingled measure
      From the fountain and the caves.
It was a miracle of rare device,   35
A sunny pleasure dome with caves of ice!

    A damsel with a dulcimer
    In a vision once I saw:
    It was an Abyssinian maid,
    And on her dulcimer she played,   40
    Singing of Mount Abora.
    Could I revive within me
    Her symphony and song,
    To such a deep delight 'twould win me,
That with music loud and long,   45
I would build that dome in air,
That sunny dome! those caves of ice!
And all who heard should see them there,
And all should cry, Beware! Beware!
His flashing eyes, his floating hair!   50
Weave a circle round him thrice,
And close your eyes with holy dread,
For he on honey-dew hath fed,
And drunk the milk of Paradise.

[c. 1797–98—Great Britain]

---

37. *dulcimer:* a harplike instrument.   **51.** *Weave a circle round him thrice:* a ritual to guard the inspired poet from intrusion.   **54.** *Paradise:* Lines 50ff. ring of Plato's description of inspired poets (*Ion*): "like Bacchic maidens who draw milk and honey from the rivers when they are under the influence of Dionysus but not when they are in their right minds."

Questions

1. Assonance and alliteration are both pronounced here. Pick out several examples of each. What is their combined effect?
2. What is the effect of rhyme here along with the poem's relatively short lines and heavy metrical beat?
3. Does the poem move easily or with difficulty? What is the effect of its medial consonants and vowels in this regard?
4. What special effects does Coleridge achieve via sound? For instance, what are the effects of the plosives (*b* and *p*) and dentals (*d* and *t*) in lines 17–22?
5. Incantatory (chantlike) and lyrical (songlike), "Kubla Khan" is very possibly the most aurally rich poem in the language. What function does this richness serve? What is the overall effect of the poem's sound patterns, and what is the relation between its aural richness and the vision of human life or potentiality it embodies? How, then, does form here speak content?

Writing Assignments

1. In a paper, contrast Auden's "Musée des Beaux Arts" (p. 364) and "Kubla Khan." How do their visions of human life, at least in potential, differ? How do the differences of their sound patterns help to concretize and set off the understanding or vision of each poem?
2. Pick out any aspect of the sound of "Kubla Khan"—or several aspects, if you choose—and write an essay pointing out the effect of the aspect(s) you have chosen. Then discuss why this particular effect is relevant by considering what it does in the poem.

DOVER BEACH
— Matthew Arnold —

The sea is calm tonight.
The tide is full, the moon lies fair
Upon the straits; on the French coast the light
Gleams and is gone; the cliffs of England stand,
Glimmering and vast, out in the tranquil bay.   5
Come to the window, sweet is the night-air!
Only, from the long line of spray
Where the sea meets the moon-blanched land,
Listen! you hear the grating roar
Of pebbles which the waves draw back, and fling,   10
At their return, up the high strand,
Begin, and cease, and then again begin,
With tremulous cadence slow, and bring
The eternal note of sadness in.

Sophocles long ago   15
Heard it on the Aegean, and it brought

Into his mind the turbid ebb and flow
Of human misery; we
Find also in the sound a thought,
Hearing it by this distant northern sea.   20

The Sea of Faith
Was once, too, at the full, and round earth's shore
Lay like the folds of a bright girdle furled.
But now I only hear
Its melancholy, long, withdrawing roar,   25
Retreating, to the breath
Of the night-wind, down the vast edges drear
And naked shingles of the world.

Ah, love, let us be true
To one another! for the world, which seems   30
To lie before us like a land of dreams,
So various, so beautiful, so new,
Hath really neither joy, nor love, nor light,
Nor certitude, nor peace, nor help for pain;
And we are here as on a darkling plain   35
Swept with confused alarms of struggle and flight,
Where ignorant armies clash by night.

[1867—Great Britain]

Questions

1. What is the setting of this poem? To whom is its speaker speaking? What is the poem's situation?
2. Generally, the heavier the concentration of rhyme, alliteration, and assonance, the more lyrical a poem will be. What of "Dover Beach" in this regard? Is it lyrical throughout, or are there some passages that seem more lyrical and others less so? Explain.
3. Comment on the syntax of lines 10–12. How does syntax here imitate the movement of the waves and impart a muscular sense of that movement?
4. Comment on the consonant and vowel sounds of line 25. How do these sounds impart aurally a sense of what the line means otherwise?
5. Some of the poem's lines do not rhyme and some show off-rhyme. To what effect?
6. The third stanza of "Dover Beach" is built on an extended metaphor. What is that metaphor? How is it extended? The metaphor gives expression to the core meaning of the poem. What is that meaning?

DOVER BEACH.   **23.** *like the folds of a bright girdle furled:* like a beautiful sash, girdling and giving support. **28.** *shingles:* beaches composed of stones and pebbles.

Writing Assignments

1. Write a paragraph or more on some special effect in "Dover Beach" (for example, look at lines 10–14 or 24–28). How is the effect attained? In answering, consider syntax, sound, and rhythm.
2. Write a critique of "Dover Beach." Most critics consider it to be Arnold's one great poem. Do you agree? If so, why? If not, why not?
3. In an essay, discuss the vision of things embodied in "Dover Beach," relating what the poem says to how it says it. That is, analyze the extended metaphor at the heart of the poem, explicate the implications of its concluding imagery, and consider the effects of the poem's syntax and sound.

AT A SUMMER HOTEL
— Isabella Gardner —

I am here with my beautiful bountiful womanful child
to be soothed by the sea not roused by these roses roving wild.
My girl is gold in the sun and bold in the dazzling water,
She drowses on the blond sand and in the daisy fields my daughter
dreams. Uneasy in the drafty shade I rock on the veranda   5
reminded of Europa Persephone Miranda.

[1979—U.S.A.]

Questions

1. What can be inferred about the poem's setting, situation, and speaker?
2. Why is the speaker "Uneasy" about her child? How is her uneasiness reflected by her references to "Europa" and "Persephone," and perhaps eased by her thought of "Miranda"?
3. What words alliterate in the poem? What sounds repeat? What words exhibit assonance? What words exhibit consonance?
4. What special effects are brought about by the poem's sound? What is the general effect of its sound? How is sound here an aspect of sense?
5. What is the effect of the poem's final rhyme? In what way does it, along with the reference to Miranda, bring the poem to closure with an intimation of a possible resolution to the speaker's uneasiness?

Writing Assignments

1. In a paragraph, discuss the poem's concluding rhyme. How does it feel to you? What does it make you feel? How does it function? How does its function relate to that of the reference to Miranda?

AT A SUMMER HOTEL.   **6.** *Europa Persephone Miranda:* In Greek mythology, Europa is abducted and raped by Zeus; similarly, Persephone is abducted by Hades, god of the underworld. Miranda is a beautiful young woman in Shakespeare's *The Tempest*. The bestial Caliban attempts to rape her, but his attempt is thwarted. The play ends with Miranda betrothed to her beloved, Ferdinand.

2. Write a paper comparing and contrasting "At a Summer Hotel" and "Musée des Beaux Arts" (p. 364). Both have very long lines, but one of the two poems is highly lyrical and the other is prosaic. What in the sound patterns of each poem accounts for their markedly different effects?

[IT WAS NOT DEATH]
— Emily Dickinson —

It was not Death, for I stood up,
And all the Dead, lie down—
It was not Night, for all the Bells
Put out their Tongues, for Noon.

It was not Frost, for on my Flesh   5
I felt Siroccos—crawl—
Nor Fire—for just my Marble feet
Could keep a Chancel, cool—

And yet, it tasted, like them all,
The Figures I have seen   10
Set orderly, for Burial,
Reminded me, of mine—

As if my life were shaven,
And fitted to a frame,
And could not breathe without a key,   15
And 'twas like Midnight, some—

When everything that ticked—has stopped—
And Space stares all around—
Or Grisly frosts—first Autumn morns,
Repeal the Beating Ground—   20

But, most, like Chaos—Stopless—cool—
Without a Chance, or Spar—
Or even a Report of Land—
To justify—Despair.

[c. 1862—U.S.A.]

Questions

1. What is gained by the speaker's not naming the situation that gave rise to the feeling expressed here? Where, thus, does the poem's emphasis fall?
2. Are the lines of "[It Was Not Death]" enjambed or end-stopped? How would you describe the poem's syntax?

3. Syntax and end-line treatment both work toward the same end here. What is their combined effect? What kind of tone do they produce?
4. What is the one clear instance of consonance here? What are the poem's off-rhymes?
5. What is the effect of consonance and off-rhyme? What is the effect of the poem's few rhymes (lines 6 and 9, 18 and 20) in this context of off-rhyme and consonance?
6. How are the poem's sound patterns at one with its imagery? What feeling do sound, rhythm, and imagery combine to convey?

Writing Assignments

1. In a paragraph or two, define the tone of "[It Was Not Death]" and suggest how it is created.
2. Write an essay in which you argue that form and content are one in the poem at hand. That is, discuss the meaning of the poem in terms of its syntax, rhythm, line division, imagery, and sound.

DON JUAN
— George Gordon, Lord Byron —
from Canto II

18

"Farewell, my Spain! a long farewell!" he cried,
   "Perhaps I may revisit thee no more,
But die, as many an exiled heart hath died,
   Of its own thirst to see again thy shore: 140
Farewell, where Guadalquiver's waters glide!
   Farewell, my mother! and, since all is o'er,
Farewell, too, dearest Julia!—(here he drew
Her letter out again, and read it through).

19

"And oh! if e'er I should forget, I swear—   145
   But that's impossible, and cannot be—
Sooner shall this blue ocean melt to air,
   Sooner shall earth resolve itself to sea,
Than I resign thine image, oh, my fair!
   Or think of anything, excepting thee;   150
A mind diseased no remedy can physic—
(Here the ship gave a lurch, and he grew seasick.)

DON JUAN.   Everything in quotes is spoken by Don Juan, on board a ship sailing from Spain into exile because of his love for Julia. Juan would play the titanic hero, the undying lover, and so on. For the reason indicated, he fails.   **144.** *Her letter:* The letter is a farewell love note sent by Julia, a married woman with whom the young Juan was discovered (thus his exile).

20

"Sooner shall heaven kiss earth—(here he fell sicker)
    Oh, Julia! what is every other woe?—
(For God's sake let me have a glass of liquor;   155
    Pedro, Battista, help me down below.)
Julia, my love—(you rascal, Pedro, quicker)—
    Oh, Julia!—(this cursed vessel pitches so)—
Beloved Julia, hear me still beseeching!"
(Here he grew inarticulate with retching.)   160

21

He felt that chilling heaviness of heart,
    Or rather stomach, which, alas! attends,
Beyond the best apothecary's art,
    The loss of love, the treachery of friends,
Or death of those we dote on, when a part   165
    Of 'us dies with them as each fond hope ends:
No doubt he would have been much more pathetic,
But the sea acted as a strong emetic.

[1824—Great Britain]

Questions

1. What, overall, is the narrator's tone in these stanzas? How is this tone established? How does it affect our view of Juan?
2. In what ways do setting and situation contribute to the comedy here? What of diction in this regard?
3. What is funny about this passage? Why?
4. In what ways does rhyme contribute to the fun? What is it about the concluding couplets of stanzas 19, 20, and 21 especially that marks a comic intent and that is just plain funny?

Writing Assignments

1. (a) Write a paragraph on the narrator's tone and its effect with respect to the humor of this passage from *Don Juan.*
   (b) In a separate paragraph, state your response to this passage and the reasons why you so respond.
2. In a paragraph or more, contrast stanzas 18 and 20 as to rhythm, sound, and tone. What makes stanza 18 seem earnest and stanza 20 comic?
3. Write a paper on Byron's comic genius as witnessed in this passage. What is funny? Why? What is the point of the humor? How does form contribute to the comic mood and effect? Be sure to consider Byron's rhyming in connection with this last question.

CHAPTER

7

TRADITIONAL DESIGNS

FORM AND CONTENT

Form is a function of content and content of form. This principle has guided us throughout our study of poetry point by point. We have seen, that is, how meaning is conveyed in poetry by imagery, diction, figuration, rhythm, and sound. "Poets mold from the arbitrary givens of language a unity of form and content," as I said in the last chapter, "achieving [thus] a language potent and dense with meaning." In a genuine work of art, form and content always prove inseparable.

Sometimes, however, a poet will deliberately violate some aspect or expectation of an element of a poem's form and thereby achieve expression. We saw this, for instance, when we took up meter and found that one of the advantages afforded by a metrical norm is that it allows for meaningful deviation, as well as when we considered how the expectations aroused by rhyme can be violated to achieve certain effects. There is something of a paradox here: I am suggesting that the union of form and content can sometimes be attained by a calculated divergence of the two. But if the divergence is itself meaningful, then form and content remain indivisible.

The principle of the unity of form and content—however attained—can be discerned in poems with respect to any and all of the elements that go into their making, but it is perhaps most clearly manifested by the topic of this chapter: traditional designs, or verbal patterns defined by rhyme and sometimes by meter as well. All such designs have innate qualities exploited by the poet—if, that is, the poem succeeds—either directly or by calculated deviation. Whether or not a poem's design is meaningful and one with content is something you as reader must determine. To make the judgment, you will need to know the potentialities of the various traditional designs. This chapter will examine the most common stanzas and fixed forms from the perspective of potentiality.

RHYME SCHEMES, STANZAS, AND FIXED FORMS

Before we turn to the various traditional designs, however, I should clarify what stanzas and fixed forms are. To do so, we must begin with what a rhyme scheme is. A **rhyme scheme** is simply the pattern of end-rhymes (rhymes at the end of lines) found in a poem that rhymes. Rhyme schemes are signified by letters: like letters indicate what lines, because of the words with which they end, rhyme with what other lines. For example, *abab* would indicate that the first and third lines of a poem rhyme and the second and fourth lines, as in the following by Thomas Love Peacock:

> The mountain sheep were sweeter;
> The valley sheep were fatter.
> We therefore deemed it meeter
> To carry off the latter.

> [1828—Great Britain]

Also, a notation like *abab/cdcd/efef* indicates a likeness in the *pattern* of rhyme but a difference in the specific rhyme sounds of each four-line unit. (If the rhymes remained the same, the notation would be: *abab/abab/abab.*) Finally, capital letters are used to indicate the repetition of an entire line word for word: for instance, *abaB/cdcD* would indicate that the fourth line of each stanza is exactly the same as the second line of each.

Both traditional stanzas and fixed forms have rhyme schemes. A poem written in **stanzas**—which are demarked by spacing—will usually have a recurrent pattern of rhyme and so the same number of lines per stanza, though lines may vary in length. (Some unrhymed poems, however, especially many written in our century, are divided into stanzas; and some rhymed poems are composed of stanzas variable as to the number of lines in each.) Some stanza forms also call for a specific meter; others do not. No stanzaic design prescribes the number of stanzas a poem must contain; a stanzaic poem (that is, a poem in stanzas) can consist of as few as two stanzas and as many as it is possible to write. Fixed forms are much more prescriptive. A poem in a **fixed form** is a poem that adheres to a prescribed rhyme scheme, a set number of lines, a set number of stanzas if stanzaic, often a specific meter, and sometimes a specific pattern of repeated lines. The sonnet, the villanelle, the limerick are all examples of fixed forms. The prescribed rhyme scheme of the limerick, for instance, is *aabba;* further, the first, second, and fifth lines must be anapestic trimeters (or some variant thereof), and the third and fourth lines must be anapestic dimeters (or, again, some variant thereof). See how the following example meets these stipulations.

RELATIVITY

— Anonymous —

> There was a young lady named Bright,
> Who travelled much faster than light;

> She started one day
> In the relative way,
> And returned on the previous night.

No one has to write a limerick, of course, or a sonnet, or whatever. But if one wishes to write a limerick, say, then the prescribed form must be respected. For if it is not, then the resulting poem will simply not be a limerick by definition. To be sure, meaningful deviation from the givens of any fixed form, as from any other formal aspect of a poem, is always possible. Here is a good example with respect to the limerick.

FORM AND CONTENT
— Anonymous —

> There was a young man from Japan
> Whose limericks never would scan;
>   When they said it was so,
>   He replied, "Yes, I know,
> But I always try to get as many words into the last line as ever I
>   possibly can."

Clearly, here is another instance of meaningful deviation. But note that the formal requirements of the limerick are observed by and large; they must be for the deviation to have effect and, indeed, to be possible in the first place.

Every stanzaic pattern and fixed form carries certain potentialities (and not others). One type of stanza, for instance, might be particularly suited to narration and another to lyric lament; one fixed form might be suited to humor and another to the expression of inner conflict. The poet chooses the design employed in light of content. The reader, in turn, must know the potentialities of the various designs to judge how one or another helps to express content, whether a design is respected or deviated from. The next section, on the sonnet, should help concretize the meaning of potentiality and make clear the kind of awareness we need to bring to a poem traditional in design.

THE SONNET

Of all the fixed forms established over the centuries, none has proved as enduring and as pliable as the **sonnet**—a fourteen-line poem usually in iambic pentameter. There are a number of types of sonnet, foremost among which are the **Shakespearean** and the **Petrarchan** (each named after its most celebrated practitioner). The rhyme schemes and formal divisions of each are:

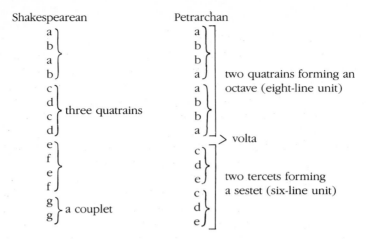

Potentialities

Each of these forms has unique potentialities. Just by looking at its abstracted rhyme schemes, you could perhaps tell that the fundamental potential of the Shakespearean form is three steps in an argument and a summation or three parallel statements and a conclusion, the summation or conclusion usually entailing a pointed reversal of some sort (which is the inherent inclination of the closed couplet, as we shall see shortly). By virtue of its division into octave (eight lines) and sestet (six lines), the Petrarchan sonnet offers more wide-ranging possibilities: question and answer; generalization and particularization, or the reverse; statement and modification or full counterstatement. Contrasts are also possible between the quatrains of the octave and even between the tercets of the sestet. The form, thus, is ideally suited to the expression of conflict and conflicted feelings. (Note that there are many Petrarchan sonnets in which the rhyme scheme of the sestet is varied. The *cde/cde* pattern is the norm to the extent that there is a norm.)

The Shakespearean Sonnet

We have already had a good example of the Shakespearean sonnet in the one that begins, "That time of year thou mayst in me behold" (pp. 272–73), which consists of three parallel statements in the three quatrains and a somewhat startling conclusion in the couplet. The alternative potential of three steps in an argument leading to a summation entailing a reversal of some sort is realized in the following sonnet.

SONNET 129

— William Shakespeare —

Th' expense of spirit in a waste of shame
Is lust in action; and till action, lust

SONNET 129.   **1.** *Th' expense . . . shame:* Without precluding other readings, I will suggest a possible gloss for this terribly knotty and much disputed line. "Spirit" commonly meant "semen" in the Renaissance,

Is perjured, murderous, bloody, full of blame,
Savage, extreme, rude, cruel, not to trust;
Enjoyed no sooner but despisèd straight: 5
Past reason hunted; and no sooner had,
Past reason hated, as a swallowed bait,
On purpose laid to make the taker mad:
Mad in pursuit, and in possession so;
Had, having, and in quest to have, extreme;   10
A bliss in proof, and proved, a very woe;
Before, a joy proposed; behind, a dream.
All this the world well knows; yet none knows well
To shun the heaven that leads men to this hell.

[1609—Great Britain]

At first glance, this seems to be a little moral lecture against lust and its effects in the "quest," in the "having," and in the "had." But the sonnet is far too knotty and inept, or seemingly so, for the purposes of a moralist. Note, for instance, the enigma of the first line and the faulty sequence of the tenth; note, as well, the haltingness of the rhythm of the whole poem; and note the anticlimaxes and their effect (lines 3, 4, and 10 all end with their weakest epithets). No, the poem is not a moral lecture but a dramatic enactment of a very human, highly conflicted state of mind, a state that cannot find adequate expression in mere words. Thus, the anticlimaxes—which in part convey the ambivalence of the speaker and also suggest that his feelings outpace his words at every turn, as feelings usually do. Thus, too, the haltingness of the poem, its knottiness, and its frequent illogicality (the sequence of line 10, for instance). All betray a deeply conflicted nature. To be sure, the speaker struggles to make reason prevail, to guide his actions by the sure knowledge gained through past experience. So he casts his thoughts into a logical pattern, each quatrain being a progressive step in an internal debate leading to the summary couplet. But his argument is not logical in substance, and everywhere we feel that he knows that the bait will once again prove too sweet to be resisted, whatever the arguments against taking it (thus the speaker's conflict, which is between will and desire). His only solace is that what he knows of himself, he knows also to be true of the rest of mankind. His attempt at reasoning with himself having failed, he settles for the meager comfort of rationalization—the summary of the couplet amounts to nothing more than this.

The Petrarchan Sonnet

In the hands of Shakespeare, the sonnet named after him proved a magnificent instrument. He made it sound a wide range of human emotions and conflicts by

---

and ejaculation was commonly spoken of as an "expending" or a "spending"; "shame" is the base meaning of the word "pudendum," the anatomical word for the female genitals. These overtones, together with the suggestion of buying in the word "expense," connote that someone's been a-whoring—engaged in an act not worth the shame.   **11.** *in proof:* in the experience.

turning its pattern (form) to his various purposes (content). Surprisingly, however, it has been the Petrarchan sonnet—which is much more difficult in terms of rhyme than the Shakespearean—that the major practitioners of the sonnet after Shakespeare chose: namely, Milton, Wordsworth, and Hopkins. The reason the Petrarchan sonnet has been the dominant form, I believe, has to do with its many structural divisions. Allowing for three and sometimes even four contrasting movements, the form is well suited to the expression of conflict, for instance, or the subtle shades of human feeling. Certainly, division is the life of the Petrarchan sonnet, as Hopkins asserted when discussing the form:

> Now it seems to me that this division [between octave and sestet] is the real characteristic of the sonnet and that what is not so marked off and moreover has not the octet [another word for "octave"] again divided into quatrains is not to be called a sonnet at all. (71)

The following sonnet (Petrarchan) is a good example of Hopkins's analysis. Note especially the contrast between the quatrains and the shift (volta) into the sestet. The meaning of the poem lies in the contrasts made possible by its formal design; to grasp the poem fully, therefore, one must understand that design.

GOD'S GRANDEUR
— G. M. Hopkins —

The world is charged with the grandeur of God.
　It will flame out, like shining from shook foil;
　It gathers to a greatness, like the ooze of oil
Crushed. Why do men then now not reck his rod?
Generations have trod, have trod, have trod;　　　　　　5
　And all is seared with trade; bleared, smeared with toil;
　And wears man's smudge and shares man's smell: the soil
Is bare now, nor can foot feel, being shod.

And for all this, nature is never spent;
　There lives the dearest freshness deep down things;　　10
And though the last lights off the black West went
　Oh, morning, at the brown brink eastward, springs—
Because the Holy Ghost over the bent
　World broods with warm breast and with ah! bright wings.

[c. 1877—Great Britain]

GOD'S GRANDEUR. **1.** *charged:* as a battery is charged. **2.** *shook foil:* In the Leyden jar experiment, a piece of gold foil suspended in a bell jar in which a vacuum has been created will, if fur is rubbed on the outside of the jar, spark with static electricity. **4.** *Crushed:* Highly viscous oil will, if pressed ("crushed") with a finger, gather back on itself because of its surface tension. **6.** *seared . . . toil:* The point of contrast is that the very things—"flame" and "oil"—that in their natural state reveal God serve in the hands of man to conceal Him (thus "seared" and "bleared, smeared"). **9.** *spent:* as a battery is said to be "spent" (see, too, Wordsworth's "Getting and spending" in the next poem). **14.** *broods:* as a bird (specifically, a dove) broods on an egg.

Meaningful Deviation

Again, we cannot overlook the possibility of meaningful deviation. Wordsworth, for instance, deviates most meaningfully from the givens of the Petrarchan form and its expectations in the next poem (against which "God's Grandeur" should be read—the two poems make like judgments of the modern world, though they differ in final stance). Observe in particular what happens between the octave and the sestet.

THE WORLD IS TOO MUCH WITH US
— William Wordsworth —

The world is too much with us; late and soon,
Getting and spending, we lay waste our powers;
Little we see in Nature that is ours;
We have given our hearts away, a sordid boon!
This Sea that bares her bosom to the moon,   5
The winds that will be howling at all hours,
And are up-gathered now like sleeping flowers,
For this, for everything, we are out of tune;
It moves us not.—Great God! I'd rather be
A Pagan suckled in a creed outworn;   10
So might I, standing on this pleasant lea,
Have glimpses that would make me less forlorn;
Have sight of Proteus rising from the sea;
Or hear old Triton blow his wreathèd horn.

[1807—Great Britain]

The octave—the quatrains of which are contrasting—rises to a climax with the sweeping indictment of its eighth line and then falls into anticlimax with the tagged-on "It moves us not." If we know the form and come to Wordsworth's sonnet with the appropriate expectations, this slopping over of the octave into the sestet causes us to let down our guard. We expect a volta but get, it seems, its opposite. So we relax for just a moment. Then Wordsworth lets us have it: the voice rises to the pitch of passion with the delayed volta "Great God!"—all the more jarring because delayed and thus unexpected. By this subtle deviation, Wordsworth gains tremendous power.

The next sonnet is much more deviant, though it is clearly a Petrarchan sonnet in terms of rhyme (the *cdcdcd* scheme of the sestet is a common variant). Written late in the poet's life, the poem concerns his spiritual struggles and the emotional

---

THE WORLD IS TOO MUCH WITH US.   **13.** *Proteus:* a sea deity capable of assuming different shapes.   **14.** *Triton:* a sea deity usually represented as blowing on a conch shell.

collapse they have led to. As you read the poem, watch its structural divisions and what is done with them to see how form here is made to embody the poet's state of feeling.

[THOU ART INDEED JUST, LORD]
— G. M. Hopkins —

Justus quidem tu es, Domine, si disputem tecum:
verumtamen justa loquar ad te:
Quare via impiorum prosperatur? etc.

Thou art indeed just, Lord, if I contend
With thee; but, sir, so what I plead is just.
Why do sinners' ways prosper? and why must
Disappointment all I endeavour end?
    Wert thou my enemy, O thou my friend,   5
How wouldst thou worse, I wonder, than thou dost
Defeat, thwart me? Oh, the sots and thralls of lust
Do in spare hours more thrive than I that spend,
Sir, life upon thy cause. See, banks and brakes
Now, leavèd how thick! lacèd they are again   10
With fretty chervil, look, and fresh wind shakes
Them; birds build—but not I build; no, but strain,
Time's eunuch, and not breed one work that wakes.
Mine, O thou lord of life, send my roots rain.

[c. 1889—Great Britain]

Beginning by paraphrasing Jeremiah's question, though with two significant differences—Hopkins's God seems sterner ("sir") than Jeremiah's (who calls God by the familiar *tu*), and Hopkins's concern is much more personal ("I")—Hopkins makes the Petrarchan form implode by collapsing the octave into the sestet. This collapse is purposeful: it is dramatically at one with the emotional collapse of the poet himself enacted in the latter part of the poem. The formal collapse, then, gives shape to the corresponding emotional collapse, thus rendering form and content inseparable.

[THOU ART INDEED JUST, LORD]. *Epigraph:* "Righteous art thou, O Lord, when I complain to thee; yet I would plead my case before thee. Why does the way of the wicked prosper?" (Jeremiah 12:1). What follows in Jeremiah is also relevant: "Why do all who are treacherous thrive? Thou plantest them and they take root; they grow and bring forth fruit; thou art near in their mouth and far from their heart." **9.** *brakes:* clumps of fern. **11.** *fretty:* fretted. Chervil is a spring herb.

The poem is a perfect Petrarchan sonnet because its form has been made a vehicle of content.

Inept Deviation

Deviation is not always meaningful, of course; there is always the possibility of ineptness. Look at the well-known sonnet that follows in this regard. It may be well known, but it is not a successful poem when judged in light of the aesthetic criteria we have established in this chapter.

SONNETS FROM THE PORTUGUESE, NO. 43

— Elizabeth Barrett Browning —

How do I love thee? Let me count the ways.
I love thee to the depth and breadth and height
My soul can reach, when feeling out of sight
For the ends of Being and ideal Grace.
I love thee to the level of everyday's   5
Most quiet need, by sun and candle light.
I love thee freely, as men strive for Right;
I love thee purely, as they turn from Praise.
I love thee with the passion put to use
In my old griefs, and with my childhood's faith.   10
I love thee with a love I seemed to lose
With my lost saints—I love thee with the breath,
Smiles, tears, of all my life!—and, if God choose,
I shall but love thee better after death.

[1850—Great Britain]

This is a pleasant poem, certainly, and one of some historical interest. Like Matthew Arnold in "Dover Beach" (pp. 367–68), Elizabeth Barrett Browning gives voice to the Victorian spiritualization of sexual love and the cause thereof (the loss of faith) in the lines "I love thee with a love I seemed to lose / With my lost saints." But what does the poet do with the structural divisions of the form she chose to work in? Nothing. There are no contrasts here at all: the quatrains that form the octave are to the same burden, and so too are the octave and the sestet. Hopkins deviates from the expected divisions and contrasts of the Petrarchan form meaningfully, making form serve content; Browning also deviates, but not meaningfully. That is, there is no particular reason why her poem should have the shape it does. This at least in part explains why her sonnet, though appealing in some ways and interesting in others, seems flaccid overall and not compelling. Its formal design is arbitrary and of no relevance to the poem's content. No poem of which this is true can be called truly successful.

OTHER FIXED FORMS

Aside from the sonnet, there are many other fixed forms, such as the sestina, the rondeau, the rondel, the triolet, the limerick, the villanelle. There are far too many for us to go into each here. Nor do we really need to, given that our concern is less with specific traditional designs than with the principle of the relationship of form and content. We have applied this principle when looking at the sonnet; now let us apply it once more in connection with one other fixed form. Take the **villanelle,** an extremely complex form that has attracted many great poets despite its complexity (or because of it). The rhyme scheme of the villanelle is *AbA'/abA/abA'/abA/abA'/ abAA'* (lines *A* and *A',* which rhyme, repeat exactly as the poem unfolds). Because of its formal complexity, the villanelle has often been used for comic poems, which seem to thrive on complex rhyme schemes and repetition. But it can be turned to other ends, as it is in Dylan Thomas's justly famous poem about the imminent death of his father (the poem's situation).

DO NOT GO GENTLE INTO THAT GOOD NIGHT
— Dylan Thomas —

Do not go gentle into that good night,
Old age should burn and rave at close of day;
Rage, rage against the dying of the light.

Though wise men at their end know dark is right,
Because their words had forked no lightning they   5
Do not go gentle into that good night.

Good men, the last wave by, crying how bright
Their frail deeds might have danced in a green bay,
Rage, rage against the dying of the light.

Wild men who caught and sang the sun in flight,   10
And learn, too late, they grieved it on its way,
Do not go gentle into that good night.

Grave men, near death, who see with blinding sight
Blind eyes could blaze like meteors and be gay,
Rage, rage against the dying of the light.   15

And you, my father, there on the sad height,
Curse, bless, me now with your fierce tears, I pray.
Do not go gentle into that good night.
Rage, rage against the dying of the light.

[1952—Great Britain]

Thomas's poem is paradoxical: he calls death a "good night" and "right," yet insists that one must resist it. This paradox is one with which we are all faced: to affirm life, we must rage against death and yet accept it as right because it is an aspect of life. Thomas expresses this paradoxical facet of human awareness in the texture of his almost surrealistic imagery and especially by way of his chosen form. Because of the overriding comic potential of the villanelle, the form serves to lighten the poem's tone despite its serious subject, thereby creating a tension between form and content that captures and embodies the paradoxical attitude toward life and death that the poet would have his father take. The principle, once more, is that for a poem to succeed fully, its formal design along with all other aspects of its form (imagery, rhythm, and so forth) must participate in its meaning. In "Do Not Go Gentle," Thomas achieves that elusive union.

STANZAIC PATTERNS

Along with fixed forms, there are a number of fixed stanzaic patterns found in English poetry, most of which are defined by rhyme and some by meter as well. Stanzas—yet another kind of concretion (as are designs of any sort)—should be thought of as building blocks constructing the larger edifice of the whole poem. But what is most important to grasp is, again, the idea of potentiality, or what purposes a given stanzaic form can be put to because of its own innate qualities. Keeping potentiality in mind, we shall focus on the four most recurrent stanza forms in English poetry, each of which has its own distinct character.

Terza Rima

Terza rima stanzas are tercets (three-line units) marked by interlocking rhymes: *aba/bcb/cdc/ded* and so on. This rhyme pattern creates a marked pull forward, the *b* rhyme pulling us on from stanza one to stanza two, the *c* rhyme from stanza two to stanza three, and so forth. For this reason, the form is suited to narrative poetry, though it also has a lyric potential. For narrative generally needs a strong forward motion, and that is the innate effect of terza rima. No doubt that is why Dante chose terza rima for *The Divine Comedy,* one of the greatest narrative poems in any language. As I have suggested, the form also has lyric possibilities, or can serve the ends of a lyric poet if a sense of forward motion is appropriate to a poem for whatever reason. In this regard, look at the following poem with an eye to its rhyme scheme and stanzaic design, and how that design acts as a kind of magnet pulling us on, just as the poem's speaker is pulled through the night by some inner necessity.

ACQUAINTED WITH THE NIGHT
— Robert Frost —

I have been one acquainted with the night.
I have walked out in rain—and back in rain.
I have outwalked the furthest city light.

I have looked down the saddest city lane.
I have passed by the watchman on his beat   5
And dropped my eyes, unwilling to explain.

I have stood still and stopped the sound of feet
When far away an interrupted cry
Came over houses from another street,

But not to call me back or say good-by;   10
And further still at an unearthly height
One luminary clock against the sky

Proclaimed the time was neither wrong nor right.
I have been one acquainted with the night.

[1928—U.S.A.]

Drawn past "the furthest city light"—beyond, that is, all human attempts at order-ing, like the city—the speaker is one who has seen the dark side of things. Sadly, that side is to be found not outside the city and all it represents but within the city, in its "saddest lane" and in the "interrupted cry / . . . from another street." The poem brings into question, then, our human attempts at finding or forging an order for ourselves. But "the time was neither wrong nor right," says the clock, suggesting that the problem of order is recurrent and that it must be faced anew by each generation. Frost found his answer in traditional forms of all kinds, which he called his "stay against confusion." In the present case, that stay is the terza rima stanza, with reference to the sonnet (the poem has fourteen lines) providing a further degree of solidity. So, though the poem questions our ability to order at this time, its design suggests the possibility that the mind can impose order at any time. Also, as I have suggested, Frost's terza rima design imparts muscularly a sense of the speaker's being pulled by some internal force to an understanding that "the time was neither wrong nor right," to, that is, an appreciation of the task to which each human generation is set.

The Spenserian Stanza

Named after Edmund Spenser, who devised the form, the **Spenserian stanza** is rather elaborate: it is composed of nine lines rhymed *ababbcbcc,* with the first eight lines in iambic pentameter and the ninth line in iambic hexameter (such a line is called an **alexandrine**). A good narrative stanza because of its length (a full action can be encompassed in a single stanza) and forward thrust, it is especially suited to descriptive poetry or to poetry that involves a good deal of description along with narration. Its sheer luxuriance of sound—with its four *b* and three *c* rhymes—lends itself to descriptive purposes. When handled well, the interweaving rhymes of the stanza add a dimension of tonal depth and coloration that works toward descriptive ends.

That the stanza is so well suited to descriptive purposes may be why it became a favorite among such romantic poets as Wordsworth, Byron, Shelley, Keats, and Tennyson. The stanza is supple and rich in sound, and its sound as it cumulates serves to flesh out description. Take, for instance, the following stanzas from Byron's *Childe Harold,* stanzas whose tonal richness echoes first the opulence of the dance and then the clang and discord of the first moments of battle.

CHILDE HAROLD'S PILGRIMAGE
— George Gordon, Lord Byron —
from Canto III

21

There was a sound of revelry by night,
And Belgium's capital had gathered then
Her Beauty and her Chivalry, and bright
The lamps shone o'er fair women and brave men;
A thousand hearts beat happily; and when   185
Music arose with its voluptuous swell,
Soft eyes looked love to eyes which spake again,
And all went merry as a marriage bell—
But hush! hark! a deep sound strikes like a rising knell!

22

Did ye not hear it?—No; 'twas but the wind,   190
Or the car rattling o'er the stony street;
On with the dance! let joy be unconfined;
No sleep till morn, when Youth and Pleasure meet
To chase the glowing Hours with flying feet—
But hark!—that heavy sound breaks in once more,   195
As if the clouds its echo would repeat;
And nearer, clearer, deadlier than before!
Arm! Arm! it is—it is—the cannon's opening roar!

24

Ah! then and there was hurrying to and fro,
And gathering tears, and tremblings of distress,
And cheeks all pale, which but an hour ago   210
Blushed at the praise of their own loveliness;
And there were sudden partings, such as press

CHILDE HAROLD'S PILGRIMAGE.   **181.** *sound of revelry:* Byron here describes the eve of the Battle of Waterloo.

The life from out young hearts, and choking sighs
Which ne'er might be repeated; who could guess
If ever more should meet those mutual eyes,   215
Since upon night so sweet such awful morn could rise!

25

And there was mounting in hot haste: the steed,
The mustering squadron, and the clattering car,
Went pouring forward with impetuous speed,
And swiftly forming in the ranks of war;   220
And the deep thunder peal on peal afar;
And near, the beat of the alarming drum
Roused up the soldier ere the morning star;
While thronged the citizens with terror dumb,
Or whispering, with white lips—"The foe! They come! they come!"   225

[1816—Great Britain]

Ottava Rima

The main potentiality of the **ottava rima** stanza, which rhymes *ababab cc,* is suggested by the couplet with which it closes: wit, humor, satirical thrust (as we will see shortly, this is always a potential of the closed and/or closing couplet). It is for this potential that Byron chose ottava rima for his long comic narrative *Don Juan.* (Like the Spenserian stanza, the ottava rima stanza is long enough for narrative purposes.) Two stanzas from Canto I should suffice to illustrate the innate qualities of the form. The first concerns a search conducted by Julia's husband, Alfonso, for her suspected lover, Don Juan. Finding nothing, Alfonso stands at Julia's mercy—the substance of the second stanza until the last.

DON JUAN
— George Gordon, Lord Byron —
from Canto I

144

Under the bed they searched, and there they found—   1145
  No matter what—it was not what they sought;
They opened windows, gazing if the ground
  Had signs or footmarks, but the earth said nought;
And then they stared each other's faces round:
  'Tis odd, not one of all these seekers thought,   1150

And seems to me almost a sort of blunder,
Of looking *in* the bed as well as under.

180

Alfonso closed his speech, and begged her pardon,
   Which Julia half withheld, and then half granted,
And laid conditions, he thought very hard on,   1435
   Denying several little things he wanted:
He stood like Adam lingering near his garden,
   With useless penitence perplexed and haunted,
Beseeching she no further would refuse,
When, lo! he stumbled o'er a pair of shoes.   1440

[1819—Great Britain]

The In-Memoriam Stanza

The single most frequent stanzaic form in English poetry is the **quatrain,** a four-line stanza that can rhyme *aabb, abab, aaba, abcb,* or *abba*. The last—called the **In-Memoriam stanza**—is particularly important and particularly instructive with regard to the concept of potentiality. Named after a long poem by Tennyson in which it is exploited in every way possible, the stanza is also called the "envelope" stanza, suggesting something of its nature: having no sense of forward motion whatsoever, the stanza has an innate sense of enclosure and inwardness about it. Too short and halting for the purposes of narration, too plain and unadorned for elaborate tonal effects, the stanza is wonderfully suited for little bursts of lyric passion or quiet moments of meditation. That is why Tennyson turned to the form when he poured out the lyrics that compose *In Memoriam,* an intensely personal poem expressing in bursts the poet's grief over the death of his dearest friend. The following lyric from *In Memoriam,* imbued with a sense of deep personal grief, is remarkable for its inwardness and aura of authentic feeling.

IN MEMORIAM
— Alfred, Lord Tennyson —

No. 7

Dark house, by which once more I stand
   Here in the long unlovely street,
   Doors, where my heart was used to beat
So quickly, waiting for a hand,

A hand that can be clasped no more—   5
   Behold me, for I cannot sleep,

And like a guilty thing I creep
At earliest morning to the door.

He is not here; but far away
   The noise of life begins again,   10
   And ghastly through the drizzling rain
On the bald street breaks the blank day.

[1859—Great Britain]

As for the meditative potential of the stanza, consider the next poem, as quiet and inward as meditation itself.

PLAYBOY

— Richard Wilbur —

High on his stockroom ladder like a dunce
The stock-boy sits, and studies like a sage
The subject matter of one glossy page,
As lost in curves as Archimedes once.

Sometimes, without a glance, he feeds himself.   5
The left hand, like a mother-bird in flight,
Brings him a sandwich for a sidelong bite,
And then returns it to a dusty shelf.

What so engrosses him? The wild décor
Of this pink-papered alcove into which   10
A naked girl has stumbled, with its rich
Welter of pelts and pillows on the floor,

Amidst which, kneeling in a supple pose,
She lifts a goblet in her farther hand,
As if about to toast a flower-stand   15
Above which hovers an exploding rose

Fired from a long-necked crystal vase that rests
Upon a tasseled and vermilion cloth
One taste of which would shrivel up a moth?
Or is he pondering her perfect breasts?   20

Nothing escapes him of her body's grace
Or of her floodlit skin, so sleek and warm
And yet so strangely like a uniform,
But what now grips his fancy is her face,

And how the cunning picture holds her still   25
At just that smiling instant when her soul,
Grown sweetly faint, and swept beyond control,
Consents to his inexorable will.

[1969—U.S.A.]

Actually, meditation is twofold here: high on his ladder (the poem's setting), the stock-boy ponders while the speaker meditates on the stock-boy's pondering. The sense of internalization of the poem's stanza form, then, is doubly appropriate. But the poem's form also implies irony. The speaker is engaged in genuine meditation, but the young man, mechanically eating a sandwich as he studies *Playboy* (the poem's situation), is shallow and empty-headed, with nothing even resembling a thought in his head. The inwardness of the stanza, thus, functions with respect both to the speaker and to the boy. It reflects the speaker's contemplative frame of mind and, by contrast, the boy's sublime mindlessness.

COUPLETS: OPEN AND CLOSED

A **couplet** is composed of two contiguous lines that rhyme. For instance:

ON HIS BOOKS
— Hilaire Belloc —

When I am dead, I hope it may be said:
"His sins were scarlet, but his books were read."

[1944—Great Britain]

Not a lot can be done in a single couplet. But a single couplet is ideal for an **epigram**—a concise statement, usually witty or satirical, that makes a single point and that usually has a punch to it (in context, the punch lines of most jokes are epigrammatic). The couplet above is a good example of the inherent potential of the single, self-contained couplet, which seems almost to want to end with a punch, or which seems by its nature to be epigrammatic. Belloc's design is right for his subject.

Longer poems, too, can be composed of couplets (denoted *aabbccddee* . . .). Because such poems can be of any length, they are not exactly "fixed" in form, nor are they stanzaic (the larger units of poems in couplets are called **verse paragraphs** rather than stanzas). Still, a poem composed of couplets clearly has a design defined by rhyme, whether the couplets are open or closed. These are the two types of couplet, types that differ considerably in potential.

Open Couplets

A poem in open couplets can be in any meter or even in free verse. What defines **open couplets** is that their grammar and syntax can be such that one couplet can move into the next without pause; to put this the other way round, each couplet of a poem in open couplets is *not* necessarily a grammatically self-contained unit. The attraction of open couplets is that they can serve to structure, to give shape and a sense of continuity; yet, handled well, they are unobtrusive. The form also allows for speechlike effects of pace and pause, making it a fine vehicle especially for monologues. "To His Coy Mistress" (pp. 256–57) and "My Last Duchess" (pp. 235–36), both of which are in open couplets, are excellent examples of the potentialities of the form. Listen again to the opening lines of the latter and note how naturally the passage moves and how fluidly. It seems natural and speechlike because the rhyming is unobtrusive; it seems fluid—fluidity here reflecting the character of the Duke—because of the pull of the rhyme along with the many graceful enjambments.

That's my last duchess painted on the wall,
Looking as if she were alive. I call
That piece a wonder, now: Frà Pandolf's hands
Worked busily a day, and there she stands.
Will't please you sit and look at her? I said   5
"Frà Pandolf" by design, for never read
Strangers like you that pictured countenance,
The depth and passion of its earnest glance,
But to myself they turned (since none puts by
The curtain I have drawn for you, but I)   10
And seemed as they would ask me, if they durst,
How such a glance came there; so, not the first
Are you to turn and ask thus.

Closed Couplets

A **closed couplet** is a self-contained grammatical unit expressing a complete thought. The Belloc couplet on page 389 is closed, as is the following satirical piece:

a politician

— E. E. Cummings —

a politician is an arse upon
which everyone has sat except a man

[1944—U.S.A.]

Again, note the pithy quality of the closed couplet and the way it tends to surprise and so to end with a punch. We saw the same potentialities, recall, when we looked at the Shakespearean sonnet and the ottava rima stanza, both of which end in closed couplets and achieve thereby a sense of closure as well as surprise (comic or otherwise).

Like open couplets, closed couplets can be used to fashion longer poems in any meter or, theoretically, in free verse. But there is one type of closed couplet whose meter is specified, a type of special importance in English poetry: the **heroic couplet.** The heroic couplet is a closed couplet in iambic pentameter (both meter and rhyme define the form) used as the basic building block of a longer poem (that is, longer than a single couplet). Because most of the finest poems in heroic couplets date from the late seventeenth and the eighteenth centuries, we shall turn to this era for illustration. As you read the following selections, try to determine what the form is best suited for.

AN ESSAY ON MAN
— Alexander Pope —
from Book II

> Know then thyself, presume not God to scan;
> The proper study of mankind is Man.
> Placed on this isthmus of a middle state,
> A being darkly wise, and rudely great:
> With too much knowledge for the skeptic side,　　　　5
> With too much weakness for the Stoic's pride,
> He hangs between; in doubt to act, or rest,
> In doubt to deem himself a god, or beast;
> In doubt his mind or body to prefer,
> Born but to die, and reasoning but to err;　　　　10
> Alike in ignorance, his reason such,
> Whether he thinks too little, or too much:
> Chaos of thought and passion, all confused;
> Still by himself abused, or disabused;
> Created half to rise, and half to fall;　　　　15
> Great lord of all things, yet a prey to all;
> Sole judge of truth, in endless error hurled:
> The glory, jest, and riddle of the world!

[1733—Great Britain]

TO MY DEAR AND LOVING HUSBAND
— Anne Bradstreet —

If ever two were one, then surely we.
If ever man were loved by wife, then thee;
If ever wife was happy in a man,
Compare with me ye women if you can.
I prize thy love more than whole mines of gold,   5
Or all the riches that the East doth hold.
My love is such that rivers cannot quench,
Nor ought but love from thee give recompense.
Thy love is such I can no way repay;
The heavens reward thee manifold, I pray.   10
Then while we live, in love let's so persever,
That when we live no more we may live ever.

[1678—U.S.A.]

THE RAPE OF THE LOCK
— Alexander Pope —

from Canto V

Some thought it mounted to the Lunar Sphere,
Since all things lost on Earth, are treasur'd there.
There Heroes' Wits are kept in pondrous Vases,
And Beaus' in *Snuff-boxes* and *Tweezer-Cases*.
There broken Vows, and Death-bed Alms are found,   5
And Lovers' Hearts with Ends of Riband bound;
The Courtier's Promises, and Sick Man's Pray'rs,
The Smiles of Harlots, and the Tears of Heirs,
Cages for Gnats, and Chains to Yoak a Flea;
Dry'd Butterflies, and Tomes of Casuistry.   10

[1712—Great Britain]

What, then, is the form best suited for? It would not do, I think, to express epic grandeur or the depth of abandoned passion. Rather, because it requires keen powers of linguistic and logical precision, it is a fit vehicle for another kind of passion: the intellect's passion for ideas, as the first Pope passage suggests. The

---

THE RAPE OF THE LOCK. **1.** *it:* the stolen lock of hair that the poem concerns. *Lunar Sphere:* the moon, held in folk mythology to be the repository of lost things.

heroic couplet also has the potential for a fine elegance and grace, a potential that springs from the sense of balance innate to the form, as can be seen from Anne Bradstreet's graceful lines. Most of all, the form is a superb vehicle for wit and satire—the potential evidenced by the passage from "The Rape of the Lock"—because of the epigrammatic nature of the closed couplet and the punch it can so readily deliver. That the heroic couplet was the dominant poetic mode of the eighteenth century—which veered toward the intellectual, prized elegance and grace, and produced our greatest satires—suggests that form is not only a vehicle of an artist's outlook and sensibility but an indicator of the spirit of the times as well.

SUMMARY SUGGESTIONS: UNDERSTANDING TRADITIONAL DESIGNS

1. When focusing on a poem's formal design, first jot down the rhyme scheme of a stanza if the poem is in stanzas or of the whole poem if it is in a fixed form. Use letters to do this, with each repeated letter representing a rhyme. Then determine what kind of stanza or form you are dealing with.

2. Now look at the poem with the potentialities we have discussed in mind. Try, that is, to determine in what ways the innate qualities of the stanza or form are made use of.

3. Always, however, allow for meaningful deviation. If a given poem deviates from the expectations of its form, ask why. What is the poem doing? What special emphasis or meaning does the deviation establish? Sometimes, to be sure, a seeming deviation is not meaningful but merely the result of lack of skill (and so not a deviation at all). To make such a judgment, which is a matter of critical evaluation, you must bring to bear all your knowledge of the poem's particular design and all your understanding of the relationship of formal designs and content generally.

4. If the design is not one we have considered, try to determine its potentialities on your own. Then read the poem with those potentialities in mind. The poem either will or will not bear out your judgment. If it does, then you are on the track. If it does not, then you must determine whether it is deviant or inept, or whether it fulfills a potential that you did not see.

5. In any case, what you must finally do is to relate the poem's design to meaning, form to content. Why this design rather than another? How do its inherent qualities bear on meaning? What meaning can you ascribe to the design that fits everything else you think and feel about the poem? By answering questions like these, you will come to a fuller appreciation of a given poem and a wider understanding of the nature of poetry itself.

WRITING ON TRADITIONAL DESIGNS

The aim of writing about the formal design of a poem is to demonstrate the nature of the relationship of the poem's design and meaning, or to show how its design participates in the meaning overall. In a paper on a poem's structure, therefore, your thesis will necessarily entail the relationship between that structure and its meaning: for example, a viable thesis statement for a paper on the design of Shakespeare's Sonnet 129 (pp. 367–77) would be, "Taking the logical form of a three-tiered argument with a summation, Sonnet 129 demonstrates by way of contrast between form and content how weak logic is in the face of desire and passion." Your support would entail an analysis of the poem focused in this case on the contrast between the sonnet's logical form and the driving, unrelenting passions of the speaker, which defy law and logic.

In beginning to think about the relationship of formal design and content, first construct a poem's meaning by considering all of its elements other than design. Examine its imagery and diction; consider what the poem reveals about the speaker; locate its setting, if possible, and determine the poem's situation, if it has one; interpret its figuration; and see what you can make of its rhythm and sound. Having constructed the poem's meaning to your own satisfaction in this prewriting stage, then go about relating that meaning to the poem's formal design. As you do, do not forget that the relationship might be inverse: that is, the meaning might lie in some deviation from the norm. Some poems, to be sure, will not yield to your inquiry, either because they are flawed (but this judgment itself can provide a thesis) or because you have missed something. But be assured that in every truly great poem there is a relationship to be discovered. So persevere. If need be, however, choose another poem and carry it through the process I have outlined. If you give yourself time for real thought and feeling, you will find a poem that opens up for you.

To consolidate, let's consider how design and content are related in one poem more, this a poem with which you are already familiar in that it is one of the two model works we took up at the beginning of this book. You might wish to look back at that consideration before proceeding (pp. 3–4).

THE ROAD NOT TAKEN
— Robert Frost —

Two roads diverged in a yellow wood,
And sorry I could not travel both
And be one traveler, long I stood
And looked down one as far as I could
To where it bent in the undergrowth;   5

Then took the other, as just as fair,
And having perhaps the better claim,
Because it was grassy and wanted wear;
Though as for that, the passing there
Had worn them really about the same,   10

And both that morning equally lay
In leaves no step had trodden black.
Oh, I kept the first for another day!

Yet knowing how way leads on to way,
I doubted if I should ever come back.   15

I shall be telling this with a sigh
Somewhere ages and ages hence:
Two roads diverged in a wood, and I—
I took the one less traveled by,
And that has made all the difference.   20

[1916—U.S.A.]

Recall the main point established when we last looked at this poem: that its speaker is not the individualist he might appear to be from the line "I took the one less traveled by," for in fact the two roads were exactly the same and what he actually says is that sometime in the distant future he *will* say "I took the one less traveled by"—disremembering the truth, thus, and rationalizing his choice. Now, turning to the poem's design, I note the obvious: that the poem is in stanzas (rhymed *abaab*). And the uniformity of a stanzaic design, it strikes me, runs counter to a truly individualistic ethos. So, what is suggested by the poem's design reinforces what we come to understand about its speaker through all its other elements: that he is not really an individualist blazing a trail but only someone like us faced with the common problem of choice and its basis. In other words, the very regularity of the poem's stanzas serves to undercut its closing assertion and so to alert us to what is actually being said.

This could be your thesis. To demonstrate it, you would need to discuss the poem in detail and establish its meaning. Then you could move on to show how the poem's design reflects that meaning. As always, you would need a viable beginning, stating the object of your paper: to show the relationship of meaning and design in "The Road Not Taken" or, more specifically, how the stanzaic design of the poem echoes what we come to understand about the speaker otherwise. Then you could consider what it is we come to understand from a close reading of the poem. Having done so, you could turn to the stanzaic design and show how it participates in the meaning. Your conclusion could fan out to a generalization given rise to by the poem and its design as to how we fool ourselves into believing that our own choices in life and the paths we consequently take are unique. Such is the kind of procedure that writing on formal designs entails. If you keep the procedure outlined here in mind, this admittedly difficult undertaking should prove easier and could prove especially rewarding.

POEMS FOR STUDY AND WRITING ASSIGNMENTS

IDEA, SONNET 61

— Michael Drayton —

Since there's no help, come let us kiss and part;
Nay, I have done, you get no more of me,
And I am glad, yea glad with all my heart
That thus so cleanly I myself can free;
Shake hands forever, cancel all our vows,   5
And when we meet at any time again,
Be it not seen in either of our brows
That we one jot of former love retain.
Now at the last gasp of love's latest breath,
When, his pulse failing, passion speechless lies,   10
When faith is kneeling by his bed of death,
And innocence is closing up his eyes,
    Now if thou wouldst, when all have given him over,
    From death to life thou mightst him yet recover.

[1619—Great Britain]

Questions

1. What is the rhyme scheme of this poem? What kind of fixed form is in it?
2. What is the poem's situation? What conflicted feelings does this situation arouse in the speaker?
3. In what way is this poem deviant with respect to its specific form? What does the deviation here serve to do?
4. How are the speaker's conflicted feelings reflected by the poem's formal design? How, then, does the poem's design correspond with its meaning?

Writing Assignments

1. Write a paragraph addressed to question 2 above. First establish the poem's situation; then discuss the conflicted feelings of the speaker. You might conclude with a statement as to how the design of the poem helps express those feelings.
2. In a short essay, analyze Drayton's poem with regard to its fixed form. How does the poem adhere to the type from which it originates? How does it deviate from that type? In what way is the deviation meaningful, resulting in a structure overall that follows the twists and turns of the speaker's emotions?

SURPRISED BY JOY
— William Wordsworth —

Surprised by joy—impatient as the Wind
I turned to share the transport—Oh! with whom
But thee, deep buried in the silent tomb,
That spot which no vicissitude can find?
Love, faithful love, recalled thee to my mind—   5
But how could I forget thee? Through what power,
Even for the least division of an hour,
Have I been so beguiled as to be blind
To my most grievous loss!—That thought's return
Was the worst pang that sorrow ever bore,   10
Save one, one only, when I stood forlorn,
Knowing my heart's best treasure was no more;
That neither present time, nor years unborn
Could to my sight that heavenly face restore.

[1815—Great Britain]

Questions

1. Paraphrase the poem in order to clarify to yourself its shifts in time and perspective.
2. "Surprised by Joy" presents us with *two* situations. What are they? What setting is here suggested?
3. What is the rhyme scheme of the poem? What is the name of its form?
4. How is this traditional design used? In what way is the poem's deviation from the expectations of its form meaningful?
5. What is expressed through the poem's formal design? How are its design and content one?

Writing Assignments

1. (a) In a paragraph, state what "Surprised by Joy" tells us about the psychology of grief.
   (b) In a separate paragraph, discuss your response to the poem and state why you so respond.
2. Write a paper addressed to question 5 above. Your thesis should be a statement as to the nature of the relationship of design and content in "Surprised by Joy"; your support should entail a discussion of your understanding of the meaning of the poem as borne out by its other elements and how its formal design participates in that meaning.

SURPRISED BY JOY.   **3.** *thee:* the poet's daughter Catherine, who died in 1812 at age four.

ONE ART

— Elizabeth Bishop —

The art of losing isn't hard to master;
so many things seem filled with the intent
to be lost that their loss is no disaster.

Lose something every day. Accept the fluster
of lost door keys, the hour badly spent.   5
The art of losing isn't hard to master.

Then practice losing farther, losing faster:
places, and names, and where it was you meant
to travel. None of these will bring disaster.

I lost my mother's watch. And look! my last, or   10
next-to-last, of three loved houses went.
The art of losing isn't hard to master.

I lost two cities, lovely ones. And, vaster,
some realms I owned, two rivers, a continent.
I miss them, but it wasn't a disaster.   15

—Even losing you (the joking voice, a gesture
I love) I shan't have lied. It's evident
the art of losing's not too hard to master
though it may look like (*Write* it!) like disaster.

[1976—U.S.A.]

Questions

1. Jot down the poem's rhyme scheme and note which lines repeat exactly. What is the name of this traditional form?
2. Where does the poet deviate from the expectations of her chosen form in the first fifteen lines? To what effect?
3. What is the tone of the first fifteen lines? How does the poem's formal design help to condition tone here?
4. What situation do the last four lines suggest? Even if only slightly, these lines differ in tone from the rest of the poem. How so? What is the effect of the contrast?
5. Yet the speaker would dissemble and hide her feelings. How does the poem's design itself suggest as much? What does it tell us about the speaker?
6. How do the last four lines deviate from the expectations aroused by the poem's form? What does the deviation reveal about the speaker's real feelings?

Writing Assignments

1. In a paragraph or more, consider the formal design of "One Art" in relation to its tone. What tone predominates in the poem? How does its design help to create that tone? What tonal contrast, even if slight, can be heard at the end? How do the deviations at the end from the norm of the design that the poem is cast into help us to hear this contrasting note?

2. Write an essay about the speaker of "One Art." What is happening in her life that the poem is addressed to? What are her responses? What kind of person would she be? What kind of person is she? Be sure to consider the poem's tone(s) and formal design in discussing its speaker. For it is through these mainly that we come to understand her.

3. Focusing on the poem's design, write a critique of "One Art." Consider first in what ways, if any, the poem's design participates in its meaning. Then critically evaluate the poem in light of your conclusions about the relationship, or the lack thereof, between its content and specific design.

ODE TO THE WEST WIND
— Percy Bysshe Shelley —
Section 5

Make me thy lyre, even as the forest is:
What if my leaves are falling like its own!
The tumult of thy mighty harmonies

Will take from both a deep, autumnal tone,
Sweet though in sadness. Be thou, Spirit fierce,   5
My spirit! Be thou me, impetuous one!

Drive my dead thoughts over the universe
Like withered leaves to quicken a new birth!
And, by the incantation of this verse,

Scatter, as from an unextinguished hearth   10
Ashes and sparks, my words among mankind!
Be through my lips to unawakened earth

The trumpet of a prophecy! O Wind,
If Winter comes, can Spring be far behind?

[1820—Great Britain]

ODE TO THE WEST WIND.   **1.** *thy:* the west wind.

Questions

1. What stanzaic form marks this passage?
2. What do "Winter" and "Spring" here symbolize? In what way do their symbolic meanings tie in with the phrase "Sweet though in sadness"? How do their symbolic meanings help account for Shelley's off-rhymes?
3. What is the basic effect here of the stanza form used? How does Shelley's choice of stanza relate to the wind he invokes?
4. "Sweet though in sadness" suggests ambivalence. How does the design of the passage and the way it moves because of its design help to lend a sense that all ambivalence dissolves in the face of the prophecy that the passage relentlessly pulls us to?

Writing Assignments

1. Write a paragraph or short paper on the relationship of form and content in this passage from "Ode to the West Wind." To do so you will have to define the form and its potentialities; then discuss the passage in light of those potentialities.
2. Read "Ode to the West Wind" in its entirety (pp. 506–08) and do some research about the poem. What do its critics have to say, especially about the relation in it of content and design, as well as other of its formal attributes? Now write a critical paper incorporating your research on the relationship of the poem's form—especially its formal design—and its content.

from THE EVE OF ST. AGNES
— John Keats —

1

St. Agnes' Eve—Ah, bitter chill it was!
The owl, for all his feathers, was a-cold;
The hare limped trembling through the frozen grass,
And silent was the flock in woolly fold:
Numb were the Beadsman's fingers, while he told   5
His rosary, and while his frosted breath,
Like pious incense from a censer old,
Seemed taking flight for heaven, without a death,
Past the sweet Virgin's picture, while his prayer he saith.

THE EVE OF ST. AGNES.   *St. Agnes:* the patron saint of virgins. According to legend, a young girl who performs the right rituals will have a dream-vision of her future husband on the eve before St. Agnes's Day (January 21). Marked by contrast, these introductory stanzas lead to a story about such a girl and her beloved. **5.** *Beadsman:* one paid to pray for his benefactor. He "tells" (counts) the beads of his rosary.

2

His prayer he saith, this patient, holy man;   10
Then takes his lamp, and riseth from his knees,
And back returneth, meager, barefoot, wan,
Along the chapel aisle by slow degrees:
The sculptured dead, on each side, seem to freeze,
Imprisoned in black, purgatorial rails: 15
Knights, ladies, praying in dumb orat'ries,
He passeth by; and his weak spirit fails
To think how they may ache in icy hoods and mails.

3

Northward he turneth through a little door,
And scarce three steps, ere Music's golden tongue   20
Flattered to tears this aged man and poor;
But no—already had his deathbell rung:
The joys of all his life were said and sung:
His was harsh penance on St. Agnes' Eve:
Another way he went, and soon among   25
Rough ashes sat he for his soul's reprieve,
And all night kept awake, for sinner's sake to grieve.

4

That ancient Beadsman heard the prelude soft;
And so it chanced, for many a door was wide,
From hurry to and fro. Soon, up aloft,   30
The silver, snarling trumpets 'gan to chide:
The level chambers, ready with their pride,
Were glowing to receive a thousand guests:
The carvèd angels, ever eager-eyed,
Stared, where upon their heads the cornice rests,   35
With hair blown back, and wings put cross-wise on their breasts.

[1820—Great Britain]

---

14. *sculptured dead:* the stone sculptures (friezes) depicting the dead lying within the sarcophagi on which the sculptures lie. **15.** *rails:* the railings around the sarcophagi, railings that here seem like prison bars holding the spirits of the dead in purgatory. **16.** *Knights, ladies . . . dumb orat'ries:* statues of dead knights and ladies entombed in these "dumb orat'ries" (silent chapels), statues that, like the friezes of line 14, suggest purgatorial penance to the Beadsman. **18.** *To think how they:* i.e., when he thinks how the spirits. *Mails:* flexible armor made of overlapping scales or rings. **21.** *Flattered:* beguiled. **32.** *pride:* ostentatious display. **34.** *carvèd angels:* decorations located right under the cornice, or moulding, of the room described.

Questions

1. Look at the rhyme scheme and meter here. What is the stanzaic form?
2. Contrast the first three stanzas and the fourth as to imagery, movement, texture, and sound. The fourth stanza, more typical of the poem as a whole than the first three, throws the first three stanzas into relief. How so?
3. What innate potential of the stanza form here is exploited in the fourth stanza? What might we conclude just from the fourth stanza about why Keats chose this stanza form for "The Eve of St. Agnes"?
4. In what way is the poem's stanza form in contrast with the setting and situation described in the first three stanzas? What does this contrast serve to do?

Writing Assignments

1. Write a paragraph on the inverse relationship of the stanza form and the content of the first three stanzas. Be sure to consider how this inverse relationship helps to heighten our sense of cold and decrepitude.
2. Go to the library and read the whole of "The Eve of St. Agnes." Then write an essay on its stanzaic design. Why did Keats choose this design? How does it serve his ends? In what different ways does he use it? How are form and content related—either directly or inversely—passage by passage? These are the questions you should take up and explore.

ABOUT MY STUDENTS
— John Fandel —

Against the pleated pillars of Old Main,
    Like caryatids in plaids, the coeds lean,
    Loafing in wisdom's porticoes between
Lectures on Aristotle and the Dane.

The heroes of their gaze accord the spring   5
    In rolled-up sleeves, all similar in sweet ease
    And pastimes lackadaisical as the breeze
That stalled the canvas of Mycenae's King.

Ten-minute freedoms in the outdoor sun
    Accommodate their restlessness in class   10
      Where they sit doodling, while professors mass
The facts about Thermopylae and Verdun.

ABOUT MY STUDENTS.   **2.** *caryatids:* statues of draped female figures used to support, like columns, the portico of a building of classic design.   **4.** *the Dane:* Hamlet.   **5.** *accord:* are in harmony with.   **8.** *Mycenae's King:* Agamemnon, commander of the Greek forces in the Trojan War. Because the fleet was stalled by a northern breeze, Agamemnon, acting under advisement, sacrificed his daughter Iphigenia to the gods.   **12.** *Thermopylae and Verdun:* the two great battles that frame Western history.

Among their lolling youth my daydreams flit:
  How I, like they, lived once from bell to bell.
  No old accumulated notes can tell   15
Them life is stranger than they fancy it.

[1959—U.S.A.]

Questions

1. What is the stanza form here?
2. How does the poem move? What are its mood and tone? How are the poem's movement, mood, and tone affected by its stanza form?
3. What in the poem validates its final statement (line 16)?
4. What do we learn about the poem's speaker? What does its final line reveal? What is revealed through the poem's stanza form, or its effect?
5. In what ways is the poem's stanzaic design right for the feelings expressed here? What relation does that design bear to content?

Writing Assignments

1. Write a short paper addressed to question 2 above. First describe the poem's stanza form and its potentialities. Then apply what you say to the poem itself, relating its design to movement, mood, and tone as well as to anything else you observe in the poem that seems to you related to its design.
2. In an essay, discuss the speaker of "About My Students." What do we learn about him? How do we learn what we learn? In addressing the second question, discuss the poem's stanzaic design and what it reveals about the speaker given the way the design is treated.

BELLS FOR JOHN WHITESIDE'S DAUGHTER
— John Crowe Ransom —

There was such speed in her little body,
And such lightness in her footfall,
It is no wonder her brown study
Astonishes us all.

Her wars were bruited in our high window.   5
We looked among orchard trees and beyond
Where she took arms against her shadow,
Or harried unto the pond

The lazy geese, like a snow cloud
Dripping their snow on the green grass,   10

BELLS FOR JOHN WHITESIDE'S DAUGHTER. **3.** *brown study:* serious expression.

Tricking and stopping, sleepy and proud,
Who cried in goose, Alas,

For the tireless heart within the little
Lady with rod that made them rise
From their noon apple-dreams and scuttle   15
Goose-fashion under the skies!

But now go the bells, and we are ready,
In one house we are sternly stopped
To say we are vexed at her brown study,
Lying so primly propped.   20

[1924—U.S.A.]

Questions

1. Grammatically self-contained as well as interlinked stanzas are usually used by poets as logical and emotional units of expression. How is this demonstrated by the poem above?
2. Except for those of stanza three, the lines of the stanzas alternate between off-rhyme and full rhyme. What is the effect of this mixture?
3. Each stanza here ends with a line shorter than the other lines in the stanza. What is the effect of this shortening both visually and aurally (that is, when the poem is read aloud)? How is this aspect of the poem's form related to its content?
4. You articulated the poem's structure in answering question 1 above. Now relate what you said to the poem's content. How does form express content here?

Writing Assignments

1. Whatever a poem's formal design—be it traditional or innovative, strict or free—that design will somehow participate in the meaning if the poem succeeds. Taking this statement as your thesis, write a short paper arguing that "Bells for John Whiteside's Daughter" fulfills this criterion of poetic success. Discuss *how* the poem does so and, thus, what the significance of its design is.
2. Write an essay analyzing "Bells for John Whiteside's Daughter" in all of its formal aspects. Your main concern will be *how* the poem means. What are the effects of its formal design, its meter, its line treatment and the shortening of every fourth line, its imagery and its imagistic contrasts, its contrasting tones, its off-rhymes, and so forth? Such will be your considerations as you bring to bear everything you observe about the poem's form to explicate its meaning. Your goal will be to show how every aspect of the poem's form relates to and indeed creates its meaning.

CHAPTER

�֎ 8 ✲

PULLING IT ALL TOGETHER

Reading is a dynamic activity, an experience that takes shape in the dialectic of reader and text in its entirety. One experiences a text, that is, in all of its aspects and complexity at once, and not element by element. Necessarily, of course, we have worked sequentially and discussed poems piecemeal, focusing first on one element and then on another. But now let us consider a poem from every angle. The explication that follows is meant to show you what writing on a poem with all of its various aspects taken into account entails and also how one goes about reading a poem in all of its intricacy.

A VALEDICTION FORBIDDING MOURNING
— Adrienne Rich —

My swirling wants. Your frozen lips.
The grammar turned and attacked me.
Themes, written under duress.
Emptiness of the notations.

They gave me a drug that slowed the healing of wounds.   5

I want you to see this before I leave:
the experience of repetition as death
the failure of criticism to locate the pain

A VALEDICTION FORBIDDING MOURNING.   The title refers to John Donne's poem by the same name (pp. 464–65). **5.** *They gave me . . . of wounds:* As well as alluding to Donne, Rich alludes at several points to T. S. Eliot's *The Waste Land.* In this line, for instance, there is an echo of the end of Eliot's poem, in which the fisher king Anfortas lies wounded, waiting for what will magically heal him: the simple question "What is wrong?" The "drug" Rich speaks of slows "the healing of wounds" because it numbs and so keeps one from asking this question, from feeling and facing the wound.

the poster in the bus that said:
my bleeding is under control.   10

A red plant in a cemetery of plastic wreaths.

A last attempt: the language is a dialect called metaphor.
These images go unglossed: hair, glacier, flashlight.
When I think of a landscape I am thinking of a time.
When I talk of taking a trip I mean forever.   15
I could say: those mountains have a meaning
but further than that I could not say.

To do something very common, in my own way.

[1971—U.S.A.]

Language and Self-definition

Comparison and contrast leading to thesis

Adrienne Rich's title, "A Valediction Forbidding Mourning," refers, clearly, to John Donne's poem by the same name. But there the likeness ends. With its lively conceits and elaborate metaphorical extension, Donne's poem expresses supreme confidence in language and in the purposes of the self. Fragmented in its syntax, in the way it moves and sounds, and even in the way it looks on the page, with three lines (5, 11, and 18) separated out and made to

Two-part thesis

stand in isolation, Rich's poem, in contrast, expresses the failure of its speaker to find self-definition and the failure of language (metaphor) with respect to such definition. But the poem also concerns a breaking with the past and the possibility on the part of the speaker of forging a new life by finding a language adequate to her needs.

Transition

That breaking is announced by the title, which serves to establish the poem's situation: the parting of lovers (the one of "swirling wants" from the one of "frozen lips"). The situation is Donne's. Unlike

Contrast leading to . . .

Donne's speaker, however, Rich's is "taking a trip . . . forever." Donne forbids mourning because his lovers, though they are to be separated physically, cannot be separated spiritually; Rich forbids mourning because hers are to make a clean break.

. . . topic sentences

Donne's emphasis is on continuance; Rich's is on freedom, the desire for which her speaker attempts to explain. Her explanation has to do with self and with language, of which the self is made (we conceive of self through language, so the existence of self depends on language).

Support

Thus, when the speaker says "grammar," she means herself, hitherto defined by other people's language (whose "grammar turned and attacked" her), especially that of the man she is leaving. Up until now she has not

Support

been her own person. She has allowed her life to be scripted by him, but all he has done is to write a college theme, cramped because "written under duress" (like assignments), lacking in all conviction and genuine feeling, and as empty as most term-paper footnotes. (Note how the language metaphor is extended through the first four

Support

lines.) Because his lips have been frozen, he could never speak the right word to meet

Transition

her needs. Having come to experience her life as repetition and "repetition as death," she must break out of this sterile relationship and feel what she must.

Topic
sentence

Support

What she must feel first is the depth of her pain. In a long, weary line (line 5) marked by low-pitched vowel sounds that in their heaviness reflect the feeling of being drugged, the speaker sums up her life until this moment of departure: drugged--perhaps by the repetitions of her relationship, perhaps literally by tranquilizers--she has not felt much of anything, much less her deep psychic and spiritual wounds. So how could they be healed? Like the people in

Support

T. S. Eliot's The Waste Land, of which Rich's poem is reminiscent in several ways, she has been isolated from herself. Trapped in the frozen patterns of a language that has only concealed and so only given the illusion of meaning, trapped in the grammar of conventional expectations, she has lost touch with her own needs.

Topic
sentence

Yet, "swirling," those needs have finally surfaced. She must, therefore,

Support

sever this relationship, which has been a relationship in name only. The very syntax of the first line suggests the separateness of the two "lovers," the "me" and the "you" isolated in fragmented sentences and set in opposition by the strong mid-line caesura.

Support

But however much the speaker mistrusts language because it has imprisoned her in received definitions, one of the needs ("I want") that she now feels is to explain why she is leaving. As she begins to try again to explain (line 6), a tone of tenderness enters, and even of pity at his

dumbfoundedness, and of urgency. She would
articulate both to him and to herself what
has brought her to this leave-taking.

Transition   It is the death of possibility, the
stifling of growth, the "experience of
repetition as death"--which all the
rationalizations of the socialized intellect
cannot justify or ease. The pain has been

Support there, however concealed; the wound has been
bleeding internally, however much denied by
the routines of everyday behavior and the
truth-denying language of the culture
generally--the language of commercialism,
which saps and devitalizes language and in
so doing cuts us off from ourselves and from
understanding our needs. (The language
metaphor extended in lines 1-4 is further
extended in lines 9 and 10.) The bus poster

Support for menstruation pills provides a symbolic
focal point with respect to such language:
in saying "my bleeding is under control" it
really says, "Woman, do not bleed; woman, do

Topic sentences not need." It is from all this dissembling
and deception that the speaker would break
out, like a potted plant breaking the pot
that restricts its growth. Her need is for
something real, something felt, even for
pain and bleeding if necessary--"A red plant
in a cemetery of plastic wreaths."

Transition   But how to express in the language of
explanation the swirling of the heart?

Support Rich's speaker attempts to do so three
times, in four and then five and then six
lines, as though trying harder with each

Support

attempt. Still, she finds it impossible to
say just what she means. Her unglossed
images remain unglossed. Yet they have a
peculiar resonance, as do her metaphors, and
a sense of urgency. The swirling heart

Support

cries to be free, to have world enough and
time to make its own choices. Thus, the
trip is to be "forever"; the break must be
clean. Thus, too, the "meaning" of "those
mountains," that meaning being freedom——
"In the mountains, there you feel free,"
says a female speaker in Eliot's The Waste

Topic
sentence

Land. Rich's speaker has been in an
emotional waste land, but she has awakened
to the possibility of a fuller life. More
than that she cannot say.

Topic
sentence

Partly about language, the poem also
concerns growth, the pain of endings, the
promise of a beginning. However stifled in

Support

the past, Rich's speaker is in process in
the present tense of the poem. Though she

Support

hasn't arrived anywhere, she has begun to
allow herself to feel. To be sure, she has

Support

only begun. While imitating the swirling of
the heart, the fragmented form of the poem
also suggests that the person of the speaker
is not whole. And she has far to go before
she is fully in touch with herself. The
tonal dryness of much of the poem——created,
in part, by severe end-stopping along with
syntactical and rhythmical fragmentation——
sounds a dichotomy between understanding and

Support

feeling. Nevertheless, she has made a
start, tentatively, gropingly. Her

tentativeness expresses itself in her
grammar——"To do" instead of "I shall do."
Yet there is also to be heard a firmness of
resolve in her end—stopping and especially
in the simplicity of the last line and the
tonal quality of its last phrase, which
strikes a note almost of joy: "in my own
way." The bright, high—pitched a̅ of "way,"
the strong ending (on an accented syllable),
and the sense of closure caused by the rhyme
(the only rhyme in the poem) make the phrase
convincing as to her intent. We can

Conclusion conclude, therefore, that however painful it
is to make an end, she will leave; she will
struggle to shed the language that has kept
her from growing and grope toward fulfilling
in herself the "common" need: the need for
self—definition.

THREE POETS: THEIR RANGE AND RICHNESS

The more one reads a poet, the more one comes to understand his or her characteristic patterns and themes. And the more one understands what is characteristic of a poet, the more easily and fully one can read any single poem by that poet. Certainly, to see a poem in the context of a wide range of the poet's work is to enrich the experience of reading the poem and to facilitate its interpretation. For these reasons, I conclude this chapter with a relatively large number of poems by three important American poets: Emily Dickinson, Robert Frost, and William Carlos Williams.

You would do well to choose one of these poets and read everything in the present and preceding chapters by the poet you choose. If you do so with deliberation, you should be in a good position to interpret any single poem by that poet fully— as I have just interpreted Adrienne Rich's "Valediction" —and to both evaluate and appreciate the poet's range and richness.

EMILY DICKINSON
(1830–1886)

[I Never Lost as Much But Twice]

I never lost as much but twice,
And that was in the sod.
Twice have I stood a beggar
Before the door of God!

Angels—twice descending   5
Reimbursed my store—
Burglar! Banker—Father!
I am poor once more!

[Where Bells No More Affright the Morn]

Where bells no more affright the morn—
Where scrabble never comes—
Where very nimble Gentlemen
Are forced to keep their rooms—

Where tired Children placid sleep   5
Thro' Centuries of noon
This place is Bliss—this town is Heaven—
Please, Pater, pretty soon!

"Oh could we climb where Moses stood,
And view the Landscape o'er"   10
Not Father's bells—nor Factories,
Could scare us any more!

[I'm "Wife"]

I'm "wife"—I've finished that—
That other state—
I'm Czar—I'm "Woman" now—
It's safer so—

How odd the Girl's life looks   5
Behind this soft Eclipse—
I think that Earth feels so
To folks in Heaven—now—

This being comfort—then
That other kind—was pain—   10

But why compare?
I'm "Wife"! Stop there!

[What Is—"Paradise"]

What is—"Paradise"—
Who live there—
Are they "Farmers"—
Do they "hoe"—
Do they know that this is "Amherst"—   5
And that I—am coming—too—

Do they wear "new shoes"—in "Eden"—
Is it always pleasant—there—
Won't they scold us—when we're homesick—
Or tell God—how cross we are—   10

You are sure there's such a person
As "a Father"—in the sky—
So if I get lost—there—ever—
Or do what the Nurse calls "die"—
I shan't walk the "Jasper"—barefoot—   15
Ransomed folks—won't laugh at me—
Maybe—"Eden" a'n't so lonesome
As New England used to be!

[Safe in Their Alabaster Chambers]

Safe in their Alabaster Chambers—
Untouched by Morning
And untouched by Noon—
Sleep the meek members of the Resurrection—
Rafter of satin,   5
And Roof of stone.

Light laughs the breeze
In her Castle above them—
Babbles the Bee in a stolid Ear,
Pipe the Sweet Birds in ignorant cadence—   10
Ah, what sagacity perished here!

[WHAT IS—"PARADISE"].   **15.** *"Jasper":* the roadway into heaven.   **16.** *Ransomed folks:* those already in heaven, ransomed from death by Christ's sacrifice.

[I Like a Look of Agony]

I like a look of Agony,
Because I know it's true—
Men do not sham Convulsion,
Nor simulate, a Throe—

The Eyes glaze once—and that is Death—   5
Impossible to feign
The Beads upon the Forehead
By homely Anguish strung.

[Wild Nights!]

Wild Nights—Wild Nights!
Were I with thee
Wild Nights should be
Our luxury!

Futile—the Winds—   5
To a Heart in port—
Done with the Compass—
Done with the Chart!

Rowing in Eden—
Ah, the Sea!   10
Might I but moor—Tonight—
In Thee!

[Over the Fence]

Over the fence—
Strawberries—grow—
Over the fence—
I could climb—if I tried, I know—
Berries are nice!   5

But—if I stained my Apron—
God would certainly scold!
Oh, dear,—I guess if He were a Boy—
He'd—climb—if He could!

[There's a Certain Slant of Light]

There's a certain Slant of light,
Winter Afternoons—

That oppresses, like the Heft
Of Cathedral Tunes—

Heavenly Hurt, it gives us—   5
We can find no scar,
But internal difference,
Where the Meanings, are—

None may teach it—Any—
'Tis the Seal Despair—   10
An imperial affliction
Sent us of the Air—

When it comes, the Landscape listens—
Shadows—hold their breath—
When it goes, 'tis like the Distance   15
On the look of Death—

[I'm Nobody! Who Are You?]

I'm Nobody! Who are you?
Are you—Nobody—Too?
Then there's a pair of us?
Don't tell! they'd advertise—you know!

How dreary—to be—Somebody!   5
How public—like a Frog—
To tell one's name—the livelong June—
To an admiring Bog!

[I Know That He Exists]

I know that He exists.
Somewhere—in Silence—
He has hid his rare life
From our gross eyes.

'Tis an instant's play.   5
'Tis a fond Ambush—
Just to make Bliss
Earn her own surprise!

But—should the play
Prove piercing earnest—   10
Should the glee—glaze—
In Death's—stiff—stare—

Would not the fun
Look too expensive!
Would not the jest—   15
Have crawled too far!

[After Great Pain]

After great pain, a formal feeling comes—
The Nerves sit ceremonious, like Tombs—
The stiff Heart questions was it He, that bore,
And Yesterday, or Centuries before?

The Feet, mechanical, go round—   5
Of Ground, or Air, or Ought°—   *nothing*
A Wooden way
Regardless grown,
A Quartz contentment, like a stone—

This is the Hour of Lead—   10
Remembered, if outlived,
As Freezing persons, recollect the Snow—
First—Chill—then Stupor—then the letting go—

[I Died for Beauty]

I died for Beauty—but was scarce
Adjusted in the Tomb
When One who died for Truth, was lain
In an adjoining Room—

He questioned softly "Why I failed"?   5
"For Beauty," I replied—
"And I—for Truth—Themself are One—
We Brethren, are," He said—

And so, as Kinsmen, met a Night—
We talked between the Rooms—   10
Until the Moss had reached our lips—
And covered up—our names—

[I Heard a Fly Buzz]

I heard a Fly buzz—when I died—
The Stillness in the Room

Was like the Stillness in the Air—
Between the Heaves of Storm—

The Eyes around—had wrung them dry—   5
And Breaths were gathering firm
For that last Onset—when the King
Be witnessed—in the Room—

I willed my Keepsakes—Signed away
What portion of me be   10
Assignable—and then it was
There interposed a Fly—

With Blue—uncertain stumbling Buzz—
Between the light—and me—
And then the Windows failed—and then   15
I could not see to see—

[The Heart Asks Pleasure]

The Heart asks Pleasure—first—
And then—Excuse from Pain—
And then—those little Anodynes
That deaden suffering—

And then—to go to sleep—   5
And then—if it should be
The will of its Inquisitor
The privilege to die—

[I Like to See It Lap the Miles]

I like to see it lap the Miles—
And lick the Valleys up—
And stop to feed itself at Tanks—
And then—prodigious step

Around a Pile of Mountains—   5
And supercilious peer
In Shanties—by the sides of Roads—
And then a Quarry pare

To fit its sides
And crawl between
Complaining all the while   10

In horrid—hooting stanza—
Then chase itself down Hill—

And neigh like Boanerges—
Then—prompter than a Star   15
Stop—docile and omnipotent
At its own stable door—

[We Talked as Girls Do]

We talked as Girls do—
Fond, and late—
We speculated fair, on every subject, but the Grave—
Of ours, none affair—

We handled Destinies, as cool—   5
As we—Disposers—be—
And God, a Quiet Party
To our Authority—

But fondest, dwelt upon Ourself
As we eventual—be—   10
When Girls to Women, softly raised
We—occupy—Degree—

We parted with a contract
To cherish, and to write
But Heaven made both, impossible   15
Before another night.

[The Brain]

The Brain—is wider than the Sky—
For—put them side by side—
The one the other will contain
With ease—and You—beside—

The Brain is deeper than the sea—   5
For—hold them—Blue to Blue—
The one the other will absorb—
As Sponges—Buckets—do—

The Brain is just the weight of God—
For—Heft them—Pound for Pound—   10

[I LIKE TO SEE IT LAP THE MILES].   **14.** *Boanerges:* any loud preacher or orator.

And they will differ—if they do—
As Syllable from Sound—

[Me from Myself]

Me from Myself—to banish—
Had I Art—
Impregnable my Fortress
Unto All Heart—

But since Myself—assault Me—   5
How have I peace
Except by subjugating
Consciousness?

And since We're mutual Monarch
How this be   10
Except by Abdication—
Me—of Me?

[Because I Could Not Stop for Death]

Because I could not stop for Death—
He kindly stopped for me—
The Carriage held but just Ourselves—
And Immortality.

We slowly drove—He knew no haste   5
And I had put away
My labor and my leisure too,
For His Civility—

We passed the School, where Children strove
At Recess—in the Ring—   10
We passed the Fields of Gazing Grain—
We passed the Setting Sun—

Or rather—He passed Us—
The Dews drew quivering and chill—
For only Gossamer,° my Gown—   *thin fabric* 15
My Tippet°—only Tulle°—   *cape, scarf / thin silk*

We paused before a House that seemed
A Swelling of the Ground—
The Roof was scarcely visible—
The Cornice—in the Ground—   20

Since then—'tis Centuries—and yet
Feels shorter than the Day
I first surmised the Horses' Heads
Were toward Eternity—

[You Said That I "Was Great"]

You said that I "was Great"—one Day—
Then "Great" it be—if that please Thee—
Or Small—or any size at all—
Nay—I'm the size suit Thee—

Tall—like the Stag—would that?   5
Or lower—like the Wren—
Or other heights of Other Ones
I've seen?

Tell which—it's dull to guess—
And I must be Rhinoceros   10
Or Mouse
At once—for Thee—

So say—if Queen it be—
Or Page—please Thee—
I'm that—or nought—   15
Or other thing—if other thing there be—
With just this Stipulus—
I suit Thee—

[My Life . . . a Loaded Gun]

My Life had stood—a Loaded Gun—
In Corners—till a Day
The Owner passed—identified—
And carried Me away—

And now We roam in Sovereign Woods—   5
And now We hunt the Doe—
And every time I speak for Him—
The Mountains straight reply—

And do I smile, such cordial light
Upon the Valley glow—   10

[MY LIFE . . . A LOADED GUN].   **9.** *smile:* An older carbine was said to be in a "smile position" when it was being loaded.

It is as a Vesuvian face
Had let its pleasure through—

And when at Night—Our good Day done—
I guard My Master's Head—
'Tis better than the Eider-Duck's   15
Deep Pillow—to have shared—

To foe of His—I'm deadly foe—
None stir the second time—
On whom I lay a Yellow Eye—
Or an emphatic Thumb—   20

Though I than He—may longer live
He longer must—than I—
For I have but the power to kill,
Without—the power to die—

See also:

[A Narrow Fellow in the Grass], page 266
[I Taste a Liquor Never Brewed], page 311
[It Was Not Death], page 370

ROBERT FROST

(1874–1963)

Mowing

There was never a sound beside the wood but one,
And that was my long scythe whispering to the ground.
What was it it whispered? I knew not well myself;
Perhaps it was something about the heat of the sun,
Something, perhaps, about the lack of sound—   5
And that was why it whispered and did not speak.
It was no dream of the gift of idle hours,
Or easy gold at the hand of fay or elf:
Anything more than the truth would have seemed too weak
To the earnest love that laid the swale in rows,   10
Not without feeble-pointed spikes of flowers
(Pale orchises), and scared a bright green snake.
The fact is the sweetest dream that labor knows.
My long scythe whispered and left the hay to make.

19. *Yellow Eye:* a bullet, yellow because of its brass casing.

Into My Own

One of my wishes is that those dark trees,
So old and firm they scarcely show the breeze,
Were not, as 'twere, the merest mask of gloom,
But stretched away unto the edge of doom.

I should not be withheld but that some day   5
Into their vastness I should steal away,
Fearless of ever finding open land,
Or highway where the slow wheel pours the sand.

I do not see why I should e'er turn back,
Or those should not set forth upon my track   10
To overtake me, who should miss me here
And long to know if still I held them dear.

They would not find me changed from him they knew—
Only more sure of all I thought was true.

Stars

How countlessly they congregate
    O'er our tumultuous snow,
Which flows in shapes as tall as trees
    When wintry winds do blow!—

As if with keenness for our fate,   5
    Our faltering few steps on
To white rest, and a place of rest
    Invisible at dawn—

And yet with neither love nor hate,
    Those stars like some snow-white   10
Minerva's snow-white marble eyes
    Without the gift of sight.

Birches

When I see birches bend to left and right
Across the lines of straighter darker trees,
I like to think some boy's been swinging them.
But swinging doesn't bend them down to stay
As ice-storms do. Often you must have seen them   5

STARS.   **11.** *Minerva:* Roman goddess of wisdom.

Loaded with ice a sunny winter morning
After a rain. They click upon themselves
As the breeze rises, and turn many-colored
As the stir cracks and crazes their enamel.
Soon the sun's warmth makes them shed crystal shells   10
Shattering and avalanching on the snow-crust—
Such heaps of broken glass to sweep away
You'd think the inner dome of heaven had fallen.
They are dragged to the withered bracken by the load.
And they seem not to break; though once they are bowed   15
So low for long, they never right themselves:
You may see their trunks arching in the woods
Years afterwards, trailing their leaves on the ground
Like girls on hands and knees that throw their hair
Before them over their heads to dry in the sun.   20
But I was going to say when Truth broke in
With all her matter-of-fact about the ice-storm
I should prefer to have some boy bend them
As he went out and in to fetch the cows—
Some boy too far from town to learn baseball,   25
Whose only play was what he found himself,
Summer or winter, and could play alone.
One by one he subdued his father's trees
By riding them down over and over again
Until he took the stiffness out of them,   30
And not one but hung limp, not one was left
For him to conquer. He learned all there was
To learn about not launching out too soon
And so not carrying the tree away
Clear to the ground. He always kept his poise   35
To the top branches, climbing carefully
With the same pains you use to fill a cup
Up to the brim, and even above the brim.
Then he flung outward, feet first, with a swish,
Kicking his way down through the air to the ground.   40
So was I once myself a swinger of birches.
And so I dream of going back to be.
It's when I'm weary of considerations,
And life is too much like a pathless wood
Where your face burns and tickles with the cobwebs   45
Broken across it, and one eye is weeping
From a twig's having lashed across it open.

I'd like to get away from earth awhile
And then come back to it and begin over.
May no fate willfully misunderstand me   50
And half grant what I wish and snatch me away
Not to return. Earth's the right place for love:
I don't know where it's likely to go better.
I'd like to go by climbing a birch tree,
And climb black branches up a snow-white trunk   55
Toward heaven, till the tree could bear no more,
But dipped its top and set me down again.
That would be good both going and coming back.
One could do worse than be a swinger of birches.

"Out, Out—"

The buzz saw snarled and rattled in the yard
And made dust and dropped stove-length sticks of wood,
Sweet-scented stuff when the breeze drew across it.
And from there those that lifted eyes could count
Five mountain ranges one behind the other   5
Under the sunset far into Vermont.
And the saw snarled and rattled, snarled and rattled,
As it ran light, or had to bear a load.
And nothing happened: day was all but done.
Call it a day, I wish they might have said   10
To please the boy by giving him the half hour
That a boy counts so much when saved from work.
His sister stood beside them in her apron
To tell them "Supper." At the word, the saw,
As if to prove saws knew what supper meant,   15
Leaped out at the boy's hand, or seemed to leap—
He must have given the hand. However it was,
Neither refused the meeting. But the hand!
The boy's first outcry was a rueful laugh,
As he swung toward them holding up the hand   20
Half in appeal, but half as if to keep
The life from spilling. Then the boy saw all—
Since he was old enough to know, big boy
Doing a man's work, though a child at heart—
He saw all spoiled. "Don't let him cut my hand off—   25

"OUT, OUT—"   The title alludes to Shakespeare's lines "Out, out, brief candle! / Life's but a walking shadow," from *Macbeth* (Act V, Scene 5, lines 23–24).

The doctor, when he comes. Don't let him, sister!"
So. But the hand was gone already.
The doctor put him in the dark of ether.
He lay and puffed his lips out with his breath.
And then—the watcher at his pulse took fright.   30
No one believed. They listened at his heart.
Little—less—nothing!—and that ended it.
No more to build on there. And they, since they
Were not the one dead, turned to their affairs.

The Oven Bird

There is a singer everyone has heard,
Loud, a mid-summer and a mid-wood bird,
Who makes the solid tree trunks sound again.
He says that leaves are old and that for flowers
Mid-summer is to spring as one to ten.   5
He says the early petal-fall is past,
When pear and cherry bloom went down in showers
On sunny days a moment overcast;
And comes that other fall we name the fall.
He says the highway dust is over all.   10
The bird would cease and be as other birds
But that he knows in singing not to sing.
The question that he frames in all but words
Is what to make of a diminished thing.

For Once, Then, Something

Others taunt me with having knelt at well-curbs
Always wrong to the light, so never seeing
Deeper down in the well than where the water
Gives me back in a shining surface picture
Me myself in the summer heaven, godlike,   5
Looking out of a wreath of fern and cloud puffs.
Once, when trying with chin against a well-curb,
I discerned, as I thought, beyond the picture,
Through the picture, a something white, uncertain,
Something more of the depths—and then I lost it.   10
Water came to rebuke the too clear water.
One drop fell from a fern, and lo, a ripple
Shook whatever it was lay there at bottom,
Blurred it, blotted it out. What was that whiteness?
Truth? A pebble of quartz? For once, then, something.   15

Nothing Gold Can Stay

Nature's first green is gold,
Her hardest hue to hold.
Her early leaf's a flower;
But only so an hour.
Then leaf subsides to leaf.   5
So Eden sank to grief,
So dawn goes down to day.
Nothing gold can stay.

To Earthward

Love at the lips was touch
As sweet as I could bear;
And once that seemed too much;
I lived on air

That crossed me from sweet things,   5
The flow of—was it musk
From hidden grapevine springs
Downhill at dusk?

I had the swirl and ache
From sprays of honeysuckle   10
That when they're gathered shake
Dew on the knuckle.

I craved strong sweets, but those
Seemed strong when I was young;
The petal of the rose   15
It was that stung.

Now no joy but lacks salt,
That is not dashed with pain
And weariness and fault;
I crave the stain   20

Of tears, the aftermark
Of almost too much love,
The sweet of bitter bark
And burning clove.

When stiff and sore and scarred   25
I take away my hand
From leaning on it hard
In grass and sand,

The hurt is not enough:
I long for weight and strength   30
To feel the earth as rough
To all my length.

Good-by and Keep Cold

This saying good-by on the edge of the dark
And the cold to an orchard so young in the bark
Reminds me of all that can happen to harm
An orchard away at the end of the farm
All winter, cut off by a hill from the house.   5
I don't want it girdled by rabbit and mouse,
I don't want it dreamily nibbled for browse
By deer, and I don't want it budded by grouse.
(If certain it wouldn't be idle to call
I'd summon grouse, rabbit, and deer to the wall   10
And warn them away with a stick for a gun.)
I don't want it stirred by the heat of the sun.
(We made it secure against being, I hope,
By setting it out on a northerly slope.)
No orchard's the worse for the wintriest storm;   15
But one thing about it, it mustn't get warm.
"How often already you've had to be told,
Keep cold, young orchard. Good-by and keep cold.
Dread fifty above more than fifty below."
I have to be gone for a season or so.   20
My business awhile is with different trees,
Less carefully nurtured, less fruitful than these,
And such as is done to their wood with an ax—
Maples and birches and tamaracks.
I wish I could promise to lie in the night   25
And think of an orchard's arboreal plight
When slowly (and nobody comes with a light)
Its heart sinks lower under the sod.
But something has to be left to God.

Dust of Snow

The way a crow
Shook down on me
The dust of snow
From a hemlock tree

Has given my heart   5
A change of mood
And saved some part
Of a day I had rued.

The Aim Was Song

Before man came to blow it right
   The wind once blew itself untaught,
And did its loudest day and night
   In any rough place where it caught.

Man came to tell it what was wrong: 5
   It hadn't found the place to blow;
It blew too hard—the aim was song.
   And listen—how it ought to go!

He took a little in his mouth,
   And held it long enough for north   10
To be converted into south,
   And then by measure blew it forth.

By measure. It was word and note,
   The wind the wind had meant to be—
A little through the lips and throat.   15
   The aim was song—the wind could see.

Desert Places

Snow falling and night falling fast, oh, fast
In a field I looked into going past,
And the ground almost covered smooth in snow,
But a few weeds and stubble showing last.

The woods around it have it—it is theirs.   5
All animals are smothered in their lairs.
I am too absent-spirited to count;
The loneliness includes me unawares.

And lonely as it is that loneliness
Will be more lonely ere it will be less—   10
A blanker whiteness of benighted snow
With no expression, nothing to express.

They cannot scare me with their empty spaces
Between stars—on stars where no human race is.

I have it in me so much nearer home   15
To scare myself with my own desert places.

Provide, Provide

The witch that came (the withered hag)
To wash the steps with pail and rag
Was once the beauty Abishag,

The picture pride of Hollywood.
Too many fall from great and good   5
For you to doubt the likelihood.

Die early and avoid the fate.
Or if predestined to die late,
Make up your mind to die in state.

Make the whole stock exchange your own!   10
If need be occupy a throne,
Where nobody can call *you* crone.

Some have relied on what they knew,
Others on being simply true.
What worked for them might work for you.   15

No memory of having starred
Atones for later disregard
Or keeps the end from being hard.

Better to go down dignified
With boughten friendship at your side   20
Than none at all. Provide, provide!

Departmental

An ant on the tablecloth
Ran into a dormant moth
Of many times his size.
He showed not the least surprise.
His business wasn't with such.   5
He gave it scarcely a touch,
And was off on his duty run.
Yet if he encountered one
Of the hive's enquiry squad
Whose work is to find out God   10
And the nature of time and space,

He would put him onto the case.
Ants are a curious race;
One crossing with hurried tread
The body of one of their dead   15
Isn't given a moment's arrest—
Seems not even impressed.
But he no doubt reports to any
With whom he crosses antennae,
And they no doubt report   20
To the higher up at court.
Then word goes forth in Formic:
"Death's come to Jerry McCormic,
Our selfless forager Jerry.
Will the special Janizary°   *elite soldier* 25
Whose office it is to bury
The dead of the commissary
Go bring him home to his people.
Lay him in state on a sepal.
Wrap him for shroud in a petal.   30
Embalm him with ichor of nettle.
This is the word of your Queen."
And presently on the scene
Appears a solemn mortician;
And taking formal position   35
With feelers calmly atwiddle,
Seizes the dead by the middle,
And heaving him high in air,
Carries him out of there.
No one stands round to stare.   40
It is nobody else's affair.

It couldn't be called ungentle.
But how thoroughly departmental.

Design

I found a dimpled spider, fat and white,
On a white heal-all, holding up a moth
Like a white piece of rigid satin cloth—
Assorted characters of death and blight
Mixed ready to begin the morning right,   5

DESIGN.   **2.** *heal-all:* a flower, usually blue, thought to have healing powers.

Like the ingredients of a witches' broth—
A snow-drop spider, a flower like a froth,
And dead wings carried like a paper kite.

What had that flower to do with being white,
The wayside blue and innocent heal-all?   10
What brought the kindred spider to that height,
Then steered the white moth thither in the night?
What but design of darkness to appall?—
If design govern in a thing so small.

See also:

WILLIAM CARLOS WILLIAMS
(1883–1963)

Portrait of a Lady

Your thighs are appletrees
whose blossoms touch the sky.
Which sky? The sky
where Watteau hung a lady's
slipper. Your knees   5
are a southern breeze—or
a gust of snow. Agh! what
sort of man was Fragonard?
—as if that answered
anything. Ah, yes—below   10
the knees, since the tune
drops that way, it is

PORTRAIT OF A LADY.   **4 and 8.** Jean Watteau (1684–1721) and Jean Fragonard (1732–1806) were both French painters in the rococo style. The hauntingly erotic painting by Watteau to which the speaker alludes depicts a beautiful young woman swinging in a swing while her left shoe goes flying into the air. Fragonard, inspired by Watteau, did a painting of a similar subject.

one of those white summer days,
the tall grass of your ankles
flickers upon the shore—   15
Which shore?—
the sand clings to my lips—
Which shore?

Agh, petals maybe. How
should I know?   20
Which shore? Which shore?
I said petals from an appletree.

Danse Russe

If when my wife is sleeping
and the baby and Kathleen
are sleeping
and the sun is a flame-white disc
in silken mists   5
above shining trees,—
if I in my north room
dance naked, grotesquely
before my mirror
waving my shirt round my head   10
and singing softly to myself:
"I am lonely, lonely.
I was born to be lonely,
I am best so!"
If I admire my arms, my face,   15
my shoulders, flanks, buttocks
against the yellow drawn shades,—

Who shall say I am not
the happy genius of my household?

The Locust Tree in Flower

Among
of
green

DANSE RUSSE.   **19.** *genius:* local spirit, household diety.

stiff
old   5
bright

broken
branch
come

white   10
sweet
May

again

Spring and All

By the road to the contagious hospital
under the surge of the blue
mottled clouds driven from the
northeast—a cold wind. Beyond, the
waste of broad, muddy fields   5
brown with dried weeds, standing and fallen

patches of standing water
the scattering of tall trees

All along the road the reddish
purplish, forked, upstanding, twiggy   10
stuff of bushes and small trees
with dead, brown leaves under them
leafless vines—

Lifeless in appearance, sluggish
dazed spring approaches—   15

They enter the new world naked,
cold, uncertain of all
save that they enter. All about them
the cold, familiar wind—

Now the grass, tomorrow   20
the stiff curl of wildcarrot leaf
One by one objects are defined—
It quickens: clarity, outline of leaf

But now the stark dignity of
entrance—Still, the profound change   25
has come upon them: rooted, they
grip down and begin to awaken

Queen-Ann's-Lace

Her body is not so white as
anemone petals nor so smooth—nor
so remote a thing. It is a field
of the wild carrot taking
the field by force; the grass   5
does not raise above it.
Here is no question of whiteness,
white as can be, with a purple mole
at the center of each flower.
Each flower is a hand's span   10
of her whiteness. Wherever
his hand has lain there is
a tiny purple blemish. Each part
is a blossom under his touch
to which the fibres of her being   15
stem one by one, each to its end,
until the whole field is a
white desire, empty, a single stem,
a cluster, flower by flower,
a pious wish to whiteness gone over—   20
or nothing.

Young Sycamore

I must tell you
this young tree
whose round and firm trunk
between the wet

pavement and the gutter   5
(where water
is trickling) rises
bodily

into the air with
one undulant   10

thrust half its height—
and then

dividing and waning
sending out
young branches on   15
all sides—

hung with cocoons
it thins
till nothing is left of it
but two   20

eccentric knotted
twigs
bending forward
hornlike at the top

Poem

As the cat
climbed over
the top of

the jamcloset
first the right   5
forefoot

carefully
then the hind
stepped down

into the pit of   10
the empty
flowerpot

This Is Just to Say

I have eaten
the plums
that were in
the icebox

and which   5
you were probably

saving
for breakfast

Forgive me
they were delicious   10
so sweet
and so cold

A Sort of a Song

Let the snake wait under
his weed
and the writing
be of words, slow and quick, sharp
to strike, quiet to wait,   5
sleepless.

—through metaphor to reconcile
the people and the stones.
Compose. (No ideas
but in things) Invent!   10
Saxifrage is my flower that splits
the rocks.

The Descent

The descent beckons
            as the ascent beckoned.
                        Memory is a kind
of accomplishment,
            a sort of renewal   5
                        even
an initiation, since the spaces it opens are new places
            inhabited by hordes
                        heretofore unrealized,
of new kinds—   10
            since their movements
                        are toward new objectives
(even though formerly they were abandoned).

No defeat is made up entirely of defeat—since

A SORT OF A SONG. **11.** *saxifrage:* Look it up and check its etymology.

the world it opens is always a place   15
   formerly
      unsuspected. A
world lost,
   a world unsuspected,
      beckons to new places   20
and no whiteness (lost) is so white as the memory
of whiteness

With evening, love wakens
   though its shadows
      which are alive by reason   25
of the sun shining—
   grow sleepy now and drop away
      from desire
Love without shadows stirs now
   beginning to awaken   30
      as night
advances.

The descent
   made up of despairs
      and without accomplishment   35
realizes a new awakening:
      which is a reversal
of despair.
   For what we cannot accomplish, what
is denied to love,   40
   what we have lost in the anticipation—
      a descent follows,
endless and indestructible

Portrait of a Woman at Her Bath

   it is a satisfaction
   a joy
   to have one of those
   in the house

   when she takes a bath   5
   she unclothes
   herself she is no
   Venus

I laugh at her
  an Inca   10
shivering at the well
the sun is

glad of a fellow to
marvel at
the birds and the flowers   15
look in

Asphodel, That Greeny Flower

from Book I

Of asphodel, that greeny flower,
    like a buttercup
          upon its branching stem—
save that it's green and wooden—
    I come, my sweet.   5
          to sing to you.
We lived long together
    a life filled,
          if you will,
with flowers. So that   10
    I was cheered
          when I came first to know
that there were flowers also
    in hell.
          Today   15
I'm filled with the fading memory of those flowers
    that we both loved,
          even to this poor
colorless thing—
    I saw it   20
          when I was a child—
little prized among the living
    but the dead see,
          asking among themselves:
What do I remember   25
    that was shaped
          as this thing is shaped?
while our eyes fill

ASPHODEL, THAT GREENY FLOWER. **14.** *hell:* Williams was close to death when he wrote this poem.

with tears.
                Of love, abiding love   30
it will be telling
        though too weak a wash of crimson
               colors it
to make it wholly credible.
        There is something   35
               something urgent
I have to say to you
        and you alone
               but it must wait
while I drink in   40
        the joy of your approach,
               perhaps for the last time.

. . . .
I have forgot
        and yet I see clearly enough
               something
central to the sky   55
        which ranges round it.
               An odor
springs from it!
        A sweetest odor!
               Honeysuckle! And now   60
there comes the buzzing of a bee!
        and a whole flood
               of sister memories!
Only give me time,
        time to recall them   65
               before I shall speak out.
Give me time,
        time.

. . . .
It is a curious odor,
        a moral odor,
               that brings me
near to you.   90
        The color
               was the first to go.
There had to come to me
        a challenge,
               your dear self,   95
mortal as I was,

                    the lily's throat
                                to the hummingbird!
Endless wealth,
            I thought,   100
                        held out its arms to me.
A thousand topics
            in an apple blossom.
                            The generous earth itself
gave us lief.   105
                The whole world
                            became my garden!

. . . .

from Book III

For our wedding, too,
                the light was wakened
                            and shone. The light!   425
the light stood before us
                waiting!
                            I thought the world
stood still.
                At the altar   430
                            so intent was I
before my vows,
                so moved by your presence
                            a girl so pale
and ready to faint   435
                that I pitied
                            and wanted to protect you.
As I think of it now,
                after a lifetime,
                            it is as if   440
a sweet-scented flower
                were poised
                            and for me did open.
Asphodel
                has no odor   445
                            save to the imagination
but it too
                celebrates the light.
                            It is late

but an odor   450
　　　　　　as from our wedding
　　　　　　　　　　has revived for me
　　and begun again to penetrate
　　　　　　　　into all crevices
　　　　　　　　　　　　of my world.   455

See also:

　The Buffalos, page 137
　The Use of Force, page 167
　The Young Housewife, page 296
　To a Poor Old Woman, page 320
　The Dance, page 336

ANTHOLOGY

CHAOS STAGGERED UP THE HILL
— A. R. Ammons —

Chaos staggered up the hill
and got the daisies dirty
that were pretty along the road:
messy chaos I said
but then in cooler mind saw   5
incipient eyes revolving in it
with possibly incipient sorrow
and had to admire how
it got along at all
in its kind of weather: 10
passing, it engulfed me
and I couldn't know dissolving
it had rhizobia with it
to make me green some other place.

[1955—U.S.A.]

THE CITY LIMITS
— A. R. Ammons —

When you consider the radiance, that it does not withhold
itself but pours its abundance without selection into every
nook and cranny not overhung or hidden; when you consider

that birds' bones make no awful noise against the light but
lie low in the light as in a high testimony; when you consider   5
the radiance, that it will look into the guiltiest

swervings of the weaving heart and bear itself upon them,
not flinching into disguise or darkening; when you consider
the abundance of such resource as illuminates the glow-blue

bodies and gold-skeined wings of flies swarming the dumped   10
guts of a natural slaughter or the coil of shit and in no
way winces from its storms of generosity; when you consider

that air or vacuum, snow or shale, squid or wolf, rose or lichen,
each is accepted into as much light as it will take, then
the heart moves roomier, the man stands and looks about, the   15

leaf does not increase itself above the grass, and the dark
work of the deepest cells is of a tune with May bushes
and fear lit by the breadth of such calmly turns to praise.

[1971—U.S.A.]

FOWLES IN THE FRITH

— Anonymous —

Fowles° in the frith,°   *birds / woods*
The fisshes in the flood,
And I mon waxe wood;°   *I must go mad*
Much sowre° I walke with   *sorrow*
For beste° of boon° and blood.   *best / bone*

[13th cen.—Great Britain]

THE CUCKOO SONG

— Anonymous —

Sumer is ycomen° in,   *coming*
Loude° sing cuckou!   *loudly*
Groweth seed and bloweth meed,
And springth the wode° now.   *wood*
Sing cuckou!   5

Ewe bleteth after lamb,
Loweth after calve cow,

FOWLES IN THE FRITH. Though we can never know the intentions of an author directly, we sometimes know for sure what was *not* intended. For example, the language of "Fowles in the Frith" was not intended to be quaint. Its language is the language of the day.
THE CUCKOO SONG. **3.** *meed:* the meadow blossoms. **7.** *Loweth after calve cow:* the cow lows after the calf.

Bulloc sterteth,° bucke verteth,°   *leaps / breaks wind*
Merye sing cuckou!
Cuckou, cuckou,   10
Wel singest thou cuckou:
Ne swik° thou never now!   *cease*

[14th cen.—Great Britain]

THE HUMBLE WISH

— Anonymous —

I Ask not wit, nor beauty do I crave,
Nor wealth, nor pompous titles wish to have;
But since 'tis doom'd, in all degrees of life,
(Whether a daughter, sister, or a wife,)
That females shall the stronger males obey,   5
And yield per force to their tyrannic sway;
Since this, I say, is ev'ry woman's fate,
Give me a mind to suit my slavish state.

[18th cen.—Great Britain]

AT NORTH FARM

— John Ashbery —

Somewhere someone is traveling furiously toward you,
At incredible speed, traveling day and night,
Through blizzards and desert heat, across torrents, through narrow passes.
But will he know where to find you,
Recognize you when he sees you,   5
Give you the thing he has for you?

Hardly anything grows here,
Yet the granaries are bursting with meal,
The sacks of meal piled to the rafters.
The streams run with sweetness, fattening fish;   10
Birds darken the sky. Is it enough
That the dish of milk is set out at night,
That we think of him sometimes,
Sometimes and always, with mixed feelings?

[1981—U.S.A.]

ON HER LOVING TWO EQUALLY
— Aphra Behn —

I

How strong does my passion flow,
Divided equally twixt two?
Damon had ne'er subdued my heart
Had not Alexis took his part;
Nor could Alexis powerful prove,   5
Without my Damon's aid, to gain my love.

II

When my Alexis present is,
Then I for Damon sigh and mourn;
But when Alexis I do miss,
Damon gains nothing but my scorn.   10
But if it chance they both are by,
For both alike I languish, sigh, and die.

III

Cure then, thou mighty wingéd god,
This restless fever in my blood;
One golden-pointed dart take back: 15
But which, O Cupid, wilt thou take?
If Damon's, all my hopes are crossed;
Or that of my Alexis, I am lost.

[1684—Great Britain]

THE DREAM SONGS
— John Berryman —

No. 1

Huffy Henry hid   the day,
unappeasable Henry sulked.
I see his point,—a trying to put things over,
It was the thought that they thought

ON HER LOVING TWO EQUALLY.   **13.** *wingéd god:* Cupid, whose golden darts represent true love.   **17.** *crossed:* ruined.

they could *do* it made Henry wicked & away.   5
But he should have come out and talked.

All the world like a woolen lover
once did seem on Henry's side.
Then came a departure.
Thereafter nothing fell out as it might or ought.   10
I don't see how Henry, pried
open for all the world to see, survived.

What he has now to say is a long
wonder the world can bear & be.
Once in a sycamore I was glad   15
all at the top, and I sang.
Hard on the land wears the strong sea
and empty grows every bed.

[1964—U.S.A.]

No. 14

Life, friends, is boring. We must not say so.
After all, the sky flashes, the great sea yearns,
we ourselves flash and yearn,
and moreover my mother told me as a boy
(repeatedly) "Ever to confess you're bored   5
means you have no

Inner Resources." I conclude now I have no
inner resources, because I am heavy bored.
Peoples bore me,
literature bores me, especially great literature,   10
Henry bores me, with his plights & gripes
as bad as achilles,

who loves people and valiant art, which bores me.
And the tranquil hills, & gin, look like a drag
and somehow a dog   15
has taken itself & its tail considerably away

THE DREAM SONGS, 1.   **5.** *do it:* comfort Henry. "They" refers to friends and relatives gathered for the funeral of the departed one.   **7.** *woolen lover:* security blanket.   **9.** *departure:* Though Henry is a persona, the "departure" can be identified as that of Berryman's father, who committed suicide.
THE DREAM SONGS, 14.   **12.** *achilles:* Achilles retired from fighting during the Trojan War because of a slight from Agamemnon, the Greeks' general.

into mountains or sea or sky, leaving
behind: me, wag.

[1964—U.S.A.]

INFANT SORROW
— William Blake —

My mother groand! my father wept.
Into the dangerous world I leapt:
Helpless, naked, piping loud;
Like a fiend hid in a cloud.

Struggling in my father's hands,   5
Striving against my swadling bands,
Bound and weary I thought best
To sulk upon my mother's breast.

[1794—Great Britain]

THE TYGER
— William Blake —

Tyger! Tyger! burning bright
In the forests of the night,
What immortal hand or eye
Could frame thy fearful symmetry?

In what distant deeps or skies   5
Burnt the fire of thine eyes?
On what wings dare he aspire?
What the hand, dare seize the fire?

And what shoulder, & what art,
Could twist the sinews of thy heart?   10
And when thy heart began to beat,
What dread hand? & what dread feet?

What the hammer? what the chain?
In what furnace was thy brain?
What the anvil? what dread grasp   15
Dare its deadly terrors clasp?

When the stars threw down their spears,
And water'd heaven with their tears,
Did he smile his work to see?
Did he who made the Lamb make thee?   20

Tyger! Tyger! burning bright
In the forests of the night,
What immortal hand or eye
Dare frame thy fearful symmetry?

[1794—Great Britain]

A POISON TREE
— William Blake —

I was angry with my friend:
I told my wrath, my wrath did end.
I was angry with my foe:
I told it not, my wrath did grow.

And I waterd it in fears,   5
Night & morning with my tears;
And I sunnèd it with smiles,
And with soft deceitful wiles.

And it grew both day and night,
Till it bore an apple bright.   10
And my foe beheld it shine,
And he knew that it was mine,

And into my garden stole,
When the night had veild the pole;
In the morning glad I see   15
My foe outstretchd beneath the tree.

[1794—Great Britain]

THE GARDEN OF LOVE
— William Blake —

I went to the Garden of Love,
And saw what I never had seen:

A Chapel was built in the midst,
Where I used to play on the green.

And the gates of this Chapel were shut,   5
And "Thou shalt not" writ over the door;
So I turn'd to the Garden of Love,
That so many sweet flowers bore,

And I saw it was filled with graves,
And tomb-stones where flowers should be: 10
And Priests in black gowns were walking their rounds,
And binding with briars my joys & desires.

[1794—Great Britain]

JUAN'S SONG
— Louise Bogan —

When beauty breaks and falls asunder,
I feel no grief for it, but wonder.
When love, like a frail shell, lies broken,
I keep no chip of it for token.
I never had a man for friend   5
Who did not know that love must end.
I never had a girl for lover
Who could discern when love was over.
What the wise doubt, the fool believes—
Who is it, then, that love deceives.   10

[1954—U.S.A.]

A BLACK MAN TALKS OF REAPING
— Arna Bontemps —

I have sown beside all waters in my day.
I planted deep, within my heart the fear
that wind or fowl would take the grain away.
I planted safe against this stark, lean year.

I scattered seed enough to plant the land   5
in rows from Canada to Mexico
but for my reaping only what the hand
can hold at once is all that I can show.

Yet what I sowed and what the orchard yields
my brother's sons are gathering stalk and root;   10
small wonder then my children glean in fields
they have not sown, and feed on bitter fruit.

[1940—U.S.A.]

A LETTER TO HER HUSBAND, ABSENT UPON PUBLIC EMPLOYMENT
— Anne Bradstreet —

My head, my heart, mine eyes, my life, nay, more,
My joy, my magazine of earthly store,
If two be one, as surely thou and I,
How stayest thou there, whilst I at Ipswich lie?
So many steps, head from the heart to sever,   5
If but a neck, soon should we be together.
I, like the Earth this season, mourn in black,
My sun is gone so far in's zodiac,
Whom whilst I 'joyed, nor storms, nor frost I felt,
His warmth such frigid colds did cause to melt.   10
My chilled limbs now numbed lie forlorn:
Return, return, sweet Sol, from Capricorn;
In this dead time, alas, what can I more
Than view those fruits which through thy heat I bore?
Which sweet contentment yield me for a space,   15
True living pictures of their father's face.
O strange effect! now thou art southward gone,
I weary grow the tedious day so long;
But when thou northward to me shalt return,
I wish my Sun may never set, but burn   20
Within the Cancer of my glowing breast,
The welcome house of him my dearest guest.
Where ever, ever stay, and go not thence,
Till nature's sad decree shall call thee hence;
Flesh of thy flesh, bone of thy bone,   25
I here, thou there, yet both but one.

[1678—U.S.A.]

A LETTER TO HER HUSBAND.   **2.** *magazine:* warehouse.   **4.** *Ipswich:* a town north of Boston.   **8.** *zodiac:* the path of the sun and the planets. In this constellation, "My sun" refers to the speaker's husband.   **12.** *Sol; Capricorn:* Sol is the sun; Capricorn is a winter sign in the zodiac.   **21.** *Cancer:* a summer sign in the zodiac.

SONG

— Emily Brontë —

The linnet in the rocky dells,
  The moor-lark in the air,
The bee among the heather bells
  That hide my lady fair:

The wild deer browse above her breast;   5
  The wild birds raise their brood;
And they, her smiles of love caressed,
  Have left her solitude.

I ween that, when the grave's dark wall
  Did first her form retain,   10
They thought their hearts could ne'er recall
  The light of joy again.

They thought the tide of grief would flow
  Unchecked through future years;
But where is all their anguish now,   15
  And where are all their tears?

Well, let them fight for honor's breath,
  Or pleasure's shade pursue—
The dweller in the land of death
  Is changed and careless too.   20

And, if their eyes should watch and weep
  Till sorrow's source were dry,
She would not, in her tranquil sleep,
  Return a single sigh.

Blow, west-wind, by the lonely mound,   25
  And murmur, summer streams!
There is no need of other sound
  To soothe my lady's dreams.

[1844—Great Britain]

THE VACANT LOT

— Gwendolyn Brooks —

Mrs. Coley's three-flat brick
Isn't here any more.

All done with seeing her fat little form
Burst out of the basement door;
And with seeing her African son-in-law 5
(Rightful heir to the throne)
With his great white strong cold squares of teeth
And his little eyes of stone;
And with seeing the squat fat daughter
Letting in the men 10
When majesty has gone for the day—
And letting them out again.

[1945—U.S.A.]

THE SONNET-BALLAD
— Gwendolyn Brooks —

Oh mother, mother, where is happiness?
They took my lover's tallness off to war.
Left me lamenting. Now I cannot guess
What I can use an empty heart-cup for.
He won't be coming back here any more. 5
Some day the war will end, but, oh, I knew
When he went walking grandly out that door
That my sweet love would have to be untrue.
Would have to be untrue. Would have to court
Coquettish death, whose impudent and strange 10
Possessive arms and beauty (of a sort)
Can make a hard man hesitate—and change.
And he will be the one to stammer, "Yes."
Oh mother, mother, where is happiness?

[1950—U.S.A.]

WE REAL COOL
— Gwendolyn Brooks —

The Pool Players.
Seven at the Golden Shovel.

We real cool. We
Left school. We

Lurk late. We
Strike straight. We

Sing sin. We   5
Thin gin. We

Jazz June. We
Die soon.

[1960—U.S.A.]

CINDERELLA
— Olga Broumas —

. . . the joy that isn't shared
I heard, dies young.
Anne Sexton, 1928–1974

Apart from my sisters, estranged
from my mother, I am a woman alone
in a house of men
who secretly
call themselves princes, alone   5
with me usually, under cover of dark.   I am the one allowed in

to the royal chambers, whose small foot conveniently
fills the slipper of glass.   The woman writer, the lady
umpire, the madam chairman, anyone's wife.
I know what I know.   10
And I once was glad
of the chance to use it, even alone
in a strange castle, doing overtime on my own, cracking
the royal code.   The princes spoke
in their fathers' language, were eager to praise me   15
my nimble tongue.   I am a woman in a state of siege, alone

as one piece of laundry, strung on a windy clothesline a
mile long. A woman co-opted by promises: the lure
of a job, the ruse of a choice, a woman forced
to bear witness, falsely   20
against my kind, as each
other sister was judged inadequate, bitchy, incompetent,
jealous, too thin, too fat.   I know what I know.
What sweet bread I make
for myself in this prosperous house   25

is dirty, what good soup I boil turns
in my mouth to mud.   Give
me my ashes.   A cold stove, a cinder-block pillow, wet
canvas shoes in my sisters', my sisters' hut.   Or I swear

I'll die young   30
like those favored before me, hand-picked each one
for her joyful heart.

[1977—U.S.A.]

PORPHYRIA'S LOVER
— Robert Browning —

The rain set early in tonight,
  The sullen wind was soon awake,
It tore the elm-tops down for spite,
  And did its worst to vex the lake:
  I listened with heart fit to break.   5
When glided in Porphyria; straight
  She shut the cold out and the storm,
And kneeled and made the cheerless grate
  Blaze up, and all the cottage warm;
  Which done, she rose, and from her form   10
Withdrew the dripping cloak and shawl,
  And laid her soiled gloves by, untied
Her hat and let the damp hair fall,
  And, last, she sat down by my side
  And called me. When no voice replied,   15
She put my arm about her waist,
  And made her smooth white shoulder bare,
And all her yellow hair displaced,
  And, stooping, made my cheek lie there,
  And spread, o'er all, her yellow hair,   20
Murmuring how she loved me—she
  Too weak, for all her heart's endeavor,
To set its struggling passion free
  From pride, and vainer ties dissever,
  And give herself to me forever.   25
But passion sometimes would prevail,
  Nor could tonight's gay feast restrain
A sudden thought of one so pale

For love of her, and all in vain:
    So, she was come through wind and rain.   30
Be sure I looked up at her eyes
    Happy and proud; at last I knew
Porphyria worshiped me: surprise
    Made my heart swell, and still it grew
    While I debated what to do.   35
That moment she was mine, mine, fair,
    Perfectly pure and good: I found
A thing to do, and all her hair
    In one long yellow string I wound
    Three times her little throat around   40
And strangled her. No pain felt she;
    I am quite sure she felt no pain.
As a shut bud that holds a bee,
    I warily oped her lids: again
    Laughed the blue eyes without a stain.   45
And I untightened next the tress
    About her neck; her cheek once more
Blushed bright beneath my burning kiss:
    I propped her head up as before,
    Only, this time my shoulder bore   50
Her head, which droops upon it still:
    The smiling rosy little head,
So glad it has its utmost will,
    That all it scorned at once is fled,
    And I, its love, am gained instead!   55
Porphyria's love: she guessed not how
    Her darling one wish would be heard.
And thus we sit together now,
    And all night long we have not stirred,
    And yet God has not said a word!   60

[1836—Great Britain]

TO A MOUSE

— Robert Burns —

On turning her up in her nest with the plough,
November, 1785

Wee, sleekit,° cow'rin, tim'rous beastie,   *sleek*

O, what a panic's in thy breastie!
Thou need na start awa sae hasty,
    Wi' bickering° brattle!°   *hurried / scamper*
I wad be laith to rin an' chase thee,   5
    Wi' murd'ring pattle!°   *plowstaff ("paddle")*

I'm truly sorry man's dominion
Has broken Nature's social union,
An' justifies that ill opinion
    Which makes thee startle   10
At me, thy poor earth-born companion,
    An' fellow-mortal!

I doubt na, whiles,° but thou may thieve;   *sometimes*
What then? poor beastie, thou maun° live!   *must*
A daimen° icker° in a thrave°   *random / corn-ear / shock* 15
    'S a sma' request:
I'll get a blessin wi' the lave,°   *rest*
    And never miss't!

Thy wee bit housie, too, in ruin!
Its silly° wa's the win's are strewin!   *frail* 20
An' naething, now, to big° a new ane,   *build*
    O' foggage° green!   *mosses*
An' bleak December's winds ensuin,
    Baith snell° an' keen!   *bitter*

Thou saw the fields laid bare and waste,   25
An' weary winter comin fast,
An' cozie here, beneath the blast,
    Thou thought to dwell,
Till crash! the cruel coulter° past   *plowshare*
    Out thro' thy cell.   30

That wee bit heap o' leaves an' stibble°   *stubble*
Has cost thee mony a weary nibble!
Now thou's turned out, for a' thy trouble,
    But° house or hald,°   *without / home ("hold")*
To thole° the winter's sleety dribble,   *endure* 35
    An' cranreuch° cauld!   *hoarfrost*

But, Mousie, thou art no thy lane,°   *not alone*
In proving foresight may be vain:
The best laid schemes o' mice an' men
    Gang° aft a-gley.°   *go / astray* 40

An' lea'e us nought but grief an' pain
            For promised joy.

Still thou art blest, compared wi' me!
The present only toucheth thee:
But och! I backward cast my e'e   45
            On prospects drear!
An' forward, tho' I canna see,
            I guess an' fear!

                    [1786—Scotland]

A RED, RED ROSE
— Robert Burns —

O My Luve's like a red, red rose,
    That's newly sprung in June;
O My Luve's like the melodie
    That's sweetly played in tune.

As fair art thou, my bonnie lass,   5
    So deep in luve am I;
And I will luve thee still, my dear,
    Till a' the seas gang dry.

Till a' the seas gang dry, my dear,
    And the rocks melt wi' the sun: 10
O I will love thee still, my dear,
    While the sands o' life shall run.

And fare thee weel, my only luve,
    And fare thee weel awhile!
And I will come again, my luve,   15
    Though it were ten thousand mile.

                    [1796—Scotland]

TO THE LADIES
— Lady Mary Chudleigh —

Wife and servant are the same,
But only differ in the name:
For when that fatal knot is tied,
Which nothing, nothing can divide:

When she the word *obey* has said,   5
And man by law supreme has made,
Then all that's kind is laid aside,
And nothing left but state and pride:
Fierce as an Eastern prince he grows,
And all his innate rigor shows: 10
Then but to look, to laugh, or speak,
Will the nuptual contract break.
Like mutes she signs alone must make,
And never any freedom take:
But still be governed by a nod,   15
And fear her husband as her God:
Him still must serve, him still obey,
And nothing act, and nothing say,
But what her haughty lord thinks fit,
Who with the power, has all the wit.   20
Then shun, oh! shun that wretched state,
And all the fawning flatt'rers hate:
Value your selves, and men despise,
You must be proud, if you'll be wise.

[1703—Great Britain]

BADGER
— John Clare —

When midnight comes a host of dogs and men
Go out and track the badger to his den,
And put a sack within the hole, and lie
Till the old grunting badger passes by.
He comes and hears—they let the strongest loose.   5
The old fox hears the noise and drops the goose.
The poacher shoots and hurries from the cry,
And the old hare half wounded buzzes by.
They get a forkèd stick to bear him down
And clap the dogs and take him to the town,   10
And bait him all the day with many dogs,
And laugh and shout and fright the scampering hogs.
He runs along and bites at all he meets:
They shout and hollo down the noisy streets.

TO THE LADIES.   **8.** *state:* marriage (cf. "wretched state," line 21).

He turns about to face the loud uproar   15
And drives the rebels to their very door.
The frequent stone is hurled where'r they go;
When badgers fight, then everyone's a foe.
The dogs are clapped and urged to join the fray;
The badger turns and drives them all away.   20
Though scarcely half as big, demure and small,
He fights with dogs for hours and beats them all.
The heavy mastiff, savage in the fray,
Lies down and licks his feet and turns away.
The bulldog knows his match and waxes cold,   25
The badger grins and never leaves his hold.
He drives the crowd and follows at their heels
And bites them through—the drunkard swears and reels.

The frighted women take the boys away,
The blackguard laughs and hurries on the fray.   30
He tries to reach the woods, an awkward race,
But sticks and cudgels quickly stop the chase.
He turns again and drives the noisy crowd
And beats the many dogs in noises loud.
He drives away and beats them every one,   35
And then they loose them all and set them on.
He falls as dead and kicked by boys and men,
Then starts and grins and drives the crowd again;
Till kicked and torn and beaten out he lies
And leaves his hold and crackles, groans, and dies.   40

[c. 1835—Ireland]

FOR DELAWD

— Lucille Clifton —

people say they have a hard time
understanding how I
go on about my business
playing my Ray Charles
hollering at the kids—   5
seem like my Afro
cut off in some old image
would show I got a long memory
and I come from a line

of black and going on women   10
who got used to making it through murdered sons
and who grief kept on pushing
who fried chicken
ironed
swept off the back steps   15
who grief kept
for their still alive sons
for their sons coming
for their sons gone
just pushing   20

[1969—U.S.A.]

THE STORY WE KNOW

— Martha Collins —

The way to begin is always the same. Hello,
Hello. Your hand, your name. So glad, Just fine,
and Good-bye at the end. That's every story we know,

and why pretend? But lunch tomorrow? No?
Yes? An omelette, salad, chilled white wine?   5
The way to begin is simple, sane, Hello,

and then it's Sunday, coffee, the *Times,* a slow
day by the fire, dinner at eight or nine
and Good-bye. In the end, this is a story we know

so well we don't turn the page, or look below   10
the picture, or follow the words to the next line:
The way to begin is always the same Hello.

But one night, through the latticed window, snow
begins to whiten the air, and the tall white pine.
Good-bye is the end of every story we know   15

that night, and when we close the curtains, oh,
we hold each other against that cold white sign
of the way we all begin and end. *Hello,*
Good-bye is the only story. We know, we know.

[1980—U.S.A.]

THE BLACK RIDERS
— Stephen Crane —

Poem 3

In the desert
I saw a creature, naked, bestial,
Who, squatting upon the ground,
Held his heart in his hands,
And ate of it.   5
I said, "Is it good, friend?"
"It is bitter—bitter," he answered;
"But I like it
Because it is bitter,
And because it is my heart."   10

[1895—U.S.A.]

WAR IS KIND
— Stephen Crane —

Poem 21

A man said to the universe:
"Sir, I exist!"
"However," replied the universe,
"The fact has not created in me
A sense of obligation."

[1899—U.S.A.]

INCIDENT
— Countee Cullen —

Once riding in old Baltimore,
  Heart-filled, head-filled with glee,
I saw a Baltimorean
  Keep looking straight at me.

Now I was eight and very small,   5
  And he was no whit bigger,

And so I smiled, but he poked out
   His tongue, and called me, "Nigger."

I saw the whole of Baltimore,
   From May until December;   10
Of all the things that happened there
   That's all that I remember.

[1925—U.S.A.]

UNCLE JIM
— Countee Cullen —

"White folks is white," says uncle Jim;
"A platitude," I sneer;
And then I tell him so is milk,
And the froth upon his beer.

His heart walled up with bitterness,   5
He smokes his pungent pipe,
And nods at me as if to say,
"Young fool, you'll soon be ripe!"

I have a friend who eats his heart
Away with grief of mine,   10
Who drinks my joy as tipplers drain
Deep goblets filled with wine.

I wonder why here at his side,
Face-in-the-grass with him,
My mind should stray the Grecian urn   15
To muse on uncle Jim.

[1927—U.S.A.]

IN JUST-
— E. E. Cummings —

in Just-
spring   when the world is mud-
luscious the little

UNCLE JIM. **15.** *Grecian urn:* a reference to "Ode on a Grecian Urn" by John Keats. Keats is the "friend" mentioned in the third stanza.

lame balloonman

whistles   far   and wee   5

and eddieandbill come
running from marbles and
piracies and it's
spring

when the world is puddle-wonderful   10

the queer
old balloonman whistles
far   and   wee
and bettyandisbel come dancing

from hop-scotch and jump-rope and   15

it's
spring
and
        the

            goat-footed   20
balloonMan   whistles
far
and
wee

[1923—U.S.A.]

COME TO THE EDGE

(After Apollinaire)

— Sylvia Dees —

Come to the edge, he said.
No, they said—
It's steep and we might fall.

Come to the edge.
No, we are afraid.   5

Come to the edge.
Why should we trust you?

Come to the edge,
Come to the edge.

So they came.   10
He pushed them

And they flew.

[1988—U.S.A.]

A VALEDICTION: FORBIDDING MOURNING
— John Donne —

As virtuous men pass mildly away,
   And whisper to their souls to go,
Whilst some of their sad friends do say
   The breath goes now, and some say, No;

So let us melt, and make no noise,   5
   No tear-floods, nor sigh-tempests move,
'Twere profanation of our joys
   To tell the laity our love.

Moving of th' earth brings harms and fears,
   Men reckon what it did and meant;   10
But trepidation of the spheres,
   Though greater far, is innocent.

Dull sublunary lovers' love
   (Whose soul° is sense) cannot admit   *essence*
Absence, because it doth remove   15
   Those things which elemented° it.   *composed*

But we by a love so much refined
   That our selves know not what it is,
Inter-assurèd of the mind,
   Care less, eyes, lips, and hands to miss.   20

Our two souls therefore, which are one,
   Though I must go, endure not yet

A VALEDICTION: FORBIDDING MOURNING. According to Sir Izaak Walton (a contemporary of Donne's), the poem was addressed to Donne's wife and written with great gravity of mind and purpose. **12.** *innocent:* Donne refers to the Ptolemaic explanation of slight changes in the positions of the stars, caused in fact by the wobbling of the earth on its axis. Unlike earthquakes ("Moving of th' earth"), which were thought to be evil omens, such "trepidation" (shuddering) was held to be "innocent" (harmless). **13.** *sublunary:* beneath the moon, and therefore mundane (of the earth).

A breach, but an expansion,
    Like gold to airy thinness beat.

If they be two, they are two so   25
    As stiff twin compasses are two;
Thy soul, the fixed foot, makes no show
    To move, but doth, if th' other do.

And though it in the center sit,
    Yet when the other far doth roam,   30
It leans and harkens after it,
    And grows erect, as that comes home.

Such wilt thou be to me, who must
    Like th' other foot, obliquely run;
Thy firmness makes my circle just,   35
    And makes me end where I begun.

[1633—Great Britain]

HOLY SONNETS

— John Donne —

No. 7

At the round earth's imagined corners, blow
Your trumpets, angels; and arise, arise
From death, you numberless infinities
Of souls, and to your scattered bodies go;
All whom the flood did, and fire shall, o'erthrow,   5
All whom war, dearth, age, agues, tyrannies,
Despair, law, chance hath slain, and you whose eyes
Shall behold God, and never taste death's woe.
But let them sleep, Lord, and me mourn a space;
For, if above all these, my sins abound,   10
'Tis late to ask abundance of Thy grace
When we are there. Here on this lowly ground,

---

35. *circle:* The closed or complete ("just") circle—such as is made with a compass—is a symbol of unity and wholeness.
HOLY SONNETS, NO. 7. **2.** *angels:* "I saw four angels standing on the four corners of the earth, holding the four winds of the earth [Revelation 7:1]." **5.** *fire shall:* At the last trumpet call (the end of the world), "the elements shall melt with fervent heat, the earth also and the works that are therein shall be burned up [II Peter 3:10]." **8.** *death's woe:* "But I tell you of a truth, there be some standing here, which shall not taste of death, till they see the kingdom of God [Christ's words to his disciples, Luke 9:27]."

Teach me how to repent; for that's as good
As if Thou hadst sealed my pardon with Thy blood.

[1633—Great Britain]

No. 10

Death, be not proud, though some have callèd thee
Mighty and dreadful, for thou art not so;
For those whom thou think'st thou dost overthrow
Die not, poor Death, nor yet canst thou kill me.
From rest and sleep, which but thy pictures be,   5
Much pleasure; then from thee much more must flow,
And soonest our best men with thee do go,
Rest of their bones, and soul's delivery.
Thou art slave to fate, chance, kings, and desperate men,
And dost with poison, war, and sickness dwell,   10
And poppy or charms can make us sleep as well
And better than thy stroke; why swell'st thou then?
One short sleep past, we wake eternally
And death shall be no more; Death, thou shalt die.

[1633—Great Britain]

No. 14

Batter my heart, three-personed God; for You
As yet but knock, breathe, shine, and seek to mend;
That I may rise and stand, o'erthrow me, and bend
Your force to break, blow, burn, and make me new.
I, like an usurped town, to another due,   5
Labor to admit You, but O, to no end;
Reason, Your viceroy in me, me should defend,
But is captived, and proves weak or untrue.
Yet dearly I love You, and would be lovèd fain,
But am betrothed unto Your enemy.   10
Divorce me, untie or break that knot again;
Take me to You, imprison me, for I,

HOLY SONNETS, NO. 10. **8.** *soul's delivery:* i.e., our best men go with you to find rest for their bones and freedom ("delivery") for their souls. **12.** *swell'st:* puff up with pride.

Except You enthrall me, never shall be free,
Nor ever chaste, except You ravish me.

[1633—Great Britain]

PRELUDES
— T. S. Eliot —

1

The winter evening settles down
With smell of steaks in passageways.
Six o'clock.
The burnt-out ends of smoky days.
And now a gusty shower wraps   5
The grimy scraps
Of withered leaves about your feet
And newspapers from vacant lots;
The showers beat
On broken blinds and chimney-pots,   10
And at the corner of the street
A lonely cab-horse steams and stamps.
And then the lighting of the lamps.

2

The morning comes to consciousness
Of faint stale smells of beer   15
From the sawdust-trampled street
With all its muddy feet that press
To early coffee-stands.
With the other masquerades
That time resumes,   20
One thinks of all the hands
That are raising dingy shades
In a thousand furnished rooms.

3

You tossed a blanket from the bed,
You lay upon your back, and waited;   25
You dozed, and watched the night revealing
The thousand sordid images
Of which your soul was constituted;

They flickered against the ceiling.
And when all the world came back   30
And the light crept up between the shutters
And you heard the sparrows in the gutters,
You had such a vision of the street
As the street hardly understands;
Sitting along the bed's edge, where   35
You curled the papers from your hair,
Or clasped the yellow soles of feet
In the palms of both soiled hands.

4

His soul stretched tight across the skies
That fade behind a city block,   40
Or trampled by insistent feet
At four and five and six o'clock;
And short square fingers stuffing pipes,
And evening newspapers, and eyes
Assured of certain certainties,   45
The conscience of a blackened street
Impatient to assume the world.

I am moved by fancies that are curled
Around these images, and cling:
The notion of some infinitely gentle   50
Infinitely suffering thing.

Wipe your hand across your mouth, and laugh;
The worlds revolve like ancient women
Gathering fuel in vacant lots.

[1917—U.S.A.]

THE WASTE LAND
— T. S. Eliot —

from I. The Burial of the Dead

April is the cruelest month, breeding
Lilacs out of the dead land, mixing
Memory and desire, stirring
Dull roots with spring rain.

Winter kept us warm, covering   5
Earth in forgetful snow, feeding
A little life with dried tubers.
Summer surprised us, coming over the Starnbergersee
With a shower of rain; we stopped in the colonnade,
And went on in sunlight, into the Hofgarten,   10
And drank coffee, and talked for an hour.
Bin gar keine Russin, stamm' aus Litauen, echt deutsch.
And when we were children, staying at the archduke's,
My cousin's, he took me out on a sled,
And I was frightened. He said, Marie,   15
Marie, hold on tight. And down we went.
In the mountains, there you feel free.
I read, much of the night, and go south in the winter.

What are the roots that clutch, what branches grow
Out of this stony rubbish? Son of man,   20
You cannot say, or guess, for you know only
A heap of broken images, where the sun beats,
And the dead tree gives no shelter, the cricket no relief,
And the dry stone no sound of water. Only
There is shadow under this red rock,   25
(Come in under the shadow of this red rock),
And I will show you something different from either
Your shadow at morning striding behind you
Or your shadow at evening rising to meet you;
I will show you fear in a handful of dust.   30

.   .   .   .

Unreal City,   60
Under the brown fog of a winter dawn,
A crowd flowed over London Bridge, so many,
I had not thought death had undone so many.
Sighs, short and infrequent, were exhaled,
And each man fixed his eyes before his feet.   65
Flowed up the hill and down King William Street,
To where Saint Mary Woolnoth kept the hours
With a dead sound on the final stroke of nine.
There I saw one I knew, and stopped him, crying: "Stetson!
"You who were with me in the ships at Mylae!   70
"That corpse you planted last year in your garden,

THE WASTE LAND, I.   **8.** *Starnbergersee:* a lake near Munich, Germany.   **12.** *Bin gar keine* . . . *:* "I am by no means a Russian, I come from Lithuania, am really German."

"Has it begun to sprout? Will it bloom this year?
"Or has the sudden frost disturbed its bed?
"Oh keep the Dog far hence, that's friend to men,
"Or with his nails he'll dig it up again!   75
"You! hypocrite lecteur!—mon semblable,—mon frère!"

from III. The Fire Sermon

The time is now propitious, as he guesses,   235
The meal is ended, she is bored and tired,
Endeavors to engage her in caresses
Which still are unreproved, if undesired.
Flushed and decided, he assaults at once;
Exploring hands encounter no defense;   240
His vanity requires no response,
And makes a welcome of indifference.

.   .   .   .

Bestows one final patronizing kiss,
And gropes his way, finding the stairs unlit . . .

She turns and looks a moment in the glass,
Hardly aware of her departed lover;   250
Her brain allows one half-formed thought to pass;
"Well now that's done: and I'm glad it's over."
When lovely woman stoops to folly and
Paces about her room again, alone,
She smoothes her hair with automatic hand,   255
And puts a record on the gramophone.

[1922—U.S.A.]

WOMAN

— Nikki Giovanni —

she wanted to be a blade
of grass amid the fields
but he wouldn't agree
to be the dandelion

she wanted to be a robin singing   5
through the leaves

---

76. "Hypocrite reader—my likeness—my brother."
THE WASTE LAND, III.   **253–56.** *When lovely woman* . . . : cf. Goldsmith, "When Lovely Woman Stoops to
Folly," p. 472.

but he refused to be
her tree

she spun herself into a web
and   looking for a place to rest   10
turned to him
but he stood straight
declining to be her corner

she tried to be a book
but he wouldn't read   15

she turned herself into a bulb
but he wouldn't let her grow

she decided to become
a woman
and though he still refused   20
to be a man
she decided it was all
right

[1978—U.S.A.]

GRATITUDE
— Louise Glück —

Do not think I am not grateful for your small
kindness to me.
I like small kindnesses.
In fact I actually prefer them to the more
substantial kindness, that is always eying you,   5
like a large animal on a rug,
until your whole life reduces
to nothing but waking up morning after morning
cramped, and the bright sun shining on its tusks.

[1968—U.S.A.]

ILLUMINATIONS
— Louise Glück —

1

My son squats in the snow in his blue snowsuit.
All around him stubble, the brown

degraded bushes. In the morning air
they seem to stiffen into words.
And, between, the white steady silence.   5
A wren hops on the airstrip
under the sill, drills
for sustenance, then spreads
its short wings, shadows
dropping from them.   10

2

Last winter he could barely speak.
I moved his crib to face the window:
in the dark mornings
he would stand and grip the bars
until the walls appeared,   15
calling *light, light,*
that one syllable, in
demand or recognition.

3

He sits at the kitchen window
with his cup of apple juice.   20
Each tree forms where he left it,
leafless, trapped on his breath.
How clear their edges are,
no limb obscured by motion,
as the sun rises   25
cold and single over the map of language.

[1980—U.S.A.]

WHEN LOVELY WOMAN STOOPS TO FOLLY
— Oliver Goldsmith —

When lovely woman stoops to folly,
   And finds too late that men betray,
What charm can soothe her melancholy,
   What art can wash her guilt away?

The only art her guilt to cover,   5
   To hide her shame from every eye,
To give repentance to her lover,
   And wring his bosom—is to die.

[1766—Great Britain]

DOWN, WANTON, DOWN
— Robert Graves —

Down, wanton, down! Have you no shame
That at the whisper of Love's name,
Or Beauty's, presto! up you raise
Your angry head and stand at gaze?

Poor bombard-captain, sworn to reach   5
The ravelin and effect a breach—
Indifferent what you storm or why,
So be that in the breach you die!

Love may be blind, but Love at least
Knows what is man and what mere beast;   10
Or Beauty wayward, but requires
More delicacy from her squires.

Tell me, my witless, whose one boast
Could be your staunchness at the post,
When were you made a man of parts   15
To think fine and profess the arts?

Will many-gifted Beauty come
Bowing to your bald rule of thumb,
Or Love swear loyalty to your crown?
Be gone, have done! Down, wanton, down!   20

[1933—Great Britain]

ON THE MOVE
— Thom Gunn —

"Man, you gotta Go."

The blue jay scuffling in the bushes follows
Some hidden purpose, and the gust of birds
That spurts across the field, the wheeling swallows,
Have nested in the trees and undergrowth.
Seeking their instinct, or their poise, or both,   5
One moves with an uncertain violence
Under the dust thrown by a baffled sense
Or the dull thunder of approximate words.

On motorcycles, up the road, they come:
Small, black, as flies hanging in heat, the Boys,   10
Until the distance throws them forth, their hum
Bulges to thunder held by calf and thigh.
In goggles, donned impersonality,
In gleaming jackets trophied with the dust,
They strap in doubt—by hiding it, robust—   15
And almost hear a meaning in their noise.

Exact conclusion of their hardiness
Has no shape yet, but from known whereabouts
They ride, direction where the tires press.
They scare a flight of birds across the field: 20
Much that is natural, to the will must yield.
Men manufacture both machine and soul,
And use what they imperfectly control
To dare a future from the taken routes.

It is a part solution, after all.   25
One is not necessarily discord
On earth; or damned because, half animal,
One lacks direct instinct, because one wakes
Afloat on movement that divides and breaks.
One joins the movement in a valueless world,   30
Choosing it, till, both hurler and the hurled,
One moves as well, always toward, toward.

A minute holds them, who have come to go:
The self-defined, astride the created will
They burst away; the towns they travel through   35
Are home for neither bird nor holiness,
For birds and saints complete their purposes.
At worst, one is in motion; and at best,
Reaching no absolute, in which to rest,
One is always nearer by not keeping still.   40

[1957—U.S.A.]

LIFE AND DEATH AT SUNRISE
— Thomas Hardy —

The hills uncap their tops
Of woodland, pasture, copse,

And look on the layers of mist
At their foot that still persist:
They are like awakened sleepers on one elbow lifted,   5
Who gaze around to learn if things during night have shifted.

A waggon creaks up from the fog
With a laboured leisurely jog;
Then a horseman from off the hill-tip
Comes clapping down into the dip;   10
While woodlarks, finches, sparrows, try to entune at one time,
And cocks and hens and cows and bulls take up the chime.

With a shouldered basket and flagon
A man meets the one with the waggon,
And both the men halt of long use.   15
"Well," the waggoner says, "what's the news?"
"—'Tis a boy this time. You've just met the doctor trotting back.
She's doing very well. And we think we shall call him 'Jack.'

"And what have you got covered there?"
He nods to the waggon and mare.   20
"Oh, a coffin for old John Thinn:
We are just going to put him in."
"—So he's gone at last. He always had a good constitution."
"—He was ninety-odd. He could call up the French Revolution."

[1925—Great Britain]

LONG DISTANCE, II

— Tony Harrison —

Though my mother was already two years dead
Dad kept her slippers warming by the gas,
put hot water bottles her side of the bed
and still went to renew her transport pass.

You couldn't just drop in. You had to phone.   5
He'd put you off an hour to give him time
to clear away her things and look alone
as though his still raw love were such a crime.

He couldn't risk my blight of disbelief
though sure that very soon he'd hear her key   10

scrape in the rusted lock and end his grief.
He *knew* she'd just popped out to get the tea.

I believe life ends with death, and that is all.
You haven't both gone shopping; just the same,
in my new black leather phone book there's your name   15
and the disconnected number I still call.

[1975—Great Britain]

PIED BEAUTY

— G. M. Hopkins —

Glory be to God for dappled things—
   For skies of couple-colour as a brinded cow;
     For rose-moles all in stipple upon trout that swim;
Fresh-firecoal chestnut-falls; finches' wings;
   Landscape plotted and pieced—fold, fallow, and plough;   5
     And áll trádes, their gear and tackle and trim.

All things counter, original, spare, strange;
   Whatever is fickle, freckled (who knows how?)
     With swift, slow; sweet, sour; adazzle, dim;
He fathers-forth whose beauty is past change: 10
          Praise him.

[c. 1877—Great Britain]

SPRING AND FALL

to a young child

— G. M. Hopkins —

Márgarét, áre you gríeving
Over Goldengrove unleaving?
Leáves, líke the things of man, you
With your fresh thoughts care for, can you?

Áh! ás the heart grows older   5
It will come to such sights colder
By and by, nor spare a sigh
Though worlds of wanwood leafmeal lie;
And yet you *will* weep and know why.
Now no matter, child, the name: 10

Sórrow's spríngs áre the same.
Nor mouth had, no nor mind, expressed
What heart heard of, ghost guessed:
It ís the blight man was born for,
It is Margaret you mourn for.   15

[c. 1880—Great Britain]

[NO WORST, THERE IS NONE]
— G. M. Hopkins —

No worst, there is none. Pitched past pitch of grief,
More pangs will, schooled at forepangs, wilder wring.
Comforter, where, where is your comforting?
Mary, mother of us, where is your relief?
My cries heave, herds-long; huddle in a main, a chief-   5
woe, world-sorrow; on an age-old anvil wince and sing—
Then lull, then leave off. Fury had shrieked "No ling-
ering! Let me be fell:° force° I must be brief."   *deadly / perforce*
O the mind, mind has mountains; cliffs of fall
Frightful, sheer, no-man-fathomed. Hold them cheap   10
May who ne'er hung there. Nor does long our small
Durance deal with that steep or deep. Here! creep,
Wretch, under a comfort serves in a whirlwind: all
Life death does end and each day dies with sleep.

[c. 1885—Great Britain]

DEATH OF A VERMONT FARM WOMAN
— Barbara Howes —

Is it time now to go away?
July is nearly over; hay
Fattens the barn, the herds are strong,
Our old fields prosper; these long
Green evenings will keep death at bay.   5

Last winter lingered; it was May
Before a flowering lilac spray
Barred cold for ever. I was wrong.
        Is it time now?

Six decades vanished in a day!   10
I bore four sons: one lives; they

Were all good men; three dying young
Was hard on us. I have looked long
For these hills to show me where peace lay.
Is it time now?   15

[1954—U.S.A.]

THEME FOR ENGLISH B
— Langston Hughes —

The instructor said,

Go home and write
a page tonight.
And let that page come out of you—
Then, it will be true.   5

I wonder if it's that simple?
I am twenty-two, colored, born in Winston-Salem.
I went to school there, then Durham, then here
to this college on the hill above Harlem.
I am the only colored student in my class.   10
The steps from the hill lead down into Harlem,
through a park, then I cross St. Nicholas,
Eighth Avenue, Seventh, and I come to the Y,
the Harlem Branch Y, where I take the elevator
up to my room, sit down, and write this page: 15

It's not easy to know what is true for you or me
at twenty-two, my age. But I guess I'm what
I feel and see and hear, Harlem, I hear you:
hear you, hear me—we two—you, me, talk on this page.
(I hear New York, too.) Me—who?   20

Well, I like to eat, sleep, drink, and be in love.
I like to work, read, learn, and understand life.
I like a pipe for a Christmas present,
or records—Bessie, bop, or Bach.
I guess being colored doesn't make me *not* like   25
the same things other folks like who are other races.
So will my page be colored that I write?

THEME FOR ENGLISH B.   **7 and 8.** *Winston-Salem* and *Durham:* cities in North Carolina.   **9.** *college:* Columbia University.   **12.** *St. Nicholas:* a street east of Columbia.   **24.** *Bessie:* Bessie Smith, blues singer (1898?–1937).

Being me, it will not be white.
But it will be
a part of you, instructor.   30
You are white—
yet a part of me, as I am a part of you.
That's American.
Sometimes perhaps you don't want to be a part of me.
Nor do I often want to be a part of you.   35
But we are, that's true!

As I learn from you,
I guess you learn from me—
although you're older—and white—
and somewhat more free.   40

This is my page for English B.

[1959—U.S.A.]

A SICK CHILD
— Randall Jarrell —

The postman comes when I am still in bed.
"Postman, what do you have for me today?"
I say to him. (But really I'm in bed.)
Then he says—what shall I have him say?

"This letter says that you are president   5
Of—this word here; it's a republic."
Tell them I can't answer right away.
"It's your duty." No, I'd rather just be sick.

Then he tells me there are letters saying everything
That I can think of that I want for them to say.   10
I say, "Well, thank you very much. Good-bye."
He is ashamed, and turns and walks away.

If I can think of it, it isn't what I want.
I want . . . I want a ship from some near star
To land in the yard, and beings to come out   15
And think to me: "So this is where you are!

Come." Except that they won't do,
I thought of them. . . . And yet somewhere there must be

Something that's different from everything.
All that I've never thought of—think of me!   20

[1945—U.S.A.]

PENIS ENVY
— Erica Jong —

I envy men who can yearn
with infinite emptiness
toward the body of a woman,

hoping that the yearning
will make a child,   5
that the emptiness itself
will fertilize the darkness.

Women have no illusions about this,
being at once
houses, tunnels,   10
cups & cupbearers,
knowing emptiness as a temporary state
between two fullnesses,
& seeing no romance in it.

If I were a man   15
doomed to that infinite emptiness,
& having no choice in the matter,
I would, like the rest, no doubt,
find a woman
& christen her moonbelly,   20
madonna, gold-haired goddess
& make her the tent of my longing,
the silk parachute of my lust,
the blue-eyed icon of my sacred sexual itch,
the mother of my hunger.   25

But since I am a woman,
I must not only inspire the poem
but also type it,
not only conceive the child
but also bear it,   30
not only bear the child
but also bathe it,
not only bathe the child

but also feed it,
not only feed the child   35
but also carry it
everywhere, everywhere . . .

while men write poems
on the mysteries of motherhood.

I envy men who can yearn   40
with infinite emptiness.

[1976—U.S.A.]

ON MY FIRST SON
— Ben Jonson —

Farewell, thou child of my right hand, and joy;
My sin was too much hope of thee, loved boy:
Seven years thou'wert lent to me, and I thee pay,
Exacted by thy fate, on the just day.
O could I lose all father now! for why   5
Will man lament the state he should envý,
To have so soon 'scaped world's and flesh's rage,
And, if no other misery, yet age?
Rest in soft peace, and asked, say, "Here doth lie
Ben Jonson his best piece of poetry."   10
For whose sake henceforth all his vows be such
As what he loves may never like too much.

[1616—Great Britain]

ON FIRST LOOKING INTO CHAPMAN'S HOMER
— John Keats —

Much have I traveled in the realms of gold,
    And many goodly states and kingdoms seen;
    Round many western islands have I been
Which bards in fealty° to Apollo hold.   *allegiance*
Oft of one wide expanse had I been told   5

ON MY FIRST SON.   **1.** *child of my right hand:* the literal translation of the Hebrew name "Benjamin," the boy's first name.   **4.** *just day:* Jonson's son died on his seventh birthday in 1603.   **5.** *lose all father:* give up any thoughts of being a father.   **12.** *too much:* cf. line 2.
ON FIRST LOOKING INTO CHAPMAN'S HOMER.   *Chapman's Homer:* translation of the *Iliad* by George Chapman (1559?–1634).   **4.** *Apollo:* the Greek god of poetic inspiration.

That deep-browed Homer ruled as his demesne;°   *domain*
Yet did I never breathe its pure serene°   *atmosphere*
Till I heard Chapman speak out loud and bold:
Then felt I like some watcher of the skies
   When a new planet swims into his ken;   10
Or like stout Cortez when with eagle eyes
   He stared at the Pacific—and all his men
Looked at each other with a wild surmise—
   Silent, upon a peak in Darien.

[1816—Great Britain]

WHEN I HAVE FEARS
— John Keats —

When I have fears that I may cease to be
   Before my pen has gleaned my teeming brain,
Before high-pilèd books, in charact'ry,°   *written symbols*
   Hold like rich garners the full-ripened grain;
When I behold, upon the night's starred face,   5
   Huge cloudy symbols of a high romance,
And think that I may never live to trace
   Their shadows, with the magic hand of chance;
And when I feel, fair creature of an hour,
   That I shall never look upon thee more,   10
Never have relish in the faery° power   *magical*
   Of unreflecting love!—then on the shore
Of the wide world I stand alone, and think
Till Love and Fame to nothingness do sink.

[c. 1819—Great Britain]

TO AUTUMN
— John Keats —

1

Season of mists and mellow fruitfulness,
   Close bosom-friend of the maturing sun;

11. *Cortez:* the Spanish conqueror of Mexico. Keats confused him with Balboa, who first sighted the Pacific from the heights of Darien, in Panama. Although the confusion matters not at all to the poem, it has a certain charm, for it suggests that the poem was written by a young man in the heat of discovery.

Conspiring with him how to load and bless
    With fruit the vines that round the thatch-eaves run;
To bend with apples the mossed cottage-trees,
    And fill all fruit with ripeness to the core;   5
        To swell the gourd, and plump the hazel shells
With a sweet kernel; to set budding more,
    And still more, later flowers for the bees,
    Until they think warm days will never cease,   10
        For Summer has o'er-brimmed their clammy cells.

2

Who hath not seen thee oft amid thy store?
    Sometimes whoever seeks abroad may find
Thee sitting careless on a granary floor,
    Thy hair soft-lifted by the winnowing wind;   15
Or on a half-reaped furrow sound asleep,
    Drowsed with the fume of poppies, while thy hook
        Spares the next swath and all its twinèd flowers:
And sometimes like a gleaner thou dost keep
    Steady thy laden head across a brook;   20
    Or by a cider-press, with patient look,
        Thou watchest the last oozings hours by hours.

3

Where are the songs of Spring? Aye, where are they?
    Think not of them, thou hast thy music too—
While barred clouds bloom the soft-dying day,   25
    And touch the stubble-plains with rosy hue;
Then in a wailful choir the small gnats mourn
    Among the river sallows, borne aloft
        Or sinking as the light wind lives or dies;
And full-grown lambs loud bleat from hilly bourn;   30
    Hedge crickets sing; and now with treble soft
    The redbreast whistles from a garden croft;
        And gathering swallows twitter in the skies.

[1820—Great Britain]

TO AUTUMN: **15.** *winnowing:* blowing the grain clear from the chaff.   **17.** *hook:* a scythe—a small curved blade used for cutting grain.   **28.** *sallows:* willow trees.   **30.** *bourn:* region, locale.   **32.** *croft:* an enclosed plot of farmland.

THE INTRUDER

— Carolyn Kizer —

My mother—preferring the strange to the tame:
Dove-note, bone marrow, deer dung,
Frog's belly distended with finny young,
Leaf-mould wilderness, hare-bell, toadstool,
Odd, small snakes roving through the leaves,   5
Metallic beetles rambling over stones: all
Wild and natural!—flashed out her instinctive love, and quick, she
Picked up the fluttering, bleeding bat the cat laid at her feet,
And held the little horror to the mirror, where
He gazed on himself, and shrieked like an old screen door far off.   10

Depended from her pinched thumb, each wing
Came clattering down like a small black shutter.
Still tranquil, she began, "It's rather sweet. . . ."
The soft mouse body, the hard feral glint
In the caught eyes. Then we saw,   15
And recoiled: lice, pallid, yellow,
Nested within the wing-pits, cosily sucked and snoozed.
The thing dropped from her hands, and with its thud,
Swiftly, the cat, with a clean careful mouth
Closed on the soiled webs, growling, took them out to the back stoop.   20

But still, dark blood, a sticky puddle on the floor
Remained, of all my mother's tender, wounding passion
For a whole wild, lost, betrayed and secret life
Among its dens and burrows, its clean stones,
Whose denizens can turn upon the world   25
With spitting tongue, an odor, talon, claw,
To sting or soil benevolence, alien
As our clumsy traps, our random scatter of shot.
She swept to the kitchen. Turning on the tap,
She washed and washed the pity from her hands.   30

[1969—U.S.A.]

THE WARDEN SAID TO ME

— Etheridge Knight —

The warden said to me the other day
(innocently, I think), "Say, etheridge,

why come the black boys don't run off
like the white boys do?"
I lowered my jaw and scratched my head   5
and said (innocently, I think), "Well, suh,
I ain't for sure, but I reckon it's cause
we ain't got no wheres to run to."

[1968—U.S.A.]

WOODCHUCKS
— Maxine Kumin —

Gassing the woodchucks didn't turn out right.
The knockout bomb from the Feed and Grain Exchange
was featured as merciful, quick at the bone
and the case we had against them was airtight,
both exits shoehorned shut with puddingstone,   5
but they had a sub-sub-basement out of range.

Next morning they turned up again, no worse
for the cyanide than we for our cigarettes
and state-store Scotch, all of us up to scratch.
They brought down the marigolds as a matter of course   10
and then took over the vegetable patch
nipping the broccoli shoots, beheading the carrots.

The food from our mouths, I said, righteously thrilling
to the feel of the .22, the bullets' neat noses.
I, a lapsed pacifist fallen from grace   15
puffed with Darwinian pieties for killing,
now drew a bead on the littlest woodchuck's face.
He died down in the everbearing roses.

Ten minutes later I dropped the mother. She
flipflopped in the air and fell, her needle teeth   20
still hooked in a leaf of early Swiss chard.
Another baby next. O one-two-three
the murderer inside me rose up hard,
the hawkeye killer came on stage forthwith.

There's one chuck left. Old wily fellow, he keeps   25
me cocked and ready day after day after day.

WOODCHUCKS. **16.** *Darwinian pieties:* a reference to "the survival of the fittest," Darwin's mechanism of
evolution.

All night I hunt his humped-up form. I dream
I sight along the barrel in my sleep.
If only they'd all consented to die unseen
gassed underground the quiet Nazi way.   30

[1972—U.S.A.]

WANTS

— Philip Larkin —

Beyond all this, the wish to be alone:
However the sky grows dark with invitation-cards
However we follow the printed directions of sex
However the family is photographed under the flagstaff—
Beyond all this, the wish to be alone.   5

Beneath it all, desire of oblivion runs:
Despite the artful tensions of the calendar,
The life insurance, the tabled fertility rites,
The costly aversion of the eyes from death—
Beneath it all, desire of oblivion runs.   10

[1955—Great Britain]

CHERRY ROBBERS

— D. H. Lawrence —

Under the long dark boughs, like jewels red
    In the hair of an Eastern girl
Hang strings of crimson cherries, as if had bled
    Blood-drops beneath each curl.

Under the glistening cherries, with folded wings   5
    Three dead birds lie:
Pale-breasted throstles and a blackbird, robberlings
    Stained with red dye.

Against the haystack a girl stands laughing at me,
    Cherries hung round her ears.   10
Offers me her scarlet fruit: I will see
    If she has any tears.

[1913—Great Britain]

BAVARIAN GENTIANS
— D. H. Lawrence —

Not every man has gentians in his house
in Soft September, at slow, sad Michaelmas.

Bavarian gentians, big and dark, only dark
darkening the daytime, torch-like with the smoking blueness of Pluto's gloom,
ribbed and torch-like, with their blaze of darkness spread blue   5
down flattening into points, flattened under the sweep of white day
torch-flower of the blue-smoking darkness, Pluto's dark-blue daze,
black lamps from the halls of Dis, burning dark blue,
giving off darkness, blue darkness, as Demeter's pale lamps give off light,
lead me then, lead the way.   10

Reach me a gentian, give me a torch!
let me guide myself with the blue, forked torch of this flower
down the darker and darker stairs, where blue is darkened on blueness
even where Persephone goes, just now, from the frosted September
to the sightless realm where darkness is awake upon the dark   15
and Persephone herself is but a voice
or a darkness invisible enfolded in the deeper dark
of the arms Plutonic, and pierced with the passion of dense gloom,
among the splendor of torches of darkness, shedding darkness on the lost
    bride and her groom.

[1932—Great Britain]

FOR SALE
— Robert Lowell —

Poor sheepish plaything,
organized with prodigal animosity,
lived in just a year—
my Father's cottage at Beverly Farms
was on the market the month he died.   5
Empty, open, intimate,

BAVARIAN GENTIANS. *Bavarian Gentians:* dark blue fall flowers. **2.** *Michaelmas:* the feast of St. Michael, September 29. **4.** *Pluto:* Roman god of the underworld. **8.** *Dis:* another name for Pluto. **9.** *Demeter:* Persephone's mother, goddess of nature's growing cycle. **14.** *Persephone:* Abducted by Pluto, Persephone became goddess of the underworld for six months out of every year. According to the myth, she returns every spring to her mother and departs every fall to Pluto's dark underworld.

its town-house furniture
had an on tiptoe air
of waiting for the mover
on the heels of the undertaker.   10
Ready, afraid
of living alone till eighty,
Mother mooned in a window,
as if she had stayed on a train
one stop past her destination.   15

[1956—U.S.A.]

MIDWAY
— Naomi Long Madgett —

I've come this far to freedom and I won't turn back.
I'm climbing to the highway from my old dirt track.
   I'm coming and I'm going
   And I'm stretching and I'm growing
And I'll reap what I've been sowing or my skin's not black.   5

I've prayed and slaved and waited, and I've sung my song.
You've bled me and you've starved me, but I've still grown strong.
   You've lashed me and you've treed me
   And you've everything but freed me
But in time you'll know you need me, and it won't be long.   10

I've seen the daylight breaking high above the bough.
I've found my destination and I've made my vow;
   So whether you abhor me
   Or deride me or ignore me,
Mighty mountains loom before me and I won't stop now!   15

[1965—U.S.A.]

THE PASSIONATE SHEPHERD TO HIS LOVE
— Christopher Marlowe —

Come live with me and be my love,
And we will all the pleasures prove°   *try*

THE PASSIONATE SHEPHERD TO HIS LOVE.   cf. Raleigh's "The Nymph's Reply to the Shepherd," p. 499.

That valleys, groves, hills, and fields,
Woods, or steepy mountain yields.

And we will sit upon the rocks,   5
Seeing the shepherds feed their flocks,
By shallow rivers to whose falls
Melodious birds sing madrigals.

And I will make thee beds of roses
And a thousand fragrant posies,   10
A cap of flowers, and kirtle
Embroidered all with leaves of myrtle;

A gown made of the finest wool
Which from our pretty lambs we pull;
Fair lined slippers for the cold,   15
With buckles of the purest gold;

A belt of straw and ivy buds,
With coral clasps and amber studs:
And if these pleasures may thee move,
Come live with me, and be my love.   20

The shepherds' swains shall dance and sing
For thy delight each May morning:
If these delights thy mind may move,
Then live with me and be my love.

[1599—Great Britain]

HOW SOON HATH TIME
— John Milton —

How soon hath Time, the subtle thief of youth,
    Stoln on his wing my three and twentieth year!
    My hasting days fly on with full career,
    But my late spring no bud or blossom show'th.
Perhaps my semblance might deceive the truth,   5
    That I to manhood am arrived so near,
    And inward ripeness doth much less appear,
    That some more timely-happy spirits endu'th.°   *endow*
Yet be it less or more, or soon or slow,

---

11. *kirtle:* outer petticoat, skirt.

It shall be still° in strictest measure even   *always*   10
    To that same lot, however mean or high,
Toward which Time leads me, and the will of Heaven;
    All is, if I have grace to use it so,
    As ever in my great Taskmaster's eye.

[1631—Great Britain]

GYPSY BRIDE
— Elizabeth Moore —

Saucers must be polished in a long round row,
    Floors are always looking for a broom,
Hearts be tightly buttoned up in calico,
    Just as souls are buttoned in a room.

Close the door, my heart, nor let it be ajar,   5
    Shut the sky-line out, and pull the shade,
I might leave the hearth to go and pick a star,
    And I have fresh butter to be made.

I am not complaining; he is good to me,
    He would make me happy, if he could,   10
But he brings me gold-fish, when I want the sea,
    And door-step trees to me who wants a wood.

[1927—U.S.A.]

POETRY
— Marianne Moore —

I, too, dislike it: there are things that are important beyond all this fiddle.
    Reading it, however, with a perfect contempt for it, one discovers in
    it after all, a place for the genuine.
        Hands that can grasp, eyes
        that can dilate, hair that can rise   5
            if it must, these things are important not because a

---

HOW SOON HATH TIME.   **10.** *even:* equal, like the measures of a piece of music.   **14.** *Taskmaster's eye:*
The sonnet concludes with a pledge to fulfill in due course the Gospel command to labor.

high-sounding interpretation can be put upon them but because they are
  useful. When they become so derivative as to become unintelligible,
  the same thing may be said for all of us, that we
    do not admire what   10
    we cannot understand: the bat
      holding on upside down or in quest of something to

eat, elephants pushing, a wild horse taking a roll, a tireless wolf under
  a tree, the immovable critic twitching his skin like a horse that feels
    a flea, the base-   15
  ball fan, the statistician—
    nor is it valid
      to discriminate against "business documents and

school-books"; all these phenomena are important. One must make a distinction

however: when dragged into prominence by half poets, the result is not poetry, 20
nor till the poets among us can be
  "literalists of
  the imagination"—above
    insolence and triviality and can present

for inspection, "imaginary gardens with real toads in them," shall we have 25
  it. In the meantime, if you demand on the one hand,
  the raw material of poetry in
    all its rawness and
    that which is on the other hand
      genuine, you are interested in poetry.   30

[1921—U.S.A.]

THE ANIMALS

— Edwin Muir —

They do not live in the world,
Are not in time and space.
From birth to death hurled
No word do they have, not one
To plant a foot upon,   5
Were never in any place.

POETRY. **18–19.** *business documents . . . school-books:* a reference to the following from Leo Tolstoy's *Diary:* "Where the boundary between prose and poetry lies, I shall never be able to understand. The question is raised in manuals of style, yet the answer to it lies beyond me. Poetry is verse: prose is not verse. Or else poetry is everything with the exception of business documents and school books."

For with names the world was called
Out of the empty air,
With names was built and walled,
Line and circle and square,   10
Dust and emerald;
Snatched from deceiving death
By the articulate breath.

But these have never trod
Twice the familiar track,   15
Never never turned back
Into the memoried day.
All is new and near
In the unchanging Here
Of the fifth great day of God,   20
That shall remain the same,
Never shall pass away.

On the sixth day we came.

[1949—Great Britain]

WHY I AM NOT A PAINTER
— Frank O'Hara —

I am not a painter, I am a poet.
Why? I think I would rather be
a painter, but I am not. Well,

for instance, Mike Goldberg
is starting a painting. I drop in.   5
"Sit down and have a drink" he
says. I drink; we drink. I look
up. "You have SARDINES in it."
"Yes, it needed something there."
"Oh." I go and the days go by   10
and I drop in again. The painting
is going on, and I go, and the days
go by. I drop in. The painting is
finished. "Where's SARDINES?"
All that's left is just   15
letters, "It was too much," Mike says.

THE ANIMALS.   **20.** *fifth great day:* the fifth day of creation (see Genesis 1:20–25).
WHY I AM NOT A PAINTER.   **4.** *Mike Goldberg:* a New York artist (b. 1924).

But me? One day I am thinking of
a color: orange. I write a line
about orange. Pretty soon it is a
whole page of words, not lines.   20
Then another page. There should be
so much more, not of orange, of
words, of how terrible orange is
and life. Days go by. It is even in
prose, I am a real poet. My poem   25
is finished and I haven't mentioned
orange yet. It's twelve poems, I call
it ORANGES. And one day in a gallery
I see Mike's painting, called SARDINES.

[1971—U.S.A.]

THE CONNOISSEUSE OF SLUGS
— Sharon Olds —

When I was a connoisseuse of slugs
I would part the ivy leaves, and look for the
naked jelly of those gold bodies,
translucent strangers glistening along the
stones, slowly, their gelatinous bodies   5
at my mercy. Made mostly of water, they would shrivel
to nothing if they were sprinkled with salt,
but I was not interested in that. What I liked
was to draw aside the ivy, breathe the
odor of the wall, and stand there in silence   10
until the slug forgot I was there
and sent its antennae up out of its
head, the glimmering umber horns
rising like telescopes, until finally the
sensitive knobs would pop out the ends,   15
delicate and intimate. Years later,
when I first saw a naked man,
I gasped with pleasure to see that quiet
mystery reenacted, the slow
elegant being coming out of hiding and   20
gleaming in the dark air, eager and so
trusting you could weep.

[1983—U.S.A.]

THE SHAPE OF THINGS
— Terence Paré —

In high school,
I learned to shape opinions
into squares:
the building blocks
of matter,   5
of life,
of history—
stackable, storeable, neat
like Tupperware.
I made a world of toys.   10

In college,
I learned in circles
(a rounded education):
the Platonic sphere,
the cycles of things,   15
Hegel's spiral.
I squeezed the universe into a ball,
rolled it toward the overwhelming question,
and it rolled right back again,
undisturbed.   20

These days, I think
in wavy lines and arcs:
the koala bear's opposable thumb,
a lick of moon, the sleeping cat,
my lover's hair spilled over the pillow;   25
sloppy fluid things
that don't add up—
tigers in the snow!
Chaotic, mostly living,
they'll die   30
or burst from time to time
like stars.

[1985—U.S.A.]

THE SHAPE OF THINGS.   **17–20.** *I squeezed the universe* . . . . : a reference to T. S. Eliot's "The Lovesong of J. Alfred Prufrock": "To have squeezed the universe into a ball / To roll it toward some overwhelming question."

UNFORTUNATE COINCIDENCE
— Dorothy Parker —

By the time you swear you're his,
   Shivering and sighing,
And he vows his passion is
   Infinite, undying—
Lady, make a note of this: 5
   One of you is lying

[1926—U.S.A.]

THE FLAW IN PAGANISM
— Dorothy Parker —

Drink and dance and laugh and lie,
   Love, the reeling midnight through,
For tomorrow we shall die!
   (But, alas, we never do.)

[1933—U.S.A.]

TO MY EXCELLENT LUCASIA, ON OUR FRIENDSHIP
— Katherine Phillips —

I did not live until this time
   Crown'd my felicity,
When I could say without a crime,
   I am not thine, but Thee.

This carcase breath'd, and walkt, and slept,   5
   So that the World believ'd
There was a soul the motions kept;
   But they were all deceiv'd.

For as a watch by art is wound
   To motion, such was mine: 10
But never had Orinda found
   A soul till she found thine;

Which now inspires, cures and supplies,
   And guides my darkened breast:

TO MY EXCELLENT LUCASIA. **11.** *Orinda:* name of the woman speaking the poem; Phillips habitually used this name to refer to herself in poetry.

For thou art all that I can prize,   15
  My Joy, my Life, my Rest.

No bridegroom's nor crown-conqueror's mirth
  To mine compar'd can be:
They have but pieces of this Earth,
  I've all the World in thee.   20

Then let our flames still light and shine,
  And no false fear control,
As innocent as our design,
  Immortal as our soul.

[1667—Great Britain]

THE FRIEND
— Marge Piercy —

We sat across the table.
he said, cut off your hands.
they are always poking at things.
they might touch me.
I said yes.   5

Food grew cold on the table.
he said, burn your body.
it is not clean and smells like sex.
it rubs my mind sore.
I said yes.   10

I love you, I said.
that's very nice, he said
I like to be loved,
that makes me happy.
Have you cut off your hands yet?   15

[1969—U.S.A.]

[NATURE AND NATURE'S LAWS]
— Alexander Pope —

Nature and Nature's Laws lay hid in Night:
God said, *Let* NEWTON *be:* And all was Light!

[1730—Great Britain]

[WHOSE DOG?]
— Alexander Pope —

[Engraved on a dog collar Pope gave to the Prince of Wales]

I AM his Highness Dog at Kew;
Pray tell me Sir, whose Dog are you?

[1736—Great Britain]

ANCIENT MUSIC
— Ezra Pound —

Winter is icummen in,
   Lhude sing Goddamm,
    Raineth drop and staineth slop,
And how the wind doth ramm!
        Sing: Goddamm.   5
Skiddeth bus and sloppeth us,
An ague hath my ham.
Freezeth river, turneth liver,
        Damn you, sing: Goddamm.
Goddamm, Goddamm, 'tis why I am, Goddamm,   10
       So 'gainst the winter's balm.
Sing goddamm, damm, sing Goddamm,
Sing goddamm, sing goddamm, DAMM.

[1915—U.S.A.]

A BETTER ANSWER
— Matthew Prior —

I.

DEAR Cloe, how blubber'd is that pretty Face?
   Thy Cheek all on Fire, and Thy Hair all uncurl'd:
Pr'ythee quit this Caprice; and (as Old Falstaf says)
   Let Us e'en talk a little like Folks of This World.

[whose dog?] **1.** *Kew:* a royal residence.
ancient music.   cf. "The Cuckoo Song," pp. 443–44.

II.

How can'st Thou presume, Thou hast leave to destroy   5
    The Beauties, which Venus but lent to Thy keeping?
Those Looks were design'd to inspire Love and Joy:
    More ord'nary Eyes may serve People for weeping.

III.

To be vext at a Trifle or two that I writ,
    Your Judgment at once, and my Passion You wrong: 10
You take that for Fact, which will scarce be found Wit:
    Od's Life! must One swear to the Truth of a Song?

IV.

What I speak, my fair Cloe, and what I write, shews
    The Diff'rence there is betwixt Nature and Art:
I court others in Verse; but I love Thee in Prose: 15
    And They have my Whimsies; but Thou hast my Heart.

V.

The God of us Verse-men (You know Child) the Sun,
    How after his Journeys He sets up his Rest:
If at Morning o'er Earth 'tis his Fancy to run;
    At Night he reclines on his Thetis's Breast.   20

VI.

So when I am weary'd with wand'ring all Day;
    To Thee my Delight in the Evening I come:
No Matter what Beauties I saw in my Way:
    They were but my Visits; but Thou art my Home.

VII.

Then finish, Dear Cloe, this Pastoral War;   25
    And let us like Horace and Lydia agree:
For Thou art a Girl as much brighter than Her,
    As He was a Poet sublimer than Me.

[1718—Great Britain]

A BETTER ANSWER. **17.** *The God:* Apollo, patron of poetry as well as god of the sun. **20.** *Thetis:* a goddess of the sea. **26.** *Horace and Lydia:* a great Roman poet and his ideal beloved.

THE NYMPH'S REPLY TO THE SHEPHERD
— Sir Walter Raleigh —

If all the world and love were young,
And truth in every shepherd's tongue,
These pretty pleasures might me move
To live with thee and be thy love.

Time drives the flocks from field to fold   5
When rivers rage and rocks grow cold,
And Philomel becometh dumb;
The rest complains of cares to come.

The flowers do fade, and wanton fields
To wayward winter reckoning yields;   10
A honey tongue, a heart of gall,
Is fancy's spring, but sorrow's fall.

Thy gowns, thy shoes, thy beds of roses,
Thy cap, thy kirtle, and thy posies
Soon break, soon wither, soon forgotten—   15
In folly ripe, in reason rotten.

Thy belt of straw and ivy buds,
Thy coral clasps and amber studs,
All these in me no means can move
To come to thee and be thy love.   20

But could youth last and love still breed,
Had joys no date nor age no need,
Then these delights my mind might move
To live with thee and be thy love.

[1600—Great Britain]

SURVEY OF LITERATURE
— John Crowe Ransom —

In all the good Greek of Plato
I lack my roastbeef and potato.

THE NYMPH'S REPLY.   cf. Marlowe's "The Passionate Shepherd to His Love," pp. 488–89.   **7.** *Philomel:* the nightingale, the bird of love.   **22.** *no date:* no ending.

A better man was Aristotle,
Pulling steady on the bottle.

I dip my hat to Chaucer,   5
Swilling soup from his saucer,

And to Master Shakespeare
Who wrote big on small beer.

The abstemious Wordsworth
Subsisted on a curd's-worth,   10

But a slick one was Tennyson,
Putting gravy on his venison.

What these men had to eat and drink
Is what we say and what we think.

The influence of Milton   15
Came wry out of Stilton.

Sing a song for Percy Shelley,
Drowned in pale lemon jelly,

And for precious John Keats,
Dripping blood of pickled beets.   20

Then there was poor Willie Blake,
He foundered on sweet cake.

God have mercy on the sinner
Who must write with no dinner,

No gravy and no grub,   25
No pewter and no pub,

No belly and no bowels,
Only consonants and vowels.

[1945—U.S.A.]

IDEAL LANDSCAPE
— Adrienne Rich —

We had to take the world as it was given:
The nursemaid sitting passive in the park
Was rarely by a changeling prince accosted.
The mornings happened similar and stark

In rooms of selfhood where we woke and lay   5
Watching today unfold like yesterday.

Our friends were not unearthly beautiful.
Nor spoke with tongues of gold; our lovers blundered
Now and again when most we sought perfection,
Or hid in cupboards when the heavens thundered.   10
The human rose to haunt us everywhere,
Raw, flawed, and asking more than we could bear.

And always time was rushing like a tram
Through streets of a foreign city, streets we saw
Opening into great and sunny squares   15
We could not find again, no map could show—
Never those fountains tossed in that same light,
Those gilded trees, those statues green and white.

[1955—U.S.A.]

RICHARD CORY

— E. A. Robinson —

Whenever Richard Cory went down town,
We people on the pavement looked at him:
He was a gentleman from sole to crown,
Clean favored, and imperially slim.

And he was always quietly arrayed,   5
And he was always human when he talked;
But still he fluttered pulses when he said,
"Good-morning," and he glittered when he walked.

And he was rich—yes, richer than a king—
And admirably schooled in every grace: 10
In fine, we thought that he was everything
To make us wish that we were in his place.

So on we worked, and waited for the light,
And went without the meat, and cursed the bread;
And Richard Cory, one calm summer night,   15
Went home and put a bullet through his head.

[1897—U.S.A.]

"LONG LIVE THE WEEDS"
— Theodore Roethke —

Long live the weeds that overwhelm
My narrow vegetable realm!
The bitter rock, the barren soil
That force the son of man to toil;
All things unholy, marred by curse,   5
The ugly of the universe.
The rough, the wicked, and the wild
That keep the spirit undefiled.
With these I match my little wit
And earn the right to stand or sit,   10
Hope, love, create, or drink and die:
These shape the creature that is I.

[1941—U.S.A.]

SONG
— Christina Rossetti —

She sat and sang alway
    By the green margin of a stream,
Watching the fishes leap and play
    Beneath the glad sunbeam.

I sat and wept away   5
    Beneath the moon's most shadowy beam,
Watching the blossoms of the May
    Weep leaves into the stream.

I wept for memory;
    She sang for hope that is so fair: 10
My tears were swallowed by the sea;
    Her songs died on the air.

[1862—Great Britain]

"LONG LIVE THE WEEDS."   The title comes from Hopkins's "Inversnaid": "Long live the weeds and the wilderness yet."

DEATH OF A PSYCHIATRIST
— May Sarton —

1

Now the long lucid listening is done,
Where shame and anguish were subtly opposed:
His patients mourn this father as their own.

Each was accepted whole and wholly known,
Down to the deepest naked need exposed.   5
Now the long lucid listening is done.

For the raw babe, he was a healing zone.
The cry was heard; the rage was not refused.
Each has a father to mourn as his own.

When someone sees at last, the shame is gone;   10
When someone hears, anguish may be composed,
And the long lucid listening is done.

The ghostly child goes forth once more alone,
And scars remain, but the deep wound is closed.
Each has a father to mourn as his own.   15

A guiltless loss, this shines like a sun,
And love remains, but the deep wound is closed.
Each has a father to mourn as his own,
Now the long lucid listening is done.

2

It was not listening alone, but hearing,   20
For he remembered every crucial word
And gave one back oneself because he heard.

Who listens so, does more than listen well.
He goes down with his patient into Hell.

It was not listening alone, but healing.   25
We knew a total, yet detached response,
Harsh laugh, sane and ironical at once.

Who listens so, does more than merely pity,
Restores the soul to its lost dignity.

It was not listening alone, but sharing,   30
And I remember how he bowed his head
Before a poem. "Read it again," he said.

Then, in the richest silence he could give,
I saw the poem born, knew it would live.

It was not listening alone, but being.   35
We saw a face so deeply lined and taut
It wore the passion of dispassionate thought.

Because he cared, he heard; because he heard,
He lifted, shared, and healed without a word.

[1966—U.S.A.]

SONNET 65
— William Shakespeare —

Since brass, nor stone, nor earth, nor boundless sea,
But sad mortality o'ersways their power,
How with this rage shall beauty hold a plea,
Whose action is no stronger than a flower?
Oh, how shall summer's honey breath hold out   5
Against the wrackful siege of battering days,
When rocks impregnable are not so stout,
Nor gates of steel so strong, but Time decays?
O fearful meditation! Where, alack,
Shall Time's best jewel from Time's chest lie hid?   10
Or what strong hand can hold his swift foot back?
Or who his spoil of beauty can forbid?
    Oh, none, unless this miracle have might,
    That in black ink my love may still shine bright.

[1609—Great Britain]

SONNET 146
— William Shakespeare —

Poor soul, the center of my sinful earth,
Lord of these rebel powers that thee array,

SONNET 146. **2.** *array:* clothe, adorn with dress.

Why dost thou pine within and suffer dearth,
Painting thy outward walls so costly gay?
Why so large cost, having so short a lease, 5
Dost thou upon thy fading mansion spend?
Shall worms, inheritors of this excess,
Eat up thy charge? Is this thy body's end?
Then, soul, live thou upon thy servant's loss,
And let that pine to aggravate thy store; 10
Buy terms divine in selling hours of dross;
Within be fed, without be rich no more.
So shalt thou feed on death, that feeds on men,
And death once dead, there's no more dying then.

[1609—Great Britain]

OZYMANDIAS

— Percy Bysshe Shelley —

I met a traveler from an antique land
Who said: Two vast and trunkless legs of stone
Stand in the desert . . . Near them, on the sand,
Half sunk, a shattered visage lies, whose frown,
And wrinkled lip, and sneer of cold command, 5
Tell that its sculptor well those passions read
Which yet survive, stamped on these lifeless things,
The hand that mocked them, and the heart that fed:
And on the pedestal these words appear:
"My name is Ozymandias, king of kings: 10
Look on my works, ye Mighty, and despair!"
Nothing beside remains. Round the decay
Of that colossal wreck, boundless and bare
The lone and level sands stretch far away.

[1818—Great Britain]

---

10. *that:* the body. *pine:* decay. *aggravate:* increase. *thy store:* the riches of the soul.   **11.** *terms:* periods of time. *dross:* waste matter, refuse.
OZYMANDIAS.   *Ozymandias:* Greek name for the Egyptian monarch Ramses II (13th cent. B.C.), a builder of such things as are described in the poem.

ODE TO THE WEST WIND

— Percy Bysshe Shelley —

1

O wild West Wind, thou breath of Autumn's being,
Thou, from whose unseen presence the leaves dead
Are driven, like ghosts from an enchanter fleeing,

Yellow, and black, and pale, and hectic red,
Pestilence-stricken multitudes: O thou,   5
Who chariotest to their dark wintry bed

The wingèd seeds, where they lie cold and low,
Each like a corpse within its grave, until
Thine azure sister of the Spring shall blow

Her clarion o'er the dreaming earth, and fill   10
(Driving sweet buds like flocks to feed in air)
With living hues and odors plain and hill:

Wild Spirit, which art moving everywhere;
Destroyer and preserver; hear, oh, hear!

2

Thou on whose stream, mid the steep sky's commotion,   15
Loose clouds like earth's decaying leaves are shed,
Shook from the tangled boughs of Heaven and Ocean,

Angels of rain and lightning: there are spread
On the blue surface of thine aëry surge,
Like the bright hair uplifted from the head   20

Of some fierce Maenad, even from the dim verge
Of the horizon to the zenith's height,
The locks of the approaching storm. Thou dirge

Of the dying year, to which this closing night
Will be the dome of a vast sepulcher,   25
Vaulted with all thy congregated might

Of vapors, from whose solid atmosphere
Black rain, and fire, and hail will burst: oh, hear!

ODE TO THE WEST WIND. *Wind:* As in many romantic poems, the wind here serves to inspire (which means, etymologically, "to breathe into") the poet and to rouse him from apathy to spiritual excitement.   **10.** *clarion:* trumpet call.   **18.** *Angels:* from the Greek meaning "divine messengers."   **21.** *Maenad:* a frenzied worshiper of Dionysus, a vegetation deity who dies each fall to be resurrected in the spring.

3

Thou who didst waken from his summer dreams
The blue Mediterranean, where he lay,   30
Lulled by the coil of his crystalline streams,

Beside a pumice isle in Baiae's bay,
And saw in sleep old palaces and towers
Quivering within the wave's intenser day,

All overgrown with azure moss and flowers   35
So sweet, the sense faints picturing them! Thou
For whose path the Atlantic's level powers

Cleave themselves into chasms, while far below
The sea-blooms and the oozy woods which wear
The sapless foliage of the ocean, know   40

Thy voice, and suddenly grow gray with fear,
And tremble and despoil themselves: oh, hear!

4

If I were a dead leaf thou mightest bear;
If I were a swift cloud to fly with thee;
A wave to pant beneath thy power, and share   45

The impulse of thy strength, only less free
Than thou, O uncontrollable! If even
I were as in my boyhood, and could be

The comrade of thy wanderings over Heaven,
As then, when to outstrip thy skyey speed   50
Scarce seemed a vision; I would ne'er have striven

As thus with thee in prayer in my sore need.
Oh, lift me as a wave, a leaf, a cloud!
I fall upon the thorns of life! I bleed!

A heavy weight of hours has chained and bowed   55
One too like thee: tameless, and swift, and proud.

5

Make me thy lyre, even as the forest is:
What if my leaves are falling like its own!
The tumult of thy mighty harmonies

32. *Baiae's bay:* near Naples, Italy.   **41–42.** "The vegetation at the bottom of the sea . . . sympathizes with that of the land in the change of seasons"—Shelley's note.   **57.** *lyre:* i.e., Eolian lyre, or wind harp (a musical device fashioned to respond to the wind).

Will take from both a deep, autumnal tone,   60
Sweet though in sadness. Be thou, Spirit fierce,
My spirit! Be thou me, impetuous one!

Drive my dead thoughts over the universe
Like withered leaves to quicken a new birth!
And, by the incantation of this verse,   65

Scatter, as from an unextinguished hearth
Ashes and sparks, my words among mankind!
Be through my lips to unawakened earth

The trumpet of a prophecy! O Wind,
If Winter comes, can Spring be far behind?   70

[1820—Great Britain]

THE EMPEROR OF ICE-CREAM
— Wallace Stevens —

Call the roller of big cigars,
The muscular one, and bid him whip
In kitchen cups concupiscent° curds.   *ardently desired*
Let the wenches dawdle in such dress
As they are used to wear, and let the boys   5
Bring flowers in last month's newspapers.
Let be be finale of seem.
The only emperor is the emperor of ice-cream.

Take from the dresser of deal,
Lacking the three glass knobs, that sheet   10
On which she embroidered fantails once
And spread it so as to cover her face.
If her horny feet protrude, they come
To show how cold she is, and dumb.
Let the lamp affix its beam.   15
The only emperor is the emperor of ice-cream.

[1923—U.S.A.]

---

69. *prophecy:* a reference to line 10 and to the trumpet call of the apocalypse.

THE PLEASURES OF MERELY CIRCULATING
— Wallace Stevens —

The garden flew round with the angel,
The angel flew round with the clouds,
And the clouds flew round and the clouds flew round
And the clouds flew round with the clouds.

Is there any secret in skulls,   5
The cattle skulls in the woods?
Do the drummers in black hoods
Rumble anything out of their drums?

Mrs. Anderson's Swedish baby
Might well have been German or Spanish,   10
Yet that things go round and again go round
Has rather a classical sound.

[1935—U.S.A.]

QUESTION
— May Swenson —

Body my house
my horse my hound
what will I do
when you are fallen

Where will I sleep   5
How will I ride
What will I hunt

Where can I go
without my mount
all eager and quick   10
How will I know
in thicket ahead
is danger or treasure
when Body my good
bright dog is dead   15

How will it be
to lie in the sky

without roof or door
and wind for an eye

With cloud for shift   20
how will I hide?

[1954—U.S.A.]

A DESCRIPTION OF A CITY SHOWER
— Jonathan Swift —

Careful Observers may fortel the Hour
(By sure Prognosticks) when to dread a Show'r:
While Rain depends,° the pensive Cat gives o'er   *impends*
Her Frolicks, and purses her Tail no more.
Returning Home at Night, you'll find the Sink°   *sewer* 5
Strike your offended Sense with double Stink.
If you be wise, then go not far to dine,
You'll spend in Coach-hire more than save in Wine.
A coming Show'r your shooting Corns presage,
Old Aches throb, your hollow Tooth will rage.   10
Sauntring in Coffee-house is *Dulman* seen;
He damns the Climate, and complains of Spleen.
    Meanwhile the South° rising with dabbled° Wings,   *i.e., wind / splashed*
A Sable Cloud a-thwart the Welkin° flings,   *sky*
That swill'd more Liquor than it could contain,   15
And like a Drunkard gives it up again.
Brisk *Susan* whips her Linen from the Rope,
While the first drizzling Show'r is born aslope,
Such is that Sprinkling which some careless Quean°   *slut*
Flirts on you from her Mop, but not so clean.   20
You fly, invoke the Gods; then turning, stop
To rail; she singing, still whirls on her Mop.
Not yet the Dust had shun'd th' unequal Strife,
But aided by the Wind, fought still for Life;
And wafted with its Foe by violent Gust,   25
'Twas doubtful which was Rain, and which was Dust.
Ah! where must needy Poet seek for Aid,

A DESCRIPTION OF A CITY SHOWER. **11.** *Dulman:* a type name meaning "dull man."

When Dust and Rain at once his Coat invade;
His only Coat, where Dust confus'd with Rain,
Roughen the Nap, and leave a mingled Stain.   30
    Now in contiguous Drops the Flood comes down,
Threat'ning with Deluge this *devoted* Town.
To Shops in Crouds the dagged Females fly,
Pretend to cheapen° Goods, but nothing buy.   *shop for*
The Templer spruce, while ev'ry Spout's a-broach,°   *astir*   35
Stays till 'tis fair, yet seems to call a Coach.
The tuck'd-up Sempstress walks with hasty Strides,
While Streams run down her oil'd Umbrella's Sides.
Here various Kinds by various Fortunes led,
Commence Acquaintance underneath a Shed.   40
Triumphant Tories, and desponding Whigs,
Forget their Fewds, and join to save their Wigs.
Box'd in a Chair the Beau impatient sits,
While Spouts run clatt'ring o'er the Roof by Fits;
And ever and anon with frightful Din   45
The Leather sounds, he trembles from within.
So when *Troy* Chair-men bore the Wooden Steed,
Pregnant with *Greeks,* impatient to be freed,
(Those Bully *Greeks,* who, as the Moderns do,
Instead of paying Chair-men, run them thro')   50
Laoco'n struck the Outside with his Spear,
And each imprison'd Hero quak'd for Fear.
    Now from all Parts the swelling Kennels flow,
And bear their Trophies with them as they go:
Filth of all Hues and Odours seem to tell   55
What Street they sail'd from, by their Sight and Smell.
They, as each Torrent drives, with rapid Force
From *Smithfield,* or St. *Pulchre's* shape their Course,
And in huge Confluent join at *Snow-Hill* Ridge,
Fall from the *Conduit* prone to *Holborn-Bridge.*   60
Sweepings from Butchers Stalls, Dung, Guts, and Blood, ⎫
Drown'd Puppies, stinking Sprats, all drench'd in Mud, ⎬
Dead Cats and Turnip-Tops come tumbling down the Flood. ⎭

[1710—Great Britain]

---

33. *dagged:* spattered with mud.   **35.** *Templer spruce:* a young man studying for the law.   **41.** *Tories*
. . . *Whigs:* the rival political parties of the day.   **43.** *chair:* sedan chair, carried by servants.   **46.** *Leather:*
sedan chairs were made of leather.   **50.** *run them thro':* i.e., with swords.   **53.** *Kennels:* open gutters in
the middle of the street.

"THERE WILL COME SOFT RAINS"
(War Time)
— Sara Teasdale —

There will come soft rains and the smell of the ground,
And swallows circling with their shimmering sound;

And frogs in the pools singing at night,
And wild plum-trees in tremulous white;

Robins will wear their feathery fire   5
Whistling their whims on a low fence-wire;

And not one will know of the war, not one
Will care at last when it is done.

Not one would mind, neither bird nor tree
If mankind perished utterly;   10

And Spring herself, when she woke at dawn,
Would scarcely know that we were gone.

[1920—U.S.A.]

BREAK, BREAK, BREAK
— Alfred, Lord Tennyson —

Break, break, break,
  On thy cold gray stones, O Sea!
And I would that my tongue could utter
  The thoughts that arise in me.

O, well for the fisherman's boy,   5
  That he shouts with his sister at play!
O, well for the sailor lad,
  That he sings in his boat on the bay!

And the stately ships go on
  To their haven under the hill;   10
But O for the touch of a vanished hand,
  And the sound of a voice that is still!

Break, break, break,
  At the foot of thy crags, O Sea!

But the tender grace of a day that is dead   15
  Will never come back to me.

[1842—Great Britain]

IN MEMORIAM
— Alfred, Lord Tennyson —

No. 55

The wish, that of the living whole
  No life may fail beyond the grave,
  Derives it not from what we have
The likest God within the soul?

Are God and Nature then at strife,   5
  That Nature lends such evil dreams?
  So careful of the type° she seems,   *species*
So careless of the single life,

That I, considering everywhere
  Her secret meaning in her deeds,   10
  And finding that of fifty seeds
She often brings but one to bear,

I falter where I firmly trod,
  And falling with my weight of cares
  Upon the great world's altar-stairs   15
That slope through darkness up to God,

I stretch lame hands of faith, and grope,
  And gather dust and chaff, and call
  To what I feel is Lord of all,
And faintly trust the larger hope.   20

No. 56

"So careful of the type?" but no.
  From scarpèd cliff and quarried stone
  She cries, "A thousand types are gone;
I care for nothing, all shall go.

IN MEMORIAM, 56. **2.** *scarpèd:* cut away so that the strata are exposed. **3.** *She:* Nature.

"Thou makest thine appeal to me: 5
    I bring to life, I bring to death;
    The spirit does but mean the breath:
I know no more." And he, shall he,

Man, her last work, who seemed so fair,
    Such splendid purpose in his eyes,   10
    Who rolled the psalm to wintry skies,
Who built him fanes° of fruitless prayer,   *temples, churches*

Who trusted God was love indeed
    And love Creation's final law—
    Though Nature, red in tooth and claw   15
With ravine, shrieked against his creed—

Who loved, who suffered countless ills,
    Who battled for the True, the Just,
    Be blown about the desert dust,
Or sealed within the iron hills?   20

No more? A monster then, a dream,
    A discord. Dragons of the prime,
    That tare each other in their slime,
Were mellow music matched with him.

O life as futile, then, as frail!   25
    O for thy voice to soothe and bless!
    What hope of answer, or redress?
Behind the veil, behind the veil.

[1850—Great Britain]

THE EAGLE: A FRAGMENT
— Alfred, Lord Tennyson —

He clasps the crag with crooked hands;
Close to the sun in lonely lands,
Ringed with the azure world, he stands.

The wrinkled sea beneath him crawls:
He watches from his mountain walls,   5
And like a thunderbolt he falls.

[1851—Great Britain]

23. *tare:* tore (archaic).

A REFUSAL TO MOURN THE DEATH, BY FIRE, OF A CHILD IN LONDON
— Dylan Thomas —

Never until the mankind making
Bird beast and flower
Fathering and all humbling darkness
Tells with silence the last light breaking
And the still hour   5
Is come of the sea tumbling in harness

And I must enter again the round
Zion of the water bead
And the synagogue of the ear of corn
Shall I let pray the shadow of a sound   10
Or sow my salt seed
In the least valley of sackcloth to mourn

The majesty and burning of the child's death.
I shall not murder
The mankind of her going with a grave truth   15
Nor blaspheme down the stations of the breath
With any further
Elegy of innocence and youth.

Deep with the first dead lies London's daughter,
Robed in the long friends,   20
The grains beyond age, the dark veins of her mother,
Secret by the unmourning water
Of the riding Thames.
After the first death, there is no other.

[1946—Great Britain]

TWO HEARTS
— Anne Waldman —

She's got my heart and I've got hers
It was fair, we fell in love

I hold hers precious and mine she would miss
There never was anything like this
Her heart in my brain keeps us one   5
My heart in her guides thoughts and feelings
She loves my heart for once it was hers
I love hers because it lived in me
I once wounded her, it was misunderstanding
And then my heart hurt for her heart   10
For as from me on her hurt did sit
So I felt still in me her hurt hurt, it
Both of us hurt simultaneously and then we saw how
We're stuck with each other's hearts now.

[1980—U.S.A.]

MEDITERRANEAN BEACH, DAY AFTER STORM
— Robert Penn Warren —

How instant joy, how clang
And whang the sun, how
Whoop the sea, and oh,
Sun, sing, as whiter than
Rage of snow, let sea the spume   5
fling.

Let sea the spume, white, fling,
White on blue wild
With wind, let sun
Sing, while the world   10
Scuds, clouds boom and belly,
Creak like snails, whiter than,
Brighter than,
Spume in sun-song, oho!
The wind is bright.   15

Wind the hearts winds
In constant coil, turning
In the—forever—light.

Give me your hand.

[1985—U.S.A.]

ON BEING BROUGHT FROM AFRICA TO AMERICA
— Phyllis Wheatley —

'Twas mercy brought me from my *Pagan* land,
Taught my benighted soul to understand
That there's a God, that there's a *Saviour* too:
Once I redemption neither sought nor knew.
Some view our sable race with scornful eye,   5
"Their colour is a diabolic die."
Remember, *Christians, Negroes,* black as *Cain,*
May be refin'd, and join th' angelic train.

[1773—U.S.A.]

BEAT! BEAT! DRUMS!
— Walt Whitman —

Beat! beat! drums!—blow! bugles! blow!
Through the windows—through doors—burst like a ruthless force,
Into the solemn church, and scatter the congregation,
Into the school where the scholar is studying;
Leave not the bridegroom quiet—no happiness must he have now with his
    bride,   5

Nor the peaceful farmer any peace, ploughing his field or gathering his grain,
So fierce you whirr and pound you drums—so shrill you bugles blow.

Beat! beat! drums!—blow! bugles! blow!
Over the traffic of cities—over the rumble of wheels in the streets;
Are beds prepared for sleepers at night in the houses? no sleepers must sleep
    in those beds,   10
No bargainers' bargains by day—no brokers or speculators—would they con-
    tinue?
Would the talkers be talking? would the singer attempt to sing?
Would the lawyer rise in the court to state his case before the judge?
Then rattle quicker, heavier drums—you bugles wilder blow.

Beat! beat! drums!—blow! bugles! blow!   15
Make no parley—stop for no expostulation,
Mind not the timid—mind not the weeper or prayer,
Mind not the old man beseeching the young man,
Let not the child's voice be heard, nor the mother's entreaties,

Make even the trestles to shake the dead where they lie awaiting the hearses,   20
So strong you thump O terrible drums—so loud you bugles blow.

[1867—U.S.A.]

THE PARDON
— RICHARD WILBUR —

My dog lay dead five days without a grave
In the thick of summer, hid in a clump of pine
And a jungle of grass and honeysuckle-vine.
I who had loved him while he kept alive

Went only close enough to where he was   5
To sniff the heavy honeysuckle-smell
Twined with another odor heavier still
And hear the flies' intolerable buzz.

Well, I was ten and very much afraid.
In my kind world the dead were out of range   10
And I could not forgive the sad or strange
In beast or man. My father took the spade

And buried him. Last night I saw the grass
Slowly divide (it was the same scene
But now it glowed a fierce and mortal green)   15
And saw the dog emerging. I confess

I felt afraid again, but still he came
In the carnal sun, clothed in a hymn of flies,
And death was breeding in his lively eyes.
I started in to cry and call his name,   20

Asking forgiveness of his tongueless head.
. . . I dreamt the past was never past redeeming:
But whether this was false or honest dreaming
I beg death's pardon now. And mourn the dead.

[1950—U.S.A.]

STRANGE FITS OF PASSION HAVE I KNOWN
— William Wordsworth —

Strange fits of passion have I known:
And I will dare to tell,

But in the Lover's ear alone,
What once to me befel.

When she I loved looked every day   5
Fresh as a rose in June,
I to her cottage bent my way,
Beneath an evening moon.

Upon the moon I fixed my eye,
All over the wide lea;   10
With quickening pace my horse drew nigh
Those paths so dear to me.

And now we reached the orchard-plot;
And, as we climbed the hill,
The sinking moon to Lucy's cot   15
Came near, and nearer still.

In one of those sweet dreams I slept,
Kind Nature's gentlest boon!
And all the while my eyes I kept
On the descending moon.   20

My horse moved on; hoof after hoof
He raised, and never stopped:
When down behind the cottage roof,
At once, the bright moon dropped.

What fond and wayward thoughts will slide   25
Into a Lover's head!
"O mercy!" to myself I cried,
"If Lucy should be dead!"

[1800—Great Britain]

NUTTING

— William Wordsworth —

——————————It seems a day
(I speak of one from many singled out)
One of those heavenly days that cannot die;
When, in the eagerness of boyish hope,
I left our cottage-threshold, sallying forth   5
With a huge wallet o'er my shoulder slung,
A nutting-crook in hand; and turned my steps

Tow'rd some far-distant wood, a Figure quaint,
Tricked out in proud disguise of cast-off weeds°   *clothes*
Which for that service had been husbanded,   10
By exhortation of my frugal Dame—
Motley accoutrement, of power to smile
At thorns, and brakes, and brambles,—and, in truth,
More raggèd than need was! O'er pathless rocks,
Through beds of matted fern, and tangled thickets,   15
Forcing my way, I came to one dear nook
Unvisited, where not a broken bough
Drooped with its withered leaves, ungracious sign
Of devastation; but the hazels rose
Tall and erect, with tempting clusters hung,   20
A virgin scene!—A little while I stood,
Breathing with such suppression of the heart
As joy delights in; and, with wise restraint
Voluptuous, fearless of a rival, eyed
The banquet;—or beneath the trees I sate   25
Among the flowers, and with the flowers I played;
A temper known to those, who, after long
And weary expectation, have been blest
With sudden happiness beyond all hope.
Perhaps it was a bower beneath whose leaves   30
The violets of five seasons re-appear
And fade, unseen by any human eye;
Where fairy water-breaks do murmur on
For ever; and I saw the sparkling foam,
And—with my cheek on one of those green stones   35
That, fleeced with moss, under the shady trees,
Lay round me, scattered like a flock of sheep—
I heard the murmur and the murmuring sound,
In that sweet mood when pleasure loves to pay
Tribute to ease; and, of its joy secure,   40
The heart luxuriates with indifferent things,
Wasting its kindliness on stocks and stones,
And on the vacant air. Then up I rose,
And dragged to earth both branch and bough, with crash
And merciless ravage: and the shady nook   45
Of hazels, and the green and mossy bower,
Deformed and sullied, patiently gave up

NUTTING.   **33.** *fairy water-breaks:* places where the flow of a stream is broken by rocks.   **42.** *stocks:* tree stumps.

Their quiet being: and, unless I now
Confound my present feelings with the past;
Ere from the mutilated bower I turned   50
Exulting, rich beyond the wealth of kings,
I felt a sense of pain when I beheld
The silent trees, and saw the intruding sky.—
Then, dearest Maiden, move along these shades
In gentleness of heart; with gentle hand   55
Touch—for there is a spirit in the woods.

[1800—Great Britain]

COMPOSED UPON WESTMINSTER BRIDGE, SEPTEMBER 3, 1802

— William Wordsworth —

Earth has not anything to show more fair:
Dull would he be of soul who could pass by
A sight so touching in its majesty;
This City now doth, like a garment, wear
The beauty of the morning; silent, bare,   5
Ships, towers, domes, theaters, and temples lie
Open unto the fields, and to the sky;
All bright and glittering in the smokeless air.
Never did sun more beautifully steep
In his first splendor, valley, rock, or hill;   10
Ne'er saw I, never felt, a calm so deep!
The river glideth at his own sweet will:
Dear God! the very houses seem asleep;
And all that mighty heart is lying still!

[1807—Great Britain]

THAT THE NIGHT COME

— W. B. Yeats —

She lived in storm and strife,
Her soul had such desire
For what proud death may bring
That it could not endure
The common good of life,   5
But lived as 'twere a king
That packed his marriage day

With banneret and pennon,
Trumpet and kettledrum,
And the outrageous cannon,   10
To bundle time away
That the night come.

[1914—Ireland]

TO A FRIEND WHOSE WORK HAS COME TO NOTHING
— W. B. Yeats —

Now all the truth is out,
Be secret and take defeat
From any brazen throat,
For how can you compete,
Being honor bred, with one   5
Who, were it proved he lies,
Were neither shamed in his own
Nor in his neighbours' eyes?
Bred to a harder thing
Than Triumph, turn away   10
And like a laughing string
Whereon mad fingers play
Amid a place of stone,
Be secret and exult,
Because of all things known   15
That is most difficult.

[1914—Ireland]

THE MERMAID
— W. B. Yeats —

A mermaid found a swimming lad,
Picked him for her own,
Pressed his body to her body,
Laughed; and plunging down
Forgot in cruel happiness   5
That even lovers drown.

[1928—Ireland]

TO A FRIEND WHOSE WORK HAS COME TO NOTHING.   *Friend:* Yeats refers to his friend Lady Gregory, who had failed in her effort to secure an art museum for Dublin.

A DIALOGUE OF SELF AND SOUL
— W. B. Yeats —
Part 2

MY SELF. A living man is blind and drinks his drop.
   What matter if the ditches are impure?
   What matter if I live it all once more?
   Endure that toil of growing up;
   The ignominy of boyhood; the distress   5
   Of boyhood changing into man;
   The unfinished man and his pain
   Brought face to face with his own clumsiness;

   The finished man among his enemies?—
   How in the name of Heaven can he escape   10
   That defiling and disfigured shape
   The mirror of malicious eyes
   Casts upon his eyes until at last
   He thinks that shape must be his shape?
   And what's the good of an escape   15
   If honor find him in the wintry blast?

   I am content to live it all again
   And yet again, if it be life to pitch
   Into the frog-spawn of a blind man's ditch,
   A blind man battering blind men;   20
   Or into that most fecund ditch of all,
   The folly that man does
   Or must suffer, if he woos
   A proud woman not kindred of his soul.

   I am content to follow to its source   25
   Every event in action or in thought;
   Measure the lot; forgive myself the lot!
   When such as I cast out remorse
   So great a sweetness flows into the breast
   We must laugh and we must sing,   30
   We are blest by everything,
   Everything we look upon is blest.

[1929—Ireland]

LAPIS LAZULI
— W. B. Yeats —

I have heard that hysterical women say
They are sick of the palette and fiddle-bow,
Of poets that are always gay,
For everybody knows or else should know
That if nothing drastic is done   5
Aeroplane and Zeppelin will come out,
Pitch like King Billy bomb-balls in
Until the town lie beaten flat.

All perform their tragic play,
There struts Hamlet, there is Lear,   10
That's Ophelia, that Cordelia;
Yet they, should the last scene be there,
The great stage curtain about to drop,
If worthy their prominent part in the play,
Do not break up their lines to weep.   15
They know that Hamlet and Lear are gay;
Gaiety transfiguring all that dread.
All men have aimed at, found and lost;
Black out; Heaven blazing into the head:
Tragedy wrought to its uttermost.   20
Though Hamlet rambles and Lear rages,
And all the drop-scenes drop at once
Upon a hundred thousand stages,
It cannot grow by an inch or an ounce.

On their own feet they came, or on shipboard,   25
Camelback, horseback, ass-back, mule-back,
Old civilizations put to the sword.
Then they and their wisdom went to rack:
No handiwork of Callimachus,
Who handled marble as if it were bronze,   30

LAPIS LAZULI.   Yeats wrote to his friend Dorothy Wellesley: "I notice that you have much lapis lazuli [a beautiful dark blue stone]; someone has sent me a present of a great piece carved by some Chinese sculptor into the semblance of a mountain with temple, trees, paths, and an ascetic and pupil about to climb the mountain. Ascetic, pupil, hard stone, eternal theme of the sensual east. The heroic cry in the midst of despair. But no, I am wrong, the east has its solutions always and therefore knows nothing of tragedy. It is we, not the east, that must raise the heroic cry." **6. *Aeroplane:*** The poem was written on the eve of World War II.   **7. *King Billy:*** The reference is to William III, who defeated the army of King James II at the Battle of the Boyne in 1690.   **29. *Callimachus:*** a famous Greek sculptor, whose work survives only in descriptions of contemporaries.

Made draperies that seemed to rise
When sea-wind swept the corner, stands;
His long lamp-chimney shaped like the stem
Of a slender palm, stood but a day;
All things fall and are built again,   35
And those that build them again are gay.

Two Chinamen, behind them a third,
Are carved in lapis lazuli,
Over them flies a long-legged bird,
A symbol of longevity;   40
The third, doubtless a serving-man,
Carries a musical instrument.

Every discoloration of the stone,
Every accidental crack or dent,
Seems a water-course or an avalanche,   45
Or lofty slope where it still snows
Though doubtless plum or cherry-branch
Sweetens the little half-way house
Those Chinamen climb towards, and I
Delight to imagine them seated there;   50
There, on the mountain and the sky,
On all the tragic scene they stare.
One asks for mournful melodies;
Accomplished fingers begin to play.
Their eyes mid many wrinkles, their eyes,   55
Their ancient, glittering eyes, are gay.

[1938—Ireland]

SECTION IV

DRAMA

WHAT PLAYS ARE

The word "play" refers both to a written text or script, which supplies the words for actors to speak as well as various directions as to performance, and to the performance itself. So, one can read a play and one can go to see a play. However, reading a play and seeing it are quite different experiences. As we will discuss shortly, the elements composing the written texts of plays are by and large the same as those we have encountered already when looking at fiction and poetry. But performance adds another dimension and entails other elements and ways of meaning unique to the theater (or movies and television drama).

Take lighting. An element of drama as we know it, lighting can be an important agent in the creation of mood and therefore can contribute to our understanding of the meaning or theme of a play as produced. But lighting contributes thus mainly in performance. Even an elaborate description in the stage directions of a play as to what the lighting is to be does not carry the weight and impact of actually seeing the light change color, or dim, or brighten. The same is true of all other aspects of performance. The *way* words are spoken by the actors, for example, very much affects meaning, as do blocking (the physical movement on stage), scenery, costuming, and so forth. All are agents of meaning that come into their own only in performance. In other words, the play as text is only part of the story of drama (which comes from the Greek meaning "to do" or "to act"); the play as performance is the rest.

As performed, a play is a collaborative effort on the parts of many people: the playwright (or the builder of plays—*wright* comes from a word meaning "builder"), the producer, the director, the actors, the designers of lighting, sets, and costumes, and so on. The playwright writes the play, but what an audience finally sees is the result of the collective interpretation of many minds. Still, the text is basic, for everything else depends on it. And a play in the sense of "script" can be read like any other text, though reading a play fully involves certain special mental activities. We shall consider what these activities are a little later. For now, just be aware that the word "play" has two senses, and the sense that will apply for the most part in our considerations is "script," the written text on which all else is based.

TYPES OF PLAYS

The first thing to note about plays of any type is that they can be and have been written in both prose and verse. However, though plays written in prose are usually more like fiction and plays in verse are more like poetry, both are still more like each other than like anything else. That is, whether in prose or verse, plays are plays with respect to dramatic structure and effect. As to specific types, plays have been divided into any number of categories: tragedy and comedy, of course, but also tragicomedy, melodrama, farce, social or problem plays, the comedy of manners, situation plays, and so forth. For our purposes, four categories should suffice: tragedy, comedy, realism, and nonrealism. We will take up each type in turn, focusing on its defining characteristics.

Tragedy

Aristotle, the first theater critic, divided plays into two types only, the two he was familiar with from the theater of ancient Athens: tragedy and comedy. Tragedy, according to Aristotle, is "an imitation of an action that is serious, complete, and of a certain magnitude" (23). By "serious" Aristotle meant that a tragedy must be elevated or noble in style and subject matter alike, involving highborn rather than ordinary people; by "complete" he meant that a tragedy must proceed logically, with all its incidents in causal relationship (in other words, a tragedy must have a sound plot); and by "a certain magnitude" he meant simply that the plot must be easily remembered in its totality. Further, Aristotle held that the action of a tragedy, or the kind of real-life event that a tragedy imitates or represents, must concern the fall of a person of eminence from greatness and prosperity to lowliness and adversity due to some "error or frailty" (45) on the part of the tragic protagonist. For instance, in part because of his unbridled thirst for knowledge of his parentage, Oedipus, the king of Thebes, winds up at the end of *Oedipus Rex* a blind man about to become a wandering beggar.

Aristotle's sense of tragedy endured more or less until the late nineteenth century. However, from the Renaissance on, it has generally been felt that tragedy must necessarily end in death, which Aristotle did not hold; and, from the Renaissance on, tragic heroes have not necessarily fallen only because of their own errors or frailties but sometimes because of overwhelming external forces. Shakespeare's Othello falls because of a frailty inflamed by Iago—his (Othello's) jealousy; Hamlet, on the other hand, is led to tragedy by the murder of his father, which has nothing to do with anything internal to Hamlet. Still, from Sophocles to Shakespeare right on down to Ibsen, tragedy was felt necessarily to concern the fall of the great rather than the tribulations of the ordinary.

Starting with Ibsen, a new sense of tragedy emerges in Western literature, a sense that remains intact today. Tragedy since Ibsen mainly concerns the lives of ordinary men and women brought to some catastrophe (usually, but not necessarily, entailing death) by their own flaws, perhaps, or by external forces, or most often by a combination of the two. In concerning ordinary people, modern tragedy shows the effects of realism, which has affected all literary genres in our century. Arthur Miller's *Death of a Salesman* well exemplifies the modern sense of tragedy in all of these regards. Its protagonist, Willy Loman, is a nobody, as his name suggests. Because of his own lack of daring, his life has not amounted to much. This one comes painfully to realize as external forces (the changing business climate) bring Willy down. Scene by scene, the play builds to Willy's suicide, the climax of his mounting desperation and sense of failure. Miller's plot, which Aristotle would have found "of a certain magnitude," leaves one feeling grief for Willy not only in his death but also in his life, which seems to touch all of us in our ordinary, everyday world.

But Miller's play leaves us with another feeling as well—a sense of the dignity of human life, of every life played to completion. Aristotle believed that the effect of tragedy is to raise in the viewer feelings of "pity and fear" (23) and its function is to purge those feelings and by so doing yield the highest kind of pleasure. That has never seemed quite right to me for a number of reasons, perhaps the most important being that there are many great tragedies that do not purge pity and fear at all (for example, *Hamlet* and *Death of a Salesman*). Yes, tragedy raises the emotions of pity and fear, but I do not think that it then turns round to dissipate these most human of feelings. Nor should it. For it is pity and fear that tie us to our fellow beings and lead us to see the tragic side of things. And rather than coming from purgation, the pleasure of tragedy comes from this way of seeing; that is, the pleasure of tragedy derives from its making us see life as tragedy and thus feel life's potential grandeur. Every great tragedy, I believe, leaves us with a sense of dignity and grandeur. Lacking this sense, many would-be tragedies become merely voyeuristic and morbid, appealing to our lowest appetites (for example, for violence) and leaving us unmoved, unengaged, and empty. When you read *Oedipus Rex* and/or *Hamlet,* which follow in turn after this introduction, see what you feel at the end. Do you feel depressed because of the terrible events depicted in the play—in which case you shouldn't find it very pleasurable? Or do you feel somehow uplifted, full of a sense of the dignity of humankind—in which case your justified pleasure, I think you will find, comes from your elevated vision of human suffering? In that both *Oedipus Rex* and *Hamlet* are great tragedies, I have no doubt that the latter will be your response.

Comedy

Aristotle left a treatise on tragedy and another on comedy. The latter, alas, has been lost to history. We can only guess, therefore, how Aristotle would have defined comedy. But the Greek word for comedy, *komos*—meaning "revel," "celebration," "merrymaking"—gives us a good lead, especially when taken with the plays of Aristophanes, the great Greek comic playwright of Aristotle's day. The satiric plays of Aristophanes put us in a merrymaking mood because they are funny. They make us laugh. It is highly likely, then, that, whatever else he said about comedy, Aristotle took laughter as central to his definition.

To be sure, laughter has not always been associated with the word "comedy." In the Middle Ages, which spanned roughly a thousand years of the history of the West, comedy was thought of simply as the reverse of tragedy; that is, a comedy was held to be anything that exhibits an upward movement (as opposed to a fall) from adversity to prosperity. It is in this sense that Dante's great poem *The Divine Comedy* is a comedy. But for us, as for the ancient Greeks, the idea of comedy is inseparable from laughter. The smiling mask of comedy as opposed to the frowning mask of tragedy points to the heart of the matter.

Why, though, do we laugh? There have been dozens of theories of laughter over the centuries, but so far, although many of the things that make us laugh have been isolated and examined satisfactorily, no one has yet come up with a compelling theory of why we laugh at those things. All I can say on this score is, "Thank God we laugh." For laughter, most of us agree, is our greatest asset in coping with life. And how good a good laugh feels: it purges us—perhaps of pity and fear (Aristotle's concept of the function of tragedy is perhaps better suited to comedy)—and leaves us in a mirthful, celebratory frame of mind. Tragedy engenders in us a feeling of the grandeur of human life *because* of suffering and death; comedy engenders the feeling that life should be celebrated *in its entirety,* absurdities and all. Dignity is the mark of tragedy; the mark of comedy is mirthful celebration. Thus, many comedies end in the celebration of one or more marriages, which signify inclusion into the community (tragedy usually involves exclusion) and a sense of general celebration; and most end with things being put right and a sense of general delight. The mood is contagious.

But to return to laughter, though I cannot tell you why we laugh, I can suggest more or less what makes us laugh. The causes of laughter can be boiled down to three categories: language, physical action, and the complications of a plot or the intricacies of a situation. A good joke or pun exemplifies the ability of language to make us laugh, as does the routine of any good stand-up comedian. Such a routine is all words and nothing but words. In plays, language is also a prime source of humor. If we find what characters say to be funny, we laugh at the sheer wit of their words. We also laugh at the buffoonery of clowns as they knock into each other and fall on their faces, as well as at pies thrown into people's faces, and so forth and so on. This second source of humor—that is, physical action—was incorporated into comedy from the first. Aristophanes, for instance, though a great satirist whose humor depends largely on language, incorporated physical humor as well into his plays. In his *The Clouds,* no less a personage than Socrates swings across the stage in a basket as he proclaims himself able to walk on air; and in *Lysistrata,* a chorus of men, deprived of sexual gratification by their rebellious wives, appear on the stage wearing huge phalluses, indicating their frustration. These examples suggest that low-down slapstick is in no way at odds with the most sophisticated of verbal humor. Great comic dramatists have never made the strict distinctions that critics are prone to pronounce. In any case, the third source of laughter—complications of plot or situation—does not appear until the third century B.C. with the plays of the Greek playwright Menander. Most "situation" comedies on television follow the pattern established by Menander and copied by the later Roman playwrights Plautus and Terence. Such comedies proceed by someone's doing something (think of Lucy, for instance) that then gives rise to a series of events each more tangled than the last. (In connection with television comedies, "situation" refers to the fact that each episode starts with the same general state of affairs. But once an episode gets moving, the plot thickens.) The humor lies in the entanglement, which of necessity, because we are dealing with comedy, resolves itself at the last. Though related, comedy springing from the intricacies of situation alone is much later in origin, appearing fully only in the eighteenth century. Dating from the late nineteenth century, Oscar Wilde's *The Importance of Being Earnest* is the best possible example. Here, absolutely nothing happens; but the situation in which we find the play's characters grows more and more complex, with each added complexity seeming funnier and funnier. The play also exhibits wonderful verbal humor, which, along with the intricacy of its situation, helps make it a high comedy throughout.

"Funnier and funnier," I say, as I speak of "high comedy." Yet, as most teachers would agree, there is nothing harder to teach than comedy. Is the reason for this that most students simply don't have a sense of humor? No, I don't think so. Rather, I believe the cause to be that most students think of the college classroom as a "serious" place, not the place for the frivolity of laughter, despite the fact that we all love to laugh and take readily on our own to what is humorous. Well, against the charge of frivolity I maintain that comedy is serious business and that laughter is no less important nor less worthy of exploration than graver matters. In other words, a great comedy is just as great and just as worthy of study as a great tragedy. Both express aspects of the human condition, and both show us equally, though in opposite ways, possible human responses to the world. We should not distinguish between what is serious and what is comic, therefore, but between what is comic and (for want of a better word) what is grave. I urge you, thus, to let yourself go when comedy is the topic and laugh as freely in class as you do out of class. Remember, as the ancient Greeks held, "laughter is the greatest gift of the gods."

Realism

Appearing toward the end of the nineteenth century, realism cuts across both tragedy and comedy. That is, there are realistic plays that are tragedies and others that are comedies. Ibsen's *Ghosts,* for instance, is a realistic tragedy; and most of George Bernard Shaw's plays are realistic comedies. Nevertheless, realism constitutes a valid category unto itself. For, whether tragic, comic, both, or neither, realistic plays all share the same object: to create the illusion of life, or to seem when performed as much like life as possible. That was not the concern of Sophocles or Shakespeare. It was the central concern, however, of such latter-day playwrights as Ibsen, Shaw, and Maksim Gorki. Therefore, it is sensible to group plays by these relatively recent writers under the heading of "realism."

In the context of the last hundred years or so, "realism" as applied to drama means the imitation on the stage of ordinary people in ordinary settings behaving in ways that seem true to life. The realistic playwright holds a mirror up to life as *we* know it—that is, middle-class life in a middle-class world—and creates the illusion that what we are seeing is actually happening. In order to create such an illusion, realistic plays call for elaborate sets that really look like what they represent, a natural as opposed to the grand acting style, and a text whose language is that of the people represented (ordinary middle-class people)—that is, contemporary, collo-quial prose (as opposed to verse). Asides, soliloquies, flashbacks—anything not felt to be lifelike is banished. Characters talk only to each other and never to the audience, and the action proceeds in a normal chronological sequence. Realistic plays, thus, put the audience in the position of eavesdroppers looking into a room through a wall that by convention can be seen through by the audience but not by the characters. As to content, most realistic plays concern contemporary issues and social problems, to which the style of realism is suited. For instance, Ibsen deals with water pollution in *An Enemy of the People* and women's rights in *A Doll's House,* Gorki with the slums in *The Lower Depths,* and Shaw with prostitution in *Mrs. Warren's Profession.* It is because realistic plays usually deal with such issues that they are sometimes referred to as "social dramas" or "problem plays." In sum, the realistic play, which never calls attention to the fact that it is a play, generally concerns some social issue in such a way as to create the illusion that it (the play) is a self-contained world as real as reality itself (middle-class reality, that is).

The reasons for the rise and influence of realism in the drama are complex. Certainly, the state of the theater toward the end of the nineteenth century provided a strong impetus to playwrights of merit to write plays opposite in character from those then in fashion. When Ibsen came on the scene, what passed for theater was merely escapist entertainment with exaggerated characters (the villain, the hero, the pretty young maid), insignificant plots irrelevant to anyone's actual life, and an acting tradition marked by flamboyance and histrionics. It is no wonder that Ibsen and others like him set out to construct plays that point by point would be the opposite of what then passed for drama. Another reason for the emergence of realism in the theater has to do with the prestige and influence of science. Indeed, this is a key reason why realism came to affect all the arts. Whether rightly or not, it was felt by talented young playwrights that plays should be more scientific, which meant that they should dissect life as we know it, with no heroes as such or villains but just people caught in conflicts that mirror those of our world. But perhaps the most important reason for the influence of realism is that, who knows why, several great playwrights appeared at about the same time. Because they were men of genius, they set out to reform the theater; they turned to realism because of the other reasons just discussed.

Before we move on to our final category, a word of caution about dealing with realistic plays: do not confuse realism with reality. A realistic play is no more real than any other work of art. It is a play, after all, and not in fact a slice of life. Indeed, one could make a case that, because it creates the illusion of reality, a realistic play is less real than a play that makes no pretense to seem real. For, in reality, both are plays and nothing else. And realistic plays are no less conventional than any other type. If they seem less conventional, it is only because we have all been trained in the conventions of realism and so accept them without thought. At any rate, my point, simply, is that plays are plays, including those that create the illusion of reality; and those that do not attempt this illusion are no less real for not doing so. Whatever kind of play you are dealing with, the word "real" should be reserved to define something about the play's substance: for instance, Oedipus, though certainly not realistically drawn, seems terribly real because Sophocles communicates through him fundamental human truths. Conversely, there have been thousands of realistic plays that, in terms of substance, are not at all real in that they feed on trivialities and convey not even an inkling of anything that is true. In a word, "realistic" should be used only to suggest a certain kind of play with a certain kind of subject matter and not as an adjective of praise and approbation.

Nonrealism

In a sense, all plays until the late nineteenth century are nonrealistic. When Oedipus, masked, speaks with a masked chorus, or when Hamlet reveals his deepest thoughts in soliloquy, we are not meant to think that in the time of Sophocles people wore masks in daily life and went around in choruses chanting, or that in Elizabethan England human beings talked aloud to themselves when thinking. Rather, we are meant to see the masks, the chorus, the soliloquy as stage conventions that allow certain things to be accomplished. Of course, neither Sophocles nor Shakespeare wanted us to pretend that their plays were not plays. They would have found the notion absurd. The term "nonrealistic," therefore, has no useful application beyond our century. That is, it is meaningful only in the context of realism, in which context the term indicates a movement among various playwrights of the present century against the relatively new conventions of the realistic stage.

What is most important to grasp about nonrealistic plays is that they do not attempt to hold the mirror up to everyday life or to create the illusion of "real" life. Many such plays, in fact, seem designed to do just the opposite: openly and flamboyantly to declare by whatever means that what we are reading or watching is a play. Eugene O'Neill, for instance, although he also wrote realistic plays, wrote plays in which the characters wear masks, speak in asides to the audience and some-times in chorus, and use language that is often highly poetic. In other nonrealistic or even antirealistic plays, sets are used to suggest multiple times and places, lighting to suggest flashbacks or dream sequences, and costumes to indicate the characters' internal states of being. Usually written for new types of stage and staging—theater in the round, for example—nonrealistic plays by such playwrights as Luigi Pirandello, Bertolt Brecht, Eugène Ionesco, and Samuel Beckett often proceed in ways other than chronological, contain nameless characters who act without motivation, and, as easily as not, fall into verse or pure nonsense. Then, too, these plays frequently have minimal sets or are produced on a bare stage. For instance, the most famous of all nonrealistic plays, Beckett's *Waiting for Godot,* specifies for set simply "A country road. A tree." In the first act, the tree is barren; in the second, it has sprouted a single leaf. As well as being minimal, Beckett's set is highly symbolic, symbolism being a central characteristic of nonrealistic plays. To be sure, realistic plays, too, usually contain symbols, but their symbols are by and large fairly well concealed. In contrast, the symbolism in a play like *Waiting for Godot,* however difficult to interpret, stares one in the face. To take another example, in Ionesco's *Rhinoceros* there is little doubt that the turning of the characters into rhinos is symbolic, though what exactly is symbolized might elude us. Both Beckett and Ionesco, incidentally, are commonly thought of as representative of the "theater of the absurd." Both would no doubt protest, but their plays are so nonrealistic that they communicate to many people the idea that nothing is real and that life, consequently, is absurd.

One final type of play that must be considered here is the type that falls somewhere between the realistic and the nonrealistic. Such is the case with many plays written since the Second World War. Tennessee Williams's *The Glass Menagerie* is a clear example. Usually classified as a "tragicomedy" (that is, a play with both comic and tragic dimensions), *The Glass Menagerie* is a mix of realistic and nonrealistic elements. For the most part, the characterization, the language, the plot, and the setting smack of ordinary life, of day-to-day existence as most people experience it. But one of the characters in the play also acts as a narrator, addressing the audience directly and thus reminding us that we are seeing a play and not a slice of life. Then, too, both lighting and music are used symbolically, sometimes signifying the moods of characters and sometimes providing mute commentary (often ironic) on their hopes and remembrances. Finally, and most obviously nonrealistic, Williams uses a device he calls "the screen" (by which he means a back wall of the set) on which are flashed continually phrases or images that sum up or comment on the segment of the play before us. Through combining techniques, Williams gives us a feel both for the external lives of his characters and for their internal lives, their private feelings, memories, and dreams. That is a great deal, and that, I believe, is why the play is as highly regarded as it is.

THE ELEMENTS OF DRAMA

The play as written text is composed of many of the elements we have studied in connection with both fiction and poetry. The play as drama, on the other hand (that is, in performance), involves other elements as well, elements unique to the drama. Even when reading a play, you should be aware of these other elements as they come into play. For, again, plays are written to be performed. One cannot understand a play in its entirety, therefore, without taking into account its performance elements. I shall now briefly discuss each of the elements that plays share with the other genres of literature; then we shall consider those that are unique to the drama. (The page numbers refer to the sections in which full consideration of the shared element in question can be found.)

Plot and Situation (pp. 68–70)

Like short stories, short plays—by which is usually meant one-act plays—are built on either a plot or a situation. The causally linked actions and interactions of characters (plot) or their interactions alone (situation) provide a vehicle for whatever theme the play concerns. The same is true of full-length plays, though they are bound to be more complex simply because of their length. Perhaps an equation will clarify the distinction: one-act plays are to short stories as full-length plays are to novels. Like the novel, the full-length play may have more than one plot working at the same time, or perhaps a main plot and one or more subplots. The double plots or the main plot and subplots of a longer play, of course, will be related. And all will converge and get resolved somehow or another in the **denouement** (which literally means "unraveling") or climax at the end. *Hamlet* provides a classic example. Its main plot concerns the revenge Hamlet must take for the murder of his father. In seeking revenge, Hamlet mistakenly kills Polonius, the father of Laertes and Ophelia. Two subplots thus emerge, one springing from Laertes's consuming desire for revenge in his turn and one involving what happens to Ophelia because of her father's death. Note that both subplots develop out of the main plot and, thus, are dependent on it. As to resolution, all plots and subplots resolve in *Hamlet* in the last act through death. A full-length play may also be based on a situation if the situation is of sufficient complexity as to be able to be carried out at such length. In Wilde's *The Importance of Being Earnest,* for example, the many confusions as to names and identities serve to sustain our interest (as well as to make the play uproarious) as we attend to the interactions of the characters.

One thing more that you should be aware of about plays with respect to plot has to do with conflict. Although the plots of most stories do entail conflict, stories can get by without it, and in many stories conflict is muted or secondary. In plays, on the other hand, conflict of some sort—whether comic or grave—is usually central. For plays present us with people alone, usually interacting with each other through dialogue and sometimes talking to themselves in soliloquy. All but inevitably, therefore, some kind of conflict emerges: whether between a character and the world around, natural or social; or between one character and another (usually referred to as the protagonist and the antagonist); or between opposing sides within a single character. In short plays, conflict is limited by and large to one of these kinds; in longer plays, all might come into play. Hamlet's conflicts, for instance, are multiple: Hamlet is in conflict with most of the play's other characters; with society and its codes and even, perhaps, with nature (another character suggests as much with respect of Hamlet's mourning); and, most of all, with himself, which he expresses in his solilo-quies. Much of the meaning of the play lies in these various conflicts and Hamlet's progress toward resolving them. Indeed, conflict is the life of drama. Thus, whether you are reading or seeing a play, it is important to identify the conflicts it presents and to follow each as it moves toward resolution.

Characterization (pp. 98–101)

Like characters in fiction, characters in plays can be stock, flat, or round. Also, round characters in plays, like those in fiction, can (and almost always do) either grow in some way and for some reason (for example, by attaining knowledge, as in *Oedipus Rex*) or disintegrate because of external and/or internal forces (the fate of Laura in *The Glass Menagerie*). The main difference between characters in plays and those in fiction has to do with characterization. In fiction, the narrator may tell us a good deal about the characters in the story or novel we are reading. For the most part (but not entirely, for there are plays with narrators—see the next section), this means of characterization is not available to the playwright. In most plays, therefore, characterization depends wholly on what characters say, how they say it, and how they act and interact. Inference, then, is doubly important when it comes to plays, especially reading them. On this score, plays are analogous to poems. In reading a poem, as we have seen, one must pay careful attention to diction, tone, rhythm, and so forth, as well as to what the speaker says, why, and to whom. The same is true as to characters in plays. Since no one can tell us anything directly about a character, we must attend closely to diction, tone, character interaction, and so on for full comprehension.

One other matter concerning characters that you should note is that, like plays themselves, characters in plays can be realistic or nonrealistic. You should always distinguish between the two because one's reception of a play often rests on one's expectations of it. In other words, do not bring to a nonrealistic play the expectations you would bring to a realistic play, just as you would not bring to a tragedy the expectations you would to a comedy. Character consistency and development, for instance, are not concerns of nonrealistic plays and so should not be your concerns when reading or seeing such a play. Your attention should be elsewhere.

Narration and Point of View (pp. 121–25)

There are plays with narrators: for example, Thornton Wilder's *Our Town* and Tennessee Williams's *The Glass Menagerie.* Such plays are by definition nonrealistic, at least in part. What is true of narrators and narration in fiction applies equally to both in plays. A narrator in a play can narrate in the third person or the first. In the case of the latter, the narrator is a character in the play and must be thought of accordingly. Narrative point of view, of course, is a consideration only if a play has a narrator. But very few do. For the most part, all the information conveyed in plays is conveyed by and only by the characters interacting with each other (some commentators refer to this mode of delivery as the "dramatic point of view").

Mood, Irony, and Style (pp. 150–54)

No less than writers of prose fiction, playwrights create mood and thus meaning through irony and style. Dramatic irony—which springs from the audience's knowing more than a character—is particularly suited to plays, *Oedipus Rex* providing the classic example. Indeed, the very term "dramatic irony" comes from the theater in the first place. In plays, as in stories and poems, irony helps shape our mood and thereby our response. *The Glass Menagerie,* for instance, contains many ironies, which can be played up or down by a director. When the ironies are stressed, the play is more satirical and comic; when they are passed over, the play becomes more tragic. The general style of a play (that is, its language) also affects mood, as the specific styles of individual characters affect characterization. For instance, the bare, plain language of Arthur Miller's *Death of a Salesman,* reflecting the barrenness of its protagonist's (Willy Loman's) inner life, works to create a bleak mood and so to communicate the bleakness of Willy's existence. In contrast, Hamlet's heavily metaphorical style, marked also by puns and often by a complex syntax, serves both to establish Hamlet as a unique person in our minds and to portray him as a man whose inner life is dense and rich.

Setting and Symbolism (pp. 179–84, 295–300)

Setting tells us much about characters and the world they inhabit by locating both as to time and place. We have seen this when considering both stories and poems; it is true as well of plays. The setting of *The Importance of Being Earnest,* for instance, suggests at the outset—at least to anyone who knows something about well-to-do Britishers at the end of the last century—that the play's characters will be highly refined in the social graces and completely idle, and that their world will be one of pastimes and chitchat. This proves to be the case, as Wilde, capitalizing on his material, performs a miracle before our eyes: that is, making something from nothing. Setting also affects mood. Consider the beginning of *Hamlet.* By virtue of both time and place, the opening scene on the ramparts at midnight creates a mood of foreboding, which intimates the nature of the action to come. The darkness of the opening scene is possibly also symbolic, objectifying the sense of the dark reaches of the self that Hamlet is to experience. As we have seen previously, setting is often symbolic in ways like this.

As to other kinds of symbolism, what is true of symbolism in any context is true of symbolism in plays. The symbols of plays may be conventional or created, for instance, and symbols are recognized and interpreted in plays in the same way as in poems and stories. Take Hamlet's wearing of black, which outwardly symbolizes his inner grief. This is a conventional symbol that we recognize and understand by the cultural context (for black is not a symbol of mourning in all cultures). The many references in *Hamlet* to ears, on the other hand, become symbolic because of the literary context alone; in the context of a murder accomplished by poison poured into the victim's ear, references to the ear carry special meaning. The ear becomes in *Hamlet* a created symbol reminding us again and again of the murder of Hamlet's father and what remains for Hamlet to do. To understand fully the symbols found in plays, what you need to do is to relate anything you think might be symbolic to the primary action or situation of the play you are considering. If a relationship exists, then you have no doubt found something of symbolic weight and, thus, special significance in the play in question.

Voice, Tone, and Diction (pp. 239–44)

When reading a play, be alert to how things are said, or to what we called "voice" and thence "tone of voice" when examining poems. Because plays consist mainly of people speaking, these elements are particularly important to keep in mind when reading a play. Stage directions, which are equivalent to what narrators might tell us, can be helpful in directing the reader in this regard: for instance, a stage direction might say, "to be said moodily" or "angrily" or "mockingly," just as a fictional narrator might say, " 'Blah, blah, blah,' she said, warmly." But more often than not, stage directions of this sort are lacking. Even when there are stage directions, but especially when there are not, one must pay close attention to matters of diction, rhythm, and so on. These are what actors base their interpretations on and what a reader, mentally acting out a play, must take into account as well.

Meter and Rhythm (pp. 322–33)

As I have indicated previously, plays can be in verse as well as prose. *Hamlet,* for instance, is in blank verse. When a play is in verse, some attention should be paid to meter—how it is used and to what end. The questions to ask of the verse of a play in verse are: what kind of rhythm does the meter produce point by point and overall, and how do a play's rhythms affect its meaning? The rhythms of *Hamlet,* for example, are frequently nervous and tense, as is the following exchange between Bernardo and Francisco that opens the play:

> BER. Who's there?
> FRAN. Nay, answer me. Stand and unfold yourself.
> BER. Long live the king!
> FRAN. Bernardo?
> BER. He.

Created by a fragmentation of the blank verse line, the nervous tension in the rhythm here and elsewhere suggests, in the words of Marcellus, that "Something is rotten in the state of Denmark" (Act I, Scene 4).

Production Elements

So much for the elements that plays share with the other literary genres. Now let us move to what I have called the "production elements," that is, to those elements that are unique to drama, elements that come into being when plays are produced and performed on a stage (or a screen) before an audience.

All the production elements of drama derive from the presence of actors and sets. When "tone of voice" is spoken of in connection with a performance, for instance, what is referred to is literal, the actual tones of voice in which actors speak lines. To the extent that tone is meaning, the meaning of lines as spoken, therefore—or at least the actors' interpretation of their meaning—is conveyed directly, which is true of no other genre. Sets, costumes, and props of whatever sort (masks, for instance) also convey meaning directly. For example, the masks worn in Greek drama tell us immediately about the inner states of the characters; and a good set brings a setting to life, locating the time and place of a play concretely and thus vividly. Sets can also help to create one or another mood, depending on the set. As anyone who has seen more than one production of the same play will attest, different sets can create very different moods and so convey quite different interpretations of the play.

Movement and gesture are also elements unique to drama, elements that are interpretative on the part of actors and that help them communicate to an audience visually, as we communicate to each other all the time. Equally unique to the theater, along with other visual media (television and the movies), is what is called the **stage symbol**—a symbol of whatever sort that comes into existence primarily in performance. Take Laurence Olivier's film version of *Hamlet,* in which there are many shots of towers and tunnels. Glancingly, these visual images come to be Freudian symbols that tie in with Olivier's interpretation of the play as concerning Hamlet's Oedipus complex. Repeated at significant moments, a sound or sounds can also be symbolic, and so can light, as I suggested when speaking of the use of lighting in *The Glass Menagerie,* in which light is used to create an atmosphere of memory as well as to indicate symbolically the moods and changes in mood of the play's characters. Nonrealistic plays, incidentally, are often rich in stage symbols; but they are to be found as well in all other types of play.

Theme

All of these last elements are unique to performance, though you should try to imagine them as you read a play. But whatever the elements a given play is constructed from, all serve exactly the same end as those of fiction or poetry: the exploration and communication of a theme or interlocking themes. The same ultimate questions, then, should be asked of plays as of stories and poems: What is the meaning of the work as a whole? What does it say through its combination of specific elements? What are we left to ponder? What ideas about life does it dramatize? The one difference between the stories and poems we have studied and the full-length play is that the latter (like the novel) is much longer and so can accommodate more than a single theme. In reading a full-length play, therefore, be aware that it probably has several interlocking themes, with perhaps one dominant theme from which the others derive. In Ibsen's *A Doll's House,* for instance, there are at least four related themes explored concurrently: one entailing marriage; another, sexism; a third, social convention; and the fourth—the master theme—the right of the individual to become as much as he or she can be. I call the fourth the "master theme" because it is what ties the others together, for each has something to do with the question of human rights. In sum, to understand *A Doll's House* or any other play (or story or peom), you must come to grips with what its elements serve to embody—its theme(s), or what it has to say about its subject matter.

READING PLAYS

Ideally, plays should be seen in performance. But plays are also written texts, and reading a play offers certain advantages over seeing it. One advantage has to do with what we were just considering, that is, theme: because a reader can take the time to mull over each element of a play as it presents itself and stop to turn back when necessary to check on details and check out ideas, the reader can come to a fuller understanding of the play's theme(s) than can someone who has seen it one time through. Then, too, a play as performed is a collective interpretation on the parts of the director, actors, set designer, and so forth. When a play is read, there is no such mediation. You, the reader, are director, actors, designer all in one, left to interpret the play according to your own lights. For the active reader, this is a great plus.

But reading a play is not quite the same as reading a story or a poem. Remember, a play is written to be performed. Therefore, the reader *must* become director, actors, and designer. That is, approach the reading of a play with performance in mind. Envision at every turn the physical action suggested by the dialogue and stage directions. Imagine sets, lighting, and costumes as you construct in your mind's eye a stage for the play to be performed on. Of course, you should also pay as close attention to matters of diction and tone as you would when reading a poem so as to catch any hints as to the tone of voice of a given passage. And pay as much attention to plot and characterization as you would when reading a story as you work your way to an articulation of the theme or themes of the play at hand.

You should be prepared, too, to open yourself to conventions you may not be familiar with, to determine their function, and to read accordingly. For instance, the chorus in Greek tragedy, the soliloquy in Shakespeare, and the missing wall in Ibsen are all stage conventions that need to be viewed in light of their functions. If you are reading a play by Sophocles, you need to understand that the chorus stands for the common people and, by convention, gives them voice; if Shakespeare is at hand, then you need to know that the soliloquy was not intended to be taken realistically but is a convention that allows characters to express their thoughts and feelings; and if Ibsen is in question, you must grasp that the invisible wall—a convention we still accept readily—allows for the illusion of reality that realistic plays seek to create. You could also acquaint yourself with the kind of stage a given play was written for: *Oedipus Rex,* for instance, was originally performed in an open-air arena with no sets; *Hamlet* was also performed in an open-air theater, but one with a stage that thrust out into the audience and a semblance of a set; *A Doll's House* was written for a theater that we still know today—an indoor theater with a proscenium arch separating actors and audience and with full realistic sets. Part of imagining each of these plays is imagining it on a stage appropriate to it. Finally, try to determine at the outset what expectations are appropriate to a given play. If a play is realistic, say, bring one set of expectations to it: for instance, expect characters to behave like people you know, and if they don't, then question why not. If a play is nonrealistic, however, then you should bring to it an entirely different set of expectations: when you are not asked to accept the characters as "real," don't expect them to be or judge them on the basis of realism.

Now let's turn our attention to the thing itself, that is, to a play—and one of much dramatic interest. As you read the one-act play that follows, try consciously to apply the various things we have considered about reading plays. Because this play is realistic, bring to it the expectations appropriate to realism.

TRIFLES

──────────────── ✳ SUSAN GLASPELL ✳ ────────────────

CHARACTERS

GEORGE HENDERSON, *County Attorney*
HENRY PETERS, *Sheriff*
LEWIS HALE, *A Neighboring Farmer*
MRS. PETERS
MRS. HALE

SCENE: *The kitchen in the now abandoned farmhouse of* JOHN WRIGHT, *a gloomy kitchen, and left without having been put in order—unwashed pans under the sink, a loaf of bread outside the bread-box, a dish-towel on the table—other signs of incompleted work. At the rear the outer door opens and the* SHERIFF *comes in followed by the* COUNTY ATTORNEY *and* HALE. *The* SHERIFF *and* HALE *are men in middle life, the* COUNTY ATTORNEY *is a young man; all are much bundled up and go at once to the stove. They are followed by the two women—the* SHERIFF'S WIFE *first; she is a slight wiry woman, a thin nervous face.* MRS. HALE *is larger and would ordinarily be called more comfortable looking, but she is disturbed now and looks fearfully about as she enters. The women have come in slowly, and stand close together near the door.*

COUNTY ATTORNEY. [*Rubbing his hands.*] This feels good. Come up to the fire, ladies.

MRS. PETERS. [*After taking a step forward.*] I'm not—cold.

SHERIFF. [*Unbuttoning his overcoat and stepping away from the stove as if to mark the beginning of official business.*] Now, Mr. Hale, before we move things about, you explain to Mr. Henderson just what you saw when you came here yesterday morning.

COUNTY ATTORNEY. By the way, has anything been moved? Are things just as you left them yesterday?

SHERIFF. [*Looking about.*] It's just the same. When it dropped below zero last night I thought I'd better send Frank out this morning to make a fire for us—no use getting pneumonia with a big case on, but I told him not to touch anything except the stove—and you know Frank.

COUNTY ATTORNEY. Somebody should have been left here yesterday.

SHERIFF. Oh—yesterday. When I had to send Frank to Morris Center for that man who went crazy—I want you to know I had my hands full yesterday. I knew you could get back from Omaha by today and as long as I went over everything here myself—

COUNTY ATTORNEY. Well, Mr. Hale, tell just what happened when you came here yesterday morning.

HALE. Harry and I had started to town with a load of potatoes. We came along the road from my place and as I got here I said, "I'm going to see if I can't get John Wright to go in with me on a party telephone." I spoke to Wright about it once before and he put me off, saying folks talked too much anyway, and all he asked was peace and quiet—I guess you know about how much he talked himself; but I thought maybe if I went to the house and talked about it before his wife, though I said to Harry that I didn't know as what his wife wanted made much difference to John—

COUNTY ATTORNEY. Let's talk about that later, Mr. Hale. I do want to talk about that, but tell now just what happened when you got to the house.

HALE. I didn't hear or see anything; I knocked at the door, and still it was all quiet inside. I knew they must be up, it was past eight o'clock. So I knocked again, and I thought I heard somebody say, "Come in." I wasn't sure, I'm not sure yet, but I opened the door—this door [*indicating the door by which the two women are still standing*] and there in that rocker—[*pointing to it*] sat Mrs. Wright.

[*They all look at the rocker.*]

COUNTY ATTORNEY. What—was she doing?

HALE. She was rockin' back and forth. She had her apron in her hand and was kind of—pleating it.

COUNTY ATTORNEY. And how did she—look?

HALE. Well, she looked queer.

COUNTY ATTORNEY. How do you mean—queer?

HALE. Well, as if she didn't know what she was going to do next. And kind of done up.

COUNTY ATTORNEY. How did she seem to feel about your coming?

HALE. Why, I don't think she minded—one way or other. She didn't pay much attention. I said, "How do, Mrs. Wright, it's cold, ain't it?" And she said, "Is it?"—and went on kind of pleating at her apron. Well, I was surprised; she didn't ask me to come up to the stove, or to set down, but just sat there, not even looking at me, so I said, "I want to see John." And then she—laughed. I guess you would call it a laugh. I thought of Harry and the team outside, so I said a little sharp: "Can't I see John?" "No," she says, kind o' dull like. "Ain't he home?" says I. "Yes," says she, "he's home." "Then why can't I see him?" I asked her, out of patience. " 'Cause he's dead," says she. *"Dead?"* says I. She just nodded her head, not getting a bit excited, but rockin' back and forth. "Why—where is he?" says I, not knowing what to say. She just pointed upstairs—like that [*himself pointing to the room above*]. I got up, with the idea of going up there. I walked from there to here— then I says, "Why, what did he die of?" "He died of a rope round his neck," says she, and just went on pleatin' at her apron. Well, I went out and called Harry. I thought I might—need help. We went upstairs and there he was lyin'—

COUNTY ATTORNEY. I think I'd rather have you go into that upstairs, where you can point it all out. Just go on now with the rest of the story.

HALE. Well, my first thought was to get that rope off. It looked . . . [*Stops, his face twitches*] . . . but Harry, he went up to him, and he said, "No, he's dead all right, and we'd better not touch anything." So we went back downstairs. She was still sitting that same way. "Has anybody been notified?" I asked. "No," says she, uncon-cerned. "Who did this, Mrs. Wright?" said Harry. He said it businesslike—and she stopped pleatin' of her apron. "I don't know," she says. "You don't *know?*" says Harry. "No," says she. "Weren't you sleepin' in the bed with him?" says Harry. "Yes," says she, "but I was on the inside." "Somebody slipped a rope round his neck and strangled him and you didn't wake up?" says Harry. "I didn't wake up," she said after him. We must 'a looked as if we didn't see how that could be, for after a minute she said, "I sleep sound." Harry was going to ask her more questions but I said maybe we ought to let her tell her story first to the coroner, or the sheriff, so Harry went fast as he could to Rivers' place, where there's a telephone.

COUNTY ATTORNEY. And what did Mrs. Wright do when she knew that you had gone for the coroner?

HALE. She moved from that chair to this one over here [*pointing to a small chair in the corner*] and just sat there with her hands held together and looking down. I got a feeling that I ought to make some conversation, so I said I had come in to see if John wanted to put in a telephone, and at that she started to laugh, and then she stopped and looked at me—scared. [*The* COUNTY ATTORNEY, *who has had his notebook out, makes a note.*] I dunno, maybe, it wasn't scared. I wouldn't like to say it was. Soon Harry got back, and then Dr. Lloyd came, and you, Mr. Peters, and so I guess that's all I know that you don't.

COUNTY ATTORNEY. [*Looking around.*] I guess we'll go upstairs first—and then out to the barn and around there. [*To the* SHERIFF.] You're convinced that there was nothing important here—nothing that would point to any motive.

SHERIFF. Nothing here but kitchen things.

[*The* COUNTY ATTORNEY, *after again looking around the kitchen, opens the door of a cupboard closet. He gets up on a chair and looks on a shelf. Pulls his hand away, sticky.*]

COUNTY ATTORNEY. Here's a nice mess.

[*The women draw nearer.*]

MRS. PETERS. [*To the other woman.*] Oh, her fruit; it did freeze. [*To the* LAWYER.] She worried about that when it turned so cold. She said the fire'd go out and her jars would break.

SHERIFF. Well, can you beat the women! Held for murder and worryin' about her preserves.

COUNTY ATTORNEY. I guess before we're through she may have something more serious than preserves to worry about.

HALE. Well, women are used to worrying over trifles.

[*The two women move a little closer together.*]

COUNTY ATTORNEY. [*With the gallantry of a young politician.*] And yet, for all their worries, what would we do without the ladies? [*The women do not unbend. He goes to the sink, takes a dipperful of water from the pail and pouring it into a basin, washes his hands. Starts to wipe them on the roller-towel, turns it for a cleaner place.*] Dirty towels! [*Kicks his foot against the pans under the sink.*] Not much of a housekeeper, would you say, ladies?

MRS. HALE. [*Stiffly.*] There's a great deal of work to be done on a farm.

COUNTY ATTORNEY. To be sure. And yet [*with a little bow to her*] I know there are some Dickson county farmhouses which do not have such roller towels.

[*He gives it a pull to expose its full length again.*]

MRS. HALE. Those towels get dirty awful quick. Men's hands aren't always as clean as they might be.

COUNTY ATTORNEY. Ah, loyal to your sex, I see. But you and Mrs. Wright were neighbors. I suppose you were friends, too.

MRS. HALE. [*Shaking her head.*] I've not seen much of her of late years. I've not been in this house—it's more than a year.

COUNTY ATTORNEY. And why was that? You didn't like her?

MRS. HALE. I liked her all well enough. Farmers' wives have their hands full, Mr. Henderson. And then—

COUNTY ATTORNEY. Yes—?

MRS. HALE. [*Looking about.*] It never seemed a very cheerful place.

COUNTY ATTORNEY. No—it's not cheerful. I shouldn't say she had the homemaking instinct.

MRS. HALE. Well, I don't know as Wright had, either.

COUNTY ATTORNEY. You mean that they didn't get on very well?

MRS. HALE. No, I don't mean anything. But I don't think a place'd be any cheerfuller for John Wright's being in it.

COUNTY ATTORNEY. I'd like to talk more of that a little later. I want to get the lay of things upstairs now.

[*He goes to the left, where three steps lead to a stair door.*]

SHERIFF. I suppose anything Mrs. Peters does'll be all right. She was to take in some clothes for her, you know, and a few little things. We left in such a hurry yesterday.

COUNTY ATTORNEY. Yes, but I would like to see what you take, Mrs. Peters, and keep an eye out for anything that might be of use to us.

MRS. PETERS. Yes, Mr. Henderson.

[*The women listen to the men's steps on the stairs, then look about the kitchen.*]

MRS. HALE. I'd hate to have men coming into my kitchen, snooping around and criticizing.

[*She arranges the pans under sink which the* LAWYER *had shoved out of place.*]

MRS. PETERS. Of course it's no more than their duty.

MRS. HALE. Duty's all right, but I guess that deputy sheriff that came out to make the fire might have got a little of this on. [*Gives the roller towel a pull.*] Wish I'd thought of that sooner. Seems mean to talk about her for not having things slicked up when she had to come away in such a hurry.

MRS. PETERS. [*Who has gone to a small table in the left rear corner of the room, and lifted one end of a towel that covers a pan.*] She had bread set.

[*Stands still.*]

MRS. HALE. [*Eyes fixed on a loaf of bread beside the breadbox, which is on a low shelf at the other side of the room. Moves slowly toward it.*] She was going to put this in there. [*Picks up loaf, then abruptly drops it. In a manner of returning to familiar things.*] It's a shame about her fruit. I wonder if it's all gone. [*Gets up on the chair and looks.*] I think there's some here that's all right, Mrs. Peters. Yes— here; [*Holding it toward the window*] this is cherries, too. [*Looking again.*] I declare I believe that's the only one. [*Gets down, bottle in her hand. Goes to the sink and wipes it off on the outside.*] She'll feel awful bad after all her hard work in the hot weather. I remember the afternoon I put up my cherries last summer.

[*She puts the bottle on the big kitchen table, center of the room. With a sigh, is about to sit down in the rocking-chair. Before she is seated realizes what chair it is; with a slow look at it, steps back. The chair which she has touched rocks back and forth.*]

MRS. PETERS. Well, I must get those things from the front room closet. [*She goes to the door at the right, but after looking into the other room, steps back.*] You coming with me, Mrs. Hale? You could help me carry them.

[*They go in the other room; reappear,* MRS. PETERS *carrying a dress and skirt,* MRS. HALE *following with a pair of shoes.*]

MRS. PETERS. My, it's cold in there.

[*She puts the clothes on the big table and hurries to the stove.*]

MRS. HALE. [*Examining the skirt.*] Wright was close. I think maybe that's why she kept so much to herself. She didn't even belong to the Ladies Aid. I suppose she felt she couldn't do her part, and then you don't enjoy things when you feel shabby. She used to wear pretty clothes and be lively, when she was Minnie Foster, one of the town girls singing in the choir. But that—oh, that was thirty years ago. This all you was to take in?

MRS. PETERS. She said she wanted an apron. Funny thing to want, for there isn't much to get you dirty in jail, goodness knows. But I suppose just to make her feel more natural. She said they was in the top drawer in this cupboard. Yes, here. And then her little shawl that always hung behind the door. [*Opens stair door and looks.*] Yes, here it is.

[*Quickly shuts door leading upstairs.*]

MRS. HALE. [*Abruptly moving toward her.*] Mrs. Peters?

MRS. PETERS. Yes, Mrs. Hale?

MRS. HALE. Do you think she did it?

MRS. PETERS. [*In a frightened voice.*] Oh, I don't know.

MRS. HALE. Well, I don't think she did. Asking for an apron and her little shawl. Worrying about her fruit.

MRS. PETERS. [*Starts to speak, glances up, where footsteps are heard in the room above. In a low voice.*] Mr. Peters says it looks bad for her. Mr. Henderson is awful sarcastic in a speech and he'll make fun of her sayin' she didn't wake up.

MRS. HALE. Well, I guess John Wright didn't wake when they was slipping that rope under his neck.

MRS. PETERS. No, it's strange. It must have been done awful crafty and still. They say it was such a—funny way to kill a man, rigging it all up like that.

MRS. HALE. That's just what Mr. Hale said. There was a gun in the house. He says that's what he can't understand.

MRS. PETERS. Mr. Henderson said coming out that what was needed for the case was a motive; something to show anger, or—sudden feeling.

MRS. HALE. [*Who is standing by the table.*] Well, I don't see any signs of anger around here. [*She puts her hand on the dish towel which lies on the table, stands looking down at table, one half of which is clean, the other half messy.*] It's wiped to here. [*Makes a move as if to finish work, then turns and looks at loaf of bread outside the breadbox. Drops towel. In that voice of coming back to familiar things.*] Wonder how they are finding things upstairs. I hope she had it a little more red-up up there. You know, it seems kind of *sneaking*. Locking her up in town and then coming out here and trying to get her own house to turn against her!

MRS. PETERS. But Mrs. Hale, the law is the law.

MRS. HALE. I s'pose 'tis. [*Unbuttoning her coat.*] Better loosen up your things, Mrs. Peters. You won't feel them when you go out.

[MRS. PETERS *takes off her fur tippet, goes to hang it on hook at back of room, stands looking at the under part of the small corner table.*]

MRS. PETERS. She was piecing a quilt.

[*She brings the large sewing basket and they look at the bright pieces.*]

MRS. HALE. It's log cabin pattern. Pretty, isn't it? I wonder if she was goin' to quilt it or just knot it?

[*Footsteps have been heard coming down the stairs. The* SHERIFF *enters followed by* HALE *and the* COUNTY ATTORNEY.]

SHERIFF. They wonder if she was going to quilt it or just knot it!

[*The men laugh, the women look abashed.*]

COUNTY ATTORNEY. [*Rubbing his hands over the stove.*] Frank's fire didn't do much up there, did it? Well, let's go out to the barn and get that cleared up.

[*The men go outside.*]

MRS. HALE. [*Resentfully.*] I don't know as there's anything so strange, our takin' up our time with little things while we're waiting for them to get the evidence. [*She sits down at the big table smoothing out a block with decision.*] I don't see as it's anything to laugh about.

MRS. PETERS. [*Apologetically.*] Of course they've got awful important things on their minds.

[*Pulls up a chair and joins* MRS. HALE *at the table.*]

MRS. HALE. [*Examining another block.*] Mrs. Peters, look at this one. Here, this is the one she was working on, and look at the sewing! All the rest of it has been so nice and even. And look at this! It's all over the place! Why, it looks as if she didn't know what she was about!

[*After she has said this they look at each other, then start to glance back at the door. After an instant* MRS. HALE *has pulled at a knot and ripped the sewing.*]

MRS. PETERS. Oh, what are you doing, Mrs. Hale?

MRS. HALE. [*Mildly.*] Just pulling out a stitch or two that's not sewed very good. [*Threading a needle.*] Bad sewing always made me fidgety.

MRS. PETERS. [*Nervously.*] I don't think we ought to touch things.

MRS. HALE. I'll just finish up this end. [*Suddenly stopping and leaning forward.*] Mrs. Peters?

MRS. PETERS. Yes, Mrs. Hale?

MRS. HALE. What do you suppose she was so nervous about?

MRS. PETERS. Oh—I don't know. I don't know as she was nervous. I sometimes sew awful queer when I'm just tired. [MRS. HALE *starts to say something, looks at* MRS. PETERS, *then goes on sewing.*] Well I must get these things wrapped up. They may be through sooner than we think. [*Putting apron and other things together.*] I wonder where I can find a piece of paper, and string.

MRS. HALE. In that cupboard, maybe.

MRS. PETERS. [*Looking in cupboard.*] Why, here's a bird-cage. [*Holds it up.*] Did she have a bird, Mrs. Hale?

MRS. HALE. Why, I don't know whether she did or not—I've not been here for so long. There was a man around last year selling canaries cheap, but I don't know as she took one; maybe she did. She used to sing real pretty herself.

MRS. PETERS. [*Glancing around.*] Seems funny to think of a bird here. But she must have had one, or why would she have a cage? I wonder what happened to it.

MRS. HALE. I s'pose maybe the cat got it.

MRS. PETERS. No, she didn't have a cat. She's got that feeling some people have about cats—being afraid of them. My cat got in her room and she was real upset and asked me to take it out.

MRS. HALE. My sister Bessie was like that. Queer, ain't it?

MRS. PETERS. [*Examining the cage.*] Why, look at this door. It's broke. One hinge is pulled apart.

MRS. HALE. [*Looking too.*] Looks as if someone must have been rough with it.

MRS. PETERS. Why, yes.

[*She brings the cage forward and puts it on the table.*]

MRS. HALE. I wish if they're going to find any evidence they'd be about it. I don't like this place.

MRS. PETERS. But I'm awful glad you came with me, Mrs. Hale. It would be lonesome for me sitting here alone.

MRS. HALE. It would, wouldn't it? [*Dropping her sewing.*] But I tell you what I do wish, Mrs. Peters. I wish I had come over sometimes when *she* was here. I— [*looking around the room*]—wish I had.

MRS. PETERS. But of course you were awful busy, Mrs. Hale—your house and your children.

MRS. HALE. I could've come. I stayed away because it weren't cheerful—and that's why I ought to have come. I—I've never liked this place. Maybe because it's down in a hollow and you don't see the road. I dunno what it is, but it's a lonesome place and always was. I wish I had come over to see Minnie Foster sometimes. I can see now—

[*Shakes her head.*]

MRS. PETERS. Well, you mustn't reproach yourself, Mrs. Hale. Somehow we just don't see how it is with other folks until—something comes up.

MRS. HALE. Not having children makes less work—but it makes a quiet house, and Wright out to work all day, and no company when he did come in. Did you know John Wright, Mrs. Peters?

MRS. PETERS. Not to know him; I've seen him in town. They say he was a good man.

MRS. HALE. Yes—good; he didn't drink, and kept his word as well as most, I guess, and paid his debts. But he was a hard man, Mrs. Peters. Just to pass the time of day with him—[*Shivers.*] Like a raw wind that gets to the bone. [*Pauses, her eye falling on the cage.*] I should think she would 'a wanted a bird. But what do you suppose went with it?

MRS. PETERS. I don't know, unless it got sick and died.

[*She reaches over and swings the broken door, swings it again, both women watch it.*]

MRS. HALE. You weren't raised round here, were you? [*Mrs. Peters shakes her head.*] You didn't know—her?

MRS. PETERS. Not till they brought her yesterday.

MRS. HALE. She—come to think of it, she was kind of like a bird herself—real sweet and pretty, but kind of timid and—fluttery. How—she—did—change. [*Silence; then as if struck by a happy thought and relieved to get back to everyday things.*] Tell you what, Mrs. Peters, why don't you take the quilt in with you? It might take up her mind.

MRS. PETERS. Why, I think that's a real nice idea, Mrs. Hale. There couldn't possibly be any objection to it, could there? Now, just what would I take? I wonder if her patches are in here—and her things.

[*They look in the sewing basket.*]

MRS. HALE. Here's some red. I expect this has got sewing things in it. [*Brings out a fancy box.*] What a pretty box. Looks like something somebody would give you. Maybe her scissors are in here. [*Opens box. Suddenly puts her hand to her nose.*] Why—[MRS. PETERS *bends nearer, then turns her face away.*] There's something wrapped up in this piece of silk.

MRS. PETERS. Why, this isn't her scissors.

MRS. HALE. [*Lifting the silk.*] Oh, Mrs. Peters—it's—

[MRS. PETERS *bends closer.*]

MRS. PETERS. It's the bird.

MRS. HALE. [*Jumping up.*] But, Mrs. Peters—look at it! Its neck! Look at its neck! It's all—other side *to.*

MRS. PETERS. Somebody—wrung—its—neck.

[*Their eyes meet. A look of growing comprehension, of horror. Steps are heard outside.* MRS. HALE *slips box under quilt pieces, and sinks into her chair. Enter* SHERIFF *and* COUNTY ATTORNEY. MRS. PETERS *rises.*]

COUNTY ATTORNEY. [*As one turning from serious things to little pleasantries.*] Well, ladies, have you decided whether she was going to quilt it or knot it?

MRS. PETERS. We think she was going to—knot it.

COUNTY ATTORNEY. Well, that's interesting, I'm sure. [*Seeing the bird-cage.*] Has the bird flown?

MRS. HALE. [*Putting more quilt pieces over the box.*] We think the—cat got it.

COUNTY ATTORNEY. [*Preoccupied.*] Is there a cat?

[MRS. HALE *glances in a quick covert way at* MRS. PETERS.]

MRS. PETERS. Well, not *now.* They're superstitious, you know. They leave.

COUNTY ATTORNEY. [*To* SHERIFF PETERS, *continuing an interrupted conversation.*] No sign at all of anyone having come from the outside. Their own rope. Now let's go up again and go over it piece by piece. [*They start upstairs.*] It would have to have been someone who knew just the—

[MRS. PETERS *sits down. The two women sit there not looking at one another, but as if peering into something and at the same time holding back. When they talk now it is in the manner of feeling their way over strange ground, as if afraid of what they are saying, but as if they cannot help saying it.*]

MRS. HALE. She liked the bird. She was going to bury it in that pretty box.

MRS. PETERS. [*In a whisper.*] When I was a girl—my kitten—there was a boy took a hatchet, and before my eyes—and before I could get there—[*Covers her face an instant.*] If they hadn't held me back I would have—[*Catches herself, looks upstairs where steps are heard, falters weakly*]—hurt him.

MRS. HALE. [*With a slow look around her.*] I wonder how it would seem never to have had any children around. [*Pause.*] No, Wright wouldn't like the bird—a thing that sang. She used to sing. He killed that, too.

MRS. PETERS. [*Moving uneasily.*] We don't know who killed the bird.

MRS. HALE. I knew John Wright.

MRS. PETERS. It was an awful thing was done in this house that night, Mrs. Hale. Killing a man while he slept, slipping a rope around his neck that choked the life out of him.

MRS. HALE. His neck. Choked the life out of him.

[*Her hand goes out and rests on the bird-cage.*]

MRS. PETERS. [*With rising voice.*] We don't know who killed him. We don't *know.*

MRS. HALE. [*Her own feeling not interrupted.*] If there'd been years and years of nothing, then a bird to sing to you, it would be awful—still, after the bird was still.

MRS. PETERS. [*Something within her speaking.*] I know what stillness is. When we homesteaded in Dakota, and my first baby died—after he was two years old, and me with no other then—

MRS. HALE. [*Moving.*] How soon do you suppose they'll be through, looking for the evidence?

MRS. PETERS. I know what stillness is. [*Pulling herself back.*] The law has got to punish crime, Mrs. Hale.

MRS. HALE. [*Not as if answering that.*] I wish you'd seen Minnie Foster when she wore a white dress with blue ribbons and stood up there in the choir and sang. [*A look around the room.*] Oh, I *wish* I'd come over here once in a while! That was a crime! That was a crime! Who's going to punish that?

MRS. PETERS. [*Looking upstairs.*] We mustn't—take on.

MRS. HALE. I might have known she needed help! I know how things can be—for women. I tell you, it's queer, Mrs. Peters. We live close together and we live far apart. We all go through the same things—it's all just a different kind of the same thing. [*Brushes her eyes, noticing the bottle of fruit, reaches out for it.*] If I was you I wouldn't tell her her fruit was gone. Tell her it *ain't.* Tell her it's all right. Take this in to prove it to her. She—she may never know whether it was broke or not.

MRS. PETERS. [*Takes the bottle, looks about for something to wrap it in; takes petticoat from the clothes brought from the other room, very nervously begins winding this around the bottle. In a false voice.*] My, it's a good thing the men couldn't hear us. Wouldn't they just laugh! Getting all stirred up over a little thing like a—dead canary. As if that could have anything to do with—with—wouldn't they *laugh!*

[*The men are heard coming down stairs.*]

MRS. HALE. [*Under her breath.*] Maybe they would—maybe they wouldn't.

COUNTY ATTORNEY. No, Peters, it's all perfectly clear except a reason for doing it. But you know juries when it comes to women. If there was some definite thing. Something to show—something to make a story about—a thing that would connect up with this strange way of doing it—

[*The women's eyes meet for an instant. Enter HALE from outer door.*]

HALE. Well, I've got the team around. Pretty cold out there.

COUNTY ATTORNEY. I'm going to stay here a while by myself. [*To the SHERIFF.*] You can send Frank out for me, can't you? I want to go over everything. I'm not satisfied that we can't do better.

SHERIFF. Do you want to see what Mrs. Peters is going to take in?

[*The LAWYER goes to the table, picks up the apron, laughs.*]

COUNTY ATTORNEY. Oh, I guess they're not very dangerous things the ladies have picked out. [*Moves a few things about, disturbing the quilt pieces which cover the box. Steps back.*] No, Mrs. Peters doesn't need supervising. For that matter, a sheriff's wife is married to the law. Ever think of it that way, Mrs. Peters?

MRS. PETERS. Not—just that way.

SHERIFF. [*Chuckling.*] Married to the law. [*Moves toward the other room.*] I just want you to come in here a minute, George. We ought to take a look at these windows.

COUNTY ATTORNEY. [*Scoffingly.*] Oh, windows!

SHERIFF. We'll be right out, Mr. Hale.

[Hale *goes outside. The* SHERIFF *follows the* COUNTY ATTORNEY *into the other room. Then* MRS. HALE *rises, hands tight together, looking intensely at* MRS. PETERS, *whose eyes make a slow turn, finally meeting* MRS. HALE'S. *A moment* MRS. HALE *holds her, then her own eyes point the way to where the box is concealed. Suddenly* MRS. PETERS *throws back quilt pieces and tries to put the box in the bag she is wearing. It is too big. She opens box, starts to take bird out, cannot touch it, goes to pieces, stands there helpless. Sound of a knob turning in the other room.* MRS. HALE *snatches the box and puts it in the pocket of her big coat. Enter* COUNTY ATTORNEY *and* SHERIFF.]

COUNTY ATTORNEY. [*Facetiously.*] Well, Henry, at least we found out that she was not going to quilt it. She was going to—what is it you call it, ladies?

MRS. HALE. [*Her hand against her pocket.*] We call it—knot it, Mr. Henderson.

(*CURTAIN*)

[1916—U.S.A.]

Shortly after "Trifles" was first staged, Glaspell recast it into a short story entitled "A Jury of Her Peers." Though "Trifles" is a fine title, ironic and symbolic at once, the alternative title helps clarify the unexpressed judgment that Mrs. Peters and Mrs. Hale make as to the guilt or innocence of Mrs. Wright. Oh, they know that she murdered her husband, at least they do by the time they make their judgment. The question is why she did so. Their conclusion is self-defense; therefore, they suppress the evidence.

Now, what leads the two women to this conclusion? Of the common elements we have discussed (those that plays share with other genres), the main element here is characterization; the set is the main production element. The set serves primarily to establish mood. Mrs. Wright's kitchen is "gloomy," we are told, and its visual gloom, which we must imagine as we read, communicates something central about the the Wrights—that their lives were steeped in gloom. Also, note, in the world of this play the kitchen is the female room, the one room in the house in which females rule. That fact is of symbolic importance as the play builds to its climax. As to characterization, what is most fascinating about "Trifles" is that the characters we come to know best, or who are most fully characterized, never appear on stage. We learn little, really, about the characters we see: the two women are basically flat characters and the men border on the stock. But we learn a good deal about Mr. and Mrs. Wright, in part by way of contrast. We learn that she was like a bird herself before she was married, beautiful and full of joy; everything said about Mr. Wright, on the other hand, goes to convince us that he was a joyless man who had little to say to or share with his fellow creatures. And, spreading gloom by his mere presence, he slowly, year by year, crushed the vitality of his wife. The characterization, note, is accomplished entirely by the statements and responses of other characters. Such is frequently the case in plays, most of which, as I have pointed out, do not have narrators to fill us in.

So, the two women are led to their conclusion by what they come to understand about the lives of the Wrights. That understanding is sharpened and made evident by the discovery of the broken bird cage and the dead bird. Both function literally, to exemplify Mr. Wright's abrasiveness and cruelty, and also symbolically, suggesting that Minnie Foster was imprisoned by her marriage and that her spirit was crushed by her husband no less than the canary was crushed to death by his hand. The bird cage and the dead bird—both stage symbols—represent Minnie's life with this unnatural man who was capable only of negation and destruction.

But was he indeed unnatural, aberrant, an isolated case, or, with respect to his treatment of his wife, was he perhaps typical—albeit extreme—of men in his culture? Through what we come to construe of its action in the past, to be sure, the play depicts but a single marriage and a single instance of male abuse. However, it suggests through its situation in the present—which is central to the meaning of the play—that it's a man's world and that the position of women in this world is intolerable. Here we have arrived at the play's theme: what "Trifles" explores in both past (via the relationship of Minnie and her husband) and present (via the attitudes expressed by the men about the women) is the subjugation of women in a male-oriented society. Clearly, the males in the play treat the females (the wives of two of the males) miserably. Witness the jokes the males feel free to make in their condescension and derision. In a world in which such gratuitous belittling of women is not only tolerated but the rule, it is no wonder that Mrs. Hale and Mrs. Peters are guarded and mistrustful even alone with each other. But, with a true act of courage, each overcomes her mistrust and fear of the other as the play takes a marvelously ironic turn. With their kitchen interests and their sewing, they are seen by the men as being of no possible help when it comes to man's work—here, the solving of the murder. The irony is that it is the women, by their attention to the very trifles scorned by the men ("women are used to worrying over trifles," says Mr. Hale), who solve the murder. This fine irony is instrumental in establishing the play's closing mood—a quiet sense of triumph. For the men have found no evidence and fear the case will be lost; the women have not only found the evidence but, rational as well as intuitive, have drawn conclusions from it that lead them to keep it from the men. The women, including Mrs. Wright, win the day.

Most of what I say here I say with regard to the play as text. After all, *we* are dealing with a text and not a production. Still, in speaking of the set as well as of the bird cage and dead bird, I also consider those production elements that are particularly important to the play, elements that call for a kind of sleight of mind to be realized from the text alone. But it is possible, by focusing intensely on the play, to imagine its set in all its gloom and feel both the pathos and symbolic import of the cage and dead canary by envisioning them in the mind's eye. Reading a play as fully as possible requires this special act of the imagination. As you read any of the plays gathered hereafter, it is essential that you bring your imagination to bear in this way and through it create from the text a living play.

WRITING ON PLAYS

What I have written about "Trifles" should give you a good idea as to what writing about plays entails: in sum, it entails a consideration of the elements of a play and how each contributes to the play's meaning, its theme. So I consider characterization in "Trifles," its set, and the functions of each; its moods, how they are established (by the set at the beginning and irony at the end) and what they reveal; its stage symbols of broken cage and dead canary, and their meanings; and, finally, its theme, which embraces everything in the play, both past and present. To be sure, I cover a good deal of ground in just a few paragraphs, for my intent was simply to give a quick synopsis of the elements of the play and their meaning. As a rule, however, only one or maybe two elements should be taken and examined in detail, with emphasis placed on their relationship to theme; or you could focus on the theme itself, bringing to bear anything in the play you are writing on that supports your interpretation of its meaning. But this is no different from writing on stories or poems. Everything said about writing in connection with fiction and poetry, therefore, is pertinent to writing about plays.

Any of what I called earlier the "common elements" could be a rewarding subject for a paper on a given play. The element chosen, of course, must be prominent in the play. For instance, plot would not be a particularly appropriate choice with respect to "Trifles," for in terms of time present the play presents us with a situation rather than a plot. But a fascinating paper could be written on plot in connection with *A Doll's House,* whose plot seems to move with a sense of inevitability to Nora's slamming the door. What makes the plot here a particularly good subject for a paper is that the plot is close to what is perhaps the play's main theme: the stifling nature of social convention and the need on the part of the individual to break out of merely conventional thinking and behavior in order to grow. Everything that happens to Nora moves her step by step to her final action. And we come to understand through what happens how Nora has been kept a child by the social conventions she has internalized—the conventions of marriage, for instance, and of male dominance. Understanding thus, we can take Nora's final action only as a triumph. In other words, the play's plot moves us finally to an attitude about convention and human freedom, the freedom to grow. Its plot, then, helps to communicate the play's dominant theme and to move us to assent to its validity. This would make a fine thesis for a paper on Ibsen's ground-breaking drama.

So would a thesis involving mood in "Trifles," which would lead to a discussion of the function of the play's set and the dramatic irony springing from the word "trifles" and the women's seeing what the men overlook. Even a single word can be topic enough if the word repeats significantly in various contexts. For example, a student of mine wrote a superb paper on the word "ear" in *Hamlet.* If you should read *Hamlet,* you might keep an eye out for the word. It recurs often and in interesting ways. In the paper in question, the student first established the recurrence of the word, then considered several passages in which the word figures prominently, and finally related what he had said to the central fact of the play and the source of one of its main themes (the problem of revenge in a Christian world)—that is, the murder by Hamlet's uncle of the king, Hamlet's father (by way of poison in the *ear*).

Various production elements can serve, too, as a source of topics. Granted, these are more difficult to deal with because they are not exactly in a play, or its text, but are only suggested in stage directions (and often not even that). Yet one can imagine lighting appropriate to *Hamlet,* for instance. Having so imagined, you could write an interesting paper on your conception of the lighting and why it is appropriate (that is, its meaning or symbolic weight). Or take *The Glass Menagerie* again. Here, lighting is specified in detail in the stage directions. A fine paper could result from a consideration of Williams's symbolic use of lighting and its relation to characterization, mood, and the play's thematic core. Or, to take one last example, the set and the props (bird cage and dead canary) in "Trifles" could be taken and examined as stage symbols. Having discussed the symbolic meanings of each, you would then move on to a consideration of how these symbols relate to the play's theme—the subjugation of women.

Whatever you choose to focus on, remember that in one way or another you must show how the meaning of the play you are discussing is shaped and emphasized by your focal element. If, however, you choose to write a paper on the thematic core of the play, be aware of the major difference between short stories and lyric poems on the one hand and full-length plays on the other. By virtue of their length alone, full-length plays generally have a broader scope than is possible in stories or short poems. That is, a play longer than one act will probably have not one theme but several interconnected themes. If this is the case, one thing to do is to state what a play's themes are and then to demonstrate how they are related, or what broader theme emerges from the way in which the secondary themes relate to each other. For instance, there are at least four themes in Ibsen's *A Doll's House,* which I enumerated when addressing the subject of theme two subsections back. But one is the "master theme" (as I called it earlier), uniting all the others. The theme entailing the rights of the individual subsumes the consequently secondary themes concerning marriage, sexism, and social convention. For it is through exploration of these themes that the play as a whole explores the larger theme of human rights. That would be a viable thesis. But it would be just as possible to take a subsidiary theme and follow its development through the play to its climax. One such theme in *Hamlet,* for instance, is the nature of the self, an idea new to the Renaissance. Though subsidiary, this theme, announced by Polonius when he counsels his son "to thine own self be true" (Act I, Scene 3), is certainly compelling and could be fascinating to pursue.

The following paper should concretize what I have been saying more or less in the abstract. This paper—on the symbolism in "Trifles"—demonstrates what writing on a single element of a play calls for as well as how an interpretation of a play overall can be arrived at through close attention to a single element if that element is a prominent means in the play.

Symbolism in "Trifles"

Funnel
beginning

People who are used to reading stories and poems understand the nature of verbal symbols--that is, symbols that are established by repeated verbal reference and interpreted in light of the text as a whole. Such symbols are to be found in plays, too. But drama presents another kind of symbol as well, a kind unique to performance: the "stage symbol," which, though also to be interpreted in light of the context as a whole, is recognized by its

Thesis   strong visual presence. This type of symbol is to be found powerfully in Susan Glaspell's "Trifles."

Transition

Topic
sentence (a)

Support

Topic
sentence (b)

Support

Support

Topic
sentences

The first thing an audience seeing the play is confronted with is its set, a drab, "gloomy" kitchen last occupied by Mr. and Mrs. Wright. One function of this set is to suggest the drabness of the lives of the Wrights due to Mr. Wright's negative, abrasive nature. If it did no more than visually communicate this drabness, the set would be symbolic, carrying meaning over and above the literal. But the set is symbolic in a more subtle way as well. When "Trifles" was written (1916), what was the kitchen? It was the domain of the female, the one room that was hers. The kitchen we see on stage, then, was Mrs. Wright's province (thus the business about the broken bottles of fruit) and, during the course of the play, is that of Mrs. Hale and Mrs. Peters, whose presence dominates the play as it unfolds. The set, thus, represents the world of the female, or is symbolic of the feminine mind or spirit as against the masculine. Now, what is noteworthy about the kitchen in "Trifles" is that the clues to the murder are to be found there and not in the bedroom, which occupies the attention of the men of the play. The irony that the kitchen holds the truth underscores the triumph of the women in their male–dominated world. We might even go so far as to say that the kitchen wins out over the bedroom, which would be to say symbolically that the women prove superior to the men.

Two other stage symbols are prominent

in "Trifles"—the broken bird cage and the dead canary. Together, these props carry two separate symbolic meanings. First, they

Support

are the vital clues to the murder, or its motivation. Seeing the broken cage, we suddenly picture Mr. Wright, in a fit of rage and meanness, breaking the door open, thrusting his hand into the cage, and crushing the canary in his fingers. The dead bird itself is the clinching bit of evidence needed to supply the motive: Mr. Wright pushed his wife too far this time; she had taken a lifetime of misery from him, but this last act, this last negation of her pleasure and joy, was the motive for murder (which was accomplished in an appropriate way, given that Mr. Wright had wrung the bird's neck—strangulation). All of this

Support

Mrs. Hale and Mrs. Peters read aright. They see that the cage and canary are symbols (as clues generally are) telling the story of what motivated the murder they are confronted with.

Transition and topic sentence

Further, the cage and dead canary come to symbolize Mrs. Wright's existence with her life-denying husband, and so supply another aspect of her motivation, or what led her to the point of snapping when the canary was killed. She herself, we should

Support

remember, is compared with a bird by Mrs. Hale, who tells Mrs. Peters (and us) what Minnie Foster was like thirty years ago, before her marriage. She was pretty, well dressed, joyful, and she sang "like a bird"

Support

in the choir. Why she married the man she
did we are not told. But from what is said,
as well as from the stage symbols of cage
and canary, we can construe what happened
once she was married: Mr. Wright (is there
an ironic pun here?) imprisoned her in the
cage of his house and slowly choked the life
out of her. The dead canary as visual
symbol speaks of the waste of Mrs. Wright's
life.

Topic
sentence

From these symbolic meanings—various,
but all to the same point—we can conclude
that "Trifles" examines the intolerable
position of women at the beginning of this

Support

century. Its set, for instance, points to
the relegation of women to a secondary role
in a world bound and circumscribed by the
dictates of men. And set, cage, and canary

Support

all speak of the trap that marriage could
be, though the very thing that women were
supposed to define themselves by (which is
perhaps the reason Minnie Foster married Mr.

Conclusion

Wright). Clearly, Susan Glaspell was an
early feminist and a prophet of the
revolution to come.

PULLING IT ALL TOGETHER

The sample essay that you have just read exemplifies writing on a single element. The type of paper focused on a play's theme(s) is exemplified by what follows. Because writing on a theme usually involves the discussion of a number of elements for support, this second sample essay should also serve to do what the essays found in Sections II and III under the heading "Pulling It All Together" are meant to do: to show you how to write about a text in its entirety, or to draw on its many aspects in order to support your thesis and further your argument.

Mr. Right: Sexism and Feminism
in Susan Glaspell's "Trifles"

Funnel
beginning
The feminist movement in this century
has taken us a long way. By showing us
where women started, Susan Glaspell's play
"Trifles" gives us a way to measure just how
far that is. Concerning the subjugation of
women in a male–dominated world, the play

Thesis
makes vivid what women had to endure before
they finally rose up and asserted their
rights. The play itself, of course, is one
such act of assertion.

Topic
sentences
Though short, "Trifles" presents us
with both a plot and a situation. The plot,
which begins in the distant past with the
young womanhood of Minnie Foster and brings
us up to the murder of Mr. Wright the night
before the play takes place, involves
everything we can construe about Minnie's
life and thence her motivation for murdering

Support
her husband. What we learn through the
dialogue of Mrs. Hale and Mrs. Peters is
that before her marriage Minnie was a
lovely, joyful creature, who sang "like a
bird" (the simile is deliberate, as we shall
see shortly). Then, for reasons not given,

Support
she married Mr. Wright, but unlike the Mr.
Right of the mythology of marriage, this one
proved all wrong. The very mood established
by the play's "gloomy" set tells us that
Mrs. Wright's was an unhappy life. In a
contrast relationship with what we learn
about Mrs. Wright when young, what we learn

Support

about Mr. Wright convinces us that he imprisoned his wife and slowly choked the life out of her. This is the import of the two stage symbols introduced in the latter half of the play—broken bird cage and dead canary. They are visual tokens of Mrs. Wright's life with Mr. Wright that speak . . ., no, scream of her motivation (her thirty-year imprisonment in the cage of his house and her slow strangulation) as well as being clues to the precipitating event (Mr. Wright's killing of the canary) that brought the murder about.

Transition

In and of itself, this plot could not be taken as reflecting marriage in general.

Topic sentence

Still, what we learn about the Wrights' marriage does suggest the subjugation, at the time of the play, of women by marriage, at least when the play's plot is taken with

Support

its situation. That situation, which occurs in time present, is what we watch on stage: two women, relegated to the kitchen— symbolic here of the male view of female capacities—chatting and sewing and occasionally interacting with the men. What

Support

is most arresting about this situation is how it quietly but forcefully demonstrates the plight of women (thus, the situation echoes the plot). Not only are the women relegated to the kitchen but they are condescended to, snickered at, and summarily dismissed by the men. The way the men act

Support

is disgraceful, yet the women endure in silence. And these, we have every reason to believe, are just ordinary, average men, and not monsters like Mr. Wright. Mr. Right, it would seem, is nowhere to be found.

Topic sentence

At any rate, the play's situation gives rise to the most delicious irony (dramatic because the men are unaware of it), and from its irony springs the play's final mood.

Support

"Well, women are used to worrying over trifles," says Mr. Hale, condescendingly. But it is through their attention to trifles that the women solve the murder, whereas the men in all their pomposity don't have a

Support

clue. That the women suppress their information tells us, in part, that they have judged Mrs. Wright not guilty by reason of self-defense but also, in part, that on some level they scorn the men because they (the women) realize their plight in this man's world. The women do not gloat, but for the audience the irony sets a mood of quiet triumph. This is the feeling that most comes across as the play ends, a feeling that marks the play as an early feminist work, an act of assertion, as I have suggested, on the part of a female (Susan Glaspell) in a world in which the plight of the female was invisible.

Yes, we have come a long way since that time. Surely, no female today would put up with a husband like Mr. Wright or take the nonsense that Mrs. Hale and Mrs. Peters accept without a word or dream of the phantom Mr. Right. Oh, no? What about battered wives, sexual harassment, and the

statistical fact that the great majority of
teenage girls continue to believe in a Mr.
Right? Because of women like Susan
Glaspell, women are now better able to
assert themselves and their talents than in
1916, when "Trifles" was written. But, though
we may have come a long way, we still have a long
way to go.

Reverse
funnel
ending

PLAYS FOR STUDY AND WRITING ASSIGNMENTS

OEDIPUS REX

———————————— ❊ SOPHOCLES ❊ ————————————

Translated by Dudley Fitts and Robert Fitzgerald

CHARACTERS

OEDIPUS
A PRIEST
KREON
TEIRESIAS
IOKASTÊ
MESSENGER
SHEPHERD OF LAÏOS
SECOND MESSENGER
CHORUS OF THEBAN ELDERS

The Scene. Before the palace of OEDIPUS, *King of Thebes. A central door and two lateral doors open onto a platform which runs the length of the façade. On the platform, right and left, are altars; and three steps lead down into the* "orchêstra," *or chorus-ground. At the beginning of the action these steps are crowded by suppliants who have brought branches and chaplets of olive leaves and who sit in various attitudes of despair.*

[OEDIPUS *enters.*]

PROLOGUE

OEDIPUS. My children, generations of the living
  In the line of Kadmos, nursed at his ancient hearth:
  Why have you strewn yourselves before these altars
  In supplication, with your boughs and garlands?
  The breath of incense rises from the city
  With a sound of prayer and lamentation.
                          Children,
  I would not have you speak through messengers,
  And therefore I have come myself to hear you—
  I, Oedipus, who bear the famous name.

[*To a* PRIEST]

> You, there, since you are eldest in the company,   10
> Speak for them all, tell me what preys upon you,
> Whether you come in dread, or crave some blessing:
> Tell me, and never doubt that I will help you
> In every way I can; I should be heartless
> Were I not moved to find you suppliant here.

PRIEST.   Great Oedipus, O powerful King of Thebes!
> You see how all the ages of our people
> Cling to your altar steps: here are boys
> Who can barely stand alone, and here are priests
> By weight of age, as I am a priest of God,   20
> And young men chosen from those yet unmarried;
> As for the others, all that multitude,
> They wait with olive chaplets in the squares,
> At the two shrines of Pallas, and where Apollo
> Speaks in the glowing embers.
>   Your own eyes
> Must tell you: Thebes is tossed on a murdering sea
> And can not lift her head from the death surge.
> A rust consumes the buds and fruits of the earth;
> The herds are sick; children die unborn,
> And labor is vain. The god of plague and pyre   30
> Raids like detestable lightning through the city,
> And all the house of Kadmos is laid waste,
> All emptied, and all darkened: Death alone
> Battens upon the misery of Thebes.
>
> You are not one of the immortal gods, we know;
> Yet we have come to you to make our prayer
> As to the man surest in mortal ways
> And wisest in the ways of God. You saved us
> From the Sphinx, that flinty singer, and the tribute
> We paid to her so long; yet you were never   40
> Better informed than we, nor could we teach you:
> A god's touch, it seems, enabled you to help us.
>
> Therefore, O mighty power, we turn to you:
> Find us our safety, find us a remedy,

---

39. *Sphinx:* a creature with a woman's head, a lion's body, and wings who devoured anyone who could not solve her riddle: "What goes on four legs in the morning, two in the afternoon, and three in the evening?" Oedipus solved the riddle—man, who crawls on all fours in infancy, walks upright thereafter until old age, and finally needs a cane—and so brought the Sphinx's reign of terror to an end. Oedipus was rewarded for freeing Thebes from the Sphinx by being made king and given the hand of Iokastê, recently widowed by the untimely death of Laïos.

Whether by counsel of the gods or of men.
A king of wisdom tested in the past
Can act in a time of troubles, and act well.
Noblest of men, restore
Life to your city! Think how all men call you
Liberator for your boldness long ago;   50
Ah, when your years of kingship are remembered,
Let them not say *We rose, but later fell*—
Keep the State from going down in the storm!
Once, years ago, with happy augury,
You brought us fortune; be the same again!
No man questions your power to rule the land:
But rule over men, not over a dead city!
Ships are only hulls, high walls are nothing,
When no life moves in the empty passageways.
OEDIPUS. Poor children! You may be sure I know   60
All that you longed for in your coming here.
I know that you are deathly sick; and yet,
Sick as you are, not one is as sick as I.
Each of you suffers in himself alone
His anguish, not another's; but my spirit
Groans for the city, for myself, for you.

I was not sleeping, you are not waking me.
No, I have been in tears for a long while
And in my restless thought walked many ways.
In all my search I found one remedy,   70
And I have adopted it: I have sent Kreon,
Son of Menoikeus, brother of the Queen,
To Delphi, Apollo's place of revelation,
To learn there, if he can,
What act or pledge of mine may save the city.
I have counted the days, and now, this very day,
I am troubled, for he has overstayed his time.
What is he doing? He has been gone too long.
Yet whenever he comes back, I should do ill
Not to take any action the god orders.   80
PRIEST.   It is a timely promise. At this instant
They tell me Kreon is here.
OEDIPUS.   O Lord Apollo!
May his news be fair as his face is radiant!
PRIEST. Good news, I gather: he is crowned with bay,
The chaplet is thick with berries.
OEDIPUS.   We shall soon know;
He is near enough to hear us now.

[*Enter* KREON.]

O Prince:
Brother: son of Menoikeus:
What answer do you bring us from the God?
KREON. A strong one. I can tell you, great afflictions
    Will turn out well, if they are taken well.   90
OEDIPUS. What was the oracle? These vague words
    Leave me still hanging between hope and fear.
KREON. Is it your pleasure to hear me with all these
    Gathered around us? I am prepared to speak,
    But should we not go in?
OEDIPUS.   Speak to them all.
    It is for them I suffer, more than for myself.
KREON. Then I will tell you what I heard at Delphi.

In plain words
The god commands us to expel from the land of Thebes
An old defilement we are sheltering.   100
It is a deathly thing, beyond cure;
We must not let it feed upon us longer.
OEDIPUS. What defilement? How shall we rid ourselves of it?
KREON. By exile or death, blood for blood. It was
    Murder that brought the plague-wind on the city.
OEDIPUS. Murder of whom? Surely the god has named him?
KREON. My lord: Laïos once ruled this land,
    Before you came to govern us.
OEDIPUS.   I know;
    I learned of him from others; I never saw him.
KREON. He was murdered; and Apollo commands us now   110
    To take revenge upon whoever killed him.
OEDIPUS. Upon whom? Where are they? Where shall we find a clue
    To solve that crime, after so many years?
KREON. Here in this land, he said. Search reveals
    Things that escape an inattentive man.
OEDIPUS. Tell me: Was Laïos murdered in his house,
    Or in the fields, or in some foreign country?
KREON. He said he planned to make a pilgrimage.
    He did not come home again.
OEDIPUS.   And was there no one,
    No witness, no companion, to tell what happened?   120
KREON. They were all killed but one, and he got away
    So frightened that he could remember one thing only.
OEDIPUS. What was that one thing? One may be the key
    To everything, if we resolve to use it.

KREON. He said that a band of highwaymen attacked them,
   Outnumbered them, and overwhelmed the King.
OEDIPUS. Strange, that a highwayman should be so daring—
   Unless some faction here bribed him to do it.
KREON. We thought of that. But after Laïos' death
   New troubles arose and we had no avenger.   130
OEDIPUS. What troubles could prevent your hunting down the killers?
KREON. The riddling Sphinx's song
   Made us deaf to all mysteries but her own.
OEDIPUS. Then once more I must bring what is dark to light.
   It is most fitting that Apollo shows,
   As you do, this compunction for the dead.
   You shall see how I stand by you, as I should,
   Avenging this country and the god as well,
   And not as though it were for some distant friend,
   But for my own sake, to be rid of evil.   140
   Whoever killed King Laïos might—who knows?—
   Lay violent hands even on me—and soon.
   I act for the murdered king in my own interest.

   Come, then, my children: leave the altar steps,
   Lift up your olive boughs!
                         One of you go
   And summon the people of Kadmos to gather here.
   I will do all that I can; you may tell them that.

[*Exit a Page.*]

   So, with the help of God.
   We shall be saved—or else indeed we are lost.
PRIEST. Let us rise, children. It was for this we came,   150
   And now the King has promised it.
   Phoibos has sent us an oracle; may he descend
   Himself to save us and drive out the plague.

[*Exeunt* OEDIPUS *and* KREON *into the palace by the central door. The* PRIEST *and the
Suppliants disperse right and left. After a short pause the* CHORUS *enters the* orchêstra.]

PÁRODOS[*]

CHORUS. What is God singing in his profound   STROPHE 1[**]
   Delphi of gold and shadow?
   What oracle for Thebes, the sunwhipped city?

[*] *Párodos*: the first ode chanted by the chorus after entering the arena.
[**] *Strophe/Antistrophe*: divisions of the choral ode and opposite steps in the dance that accompanied the
choral recitation. The contrasting steps in the dance echo contrasting subjects in the ode itself.

Fear unjoints me, the roots of my heart tremble.

Now I remember, O Healer, your power and wonder:
Will you send doom like a sudden cloud, or weave it
Like nightfall of the past?

Speak, speak to us, issue of holy sound;
Dearest to our Expectancy: be tender!

Let me pray to Athenê, the immortal daughter of Zeus,   ANTISTROPHE 1** 10
And to Artemis her sister
Who keeps her famous throne in the market ring,
And to Apollo, archer from distant heaven—

O gods, descend! Like three streams leap against
The fires of our grief, the fires of darkness;
Be swift to bring us rest!

As in the old time from the brilliant house
Of air you stepped to save us, come again!

Now our afflictions have no end   STROPHE 2
Now all our stricken host lies down   20
And no man fights off death with his mind;

The noble plowland bears no grain,
And groaning mothers can not bear—

See, how our lives like birds take wing,
Like sparks that fly when a fire soars,
To the shore of the god of evening.

The plague burns on, it is pitiless,   ANTISTROPHE 2
Though pallid children laden with death
Lie unwept in the stony ways,

And old gray women by every path   30
Flock to the strand about the altars

There to strike their breasts and cry
Worship of Phoibos in wailing prayers:
Be kind, God's golden child!

There are no swords in this attack by fire,   STROPHE 3
No shields, but we are ringed with cries.

Send the besieger plunging from our homes
Into the vast sea-room of the Atlantic
Or into the waves that foam eastward of Thrace—
For the day ravages what the night spares—   40

Destroy our enemy, lord of the thunder!
Let him be riven by lightning from heaven!

Phoibos Apollo, stretch the sun's bowstring,   ANTISTROPHE 3
That golden cord, until it sing for us,
Flashing arrows in heaven!
                    Artemis, Huntress,
Race with flaring lights upon our mountains!

O scarlet god, O golden-banded brow,
O Theban Bacchos in a storm of Maenads,

[*Enter* OEDIPUS, *center.*]

Whirl upon Death, that all the Undying hate!
Come with blinding torches, come in joy!   50

SCENE I

OEDIPUS. Is this your prayer? It may be answered. Come,
Listen to me, act as the crisis demands,
And you shall have relief from all these evils.

Until now I was a stranger to this tale,
As I had been a stranger to the crime.
Could I track down the murderer without a clue?
But now, friends,
As one who became a citizen after the murder,
I make this proclamation to all Thebans:

If any man knows by whose hand Laïos, son of Labdakos,   10
Met his death, I direct that man to tell me everything,
No matter what he fears for having so long withheld it.
Let it stand as promised that no further trouble
Will come to him, but he may leave the land in safety.

Moreover: If anyone knows the murderer to be foreign,
Let him not keep silent: he shall have his reward from me.
However, if he does conceal it; if any man
Fearing for his friend or for himself disobeys this edict,
Hear what I propose to do:

I solemnly forbid the people of this country,   20
Where power and throne are mine, ever to receive that man
Or speak to him, no matter who he is, or let him
Join in sacrifice, lustration, or in prayer.
I decree that he be driven from every house,
Being, as he is, corruption itself to us: the Delphic
Voice of Apollo has pronounced this revelation.
Thus I associate myself with the oracle
And take the side of the murdered king.

As for the criminal, I pray to God—
Whether it be a lurking thief, or one of a number—   30
I pray that that man's life be consumed in evil and wretchedness.
And as for me, this curse applies no less
If it should turn out that the culprit is my guest here,
Sharing my hearth.
                              You have heard the penalty.

I lay it on you now to attend to this
For my sake, for Apollo's, for the sick
Sterile city that heaven has abandoned.
Suppose the oracle had given you no command:
Should this defilement go uncleansed for ever?
You should have found the murderer: your king,   40
A noble king, had been destroyed!
                              Now I,
Having the power that he held before me,
Having his bed, begetting children there
Upon his wife, as he would have, had he lived—
Their son would have been my children's brother,
If Laïos had had luck in fatherhood!
(And now his bad fortune has struck him down)—
I say I take the son's part, just as though
I were his son, to press the fight for him
And see it won! I'll find the hand that brought   50
Death to Labdakos' and Polydoros' child,
Heir of Kadmos' and Agenor's line.
And as for those who fail me,
May the gods deny them the fruit of the earth,
Fruit of the womb, and may they rot utterly!
Let them be wretched as we are wretched, and worse!
For you, for loyal Thebans, and for all
Who find my actions right, I pray the favor
Of justice, and of all the immortal gods.

CHORAGOS.* Since I am under oath, my lord, I swear   60
   I did not do the murder, I can not name
   The murderer. Phoibos ordained the search;
   Why did he not say who the culprit was?
OEDIPUS. An honest question. But no man in the world
   Can make the gods do more than the gods will.
CHORAGOS. There is an alternative, I think—
OEDIPUS.   Tell me.
   Any or all, you must not fail to tell me.
CHORAGOS. A lord clairvoyant to the lord Apollo,
   As we all know, is the skilled Teiresias.
   One might learn much about this from him, Oedipus.   70
OEDIPUS. I am not wasting time:
   Kreon spoke of this, and I have sent for him—
   Twice, in fact; it is strange that he is not here.
CHORAGOS. The other matter—that old report—seems useless.
OEDIPUS. What was that? I am interested in all reports.
CHORAGOS. The King was said to have been killed by highwaymen.
OEDIPUS. I know. But we have no witnesses to that.
CHORAGOS. If the killer can feel a particle of dread,
   Your curse will bring him out of hiding!
OEDIPUS.   No.
   The man who dared that act will fear no curse.   80

[*Enter the blind seer* TEIRESIAS, *led by a Page.*]

CHORAGOS. But there is one man who may detect the criminal.
   This is Teiresias, this is the holy prophet
   In whom, alone of all men, truth was born.
OEDIPUS. Teiresias: seer: student of mysteries,
   Of all that's taught and all that no man tells,
   Secrets of Heaven and secrets of the earth:
   Blind though you are, you know the city lies
   Sick with plague; and from this plague, my lord,
   We find that you alone can guard or save us.

   Possibly you did not hear the messengers?   90
   Apollo, when we sent to him,
   Sent us back word that this great pestilence
   Would lift, but only if we established clearly

Choragos: leader of and spokesman for the chorus.
62. *Phoibos*: Apollo, god of the sun in Greek mythology.

The identity of those who murdered Laïos.
They must be killed or exiled.
                                    Can you use
Birdflight or any art of divination
To purify yourself, and Thebes, and me
From this contagion? We are in your hands.
There is no fairer duty
Than that of helping others in distress.   100
TEIRESIAS. How dreadful knowledge of the truth can be
    When there's no help in truth! I knew this well
    But did not act on it: else I should not have come.
OEDIPUS. What is troubling you? Why are your eyes so cold?
TEIRESIAS. Let me go home. Bear your own fate, and I'll
    Bear mine. It is better so: trust what I say.
OEDIPUS. What you say is ungracious and unhelpful
    To your native country. Do not refuse to speak.
TEIRESIAS. When it comes to speech, your own is neither temperate
    Nor opportune. I wish to be more prudent.   110
OEDIPUS. In God's name, we all beg you—
TEIRESIAS.   You are all ignorant.
    No; I will never tell you what I know.
    Now it is my misery; then, it would be yours.
OEDIPUS. What! You do know something, and will not tell us?
    You would betray us all and wreck the State?
TEIRESIAS. I do not intend to torture myself, or you.
    Why persist in asking? You will not persuade me.
OEDIPUS. What a wicked old man you are! You'd try a stone's
    Patience! Out with it! Have you no feeling at all?
TEIRESIAS. You call me unfeeling. If you could only see   120
    The nature of your own feelings . . .
OEDIPUS.   Why,
    Who would not feel as I do? Who could endure
    Your arrogance toward the city?
TEIRESIAS.   What does it matter?
    Whether I speak or not, it is bound to come.
OEDIPUS. Then, if 'it' is bound to come, you are bound to tell me.
TEIRESIAS. No, I will not go on. Rage as you please.
OEDIPUS. Rage? Why not!
                        And I'll tell you what I think:
    You planned it, you had it done, you all but
    Killed him with your own hands: if you had eyes,
    I'd say the crime was yours, and yours alone.   130
TEIRESIAS. So? I charge you, then,
    Abide by the proclamation you have made:
    From this day forth

Never speak again to these men or to me;
  You yourself are the pollution of this country.
OEDIPUS. You dare say that! Can you possibly think you have
  Some way of going free, after such insolence?
TEIRESIAS. I have gone free. It is the truth sustains me.
OEDIPUS. Who taught you shamelessness? It was not your craft.
TEIRESIAS. You did. You made me speak. I did not want to.   140
OEDIPUS. Speak what? Let me hear it again more clearly.
TEIRESIAS. Was it not clear before? Are you tempting me?
OEDIPUS. I did not understand it. Say it again.
TEIRESIAS. I say that you are the murderer whom you seek.
OEDIPUS. Now twice you have spat out infamy. You'll pay for it!
TEIRESIAS. Would you care for more? Do you wish to be really angry?
OEDIPUS. Say what you will. Whatever you say is worthless.
TEIRESIAS. I say you live in hideous shame with those
  Most dear to you. You can not see the evil.
OEDIPUS. Can you go on babbling like this for ever?   150
TEIRESIAS. I can, if there is power in truth.
OEDIPUS.   There is:
  But not for you, not for you,
  You sightless, witless, senseless, mad old man!
TEIRESIAS. You are the madman. There is no one here
  Who will not curse you soon, as you curse me.
OEDIPUS. You child of total night! I would not touch you;
  Neither would any man who sees the sun.
TEIRESIAS. True: it is not from you my fate will come.
  That lies within Apollo's competence,
  As it is his concern.
OEDIPUS.   Tell me, who made   160
  These fine discoveries? Kreon? or someone else?
TEIRESIAS. Kreon is no threat. You weave your own doom.
OEDIPUS. Wealth, power, craft of statesmanship!
  Kingly position, everywhere admired!
  What savage envy is stored up against these,
  If Kreon, whom I trusted, Kreon my friend,
  For this great office which the city once
  Put in my hands unsought—if for this power
  Kreon desires in secret to destroy me!

  He has bought this decrepit fortune-teller, this   170
  Collector of dirty pennies, this prophet fraud—
  Why, he is no more clairvoyant than I am!
                                    Tell us:
  Has your mystic mummery ever approached the truth?
  When that hellcat the Sphinx was performing here,

What help were you to these people?
Her magic was not for the first man who came along:
It demanded a real exorcist. Your birds—
What good were they? or the gods, for the matter of that?
But I came by,
Oedipus, the simple man, who knows nothing—   180
I thought it out for myself, no birds helped me!
And this is the man you think you can destroy.
That you may be close to Kreon when he's king!
Well, you and your friend Kreon, it seems to me,
Will suffer most. If you were not an old man,
You would have paid already for your plot.
CHORAGOS. We can not see that his words or yours
    Have been spoken except in anger, Oedipus,
    And of anger we have no need. How to accomplish
    The god's will best: that is what most concerns us.   190
TEIRESIAS. You are a king. But where argument's concerned
    I am your man, as much a king as you.
    I am not your servant, but Apollo's
    I have no need of Kreon's name.

    Listen to me. You mock my blindness, do you?
    But I say that you, with both your eyes, are blind:
    You can not see the wretchedness of your life,
    Nor in whose house you live, no, nor with whom.
    Who are your father and mother? Can you tell me?
    You do not even know the blind wrongs   200
    That you have done them, on earth and in the world below.
    But the double lash of your parents' curse will whip you
    Out of this land some day, with only night
    Upon your precious eyes.
    Your cries then—where will they not be heard?
    What fastness of Kithairon will not echo them?
    And that bridal-descant of yours—you'll know it then,
    The song they sang when you came here to Thebes
    And found your misguided berthing.
    All this, and more, that you can not guess at now,   210
    Will bring you to yourself among your children.

    Be angry, then. Curse Kreon. Curse my words.
    I tell you, no man that walks upon the earth
    Shall be rooted out more horribly than you.
OEDIPUS. Am I to bear this from him?—Damnation
    Take you! Out of this place! Out of my sight!

TEIRESIAS. I would not have come at all if you had not asked me.

OEDIPUS. Could I have told that you'd talk nonsense, that
   You'd come here to make a fool of yourself, and of me?

TEIRESIAS. A fool? Your parents thought me sane enough.   220

OEDIPUS. My parents again!—Wait: who were my parents?

TEIRESIAS. This day will give you a father, and break your heart.

OEDIPUS. Your infantile riddles! Your damned abracadabra!

TEIRESIAS. You were a great man once at solving riddles.

OEDIPUS. Mock me with that if you like; you will find it true.

TEIRESIAS. It was true enough. It brought about your ruin.

OEDIPUS. But if it saved this town?

TEIRESIAS. [*To the Page*]   Boy, give me your hand.

OEDIPUS. Yes, boy; lead him away.

                 —While you are here
   We can do nothing. Go; leave us in peace.

TEIRESIAS. I will go when I have said what I have to say.   230
   How can you hurt me? And I tell you again:
   The man you have been looking for all this time,
   The damned man, the murderer of Laïos,
   That man is in Thebes. To your mind he is foreign-born,
   But it will soon be shown that he is a Theban,
   A revelation that will fail to please.

                A blind man,
   Who has his eyes now; a penniless man, who is rich now;
   And he will go tapping the strange earth with his staff.
   To the childen with whom he lives now he will be
   Brother and father—the very same; to her   240
   Who bore him, son and husband—the very same
   Who came to his father's bed, wet with his father's blood.

   Enough. Go think that over.
   If later you find error in what I have said,
   You may say that I have no skill in prophecy.

[*Exit* TEIRESIAS, *led by his Page.* OEDIPUS *goes into the palace.*]

ODE I

CHORUS. The Delphic stone of prophecies   STROPHE 1
   Remembers ancient regicide
   And a still bloody hand.

   That killer's hour of flight has come.
   He must be stronger than riderless
   Coursers of untiring wind,

For the son of Zeus armed with his father's thunder
Leaps in lightning after him;
And the Furies hold his track, the sad Furies.

Holy Parnassos' peak of snow   ANTISTROPHE 1   10
Flashes and blinds that secret man,
That all shall hunt him down:
Though he may roam the forest shade
Like a bull gone wild from pasture
To rage through glooms of stone.
Doom comes down on him; flight will not avail him;
For the world's heart calls him desolate,
And the immortal voices follow, for ever follow.

But now a wilder thing is heard   STROPHE 2
From the old man skilled at hearing Fate in the wing-beat of a bird.   20
Bewildered as a blown bird, my soul hovers and can not find
Foothold in this debate, or any reason or rest of mind.
But no man ever brought—none can bring
Proof of strife between Thebes' royal house,
Labdakos' line, and the son of Polybos;
And never until now has any man brought word
Of Laïos' dark death staining Oedipus the King.

Divine Zeus and Apollo hold   ANTISTROPHE 2
Perfect intelligence alone of all tales ever told;
And well though this diviner works, he works in his own night;   30
No man can judge that rough unknown or trust in second sight,
For wisdom changes hands among the wise.
Shall I believe my great lord criminal
At a raging word that a blind old man let fall?
I saw him, when the carrion woman faced him of old,
Prove his heroic mind. These evil words are lies.

SCENE II

KREON. Men of Thebes:
  I am told that heavy accusations
  Have been brought against me by King Oedipus.
  I am not the kind of man to bear this tamely.

  If in these present difficulties
  He holds me accountable for any harm to him
  Through anything I have said or done—why, then,
  I do not value life in this dishonor.

It is not as though this rumor touched upon
Some private indiscretion. The matter is grave.   10
The fact is that I am being called disloyal
To the State, to my fellow citizens, to my friends.
CHORAGOS. He may have spoken in anger, not from his mind.
KREON. But did you not hear him say I was the one
  Who seduced the old prophet into lying?
CHORAGOS. The thing was said; I do not know how seriously.
KREON. But you were watching him! Were his eyes steady?
  Did he look like a man in his right mind?
CHORAGOS.   I do not know.
  I can not judge the behavior of great men.
  But here is the King himself.

[*Enter* OEDIPUS.]

OEDIPUS.   So you dared come back.   20
  Why? How brazen of you to come to my house,
  You murderer!
             Do you think I do not know
  That you plotted to kill me, plotted to steal my throne?
  Tell me, in God's name: am I coward, a fool,
  That you should dream you could accomplish this?
  A fool who could not see your slippery game?
  A coward, not to fight back when I saw it?
  You are the fool, Kreon, are you not? hoping
  Without support or friends to get a throne?
  Thrones may be won or bought: you could do neither.   30
KREON. Now listen to me. You have talked; let me talk, too.
  You can not judge unless you know the facts.
OEDIPUS. You speak well: there is one fact; but I find it hard
  To learn from the deadliest enemy I have.
KREON. That above all I must dispute with you.
OEDIPUS. That above all I will not hear you deny.
KREON. If you think there is anything good in being stubborn
  Against all reason, then I say you are wrong.
OEDIPUS. If you think a man can sin against his own kind
  And not be punished for it, I say you are mad.   40
KREON. I agree. But tell me: what have I done to you?
OEDIPUS. You advised me to send for that wizard, did you not?
KREON. I did. I should do it again.
OEDIPUS.   Very well. Now tell me:
  How long has it been since Laïos—
KREON.   What of Laïos?
OEDIPUS. Since he vanished in that onset by the road?

KREON. It was long ago, a long time.

OEDIPUS.   And this prophet,
   Was he practicing here then?

KREON.   He was; and with honor, as now.

OEDIPUS. Did he speak of me at that time?

KREON.   He never did;
   At least, not when I was present.

OEDIPUS.   But . . . the enquiry?
   I suppose you held one?

KREON.   We did, but we learned nothing.   50

OEDIPUS. Why did the prophet not speak against me then?

KREON. I do not know; and I am the kind of man
   Who holds his tongue when he has no facts to go on.

OEDIPUS. There's one fact that you know, and you could tell it.

KREON. What fact is that? If I know it, you shall have it.

OEDIPUS. If he were not involved with you, he could not say
   That it was I who murdered Laïos.

KREON. If he says that, you are the one that knows it!—
   But now it is my turn to question you.

OEDIPUS. Put your questions. I am no murderer.   60

KREON. First, then: You married my sister?

OEDIPUS.   I married your sister.

KREON. And you rule the kingdom equally with her?

OEDIPUS. Everything that she wants she has from me.

KREON. And I am the third, equal to both of you?

OEDIPUS. That is why I call you a bad friend.

KREON. No. Reason it out, as I have done.
   Think of this first: Would any sane man prefer
   Power, with all a king's anxieties,
   To that same power and the grace of sleep?
   Certainly not I.   70
   I have never longed for the king's power—only his rights.
   Would any wise man differ from me in this?
   As matters stand, I have my way in everything
   With your consent, and no responsibilities.
   If I were king, I should be a slave to policy.
   How could I desire a sceptre more
   Than what is now mine—untroubled influence?
   No, I have not gone mad; I need no honors,
   Except those with the perquisites I have now.
   I am welcome everywhere; every man salutes me,   80
   And those who want your favor seek my ear,
   Since I know how to manage what they ask.
   Should I exchange this ease for that anxiety?

Besides, no sober mind is treasonable.
I hate anarchy
And never would deal with any man who likes it.

Test what I have said. Go to the priestess
At Delphi, ask if I quoted her correctly.
And as for this other thing: if I am found
Guilty of treason with Teiresias,   90
Then sentence me to death. You have my word
It is a sentence I should cast my vote for—
But not without evidence!
                              You do wrong
When you take good men for bad, bad men for good.
A true friend thrown aside—why, life itself
Is not more precious!
                              In time you will know this well:
For time, and time alone, will show the just man,
Though scoundrels are discovered in a day.
CHORAGOS. This is well said, and a prudent man would ponder it.
   Judgments too quickly formed are dangerous.   100
OEDIPUS. But is he not quick in his duplicity?
   And shall I not be quick to parry him?
   Would you have me stand still, holding my peace, and let
   This man win everything, through my inaction?
KREON. And you want—what is it, then? To banish me?
OEDIPUS. No, not exile. It is your death I want,
   So that all the world may see what treason means.
KREON. You will persist, then? You will not believe me?
OEDIPUS. How can I believe you?
KREON.   Then you are a fool.
OEDIPUS. To save myself?
KREON.   In justice, think of me.   110
OEDIPUS. You are evil incarnate.
KREON.   But suppose that you are wrong?
OEDIPUS. Still I must rule.
KREON.   But not if you rule badly.
OEDIPUS. O city, city!
KREON.   It is my city, too!
CHORAGOS. Now, my lords, be still. I see the Queen,
   Iokastê, coming from her palace chambers;
   And it is time she came, for the sake of you both.
   This dreadful quarrel can be resolved through her.

[*Enter* IOKASTÊ.]

IOKASTÊ. Poor foolish men, what wicked din is this?
With Thebes sick to death, is it not shameful
That you should rake some private quarrel up?   120

[*To* OEDIPUS]

Come into the house
                         —And you, Kreon, go now:
Let us have no more of this tumult over nothing.
KREON. Nothing? No, sister: what your husband plans for me
Is one of two great evils: exile or death.
OEDIPUS. He is right.
                         Why, woman I have caught him squarely
Plotting against my life.
KREON.   No! Let me die
Accurst if ever I have wished you harm!
IOKASTÊ. Ah, believe it, Oedipus!
In the name of the gods, respect this oath of his
For my sake, for the sake of these people here!   130

CHORAGOS. Open your mind to her, my lord. Be ruled by her,   STROPHE 1
      I beg you!
OEDIPUS. What would you have me do?
CHORAGOS. Respect Kreon's word. He has never spoken like a fool,
And now he has sworn an oath.
OEDIPUS. You know what you ask?
CHORAGOS.   I do.
OEDIPUS.   Speak on, then.
CHORAGOS. A friend so sworn should not be baited so,
In blind malice, and without final proof.
OEDIPUS. You are aware, I hope, that what you say
Means death for me, or exile at the least.

CHORAGOS.   STROPHE 2
No, I swear by Helios, first in Heaven!   140
   May I die friendless and accurst,
The worst of deaths, if ever I meant that!
      It is the withering fields
        That hurt my sick heart:
      Must we bear all these ills,
        And now your bad blood as well?
OEDIPUS. Then let him go. And let me die, if I must,
Or be driven by him in shame from the land of Thebes.
It is your unhappiness, and not his talk,
That touches me.
                         As for him—   150

Wherever he goes, hatred will follow him.

KREON. Ugly in yielding, as you were ugly in rage!
Natures like yours chiefly torment themselves.

OEDIPUS. Can you not go? Can you not leave me?

KREON.   I can.
You do not know me; but the city knows me,
And in its eyes I am just, if not in yours.

[*Exit* KREON.]

CHORAGOS.   Lady Iokastê, did you not ask the King to go to   ANTISTROPHE 1
        his chambers?

IOKASTÊ. First tell me what has happened.

CHORAGOS. There was suspicion without evidence; yet it rankled
As even false charges will.   160

IOKASTÊ.   On both sides?

CHORAGOS.   On both.

IOKASTÊ.   But what was said?

CHORAGOS. Oh let it rest, let it be done with!
Have we not suffered enough?

OEDIPUS. You see to what your decency has brought you:
You have made difficulties where my heart saw none.

CHORAGOS. Oedipus, it is not once only I have told you—   ANTISTROPHE 2
        You must know I should count myself unwise
To the point of madness, should I now forsake you—
            You, under whose hand,
                In the storm of another time,   170
            Our dear land sailed out free.
                But now stand fast at the helm!

IOKASTÊ. In God's name, Oedipus, inform your wife as well:
Why are you so set in this hard anger?

OEDIPUS. I will tell you, for none of these men deserves
My confidence as you do. It is Kreon's work,
His treachery, his plotting against me.

IOKASTÊ. Go on, if you can make this clear to me.

OEDIPUS. He charges me with the murder of Laïos.

IOKASTÊ. Has he some knowledge? Or does he speak from hearsay?   180

OEDIPUS He would not commit himself to such a charge,
But he has brought in that damnable soothsayer
To tell his story.

IOKASTÊ.   Set your mind at rest.
If it is a question of soothsayers, I tell you
That you will find no man whose craft gives knowledge
Of the unknowable.
                    Here is my proof:

An oracle was reported to Laïos once
(I will not say from Phoibos himself, but from
His appointed ministers, at any rate)
That his doom would be death at the hands of his own son—   190
His son, born of his flesh and of mine!

Now, you remember the story: Laïos was killed
By marauding strangers where three highways meet;
But his child had not been three days in this world
Before the King had pierced the baby's ankles
And left him to die on a lonely mountainside.

Thus, Apollo never caused that child
To kill his father, and it was not Laïos' fate
To die at the hands of his son, as he had feared.
This is what prophets and prophecies are worth!   200
Have no dread of them.
                    It is God himself
Who can show us what he wills, in his own way.
OEDIPUS. How strange a shadowy memory crossed my mind,
    Just now while you were speaking; it chilled my heart.
IOKASTÊ. What do you mean? What memory do you speak of?
OEDIPUS. If I understand you, Laïos was killed
    At a place where three roads meet.
IOKASTÊ.   So it was said:
    We have no later story.
OEDIPUS.   Where did it happen?
Iokastê. Phokis, it is called: at a place where the Theban Way
    Divides into the roads toward Delphi and Daulia.   210
OEDIPUS. When?
Iokastê.   We had the news not long before you came
    And proved the right to your succession here.
OEDIPUS. Ah, what net has God been weaving for me?
IOKASTÊ. Oedipus! Why does this trouble you?
OEDIPUS.   Do not ask me yet.
    First, tell me how Laïos looked, and tell me
    How old he was.
Iokastê.   He was tall, his hair just touched
    With white; his form was not unlike your own.
OEDIPUS. I think that I myself may be accurst
    By my own ignorant edict.
IOKASTÊ.   You speak strangely.
    It makes me tremble to look at you, my King.   220
OEDIPUS. I am not sure that the blind man can not see.
    But I should know better if you were to tell me—

IOKASTÊ. Anything—though I dread to hear you ask it.
OEDIPUS. Was the King lightly escorted, or did he ride
 With a large company, as a ruler should?
IOKASTÊ. There were five men with him in all: one was a herald;
 And a single chariot, which he was driving.
OEDIPUS. Alas, that makes it plain enough!
          But who—
 Who told you how it happened?
IOKASTÊ.   A household servant,
 The only one to escape.
OEDIPUS.   And is he still   230
 A servant of ours?
IOKASTÊ.   No; for when he came back at last
 And found you enthroned in the place of the dead king,
 He came to me, touched my hand with his, and begged
 That I would send him away to the frontier district
 Where only the shepherds go—
 As far away from the city as I could send him.
 I granted his prayer; for although the man was a slave,
 He had earned more than this favor at my hands.
OEDIPUS. Can he be called back quickly?
IOKASTÊ.   Easily.
 But why?
OEDIPUS. I have taken too much upon myself   240
 Without enquiry; therefore I wish to consult him.
IOKASTÊ. Then he shall come.
        But am I not one also
 To whom you might confide these fears of yours?
OEDIPUS. That is your right; it will not be denied you,
 Now least of all; for I have reached a pitch
 Of wild foreboding. Is there anyone
 To whom I should sooner speak?

 Polybos of Corinth is my father.
 My mother is a Dorian: Meropê.
 I grew up chief among the men of Corinth   250
 Until a strange thing happened—
 Not worth my passion, it may be, but strange.

 At a feast, a drunken man maundering in his cups
 Cries out that I am not my father's son!
 I contained myself that night, though I felt anger
 And a sinking heart. The next day I visited
 My father and mother, and questioned them. They stormed,
 Calling it all the slanderous rant of a fool;

And this relieved me. Yet the suspicion
Remained always aching in my mind;   260
I knew there was talk; I could not rest;
And finally, saying nothing to my parents,
I went to the shrine at Delphi.

The god dismissed my question without reply;
He spoke of other things.

      Some were clear,
Full of wretchedness, dreadful, unbearable:
As that I should lie with my own mother, breed
Children from whom all men would turn their eyes;
And that I should be my father's murderer.

I heard all this, and fled. And from that day   270
Corinth to me was only in the stars
Descending in that quarter of the sky,
As I wandered farther and farther on my way
To a land where I should never see the evil
Sung by the oracle. And I came to this country
Where, so you say, King Laïos was killed.
I will tell you all that happened there, my lady.

There were three highways
Coming together at a place I passed;
And there a herald came towards me, and a chariot   280
Drawn by horses, with a man such as you describe
Seated in it. The groom leading the horses
Forced me off the road at his lord's command;
But as this charioteer lurched over towards me
I struck him in my rage. The old man saw me
And brought his double goad down upon my head
As I came abreast.

    He was paid back, and more!
Swinging my club in this right hand I knocked him
Out of his car, and he rolled on the ground.

        I killed him.
I killed them all.   290
Now if that stranger and Laïos were—kin,
Where is a man more miserable than I?
More hated by the gods? Citizen and alien alike
Must never shelter me or speak to me—
I must be shunned by all.

      And I myself
Pronounced this malediction upon myself!

Think of it: I have touched you with these hands,
These hands that killed your husband. What defilement!

Am I all evil, then? It must be so,
Since I must flee from Thebes, yet never again   300
See my own countrymen, my own country,
For fear of joining my mother in marriage
And killing Polybos, my father.
                                 Ah,
If I was created so, born to this fate,
Who could deny the savagery of God?

O holy majesty of heavenly powers!
May I never see that day! Never!
Rather let me vanish from the race of men
Than know the abomination destined me!
CHORAGOS. We too, my lord, have felt dismay at this.   310
   But there is hope: you have yet to hear the shepherd.
OEDIPUS. Indeed, I fear no other hope is left me.
IOKASTÊ. What do you hope from him when he comes?
OEDIPUS.   This much:
   If his account of the murder tallies with yours,
   Then I am cleared.
IOKASTÊ.   What was it that I said
   Of such importance?
OEDIPUS.   Why, "marauders," you said,
   Killed the King, according to this man's story.
   If he maintains that still, if there were several,
   Clearly the guilt is not mine: I was alone.
   But if he says one man, singlehanded, did it,   320
   Then the evidence all points to me.
IOKASTÊ.   You may be sure that he said there were several;
   And can he call back that story now? He can not.
   The whole city heard it as plainly as I.
   But suppose he alters some detail of it:
   He can not ever show that Laïos' death
   Fulfilled the oracle: for Apollo said
   My child was doomed to kill him; and my child—
   Poor baby!—it was my child that died first.

No. From now on, where oracles are concerned,   330
I would not waste a second thought on any.
OEDIPUS. You may be right.
                    But come: let someone go
For the shepherd at once. This matter must be settled.

IOKASTÊ.   I will send for him.
I would not wish to cross you in anything,
And surely not in this.—Let us go in.

[*Exeunt into the palace.*]

ODE II

CHORUS. Let me be reverent in the ways of right,	STROPHE 1

CHORUS. Let me be reverent in the ways of right,   STROPHE 1
     Lowly the paths I journey on;
     Let all my words and actions keep
     The laws of the pure universe
     From highest Heaven handed down.
     For Heaven is their bright nurse,
     Those generations of the realms of light;
     Ah, never of mortal kind were they begot,
     Nor are they slaves of memory, lost in sleep:
     Their Father is greater than Time, and ages not.   10

     The tyrant is a child of Pride   ANTISTROPHE 1
     Who drinks from his great sickening cup
     Recklessness and vanity,
     Until from his high crest headlong
     He plummets to the dust of hope.
     That strong man is not strong.
     But let no fair ambition be denied;
     May God protect the wrestler for the State
     In government, in comely policy,
     Who will fear God, and on His ordinance wait.   20

     Haughtiness and the high hand of disdain   STROPHE 2
     Tempt and outrage God's holy law;
     And any mortal who dares hold
     No immortal Power in awe
     Will be caught up in a net of pain:
     The price for which his levity is sold.
     Let each man take due earnings, then,
     And keep his hands from holy things,
     And from blasphemy stand apart—
     Else the crackling blast of heaven   30
     Blows on his head, and on his desperate heart.
     Though fools will honor impious men,
     In their cities no tragic poet sings.

     Shall we lose faith in Delphi's obscurities,   ANTISTROPHE 2
     We who have heard the world's core

Discredited, and the sacred wood
Of Zeus at Elis praised no more?
The deeds and the strange prophecies
Must make a pattern yet to be understood.
Zeus, if indeed you are lord of all,   40
Throned in light over night and day,
Mirror this in your endless mind:
Our masters call the oracle
Words on the wind, and the Delphic vision blind!
Their hearts no longer know Apollo,
And reverence for the gods has died away.

SCENE III

[*Enter* IOKASTÊ.]

IOKASTÊ.   Princes of Thebes, it has occurred to me
  To visit the altars of the gods, bearing
  These branches as a suppliant, and this incense.
  Our king is not himself: his noble soul
  Is overwrought with fantasies of dread,
  Else he would consider
  The new prophecies in the light of the old.
  He will listen to any voice that speaks disaster,
  And my advice goes for nothing.

[*She approaches the altar, right.*]

                              To you, then, Apollo,
  Lycéan lord, since you are nearest, I turn in prayer.   10

  Receive these offerings, and grant us deliverance
  From defilement. Our hearts are heavy with fear
  When we see our leader distracted, as helpless sailors
  Are terrified by the confusion of their helmsman.

[*Enter* MESSENGER.]

MESSENGER. Friends, no doubt you can direct me:
  Where shall I find the house of Oedipus,
  Or, better still, where is the King himself?
CHORAGOS. It is this very place, stranger; he is inside.
  This is his wife and mother of his children.
MESSENGER. I wish her happiness in a happy house,   20
  Blest in all the fulfillment of her marriage.
IOKASTÊ. I wish as much for you: your courtesy
  Deserves a like good fortune. But now, tell me:
  Why have you come? What have you to say to us?

MESSENGER. Good news, my lady, for your house and your husband.

IOKASTÊ. What news? Who sent you here?

MESSENGER.   I am from Corinth.
   The news I bring ought to mean joy for you,
   Though it may be you will find some grief in it.

IOKASTÊ. What is it? How can it touch us in both ways?

MESSENGER. The word is that the people of the Isthmus   30
   Intend to call Oedipus to be their king.

IOKASTÊ. But old King Polybos—is he not reigning still?

MESSENGER. No. Death holds him in his sepulchre.

IOKASTÊ. What are you saying? Polybos is dead?

MESSENGER. If I am not telling the truth, may I die myself.

IOKASTÊ. [*To a Maidservant*]
   Go in, go quickly; tell this to your master.

   O riddlers of God's will, where are you now!
   This was the man whom Oedipus, long ago,
   Feared so, fled so, in dread of destroying him—
   But it was another fate by which he died.   40

[*Enter* OEDIPUS, *center.*]

OEDIPUS. Dearest Iokastê, why have you sent for me?

IOKASTÊ. Listen to what this man says, and then tell me
   What has become of the solemn prophecies.

OEDIPUS. Who is this man? What is his news for me?

IOKASTÊ. He has come from Corinth to announce your father's death!

OEDIPUS. Is it true, stranger? Tell me in your own words.

MESSENGER. I can not say it more clearly: the King is dead.

OEDIPUS. Was it by treason? Or by an attack of illness?

MESSENGER. A little thing brings old men to their rest.

OEDIPUS. It was sickness, then?

MESSENGER.   Yes, and his many years.   50

OEDIPUS. Ah!
   Why should a man respect the Pythian hearth, or
   Give heed to the birds that jangle above his head?
   They prophesied that I should kill Polybos,
   Kill my own father; but he is dead and buried,
   And I am here—I never touched him, never,
   Unless he died of grief for my departure,
   And thus, in a sense, through me. No. Polybos
   Has packed the oracles off with him underground.
   They are empty words.

IOKASTÊ.   Had I not told you so?

OEDIPUS. You had; it was my faint heart that betrayed me.   60

IOKASTÊ. From now on never think of those things again.

OEDIPUS. And yet—must I not fear my mother's bed?

IOKASTÊ. Why should anyone in this world be afraid,
   Since Fate rules us and nothing can be foreseen?
   A man should live only for the present day.
   Have no more fear of sleeping with your mother:
   How many men, in dreams, have lain with their mothers!
   No reasonable man is troubled by such things.

OEDIPUS. That is true; only—
   If only my mother were not still alive!   70
   But she is alive. I can not help my dread.

IOKASTÊ. Yet this news of your father's death is wonderful.

OEDIPUS. Wonderful. But I fear the living woman.

MESSENGER. Tell me, who is this woman you fear?

OEDIPUS. It is Meropê, man; the wife of King Polybos.

MESSENGER. Meropê? Why should you be afraid of her?

OEDIPUS. An oracle of the gods, a dreadful saying.

MESSENGER. Can you tell me about it or are you sworn to silence?

OEDIPUS. I can tell you, and I will.
   Apollo said through his prophet that I was the man   80
   Who should marry his own mother, shed his father's blood
   With his own hands. And so, for all these years
   I have kept clear of Corinth, and no harm has come—
   Though it would have been sweet to see my parents again.

MESSENGER. And is this the fear that drove you out of Corinth?

OEDIPUS. Would you have me kill my father?

MESSENGER.   As for that
   You must be reassured by the news I gave you.

OEDIPUS. If you could reassure me, I would reward you.

MESSENGER. I had that in mind, I will confess: I thought
   I could count on you when you returned to Corinth.   90

OEDIPUS. No: I will never go near my parents again.

MESSENGER. Ah, son, you still do not know what you are doing—

OEDIPUS. What do you mean? In the name of God tell me!

MESSENGER. —If these are your reasons for not going home.

OEDIPUS. I tell you, I fear the oracle may come true.

MESSENGER. And guilt may come upon you through your parents?

OEDIPUS. That is the dread that is always in my heart.

MESSENGER. Can you not see that all your fears are groundless?

OEDIPUS. Groundless? Am I not my parents' son?

MESSENGER. Polybos was not your father.

OEDIPUS.   Not my father?   100

MESSENGER. No more your father than the man speaking to you.

OEDIPUS. But you are nothing to me!

MESSENGER.   Neither was he.

OEDIPUS. Then why did he call me son?

MESSENGER.   I will tell you:
  Long ago he had you from my hands, as a gift.
OEDIPUS. Then how could he love me so, if I was not his?
MESSENGER. He had no children, and his heart turned to you.
OEDIPUS. What of you? Did you buy me? Did you find me by chance?
MESSENGER. I came upon you in the woody vales of Kithairon.
OEDIPUS. And what were you doing there?
MESSENGER.   Tending my flocks.
OEDIPUS. A wandering shepherd?
MESSENGER.   But your savior, son, that day.   110
OEDIPUS. From what did you save me?
MESSENGER.   Your ankles should tell you that.
OEDIPUS. Ah, stranger, why do you speak of that childhood pain?
MESSENGER. I pulled the skewer that pinned your feet together.
OEDIPUS. I have had the mark as long as I can remember.
MESSENGER. That was why you were given the name you bear.
OEDIPUS. God! Was it my father or my mother who did it?
  Tell me!
MESSENGER. I do not know. The man who gave you to me
  Can tell you better than I.
OEDIPUS. It was not you that found me, but another?
MESSENGER. It was another shepherd gave you to me.   120
OEDIPUS. Who was he? Can you tell me who he was?
MESSENGER. I think he was said to be one of Laïos' people.
OEDIPUS. You mean the Laïos who was king here years ago?
MESSENGER. Yes; King Laïos; and the man was one of his herdsmen.
OEDIPUS. Is he still alive? Can I see him?
MESSENGER.   These men here
  Know best about such things.
OEDIPUS.   Does anyone here
  Know this shepherd that he is talking about?
  Have you seen him in the fields, or in the town?
  If you have, tell me. It is time things were made plain.
CHORAGOS. I think the man he means is that same shepherd   130
  You have already asked to see. Iokastê perhaps
  Could tell you something.
OEDIPUS.   Do you know anything
  About him, Lady? Is he the man we have summoned?
  Is that the man the shepherd means?
IOKASTÊ.   Why think of him?
  Forget this herdsman. Forget it all.
  This talk is a waste of time.
OEDIPUS   How can you say that?

---

115. *name*: Oedipus means "swollen foot" in Greek.

When the clues to my true birth are in my hands?
IOKASTÊ. For God's love, let us have no more questioning!
  Is your life nothing to you?
  My own is pain enough for me to bear.   140
OEDIPUS. You need not worry. Suppose my mother a slave,
  And born of slaves: no baseness can touch you.
IOKASTÊ. Listen to me, I beg you: do not do this thing!
OEDIPUS. I will not listen; the truth must be made known.
IOKASTÊ. Everything that I say is for your own good!
OEDIPUS.   My own good
  Snaps my patience, then; I want none of it.
IOKASTÊ. You are fatally wrong! May you never learn who you are!
OEDIPUS. Go, one of you, and bring the shepherd here.
  Let us leave this woman to brag of her royal name.
IOKASTÊ. Ah, miserable!   150
  That is the only word I have for you now.
  That is the only word I can ever have.

[*Exit into the palace.*]

CHORAGOS. Why has she left us, Oedipus? Why has she gone
  In such a passion of sorrow? I fear this silence:
  Something dreadful may come of it.
OEDIPUS.   Let it come!
  However base my birth, I must know about it.
  The Queen, like a woman, is perhaps ashamed
  To think of my own origin. But I
  Am a child of Luck; I can not be dishonored.
  Luck is my mother; the passing months, my brothers,   160
  Have seen me rich and poor.
                      If this be so,
  How could I wish that I were someone else?
  How could I not be glad to know my birth?

ODE III

CHORUS. If ever the coming time were known   STROPHE
  To my heart's pondering,
  Kithairon, now by Heaven I see the torches
  At the festival of the next full moon,
  And see the dance, and hear the choir sing
  A grace to your gentle shade:
  Mountain where Oedipus was found,
  O mountain guard of a noble race!
  May the god who heals us lend his aid,

And let that glory come to pass   10
For our king's cradling-ground.

Of the nymphs that flower beyond the years,   ANTISTROPHE
Who bore you, royal child,
To Pan of the hills or the timberline Apollo,
Cold in delight where the upland clears,
Or Hermês for whom Kyllenê's heights are piled?
Or flushed as evening cloud,
Great Dionysos, roamer of mountains,
He—was it he who found you there,
And caught you up in his own proud   20
Arms from the sweet god-ravisher
Who laughed by the Muses' fountains?

SCENE IV

OEDIPUS. Sirs: though I do not know the man,
    I think I see him coming, this shepherd we want:
    He is old, like our friend here, and the men
    Bringing him seem to be servants of my house.
    But you can tell, if you have ever seen him.

[*Enter* SHEPHERD *escorted by servants.*]

CHORAGOS. I know him, he was Laïos' man. You can trust him.
OEDIPUS. Tell me first, you from Corinth: is this the shepherd
    We were discussing?
MESSENGER.   This is the very man.
OEDIPUS. [*To* SHEPHERD]
    Come here. No, look at me. You must answer
    Everything I ask.—You belonged to Laïos?   10
SHEPHERD. Yes: born his slave, brought up in his house.
OEDIPUS. Tell me: what kind of work did you do for him?
SHEPHERD. I was a shepherd of his, most of my life.
OEDIPUS. Where mainly did you go for pasturage?
SHEPHERD. Sometimes Kithairon, sometimes the hills near-by.
OEDIPUS. Do you remember ever seeing this man out there?
SHEPHERD. What would he be doing there? This man?
OEDIPUS. This man standing here. Have you seen him before?
SHEPHERD. No. At least, not to my recollection.
MESSENGER. And that is not strange, my lord. But I'll refresh   20
    His memory: he must remember when we two
    Spent three whole seasons together, March to September,
    On Kithairon or thereabouts. He had two flocks;

I had one. Each autumn I'd drive mine home
And he would go back with his to Laïos' sheepfold.—
Is this not true, just as I have described it?
SHEPHERD. True, yes; but it was all so long ago.
MESSENGER. Well, then: do you remember, back in those days,
That you gave me a baby boy to bring up as my own?
SHEPHERD. What if I did? What are you trying to say?   30
MESSENGER. King Oedipus was once that little child.
SHEPHERD. Damn you, hold your tongue!
OEDIPUS.   No more of that!
It is your tongue that needs watching, not this man's.
SHEPHERD. My King, my Master, what is it I have done wrong?
OEDIPUS. You have not answered his question about the boy.
SHEPHERD. He does not know . . . He is only making trouble . . .
OEDIPUS. Come, speak plainly, or it will go hard with you.
SHEPHERD. In God's name, do not torture an old man!
OEDIPUS. Come here, one of you; bind his arms behind him.
SHEPHERD. Unhappy king! What more do you wish to learn?   40
OEDIPUS. Did you give this man the child he speaks of?
SHEPHERD.   I did.
And I would to God I had died that very day.
OEDIPUS. You will die now unless you speak the truth.
SHEPHERD. Yet if I speak the truth, I am worse than dead.
OEDIPUS. [To Attendant]
He intends to draw it out, apparently—
SHEPHERD. No! I have told you already that I gave him the boy.
OEDIPUS. Where did you get him? From your house? From somewhere else?
SHEPHERD. Not from mine, no. A man gave him to me.
OEDIPUS. Is that man here? Whose house did he belong to?
SHEPHERD. For God's love, my King, do not ask me any more!   50
OEDIPUS. You are a dead man if I have to ask you again.
SHEPHERD. Then . . . Then the child was from the palace of Laïos.
OEDIPUS. A slave child? Or a child of his own line?
SHEPHERD. Ah, I am on the brink of dreadful speech!
OEDIPUS. And I of dreadful hearing. Yet I must hear.
SHEPHERD. If you must be told, then . . .
They said it was Laïos' child:
But it is your wife who can tell you about that.
OEDIPUS. My wife!—Did she give it to you?
SHEPHERD.   My Lord, she did.
OEDIPUS. Do you know why?
SHEPHERD   I was told to get rid of it.
OEDIPUS. O heartless mother!
SHEPHERD.   But in dread of prophecies . . .   60

OEDIPUS. Tell me.

SHEPHERD. It was said that the boy would kill his own father.

OEDIPUS. Then why did you give him over to this old man?

SHEPHERD. I pitied the baby, my King,
    And I thought that this man would take him far away
    To his own country.
                                    He saved him—but for what a fate!
    For if you are what this man says you are,
    No man living is more wretched than Oedipus.

OEDIPUS. Ah God!
    It was true!
            All the prophecies!
                        —Now,
    O Light, may I look on you for the last time!   70
    I, Oedipus,
    Oedipus, damned in his birth, in his marriage damned,
    Damned in the blood he shed with his own hand!

[*He rushes into the palace.*]

ODE IV

CHORUS. Alas for the seed of men.   STROPHE 1

    What measure shall I give these generations
    That breathe on the void and are void
    And exist and do not exist?

    Who bears more weight of joy
    Than mass of sunlight shifting in images,
    Or who shall make his thought stay on
    That down time drifts away?

    Your splendor is all fallen.

    O naked brow of wrath and tears,   10
    O change of Oedipus!
    I who saw your days call no man blest—
    Your great days like ghósts góne.

    That mind was a strong bow.   ANTISTROPHE 1

    Deep, how deep you drew it then, hard archer,
    At a dim fearful range,
    And brought dear glory down!

You overcame the stranger—
The virgin with her hooking lion claws—
And though death sang, stood like a tower   20
To make pale Thebes take heart.

Fortress against our sorrow!

True king, giver of laws,
Majestic Oedipus!
No prince in Thebes had ever such renown,
No prince won such grace of power.

And now of all men ever known   STROPHE 2
Most pitiful is this man's story:
His fortunes are most changed, his state
Fallen to a low slave's   30
Ground under bitter fate.

O Oedipus, most royal one!
The great door that expelled you to the light
Gave at night—ah, gave night to your glory:
As to the father, to the fathering son.

All understood too late.

How could that queen whom Laïos won,
The garden that he harrowed at his height,
Be silent when that act was done?

But all eyes fail before time's eye,   ANTISTROPHE 2   40
All actions come to justice there.
Though never willed, though far down the deep past,
Your bed, your dread sirings,
Are brought to book at last.

Child by Laïos doomed to die,
Then doomed to lose that fortunate little death,
Would God you never took breath in this air
That with my wailing lips I take to cry:

For I weep the world's outcast.
I was blind, and now I can tell why: 50
Asleep, for you had given ease of breath
To Thebes, while the false years went by.

ÉXODOS*

[Enter, from the palace, SECOND MESSENGER.]

SECOND MESSENGER.   Elders of Thebes, most honored in this land,
    What horrors are yours to see and hear, what weight
    Of sorrow to be endured, if, true to your birth,
    You venerate the line of Labdakos!
    I think neither Istros nor Phasis, those great rivers,
    Could purify this place of all the evil
    It shelters now, or soon must bring to light—
    Evil not done unconsciously, but willed.

    The greatest griefs are those we cause ourselves
CHORAGOS.   Surely, friend, we have grief enough already;   10
    What new sorrow do you mean?
SECOND MESSENGER.   The Queen is dead.
CHORAGOS.   O miserable Queen! But at whose hand?
SECOND MESSENGER.   Her own.
    The full horror of what happened you can not know,
    For you did not see it; but I, who did, will tell you
    As clearly as I can how she met her death.

    When she had left us,
    In passionate silence, passing through the court,
    She ran to her apartment in the house,
    Her hair clutched by the fingers of both hands.
    She closed the doors behind her; then, by that bed   20
    Where long ago the fatal son was conceived—
    That son who should bring about his father's death—
    We heard her call upon Laïos, dead so many years,
    And heard her wail for the double fruit of her marriage,
    A husband by her husband, children by her child.

    Exactly how she died I do not know:
    For Oedipus burst in moaning and would not let us
    Keep vigil to the end: it was by him
    As he stormed about the room that our eyes were caught.
    From one to another of us he went, begging a sword,   30
    Hunting the wife who was not his wife, the mother
    Whose womb had carried his own children and himself.
    I do not know: it was none of us aided him,
    But surely one of the gods was in control!
    For with a dreadful cry

Éxodos: the scene that follows the last choral ode in ancient Greek drama and contains the denouement or resolution of a tragedy's issues and plot.

He hurled his weight, as though wrenched out of himself,
At the twin doors: the bolts gave, and he rushed in.
And there we saw her hanging, her body swaying
From the cruel cord she had noosed about her neck.
A great sob broke from him, heartbreaking to hear,   40
As he loosed the rope and lowered her to the ground.

I would blot out from my mind what happened next!
For the King ripped from her gown the golden brooches
That were her ornament, and raised them, and plunged them down
Straight into his own eyeballs, crying, "No more,
No more shall you look on the misery about me,
The horrors of my own doing! Too long you have known
The faces of those whom I should never have seen,
Too long been blind to those for whom I was searching!
From this hour, go in darkness!" And as he spoke,   50
He struck at his eyes—not once, but many times;
And the blood spattered his beard,
Bursting from his ruined sockets like red hail.

So from the unhappiness of two this evil has sprung,
A curse on the man and woman alike. The old
Happiness of the house of Labdakos
Was happiness enough: where is it today?
It is all wailing and ruin, disgrace, death—all
The misery of mankind that has a name—
And it is wholly and for ever theirs.   60
CHORAGOS. Is he in agony still? Is there no rest for him?
SECOND MESSENGER. He is calling for someone to open the doors wide
    So that all the children of Kadmos may look upon
    His father's murderer, his mother's—no,
    I can not say it!
                    And then he will leave Thebes,
    Self-exiled, in order that the curse
    Which he himself pronounced may depart from the house.
    He is weak, and there is none to lead him,
    So terrible is his suffering.
                        But you will see:
    Look, the doors are opening; in a moment   70
    You will see a thing that would crush a heart of stone.

[*The central door is opened;* OEDIPUS, *blinded, is led in.*]

CHORAGOS. Dreadful indeed for men to see.
    Never have my own eyes
    Looked on a sight so full of fear.

Oedipus!
What madness came upon you, what daemon
Leaped on your life with heavier
Punishment than a mortal man can bear?
No: I can not even
Look at you, poor ruined one.   80
And I would speak, question, ponder,
If I were able. No.
You make me shudder.

OEDIPUS. God.   God.
  Is there a sorrow greater?
  Where shall I find harbor in this world?
  My voice is hurled far on a dark wind.
  What has God done to me?

CHORAGOS. Too terrible to think of, or to see.

OEDIPUS. O cloud of night,   STROPHE 1   90
  Never to be turned away: night coming on,
  I can not tell how: night like a shroud!

  My fair winds brought me here.
                              O God. Again
  The pain of the spikes where I had sight,
  The flooding pain
  Of memory, never to be gouged out.

CHORAGOS. This is not strange.
  You suffer it all twice over, remorse in pain,
  Pain in remorse.

OEDIPUS. Ah dear friend   ANTISTROPHE 1   100
  Are you faithful even yet, you alone?
  Are you still standing near me, will you stay here,
  Patient, to care for the blind?
                              The blind man!
  Yet even blind I know who it is attends me,
  By the voice's tone—
  Though my new darkness hide the comforter.

CHORAGOS. Oh fearful act!
  What god was it drove you to rake black
  Night across your eyes?

OEDIPUS. Apollo. Apollo. Dear   STROPHE 2   110
  Children, the god was Apollo.

He brought my sick, sick fate upon me.
But the blinding hand was my own!
How could I bear to see
When all my sight was horror everywhere?

CHORAGOS. Everywhere; that is true.

OEDIPUS. And now what is left?
   Images? Love? A greeting even,
   Sweet to the senses? Is there anything?
   Ah, no, friends: lead me away.   120
   Lead me away from Thebes.
                                    Lead the great wreck
   And hell of Oedipus, whom the gods hate.

CHORAGOS. Your misery, you are not blind to that.
   Would God you had never found it out!

OEDIPUS. Death take the man who unbound   ANTISTROPHE 2
   My feet on that hillside
   And delivered me from death to life! What life?
   If only I had died,
   This weight of monstrous doom
   Could not have dragged me and my darlings down.   130
CHORAGOS. I would have wished the same.

OEDIPUS. Oh never to have come here
   With my father's blood upon me! Never
   To have been the man they call his mother's husband!
   Oh accurst! Oh child of evil,
   To have entered that wretched bed—
                                    the selfsame one!
   More primal than sin itself, this fell to me.

CHORAGOS. I do not know what words to offer you.
   You were better dead than alive and blind.

OEDIPUS.   Do not counsel me any more. This punishment   140
   That I have laid upon myself is just.
   If I have eyes,
   I do not know how I could bear the sight
   Of my father, when I came to the house of Death,
   Or my mother; for I have sinned against them both
   So vilely that I could not make my peace

By strangling my own life.
                              Or do you think my children,
Born as they were born, would be sweet to my eyes?
Ah never, never! Nor this town with its high walls,
Nor the holy images of the gods.
                              For I,   150
Thrice miserable!—Oedipus, noblest of all the line
Of Kadmos, have condemned myself to enjoy
These things no more, by my own malediction
Expelling that man whom the gods declared
To be a defilement in the house of Laïos.
After exposing the rankness of my own guilt,
How could I look men frankly in the eyes?
No, I swear it,
If I could have stifled my hearing at its source,
I would have done it and made all this body   160
A tight cell of misery, blank to light and sound:
So I should have been safe in my dark mind
Beyond external evil.
                      Ah Kithairon!
Why did you shelter me? When I was cast upon you,
Why did I not die? Then I should never
Have shown the world my execrable birth.

Ah Polybos! Corinth, city that I believed
The ancient seat of my ancestors: how fair
I seemed, your child! And all the while this evil
Was cancerous within me!
                          For I am sick   170
In my own being, sick in my origin.

O three roads, dark ravine, woodland and way
Where three roads met: you, drinking my father's blood,
My own blood, spilled by my own hand: can you remember
The unspeakable things I did there, and the things
I went on from there to do?
                            O marriage, marriage!
The act that engendered me, and again the act
Performed by the son in the same bed—
                                      Ah, the net
Of incest, mingling fathers, brothers, sons,
With brides, wives, mothers: the last evil   180
That can be known by men: no tongue can say
How evil!
          No. For the love of God, conceal me

Somewhere far from Thebes; or kill me; or hurl me
Into the sea, away from men's eyes for ever.
Come, lead me. You need not fear to touch me.
Of all men, I alone can bear this guilt.

[*Enter* KREON.]

CHORAGOS. Kreon is here now. As to what you ask,
  He may decide the course to take. He only
  Is left to protect the city in your place.
OEDIPUS. Alas, how can I speak to him? What right have I   190
  To beg his courtesy whom I have deeply wronged?
KREON. I have not come to mock you, Oedipus,
  Or to reproach you, either.
  [*To Attendants*]   —You standing there:
  If you have lost all respect for man's dignity,
  At least respect the flame of Lord Helios:
  Do not allow this pollution to show itself
  Openly here, an affront to the earth
  And Heaven's rain and the light of day. No, take him
  Into the house as quickly as you can.
  For it is proper   200
  That only the close kindred see his grief.
OEDIPUS. I pray you in God's name, since your courtesy
  Ignores my dark expectation, visiting
  With mercy this man of all men most execrable:
  Give me what I ask—for your good, not for mine.
KREON. And what is it that you turn to me begging for?
OEDIPUS. Drive me out of this country as quickly as may be
  To a place where no human voice can ever greet me.
KREON. I should have done that before now—only,
  God's will had not been wholly revealed to me.   210
OEDIPUS. But his command is plain: the parricide
  Must be destroyed. I am that evil man.
KREON. That is the sense of it, yes; but as things are,
  We had best discover clearly what is to be done.
OEDIPUS. You would learn more about a man like me?
KREON. You are ready now to listen to the god.
OEDIPUS. I will listen. But it is to you
  That I must turn for help. I beg you, hear me.

  The woman in there—
  Give her whatever funeral you think proper: 220

---

195. *Helios*: another name for Apollo, god of the sun.

She is your sister.
                    —But let me go, Kreon!
Let me purge my father's Thebes of the pollution
Of my living here, and go out to the wild hills,
To Kithairon, that has won such fame with me,
The tomb my mother and father appointed for me,
And let me die there, as they willed I should.
And yet I know
Death will not ever come to me through sickness
Or in any natural way: I have been preserved
For some unthinkable fate. But let that be.   230

As for my sons, you need not care for them.
They are men, they will find some way to live.
But my poor daughters, who have shared my table,
Who never before have been parted from their father—
Take care of them, Kreon; do this for me.
And will you let me touch them with my hands
A last time, and let us weep together?
Be kind, my lord,
Great prince, be kind!
                    Could I but touch them,
They would be mine again, as when I had my eyes.   240

[*Enter Antigone and Ismene, attended.*]

Ah, God!
Is it my dearest children I hear weeping?
Has Kreon pitied me and sent my daughters?
KREON. Yes, Oedipus: I knew that they were dear to you
In the old days, and know you must love them still.
OEDIPUS. May God bless you for this—and be friendlier
Guardian to you than he has been to me!

Children, where are you?
Come quickly to my hands: they are your brother's—
Hands that have brought your father's once clear eyes   250
To this way of seeing—
                    Ah dearest ones,
I had neither sight nor knowledge then, your father
By the woman who was the source of his own life!
And I weep for you—having no strength to see you—,
I weep for you when I think of the bitterness
That men will visit upon you all your lives.
What homes, what festivals can you attend
Without being forced to depart again in tears?

And when you come to marriageable age,
Where is the man, my daughters, who would dare   260
Risk the bane that lies on all my children?
Is there any evil wanting? Your father killed
His father; sowed the womb of her who bore him;
Engendered you at the fount of his own existence!

That is what they will say of you.
                         Then, whom
Can you ever marry? There are no bridegrooms for you,
And your lives must wither away in sterile dreaming.

O Kreon, son of Menoikeus!
You are the only father my daughters have,
Since we, their parents, are both of us gone for ever.   270
They are your own blood: you will not let them
Fall into beggary and loneliness;
You will keep them from the miseries that are mine!
Take pity on them; see, they are only children,
Friendless except for you. Promise me this,
Great Prince, and give me your hand in token of it.

[KREON *clasps his right hand.*]

Children:
I could say much, if you could understand me,
But as it is, I have only this prayer for you:
Live where you can, be as happy as you can—   280
Happier, please God, than God has made your father.
KREON.   Enough. You have wept enough. Now go within.
OEDIPUS. I must; but it is hard.
KREON.   Time eases all things.
OEDIPUS. You know my mind, then?
KREON.   Say what you desire.
OEDIPUS. Send me from Thebes!
KREON.   God grant that I may!
OEDIPUS. But since God hates me . . .
KREON.   No, he will grant your wish.
Oedipus. You promise?
KREON.   I can not speak beyond my knowledge.
OEDIPUS. Then lead me in.
KREON.   Come now, and leave your children.
OEDIPUS. No! Do not take them from me!
KREON.   Think no longer
That you are in command here, but rather think   290
How, when you were, you served your own destruction.

[Exeunt into the house all but the Chorus; the CHORAGOS *chants directly to the audience.]*

CHORAGOS. Men of Thebes: look upon Oedipus.

This is the king who solved the famous riddle
And towered up, most powerful of men.
No mortal eyes but looked on him with envy,
Yet in the end ruin swept over him.

Let every man in mankind's frailty
Consider his last day; and let none
Presume on his good fortune until he find
Life, at his death, a memory without pain.   300

[c. 430 B.C.—Athens, Greece]

Questions

Prologue

1. What is the function of the Prologue? What do we learn about Oedipus here?
2. Sophocles knew that his audience would know the story of Oedipus. Thus, he was able to imbue *Oedipus Rex* with dramatic irony. What examples of such irony do you find in the Prologue (consider, for instance, lines 140–143)? What mood(s) here and as the play moves on do its many ironies create?

Scene I

1. What does Oedipus's reaction to Teiresias's refusal to speak tell us about Oedipus? How does the character trait revealed tie in with the murder of Laïos?
2. What in this scene suggests that we are but the pawns of the gods, acting out what fate has decreed? Yet, "You weave your own doom," Teiresias says to Oedipus (line 162). Is it fate or personality, then, that accounts for our actions? Or is personality itself a kind of fate?
3. Dramatic irony abounds in Scene I. Find a few examples. In what way does such irony here and elsewhere suggest that fate rules human life?
4. Why does Oedipus fail to see the truth that he forces from Teiresias? What does this failure reveal about Oedipus?
5. "How dreadful knowledge of the truth can be / When there's no help in truth," says Teiresias (lines 101–102), hoping to suppress the truth. This statement points to a central theme of Sophocles's play. What theme is that? How does it figure in the play as a whole?

Scene II

1. Contrast Oedipus and Kreon. What is reinforced by the comparison that we already know about Oedipus? Why? What else do we learn about Oedipus in this scene?
2. Is Kreon's defense convincing? Why or why not? In any case, what does the defense underscore about Oedipus?

3. Dramatic irony is to be felt with a vengeance in what Iokastê says in her speech from line 183 on. How so?
4. How do you see Iokastê? What is her mentality? What is suggested by her being proved so utterly wrong?
5. From lines 263–269, we learn that Oedipus knew the truth all along. Why didn't he and doesn't he still (in Scene II) believe it? Similarly, why doesn't he see that the prophesy made to him and what Iokastê reveals (line 183 on) are the same? Why, too, doesn't he recall that he killed several people under circumstances exactly like those of the murder of Laïos?
6. Lines 270–275 suggest the nature of fate. How so?

Scene III

1. At the beginning of the play, Oedipus is in search of a murderer. What change occurs in Scene III as to the object of his search? Why this change? What does it reveal about his unconscious awareness and possible guilt?
2. What is ironic about the "good news" (line 25) brought by the messenger and his subsequent reassurance (line 87)? How does this news, presented at about the middle of the play, momentarily change its direction of feeling? But the change is only momentary. What is the effect when the good news proves terrible?
3. In *Oedipus Rex*, Sophocles proves no less a psychologist than Freud, who coined the term "Oedipus complex." Consider lines 66–68 from a psychological perspective.
4. What does Iokastê actually believe about fate? On which side of the fate/personality dichotomy does she fall?
5. Contrast Iokastê and Oedipus. Iokastê's advice is good as far as it goes. Why can't Oedipus take it?

Scene IV

1. "Do not ask me any more," says the shepherd in Scene IV (line 50), echoing what Teiresias says near the beginning of the play. Why does Oedipus persist? Given his persistence, is not his destiny determined by personality (as opposed to fate) after all? Elaborate.
2. There is much coincidence here—for example, it was the selfsame servant who saved the infant Oedipus, accompanied Laïos the day he and all but one of his party were killed, and managed to be that one survivor. How do you respond to such coincidences? Are they merely a matter of convenience, or do they help to deepen the play's fatalism?
3. How does the Chorus in the Ode that follows Scene IV sum up the *tragedy* of Oedipus (that is, the tragic element in the play)? Would Aristotle have agreed? How so?

Éxodos

1. What might Oedipus's blinding himself (as opposed to some other act of self-mutilation) symbolically suggest? What does the blindness itself symbolize with respect to the theme of knowledge?
2. Oedipus did not know that Laïos and Iokastê were his parents; Iokastê did not know that Oedipus was her son; and their children are innocents, in no way responsible for the play's action. Yet all are engulfed by the tragedy. Does this seem just? Is justice, then, but a fiction, an ideal with no basis in our lives as we live them?
3. The play's three subsidiary themes, which can only be stated as questions, converge in

the Éxodos: Is knowledge an absolute good, to be sought at any cost, or is it only a relative good, needing the guidance of reason? Does our destiny depend on fate or on individual personality and choice? Is there justice in this world? Pick out passages that suggest each theme. A possible master theme uniting these subsidiary themes is intimated in the closing speech of the Choragos. What is that? How are the subsidiary themes united by this possible master theme and, in turn, how do they support its validity?

Writing Assignments

1. There are many coincidences in *Oedipus Rex* in relation to the life story of Oedipus. Write a paper in which you enumerate the main coincidences and then discuss their effect. How do you respond to them? How do they relate to the theme entailing fate? If something is indeed fated, is coincidence possible?
2. There are many separate conflicts in the play. In an essay, describe them climactically, building to the play's primary conflict. What is that conflict? What is the significance of its centrality?
3. What does Sophocles suggest governs human destiny—fate, personality, both, or neither? Write an essay addressed to this question. Use textual evidence as support for your thesis as to the view or views about human destiny embodied in *Oedipus Rex.*
4. Is knowledge an absolute good, or are there things better left unknown? In a paper, discuss what Sophocles intimates about this matter. You might enrich your discussion by doing some research into how the ancient Greeks in general viewed knowledge and its pursuit.
5. Is Oedipus responsible or not? Write an essay taking one position or the other (but allow for the possible validity of the position you do not take). Support your position with textual evidence and move to a consideration of the question of justice raised at the end of the play.
6. Write a paper in which you state what the master theme of *Oedipus Rex* is and go on to discuss how its subsidiary themes support the master theme and are united by it. Here again, research could be of use. Read two or three critical treatments of *Oedipus Rex,* keeping your eye out for anything said about themes and, in particular, a primary theme.
7. In an essay, discuss the use of dramatic irony by Sophocles. Exemplify that use and then suggest what dramatic irony here serves to do. For instance, what kind of mood does it help to establish? Why this mood? How does Sophocles's irony relate to any or all of the play's themes? What is its effect overall?
8. How does the play leave you feeling? Consider this question as you write a paper on the nature and function of tragedy. What is tragedy? What psychological purpose does it serve? Explore these questions via *Oedipus Rex* and your response to it as tragedy.
9. You are captured by aliens who scorn the human race as being shallow and simpleminded. Wishing to defend your species, you ask the aliens to read your handy copy of *Oedipus Rex* for a discussion the next day. What subtleties of the play and what complexities of human mentality and life dramatized in it will you point out to them? Write an essay on how you would defend the human race against the aliens' charges.
10. *Oedipus Rex* is a tragedy of an individual. But it is also a tragedy of a nation. How so? In an essay, contrast Oedipus and Kreon as to temperament and personal qualities. What kind of a king was Oedipus? What kind, do you think, will Kreon be? Support your judgments with reference to the play and conclude by suggesting how it can be seen as a "tragedy of a nation." For other support material, get a book on mythology and read about Kreon during the latter days of Thebes.

HAMLET

PRINCE OF DENMARK

—————————— ❊ WILLIAM SHAKESPEARE ❊ ——————————

CAST OF CHARACTERS

CLAUDIUS, *King of Denmark*

HAMLET, *son to the late, and nephew to the present, King*

POLONIUS, *Lord Chamberlain*

HORATIO, *friend to Hamlet*

LAERTES, *son to Polonius*

VOLTEMAND
CORNELIUS
ROSENCRANTZ } *courtiers*
GUILDENSTERN
OSRIC
A GENTLEMAN

A PRIEST

MARCELLUS } *officers*
BERNARDO

FRANCISCO, *a soldier*

REYNALDO, *servant to Polonius*

PLAYERS

TWO CLOWNS, *gravediggers*

FORTINBRAS, *Prince of Norway*

A NORWEGIAN CAPTAIN

ENGLISH AMBASSADORS

GERTRUDE, *Queen of Denmark, mother to Hamlet*

OPHELIA, *daughter to Polonius*

GHOST OF HAMLET'S FATHER

LORDS, LADIES, OFFICERS, SOLDIERS, SAILORS, MESSENGERS, ATTENDANTS

SCENE: *Elsinore*

ACT I, SCENE 1

[*Enter* BERNARDO *and* FRANCISCO, *two sentinels.*]

BERNARDO. Who's there?

FRANCISCO. Nay, answer me. Stand and unfold yourself.

HAMLET. The line numbers in this edition are somewhat unusual: as well as allowing for easy reference, each line number printed in the margin indicates that there is a footnote for something in the line numbered. Therefore, whenever there is a line number, drop your eyes down for a moment to the similarly numbered note at the bottom of the page to see what is glossed.

The text of the play and the notes are reprinted from the Pelican edition of *Hamlet,* edited by William Farnham (Viking-Penguin, 1957).

I, 1. Elsinore Castle: a sentry-post.

BERNARDO. Long live the king!

FRANCISCO. Bernardo?

BERNARDO. He.

FRANCISCO. You come most carefully upon your hour.

BERNARDO. 'Tis now struck twelve. Get thee to bed, Francisco.

FRANCISCO. For this relief much thanks. 'Tis bitter cold,
    And I am sick at heart.

BERNARDO. Have you had quiet guard?

FRANCISCO.   Not a mouse stirring.

BERNARDO. Well, good night.
    If you do meet Horatio and Marcellus,
    The rivals of my watch, bid them make haste.   13

[*Enter* HORATIO *and* MARCELLUS.]

FRANCISCO. I think I hear them. Stand, ho! Who is there?

HORATIO.   Friends to this ground.

MARCELLUS.   And liegemen to the Dane.   15

FRANCISCO.   Give you good night.

MARCELLUS.   O, farewell, honest soldier.
    Who hath relieved you?

FRANCISCO.   Bernardo hath my place.
    Give you good night.   [*Exit* FRANCISCO.]

MARCELLUS.   Holla, Bernardo!

BERNARDO.   Say—
    What, is Horatio there?

HORATIO.   A piece of him.

BERNARDO. Welcome, Horatio. Welcome, good Marcellus.

HORATIO. What, has this thing appeared again to-night?

BERNARDO. I have seen nothing.

MARCELLUS. Horatio says 'tis but our fantasy,
    And will not let belief take hold of him
    Touching this dreaded sight twice seen of us.
    Therefore I have entreated him along
    With us to watch the minutes of this night,
    That, if again this apparition come,
    He may approve our eyes and speak to it.   29

HORATIO. Tush, tush, 'twill not appear.

BERNARDO.   Sit down awhile,
    And let us once again assail your ears,
    That are so fortified against our story,
    What we two nights have seen.

HORATIO.   Well, sit we down,
    And let us hear Bernardo speak of this.

---

13. *rivals:* sharers.   **15.** *Dane:* King of Denmark.   **29.** *approve:* confirm.

BERNARDO. Last night of all,
   When yond same star that's westward from the pole   36
   Had made his course t'illume that part of heaven
   Where now it burns, Marcellus and myself,
   The bell then beating one—

[*Enter* GHOST.]

MARCELLUS. Peace, break thee off. Look where it comes again.
BERNARDO. In the same figure like the king that's dead.
MARCELLUS. Thou art a scholar; speak to it, Horatio.
BERNARDO. Looks 'a not like the king? Mark it, Horatio.
HORATIO. Most like. It harrows me with fear and wonder.
BERNARDO. It would be spoke to.
MARCELLUS.   Speak to it, Horatio.
HORATIO. What art thou that usurp'st this time of night
   Together with that fair and warlike form
   In which the majesty of buried Denmark   48
   Did sometimes march? By heaven I charge thee, speak.   49
MARCELLUS. It is offended.
BERNARDO.   See, it stalks away.
HORATIO. Stay. Speak, speak. I charge thee, speak.   [*Exit* GHOST.]
MARCELLUS. 'Tis gone and will not answer.
BERNARDO. How now, Horatio? You tremble and look pale.
   Is not this something more than fantasy?
   What think you on't?
HORATIO. Before my God, I might not this believe
   Without the sensible and true avouch
   Of mine own eyes.
MARCELLUS.   Is it not like the king?
HORATIO. As thou art to thyself.
   Such was the very armor he had on
   When he th' ambitious Norway combated.   61
   So frowned he once when, in an angry parle,   62
   He smote the sledded Polacks on the ice.
   'Tis strange.
MARCELLUS. Thus twice before, and jump at this dead hour,   65
   With martial stalk hath he gone by our watch.
HORATIO. In what particular thought to work I know not;
   But, in the gross and scope of my opinion,   68
   This bodes some strange eruption to our state.
MARCELLUS. Good now, sit down, and tell me he that knows,

---

36. *pole:* polestar.   **48.** *buried Denmark:* the buried King of Denmark.   **49.** *sometimes:* formerly.   **61.** *Norway:* King of Norway.   **62.** *parle:* parley.   **65.** *jump:* just, exactly.   **68.** *gross and scope:* gross scope, general view.

Why this same strict and most observant watch
So nightly toils the subject of the land,   72
And why such daily cast of brazen cannon
And foreign mart for implements of war,   74
Why such impress of shipwrights, whose sore task   75
Does not divide the Sunday from the week.
What might be toward that this sweaty haste   77
Doth make the night joint-laborer with the day?
Who is't that can inform me?
HORATIO.   That can I.
At least the whisper goes so. Our last king,
Whose image even but now appeared to us,
Was as you know by Fortinbras of Norway,
Thereto pricked on by a most emulate pride,   83
Dared to the combat; in which our valiant Hamlet
(For so this side of our known world esteemed him)
Did slay this Fortinbras; who, by a sealed compact
Well ratified by law and heraldry,   87
Did forfeit, with his life, all those his lands
Which he stood seized of to the conqueror;   89
Against the which a moiety competent   90
Was gagèd by our king, which had returned   91
To the inheritance of Fortinbras
Had he been vanquisher, as, by the same comart   93
And carriage of the article designed,   94
His fell to Hamlet. Now, sir, young Fortinbras,
Of unimprovèd mettle hot and full,   96
Hath in the skirts of Norway here and there
Sharked up a list of lawless resolutes   98
For food and diet to some enterprise
That hath a stomach in't; which is no other,   100
As it doth well appear unto our state,
But to recover of us by strong hand
And terms compulsatory those foresaid lands
So by his father lost; and this, I take it,
Is the main motive of our preparations,
The source of this our watch, and the chief head   106
Of this posthaste and romage in the land.   107
BERNARDO. I think it be no other but e'en so.

---

72. *toils:* makes toil; *subject:* subjects. **74.** *mart:* trading. **75.** *impress:* conscription. **77.** *toward:* in preparation. **83.** *emulate:* jealously rivalling. **87.** *law and heraldry:* law of heralds regulating combat. **89.** *seized:* possessed. **90.** *moiety competent:* sufficient portion. **91.** *gagèd:* engaged, staked. **93.** *comart:* joint bargain. **94.** *carriage:* purport. **96.** *unimprovèd:* unused. **98.** *Sharked:* snatched indiscriminately as the shark takes prey; *resolutes:* desperadoes. **100.** *stomach:* show of venturesomeness. **106.** *head:* fountainhead, source. **107.** *romage:* intense activity.

Well may it sort that this portentous figure   109
Comes armèd through our watch so like the king
That was and is the question of these wars.
HORATIO. A mote it is to trouble the mind's eye.   112
In the most high and palmy state of Rome,
A little ere the mightiest Julius fell,
The graves stood tenantless and the sheeted dead   115
Did squeak and gibber in the Roman streets;
As stars with trains of fire and dews of blood,
Disasters in the sun; and the moist star   118
Upon whose influence Neptune's empire stands
Was sick almost to doomsday with eclipse.
And even the like precurse of feared events,   121
As harbingers preceding still the fates   122
And prologue to the omen coming on,   123
Have heaven and earth together demonstrated
Unto our climatures and countrymen.   125

[*Enter* GHOST.]

But soft, behold, lo where it comes again!
I'll cross it, though it blast me—Stay, illusion.   127

[*He spreads his arms.*]

If thou hast any sound or use of voice,
Speak to me.
If there be any good thing to be done
That may to thee do ease and grace to me,
Speak to me.
If thou art privy to thy country's fate,
Which happily foreknowing may avoid,   134
O, speak!
Or if thou hast uphoarded in thy life
Extorted treasure in the womb of earth,
For which, they say, you spirits oft walk in death,

[*The cock crows.*]

Speak of it. Stay and speak. Stop it, Marcellus.
MARCELLUS. Shall I strike at it with my partisan?   140
HORATIO. Do, if it will not stand.
BERNARDO.   'Tis here.
HORATIO.   'Tis here.

---

109. *sort:* suit.   **112.** *mote:* speck of dust.   **115.** *sheeted:* in shrouds.   **118.** *Disasters:* ominous signs; *moist star:* moon.   **121.** *precurse:* foreshadowing.   **122.** *harbingers:* forerunners; *still:* constantly.   **123.** *omen:* calamity.   **125.** *climatures:* regions.   **127.** *cross it:* cross its path.   **134.** *happily:* haply, perchance.   **140.** *partisan:* pike.

MARCELLUS. 'Tis gone.   [*Exit* GHOST.]
    We do it wrong, being so majestical,
    To offer it the show of violence,
    For it is as the air invulnerable,
    And our vain blows malicious mockery.
BERNARDO. It was about to speak when the cock crew.
HORATIO. And then it started, like a guilty thing
    Upon a fearful summons. I have heard
    The cock, that is the trumpet to the morn,
    Doth with his lofty and shrill-sounding throat
    Awake the god of day, and at his warning,
    Whether in sea or fire, in earth or air,
    Th' extravagant and erring spirit hies   154
    To his confine; and of the truth herein
    This present object made probation.   156
MARCELLUS. It faded on the crowing of the cock.
    Some say that ever 'gainst that season comes   158
    Wherein our Saviour's birth is celebrated,
    This bird of dawning singeth all night long,
    And then, they say, no spirit dare stir abroad,
    The nights are wholesome, then no planets strike,   162
    No fairy takes, nor witch hath power to charm.   163
    So hallowed and so gracious is that time.
HORATIO. So have I heard and do in part believe it.
    But look, the morn in russet mantle clad
    Walks o'er the dew of yon high eastward hill.
    Break we our watch up, and by my advice
    Let us impart what we have seen to-night
    Unto young Hamlet, for upon my life
    This spirit, dumb to us, will speak to him.
    Do you consent we shall acquaint him with it,
    As needful in our loves, fitting our duty?
MARCELLUS. Let's do't, I pray, and I this morning know
    Where we shall find him most conveniently.   [*Exeunt.*]

ACT I, SCENE 2

[*Flourish. Enter* CLAUDIUS, *King of Denmark,* GERTRUDE *the Queen,* COUNCILLORS,
POLONIUS *and his son* LAERTES, HAMLET, *cum aliis including* VOLTEMAND *and* CORNELIUS.]

KING. Though yet of Hamlet our dear brother's death
    The memory be green, and that it us befitted

---

154. *extravagant:* wandering beyond bounds; *erring:* wandering.   **156.** *probation:* proof.   **158.** *'gainst:*
just before.   **162.** *strike:* work evil by influence.   **163.** *takes:* bewitches.
I, 2. Elsinore Castle: a room of state.   **s.d.** *cum aliis:* with others.

To bear our hearts in grief, and our whole kingdom
To be contracted in one brow of woe,
Yet so far hath discretion fought with nature
That we with wisest sorrow think on him
Together with remembrance of ourselves.
Therefore our sometime sister, now our queen,
Th' imperial jointress to this warlike state,   9
Have we, as 'twere with a defeated joy,
With an auspicious and a dropping eye,
With mirth in funeral and with dirge in marriage,
In equal scale weighing delight and dole,
Taken to wife. Nor have we herein barred   14
Your better wisdoms, which have freely gone
With this affair along. For all, our thanks.
Now follows, that you know, young Fortinbras,
Holding a weak supposal of our worth,
Or thinking by our late dear brother's death
Our state to be disjoint and out of frame,
Colleaguèd with this dream of his advantage,   21
He hath not failed to pester us with message
Importing the surrender of those lands
Lost by his father, with all bands of law,
To our most valiant brother. So much for him.
Now for ourself and for this time of meeting.
Thus much the business is: we have here writ
To Norway, uncle of young Fortinbras—
Who, impotent and bedrid, scarcely hears
Of this his nephew's purpose—to suppress
His further gait herein, in that the levies,   31
The lists, and full proportions are all made   32
Out of his subject; and we here dispatch
You, good Cornelius, and you, Voltemand,
For bearers of this greeting to old Norway,
Giving to you no further personal power
To business with the king, more than the scope
Of these delated articles allow.   38
     Farewell, and let your haste commend your duty.
CORNELIUS, VOLTEMAND. In that, and all things, will we show our duty.
KING. We doubt it nothing. Heartily farewell.
                              [*Exeunt* VOLTEMAND *and* CORNELIUS.]
     And now, Laertes, what's the news with you?
     You told us of some suit. What is't, Laertes?

9. *jointress:* a woman who has a jointure, or joint tenancy of an estate.   **14.** *barred:* excluded.   **21.** *Colleaguèd:* united.   **31.** *gait:* going.   **32.** *proportions:* amounts of forces and supplies.   **38.** *delated:* detailed.

You cannot speak of reason to the Dane   44
And lose your voice. What wouldst thou beg, Laertes,   45
That shall not be my offer, not thy asking?
The head is not more native to the heart,   47
The hand more instrumental to the mouth,   48
Than is the throne of Denmark to thy father.
What wouldst thou have, Laertes?
LAERTES.   My dread lord,
    Your leave and favor to return to France,
    From whence though willingly I came to Denmark
    To show my duty in your coronation,
    Yet now I must confess, that duty done,
    My thoughts and wishes bend again toward France
    And bow them to your gracious leave and pardon.
KING. Have you your father's leave? What says Polonius?
POLONIUS. He hath, my lord, wrung from me my slow leave
    By laborsome petition, and at last
    Upon his will I sealed my hard consent.
    I do beseech you give him leave to go.
KING. Take thy fair hour, Laertes. Time be thine,
    And thy best graces spend it at thy will.
    But now, my cousin Hamlet, and my son—   64
HAMLET [*aside*]. A little more than kin, and less than kind!   65
KING. How is it that the clouds still hang on you?
HAMLET. Not so, my lord. I am too much in the sun.   67
QUEEN. Good Hamlet, cast thy nighted color off,
    And let thine eye look like a friend on Denmark.
    Do not for ever with thy vailèd lids   70
    Seek for thy noble father in the dust.
    Thou know'st 'tis common. All that lives must die,
    Passing through nature to eternity.
HAMLET. Ay, madam, it is common.
QUEEN.   If it be,
    Why seems it so particular with thee?
HAMLET. Seems, madam? Nay, it is. I know not 'seems.'
    'Tis not alone my inky cloak, good mother,
    Nor customary suits of solemn black,
    Nor windy suspiration of forced breath,
    No, nor the fruitful river in the eye,
    Nor the dejected havior of the visage,

---

44. *Dane:* King of Denmark.   **45.** *lose your voice:* speak in vain.   **47.** *native:* joined by nature.
48. *instrumental:* serviceable.   **64.** *cousin:* kinsman more distant than parent, child, brother, or
sister.   **65.** *kin:* related as nephew; *kind:* kindly in feeling, as by kind, or nature, a son would be to his
father.   **67.** *sun:* sunshine of the king's undesired favor (with the punning additional meaning of "place
of a son").   **70.** *vailèd:* downcast.

Together with all forms, moods, shapes of grief,
That can denote me truly. These indeed seem,
For they are actions that a man might play,
But I have that within which passeth show—
These but the trappings and the suits of woe.
KING. 'Tis sweet and commendable in your nature, Hamlet,
To give these mourning duties to your father,
But you must know your father lost a father,
That father lost, lost his, and the survivor bound
In filial obligation for some term
To do obsequious sorrow. But to persever   92
In obstinate condolement is a course
Of impious stubbornness. 'Tis unmanly grief.
It shows a will most incorrect to heaven,
A heart unfortified, a mind impatient,
An understanding simple and unschooled.
For what we know must be and is as common
As any the most vulgar thing to sense,
Why should we in our peevish opposition
Take it to heart? Fie, 'tis a fault to heaven,
A fault against the dead, a fault to nature,
To reason most absurd, whose common theme
Is death of fathers, and who still hath cried,
From the first corse till he that died to-day,
'This must be so.' We pray you throw to earth
This unprevailing woe, and think of us
As of a father, for let the world take note
You are the most immediate to our throne,
And with no less nobility of love
Than that which dearest father bears his son
Do I impart toward you. For your intent
In going back to school in Wittenberg,
It is most retrograde to our desire,   114
And we beseech you, bend you to remain
Here in the cheer and comfort of our eye,
Our chiefest courtier, cousin, and our son.
QUEEN. Let not thy mother lose her prayers, Hamlet.
I pray thee stay with us, go not to Wittenberg.
HAMLET. I shall in all my best obey you, madam.
KING. Why, 'tis a loving and a fair reply.
Be as ourself in Denmark. Madam, come.

---

92. *obsequious:* proper to obsequies or funerals; *persever:* persevere (accented on the second syllable, as always in Shakespeare).   **114.** *retrograde:* contrary.

This gentle and unforced accord of Hamlet
Sits smiling to my heart, in grace whereof
No jocund health that Denmark drinks to-day
But the great cannon to the clouds shall tell,
And the king's rouse the heaven shall bruit again,   127
Respeaking earthly thunder. Come away.

[*Flourish. Exeunt all but* HAMLET.]

HAMLET. O that this too too sullied flesh would melt,
Thaw, and resolve itself into a dew,
Or that the Everlasting had not fixed
His canon 'gainst self-slaughter. O God, God,   132
How weary, stale, flat, and unprofitable
Seem to me all the uses of this world!
Fie on't, ah, fie, 'tis an unweeded garden
That grows to seed. Things rank and gross in nature
Possess it merely. That it should come to this,   137
But two months dead, nay, not so much, not two,
So excellent a king, that was to this
Hyperion to a satyr, so loving to my mother   140
That he might not beteem the winds of heaven   141
Visit her face too roughly. Heaven and earth,
Must I remember? Why, she would hang on him
As if increase of appetite had grown
By what it fed on, and yet within a month—
Let me not think on't; frailty, thy name is woman—
A little month, or ere those shoes were old
With which she followed my poor father's body
Like Niobe, all tears, why she, even she—   149
O God, a beast that wants discourse of reason   150
Would have mourned longer—married with my uncle,
My father's brother, but no more like my father
Than I to Hercules. Within a month,
Ere yet the salt of most unrighteous tears
Had left the flushing in her gallèd eyes,   155
She married. O, most wicked speed, to post
With such dexterity to incestuous sheets!
It is not nor it cannot come to good.
But break my heart, for I must hold my tongue.

[*Enter* HORATIO, MARCELLUS, *and* BERNARDO.]

---

127. *rouse:* toast drunk in wine; *bruit:* echo.   **132.** *canon:* law.   **137.** *merely:* completely.   **140.** *Hyperion:* the sun god.   **141.** *beteem:* allow.   **149.** *Niobe:* the proud mother who boasted of having more children than Leto and was punished when they were slain by Apollo and Artemis, children of Leto; the grieving Niobe was changed by Zeus into a stone, which continually dropped tears.   **150.** *discourse:* logical power or process.   **155.** *gallèd:* irritated.

HORATIO. Hail to your lordship!

HAMLET.   I am glad to see you well.
  Horatio—or I do forget myself.

HORATIO. The same, my lord, and your poor servant ever.

HAMLET. Sir, my good friend, I'll change that name with you.   163
  And what make you from Wittenberg, Horatio?   164
  Marcellus?

MARCELLUS. My good lord!

HAMLET. I am very glad to see you. [*to* BERNARDO] Good even, sir.
  But what, in faith, make you from Wittenberg?

HORATIO. A truant disposition, good my lord.

HAMLET. I would not hear your enemy say so,
  Nor shall you do my ear that violence
  To make it truster of your own report
  Against yourself. I know you are no truant.
  But what is your affair in Elsinore?
  We'll teach you to drink deep ere you depart.

HORATIO. My lord, I came to see your father's funeral.

HAMLET. I prithee do not mock me, fellow student.
  I think it was to see my mother's wedding.

HORATIO. Indeed, my lord, it followed hard upon.

HAMLET. Thrift, thrift, Horatio. The funeral baked meats
  Did coldly furnish forth the marriage tables.
  Would I had met my dearest foe in heaven   182
  Or ever I had seen that day, Horatio!
  My father—methinks I see my father.

HORATIO. Where, my lord?

HAMLET.   In my mind's eye, Horatio.

HORATIO. I saw him once. 'A was a goodly king.

HAMLET. 'A was a man, take him for all in all,
  I shall not look upon his like again.

HORATIO. My lord, I think I saw him yesternight.

HAMLET. Saw? who?

HORATIO. My lord, the king your father.

HAMLET.   The king my father?

HORATIO. Season your admiration for a while   192
  With an attent ear till I may deliver
  Upon the witness of these gentlemen
  This marvel to you.

HAMLET.   For God's love let me hear!

HORATIO. Two nights together had these gentlemen,
  Marcellus and Bernardo, on their watch

---

163. *change:* exchange.   **164.** *make:* do.   **182.** *dearest:* direst, bitterest.   **192.** *Season your admiration:* control your wonder.

In the dead waste and middle of the night
Been thus encountered. A figure like your father,
Armèd at point exactly, cap-a-pe,   200
Appears before them and with solemn march
Goes slow and stately by them. Thrice he walked
By their oppressed and fear-suprisèd eyes
Within his truncheon's length, whilst they, distilled   204
Almost to jelly with the act of fear,
Stand dumb and speak not to him. This to me
In dreadful secrecy impart they did,
And I with them the third night kept the watch,
Where, as they had delivered, both in time,
Form of the thing, each word made true and good,
The apparition comes. I knew your father.
These hands are not more like.
HAMLET.   But where was this?
MARCELLUS. My lord, upon the platform where we watched.
HAMLET. Did you not speak to it?
HORATIO.   My lord, I did,
    But answer made it none. Yet once methought
    It lifted up it head and did address   216
    Itself to motion like as it would speak.
    But even then the morning cock crew loud,
    And at the sound it shrunk in haste away
    And vanished from our sight.
HAMLET.   'Tis very strange.
HORATIO. As I do live, my honored lord, 'tis true,
    And we did think it writ down in our duty
    To let you know of it.
HAMLET. Indeed, indeed, sirs, but this troubles me.
    Hold you the watch to-night?
ALL.   We do, my lord.
HAMLET. Armed, say you?
ALL. Armed, my lord.
HAMLET. From top to toe?
ALL.   My lord, from head to foot.
HAMLET. Then saw you not his face?
HORATIO. O, yes, my lord. He wore his beaver up.   230
HAMLET. What, looked he frowningly?
HORATIO. A countenance more in sorrow than in anger.
HAMLET. Pale or red?
HORATIO. Nay, very pale.

---

200. *at point:* completely; *cap-a-pe:* from head to foot.   **204.** *truncheon:* military commander's baton.   **216.** *it:* its.   **230.** *beaver:* visor or movable face-guard of the helmet.

HAMLET.   And fixed his eyes upon you?
HORATIO. Most constantly.
HAMLET.   I would I had been there.
HORATIO. It would have much amazed you.
HAMLET. Very like, very like. Stayed it long?
HORATIO. While one with moderate haste might tell a hundred. 238
BOTH. Longer, longer.
HORATIO. Not when I saw't.
HAMLET.   His beard was grizzled, no? 240
HORATIO. It was as I have seen it in his life,
 A sable silvered. 242
HAMLET.   I will watch to-night.
 Perchance 'twill walk again.
HORATIO.   I warr'nt it will.
HAMLET. If it assume my noble father's person,
 I'll speak to it though hell itself should gape
 And bid me hold my peace. I pray you all,
 If you have hitherto concealed this sight,
 Let it be tenable in your silence still, 248
 And whatsomever else shall hap to-night,
 Give it an understanding but no tongue.
 I will requite your loves. So fare you well.
 Upon the platform, 'twixt eleven and twelve
 I'll visit you.
ALL.   Our duty to your honor.
HAMLET. Your loves, as mine to you. Farewell.

           [*Exeunt all but* HAMLET.]

 My father's spirit—in arms? All is not well.
 I doubt some foul play. Would the night were come! 256
 Till then sit still, my soul. Foul deeds will rise,
 Though all the earth o'erwhelm them, to men's eyes. [*Exit.*]

ACT I, SCENE 3

[*Enter* LAERTES *and* OPHELIA, *his sister.*]

LAERTES. My necessaries are embarked. Farewell.
 And, sister, as the winds give benefit
 And convoy is assistant, do not sleep, 3
 But let me hear from you.
OPHELIA.   Do you doubt that?
LAERTES. For Hamlet, and the trifling of his favor,

---

238. *tell:* count. **240.** *grizzled:* grey. **242.** *sable silvered:* black mixed with white. **248.** *tenable:* held firmly. **256.** *doubt:* suspect, fear.
I, 3. Elsinore Castle: the chambers of Polonius. **3.** *convoy:* means of transport.

Hold it a fashion and a toy in blood,
A violet in the youth of primy nature,   7
Forward, not permanent, sweet, not lasting,
The perfume and suppliance of a minute,   9
No more.

OPHELIA.   No more but so?

LAERTES.   Think it no more.
For nature crescent does not grow alone   11
In thews and bulk, but as this temple waxes   12
The inward service of the mind and soul
Grows wide withal. Perhaps he loves you now,
And now no soil nor cautel doth besmirch   15
The virtue of his will, but you must fear,   16
His greatness weighed, his will is not his own.   17
For he himself is subject to his birth.
He may not, as unvalued persons do,
Carve for himself, for on his choice depends
The safety and health of this whole state,
And therefore must his choice be circumscribed
Unto the voice and yielding of that body   23
Whereof he is the head. Then if he says he loves you,
It fits your wisdom so far to believe it
As he in his particular act and place
May give his saying deed, which is no further
Than the main voice of Denmark goes withal.
Then weigh what loss your honor may sustain
If with too credent ear you list his songs,   30
Or lose your heart, or your chaste treasure open
To his unmastered importunity.
Fear it, Ophelia, fear it, my dear sister,
And keep you in the rear of your affection,   34
Out of the shot and danger of desire.
The chariest maid is prodigal enough
If she unmask her beauty to the moon.
Virtue itself scapes not calumnious strokes.
The canker galls the infants of the spring   39
Too oft before their buttons be disclosed,   40
And in the morn and liquid dew of youth
Contagious blastments are most imminent.   42
Be wary then; best safety lies in fear.
Youth to itself rebels, though none else near.

---

7. *primy:* of the springtime.   **9.** *perfume and suppliance:* filling sweetness.   **11.** *crescent:* growing.   **12.** *this temple:* the body.   **15.** *cautel:* deceit.   **16.** *will:* desire.   **17.** *greatness weighed:* high position considered.   **23.** *yielding:* assent.   **30.** *credent:* credulous.   **34.** *affection:* feelings, which rashly lead forward into dangers.   **39.** *canker:* rose worm; *galls:* injures.   **40.** *buttons:* buds.   **42.** *blastments:* blights.

OPHELIA. I shall the effect of this good lesson keep
  As watchman to my heart, but, good my brother,
  Do not as some ungracious pastors do,
  Show me the steep and thorny way to heaven,
  Whiles like a puffed and reckless libertine
  Himself the primrose path of dalliance treads
  And recks not his own rede.   51

[*Enter* POLONIUS.]

LAERTES.   O, fear me not.
  I stay too long. But here my father comes.
  A double blessing is a double grace;
  Occasion smiles upon a second leave.
POLONIUS. Yet here, Laertes? Aboard, aboard, for shame!
  The wind sits in the shoulder of your sail,
  And you are stayed for. There—my blessing with thee,
  And these few precepts in thy memory
  Look thou character. Give thy thoughts no tongue,   59
  Nor any unproportioned thought his act.   60
  Be thou familiar, but by no means vulgar.
  Those friends thou hast, and their adoption tried,
  Grapple them unto thy soul with hoops of steel,
  But do not dull thy palm with entertainment
  Of each new-hatched, unfledged courage. Beware   65
  Of entrance to a quarrel; but being in,
  Bear't that th' opposèd may beware of thee.
  Give every man thine ear, but few thy voice;
  Take each man's censure, but reserve thy judgment.   69
  Costly thy habit as thy purse can buy,
  But not expressed in fancy; rich, not gaudy,
  For the apparel oft proclaims the man,
  And they in France of the best rank and station
  Are of a most select and generous chief in that.   74
  Neither a borrower nor a lender be,
  For loan oft loses both itself and friend,
  And borrowing dulleth edge of husbandry.   77
  This above all, to thine own self be true,
  And it must follow as the night the day
  Thou canst not then be false to any man.
  Farewell. My blessing season this in thee!   81
LAERTES. Most humbly do I take my leave, my lord.
POLONIUS. The time invites you. Go, your servants tend.   83

51. *recks:* regards; *rede:* counsel. **59.** *character:* inscribe. **60.** *unproportioned:* unadjusted to what is right. **65.** *courage:* man of spirit, young blood. **69.** *censure:* judgment. **74.** *chief:* eminence. **77.** *husbandry:* thriftiness. **81.** *season:* ripen and make fruitful. **83.** *tend:* wait.

LAERTES. Farewell, Ophelia, and remember well
    What I have said to you.
OPHELIA.   'Tis in my memory locked,
    And you yourself shall keep the key of it.
LAERTES. Farewell.   [*Exit* LAERTES.]
POLONIUS. What is't, Ophelia, he hath said to you?
OPHELIA. So please you, something touching the Lord Hamlet.
POLONIUS. Marry, well bethought.   90
    'Tis told me he hath very oft of late
    Given private time to you, and you yourself
    Have of your audience been most free and bounteous.
    If it be so—as so 'tis put on me,
    And that in way of caution—I must tell you
    You do not understand yourself so clearly
    As it behooves my daughter and your honor.
    What is between you? Give me up the truth.
OPHELIA. He hath, my lord, of late made many tenders   99
    Of his affection to me.
POLONIUS. Affection? Pooh! You speak like a green girl,
    Unsifted in such perilous circumstance.   102
    Do you believe his tenders, as you call them?
OPHELIA. I do not know, my lord, what I should think.
POLONIUS. Marry, I will teach you. Think yourself a baby
    That you have ta'en these tenders for true pay   106
    Which are not sterling. Tender yourself more dearly,
    Or (not to crack the wind of the poor phrase,   108
    Running it thus) you'll tender me a fool.
OPHELIA. My lord, he hath importuned me with love
    In honorable fashion.
POLONIUS. Ay, fashion you may call it. Go to, go to.   112
OPHELIA. And hath given countenance to his speech, my lord,
    With almost all the holy vows of heaven.
POLONIUS. Ay, springes to catch woodcocks. I do know,   115
    When the blood burns, how prodigal the soul
    Lends the tongue vows. These blazes, daughter,
    Give more light than heat, extinct in both
    Even in their promise, as it is a-making,
    You must not take for fire. From this time
    Be something scanter of your maiden presence.

---

90. *Marry:* by Mary.   **99.** *tenders:* offers.   **102.** *Unsifted:* untested.   **106–09.** *tenders . . . Tender . . . tender:* offers . . . hold in regard . . . present (a word play going through three meanings, the last use of the word yielding further complexity with its valid implications that she will show herself to him as a fool, will show him to the world as a fool, and may go so far as to present him with a baby, which would be a fool because "fool" was an Elizabethan term of endearment especially applicable to an infant as a "little innocent").   **108.** *crack . . . of:* make wheeze like a horse driven too hard.   **112.** *Go to:* go away, go on (expressing impatience).   **115.** *springes:* snares; *woodcocks:* birds believed foolish.

Set your entreatments at a higher rate 122
Than a command to parley. For Lord Hamlet, 123
Believe so much in him that he is young,
And with a larger tether may he walk
Than may be given you. In few, Ophelia,
Do not believe his vows, for they are brokers, 127
Not of that dye which their investments show, 128
But mere implorators of unholy suits,
Breathing like sanctified and pious bawds,
The better to beguile. This is for all:
I would not, in plain terms, from this time forth
Have you so slander any moment leisure 133
As to give words or talk with the Lord Hamlet.
Look to't, I charge you. Come your ways.
OPHELIA. I shall obey, my lord.   [*Exeunt.*]

ACT I, SCENE 4

[*Enter* HAMLET, HORATIO, *and* MARCELLUS.]

HAMLET. The air bites shrewdly; it is very cold. 1
HORATIO. It is a nipping and an eager air. 2
HAMLET. What hour now?
HORATIO.   I think it lacks of twelve.
MARCELLUS. No, it is struck.
HORATIO. Indeed? I heard it not. It then draws near the season
    Wherein the spirit held his wont to walk.

[*A flourish of trumpets, and two pieces goes off.*]

    What does this mean, my lord?
HAMLET. The king doth wake to-night and takes his rouse, 8
    Keeps wassail, and the swaggering upspring reels, 9
    And as he drains his draughts of Rhenish down 10
    The kettledrum and trumpet thus bray out
    The triumph of his pledge. 12
HORATIO.   Is it a custom?
HAMLET. Ay, marry, is't,
    But to my mind, though I am native here
    And to the manner born, it is custom
    More honored in the breach than the observance. 16

---

122. *entreatments:* military negotiations for surrender.   **123.** *parley:* confer with a besieger.   **127.** *brokers:* middlemen, panders.   **128.** *investments:* clothes.   **133.** *slander:* use disgracefully; *moment:* momentary. **I, 4.** The sentry-post.   **1.** *shrewdly:* wickedly.   **2.** *eager:* sharp.   **8.** *rouse:* carousal.   **9.** *upspring:* a German dance.   **10.** *Rhenish:* Rhine wine.   **12.** *triumph:* achievement, feat (in downing a cup of wine at one draught).   **16.** *More . . . observance:* better broken than observed.

This heavy-headed revel east and west
Makes us traduced and taxed of other nations.   18
They clepe us drunkards and with swinish phrase   19
Soil our addition, and indeed it takes   20
From our achievements, though performed at height,
The pith and marrow of our attribute.   22
So oft it chances in particular men
That (for some vicious mole of nature in them,   24
As in their birth, wherein they are not guilty,
Since nature cannot choose his origin)   26
By the o'ergrowth of some complexion,   27
Oft breaking down the pales and forts of reason,   28
Or by some habit that too much o'erleavens   29
The form of plausive manners—that (these men   30
Carrying, I say, the stamp of one defect,
Being nature's livery, or fortune's star)   32
Their virtues else, be they as pure as grace,
As infinite as man may undergo,
Shall in the general censure take corruption
From that particular fault. The dram of evil
Doth all the noble substance of a doubt,
To his own scandal.

[*Enter* GHOST.]

HORATIO.   Look, my lord, it comes.
HAMLET. Angels and ministers of grace defend us!
Be thou a spirit of health or goblin damned,   40
Bring with thee airs from heaven or blasts from hell,
Be thy intents wicked or charitable,
Thou com'st in such a questionable shape
That I will speak to thee. I'll call thee Hamlet,
King, father, royal Dane. O, answer me!
Let me not burst in ignorance, but tell
Why thy canonized bones, hearsèd in death,   47
Have burst their cerements, why the sepulchre   48
Wherein we saw thee quietly interred
Hath oped his ponderous and marble jaws
To cast thee up again. What may this mean
That thou, dead corse, again in complete steel,
Revisits thus the glimpses of the moon,

---

18. *taxed of:* censured by.   **19.** *clepe:* call.   **20.** *addition:* reputation, title added as a distinction.   **22.** *attribute:* reputation, what is attributed.   **24.** *mole:* blemish, flaw.   **26.** *his:* its.   **27.** *complexion:* part of the make-up, combination of humors.   **28.** *pales:* barriers, fences.   **29.** *o'erleavens:* works change throughout, as yeast ferments dough.   **30.** *plausive:* pleasing.   **32.** *livery:* characteristic equipment or provision; *star:* make-up as formed by stellar influence.   **40.** *of health:* sound, good; *goblin:* fiend.   **47.** *canonized:* buried with the established rites of the Church.   **48.** *cerements:* waxed grave-cloths.

Making night hideous, and we fools of nature   54
So horridly to shake our disposition
With thoughts beyond the reaches of our souls?
Say, why is this? wherefore? what should we do?

[GHOST *beckons.*]

HORATIO. It beckons you to go away with it,
    As if it some impartment did desire
    To you alone.
MARCELLUS.   Look with what courteous action
    It waves you to a more removèd ground.
    But do not go with it.
HORATIO.   No, by no means.
HAMLET. It will not speak. Then will I follow it.
HORATIO. Do not, my lord.
HAMLET.   Why, what should be the fear?
    I do not set my life at a pin's fee,
    And for my soul, what can it do to that,
    Being a thing immortal as itself?
    It waves me forth again. I'll follow it.
HORATIO. What if it tempt you toward the flood, my lord,
    Or to the dreadful summit of the cliff
    That beetles o'er his base into the sea,   71
    And there assume some other horrible form,
    Which might deprive your sovereignty of reason   73
    And draw you into madness? Think of it.
    The very place puts toys of desperation,   75
    Without more motive, into every brain
    That looks so many fathoms to the sea
    And hears it roar beneath.
HAMLET.   It waves me still.
    Go on. I'll follow thee.
MARCELLUS. You shall not go, my lord.
HAMLET.   Hold off your hands.
HORATIO. Be ruled. You shall not go.
HAMLET.   My fate cries out
    And makes each petty artere in this body   82
    As hardy as the Nemean lion's nerve.   83
    Still am I called. Unhand me, gentlemen.
    By heaven, I'll make a ghost of him that lets me!   85
    I say, away! Go on. I'll follow thee.   [*Exit* GHOST, *and* HAMLET.]

---

54. *fools of nature:* men made conscious of natural limitations by a supernatural manifestation. **71.**
beetles: juts out. **73.** *deprive:* take away; *sovereignty of reason:* state of being ruled by reason. **75.**
toys: fancies. **82.** *artere:* artery. **83.** *Nemean lion:* a lion slain by Hercules in the performance of one
of his twelve labors; *nerve:* sinew. **85.** *lets:* hinders.

HORATIO. He waxes desperate with imagination.
MARCELLUS. Let's follow. 'Tis not fit thus to obey him.
HORATIO. Have after. To what issue will this come?
MARCELLUS. Something is rotten in the state of Denmark.
HORATIO. Heaven will direct it.
MARCELLUS.   Nay, let's follow him.   [*Exeunt.*]

ACT I, SCENE 5

[*Enter* GHOST *and* HAMLET.]

HAMLET. Whither wilt thou lead me? Speak. I'll go no further.
GHOST. Mark me.
HAMLET.   I will.
GHOST   My hour is almost come,
   When I to sulph'rous and tormenting flames   3
   Must render up myself.
HAMLET.   Alas, poor ghost!
GHOST. Pity me not, but lend thy serious hearing
   To what I shall unfold.
HAMLET.   Speak. I am bound to hear.
GHOST. So art thou to revenge, when thou shalt hear.
HAMLET. What?
GHOST. I am thy father's spirit,
   Doomed for a certain term to walk the night,
   And for the day confined to fast in fires,   11
   Till the foul crimes done in my days of nature
   Are burnt and purged away. But that I am forbid
   To tell the secrets of my prison house,
   I could a tale unfold whose lightest word
   Would harrow up thy soul, freeze thy young blood,
   Make thy two eyes like stars start from their spheres,   17
   Thy knotted and combinèd locks to part,
   And each particular hair to stand an end   19
   Like quills upon the fretful porpentine.   20
   But this eternal blazon must not be   21
   To ears of flesh and blood. List, list, O, list!
   If thou didst ever thy dear father love—
HAMLET. O God!
GHOST. Revenge his foul and most unnatural murder.
HAMLET. Murder?

I, 5. Another part of the fortifications. **3.** *flames:* sufferings in purgatory (not hell). **11.** *fast:* do penance. **17.** *spheres:* transparent revolving shells in each of which, according to the Ptolemaic astronomy, a planet or other heavenly body was placed. **19.** *an:* on. **20.** *porpentine:* porcupine. **21.** *eternal blazon:* revelation of eternity.

GHOST. Murder most foul, as in the best it is,
　But this most foul, strange, and unnatural.
HAMLET. Haste me to know't, that I, with wings as swift
　As meditation or the thoughts of love,　　　　　　　　　　30
　May sweep to my revenge.
GHOST.　　　　　　　　　　I find thee apt,
　And duller shouldst thou be than the fat weed
　That roots itself in ease on Lethe wharf,　　　　　　　　33
　Wouldst thou not stir in this. Now, Hamlet, hear.
　'Tis given out that, sleeping in my orchard,
　A serpent stung me. So the whole ear of Denmark
　Is by a forgèd process of my death　　　　　　　　　　37
　Rankly abused. But know, thou noble youth,
　The serpent that did sting thy father's life
　Now wears his crown.
HAMLET.　　　　　　　　O my prophetic soul!
　My uncle?
GHOST. Ay, that incestuous, that adulterate beast,　　　　42
　With witchcraft of his wit, with traitorous gifts—
　O wicked wit and gifts, that have the power
　So to seduce!—won to his shameful lust
　The will of my most seeming-virtuous queen.
　O Hamlet, what a falling-off was there,
　From me, whose love was of that dignity
　That it went hand in hand even with the vow
　I made to her in marriage, and to decline
　Upon a wretch whose natural gifts were poor
　To those of mine!
　But virtue, as it never will be moved,
　Though lewdness court it in a shape of heaven,　　　　54
　So lust, though to a radiant angel linked,
　Will sate itself in a celestial bed
　And prey on garbage.
　But soft, methinks I scent the morning air.
　Brief let me be. Sleeping within my orchard,
　My custom always of the afternoon,
　Upon my secure hour thy uncle stole　　　　　　　　61
　With juice of cursed hebona in a vial,　　　　　　　　62
　And in the porches of my ears did pour
　The leperous distilment, whose effect
　Holds such an enmity with blood of man

---

30. *meditation:* thought.　　**33.** *Lethe:* the river in Hades which brings forgetfulness of past life to a spirit who drinks of it.　　**37.** *forgèd process:* falsified official report.　　**42.** *adulterate:* adulterous.　　**54.** *shape of heaven:* angelic disguise.　　**61.** *secure:* carefree, unsuspecting.　　**62.** *hebona:* some poisonous plant.

That swift as quicksilver it courses through
The natural gates and alleys of the body,
And with a sudden vigor it doth posset   68
And curd, like eager droppings into milk,   69
The thin and wholesome blood. So did it mine,
And a most instant tetter barked about   71
Most lazar-like with vile and loathsome crust   72
All my smooth body.
Thus was I sleeping by a brother's hand
Of life, of crown, of queen at once dispatched,
Cut off even in the blossoms of my sin,
Unhouseled, disappointed, unaneled,   77
No reck'ning made, but sent to my account
With all my imperfections on my head.
O, horrible! O, horrible! most horrible!
If thou hast nature in thee, bear it not.
Let not the royal bed of Denmark be
A couch for luxury and damnèd incest.   83
But howsomever thou pursues this act,
Taint not thy mind, nor let thy soul contrive
Against thy mother aught. Leave her to heaven
And to those thorns that in her bosom lodge
To prick and sting her. Fare thee well at once.
The glowworm shows the matin to be near   89
And gins to pale his uneffectual fire.
Adieu, adieu, adieu. Remember me.   [*Exit.*]
HAMLET. O all you host of heaven! O earth! What else?
And shall I couple hell? O fie! Hold, hold, my heart,
And you, my sinews, grow not instant old,
But bear me stiffly up. Remember thee?
Ay, thou poor ghost, while memory holds a seat
In this distracted globe. Remember thee?   97
Yea, from the table of my memory   98
I'll wipe away all trivial fond records,
All saws of books, all forms, all pressures past   100
That youth and observation copied there,
And thy commandment all alone shall live
Within the book and volume of my brain,
Unmixed with baser matter. Yes, by heaven!
O most pernicious woman!
O villain, villain, smiling, damnèd villain!

---

68. *posset:* curdle. **69.** *eager:* sour. **71.** *tetter:* eruption; *barked:* covered as with a bark. **72.** *lazar-like:* leper-like. **77.** *Unhouseled:* without the Sacrament; *disappointed:* unprepared spiritually; *unaneled:* without extreme unction. **83.** *luxury:* lust. **89.** *matin:* morning. **97.** *globe:* head. **98.** *table:* writing tablet, record book. **100.** *saws:* wise sayings; *forms:* mental images, concepts; *pressures:* impressions.

My tables—meet it is I set it down
That one may smile, and smile, and be a villain.
At least I am sure it may be so in Denmark.

[*Writes.*]

So, uncle, there you are. Now to my word:
It is 'Adieu, adieu, remember me.'
I have sworn't.

[*Enter* HORATIO *and* MARCELLUS.]

HORATIO. My lord, my lord!
MARCELLUS.   Lord Hamlet!
HORATIO.   Heavens secure him!
HAMLET. So be it!
MARCELLUS. Illo, ho, ho, my lord!   115
HAMLET. Hillo, ho, ho, boy! Come, bird, come.
MARCELLUS. How is't, my noble lord?
HORATIO.   What news, my lord?
HAMLET. O, wonderful!
HORATIO. Good my lord, tell it.
HAMLET.   No, you will reveal it.
HORATIO. Not I, my lord, by heaven.
MARCELLUS.   Nor I, my lord.
HAMLET. How say you then? Would heart of man once think it?
  But you'll be secret?
BOTH.   Ay, by heaven, my lord.
HAMLET. There's never a villain dwelling in all Denmark
  But he's an arrant knave.
HORATIO. There needs no ghost, my lord, come from the grave
  To tell us this.
HAMLET.   Why, right, you are in the right,
  And so, without more circumstance at all,   127
  I hold it fit that we shake hands and part:
  You, as your business and desires shall point you,
  For every man hath business and desire
  Such as it is, and for my own poor part,
  Look you, I'll go pray.
HORATIO. These are but wild and whirling words, my lord.
HAMLET. I am sorry they offend you, heartily;
  Yes, faith, heartily.
HORATIO.   There's no offense, my lord.
HAMLET. Yes, by Saint Patrick, but there is, Horatio,
  And much offense too. Touching this vision here,

115. *Illo, ho, ho:* cry of the falconer to summon his hawk.   **127.** *circumstance:* ceremony.

It is an honest ghost, that let me tell you.   138
For your desire to know what is between us,
O'ermaster't as you may. And now, good friends,
As you are friends, scholars, and soldiers,
Give me one poor request.
HORATIO. What is't, my lord? We will.
HAMLET. Never make known what you have seen to-night.
BOTH. My lord, we will not.
HAMLET.   Nay, but swear't.
HORATIO.   In faith,
My lord, not I.
MARCELLUS.   Nor I, my lord—in faith.
HAMLET. Upon my sword.   147
MARCELLUS.   We have sworn, my lord, already.
HAMLET. Indeed, upon my sword, indeed.

[GHOST *cries under the stage.*]

GHOST. Swear.
HAMLET. Ha, ha, boy, say'st thou so? Art thou there, truepenny?   150
Come on. You hear this fellow in the cellarage.
Consent to swear.
HORATIO.   Propose the oath, my lord.
HAMLET. Never to speak of this that you have seen,
Swear by my sword.
GHOST [*beneath*]. Swear.
HAMLET. Hic et ubique? Then we'll shift our ground.   156
Come hither, gentlemen,
And lay your hands again upon my sword.
Swear by my sword
Never to speak of this that you have heard.
GHOST [*beneath*]. Swear by his sword.
HAMLET. Well said, old mole! Canst work i'th' earth so fast?
A worthy pioner! Once more remove, good friends.   163
HORATIO. O day and night, but this is wondrous strange!
HAMLET. And therefore as a stranger give it welcome.
There are more things in heaven and earth, Horatio,
Than are dreamt of in your philosophy.   167
But come:
Here as before, never, so help you mercy,
How strange or odd some'er I bear myself
(As I perchance hereafter shall think meet
To put an antic disposition on),   172

138. *honest:* genuine (not a disguised demon).   **147.** *sword:* i.e. upon the cross formed by the sword hilt.   **150.** *truepenny:* honest old fellow.   **156.** *Hic et ubique:* here and everywhere.   **163.** *pioner:* pioneer, miner.   **167.** *your philosophy:* this philosophy one hears about.   **172.** *antic:* grotesque, mad.

That you, at such times seeing me, never shall,
With arms encumb'red thus, or this head-shake,   174
Or by pronouncing of some doubtful phrase,
As 'Well, well, we know,' or 'We could, an if we would,'   176
Or 'If we list to speak,' or 'There be, an if they might,'
Or such ambiguous giving out, to note
That you know aught of me—this do swear,
So grace and mercy at your most need help you.
GHOST [*beneath*]. Swear.

[*They swear.*]

HAMLET. Rest, rest, perturbèd spirit! So, gentlemen,
With all my love I do commend me to you,   183
And what so poor a man as Hamlet is
May do t'express his love and friending to you,
God willing, shall not lack. Let us go in together,
And still your fingers on your lips, I pray.   187
The time is out of joint. O cursèd spite
That ever I was born to set it right!
Nay, come, let's go together.   [*Exeunt.*]

ACT II, SCENE 1

[*Enter old* POLONIUS, *with his man* REYNALDO.]

POLONIUS. Give him this money and these notes, Reynaldo.
REYNALDO. I will, my lord.
POLONIUS. You shall do marvellous wisely, good Reynaldo,
Before you visit him, to make inquire
Of his behavior.
REYNALDO.   My lord, I did intend it.
POLONIUS. Marry, well said, very well said. Look you, sir,
Enquire me first what Danskers are in Paris,   7
And how, and who, what means, and where they keep,   8
What company, at what expense; and finding
By this encompassment and drift of question   10
That they do know my son, come you more nearer
Than your particular demands will touch it.   12
Take you as 'twere some distant knowledge of him,
As thus, 'I know his father and his friends,
And in part him'—do you mark this, Reynaldo?
REYNALDO. Ay, very well, my lord.

---

174. *encumb'red:* folded.   **176.** *an if:* if.   **183.** *commend:* entrust.   **187.** *still:* always.
II, 1. The chambers of Polonius.   **7.** *Danskers:* Danes.   **8.** *what means:* what their wealth; *keep:* dwell.   **10.** *encompassment:* circling about.   **12.** *particular demands:* definite questions.

POLONIUS. 'And in part him, but,' you may say, 'not well,
  But if't be he I mean, he's very wild
  Addicted so and so.' And there put on him
  What forgeries you please; marry, none so rank   20
  As may dishonor him—take heed of that—
  But, sir, such wanton, wild, and usual slips
  As are companions noted and most known
  To youth and liberty.
REYNALDO.   As gaming, my lord.
POLONIUS. Ay, or drinking, fencing, swearing, quarrelling,
  Drabbing. You may go so far.   26
REYNALDO. My lord, that would dishonor him.
POLONIUS. Faith, no, as you may season it in the charge. 28
  You must not put another scandal on him,
  That he is open to incontinency.   30
  That's not my meaning. But breathe his faults so quaintly 31
  That they may seem the taints of liberty,
  The flash and outbreak of a fiery mind,
  A savageness in unreclaimèd blood,   34
  Of general assault.   35
REYNALDO.   But, my good lord—
POLONIUS. Wherefore should you do this?
REYNALDO.   Ay, my lord,
  I would know that.
POLONIUS.   Marry, sir, here's my drift,
  And I believe it is a fetch of warrant.   38
  You laying these slight sullies on my son
  As 'twere a thing a little soiled i' th' working,
  Mark you,
  Your party in converse, him you would sound,
  Having ever seen in the prenominate crimes   43
  The youth you breathe of guilty, be assured
  He closes with you in this consequence: 45
  'Good sir,' or so, or 'friend,' or 'gentleman'—
  According to the phrase or the addition   47
  Of man and country—
REYNALDO.   Very good, my lord.
POLONIUS. And then, sir, does'a this—'a does—
  What was I about to say? By the mass, I was about to say something! Where
  did I leave?

---

20. *forgeries:* invented wrongdoings. **26.** *Drabbing:* whoring. **28.** *season:* soften. **30.** *incontinency:* extreme sensuality. **31.** *quaintly:* expertly, gracefully. **34.** *unreclaimèd:* untamed. **35.** *Of general assault:* assailing all young men. **38.** *fetch of warrant:* allowable trick. **43.** *Having ever:* if he has ever; *prenominate:* aforementioned. **45.** *closes with you:* follows your lead to a conclusion; *consequence:* following way. **47.** *addition:* title.

REYNALDO. At 'closes in the consequence,' at 'friend or so,' and 'gentleman.'
POLONIUS. At 'closes in the consequence'—Ay, marry!
  He closes thus: 'I know the gentleman;
  I saw him yesterday, or t' other day,
  Or then, or then, with such or such, and, as you say,
  There was 'a gaming, there o'ertook in's rouse,   57
  There falling out at tennis'; or perchance,   58
  'I saw him enter such a house of sale,'
  Videlicet, a brothel, or so forth.   60
  See you now—
  Your bait of falsehood takes this carp of truth,
  And thus do we of wisdom and of reach,   63
  With windlasses and with assays of bias,   64
  By indirections find directions out.   65
  So, by my former lecture and advice,
  Shall you my son. You have me, have you not?
REYNALDO. My lord, I have.
POLONIUS.   God bye ye, fare ye well.   68
REYNALDO. Good my lord.
POLONIUS. Observe his inclination in yourself.
REYNALDO. I shall, my lord.
POLONIUS. And let him ply his music.
REYNALDO.   Well, my lord.
POLONIUS. Farewell.   [*Exit* REYNALDO.]

[*Enter* OPHELIA.]

                How now, Ophelia, what's the matter?
OPHELIA. O my lord, my lord, I have been so affrighted!
POLONIUS. With what, i' th' name of God?
OPHELIA. My lord, as I was sewing in my closet,   76
  Lord Hamlet, with his doublet all unbraced,   77
  No hat upon his head, his stockings fouled,
  Ungartered, and down-gyvèd to his ankle,   79
  Pale as his shirt, his knees knocking each other,
  And with a look so piteous in purport
  As if he had been loosèd out of hell
  To speak of horrors—he comes before me.
POLONIUS. Mad for thy love?
OPHELIA.   My lord, I do not know,
  But truly I do fear it.
POLONIUS.   What said he?

---

57. *o'ertook:* overcome with drunkenness; *rouse:* carousal.   **58.** *falling out:* quarrelling.   **60.** *Videlicet:* namely.   **63.** *reach:* far-reaching comprehension.   **64.** *windlasses:* roundabout courses; *assays of bias:* devious attacks.   **65.** *directions:* ways of procedure.   **68.** *God bye ye:* God be with you, good-bye.   **76.** *closet:* private living-room.   **77.** *doublet:* jacket; *umbraced:* unlaced.   **79.** *down-gyvèd:* fallen down like gyves or fetters on a prisoner's legs.

OPHELIA. He took me by the wrist and held me hard.
  Then goes he to the length of all his arm,
  And with his other hand thus o'er his brow
  He falls to such perusal of my face
  As 'a would draw it. Long stayed he so.
  At last, a little shaking of mine arm
  And thrice his head thus waving up and down,
  He raised a sigh so piteous and profound
  As it did seem to shatter all his bulk
  And end his being. That done, he lets me go,
  And with his head over his shoulder turned
  He seemed to find his way without his eyes,
  For out o'doors he went without their helps
  And to the last bended their light on me.
POLONIUS. Come, go with me. I will go seek the king.
  This is the very ecstasy of love,   101
  Whose violent property fordoes itself   102
  And leads the will to desperate undertakings
  As oft as any passion under heaven
  That does afflict our natures. I am sorry.
  What, have you given him any hard words of late?
OPHELIA. No, my good lord; but as you did command
  I did repel his letters and denied
  His access to me.
POLONIUS.   That hath made him mad.
  I am sorry that with better heed and judgment
  I had not quoted him. I feared he did but trifle   111
  And meant to wrack thee; but beshrew my jealousy.   112
  By heaven, it is as proper to our age
  To cast beyond ourselves in our opinions   114
  As it is common for the younger sort
  To lack discretion. Come, go we to the king.
  This must be known, which, being kept close, might move   117
  More grief to hide than hate to utter love.   118
  Come.   [*Exeunt.*]

ACT II, SCENE 2

[*Flourish. Enter* KING *and* QUEEN, ROSENCRANTZ, *and* GUILDENSTERN *with others.*]

KING. Welcome, dear Rosencrantz and Guildenstern.
  Moreover that we much did long to see you,   2

101. *ecstasy:* madness.   **102.** *property:* quality; *fordoes:* destroys.   **111.** *quoted:* observed.   **112.** *beshrew:* curse.   **114.** *cast beyond ourselves:* find by calculation more significance in something than we ought to.   **117.** *close:* secret; *move:* cause.   **118.** *to hide . . . love:* by such hiding of love than there would be hate moved by a revelation of it (a violently condensed putting of the case which is a triumph of special statement for Polonius).
II, 2. A chamber in the Castle.   **2.** *Moreover that:* besides the fact that.

The need we have to use you did provoke
Our hasty sending. Something have you heard
Of Hamlet's transformation—so call it,
Sith nor th' exterior nor the inward man   6
Resembles that it was. What it should be,
More than his father's death, that thus hath put him
So much from th' understanding of himself,
I cannot dream of. I entreat you both
That, being of so young days brought up with him,
And sith so neighbored to his youth and havior,   12
That you vouchsafe your rest here in our court
Some little time, so by your companies
To draw him on to pleasures, and to gather
So much as from occasion you may glean,
Whether aught to us unknown afflicts him thus,
That opened lies within our remedy.   18
QUEEN. Good gentlemen, he hath much talked of you,
   And sure I am two men there are not living
   To whom he more adheres. If it will please you   21
   To show us so much gentry and good will   22
   As to expend your time with us awhile
   For the supply and profit of our hope,
   Your visitation shall receive such thanks
   As fits a king's remembrance.
ROSENCRANTZ.   Both your majesties
   Might, by the sovereign power you have of us,
   Put your dread pleasures more into command
   Than to entreaty.
GUILDENSTERN.   But we both obey,
   And here give up ourselves in the full bent   30
   To lay our service freely at your feet,
   To be commanded.
KING. Thanks, Rosencrantz and gentle Guildenstern.
QUEEN. Thanks, Guildenstern and gentle Rosencrantz.
   And I beseech you instantly to visit
   My too much changèd son.—Go, some of you,
   And bring these gentlemen where Hamlet is.
GUILDENSTERN. Heavens make our presence and our practices
   Pleasant and helpful to him!
QUEEN.   Ay, amen!
        [*Exeunt* ROSENCRANTZ *and* GUILDENSTERN *with some Attendants.*]

[*Enter* POLONIUS.]

---

6. *Sith:* since.   **12.** *youth and havior:* youthful ways of life.   **18.** *opened:* revealed.   **21.** *more adheres:* is more attached.   **22.** *gentry:* courtesy.   **30.** *in the full bent:* at the limit of bending (of a bow), to full capacity.

POLONIUS. Th' ambassadors from Norway, my good lord,
    Are joyfully returned.
KING. Thou still hast been the father of good news.   42
POLONIUS. Have I, my lord? Assure you, my good liege,
    I hold my duty as I hold my soul,
    Both to my God and to my gracious king,
    And I do think—or else this brain of mine
    Hunts not the trail of policy so sure
    As it hath used to do—that I have found
    The very cause of Hamlet's lunacy.
KING. O, speak of that! That do I long to hear.
POLONIUS. Give first admittance to th' ambassadors.
    My news shall be the fruit to that great feast.   52
KING. Thyself do grace to them and bring them in.   [*Exit* POLONIUS.]   53
    He tells me, my dear Gertrude, he hath found
    The head and source of all your son's distemper.
QUEEN. I doubt it is no other but the main,   56
    His father's death and our o'erhasty marriage.
KING. Well, we shall sift him.

[*Enter Ambassadors* VOLTEMAND *and* CORNELIUS, *with* POLONIUS.]

                    Welcome, my good friends.
    Say, Voltemand, what from our brother Norway?
VOLTEMAND. Most fair return of greetings and desires.
    Upon our first, he sent out to suppress   61
    His nephew's levies, which to him appeared
    To be a preparation 'gainst the Polack,
    But better looked into, he truly found
    It was against your highness, whereat grieved,
    That so his sickness, age, and impotence
    Was falsely borne in hand, sends out arrests   67
    On Fortinbras; which he in brief obeys,
    Receives rebuke from Norway, and in fine   69
    Makes vow before his uncle never more
    To give th' assay of arms against your majesty.   71
    Whereon old Norway, overcome with joy,
    Gives him threescore thousand crowns in annual fee
    And his commission to employ those soldiers,
    So levied as before, against the Polack,
    With an entreaty, herein further shown,

[*Gives a paper.*]

---

42. *still:* always.   **52.** *fruit:* dessert.   **53.** *grace:* honor.   **56.** *doubt:* suspect.   **61.** *our first:* our first words about the matter.   **67.** *borne in hand:* deceived.   **69.** *in fine:* in the end.   **71.** *assay:* trial.

That it might please you to give quiet pass
Through your dominions for this enterprise,
On such regards of safety and allowance   79
As therein are set down.
KING.   It likes us well;
And at our more considered time we'll read,   81
Answer, and think upon this business.
Meantime we thank you for your well-took labor.
Go to your rest; at night we'll feast together.
Most welcome home!   [*Exeunt Ambassadors.*]
POLONIUS.   This business is well ended.
My liege and madam, to expostulate   86
What majesty should be, what duty is,
Why day is day, night night, and time is time,
Were nothing but to waste night, day, and time.
Therefore, since brevity is the soul of wit,   90
And tediousness the limbs and outward flourishes,
I will be brief. Your noble son is mad.
Mad call I it, for, to define true madness,
What is't but to be nothing else but mad?
But let that go.
QUEEN.   More matter, with less art.
POLONIUS. Madam, I swear I use no art at all.
That he is mad, 'tis true: 'tis true 'tis pity,
And pity 'tis 'tis true—a foolish figure.   98
But farewell it, for I will use no art.
Mad let us grant him then, and now remains
That we find out the cause of this effect—
Or rather say, the cause of this defect,
For this effect defective comes by cause.
Thus it remains, and the remainder thus.
Perpend.   105
I have a daughter (have while she is mine),
Who in her duty and obedience, mark,
Hath given me this. Now gather, and surmise.
     [*Reads the letter.*]
'To the celestial, and my soul's idol, the most beautified Ophelia,'—
That's an ill phrase, a vile phrase; 'beautified' is a vile phrase. But you shall
hear. Thus:
     [*Reads.*]
'In her excellent white bosom, these, &c.'
QUEEN. Came this from Hamlet to her?

79. *regards:* terms. **81.** *considered time:* convenient time for consideration. **86.** *expostulate:*
discuss. **90.** *wit:* understanding. **98.** *figure:* figure in rhetoric. **105.** *Perpend:* ponder.

POLONIUS. Good madam, stay awhile. I will be faithful.
    [*Reads.*]

'Doubt thou the stars are fire;
  Doubt that the sun doth move;
Doubt truth to be a liar;   118
  But never doubt I love.

  'O dear Ophelia, I am ill at these numbers. I have not art to reckon my 120
groans, but that I love thee best, O most best, believe it. Adieu.

'Thine evermore, most dear lady,
  whilst this machine is to him, Hamlet.'   123

This in obedience hath my daughter shown me,
And more above hath his solicitings,   125
As they fell out by time, by means, and place,
All given to mine ear.
KING.   But how hath she
  Received his love?
POLONIUS.   What do you think of me?
KING. As of a man faithful and honorable.
POLONIUS. I would fain prove so. But what might you think,
  When I had seen this hot love on the wing
  (As I perceived it, I must tell you that,
  Before my daughter told me), what might you,
  Or my dear majesty your queen here, think,
  If I had played the desk or table book,   135
  Or given my heart a winking, mute and dumb,   136
  Or looked upon this love with idle sight?
  What might you think? No, I went round to work   138
  And my young mistress thus I did bespeak:
  'Lord Hamlet is a prince, out of thy star.   140
  This must not be.' And then I prescripts gave her,   141
  That she should lock herself from his resort,
  Admit no messengers, receive no tokens.
  Which done, she took the fruits of my advice,
  And he, repellèd, a short tale to make,
  Fell into a sadness, then into a fast,
  Thence to a watch, thence into a weakness,   147
  Thence to a lightness, and, by this declension,   148
  Into the madness wherein now he raves,
  And all we mourn for.
KING.   Do you think 'tis this?
QUEEN. It may be, very like.

---

118. *Doubt:* suspect. **120.** *numbers:* verses. **123.** *machine:* body; *to:* attached to. **125.** *above:* besides. **135.** *desk or table book:* i.e. silent receiver. **136.** *winking:* closing of the eyes. **138.** *round:* roundly, plainly. **140.** *star:* condition determined by stellar influence. **141.** *prescripts:* instructions. **147.** *watch:* sleepless state. **148.** *lightness:* lightheadedness.

POLONIUS. Hath there been such a time—I would fain know that—
  That I have positively said, ''Tis so,'
  When it proved otherwise?
KING.   Not that I know.
POLONIUS [*pointing to his head and shoulder*].
  Take this from this, if this be otherwise.
  If circumstances lead me, I will find
  Where truth is hid, though it were hid indeed
  Within the center.   158
KING.   How may we try it further?
POLONIUS. You know sometimes he walks four hours together
  Here in the lobby.
QUEEN.   So he does indeed.
POLONIUS. At such a time I'll loose my daughter to him.
  Be you and I behind an arras then.   162
  Mark the encounter. If he love her not,
  And be not from his reason fallen thereon,   164
  Let me be no assistant for a state
  But keep a farm and carters.
KING.   We will try it.

[*Enter* HAMLET *reading on a book.*]

QUEEN. But look where sadly the poor wretch comes reading.
POLONIUS. Away, I do beseech you both, away.
                     [*Exit* KING *and* QUEEN *with Attendants.*]
  I'll board him presently. O, give me leave.   169
  How does my good Lord Hamlet?
HAMLET. Well, God-a-mercy.   171
POLONIUS. Do you know me, my lord?
HAMLET. Excellent well. You are a fishmonger.   173
POLONIUS. Not I, my lord.
HAMLET. Then I would you were so honest a man.
POLONIUS. Honest, my lord?
HAMLET. Ay, sir. To be honest, as this world goes, is to be one man picked out
  of ten thousand.
POLONIUS. That's very true, my lord.
HAMLET. For if the sun breed maggots in a dead dog, being a good kissing carrion—   180
  Have you a daughter?
POLONIUS. I have, my lord.
HAMLET. Let her not walk i' th' sun. Conception is a blessing, but as your daughter
  may conceive, friend, look to't.

---

158. *center:* center of the earth and also of the Ptolemaic universe.   **162.** *arras:* hanging tapestry.   **164.**
thereon: on that account.   **169.** *board:* accost; *presently:* at once.   **171.** *God-a-mercy:* thank you (literally,
"God have mercy!").   **173.** *fishmonger:* seller of harlots, procurer (a cant term used here with a glance
at the fishing Polonius is doing when he offers Ophelia as bait).   **180.** *good kissing carrion:* good bit of
flesh for kissing.

POLONIUS [*aside*]. How say you by that? Still harping on my daughter. Yet he knew me not at first. 'A said I was a fishmonger. 'A is far gone, far gone. And truly in my youth I suffered much extremity for love, very near this. I'll speak to him again—What do you read, my lord?

HAMLET. Words, words, words.

POLONIUS. What is the matter, my lord?

HAMLET. Between who?   191

POLONIUS. I mean the matter that you read, my lord.

HAMLET. Slanders, sir, for the satirical rogue says here that old men have grey beards, that their faces are wrinkled, their eyes purging thick amber and plum-tree gum, and that they have a plentiful lack of wit, together with most weak hams. All which, sir, though I most powerfully and potently believe, yet I hold it not honesty to have it thus set down, for you yourself, sir, should be old as I am if, like a crab, you could go backward.

POLONIUS [*aside*]. Though this be madness, yet there is method in't.—Will you walk out of the air, my lord?

HAMLET. Into my grave?

POLONIUS. Indeed, that's out of the air. [*aside*] How pregnant sometimes his replies   202
are! a happiness that often madness hits on, which reason and sanity could   203
not so prosperously be delivered of. I will leave him and suddenly contrive the means of meeting between him and my daughter.—My honorable lord, I will most humbly take my leave of you.

HAMLET. You cannot, sir, take from me anything that I will more willingly part withal—except my life, except my life, except my life.   208

[*Enter* GUILDENSTERN *and* ROSENCRANTZ.]

POLONIUS. Fare you well, my lord.

HAMLET. These tedious old fools!

POLONIUS. You go to seek the Lord Hamlet. There he is.

ROSENCRANTZ [*to* POLONIUS]. God save you, sir!   [*Exit* POLONIUS.]

GUILDENSTERN. My honored lord!

ROSENCRANTZ. My most dear lord!

HAMLET. My excellent good friends! How dost thou, Guildenstern? Ah, Rosencrantz! Good lads, how do ye both?

ROSENCRANTZ. As the indifferent children of the earth.   217

GUILDENSTERN. Happy in that we are not over-happy.
On Fortune's cap we are not the very button.

HAMLET. Nor the soles of her shoe?

ROSENCRANTZ. Neither, my lord.

HAMLET. Then you live about her waist, or in the middle of her favors?

GUILDENSTERN. Faith, her privates we.   223

---

191. *Between who:* matter for a quarrel between what persons (Hamlet's willful misunderstanding).
202. *pregnant:* full of meaning.   **203.** *happiness:* aptness of expression.   **208.** *withal:* with.   **217.** *indifferent:* average.   **223.** *privates:* ordinary men in private, not public, life (with obvious play upon the sexual term "private parts").

HAMLET. In the secret parts of Fortune? O, most true! she is a strumpet. What news?

ROSENCRANTZ. None, my lord, but that the world's grown honest.

HAMLET. Let me question more in particular. What have you, my good friends, deserved at the hands of Fortune that she sends you to prison hither?

GUILDENSTERN. Prison, my lord?

HAMLET. Denmark's a prison.

ROSENCRANTZ. Then is the world one.

HAMLET. A goodly one; in which there are many confines, wards, and dungeons,   232
Denmark being one o'th' worst.

ROSENCRANTZ. We think not so, my lord.

HAMLET. Why, then 'tis none to you, for there is nothing either good or bad but thinking makes it so. To me it is a prison.

ROSENCRANTZ. Why, then your ambition makes it one. 'Tis too narrow for your mind.

HAMLET. O God, I could be bounded in a nutshell and count myself a king of infinite space, were it not that I have bad dreams.

GUILDENSTERN. Which dreams indeed are ambition, for the very substance of the ambitious is merely the shadow of a dream.

HAMLET. A dream itself is but a shadow.

ROSENCRANTZ. Truly, and I hold ambition of so airy and light a quality that it is but a shadow's shadow.

HAMLET. Then are our beggars bodies, and our monarchs and outstretched heroes   246
the beggars' shadows. Shall we to th' court? for, by my fay, I cannot reason.   247

BOTH. We'll wait upon you.   248

HAMLET. No such matter. I will not sort you with the rest of my servants, for, to speak to you like an honest man, I am most dreadfully attended. But in the beaten way of friendship, what make you at Elsinore?   251

ROSENCRANTZ. To visit you, my lord; no other occasion.

HAMLET. Beggar that I am, I am even poor in thanks, but I thank you; and sure, dear friends, my thanks are too dear a halfpenny. Were you not sent for? Is   254
it your own inclining? Is it a free visitation? Come, come, deal justly with me.
Come, come. Nay, speak.

GUILDENSTERN. What should we say, my lord?

HAMLET. Why, anything—but to th' purpose. You were sent for, and there is a kind of confession in your looks, which your modesties have not craft enough to color. I know the good king and queen have sent for you.

ROSENCRANTZ. To what end, my lord?

HAMLET. That you must teach me. But let me conjure you by the rights of our fellowship, by the consonancy of our youth, by the obligation of our ever-   263

---

232. *confines:* places of imprisonment; *wards:* cells.   **246.** *bodies:* solid substances, not shadows (because beggars lack ambition); *outstretched:* elongated as shadows (with a corollary implication of far-reaching with respect to the ambitions that make both heroes and monarchs into shadows).   **247.** *fay:* faith.   **248.** *wait upon:* attend.   **251.** *make:* do.   **254.** *a halfpenny:* at a halfpenny.   **263.** *consonancy:* accord (in sameness of age).

preserved love, and by what more dear a better proposer can charge you 264
withal, be even and direct with me whether you were sent for or no.   265
ROSENCRANTZ [*aside to Guildenstern*]. What say you?
HAMLET [*aside*]. Nay then, I have an eye of you.—If you love me, hold not off.
GUILDENSTERN. My lord, we were sent for.
HAMLET. I will tell you why. So shall my anticipation prevent your discovery, 269
and your secrecy to the king and queen moult no feather. I have of late— 270
but wherefore I know not—lost all my mirth, forgone all custom of exercises;
and indeed, it goes so heavily with my disposition that this goodly frame the
earth seems to me a sterile promontory; this most excellent canopy, the air,
look you, this brave o'erhanging firmament, this majestical roof fretted with 274
golden fire—why, it appeareth nothing to me but a foul and pestilent congregation of vapors. What a piece of work is a man, how noble in reason,
how infinite in faculties; in form and moving how express and admirable, in 277
action how like an angel, in apprehension how like a god: the beauty of the
world, the paragon of animals! And yet to me what is this quintessence of 279
dust? Man delights not me—nor woman neither, though by your smiling you
seem to say so.
ROSENCRANTZ. My lord, there was no such stuff in my thoughts.
HAMLET. Why did ye laugh then, when I said 'Man delights not me'?
ROSENCRANTZ. To think, my lord, if you delight not in man, what lenten entertain- 284
ment the players shall receive from you. We coted them on the way, and 285
hither are they coming to offer you service.
HAMLET. He that plays the king shall be welcome—his majesty shall have tribute
of me—, the adventurous knight shall use his foil and target, the lover shall 288
not sigh gratis, the humorous man shall end his part in peace, the clown 289
shall make those laugh whose lungs are tickle o' th' sere, and the lady shall 290
say her mind freely, or the blank verse shall halt for't. What players are they? 291
ROSENCRANTZ. Even those you were wont to take such delight in, the tragedians
of the city.
HAMLET. How chances it they travel? Their residence, both in reputation and 294
profit, was better both ways.
ROSENCRANTZ. I think their inhibition comes by the means of the late innovation. 296
HAMLET. Do they hold the same estimation they did when I was in the city? Are
they so followed?
ROSENCRANTZ. No indeed, are they not.
HAMLET. How comes it? Do they grow rusty?
ROSENCRANTZ. Nay, their endeavor keeps in the wonted pace, but there is, sir, an

---

264. *proposer:* propounder. **265.** *withal:* with; *even:* straight. **269.** *prevent:* forestall; *discovery:* disclosure. **270.** *moult no feather:* be left whole. **274.** *firmament:* sky; *fretted:* decorated with fretwork. **277.** *express:* well framed. **279.** *quintessence:* fifth or last and finest essence (an alchemical term). **284.** *lenten:* scanty. **285.** *coted:* overtook. **288.** *foil and target:* sword and shield. **289.** *humorous man:* eccentric character dominated by one of the humours. **290.** *tickle o' th' sere:* hair-triggered for the discharge of laughter ("sere": part of a gunlock). **291.** *halt:* go lame. **294.** *residence:* residing at the capital. **296.** *inhibition:* impediment to acting in residence (formal prohibition?); *innovation:* new fashion of having companies of boy actors play on the "private" stage (?), political upheaval (?).

eyrie of children, little eyases, that cry out on the top of question and are 302
most tyrannically clapped for't. These are now the fashion, and so berattle 303
the common stages (so they call them) that many wearing rapiers are afraid 304
of goosequills and dare scarce come thither. 305

HAMLET. What, are they children? Who maintains 'em? How are they escoted? 306
Will they pursue the quality no longer than they can sing? Will they not say 307
afterwards, if they should grow themselves to common players (as it is most
like, if their means are no better), their writers do them wrong to make
them exclaim against their own succession?

ROSENCRANTZ. Faith, there has been much to do on both sides, and the nation
holds it no sin to tarre them to controversy. There was, for a while, no money 312
bid for argument unless the poet and the player went to cuffs in the question. 313

HAMLET. Is't possible?

GUILDENSTERN. O, there has been much throwing about of brains.

HAMLET. Do the boys carry it away?

ROSENCRANTZ. Ay, that they do, my lord—Hercules and his load too. 317

HAMLET. It is not very strange, for my uncle is King of Denmark, and those that
would make mows at him while my father lived give twenty, forty, fifty, a 319
hundred ducats apiece for his picture in little. 'Sblood, there is something in 320
this more than natural, if philosophy could find it out.

[*A flourish.*]

GUILDENSTERN. There are the players.

HAMLET. Gentlemen, you are welcome to Elsinore. Your hands, come then. Th'
appurtenance of welcome is fashion and ceremony. Let me comply with you
in this garb, lest my extent to the players (which I tell you must show fairly 325
outwards) should more appear like entertainment than yours. You are welcome.
But my uncle-father and aunt-mother are deceived.

GUILDENSTERN. In what, my dear lord?

HAMLET. I am but mad north-north-west. When the wind is southerly I know a
hawk from a handsaw. 330

[*Enter* POLONIUS.]

POLONIUS. Well be with you, gentlemen.

HAMLET. Hark you, Guildenstern—and you too—at each ear a hearer. That great
baby you see there is not yet out of his swaddling clouts. 333

---

302. *eyrie:* nest; *eyases:* nestling hawks; *on the top of question:* above others on matter of dispute.   **303.** *berattle:* berate.   **304.** *common stages:* "public" theatres of the "common" players, who were organized in companies mainly composed of adult actors (allusion being made to the "War of the Theatres" in Shakespeare's London).   **305.** *goosequills:* pens (of satirists who made out that the London public stage showed low taste).   **306.** *escoted:* supported.   **307.** *quality:* profession of acting; *sing:* i.e. with unchanged voices.   **312.** *tarre:* incite.   **313.** *argument:* matter of a play.   **317.** *load:* i.e. the whole world (with a topical reference to the sign of the Globe Theatre, a representation of Hercules bearing the world on his shoulders).   **319.** *mows:* grimaces.   **320.** *'Sblood:* by God's blood.   **325.** *garb:* fashion; *extent:* showing of welcome.   **330.** *hawk:* mattock or pickaxe (also called "hack"; here used apparently with a play on "hawk": a bird); *handsaw:* carpenter's tool (apparently with a play on some corrupt form of "hernshaw"; heron, a bird often hunted with the hawk).   **333.** *clouts:* clothes.

ROSENCRANTZ. Happily he is the second time come to them, for they say an old   334
man is twice a child.

HAMLET. I will prophesy he comes to tell me of the players. Mark it.—You say
right, sir; a Monday morning, 'twas then indeed.

POLONIUS. My lord, I have news to tell you.

HAMLET. My lord, I have news to tell you. When Roscius was an actor in Rome—   339

POLONIUS. The actors are come hither, my lord.

HAMLET. Buzz, buzz.

POLONIUS. Upon my honor—

HAMLET. Then came each actor on his ass—

POLONIUS. The best actors in the world, either for tragedy, comedy, history, pastoral,
pastoral-comical, historical-pastoral, tragical-historical, tragical-comical-histori-
cal-pastoral; scene individable, or poem unlimited. Seneca cannot be too heavy,   346
nor Plautus too light. For the law of writ and the liberty, these are the only   347
men.

HAMLET. O Jephthah, judge of Israel, what a treasure hadst thou!   349

POLONIUS. What treasure had he, my lord?

HAMLET. Why,

'One fair daughter, and no more,
The which he lovèd passing well.'

POLONIUS [aside]. Still on my daughter.

HAMLET. Am I not i' th' right, old Jephthah?

POLONIUS. If you call me Jephthah, my lord, I have a daughter that I love passing   356
well.

HAMLET. Nay, that follows not.

POLONIUS. What follows then, my lord?

HAMLET. Why,

'As by lot, God wot,'

and then, you know,

'It came to pass, as most like it was.'

The first row of the pious chanson will show you more, for look where my   364
abridgment comes.   365

[Enter the Players.]

You are welcome, masters, welcome, all.—I am glad to see thee well.—Welcome, good friends.—O, old friend, why, thy face is valanced since I saw   367
thee last. Com'st thou to beard me in Denmark?—What, my young lady and   368
mistress? By'r Lady, your ladyship is nearer to heaven than when I saw you

---

334. *Happily:* haply, perhaps.   **339.** *Roscius:* the greatest of Roman comic actors.   **346.** *scene individable:* drama observing the unities; *poem unlimited:* drama not observing the unities; *Seneca:* Roman writer of tragedies.   **347.** *Plautus:* Roman writer of comedies; *law of writ:* orthodoxy determined by critical rules of the drama; *liberty:* freedom from such orthodoxy.   **349.** *Jephthah:* the compelled sacrificer of a dearly beloved daughter (Judges xi).   **356.** *passing:* surpassingly (verses are from a ballad on Jephthah).   **364.** *row:* stanza; *chanson:* song.   **364–65.** *my abridgment:* that which shortens my talk.   **367.** *valanced:* fringed (with a beard).   **368.** *young lady:* boy who plays women's parts.

last by the altitude of a chopine. Pray God your voice, like a piece of uncurrent 370
gold, be not cracked within the ring.—Masters, you are all welcome. We'll 371
e'en to't like French falconers, fly at anything we see. We'll have a speech
straight. Come, give us a taste of your quality. Come, a passionate speech.

PLAYER. What speech, my good lord?

HAMLET. I heard thee speak me a speech once, but it was never acted, or if it
was, not above once, for the play, I remember, pleased not the million; 'twas
caviary to the general, but it was (as I received it, and others, whose judgments 377
in such matters cried in the top of mine) an excellent play, well digested in 378
the scenes, set down with as much modesty as cunning. I remember one
said there were no sallets in the lines to make the matter savory, nor no 380
matter in the phrase that might indict the author of affectation, but called it
an honest method, as wholesome as sweet, and by very much more handsome
than fine. One speech in't I chiefly loved. 'Twas Aeneas' tale to Dido, and
thereabout of it especially where he speaks of Priam's slaughter. If it live in 384
your memory, begin at this line—let me see, let me see:

    'The rugged Pyrrhus, like th' Hyrcanian beast—' 386
'Tis not so; it begins with Pyrrhus:

    'The rugged Pyrrhus, he whose sable arms, 388
    Black as his purpose, did the night resemble
    When he lay couchèd in the ominous horse, 390
    Hath now this dread and black complexion smeared
    With heraldry more dismal. Head to foot 392
    Now is he total gules, horridly tricked 393
    With blood of fathers, mothers, daughters, sons,
    Baked and impasted with the parching streets, 395
    That lend a tyrannous and a damnèd light
    To their lord's murder. Roasted in wrath and fire,
    And thus o'ersizèd with coagulate gore, 398
    With eyes like carbuncles, the hellish Pyrrhus
    Old grandsire Priam seeks.'
So, proceed you.

POLONIUS. Fore God, my lord, well spoken, with good accent and good discretion.

PLAYER.   'Anon he finds him,
    Striking too short at Greeks. His antique sword,
    Rebellious to his arms, lies where it falls,
    Repugnant to command. Unequal matched,
    Pyrrhus at Priam drives, in rage strikes wide,

---

370. *chopine:* women's thick-soled shoe; *uncurrent:* not legal tender.   **371.** *within the ring:* from the edge through the line circling the design on the coin (with a play on "ring": a sound).   **377.** *caviary:* caviare; *general:* multitude.   **378.** *in the top of:* more authoritatively than.   **380.** *sallets:* salads, highly seasoned passages.   **384.** *Priam's slaughter:* i.e. at the fall of Troy (Aeneid II, 506 ff.).   **386.** *Hyrcanian beast:* tiger.   **388.** *sable:* black.   **390.** *ominous:* fateful; the wooden horse by which the Greeks gained entrance to Troy.   **392.** *dismal:* ill-omened.   **393.** *gules:* red (heraldic term); *tricked:* decorated in color (heraldic term).   **395.** *parching:* i.e. because Troy was burning.   **398.** *o'ersizèd:* covered as with size, a glutinous material used for filling pores of plaster, etc.; *coagulate:* clotted.

But with the whiff and wind of his fell sword   408
Th' unnervèd father falls. Then senseless Ilium,   409
Seeming to feel this blow, with flaming top
Stoops to his base, and with a hideous crash   411
Takes prisoner Pyrrhus' ear. For lo! his sword,
Which was declining on the milky head
Of reverend Priam, seemed i'th'air to stick.
So as a painted tyrant Pyrrhus stood,   415
And like a neutral to his will and matter   416
Did nothing.
But as we often see, against some storm,   418
A silence in the heavens, the rack stand still,   419
The bold winds speechless, and the orb below
As hush as death, anon the dreadful thunder
Doth rend the region, so after Pyrrhus' pause,   422
Arousèd vengeance sets him new awork,
And never did the Cyclops' hammers fall   424
On Mars' armor, forged for proof eterne,   425
With less remorse than Pyrrhus' bleeding sword
Now falls on Priam.
Out, out, thou strumpet Fortune! All you gods,
In general synod take away her power,
Break all the spokes and fellies from her wheel,   430
And bowl the round nave down the hill of heaven,   431
As low as to the fiends.'
POLONIUS. This is too long.
HAMLET. It shall to the barber's, with your beard.—Prithee say on. He's for a jig   434
  or a tale of bawdry, or he sleeps. Say on; come to Hecuba.
PLAYER.
    'But who (ah woe!) had seen the mobled queen—'   436
HAMLET. 'The mobled queen'?
POLONIUS. That's good. 'Mobled queen' is good.
PLAYER.
    'Run barefoot up and down, threat'ning the flames
    With bisson rheum; a clout upon that head   440
    Where late the diadem stood, and for a robe,
    About her lank and all o'erteemèd loins.   442
    A blanket in the alarm of fear caught up—

---

408. *fell:* cruel.   **409.** *senseless:* without feeling.   **411.** *his:* its.   **415:** *painted:* pictured.   **416.** *will and matter:* purpose and its realization (between which he stands motionless).   **418.** *against:* just before.   **419.** *rack:* clouds.   **422.** *region:* sky.   **424.** *Cyclops:* giant workmen who made armor in the smithy of Vulcan.   **425.** *proof eterne:* eternal protection.   **430.** *fellies:* segments of the rim.   **431.** *nave:* hub.   **434.** *jig:* short comic piece with singing and dancing often presented after a play.   **436.** *mobled:* muffled.   **440.** *bisson rheum:* blinding tears; *clout:* cloth.   **442.** *o'erteemèd:* overproductive of children.

Who this had seen, with tongue in venom steeped
'Gainst Fortune's state would treason have pronounced.   445
But if the gods themselves did see her then,
When she saw Pyrrhus make malicious sport
In mincing with his sword her husband's limbs,
The instant burst of clamor that she made
(Unless things mortal move them not at all)
Would have made milch the burning eyes of heaven   451
And passion in the gods.'

POLONIUS. Look, whe'r he has not turned his color, and has tears in's eyes. Prithee   453
no more.

HAMLET. 'Tis well. I'll have thee speak out the rest of this soon.—Good my lord,
will you see the players well bestowed? Do you hear? Let them be well used,   456
for they are the abstract and brief chronicles of the time. After your death
you were better have a bad epitaph than their ill report while you live.

POLONIUS. My lord, I will use them according to their desert.

HAMLET. God's bodkin, man, much better! Use every man after his desert, and   460
who shall scape whipping? Use them after your own honor and dignity. The
less they deserve, the more merit is in your bounty. Take them in.

POLONIUS. Come, sirs.

HAMLET. Follow him, friends. We'll hear a play tomorrow. [*aside to* PLAYER] Dost
thou hear me, old friend? Can you play 'The Murder of Gonzago'?

PLAYER. Ay, my lord.

HAMLET. We'll ha't to-morrow night. You could for a need study a speech of
some dozen or sixteen lines which I would set down and insert in't, could
you not?

PLAYER. Ay, my lord.

HAMLET. Very well. Follow that lord, and look you mock him not.—My good
friends, I'll leave you till night. You are welcome to Elsinore.

[*Exeunt* POLONIUS *and* PLAYERS.]

ROSENCRANTZ. Good my lord.

[*Exeunt* ROSENCRANTZ *and* GUILDENSTERN.]

HAMLET. Ay, so, God bye to you.—Now I am alone.
O, what a rogue and peasant slave am I!
Is it not monstrous that this player here,
But in a fiction, in a dream of passion,
Could force his soul so to his own conceit   477
That from her working all his visage wanned,
Tears in his eyes, distraction in his aspect,
A broken voice, and his whole function suiting   480
With forms to his conceit? And all for nothing,

---

445. *state:* government of worldly events.   **451.** *milch:* tearful (milk-giving); *eyes:* i.e. stars.   **453.** *whe'r:* whether.   **456.** *bestowed:* lodged.   **460.** *God's bodkin:* by God's little body.   **477.** *conceit:* conception, idea.   **480.** *function:* action of bodily powers.

For Hecuba!
What's Hecuba to him, or he to Hecuba,
That he should weep for her? What would he do
Had he the motive and the cue for passion
That I have? He would drown the stage with tears
And cleave the general ear with horrid speech,
Make mad the guilty and appal the free,
Confound the ignorant, and amaze indeed
The very faculties of eyes and ears.
Yet I,
A dull and muddy-mettled rascal, peak   492
Like John-a-dreams, unpregnant of my cause,   493
And can say nothing. No, not for a king,
Upon whose property and most dear life
A damned defeat was made. Am I a coward?
Who calls me villain? breaks my pate across?
Plucks off my beard and blows it in my face?
Tweaks me by the nose? gives me the lie i'th' throat
As deep as to the lungs? Who does me this?
Ha, 'swounds, I should take it, for it cannot be   501
But I am pigeon-livered and lack gall   502
To make oppression bitter, or ere this
I should ha' fatted all the region kites   504
With this slave's offal. Bloody, bawdy villain!   505
Remorseless, treacherous, lecherous, kindless villain!   506
O, vengeance!
Why, what an ass am I! This is most brave
That I, the son of a dear father murdered,
Prompted to my revenge by heaven and hell,
Must like a whore unpack my heart with words
And fall a-cursing like a very drab,
A stallion! Fie upon't, foh! About, my brains.   513
Hum—
I have heard that guilty creatures sitting at a play
Have by the very cunning of the scene
Been struck so to the soul that presently   517
They have proclaimed their malefactions.
For murder, though it have no tongue, will speak
With most miraculous organ. I'll have these players
Play something like the murder of my father
Before mine uncle. I'll observe his looks.

492. *muddy-mettled:* dull-spirited; *peak:* mope.   **493.** *John-a-dreams:* a sleepy dawdler; *unpregnant:* barren of realization.   **501.** *'swounds:* by God's wounds.   **502.** *pigeon-livered:* of dove-like gentleness.   **504.** *region kites:* kites of the air.   **505.** *offal:* guts.   **506.** *kindless:* unnatural.   **513.** *stallion:* prostitute (male or female).   **517.** *presently:* immediately.

I'll tent him to the quick. If 'a do blench,   523
I know my course. The spirit that I have seen
May be a devil, and the devil hath power
T'assume a pleasing shape, yea, and perhaps
Out of my weakness and my melancholy,
As he is very potent with such spirits,
Abuses me to damn me. I'll have grounds   529
More relative than this. The play's the thing   530
Wherein I'll catch the conscience of the king.   [*Exit.*]

ACT III, SCENE 1

[*Enter* KING, QUEEN, POLONIUS, OPHELIA, ROSENCRANTZ, GUILDENSTERN, *Lords.*]

KING. And can you by no drift of conference   1
  Get from him why he puts on this confusion,
  Grating so harshly all his days of quiet
  With turbulent and dangerous lunacy?
ROSENCRANTZ. He does confess he feels himself distracted,
  But from what cause 'a will by no means speak.
GUILDENSTERN. Nor do we find him forward to be sounded,
  But with a crafty madness keeps aloof
  When we would bring him on to some confession
  Of his true state.
QUEEN.   Did he receive you well?
ROSENCRANTZ. Most like a gentleman.
GUILDENSTERN. But with much forcing of his disposition.
ROSENCRANTZ. Niggard of question, but of our demands
  Most free in his reply.
QUEEN.   Did you assay him   14
  To any pastime?
ROSENCRANTZ. Madam, it so fell out that certain players
  We o'erraught on the way. Of these we told him,   17
  And there did seem in him a kind of joy
  To hear of it. They are here about the court,
  And, as I think, they have already order
  This night to play before him.
POLONIUS.   'Tis most true,
  And he beseeched me to entreat your majesties
  To hear and see the matter.
KING. With all my heart, and it doth much content me
  To hear him so inclined.

---

523. *tent:* probe; *blench:* flinch.   **529.** *Abuses:* deludes.   **530.** *relative:* pertinent.
III, 1. A chamber in the Castle.   **1.** *drift of conference:* direction of conversation.   **14.** *assay:* try to
win.   **17.** *o'erraught:* overtook.

Good gentlemen, give him a further edge   26
And drive his purpose into these delights.
ROSENCRANTZ. We shall, my lord.   [*Exeunt* ROSENCRANTZ *and* GUILDENSTERN.]
KING.   Sweet Gertrude, leave us too,
For we have closely sent for Hamlet hither,   29
That he, as 'twere by accident, may here
Affront Ophelia.   31
Her father and myself (lawful espials)   32
Will so bestow ourselves that, seeing unseen,
We may of their encounter frankly judge
And gather by him, as he is behaved,
If 't be th' affliction of his love or no
That thus he suffers for.
QUEEN.   I shall obey you.—
And for your part, Ophelia, I do wish
That your good beauties be the happy cause
Of Hamlet's wildness. So shall I hope your virtues
Will bring him to his wonted way again,
To both your honors.
OPHELIA.   Madam, I wish it may.   [*Exit* QUEEN.]
POLONIUS. Ophelia, walk you here.—Gracious, so please you,
We will bestow ourselves—
     [*To* OPHELIA]   Read on this book,
That show of such an exercise may color   45
Your loneliness. We are oft to blame in this,
'Tis too much proved, that with devotion's visage
And pious action we do sugar o'er
The devil himself.
KING [*aside*].   O, 'tis too true.
How smart a lash that speech doth give my conscience!
The harlot's cheek, beautied with plast'ring art,
Is not more ugly to the thing that helps it   52
Than is my deed to my most painted word.
O heavy burthen!
POLONIUS. I hear him coming. Let's withdraw, my lord.
                                        [*Exeunt* KING *and* POLONIUS.]

[*Enter* HAMLET.]

HAMLET. To be, or not to be—that is the question:
Whether 'tis nobler in the mind to suffer
The slings and arrows of outrageous fortune

---

26. *edge:* keenness of desire.   **29.** *closely:* privately.   **31.** *Affront:* come face to face with.   **32.** *espials:* spies.   **45.** *exercise:* religious exercise (the book being obviously one of devotion); *color:* give an appearance of naturalness to.   **52.** *to:* compared to.

Or to take arms against a sea of troubles
And by opposing end them. To die, to sleep—
No more—and by a sleep to say we end
The heartache, and the thousand natural shocks
That flesh is heir to. 'Tis a consummation
Devoutly to be wished. To die, to sleep—
To sleep—perchance to dream: ay, there's the rub,   65
For in that sleep of death what dreams may come
When we have shuffled off this mortal coil,   67
Must give us pause. There's the respect   68
That makes calamity of so long life.   69
For who would bear the whips and scorns of time,
Th' oppressor's wrong, the proud man's contumely
The pangs of despised love, the law's delay,
The insolence of office, and the spurns
That patient merit of th' unworthy takes,
When he himself might his quietus make   75
With a bare bodkin? Who would fardels bear,   76
To grunt and sweat under a weary life,
But that the dread of something after death,
The undiscovered country, from whose bourn   79
No traveller returns, puzzles the will,
And makes us rather bear those ills we have
Than fly to others that we know not of?
Thus conscience does make cowards of us all,
And thus the native hue of resolution
Is sicklied o'er with the pale cast of thought,
And enterprises of great pitch and moment   86
With this regard their currents turn awry   87
And lose the name of action.—Soft you now,
The fair Ophelia!—Nymph, in thy orisons   89
Be all my sins remembered.
OPHELIA.   Good my lord,
    How does your honor for this many a day?
HAMLET. I humbly thank you, well, well, well.
OPHELIA. My lord, I have remembrances of yours
    That I have longèd long to re-deliver.
    I pray you, now receive them.
HAMLET.   No, not I,
    I never gave you aught.

---

65. *rub:* obstacle (literally, obstruction encountered by a bowler's ball).   **67.** *shuffled off:* cast off as an encumbrance; *coil:* to-do, turmoil.   **68.** *respect:* consideration.   **69.** *of so long life:* so long-lived.   **75.** *quietus:* settlement (literally, release from debt).   **76.** *bodkin:* dagger; *fardels:* burdens.   **79.** *bourn:* confine, region.   **86.** *pitch:* height (of a soaring falcon's flight).   **87.** *regard:* consideration.   **89.** *orisons:* prayers (because of the book of devotion she reads).

OPHELIA. My honored lord, you know right well you did,
And with them words of so sweet breath composed
As made the things more rich. Their perfume lost,
Take these again, for to the noble mind
Rich gifts wax poor when givers prove unkind.
There, my lord.

HAMLET. Ha, ha! Are you honest?   103

OPHELIA. My lord?

HAMLET. Are you fair?

OPHELIA. What means your lordship?

HAMLET. That if you be honest and fair, your honesty should admit no discourse
to your beauty.

OPHELIA. Could beauty, my lord, have better commerce than with honesty?   109

HAMLET. Ay, truly; for the power of beauty will sooner transform honesty from
what it is to a bawd than the force of honesty can translate beauty into his
likeness. This was sometime a paradox, but now the time gives it proof. I   112
did love you once.

OPHELIA. Indeed, my lord, you made me believe so.

HAMLET. You should not have believed me, for virtue cannot so inoculate our   115
old stock but we shall relish of it. I loved you not.   116

OPHELIA. I was the more deceived.

HAMLET. Get thee to a nunnery. Why wouldst thou be a breeder of sinners? I
am myself indifferent honest, but yet I could accuse me of such things that it   119
were better my mother had not borne me: I am very proud, revengeful, ambitious, with more offenses at my beck than I have thoughts to put them in,
imagination to give them shape, or time to act them in. What should such
fellows as I do crawling between earth and heaven? We are arrant knaves all;
believe none of us. Go thy ways to a nunnery. Where's your father?

OPHELIA. At home, my lord.

HAMLET. Let the doors be shut upon him, that he may play the fool nowhere
but in's own house. Farewell.

OPHELIA. O, help him, you sweet heavens!

HAMLET. If thou dost marry, I'll give thee this plague for thy dowry: be thou as
chaste as ice, as pure as snow, thou shalt not escape calumny. Get thee to a
nunnery. Go, farewell. Or if thou wilt needs marry, marry a fool, for wise
men know well enough what monsters you make of them. To a nunnery, go,   132
and quickly too. Farewell.

OPHELIA. O heavenly powers, restore him!

HAMLET. I have heard of your paintings too, well enough. God hath given you
one face, and you make yourselves another. You jig, you amble, and you
lisp; you nickname God's creatures and make your wantonnness your ignorance.   137

---

103. *honest:* chaste.   **109.** *commerce:* intercourse.   **112.** *paradox:* idea contrary to common opinion.
115. *inoculate:* graft.   **116.** *relish:* have a flavor (because of original sin).   **119.** *indifferent honest:* moder-
ately respectable.   **132.** *monsters:* i.e. unnatural combinations of wisdom and uxorious folly.   **137.** *wantonness:* affectation; *your ignorance:* a matter for which you offer the excuse that you don't know any better.

Go to, I'll no more on't; it hath made me mad. I say we will have no more
marriage. Those that are married already—all but one—shall live. The rest
shall keep as they are. To a nunnery, go.   [*Exit.*]

OPHELIA. O, what a noble mind is here o'erthrown!
The courtier's, soldier's, scholar's, eye, tongue, sword,
Th' expectancy and rose of the fair state,   143
The glass of fashion and the mould of form,   144
Th' observed of all observers, quite, quite down!
And I, of ladies most deject and wretched,
That sucked the honey of his music vows,
Now see that noble and most sovereign reason
Like sweet bells jangled, out of time and harsh,
That unmatched form and feature of blown youth
Blasted with ecstasy. O, woe is me   151
T' have seen what I have seen, see what I see!

[*Enter* KING *and* POLONIUS.]

KING. Love? his affections do not that way tend,   153
Nor what he spake, though it lacked form a little,
Was not like madness. There's something in his soul
O'er which his melancholy sits on brood,
And I do doubt the hatch and the disclose   157
Will be some danger; which for to prevent,
I have in quick determination
Thus set it down: he shall with speed to England
For the demand of our neglected tribute.
Haply the seas, and countries different,
With variable objects, shall expel
This something-settled matter in his heart,   164
Whereon his brains still beating puts him thus
From fashion of himself. What think you on't?

POLONIUS. It shall do well. But yet do I believe
The origin and commencement of his grief
Sprung from neglected love.—How now, Ophelia?
You need not tell us what Lord Hamlet said.
We heard it all.—My lord, do as you please,
But if you hold it fit, after the play
Let his queen mother all alone entreat him
To show his grief. Let her be round with him,   174
And I'll be placed, so please you, in the ear
Of all their conference. If she find him not,
To England send him, or confine him where
Your wisdom best shall think.

---

143. *expectancy and rose:* fair hope.   **144.** *glass:* mirror.   **151.** *ecstasy:* madness.   **153.** *affections:*
emotions.   **157.** *doubt:* fear.   **164.** *something-settled:* somewhat settled.   **174.** *round:* plain-spoken.

KING.   It shall be so.
Madness in great ones must not unwatched go.   [*Exeunt.*]

ACT III, SCENE 2

[*Enter* HAMLET *and three of the* PLAYERS.]

HAMLET. Speak the speech, I pray you, as I pronounced it to you, trippingly on   1
the tongue. But if you mouth it, as many of our players do, I had as lief the
town crier spoke my lines. Nor do not saw the air too much with your hand,
thus, but use all gently, for in the very torrent, tempest, and (as I may say)
whirlwind of your passion, you must acquire and beget a temperance that
may give it smoothness. O, it offends me to the soul to hear a robustious   6
periwig-pated fellow tear a passion to tatters, to very rags, to split the ears of   7
the groundlings, who for the most part are capable of nothing but inexplicable   8
dumb shows and noise. I would have such a fellow whipped for o'erdoing   9
Termagant. It out-herods Herod. Pray you avoid it.   10

PLAYER. I warrant your honor.

HAMLET. Be not too tame neither, but let your own discretion be your tutor.
Suit the action to the word, the word to the action, with this special observance,
that you o'erstep not the modesty of nature. For anything so overdone is
from the purpose of playing, whose end, both at the first and now, was and   15
is, to hold, as 'twere, the mirror up to nature, to show virtue her own feature,
scorn her own image, and the very age and body of the time his form and
pressure. Now this overdone, or come tardy off, though it make the unskillful   18
laugh, cannot but make the judicious grieve, the censure of the which one   19
must in your allowance o'erweigh a whole theatre of others. O, there be
players that I have seen play, and heard others praise, and that highly (not to
speak it profanely), that neither having th' accent of Christians, nor the gait
of Christian, pagan, nor man, have so strutted and bellowed that I have thought
some of Nature's journeymen had made men, and not made them well, they   24
imitated humanity so abominably.

PLAYER. I hope we have reformed that indifferently with us, sir.   26

HAMLET. O, reform it altogether! And let those that play your clowns speak no
more than is set down for them, for there be of them that will themselves   28
laugh, to set on some quantity of barren spectators to laugh too, though in
the mean time some necessary question of the play be then to be considered.
That's villainous and shows a most pitiful ambition in the fool that uses it.
Go make you ready.   [*Exeunt* PLAYERS.]

III, 2. The hall of the Castle.   1. *trippingly:* easily.   6. *robustious:* boisterous.   7. *periwig-pated:* wig-wearing (after the custom of actors).   8. *groundlings:* spectators who paid least and stood on the ground in the pit or yard of the theatre.   9. *dumb shows:* brief actions without words, forecasting dramatic matter to follow (the play presented later in this scene giving an old-fashioned example).   10. *Termagant:* a Saracen "god" in medieval romance and drama; *Herod:* the raging tyrant of old Biblical plays.   15. *from:* apart from.   18. *pressure:* impressed or printed character; *come tardy off:* brought off slowly and badly.   19. *the censure of the which one:* the judgment of even one of whom.   24. *journeymen:* workmen not yet masters of their trade.   26. *indifferently:* fairly well.   28. *of them:* some of them.

[*Enter* POLONIUS, GUILDENSTERN, *and* ROSENCRANTZ.]

　　How now, my lord? Will the king hear this piece of work?
POLONIUS. And the queen too, and that presently.   34   [*Exit* POLONIUS.]
HAMLET. Bid the players make haste.
　　Will you two help to hasten them?
ROSENCRANTZ. Ay, my lord.   [*Exeunt they two.*]
HAMLET. What, ho, Horatio!

[*Enter* HORATIO.]

HORATIO. Here, sweet lord, at your service.
HAMLET. Horatio, thou art e'en as just a man
　　As e'er my conversation coped withal.   41
HORATIO. O, my dear lord—
HAMLET.　　　　　　　　　Nay, do not think I flatter.
　　For what advancement may I hope from thee,
　　That no revenue hast but thy good spirits
　　To feed and clothe thee? Why should the poor be flattered?
　　No, let the candied tongue lick absurd pomp,
　　And crook the pregnant hinges of the knee   47
　　Where thrift may follow fawning. Dost thou hear?   48
　　Since my dear soul was mistress of her choice
　　And could of men distinguish her election,
　　S' hath sealed thee for herself, for thou hast been   51
　　As one in suff'ring all that suffers nothing,
　　A man that Fortune's buffets and rewards
　　Hast ta'en with equal thanks; and blest are those
　　Whose blood and judgment are so well commeddled   55
　　That they are not a pipe for Fortune's finger
　　To sound what stop she please. Give me that man
　　That is not passion's slave, and I will wear him
　　In my heart's core, ay, in my heart of heart,
　　As I do thee. Something too much of this—
　　There is a play to-night before the king.
　　One scene of it comes near the circumstance
　　Which I have told thee, of my father's death.
　　I prithee, when thou seest that act afoot,
　　Even with the very comment of thy soul   65
　　Observe my uncle. If his occulted guilt   66
　　Do not itself unkennel in one speech,
　　It is a damnèd ghost that we have seen,   68
　　And my imaginations are as foul

---

34. *presently:* at once.　**41.** *conversation coped withal:* intercourse with men encountered.　**47.** *pregnant:* quick to move.　**48.** *thrift:* profit.　**51.** *sealed:* marked.　**55.** *blood:* passion; *commeddled:* mixed together.　**65.** *the very . . . soul:* thy deepest sagacity.　**66.** *occulted:* hidden.　**68.** *damnèd ghost:* evil spirit, devil (as thought of in II, ii, 524 ff.).

As Vulcan's stithy. Give him heedful note,   70
For I mine eyes will rivet to his face,
And after we will both our judgments join
In censure of his seeming.   73
HORATIO.   Well, my lord.
If a steal aught the while this play is playing,
And scape detecting, I will pay the theft.

[*Enter Trumpets and Kettledrums,* KING, QUEEN, POLONIUS, OPHELIA, ROSENCRANTZ,
GUILDENSTERN, *and other* LORDS *attendant.*]

HAMLET. They are coming to the play. I must be idle.   76
Get you a place.
KING. How fares our cousin Hamlet?   78
HAMLET. Excellent, i' faith, of the chameleon's dish. I eat the air, promise-crammed. 79
You cannot feed capons so.
KING. I have nothing with this answer, Hamlet. These words are not mine. 81
HAMLET. No, nor mine now. [*to* POLONIUS] My lord, you played once i' th' university,
you say?
POLONIUS. That did I, my lord, and was accounted a good actor.
HAMLET. What did you enact?
POLONIUS. I did enact Julius Caesar. I was killed i' th' Capitol; Brutus killed me.
HAMLET. It was a brute part of him to kill so capital a calf there. Be the players
ready?
ROSENCRANTZ. Ay, my lord. They stay upon your patience.   89
QUEEN. Come hither, my dear Hamlet, sit by me.
HAMLET. No, good mother. Here's metal more attractive.
POLONIUS [*to the* KING]. O ho! do you mark that?
HAMLET. Lady, shall I lie in your lap?

[*He lies at* OPHELIA's *feet.*]

OPHELIA. No, my lord.
HAMLET. I mean, my head upon your lap?
OPHELIA. Ay, my lord.
HAMLET. Do you think I meant country matters?   97
OPHELIA. I think nothing, my lord.
HAMLET. That's a fair thought to lie between maids' legs.
OPHELIA. What is, my lord?
HAMLET. Nothing.
OPHELIA. You are merry, my lord.
HAMLET. Who, I?
OPHELIA. Ay, my lord.

---

70. *stithy:* smithy.   **73.** *censure of:* sentence upon.   **76.** *be idle:* be foolish, act the madman.   **78.** *cousin:*
nephew.   **79.** *chameleon's dish:* i.e. air (which was believed the chameleon's food; Hamlet willfully
takes *fares* in the sense of "feeds").   **81.** *not mine:* not for me as the asker of my question.   **89.** *stay*
upon your patience: await your indulgence.   **97.** *country matters:* rustic goings-on, barnyard mating
(with a play upon a sexual term).

HAMLET. O God, your only jig-maker! What should a man do but be merry? For 105
look you how cheerfully my mother looks, and my father died within's two
hours.

OPHELIA. Nay, 'tis twice two months, my lord.

HAMLET. So long? Nay then, let the devil wear black, for I'll have a suit of sables. 109
O heavens! die two months ago, and not forgotten yet? Then there's hope a
great man's memory may outlive his life half a year. But, by'r Lady, 'a must
build churches then, or else shall 'a suffer not thinking on, with the hobby- 112
horse, whose epitaph is 'For O, for O, the hobby-horse is forgot!' 113

[*The trumpets sound. Dumb show follows:*]

*Enter a King and a Queen [very lovingly], the Queen embracing him, and he
her. She kneels; and makes show of protestation unto him. He takes her up,
and declines his head upon her neck. He lies him down upon a bank of flowers.
She, seeing him asleep, leaves him. Anon come in another man: takes off his
crown, kisses it, pours poison in the sleeper's ears, and leaves him. The Queen
returns, finds the King dead, makes passionate action. The poisoner, with some
three or four, come in again, seem to condole with her. The dead body is carried
away. The poisoner woos the Queen with gifts; she seems harsh awhile, but in
the end accepts love.* [*Exeunt.*]

OPHELIA. What means this, my lord?

HAMLET. Marry, this is miching mallecho; it means mischief. 115

OPHELIA. Belike this show imports the argument of the play.

[*Enter* PROLOGUE.]

HAMLET. We shall know by this fellow. The players cannot keep counsel; they'll
tell all.

OPHELIA. Will 'a tell us what this show meant?

HAMLET. Ay, or any show that you'll show him. Be not you ashamed to show,
he'll not shame to tell you what it means.

OPHELIA. You are naught, you are naught. I'll mark the play. 122

PROLOGUE. For us and for our tragedy,
Here stooping to your clemency,
We beg your hearing patiently. [*Exit.*]

HAMLET. Is this a prologue, or the posy of a ring? 126

OPHELIA. 'Tis brief, my lord.

HAMLET. As woman's love.

[*Enter two* PLAYERS *as* KING *and* QUEEN.]

KING. Full thirty times hath Phoebus' cart gone round 129
Neptune's salt wash and Tellus' orbèd ground, 130

---

105. *jig-maker:* writer of jigs (see II,ii,434). **109.** *sables:* black furs (luxurious garb, not for
mourning). **112–13.** *hobby-horse:* traditional figure strapped round the waist of a performer in May
games and morris dances. **115.** *miching mallecho:* sneaking iniquity. **122.** *naught:* indecent. **126.**
posy: brief motto in rhyme ("poesy"); *ring:* finger ring. **129.** *Phoebus' cart:* the sun's chariot. **130.**
Tellus: Roman goddess of the earth.

And thirty dozen moons with borrowed sheen   131
About the world have times twelve thirties been,
Since love our hearts, and Hymen did our hands,   133
Unite commutual in most sacred bands.   134

QUEEN. So many journeys may the sun and moon
    Make us again count o'er ere love be done!
    But woe is me, you are so sick of late,
    So far from cheer and from your former state,
    That I distrust you. Yet, though I distrust,   139
    Discomfort you, my lord, it nothing must.
    For women fear too much, even as they love,
    And women's fear and love hold quantity,   142
    In neither aught, or in extremity.
    Now what my love is, proof hath made you know,
    And as my love is sized, my fear is so.
    Where love is great, the littlest doubts are fear;
    Where little fears grow great, great love grows there.

KING. Faith, I must leave thee, love, and shortly too;
    My operant powers their functions leave to do.   149
    And thou shalt live in this fair world behind,
    Honored, beloved, and haply one as kind
    For husband shalt thou—

QUEEN.   O, confound the rest!
    Such love must needs be treason in my breast.
    In second husband let me be accurst!
    None wed the second but who killed the first.

HAMLET [*aside*]. That's wormwood.   156

QUEEN. The instances that second marriage move   157
    Are base respects of thrift, but none of love.
    A second time I kill my husband died
    When second husband kisses me in bed.

KING. I do believe you think what now you speak,
    But what we do determine oft we break.
    Purpose is but the slave to memory,   163
    Of violent birth, but poor validity,   164
    Which now like fruit unripe sticks on the tree,
    But fall unshaken when they mellow be.
    Most necessary 'tis that we forget
    To pay ourselves what to ourselves is debt.
    What to ourselves in passion we propose,
    The passion ending, doth the purpose lose.

---

131. *borrowed:* i.e. taken from the sun. **133.** *Hymen:* Greek god of marriage. **134.** *commutual:* mutually. **139.** *distrust you:* fear for you. **142.** *quantity:* proportion. **149.** *operant powers:* active bodily forces. **156.** *wormwood:* a bitter herb. **157.** *instances:* motives. **163.** *slave to:* i.e. dependent upon for life. **164.** *validity:* strength.

The violence of either grief or joy
Their own enactures with themselves destroy.   172
Where joy most revels, grief doth most lament;
Grief joys, joy grieves, on slender accident.
This world is not for aye, nor 'tis not strange
That even our loves should with our fortunes change,
For 'tis a question left us yet to prove,
Whether love lead fortune, or else fortune love.
The great man down, you mark his favorite flies,
The poor advanced makes friends of enemies;
And hitherto doth love on fortune tend,
For who not needs shall never lack a friend,
And who in want a hollow friend doth try,
Directly seasons him his enemy.   184
But, orderly to end where I begun,
Our wills and fates do so contrary run
That our devices still are overthrown;   187
Our thoughts are ours, their ends none of our own.
So think thou wilt no second husband wed,
But die thy thoughts when thy first lord is dead.
QUEEN. Nor earth to me give food, nor heaven light,
　Sport and repose lock from me day and night,
　To desperation turn my trust and hope,
　An anchor's cheer in prison be my scope,   194
　Each opposite that blanks the face of joy   195
　Meet what I would have well, and it destroy,
　Both here and hence pursue me lasting strife,   197
　If, once a widow, ever I be wife!
HAMLET. If she should break it now!
KING. 'Tis deeply sworn. Sweet, leave me here awhile.
　My spirits grow dull, and fain I would beguile
　The tedious day with sleep.
QUEEN.   Sleep rock thy brain,   [*He sleeps.*]
　And never come mischance between us twain!   [*Exit.*]
HAMLET. Madam, how like you this play?
QUEEN. The lady doth protest too much, methinks.
HAMLET. O, but she'll keep her word.
KING. Have you heard the argument? Is there no offense in't?   207
HAMLET. No, no, they do but jest, poison in jest; no offense i' th' world.
KING. What do you call the play?
HAMLET. 'The Mousetrap.' Marry, how? Tropically. This play is the image of a   210
　murder done in Vienna. Gonzago is the duke's name; his wife, Baptista. You

---

172. *enactures:* fulfillments.   **184.** *seasons him:* ripens him into.   **187.** *still:* always.   **194.** *anchor's:* hermit's.   **195.** *blanks:* blanches, makes pale.   **197.** *hence:* in the next world.   **207.** *argument:* plot summary.   **210.** *Tropically:* in the way of a trope or figure (with a play on "trapically").

shall see anon. 'Tis a knavish piece of work, but what o' that? Your majesty, and we that have free souls, it touches us not. Let the galled jade winch; our   213
withers are unwrung.   214

[*Enter* LUCIANUS.]

This is one Lucianus, nephew to the king.

OPHELIA. You are as good as a chorus, my lord.   216

HAMLET. I could interpret between you and your love, if I could see the puppets   217
dallying.

OPHELIA. You are keen, my lord, you are keen.

HAMLET. It would cost you a groaning to take off my edge.

OPHELIA. Still better, and worse.

HAMLET. So you must take your husbands.—Begin, murderer. Leave thy damnable
faces and begin. Come, the croaking raven doth bellow for revenge.

LUCIANUS. Thoughts black, hands apt, drugs fit, and time agreeing,
Confederate season, else no creature seeing,   225
Thou mixture rank, of midnight weeds collected,
With Hecate's ban thrice blasted, thrice infected,   227
Thy natural magic and dire property
On wholesome life usurps immediately.

[*Pours the poison in his ears.*]

HAMLET. 'A poisons him i' th' garden for his estate. His name's Gonzago. The
story is extant, and written in very choice Italian. You shall see anon how
the murderer gets the love of Gonzago's wife.

OPHELIA. The king rises.

HAMLET. What, frighted with false fire?   234

QUEEN. How fares my lord?

POLONIUS. Give o'er the play.

KING. Give me some light. Away!

POLONIUS. Lights, lights, lights!   [*Exeunt all but* HAMLET *and* HORATIO.]

HAMLET. Why, let the strucken deer go weep,
        The hart ungallèd play.
    For some must watch, while some must sleep;
        Thus runs the world away.
Would not this, sir, and a forest of feathers—if the rest of my fortunes turn   243
Turk with me—with two Provincial roses on my razed shoes, get me a fellowship   244
in a cry of players, sir?   245

HORATIO. Half a share.

---

213. *free:* guiltless; *galled:* sore-backed; *jade:* horse; *winch:* wince.   **214.** *withers:* shoulders.   **216.** *chorus:*
one in a play who explains the action.   **217.** *puppets:* i.e. you and your lover as in a puppet show.   **225.**
Confederate season: the occasion being my ally.   **227.** *Hecate:* goddess of witchcraft and black magic;
ban: curse.   **234.** *false fire:* a firing of a gun charged with powder but no shot, a blank-discharge.   **243.**
feathers: plumes for actors' costumes.   **243–44.** *turn Turk:* turn renegade, like a Christian turning
Mohammedan.   **244.** *Provincial roses:* ribbon rosettes; *razed:* decorated with cut patterns.   **245.** *cry:*
pack.

HAMLET. A whole one, I.
> For thou dost know, O Damon dear,
> > This realm dismantled was
> Of Jove himself; and now reigns here
> > A very, very—peacock.

HORATIO. You might have rhymed.

HAMLET. O good Horatio, I'll take the ghost's word for a thousand pound. Didst perceive?

HORATIO. Very well, my lord.

HAMLET. Upon the talk of the poisoning?

HORATIO. I did very well note him.

HAMLET. Aha! Come, some music! Come, the recorders!   258
> For if the king like not the comedy,
> Why then, belike he likes it not, perdy.   260

Come, some music!

[*Enter* ROSENCRANTZ *and* GUILDENSTERN.]

GUILDENSTERN. Good my lord, vouchsafe me a word with you.

HAMLET. Sir, a whole history.

GUILDENSTERN. The king, sir—

HAMLET. Ay, sir, what of him?

GUILDENSTERN. Is in his retirement marvellous distempered.   266

HAMLET. With drink, sir?

GUILDENSTERN. No, my lord, with choler.   268

HAMLET. Your wisdom should show itself more richer to signify this to the doctor, for me to put him to his purgation would perhaps plunge him into more choler.

GUILDENSTERN. Good my lord, put your discourse into some frame, and start not 272
so wildly from my affair.

HAMLET. I am tame, sir; pronounce.

GUILDENSTERN. The queen, your mother, in most great affliction of spirit hath sent me to you.

HAMLET. You are welcome.

GUILDENSTERN. Nay, good my lord, this courtesy is not of the right breed. If it shall please you to make me a wholesome answer, I will do your mother's commandment. If not, your pardon and my return shall be the end of my business.

HAMLET. Sir, I cannot.

ROSENCRANTZ. What, my lord?

HAMLET. Make you a wholesome answer; my wit 's diseased. But, sir, such answer as I can make, you shall command, or rather, as you say, my mother. Therefore no more, but to the matter. My mother, you say—

---

258. *recorders:* musical instruments of the flute class.   **260.** *perdy:* by God ("par dieu").   **266.** *distempered:* out of temper, vexed (twisted by Hamlet into "deranged").   **268.** *choler:* anger (twisted by Hamlet into "biliousness").   **272.** *frame:* logical order.

ROSENCRANTZ. Then thus she says: your behavior hath struck her into amazement and admiration.   288

HAMLET. O wonderful son, that can so stonish a mother! But is there no sequel at the heels of this mother's admiration? Impart.

ROSENCRANTZ. She desires to speak with you in her closet ere you go to bed.   291

HAMLET. We shall obey, were she ten times our mother. Have you any further trade with us?

ROSENCRANTZ. My lord, you once did love me.

HAMLET. And do still, by these pickers and stealers.   295

ROSENCRANTZ. Good my lord, what is your cause of distemper? You do surely bar the door upon your own liberty, if you deny your griefs to your friend.

HAMLET. Sir, I lack advancement.

ROSENCRANTZ. How can that be, when you have the voice of the king himself for your succession in Denmark?

HAMLET. Ay, sir, but 'while the grass grows'—the proverb is something musty.   301

[*Enter the* PLAYER *with recorders.*]

O, the recorders. Let me see one. To withdraw with you—why do you go   302
about to recover the wind of me, as if you would drive me into a toil?   303

GUILDENSTERN. O my lord, if my duty be too bold, my love is too unmannerly.   304

HAMLET. I do not well understand that. Will you play upon this pipe?

GUILDENSTERN. My lord, I cannot.

HAMLET. I pray you.

GUILDENSTERN. Believe me, I cannot.

HAMLET. I do beseech you.

GUILDENSTERN. I know no touch of it, my lord.

HAMLET. It is as easy as lying. Govern these ventages with your fingers and thumb,   311
give it breath with your mouth, and it will discourse most eloquent music. Look you, these are the stops.

GUILDENSTERN. But these cannot I command to any utt'rance of harmony. I have not the skill.

HAMLET. Why, look you now, how unworthy a thing you make of me! You would play upon me, you would seem to know my stops, you would pluck out the heart of my mystery, you would sound me from my lowest note to the top of my compass; and there is much music, excellent voice, in this little organ, yet cannot you make it speak. 'Sblood, do you think I am easier to be played on than a pipe? Call me what instrument you will, though you can fret me,   321
you cannot play upon me.

[*Enter* POLONIUS.]

God bless you, sir!

POLONIUS. My lord, the queen would speak with you, and presently.   324

288. *admiration:* wonder.   **291.** *closet:* private room.   **295.** *pickers and stealers:* i.e. hands.   **301.** *while the grass grows* (a proverb, ending: "the horse starves").   **302.** *recorders* (see III, ii, 258n.); *withdraw:* step aside.   **303.** *recover the wind:* come up to windward like a hunter; *toil:* snare.   **304.** *is too unmannerly:* leads me beyond the restraint of good manners.   **311.** *ventages:* holes, vents.   **321.** *fret:* irritate (with a play on the fret-fingering of certain stringed musical instruments).   **324.** *presently:* at once.

HAMLET. Do you see yonder cloud that's almost in shape of a camel?

POLONIUS. By th' mass and 'tis, like a camel indeed.

HAMLET. Methinks it is like a weasel.

POLONIUS. It is backed like a weasel.

HAMLET. Or like a whale.

POLONIUS. Very like a whale.

HAMLET. Then I will come to my mother by and by. [*aside*] They fool me to the   331
top of my bent.—I will come by and by.   332

POLONIUS. I will say so.   [*Exit.*]

HAMLET. 'By and by' is easily said. Leave me, friends.

[*Exeunt all but* HAMLET.]

'Tis now the very witching time of night,
When churchyards yawn, and hell itself breathes out
Contagion to this world. Now could I drink hot blood
And do such bitter business as the day
Would quake to look on. Soft, now to my mother.
O heart, lose not thy nature; let not ever
The soul of Nero enter this firm bosom.   341
Let me be cruel, not unnatural;
I will speak daggers to her, but use none.
My tongue and soul in this be hypocrites:
How in my words somever she be shent,   345
To give them seals never, my soul, consent!   [*Exit.*]   346

ACT III, SCENE 3

[*Enter* KING, ROSENCRANTZ, *and* GUILDENSTERN.]

KING. I like him not, nor stands it safe with us
To let his madness range. Therefore prepare you.
I your commission will forthwith dispatch,
And he to England shall along with you.
The terms of our estate may not endure   5
Hazard so near's as doth hourly grow
Out of his brows.   7

GUILDENSTERN.   We will ourselves provide.
Most holy and religious fear it is
To keep those many many bodies safe
That live and feed upon your majesty.

ROSENCRANTZ. The single and peculiar life is bound   11
With all the strength and armor of the mind
To keep itself from noyance, but much more   13

331. *by and by:* immediately.   **332.** *bent* (see II, ii, 30n.)   **341.** *Nero:* murderer of his mother.   **345.** *shent:* reproved.   **346.** *seals:* authentications in actions.
III, 3. A chamber in the Castle.   **5.** *terms:* circumstances; *estate:* royal position.   **7.** *brows:* effronteries (apparently with an implication of knitted brows).   **11.** *peculiar:* individual.   **13.** *noyance:* harm.

That spirit upon whose weal depends and rests
The lives of many. The cess of majesty   15
Dies not alone, but like a gulf doth draw   16
What's near it with it; or 'tis a massy wheel
Fixed on the summit of the highest mount,
To whose huge spokes ten thousand lesser things
Are mortised and adjoined, which when it falls,
Each small annexment, petty consequence,
Attends the boist'rous ruin. Never alone   22
Did the king sigh, but with a general groan.
KING. Arm you, I pray you, to this speedy voyage,   24
　For we will fetters put upon this fear,
　Which now goes too free-footed.
ROSENCRANTZ.   We will haste us.   [*Exeunt Gentlemen.*]

[*Enter* POLONIUS.]

POLONIUS. My lord, he's going to his mother's closet.
　Behind the arras I'll convey myself
　To hear the process. I'll warrant she'll tax him home,   29
　And, as you said, and wisely was it said,
　'Tis meet that some more audience than a mother,
　Since nature makes them partial, should o'erhear
　The speech, of vantage. Fare you well, my liege.   33
　I'll call upon you ere you go to bed
　And tell you what I know.
KING.   Thanks, dear my lord.   [*Exit* POLONIUS.]
　O, my offense is rank, it smells to heaven;
　It hath the primal eldest curse upon't,   37
　A brother's murder. Pray can I not,
　Though inclination be as sharp as will.
　My stronger guilt defeats my strong intent,
　And like a man to double business bound
　I stand in pause where I shall first begin,
　And both neglect. What if this cursèd hand
　Were thicker than itself with brother's blood,
　Is there not rain enough in the sweet heavens
　To wash it white as snow? Whereto serves mercy
　But to confront the visage of offense?   47
　And what's in prayer but this twofold force,
　To be forestallèd ere we come to fall,
　Or pardoned being down? Then I'll look up.

---

15. *cess:* cessation, decease.   **16.** *gulf:* whirlpool.   **22.** *Attends:* joins in (like a royal attendant).   **24.** *Arm:* prepare.   **29.** *process:* proceedings; *tax him home:* thrust home in reprimanding him.   **33.** *of vantage:* from an advantageous position.   **37.** *primal eldest curse:* that of Cain, who also murdered a brother. **47.** *offense:* sin.

My fault is past. But, O, what form of prayer
Can serve my turn? 'Forgive me my foul murder'?
That cannot be, since I am still possessed
Of those effects for which I did the murder,   54
My crown, mine own ambition, and my queen.
May one be pardoned and retain th' offense?
In the corrupted currents of this world
Offense's gilded hand may shove by justice,   58
And oft 'tis seen the wicked prize itself
Buys out the law. But 'tis not so above.
There is no shuffling; there the action lies   61
In his true nature, and we ourselves compelled,
Even to the teeth and forehead of our faults,   63
To give in evidence. What then? What rests?
Try what repentance can. What can it not?
Yet what can it when one cannot repent?
O wretched state! O bosom black as death!
O limèd soul, that struggling to be free   68
Art more engaged! Help, angels! Make assay.   69
Bow, stubborn knees, and, heart with strings of steel,
Be soft as sinews of the new-born babe.
All may be well.
        [*He kneels.*]

[*Enter* HAMLET.]

HAMLET. Now might I do it pat, now 'a is a-praying,   73
    And now I'll do't. And so 'a goes to heaven,
    And so am I revenged. That would be scanned.
    A villain kills my father, and for that
    I, his sole son, do this same villain send
    To heaven.
    Why, this is hire and salary, not revenge.
    'A took my father grossly, full of bread,   80
    With all his crimes broad blown, as flush as May;   81
    And how his audit stands, who knows save heaven?   82
    But in our circumstance and course of thought,
    'Tis heavy with him; and am I then revenged,
    To take him in the purging of his soul,
    When he is fit and seasoned for his passage?
    No.

54. *effects:* things acquired.   **58.** *gilded:* gold-laden.   **61.** *shuffling:* sharp practice, double-dealing; *action:* legal proceeding (in heaven's court).   **63.** *teeth and forehead:* face-to-face recognition.   **68.** *limèd:* caught in birdlime, a gluey material spread as a bird-snare.   **69.** *engaged:* embedded; *assay:* an attempt.   **73.** *pat:* opportunely.   **80.** *grossly:* in a state of gross unpreparedness; *bread:* i.e. worldly sense gratification.   **81.** *broad blown:* fully blossomed; *flush:* vigorous.   **82.** *audit:* account.

Up, sword, and know thou a more horrid hent.   88
When he is drunk asleep, or in his rage,
Or in th' incestuous pleasure of his bed,
At game a-swearing, or about some act
That has no relish of salvation in't—   92
Then trip him, that his heels may kick at heaven,
And that his soul may be as damned and black
As hell, whereto it goes. My mother stays.
This physic but prolongs thy sickly days.   [*Exit.*]
KING [*rises*].   My words fly up, my thoughts remain below.
Words without thoughts never to heaven go.   [*Exit.*]

ACT III, SCENE 4

[*Enter* QUEEN GERTRUDE *and* POLONIUS.]

POLONIUS. 'A will come straight. Look you lay home to him.   1
    Tell him his pranks have been too broad to bear with,   2
    And that your grace hath screened and stood between
    Much heat and him. I'll silence me even here.
    Pray you be round with him.   5
HAMLET [*within*]. Mother, mother, mother!
QUEEN. I'll warrant you; fear me not.
    Withdraw; I hear him coming.   [POLONIUS *hides behind the arras.*]

[*Enter* HAMLET.]

HAMLET. Now, mother, what's the matter?
QUEEN. Hamlet, thou hast thy father much offended.
HAMLET. Mother, you have my father much offended.
QUEEN. Come, come, you answer with an idle tongue.   12
HAMLET. Go, go, you question with a wicked tongue.
QUEEN. Why, how now, Hamlet?
HAMLET.   What's the matter now?
QUEEN. Have you forgot me?
HAMLET.   No, by the rood, not so!   15
    You are the queen, your husband's brother's wife,
    And (would it were not so) you are my mother.
QUEEN. Nay, then I'll set those to you that can speak.
HAMLET. Come, come, and sit you down. You shall not budge.
    You go not till I set you up a glass
    Where you may see the inmost part of you.

---

88. *more horrid hent:* grasping by me on a more horrid occasion.   **92.** *relish:* flavor.
III, 4. The private chamber of the Queen.   **1.** *lay:* thrust.   **2.** *broad:* unrestrained.   **5.** *round:* plain-spoken.   **12.** *idle:* foolish.   **15.** *rood:* cross.

QUEEN. What wilt thou do? Thou wilt not murder me?
  Help, ho!
POLONIUS [*behind*]. What, ho! help!
HAMLET [*draws*]. How now? a rat? Dead for a ducat, dead!

[*Makes a pass through the arras and kills* POLONIUS.]

POLONIUS [*behind*]. O, I am slain!
QUEEN.   O me, what hast thou done?
HAMLET. Nay, I know not. Is it the king?
QUEEN. O, what a rash and bloody deed is this!
HAMLET. A bloody deed—almost as bad, good mother,
  As kill a king, and marry with his brother.
QUEEN. As kill a king?
HAMLET.   Ay, lady, it was my word.

[*Lifts up the arras and sees* POLONIUS.]

  Thou wretched, rash, intruding fool, farewell!
  I took thee for thy better. Take thy fortune.
  Thou find'st to be too busy is some danger.—
  Leave wringing of your hands. Peace, sit you down
  And let me wring your heart, for so I shall
  If it be made of penetrable stuff,
  If damnèd custom have not brazed it so   38
  That it is proof and bulwark against sense.   39
QUEEN. What have I done that thou dar'st wag thy tongue
  In noise so rude against me?
HAMLET.   Such an act
  That blurs the grace and blush of modesty,
  Calls virtue hypocrite, takes off the rose
  From the fair forehead of an innocent love,
  And sets a blister there, makes marriage vows   45
  As false as dicers' oaths. O, such a deed
  As from the body of contraction plucks   47
  The very soul, and sweet religion makes   48
  A rhapsody of words! Heaven's face does glow,
  And this solidity and compound mass,   50
  With heated visage, as against the doom,   51
  Is thought-sick at the act.
QUEEN.   Ay me, what act,
  That roars so loud and thunders in the index?   53
HAMLET. Look here upon this picture, and on this,

38. *custom:* habit; *brazed:* hardened like brass.   39. *proof:* armor; *sense:* feeling.   45. *blister:* brand (of degradation).   47. *contraction:* the marriage contract.   48. *religion:* i.e. sacred marriage vows.   50. *compound mass:* the earth as compounded of the four elements.   51. *against:* in expectation of; *doom:* Day of Judgment.   53. *index:* table of contents preceding the body of a book.

The counterfeit presentment of two brothers.   55
See what a grace was seated on this brow:
Hyperion's curls, the front of Jove himself,   57
An eye like Mars, to threaten and command,
A station like the herald Mercury   59
New lighted on a heaven-kissing hill—
A combination and a form indeed
Where every god did seem to set his seal
To give the world assurance of a man.
This was your husband. Look you now what follows.
Here is your husband, like a mildewed ear
Blasting his wholesome brother. Have you eyes?
Could you on this fair mountain leave to feed,
And batten on this moor? Ha! have you eyes?   68
You cannot call it love, for at your age
The heyday in the blood is tame, it's humble,   70
And waits upon the judgment, and what judgment   71
Would step from this to this? Sense sure you have,   72
Else could you not have motion, but sure that sense   73
Is apoplexed, for madness would not err,   74
Nor sense to ecstasy was ne'er so thralled   75
But it reserved some quantity of choice
To serve in such a difference. What devil was't
That thus hath cozened you at hoodman-blind?   78
Eyes without feeling, feeling without sight,
Ears without hands or eyes, smelling sans all,   80
Or but a sickly part of one true sense
Could not so mope.   82
O shame, where is thy blush? Rebellious hell,
If thou canst mutine in a matron's bones,   84
To flaming youth let virtue be as wax
And melt in her own fire. Proclaim no shame
When the compulsive ardor gives the charge,   87
Since frost itself as actively doth burn,
And reason panders will.   89
QUEEN.   O Hamlet, speak no more.
Thou turn'st mine eyes into my very soul,
And there I see such black and grainèd spots   91
As will not leave their tint.   92

---

55. *counterfeit presentment:* portrayed representation.   **57.** *Hyperion:* the sun god; *front:* forehead.   **59.** *station:* attitude in standing.   **68.** *batten:* feed greedily.   **70.** *heyday:* excitement of passion.   **71.** *waits upon:* yields to.   **72.** *Sense:* feeling.   **73.** *motion:* desire, impulse.   **74.** *apoplexed:* paralyzed.   **75.** *ecstasy:* madness.   **78.** *cozened:* cheated; *hoodman-blind:* blindman's buff.   **80.** *sans:* without.   **82.** *mope:* be stupid.   **84.** *mutine:* mutiny.   **87.** *compulsive:* compelling; *gives the charge:* delivers the attack.   **89.** *panders will:* acts as procurer for desire.   **91.** *grainèd:* dyed in grain.   **92.** *tinct:* color.

HAMLET.   Nay, but to live
  In the rank sweat of an enseamèd bed,   93
  Stewed in corruption, honeying and making love
  Over the nasty sty—
QUEEN.   O, speak to me no more.
  These words like daggers enter in mine ears.
  No more, sweet Hamlet.
HAMLET.   A murderer and a villain,
  A slave that is not twentieth part the tithe   98
  Of your precedent lord, a vice of kings,   99
  A cutpurse of the empire and the rule,   100
  That from a shelf the precious diadem stole
  And put it in his pocket—
QUEEN.   No more.   102

[*Enter the* GHOST *in his nightgown.*]

HAMLET. A king of shreds and patches—
  Save me and hover o'er me with your wings,
  You heavenly guards? What would your gracious figure?
QUEEN. Alas, he's mad.
HAMLET. Do you not come your tardy son to chide,
  That, lapsed in time and passion, lets go by   108
  Th' important acting of your dread command?
  O, say!
GHOST. Do not forget. This visitation
  Is but to whet thy almost blunted purpose.
  But look, amazement on thy mother sits.
  O, step between her and her fighting soul!
  Conceit in weakest bodies strongest works.   115
  Speak to her, Hamlet.
HAMLET.   How is it with you, lady?
QUEEN. Alas, how is't with you,
  That you do bend your eye on vacancy,
  And with th' incorporal air do hold discourse?   119
  Forth at your eyes your spirits wildly peep,
  And as the sleeping soldiers in th' alarm
  Your bedded hairs like life in excrements   122
  Start up and stand an end. O gentle son,   123
  Upon the heat and flame of thy distemper   124
  Sprinkle cool patience. Whereon do you look?
HAMLET. On him, on him! Look you, how pale he glares!

---

93. *enseamèd:* grease-laden.   **98.** *tithe:* tenth part.   **99.** *vice:* clownish rogue (like the Vice of the morality plays).   **100.** *cutpurse:* skulking thief.   **102 s.d.** *nightgown:* dressing gown.   **108.** *lapsed . . . passion:* having let the moment slip and passion cool.   **115.** *Conceit:* imagination.   **119.** *incorporal:* bodiless. **122.** *excrements:* outgrowths.   **123.** *an:* on.   **124.** *distemper:* mental disorder.

His form and cause conjoined, preaching to stones,
Would make them capable.—Do not look upon me,   128
Lest with this piteous action you convert
My stern effects. Then what I have to do   130
Will want true color—tears perchance for blood.
QUEEN. To whom do you speak this?
HAMLET.   Do you see nothing there?
QUEEN. Nothing at all; yet all that is I see.
HAMLET. Nor did you nothing hear?
QUEEN.   No, nothing but ourselves.
HAMLET. Why, look you there! Look how it steals away!
My father, in his habit as he lived!
Look where he goes even now out at the portal!   [*Exit* GHOST.]
QUEEN. This is the very coinage of your brain.
This bodiless creation ecstasy   139
Is very cunning in.
HAMLET.   Ecstasy?
My pulse as yours doth temperately keep time
And makes as healthful music. It is not madness
That I have uttered. Bring me to the test,
And I the matter will reword, which madness
Would gambol from. Mother, for love of grace,   145
Lay not that flattering unction to your soul,   146
That not your trespass but my madness speaks.
It will but skin and film the ulcerous place
Whiles rank corruption, mining all within,   149
Infects unseen. Confess yourself to heaven,
Repent what's past, avoid what is to come,
And do not spread the compost on the weeds   152
To make them ranker. Forgive me this my virtue.
For in the fatness of these pursy times   154
Virtue itself of vice must pardon beg,
Yea, curb and woo for leave to do him good.   156
QUEEN. O Hamlet, thou hast cleft my heart in twain.
HAMLET. O, throw away the worser part of it,
And live the purer with the other half.
Good night—but go not to my uncle's bed.
Assume a virtue, if you have it not.
That monster custom, who all sense doth eat,
Of habits devil, is angel yet in this,
That to the use of actions fair and good
He likewise gives a frock or livery   165

---

128. *capable:* susceptible.   **130.** *effects:* manifestations of emotion and purpose.   **139.** *ecstasy:* madness.
145. *gambol:* shy (like a startled horse).   **146.** *unction:* ointment.   **149.** *mining:* undermining.   **152.**
compost: fertilizing mixture.   **154.** *fatness:* gross slackness; *pursy:* corpulent.   **156.** *curb:* bow to.   **165.**
livery: characteristic dress (accompanying the suggestion of "garb" in *habits*).

That aptly is put on. Refrain to-night,
And that shall lend a kind of easiness
To the next abstinence; the next more easy;
For use almost can change the stamp of nature,   169
And either . . . the devil, or throw him out
With wondrous potency. Once more, good night,
And when you are desirous to be blest,
I'll blessing beg of you.—For this same lord,
I do repent; but heaven hath pleased it so,
To punish me with this, and this with me,
That I must be their scourge and minister.
I will bestow him and will answer well   177
The death I gave him. So again, good night.
I must be cruel only to be kind.
Thus bad begins, and worse remains behind.   180
One word more, good lady.
QUEEN.   What shall I do?
HAMLET. Not this, by no means, that I bid you do:
Let the bloat king tempt you again to bed,   183
Pinch wanton on your cheek, call you his mouse,
And let him, for a pair of reechy kisses,   185
Or paddling in your neck with his damned fingers,
Make you to ravel all this matter out,   187
That I essentially am not in madness,
But mad in craft. 'Twere good you let him know,
For who that's but a queen, fair, sober, wise,
Would from a paddock, from a bat, a gib,   191
Such dear concernings hide? Who would do so?   192
No, in despite of sense and secrecy,
Unpeg the basket on the house's top,
Let the birds fly, and like the famous ape,   195
To try conclusions, in the basket creep   196
And break your own neck down.
QUEEN. Be thou assured, if words be made of breath,
And breath of life, I have no life to breathe
What thou hast said to me.
HAMLET. I must to England; you know that?
QUEEN.   Alack,
I had forgot. 'Tis so concluded on.
HAMLET. There's letters sealed, and my two schoolfellows,
Whom I will trust as I will adders fanged,
They bear the mandate; they must sweep my way   205

169. *use:* habit; *stamp:* impression, form.   177. *bestow:* stow, hide.   180. *behind:* to come.   183. *bloat:* bloated with sense gratification.   185. *reechy:* filthy.   187. *ravel . . . out:* disentangle.   191. *paddock:* toad; *gib:* tomcat.   192. *dear concernings:* matters of great personal significance.   195. *famous ape* (one in a story now unknown).   196. *conclusions:* experiments.   205. *mandate:* order.

And marshal me to knavery. Let it work.
For 'tis the sport to have the enginer   207
Hoist with his own petar, and 't shall go hard   208
But I will delve one yard below their mines
And blow them at the moon. O, 'tis most sweet
When in one line two crafts directly meet.
This man shall set me packing.   212
I'll lug the guts into the neighbor room.
Mother, good night. Indeed, this counsellor
Is now most still, most secret, and most grave,
Who was in life a foolish prating knave.
Come, sir, to draw toward an end with you.
Good night, mother.   [*Exit the* QUEEN. *Then exit* HAMLET, *tugging in* POLONIUS.]

ACT IV, SCENE 1

[*Enter* KING *and* QUEEN, *with* ROSENCRANTZ *and* GUILDENSTERN.]

KING. There's matter in these sighs. These profound heaves
  You must translate; 'tis fit we understand them.
  Where is your son?
QUEEN. Bestow this place on us a little while.

                    [*Exeunt* ROSENCRANTZ *and* GUILDENSTERN.]

  Ah, mine own lord, what have I seen to-night!
KING. What, Gertrude? How does Hamlet?
QUEEN. Mad as the sea and wind when both contend
  Which is the mightier. In his lawless fit,
  Behind the arras hearing something stir,
  Whips out his rapier, cries, 'A rat, a rat!'
  And in this brainish apprehension kills   11
  The unseen good old man.
KING.   O heavy deed!
  It had been so with us, had we been there.
  His liberty is full of threats to all,
  To you yourself, to us, to every one.
  Alas, how shall this bloody deed be answered?
  It will be laid to us, whose providence   17
  Should have kept short, restrained, and out of haunt   18
  This mad young man. But so much was our love
  We would not understand what was most fit,
  But, like the owner of a foul disease,

---

207. *enginer:* engineer, constructor of military engines or works.   **208.** *Hoist:* blown up; *petar:* petard, bomb or mine.   **212.** *packing:* travelling in a hurry (with a play upon his "packing" or shouldering of Polonius' body and also upon his "packing" in the sense of "plotting" or "contriving").
IV, 1. A chamber in the Castle.   **11.** *brainish apprehension:* headstrong conception.   **17.** *providence:* foresight.   **18.** *haunt:* association with others.

To keep it from divulging, let it feed   22
Even on the pith of life. Where is he gone?
QUEEN. To draw apart the body he hath killed;
  O'er whom his very madness, like some ore   25
  Among a mineral of metals base,   26
  Shows itself pure. 'A weeps for what is done.
KING. O Gertrude, come away!
  The sun no sooner shall the mountains touch
  But we will ship him hence, and this vile deed
  We must with all our majesty and skill
  Both countenance and excuse. Ho, Guildenstern!

[*Enter* ROSENCRANTZ *and* GUILDENSTERN.]

  Friends both, go join you with some further aid.
  Hamlet in madness hath Polonius slain,
  And from his mother's closet hath he dragged him.
  Go seek him out; speak fair, and bring the body
  Into the chapel. I pray you haste in this.
                   [*Exeunt* ROSENCRANTZ *and* GUILDENSTERN.]
  Come, Gertrude, we'll call up our wisest friends
  And let them know both what we mean to do
  And what's untimely done . . .
  Whose whisper o'er the world's diameter,
  As level as the cannon to his blank   42
  Transports his poisoned shot, may miss our name
  And hit the woundless air. O, come away!
  My soul is full of discord and dismay.   [*Exeunt.*]

ACT IV, SCENE 2

[*Enter* HAMLET.]

HAMLET. Safely stowed.
GENTLEMEN [*within*]. Hamlet! Lord Hamlet!
HAMLET. But soft, what noise? Who calls on Hamlet? O, here they come.

[*Enter* ROSENCRANTZ, GUILDENSTERN, *and others.*]

ROSENCRANTZ. What have you done, my lord, with the dead body?
HAMLET. Compounded it with dust, whereto 'tis kin.
ROSENCRANTZ. Tell us where 'tis, that we may take it thence
  And bear it to the chapel.

---

22. *divulging:* becoming known.   **25.** *ore:* vein of gold.   **26.** *mineral:* mine.   **42.** *As level:* with as direct
aim; *blank:* mark, central white spot on a target.
IV, 2. A passage in the Castle.

HAMLET. Do not believe it.

ROSENCRANTZ. Believe what?

HAMLET. That I can keep your counsel and not mine own. Besides, to be demanded
of a sponge, what replication should be made by the son of a king?   11

ROSENCRANTZ. Take you me for a sponge, my lord?

HAMLET. Ay, sir, that soaks up the king's countenance, his rewards, his authorities.   13
But such officers do the king best service in the end. He keeps them, like an
ape, in the corner of his jaw, first mouthed, to be last swallowed. When he
needs what you have gleaned, it is but squeezing you and, sponge, you shall
be dry again.

ROSENCRANTZ. I understand you not, my lord.

HAMLET. I am glad of it. A knavish speech sleeps in a foolish ear.   19

ROSENCRANTZ. My lord, you must tell us where the body is and go with us to the
king.

HAMLET. The body is with the king, but the king is not with the body. The king
is a thing—

GUILDENSTERN. A thing, my lord?

HAMLET. Of nothing. Bring me to him. Hide fox, and all after.   [*Exeunt.*]   25

ACT IV, SCENE 3

[*Enter* KING, *and two or three.*]

KING. I have sent to seek him and to find the body.
How dangerous is it that this man goes loose!
Yet must not we put the strong law on him;
He's loved of the distracted multitude,   4
Who like not in their judgment, but their eyes,
And where 'tis so, th' offender's scourge is weighed,   6
But never the offense. To bear all smooth and even,
This sudden sending him away must seem
Deliberate pause. Diseases desperate grown   9
By desperate appliance are relieved,
Or not at all.

[*Enter* ROSENSENCRANTZ, GUILDENSTERN, *and all the rest.*]

　　　　　How now? What hath befallen?

ROSENCRANTZ. Where the dead body is bestowed, my lord,
We cannot get from him.

KING.　　　　　But where is he?

ROSENCRANTZ. Without, my lord; guarded, to know your pleasure.

---

11. *replication:* reply.   **13.** *countenance:* favor.   **19.** *sleeps in:* means nothing to.   **25.** *Of nothing* (cf.
Prayer Book, Psalm cxliv, 4, "Man is like a thing of naught: his time passeth away like a shadow"); *Hide
. . . after* (apparently well-known words from some game of hide-and-seek).
IV, 3. A chamber in the Castle.   **4.** *distracted:* confused.   **6.** *scourge:* punishment.   **9.** *Deliberate pause:*
something done with much deliberation.

KING. Bring him before us.

ROSENCRANTZ.   Ho! Bring in the lord.

[*They enter with* HAMLET.]

KING. Now, Hamlet, where's Polonius?

HAMLET. At supper.

KING. At supper? Where?

HAMLET. Not where he eats, but where 'a is eaten. A certain convocation of politic 19
worms are e'en at him. Your worm is your only emperor for diet. We fat all 20
creatures else to fat us, and we fat ourselves for maggots. Your fat king and
your lean beggar is but variable service—two dishes, but to one table. That's 22
the end.

KING. Alas, alas!

HAMLET. A man may fish with the worm that hath eat of a king, and eat of the
fish that hath fed of that worm.

KING. What dost thou mean by this?

HAMLET. Nothing but to show you how a king may go a progress through the 28
guts of a beggar.

KING. Where is Polonius?

HAMLET. In heaven. Send thither to see. If your messenger find him not there,
seek him i' th' other place yourself. But if indeed you find him not within
this month, you shall nose him as you go up the stairs into the lobby.

KING [*to Attendants*].   Go seek him there.

HAMLET. 'A will stay till you come.   [*Exeunt Attendants.*]

KING. Hamlet, this deed, for thine especial safety,
Which we do tender as we dearly grieve   37
For that which thou hast done, must send thee hence
With fiery quickness. Therefore prepare thyself.
The bark is ready and the wind at help,
Th' associates tend, and everything is bent   41
For England.

HAMLET.   For England?

KING.   Ay, Hamlet.

HAMLET.   Good.

KING. So is it, if thou knew'st our purposes.

HAMLET. I see a cherub that sees them. But come, for England! Farewell, dear 44
mother.

KING. Thy loving father, Hamlet.

HAMLET. My mother—father and mother is man and wife, man and wife is one
flesh, and so, my mother. Come, for England!   [*Exit.*]

19–20. *politic worms:* political and craftily scheming worms (such as Polonius might well attract).   **20.**
diet: food and drink (perhaps with a play upon a famous "convocation," the Diet of Worms opened by
the Emperior Charles V on January 28, 1521, before which Luther appeared).   **22.** *variable service:* different
servings of one food.   **28.** *progress:* royal journey of state.   **37.** *tender:* hold dear; *dearly:* intensely.   **41.**
tend: wait; *bent:* set in readiness (like a bent bow).   **44.** *cherub:* one of the cherubim (angels with a
distinctive quality of knowledge).

KING. Follow him at foot; tempt him with speed aboard.   49
   Delay it not; I'll have him hence to-night.
   Away! for everything is sealed and done
   That else leans on th' affair. Pray you make haste.   52

                                         [Exeunt all but the KING.]

   And, England, if my love thou hold'st at aught—   53
   As my great power thereof may give thee sense,
   Since yet thy cicatrice looks raw and red
   After the Danish sword, and thy free awe   56
   Pays homage to us—thou mayst not coldly set   57
   Our sovereign process, which imports at full   58
   By letters congruing to that effect   59
   The present death of Hamlet. Do it, England,   60
   For like the hectic in my blood he rages,   61
   And thou must cure me. Till I know 'tis done,
   Howe'er my haps, my joys were ne'er begun.   *[Exit.]*   63

ACT IV, SCENE 4

[*Enter* FORTINBRAS *with his Army over the stage.*]

FORTINBRAS. Go, captain, from me greet the Danish king.
   Tell him that by his license Fortinbras
   Craves the conveyance of a promised march   3
   Over his kingdom. You know the rendezvous.
   If that his majesty would aught with us,
   We shall express our duty in his eye;   6
   And let him know so.
CAPTAIN.   I will do't, my lord.
FORTINBRAS. Go softly on.   *[Exeunt all but the* CAPTAIN.]   8

[*Enter* HAMLET, ROSENCRANTZ, GUILDENSTERN, *and others.*]

HAMLET. Good sir, whose powers are these?   9
CAPTAIN. They are of Norway, sir.
HAMLET. How purposed, sir, I pray you?
CAPTAIN. Against some part of Poland.
HAMLET. Who commands them, sir?
CAPTAIN. The nephew to old Norway, Fortinbras.
HAMLET. Goes it against the main of Poland, sir,   15
   Or for some frontier?

---

49. *at foot:* at heel, close.   52. *leans on:* is connected with.   53. *England:* King of England.   56. *free awe:* voluntary show of respect.   57. *set:* esteem.   58. *process:* formal command.   59. *congruing:* agreeing.   60. *present:* instant.   61. *hectic:* a continuous fever.   63. *haps:* fortunes.
IV, 4. A coastal highway.   3. *conveyance:* escort.   6. *eye:* presence.   8. *softly:* slowly.   9. *powers:* forces.
15. *main:* main body.

CAPTAIN. Truly to speak, and with no addition,   17
   We go to gain a little patch of ground
   That hath in it no profit but the name.
   To pay five ducats, five, I would not farm it,   20
   Nor will it yield to Norway or the Pole
   A ranker rate, should it be sold in fee.   22
HAMLET. Why, then the Polack never will defend it.
CAPTAIN. Yes, it is already garrisoned.
HAMLET. Two thousand souls and twenty thousand ducats
   Will not debate the question of this straw.
   This is th' imposthume of much wealth and peace,   27
   That inward breaks, and shows no cause without
   Why the man dies. I humbly thank you, sir.
CAPTAIN. God bye you, sir.   [*Exit.*]
ROSENCRANTZ.   Will't please you go, my lord?
HAMLET. I'll be with you straight. Go a little before.

                                    [*Exeunt all but* HAMLET.]
   How all occasions do inform against me   32
   And spur my dull revenge! What is a man,
   If his chief good and market of his time   34
   Be but to sleep and feed? A beast, no more.
   Sure he that made us with such large discourse,   36
   Looking before and after, gave us not
   That capability and godlike reason
   To fust in us unused. Now, whether it be   39
   Bestial oblivion, or some craven scruple   40
   Of thinking too precisely on th' event—   41
   A thought which, quartered, hath but one part wisdom
   And ever three parts coward—I do not know
   Why yet I live to say, 'This thing's to do,'
   Sith I have cause, and will, and strength, and means
   To do't. Examples gross as earth exhort me.   46
   Witness this army of such mass and charge,   47
   Led by a delicate and tender prince,
   Whose spirit, with divine ambition puffed,
   Makes mouths at the invisible event,   50
   Exposing what is mortal and unsure
   To all that fortune, death, and danger dare,
   Even for an eggshell. Rightly to be great
   Is not to stir without great argument,

---

17. *addition:* exaggeration.   **20** *To pay:* i.e. for a yearly rental of.   **22.** *ranker:* more abundant; *in fee:* outright.   **27.** *imposthume:* abscess.   **32.** *inform:* take shape.   **34.** *market of:* compensation for.   **36.** *discourse:* power of thought.   **39.** *fust:* grow mouldy.   **40.** *oblivion:* forgetfulness.   **41.** *event:* outcome (as also in l. 50).   **46.** *gross:* large and evident.   **47.** *charge:* expense.   **50.** *Makes mouths:* makes faces scornfully.

But greatly to find quarrel in a straw   55
When honor's at the stake. How stand I then,
That have a father killed, a mother stained,
Excitements of my reason and my blood,
And let all sleep, while to my shame I see
The imminent death of twenty thousand men
That for a fantasy and trick of fame   61
Go to their graves like beds, fight for a plot
Whereon the numbers cannot try the cause,   63
Which is not tomb enough and continent   64
To hide the slain? O, from this time forth,
My thoughts be bloody, or be nothing worth!   [*Exit.*]

ACT IV, SCENE 5

[*Enter* HORATIO, QUEEN GERTRUDE, *and a* GENTLEMAN.]

QUEEN. I will not speak with her.
GENTLEMAN. She is importunate, indeed distract.   2
  Her mood will needs be pitied.
QUEEN.   What would she have?
GENTLEMAN. She speaks much of her father, says she hears
  There's tricks i' th' world, and hems, and beats her heart,   5
  Spurns enviously at straws, speaks things in doubt   6
  That carry but half sense. Her speech is nothing,
  Yet the unshaped use of it doth move   8
  The hearers to collection; they aim at it,   9
  And botch the words up fit to their own thoughts,   10
  Which, as her winks and nods and gestures yield them,
  Indeed would make one think there might be thought,
  Though nothing sure, yet much unhappily.
HORATIO. 'Twere good she were spoken with, for she may strew
  Dangerous conjectures in ill-breeding minds.
QUEEN. Let her come in.   [*Exit* GENTLEMAN.]
    [*Aside*]
  To my sick soul (as sin's true nature is)
  Each toy seems prologue to some great amiss.   18
  So full of artless jealousy is guilt   19
  It spills itself in fearing to be spilt.   20

55. *greatly . . . straw:* to recognize the great argument even in some small matter.   61. *fantasy:* fanciful image; *trick:* toy.   63. *try the cause:* find space in which to settle the issue by battle.   64. *continent:* receptacle.
IV, 5. A chamber in the Castle.   2. *distract:* insane.   5. *tricks:* deceits.   6. *Spurns enviously:* kicks spitefully, takes offense; *straws:* trifles.   8. *unshapèd use:* disordered manner.   9. *collection:* attempts at shaping meaning; *aim:* guess.   10. *botch:* patch.   18. *toy:* trifle; *amiss:* calamity.   19. *artless:* unskillfully managed; *jealousy:* suspicion.   20. *spills:* destroys.

[*Enter* OPHELIA *distracted.*]

OPHELIA. Where is the beauteous majesty of Denmark?
QUEEN. How now, Ophelia?
OPHELIA. [*She sings.*]

> How should I your true-love know
>   From another one?
> By his cockle hat and staff   25
>   And his sandal shoon.   26

QUEEN. Alas, sweet lady, what imports this song?
OPHELIA. Say you? Nay, pray you mark.

> *Song.*
> He is dead and gone, lady,
>   He is dead and gone;
> At his head a grass-green turf,
>   At his heels a stone.

O, ho!

QUEEN. Nay, but Ophelia—
OPHELIA. Pray you mark.

[*Sings*] White his shroud as the mountain snow—

[*Enter* KING.]

QUEEN. Alas, look here, my lord.
OPHELIA.   *Song.*

> Larded all with sweet flowers;   38
> Which bewept to the grave did not go
>   With true-love showers.

KING. How do you, pretty lady?
OPHELIA. Well, God dild you! They say the owl was a baker's daughter. Lord, we   42
know what we are, but know not what we may be. God be at your table!
KING. Conceit upon her father.   44
OPHELIA. Pray let's have no words of this, but when they ask you what it means,
say you this:

> *Song.*
> To-morrow is Saint Valentine's day.
>   All in the morning betime,   48
> And I a maid at your window,
>   To be your Valentine.
> Then up he rose and donned his clo'es
>   And dupped the chamber door,   52

---

25. *cockle hat:* hat bearing a cockle shell, worn by a pilgrim who had been to the shrine of St. James of Compostela.   **26.** *shoon:* shoes.   **38.** *Larded:* garnished.   **42.** *dild:* yield, repay; *the owl:* an owl into which, according to a folk-tale, a baker's daughter was transformed because of her failure to show whole-hearted generosity when Christ asked for bread in the baker's shop.   **44.** *Conceit:* thought.   **48.** *betime:* early.   **52.** *dupped:* opened.

> Let in the maid, that out a maid
>   Never departed more.

KING. Pretty Ophelia!

OPHELIA. Indeed, la, without an oath, I'll make an end on't:

> [*Sings*]   By Gis and by Saint Charity,   57
>   Alack, and fie for shame!
>   Young men will do't if they come to't.
>   By Cock, they are to blame.   60
>   Quoth she, 'Before you tumbled me,
>   You promised me to wed.'

He answers:

>   'So would I'a'done, by yonder sun,
>   And thou hadst not come to my bed.'

KING. How long hath she been thus?

OPHELIA. I hope all will be well. We must be patient, but I cannot choose but weep to think they would lay him i' th' cold ground. My brother shall know of it; and so I thank you for your good counsel. Come, my coach! Good night, ladies, good night. Sweet ladies, good night, good night.   [*Exit.*]

KING. Follow her close; give her good watch, I pray you.   [*Exit* Horatio.]

> O, this is the poison of deep grief; it springs
> All from her father's death—and now behold!
> O Gertrude, Gertrude,
> When sorrows come, they come not single spies,
> But in battalions: first, her father slain;
> Next, your son gone, and he most violent author
> Of his own just remove; the people muddied,   77
> Thick and unwholesome in their thoughts and whispers
> For good Polonius' death, and we have done but greenly   79
> In hugger-mugger to inter him; poor Ophelia   80
> Divided from herself and her fair judgment,
> Without the which we are pictures or mere beasts;
> Last, and as much containing as all these,
> Her brother is in secret come from France,
> Feeds on his wonder, keeps himself in clouds,   85
> And wants not buzzers to infect his ear   86
> With pestilent speeches of his father's death,
> Wherein necessity, of matter beggared,   88
> Will nothing stick our person to arraign   89
> In ear and ear. O my dear Gertrude, this,
> Like to a murd'ring piece, in many places   91
> Gives me superfluous death.

---

57. *Gis:* Jesus.   **60.** *Cock:* God (with a perversion of the name not uncommon in oaths).   **77.** *muddied:* stirred up and confused.   **79.** *greenly:* foolishly.   **80.** *hugger-mugger:* secrecy and disorder.   **85.** *clouds:* obscurity.   **86.** *wants:* lacks; *buzzers:* whispering tale-bearers.   **88.** *of matter beggared:* unprovided with facts.   **89.** *nothing stick:* in no way hesitate; *arraign:* accuse.   **91.** *murd'ring piece:* cannon loaded with shot meant to scatter.

[*A noise within.*]
[*Enter a* MESSENGER.]

QUEEN.   Alack, what noise is this?
KING. Attend, where are my Switzers? Let them guard the door.   93
  What is the matter?
MESSENGER.   Save yourself, my lord.
  The ocean, overpeering of his list,   95
  Eats not the flats with more impiteous haste   96
  Than young Laertes, in a riotous head,   97
  O'erbears your officers. The rabble call him lord,
  And, as the world were now but to begin,
  Antiquity forgot, custom not known,
  The ratifiers and props of every word,   101
  They cry, 'Choose we! Laertes shall be king!'
  Caps, hands, and tongues applaud it to the clouds,
  'Laertes shall be king! Laertes king!'

[*A noise within.*]

QUEEN. How cheerfully on the false trail they cry!
  O, this is counter, you false Danish dogs!   106
KING. The doors are broke.

[*Enter* LAERTES *with others.*]

LAERTES. Where is this king?—Sirs, stand you all without.
ALL. No, let's come in.
LAERTES.   I pray you give me leave.
ALL. We will, we will.
LAERTES. I thank you. Keep the door.   [*Exeunt his Followers.*]
                O thou vile king,
  Give me my father.
QUEEN.   Calmly, good Laertes.
LAERTES. That drop of blood that's calm proclaims me bastard,
  Cries cuckold to my father, brands the harlot
  Even here between the chaste unsmirchèd brows
  Of my true mother.
KING.   What is the cause, Laertes,
  That thy rebellion looks so giant-like?
  Let him go, Gertrude. Do not fear our person.   118
  There's such divinity doth hedge a king
  That treason can but peep to what it would,   120
  Acts little of his will. Tell me, Laertes,

---

93. *Switzers:* hired Swiss guards. **95.** *overpeering of:* rising to look over and pass beyond; *list:* boundary. **96.** *impiteous:* pitiless. **97.** *head:* armed force. **101.** *word:* promise. **106.** *counter:* hunting backward on the trail. **118.** *fear:* fear for. **120.** *peep to:* i.e. through the barrier.

Why thou art thus incensed. Let him go, Gertrude.
Speak, man.

LAERTES. Where is my father?

KING.   Dead.

QUEEN.   But not by him.

KING. Let him demand his fill.

LAERTES. How came he dead? I'll not be juggled with.
To hell allegiance, vows to the blackest devil,
Conscience and grace to the profoundest pit!
I dare damnation. To this point I stand,
That both the worlds I give to negligence,   130
Let come what comes, only I'll be revenged
Most throughly for my father.   132

KING.   Who shall stay you?

LAERTES. My will, not all the world's.
And for my means, I'll husband them so well
They shall go far with little.

KING.   Good Laertes,
If you desire to know the certainty
Of your dear father, is't writ in your revenge
That swoopstake you will draw both friend and foe,   138
Winner and loser?

LAERTES. None but his enemies.

KING.   Will you know them then?

LAERTES. To his good friends thus wide I'll ope my arms
And like the kind life-rend'ring pelican   142
Repast them with my blood.

KING.   Why, now you speak
Like a good child and a true gentleman.
That I am guiltless of your father's death,
And am most sensibly in grief for it,   146
It shall as level to your judgment 'pear   147
As day does to your eye.

[*A noise within: 'Let her come in.'*]

LAERTES. How now? What noise is that?

[*Enter* OPHELIA.]

O heat, dry up my brains; tears seven times salt
Burn out the sense and virtue of mine eye!
By heaven, thy madness shall be paid by weight

---

130. *both the worlds:* whatever may result in this world or the next; *give to negligence:* disregard.   **132.** *throughly:* thoroughly.   **138.** *swoopstake:* sweepstake, taking all stakes on the gambling table.   **142.** *life-rend'ring:* life-yielding (because the mother pelican supposedly took blood from her breast with her bill to feed her young).   **146.** *sensibly:* feelingly.   **147.** *level:* plain.

Till our scale turn the beam. O rose of May,   153
Dear maid, kind sister, sweet Ophelia!
O heavens, is't possible a young maid's wits
Should be as mortal as an old man's life?
Nature is fine in love, and where 'tis fine,   157
It sends some precious instance of itself   158
After the thing it loves.

OPHELIA.   *Song.*
                They bore him barefaced on the bier
                    Hey non nony, nony, hey nony
                And in his grave rained many a tear—
Fare you well, my dove!

LAERTES. Hadst thou thy wits, and didst persuade revenge,
It could not move thus.

OPHELIA. You must sing 'A-down a-down, and you call him a-down-a.' O, how
the wheel becomes it! It is the false steward, that stole his master's daughter.   167

LAERTES. This nothing's more than matter.   168

OPHELIA. There's rosemary, that's for remembrance. Pray you, love, remember.
And there is pansies, that's for thoughts.

LAERTES. A document in madness, thoughts and remembrance fitted.   171

OPHELIA. There's fennel for you, and columbines. There's rue for you, and here's   172
some for me. We may call it herb of grace o'Sundays. O, you must wear
your rue with a difference. There's a daisy. I would give you some violets,   174
but they withered all when my father died. They say 'a made a good end.
[*Sings*] For bonny sweet Robin is all my joy.

LAERTES. Thought and affliction, passion, hell itself,
She turns to favor and to prettiness.   178

OPHELIA.   *Song.*
                And will 'a not come again?
                And will 'a not come again?
                    No, no, he is dead;
                    Go to thy deathbed;
                He never will come again.
                His beard was as white as snow,
                All flaxen was his poll.   185
                    He is gone, he is gone,
                    And we cast away moan.
                God 'a' mercy on his soul!
And of all Christian souls, I pray God. God bye you.   [*Exit.*]   189

LAERTES. Do you see this, O God?

---

153. *beam:* bar of a balance.   **157.** *fine:* refined to purity.   **158.** *instance:* token.   **167.** *wheel:* burden, refrain.   **168.** *more than matter:* more meaningful than sane speech.   **171.** *document:* lesson. **172.** *fennel:* symbol of flattery; *columbines:* symbol of thanklessness (?); *rue:* symbol of repentance. **174.** *daisy:* symbol of dissembling; *violets:* symbol of faithfulness.   **178.** *favor:* charm.   **185.** *poll:* head. **189.** *of:* on.

KING. Laertes, I must commune with your grief,
　　Or you deny me right. Go but apart,
　　Make choice of whom your wisest friends you will,
　　And they shall hear and judge 'twixt you and me.
　　If by direct or by collateral hand   195
　　They find us touched, we will our kingdom give,   196
　　Our crown, our life, and all that we call ours,
　　To you in satisfaction; but if not,
　　Be you content to lend your patience to us,
　　And we shall jointly labor with your soul
　　To give it due content.
LAERTES.　　　　　　　　　Let this be so.
　　His means of death, his obscure funeral—
　　No trophy, sword, nor hatchment o'er his bones,   203
　　No noble rite nor formal ostentation—   204
　　Cry to be heard, as 'twere from heaven to earth,
　　That I must call't in question.   206
KING.　　　　　　　　　　So you shall;
　　And where th' offense is, let the great axe fall.
　　I pray you go with me.   [*Exeunt.*]

ACT IV, SCENE 6

[*Enter* HORATIO *and others.*]

HORATIO. What are they that would speak with me?
GENTLEMAN. Seafaring men, sir. They say they have letters for you.
HORATIO. Let them come in.   [*Exit Attendant.*]
　　I do not know from what part of the world
　　I should be greeted, if not from Lord Hamlet.

[*Enter* SAILORS.]

SAILOR. God bless you, sir.
HORATIO. Let him bless thee too.
SAILOR. 'A shall, sir, an't please him. There's a letter for you, sir—it came from
　　th' ambassador that was bound for England—if your name be Horatio, as I
　　am let to know it is.
HORATIO [*reads the letter*]. 'Horatio, when thou shalt have overlooked this, give   11
　　these fellows some means to the king. They have letters for him. Ere we   12
　　were two days old at sea, a pirate of very warlike appointment gave us chase.   13
　　Finding ourselves too slow of sail, we put on a compelled valor, and in the

---

195. *collateral:* indirect.　**196.** *touched:* i.e. with the crime.　**203.** *trophy:* memorial; *hatchment:* coat of arms.　**204.** *ostentation:* ceremony.　**206.** *That:* so that.
IV, 6. A chamber in the Castle.　**11.** *overlooked:* surveyed, scanned.　**12.** *means:* i.e. of access.　**13.** *appointment:* equipment.

grapple I boarded them. On the instant they got clear of our ship; so I alone became their prisoner. They have dealt with me like thieves of mercy, but they knew what they did: I am to do a good turn for them. Let the king have the letters I have sent, and repair thou to me with as much speed as thou wouldest fly death. I have words to speak in thine ear will make thee dumb; yet are they much too light for the bore of the matter. These good fellows will bring thee where I am. Rosencrantz and Guildenstern hold their course for England. Of them I have much to tell thee. Farewell. 16 20

                                   'He that thou knowest thine, Hamlet.'
Come, I will give you way for these your letters,
And do't the speedier that you may direct me
To him from whom you brought them.   [*Exeunt.*]

ACT IV, SCENE 7

[*Enter* KING *and* LAERTES.]

KING. Now must your conscience my acquittance seal,
    And you must put me in your heart for friend,
    Sith you have heard, and with a knowing ear,
    That he which hath your noble father slain
    Pursued my life.
LAERTES.   It well appears. But tell me
    Why you proceeded not against these feats   6
    So crimeful and so capital in nature,   7
    As by your safety, wisdom, all things else,
    You mainly were stirred up.   9
KING.   O, for two special reasons,
    Which may to you perhaps seem much unsinewed,
    But yet to me they're strong. The queen his mother
    Lives almost by his looks, and for myself—
    My virtue or my plague, be it either which—
    She is so conjunctive to my life and soul   14
    That, as the star moves not but in his sphere,
    I could not but by her. The other motive
    Why to a public count I might not go   17
    Is the great love the general gender bear him,   18
    Who, dipping all his faults in their affection,
    Would, like the spring that turneth wood to stone,
    Convert his gyves to graces; so that my arrows,   21
    Too slightly timbered for so loud a wind,

---

16. *thieves of mercy:* merciful thieves.   **20.** *bore:* caliber (as of a gun).
IV, 7. A chamber in the Castle.   **6.** *feats:* deeds.   **7.** *capital:* punishable by death.   **9.** *mainly:* powerfully.   **14.** *conjunctive:* closely united.   **17.** *count:* trial, accounting.   **18.** *general gender:* common people.   **21.** *gyves:* fetters.

Would have reverted to my bow again,
And not where I had aimed them.

LAERTES. And so have I a noble father lost,
  A sister driven into desp'rate terms,   26
  Whose worth, if praises may go back again,   27
  Stood challenger on mount of all the age   28
  For her perfections. But my revenge will come.

KING. Break not your sleeps for that. You must not think
  That we are made of stuff so flat and dull
  That we can let our beard be shook with danger,
  And think it pastime. You shortly shall hear more.
  I loved your father, and we love ourself,
  And that, I hope, will teach you to imagine—

[*Enter a* MESSENGER *with letters.*]

  How now? What news?
MESSENGER.   Letters, my lord, from Hamlet:
  These to your majesty, this to the queen.
KING. From Hamlet? Who brought them?
MESSENGER. Sailors, my lord, they say; I saw them not.
  They were given me by Claudio; he received them
  Of him that brought them.
KING.   Laertes, you shall hear them.—
  Leave us.   [*Exit* MESSENGER.]
  [*Reads*] 'High and mighty, you shall know I am set naked on your kingdom.   43
  To-morrow shall I beg leave to see your kingly eyes; when I shall (first asking
  your pardon thereunto) recount the occasion of my sudden and more strange
  return.   Hamlet.'
  What should this mean? Are all the rest come back?
  Or is it some abuse, and no such thing?   48
LAERTES. Know you the hand?
KING.   'Tis Hamlet's character. 'Naked'!   49
  And in a postscript here, he says 'alone.'
  Can you devise me?   51
LAERTES. I am lost in it, my lord. But let him come.
  It warms the very sickness in my heart
  That I shall live and tell him to his teeth,
  'Thus diddest thou.'
KING.   If it be so, Laertes,
  (As how should it be so? how otherwise?)
  Will you be ruled by me?

---

26. *terms:* circumstances.   **27.** *back again:* i.e. to her better circumstances.   **28.** *on mount:* on a height.   **43.** *naked:* destitute.   **48.** *abuse:* imposture.   **49.** *character:* handwriting.   **51.** *devise:* explain to.

LAERTES.   Ay, my lord,
  So you will not o'errule me to a peace.
KING. To thine own peace. If he be now returned,
  As checking at his voyage, and that he means   60
  No more to undertake it, I will work him
  To an exploit now ripe in my device,
  Under the which he shall not choose but fall;
  And for his death no wind of blame shall breathe,
  But even his mother shall uncharge the practice   65
  And call it accident.
LAERTES.   My lord, I will be ruled;
  The rather if you could devise it so
  That I might be the organ.   68
KING.   It falls right.
  You have been talked of since your travel much,
  And that in Hamlet's hearing, for a quality
  Wherein they say you shine. Your sum of parts
  Did not together pluck such envy from him
  As did that one, and that, in my regard,
  Of the unworthiest siege.   74
LAERTES.   What part is that, my lord?
KING. A very riband in the cap of youth,   75
  Yet needful too, for youth no less becomes
  The light and careless livery that it wears   77
  Than settled age his sables and his weeds,   78
  Importing health and graveness. Two months since   79
  Here was a gentleman of Normandy.
  I have seen myself, and served against, the French,
  And they can well on horseback, but this gallant   82
  Had witchcraft in't. He grew unto his seat,
  And to such wondrous doing brought his horse
  As had he been incorpsed and demi-natured   85
  With the brave beast. So far he topped my thought   86
  That I, in forgery of shapes and tricks,   87
  Come short of what he did.
LAERTES.   A Norman was't?
KING. A Norman.
LAERTES. Upon my life, Lamord.
KING.   The very same.

60. *checking at:* turning aside from (like a falcon turning from its quarry for other prey).   **65.** *uncharge the practice:* acquit the stratagem of being a plot.   **68.** *organ:* instrument.   **74.** *siege:* seat, rank.   **75.** *riband:* decoration.   **77.** *livery:* distinctive attire.   **78.** *sables:* dignified robes richly furred with sable; *weeds:* distinctive garments.   **79.** *health:* welfare, prosperity.   **82.** *can well:* can perform well.   **85.** *incorpsed:* made one body; *demi-natured:* made sharer of nature half and half (as man shares with horse in the centaur).   **86.** *topped:* excelled; *thought:* imagination of possibilities.   **87.** *forgery:* invention.

LAERTES. I know him well. He is the brooch indeed   91
   And gem of all the nation.
KING. He made confession of you,   93
   And gave you such a masterly report
   For art and exercise in your defense,
   And for your rapier most especial,
   That he cried out 'twould be a sight indeed
   If one could match you. The scrimers of their nation   98
   He swore had neither motion, guard, nor eye,
   If you opposed them. Sir, this report of his
   Did Hamlet so envenom with his envy
   That he could nothing do but wish and beg
   Your sudden coming o'er to play with you.
   Now, out of this—
LAERTES.   What out of this, my lord?
KING. Laertes, was your father dear to you?
   Or are you like the painting of a sorrow,
   A face without a heart?
LAERTES.   Why ask you this?
KING. Not that I think you did not love your father,
   But that I know love is begun by time,
   And that I see, in passages of proof,   110
   Time qualifies the spark and fire of it.   111
   There lives within the very flame of love
   A kind of wick or snuff that will abate it,   113
   And nothing is at a like goodness still,   114
   For goodness, growing to a plurisy,   115
   Dies in his own too-much. That we would do
   We should do when we would, for this 'would' changes,
   And hath abatements and delays as many
   As there are tongues, are hands, are accidents,
   And then this 'should' is like a spendthrift sigh,
   That hurts by easing. But to the quick o' th' ulcer—   121
   Hamlet comes back; what would you undertake
   To show yourself your father's son in deed
   More than in words?
LAERTES.   To cut his throat i' th' church!
KING. No place indeed should murder sanctuarize;   125
   Revenge should have no bounds. But, good Laertes,
   Will you do this? Keep close within your chamber.

---

91. *brooch:* ornament. **93.** *made confession:* admitted the rival accomplishments. **98.** *scrimers:* fencers.
110. *passages of proof:* incidents of experience. **111.** *qualifies:* weakens. **113.** *snuff:* unconsumed
portion of the burned wick. **114.** *still:* always. **115.** *plurisy:* excess. **121.** *hurts:* i.e. shortens life by
drawing blood from the heart (as was believed); *quick:* sensitive flesh. **125.** *sanctuarize:* protect from
punishment, give sanctuary to.

Hamlet returned shall know you are come home.
We'll put on those shall praise your excellence   129
And set a double varnish on the fame
The Frenchman gave you, bring you in fine together   131
And wager on your heads. He, being remiss,   132
Most generous, and free from all contriving,
Will not peruse the foils, so that with ease,   134
Or with a little shuffling, you may choose
A sword unbated, and, in a pass of practice,   136
Requite him for your father.
LAERTES.   I will do't,
And for that purpose I'll anoint my sword.
I bought an unction of a mountebank,   139
So mortal that, but dip a knife in it,
Where it draws blood no cataplasm so rare,   141
Collected from all simples that have virtue   142
Under the moon, can save the thing from death
That is but scratched withal. I'll touch my point   144
With this contagion, that, if I gall him slightly,   145
It may be death.
KING.   Let's further think of this,
Weigh what convenience both of time and means
May fit us to our shape. If this should fail,   148
And that our drift look through our bad performance,   149
'Twere better not assayed. Therefore this project
Should have a back or second, that might hold
If this did blast in proof. Soft, let me see.   152
We'll make a solemn wager on your cunnings—
I ha't!
When in your motion you are hot and dry—
As make your bouts more violent to that end—
And that he calls for drink, I'll have preferred him   157
A chalice for the nonce, whereon but sipping,   158
If he by chance escape your venomed stuck,   159
Our purpose may hold there.—But stay, what noise?

[*Enter* QUEEN.]

QUEEN. One woe doth tread upon another's heel,
    So fast they follow. Your sister's drowned, Laertes.
LAERTES. Drowned! Oh, where?

---

129. *put on:* instigate.   **131.** *in fine:* finally.   **132.** *remiss:* negligent.   **134.** *peruse:* scan.   **136.** *unbated:* not blunted; *pass of practice:* thrust made effective by trickery.   **139.** *unction:* ointment; *mountebank:* quack-doctor.   **141.** *cataplasm:* poultice.   **142.** *simples:* herbs.   **144.** *withal:* with it.   **145.** *gall:* scratch.   **148.** *shape:* plan.   **149.** *drift:* intention; *look:* show.   **152.** *blast in proof:* burst during trial (like a faulty cannon).   **157.** *preferred:* offered.   **158.** *nonce:* occasion.   **159.** *stuck:* thrust.

QUEEN. There is a willow grows askant the brook,   164
   That shows his hoar leaves in the glassy stream.   165
   Therewith fantastic garlands did she make
   Of crowflowers, nettles, daisies, and long purples,
   That liberal shepherds give a grosser name,   168
   But our cold maids do dead men's fingers call them.
   There on the pendent boughs her crownet weeds   170
   Clamb'ring to hang, an envious sliver broke,
   When down her weedy trophies and herself
   Fell in the weeping brook. Her clothes spread wide,
   And mermaid-like awhile they bore her up,
   Which time she chanted snatches of old lauds,   175
   As one incapable of her own distress,   176
   Or like a creature native and indued   177
   Unto that element. But long it could not be
   Till that her garments, heavy with their drink,
   Pulled the poor wretch from her melodious lay
   To muddy death.
LAERTES.   Alas, then she is drowned?
QUEEN. Drowned, drowned.
LAERTES. Too much of water hast thou, poor Ophelia,
   And therefore I forbid my tears; but yet
   It is our trick; nature her custom holds,   185
   Let shame say what it will. When these are gone,
   The woman will be out. Adieu, my lord.   187
   I have a speech o'fire, that fain would blaze
   But that this folly drowns it.   [*Exit.*]
KING.   Let's follow, Gertrude.
   How much I had to do to calm his rage!
   Now fear I this will give it start again;
   Therefore let's follow.   [*Exeunt.*]

ACT V, SCENE 1

[*Enter two* CLOWNS.]

CLOWN. Is she to be buried in Christian burial when she willfully seeks her   1
   own salvation?
OTHER. I tell thee she is. Therefore make her grave straight. The crowner hath   3
   sate on her, and finds it Christian burial.

---

164. *askant:* alongside. **165.** *hoar:* grey. **168.** *liberal:* free-spoken, licentious. **170.** *crownet:* coronet. **175.** *lauds:* hymns. **176.** *incapable of:* insensible to. **177.** *indued:* endowed. **185.** *trick:* way (i.e. to shed tears when sorrowful). **187.** *woman:* unmanly part of nature.
V, 1. A churchyard. **s.d.** *Clowns:* rustics. **1.** *in Christian burial:* in consecrated ground with the prescribed service of the Church (a burial denied to suicides). **3.** *straight:* straightway, at once; *crowner:* coroner.

CLOWN. How can that be, unless she drowned herself in her own defense?

OTHER. Why, 'tis found so.

CLOWN. It must be *se offendendo;* it cannot be else. For here lies the point: if I   7
drown myself wittingly, it argues an act, and an act hath three branches—it
is to act, to do, and to perform. Argal, she drowned herself wittingly.   9

OTHER. Nay, but hear you, Goodman Delver.   10

CLOWN. Give me leave. Here lies the water—good. Here stands the man—good.
If the man go to this water and drown himself, it is, will he nill he, he goes,   12
mark you that. But if the water come to him and drown him, he drowns not
himself. Argal, he that is not guilty of his own death shortens not his own
life.

OTHER. But is this law?

CLOWN. Ay marry, is't—crowner's quest law.   17

OTHER. Will you ha' the truth on't? If this had not been a gentlewoman, she
should have been buried out o' Christian burial.

CLOWN. Why, there thou say'st. And the more pity that great folk should have   20
count'nance in this world to drown or hang themselves more than their even-   21
Christen. Come, my spade. There is no ancient gentlemen but gard'ners, ditch-   22
ers, and grave-makers. They hold up Adam's profession.

OTHER. Was he a gentleman?

CLOWN. 'A was the first that ever bore arms.

OTHER. Why, he had none.   26

CLOWN. What, art a heathen? How dost thou understand the Scripture? The Scripture says Adam digged. Could he dig without arms? I'll put another question
to thee. If thou answerest me not to the purpose, confess thyself—

OTHER. Go to.

CLOWN. What is he that builds stronger than either the mason, the shipwright,
or the carpenter?

OTHER. The gallows-maker, for that frame outlives a thousand tenants.

CLOWN. I like thy wit well, in good faith. The gallows does well. But how does
it well? It does well to those that do ill. Now thou dost ill to say the gallows
is built stronger than the church. Argal, the gallows may do well to thee. To't
again, come.

OTHER. Who builds stronger than a mason, a shipwright, or a carpenter?

CLOWN. Ay, tell me that, and unyoke.   39

OTHER. Marry, now I can tell.

CLOWN. To't.

OTHER. Mass, I cannot tell.   42

CLOWN. Cudgel thy brains no more about it, for your dull ass will not mend his
pace with beating. And when you are asked this question next, say 'a grave-

---

7. *se offendendo:* a clownish transformation of *"se defendendo,"* "in self-defense."   **9.** *Argal:* for *"ergo,"*
"therefore."   **10.** *Delver:* Digger.   **12.** *will he nill he:* willy-nilly.   **17.** *quest:* inquest.   **20.** *thou say'st:*
you have it right.   **21.** *count'nance:* privilege.   **21–22.** *even-Christen:* fellow Christian.   **26.** *had none:*
i.e. had no gentleman's coat of arms.   **39.** *unyoke:* i.e. unharness your powers of thought after a good
day's work.   **42.** *Mass:* by the Mass.

maker.' The houses he makes last till doomsday. Go, get thee in, and fetch
me a stoup of liquor.   [*Exit* OTHER CLOWN.]   46

[*Enter* HAMLET *and* HORATIO *as* CLOWN *digs and sings.*]

Song.

In youth when I did love, did love,
  Methought it was very sweet
To contract—O—the time for—a—my behove,   49
  O, methought there—a—was nothing—a—meet.

HAMLET. Has this fellow no feeling of his business, that'a sings at grave-making?
HORATIO. Custom hath made it in him a property of easiness.   52
HAMLET. 'Tis e'en so. The hand of little employment hath the daintier sense.   53
CLOWN.

Song.

But age with his stealing steps
  Hath clawed me in his clutch,
And hath shipped me intil the land,   56
  As if I had never been such.

[*Throws up a skull.*]

HAMLET. That skull had a tongue in it, and could sing once. How the knave
jowls it to the ground, as if'twere Cain's jawbone, that did the first murder!   59
This might be the pate of a politician, which this ass now o'erreaches; one   60
that would circumvent God, might it not?
HORATIO. It might, my lord.
HAMLET. Or of a courtier, which could say 'Good morrow, sweet lord! How dost
thou, sweet lord? This might be my Lord Such-a-one, that praised my Lord
Such-a-one's horse when 'a meant to beg it, might it not?
HORATIO. Ay, my lord.
HAMLET. Why, e'en so, and now my Lady Worm's, chapless, and knocked about   67
the mazzard with a sexton's spade. Here's fine revolution, an we had the   68
trick to see't. Did these bones cost no more the breeding but to play at
loggets with 'em? Mine ache to think on't.   70
CLOWN.

Song.

A pickaxe and a spade, a spade,
  For and a shrouding sheet;   72
O, a pit of clay for to be made
  For such a guest is meet.

[*Throws up another skull.*]

---

46. *stoup:* large mug. **49.** *behove:* behoof, benefit. **52.** *property:* peculiarity; *easiness:* easy acceptability. **53.** *daintier sense:* more delicate feeling (because the hand is less calloused). **56.** *intil:* into. **59.** *jowls:* hurls. **60.** *politician:* crafty schemer; *o'erreaches:* gets the better of (with a play upon the literal meaning). **67.** *chapless:* lacking the lower chap or jaw. **68.** *mazzard:* head. **70.** *loggets:* small pieces of wood thrown in a game. **72.** *For and:* and.

HAMLET. There's another. Why may not that be the skull of a lawyer? Where be his quiddities now, his quillities, his cases, his tenures, and his tricks? Why 76 does he suffer this mad knave now to knock him about the sconce with a 77 dirty shovel, and will not tell him of his action of battery? Hum! This fellow might be in's time a great buyer of land, with his statutes, his recognizances, 79 his fines, his double vouchers, his recoveries. Is this the fine of his fines, 80 and the recovery of his recoveries, to have his fine pate full of fine dirt? Will his vouchers vouch him no more of his purchases, and double ones too, than the length and breadth of a pair of indentures? The very conveyances of 83 his lands will scarcely lie in this box, and must th' inheritor himself have no more, ha?

HORATIO. Not a jot more, my lord.

HAMLET. Is not parchment made of sheepskins?

HORATIO. Ay, my lord, and of calveskins too.

HAMLET. They are sheep and calves which seek out assurance in that. I will speak to this fellow. Whose grave's this, sirrah?

CLOWN. Mine, sir. [*Sings*]

> O, a pit of clay for to be made
> For such a guest is meet.

HAMLET. I think it be thine indeed, for thou liest in't.

CLOWN. You lie out on't, sir, and therefore 'tis not yours. For my part, I do not lie in't, yet it is mine.

HAMLET. Thou dost lie in't, to be in't and say it is thine. 'Tis for the dead, not for the quick; therefore thou liest. 98

CLOWN. 'Tis a quick lie, sir; 'twill away again from me to you.

HAMLET. What man dost thou dig it for?

CLOWN. For no man, sir.

HAMLET. What woman then?

CLOWN. For none neither.

HAMLET. Who is to be buried in't?

CLOWN. One that was a woman, sir; but, rest her soul, she's dead.

HAMLET. How absolute the knave is! We must speak by the card, or equivocation 106 will undo us. By the Lord, Horatio, this three years I have taken note of it, the age is grown so picked that the toe of the peasant comes so near the 108 heel of the courtier he galls his kibe.—How long has thou been a grave- 109 maker?

CLOWN. Of all the days i' th' year, I came to't that day that our last king Hamlet overcame Fortinbras.

---

76. *quiddities:* subtleties (from scholastic *"quidditas,"* meaning the distinctive nature of anything); *quillities:* nice distinctions; *tenures:* holdings of property.   **77.** *sconce:* head.   **79.** *statutes, recognizances:* legal documents or bonds acknowledging debt.   **80.** *fines, recoveries:* modes of converting estate tail into fee simple; *vouchers:* persons vouched or called on to warrant a title; *fine:* end (introducing a word play involving four meanings of *"fine"*).   **83.** *pair of indentures:* deed or legal agreement in duplicate; *conveyances:* deeds.   **98.** *quick:* living.   **106.** *absolute:* positive; *by the card:* by the card on which the points of the mariner's compass are marked, absolutely to the point; *equivocation:* ambiguity.   **108.** *picked:* refined, spruce.   **109.** *galls:* chafes; *kibe:* chilblain.

HAMLET. How long is that since?

CLOWN. Cannot you tell that? Every fool can tell that. It was the very day that young Hamlet was born—he that is mad, and sent into England.

HAMLET. Ay, marry, why was he sent into England?

CLOWN. Why, because 'a was mad. 'A shall recover his wits there; or, if 'a do not, 'tis no great matter there.

HAMLET. Why?

CLOWN. 'Twill not be seen in him there. There the men are as mad as he.

HAMLET. How came he mad?

CLOWN. Very strangely, they say.

HAMLET. How strangely?

CLOWN. Faith, e'en with losing his wits.

HAMLET. Upon what ground?

CLOWN. Why, here in Denmark. I have been sexton here, man and boy, thirty years.

HAMLET. How long will a man lie i' th' earth ere he rot?

CLOWN. Faith, if 'a be not rotten before 'a die (as we have many pocky corses   129
now-a-days that will scarce hold the laying in), 'a will last you some eight year or nine year. A tanner will last you nine year.

HAMLET. Why he more than another?

CLOWN. Why, sir, his hide is so tanned with his trade that 'a will keep out water a great while, and your water is a sore decayer of your whoreson dead body. Here's a skull now hath lien you i' th' earth three-and-twenty years.

HAMLET. Whose was it?

CLOWN. A whoreson mad fellow's it was. Whose do you think it was?

HAMLET. Nay, I know not.

CLOWN. A pestilence on him for a mad rogue! 'A poured a flagon of Rhenish on   139
my head once. This same skull, sir, was—sir—Yorick's skull, the king's jester.

HAMLET. This?

CLOWN. E'en that.

HAMLET. Let me see. [*Takes the skull.*] Alas, poor Yorick! I knew him, Horatio, a fellow of infinite jest, of most excellent fancy. He hath borne me on his back a thousand times. And now how abhorred in my imagination it is! My gorge rises at it. Here hung those lips that I have kissed I know not how oft. Where be your gibes now? Your gambols, your songs, your flashes of merriment that were wont to set the table on a roar? Not one now to mock your own grinning? Quite chapfall'n? Now get you to my lady's chamber, and tell her,   149
let her paint an inch thick, to this favor she must come. Make her laugh at   150
that. Prithee, Horatio, tell me one thing.

HORATIO. What's that, my lord?

HAMLET. Dost thou think Alexander looked o' this fashion i' th' earth?

HORATIO. E'en so.

HAMLET. And smelt so? Pah!

---

129. *pocky:* rotten (literally, corrupted by pox, or syphilis).   **139.** *Rhenish:* Rhine wine.   **149.** *chapfall'n:* lacking the lower chap, or jaw (with a play on the sense "down in the mouth," "dejected").   **150.** *favor:* countenance, aspect.

[*Puts down the skull.*]

HORATIO. E'en so, my lord.

HAMLET. To what base uses we may return, Horatio! Why may not imagination trace the noble dust of Alexander till'a find it stopping a bunghole?

HORATIO. 'Twere to consider too curiously, to consider so.   159

HAMLET. No, faith, not a jot, but to follow him thither with modesty enough,   160
and likelihood to lead it; as thus: Alexander died, Alexander was buried, Alexander returneth to dust; the dust is earth; of earth we make loam; and why of that loam whereto he was converted might they not stop a beer barrel?

Imperious Caesar, dead and turned to clay,   164
Might stop a hole to keep the wind away.
O, that that earth which kept the world in awe
Should patch a wall t' expel the winter's flaw!   167
But soft, but soft awhile! Here comes the king—

[*Enter* KING, QUEEN, LAERTES, *and the Corse with Lords attendant and a* DOCTOR
OF DIVINITY *as Priest.*]

The queen, the courtiers. Who is this they follow?
And with such maimèd rites? This doth betoken
The corse they follow did with desp'rate hand
Fordo it own life. 'Twas of some estate.   172
Couch we awhile, and mark.   [*Retires with* HORATIO.]   173

LAERTES. What ceremony else?

HAMLET.   That is Laertes,
A very noble youth. Mark.

LAERTES. What ceremony else?

DOCTOR. Her obsequies have been as far enlarged
As we have warranty. Her death was doubtful,
And, but that great command o'ersways the order,
She should in ground unsanctified have lodged
Till the last trumpet. For charitable prayers,
Shards, flints, and pebbles should be thrown on her.   182
Yet here she is allowed her virgin crants,   183
Her maiden strewments, and the bringing home   184
Of bell and burial.

LAERTES. Must there no more be done?

DOCTOR.   No more be done.
We should profane the service of the dead
To sing a requiem and such rest to her
As to peace-parted souls.

LAERTES.   Lay her i' th' earth,
And from her fair and unpolluted flesh

159. *curiously:* minutely.   **160.** *modesty:* moderation.   **164.** *Imperious:* imperial.   **167.** *flaw:* gust of wind.   **172.** *Fordo:* destroy; *it:* its; *estate:* rank.   **173.** *Couch:* hide.   **182.** *Shards:* broken pieces of pottery.   **183.** *crants:* garland.   **184.** *strewments:* strewings of the grave with flowers; *bringing home:* laying to rest.

May violets spring! I tell thee, churlish priest,
A minist'ring angel shall my sister be
When thou liest howling.
HAMLET.   What, the fair Ophelia?
QUEEN. Sweets to the sweet! Farewell.
     [*Scatters flowers.*]
I hoped thou shouldst have been my Hamlet's wife.
I thought thy bride-bed to have decked, sweet maid,
And not have strewed thy grave.
LAERTES.   O, treble woe
Fall ten times treble on that cursèd head
Whose wicked deed thy most ingenious sense   199
Deprived thee of! Hold off the earth awhile,
Till I have caught her once more in mine arms.
    [*Leaps in the grave.*]
Now pile your dust upon the quick and dead
Till of this flat a mountain you have made
T' o'ertop old Pelion or the skyish head   204
Of blue Olympus.
HAMLET [*coming forward*]. What is he whose grief
Bears such an emphasis? whose phrase of sorrow
Conjures the wand'ring stars, and makes them stand   207
Like wonder-wounded hearers? This is I,
Hamlet the Dane.
    [*Leaps in after* LAERTES.]
LAERTES.   The devil take thy soul!
    [*Grapples with him.*]
HAMLET. Thou pray'st not well.
I prithee take thy fingers from my throat,
For, though I am not splenitive and rash,   212
Yet have I in me something dangerous,
Which let thy wisdom fear. Hold off thy hand.
KING. Pluck them asunder.
QUEEN.   Hamlet, Hamlet!
ALL. Gentlemen!
HORATIO.   Good my lord, be quiet.

[*Attendants part them, and they come out of the grave.*]

HAMLET. Why, I will fight with him upon this theme
  Until my eyelids will no longer wag.
QUEEN. O my son, what theme?

---

199. *most ingenious:* of quickest apprehension.   **204.** *Pelion:* a mountain in Thessaly, like Olympus and also Ossa (the allusion being to the war in which the Titans fought the gods and attempted to heap Ossa and Olympus on Pelion, or Pelion and Ossa on Olympus, in order to scale heaven).   **207.** *Conjures:* charms, puts a spell upon; *wand'ring stars:* planets.   **212.** *splenitive:* of fiery temper (the spleen being considered the seat of anger).

HAMLET. I loved Ophelia. Forty thousand brothers
    Could not with all their quantity of love
    Make up my sum. What wilt thou do for her?
KING. Oh, he is mad, Laertes.
QUEEN. For love of God, forbear him.
HAMLET. 'Swounds, show me what thou't do.
    Woo't weep? woo't fight? woo't fast? woo't tear thyself?   226
    Woo't drink up esill? eat a crocodile?   227
    I'll do't. Dost thou come here to whine?
    To outface me with leaping in her grave?
    Be buried quick with her, and so will I.   230
    And if thou prate of mountains, let them throw
    Millions of acres on us, till our ground,
    Singeing his pate against the burning zone,
    Make Ossa like a wart! Nay, an thou'lt mouth,
    I'll rant as well as thou.
QUEEN.   This is mere madness;   235
    And thus a while the fit will work on him.
    Anon, as patient as the female dove
    When that her golden couplets are disclosed,   238
    His silence will sit drooping.
HAMLET.   Hear you, sir.
    What is the reason that you use me thus?
    I loved you ever. But it is no matter,
    Let Hercules himself do what he may,
    The cat will mew, and dog will have his day.
KING. I pray thee, good Horatio, wait upon him.

                        [*Exit* HAMLET *and* HORATIO.]

      [*To* LAERTES]
    Strengthen your patience in our last night's speech.   245
    We'll put the matter to the present push.—   246
    Good Gertrude, set some watch over your son.—
    This grave shall have a living monument.
    An hour of quiet shortly shall we see;
    Till then in patience our proceeding be.   [*Exeunt.*]

ACT V, SCENE 2

[*Enter* HAMLET *and* HORATIO.]

HAMLET. So much for this, sir; now shall you see the other.
    You do remember all the circumstance?

---

226. *Woo't:* wilt (thou). **227.** *esill:* vinegar. **230.** *quick:* alive. **235.** *mere:* absolute. **238.** *couplets:*
pair of fledglings; *disclosed:* hatched. **245.** *in:* by calling to mind. **246.** *present push:* immediate trial.
V, 2. The hall of the Castle.

HORATIO. Remember it, my lord!

HAMLET. Sir, in my heart there was a kind of fighting
    That would not let me sleep. Methought I lay
    Worse than the mutines in the bilboes. Rashly,   6
    And praised be rashness for it—let us know,
    Our indiscretion sometimes serves us well
    When our deep plots do pall, and that should learn us   9
    There's a divinity that shapes our ends,
    Rough-hew them how we will—   11

HORATIO.   That is most certain.

HAMLET. Up from my cabin,
    My sea-gown scarfed about me, in the dark
    Groped I to find out them, had my desire,
    Fingered their packet, and in fine withdrew   15
    To mine own room again, making so bold,
    My fears forgetting manners, to unseal
    Their grand commission; where I found, Horatio—
    Ah, royal knavery!—an exact command,
    Larded with many several sorts of reasons,   20
    Importing Denmark's health, and England's too,   21
    With, ho! such bugs and goblins in my life,   22
    That on the supervise, no leisure bated,   23
    No, not to stay the grinding of the axe,
    My head should be struck off.

HORATIO.   Is't possible?

HAMLET. Here's the commission; read it at more leisure.
    But wilt thou hear me how I did proceed?

HORATIO. I beseech you.

HAMLET. Being thus benetted round with villainies,
    Or I could make a prologue to my brains,   30
    They had begun the play. I sat me down,
    Devised a new commission, wrote it fair.
    I once did hold it, as our statists do,   33
    A baseness to write fair, and labored much   34
    How to forget that learning, but, sir, now
    It did me yeoman's service. Wilt thou know   36
    Th' effect of what I wrote?   37

HORATIO.   Ay, good my lord.

HAMLET. An earnest conjuration from the king,
    As England was his faithful tributary,
    As love between them like the palm might flourish,

---

6. *mutines:* mutineers; *bilboes:* fetters. **9.** *pall:* fail. **11.** *Rough-hew:* shape roughly in trial form. **15.** *Fingered:* filched; *in fine:* finally. **20.** *Larded:* enriched. **21.** *Importing:* relating to. **22.** *bugs:* bugbears; *in my life:* to be encountered as dangers if I should be allowed to live. **23.** *supervise:* perusal; *bated:* deducted, allowed. **30.** *Or:* ere. **33.** *statists:* statesmen. **34.** *fair:* with professional clarity (like a clerk or a scrivener, not like a gentleman). **36.** *yeoman's service:* stout service such as yeomen footsoldiers gave as archers. **37.** *effect:* purport.

As peace should still her wheaten garland wear   41
And stand a comma 'tween their amities,   42
And many such-like as's of great charge,   43
That on the view and knowing of these contents,
Without debatement further, more or less,
He should the bearers put to sudden death,
Not shriving time allowed.   47
HORATIO.   How was this sealed?
HAMLET. Why, even in that was heaven ordinant.   48
  I had my father's signet in my purse,
  Which was the model of that Danish seal,   50
  Folded the writ up in the form of th' other,
  Subscribed it, gave't th' impression, placed it safely,   52
  The changeling never known. Now, the next day
  Was our sea-fight, and what to this was sequent   54
  Thou know'st already.
HORATIO. So Guildenstern and Rosencrantz go to't.
HAMLET. Why, man, they did make love to this employment.
  They are not near my conscience; their defeat
  Does by their own insinuation grow.   59
  'Tis dangerous when the baser nature comes
  Between the pass and fell incensèd points   61
  Of mighty opposites.
HORATIO.   Why, what a king is this!
HAMLET. Does it not, think thee, stand me now upon—   63
  He that hath killed my king, and whored my mother,
  Popped in between th' election and my hopes,   65
  Thrown out his angle for my proper life,   66
  And with such coz'nage—is't not perfect conscience   67
  To quit him with this arm? And is't not to be damned   68
  To let this canker of our nature come   69
  In further evil?
HORATIO. It must be shortly known to him from England
  What is the issue of the business there.
HAMLET. It will be short; the interim is mine,
  And a man's life's no more than to say 'one.'
  But I am very sorry, good Horatio,
  That to Laertes I forgot myself,
  For by the image of my cause I see
  The portraiture of his. I'll court his favors.

41. *wheaten garland:* adornment of fruitful agriculture.   **42.** *comma:* connective (because it indicates continuity of thought in a sentence).   **43.** *charge:* burden (with a double meaning to fit a play that makes *as's* into "asses").   **47.** *shriving time:* time for confession and absolution.   **48.** *ordinant:* controlling.   **50.** *model:* counterpart.   **52.** *impression:* i.e. of the signet.   **54.** *sequent:* subsequent.   **59.** *insinuation:* intrusion.   **61.** *pass:* thrust; *fell:* fierce.   **63.** *stand:* rest incumbent.   **65.** *election:* i.e. to the kingship (the Danish kingship being elective).   **66.** *angle:* fishing line; *proper:* own.   **67.** *coz'nage:* cozenage, trickery.   **68.** *quit:* repay.   **69.** *canker:* cancer, ulcer.

But sure the bravery of his grief did put me   79
Into a tow'ring passion.
HORATIO.   Peace, who comes here?

[*Enter* OSRIC, *a courtier.*]

OSRIC. Your lordship is right welcome back to Denmark.

HAMLET. I humbly thank you, sir. [*aside to* HORATIO] Dost know this waterfly?

HORATIO [*aside to* HAMLET]. No, my good lord.

HAMLET [*aside to* HORATIO]. Thy state is the more gracious, for 'tis a vice to know
him. He hath much land, and fertile. Let a beast be lord of beasts, and his
crib shall stand at the king's mess. 'Tis a chough, but, as I say, spacious in   86
the possession of dirt.

OSRIC. Sweet lord, if your lordship were at leisure, I should impart a thing to
you from his majesty.

HAMLET. I will receive it, sir, with all diligence of spirit. Put your bonnet to his
right use. 'Tis for the head.

OSRIC. I thank your lordship, it is very hot.

HAMLET. No, believe me, 'tis very cold; the wind is northerly.

OSRIC. It is indifferent cold, my lord, indeed.   94

HAMLET. But yet methinks it is very sultry and hot for my complexion.   95

OSRIC. Exceedingly, my lord; it is very sultry, as 'twere—I cannot tell how. But,
my lord, his majesty bade me signify to you that'a has laid a great wager on
your head. Sir, this is the matter—

HAMLET. I beseech you remember.   99

[HAMLET *moves him to put on his hat.*]

OSRIC. Nay, good my lord; for mine ease, in good faith. Sir, here is newly come   100
to court Laertes—believe me, an absolute gentleman, full of most excellent
differences, of very soft society and great showing. Indeed, to speak feelingly 102
of him, he is the card or calendar of gentry; for you shall find in him the   103
continent of what part a gentleman would see.   104

HAMLET. Sir, his definement suffers no perdition in you, though, I know, to divide 105
him inventorially would dozy th' arithmetic of memory, and yet but yaw neither   106
in respect of his quick sail. But, in the verity of extolment, I take him to be a 107
soul of great article, and his infusion of such dearth and rareness as, to make 108
true diction of him, his semblable is his mirror, and who else would trace   109
him, his umbrage, nothing more.   110

---

79. *bravery:* ostentatious display. **86.** *mess:* table; *chough:* jackdaw, chatterer. **94.** *indifferent:* somewhat. **95.** *complexion:* temperament. **99.** *remember:* i.e. remember you have done all that courtesy demands. **100.** *for mine ease:* i.e. I keep my hat off just for comfort (a conventional polite phrase). **102.** *differences:* differentiating characteristics, special qualities; *soft society:* gentle manners; *great showing:* noble appearance; *feelingly:* appropriately. **103.** *card:* map; *calendar:* guide; *gentry:* gentlemanliness. **104.** *continent:* all-containing embodiment (with an implication of geographical continent to go with *card*). **105.** *definement:* definition; *perdition:* loss. **106.** *dozy:* dizzy, stagger; *yaw:* hold to a course unsteadily like a ship that steers wild; *neither:* for all that. **107.** *in respect of:* in comparison with. **108.** *article:* scope, importance; *infusion:* essence; *dearth:* scarcity. **109.** *semblable:* likeness (i.e., only true likeness); *trace:* follow. **110.** *umbrage:* shadow.

OSRIC. Your lordship speaks most infallibly of him.

HAMLET. The concernancy, sir? Why do we wrap the gentleman in our more 112 rawer breath? 113

OSRIC. Sir?

HORATIO. Is't not possible to understand in another tongue? You will to't, sir, 115 really.

HAMLET. What imports the nomination of this gentleman? 117

OSRIC. Of Laertes?

HORATIO [*aside to* HAMLET]. His purse is empty already. All's golden words are spent.

HAMLET. Of him, sir.

OSRIC. I know you are not ignorant—

HAMLET. I would you did, sir; yet, in faith, if you did, it would not much approve 123 me. Well, sir?

OSRIC. You are not ignorant of what excellence Laertes is—

HAMLET. I dare not confess that, lest I should compare with him in excellence; 126 but to know a man well were to know himself.

OSRIC. I mean, sir, for his weapon; but in the imputation laid on him by them, in his meed he's unfellowed. 129

HAMLET. What's his weapon?

OSRIC. Rapier and dagger.

HAMLET. That's two of his weapons—but well.

OSRIC. The king, sir, hath wagered with him six Barbary horses, against the which he has impawned, as I take it, six French rapiers and poniards, with their 134 assigns, as girdle, hangers, and so. Three of the carriages, in faith, are very 135 dear to fancy, very responsive to the hilts, most delicate carriages, and of 136 very liberal conceit. 137

HAMLET. What call you the carriages?

HORATIO [*aside to* Hamlet]. I knew you must be edified by the margent ere you 139 had done.

OSRIC. The carriages, sir, are the hangers.

HAMLET. The phrase would be more germane to the matter if we could carry a cannon by our sides. I would it might be hangers till then. But on! Six Barbary horses against six French swords, their assigns, and three liberal-conceited carriages—that's the French bet against the Danish. Why is this all impawned, as you call it?

OSRIC. The king, sir, hath laid, sir, that in a dozen passes between yourself and him he shall not exceed you three hits; he hath laid on twelve for nine, and it would come to immediate trial if your lordship would vouchsafe the answer.

---

112. *concernancy:* relevance. **113.** *rawer breath:* cruder speech. **115.** *to't:* i.e. get to an understanding. **117.** *nomination:* mention. **123–24.** *approve me:* be to my credit. **126.** *compare:* compete. **129.** *meed:* worth. **134.** *impawned:* staked. **135.** *assigns:* appurtenances; *hangers:* straps by which the sword hangs from the belt. **136.** *dear to fancy:* finely designed; *responsive:* corresponding closely. **137.** *liberal conceit:* tasteful design, refined conception. **139.** *margent:* margin (i.e. explanatory notes there printed).

HAMLET. How if I answer no?

OSRIC. I mean, my lord, the opposition of your person in trial.

HAMLET. Sir, I will walk here in the hall. If it please his majesty, it is the breathing   152
time of day with me. Let the foils be brought, the gentleman willing, and the   153
king hold his purpose, I will win for him an I can; if not, I will gain nothing   154
but my shame and the odd hits.

OSRIC. Shall I redeliver you e'en so?

HAMLET. To this effect, sir, after what flourish your nature will.

OSRIC. I commend my duty to your lordship.

HAMLET. Yours, yours. [*Exit* OSRIC.] He does well to commend it himself; there
are no tongues else for's turn.

HORATIO. This lapwing runs away with the shell on his head.   161

HAMLET. 'A did comply, sir, with his dug before 'a sucked it. Thus has he, and   162
many more of the same bevy that I know the drossy age dotes on, only got   163
the tune of the time and, out of an habit of encounter, a kind of yeasty collection,
which carries them through and through the most fanned and winnowed   165
opinions; and do but blow them to their trial, the bubbles are out.

[*Enter a* LORD.]

LORD. My lord, his majesty commended him to you by young Osric, who brings
back to him that you attend him in the hall. He sends to know if your pleasure
hold to play with Laertes, or that you will take longer time.

HAMLET. I am constant to my purposes; they follow the king's pleasure. If his
fitness speaks, mine is ready; now or whensoever, provided I be so able as
now.

LORD. The king and queen and all are coming down.

HAMLET. In happy time.   174

LORD. The queen desires you to use some gentle entertainment to Laertes before   175
you fall to play.

HAMLET. She well instructs me.   [*Exit* LORD.]

HORATIO. You will lose this wager, my lord.

HAMLET. I do not think so. Since he went into France I have been in continual
practice. I shall win at the odds. But thou wouldst not think how ill all's
here about my heart. But it is no matter.

HORATIO. Nay, good my lord—

HAMLET. It is but foolery, but it is such a kind of gaingiving as would perhaps   183
trouble a woman.

HORATIO. If your mind dislike anything, obey it. I will forestall their repair hither
and say you are not fit.

HAMLET. Not a whit, we defy augury. There is special providence in the fall of a

---

152–53. *breathing time:* exercise hour.   **154.** *an:* if.   **161.** *lapwing:* a bird reputed to be so precocious as to run as soon as hatched.   **162.** *comply:* observe formalities of courtesy; *dug:* mother's nipple.   **163.** *bevy:* company; *drossy:* frivolous.   **165.** *fanned and winnowed:* select and refined.   **174.** *In happy time:* I am happy (a polite response).   **175.** *entertainment:* words of reception or greeting.   **183.** *gaingiving:* misgiving.

sparrow. If it be now, 'tis not to come; if it be not to come, it will be now; if it be not now, yet it will come. The readiness is all. Since no man of aught 189 he leaves knows, what is't to leave betimes? Let be.

[*A table prepared. Enter Trumpets, Drums, and Officers with cushions;* KING, QUEEN, OSRIC, *and all the State, with foils, daggers, and stoups of wine borne in; and* LAERTES.]

KING. Come, Hamlet, come, and take this hand from me.

[*The* KING *puts* LAERTES' *hand into* HAMLET'S.]

HAMLET. Give me your pardon, sir. I have done you wrong,
But pardon't, as you are a gentleman.
This presence knows, and you must needs have heard,   194
How I am punished with a sore distraction.
What I have done
That might your nature, honor, and exception   197
Roughly awake, I here proclaim was madness.
Was't Hamlet wronged Laertes? Never Hamlet.
If Hamlet from himself be ta'en away,
And when he's not himself does wrong Laertes,
Then Hamlet does it not, Hamlet denies it.
Who does it then? His madness. If't be so,
Hamlet is of the faction that is wronged;   204
His madness is poor Hamlet's enemy.
Sir, in this audience,
Let my disclaiming from a purposed evil
Free me so far in your most generous thoughts
That I have shot my arrow o'er the house
And hurt my brother.
LAERTES.   I am satisfied in nature,   210
Whose motive in this case should stir me most
To my revenge. But in my terms of honor   212
I stand aloof, and will no reconcilement
Till by some elder masters of known honor
I have a voice and precedent of peace   215
To keep my name ungored. But till that time   216
I do receive your offered love like love,
And will not wrong it.
HAMLET.   I embrace it freely,
And will this brother's wager frankly play.
Give us the foils. Come on.
LAERTES.   Come, one for me.

---

189. *all:* all that matters.   **194.** *presence:* assembly.   **197.** *exception:* disapproval.   **204.** *faction:* body of persons taking a side in a contention.   **210.** *nature:* natural feeling as a person.   **212.** *terms of honor:* position as a man of honor.   **215.** *voice:* authoritative statement.   **216.** *ungored:* uninjured.

HAMLET. I'll be your foil, Laertes. In mine ignorance   221
    Your skill shall, like a star i' th' darkest night,
    Stick fiery off indeed.   223
LAERTES.   You mock me, sir.
HAMLET. No, by this hand.
KING. Give them the foils, young Osric. Cousin Hamlet,
    You know the wager?
HAMLET.   Very well, my lord.
    Your grace has laid the odds o' th' weaker side.
KING. I do not fear it, I have seen you both;
    But since he is bettered, we have therefore odds.
LAERTES. This is too heavy; let me see another.
HAMLET. This likes me well. These foils have all a length?

[Prepare to play.]

OSRIC. Ay, my good lord.
KING. Set me the stoups of wine upon that table.
    If Hamlet give the first or second hit,
    Or quit in answer of the third exchange,   235
    Let all the battlements their ordnance fire.
    The king shall drink to Hamlet's better breath,
    And in the cup an union shall he throw   238
    Richer than that which four successive kings
    In Denmark's crown have worn. Give me the cups,
    And let the kettle to the trumpet speak,   241
    The trumpet to the cannoneer without,
    The cannons to the heavens, the heaven to earth,
    'Now the king drinks to Hamlet.' Come, begin.

[Trumpets the while.]

    And you, the judges, bear a wary eye.
HAMLET. Come on, sir.
LAERTES.   Come, my lord.

[They play.]

HAMLET.   One.
LAERTES.   No.
HAMLET.   Judgment?
OSRIC. A hit, a very palpable hit.

[Drum, trumpets, and shot. Flourish; a piece goes off.]

LAERTES.   Well, again.

---

221. *foil:* setting that displays a jewel advantageously (with a play upon the meaning "weapon").   **223.** *Stick fiery off:* show in brilliant relief.   **235.** *quit:* repay by a hit.   **238.** *union:* pearl.   **241.** *kettle:* kettledrum.

KING. Stay, give me drink. Hamlet, this pearl is thine.
  Here's to thy health. Give him the cup.
HAMLET. I'll play this bout first; set it by awhile.
  Come. [*They play.*] Another hit. What say you?
LAERTES. A touch, a touch; I do confess't.
KING. Our son shall win.
QUEEN.   He's fat, and scant of breath.   253
  Here, Hamlet, take my napkin, rub thy brows.   254
  The queen carouses to thy fortune, Hamlet.   255
HAMLET. Good madam!
KING.   Gertrude, do not drink.
QUEEN. I will, my lord; I pray you pardon me.

[*Drinks.*]

KING [*aside*]. It is the poisoned cup; it is too late.
HAMLET. I dare not drink yet, madam—by and by.
QUEEN. Come, let me wipe thy face.
LAERTES. My lord, I'll hit him now.
KING.   I do not think't.
LAERTES [*aside*]. And yet it is almost against my conscience.
HAMLET. Come for the third, Laertes. You but dally.
  I pray you pass with your best violence;
  I am afeard you make a wanton of me.   265
LAERTES. Say you so? Come on.

[*They play.*]

OSRIC. Nothing neither way.
LAERTES. Have at you now!

[*In scuffling they change rapiers, and both are wounded with the poisoned weapon.*]

KING.   Part them. They are incensed.
HAMLET. Nay, come—again!

[*The* QUEEN *falls.*]

OSRIC.   Look to the queen there, ho!
HORATIO. They bleed on both sides. How is it, my lord?
OSRIC. How is't, Laertes?
LAERTES. Why, as a woodcock to mine own springe, Osric.   272
  I am justly killed with mine own treachery.
HAMLET. How does the queen?
KING.   She sounds to see them bleed.   274

253. *fat:* not physically fit, out of training.   **254.** *napkin:* handkerchief.   **255.** *carouses:* drinks a toast.
265. *wanton:* pampered child.   **272.** *woodcock:* a bird reputed to be stupid and easily trapped; *springe:* trap.   **274.** *sounds:* swoons.

QUEEN. No, no, the drink, the drink! O my dear Hamlet!
  The drink, the drink! I am poisoned.

[*Dies.*]

HAMLET. O villainy! Ho! let the door be locked.
  Treachery! Seek it out.

[LAERTES *falls.*]

LAERTES. It is here, Hamlet. Hamlet, thou art slain;
  No med'cine in the world can do thee good.
  In thee there is not half an hour's life.
  The treacherous instrument is in thy hand,
  Unbated and envenomed. The foul practice   283
  Hath turned itself on me. Lo, here I lie,
  Never to rise again. Thy mother's poisoned.
  I can no more. The king, the king's to blame.
HAMLET. The point envenomed too?
  Then venom, to thy work.

[*Hurts the* KING.]

ALL. Treason! treason!
KING. O, yet defend me, friends. I am but hurt.
HAMLET. Here, thou incestuous, murd'rous, damnèd Dane,
  Drink off this potion. Is thy union here?
  Follow my mother.

[KING *dies.*]

LAERTES.   He is justly served.
  It is a poison tempered by himself.   294
  Exchange forgiveness with me, noble Hamlet.
  Mine and my father's death come not upon thee,
  Nor thine on me!

[*Dies.*]

HAMLET. Heaven make thee free of it! I follow thee.
  I am dead, Horatio. Wretched queen, adieu!
  You that look pale and tremble at this chance,
  That are but mutes or audience to this act,   301
  Had I but time—as this fell sergeant, Death,   302
  Is strict in his arrest—O, I could tell you—
  But let it be. Horatio, I am dead;
  Thou livest; report me and my cause aright
  To the unsatisfied.
HORATIO.   Never believe it.

283. *Unbated:* unblunted; *practice:* stratagem. **294.** *tempered:* mixed. **301.** *mutes:* actors in a play who speak no lines. **302.** *sergeant:* sheriff's officer.

I am more an antique Roman than a Dane.
Here's yet some liquor left.
HAMLET.   As th' art a man,
Give me the cup. Let go. By heaven, I'll ha't!
O God, Horatio, what a wounded name,
Things standing thus unknown, shall live behind me!
If thou didst ever hold me in thy heart,
Absent thee from felicity awhile,
And in this harsh world draw thy breath in pain,
To tell my story.
          [*A march afar off.*]
                    What warlike noise is this?
OSRIC. Young Fortinbras, with conquest come from Poland,
To the ambassadors of England gives
This warlike volley.
HAMLET.   O, I die, Horatio!
The potent poison quite o'ercrows my spirit.   319
I cannot live to hear the news from England,
But I do prophesy th' election lights   321
On Fortinbras. He has my dying voice.   322
So tell him, with th' occurrents, more and less,   323
Which have solicited—the rest is silence.   324

[*Dies.*]

HORATIO. Now cracks a noble heart. Good night, sweet prince,
And flights of angels sing thee to thy rest!
          [*March within.*]
Why does the drum come hither?

[*Enter* FORTINBRAS, *with the* AMBASSADORS *and with his train of Drum, Colors, and
Attendants.*]

FORTINBRAS. Where is this sight?
HORATIO.   What is it you would see?
If aught of woe or wonder, cease your search.
FORTINBRAS. This quarry cries on havoc. O proud Death,   330
What feast is toward in thine eternal cell   331
That thou so many princes at a shot
So bloodily hast struck?
AMBASSADOR.   The sight is dismal;
And our affairs from England come too late.
The ears are senseless that should give us hearing

---

319. *o'ercrows:* triumphs over (like a victor in a cockfight).   **321.** *election:* i.e. to the throne.   **322.** *voice:* vote.   **323.** *occurrents:* occurrences.   **324.** *solicited:* incited, provoked.   **330.** *quarry:* pile of dead (literally, of dead deer gathered after the hunt); *cries on:* proclaims loudly; *havoc:* indiscriminate killing and destruction such as would follow the order "havoc," or "pillage," given to an army.   **331.** *toward:* forthcoming.

To tell him his commandment is fulfilled,
That Rosencrantz and Guildenstern are dead.
Where should we have our thanks?
HORATIO.   Not from his mouth,
Had it th' ability of life to thank you.
He never gave commandment for their death.
But since, so jump upon this bloody question,   341
You from the Polack wars, and you from England,
Are here arrived, give order that these bodies
High on a stage be placèd to the view,   344
And let me speak to th' yet unknowing world
How these things came about. So shall you hear
Of carnal, bloody, and unnatural acts,
Of accidental judgments, casual slaughters,   348
Of deaths put on by cunning and forced cause,   349
And, in this upshot, purposes mistook
Fall'n on th' inventors' heads. All this can I
Truly deliver.
FORTINBRAS.   Let us haste to hear it,
And call the noblest to the audience.
For me, with sorrow I embrace my fortune.
I have some rights of memory in this kingdom,   355
Which now to claim my vantage doth invite me.   356
HORATIO. Of that I shall have also cause to speak,
And from his mouth whose voice will draw on more.   358
But let this same be presently performed,   359
Even while men's minds are wild, lest more mischance
On plots and errors happen.   361
FORTINBRAS.   Let four captains
Bear Hamlet like a soldier to the stage,
For he was likely, had he been put on,   363
To have proved most royal; and for his passage   364
The soldiers' music and the rites of war
Speak loudly for him.
Take up the bodies. Such a sight as this
Becomes the field, but here shows much amiss.
Go, bid the soldiers shoot.
          [*Exeunt marching; after the which a peal of ordinance are shot off.*]

                                        [c. 1603—Great Britain]

---

341. *jump:* precisely.   **344.** *stage:* platform.   **348.** *judgments:* retributions; *casual:* not humanly planned (reinforcing *accidental*).   **349.** *put on:* instigated.   **355.** *of memory:* traditional and kept in mind.   **356.** *vantage:* advantageous opportunity.   **358.** *more:* i.e. more voices, or votes, for the kingship.   **359.** *presently:* immediately.   **361.** *On:* on the basis of.   **363.** *put on:* set to perform in office.   **364.** *passage:* death.

Questions

Act I

1. Minor characters often provide clues to the understanding of major characters and themes. What of Horatio in this regard? What is inconsistent about Horatio's characterization? What do you make of this inconsistency?
2. Contrast King Hamlet as he is described in Scene 1 (lines 80–95) and Claudius as we see him in Scene 2. How do their types of kingship differ? How does the contrast tie in with the inconsistency in the characterization of Horatio pointed to in the last question?
3. What do you make of Polonius's advice to Laertes in Scene 3 (lines 55–81)? Is it sound? Is it apt for a modern young man or woman?
4. What, now, of Hamlet? What should we make of his dress, his youth, his inwardness? As we first encounter Hamlet, he is alienated. From what and from whom? In many ways, Hamlet seems almost an adolescent as we understand this phase of human development. What would lead one to this conclusion?
5. With respect to what King Hamlet and Claudius each represents, what might the murder of King Hamlet by Claudius symbolize? What theme—possibly the play's master theme—does this symbolism help to establish?

Act II

1. What subtheme that runs through *Hamlet* is suggested by the first scene of Act II and perhaps explains the scene's inclusion in the play? In what way is this theme relevant to another important theme in the play—the self, its definition and nature? How do both themes apply to Hamlet?
2. How does Polonius come off in Act II? How does our opinion of him as it is shaped in Act II affect in retrospect our reception of what he says in Act I—especially about the self? The way Polonius is characterized reveals skepticism on Shakespeare's part about this "self" to which we are to "be true." How so?
3. How does Claudius come off in Act II? How does he show himself to be a man of the Renaissance? Hamlet and Claudius are, ironically, much alike. How so?
4. In Scene 2, Hamlet gives full expression to Renaissance humanism. What does "humanism" mean? What is humanistic in Hamlet's terse statement about "man" (lines 276–281)? Why, after such an eloquent statement about humankind, does Hamlet turn negative?
5. Is Hamlet really mad, or is he only feigning? Why is this an interesting question with respect to how the idea of self has been understood since *Hamlet?* How do *we* conceive of self? Why might anyone who does not so conceive think the conception mad?
6. Why does Shakespeare dwell on actors and acting in *Hamlet?* What is suggested by both that ties in with the theme of self?
7. The idea that the self can consciously play a role different from what it is pervades *Hamlet*. What two characters exemplify this new possibility? Why these two?
8. Why doesn't Hamlet take revenge immediately? What is his stated reason? Are there any other reasons that can be inferred? Why does he agonize so over the revenge called for by the Ghost (see, for instance, his soliloquy in Scene 2, lines 473–531)? Should he seek revenge at all? How can revenge be reconciled with Christian morality?

Act III

1. What more do we learn about Claudius in Act III? No less than Hamlet, Claudius as character-ized brings up questions pertaining to the new concept of self. What questions are these?

2. What is at issue in Hamlet's "To be or not to be" soliloquy (Scene 1, lines 56–90)? In what way does it bring the idea of self into question?

3. Why does Hamlet act as he does toward Ophelia? Does he know that Claudius and Polonius are listening? How do you imagine the set and the stage action vis-à-vis the set? Might Hamlet's harsh words also be explained by his love of Ophelia? Why or why not?

4. Why is Hamlet so enigmatic with the players (as well as elsewhere)? What might his enigmatic form of expression symbolize with respect to the self?

5. Why doesn't Hamlet kill Claudius in the third scene? Is the reason he gives (lines 73–78) adequate or merely a rationalization? What other reason—perhaps unconscious—could he have?

6. What sexual overtones do you find in the interaction between Hamlet and Gertrude in the last scene of Act III (Scene 4)? Why these overtones? How do they relate to Hamlet's inner struggle with Claudius and to Hamlet's growth?

7. How do you respond to the killing of Polonius? How does the killing function with respect to plot as the play moves on?

Act IV

1. Claudius sends Hamlet off to England to be executed. Why England? Why doesn't Claudius simply have Hamlet killed in Denmark? What do his reasons (Scene 3, lines 1–10) show about him and his governance?

2. Why the material on Fortinbras in Scene 4? Contrast Hamlet with Fortinbras and Laertes. How do the contrasts show Hamlet to be a new type of mentality and Fortinbras and Laertes to be of an older world?

3. There is a subtheme in *Hamlet* entailing madness—madness with respect to the concept of self, Hamlet's feigning madness, and so on. How does Ophelia's madness (Scene 5) qualify all other references to madness heretofore? What, in particular, does it suggest about madness and the self?

4. Again, contrast Hamlet and Laertes, now on the subject of revenge (see Act IV, Scene 7, line 125, for the crux of the contrast). How does the contrast, along with Laertes's heedlessness, bring revenge into question once more?

5. What function does the business of the pirates as described in Hamlet's letter (Scene 6, lines 11–23) have? What does it reveal about Hamlet?

Act V

1. Are we to believe Hamlet when he reveals his feelings for Ophelia (Scene 1, lines 220–22)? What light does this revelation shed on his behavior with Ophelia in Act III?

2. How has Hamlet changed between the last time we saw him and his return in Act V? What has brought about the changes in him? What does his growth suggest about introspection and the quest for self?

3. Why, do you think, are we told of Hamlet's changing the commission and thus sending Rosencrantz and Guildenstern to their deaths? Should we feel sympathy for them? Why or why not?

4. Why the inclusion of Osric? What function does he serve?

5. Does Hamlet indeed revenge his father's murder, or is his killing of Claudius something other than an act of simple revenge? At the last, Hamlet is his own person. How does his killing Claudius suggest this? How does the fact that Hamlet's death follows soon after he comes into his own affect you?

6. What is the mood of the end of the play? What does the ending make you feel? What especially do you feel at the end about Hamlet and his death?

7. Summarize the various subthemes of *Hamlet*. How are they related to each other? Formulate fully what you see the master theme of the play to be. How do its subthemes work toward exploring this primary theme?

Writing Assignments

1. In many ways, Claudius is a representative Renaissance monarch. Write a paper in which you analyze Claudius as such. How does he differ from King Hamlet? What is Claudius's conception of kingship? What are his views of governance and the state?

2. Write an essay analyzing Hamlet as an adolescent. Consider his youth, his inwardness, and his alienation. Consider as well the questions of self and of the relation of fathers and sons that run through the play.

3. Why doesn't Hamlet take revenge immediately? Why, when he has the opportunity, doesn't he kill Claudius in Act III? Answer these questions in a paper addressed to the subject of revenge. Should Hamlet seek revenge at all? Does he take revenge finally, or is his slaying of Claudius something else? How does the revenge theme, and the sharp distinction drawn between Hamlet and Laertes by way of this theme, help paint Hamlet as a new man, a man of the Renaissance?

4. In a paper, discuss why Hamlet acts as he does toward Ophelia in Act III (Scene 1). Does he act so because he is mad? What could his motive(s) be otherwise? Does his protestation of love in Act V (Scene 1) shed any light here? Does Hamlet know that Polonius and Claudius are listening? If so, how might that account for his behavior? The question is one often debated by critics. You might do some research here and use your research to help solve the puzzle of Hamlet's motivation.

5. Write an essay contrasting Hamlet with Laertes and Fortinbras. First consider the points of contrast and then consider how the contrast shows Hamlet to be a totally different mentality from the other two. Finally, discuss the point of the contrast—that is, how it relates to the play's meaning overall.

6. In many ways, Claudius is more truly Hamlet's father than is Hamlet's blood father, the medieval King Hamlet. In a paper, compare Claudius and Hamlet, especially with respect to their understanding of and fascination with the self and the possibility of role-playing. Given the likeness, what deeper level might be found for Hamlet's conflict with Claudius (that is, deeper than that involving revenge)? Conversely, how might the likeness account for Hamlet's hesitations?

7. Hamlet seems to have changed considerably between the last time we see him in Act IV and his return in Act V. Write an essay delineating the nature of the changes sensed in him in Act V. Consider as well what has brought these changes about and how Hamlet's growth relates to the theme of self.

8. There are many highly metaphorical passages in *Hamlet,* some exhibiting metaphorical extension, as well as recurrent images and metaphors throughout. Choose an appropriate passage or recurrent figure and, in a paper, analyze the passage as to metaphor or the

recurrent figure as to its various meanings in context. Relate what you say about passage or figure to the play as a whole. Much has been written on these matters. You could turn this assignment into a research project by looking into what has been written on figurative language in *Hamlet* and incorporating what you find in your paper.

9. *Hamlet* can be read as concerning the delineation of Renaissance values and sensibility against the medieval background. Write a paper in which you examine *Hamlet* from this perspective. In doing so, enumerate the play's various subthemes and discuss how each relates to the medieval/Renaissance opposition in the play.

THE IMPORTANCE OF BEING EARNEST
————————————— ❋ OSCAR WILDE ❋ —————————————

CHARACTERS

JOHN WORTHING, J.P.
ALGERNON MONCRIEFF
REV. CANON CHASUBLE, D.D.
MERRIMAN, *Butler*
LANE, *Manservant*
LADY BRACKNELL
HON. GWENDOLEN FAIRFAX
CECILY CARDEW
MISS PRISM, *Governess*

THE SCENES OF THE PLAY

ACT I.
Algernon Moncrieff's Flat in Half-Moon Street, W.

ACT II.
The Garden at the Manor House, Woolton

ACT III.
Drawing-Room of the Manor House, Woolton

TIME—*The Present*   PLACE—*London*

ACT I

SCENE

Morning-room in ALGERNON'S *flat in Half-Moon Street. The room is luxuriously and artistically furnished. The sound of a piano is heard in the adjoining room.*

[LANE *is arranging afternoon tea on the table, and after the music has ceased,* ALGERNON *enters.*]

ALGERNON. Did you hear what I was playing, Lane?
LANE. I didn't think it polite to listen, sir.
ALGERNON. I'm sorry for that, for your sake. I don't play accurately—anyone can play accurately—but I play with wonderful expression. As far as the piano is concerned, sentiment is my forte. I keep science for Life.
LANE. Yes, sir.
ALGERNON. And, speaking of the science of Life, have you got the cucumber sandwiches cut for Lady Bracknell?

LANE. Yes, sir. [*Hands them on a salver.*]

ALGERNON [*inspects them, takes two, and sits down on the sofa*]. Oh! . . . by the way, Lane, I see from your book that on Thursday night, when Lord Shoreman and Mr. Worthing were dining with me, eight bottles of champagne are entered as having been consumed.

LANE. Yes, sir; eight bottles and a pint.

ALGERNON. Why is it that in a bachelor's establishment the servants invariably drink the champagne? I ask merely for information.

LANE. I attribute it to the superior quality of the wine, sir. I have often observed that in married households the champagne is rarely of a first-rate brand.

ALGERNON. Good Heavens! Is marriage so demoralizing as that?

LANE. I believe it *is* a very pleasant state, sir. I had had very little experience of it myself up to the present. I have only been married once. That was in consequence of a misunderstanding between myself and a young woman.

ALGERNON [*languidly*]. I don't know that I am much interested in your family life, Lane.

LANE. No, sir; it is not a very interesting subject. I never think of it myself.

ALGERNON. Very natural, I am sure. That will do, Lane, thank you.

LANE. Thank you, sir. [LANE *goes out.*]

ALGERNON. Lane's views on marriage seem somewhat lax. Really, if the lower orders don't set us a good example, what on earth is the use of them? They seem, as a class, to have absolutely no sense of moral responsibility. [*Enter* LANE.]

LANE. Mr. Ernest Worthing. [Enter JACK. LANE *goes out.*]

ALGERNON. How are you, my dear Ernest? What brings you up to town?

JACK. Oh, pleasure, pleasure! What else should bring one anywhere? Eating as usual, I see, Algy!

ALGERNON [*stiffly*]. I believe it is customary in good society to take some slight refreshment at five o'clock. Where have you been since last Thursday?

JACK [*sitting down on the sofa*]. In the country.

ALGERNON. What on earth do you do there?

JACK [*pulling off his gloves*]. When one is in town one amuses oneself. When one is in the country one amuses other people. It is excessively boring.

ALGERNON. And who are the people you amuse?

JACK [*airily*]. Oh, neighbors, neighbors.

ALGERNON. Got nice neighbors in your part of Shropshire?

JACK. Perfectly horrid! Never speak to one of them.

ALGERNON. How immensely you must amuse them! [*Goes over and takes sandwich.*] By the way, Shropshire is your country, is it not?

JACK. Eh? Shropshire? Yes, of course. Hallo! Why all these cups? Why cucumber sandwiches? Why such reckless extravagance in one so young? Who is coming to tea?

ALGERNON. Oh! merely Aunt Augusta and Gwendolen.

JACK. How perfectly delightful!

ALGERNON. Yes, that is all very well; but I am afraid Aunt Augusta won't quite approve of your being here.

JACK. May I ask why?

ALGERNON. My dear fellow, the way you flirt with Gwendolen is perfectly disgraceful. It is almost as bad as the way Gwendolen flirts with you.

JACK. I am in love with Gwendolen. I have come up to town expressly to propose to her.

ALGERNON. I thought you had come for pleasure? . . . I call that business.

JACK. How utterly unromantic you are!

ALGERNON. I really don't see anything romantic in proposing. It is very romantic to be in love. But there is nothing romantic about a definite proposal. Why, one may be accepted. One usually is, I believe. Then the excitement is all over. The very essence of romance is uncertainty. If ever I get married, I'll certainly try to forget the fact.

JACK. I have no doubt about that, dear Algy. The Divorce Court was specially invented for people whose memories are so curiously constituted.

ALGERNON. Oh! there is no use speculating on that subject. Divorces are made in Heaven—[JACK *puts out his hand to take a sandwich.* ALGERNON *at once interferes.*] Please don't touch the cucumber sandwiches. They are ordered specially for Aunt Augusta. [*Takes one and eats it.*]

JACK. Well, you have been eating them all the time.

ALGERNON. That is quite a different matter. She is my aunt. [*Takes plate from below.*] Have some bread and butter. The bread and butter is for Gwendolen. Gwendolen is devoted to bread and butter.

JACK [*advancing to table and helping himself*]. And very good bread and butter it is, too.

ALGERNON. Well, my dear fellow, you need not eat as if you were going to eat it all. You behave as if you were married to her already. You are not married to her already, and I don't think you will ever be.

JACK. Why on earth do you say that?

ALGERNON. Well, in the first place girls never marry the men they flirt with. Girls don't think it right.

JACK. Oh, that is nonsense!

ALGERNON. It isn't. It is a great truth. It accounts for the extraordinary number of bachelors that one sees all over the place. In the second place, I don't give my consent.

JACK. Your consent!

ALGERNON. My dear fellow, Gwendolen is my first cousin. And before I allow you to marry her, you will have to clear up the whole question of Cecily. [*Rings bell.*]

JACK. Cecily! What on earth do you mean? What do you mean, Algy, by Cecily? I don't know anyone of the name of Cecily. [*Enter* LANE.]

ALGERNON. Bring me that cigarette case Mr. Worthing left in the smoking-room the last time he dined here.

LANE. Yes, sir. [LANE *goes out.*]

JACK. Do you mean to say you have had my cigarette case all this time? I wish to goodness you had let me know. I have been writing frantic letters to Scotland Yard about it. I was very nearly offering a large reward.

ALGERNON. Well, I wish you would offer one. I happen to be more than usually hard up.

JACK. There is no good offering a large reward now that the thing is found. [*Enter* LANE *with the cigarette case on a salver.* ALGERNON *takes it at once.* LANE *goes out.*]

ALGERNON. I think that is rather mean of you, Ernest, I must say. [*Opens case and examines it.*] However, it makes no matter, for, now that I look at the inscription, I find that the thing isn't yours after all.

JACK. Of course it's mine. [*Moving to him.*] You have seen me with it a hundred times, and you have no right whatsoever to read what is written inside. It is a very ungentlemanly thing to read a private cigarette case.

ALGERNON. Oh! it is absurd to have a hard-and-fast rule about what one should read and what one shouldn't. More than half of modern culture depends on what one shouldn't read.

JACK. I am quite aware of the fact, and I don't propose to discuss modern culture. It isn't the sort of thing one should talk of in private. I simply want my cigarette case back.

ALGERNON. Yes; but this isn't your cigarette case. This cigarette case is a present from someone of the name of Cecily, and you said you didn't know anyone of that name.

JACK. Well, if you want to know, Cecily happens to be my aunt.

ALGERNON. Your aunt!

JACK. Yes. Charming old lady she is, too. Lives at Tunbridge Wells. Just give it back to me, Algy.

ALGERNON [*retreating to back of sofa*]. But why does she call herself little Cecily if she is your aunt and lives at Tunbridge Wells? [*Reading.*] "From little Cecily with her fondest love."

JACK [*moving to sofa and kneeling upon it*]. My dear fellow, what on earth is there in that? Some aunts are tall, some aunts are not tall. That is a matter that surely an aunt may be allowed to decide for herself. You seem to think that every aunt should be exactly like your aunt! That is absurd! For Heaven's sake give me back my cigarette case. [*Follows* ALGERNON *round the room.*]

ALGERNON. Yes. But why does your aunt call you her uncle? "From little Cecily, with her fondest love to her dear Uncle Jack." There is no objection, I admit, to an aunt being a small aunt, but why an aunt, no matter what her size may be, should call her own nephew her uncle, I can't quite make out. Besides, your name isn't Jack at all; it's Ernest.

JACK. It isn't Ernest; it's Jack.

ALGERNON. You have always told me it was Ernest. I have introduced you to everyone as Ernest. You answer to the name of Ernest. You look as if your name was Ernest. You are the most earnest-looking person I ever saw in my life. It is perfectly absurd your saying that your name isn't Ernest. It's on your cards. Here is one of them. [*Taking it from case.*] "Mr Ernest Worthing, B 4, The Albany." I'll keep this as a proof your name is Ernest if ever you attempt to deny it to me, or to Gwendolen, or to anyone else. [*Puts the card in his pocket.*]

JACK. Well, my name is Ernest in town and Jack in the country, and the cigarette case was given to me in the country.

ALGERNON. Yes, but that does not account for the fact that your small Aunt Cecily, who lives at Tunbridge Wells, calls you her dear uncle. Come, old boy, you had much better have the thing out at once.

JACK. My dear Algy, you talk exactly as if you were a dentist. It is very vulgar to talk like a dentist when one isn't a dentist. It produces a false impression.

ALGERNON. Well, that is exactly what dentists always do. Now, go on! Tell me the whole thing. I may mention that I have always suspected you of being a confirmed and secret Bunburyist; and I am quite sure of it now.

JACK. Bunburyist? What on earth do you mean by a Bunburyist?

ALGERNON. I'll reveal to you the meaning of that incomparable expression as soon as you are kind enough to inform me why you are Ernest in town and Jack in the country.

JACK. Well, produce my cigarette case first.

ALGERNON. Here it is. [*Hands cigarette case.*] Now produce your explanation, and pray make it improbable. [*Sits on sofa.*]

JACK. My dear fellow, there is nothing improbable about my explanation at all. In fact it's perfectly ordinary. Old Mr. Thomas Cardew, who adopted me when I was a little boy, made me in his will guardian to his grand-daughter, Miss Cecily Cardew. Cecily, who addresses me as her uncle from motives of respect that you could not possibly appreciate, lives at my place in the country under the charge of her admirable governess, Miss Prism.

ALGERNON. Where is that place in the country, by the way?

JACK. That is nothing to you, dear boy. You are not going to be invited. . . . I may tell you candidly that the place is not in Shropshire.

ALGERNON. I suspected that, my dear fellow! I have Bunburyed all over Shropshire on two separate occasions. Now, go on. Why are you Ernest in town and Jack in the country?

JACK. My dear Algy, I don't know whether you will be able to understand my real motives. You are hardly serious enough. When one is placed in the position of guardian, one has to adopt a very high moral tone on all subjects. It's one's duty to do so. And as a high moral tone can hardly be said to conduce very much to either one's health or one's happiness, in order to get up to town I have always pretended to have a younger brother of the name of Ernest, who lives in the Albany, and gets into the most dreadful scrapes. That, my dear Algy, is the whole truth pure and simple.

ALGERNON. The truth is rarely pure and never simple. Modern life would be very tedious if it were either, and modern literature a complete impossibility!

JACK. That wouldn't be at all a bad thing.

ALGERNON. Literary criticism is not your forte, my dear fellow. Don't try it. You should leave that to people who haven't been at a University. They do it so well in the daily papers. What you really are is a Bunburyist. I was quite right in saying you were a Bunburyist. You are one of the most advanced Bunburyists I know.

JACK. What on earth do you mean?

ALGERNON. You have invented a very useful younger brother called Ernest, in order that you may be able to come up to town as often as you like. I have invented an invaluable permanent invalid called Bunbury, in order that I may be able to go down into the country whenever I choose. Bunbury is perfectly invaluable. If it wasn't for Bunbury's extraordinary bad health, for instance, I wouldn't be able to dine with you at Willis' tonight, for I have been really engaged to Aunt Augusta for more than a week.

JACK. I haven't asked you to dine with me anywhere tonight.

ALGERNON. I know. You are absolutely careless about sending out invitations. It is very foolish of you. Nothing annoys people so much as not receiving invitations.

JACK. You had much better dine with your Aunt Augusta.

ALGERNON. I haven't the smallest intention of doing anything of the kind. To begin with, I dined there on Monday, and once a week is quite enough to dine with one's own relatives. In the second place, whenever I do dine there I am always treated as a member of the family, and sent down with either no woman at all, or two. In the third place, I know perfectly well whom she will place me next, tonight. She will place me next Mary Farquhar, who always flirts with her own husband across the dinnertable. That is not very pleasant. Indeed, it is not even decent . . . and that sort of thing is enormously on the increase. The amount of women in London who flirt with their own husbands is perfectly scandalous. It looks so bad. It is simply washing one's clean linen in public. Besides, now that I know you to be a confirmed Bunburyist I naturally want to talk to you about Bunburying. I want to tell you the rules.

JACK. I'm not a Bunburyist at all. If Gwendolen accepts me, I am going to kill my brother, indeed I think I'll kill him in any case. Cecily is a little too much interested in him. It is rather a bore. So I am going to get rid of Ernest. And I strongly advise you to do the same with Mr. . . . with your invalid friend who has the absurd name.

ALGERNON. Nothing will induce me to part with Bunbury, and if you ever get married, which seems to be extremely problematic, you will be very glad to know Bunbury. A man who marries without knowing Bunbury has a very tedious time of it.

JACK. That is nonsense. If I marry a charming girl like Gwendolen, and she is the only girl I ever saw in my life that I would marry, I certainly won't want to know Bunbury.

ALGERNON. Then your wife will. You don't seem to realize, that in married life three is company and two is none.

JACK [*sententiously*]. That, my dear young friend, is the theory that the corrupt French Drama has been propounding for the last fifty years.

ALGERNON. Yes; and that the happy English home has proved in half the time.

JACK. For heaven's sake, don't try to be cynical. It's perfectly easy to be cynical.

ALGERNON. My dear fellow, it isn't easy to be anything now-a-days. There's such a lot of beastly competition about. [*The sound of an electric bell is heard.*] Ah! that must be Aunt Augusta. Only relatives, or creditors, ever ring in that Wagnerian manner. Now, if I get her out of the way for ten minutes, so that you can have an opportunity for proposing to Gwendolen, may I dine with you tonight at Willis'?

JACK. I suppose so, if you want to.

ALGERNON. Yes, but you must be serious about it. I hate people who are not serious about meals. It is so shallow of them. [*Enter* LANE.]

LANE. Lady Bracknell and Miss Fairfax. [ALGERNON *goes forward to meet them. Enter* LADY BRACKNELL *and* GWENDOLEN.]

LADY BRACKNELL. Good afternoon, dear Algernon, I hope you are behaving very well.

ALGERNON.. I'm feeling very well, Aunt Augusta.

LADY BRACKNELL. That's not quite the same thing. In fact the two things rarely go together. [*Sees* JACK *and bows to him with icy coldness.*]

ALGERNON [*to* GWENDOLEN]. Dear me, you are smart!

GWENDOLEN. I am always smart! Aren't I, Mr. Worthing?

JACK. You're quite perfect, Miss Fairfax.

GWENDOLEN. Oh! I hope not that. It would leave no room for developments, and I intend to develop in *many directions.* [GWENDOLEN *and* JACK *sit down together in the corner.*]

LADY BRACKNELL. I'm sorry if we are a little late, Algernon, but I was obliged to call on dear Lady Harbury. I hadn't been there since her poor husband's death. I never saw a woman so altered; she looks quite twenty years younger. And now I'll have a cup of tea, and one of those nice cucumber sandwiches you promised me.

ALGERNON. Certainly, Aunt Augusta. [*Goes over to tea-table.*]

LADY BRACKNELL. Won't you come and sit here, Gwendolen?

GWENDOLEN. Thanks, mamma, I'm quite comfortable where I am.

ALGERNON [*picking up empty plate in horror*]. Good heavens! Lane! Why are there no cucumber sandwiches? I ordered them specially.

LANE [*gravely*]. There were no cucumbers in the market this morning, sir. I went down twice.

ALGERNON. No cucumbers!

LANE. No, sir. Not even for ready money.

ALGERNON. That will do, Lane, thank you.

LANE. Thank you, sir. [*Goes out.*]

ALGERNON. I am greatly distressed, Aunt Augusta, about there being no cucumbers, not even for ready money.

LADY BRACKNELL. It really makes no matter, Algernon. I had some crumpets with Lady Harbury, who seems to me to be living entirely for pleasure now.

ALGERNON. I hear her hair has turned quite gold from grief.

LADY BRACKNELL. It certainly has changed its color. From what cause I, of course, cannot say. [ALGERNON *crosses and hands tea.*] Thank you. I've quite a treat for you tonight, Algernon. I am going to send you down with Mary Farquhar. She is such a nice woman, and so attentive to her husband. It's delightful to watch them.

ALGERNON. I am afraid, Aunt Augusta, I shall have to give up the pleasure of dining with you tonight after all.

LADY BRACKNELL [*frowning*]. I hope not, Algernon. It would put my table completely out. Your uncle would have to dine upstairs. Fortunately he is accustomed to that.

ALGERNON. It is a great bore, and, I need hardly say, a terrible disappointment to me, but the fact is I have just had a telegram to say that my poor friend Bunbury is very ill again. [*Exchanges glances with* JACK.] They seem to think I should be with him.

LADY BRACKNELL. It is very strange. This Mr. Bunbury seems to suffer from curiously bad health.

ALGERNON. Yes; poor Bunbury is a dreadful invalid.

LADY BRACKNELL. Well, I must say, Algernon, that I think it is high time that Mr. Bunbury made up his mind whether he was going to live or to die.This shilly-shallying with the question is absurd. Nor do I in any way approve of the modern sympathy with invalids. I consider it morbid. Illness of any kind is hardly a thing to be encouraged in others. Health is the primary duty of life. I am always telling that to your poor uncle, but he never seems to take much notice . . . as far as any improvement in his ailment goes. I should be much obliged if you would ask Mr. Bunbury, from me, to be kind enough not to have a relapse on Saturday, for I rely on you to arrange my music for me. It is my last reception and one wants something that will encourage conversation, particularly at the end of the season when everyone has practically said whatever they had to say, which, in most cases, was probably not much.

ALGERNON. I'll speak to Bunbury, Aunt Augusta, if he is still conscious, and I think I can promise you he'll be all right by Saturday. You see, if one plays good music, people don't listen, and if one plays bad music people don't talk. But I'll run over the program I've drawn out, if you will kindly come into the next room for a moment.

LADY BRACKNELL. Thank you, Algernon. It is very thoughtful of you. [*Rising, and following* ALGERNON.] I'm sure the program will be delightful, after a few expurgations. French songs I cannot possibly allow. People always seem to think that they are improper, and either look shocked, which is vulgar, or laugh, which is worse. But German sounds a thoroughly respectable language, and indeed, I believe is so. Gwendolen, you will accompany me.

GWENDOLEN. Certainly, mamma. [LADY BRACKNELL *and* ALGERNON *go into the music-room,* GWENDOLEN *remains behind.*]

JACK. Charming day it has been, Miss Fairfax.

GWENDOLEN. Pray don't talk to me about the weather, Mr. Worthing. Whenever people talk to me about the weather, I always feel quite certain that they mean something else. And that makes me so nervous.

JACK. I do mean something else.

GWENDOLEN. I thought so. In fact, I am never wrong.

JACK. And I would like to be allowed to take advantage of Lady Bracknell's temporary absence . . .

GWENDOLEN. I would certainly advise you to do so. Mamma has a way of coming back suddenly into a room that I have often had to speak to her about.

JACK [*nervously*]. Miss Fairfax, ever since I met you I have admired you more than any girl . . . I have ever met since . . . I met you.

GWENDOLEN. Yes, I am quite aware of the fact. And I often wish that in public, at any rate, you had been more demonstrative. For me you have always had an irresistible fascination. Even before I met you I was far from indifferent to you. [JACK *looks at her in amazement.*] We live, as I hope you know, Mr. Worthing, in an age of ideals. The fact is constantly mentioned in the more expensive monthly magazines, and has reached the provincial pulpits I am told: and my ideal has always been to love some one of the name of Ernest. There is something in that name that inspires absolute confidence. The moment Algernon first mentioned to me that he had a friend called Ernest, I knew I was destined to love you.

JACK. You really love me, Gwendolen?

GWENDOLEN. Passionately!

JACK. Darling! You don't know how happy you've made me.

GWENDOLEN. My own Ernest!

JACK. But you don't really mean to say that you couldn't love me if my name wasn't Ernest?

GWENDOLEN. But your name is Ernest.

JACK. Yes, I know it is. But supposing it was something else? Do you mean to say you couldn't love me then?

GWENDOLEN [*glibly*]. Ah! that is clearly a metaphysical speculation, and like most metaphysical speculations has very little reference at all to the actual facts of real life, as we know them.

JACK. Personally, darling, to speak quite candidly, I don't much care about the name of Ernest . . . I don't think that name suits me at all.

GWENDOLEN. It suits you perfectly. It is a divine name. It has a music of its own. It produces vibrations.

JACK. Well, really, Gwendolen, I must say that I think there are lots of other much nicer names. I think, Jack, for instance, a charming name.

GWENDOLEN. Jack? . . . No, there is very little music in the name Jack, if any at all, indeed. It does not thrill. It produces absolutely no vibrations. . . . I have known several Jacks, and they all, without exception, were more than usually plain. Besides, Jack is a notorious domesticity for John! And I pity any woman who is married to a man called John. She would probably never be allowed to know the entrancing pleasure of a single moment's solitude. The only really safe name is Ernest.

JACK. Gwendolen, I must get christened at once—I mean we must get married at once. There is no time to be lost.

GWENDOLEN. Married, Mr. Worthing?

JACK [*astounded*]. Well . . . surely. You know that I love you, and you led me to believe, Miss Fairfax, that you were not absolutely indifferent to me.

GWENDOLEN. I adore you. But you haven't proposed to me yet. Nothing has been said at all about marriage. The subject has not even been touched on.

JACK. Well . . . may I propose to you now?

GWENDOLEN. I think it would be an admirable opportunity. And to spare you any possible disappointment, Mr. Worthing, I think it only fair to tell you quite frankly beforehand that I am fully determined to accept you.

JACK. Gwendolen!

GWENDOLEN. Yes, Mr. Worthing, what have you got to say to me?

JACK. You know what I have got to say to you.

GWENDOLEN. Yes, but you don't say it.

JACK. Gwendolen, will you marry me? [*Goes on his knees.*]

GWENDOLEN. Of course I will, darling. How long you have been about it! I am afraid you have had very little experience in how to propose.

JACK. My own one, I have never loved anyone in the world but you.

GWENDOLEN. Yes, but men often propose for practice. I know my brother Gerald does. All my girl-friends tell me so. What wonderfully blue eyes you have, Ernest! They are quite, quite blue. I hope you will always look at me just like that, especially when there are other people present. [*Enter* LADY BRACKNELL.]

LADY BRACKNELL. Mr. Worthing! Rise, sir, from this semi-recumbent posture. It is most indecorous.

GWENDOLEN. Mamma! [*He tries to rise; she restrains him.*] I must beg you to retire. This is no place for you. Besides, Mr. Worthing has not quite finished yet.

LADY BRACKNELL. Finished what, may I ask?

GWENDOLEN. I am engaged to Mr. Worthing, mamma. [*They rise together.*]

LADY BRACKNELL. Pardon me, you are not engaged to anyone. When you do become engaged to some one, I, or your father, should his health permit him, will inform you of the fact. An engagement should come on a young girl as a surprise, pleasant or unpleasant, as the case may be. It is hardly a matter that she could be allowed to arrange for herself. . . . And now I have a few questions to put to you, Mr. Worthing. While I am making these inquiries, you, Gwendolen, will wait for me below in the carriage.

GWENDOLEN [*reproachfully*]. Mamma!

LADY BRACKNELL. In the carriage, Gwendolen! [GWENDOLEN *goes to the door. She and* JACK *blow kisses to each other behind* LADY BRACKNELL'S *back.* LADY BRACKNELL *looks vaguely about as if she could not understand what the noise was. Finally turns round.*] Gwendolen, the carriage!

GWENDOLEN. Yes, mamma. [*Goes out, looking back at* JACK.]

LADY BRACKNELL [*sitting down*]. You can take a seat, Mr. Worthing. [*Looks in her pocket for note-book and pencil.*]

JACK. Thank you, Lady Bracknell, I prefer standing.

LADY BRACKNELL [*pencil and note-book in hand*]. I feel bound to tell you that you are not down on my list of eligible young men, although I have the same list as the dear Duchess of Bolton has. We work together, in fact. However, I am quite ready to enter your name, should your answers be what a really affectionate mother requires. Do you smoke?

JACK. Well, yes, I must admit I smoke.

LADY BRACKNELL. I am glad to hear it. A man should always have an occupation of some kind. There are far too many idle men in London as it is. How old are you?

JACK. Twenty-nine.

LADY BRACKNELL. A very good age to be married at. I have always been of opinion that a man who desires to get married should know either everything or nothing. Which do you know?

JACK [*after some hesitation*]. I know nothing, Lady Bracknell.

LADY BRACKNELL. I am pleased to hear it. I do not approve of anything that tampers with natural ignorance. Ignorance is like a delicate exotic fruit; touch it and the bloom is gone. The whole theory of modern education is radically unsound. Fortunately in England, at any rate, education produces no effect whatsoever. If it did, it would prove a serious danger to the upper classes, and probably lead to acts of violence in Grosvenor Square. What is your income?

JACK. Between seven and eight thousand a year.

LADY BRACKNELL [*makes a note in her book*]. In land, or investments?

JACK. In investments, chiefly.

LADY BRACKNELL. That is satisfactory. What between the duties expected of one during one's life-time, and the duties exacted from one after one's death, land has ceased to be either a profit or a pleasure. It gives one position, and prevents one from keeping it up. That's all that can be said about land.

JACK. I have a country house with some land, of course, attached to it, about fifteen hundred acres, I believe; but I don't depend on that for my real income. In fact, as far as I can make out, the poachers are the only people who make anything out of it.

LADY BRACKNELL. A country house! How many bedrooms? Well, that point can be cleared up afterwards. You have a town house, I hope? A girl with a simple, unspoiled nature, like Gwendolen, could hardly be expected to reside in the country.

JACK. Well, I own a house in Belgrave Square, but it is let by the year to Lady Bloxham. Of course, I can get it back whenever I like, at six months' notice.

LADY BRACKNELL. Lady Bloxham? I don't know her.

JACK. Oh, she goes about very little. She is a lady considerably advanced in years.

LADY BRACKNELL. Ah, now-a-days that is no guarantee of respectability of character. What number in Belgrave Square?

JACK. 149.

LADY BRACKNELL [*shaking her head*]. The unfashionable side. I thought there was something. However, that could easily be altered.

JACK. Do you mean the fashion, or the side?

LADY BRACKNELL [*sternly*]. Both, if necessary, I presume. What are your politics?

JACK. Well, I am afraid I really have none. I am a Liberal Unionist.

LADY BRACKNELL. Oh, they count as Tories. They dine with us. Or come in the evening, at any rate. Now to minor matters. Are your parents living?

JACK. I have lost both my parents.

LADY BRACKNELL. Both? . . . That seems like carelessness. Who was your father? He was evidently a man of some wealth. Was he born in what the Radical papers call the purple of commerce, or did he rise from the ranks of the aristocracy?

JACK. I am afraid I really don't know. The fact is, Lady Bracknell, I said I had lost my parents. It would be nearer the truth to say that my parents seem to have lost me . . . I don't actually know who I am by birth. I was . . . well, I was found.

LADY BRACKNELL. Found!

JACK. The late Mr. Thomas Cardew, an old gentleman of a very charitable and kindly disposition, found me, and gave me the name of Worthing, because he happened to have a first-class ticket for Worthing in his pocket at the time. Worthing is a place in Sussex. It is a seaside resort.

LADY BRACKNELL. Where did the charitable gentleman who had a first-class ticket for this seaside resort find you?

JACK [*gravely*]. In a hand-bag.

LADY BRACKNELL. A hand-bag?

JACK [*very seriously*]. Yes, Lady Bracknell. I was in a hand-bag—a somewhat large, black leather hand-bag, with handles to it—an ordinary hand-bag in fact.

LADY BRACKNELL. In what locality did this Mr. James, or Thomas, Cardew come across this ordinary hand-bag?

JACK. In the cloak-room at Victoria Station. It was given to him in mistake for his own.

LADY BRACKNELL. The cloak-room at Victoria Station?

JACK. The Brighton line.

LADY BRACKNELL. The line is immaterial. Mr. Worthing, I confess I feel somewhat bewildered by what you have just told me. To be born, or at any rate bred, in a hand-bag, whether it had handles or not, seems to me to display a contempt for the ordinary decencies of family life that remind one of the worst excesses of the French Revolution. And I presume you know what that unfortunate movement led to? As for the particular locality in which the hand-bag was found, a cloak-room at a railway station might serve to conceal a social indiscretion—has probably, indeed, been used for that purpose before now—but it could hardly be regarded as an assured basis for a recognized position in good society.

JACK. May I ask you then what you would advise me to do? I need hardly say I would do anything in the world to ensure Gwendolen's happiness.

LADY BRACKNELL. I would strongly advise you, Mr. Worthing, to try and acquire some relations as soon as possible, and to make a definite effort to produce at any rate one parent, of either sex, before the season is quite over.

JACK. Well, I don't see how I could possibly manage to do that. I can produce the hand-bag at any moment. It is in my dressing-room at home. I really think that should satisfy you, Lady Bracknell.

LADY BRACKNELL. Me, sir! What has it to do with me? You can hardly imagine that I and Lord Bracknell would dream of allowing our only daughter—a girl brought up with the utmost care—to marry into a cloak-room, and form an alliance with a parcel? Good morning, Mr. Worthing! [LADY BRACKNELL *sweeps out in majestic indignation.*]

JACK. Good morning! [ALGERNON, *from the other room, strikes up the Wedding March.* JACK *looks perfectly furious, and goes to the door.*] For goodness' sake don't play that ghastly tune, Algy! How idiotic you are! [*The music stops, and* ALGERNON *enters cheerily.*]

ALGERNON. Didn't it go off all right, old boy? You don't mean to say Gwendolen refused you? I know it is a way she has. She is always refusing people. I think it is most ill-natured of her.

JACK. Oh, Gwendolen is as right as a trivet. As far as she is concerned, we are engaged.

Her mother is perfectly unbearable. Never met such a Gorgon . . . I don't really know what a Gorgon is like, but I am quite sure that Lady Bracknell is one. In any case, she is a monster, without being a myth, which is rather unfair. . . . I beg your pardon, Algy, I suppose I shouldn't talk about your own aunt in that way before you.

ALGERNON. My dear boy, I love hearing my relations abused. It is the only thing that makes me put up with them at all. Relations are simply a tedious pack of people, who haven't got the remotest knowledge of how to live, nor the smallest instinct about when to die.

JACK. Oh, that is nonsense!

ALGERNON. It isn't!

JACK. Well, I won't argue about the matter. You always want to argue about things.

ALGERNON. That is exactly what things were originally made for.

JACK. Upon my word, if I thought that, I'd shoot myself. . . . [*A pause.*] You don't think there is any chance of Gwendolen becoming like her mother in about a hundred and fifty years, do you, Algy?

ALGERNON. All women become like their mothers. That is their tragedy. No man does. That's his.

JACK. Is that clever?

ALGERNON. It is perfectly phrased! and quite as true as any observation in civilized life should be.

JACK. I am sick to death of cleverness. Everybody is clever now-a-days. You can't go anywhere without meeting clever people. The thing has become an absolute public nuisance. I wish to goodness we had a few fools left.

ALGERNON. We have.

JACK. I should extremely like to meet them. What do they talk about?

ALGERNON. The fools? Oh! about the clever people, of course.

JACK. What fools!

ALGERNON. By the way, did you tell Gwendolen the truth about your being Ernest in town, and Jack in the country?

JACK [*in a very patronizing manner*]. My dear fellow, the truth isn't quite the sort of thing one tells to a nice, sweet, refined girl. What extraordinary ideas you have about the way to behave to a woman!

ALGERNON. The only way to behave to a woman is to make love to her, if she is pretty, and to someone else if she is plain.

JACK. Oh, that is nonsense.

ALGERNON. What about your brother? What about the profligate Ernest?

JACK. Oh, before the end of the week I shall have got rid of him. I'll say he died in Paris of apoplexy. Lots of people die of apoplexy, quite suddenly, don't they?

ALGERNON. Yes, but it's hereditary, my dear fellow. It's a sort of thing that runs in families. You had much better say a severe chill.

JACK. You are sure a severe chill isn't hereditary, or anything of that kind?

ALGERNON. Of course it isn't!

JACK. Very well, then. My poor brother Ernest is carried off suddenly in Paris, by a severe chill. That gets rid of him.

ALGERNON. But I thought you said that . . . Miss Cardew was a little too much interested in your poor brother Ernest? Won't she feel his loss a good deal?

JACK. Oh, that is all right. Cecily is not a silly, romantic girl, I am glad to say. She has got a capital appetite, goes for long walks, and pays no attention at all to her lessons.

ALGERNON. I would rather like to see Cecily.

JACK. I will take very good care you never do. She is excessively pretty, and she is only just eighteen.

ALGERNON. Have you told Gwendolen yet that you have an excessively pretty ward who is only just eighteen?

JACK. Oh! one doesn't blurt these things out to people. Cecily and Gwendolen are perfectly certain to be extremely great friends. I'll bet you anything you like that half an hour after they have met, they will be calling each other sister.

ALGERNON. Women only do that when they have called each other a lot of other things first. Now, my dear boy, if we want to get a good table at Willis', we really must go and dress. Do you know it is nearly seven?

JACK [*irritably*]. Oh! it always is nearly seven.

ALGERNON. Well, I'm hungry.

JACK. I never knew you when you weren't. . . .

ALGERNON. What shall we do after dinner? Go to a theater?

JACK. Oh, no! I loathe listening.

ALGERNON. Well, let us go to the Club?

JACK. Oh, no! I hate talking.

ALGERNON. Well, we might trot round to the Empire at ten?

JACK. Oh, no! I can't bear looking at things. It is so silly.

ALGERNON. Well, what shall we do?

JACK. Nothing!

ALGERNON. It is awfully hard work doing nothing. However, I don't mind hard work where there is no definite object of any kind. [*Enter* LANE.]

LANE. Miss Fairfax. [*Enter* GWENDOLEN. LANE *goes out.*]

ALGERNON. Gwendolen, upon my word!

GWENDOLEN. Algy, kindly turn your back. I have something very particular to say to Mr. Worthing.

ALGERNON. Really, Gwendolen, I don't think I can allow this at all.

GWENDOLEN. Algy, you always adopt a strictly immoral attitude towards life. You are not quite old enough to do that. [ALGERNON *retires to the fireplace.*]

JACK. My own darling!

GWENDOLEN. Ernest, we may never be married. From the expression on mamma's face I fear we never shall. Few parents now-a-days pay any regard to what their children say to them. The old-fashioned respect for the young is fast dying out. Whatever influence I ever had over mamma, I lost at the age of three. But although she may prevent us from becoming man and wife, and I may marry someone else, and marry often, nothing that she can possibly do can alter my eternal devotion to you.

JACK. Dear Gwendolen.

GWENDOLEN. The story of your romantic origin, as related to me by mamma, with unpleasing comments, has naturally stirred the deeper fibers of my nature. Your Christian name has an irresistible fascination. The simplicity of your character makes you exquisitely incomprehensible to me. Your town address at the Albany I have. What is your address in the country?

JACK. The Manor House, Woolton, Hertfordshire. [ALGERNON, *who has been carefully listening, smiles to himself, and writes the address on his shirt-cuff. Then picks up the Railway Guide.*]

GWENDOLEN. There is a good postal service, I suppose? It may be necessary to do something desperate. That, of course, will require serious consideration. I will communicate with you daily.

JACK. My own one!

GWENDOLEN. How long do you remain in town?

JACK. Till Monday.

GWENDOLEN. Good! Algy, you may turn round now.

ALGERNON. Thanks, I've turned round already.

GWENDOLEN. You may also ring the bell.

JACK. You will let me see you to your carriage, my own darling?

GWENDOLEN. Certainly.

JACK [*to* LANE, *who now enters*]. I will see Miss Fairfax out.

LANE. Yes, sir. [JACK *and* GWENDOLEN *go off.* LANE *presents several letters on a salver to* ALGERNON. *It is to be surmised that they are bills, as* ALGERNON, *after looking at the envelopes, tears them up.*]

ALGERNON. A glass of sherry, Lane.

LANE. Yes, sir.

ALGERNON. Tomorrow, Lane, I'm going Bunburying.

LANE. Yes, sir.

ALGERNON. I shall probably not be back till Monday. You can put up my dress clothes, my smoking jacket, and all the Bunbury suits . . .

LANE. Yes, sir. [*Handing sherry.*]

ALGERNON. I hope tomorrow will be a fine day, Lane.

LANE. It never is, sir.

ALGERNON. Lane, you're a perfect pessimist.

LANE. I do my best to give satisfaction, sir. [*Enter* JACK. LANE *goes off.*]

JACK. There's a sensible, intellectual girl! the only girl I ever cared for in my life. [ALGERNON *is laughing immoderately.*] What on earth are you so amused at?

ALGERNON. Oh, I'm a little anxious about poor Bunbury, that's all.

JACK. If you don't take care, your friend Bunbury will get you into a serious scrape some day.

ALGERNON. I love scrapes. They are the only things that are never serious.

JACK. Oh, that's nonsense, Algy. You never talk anything but nonsense.

ALGERNON. Nobody ever does. [JACK *looks indignantly at him, and leaves the room.* ALGERNON *lights a cigarette, reads his shirt-cuff, and smiles.*]

ACT DROP

ACT II

SCENE

Garden at the Manor House. A flight of gray stone steps leads up to the house. The garden, an old-fashioned one, full of roses. Time of year, July. Basket chairs, and a table covered with books, are set under a large yew tree.

[Miss Prism *discovered seated at the table.* Cecily *is at the back watering flowers.*]

Miss Prism [*calling*]. Cecily, Cecily! Surely such a utilitarian occupation as the watering of flowers is rather Moulton's duty than yours? Especially at a moment when intellectual pleasures await you. Your German grammar is on the table. Pray, open it at page fifteen. We will repeat yesterday's lesson.

Cecily [*coming over very slowly*]. But I don't like German. It isn't at all a becoming language. I know perfectly well that I look quite plain after my German lesson.

Miss Prism. Child, you know how anxious your guardian is that you should improve yourself in every way. He laid particular stress on your German, as he was leaving for town yesterday. Indeed, he always lays stress on your German when he is leaving for town.

Cecily. Dear Uncle Jack is so very serious! Sometimes he is so serious that I think he cannot be quite well.

Miss Prism [*drawing her self up*]. Your guardian enjoys the best of health, and his gravity of demeanor is especially to be commended in one so comparatively young as he is. I know no one who has a higher sense of duty and responsibility.

Cecily. I suppose that is why he often looks a little bored when we three are together.

Miss Prism. Cecily! I am surprised at you. Mr. Worthing has many troubles in his life. Idle merriment and triviality would be out of place in his conversation. You must remember his constant anxiety about that unfortunate young man, his brother.

Cecily. I wish Uncle Jack would allow that unfortunate young man, his brother, to come down here sometimes. We might have a good influence over him, Miss Prism. I am sure you certainly would. You know German, and geology, and things of that kind influence a man very much. [Cecily *begins to write in her diary.*]

Miss Prism [*shaking her head*]. I do not think that even I could produce any effect on a character that, according to his own brother's admission, is irretrievably weak and vacillating. Indeed, I am not sure that I would desire to reclaim him. I am not in favor of this modern mania for turning bad people into good people at a moment's notice. As a man sows so let him reap. You must put away your diary, Cecily. I really don't see why you should keep a diary at all.

Cecily. I keep a diary in order to enter the wonderful secrets of my life. If I didn't write them down I should probably forget all about them.

Miss Prism. Memory, my dear Cecily, is the diary that we all carry about with us.

Cecily. Yes, but it usually chronicles the things that have never happened, and couldn't possibly have happened. I believe that Memory is responsible for nearly all the three-volume novels that Mudie[1] sends us.

---

[1]*Mudie:* Mudie's Lending Library.

MISS PRISM. Do not speak slightingly of the three-volume novel, Cecily. I wrote one myself in earlier days.

CECILY. Did you really, Miss Prism? How wonderfully clever you are! I hope it did not end happily? I don't like novels that end happily. They depress me so much.

MISS PRISM. The good ended happily, and the bad unhappily. That is what Fiction means.

CECILY. I suppose so. But it seems very unfair. And was your novel ever published?

MISS PRISM. Alas! no. The manuscript unfortunately was abandoned. I use the word in the sense of lost or mislaid. To your work, child, these speculations are profitless.

CECILY [*smiling*]. But I see dear Dr. Chasuble coming up through the garden.

MISS PRISM [*rising and advancing*]. Dr. Chasuble! This is indeed a pleasure. [*Enter* CANON CHASUBLE.]

CHASUBLE. And how are we this morning? Miss Prism, you are, I trust, well?

CECILY. Miss Prism has just been complaining of a slight headache. I think it would do her so much good to have a short stroll with you in the park, Dr. Chasuble.

MISS PRISM. Cecily, I have not mentioned anything about a headache.

CECILY. No, dear Miss Prism, I know that, but I felt instinctively that you had a headache. Indeed I was thinking about that, and not about my German lesson when the Rector came in.

CHASUBLE. I hope, Cecily, you are not inattentive.

CECILY. Oh, I am afraid I am.

CHASUBLE. That is strange. Were I fortunate enough to be Miss Prism's pupil, I would hang upon her lips. [MISS PRISM *glares*.] I spoke metaphorically.—My metaphor was drawn from bees. Ahem! Mr. Worthing, I suppose, has not returned from town yet?

MISS PRISM. We do not expect him till Monday afternoon.

CHASUBLE. Ah yes, he usually likes to spend his Sunday in London. He is not one of those whose sole aim is enjoyment, as, by all accounts, that unfortunate young man, his brother, seems to be. But I must not disturb Egeria[2] and her pupil any longer.

MISS PRISM. Egeria? My name is Laetitia, Doctor.

CHASUBLE [*bowing*]. A classical allusion merely, drawn from the Pagan authors. I shall see you both no doubt at Evensong.

MISS PRISM. I think, dear Doctor, I will have a stroll with you. I find I have a headache after all, and a walk might do it good.

CHASUBLE. With pleasure, Miss Prism, with pleasure. We might go so far as the schools and back.

MISS PRISM. That would be delightful. Cecily, you will read your Political Economy in my absence. The chapter on the Fall of the Rupee you may omit. It is somewhat too sensational. Even these metallic problems have their melodramatic side. [*Goes down the garden with* DR. CHASUBLE.]

CECILY [*picks up books and throws them back on table*]. Horrid Political Economy!

[2] *Egeria:* a Roman nymph known for her intellect.

Horrid Geography! Horrid, horrid German! [*Enter* MERRIMAN *with a card on a salver.*]

MERRIMAN. Mr. Ernest Worthing has just driven over from the station. He has brought his luggage with him.

CECILY [*takes the card and reads it*]. "Mr. Ernest Worthing, B 4, The Albany, W." Uncle Jack's brother! Did you tell him Mr. Worthing was in town?

MERRIMAN. Yes, Miss. He seemed very much disappointed. I mentioned that you and Miss Prism were in the garden. He said he was anxious to speak to you privately for a moment.

CECILY. Ask Mr. Ernest Worthing to come here. I suppose you had better talk to the housekeeper about a room for him.

MERRIMAN. Yes, Miss. [MERRIMAN *goes off.*]

CECILY. I have never met any really wicked person before. I feel rather frightened. I am so afraid he will look just like everyone else. [*Enter* ALGERNON, *very gay and debonair.*] He does!

ALGERNON [*raising his hat*]. You are my little Cousin Cecily, I'm sure.

CECILY. You are under some strange mistake. I am not little. In fact, I am more than usually tall for my age. [ALGERNON *is rather taken aback.*] But I am your Cousin Cecily. You, I see from your card, are Uncle Jack's brother, my Cousin Ernest, my wicked Cousin Ernest.

ALGERNON. Oh! I am not really wicked at all, Cousin Cecily. You mustn't think that I am wicked.

CECILY. If you are not, then you have certainly been deceiving us all in a very inexcusable manner. I hope you have not been leading a double life, pretending to be wicked and being really good all the time. That would be hypocrisy.

ALGERNON [*looks at her in amazement*]. Oh! of course I have been rather reckless.

CECILY. I am glad to hear it.

ALGERNON. In fact, now you mention the subject, I have been very bad in my own small way.

CECILY. I don't think you should be so proud of that, though I am sure it must have been very pleasant.

ALGERNON. It is much pleasanter being here with you.

CECILY. I can't understand how you are here at all. Uncle Jack won't be back till Monday afternoon.

ALGERNON. That is a great disappointment. I am obliged to go up by the first train on Monday morning. I have a business appointment that I am anxious . . . to miss.

CECILY. Couldn't you miss it anywhere but in London?

ALGERNON. No; the appointment is in London.

CECILY. Well, I know, of course, how important it is not to keep a business engagement, if one wants to retain any sense of the beauty of life, but still I think you had better wait till Uncle Jack arrives. I know he wants to speak to you about your emigrating.

ALGERNON. About my what?

CECILY. Your emigrating. He has gone up to buy your outfit.

ALGERNON. I certainly wouldn't let Jack buy my outfit. He has no taste in neckties at all.

CECILY. I don't think you will require neckties. Uncle Jack is sending you to Australia.

ALGERNON. Australia! I'd sooner die.

CECILY. Well, he said at dinner on Wednesday night, that you would have to choose between this world, the next world, and Australia.

ALGERNON. Oh, well! The accounts I have received of Australia and the next world, are not particularly encouraging. This world is good enough for me, Cousin Cecily.

CECILY. Yes, but are you good enough for it?

ALGERNON. I'm afraid I'm not that. That is why I want you to reform me. You might make that your mission, if you don't mind, Cousin Cecily.

CECILY. I'm afraid I've not time, this afternoon.

ALGERNON. Well, would you mind reforming myself this afternoon?

CECILY. That is rather Quixotic of you. But I think you should try.

ALGERNON. I will. I feel better already.

CECILY. You are looking a little worse.

ALGERNON. That is because I am hungry.

CECILY. How thoughtless of me. I should have remembered that when one is going to lead an entirely new life, one requires regular and wholesome meals. Won't you come in?

ALGERNON. Thank you. Might I have a button-hole first? I never have any appetite unless I have a button-hole first.

CECILY. A Maréchal Niel? [*Picks up scissors.*]

ALGERNON. No, I'd sooner have a pink rose.

CECILY. Why? [*Cuts a flower.*]

ALGERNON. Because you are like a pink rose, Cousin Cecily.

CECILY. I don't think it can be right for you to talk to me like that. Miss Prism never says such things to me.

ALGERNON. Then Miss Prism is a short-sighted old lady. [CECILY *puts the rose in his button-hole.*] You are the prettiest girl I ever saw.

CECILY. Miss Prism says that all good looks are a snare.

ALGERNON. They are a snare that every sensible man would like to be caught in.

CECILY. Oh! I don't think I would care to catch a sensible man. I shouldn't know what to talk to him about. [*They pass into the house.* MISS PRISM *and* DR. CHASUBLE *return.*]

MISS PRISM. You are too much alone, dear Dr. Chasuble. You should get married. A misanthrope I can understand—a womanthrope, never!

CHASUBLE [*with a scholar's shudder*]. Believe me, I do not deserve so neologistic a phrase. The precept as well as the practice of the Primitive Church was distinctly against matrimony.

MISS PRISM [*sententiously*]. That is obviously the reason why the Primitive Church has not lasted up to the present day. And you do not seem to realize, dear Doctor, that by persistently remaining single, a man converts himself into a permanent public temptation. Men should be careful; this very celibacy leads weaker vessels astray.

CHASUBLE. But is a man not equally attractive when married?

MISS PRISM. No married man is ever attractive except to his wife.

CHASUBLE. And often, I've been told, not even to her.

MISS PRISM. That depends on the intellectual sympathies of the woman. Maturity can always be depended on. Ripeness can be trusted. Young women are green. [DR. CHASUBLE *starts.*] I spoke horticulturally. My metaphor was drawn from fruits. But where is Cecily?

CHASUBLE. Perhaps she followed us to the schools. [*Enter* JACK *slowly from the back of the garden. He is dressed in the deepest mourning, with crape hat-band and black gloves.*]

MISS PRISM. Mr. Worthing!

CHASUBLE. Mr. Worthing?

MISS PRISM. This is indeed a surpirse. We did not look for you till Monday afternoon.

JACK [*shakes* MISS PRISM's *hand in a tragic manner*]. I have returned sooner than I expected. Dr. Chasuble, I hope you are well?

CHASUBLE. Dear Mr. Worthing, I trust this garb of woe does not betoken some terrible calamity?

JACK. My brother.

MISS PRISM. More shameful debts and extravagance?

CHASUBLE. Still leading his life of pleasure?

JACK [*shaking his head*]. Dead.

CHASUBLE. Your brother Ernest dead?

JACK. Quite dead.

MISS PRISM. What a lesson for him! I trust he will profit by it.

CHASUBLE. Mr. Worthing, I offer you my sincere condolence. You have at least the consolation of knowing that you were always the most generous and forgiving of brothers.

JACK. Poor Ernest! He had many faults, but it is a sad, sad blow.

CHASUBLE. Very sad indeed. Were you with him at the end?

JACK. No. He died abroad; in Paris, in fact. I had a telegram last night from the manager of the Grand Hotel.

CHASUBLE. Was the cause of death mentioned?

JACK. A severe chill, it seems.

MISS PRISM. As a man sows, so shall he reap.

CHASUBLE [*raising his hand*]. Charity, dear Miss Prism, charity! None of us are perfect. I myself am peculiarly susceptible to drafts. Will the interment take place here?

JACK. No. He seems to have expressed a desire to be buried in Paris.

CHASUBLE. In Paris! [*Shakes his head.*] I fear that hardly points to any very serious state of mind at the last. You would no doubt wish me to make some slight allusion to this tragic domestic affliction next Sunday. [JACK *presses his hand convulsively.*] My sermon on the meaning of the manna in the wilderness can be adapted to almost any occasion, joyful, or, as in the present case, distressing. [*All sigh.*] I have preached it at harvest celebrations, christenings, confirmations, on days of humiliation and festal days. The last time I delivered it was in the Cathedral, as a charity sermon on behalf of the Society for the Prevention of Discontentment among the Upper Orders. The Bishop, who was present, was much struck by some of the analogies I drew.

JACK. Ah, that reminds me, you mentioned christenings I think, Dr. Chasuble? I suppose you know how to christen all right? [DR. CHASUBLE *looks astounded.*] I mean, of course, you are continually christening, aren't you?

MISS PRISM. It is, I regret to say, one of the Rector's most constant duties in this parish. I have often spoken to the poorer classes on the subject. But they don't seem to know what thrift is.

CHASUBLE. But is there any particular infant in whom you are interested, Mr. Worthing? Your brother was, I believe, unmarried, was he not?

JACK. Oh, yes.

MISS PRISM [*bitterly*]. People who live entirely for pleasure usually are.

JACK. But it is not for any child, dear Doctor. I am very fond of children. No! the fact is, I would like to be christened myself, this afternoon, if you have nothing better to do.

CHASUBLE. But surely, Mr. Worthing, you have been christened already?

JACK. I don't remember anything about it.

CHASUBLE. But have you any grave doubts on the subject?

JACK. I certainly intend to have. Of course, I don't know if the thing would bother you in any way, or if you think I am a little too old now.

CHASUBLE. Not at all. The sprinkling, and, indeed, the immersion of adults is a perfectly canonical practice.

JACK. Immersion!

CHASUBLE. You need have no apprehensions. Sprinkling is all that is necessary, or indeed I think advisable. Our weather is so changeable. At what hour would you wish the ceremony performed?

JACK. Oh, I might trot around about five if that would suit you.

CHASUBLE. Perfectly, perfectly! In fact I have two similar ceremonies to perform at that time. A case of twins that occurred recently in one of the outlying cottages on your own estate. Poor Jenkins the carter, a most hard-working man.

JACK. Oh! I don't see much fun in being christened along with other babies. It would be childish. Would half-past five do?

CHASUBLE. Admirably! Admirably! Admirably! [*Takes out watch.*] And now, dear Mr. Worthing, I will not intrude any longer into a house of sorrow. I would merely beg you not to be too much bowed down by grief. What seem to us bitter trials at the moment are often blessings in disguise.

MISS PRISM. This seems to me a blessing of an extremely obvious kind. [*Enter* CECILY *from the house.*]

CECILY. Uncle Jack! Oh, I am pleased to see you back. But what horrid clothes you have on! Do go and change them.

MISS PRISM. Cecily!

CHASUBLE. My child! my child! [CECILY *goes towards* JACK; *he kisses her brow in a melancholy manner.*]

CECILY. What is the matter, Uncle Jack? Do look happy! You look as if you had a toothache and I have a surprise for you. Who do you think is in the dining-room? Your brother!

JACK. Who?

CECILY. Your brother Ernest. He arrived about half an hour ago.

JACK. What nonsense! I haven't got a brother.

CECILY. Oh, don't say that. However badly he may have behaved to you in the past he is still your brother. You couldn't be so heartless as to disown him. I'll tell him to come out. And you will shake hands with him, won't you, Uncle Jack? [*Runs back into the house.*]

CHASUBLE. These are very joyful tidings.

MISS PRISM. After we had all been resigned to his loss, his sudden return seems to me peculiarly distressing.

JACK. My brother is in the dining-room? I don't know what it all means. I think it is perfectly absurd. [*Enter* ALGERNON *and* CECILY *hand in hand. They come slowly up to* JACK.]

JACK. Good heavens! [*Motions* ALGERNON *away.*]

ALGERNON. Brother John, I have come down from town to tell you that I am very sorry for all the trouble I have given you, and that I intend to lead a better life in the future. [JACK *glares at him and does not take his hand.*]

CECILY. Uncle Jack, you are not going to refuse your own brother's hand?

JACK. Nothing will induce me to take his hand. I think his coming down here disgraceful. He knows perfectly well why.

CECILY. Uncle Jack, do be nice. There is some good in everyone. Ernest has just been telling me about his poor invalid friend, Mr. Bunbury, whom he goes to visit so often. And surely there must be much good in one who is kind to an invalid, and leaves the pleasures of London to sit by a bed of pain.

JACK. Oh, he has been talking about Bunbury, has he?

CECILY. Yes, he has told me all about poor Mr. Bunbury, and his terrible state of health.

JACK. Bunbury! Well, I won't have him talk to you about Bunbury or about anything else. It is enough to drive one perfectly frantic.

ALGERNON. Of course I admit that the faults were all on my side. But I must say that I think that Brother John's coldness to me is peculiarly painful. I expected a more enthusiastic welcome, especially considering it is the first time I have come here.

CECILY. Uncle Jack, if you don't shake hands with Ernest I will never forgive you.

JACK. Never forgive me?

CECILY. Never, never, never!

JACK. Well, this is the last time I shall ever do it. [*Shakes hands with* ALGERNON *and glares.*]

CHASUBLE. It's pleasant, is it not, to see so perfect a reconciliation? I think we might leave the two brothers together.

MISS PRISM. Cecily, you will come with us.

CECILY. Certainly, Miss Prism. My little task of reconciliation is over.

CHASUBLE. You have done a beautiful action today, dear child.

MISS PRISM. We must not be premature in our judgments.

CECILY. I feel very happy. [*They all go off.*]

JACK. You young scoundrel, Algy, you must get out of this place as soon as possible. I don't allow any Bunburying here. [*Enter* MERRIMAN.]

MERRIMAN. I have put Mr. Ernest's things in the room next to yours, sir. I suppose that is all right?

JACK. What?

MERRIMAN. Mr. Ernest's luggage, sir. I have unpacked it and put it in the room next to your own.

JACK. His luggage?

MERRIMAN. Yes, sir. Three portmanteaus, a dressing-case, two hat-boxes, and a large luncheon-basket.

ALGERNON. I am afraid I can't stay more than a week this time.

JACK. Merriman, order the dog-cart at once. Mr. Ernest has been suddenly called back to town.

MERRIMAN. Yes, sir. [*Goes back into the house.*]

ALGERNON. What a fearful liar you are, Jack. I have not been called back to town at all.

JACK. Yes, you have.

ALGERNON. I haven't heard anyone call me.

JACK. Your duty as a gentleman calls you back.

ALGERNON. My duty as a gentleman has never interfered with my pleasures in the smallest degree.

JACK. I can quite understand that.

ALGERNON. Well, Cecily is a darling.

JACK. You are not to talk of Miss Cardew like that. I don't like it.

ALGERNON. Well, I don't like your clothes. You look perfectly ridiculous in them. Why on earth don't you go up and change? It is perfectly childish to be in deep mourning for a man who is actually staying for a whole week with you in your house as a guest. I call it grotesque.

JACK. You are certainly not staying with me for a whole week as a guest or anything else. You have got to leave . . . by the four-five train.

ALGERNON. I certainly won't leave you so long as you are in mourning. It would be most unfriendly. If I were in mourning you would stay with me, I suppose. I should think it very unkind if you didn't.

JACK. Well, will you go if I change my clothes?

ALGERNON. Yes, if you are not too long. I never saw anybody take so long to dress, and with such little result.

JACK. Well, at any rate, that is better than being always over-dressed as you are.

ALGERNON. If I am occasionally a little over-dressed, I make up for it by being always immensely over-educated.

JACK. Your vanity is ridiculous, your conduct an outrage, and your presence in my garden utterly absurd. However, you have got to catch the four-five, and I hope you will have a pleasant journey back to town. This Bunburying, as you call it, has not been a great success for you. [*Goes into the house.*]

ALGERNON. I think it has been a great success. I'm in love with Cecily, and that is everything. [*Enter* CECILY *at the back of the garden. She picks up the can and begins to water the flowers.*] But I must see her before I go, and make arrangements for another Bunbury. Ah, there she is.

CECILY. Oh, I merely came back to water the roses. I thought you were with Uncle Jack.

ALGERNON. He's gone to order the dog-cart for me.

CECILY. Oh, is he going to take you for a nice drive?

ALGERNON. He's going to send me away.

CECILY. Then have we got to part?

ALGERNON. I am afraid so. It's a very painful parting.

CECILY. It is always painful to part from people whom one has known for a very brief space of time. The absence of old friends one can endure with equanimity. But even a momentary separation from anyone to whom one has just been introduced is almost unbearable.

ALGERNON. Thank you. [*Enter* MERRIMAN.]

MERRIMAN. The dog-cart is at the door, sir. [ALGERNON *looks appealingly at* CECILY.]

CECILY. It can wait, Merriman . . . for . . . five minutes.

MERRIMAN. Yes, Miss. [*Exit* MERRIMAN.]

ALGERNON. I hope, Cecily, I shall not offend you if I state quite frankly and openly that you seem to me to be in every way the visible personification of absolute perfection.

CECILY. I think your frankness does you great credit, Ernest. If you will allow me I will copy your remarks into my diary. [*Goes over to table and begins writing in diary.*]

ALGERNON. Do you really keep a diary? I'd give anything to look at it. May I?

CECILY. Oh, no. [*Puts her hand over it.*] You see, it is simply a very young girl's record of her own thoughts and impressions, and consequently meant for publication. When it appears in volume form I hope you will order a copy. But pray, Ernest, don't stop. I delight in taking down from dictation. I have reached "absolute perfection." You can go on. I am quite ready for more.

ALGERNON [*somewhat taken aback.*]. Ahem! Ahem!

CECILY. Oh, don't cough, Ernest. When one is dictating one should speak fluently and not cough. Besides, I don't know how to spell a cough. [*Writes as* ALGERNON *speaks.*]

ALGERNON [*speaking very rapidly*]. Cecily, ever since I first looked upon your wonderful and incomparable beauty, I have dared to love you wildly, passionately, devotedly, hopelessly.

CECILY. I don't think that you should tell me that you love me wildly, passionately, devotedly, hopelessly. Hopelessly doesn't seem to make much sense, does it?

ALGERNON. Cecily! [*Enter* MERRIMAN.]

MERRIMAN. The dog-cart is waiting, sir.

ALGERNON. Tell it to come round next week, at the same hour.

MERRIMAN [*looks at* CECILY, *who makes no sign*]. Yes, sir. [MERRIMAN *retires.*]

CECILY. Uncle Jack would be very much annoyed if he knew you were staying on till next week, at the same hour.

ALGERNON. Oh, I don't care about Jack. I don't care for anybody in the whole world but you. I love you, Cecily. You will marry me, won't you?

CECILY. You silly you! Of course. Why, we have been engaged for the last three months.

ALGERNON. For the last three months?

CECILY. Yes, it will be exactly three months on Thursday.

ALGERNON. But how did we become engaged?

CECILY. Well, ever since dear Uncle Jack first confessed to us that he had a younger brother who was very wicked and bad, you of course have formed the chief topic of conversation between myself and Miss Prism. And of course a man who is much talked about is always very attractive. One feels there must be something in him after all. I daresay it was foolish of me, but I feel in love with you, Ernest.

ALGERNON. Darling! And when was the engagement actually settled?

CECILY. On the 4th of February last. Worn out by your entire ignorance of my existence, I determined to end the matter one way or the other, and after a long struggle with myself I accepted you under this dear old tree here. The next day I bought this little ring in your name, and this is the little bangle with the true lovers' knot I promised you always to wear.

ALGERNON. Did I give you this? It's very pretty, isn't it?

CECILY. Yes, you've wonderfully good taste, Ernest. It's the excuse I've always given for your leading such a bad life. And this is the box in which I keep all your dear letters. [*Kneels at table, opens box, and produces letters tied up with blue ribbon.*]

ALGERNON. My letters! But my own sweet Cecily, I have never written you any letters.

CECILY. You need hardly remind me of that, Ernest. I remember only too well that I was forced to write your letters for you. I wrote always three times a week, and sometimes oftener.

ALGERNON. Oh, do let me read them, Cecily?

CECILY. Oh, I couldn't possibly. They would make you far too conceited. [*Replaces box.*] The three you wrote me after I had broken off the engagement are so beautiful, and so badly spelled, that even now I can hardly read them without crying a little.

ALGERNON. But was our engagement ever broken off?

CECILY. Of course it was. On the 22nd of last March. You can see the entry if you like. [*Shows diary.*] "Today I broke off my engagement with Ernest. I feel it is better to do so. The weather still continues charming."

ALGERNON. But why on earth did you break it off? What had I done? I had done nothing at all. Cecily, I am very much hurt indeed to hear you broke it off. Particularly when the weather was so charming.

CECILY. It would hardly have been a really serious engagement if it hadn't been broken off at least once. But I forgave you before the week was out.

ALGERNON [*crossing to her, and kneeling*]. What a perfect angel you are, Cecily.

CECILY. You dear romantic boy. [*He kisses her, she puts her fingers through his hair.*] I hope your hair curls naturally, does it?

ALGERNON. Yes, darling, with a little help from others.

CECILY. I am so glad.

ALGERNON. You'll never break off our engagement again, Cecily?

CECILY. I don't think I could break it off now that I have actually met you. Besides, of course, there is the question of your name.

ALGERNON. Yes, of course. [*Nervously.*]

CECILY. You must not laugh at me, darling, but it had always been a girlish dream of mine to love some one whose name was Ernest. [ALGERNON *rises,* CECILY *also.*] There is something in that name that seems to inspire absolute confidence. I pity any poor married woman whose husband is not called Ernest.

ALGERNON. But, my dear child, do you mean to say you could not love me if I had some other name?

CECILY. But what name?

ALGERNON. Oh, any name you like—Algernon, for instance. . . .

CECILY. But I don't like the name of Algernon.

ALGERNON. Well, my own dear, sweet, loving little darling, I really can't see why you should object to the name Algernon. It is not at all a bad name. In fact, it is rather an aristocratic name. Half of the chaps who get into the Bankruptcy Court are called Algernon. But seriously, Cecily . . . [*moving to her*] . . . if my name was Algy, couldn't you love me?

CECILY [*rising*]. I might respect you, Ernest, I might admire your character, but I fear that I should not be able to give you my undivided attention.

ALGERNON. Ahem! Cecily! [*Picking up hat.*] Your Rector here is, I suppose, thoroughly experienced in the practice of all the rites and ceremonials of the church?

CECILY. Oh, yes. Dr. Chasuble is a most learned man. He has never written a single book, so you can imagine how much he knows.

ALGERNON. I must see him at once on a most important christening—I mean on most important business.

CECILY. Oh!

ALGERNON. I sha'n't be away more than half an hour.

CECILY. Considering that we have been engaged since February the 14th, and that I only met you to-day for the first time, I think it is rather hard that you should leave me for so long a period as half an hour. Couldn't you make it twenty minutes?

ALGERNON. I'll be back in no time. [*Kisses her and rushes down the garden.*]

CECILY. What an impetuous boy he is. I like his hair so much. I must enter his proposal in my diary. [*Enter* MERRIMAN.]

MERRIMAN. A Miss Fairfax has just called to see Mr. Worthing. On very important business, Miss Fairfax states.

CECILY. Isn't Mr. Worthing in his library?

MERRIMAN. Mr. Worthing went over in the direction of the Rectory some time ago.

CECILY. Pray ask the lady to come out here; Mr. Worthing is sure to be back soon. And you can bring tea.

MERRIMAN. Yes, miss. [*Goes out.*]

CECILY. Miss Fairfax! I suppose one of the many good elderly women who are associated with Uncle Jack in some of his philanthropic work in London. I don't quite like women who are interested in philanthropic work. I think it is so forward of them. [*Enter* MERRIMAN.]

MERRIMAN. Miss Fairfax. [*Enter* GWENDOLEN. *Exit* MERRIMAN.]

CECILY [*advancing to meet her*]. Pray let me introduce myself to you. My name is Cecily Cardew.

GWENDOLEN. Cecily Cardew? [*Moving to her and shaking hands.*] What a very sweet name! Something tells me that we are going to be great friends. I like you already more than I can say. My first impressions of people are never wrong.

CECILY. How nice of you to like me so much after we have known each other such a comparatively short time. Pray sit down.

GWENDOLEN [*still standing up*]. I may call you Cecily, may I not?

CECILY. With pleasure!

GWENDOLEN. And you will always call me Gwendolen, won't you?

CECILY. If you wish.

GWENDOLEN. Then that is all quite settled, is it not?

CECILY. I hope so. [*A pause. They both sit down together.*]

GWENDOLEN. Perhaps this might be a favorable opportunity for my mentioning who I am. My father is Lord Bracknell. You have never heard of papa, I suppose?

CECILY. I don't think so.

GWENDOLEN. Outside the family circle, papa, I am glad to say, is entirely unknown. I think that is quite as it should be. The home seems to me to be the proper sphere for the man. And certainly once a man begins to neglect his domestic duties he becomes painfully effeminate, does he not? And I don't like that. It makes men so very attractive. Cecily, mamma, whose views on education are remarkably strict, has brought me up to be extremely short-sighted; it is part of her system; so do you mind my looking at you through my glasses?

CECILY. Oh, not at all, Gwendolen. I am very fond of being looked at.

GWENDOLEN [*after examining* CECILY *carefully through a lorgnette*]. You are here on a short visit, I suppose.

CECILY. Oh, no, I live here.

GWENDOLEN [*severely*]. Really? Your mother, no doubt, or some female relative of advanced years, resides here also?

CECILY. Oh, no. I have no mother, nor, in fact, any relations.

GWENDOLEN. Indeed?

CECILY. My dear guardian, with the assistance of Miss Prism, has the arduous task of looking after me.

GWENDOLEN. Your guardian?

CECILY. Yes, I am Mr. Worthing's ward.

GWENDOLEN. Oh! It is strange he never mentioned to me that he had a ward. How secretive of him! He grows more interesting hourly. I am not sure, however, that the news inspires me with feelings of unmixed delight. [*Rising and going to her.*] I am very fond of you, Cecily. I have liked you ever since I met you. But I am bound to state that now that I know that you are Mr. Worthing's ward, I cannot help expressing a wish you were—well, just a little older than you seem to be—and not quite so very alluring in appearance. In fact, if I may speak candidly—

CECILY. Pray do! I think that whenever one has anything unpleasant to say, one should always be quite candid.

GWENDOLEN. Well, to speak with perfect candor, Cecily, I wish that you were fully forty-two, and more than usually plain for your age. Ernest has a strong upright nature. He is the very soul of truth and honor. Disloyalty would be as impossible to him as deception. But even men of the noblest possible moral character are extremely susceptible to the influence of the physical charms of others. Modern, no less than Ancient History, supplies us with many most painful examples of what I refer to. If it were not so, indeed, History would be quite unreadable.

CECILY. I beg your pardon, Gwendolen, did you say Ernest?

GWENDOLEN. Yes.

CECILY. Oh, but it is not Mr. Ernest Worthing who is my guardian. It is his brother— his elder brother.

GWENDOLEN [*sitting down again*]. Ernest never mentioned to me that he had a brother.

CECILY. I am sorry to say they have not been on good terms for a long time.

GWENDOLEN. Ah! that accounts for it. And now that I think of it I have never heard any man mention his brother. The subject seems distasteful to most men. Cecily, you have lifted a load from my mind. I was growing almost anxious. It would have been terrible if any cloud had come across a friendship like ours, would it not? Of course you are quite, quite sure that it is not Mr. Ernest Worthing who is your guardian?

CECILY. Quite sure. [*A pause.*] In fact, I am going to be his.

GWENDOLEN [*enquiringly*]. I beg your pardon?

CECILY [*rather shy and confidingly*]. Dearest Gwendolen, there is no reason why I should make a secret of it to you. Our little county newspaper is sure to chronicle the fact next week. Mr. Ernest Worthing and I are engaged to be married.

GWENDOLEN [*quite politely, rising*]. My darling Cecily, I think there must be some slight error. Mr. Ernest Worthing is engaged to me. The announcement will appear in the *Morning Post* on Saturday at the latest.

CECILY [*very politely, rising*]. I am afraid you must be under some misconception. Ernest proposed to me exactly ten minutes ago. [*Shows diary.*]

GWENDOLEN [*examines diary through her lorgnette carefully*]. It is certainly very curious, for he asked me to be his wife yesterday afternoon at 5:30. If you would care to verify the incident, pray do so. [*Produces diary of her own.*] I never travel without my diary. One should always have something sensational to read in the train. I am so sorry, dear Cecily, if it is any disappointment to you, but I am afraid *I* have the prior claim.

CECILY. It would distress me more than I can tell you, dear Gwendolen, if it caused you any mental or physical anguish, but I feel bound to point out that since Ernest proposed to you he clearly has changed his mind.

GWENDOLEN [*meditatively*]. If the poor fellow has been entrapped into any foolish promise I shall consider it my duty to rescue him at once, and with a firm hand.

CECILY [*thoughtfully and sadly*]. Whatever unfortunate entanglement my dear boy may have got into, I will never reproach him with it after we are married.

GWENDOLEN.   Do you allude to me, Miss Cardew, as an entanglement? You are presumptuous. On an occasion of this kind it becomes more than a moral duty to speak one's mind. It becomes a pleasure.

CECILY.   Do you suggest, Miss Fairfax, that I entrapped Ernest into an engagement? How dare you? This is no time for wearing the shallow mask of manners. When I see a spade I call it a spade.

GWENDOLEN [*satirically*].   I am glad to say that I have never seen a spade. It is obvious that our social spheres have been widely different. [*Enter* MERRIMAN, *followed by the footman. He carries a salver, tablecloth, and plate-stand.* CECILY *is about to retort. The presence of the servants exercises a restraining influence, under which both girls chafe.*]

MERRIMAN.   Shall I lay tea here as usual, miss?

CECILY [*sternly, in a calm voice*]. Yes, as usual. [MERRIMAN *begins to clear and lay cloth. A long pause.* CECILY *and* GWENDOLEN *glare at each other.*]

GWENDOLEN.   Are there many interesting walks in the vicinity, Miss Cardew?

CECILY.   Oh, yes, a great many. From the top of one of the hills quite close one can see five counties.

GWENDOLEN.   Five counties! I don't think I should like that. I hate crowds.

CECILY [*sweetly*].   I suppose that is why you live in town? [GWENDOLEN *bites her lip, and beats her foot nervously with her parasol.*]

GWENDOLEN [*looking round*].   Quite a well-kept garden this is, Miss Cardew.

CECILY.   So glad you like it, Miss Fairfax.

GWENDOLEN.   I had no idea there were any flowers in the country.

CECILY.   Oh, flowers are as common here, Miss Fairfax, as people are in London.

GWENDOLEN.   Personally, I cannot understand how anybody manages to exist in the country, if anybody who is anybody does. The country always bores me to death.

CECILY.   Ah! This is what the newspapers call agricultural depression, is it not? I believe the aristocracy are suffering very much from it just at present. It is almost an epidemic amongst them, I have been told. May I offer you some tea, Miss Fairfax?

GWENDOLEN [*with elaborate politeness*].   Thank you. [*Aside.*] Detestable girl! But I require tea!

CECILY [*sweetly*].   Sugar?

GWENDOLEN [*superciliously*].   No, thank you. Sugar is not fashionable any more. [CECILY *looks angrily at her, takes up the tongs and puts four lumps of sugar into the cup.*]

CECILY [*severely*].   Cake or bread and butter?

GWENDOLEN [*in a bored manner*].   Bread and butter, please. Cake is rarely seen at the best houses nowadays.

CECILY [*cuts a very large slice of cake, and puts it on the tray*].   Hand that to Miss Fairfax. [MERRIMAN *does so, and goes out with footman.* GWENDOLEN *drinks the tea and makes a grimace. Puts down cup at once, reaches out her hand to the bread and butter, looks at it, and finds it is cake. Rises in indignation.*]

GWENDOLEN.   You have filled my tea with lumps of sugar, and though I asked most distinctly for bread and butter, you have given me cake. I am known for the gentleness of my disposition, and the extraordinary sweetness of my nature, but I warn you, Miss Cardew, you may go too far.

CECILY [*rising*]. To save my poor, innocent, trusting boy from the machinations of any other girl there are no lengths to which I would not go.

GWENDOLEN. From the moment I saw you I distrusted you. I felt that you were false and deceitful. I am never deceived in such matters. My first impressions of people are invariably right.

CECILY. It seems to me, Miss Fairfax, that I am trespassing on your valuable time. No doubt you have many other calls of a similar character to make in the neighborhood. [*Enter* JACK.]

GWENDOLEN [*catching sight of him*]. Ernest! My own Ernest!

JACK. Gwendolen! Darling! [*Offers to kiss her.*]

GWENDOLEN [*drawing back*]. A moment! May I ask if you are engaged to be married to this young lady? [*Points to* CECILY.]

JACK [*laughing*]. To dear little Cecily! Of course not! What could have put such an idea into your pretty little head?

GWENDOLEN. Thank you. You may. [*Offers her cheek.*]

CECILY [*very sweetly*]. I knew there must be some misunderstanding, Miss Fairfax. The gentleman whose arm is at present around your waist is my dear guardian, Mr. John Worthing.

GWENDOLEN. I beg your pardon?

CECILY. This is Uncle Jack.

GWENDOLEN. [*receding*]. Jack! Oh! [*Enter* ALGERNON.]

CECILY. Here is Ernest.

ALGERNON [*goes straight over to* CECILY *without noticing anyone else*]. My own love! [*Offers to kiss her.*]

CECILY [*drawing back*]. A moment, Ernest! May I ask you—are you engaged to be married to this young lady?

ALGERNON [*looking round*]. To what young lady? Good heavens! Gwendolen!

CECILY. Yes, to good heavens, Gwendolen, I mean to Gwendolen.

ALGERNON [*laughing*]. Of course not! What could have put such an idea into your pretty little head?

CECILY. Thank you. [*Presenting her cheek to be kissed.*] You may. [ALGERNON *kisses her.*]

GWENDOLEN. I felt there was some slight error, Miss Cardew. The gentleman who is now embracing you is my cousin, Mr. Algernon Moncrieff.

CECILY [*breaking away from* ALGERNON]. Algernon Moncrieff! Oh! [*The two girls move towards each other and put their arms round each other's waists as if for protection.*]

CECILY. Are you called Algernon?

ALGERNON. I cannot deny it.

CECILY. Oh!

GWENDOLEN. Is your name really John?

JACK [*standing rather proudly*]. I could deny it if I liked. I could deny anything if I liked. But my name certainly is John. It has been John for years.

CECILY [*to* GWENDOLEN]. A gross deception has been practised on both of us.

GWENDOLEN. My poor wounded Cecily!

CECILY. My sweet, wronged Gwendolen!

GWENDOLEN [*slowly and seriously*]. You will call me sister, will you not? [*They embrace.* JACK *and* ALGERNON *groan and walk up and down.*]

CECILY [*rather brightly*]. There is just one question I would like to be allowed to ask my guardian.

GWENDOLEN. An admirable idea! Mr. Worthing, there is just one question I would like to be permitted to put to you. Where is your brother Ernest? We are both engaged to be married to your brother Ernest, so it is a matter of some importance to us to know where your brother Ernest is at present.

JACK [*slowly and hesitatingly*]. Gwendolen—Cecily—it is very painful for me to be forced to speak the truth. It is the first time in my life that I have ever been reduced to such a painful position, and I am really quite inexperienced in doing anything of the kind. However I will tell you quite frankly that I have no brother Ernest. I have no brother at all. I never had a brother in my life, and I certainly have not the smallest intention of ever having one in the future.

CECILY [*surprised*]. No brother at all?

JACK [*cheerily*]. None!

GWENDOLEN [*severely*]. Had you never a brother of any kind?

JACK [*pleasantly*]. Never. Not even of any kind.

GWENDOLEN. I am afraid it is quite clear, Cecily, that neither of us is engaged to be married to anyone.

CECILY. It is not a very pleasant position for a young girl suddenly to find herself in. Is it?

GWENDOLEN. Let us go into the house. They will hardly venture to come after us there.

CECILY. No, men are so cowardly, aren't they? [*They retire into the house with scornful looks.*]

JACK. This ghastly state of things is what you call Bunburying, I suppose?

ALGERNON. Yes, and a perfectly wonderful Bunbury it is. The most wonderful Bunbury I ever had in my life.

JACK. Well, you've no right whatsoever to Bunbury here.

ALGERNON. That is absurd. One has a right to Bunbury anywhere one chooses. Every serious Bunburyist knows that.

JACK. Serious Bunburyist! Good heavens!

ALGERNON. Well, one must be serious about something, if one wants to have any amusement in life. I happen to be serious about Bunburying. What on earth you are serious about I haven't got the remotest idea. About everything, I should fancy. You have such an absolutely trivial nature.

JACK. Well, the only small satisfaction I have in the whole of this wretched business is that your friend Bunbury is quite exploded. You won't be able to run down to the country quite so often as you used to, dear Algy. And a very good thing, too.

ALGERNON. Your brother is a little off color, isn't he, dear Jack? You won't be able to disappear to London quite so frequently as your wicked custom was. And not a bad thing, either.

JACK. As for your conduct towards Miss Cardew, I must say that your taking in a sweet, simple, innocent girl like that is quite inexcusable. To say nothing of the fact that she is my ward.

ALGERNON. I can see no possible defense at all for your deceiving a brilliant, clever, thoroughly experienced young lady like Miss Fairfax. To say nothing of the fact that she is my cousin.

JACK. I wanted to be engaged to Gwendolen, that is all. I love her.

ALGERNON. Well, I simply wanted to be engaged to Cecily. I adore her.

JACK. There is certainly no chance of your marrying Miss Cardew.

ALGERNON. I don't think there is much likelihood, Jack, of you and Miss Fairfax being united.

JACK. Well, that is no business of yours.

ALGERNON. If it was my business, I wouldn't talk about it. [*Begins to eat muffins.*] It is very vulgar to talk about one's business. Only people like stockbrokers do that, and then merely at dinner parties.

JACK. How you can sit there, calmly eating muffins, when we are in this horrible trouble, I can't make out. You seem to me to be perfectly heartless.

ALGERNON. Well, I can't eat muffins in an agitated manner. The butter would probably get on my cuffs. One should always eat muffins quite calmly. It is the only way to eat them.

JACK. I say it's perfectly heartless your eating muffins at all, under the circumstances.

ALGERNON. When I am in trouble, eating is the only thing that consoles me. Indeed, when I am in really great trouble, as anyone who knows me intimately will tell you, I refuse everything except food and drink. At the present moment I am eating muffins because I am unhappy. Besides, I am particularly fond of muffins. [*Rising.*]

JACK [*rising*]. Well, that is no reason why you should eat them all in that greedy way. [*Takes muffins from* ALGERNON.]

ALGERNON [*offering tea-cake*]. I wish you would have tea-cake instead. I don't like tea-cake.

JACK. Good heavens! I suppose a man may eat his own muffins in his own garden.

ALGERNON. But you have just said it was perfectly heartless to eat muffins.

JACK. I said it was perfectly heartless of you, under the circumstances. That is a very different thing.

ALGERNON. That may be. But the muffins are the same. [*He seizes the muffin-dish from* JACK.]

JACK. Algy, I wish to goodness you would go.

ALGERNON. You can't possibly ask me to go without having some dinner. It's absurd. I never go without my dinner. No one ever does, except vegetarians and people like that. Besides I have just made arrangements with Dr. Chasuble to be christened at a quarter to six under the name of Ernest.

JACK. My dear fellow, the sooner you give up that nonsense the better. I made arrangements this morning with Dr. Chasuble to be christened myself at 5:30, and I naturally will take the name of Ernest. Gwendolen would wish it. We can't both be christened Ernest. It's absurd. Besides, I have a perfect right to be christened if I like. There is no evidence at all that I ever have been christened by anybody. I should think it extremely probable I never was, and so does Dr. Chasuble. It is entirely different in your case. You have been christened already.

ALGERNON. Yes, but I have not been christened for years.

JACK. Yes, but you have been christened. That is the important thing.

ALGERNON. Quite so. So I know my constitution can stand it. If you are not quite sure about your ever having been christened, I must say I think it rather dangerous your venturing on it now. It might make you very unwell. You can hardly have forgotten that someone very closely connected with you was very nearly carried off this week in Paris by a severe chill.

JACK. Yes, but you said yourself that a severe chill was not hereditary.

ALGERNON. It usedn't to be, I know—but I daresay it is now. Science is always making wonderul improvements in things.

JACK [*picking up the muffin-dish*]. Oh, that is nonsense; you are always talking nonsense.

ALGERNON. Jack, you are at the muffins again! I wish you wouldn't. There are only two left. [*Takes them.*] I told you I was particularly fond of muffins.

JACK. But I hate tea-cake.

ALGERNON. Why on earth then do you allow tea-cake to be served up for your guests? What ideas you have of hospitality!

JACK. Algernon! I have already told you to go. I don't want you here. Why don't you go?

ALGERNON. I haven't quite finished my tea yet, and there is still one muffin left. [JACK *groans, and sinks into a chair.* ALGERNON *still continues eating.*]

ACT DROP

ACT III

SCENE

Morning-room at the Manor House

[GWENDOLEN *and* CECILY *are at the window, looking out into the garden.*]

GWENDOLEN. The fact that they did not follow us at once into the house, as anyone else would have done, seems to me to show that they have some sense of shame left.

CECILY. They have been eating muffins. That looks like repentance.

GWENDOLEN [*after a pause*]. They don't seem to notice us at all. Couldn't you cough?

CECILY. But I haven't a cough.

GWENDOLEN. They're looking at us. What effrontery!

CECILY. They're approaching. That's very forward of them.

CECILY. Certainly. It's the only thing to do now. [*Enter* JACK, *followed by* ALGERNON. *They whistle some dreadful popular air from a British opera.*]

GWENDOLEN. This dignified silence seems to produce an unpleasant effect.

CECILY. A most distasteful one.

GWENDOLEN. But we will not be the first to speak.

CECILY. Certainly not.

GWENDOLEN. Mr. Worthing, I have something very particular to ask you. Much depends on your reply.

CECILY. Gwendolen, your common sense is invaluable. Mr. Moncrieff, kindly answer me the following question. Why did you pretend to be my guardian's brother?

ALGERNON. In order that I might have an opportunity of meeting you.

CECILY [*to* GWENDOLEN]. That certainly seems a satisfactory explanation, does it not?

GWENDOLEN. Yes, dear, if you can believe him.

CECILY. I don't. But that does not affect the wonderful beauty of his answer.

GWENDOLEN. True. In matters of grave importance, style, not sincerity, is the vital thing. Mr. Worthing, what explanation can you offer to me for pretending to have a brother? Was it in order that you might have an opportunity of coming up to town to see me as often as possible?

JACK. Can you doubt it, Miss Fairfax?

GWENDOLEN. I have the gravest doubts upon the subject. But I intend to crush them. This is not the moment for German scepticism. [*Moving to* CECILY.] Their explanations appear to be quite satisfactory, especially Mr. Worthing's. That seems to me to have the stamp of truth upon it.

CECILY. I am more than content with what Mr. Moncrieff said. His voice alone inspires one with absolute credulity.

GWENDOLEN. Then you think we should forgive them?

CECILY. Yes. I mean no.

GWENDOLEN. True! I had forgotten. There are principles at stake that one cannot surrender. Which of us should tell them? The task is not a pleasant one.

CECILY. Could we not both speak at the same time?

GWENDOLEN. An excellent idea! I nearly always speak at the same time as other people. Will you take time from me?

CECILY. Certainly. [GWENDOLEN *beats time with uplifted finger.*]

GWENDOLEN AND CECILY [*speaking together*]. Your Christian names are still an insuperable barrier. That is all!

JACK AND ALGERNON [*speaking together*]. Our Christian names! Is that all? But we are going to be christened this afternoon.

GWENDOLEN [*to* JACK]. For my sake you are prepared to do this terrible thing?

JACK. I am.

CECILY [*to* ALGERNON]. To please me you are ready to face this fearful ordeal?

ALGERNON. I am!

GWENDOLEN. How absurd to talk of the equality of the sexes! Where questions of self-sacrifice are concerned, men are infinitely beyond us.

JACK. We are. [*Clasps hands with* ALGERNON.]

CECILY. They have moments of physical courage of which we women know absolutely nothing.

GWENDOLEN [*to* JACK]. Darling!

ALGERNON [*to* CECILY]. Darling! [*They fall into each other's arms. Enter* MERRIMAN. *When he enters he coughs loudly, seeing the situation.*]

MERRIMAN. Ahem! Ahem! Lady Bracknell!

JACK. Good heavens! [*Enter* LADY BRACKNELL. *The couples separate in alarm. Exit* MERRIMAN.]

LADY BRACKNELL. Gwendolen! What does this mean?

GWENDOLEN. Merely that I am engaged to be married to Mr. Worthing, mamma.

LADY BRACKNELL. Come here. Sit down immediately. Hesitation of any kind is a sign of mental decay in the young, of physical weakness in the old. [*Turns to* JACK.] Apprised, sir, of my daughter's sudden flight by her trusty maid, whose confidence I purchased by means of a small coin, I followed her at once by a luggage train. Her unhappy father is, I am glad to say, under the impression that she is attending a more than usually lengthy lecture by the University Extension Scheme on the Influence of a Permanent Income Tax on Thought. I do not propose to undeceive him. Indeed I have never undeceived him on any question. I would consider it wrong. But of course, you will clearly understand that all communication between yourself and my daughter must cease immediately from this moment. On this point, as indeed on all points, I am firm.

JACK. I am engaged to be married to Gwendolen, Lady Bracknell!

LADY BRACKNELL. You are nothing of the kind, sir. And now, as regards Algernon! . . . Algernon!

ALGERNON. Yes, Aunt Augusta.

LADY BRACKNELL. May I ask if it is in this house that your invalid friend Mr. Bunbury resides?

ALGERNON [*stammering*]. Oh, no! Bunbury doesn't live here. Bunbury is somewhere else at present. In fact, Bunbury is dead.

LADY BRACKNELL. Dead! When did Mr. Bunbury die? His death must have been extremely sudden.

ALGERNON [*airily*]. Oh, I killed Bunbury this afternoon. I mean poor Bunbury died this afternoon.

LADY BRACKNELL. What did he die of?

ALGERNON. Bunbury? Oh, he was quite exploded.

LADY BRACKNELL. Exploded! Was he the victim of a revolutionary outrage? I was not aware that Mr. Bunbury was interested in social legislation. If so, he is well punished for his morbidity.

ALGERNON. My dear Aunt Augusta, I mean he was found out! The doctors found out that Bunbury could not live, that is what I mean—so Bunbury died.

LADY BRACKNELL. He seems to have had great confidence in the opinion of his physicians. I am glad, however, that he made up his mind at the last to some definite course of action, and acted under proper medical advice. And now that we have finally got rid of this Mr. Bunbury, may I ask, Mr. Worthing, who is that young person whose hand my nephew Algernon is now holding in what seems to me a peculiarly unnecessary manner?

JACK. That lady is Miss Cecily Cardew, my ward. [LADY BRACKNELL *bows coldly to* CECILY.]

ALGERNON. I am engaged to be married to Cecily, Aunt Augusta.

LADY BRACKNELL. I beg your pardon?

CECILY. Mr. Moncrieff and I are engaged to be married, Lady Bracknell.

LADY BRACKNELL [*with a shiver, crossing to the sofa and sitting down*]. I do not know whether there is anything peculiarly exciting in the air in this particular part of Hertfordshire, but the number of engagements that go on seems to me considerably above the proper average that statistics have laid down for our guidance. I think some preliminary enquiry on my part would not be out of place. Mr. Worthing, is Miss Cardew at all connected with any of the larger railway stations in London? I merely desire information. Until yesterday I had no idea that there were any families or persons whose origin was a Terminus. [JACK *looks perfectly furious, but restrains himself.*]

JACK [*in a clear, cold voice*]. Miss Cardew is the granddaughter of the late Mr. Thomas Cardew of 149, Belgrave Square, S.W.; Gervase Park, Dorking, Surrey; and the Sporran, Fifeshire, N.B.

LADY BRACKNELL. That sounds not unsatisfactory. Three addresses always inspire confidence, even in tradesmen. But what proof have I of their authenticity?

JACK. I have carefully preserved the Court Guide of the period. They are open to your inspection, Lady Bracknell.

LADY BRACKNELL [*grimly*]. I have known strange errors in that publication.

JACK. Miss Cardew's family solicitors are Messrs. Markby, Markby, and Markby.

LADY BRACKNELL. Markby, Markby, and Markby? A firm of the very highest position in their profession. Indeed I am told that one of the Markbys is occasionally to be seen at dinner parties. So far I am satisfied.

JACK [*very irritably*]. How extremely kind of you, Lady Bracknell! I have also in my possession, you will be pleased to hear, certificates of Miss Cardew's birth, baptism, whooping cough registration, vaccination, confirmation, and the measles—both the German and the English variety.

LADY BRACKNELL. Ah! A life crowded with incident, I see; though perhaps somewhat too exciting for a young girl. I am not myself in favor of premature experiences. [*Rises, looks at her watch.*] Gwendolen! the time approaches for our departure. We have not a moment to lose. As a matter of form, Mr. Worthing, I had better ask you if Miss Cardew has any little fortune?

JACK. Oh, about a hundred and thirty thousand pounds in the Funds. That is all. Good-bye, Lady Bracknell. So pleased to have seen you.

LADY BRACKNELL [*sitting down again*]. A moment, Mr. Worthing. A hundred and thirty thousand pounds! And in the Funds! Miss Cardew seems to me a most attractive young lady, now that I look at her. Few girls of the present day have any really solid qualities, any of the qualities that last, and improve with time. We live, I regret to say, in an age of surfaces. [*To* CECILY.] Come over here, dear. [CECILY *goes across.*] Pretty child! your dress is sadly simple, and your hair seems almost as Nature might have left it. But we can soon alter all that. A thoroughly experienced French maid produces a really marvelous result in a very brief space of time. I remember recommending one to young Lady Lancing, and after three months her own husband did not know her.

JACK [*aside*]. And after six months nobody knew her.

LADY BRACKNELL [*glares at* JACK *for a few moments. Then bends, with a practised smile, to* CECILY]. Kindly turn round, sweet child. [CECILY *turns completely round.*] No, the side view is what I want. [CECILY *presents her profile.*] Yes, quite as I expected. There are distinct social possibilities in your profile. The two weak points in our age are its want of principle and its want of profile. The chin a little higher, dear. Style largely depends on the way the chin is worn. They are worn very high, just at present. Algernon!

ALGERNON. Yes, Aunt Augusta!

LADY BRACKNELL. There are distinct social possibilities in Miss Cardew's profile.

ALGERNON. Cecily is the sweetest, dearest, prettiest girl in the whole world. And I don't care twopence about social possibilities.

LADY BRACKNELL. Never speak disrespectfully of society, Algernon. Only people who can't get into it do that. [*To* CECILY.] Dear child, of course you know that Algernon has nothing but his debts to depend upon. But I do not approve of mercenary marriages. When I married Lord Bracknell I had no fortune of any kind. But I never dreamed for a moment of allowing that to stand in my way. Well, I suppose I must give my consent.

ALGERNON. Thank you, Aunt Augusta.

LADY BRACKNELL. Cecily, you may kiss me!

CECILY [*kisses her*]. Thank you, Lady Bracknell.

LADY BRACKNELL. You may also address me as Aunt Augusta for the future.

CECILY. Thank you, Aunt Augusta.

LADY BRACKNELL. The marriage, I think, had better take place quite soon.

ALGERNON. Thank you, Aunt Augusta.

CECILY. Thank you, Aunt Augusta.

LADY BRACKNELL. To speak frankly, I am not in favor of long engagements. They give people the opportunity of finding out each other's character before marriage, which I think is never advisable.

JACK. I beg your pardon for interrupting you, Lady Bracknell, but this engagement is quite out of the question. I am Miss Cardew's guardian, and she cannot marry without my consent until she comes of age. That consent I absolutely decline to give.

LADY BRACKNELL. Upon what grounds, may I ask? Algernon is an extremely, I may almost say an ostentatiously, eligible young man. He has nothing, but he looks everything. What more can one desire?

JACK. It pains me very much to have to speak frankly to you, Lady Bracknell, about your nephew, but the fact is that I do not approve at all of his moral character. I suspect him of being untruthful. [ALGERNON *and* CECILY *look at him in indignant amazement.*]

LADY BRACKNELL. Untruthful! My nephew Algernon? Impossible! He is an Oxonian.[3]

JACK. I fear there can be no possible doubt about the matter. This afternoon, during my temporary absence in London on an important question of romance, he obtained

---

[3] *Oxonian:* someone who has attended Oxford University.

admission to my house by means of the false pretense of being my brother. Under an assumed name he drank, I've just been informed by my butler, an entire pint bottle of my Perrier-Jouet, Brut, '89, a wine I was specially reserving for myself. Continuing his disgraceful deception, he succeeded in the course of the afternoon in alienating the affections of my only ward. He subsequently stayed to tea, and devoured every single muffin. And what makes his conduct all the more heartless is, that he was perfectly well aware from the first that I have no brother, that I never had a brother, and that I don't intend to have a brother, not even of any kind. I distinctly told him so myself yesterday afternoon.

LADY BRACKNELL. Ahem! Mr. Worthing, after careful consideration I have decided entirely to overlook my nephew's conduct to you.

JACK. That is very generous of you, Lady Bracknell. My own decision, however, is unalterable. I decline to give my consent.

LADY BRACKNELL [*to* CECILY]. Come here, sweet child. [CECILY *goes over.*] How old are you, dear?

CECILY. Well, I am really only eighteen, but I always admit to twenty when I go to evening parties.

LADY BRACKNELL. You are perfectly right in making some slight alteration. Indeed, no woman should ever be quite accurate about her age. It looks so calculating. . . . [*In a meditative manner.*] Eighteen, but admitting to twenty at evening parties. Well, it will not be very long before you are of age and free from the restraints of tutelage. So I don't think your guardian's consent is, after all, a matter of any importance.

JACK. Pray excuse me, Lady Bracknell, for interrupting you again, but it is only fair to tell you that according to the terms of her grandfather's will Miss Cardew does not come legally of age till she is thirty-five.

LADY BRACKNELL. That does not seem to me to be a grave objection. Thirty-five is a very attractive age. London society is full of women of the very highest birth who have, of their own free choice, remained thirty-five for years. Lady Dumbleton is an instance in point. To my own knowledge she has been thirty-five ever since she arrived at the age of forty, which was many years ago now. I see no reason why our dear Cecily should not be even still more attractive at the age you mention than she is at present. There will be a large accumulation of property.

CECILY. Algy, could you wait for me till I was thirty-five?

ALGERNON. Of course I could, Cecily. You know I could.

CECILY. Yes, I felt it instinctively, but I couldn't wait all that time. I hate waiting even five minutes for anybody. It always makes me rather cross. I am not punctual myself, I know, but I do like punctuality in others, and waiting, even to be married, is quite out of the question.

ALGERNON. Then what is to be done, Cecily?

CECILY. I don't know, Mr. Moncrieff.

LADY BRACKNELL. My dear Mr. Worthing, as Miss Cardew states positively that she cannot wait till she is thirty-five—a remark which I am bound to say seems to me to show a somewhat impatient nature—I would beg of you to reconsider your decision.

JACK. But my dear Lady Bracknell, the matter is entirely in your own hands. The moment you consent to my marriage to Gwendolen, I will most gladly allow your nephew to form an alliance with my ward.

LADY BRACKNELL [*rising and drawing herself up*]. You must be quite aware that what you propose is out of the question.

JACK. Then a passionate celibacy is all that any of us can look forward to.

LADY BRACKNELL. This is not the destiny I propose for Gwendolen. Algernon, of course, can choose for himself. [*Pulls out her watch.*] Come, dear, [GWENDOLEN *rises.*] we have already missed five, if not six, trains. To miss any more might expose us to comment on the platform. [*Enter* DR. CHASUBLE.]

CHASUBLE. Everything is quite ready for the christenings.

LADY BRACKNELL. The christenings, sir! Is not that somewhat premature?

CHASUBLE [*looking rather puzzled, and pointing to* JACK *and* ALGERNON]. Both these gentlemen have expressed a desire for immediate baptism.

LADY BRACKNELL. At their age? The idea is grotesque and irreligious! Algernon, I forbid you to be baptized. I will not hear of such excesses. Lord Bracknell would be highly displeased if he learned that that was the way in which you wasted your time and money.

CHASUBLE. Am I to understand then that there are to be no christenings at all this afternoon?

JACK. I don't think that, as things are now, it would be of much practical value to either of us, Dr. Chasuble.

CHASUBLE. I am grieved to hear such sentiments from you, Mr. Worthing. They savor of the heretical views of the Anabaptists, views that I have completely refuted in four of my unpublished sermons. However, as your present mood seems to be one peculiarly secular, I will return to the church at once. Indeed, I have just been informed by the pew-opener that for the last hour and a half Miss Prism has been waiting for me in the vestry.

LADY BRACKNELL [*starting*]. Miss Prism! Did I hear you mention a Miss Prism?

CHASUBLE. Yes, Lady Bracknell. I am on my way to join her.

LADY BRACKNELL. Pray allow me to detain you for a moment. This matter may prove to be one of vital importance to Lord Bracknell and myself. Is this Miss Prism a female of repellent aspect, remotely connected with education?

CHASUBLE [*somewhat indignantly*]. She is the most cultivated of ladies, and the very picture of respectability.

LADY BRACKNELL. It is obviously the same person. May I ask what position she holds in your household?

CHASUBLE [*severely*]. I am a celibate, madam.

JACK [*interposing*]. Miss Prism, Lady Bracknell, has been for the last three years Miss Cardew's esteemed governess and valued companion.

LADY BRACKNELL. In spite of what I hear of her, I must see her at once. Let her be sent for.

CHASUBLE [*looking off*]. She approaches; she is nigh. [*Enter* MISS PRISM *hurriedly.*]

MISS PRISM. I was told you expected me in the vestry, dear Canon. I have been waiting for you there for an hour and three-quarters. [*Catches sight of* LADY BRACKNELL, *who has fixed her with a stony glare.* MISS PRISM *grows pale and quails. She looks anxiously round as if desirous to escape.*]

LADY BRACKNELL [*in a severe, judicial voice*]. Prism! [MISS PRISM *bows her head in shame.*] Come here, Prism! [MISS PRISM *approaches in a humble manner.*] Prism! Where is that baby? [*General consternation. The* CANON *starts back in horror.* ALGERNON *and* JACK *pretend to be anxious to shield* CECILY *and* GWENDOLEN *from hearing the details of a terrible public scandal.*] Twenty-eight years ago, Prism, you left Lord Bracknell's house, Number 104, Upper Grosvenor Street, in charge of a perambulator that contained a baby, of the male sex. You never returned. A few weeks later, through the elaborate investigations of the Metropolitan police, the perambulator was discovered at midnight, standing by itself in a remote corner of Bayswater. It contained the manuscript of a three-volume novel of more than usually revolting sentimentality. [MISS PRISM *starts in involuntary indignation.*] But the baby was not there! [*Everyone looks at* MISS PRISM.] Prism, where is that baby? [*A pause.*]

MISS PRISM. Lady Bracknell, I admit with shame that I do not know. I only wish I did. The plain facts of the case are these. On the morning of the day you mention, a day that is forever branded on my memory, I prepared as usual to take the baby out in its perambulator. I had also with me a somewhat old but capacious hand-bag in which I had intended to place the manuscript of a work of fiction that I had written during my few unoccupied hours. In a moment of mental abstraction, for which I never can forgive myself, I deposited the manuscript in the bassinette, and placed the baby in the hand-bag.

JACK [*who has been listening attentively*]. But where did you deposit the hand-bag?

MISS PRISM. Do not ask me, Mr. Worthing.

JACK. Miss Prism, this is a matter of no small importance to me. I insist on knowing where you deposited the hand-bag that contained that infant.

MISS PRISM. I left it in the cloak-room of one of the larger railway stations in London.

JACK. What railway station?

MISS PRISM [*quite crushed*]. Victoria. The Brighton line. [*Sinks into a chair.*]

JACK. I must retire to my room for a moment. Gwendolen, wait here for me.

GWENDOLEN. If you are not too long, I will wait here for you all my life. [*Exit* JACK *in great excitement.*]

CHASUBLE. What do you think this means, Lady Bracknell?

LADY BRACKNELL. I dare not even suspect, Dr. Chasuble. I need hardly tell you that in families of high position strange coincidences are not supposed to occur. They are hardly considered the thing. [*Noises heard overhead as if someone was throwing trunks about. Everybody looks up.*]

CECILY. Uncle Jack seems strangely agitated.

CHASUBLE. Your guardian has a very emotional nature.

LADY BRACKNELL. This noise is extremely unpleasant. It sounds is if he was having an argument. I dislike arguments of any kind. They are always vulgar, and often convincing.

CHASUBLE [*looking up*]. It has stopped now. [*The noise is redoubled.*].

LADY BRACKNELL. I wish he would arrive at some conclusion.

GWENDOLEN. This suspense is terrible. I hope it will last. [*Enter* JACK *with a hand-bag of black leather in his hand.*]

JACK [*rushing over to* MISS PRISM]. Is this the hand-bag, Miss Prism? Examine it carefully before you speak. The happiness of more than one life depends on your answer.

MISS PRISM [*calmly*]. It seems to be mine. Yes, here is the injury it received through the upsetting of a Gower Street omnibus in younger and happier days. Here is the stain on the lining caused by the explosion of a temperance beverage, an incident that occurred at Leamington. And here, on the lock, are my initials. I had forgotten that in an extravagant mood I had had them placed there. The bag is undoubtedly mine. I am delighted to have it so unexpectedly restored to me. It has been a great inconvenience being without it all these years.

JACK [*in a pathetic voice*]. Miss Prism, more is restored to you than this hand-bag. I was the baby you placed in it.

MISS PRISM [*amazed*]. You?

JACK [*embracing her*]. Yes . . . mother!

MISS PRISM [*recoiling in indignant astonishment*]. Mr. Worthing! I am unmarried!

JACK. Unmarried! I do not deny that is a serious blow. But after all, who has the right to cast a stone against one who has suffered? Cannot repentance wipe out an act of folly? Why should there be one law for men and another for women? Mother, I forgive you. [*Tries to embrace her again.*]

MISS PRISM [*still more indignant*]. Mr. Worthing, there is some error. [*Pointing to* LADY BRACKNELL.] There is the lady who can tell you who you really are.

JACK [*after a pause*]. Lady Bracknell, I hate to seem inquisitive, but would you kindly inform me who I am?

LADY BRACKNELL. I am afraid that the news I have to give you will not altogether please you. You are the son of my poor sister, Mrs. Moncrieff, and consequently Algernon's elder brother.

JACK. Algy's elder brother! Then I have a brother after all. I knew I had a brother! I always said I had a brother! Cecily—how could you have ever doubted that I had a brother? [*Seizes hold of* ALGERNON.] Dr. Chasuble, my unfortunate brother. Miss Prism, my unfortunate brother. Gwendolen, my unfortunate brother. Algy, you young scoundrel, you will have to treat me with more respect in the future. You have never behaved to me like a brother in all your life.

ALGERNON. Well, not till today, old boy, I admit. I did my best, however, though I was out of practice. [*Shakes hands.*]

GWENDOLEN [*to* JACK]. My own! But what own are you? What is your Christian name, now that you have become someone else?

JACK. Good heavens! . . . I had quite forgotten that point. Your decision on the subject of my name is irrevocable, I suppose?

GWENDOLEN. I never change, except in my affections.

CECILY. What a noble nature you have, Gwendolen!

JACK. Then the question had better be cleared up at once. Aunt Augusta, a moment.

At the time when Miss Prism left me in the hand-bag, had I been christened already?

LADY BRACKNELL. Every luxury that money could buy, including christening, had been lavished on you by your fond and doting parents.

JACK. Then I was christened! That is settled. Now, what name was I given? Let me know the worst.

LADY BRACKNELL. Being the eldest son you were naturally christened after your father.

JACK [*irritably*]. Yet, but what was my father's Christian name?

LADY BRACKNELL [*meditatively*]. I cannot at the present moment recall what the General's Christian name was. But I have no doubt he had one. He was eccentric, I admit. But only in later years. And that was the result of the Indian climate, and marriage, and indigestion, and other things of that kind.

JACK. Algy! Can't you recollect what our father's Christian name was?

ALGERNON. My dear boy, we were never even on speaking terms. He died before I was a year old.

JACK. His name would appear in the Army Lists of the period, I suppose, Aunt Augusta?

LADY BRACKNELL. The General was essentially a man of peace, except in his domestic life. But I have no doubt his name would appear in any military directory.

JACK. The Army Lists of the last forty years are here. These delightful records should have been my constant study. [*Rushes to bookcase and tears the books out.*] M. Generals . . . Mallam, Maxbohm, Magley, what ghastly names they have—Marksby, Migsby, Mobbs, Moncrieff! Lieutenant 1840, Captain, Lieutenant-Colonel, Colonel, General 1869, Christian names, Ernest John. [*Puts book very quietly down and speaks quite calmly.*] I always told you, Gwendolen, my name was Ernest, didn't I? Well, it is Ernest after all. I mean it naturally is Ernest.

LADY BRACKNELL. Yes, I remember that the General was called Ernest. I knew I had some particular reason for disliking the name.

GWENDOLEN. Ernest! My own Ernest! I felt from the first that you could have no other name!

JACK. Gwendolen, it is a terrible thing for a man to find out suddenly that all his life he has been speaking nothing but the truth. Can you forgive me?

GWENDOLEN. I can. For I feel that you are sure to change.

JACK. My own one!

CHASUBLE [*to* MISS PRISM]. Laetitia! [*Embraces her.*]

MISS PRISM [*enthusiastically*]. Frederick! At last!

ALGERNON. Cecily! [*Embraces her.*] At last!

JACK. Gwendolen! [*Embraces her.*]. At last!

LADY BRACKNELL. My nephew, you seem to be displaying signs of triviality.

JACK. On the contrary, Aunt Augusta, I've now realized for the first time in my life the vital Importance of Being Ernest.

TABLEAU
CURTAIN

[1895—Great Britain]

Questions

Act I

1. By what means are Algernon and Jack delineated in Act I? In what ways are they alike? How do they differ?
2. Describe Lady Bracknell. How is she characterized (i.e., by what means)? What is your response to her?
3. What did you find funny in Act I? What are the sources of humor here?
4. What dominant theme emerges from Act I? How does this theme tie in with the play's focus on social life and behavior?
5. A comedy of manners, *The Importance of Being Earnest* is clearly character-centered, as a situation play is almost bound to be. How does its being character-centered tie in with the play's focus?

Act II

1. What seed is planted early in Act II that will lead to a reversal of the play's situation in Act III?
2. What change do we witness in Algernon in Act II? How does this change bear on the play's major theme as established in Act I? How do Miss Prism and Rev. Chasuble tie in whith this theme as well as with the play's focus on life in society?
3. Compare Cecily and Gwendolen. To what extent are they differentiated?
4. Lady Bracknell, Prism, and Chasuble are all stock characters. How so? What kind of characters are Cecily and Gwendolen, Algernon and Jack? In what way are they all appropriate types to comedy? Why?
5. The play's situation takes shape in Act II. Describe that situation. Why is it funny?
6. What made you laugh in Act II? What source of humor is predominant here?

Act III

1. What are the sources of humor in Act III? What is the main source?
2. What coincidence does the third act turn on? Does the coincidence seem to demand justification? Why so or not so?
3. It could be argued that *Oedipus Rex* and *The Importance of Being Earnest* are much alike in terms of the way in which each comes to resolution. How so? The same material, then, can give rise to tragedy or comedy. How do you account for this?
4. At the beginning of Act III, Gwendolen says "style, not sincerity, is the vital thing." How does this define the interests of the play itself? How does it relate to the play's social concerns?
5. Wilde's play concludes with no less than three betrothals. What does this serve to do with respect to mood? What does it symbolize? How does it bring the play's primary theme to a climax?

Writing Assignments

1. What did you find funny in this play? Write a paper detailing what made you laugh and why. In other words, analyze the sources of humor in the play.

2. In an essay, consider the types of character to be found in the play at hand. Establish what those types are and consider why they are appropriate to comedy.

3. Why is the play's situation funny? Write a paper in answer to this question. In answering, consider the effects of coincidence and surprise, and how both are used in comedy.

4. *Oedipus Rex* and *The Importance of Being Earnest* are startlingly alike as to the way in which each comes to resolution. Write a paper discussing this similarity. What is it? What do you make of it? What fundamental human truth does it suggest?

5. Wilde's play is a "comedy of manners," that is, a play in which social life is either satirized or comically celebrated. Which is true of *The Importance of Being Earnest?* What does the play say, finally, about our collective life in society? Discuss, using textual evidence at all points to support your argument.

6. Deprecating his own genius as always, Woody Allen recently said that he prefers tragedy to comedy because tragedy intensifies while comedy diffuses. What are your ideas on the matter? Write a paper on comedy as against tragedy expressing your views. Use *The Importance of Being Earnest* and any tragedy you have read as your focal points.

A DOLL'S HOUSE

❈ HENRIK IBSEN ❈

Translated by R. Farquharson Sharp

CHARACTERS

TORVALD HELMER, *a lawyer and bank manager*
NORA, *his wife*
DOCTOR RANK
MRS. CHRISTINE LINDE
NILS KROGSTAD, *a lawyer and bank clerk*
IVAR, BOB, *and* EMMY, *the Helmers' three young children*
ANNE, *their nurse*
HELEN, *a housemaid*
A PORTER

The action takes place in HELMER'S *apartment.*

ACT 1

SCENE.—*A room furnished comfortably and tastefully, but not extravagantly. At the back, a door to the right leads to the entrance hall, another to the left leads to* HELMER'S *study. Between the doors stands a piano. In the middle of the left-hand wall is a door, and beyond it a window. Near the window are a round table, armchairs and a small sofa. In the right-hand wall, at the farther end, another door; and on the same side, nearer the footlights, a stove, two easy chairs and a rocking-chair; between the stove and the door, a small table. Engravings on the walls; a cabinet with china and other small objects; a small book-case with well-bound books. The floors are carpeted, and a fire burns in the stove. It is winter.*

A bell rings in the hall; shortly afterwards the door is heard to open. Enter NORA, *humming a tune and in high spirits. She is in out-door dress and carries a number of parcels; these she lays on the table to the right. She leaves the outer door open after her, and through it is seen a* PORTER *who is carrying a Christmas Tree and a basket, which he gives to the* MAID *who has opened the door.*

NORA. Hide the Christmas Tree carefully, Helen. Be sure the children do not see it till this evening, when it is dressed. [*to the* PORTER, *taking out her purse.*] How much?

PORTER. Sixpence.

NORA. There is a shilling. No, keep the change. [*The* PORTER *thanks her, and goes out.* NORA *shuts the door. She is laughing to herself, as she takes off her hat and coat. She takes a packet of macaroons from her pocket and eats one or two; then goes cautiously to her husband's door and listens.*] Yes, he is in.

[*Still humming, she goes to the table on the right.*]

HELMER. [*calls out from his room*] Is that my little lark twittering out there?

NORA. [*busy opening some of the parcels*] Yes, it is!

HELMER. Is my little squirrel bustling about?

NORA. Yes!

HELMER. When did my squirrel come home?

NORA. Just now. [*puts the bag of macaroons into her pocket and wipes her mouth.*] Come in here, Torvald, and see what I have bought.

HELMER. Don't disturb me. [*A little later, he opens the door and looks into the room, pen in hand.*] Bought, did you say? All these things? Has my little spendthrift been wasting money again?

NORA. Yes, but, Torvald, this year we really can let ourselves go a little. This is the first Christmas that we have not needed to economise.

HELMER. Still, you know, we can't spend money recklessly.

NORA. Yes, Torvald, we may be a wee bit more reckless now, mayn't we? Just a tiny wee bit! You are going to have a big salary and earn lots and lots of money.

HELMER. Yes, after the New Year; but then it will be a whole quarter before the salary is due.

NORA. Pooh! we can borrow till then.

HELMER. Nora! [*goes up to her and takes her playfully by the ear.*] The same little featherhead! Suppose, now, that I borrowed fifty pounds to-day, and you spent it all in the Christmas week, and then on New Year's Eve a slate fell on my head and killed me, and——

NORA. [*putting her hands over his mouth*] Oh! don't say such horrid things.

HELMER. Still, suppose that happened—what then?

NORA. If that were to happen, I don't suppose I should care whether I owed money or not.

HELMER. Yes, but what about the people who had lent it?

NORA. They? Who would bother about them? I should not know who they were.

HELMER. That is like a woman! But seriously, Nora, you know what I think about that. No debt, no borrowing. There can be no freedom or beauty about a home life that depends on borrowing and debt. We two have kept bravely on the straight road so far, and we will go on the same way for the short time longer that there need be any struggle.

NORA. [*moving towards the stove*] As you please, Torvald.

HELMER. [*following her*] Come, come, my little skylark must not droop her wings. What is this! Is my little squirrel out of temper? [*taking out his purse.*] Nora, what do you think I have got here?

NORA. [*turning around quickly*] Money!

HELMER. There you are. [*gives her some money*] Do you think I don't know what a lot is wanted for housekeeping at Christmas-time?

NORA. [*counting*] Ten shillings—a pound—two pounds! Thank you, thank you, Torvald; that will keep me going for a long time.

HELMER. Indeed it must.

NORA. Yes, yes, it will. But come here and let me show you what I have bought. And all so cheap! Look, here is a new suit for Ivar, and a sword; and a horse and a trumpet for Bob; and a doll and dolly's bedstead for Emmy—they are very plain, but anyway she will soon break them in pieces. And here are dress-lengths and handkerchiefs for the maids; old Anne ought really to have something better.

HELMER. And what is in this parcel?

NORA. [*crying out*] No, no! you mustn't see that till this evening.

HELMER. Very well. But now tell me, you extravagant little person, what would you like for yourself?

NORA. For myself? Oh, I am sure I don't want anything.

HELMER. Yes, but you must. Tell me something reasonable that you would particularly like to have.

NORA. No, I really can't think of anything—unless, Torvald——

HELMER. Well?

NORA. [*playing with his coat buttons, and without raising her eyes to his*] If you really want to give me something, you might—you might——

HELMER. Well, out with it!

NORA. [*speaking quickly*] You might give me money, Torvald. Only just as much as you can afford; and then one of these days I will buy something with it.

HELMER. But, Nora——

NORA. Oh, do! dear Torvald; please, please do! Then I will wrap it up in beautiful gilt paper and hang it on the Christmas Tree. Wouldn't that be fun?

HELMER. What are little people called that are always wasting money?

NORA. Spendthrifts—I know. Let us do as you suggest, Torvald, and then I shall have time to think what I am most in want of. That is a very sensible plan, isn't it?

HELMER. [*smiling*] Indeed it is—that is to say, if you were really to save out of the money I give you, and then really buy something for yourself. But if you spend it all on the housekeeping and any number of unnecessary things, then I merely have to pay up again.

NORA. Oh but, Torvald——

HELMER. You can't deny it, my dear little Nora. [*puts his arm around her waist*] It's a sweet little spendthrift, but she uses up a deal of money. One would hardly believe how expensive such little persons are!

NORA. It's a shame to say that. I do really save all I can.

HELMER. [*laughing*] That's very true—all you can. But you can't save anything!

NORA. [*smiling quietly and happily*] You haven't any idea how many expenses we skylarks and squirrels have, Torvald.

HELMER. You are an odd little soul. Very like your father. You always find some new way of wheedling money out of me, and, as soon as you have got it, it seems to melt in your hands. You never know where it has gone. Still, one must take you as you are. It is in the blood; for indeed it is true that you can inherit these things, Nora.

NORA. Ah, I wish I had inherited many of papa's qualities.

HELMER. And I would not wish you to be anything but just what you are, my sweet little skylark. But, do you know, it strikes me that you are looking rather—what shall I say—rather uneasy to-day? *guilty*

NORA. Do I?

HELMER. You do, really. Look straight at me.

NORA. [*looks at him*] Well?

HELMER. [*wagging his finger at her*] Hasn't Miss Sweet-Tooth been breaking rules in town to-day? *he treats her like child*

NORA. No; what makes you think that?

HELMER. Hasn't she paid a visit to the confectioner's?

NORA. No, I assure you, Torvald——

HELMER. Not been nibbling sweets?

NORA. No, certainly not——

HELMER. Not even taken a bite at a macaroon or two?

NORA. No, Torvald, I assure you really——

HELMER. There, there, of course I was only joking.

NORA. [*going to the table on the right*] I should not think of going against your wishes.

HELMER. No, I am sure of that! besides, you gave me your word—— [*going up to her*] Keep your little Christmas secrets to yourself, my darling. They will all be revealed to-night when the Christmas Tree is lit, no doubt. *premonition*

NORA. Did you remember to invite Doctor Rank?

HELMER. No. But there is no need; as a matter of course he will come to dinner with us. However, I will ask him when he comes in this morning. I have ordered some good wine. Nora, you can't think how I am looking forward to this evening.

NORA. So am I! And how the children will enjoy themselves, Torvald!

HELMER. It is splendid to feel that one has a perfectly safe appointment, and a big enough income. It's delightful to think of, isn't it?

NORA. It's wonderful!

HELMER. Do you remember last Christmas? For a full three weeks beforehand you shut yourself up every evening till long after midnight, making ornaments for the Christmas Tree and all the other fine things that were to be a surprise to us. It was the dullest three weeks I ever spent!

NORA. I didn't find it dull.

HELMER. [*smiling*] But there was precious little result, Nora.

NORA. Oh, you shouldn't tease me about that again. How could I help the cat's going in and tearing everything to pieces? *another lie*

HELMER. Of course you couldn't, poor little girl. You had the best of intentions to please us all, and that's the main thing. But it is a good thing that our hard times are over.

NORA. Yes, it is really wonderful.

HELMER. This time I needn't sit here and be dull all alone, and you needn't ruin your dear eyes and your pretty little hands——

NORA. [*clapping her hands*] No, Torvald, I needn't any longer, need I! It's wonderfully lovely to hear you say so! [*taking his arm*] Now I will tell you how I have been thinking we ought to arrange things, Torvald. As soon as Christmas is over——

[*A bell rings in the hall.*] There's the bell. [*She tidies the room a little.*] There's someone at the door. What a nuisance!

HELMER. If it is a caller, remember I am not at home.

MAID. [*in the doorway*] A lady to see you, ma'am—a stranger.

NORA. Ask her to come in.

MAID. [*to* HELMER] The doctor came at the same time, sir.

HELMER. Did he go straight into my room?

MAID. Yes, sir.

[HELMER *goes into his room. The* MAID *ushers in* MRS. LINDE, *who is in travelling dress, and shuts the door.*]

MRS. LINDE. [*in a dejected and timid voice*] How do you do, Nora?

NORA. [*doubtfully*] How do you do——

MRS. LINDE. You don't recognise me, I suppose.

NORA. No, I don't know—yes, to be sure, I seem to—— [*suddenly*] Yes! Christine! Is it really you?

MRS. LINDE. Yes, it is I.

NORA. Christine! To think of my not recognising you! And yet how could I—— [*in a gentle voice*] How you have altered, Christine!

MRS. LINDE. Yes, I have indeed. In nine, ten long years——

NORA. Is it so long since we met? I suppose it is. The last eight years have been a happy time for me, I can tell you. And so now you have come into the town, and have taken this long journey in winter—that was plucky of you.

MRS. LINDE. I arrived by steamer this morning.

NORA. To have some fun at Christmas-time, of course. How delightful! We will have such fun together! But take off your things. You are not cold, I hope. [*helps her*] Now we will sit down by the stove, and be cosy. No, take this armchair; I will sit here in the rocking-chair. [*takes her hands*] Now you look like your old self again; it was only the first moment—— You are a little paler, Christine, and perhaps a little thinner.

MRS. LINDE. And much, much older, Nora.

NORA. Perhaps a little older; very, very little; certainly not much. [*stops suddenly and speaks seriously*] What a thoughtless creature I am, chattering away like this. My poor, dear Christine, do forgive me.

MRS. LINDE. What do you mean, Nora?

NORA. [*gently*] Poor Christine, you are a widow. *— what does that have to do with anything? it was so long ago*

MRS. LINDE. Yes; it is three years ago now.

NORA. Yes, I knew; I saw it in the papers. I assure you, Christine, I meant ever so often to write to you at the time, but I always put it off and something always prevented me.

MRS. LINDE. I quite understand, dear.

NORA. It was very bad of me, Christine. Poor thing, how you must have suffered. And he left you nothing? *— only thinking about money*

MRS. LINDE. No.

NORA. And no children?

MRS. LINDE. No.

NORA. Nothing at all, then?

MRS. LINDE. Not even any sorrow or grief to live upon.

NORA. [*looking incredulously at her*] But, Christine, is that possible?

MRS. LINDE. [*smiles sadly and strokes her hair*] It sometimes happens, Nora.

NORA. So you are quite alone. How dreadfully sad that must be. I have three lovely children. You can't see them just now, for they are out with their nurse. But now you must tell me all about it.

MRS. LINDE. No, no; I want to hear you.

NORA. No, you must begin. I mustn't be selfish to-day; to-day I must only think of your affairs. But there is one thing I must tell you. Do you know we have just had a great piece of good luck? *— switches from not being selfish, listening to Linde's problems, to telling her own good fortune*

MRS. LINDE. No, what is it?

NORA. Just fancy, my husband has been made manager of the Bank!

MRS. LINDE. Your husband? What good luck!

NORA. Yes, tremendous! A barrister's profession is such an uncertain thing, especially if he won't undertake unsavoury cases; and naturally Torvald has never been willing to do that, and I quite agree with him. You may imagine how pleased we are! He is to take up his work in the Bank at the New Year, and then he will have a big salary and lots of commissions. For the future we can live quite differently— we can do just as we like. I feel so relieved and so happy. Christine! It will be splendid to have heaps of money and not need to have any anxiety, won't it?

MRS. LINDE. Yes, anyhow I think it would be delightful to have what one needs.

NORA. No, not only what one needs, but heaps and heaps of money.

MRS. LINDE. [*smiling*] Nora, Nora, haven't you learnt sense yet? In our schooldays you were a great spendthrift.

NORA. [*laughing*] Yes, that is what Torvald says now. [*wags her finger at her*] But "Nora, Nora" is not so silly as you think. We have not been in a position for me to waste money. We have both had to work.

MRS. LINDE. You too?

NORA. Yes; odds and ends, needlework, crochet-work, embroidery, and that kind of thing. [*dropping her voice*] And other things as well. You know Torvald left his office when we were married? There was no prospect of promotion there, and he had to try and earn more than before. But during the first year he overworked himself dreadfully. You see, he had to make money every way he could, and he worked early and late; but he couldn't stand it, and fell dreadfully ill, and the doctors said it was necessary for him to go south.

MRS. LINDE. You spent a whole year in Italy didn't you?

NORA. Yes. It was no easy matter to get away, I can tell you. It was just after Ivar was born; but naturally we had to go. It was a wonderfully beautiful journey, and it saved Torvald's life. But it cost a tremendous lot of money, Christine.

MRS. LINDE. So I should think.

NORA. It cost about two hundred and fifty pounds. That's a lot, isn't it?

MRS. LINDE. Yes, and in emergencies like that it is lucky to have the money.

NORA. I ought to tell you that we had it from papa.

MRS. LINDE. Oh, I see. It was just about that time that he died, wasn't it?

NORA. Yes; and, just think of it, I couldn't go and nurse him. I was expecting little Ivar's birth every day and I had my poor sick Torvald to look after. My dear, kind father—I never saw him again, Christine. That was the saddest time I have known since our marriage.

MRS. LINDE. I know how fond you were of him. And then you went off to Italy?

NORA. Yes; you see we had money then, and the doctors insisted on our going, so we started a month later.

MRS. LINDE. And your husband came back quite well?

NORA. As sound as a bell!

MRS. LINDE. But—the doctor?

NORA. What doctor?

MRS. LINDE. I thought your maid said the gentleman who arrived here just as I did was the doctor?

NORA. Yes, that was Doctor Rank, but he doesn't come here professionally. He is our greatest friend, and comes in at least once every day. No, Torvald has not had an hour's illness since then, and our children are strong and healthy and so am I. [*jumps up and claps her hands*] Christine! Christine! it's good to be alive and happy!—— But how horrid of me; I am talking of nothing but my own affairs. [*Sits on a stool near her, and rests her arms on her knees*] You mustn't be angry with me. Tell me, is it really true that you did not love your husband? Why did you marry him?

MRS. LINDE. My mother was alive then, and was bedridden and helpless, and I had to provide for my two younger brothers; so I did not think I was justified in refusing his offer.

NORA. No, perhaps you were quite right. He was rich at that time, then?

MRS. LINDE. I believe he was quite well off. But his business was a precarious one; and, when he died, it all went to pieces and there was nothing left.

NORA. And then?——

MRS. LINDE. Well, I had to turn my hand to anything I could find—first a small shop, then a small school, and so on. The last three years have seemed like one long working-day, with no rest. Now it is at an end, Nora. My poor mother needs me no more, for she is gone; and the boys do not need me either; they have got situations and can shift for themselves.

NORA. What a relief you must feel it——

MRS. LINDE. No, indeed; I only feel my life unspeakably empty. No one to live for any more. [*gets up restlessly*] That was why I could not stand the life in my little backwater any longer. I hope it may be easier here to find something which will busy me and occupy my thoughts. If only I could have the good luck to get some regular work—office work of some kind——

NORA. But, Christine, that is so frightfully tiring, and you look tired out now. You had far better go away to some watering-place.

MRS. LINDE. [*walking to the window*] I have no father to give me money for a journey, Nora.

NORA. [*rising*] Oh, don't be angry with me.

MRS. LINDE. [*going up to her*] It is you that must not be angry with me, dear. The worst of a position like mine is that it makes one so bitter. No one to work for, and yet obliged to be always on the look-out for chances. One must live, and so one becomes selfish. When you told me of the happy turn your fortunes have taken—you will hardly believe it—I was delighted not so much on your account as on my own.

NORA. How do you mean?—Oh, I understand. You mean that perhaps Torvald could get you something to do. *- I think Linde had it in her mind all along*

MRS. LINDE. Yes, that was what I was thinking of.

NORA. He must, Christine. Just leave it to me; I will broach the subject very cleverly—I will think of something that will please him very much. It will make me so happy to be of some use to you.

MRS. LINDE. How kind you are, Nora, to be so anxious to help me! It is doubly kind in you, for you know so little of the burdens and troubles of life.

NORA. I——? I know so little of them?

MRS. LINDE. [*smiling*] My dear! Small household cares and that sort of thing!—You are a child, Nora.

NORA. [*tosses her head and crosses the stage*] You ought not to be so superior.

MRS. LINDE. No?

NORA. You are just like the others. They all think that I am incapable of anything really serious—— *what others? her husband?*

MRS. LINDE. Come, come——

NORA. —that I have gone through nothing in this world of cares.

MRS. LINDE. But, my dear Nora, you have just told me all your troubles.

NORA. Pooh!—those were trifles. [*lowering her voice*] I have not told you the important thing.

MRS. LINDE. The important thing? What do you mean?

NORA. You look down upon me altogether, Christine—but you ought not to. You are proud, aren't you, of having worked so hard and so long for your mother?

MRS. LINDE. Indeed, I don't look down on any one. But it is true that I am both proud and glad to think that I was privileged to make the end of my mother's life almost free from care.

NORA. And you are proud to think of what you have done for your brothers.

MRS. LINDE. I think I have the right to be.

NORA. I think so, too. But now, listen to this; I too have something to be proud of and glad of. *she is justifying what she has done*

MRS. LINDE. I have no doubt you have. But what do you refer to?

NORA. Speak low. Suppose Torvald were to hear! He mustn't on any account—no one in the world must know, Christine, except you.

MRS. LINDE. But what is it?

NORA. Come here. [*pulls her down on the sofa beside her*] Now I will show you that I too have something to be proud and glad of. It was I who saved Torvald's life.

MRS. LINDE. "Saved"? How?

NORA. I told you about our trip to Italy. Torvald would never have recovered if he had not gone there——

MRS. LINDE. Yes, but your father gave you the necessary funds.

NORA. [*smiling*] Yes, that is what Torvald and all the others think, but——

MRS. LINDE. But——

NORA. Papa didn't give us a shilling. It was I who procured the money. *how?*

MRS. LINDE. You? All that large sum?

NORA. Two hundred and fifty pounds. What do you think of that?

MRS. LINDE. But, Nora, how could you possibly do it? Did you win a prize in the Lottery?

NORA. [*contemptuously*] In the Lottery? There would have been no credit in that.

MRS. LINDE. But where did you get it from, then?

NORA. [*humming and smiling with an air of mystery*] Hm, hm! Aha!

MRS. LINDE. Because you couldn't have borrowed it.

NORA. Couldn't I? Why not?

MRS. LINDE. No, a wife cannot borrow without her husband's consent.

NORA. [*tossing her head*] Oh, if it is a wife who has any head for business—a wife who has the wit to be a little bit clever—— *she didn't borrow from bank*
considers herself clever

MRS. LINDE. I don't understand it at all, Nora.

NORA. There is no need you should. I never said I had borrowed the money. I may have got it some other way. [*lies back on the sofa*] Perhaps got it from some other admirer. When anyone is as attractive as I am—— *prostitution?*

MRS. LINDE. You are a mad creature.

NORA. Now, you know you're full of curiosity, Christine.

MRS. LINDE. Listen to me, Nora dear. Haven't you been a little bit imprudent?

NORA. [*sits up straight*] Is it imprudent to save your husband's life?

MRS. LINDE. It seems to me imprudent, without his knowledge, to——

NORA. But it was absolutely necessary that he should not know! My goodness, can't you understand that? It was necessary he should have no idea what a dangerous condition he was in. It was to me that the doctors came and said that his life was in danger, and that the only thing to save him was to live in the south. Do you suppose I didn't try, first of all, to get what I wanted as if it were for myself? I told him how much I should love to travel abroad like other young wives; I tried tears and entreaties with him; I told him that he ought to remember the condition I was in, and that he ought to be kind and indulgent to me; I even hinted that he might raise a loan. That nearly made him angry, Christine. He said I was thoughtless, and that it was his duty as my husband not to indulge me in my whims and caprices—as I believe he called them. Very well I thought, you must be saved—and that was how I came to devise a way out of the difficulty——

Torvald's attitude

MRS. LINDE. And did your husband never get to know from your father that the money had not come from him?

NORA. No, never. Papa died just at that time. I had meant to let him into the secret and beg him never to reveal it. But he was so ill then—alas, there never was any need to tell him.

Mrs. Linde. And since then have you never told your secret to your husband?

Nora. Good Heavens, no! How could you think so? A man who has such strong opinions about these things! And besides, how painful and humiliating it would be for Torvald, with his manly independence, to know that he owed me anything! It would upset our mutual relations altogether; our beautiful happy home would no longer be what it is now.

Mrs. Linde. Do you mean never to tell him about it?

Nora. [*meditatively, and with a half smile*] Yes—some day, perhaps, after many years, when I am no longer as nice-looking as I am now. Don't laugh at me! I mean of course, when Torvald is no longer as devoted to me as he is now; when my dancing and dressing-up and reciting have palled on him; then it may be a good thing to have something in reserve—— [*breaking off*] What nonsense! That time will never come. Now, what do you think of my great secret, Christine? Do you still think I am of no use? I can tell you, too, that this affair has caused me a lot of worry. It has been by no means easy for me to meet my engagements punctually. I may tell you that there is something that is called, in business, quarterly interest, and another thing called payment in instalments, and it is always so dreadfully difficult to manage them. I have had to save a little here and there, where I could, you understand. I have not been able to put aside much from my housekeeping money, for Torvald must have a good table. I couldn't let my children be shabbily dressed; I have felt obliged to use up all he gave me for them, the sweet little darlings!

Mrs. Linde. So it has all had to come out of your own necessaries of life, poor Nora?

Nora. Of course. Besides, I was the one responsible for it. Whenever Torvald has given me the money for new dresses and such things, I have never spent more than half of it; I have always bought the simplest and cheapest things. Thank Heaven, any clothes look well on me, and so Torvald has never noticed it. But it was often very hard on me, Christine—because it is delightful to be really well dressed, isn't it?

Mrs. Linde. Quite so.

Nora. Well, then I have found other ways of earning money. Last winter I was lucky enough to get a lot of copying to do; so I locked myself up and sat writing every evening until quite late at night. Many a time I was desperately tired; but all the same it was a tremendous pleasure to sit there working and earning money. It was like being a man.

Mrs. Linde. How much have you been able to pay off in that way?

Nora. I can't tell you exactly. You see, it is very difficult to keep an account of a business matter of that kind. I only know that I have paid every penny that I could scrape together. Many a time I was at my wits' end. [*smiles*] Then I used to sit here and imagine that a rich old gentleman had fallen in love with me——

Mrs. Linde. What! Who was it?

Nora. Be quiet!—that he had died; and that when his will was opened it contained, written in big letters, the instruction: "The lovely Mrs. Nora Helmer is to have all I possess paid over to her at once in cash."

MRS. LINDE. But, my dear Nora—who could the man be? *she is soo dense*

NORA. Good gracious, can't you understand? There was no old gentleman at all; it was only something that I used to sit here and imagine, when I couldn't think of any way of procuring money. But it's all the same now; the tiresome old person can stay where he is, as far as I am concerned; I don't care about him or his will either, for I am free from care now. [*jumps up*] My goodness, it's delightful to think of, Christine! Free from care! To be able to be free from care, quite free from care; to be able to play and romp with the children; to be able to keep the house beautifully and have everything just as Torvald likes it! And, think of it, soon the spring will come and the big blue sky! Perhaps we shall be able to take a little trip—perhaps I shall see the sea again! Oh, it's a wonderful thing to be alive and be happy. [*A bell is heard in the hall.*] *She keeps saying that*

is her debt paid, or it just she has orvald's money

MRS. LINDE. [*rising*] There is the bell; perhaps I had better go.

NORA. No, don't go; no one will come in here; it is sure to be for Torvald.

SERVANT. [*at the hall door*] Excuse me, ma'am—there is a gentleman to see the master, and as the doctor is with him——

NORA. Who is it?

KROGSTAD. [*at the door*] It is I, Mrs. Helmer. [MRS. LINDE *starts, trembles, and turns to the window.*]

NORA. [*takes a step towards him, and speaks in a strained, low voice*] You? What is it? What do you want to see my husband about?

KROGSTAD. Bank business—in a way. I have a small post in the Bank, and I hear your husband is to be our chief now——

NORA. Then it is—— *is he going to blackmail her + he lent her money? mistress*

KROGSTAD. Nothing but dry business matters, Mrs. Helmer; absolutely nothing else. *prostitution?*

NORA. Be so good as to go into the study, then. [*She bows indifferently to him and shuts the door into the hall; then comes back and makes up the fire in the stove.*]

MRS. LINDE. Nora—who was that man?

NORA. A lawyer, of the name of Krogstad.

MRS. LINDE. Then it really was he.

NORA. Do you know the man?

MRS. LINDE. I used to—many years ago. At one time he was a solicitor's clerk in our town. *what is her relation to him*

NORA. Yes, he was.

MRS. LINDE. He is greatly altered.

NORA. He made a very unhappy marriage.

MRS. LINDE. He is a widower now, isn't he?

NORA. With several children. There now, it is burning up.

[*Shuts the door of the stove and moves the rocking-chair aside.*]

MRS. LINDE. They say he carries on various kinds of business. *what is she hinting at?*

NORA. Really! Perhaps he does; I don't know anything about it. But don't let us think of business; it is so tiresome. *another lie*

DOCTOR RANK. [*comes out of* HELMER'S *study. Before he shuts the door he calls to him.*] No, my dear fellow, I won't disturb you; I would rather go into your wife

for a little while. [*shuts the door and sees* MRS. LINDE] I beg your pardon; I am
afraid I am disturbing you too.

NORA. No, not at all. [*introducing him*] Doctor Rank, Mrs. Linde.

RANK. I have often heard Mrs. Linde's name mentioned here. I think I passed you
on the stairs when I arrived, Mrs. Linde?

MRS. LINDE. Yes, I go up very slowly; I can't manage stairs well.

RANK. Ah! some slight internal weakness?

MRS. LINDE. No, the fact is I have been overworking myself.

RANK. Nothing more than that? Then I suppose you have come to town to amuse
yourself with our entertainments?

MRS. LINDE. I have come to look for work.

RANK. Is that a good cure for overwork?

MRS. LINDE. One must live, Doctor Rank.

RANK. Yes, the general opinion seems to be that it is necessary.

NORA. Look here, Doctor Rank—you know you want to live.

RANK. Certainly. However wretched I may feel, I want to prolong the agony as long
as possible. All my patients are like that. And so are those who are morally diseased;
one of them, and a bad case too, is at this very moment with Helmer——

MRS. LINDE. [*sadly*] Ah!

NORA. Whom do you mean?

RANK. A lawyer of the name of Krogstad, a fellow you don't know at all. He suffers
from a diseased moral character, Mrs. Helmer; but even he began talking of its
being highly important that he should live.

NORA. Did he? What did he want to speak to Torvald about?

RANK. I have no idea; I only heard that it was something about the Bank.

NORA. I didn't know this—what's his name—Krogstad had anything to do with the
Bank.

RANK. Yes, he has some sort of appointment there. [*to* MRS. LINDE] I don't know
whether you find also in your part of the world that there are certain people
who go zealously snuffing about to smell out moral corruption, and, as soon as
they have found some, put the person concerned into some lucrative position
where they can keep their eye on him. Healthy natures are left out in the cold.

MRS. LINDE. Still I think the sick are those who most need taking care of.

RANK. [*shrugging his shoulders*] Yes, there you are. That is the sentiment that is turning
Society into a sickhouse.

[NORA, *who has been absorbed in her thoughts, breaks out into smothered laughter
and claps her hands.*]

RANK. Why do you laugh at that? Have you any notion what Society really is?

NORA. What do I care about tiresome Society? I am laughing at something quite
different, something extremely amusing. Tell me, Doctor Rank, are all the people
who are employed in the Bank dependent on Torvald now?

RANK. Is that what you find so extremely amusing?

NORA. [*smiling and humming*] That's my affair! [*walking about the room*] It's perfectly
glorious to think that we have—that Torvald has so much power over so many

people. [*takes the packet from her pocket*] Doctor Rank, what do you say to a macaroon? *rebeling against Torvald*

RANK. What, macaroons? I thought they were forbidden here.

NORA. Yes, but these are some Christine gave me. *How she does lie*

MRS. LINDE. What! I?——

NORA. Oh, well, don't be alarmed! You couldn't know that Torvald had forbidden them. I must tell you that he is afraid they will spoil my teeth. But, bah!—once in a way—— That's so, isn't it, Doctor Rank? By your leave? [*puts a macaroon into his mouth*] You must have one too, Christine. And I shall have one, just a little one—or at most two. [*walking about*] I am tremendously happy. There is just one thing in the world now that I should dearly love to do.

RANK. Well, what is that?

NORA. It's something I should dearly love to say, if Torvald could hear me.

RANK. Well, why can't you say it?

NORA. No, I daren't; it's so shocking.

MRS. LINDE. Shocking?

RANK. Well, I should not advise you to say it. Still, with us you might. What is it you would so much like to say if Torvald could hear you?

NORA. I should just love to say—Well, I'm damned! — *is this rebellion? what's the point?*

RANK. Are you mad?

MRS. LINDE. Nora, dear——!

RANK. Say it, here he is! — *Why should she say it?*

NORA. [*hiding the packet*] Hush! Hush! Hush!

[HELMER *comes out of his room, with his coat over his arm and his hat in his hands.*]

NORA. Well, Torvald dear, have you got rid of him?

HELMER. Yes, he has just gone.

NORA. Let me introduce you—this is Christine, who has come to town.

HELMER. Christine——? Excuse me, but I don't know——

NORA. Mrs. Linde, dear; Christine Linde.

HELMER. Of course. A school friend of my wife's, I presume?

MRS. LINDE. Yes, we have known each other since then.

NORA. And just think, she has taken a long journey in order to see you. *Why does she make up stories like playing dolls*

HELMER. What do you mean?

MRS. LINDE. No, really, I——

NORA. Christine is tremendously clever at book-keeping, and she is frightfully anxious to work under some clever man, so as to perfect herself——

HELMER. Very sensible, Mrs. Linde.

NORA. And when she heard you had been appointed manager of the Bank—the news was telegraphed, you know—she travelled here as quick as she could. Torvald, I am sure you will be able to do something for Christine, for my sake, won't you?

HELMER. Well, it is not altogether impossible. I presume you are a widow, Mrs. Linde?

MRS. LINDE. Yes.

HELMER. And have had some experience of book-keeping?

MRS. LINDE. Yes, a fair amount.

HELMER. Ah! well, it's very likely I may be able to find something for you——

NORA. [*clapping her hands*] What did I tell you? What did I tell you?

HELMER. You have just come at a fortunate moment, Mrs. Linde.

MRS. LINDE. How am I to thank you?

HELMER. There is no need. [*puts on his coat*] But to-day you must excuse me——

RANK. Wait a minute; I will come with you.

[*Brings his fur coat from the hall and warms it at the fire.*]

NORA. Don't be long away, Torvald dear.

HELMER. About an hour, not more.

NORA. Are you going too, Christine?

MRS. LINDE. [*putting on her cloak*] Yes, I must go and look for a room.

HELMER. Oh, well then, we can walk down the street together.

NORA. [*helping her*] What a pity it is we are so short of space here: I am afraid it is impossible for us——

MRS. LINDE. Please don't think of it! Good-bye, Nora dear, and many thanks.

NORA. Good-bye for the present. Of course you will come back this evening. And you too, Dr. Rank. What do you say? If you are well enough? Oh, you must be! Wrap yourself up well.

[*They go to the door all talking together. Children's voices are heard on the staircase.*]

NORA. There they are. There they are! [*She runs to open the door. The* NURSE *comes in with the children.*] Come in! Come in! [*stoops and kisses them*] Oh, you sweet blessings! Look at them, Christine! Aren't they darlings?

RANK. Don't let us stand here in the draught.

HELMER. Come along, Mrs. Linde; the place will only be bearable for a mother now!

[RANK, HELMER *and* MRS. LINDE *go downstairs. The* NURSE *comes forward with the children;* NORA *shuts the hall door.*]

NORA. How fresh and well you look! Such red cheeks!—like apples and roses. [*The children all talk at once while she speaks to them.*] Have you had great fun? That's splendid! What, you pulled both Emmy and Bob along on the sledge?—both at once?—that *was* good. You are a clever boy, Ivar. Let me take her for a little, Anne. My sweet little baby doll! [*takes the baby from the* MAID *and dances it up and down*] Yes, yes, mother will dance with Bob too. What! Have you been snowballing? I wish I had been there too! No, no, I will take their things off, Anne; please let me do it, it is such fun. Go in now, you look half frozen. There is some coffee for you on the stove.

[*The* NURSE *goes into the room on the left.* NORA *takes off the children's things and throws them about, while they all talk to her at once.*]

NORA. Really! Did a big dog run after you? But it didn't bite you? No, dogs don't bite nice little dolly children. You mustn't look at the parcels, Ivar. What are they? Ah, I daresay you would like to know. No, no—it's something nasty! Come, let us have a game! What shall we play at? Hide and Seek? Yes, we'll play Hide and Seek. Bob shall hide first. Must I hide? Very well, I'll hide first.

[*She and the children laugh and shout, and romp in and out of the room; at last* NORA *hides under the table, the children rush in and look for her, but do not see her; they hear her smothered laughter, run to the table, lift up the cloth and find her. Shouts of laughter. She crawls forward and pretends to frighten them. Fresh laughter. Meanwhile there has been a knock at the hall door, but none of them has noticed it. The door is half opened, and* KROGSTAD *appears. He waits a little; the game goes on.*]

KROGSTAD. Excuse me, Mrs. Helmer.

NORA. [*with a stifled cry, turns round and gets up on to her knees*] Ah! what do you want?

KROGSTAD. Excuse me, the outer door was ajar; I suppose someone forgot to shut it.

NORA. [*rising*] My husband is out, Mr. Krogstad.

KROGSTAD. I know that.

NORA. What do you want here, then?

KROGSTAD. A word with you. ~~She going to ask for sexual favor~~

NORA. With me?—— [*to the children, gently*] Go in to nurse. What? No, the strange man won't do mother any harm. When he has gone we will have another game. [*She takes the children into the room on the left, and shuts the door after them.*] You want to speak to me?

KROGSTAD. Yes, I do.

NORA. To-day? It is not the first of the month yet.

KROGSTAD. No, it is Christmas Eve, and it will depend on yourself what sort of a Christmas you will spend.

NORA. What do you want? To-day it is absolutely impossible for me——

KROGSTAD. We won't talk about that till later on. This is something different. I presume you can give me a moment? *sexual favors in addition to monthly payment*

NORA. Yes—yes, I can—although——

KROGSTAD. Good. I was in Olsen's Restaurant and saw your husband going down the street——

NORA. Yes?

KROGSTAD. With a lady.

NORA. What then?

KROGSTAD. May I make so bold as to ask if it was Mrs. Linde?

NORA. It was.

KROGSTAD. Just arrived in town?

NORA. Yes, to-day.

KROGSTAD. She is a great friend of yours, isn't she?

NORA. She is. But I don't see——

KROGSTAD. I knew her too, once upon a time.

NORA. I am aware of that.

KROGSTAD. Are you? So you know all about it; I thought as much. Then I can ask

all about what? What does Mrs. Linde have to do with anything, her connection

you, without beating about the bush—is Mrs. Linde to have an appointment in the Bank?

NORA. What right have you to question me, Mr. Krogstad?—You, one of my husband's subordinates! But since you ask, you shall know. Yes, Mrs. Linde is to have an appointment. And it was I who pleaded her cause, Mr. Krogstad, let me tell you that.

KROGSTAD. I was right in what I thought, then.

NORA. [*walking up and down the stage*] Sometimes one has a tiny little bit of influence, I should hope. Because one is a woman, it does not necessarily follow that——. When anyone is in a subordinate position, Mr. Krogstad, they should really be careful to avoid offending anyone who—who——

KROGSTAD. Who has influence?   *gloating of her influence over him*

NORA. Exactly.

KROGSTAD. [*changing his tone*] Mrs. Helmer, you will be so good as to use your influence on my behalf.

NORA. What? What do you mean?

KROGSTAD. You will be so kind as to see that I am allowed to keep my subordinate position in the Bank.

NORA. What do you mean by that? Who proposes to take your post away from you?

KROGSTAD. Oh, there is no necessity to keep up the pretence of ignorance. I can quite understand that your friend is not very anxious to expose herself to the chance of rubbing shoulders with me; and I quite understand, too, whom I have to thank for being turned out.

what?

NORA. But I assure you——

KROGSTAD. Very likely; but, to come to the point, the time has come when I should advise you to use your influence to prevent that.

NORA. But, Mr. Krogstad, I *have* no influence.

KROGSTAD. Haven't you? I thought you said yourself just now——

NORA. Naturally I did not mean you to put that construction on it. I! What should make you think I have any influence of that kind with my husband?

KROGSTAD. Oh, I have known your husband from our student days. I don't suppose he is any more unassailable than other husbands.

NORA. If you speak slightingly of my husband, I shall turn you out of the house.

KROGSTAD. You are bold, Mrs. Helmer.

NORA. I am not afraid of you any longer. As soon as the New Year comes, I shall in a very short time be free of the whole thing.

KROGSTAD. [*controlling himself*] Listen to me, Mrs. Helmer. If necessary, I am prepared to fight for my small post in the Bank as if I were fighting for my life.

NORA. So it seems.

KROGSTAD. It is not only for the sake of the money; indeed, that weighs least with me in the matter. There is another reason—well, I may as well tell you. My position is this. I daresay you know, like everybody else, that once, many years ago, I was guilty of an indiscretion.   *what did he do?*

NORA. I think I have heard something of the kind.

KROGSTAD. The matter never came into court; but every way seemed to be closed to

loan sharking?

me after that. So I took to the business that you know of. I had to do something; and, honestly, I don't think I've been one of the worst. But now I must cut myself free from all that. My sons are growing up; for their sake I must try and win back as much respect as I can in the town. This post in the Bank was like the first step up for me—and now your husband is going to kick me downstairs again into the mud.

NORA. But you must believe me, Mr. Krogstad; it is not in my power to help you at all.

KROGSTAD. Then it is because you haven't the will; but I have means to compel you.

NORA. You don't mean that you will tell my husband that I owe you money?

KROGSTAD. Hm!—suppose I were to tell him?

NORA. It would be perfectly infamous of you. [*Sobbing*] To think of his learning my secret, which has been my joy and pride, in such an ugly, clumsy way—that he should learn it from you! And it would put me in a horribly disagreeable position——

why is some-thing to be proud of

KROGSTAD. Only disagreeable?

NORA. [*impetuously*] Well, do it, then!—and it will be the worse for you. My husband will see for himself what a blackguard you are, and you certainly won't keep your post then.

KROGSTAD. I asked you if it was only a disagreeable scene at home that you were afraid of?

NORA. If my husband does get to know of it, of course he will at once pay you what is still owing, and we shall have nothing more to do with you.

KROGSTAD. [*coming a step nearer*] Listen to me, Mrs. Helmer. Either you have a very bad memory or you know very little of business. I shall be obliged to remind you of a few details.

NORA. What do you mean?

KROGSTAD. When your husband was ill, you came to me to borrow two hundred and fifty pounds.

NORA. I didn't know any one else to go to.

KROGSTAD. I promised to get you that amount——

NORA. Yes, and you did so.

KROGSTAD. I promised to get you that amount, on certain conditions. Your mind was so taken up with your husband's illness, and you were so anxious to get the money for your journey, that you seem to have paid no attention to the conditions of our bargain. Therefore it will not be amiss if I remind you of them. Now, I promised to get the money on the security of a bond which I drew up.

NORA. Yes, and which I signed.

KROGSTAD. Good. But below your signature there were a few lines constituting your father a surety for the money; those lines your father should have signed.

NORA. Should? He did sign them. *another lie*

KROGSTAD. I had left the date blank; that is to say your father should himself have inserted the date on which he signed the paper. Do you remember that?

NORA. Yes, I think I remember——

KROGSTAD. Then I gave you the bond to send by post to your father. Is that not so?

Was her father a surety because she knew he was going to die?

NORA. Yes.

KROGSTAD. And you naturally did so at once, because five or six days afterwards you brought me the bond with your father's signature. And then I gave you the money.

NORA. Well, haven't I been paying it off regularly?

KROGSTAD. Fairly so, yes. But—to come back to the matter in hand—that must have been a very trying time for you, Mrs. Helmer?

NORA. It was, indeed.

KROGSTAD. Your father was very ill, wasn't he?

NORA. He was very near his end.

KROGSTAD. And died soon afterwards?

NORA. Yes.

KROGSTAD. Tell me, Mrs. Helmer, can you by any chance remember what day your father died?—on what day of the month, I mean.

NORA. Papa died on the 29th of September.

KROGSTAD. That is correct; I have ascertained it for myself. And, as that is so, there is a discrepancy [*taking a paper from his pocket*] which I cannot account for.

NORA. What discrepancy? I don't know——

KROGSTAD. The discrepancy consists, Mrs. Helmer, in the fact that your father signed this bond three days after his death.

NORA. What do you mean? I don't understand——

KROGSTAD. Your father died on the 29th of September. But, look here; your father has dated his signature the 2nd of October. It is a discrepancy, isn't it? [NORA *is silent.*] Can you explain it to me? [NORA *is still silent.*] It is a remarkable thing, too, that the words "2nd of October," as well as the year, are not written in your father's handwriting but in one that I think I know. Well, of course it can be explained; your father may have forgotten to date his signature, and someone else may have dated it haphazard before they knew of his death. There is no harm in that. It all depends on the signature of the name; and *that* is genuine, I suppose, Mrs. Helmer? It was your father himself who signed his name here?

NORA. [*after a short pause, throws her head up and looks defiantly at him*] No, it was not. It was I that wrote papa's name.

KROGSTAD. Are you aware that is a dangerous confession?

NORA. In what way? You shall have your money soon.

KROGSTAD. Let me ask you a question; why did you not send the paper to your father?

NORA. It was impossible; papa was so ill. If I had asked him for his signature, I should have had to tell him what the money was to be used for; and when he was so ill himself I couldn't tell him that my husband's life was in danger—it was impossible.

KROGSTAD. It would have been better for you if you had given up your trip abroad.

NORA. No, that was impossible. That trip was to save my husband's life; I couldn't give that up.

KROGSTAD. But did it never occur to you that you were committing a fraud on me? *Why is he so concerned about it? Is he just using this as blackmai*

NORA. I couldn't take that into account; I didn't trouble myself about you at all. I couldn't bear you, because you put so many heartless difficulties in my way, although you knew what a dangerous condition my husband was in.

KROGSTAD. Mrs. Helmer, you evidently do not realise clearly what it is that you have been guilty of. But I can assure you that my one false step, which lost me all my reputation, was nothing more or nothing worse than what you have done.

NORA. You? Do you ask me to believe that you were brave enough to run a risk to save your wife's life?

KROGSTAD. The law cares nothing about motives.

NORA. Then it must be a very foolish law.

KROGSTAD. Foolish or not, it is the law by which you will be judged, if I produce this paper in court.

NORA. I don't believe it. Is a daughter not to be allowed to spare her dying father anxiety and care? Is a wife not to be allowed to save her husband's life? I don't know much about law; but I am certain that there must be laws permitting such things as that. Have you no knowledge of such laws—you who are a lawyer? You must be a very poor lawyer, Mr. Krogstad.

KROGSTAD. Maybe. But matters of business—such business as you and I have had together—do you think I don't understand that? Very well. Do as you please. But let me tell you this—if I lose my position a second time, you shall lose yours with me. *what is her position: mother, wife*

[*He bows, and goes out through the hall.*]

NORA. [*appears buried in thought for a short time, then tosses her head*] Nonsense! Trying to frighten me like that!—I am not so silly as he thinks. [*begins to busy herself putting the children's things in order*] And yet——? No, it's impossible! I did it for love's sake.

THE CHILDREN. [*in the doorway on the left*] Mother, the stranger man has gone out through the gate.

NORA. Yes, dears, I know. But, don't tell anyone about the stranger man. Do you hear? Not even papa.

CHILDREN. No, mother; but will you come and play again?

NORA. No, no—not now.

CHILDREN. But, mother, you promised us.

NORA. Yes, but I can't now. Run away in; I have such a lot to do. Run away in, my sweet little darlings. [*She gets them into the room by degrees and shuts the door on them; then sits down on the sofa, takes up a piece of needlework and sews a few stitches, but soon stops.*] No! [*throws down the work, gets up, goes to the hall door and calls out*] Helen! bring the Tree in. [*goes to the table on the left, opens a drawer, and stops again*] No, no! it is quite impossible!

MAID. [*coming in with the Tree*] Where shall I put it, ma'am?

NORA. Here, in the middle of the floor.

MAID. Shall I get you anything else?

NORA. No, thank you. I have all I want.

[*Exit* MAID.]

[handwritten note in left margin: she is such a flit trys to make everything right by playing the Doll]

NORA. [*begins dressing the tree*] A candle here—and flowers here——. The horrible man! It's all nonsense—there's nothing wrong. The Tree shall be splendid! I will do everything I can think of to please you, Torvald!—I will sing for you, dance for you— [HELMER *comes in with some papers under his arm*] Oh! are you back already?

HELMER. Yes. Has anyone been here?

NORA. Here? No. *[handwritten: another lie]*

HELMER. That is strange. I saw Krogstad going out of the gate.

NORA. Did you? Oh yes, I forgot, Krogstad was here for a moment.

HELMER. Nora, I can see from your manner that he has been here begging you to say a good word for him.

NORA. Yes.

HELMER. And you were to appear to do it of your own accord; you were to conceal from me the fact of his having been here; didn't he beg that of you too?

NORA. Yes, Torvald, but—— *[handwritten: another lie]*

HELMER. Nora, Nora, and you would be a party to that sort of thing? To have any talk with a man like that, and give him any sort of promise? And to tell me a lie into the bargain? *[handwritten: that isn't the only talk & promise she has made with him]*

NORA. A lie——?

HELMER. Didn't you tell me no one had been here? [*shakes his finger at her*] My little song-bird must never do that again. A song-bird must have a clean beak to chirp with—no false notes! [*puts his arm round her waist*] That is so, isn't it? Yes, I am sure it is. [*lets her go*] We will say no more about it. [*sits down by the stove*] How warm and snug it is here!

[*Turns over his papers.*]

NORA. [*after a short pause, during which she busies herself with the Christmas Tree*] Torvald!

HELMER. Yes.

NORA. I am looking forward tremendously to the fancy dress ball at the Stenborgs' the day after to-morrow.

HELMER. And I am tremendously curious to see what you are going to surprise me with.

NORA. It was very silly of me to want to do that. *[handwritten: to do what? surprise him?]*

HELMER. What do you mean?

NORA. I can't hit upon anything that will do; everything I think of seems so silly and insignificant.

HELMER. Does my little Nora acknowledge that at last?

NORA. [*standing behind his chair with her arms on the back of it*] Are you very busy, Torvald?

HELMER. Well——

NORA. What are all those papers?

HELMER. Bank business.

NORA. Already?

HELMER. I have got authority from the retiring manager to undertake the necessary changes in the staff and in the rearrangement of the work; and I must make use of the Christmas week for that, so as to have everything in order for the new year.

She is trying to manipulate him again

NORA. Then that was why this poor Krogstad——

HELMER. Hm!

NORA. [*leans against the back of his chair and strokes his hair*] If you hadn't been so busy I should have asked you a tremendously big favour, Torvald.

HELMER. What is that? Tell me.

NORA. There is no one has such good taste as you. And I do so want to look nice at the fancy-dress ball. Torvald, couldn't you take me in hand and decide what I shall go as, and what sort of a dress I shall wear? *she manipulates him by making herself into a doll*

HELMER. Aha! so my obstinate little woman is obliged to get someone to come to her rescue?

NORA. Yes, Torvald, I can't get along a bit without your help.

HELMER. Very well, I will think it over, we shall manage to hit upon something.

NORA. That is nice of you. [*goes to the Christmas Tree. A short pause.*] How pretty the red flowers look——. But, tell me, was it really something very bad that this Krogstad was guilty of?

HELMER. He forged someone's name. Have you any idea what that means?

NORA. Isn't it possible that he was driven to do it by necessity?

HELMER. Yes; or, as in so many cases, by imprudence. I am not so heartless as to condemn a man altogether because of a single false step of that kind.

NORA. No you wouldn't, would you, Torvald?

HELMER. Many a man has been able to retrieve his character, if he has openly confessed his fault and taken his punishment.

NORA. Punishment——?

HELMER. But Krogstad did nothing of that sort; he got himself out of it by a cunning trick, and that is why he has gone under altogether.

NORA. But do you think it would——?

HELMER. Just think how a guilty man like that has to lie and play the hypocrite with everyone, how he has to wear a mask in the presence of those near and dear to him, even before his own wife and children. And about the children—that is the most terrible part of it all, Nora. *She has been guilty of wearing a mask*

NORA. How?

HELMER. Because such an atmosphere of lies infects and poisons the whole life of a home. Each breath the children take in such a house is full of the germs of evil.

NORA. [*coming nearer him*] Are you sure of that?

HELMER. My dear, I have often seen it in the course of my life as a lawyer. Almost everyone who has gone to the bad early in life has had a deceitful mother.

NORA. Why do you only say—mother?

HELMER. It seems most commonly to be the mother's influence, though naturally a bad father's would have the same result. Every lawyer is familiar with the fact. This Krogstad, now, has been persistently poisoning his own children with lies and dissimulation; that is why I say he has lost all moral character. [*holds out his hands to her*] That is why my sweet little Nora must promise me not to plead his

[handwritten: She is very guilty]

cause. Give me your hand on it. Come, come, what is this? Give me your hand. There now, that's settled. I assure you it would be quite impossible for me to work with him; I literally feel physically ill when I am in the company of such people. *[handwritten: Nora is in for it now]*

NORA. [*takes her hand out of his and goes to the opposite side of the Christmas Tree*] How hot it is in here; and I have such a lot to do.

HELMER. [*getting up and putting his papers in order*] Yes, and I must try and read through some of these before dinner; and I must think about your costume, too. And it is just possible I may have something ready in gold paper to hang up on the Tree. [*Puts his hand on her head.*] My precious little singing-bird!

[*He goes into his room and shuts the door after him.*]

NORA. [*after a pause, whispers*] No, no—it isn't true. It's impossible; it must be impossible.

[*The* NURSE *opens the door on the left.*]

NURSE. The little ones are begging so hard to be allowed to come in to mamma.
NORA. No, no, no! Don't let them come in to me! You stay with them, Anne.
NURSE. Very well, ma'am.

[*Shuts the door.*]

NORA. [*pale with terror*] Deprave my little children? Poison my home? [*a short pause. Then she tosses her head.*] It's not true. It can't possibly be true.

ACT 2

THE SAME SCENE.—*The Christmas Tree is in the corner by the piano, stripped of its ornaments and with burnt-down candle-ends on its dishevelled branches.* NORA'S *cloak and hat are lying on the sofa. She is alone in the room, walking about uneasily. She stops by the sofa and takes up her cloak.*

Nora. [*drops the cloak*] Someone is coming now! [*goes to the door and listens*] No—it is no one. Of course, no one will come to-day, Christmas Day—nor tomorrow either. But, perhaps— [*opens the door and looks out*] No, nothing in the letter-box; it is quite empty. [*comes forward*] What rubbish! of course he can't be in earnest about it. Such a thing couldn't happen; it is impossible—I have three little children.

[*Enter the* NURSE *from the room on the left, carrying a big cardboard box.*]

NURSE. At last I have found the box with the fancy dress.
NORA. Thanks; put it on the table.
NURSE. [*doing so*] But it is very much in want of mending.
NORA. I should like to tear it into a hundred thousand pieces.
NURSE. What an idea! It can easily be put in order—just a little patience.
NORA. Yes, I will go and get Mrs. Linde to come and help me with it.

[handwritten in left margin: Nora's spirit is becoming depraved and hardened and guilty like Krogstad's]

NURSE. What, out again? In this horrible weather? You will catch cold, ma'am, and make yourself ill.

NORA. Well, worse than that might happen. How are the children?

NURSE. The poor little souls are playing with their Christmas presents, but——

NORA. Do they ask much for me?

NURSE. You see, they are so accustomed to have their mamma with them.

NORA. Yes, but, nurse, I shall not be able to be so much with them now as I was before. *She's afraid of poisoning them, but perhaps they do better with her*

NURSE. Oh well, young children easily get accustomed to anything.

NORA. Do you think so? Do you think they would forget their mother if she went away altogether?

NURSE. Good heavens!—went away altogether?

NORA. Nurse, I want you to tell me something I have often wondered about—how could you have the heart to put your own child out among strangers?

NURSE. I was obliged to, if I wanted to be little Nora's nurse.

NORA. Yes, but how could you be willing to do it?

NURSE. What, when I was going to get such a good place by it? A poor girl who has got into trouble should be glad to. Besides, that wicked man didn't do a single thing for me. *Was nurse raped? divorced, got into trouble w/ boyfriend?*

NORA. But I suppose your daughter has quite forgotten you.

NURSE. No, indeed she hasn't. She wrote to me when she was confirmed, and when she was married.

NORA. [*putting her arms round her neck*] Dear old Anne, you were a good mother to me when I was little.

NURSE. Little Nora, poor dear, had no other mother but me.

NORA. And if my little ones had no other mother, I am sure you would—— What nonsense I am talking! [*opens the box*] Go in to them. Now I must——. You will see to-morrow how charming I shall look.

NURSE. I am sure there will be no one at the ball so charming as you, ma'am.

[*Goes into the room on the left.*]

NORA. [*begins to unpack the box, but soon pushes it away from her*] If only I dared go out. If only no one would come. If only I could be sure nothing would happen here in the meantime. Stuff and nonsense! No one will come. Only I mustn't think about it. I will brush my muff. What lovely, lovely gloves! Out of my thoughts, out of my thoughts! One, two, three, four, five, six—— [*screams.*] Ah! there is someone coming——. *how paranoid she's become*

[*Makes a movement towards the door, but stands irresolute.*]

[*Enter* MRS. LINDE *from the hall, where she has taken off her cloak and hat.*]

NORA. Oh, it's you, Christine. There is no one else out there, is there? How good of you to come!

MRS. LINDE. I heard you were up asking for me.

NORA. Yes, I was passing by. As a matter of fact, it is something you could help me

with. Let us sit down here on the sofa. Look here. To-morrow evening there is to
be a fancy-dress ball at the Stenborgs', who live above us; and Torvald wants me
to go as a Neapolitan fisher-girl, and dance the Tarantella that I learnt at Capri.

MRS. LINDE. I see; you are going to keep up the character.

NORA. Yes, Torvald wants me to. Look, here is the dress; Torvald had it made for
me there, but now it is all so torn, and I haven't any idea——

MRS. LINDE. We will easily put that right. It is only some of the trimming come
unsewn here and there. Needle and thread? Now then, that's all we want.

NORA. It *is* nice of you. *Doesn't Nora know how to sew?*

MRS. LINDE. [*seeing*] So you are going to be dressed up to-morrow, Nora. I will tell
you what—I shall come in for a moment and see you in your fine feathers. But I
have completely forgotten to thank you for a delightful evening yesterday.

NORA. [*gets up, and crosses the stage*] Well I don't think yesterday was as pleasant as
usual. You ought to have come to town a little earlier, Christine. Certainly Torvald
does understand how to make a house dainty and attractive.

MRS. LINDE. And so do you, it seems to me; you are not your father's daughter for
nothing. But tell me, is Doctor Rank always as depressed as he was yesterday?

NORA. No; yesterday it was very noticeable, I must tell you that he suffers from a
very dangerous disease. He has consumption of the spine, poor creature. His
father was a horrible man who committed all sorts of excesses; and that is why
his son was sickly from childhood, do you understand? *parent to child*

MRS. LINDE. [*dropping her sewing*] But, my dearest Nora, how do you know anything
about such things?

NORA. [*walking about*] Pooh! When you have three children, you get visits now and
then from—from married women, who know something of medical matters, and
they talk about one thing and another.

MRS. LINDE. [*goes on sewing. A short silence*] Does Doctor Rank come here every
day?

NORA. Every day regularly. He is Torvald's most intimate friend, and a great friend
of mine too. He is just like one of the family.

MRS. LINDE. But tell me this—is he perfectly sincere? I mean, isn't he the kind of
man that is very anxious to make himself agreeable?

NORA. Not in the least. What makes you think that?

MRS. LINDE. When you introduced him to me yesterday, he declared he had often
heard my name mentioned in this house; but afterwards I noticed that your husband
hadn't the slightest idea who I was. So how could Doctor Rank——?

NORA. That is quite right, Christine. Torvald is so absurdly fond of me that he wants
me absolutely to himself, as he says. At first he used to seem almost jealous if I
mentioned any of the dear folk at home, so naturally I gave up doing so. But I
often talk about such things with Doctor Rank, because he likes hearing about
them. *Sounds fishy. Is this another lie?*

MRS. LINDE. Listen to me, Nora. You are still very like a child in many things, and I
am older than you in many ways and have a little more experience. Let me tell
you this—you ought to make an end of it with Doctor Rank.

NORA. What ought I to make an end of?

MRS. LINDE. Of two things, I think. Yesterday you talked some nonsense about a rich admirer who was to leave you money——

NORA. An admirer who doesn't exist, unfortunately! But what then?

MRS. LINDE. Is Doctor Rank a man of means?

NORA. Yes, he is.

MRS. LINDE. And has no one to provide for?

NORA. No, no one; but——

MRS. LINDE. And comes here every day?

NORA. Yes, I told you so.

MRS. LINDE. But how can this well-bred man be so tactless?

NORA. I don't understand you at all.

MRS. LINDE. Don't prevaricate, Nora. Do you suppose I don't guess who lent you the two hundred and fifty pounds?

NORA. Are you out of your senses? How can you think of such a thing! A friend of ours, who comes here every day! Do you realise what a horribly painful position that would be?

MRS. LINDE. Then it really isn't he?

NORA. No, certainly not. It would never have entered into my head for a moment. Besides, he had no money to lend then; he came into his money afterwards.

MRS. LINDE. Well, I think that was lucky for you, my dear Nora.

NORA. No, it would never have come into my head to ask Doctor Rank. Although I am quite sure that if I had asked him——

MRS. LINDE. But of course you won't.

NORA. Of course not. I have no reason to think it could possibly be necessary. But I am quite sure that if I told Doctor Rank——

MRS. LINDE. Behind your husband's back?

NORA. I must make an end of it with the other one, and that will be behind his back too. I *must* make an end of it with him.

MRS. LINDE. Yes, that is what I told you yesterday, but——

NORA. [*walking up and down*] A man can put a thing like that straight much easier than a woman——

MRS. LINDE. One's husband, yes. ‑ what?

NORA. Nonsense! [*standing still*] When you pay off a debt you get your bond back, don't you?

MRS. LINDE. Yes, as a matter of course.

NORA. And can tear it into a hundred thousand pieces, and burn it up—the nasty dirty paper!

MRS. LINDE. [*looks hard at her, lays down her sewing and gets up slowly*] Nora, you are concealing something from me.

NORA. Do I look as if I were?

MRS. LINDE. Something has happened to you since yesterday morning. Nora, what is it?

NORA. [*going nearer to her*] Christine! [*listens*] Hush! there's Torvald come home. Do you mind going in to the children for the present? Torvald can't bear to see dressmaking going on. Let Anne help you.

MRS. LINDE. [*gathering some of the things together*] Certainly—but I am not going away from here till we have had it out with one another.

[*She goes into the room on the left, as* HELMER *comes in from the hall.*]

NORA. [*going up to* HELMER] I have wanted you so much, Torvald dear.

HELMER. Was that the dressmaker?

NORA. No, it was Christine; she is helping me to put my dress in order. You will see I shall look quite smart.

HELMER. Wasn't that a happy thought of mine, now?

NORA. Splendid! But don't you think it is nice of me, too, to do as you wish?

HELMER. Nice?—because you do as your husband wishes? Well, well, you little rogue. I am sure you did not mean it in that way. But I am not going to disturb you; you will want to be trying on your dress, I expect.

her husband takes her for granted

NORA. I suppose you are going to work.

HELMER. Yes. [*shows her a bundle of papers*] Look at that. I have just been into the bank.   [*Turns to go into his room*]

NORA. Torvald.

HELMER. Yes.

NORA. If your little squirrel were to ask you for something very, very prettily——?

HELMER. What then?

NORA. Would you do it?

HELMER. I should like to hear what it is, first.

NORA. Your squirrel would run about and do all her tricks if you would be nice, and do what she wants.

HELMER. Speak plainly.

NORA. Your skylark would chirp about in every room, with her song rising and falling——

HELMER. Well, my skylark does that anyhow.

NORA. I would play the fairy and dance for you in the moonlight, Torvald.

what is it with her playacting? like a child

HELMER. Nora—you surely don't mean that request you made of me this morning?

NORA. [*going near him*] Yes, Torvald, I beg you so earnestly——

HELMER. Have you really the courage to open up that question again?

NORA. Yes, dear, you *must* do as I ask; you *must* let Krogstad keep his post in the Bank.

HELMER. My dear Nora, it is his post that I have arranged Mrs. Linde shall have.

NORA. Yes, you have been awfully kind about that; but you could just as well dismiss some other clerk instead of Krogstad.

HELMER. This is simply incredible obstinacy! Because you chose to give him a thoughtless promise that you would speak for him. I am expected to——

NORA. That isn't the reason, Torvald. It is for your own sake. This fellow writes in the most scurrilous newspapers; you have told me so yourself. He can do you an unspeakable amount of harm. I am frightened to death of him——

HELMER. Ah, I understand; it is recollections of the past that scare you.

NORA. What do you mean?

HELMER. Naturally you are thinking of your father.

NORA. Yes—yes, of course. Just recall to your mind what these malicious creatures wrote in the papers about papa, and how horribly they slandered him. I believe they would have procured his dismissal if the Department had not sent you over to inquire into it, and if you had not been so kindly disposed and helpful to him. *what did he do?   father to daughter*

HELMER. My little Nora, there is an important difference between your father and me. Your father's reputation as a public official was not above suspicion. Mine is, and I hope it will continue to be so, as long as I hold my office.

NORA. You never can tell what mischief these men may contrive. We ought to be so well off, so snug and happy here in our peaceful home, and have no cares—you and I and the children, Torvald! That is why I beg you so earnestly——

HELMER. And it is just by interceding for him that you make it impossible for me to keep him. It is already known at the Bank that I mean to dismiss Krogstad. Is it to get about now that the new manager has changed his mind at his wife's bidding——

NORA. And what if it did?

HELMER. Of course!—if only this obstinate little person can get her way! Do you suppose I am going to make myself ridiculous before my whole staff, to let people think that I am a man to be swayed by all sorts of outside influence? I should very soon feel the consequences of it, I can tell you! And besides, there is one thing that makes it quite impossible for me to have Krogstad in the Bank as long as I am manager.

NORA. Whatever is that?

HELMER. His moral failings I might perhaps have overlooked, if necessary——

NORA. Yes, you could—couldn't you.

HELMER. And I hear he is a good worker, too. But I knew him when we were boys. It was one of those rash friendships that so often prove an incubus in after life. I may as well tell you plainly, we were once on very intimate terms with one another. But this tactless fellow lays no restraint on himself when other people are present. On the contrary, he thinks it gives him the right to adopt a familiar tone with me, and every minute it is "I say, Helmer, old fellow!" and that sort of thing. I assure you it is extremely painful for me. He would make my position in the Bank intolerable.

NORA. Torvald, I don't believe you mean that.

HELMER. Don't you? Why not?

NORA. Because it is such a narrow-minded way of looking at things.

HELMER. What are you saying? Narrow-minded? Do you think I am narrow-minded?

NORA. No, just the opposite, dear—and it is exactly for that reason.

HELMER. It's the same thing. You say my point of view is narrow-minded, so I must be so too. Narrow-minded! Very well—I must put an end to this. [*Goes to the hall-door and calls.*] Helen!

NORA. What are you going to do?

HELMER. [*looking among his papers*] Settle it. [*Enter* MAID.] Look here; take this letter and go downstairs with it at once. Find a messenger and tell him to deliver it, and be quick. The address is on it, and here is the money.

MAID. Very well, sir.

[*Exit with the letter.*]

HELMER. [*putting his papers together*] Now then, little Miss Obstinate.

NORA. [*breathlessly*] Torvald—what was that letter?

HELMER. Krogstad's dismissal.

NORA. Call her back, Torvald! There is still time. Oh Torvald, call her back! Do it for my sake—for your own sake—for the children's sake! Do you hear me, Torvald? Call her back! You don't know what that letter can bring upon us.

HELMER. It's too late.

NORA. Yes, it's too late.

HELMER. My dear Nora, I can forgive the anxiety you are in, although really it is an insult to me. It is, indeed. Isn't it an insult to think that I should be afraid of a starving quill-driver's vengeance? But I forgive you nevertheless, because it is such eloquent witness to your great love for me. [*takes her in his arms*] And that is as it should be, my own darling Nora. Come what will, you may be sure I shall have both courage and strength if they be needed. You will see I am man enough to take everything upon myself.

NORA. [*in a horror-stricken voice*] What do you mean by that?

HELMER. Everything, I say——

NORA. [*recovering herself*] You will never have to do that.

HELMER. That's right. Well, we will share it, Nora, as man and wife should. That is how it shall be. [*caressing her*] Are you content now? There! there!—not these frightened dove's eyes! The whole thing is only the wildest fancy!—Now, you must go and play through the Tarantella and practise with your tambourine. I shall go into the inner office and shut the door, and I shall hear nothing; you can make as much noise as you please. [*turns back at the door*] And when Rank comes, tell him where he will find me.

[*Nods to her, takes his papers and goes into his room, and shuts the door after him.*]

NORA. [*bewildered with anxiety, stands as if rooted to the spot, and whispers*] He is capable of doing it. He will do it. He will do it in spite of everything.—No, not that! Never, never! Anything rather than that! Oh, for some help, some way out of it! [*The door-bell rings.*] Doctor Rank! Anything rather than that—anything, whatever it is!

[*She puts her hands over her face, pulls herself together, goes to the door and opens it. RANK is standing without, hanging up his coat. During the following dialogue it begins to grow dark.*]

NORA Good-day, Doctor Rank. I knew your ring. But you mustn't go into Torvald now; I think he is busy with something.

RANK. And you?

NORA. [*brings him in and shuts the door after him*] Oh, you know very well I always have time for you.

RANK. Thank you. I shall make use of as much of it as I can.

NORA. What do you mean by that? As much of it as you can?

RANK. Well, does that alarm you? *is he making a pass at her?*

NORA. It was such a strange way of putting it. Is anything likely to happen?

RANK. Nothing but what I have long been prepared for. But I certainly didn't expect it to happen so soon.

NORA. [*gripping him by the arm*] What have you found out? Doctor Rank, you must tell me.

RANK. [*sitting down by the stove*] It is all up with me. And it can't be helped.

NORA. [*with a sigh of relief*] Is it about yourself?

RANK. Who else? It is no use lying to one's self. I am the most wretched of all my patients, Mrs. Helmer. Lately I have been taking stock of my internal economy. Bankrupt! Probably within a month I shall lie rotting in the churchyard.

NORA. What an ugly thing to say!

RANK. The thing itself is cursedly ugly, and the worst of it is that I shall have to face so much more that is ugly before that. I shall only make one more examination of myself; when I have done that, I shall know pretty certainly when it will be that the horrors of dissolution will begin. There is something I want to tell you. Helmer's refined nature gives him an unconquerable disgust at everything that is ugly; I won't have him in my sick-room.

NORA. Oh, but, Doctor Rank——

RANK. I won't have him there. Not on any account. I bar my door to him. As soon as I am quite certain that the worst has come, I shall send you my card with a black cross on it, and then you will know that the loathsome end has begun.

NORA. You are quite absurd to-day. And I wanted you so much to be in a really good humour.

RANK. With death stalking beside me?—To have to pay this penalty for another man's sin! Is there any justice in that! And in every single family, in one way or another, some such inexorable retribution is being exacted——

NORA. [*putting her hands over her ears*] Rubbish! Do talk of something cheerful.

RANK. Oh, it's a mere laughing matter, the whole thing. My poor innocent spine has to suffer for my father's youthful amusements.

NORA. [*sitting at the table on the left*] I suppose you mean that he was too partial to asparagus and pâté de foie gras, don't you.

RANK. Yes, and to truffles.

NORA. Truffles, yes. And oysters too, I suppose?

RANK. Oysters, of course, that goes without saying.

NORA. And heaps of port and champagne. It is sad that all these nice things should take their revenge on our bones.

RANK. Especially that they should revenge themselves on the unlucky bones of those who have not had the satisfaction of enjoying them.

NORA. Yes, that's the saddest part of it all.

RANK. [*with a searching look at her*] Hm!——

NORA. [*after a short pause*] Why did you smile?

RANK. No, it was you that laughed.

NORA. No, it was you that smiled, Doctor Rank!

RANK. [*rising*] You are a greater rascal than I thought.

NORA. I am in a silly mood to-day.

RANK. So it seems.

NORA. [*putting her hands on his shoulders*] Dear, dear Doctor Rank, death mustn't take you away from Torvald and me.

RANK. It is a loss you would easily recover from. Those who are gone are soon forgotten.

NORA. [*looking at him anxiously*] Do you believe that?

RANK. People form new ties, and then——

NORA. Who will form new ties?

RANK. Both you and Helmer, when I am gone. You yourself are already on the high road to it, I think. What did that Mrs. Linde want here last night?

NORA. Oho!—you don't mean to say you are jealous of poor Christine?

RANK. Yes, I am. She will be my successor in this house. When I am done for, this woman will—

NORA. Hush! don't speak so loud. She is in that room.

RANK. To-day again. There, you see.

NORA. She has only come to sew my dress for me. Bless my soul, how unreasonable you are! [*sits down on the sofa*] Be nice now, Doctor Rank, and to-morrow you will see how beautifully I shall dance, and you can imagine I am doing it all for you—and for Torvald too, of course. [*takes various things out of the box*] Doctor Rank, come and sit down here, and I will show you something.

RANK. [*sitting down*] What is it?

NORA. Just look at those!

RANK. Silk stockings.

NORA. Flesh-coloured. Aren't they lovely? It is so dark here now, but to-morrow—. No, no, no! you must only look at the feet. Oh well, you may have leave to look at the legs too.

RANK. Hm!—

NORA. Why are you looking so critical? Don't you think they will fit me?

RANK. I have no means of forming an opinion about that.

NORA. [*looks at him for a moment*] For shame! [*hits him lightly on the ear with the stockings*] That's to punish you. [*folds them up again*]

RANK. And what other nice things am I to be allowed to see?

NORA. Not a single thing more, for being so naughty. [*She looks among the things, humming to herself.*]

RANK. [*after a short silence*] When I am sitting here, talking to you as intimately as this, I cannot imagine for a moment what would have become of me if I had never come into this house.

NORA. [*smiling*] I believe you do feel thoroughly at home with us.

RANK. [*in a lower voice, looking straight in front of him*] And to be obliged to leave it all——

NORA. Nonsense, you are not going to leave it.

RANK. [*as before*] And not be able to leave behind one the slightest token of one's gratitude, scarcely even a fleeting regret—nothing but an empty place which the first comer can fill as well as any other.

NORA. And if I asked you now for a—? No!

RANK. For what?

NORA. For a big proof of your friendship——

RANK. Yes, yes!

NORA. I mean a tremendously big favour——

RANK. Would you really make me so happy for once?

NORA. Ah, but you don't know what it is yet.

RANK. No—but tell me.

NORA. I really can't, Doctor Rank. It is something out of all reason; it means advice, and help, and a favour——

RANK. The bigger a thing it is the better. I can't conceive what it is you mean. Do tell me. Haven't I your confidence?

NORA. More than anyone else. I know you are my truest and best friend, and so I will tell you what it is. Well, Doctor Rank, it is something you must help me to prevent. You know how devotedly, how inexpressibly deeply Torvald loves me; he would never for a moment hesitate to give his life for me.

RANK. [*leaning towards her*] Nora—do you think he is the only one——?

NORA. [*with a slight start*] The only one—?

RANK. The only one who would gladly give his life for your sake.

NORA. [*sadly*] Is that it?   *He is in love with her?*

RANK. I was determined you should know it before I went away, and there will never be a better opportunity than this. Now you know it, Nora. And now you know, too, that you can trust me as you would trust no one else.

NORA. [*rises, deliberately and quietly*] Let me pass.

RANK. [*makes room for her to pass him, but sits still*] Nora!

NORA. [*at the hall door*] Helen, bring in the lamp. [*goes over to the stove*] Dear Doctor Rank, that was really horrid of you.

RANK. To have loved you as much as anyone else does? Was that horrid?

NORA. No, but to go and tell me so. There was really no need——

RANK. What do you mean? Did you know——? [MAID *enters with lamp, puts it down on the table, and goes out.*] Nora—Mrs. Helmer—tell me, had you any idea of this?

NORA. Oh, how do I know whether I had or whether I hadn't? I really can't tell you—To think you could be so clumsy, Doctor Rank! We were getting on so nicely.

RANK. Well, at all events you know now that you can command me, body and soul. So won't you speak out?

NORA. [*looking at him*] After what happened?

RANK. I beg you to let me know what it is.

NORA. I can't tell you anything now.

RANK. Yes, yes. You mustn't punish me in that way. Let me have permission to do for you whatever a man may do.

NORA. You can do nothing for me now. Besides, I really don't need any help at all.

You will find that the whole thing is merely fancy on my part. It really is so—of course it is! [*Sits down in the rocking-chair, and looks at him with a smile*] You are a nice sort of man, Doctor Rank!—don't you feel ashamed of yourself, now the lamp has come?

RANK. Not a bit. But perhaps I had better go—for ever?

NORA. No, indeed, you shall not. Of course you must come here just as before. You know very well Torvald can't do without you.

RANK. Yes, but you?

NORA. Oh, I am always tremendously pleased when you come.

RANK. It is just that, that put me on the wrong track. You are a riddle to me. I have often thought that you would almost as soon be in my company as in Helmer's.

NORA. Yes—you see there are some people one loves best, and others whom one would almost always rather have as companions.

RANK. Yes, there is something in that.

NORA. When I was at home, of course I loved papa best. But I always thought it tremendous fun if I could steal down into the maid's room, because they never moralised at all, and talked to each other about such entertaining things.

RANK. I see—it is *their* place I have taken.

NORA. [*jumping up and going to him*] Oh, dear, nice Doctor Rank, I never meant that at all. But surely you can understand that being with Torvald is a little like being with papa——

[*Enter* MAID *from the hall*]

MAID. If you please, ma'am. [*whispers and hands her a card*]

NORA. [*glancing at the card*] Oh! [*puts it in her pocket*]

RANK. Is there anything wrong?

NORA. No, no, not in the least. It is only something—it is my new dress——

RANK. What? Your dress is lying there.

NORA. Oh, yes, that one; but this is another. I ordered it. Torvald mustn't know about it——

RANK. Oho! Then that was the great secret.

NORA. Of course. Just go in to him; he is sitting in the inner room. Keep him as long as——

RANK. Make your mind easy; I won't let him escape. [*goes into* HELMER'S *room*]

NORA. [*to the* MAID] And he is standing waiting in the kitchen?

MAID. Yes; he came up the back stairs.

NORA. But didn't you tell him no one was in?

MAID. Yes, but it was no good.

NORA. He won't go away?

MAID. No; he says he won't until he has seen you, ma'am.

NORA. Well, let him come in—but quietly, Helen, you mustn't say anything about it to anyone. It is a surprise for my husband.

MAID. Yes, ma'am, I quite understand.   [*Exit.*]

NORA. This dreadful thing is going to happen! It will happen in spite of me! No, no, no, it can't happen—it shan't happen!

[*She bolts the door of* HELMER'S *room. The* MAID *opens the hall door for* KROGSTAD *and shuts it after him. He is wearing a fur coat, high boots and a fur cap.*]

he seems to be well off

NORA. [*advancing towards him*] Speak low—my husband is at home.

KROGSTAD. No matter about that.

NORA. What do you want of me?

KROGSTAD. An explanation of something.

NORA. Make haste then. What is it?

KROGSTAD. You know, I suppose, that I have got my dismissal.

NORA. I couldn't prevent it, Mr. Krogstad. I fought as hard as I could on your side, but it was no good.

KROGSTAD. Does your husband love you so little, then? He knows what I can expose you to, and yet he ventures——

NORA. How can you suppose that he has any knowledge of the sort?

KROGSTAD. I didn't suppose so at all. It would not be the least like our dear Torvald Helmer to show so much courage—

NORA. Mr. Krogstad, a little respect for my husband, please.

KROGSTAD. Certainly—all the respect he deserves. But since you have kept the matter so carefully to yourself, I make bold to suppose that you have a little clearer idea, than you had yesterday, of what it actually is that you have done?

NORA. More than you could ever teach me.

KROGSTAD. Yes, such a bad lawyer as I am.

NORA. What is it you want of me?

KROGSTAD. Only to see how you were, Mrs. Helmer. I have been thinking about you all day long. A mere cashier, a quill-driver, a—well, a man like me—even he has a little of what is called feeling, you know.

NORA. Show it, then; think of my little children.

KROGSTAD. Have you and your husband thought of mine? But never mind about that. I only wanted to tell you that you need not take this matter too seriously. In the first place there will be no accusation made on my part.

NORA. No, of course not; I was sure of that.

KROGSTAD. The whole thing can be arranged amicably; there is no reason why anyone should know anything about it. It will remain a secret between us three.

NORA. My husband must never get to know anything about it.

KROGSTAD. How will you be able to prevent it? Am I to understand that you can pay the balance that is owing?

NORA. No, not just at present.

KROGSTAD. Or perhaps that you have some expedient for raising the money soon?

NORA. No expedient that I mean to make use of.

KROGSTAD. Well, in any case, it would have been of no use to you now. If you stood there with ever so much money in your hand, I would never part with your bond.

NORA. Tell me what purpose you mean to put it to.

KROGSTAD. I shall only preserve it—keep it in my possession. No one who is not concerned in the matter shall have the slightest hint of it. So that if the thought of it has driven you to any desperate resolution——

NORA. It has.

KROGSTAD. If you had it in your mind to run away from your home——

NORA. I had.

KROGSTAD. Or even something worse——

NORA. How could you know that?

KROGSTAD. Give up the idea.

NORA. How did you know I had thought of *that?*

KROGSTAD. Most of us think of that at first. I did, too—but I hadn't the courage.

NORA. [*faintly*] No more had I.

KROGSTAD. [*in a tone of relief*] No, that's it, isn't it—you hadn't the courage either?

NORA. No, I haven't—I haven't.

KROGSTAD. Besides, it would have been a great piece of folly. Once the first storm at home is over—. I have a letter for your husband in my pocket.

NORA. Telling him everything?

KROGSTAD. In as lenient a manner as I possibly could.

NORA. [*quickly*] He mustn't get the letter. Tear it up. I will find some means of getting money.

KROGSTAD. Excuse me, Mrs. Helmer, but I think I told you just now——

NORA. I am not speaking of what I owe you. Tell me what sum you are asking my husband for, and I will get the money.

KROGSTAD. I am not asking your husband for a penny.

NORA. What do you want, then?

KROGSTAD. I will tell you. I want to rehabilitate myself, Mrs. Helmer; I want to get on; and in that your husband must help me. For the last year and a half I have not had a hand in anything dishonourable, and all that time I have been struggling in most restricted circumstances. I was content to work my way up step by step. Now I am turned out, and I am not going to be satisfied with merely being taken into favour again. I want to get on, I tell you. I want to get into the Bank again, in a higher position. Your husband must make a place for me——

NORA. That he will never do!

KROGSTAD. He will; I know him; he dare not protest. And as soon as I am in there again with him, then you will see! Within a year I shall be the manager's right hand. It will be Nils Krogstad and not Torvald Helmer who manages the Bank.

NORA. That's a thing you will never see!

KROGSTAD. Do you mean that you will——?

NORA. I have courage enough for it now.

KROGSTAD. Oh, you can't frighten me. A fine, spoilt lady like you——

NORA. You will see, you will see.

KROGSTAD. Under the ice, perhaps? Down into the cold, coal-black water? And then, in the spring, to float up to the surface, all horrible and unrecognisable, with your hair fallen out——

NORA. You can't frighten me.

KROGSTAD. Nor you me. People don't do such things, Mrs. Helmer. Besides, what use would it be? I should have him completely in my power all the same.

NORA. Afterwards? When I am no longer——

KROGSTAD. Have you forgotten that it is I who have the keeping of your reputation? [NORA *stands speechlessly looking at him.*] Well, now, I have warned you. Do not do anything foolish. When Helmer has had my letter, I shall expect a message from him. And be sure you remember that it is your husband himself who has forced me into such ways as this again. I will never forgive him for that. Good-bye, Mrs. Helmer. [*Exit through the hall*]

NORA. [*goes to the hall door, opens it slightly and listens*] He is going. He is not putting the letter in the box. Oh no, no! that's impossible! [*opens the door by degrees*] What is that? He is standing outside. He is not going downstairs. Is he hesitating? Can he——

[A *letter drops into the box; then* KROGSTAD'S *footsteps are heard, till they die away as he goes downstairs.* NORA *utters a stifled cry and runs across the room to the table by the sofa. A short pause.*]

NORA. In the letter-box. [*steals across to the hall door*] There it lies—Torvald, Torvald, there is no hope for us now!

[MRS. LINDE *comes in from the room on the left, carrying the dress.*]

MRS. LINDE. There, I can't see anything more to mend now. Would you like to try it on——?

NORA. [*in a hoarse whisper*] Christine, come here.

MRS. LINDE. [*throwing the dress down on the sofa*] What is the matter with you? You look so agitated!

NORA. Come here. Do you see that letter? There, look—you can see it through the glass in the letter-box.

MRS. LINDE. Yes, I see it.

NORA. That letter is from Krogstad.

MRS. LINDE. Nora—it was Krogstad who lent you the money!

NORA. Yes, and now Torvald will know all about it.

MRS. LINDE. Believe me, Nora, that's the best thing for both of you.

NORA. You don't know all. I forged a name.

MRS. LINDE. Good heavens——!

NORA. I only want to say this to you, Christine—you must be my witness.

MRS. LINDE. Your witness? What do you mean? What am I to—?

NORA. If I should go out of my mind—and it might easily happen——

MRS. LINDE. Nora!

NORA. Or if anything else should happen to me—anything, for instance, that might prevent my being here—

MRS. LINDE. Nora! Nora! you are quite out of your mind.

NORA. And if it should happen that there were someone who wanted to take all the responsibility, all the blame, you understand——

MRS. LINDE. Yes, yes—but how can you suppose—?

NORA. Then you must be my witness, that it is not true, Christine. I am not out of my mind at all; I am in my right senses now, and I tell you no one else has known anything about it; I, and I alone, did the whole thing. Remember that.

MRS. LINDE. I will, indeed. But I don't understand all this.

NORA. How should you understand it? A wonderful thing is going to happen.

MRS. LINDE. A wonderful thing?

NORA. Yes, a wonderful thing!—But it is so terrible, Christine; it *mustn't* happen, not for all the world.

MRS. LINDE. I will go at once and see Krogstad.

NORA. Don't go to him; he will do you some harm.

MRS. LINDE. There was a time when he would gladly do anything for my sake.

NORA. He?

MRS. LINDE. Where does he live?

NORA. How should I know—? Yes [*feeling in her pocket*] here is his card. But the letter, the letter——!

HELMER. [*calls from his room, knocking at the door*] Nora!

NORA. [*calls out anxiously*] Oh, what's that? What do you want?

HELMER. Don't be so frightened. We are not coming in; you have locked the door. Are you trying on your dress?

NORA. Yes, that's it. I look so nice, Torvald.

MRS. LINDE. [*who has read the card*] I see he lives at the corner here.

NORA. Yes, but it's no use. It is hopeless. The letter is lying there in the box.

MRS. LINDE. And your husband keeps the key?

NORA. Yes, always.

MRS. LINDE. Krogstad must ask for his letter back unread, he must find some pretence——

NORA. But it is just at this time that Torvald generally——

MRS. LINDE. You must delay him. Go in to him in the meantime. I will come back as soon as I can.

[*She goes out hurridly through the hall door.*]

NORA. [*goes to* HELMER'S *door, opens it and peeps in*] Torvald!

HELMER. [*from the inner room*] Well? May I venture at last to come into my own room again? Come along, Rank, now you will see— [*halting in the doorway*] But what is this?

NORA. What is what, dear?

HELMER. Rank led me to expect a splendid transformation.

RANK. [*in the doorway*] I understood so, but evidently I was mistaken.

NORA. Yes, nobody is to have the chance of admiring me in my dress until to-morrow.

HELMER. But, my dear Nora, you look so worn out. Have you been practising too much?

NORA. No, I have not practised at all.

HELMER. But you will need to—

NORA. Yes, indeed I shall, Torvald. But I can't get on a bit without you to help me; I have absolutely forgotten the whole thing.

HELMER. Oh, we will soon work it up again.

NORA. Yes, help me, Torvald. Promise that you will! I am so nervous about it—all the people—. You must give yourself up to me entirely this evening. Not the tiniest bit of business—you mustn't even take a pen in your hand. Will you promise, Torvald dear?

HELMER. I promise. This evening I will be wholly and absolutely at your service, you helpless little mortal. Ah, by the way, first of all I will just—

[*Goes towards the hall door*]

NORA. What are you going to do there?

HELMER. Only see if any letters have come.

NORA. No, no! don't do that, Torvald!

HELMER. Why not?

NORA. Torvald, please don't. There is nothing there.

HELMER. Well, let me look. [*Turns to go to the letter-box.* NORA, *at the piano, plays the first bars of the Tarantella.* HELMER *stops in the doorway.*] Aha!

NORA. I can't dance to-morrow if I don't practice with you.

HELMER. [*going up to her*] Are you really so afraid of it, dear.

NORA. Yes, so dreadfully afraid of it. Let me practise at once; there is time now, before we go to dinner. Sit down and play for me, Torvald dear; criticise me, and correct me as you play.

HELMER. With great pleasure, if you wish me to.

[*Sits down at the piano.*]

NORA. [*takes out of the box a tambourine and a long variegated shawl. She hastily drapes the shawl round her. Then she springs to the front of the stage and calls out.*] Now play for me! I am going to dance!

[HELMER *plays and* NORA *dances.* RANK *stands by the piano behind* HELMER *and looks on.*]

HELMER. [*as he plays*] Slower, slower!

NORA. I can't do it any other way.

HELMER. Not so violently, Nora!

NORA. This is the way.

HELMER. [*stops playing*] No, no—that is not a bit right.

NORA. [*laughing and swinging the tambourine*] Didn't I tell you so?

RANK. Let me play for her.

HELMER. [*getting up*] Yes, do. I can correct her better then.

[RANK *sits down at the piano and plays.* NORA *dances more and more wildly.* HELMER *has taken up a position beside the stove, and during her dance gives her frequent instructions. She does not seem to hear him; her hair comes down and falls over her shoulders; she pays no attention to it, but goes on dancing. Enter* MRS. LINDE.]

MRS. LINDE. [*standing as if spell-bound in the doorway*] Oh!——

NORA. [*as she dances*] Such fun, Christine!

HELMER. My dear darling Nora, you are dancing as if your life depended on it.

NORA. So it does.

HELMER. Stop, Rank; this is sheer madness. Stop, I tell you! [RANK *stops playing, and* NORA *suddenly stands still.* HELMER *goes up to her.*] I could never have believed it. You have forgotten everything I taught you.

NORA. [*throwing away the tambourine*] There, you see.

HELMER. You will want a lot of coaching.

NORA. Yes, you see how much I need it. You must coach me up to the last minute. Promise me that, Torvald!

HELMER. You can depend on me.

NORA. You must not think of anything but me, either to-day or to-morrow; you mustn't open a single letter—not even open the letter-box——

HELMER. Ah, you are still afraid of that fellow——

NORA. Yes, indeed I am.

HELMER. Nora, I can tell from your looks that there is a letter from him lying there.

NORA. I don't know; I think there is; but you must not read anything of that kind now. Nothing horrid must come between us till this is all over.

RANK. [*whispers to* HELMER] You mustn't contradict her.

HELMER. [*taking her in his arms*] The child shall have her way. But to-morrow night, after you have danced——

NORA. Then you will be free.

[*The* MAID *appears in the doorway to the right.*]

MAID. Dinner is served, ma'am.

NORA. We will have champagne, Helen.

MAID. Very good, ma'am.   [*Exit.*]

HELMER. Hullo!—are we going to have a banquet?

NORA. Yes, a champagne banquet till the small hours. [*calls out*] And a few macaroons, Helen—lots, just for once!

HELMER. Come, come, don't be so wild and nervous. Be my own little skylark, as you used.

NORA. Yes, dear, I will. But go in now and you too, Doctor Rank. Christine, you must help me to do up my hair.

RANK. [*whispers to* HELMER *as they go out*] I suppose there is nothing—she is not expecting anything?

HELMER. Far from it, my dear fellow; it is simply nothing more than this childish nervousness I was telling you of.

[*They go into the right-hand room.*]

NORA. Well!

MRS. LINDE. Gone out of town.

NORA. I could tell from your face.

MRS. LINDE. He is coming home to-morrow evening. I wrote a note for him.

NORA. You should have let it alone; you must prevent nothing. After all, it is splendid to be waiting for a wonderful thing to happen.

MRS. LINDE. What is it that you are waiting for?

NORA. Oh, you wouldn't understand. Go in to them, I will come in a moment. [MRS. LINDE *goes into the dining-room.* NORA *stands still for a little while, as if to compose herself. Then she looks at her watch.*] Five o'clock. Seven hours till midnight; and then four-and-twenty hours till the next midnight. Then the Tarantella will be over. Twenty-four and seven? Thirty-one hours to live.

HELMER. [*from the doorway on the right*] Where's my little skylark?

NORA. [*going to him with her arms outstretched*] Here she is!

ACT 3

THE SAME SCENE. *The table has been placed in the middle of the stage, with chairs round it. A lamp is burning on the table. The door into the hall stands open. Dance music is heard in the room above.* MRS. LINDE *is sitting at the table idly turning over the leaves of a book; she tries to read, but does not seem able to collect her thoughts. Every now and then she listens intently for a sound at the outer door.*

MRS. LINDE. [*looking at her watch*] Not yet—and the time is nearly up. If only he does not—. [*listens again*] Ah, there he is. [*Goes into the hall and opens the outer door carefully. Light footsteps are heard on the stairs. She whispers.*] Come in. There is no one here.

KROGSTAD. [*in the doorway*] I found a note from you at home. What does this mean?

MRS. LINDE. It is absolutely necessary that I should have a talk with you.

KROGSTAD. Really? And is it absolutely necessary that it should be here?

MRS. LINDE. It is impossible where I live; there is no private entrance to my rooms. Come in; we are quite alone. The maid is asleep, and the Helmers are at the dance upstairs.

KROGSTAD. [*coming into the room*] Are the Helmers really at a dance to-night?

MRS. LINDE. Yes, why not?

KROGSTAD. Certainly—why not?

MRS. LINDE. Now, Nils, let us have a talk.

KROGSTAD. Can we two have anything to talk about?

MRS. LINDE. We have a great deal to talk about.

KROGSTAD. I shouldn't have thought so.

MRS. LINDE. No, you have never properly understood me.

KROGSTAD. Was there anything else to understand except what was obvious to all the world—a heartless woman jilts a man when a more lucrative chance turns up?

MRS. LINDE. Do you believe I am as absolutely heartless as all that? And do you believe that I did it with a light heart?

KROGSTAD. Didn't you?

MRS. LINDE. Nils, did you really think that?

KROGSTAD. If it were as you say, why did you write to me as you did at the time?

Mrs. Linde. I could do nothing else. As I had to break with you, it was my duty also to put an end to all that you felt for me.

Krogstad. [*wringing his hands*] So that was it. And all this—only for the sake of money!

Mrs. Linde. You must not forget that I had a helpless mother and two little brothers. We couldn't wait for you, Nils; your prospects seemed hopeless then.

Krogstad. That may be so, but you had no right to throw me over for any one else's sake.

Mrs. Linde. Indeed I don't know. Many a time did I ask myself if I had the right to do it.

Krogstad. [*more gently*] When I lost you, it was as if all the solid ground went from under my feet. Look at me now—I am a shipwrecked man clinging to a bit of wreckage.

Mrs. Linde. But help may be near.

Krogstad. It *was* near; but then you came and stood in my way.

Mrs. Linde. Unintentionally, Nils. It was only to-day that I learnt it was your place I was going to take in the Bank.

Krogstad. I believe you, if you say so. But now that you know it, are you not going to give it up to me?

Mrs. Linde. No, because that would not benefit you in the least.

Krogstad. Oh, benefit, benefit—I would have done it whether or no.

Mrs. Linde. I have learnt to act prudently. Life, and hard, bitter necessity have taught me that.

Krogstad. And life has taught me not to believe in fine speeches.

Mrs. Linde. Then life has taught you something very reasonable. But deeds you must believe in?

Krogstad. What do you mean by that?

Mrs. Linde. You said you were like a shipwrecked man clinging to some wreckage.

Krogstad. I had good reason to say so.

Mrs. Linde. Well, I am like a shipwrecked woman clinging to some wreckage—no one to mourn for, no one to care for.

Krogstad. It was your own choice.

Mrs. Linde. There was no other choice—then.

Krogstad. Well, what now?

Mrs. Linde. Nils, how would it be if we two shipwrecked people could join forces?

Krogstad. What are you saying?

Mrs. Linde. Two on the same piece of wreckage would stand a better chance than each on their own.

Krogstad. Christine!

Mrs. Linde. What do you suppose brought me to town?

Krogstad. Do you mean that you gave me a thought?

Mrs. Linde. I could not endure life without work. All my life, as long as I can remember, I have worked, and it has been my greatest and only pleasure. But now I am quite alone in the world—my life is so dreadfully empty and I feel so forsaken. There is not the least pleasure in working for one's self. Nils, give me someone and something to work for.

KROGSTAD. I don't trust that. It is nothing but a woman's overstrained sense of generosity that prompts you to make such an offer of yourself.

MRS. LINDE. Have you ever noticed anything of the sort in me?

KROGSTAD. Could you really do it? Tell me—do you know all about my past life?

MRS. LINDE. Yes.

KROGSTAD. And do you know what they think of me here?

MRS. LINDE. You seemed to me to imply that with me you might have been quite another man.

KROGSTAD. I am certain of it.

MRS. LINDE. Is it too late now?

KROGSTAD. Christine, are you saying this deliberately? Yes, I am sure you are. I see it in your face. Have you really the courage, then—?

MRS. LINDE. I want to be a mother to someone, and your children need a mother. We two need each other. Nils, I have faith in your real character—I can dare anything together with you.

KROGSTAD. [*grasps her hands*] Thanks, thanks, Christine! Now I shall find a way to clear myself in the eyes of the world. Ah, but I forgot——

MRS. LINDE. [*listening*] Hush! The Tarantella! Go, go!

KROGSTAD. Why? What is it?

MRS. LINDE. Do you hear them up there? When that is over, we may expect them back.

KROGSTAD. Yes, yes—I will go. But it is all no use. Of course you are not aware what steps I have taken in the matter of the Helmers.

MRS. LINDE. Yes, I know all about that.

KROGSTAD. And in spite of that have you the courage to—?

MRS. LINDE. I understand very well to what lengths a man like you might be driven by despair.

KROGSTAD. If I could only undo what I have done!

MRS. LINDE. You can. Your letter is lying in the letter-box now.

KROGSTAD. Are you sure of that?

MRS. LINDE. Quite sure, but——

KROGSTAD. [*with a searching look at her*] Is that what it all means?—that you want to save your friend at any cost? Tell me frankly. Is that it?

MRS. LINDE. Nils, a woman who has once sold herself for another's sake, doesn't do it a second time.

KROGSTAD. I will ask for my letter back.

MRS. LINDE. No, no.

KROGSTAD. Yes, of course I will. I will wait here till Helmer comes; I will tell him he must give me my letter back—that it only concerns my dismissal—that he is not to read it——

MRS. LINDE. No, Nils, you must not recall your letter.

KROGSTAD. But, tell me, wasn't it for that very purpose that you asked me to meet you here?

MRS. LINDE. In my first moment of fright, it was. But twenty-four hours have elapsed since then, and in that time I have witnessed incredible things in this house. Helmer must know all about it. This unhappy secret must be disclosed; they must have a complete understanding between them, which is impossible with all this concealment and falsehood going on.

KROGSTAD. Very well, if you will take the responsibility. But there is one thing I can do in any case, and I shall do it at once.

MRS. LINDE. [*listening*] You must be quick and go! The dance is over; we are not safe a moment longer.

KROGSTAD. I will wait for you below.

MRS. LINDE. Yes, do. You must see me back to my door.

KROGSTAD. I have never had such an amazing piece of good fortune in my life.

[*Goes out through the outer door. The door between the room and the hall remains open.*]

MRS. LINDE. [*tidying up the room and laying her hat and cloak ready*] What a difference! what a difference! Someone to work for and live for—a home to bring comfort into. That I will do, indeed. I wish they would be quick and come— [*listens*] Ah, there they are now. I must put on my things.

[*Takes up her hat and cloak.* HELMER's *and* NORA's *voices are heard outside; a key is turned, and* HELMER *brings* NORA *almost by force into the hall. She is in an Italian costume with a large black shawl round her; he is in evening dress and a black domino which is flying open.*]

NORA. [*hanging back in the doorway, and struggling with him*] No, no, no!—don't take me in. I want to go upstairs again; I don't want to leave so early.

HELMER. But, my dearest Nora——

NORA. Please, Torvald dear—please, *please*—only an hour more.

HELMER. Not a single minute, my sweet Nora. You know that was our agreement. Come along into the room; you are catching cold standing there.

[*He brings her gently into the room, in spite of her resistance.*]

MRS. LINDE. Good evening.

NORA. Christine!

HELMER. You here, so late, Mrs. Linde?

MRS. LINDE. Yes, you must excuse me; I was so anxious to see Nora in her dress.

NORA. Have you been sitting here waiting for me?

MRS. LINDE. Yes, unfortunately I came too late, you had already gone upstairs; and I thought I couldn't go away again without having seen you.

HELMER. [*taking off* NORA's *shawl*] Yes, take a good look at her. I think she is worth looking at. Isn't she charming, Mrs. Linde?

MRS. LINDE. Yes, indeed she is.

HELMER. Doesn't she look remarkably pretty? Everyone thought so at the dance. But she is terribly self-willed, this sweet little person. What are we to do with her? You will hardly believe that I had almost to bring her away by force.

NORA. Torvald, you will repent not having let me stay, even if it were only for half an hour.

HELMER. Listen to her, Mrs. Linde! She had danced her Tarantella, and it had been a tremendous success, as it deserved—although possibly the performance was a trifle too realistic—a little more so, I mean, than was strictly compatible with the limitations of art. But never mind about that! The chief thing is, she had made a success—she had made a tremendous success. Do you think I was going to let her remain there after that, and spoil the effect? No indeed! I took my charming little Capri maiden—my capricious little Capri maiden, I should say—on my arm; took one quick turn round the room; a curtsey on either side, and, as they say in novels, the beautiful apparition disappeared. An exit ought always to be effective, Mrs. Linde; but that is what I cannot make Nora understand. Pooh! this room is hot. [*throws his domino on a chair and opens the door of his room*] Hullo! it's all dark in here. Oh, of course—excuse me——.

[*He goes in and lights some candles.*]

NORA. [*in a hurried and breathless whisper*] Well?

MRS. LINDE. [*in a low voice*] I have had a talk with him.

NORA. Yes, and——

MRS. LINDE. Nora, you must tell your husband all about it.

NORA. [*in an expressionless voice*] I knew it.

MRS. LINDE. You have nothing to be afraid of as far as Krogstad is concerned; but you must tell him.

NORA. I won't tell him.

MRS. LINDE. Then the letter will.

NORA. Thank you, Christine. Now I know what I must do. Hush——!

HELMER. [*coming in again*] Well, Mrs. Linde, have you admired her?

MRS. LINDE. Yes, and now I will say good-night.

HELMER. What, already? Is this yours, this knitting?

MRS. LINDE. [*taking it*] Yes, thank you, I had very nearly forgotten it.

HELMER. So you knit?

MRS. LINDE. Of course.

HELMER. Do you know, you ought to embroider.

MRS. LINDE. Really? Why?

HELMER. Yes, it's far more becoming. Let me show you. You hold the embroidery thus in your left hand, and use the needle with the right—like this—with a long, easy sweep. Do you see?

MRS. LINDE. Yes, perhaps——

HELMER. But in the case of knitting—that can never be anything but ungraceful; look here—the arms close together, the knitting-needles going up and down—it has a sort of Chinese effect—. That was really excellent champagne they gave us.

MRS. LINDE. Well,—good-night, Nora, and don't be self-willed any more.

HELMER. That's right, Mrs. Linde.

MRS. LINDE Good-night, Mr. Helmer.

HELMER. [*accompanying her to the door*] Good-night, good-night. I hope you will get home all right. I should be very happy to—but you haven't any great distance to go. Good-night, good-night. [*She goes out; he shuts the door after her, and comes in again.*] Ah!—at last we have got rid of her. She is a frightful bore, that woman.

NORA. Aren't you very tired, Torvald?

HELMER. No, not in the least.

NORA. Nor sleepy?

HELMER. Not a bit. On the contrary, I feel extraordinarily lively. And you?—you really look both tired and sleepy.

NORA. Yes, I am very tired. I want to go to sleep at once.

HELMER. There, you see it was quite right of me not to let you stay there any longer.

NORA. Everything you do is quite right, Torvald.

HELMER. [*kissing her on the forehead*] Now my little skylark is speaking reasonably. Did you notice what good spirits Rank was in this evening?

NORA. Really? Was he? I didn't speak to him at all.

HELMER. And I very little, but I have not for a long time seen him in such good form. [*looks for a while at her and then goes nearer to her*] It is delightful to be at home by ourselves again, to be all alone with you—you fascinating, charming little darling!

NORA. Don't look at me like that, Torvald.

HELMER. Why shouldn't I look at my dearest treasure?—at all the beauty that is mine, all my very own?

NORA. [*going to the other side of the table*] You mustn't say things like that to me to-night.

HELMER. [*following her*] You have still got the Tarantella in your blood, I see. And it makes you more captivating than ever. Listen—the guests are beginning to go now. [*in a lower voice*] Nora—soon the whole house will be quiet.

NORA. Yes, I hope so.

HELMER. Yes, my own darling Nora. Do you know, when I am out at a party with you like this, why I speak so little to you, keep away from you, and only send a stolen glance in your direction now and then?—do you know why I do that? It is because I make believe to myself that we are secretly in love, and you are my secretly promised bride, and that no one suspects there is anything between us.

NORA. Yes, yes—I know very well your thoughts are with me all the time.

HELMER. And when we are leaving, and I am putting the shawl over your beautiful young shoulders—on your lovely neck—then I imagine that you are my young bride and that we have just come from the wedding, and I am bringing you for the first time into our home—to be alone with you for the first time—quite alone with my shy little darling! All this evening I have longed for nothing but you. When I watched the seductive figures of the Tarantella, my blood was on fire; I could endure it no longer, and that was why I brought you down so early——

NORA. Go away, Torvald! You must let me go. I won't——

HELMER. What's that? You're joking, my little Nora! You won't—you won't? Am I not your husband—?

[*A knock is heard at the outer door.*]

NORA. [*staring*] Did you hear——?

HELMER. [*going into the hall*] Who is it?

RANK. [*outside*] It is I. May I come in for a moment?

HELMER. [*in a fretful whisper*] Oh, what does he want now? [*aloud*] Wait a minute! [*unlocks the door*] Come, that's kind of you not to pass by our door.

RANK. I thought I heard your voice, and felt as if I should like to look in. [*with a swift glance round*] Ah, yes!—these dear familiar rooms. You are very happy and cosy in here, you two.

HELMER. It seems to me that you looked after yourself pretty well upstairs too.

RANK. Excellently. Why shouldn't I? Why shouldn't one enjoy everything in this world?—at any rate as much as one can, and as long as one can. The wine was capital——

HELMER. Especially the champagne.

RANK. So you noticed that too? It is almost incredible how much I managed to put away!

NORA. Torvald drank a great deal of champagne tonight, too.

RANK. Did he?

NORA. Yes, and he is always in such good spirits afterwards.

RANK. Well, why should one not enjoy a merry evening after a well-spent day?

HELMER. Well spent? I am afraid I can't take credit for that.

RANK. [*clapping him on the back*] But I can, you know!

NORA. Doctor Rank, you must have been occupied with some scientific investigation to-day.

RANK. Exactly.

HELMER. Just listen!—little Nora talking about scientific investigations!

NORA. And may I congratulate you on the result?

RANK. Indeed you may.

NORA. Was it favourable, then?

RANK. The best possible, for both doctor and patient—certainty.

NORA. [*quickly and searchingly*] Certainty?

RANK. Absolute certainty. So wasn't I entitled to make a merry evening of it after that?

NORA. Yes, you certainly were, Doctor Rank.

HELMER. I think so too, so long as you don't have to pay for it in the morning.

RANK. Oh well, one can't have anything in this life without paying for it.

NORA. Doctor Rank—are you fond of fancy-dress balls?

RANK. Yes, if there is a fine lot of pretty costumes.

NORA. Tell me—what shall we two wear at the next?

HELMER. Little featherbrain!—are you thinking of the next already?

RANK. We two? Yes, I can tell you. You shall go as a good fairy——

HELMER. Yes, but what do you suggest as an appropriate costume for that?

RANK. Let your wife go dressed just as she is in everyday life.

HELMER. That was really very prettily turned. But can't you tell us what you will be?

RANK. Yes, my dear friend, I have quite made up my mind about that.

HELMER. Well?

RANK. At the next fancy dress ball I shall be invisible.

HELMER. That's a good joke!

RANK. There is a big black hat—have you never heard of hats that make you invisible? If you put one on, no one can see you.

HELMER. [*suppressing a smile*] Yes, you are quite right.

RANK. But I am clean forgetting what I came for. Helmer, give me a cigar—one of the dark Havanas.

HELMER. With the greatest pleasure. [*offers him his case*]

RANK. [*takes a cigar and cuts off the end*] Thanks.

NORA. [*striking a match*] Let me give you a light.

RANK. Thank you. [*She holds the match for him to light his cigar.*] And now good-bye!

HELMER. Good-bye, good-bye, dear old man!

NORA. Sleep well, Doctor Rank.

RANK. Thank you for that wish.

NORA. Wish me the same.

RANK. You? Well, if you want me to sleep well! And thanks for the light.

[*He nods to them both and goes out.*]

HELMER. [*in a subdued voice*] He has drunk more than he ought.

NORA. [*absently*] Maybe. [HELMER *takes a bunch of keys out of his pocket and goes into the hall.*] Torvald! what are you going to do there?

HELMER. Empty the letter-box; it is quite full; there will be no room to put the newspaper in to-morrow morning.

NORA. Are you going to work to-night?

HELMER. You know quite well I'm not. What is this? Some one has been at the lock.

NORA. At the lock—?

HELMER. Yes, someone has. What can it mean? I should never have thought the maid—. Here is a broken hairpin. Nora, it is one of yours.

NORA. [*quickly*] Then it must have been the children—

HELMER. Then you must get them out of those ways. There, at last I have got it open. [*Takes out the contents of the letter-box, and calls to the kitchen.*] Helen!— Helen, put out the light over the front door. [*Goes back into the room and shuts the door into the hall. He holds out his hand full of letters.*] Look at that—look what a heap of them there are. [*turning them over*] What on earth is that?

NORA. [*at the window*] The letter—No! Torvald, no!

HELMER. Two cards—of Rank's.

NORA. Of Doctor Rank's?

HELMER. [*looking at them*] Doctor Rank. They were on the top. He must have put them in when he went out.

NORA. Is there anything written on them?

HELMER. There is a black cross over the name. Look there—what an uncomfortable idea! It looks as if he were announcing his own death.

NORA. It is just what he is doing.

HELMER. What? Do you know anything about it? Has he said anything to you?

NORA. Yes. He told me that when the cards came it would be his leave-taking from us. He means to shut himself up and die.

HELMER. My poor old friend. Certainly I knew we should not have him very long with us. But so soon! And so he hides himself away like a wounded animal.

NORA. If it has to happen, it is best it should be without a word—don't you think so, Torvald?

HELMER. [*walking up and down*] He had so grown into our lives. I can't think of him as having gone out of them. He, with his sufferings and his loneliness, was like a cloudy background to our sunlit happiness. Well, perhaps it is best so. For him, anyway. [*standing still*] And perhaps for us too, Nora. We two are thrown quite upon each other now. [*puts his arms round her*] My darling wife, I don't feel as if I could hold you tight enough. Do you know, Nora, I have often wished that you might be threatened by some great danger, so that I might risk my life's blood, and everything, for your sake.

NORA. [*disengages herself, and says firmly and decidedly*] Now you must read your letters, Torvald.

HELMER. No, no; not to-night. I want to be with you, my darling wife.

NORA. With the thought of your friend's death——

HELMER. You are right, it has affected us both. Something ugly has come between us—the thought of the horrors of death. We must try and rid our minds of that. Until then—we will each go to our own room.

NORA. [*hanging on his neck*] Good-night, Torvald—Good-night!

Helmer. [*kissing her on the forehead*]. Good-night, my little singing-bird. Sleep sound, Nora. Now I will read my letters through.

> [*He takes his letters and goes into his room, shutting the door after him.*]

NORA. [*gropes distractedly about, seizes* HELMER'S *domino, throws it round her, while she says in quick, hoarse, spasmodic whispers*] Never to see him again. Never! Never! [*puts her shawl over her head*] Never to see my children again either— never again. Never! Never!—Ah! the icy, black water—the unfathomable depths— If only it were over! He has got it now—now he is reading it. Good-by, Torvald and my children!

[*She is about to rush through the hall, when* HELMER *opens his door hurriedly and stands with an open letter in his hand.*]

HELMER. Nora!

NORA. Ah!——

HELMER. What is this? Do you know what is in this letter?

NORA. Yes, I know. Let me go! Let me get out!

HELMER. [*holding her back*] Where are you going?

NORA. [*trying to get free*] You shan't save me, Torvald!

HELMER. [*reeling*] True? Is this true, that I read here? Horrible! No, no—it is impossible that it can be true.

NORA. It is true. I have loved you above everything else in the world.

HELMER. Oh, don't let us have any silly excuses.

NORA. [*taking a step towards him*] Torvald——!

HELMER. Miserable creature—what have you done?

NORA. Let me go. You shall not suffer for my sake. You shall not take it upon yourself.

HELMER. No tragedy airs, please. [*locks the hall door*] Here you shall stay and give me an explanation. Do you understand what you have done? Answer me? Do you understand what you have done?

NORA. [*looks steadily at him and says with a growing look of coldness in her face*] Yes, now I am beginning to understand thoroughly.

HELMER. [*walking about the room*] What a horrible awakening! All these eight years—she who was my joy and pride—a hypocrite, a liar—worse, worse—a criminal! The unutterable ugliness of it all! For shame! For shame! [NORA *is silent and looks steadily at him. He stops in front of her.*] I ought to have suspected that something of the sort would happen. I ought to have foreseen it. All your father's want of principle—be silent!—all your father's want of principle has come out in you. No religion, no morality, no sense of duty—. How I am punished for having winked at what he did! I did it for your sake, and this is how you repay me.

NORA. Yes, that's just it.

HELMER. Now you have destroyed all my happiness. You have ruined all my future. It is horrible to think of! I am in the power of an unscrupulous man; he can do what he likes with me, ask anything he likes of me, give me any orders he pleases—I dare not refuse. And I must sink to such miserable depths because of a thoughtless woman!

NORA. When I am out of the way, you will be free.

HELMER. No fine speeches, please. Your father had always plenty of those ready, too. What good would it be to me if you were out of the way, as you say? Not the slightest. He can make the affair known everywhere; and if he does, I may be falsely suspected of having been a party to your criminal action. Very likely people will think I was behind it all—that it was I who prompted you! And I have to thank you for all this—you whom I have cherished during the whole of our married life. Do you understand now what it is you have done for me?

NORA [*coldly and quietly*] Yes.

HELMER. It is so incredible that I can't take it in. But we must come to some understanding. Take off that shawl. Take it off, I tell you. I must try and appease him some way or another. The matter must be hushed up at any cost. And as for you and me, it must appear as if everything between us were just as before—but naturally only in the eyes of the world. You will still remain in my house, that is a matter of course. But I shall not allow you to bring up the children; I dare not trust them to you. To think that I should be obliged to say so to one whom I have loved so dearly, and whom I still——. No, that is all over. From this moment happiness is not the question; all that concerns us is to save the remains, the fragments, the appearance——

[*A ring is heard at the front-door bell.*]

HELMER. [*with a start*] What is that? so late! Can the worst——? Can he——? Hide yourself, Nora. Say you are ill.

[NORA *stands motionless.* HELMER *goes and unlocks the hall door.*]

MAID. [*half-dressed, comes to the door*] A letter for the mistress.

HELMER. Give it to me. [*takes the letter, and shuts the door*] Yes, it is from him. You shall not have it; I will read it myself.

NORA. Yes, read it.

HELMER. [*standing by the lamp*] I scarcely have the courage to do it. It may mean ruin for both of us. No, I must know. [*tears open the letter, runs his eye over a few lines, looks at a paper enclosed and gives a shout of joy*] Nora! [*She looks at him questioningly.*] Nora!—No, I must read it once again—. Yes, it is true! I am saved! Nora, I am saved!

NORA. And I?

HELMER. You too, of course; we are both saved, both you and I. Look, he sends you your bond back. He says he regrets and repents—that a happy change in his life—never mind what he says! We are saved, Nora! No one can do anything to you. Oh, Nora, Nora!—no, first I must destroy these hateful things. Let me see——. [*takes a look at the bond*] No, no, I won't look at it. The whole thing shall be nothing but a bad dream to me. [*tears up the bond and both letters, throws them all into the stove, and watches them burn*] There—now it doesn't exist any longer. He says that since Christmas Eve you——. These must have been three dreadful days for you, Nora.

NORA. I have fought a hard fight these three days.

HELMER. And suffered agonies, and seen no way out but——. No, we won't call any of the horrors to mind. We will only shout with joy, and keep saying "It's all over! It's all over!" Listen to me, Nora. You don't seem to realise that it is all over. What is this?—such a cold, set face! My poor little Nora, I quite understand; you don't feel as if you could believe that I have forgiven you. But it is true, Nora, I swear it; I have forgiven you everything. I know that what you did, you did out of love for me.

NORA. That is true.

HELMER. You have loved me as a wife ought to love her husband. Only you had not sufficient knowledge to judge of the means you used. But do you suppose you are any the less dear to me, because you don't understand how to act on your own responsibility? No, no; only lean on me; I will advise you and direct you. I should not be a man if this womanly helplessness did not just give you a double attractiveness in my eyes. You must not think any more about the hard things I said in my first moment of consternation, when I thought everything was going to overwhelm me. I have forgiven you, Nora; I swear to you I have forgiven you.

NORA. Thank you for your forgiveness.

[*She goes out through the door to the right.*]

HELMER. No, don't go——. [*looks in*] What are you doing in there?

NORA. [*from within*] Taking off my fancy dress.

HELMER. [*standing at the open door*] Yes, do. Try and calm yourself, and make your mind easy again, my frightened little singing-bird. Be at rest, and feel secure; I have broad wings to shelter you under. [*walks up and down by the door*] How warm and cosy our home is, Nora. Here is shelter for you; here I will protect you like a hunted dove that I have saved from a hawk's claws. I will bring peace to your poor beating heart. It will come, little by little, Nora, believe me. Tomorrow morning you will look upon it all quite differently; soon everything will be just as it was before. Very soon you won't need me to assure you that I have forgiven you; you will yourself feel the certainty that I have done so. Can you suppose I should ever think of such a thing as repudiating you, or even reproaching you? You have no idea what a true man's heart is like, Nora. There is something so indescribably sweet and satisfying, to a man, in the knowledge that he has forgiven his wife—forgiven her freely, and with all his heart. It seems as if that had made her, as it were, doubly his own; he has given her a new life, so to speak; and she has in a way become both wife and child to him. So you shall be for me after this, my little scared, helpless darling. Have no anxiety about anything, Nora; only be frank and open with me, and I will serve as will and conscience both to you——. What is this? Not gone to bed? Have you changed your things?

NORA. [*in everyday dress*] Yes, Torvald, I have changed my things now.

HELMER. But what for?—so late as this.

NORA. I shall not sleep to-night.

HELMER. But, my dear Nora——

NORA. [*looking at her watch*] It is not so very late. Sit down here, Torvald. You and I have much to say to one another.

[*She sits down at one side of the table.*]

HELMER. Nora—what is this?—this cold, set face?

NORA. Sit down. It will take some time; I have a lot to talk over with you.

HELMER. [*sits down at the opposite side of the table*] You alarm me, Nora!—and I don't understand you.

NORA. No, that is just it. You don't understand me, and I have never understood you either—before to-night. No, you mustn't interrupt me. You must simply listen to what I say. Torvald, this is a settling of accounts.

HELMER. What do you mean by that?

NORA. [*after a short silence*] Isn't there one thing that strikes you as strange in our sitting here like this?

HELMER. What is that?

NORA. We have been married now eight years. Does it not occur to you that this is the first time we two, you and I, husband and wife, have had a serious conversation?

HELMER. What do you mean by serious?

NORA. In all these eight years—longer than that—from the very beginning of our acquaintance, we have never exchanged a word on any serious subject.

HELMER. Was it likely that I would be continually and for ever telling you about worries that you could not help me to bear?

NORA. I am not speaking about business matters. I say that we have never sat down in earnest together to try and get at the bottom of anything.

HELMER. But, dearest Nora, would it have been any good to you?

NORA. That is just it; you have never understood me. I have been greatly wronged, Torvald—first by papa and then by you.

HELMER. What! By us two—by us two, who have loved you better than anyone else in the world?

NORA. [*shaking her head*] You have never loved me. You have only thought it pleasant to be in love with me.

HELMER. Nora, what do I hear you saying?

NORA. It is perfectly true, Torvald. When I was at home with papa, he told me his opinion about everything, and so I had the same opinions; and if I differed from him I concealed the fact, because he would not have liked it. He called me his doll-child, and he played with me just as I used to play with my dolls. And when I came to live with you——

HELMER. What sort of an expression is that to use about our marriage?

NORA. [*undisturbed*] I mean that I was simply transferred from papa's hands into yours. You arranged everything according to your own taste, and so I got the same tastes as you—or else I pretended to, I am really not quite sure which—I think sometimes the one and sometimes the other. When I look back on it, it seems to me as if I had been living here like a poor woman—just from hand to mouth. I have existed merely to perform tricks for you, Torvald. But you would have it so. You and papa have committed a great sin against me. It is your fault that I have made nothing of my life. *is it really?*

HELMER. How unreasonable and how ungrateful you are, Nora! Have you not been happy here?

NORA. No, I have never been happy. I thought I was, but it has never really been so.

HELMER. Not—not happy!

NORA. No, only merry. And you have always been so kind to me. But our home has been nothing but a playroom. I have been your doll-wife, just as at home I was papa's doll-child; and here the children have been my dolls. I thought it great fun when you played with me, just as they thought it great fun when I played with them. That is what our marriage has been, Torvald.

HELMER. There is some truth in what you say—exaggerated and strained as your view of it is. But for the future it shall be different. Playtime shall be over, and lesson-time shall begin.

NORA. Whose lesson? Mine, or the children's?

HELMER. Both yours and the children's, my darling Nora.

NORA. Alas, Torvald, you are not the man to educate me into being a proper wife for you.

HELMER. And you can say that!

NORA. And I—how am I fitted to bring up the children?

HELMER. Nora!

NORA. Didn't you say so yourself a little while ago—that you dare not trust me to bring them up?

HELMER. In a moment of anger! Why do you pay any heed to that?

NORA. Indeed, you were perfectly right. I am not fit for the task. There is another task I must undertake first. I must try and educate myself—you are not the man to help me in that. I must do that for myself. And that is why I am going to leave you now.

HELMER. [*springing up*] What do you say?

NORA. I must stand quite alone, if I am to understand myself and everything about me. It is for that reason that I cannot remain with you any longer.

HELMER. Nora! Nora!

NORA. I am going away from here now, at once. I am sure Christine will take me in for the night——

HELMER. You are out of your mind! I won't allow it! I forbid you!

NORA. It is no use forbidding me anything any longer. I will take with me what belongs to myself. I will take nothing from you, either now or later.

HELMER. What sort of madness is this!

NORA. To-morrow I shall go home—I mean, to my old home. It will be easiest for me to find something to do there.

HELMER. You blind, foolish woman!

NORA. I must try and get some sense, Torvald.

HELMER. To desert your home, your husband and your children! And you don't consider what people will say! *that's what is important to him*

NORA. I cannot consider that at all. I only know that it is necessary for me.

HELMER. It's shocking. This is how you would neglect your most sacred duties.

NORA. What do you consider my most sacred duties?

HELMER. Do I need to tell you that? Are they not your duties to your husband and your children?

NORA. I have other duties just as sacred. *how does she get these ideas?*

HELMER. That you have not. What duties could those be?

NORA. Duties to myself.

HELMER. Before all else, you are a wife and a mother.

NORA. I don't believe that any longer. I believe that before all else I am a reasonable human being, just as you are—or, at all events, that I must try and become one. I know quite well, Torvald, that most people would think you right, and that views of that kind are to be found in books; but I can no longer content myself with what most people say, or with what is found in books. I must think over things for myself and get to understand them.

HELMER. Can you not understand your place in your own home? Have you not a reliable guide in such matters as that?—have you no religion?

NORA. I am afraid, Torvald, I do not exactly know what religion is.

HELMER. What are you saying?

is Nora a U.U.

how does she get these ideas?

NORA. I know nothing but what the clergyman said when I went to be confirmed. He told us that religion was this, and that, and the other. When I am away from all this, and am alone, I will look into that matter too. I will see if what the clergyman said is true, or at all events if it is true for me.

HELMER. This is unheard of in a girl of your age! But if religion cannot lead you aright, let me try and awaken your conscience. I suppose you have some moral sense? Or—answer me—am I to think you have none?

NORA. I assure you, Torvald, that is not an easy question to answer. I really don't know. The thing perplexes me altogether. I only know that you and I look at it in quite a different light. I am learning, too, that the law is quite another thing from what I supposed; but I find it impossible to convince myself that the law is right. According to it a woman has no right to spare her old dying father, or to save her husband's life. I can't believe that.

HELMER. You talk like a child. You don't understand the conditions of the world in which you live.

NORA. No, I don't. But now I am going to try. I am going to see if I can make out who is right, the world or I.   *Very philosophical ideas*

HELMER. You are ill, Nora; you are delirious; I almost think you are out of your mind.

NORA. I have never felt my mind so clear and certain as to-night.

HELMER. And is it with a clear and certain mind that you forsake your husband and your children?

NORA. Yes, it is.

HELMER. Then there is only one possible explanation.

NORA. What is that?

HELMER. You do not love me any more.   *why is that the only explanation?*

NORA. No, that is just it.

HELMER. Nora!—and you can say that?

NORA. It gives me great pain, Torvald, for you have always been so kind to me, but I cannot help it. I do not love you any more.

HELMER. [*regaining his composure*] Is that a clear and certain conviction too?

NORA. Yes, absolutely clear and certain. That is the reason why I will not stay here any longer.

HELMER. And can you tell me what I have done to forfeit your love?

NORA. Yes, indeed I can. It was to-night, when the wonderful thing did not happen; then I saw you were not the man I had thought you.

HELMER. Explain yourself better—I don't understand you.

NORA. I have waited so patiently for eight years; for, goodness knows, I knew very well that wonderful things don't happen every day. Then this horrible misfortune came upon me; and then I felt quite certain that the wonderful thing was going to happen at last. When Krogstad's letter was lying out there, never for a moment did I imagine that you would consent to accept this man's conditions. I was so absolutely certain that you would say to him: Publish the thing to the whole world. And when that was done——

HELMER. Yes, what then?—when I had exposed my wife to shame and disgrace?

NORA. When that was done, I was so absolutely certain, you would come forward and take everything upon yourself, and say: I am the guilty one.

HELMER. Nora——!

NORA. You mean that I would never have accepted such a sacrifice on your part? No, of course not. But what would my assurances have been worth against yours? That was the wonderful thing which I hoped for and feared; and it was to prevent that, that I wanted to kill myself.

HELMER. I would gladly work night and day for you, Nora—bear sorrow and want for your sake. But no man would sacrifice his honour for the one he loves.

NORA. It is a thing hundreds of thousands of women have done.

HELMER. Oh, you think and talk like a heedless child.

NORA. Maybe. But you neither think nor talk like the man I could bind myself to. As soon as your fear was over—and it was not fear for what threatened me, but for what might happen to you—when the whole thing was past, as far as you were concerned it was exactly as if nothing at all had happened. Exactly as before, I was your little skylark, your doll, which you would in future treat with doubly gentle care, because it was so brittle and fragile. [*getting up*] Torvald—it was then it dawned upon me that for eight years I had been living here with a strange man, and had borne him three children——. Oh, I can't bear to think of it! I could tear myself into little bits!

HELMER. [*sadly*] I see, I see. An abyss has opened between us—there is no denying it. But, Nora, would it not be possible to fill it up?

NORA. As I am now, I am no wife for you.

HELMER. I have it in me to become a different man.

NORA. Perhaps—if your doll is taken away from you.

HELMER. But to part!—to part from you! No, no, Nora, I can't understand that idea.

NORA. [*going out to the right*] That makes it all the more certain that it must be done.

[*She comes back with her cloak and hat and a small bag which she puts on a chair by the table.*]

HELMER. Nora, Nora, not now! Wait till to-morrow.

NORA. [*putting on her cloak*] I cannot spend the night in a strange man's room.

HELMER. But can't we live here like brother and sister——?

NORA. [*putting on her hat*] You know very well that would not last long. [*puts the shawl round her*] Good-bye, Torvald. I won't see the little ones. I know they are in better hands than mine. As I am now, I can be of no use to them.

HELMER. But some day, Nora—some day?

NORA. How can I tell? I have no idea what is going to become of me.

HELMER. But you are my wife, whatever becomes of you.

NORA. Listen, Torvald. I have heard that when a wife deserts her husband's house, as I am doing now, he is legally freed from all obligations towards her. In any case I set you free from all your obligations. You are not to feel yourself bound in the slightest way, any more than I shall. There must be perfect freedom on both sides. See here is your ring back. Give me mine.

HELMER. That too?

NORA. That too.

HELMER. Here it is.

NORA. That's right. Now it is all over. I have put the keys here. The maids know all about everything in the house—better than I do. To-morrow, after I have left her, Christine will come here and pack up my own things that I brought with me from home. I will have them sent after me.

HELMER. All over! All over!—Nora, shall you never think of me again?

NORA. I know I shall often think of you and the children and this house.

HELMER. May I write to you, Nora?

NORA. No—never. You must not do that.

HELMER. But at least let me send you——

NORA. Nothing—nothing—

HELMER. Let me help you if you are in want.

NORA. No. I can receive nothing from a stranger.

HELMER. Nora—can I never be anything more than a stranger to you?

NORA. [*taking her bag*] Ah, Torvald, the most wonderful thing of all would have to happen.

HELMER. Tell me what that would be!

NORA. Both you and I would have to be so changed that——. Oh, Torvald, I don't believe any longer in wonderful things happening.

HELMER. But I will believe in it. Tell me? So changed that——?

NORA. That our life together would be a real wedlock. Good-bye.

[*She goes out through the hall.*]

HELMER. [*sinks down on a chair at the door and buries his face in his hands*] Nora! Nora! [*looks round, and rises*] Empty. She is gone. [*A hope flashes across his mind.*] The most wonderful thing of all——?

What is it?

[*The sound of a door slamming is heard from below.*]

[1879—Norway]

Questions

Act 1

1. What does the set as described tell us about the Helmers? What does it tell us about the play?

2. What does the setting—Norway at Christmastime at the end of the nineteenth century— suggest as to the social background of the play's characters? What might Norway in winter symbolize specifically about the society we find Nora in?

3. What kind of a man is Torvald? What are his character traits?

4. How does Nora come off in Act 1?

5. What is the function of Mrs. Linde? What is ironic about Nora's helping her obtain a position at the Bank? What kind of irony is this—verbal, circumstantial, or dramatic?

6. Describe Nora and Torvald's relationship. How does he treat her? What role does she play with him? Does she play it knowingly or unconsciously?

7. Money is a central issue in Act 1. What position is Nora put in because of money? Why can't a woman borrow without her husband's signature? Does this seem right? What does Torvald's being made "manager of the Bank" symbolize?

Act 2

1. What does Dr. Rank mean when he says, "My poor innocent spine has to suffer for my father's youthful amusements"? What more do we learn about Nora from her response, "I suppose you mean that he was too partial to asparagus"?

2. Nora could get out of her troubles by appealing to Dr. Rank, which she almost does. But, finally, she doesn't. Why? What does her not asking tell us about her?

3. Is Krogstad a villain, or at least as much of a villain as realism allows? Or is he just a man who is trapped by his society's rigid codes and conventions? Elaborate.

4. Ironically, Krogstad and Nora are much alike. How so?

5. Why is Nora so frightened that Torvald will find her out? Yet, hoping against hope, she thinks that a "wonderful thing" might happen when Torvald reads Krogstad's letter. What does she hope might happen?

6. What does the locked letter-box symbolize here? What, the Tarantella? In what ways are these symbols contrasting? How do they tie in with the play's more general symbolic opposition of north and south, Norway and Italy?

Act 3

1. How has Nora's life during her marriage been that of a doll in a doll's house?

2. Realistic plays cannot bear much in the way of coincidence. Is the coincidence of Mrs. Linde's having been Krogstad's former lover too much? Why or why not?

3. Nor can realistic plays bear unexpected revelations or changes that seem to come from left field. Is the change in Nora too sudden, or is it well grounded in what we learn about her in the past as well as in her present circumstance? How does Mrs. Linde help persuade us that Nora's change is probable? How does Nora's changed attitude about the law both reflect her growth and give it underpinning?

4. What that is new do we learn about Torvald in Act 3? What does his response to the news of the impending death of Dr. Rank show? What does his thinking of "appearance" in response to Krogstad's first letter reveal? What is his conception of "honour"?

5. What does Nora realize about Torvald and her marriage to him? Why is the realization so powerful as to precipitate Nora's awakening?

6. What does the play say about marriage, sexism, and social convention? How do these themes tie in with the master theme of the right of the individual to become as much as that individual can be?

7. What is the mood at the end of the play? It has been said that when, on the first night of the first production of *A Doll's House,* Nora slammed the door, the feminist revolution began. How so? But does the main theme of the play concern women alone or men as well? How so?

Writing Assignments

1. Write an essay on the themes of *A Doll's House:* what they are, how they emerge, and how they are united.

2. At the end of the play, Nora distinguishes between being "happy" and "merry," and between loving and being "in love." In a paper, elaborate on these distinctions, using *A Doll's House* to explore and exemplify what Nora is getting at.

3. All the business in the play concerning money comes to a kind of summation in the third act when Torvald says, "Why shouldn't I look at my treasure?—at all the beauty that is mine, all my very own?" Taking off from this quotation, write a paper about the symbolic significance of money in the world of *A Doll's House* (as well as in ours). What is the significance of money in Nora's life? What is its significance to Torvald, the banker? How does money warp values and relationships in the play?

4. Nora's awakening seems rather dramatic. Actually, however, it is well grounded. In an essay, enumerate and discuss those aspects of the play that serve to make Nora's change credible.

5. Imagine that you are a reviewer who has just attended the opening of A Doll's House. After you have determined what your persona should be (that is, you as a nineteenth-century Norwegian), write a full review of the play, detailing your response to it and the reasons why you so respond. Assume an audience that is not familiar with A Doll's House.

6. The two major symbols in A Doll's House are north (Norway) and south (Italy). Discuss in a paper the various meanings of these multifaceted symbols and suggest what other symbols (verbal or stage) in the play can be seen in terms of this polar opposition.

7. A Doll's House is a relatively early example of dramatic realism. Does it still seem realistic today? In an essay, discuss what seems realistic to you and anything that may not. Be sure to consider Nora's transformation in this regard.

8. What is the play's mood as it closes? What do you make of the way it closes? What, do you think, Ibsen's intention was in ending the play this way? Write a paper in which you explore these questions. Bring to bear your own feelings and responses as well as textual evidence.

THE GLASS MENAGERIE

✳ TENNESSEE WILLIAMS ✳

Nobody, not even the rain, has such small hands.
—E. E. CUMMINGS

SCENE   *An Alley in St. Louis*

PART I.   *Preparation for a Gentleman Caller*
PART II.   *The Gentleman calls.*

TIME: *Now and the Past.*

THE CHARACTERS

AMANDA WINGFIELD (*the mother*): A little woman of great but confused vitality clinging frantically to another time and place. Her characterization must be carefully created, not copied from type. She is not paranoiac, but her life is paranoia. There is much to admire in Amanda, and as much to love and pity as there is to laugh at. Certainly she has endurance and a kind of heroism, and though her foolishness makes her unwittingly cruel at times, there is tenderness in her slight person.

LAURA WINGFIELD (*her daughter*): Amanda, having failed to establish contact with reality, continues to live vitally in her illusions, but Laura's situation is even graver. A childhood illness has left her crippled, one leg slightly shorter than the other, and held in a brace. This defect need not be more than suggested on the stage. Stemming from this, Laura's separation increases till she is like a piece of her own glass collection, too exquisitely fragile to move from the shelf.

TOM WINGFIELD (*her son*): And the narrator of the play. A poet with a job in a warehouse. His nature is not remorseless, but to escape from a trap he has to act without pity.

JIM O'CONNOR (*the gentleman caller*): A nice, ordinary, young man.

SCENE I

The Wingfield apartment is in the rear of the building, one of those vast hive-like conglomerations of cellular living-units that flower as warty growths in overcrowded urban centers of lower middle-class population and are symptomatic of the impulse of this largest and fundamentally enslaved section of American society to avoid fluidity and differentiation and to exist and function as one interfused mass of automatism.

The apartment faces an alley and is entered by a fire escape, a structure whose name is a touch of accidental poetic truth, for all of these huge buildings are always burning with the slow and implacable fires of human desperation. The fire escape is part of what we see—that is, the landing of it and steps descending from it.

The scene is memory and is therefore nonrealistic. Memory takes a lot of poetic

814

license. It omits some details; others are exaggerated, according to the emotional value of the articles it touches, for memory is seated predominantly in the heart. The interior is therefore rather dim and poetic.

At the rise of the curtain, the audience is faced with the dark, grim rear wall of the Wingfield tenement. This building is flanked on both sides by dark, narrow alleys which run into murky canyons of tangled clotheslines, garbage cans, and the sinister latticework of neighboring fire escapes. It is up and down these side alleys that exterior entrances and exits are made during the play. At the end of TOM'S *opening commentary, the dark tenement wall slowly becomes transparent and reveals the interior of the ground-floor Wingfield apartment.*

Nearest the audience is the living room, which also serves as a sleeping room for LAURA, *the sofa unfolding to make her bed. Just beyond, separated from the living room by a wide arch or second proscenium with transparent faded portieres (or second curtain), is the dining room. In an old-fashioned whatnot in the living room are seen scores of transparent glass animals. A blown-up photograph of the father hangs on the wall of the living room, to the left of the archway. It is the face of a very handsome young man in a doughboy's First World War cap. He is gallantly smiling, ineluctably smiling, as if to say "I will be smiling forever."*

Also hanging on the wall, near the photograph, are a typewriter keyboard chart and a Gregg shorthand diagram. An upright typewriter on a small table stands beneath the charts.

The audience hears and sees the opening scene in the dining room through both the transparent fourth wall of the building and the transparent gauze portieres of the dining-room arch. It is during this revealing scene that the fourth wall slowly ascends, out of sight. This transparent exterior wall is not brought down again until the very end of the play, during TOM'S *final speech.*

The narrator is an undisguised convention of the play. He takes whatever license with dramatic convention is convenient to his purposes.

TOM *enters, dressed as a merchant sailor, and strolls across to the fire escape. There he stops and lights a cigarette. He addresses the audience.*

TOM. Yes, I have tricks in my pocket, I have things up my sleeve. But I am the opposite of a stage magician. He gives you illusion that has the appearance of truth. I give you truth in the pleasant disguise of illusion.

To begin with, I turn back time. I reverse it to that quaint period, the thirties, when the huge middle class of America was matriculating in a school for the blind. Their eyes had failed them, or they had failed their eyes, and so they were having their fingers pressed forcibly down on the fiery Braille alphabet of a dissolving economy.

In Spain there was revolution. Here there was only shouting and confusion. In Spain there was Guernica.[1] Here there were disturbances of labor, sometimes pretty violent, in otherwise peaceful cities such as Chicago, Cleveland, Saint Louis . . .

---

[1] A Spanish town bombed in 1937 by fascists in connection with the Spanish Civil War.

This is the social background of the play. [*Music begins to play.*]

The play is memory. Being a memory play, it is dimly lighted, it is sentimental, it is not realistic. In memory everything seems to happen to music. That explains the fiddle in the wings.

I am the narrator of the play, and also a character in it. The other characters are my mother, Amanda, my sister, Laura, and a gentleman caller who appears in the final scenes. He is the most realistic character in the play, being an emissary from a world of reality that we were somehow set apart from. But since I have a poet's weakness for symbols, I am using this character also as a symbol; he is the long-delayed but always expected something that we live for.

There is a fifth character in the play who doesn't appear except in this larger-than-life-size photograph over the mantel. This is our father who left us a long time ago. He was a telephone man who fell in love with long distances; he gave up his job with the telephone company and skipped the light fantastic out of town . . .

The last we heard of him was a picture postcard from Mazatlan, on the Pacific coast of Mexico, containing a message of two words: "Hello—Goodbye!" and no address.

I think the rest of the play will explain itself. . . . [AMANDA'S *voice becomes audible through the portieres.*] [*Legend on screen:* "Ou sont les neiges d'antan?"[2]] [TOM *divides the portieres and enters the dining room.* AMANDA *and* LAURA *are seated at a drop-leaf table. Eating is indicated by gestures without food or utensils.* AMANDA *faces the audience.* TOM *and* Laura *are seated in profile. The interior is lit up softly and through the scrim we see* AMANDA *and* LAURA *seated at the table.*]

AMANDA [*calling*]. Tom?

TOM. Yes, Mother.

AMANDA. We can't say grace until you come to the table!

TOM. Coming, Mother. [*He bows slightly and withdraws, reappearing a few moments later in his place at the table.*]

AMANDA [*to her son*]. Honey, don't *push* with your *fingers*. If you have to push with something, the thing to push with is a crust of bread. And chew—chew! Animals have secretions in their stomachs which enable them to digest food without mastication, but human beings are supposed to chew their food before they swallow it down. Eat food leisurely, son, and really enjoy it. A well-cooked meal has lots of delicate flavors that have to be held in the mouth for appreciation. So chew your food and give your salivary glands a chance to function! [TOM *deliberately lays his imaginary fork down and pushes his chair back from the table.*]

TOM. I haven't enjoyed one bite of this dinner because of your constant directions on how to eat it. It's you that make me rush through meals with your hawklike attention to every bite I take. Sickening—spoils my appetite—all this discussion of—animals' secretion—salivary glands—mastication!

---

[2] A quotation from the French poet François Villon (1431–1463?): "Where are the snows of yester-year?"

AMANDA [*lightly*]. Temperament like a Metropolitan star! [TOM *rises and walks toward the living room.*] You're not excused from the table.

TOM. I'm getting a cigarette.

AMANDA. You smoke too much. [LAURA *rises.*]

LAURA. I'll bring in the blanc mange. [TOM *remains standing with his cigarette by the portieres.*]

AMANDA [*rising*]. No, sister, no, sister—you be the lady this time and I'll be the darky.

LAURA. I'm already up.

AMANDA. Resume your seat, little sister—I want you to stay fresh and pretty—for gentlemen callers!

LAURA [*sitting down*]. I'm not expecting any gentlemen callers.

AMANDA [*crossing out to the kitchenette, airily*]. Sometimes they come when they are least expected! Why, I remember one Sunday afternoon in Blue Mountain— [*She enters the kitchenette.*]

TOM. I know what's coming!

LAURA. Yes. But let her tell it.

TOM. Again?

LAURA. She loves to tell it. [AMANDA *returns with a bowl of dessert.*]

AMANDA. One Sunday afternoon in Blue Mountain—your mother received—*seventeen!*—gentlemen callers! Why, sometimes there weren't chairs enough to accommodate them all. We had to send the nigger over to bring in folding chairs from the parish house.

TOM [*remaining at the portieres*]. How did you entertain those gentlemen callers?

AMANDA. I understood the art of conversation!

TOM. I bet you could talk.

AMANDA. Girls in those days *knew* how to talk, I can tell you.

TOM. Yes? [*Image on screen: Amanda as a girl on a porch, greeting callers.*]

AMANDA. They knew how to entertain their gentlemen callers. It wasn't enough for a girl to be possessed of a pretty face and a graceful figure—although I wasn't slighted in either respect. She also needed to have a nimble wit and a tongue to meet all occasions.

TOM. What did you talk about?

AMANDA. Things of importance going on in the world! Never anything coarse or common or vulgar. [*She addresses* TOM *as though he were seated in the vacant chair at the table though he remains by the portieres. He plays this scene as though reading from a script.*] My callers were gentlemen—all! Among my callers were some of the most prominent young planters of the Mississippi Delta—planters and sons of planters! [TOM *motions for music and a spot of light on* AMANDA. *Her eyes lift, her face glows, her voice becomes rich and elegiac.*] [*Screen legend:* "Ou sont les neiges d'antan?"] There was young Champ Laughlin who later became vice-president of the Delta Planters Bank. Hadley Stevenson who was drowned in Moon Lake and left his widow one hundred and fifty thousand in Government bonds. There were the Cutrere brothers, Wesley and Bates. Bates was one of my bright particular beaux! He got in a quarrel with that wild Wainwright boy. They shot it out on the floor of Moon Lake Casino. Bates was shot through the stomach. Died in the ambulance on his way to Memphis. His widow was also well provided-for, came into eight or ten thousand acres, that's all. She married him on the rebound—never loved her—carried my picture on him the night he died! And there was that boy that every girl in the Delta had set her cap for! That beautiful, brilliant young Fitzhugh boy from Greene County!

TOM. What did he leave his widow?

AMANDA. He never married! Gracious, you talk as though all of my old admirers had turned up their toes to the daisies!

TOM. Isn't this the first you've mentioned that still survives?

AMANDA. That Fitzhugh boy went North and made a fortune—came to be known as the Wolf of Wall Street! He had the Midas touch, whatever he touched turned to gold! And I could have been Mrs. Duncan J. Fitzhugh, mind you! But—I picked your *father!*

LAURA [*rising*]. Mother, let me clear the table.

AMANDA. No, dear, you go in front and study your typewriter chart. Or practice your shorthand a little. Stay fresh and pretty!—It's almost time for our gentlemen callers to start arriving. [*She flounces girlishly toward the kitchenette.*] How many do you suppose we're going to entertain this afternoon? [TOM *throws down the paper and jumps up with a groan.*]

LAURA [*alone in the dining room*]. I don't believe we're going to receive any, Mother.

AMANDA [*reappearing, airily*]. What? No one—not one? You must be joking! [LAURA *nervously echoes her laugh. She slips in a fugitive manner through the half-open portieres and draws them gently behind her. A shaft of very clear light is thrown on her face against the faded tapestry of the curtains. Faintly the music of "The Glass Menagerie" is heard as she continues, lightly.*] Not one gentleman caller? It can't be true! There must be a flood, there must have been a tornado!

LAURA. It isn't a flood, it's not a tornado, Mother. I'm just not popular like you were in Blue Mountain. . . . [TOM *utters another groan.* LAURA *glances at him with a faint, apologetic smile. Her voice catches a little.*] Mother's afraid I'm going to be an old maid. [*The scene dims out with the "Glass Menagerie" music.*]

SCENE II

On the dark stage the screen is lighted with the image of blue roses. Gradually LAURA's *figure becomes apparent and the screen goes out. The music subsides.*

LAURA *is seated in the delicate ivory chair at the small claw-foot table. She wears a dress of soft violet material for a kimono—her hair is tied back from her forehead with a ribbon. She is washing and polishing her collection of glass.* AMANDA *appears on the fire escape steps. At the sound of her ascent,* LAURA *catches her breath, thrusts the bowl of ornaments away, and sets herself stiffly before the diagram of the typewriter keyboard as though it held her spellbound. Something has happened to* AMANDA. *It is written in her face as she climbs to the landing: a look that is grim and hopeless and a little absurd. She has on one of those cheap or imitation velvety-looking cloth coats with imitation fur collar. Her hat is five or six years old, one of those dreadful cloche hats that were worn in the late Twenties, and she is clutching an enormous black patent-leather pocketbook with nickel clasps and initials. This is her full-dress outfit, the one she usually wears to the D.A.R.[3] Before entering she looks through the door. She purses her lips, opens her eyes very wide, rolls them upward and shakes her head. Then she slowly lets herself in the door. Seeing her mother's expression* LAURA *touches her lips with a nervous gesture.*

LAURA. Hello, Mother, I was—[*She makes a nervous gesture toward the chart on the wall.* AMANDA *leans against the shut door and stares at* LAURA *with a martyred look.*]

AMANDA. Deception? Deception? [*She slowly removes her hat and gloves; continuing the sweet suffering stare. She lets the hat and gloves fall on the floor—a bit of acting.*]

LAURA [*shakily*]. How was the D.A.R. meeting? [AMANDA *slowly opens her purse and removes a dainty white handkerchief which she shakes out delicately and delicately touches to her lips and nostrils.*] Didn't you go to the D.A.R. meeting, Mother?

AMANDA [*faintly, almost inaudibly*]. —No.—No. [*then more forcibly*] I did not have the strength—to go to the D.A.R. In fact, I did not have the courage! I wanted to find a hole in the ground and hide myself in it forever! [*She crosses slowly to the wall and removes the diagram of the typewriter keyboard. She holds it in front of her for a second, staring at it sweetly and sorrowfully—then bites her lips and tears it in two pieces.*]

LAURA [*faintly*]. Why did you do that, Mother? [AMANDA *repeats the same procedure with the chart of the Gregg Alphabet.*] Why are you—

AMANDA. Why? Why? How old are you, Laura?

LAURA. Mother, you know my age.

AMANDA. I thought that you were an adult; it seems that I was mistaken. [*She crosses slowly to the sofa and sinks down and stares at* LAURA.]

LAURA. Please don't stare at me, Mother. [AMANDA *closes her eyes and lowers her head. There is a ten-second pause.*]

AMANDA. What are we going to do, what is going to become of us, what is the future? [*There is another pause.*]

LAURA. Has something happened, Mother? [AMANDA *draws a long breath, takes out the handkerchief again, goes through the dabbing process.*] Mother, has—something happened?

AMANDA. I'll be all right in a minute, I'm just bewildered—[*She hesitates.*]—by life. . . .

LAURA. Mother, I wish that you would tell me what's happened!

AMANDA. As you know, I was supposed to be inducted into my office at the D.A.R. this afternoon. [*Screen image:* A swarm of typewriters.] But I stopped off at Rubicam's Business College to speak to your teachers about your having a cold and ask them what progress they thought you were making down there.

LAURA. Oh. . . .

AMANDA. I went to the typing instructor and introduced myself as your mother. She

---

[3] The Daughters of the American Revolution.

didn't know who you were. "Wingfield," she said, "We don't have any such student enrolled at the school!" I assured her she did, that you had been going to classes since early in January. "I wonder," she said, "If you could be talking about that terribly shy little girl who dropped out of school after only a few days' attendance?" "No," I said, "Laura, my daughter, has been going to school every day for the past six weeks!" "Excuse me," she said. She took the attendance book out and there was your name, unmistakably printed, and all the dates you were absent until they decided that you had dropped out of school. I still said, "No, there must have been some mistake! There must have been some mix-up in the records!" And she said, "No—I remember her perfectly now. Her hands shook so that she couldn't hit the right keys! The first time we gave a speed test, she broke down completely—was sick at the stomach and almost had to be carried into the wash room! After that morning she never showed up any more. We phoned the house but never got any answer"—While I was working at Famous-Barr, I suppose, demonstrating those— [*She indicates a brassiere with her hands.*] Oh, I felt so weak I could barely keep on my feet! I had to sit down while they got me a glass of water! Fifty dollars' tuition, all of our plans—my hopes and ambitions for you— just gone up the spout, just gone up the spout like that. [LAURA *draws a long breath and gets awkwardly to her feet. She crosses to the Victrola and winds it up.*] What are you doing?

LAURA. Oh! [*She releases the handle and returns to her seat.*]

AMANDA. Laura, where have you been going when you've gone out pretending that you were going to business college?

LAURA. I've just been going out walking.

AMANDA. That's not true.

LAURA. It is. I just went walking.

AMANDA. Walking? Walking? In winter? Deliberately courting pneumonia in that light coat? Where did you walk to, Laura?

LAURA. All sorts of places—mostly in the park.

AMANDA. Even after you'd started catching that cold?

LAURA. It was the lesser of two evils, Mother. [*Screen image:* Winter scene in a park.] I couldn't go back there. I—threw up—on the floor!

AMANDA. From half past seven till after five every day you mean to tell me you walked around in the park, because you wanted to make me think that you were still going to Rubicam's Business College?

LAURA. It wasn't as bad as it sounds. I went inside places to get warmed up.

AMANDA. Inside where?

LAURA. I went in the art museum and the bird houses at the Zoo. I visited the penguins every day! Sometimes I did without lunch and went to the movies. Lately I've been spending most of my afternoons in the Jewel Box, that big glass house where they raise the tropical flowers.

AMANDA. You did all this to deceive me, just for deception? [LAURA *looks down.*] Why?

LAURA. Mother, when you're disappointed, you get that awful suffering look on your face, like the picture of Jesus' mother in the museum!

AMANDA. Hush!

LAURA. I couldn't face it. [*There is a pause. A whisper of strings is heard. Legend on screen:* "The Crust of Humility."]

AMANDA [*hopelessly fingering the huge pocketbook*]. So what are we going to do the rest of our lives? Stay home and watch the parades go by? Amuse ourselves with the glass menagerie, darling? Eternally play those worn-out phonograph records your father left as a painful reminder of him? We won't have a business career— we've given that up because it gave us nervous indigestion! [*She laughs wearily.*] What is there left but dependency all our lives? I know so well what becomes of unmarried women who aren't prepared to occupy a position. I've seen such pitiful cases in the South—barely tolerated spinsters living upon the grudging patronage of sister's or brother's wife—stuck away in some little mousetrap of a room— encouraged by one in-law to visit another—little birdlike women without any nest—eating the crust of humility all their life! Is that the future that we've mapped out for ourselves? I swear it's the only alternative I can think of! [*She pauses.*] It isn't a very pleasant alternative, is it? [*She pauses again.*] Of course—some girls *do marry*. [LAURA *twists her hands nervously.*] Haven't you ever liked some boy?

LAURA. Yes. I liked one once. [*She rises.*] I came across his picture a while ago.

AMANDA [*with some interest*]. He gave you his picture?

LAURA. No, it's in the yearbook.

AMANDA [*disappointed*]. Oh—a high school boy. [*Screen image:* Jim as the high school hero bearing a silver cup.]

LAURA. Yes. His name was Jim. [*She lifts the heavy annual from the claw-foot table.*] Here he is in *The Pirates of Penzance*.

AMANDA [*absently*]. The what?

LAURA. The operetta the senior class put on. He had a wonderful voice and we sat across the aisle from each other Mondays, Wednesdays and Fridays in the Aud. Here he is with the silver cup for debating! See his grin?

AMANDA [*absently*]. He must have had a jolly disposition.

LAURA. He used to call me—Blue Roses. [*Screen image:* Blue roses.]

AMANDA. Why did he call you such a name as that?

LAURA. When I had that attack of pleurosis—he asked me what was the matter when I came back. I said pleurosis—he thought that I said Blue Roses! So that's what he always called me after that. Whenever he saw me, he'd holler, "Hello, Blue Roses!" I didn't care for the girl that he went out with. Emily Meisenbach. Emily was the best-dressed girl at Soldan. She never struck me, though, as being sincere . . . It says in the Personal Section—they're engaged. That's—six years ago! They must be married by now.

AMANDA. Girls that aren't cut out for business careers usually wind up married to some nice man. [*She gets up with a spark of revival.*] Sister, that's what you'll do! [LAURA *utters a startled, doubtful laugh. She reaches quickly for a piece of glass.*]

LAURA. But, Mother—

AMANDA. Yes? [*She goes over to the photograph.*]

LAURA [*in a tone of frightened apology*]. I'm—crippled!

AMANDA. Nonsense! Laura, I've told you never, never to use that word. Why, you're not crippled, you just have a little defect—hardly noticeable, even! When people have some slight disadvantage like that, they cultivate other things to make up for it—develop charm—and vivacity—and—*charm!* That's all you have to do! [*She turns again to the photograph.*] One thing your father had *plenty of*—was *charm!* [TOM *motions to the fiddle in the wings. The scene fades out with music.*]

SCENE III

Legend on screen: "After the fiasco—"

TOM *speaks from the fire escape landing.*

TOM. After the fiasco at Rubicam's Business College, the idea of getting a gentleman caller for Laura began to play a more and more important part in Mother's calculations. It became an obsession. Like some archetype of the universal unconscious, the image of the gentleman caller haunted our small apartment. . . . [*Screen image:* A young man at the door of a house with flowers.] An evening at home rarely passed without some allusion to this image, this specter, this hope. . . . Even when he wasn't mentioned, his presence hung in Mother's preoccupied look and in my sister's frightened, apologetic manner—hung like a sentence passed upon the Wingfields! Mother was a woman of action as well as words. She began to take logical steps in the planned direction. Late that winter and in the early spring—realizing that extra money would be needed to properly feather the nest and plume the bird—she conducted a vigorous campaign on the telephone, roping in subscribers to one of those magazines for matrons called *The Homemaker's Companion,* the type of journal that features the serialized sublimations of ladies of letters who think in terms of delicate cuplike breasts, slim, tapering waists, rich, creamy thighs, eyes like wood smoke in autumn, fingers that soothe and caress like strains of music, bodies as powerful as Etruscan sculpture. [*Screen image:* The cover of a glamor magazine.] [AMANDA *enters with the telephone on a long extension cord. She is spotlighted in the dim stage.*]
AMANDA. Ida Scott? This is Amanda Wingfield! We *missed* you at the D.A.R. last Monday! I said to myself: She's probably suffering with that sinus condition! How is that sinus condition? Horrors! Heaven have mercy—You're a Christian martyr, yes, that's what you are, a Christian martyr! Well, I just now happened to notice that your subscription to the *Companion's* about to expire! Yes, it expires with the next issue, honey!—just when that wonderful new serial by Bessie Mae Hopper is getting off to such an exciting start. Oh, honey, it's something that you can't miss! You remember how *Gone with the Wind* took everybody by storm? You simply couldn't go out if you hadn't read it. All everybody *talked* was Scarlett O'Hara. Well, this is a book that critics already compare to *Gone with the Wind.* It's the *Gone with the Wind* of the post-World-War generation!—What?—Burning?—Oh, honey, don't let them burn, go take a look in the oven and I'll hold the wire! Heavens—I think she's hung up! [*The scene dims out.*] [*Legend on screen:* "You think I'm in love with Continental Shoemakers?"] [*Before the lights come up again, the violent voices of* TOM *and* AMANDA *are heard. They are quarreling*

behind the portieres. In front of them stands LAURA *with clenched hands and panicky expression. A clear pool of light is on her figure throughout this scene.*]

TOM. What in Christ's name am I—

AMANDA [*shrilly*]. Don't you use that—

TOM. —supposed to do!

AMANDA. —expression! Not in my—

TOM. Ohhh!

AMANDA. —presence! Have you gone out of your senses?

TOM. I have, that's true, *driven* out!

AMANDA. What is the matter with you, you—big—big—IDIOT!

TOM. Look!—I've got *no thing,* no single thing—

AMANDA. Lower your voice!

TOM. —in my life here that I can call my OWN! Everything is—

AMANDA. Stop that shouting!

TOM. Yesterday you confiscated my books! You had the nerve to—

AMANDA. I took that horrible novel back to the library—yes! That hideous book by that insane Mr. Lawrence. [TOM *laughs wildly.*] I cannot control the output of diseased minds or people who cater to them— [TOM *laughs still more wildly.*] BUT I WON'T ALLOW SUCH FILTH BROUGHT INTO MY HOUSE! No, no, no, no, no!

TOM. House, house! Who pays rent on it, who makes a slave of himself to—

AMANDA [*fairly screeching*]. Don't you DARE to—

TOM. No, no, *I* mustn't say things! *I've* got to just—

AMANDA. Let me tell you—

TOM. I don't want to hear any more! [*He tears the portieres open. The dining-room area is lit with a turgid smoky red glow. Now we see* AMANDA; *her hair is in metal curlers and she is wearing a very old bathrobe, much too large for her slight figure, a relic of the faithless Mr. Wingfield. The upright typewriter now stands on the drop-leaf table, along with a wild disarray of manuscripts. The quarrel was probably precipitated by* AMANDA's *interruption of* TOM's *creative labor. A chair lies overthrown on the floor. Their gesticulating shadows are cast on the ceiling by the fiery glow.*]

AMANDA. You *will* hear more, you—

TOM. No, I won't hear more, I'm going out!

AMANDA. You come right back in—

TOM. Out, out, out! Because I'm—

AMANDA. Come back here, Tom Wingfield! I'm not through talking to you!

TOM. Oh, go—

LAURA [*desperately*]. —Tom!

AMANDA. You're going to listen, and no more insolence from you! I'm at the end of my patience! [*He comes back toward her.*]

TOM. What do you think I'm at? Aren't I supposed to have any patience to reach the end of, Mother? I know, I know. It seems unimportant to you, what I'm *doing*— what I *want* to do—having a little *difference* between them! You don't think that—

AMANDA. I think you've been doing things that you're ashamed of. That's why you act like this. I don't believe that you go every night to the movies. Nobody goes to the movies night after night. Nobody in their right minds goes to the movies as often as you pretend to. People don't go to the movies at nearly midnight, and movies don't let out at two A.M. Come in stumbling. Muttering to yourself like a maniac! You get three hours' sleep and then go to work. Oh, I can picture the way you're doing down there. Moping, doping, because you're in no condition.

TOM [*wildly*]. No, I'm in no condition!

AMANDA. What right have you got to jeopardize your job? Jeopardize the security of us all? How do you think we'd manage if you were—

TOM. Listen! You think I'm crazy about the *warehouse?* [*He bends fiercely toward her slight figure.*] You think I'm in love with the Continental Shoemakers? You think I want to spend fifty-five *years* down there in that—*celotex interior!* with—*fluorescent—tubes!* Look I'd rather somebody picked up a crowbar and battered out my brains—than go back mornings! I *go!* Every time you come in yelling that Goddamn *"Rise and Shine!" "Rise and Shine!"* I say to myself, "How *lucky dead* people are!" But I get up. I *go!* For sixty-five dollars a month I give up all that I dream of doing and being *ever!* And you say self—*self's* all I ever think of. Why, listen, if self is what I thought of, Mother, I'd be where he is—GONE! [*He points to his father's picture.*] As far as the system of transportation reaches! [*He starts past her. She grabs his arm.*] Don't grab at me, Mother!

AMANDA. Where are you going?

TOM. I'm going to the *movies!*

AMANDA. I don't believe that lie!

[TOM *crouches toward her, overtowering her tiny figure. She backs away, gasping.*]

TOM. I'm going to opium dens! Yes, opium dens, dens of vice and criminals' hangouts, Mother. I've joined the Hogan Gang, I'm a hired assassin, I carry a tommy gun in a violin case! I run a string of cat houses in the Valley! They call me Killer, Killer Wingfield, I'm leading a double-life, a simple, honest warehouse worker by day, by night a dynamic *czar* of the *underworld, Mother.* I go to gambling casinos, I spin away fortunes on the roulette table! I wear a patch over one eye and a false mustache, sometimes I put on green whiskers. On those occasions they call me— *El Diablo!* Oh, I could tell you many things to make you sleepless! My enemies plan to dynamite this place. They're going to blow us all sky-high some night! I'll be glad, very happy, and so will you! You'll go up, up on a broomstick, over Blue Mountain with seventeen gentlemen callers! You ugly—babbling old—*witch.* . . . [*He goes through a series of violent, clumsy movements, seizing his overcoat, lunging to the door, pulling it fiercely open. The women watch him, aghast. His arm catches in the sleeve of the coat as he struggles to pull it on. For a moment he is pinioned by the bulky garment. With an outraged groan he tears the coat off again, splitting the shoulder of it, and hurls it across the room. It strikes against the shelf of* LAURA'S *glass collection, and there is a tinkle of shattering glass.* LAURA *cries out as if wounded.*] [*Music.*] [*Screen legend:* "The Glass Menagerie."]

LAURA [*shrilly*]. My glass!—menagerie. . . . [*She covers her face and turns away.*]

[*But* AMANDA *is still stunned and stupefied by the "ugly witch" so that she barely notices this occurrence. Now she recovers her speech.*]

AMANDA [*in an awful voice*]. I won't speak to you—until you apologize!

[*She crosses through the portieres and draws them together behind her.* TOM *is left with* LAURA. LAURA *clings weakly to the mantel with her face averted.* TOM *stares at her stupidly for a moment. Then he crosses to the shelf. He drops awkwardly on his knees to collect the fallen glass, glancing at* LAURA *as if he would speak but couldn't.*]
[*"The Glass Menagerie" music steals in as the scene dims out.*]

SCENE IV

The interior of the apartment is dark. There is a faint light in the alley. A deep-voiced bell in a church is tolling the hour of five.

    TOM *appears at the top of the alley. After each solemn boom of the bell in the tower, he shakes a little noisemaker or rattle as if to express the tiny spasm of man in contrast to the sustained power and dignity of the Almighty. This and the unsteadiness of his advance make it evident that he has been drinking. As he climbs the few steps to the fire escape landing light steals up inside.* LAURA *appears in the front room in a nightdress. She notices that* TOM's *bed is empty.* TOM *fishes in his pockets for his door key, removing a motley assortment of articles in this search, including a shower of movie ticket stubs and an empty bottle. At last he finds the key, but just as he is about to insert it, it slips from his fingers. He strikes a match and crouches below the door.*

TOM [*bitterly*]. One crack—and it falls through! [LAURA *opens the door.*]
LAURA. Tom! Tom, what are you doing?
TOM. Looking for a door key.
LAURA. Where have you been all this time?
TOM. I have been to the movies.
LAURA. All this time at the movies?
TOM. There was a very long program. There was a Garbo picture and a Mickey Mouse and a travelogue and a newsreel and a preview of coming attractions. And there was an organ solo and a collection for the Milk Fund—simultaneously—which ended up in a terrible fight between a fat lady and an usher!
LAURA [*innocently*]. Did you have to stay through everything?
TOM. Of course! And, oh, I forgot! There was a big stage show! The headliner on this stage show was Malvolio the Magician. He performed wonderful tricks, many of them such as pouring water back and forth between pitchers. First it turned to wine and then it turned to beer and then it turned to whiskey. I know it was whiskey it finally turned to because he needed somebody to come up out of the audience to help him, and I came up—both shows! It was Kentucky Straight Bourbon. A very generous fellow, he gave souvenirs. [*He pulls from his pocket a shimmering rainbow-colored scarf.*] He gave me this. This is his magic scarf. You can have it, Laura. You wave it over a canary cage and you get a bowl of goldfish. You wave it over the goldfish bowl and they fly away canaries. . . . But the wonderfullest trick of all was the coffin trick. We nailed him into a coffin and he got out of the coffin without removing one nail. [*He has come inside.*] There is a trick that would

come in handy for me—get me out of this two-by-four situation! [*He flops onto the bed and starts removing his shoes.*]

LAURA. Tom—shhh!

TOM. What're you shushing me for?

LAURA. You'll wake up Mother.

TOM. Goody, goody! Pay'er back for all those "Rise an' Shines." [*He lies down, groaning.*] You know it don't take much intelligence to get yourself into a nailed-up coffin, Laura. But who in hell ever got himself out of one without removing one nail?

[*As if in answer, the father's grinning photograph lights up. The scene dims out.*] [*Immediately following, the church bell is heard striking six. At the sixth stroke the alarm clock goes off in* AMANDA's *room, and after a few moments we hear her calling: "Rise and Shine! Rise and Shine!* LAURA *go tell your brother to rise and shine!"*]

TOM [*sitting up slowly*]. I'll rise—but I won't shine. [*The light increases.*]

AMANDA. Laura, tell your brother his coffee is ready. [*Laura slips into the front room.*]

LAURA. Tom—It's nearly seven. Don't make Mother nervous. [*He stares at her stupidly.*] [*beseechingly:*] Tom, speak to Mother this morning. Make up with her, apologize, speak to her!

TOM. She won't to me. It's her that started not speaking.

LAURA. If you just say you're sorry she'll start speaking.

TOM. Her not speaking—is that such a tragedy?

LAURA. Please—please!

AMANDA [*calling from the kitchenette*]. Laura, are you going to do what I asked you to do, or do I have to get dressed and go out myself?

LAURA. Going, going—soon as I get on my coat! [*She pulls on a shapeless felt hat with a nervous, jerky movement, pleadingly glancing at* TOM. *She rushes awkwardly for her coat. The coat is one of* AMANDA's *inaccurately made-over, the sleeves too short for* LAURA.] Butter and what else?

AMANDA [*entering from the kitchenette*]. Just butter. Tell them to charge it.

LAURA. Mother, they make such faces when I do that.

AMANDA. Sticks and stones can break our bones, but the expression on Mr. Garfinkel's face won't harm us! Tell your brother his coffee is getting cold.

LAURA [*at the door*]. Do what I asked you, will you, will you, Tom? [*He looks sullenly away.*]

AMANDA. Laura, go now or just don't go at all!

LAURA [*rushing out*]. Going—going! [*A second later she cries out.* TOM *springs up and crosses to the door.* TOM *opens the door.*]

TOM. Laura?

LAURA. I'm all right. I slipped, but I'm all right.

AMANDA [*peering anxiously after her*]. If anyone breaks a leg on those fire-escape steps, the landlord ought to be sued for every cent he possesses!

[*She shuts the door. Now she remembers she isn't speaking to* TOM *and returns to the other room.*] [*As* TOM *comes listlessly for his coffee, she turns her back to him* *and stands rigidly facing the window on the gloomy gray vault of the areaway. Its light on her face with its aged but childish features is cruelly sharp, satirical as a Daumier print.] [The music of "Ave Maria" is heard softly.] [*TOM *glances sheepishly but sullenly at her averted figure and slumps at the table. The coffee is scalding hot; he sips it and gasps and spits it back in the cup. At his gasp,* AMANDA *catches her breath and half turns. Then she catches herself and turns back to the window.* TOM *blows on his coffee, glancing sidewise at his mother. She clears her throat.* TOM *clears his. He starts to rise, sinks back down again, scratches his head, clears his throat again.* AMANDA *coughs.* TOM *raises his cup in both hands to blow on it, his eyes staring over the rim of it at his mother for several moments. Then he slowly sets the cup down and awkwardly and hesitantly rises from the chair.]*

TOM [*hoarsely*]. Mother. I—I apologize, Mother. [AMANDA *draws a quick, shuddering breath. Her face works grotesquely. She breaks into childlike tears.*] I'm sorry for what I said, for everything that I said, I didn't mean it.

AMANDA [*sobbingly*]. My devotion has made me a witch and so I make myself hateful to my children!

TOM. No, you *don't*.

AMANDA. I worry so much, don't sleep, it makes me nervous!

TOM [*gently*]. I understand that.

AMANDA. I've had to put up a solitary battle all these years. But you're my right-hand bower! Don't fall down, don't fail!

TOM [*gently*]. I try, Mother.

AMANDA [*with great enthusiasm*]. Try and you will *succeed!* [*The notion makes her breathless.*] Why, you—you're just *full* of natural endowments! Both of my children— they're *unusual* children! Don't you think I know it? I'm so—*proud!* Happy and— feel I've—so much to be thankful for but—promise me one thing, son!

TOM. What, Mother?

AMANDA. Promise, son, you'll—never be a drunkard!

TOM [*turns to her grinning*]. I will never be a drunkard, Mother.

AMANDA. That's what frightened me so, that you'd be drinking! Eat a bowl of Purina!

TOM. Just coffee, Mother.

AMANDA. Shredded wheat biscuit?

TOM. No. No, Mother, just coffee.

AMANDA. You can't put in a day's work on an empty stomach. You've got ten minutes— don't gulp! Drinking too-hot liquids makes cancer of the stomach. . . . Put cream in.

TOM. No, thank you.

AMANDA. To cool it.

TOM. No! No, thank you, I want it black.

AMANDA. I know, but it's not good for you. We have to do all that we can to build ourselves up. In these trying times we live in, all that we have to cling to is— each other. . . . That's why it's important to—Tom, I—I sent out your sister so I could discuss something with you. If you hadn't spoken I would have spoken to you. [*She sits down.*]

TOM [*gently*]. What is it, Mother, that you want to discuss?

AMANDA. *Laura!* [TOM *puts his cup down slowly*] [*Legend on screen:* "Laura." *Music: "The Glass Menagerie."*]

TOM. —Oh.—Laura . . .

AMANDA [*touching his sleeve*]. You know how Laura is. So quiet but—still water runs deep! She notices things and I think she—broods about them. [TOM *looks up.*] A few days ago I came in and she was crying.

TOM. What about?

AMANDA. You.

TOM. Me?

AMANDA. She has an idea that you're not happy here.

TOM. What gave her that idea?

AMANDA. What gives her any idea? However, you do act strangely. I—I'm not criticizing, understand *that!* I know your ambitions do not lie in the warehouse, that like everybody in the whole wide world—you've had to—make sacrifices, but—Tom— Tom—life's not easy, it calls for—Spartan endurance! There's so many things in my heart that I cannot describe to you! I've never told you but I—*loved* your father. . . .

TOM [*gently*]. I know that, Mother.

AMANDA. And you—when I see you taking after his ways! Staying out late—and— well, you *had* been drinking the night you were in that—terrifying condition! Laura says that you hate the apartment and that you go out nights to get away from it! Is that true, Tom?

TOM. No. You say there's so much in your heart that you can't describe to me. That's true of me, too. There's so much in my heart that I can't describe to *you!* So let's respect each other's—

AMANDA. But, why—*why,* Tom—are you always so *restless?* Where do you *go* to, nights?

TOM. I—go to the movies.

AMANDA. Why do you go to the movies so much, Tom?

TOM. I go to the movies because—I like adventure. Adventure is something I don't have much of at work, so I go to the movies.

AMANDA. But, Tom, you go the movies *entirely* too *much!*

TOM. I like a lot of adventure. [AMANDA *looks baffled, then hurt. As the familiar inquisition resumes,* TOM *becomes hard and impatient again.* AMANDA *slips back into her querulous attitude toward him.*] [*Image on screen:* A sailing vessel with Jolly Roger.]

AMANDA. Most young men find adventure in their careers.

TOM. Then most young men are not employed in a warehouse.

AMANDA. The world is full of young men employed in warehouses and offices and factories.

TOM. Do all of them find adventure in their careers?

AMANDA. They do or they do without it! Not everybody has a craze for adventure.

TOM. Man is by instinct a lover, a hunter, a fighter, and none of those instincts are given much play at the warehouse!

AMANDA. Man is by instinct! Don't quote instinct to me! Instinct is something that people have got away from! It belongs to animals! Christian adults don't want it!

TOM. What do Christian adults want, then, Mother?

AMANDA. Superior things! Things of the mind and the spirit! Only animals have to satisfy instincts! Surely your aims are somewhat higher than theirs! Than monkeys— pigs—

TOM. I reckon they're not.

AMANDA. You're joking. However, that isn't what I wanted to discuss.

TOM [*rising*]. I haven't much time.

AMANDA [*pushing his shoulders*]. Sit down.

TOM. You want me to punch in red at the warehouse, Mother?

AMANDA. You have five minutes. I want to talk about Laura. [*Screen legend:* "Plans and Provisions."]

TOM. All right! What about Laura?

AMANDA. We have to be making some plans and provisions for her. She's older than you, two years, and nothing has happened. She just drifts along doing nothing. It frightens me terribly how she just drifts along.

TOM. I guess she's the type that people call home girls.

AMANDA. There's no such type, and if there is, it's a pity! That is unless the home is hers, with a husband!

TOM. What?

AMANDA. Oh, I can see the handwriting on the wall as plain as I see the nose in front of my face! It's terrifying! More and more you remind me of your father! He was out all hours without explanation!—Then *left! Goodbye!* And me with the bag to hold. I saw that letter you got from the Merchant Marine. I know what you're dreaming of. I'm not standing here blindfolded. [*She pauses.*] Very well, then. Then *do* it! But not till there's somebody to take your place.

TOM. What do you mean?

AMANDA. I mean that as soon as Laura has got somebody to take care of her, married, a home of her own, independent—why, then you'll be free to go wherever you please, on land, on sea, whichever way the wind blows you! But until that time you've got to look out for your sister. I don't say me because I'm old and don't matter! I say for your sister because she's young and dependent.

I put her in business college—a dismal failure! Frightened her so it made her sick at the stomach. I took her over to the Young People's League at the church. Another fiasco. She spoke to nobody, nobody spoke to her. Now all she does is fool with those pieces of glass and play those worn-out records. What kind of a life is that for a girl to lead?

TOM. What can I do about it?

AMANDA. Overcome selfishness! Self, self, self is all that you ever think of! [TOM *springs up and crosses to get his coat. It is ugly and bulky. He pulls on a cap with earmuffs.*] Where is your muffler? Put your wool muffler on! [*He snatches it angrily from the closet, tosses it around his neck and pulls both ends tight.*] Tom! I haven't said what I had in mind to ask you.

TOM. I'm too late to—

AMANDA [*catching his arm—very importunately; then shyly*]. Down at the warehouse, aren't there some—nice young men?

TOM. No!

AMANDA. There *must* be—*some* . . .

TOM. Mother—[*He gestures.*]

AMANDA. Find out one that's clean-living—doesn't drink and ask him out for sister!

TOM. What?

AMANDA. For *sister!* To *meet!* Get *acquainted!*

TOM [*stamping to the door*]. Oh, my *go-osh!*

AMANDA. Will you? [*He opens the door. She says, imploringly:*] Will you? [*He starts down the fire escape.*] Will you? *Will* you, dear?

TOM [*calling back*]. Yes! [AMANDA *closes the door hesitantly and with a troubled but faintly hopeful expression.*] [*Screen image:* The cover of a glamor magazine.] [*The spotlight picks up* AMANDA *at the phone.*]

AMANDA. Ella Cartwright? This is Amanda Wingfield! How are you, honey? How is that kidney condition? [*There is a five-second pause.*] Horrors! [*There is another pause.*] You're a Christian martyr, yes, honey, that's what you are, a Christian martyr! Well, I just now happened to notice in my little red book that your subscription to the *Companion* has just run out! I knew that you wouldn't want to miss out on the wonderful serial starting in this new issue. It's by Bessie Mae Hopper, the first thing she's written since *Honeymoon for Three.* Wasn't that a strange and interesting story? Well, this one is even lovelier, I believe. It has a sophisticated, society background. It's all about the horsey set on Long Island! [*The light fades out.*]

SCENE V

Legend on the screen: "Annunciation."

> *Music is heard as the light slowly comes on.*

> *It is early dusk of a spring evening. Supper has just been finished in the Wingfield apartment.* AMANDA *and* LAURA, *in light-colored dresses, are removing dishes from the table in the dining room, which is shadowy, their movements formalized almost as a dance or ritual, their moving forms as pale and silent as moths.* TOM, *in white shirt and trousers, rises from the table and crosses toward the fire escape.*

AMANDA [*as he passes her*]. Son, will you do me a favor?

TOM. What?

AMANDA. Comb your hair! You look so pretty when your hair is combed! [TOM *slouches on the sofa with the evening paper. Its enormous headline reads: "Franco Triumphs."*[4]]

There is only one respect in which I would like you to emulate your father.

TOM. What respect is that?

AMANDA. The care he always took of his appearance. He never allowed himself to look untidy. [*He throws down the paper and crosses to the fire escape.*] Where are you going?

---

[4] Francisco Franco (1892–1975), who led the fascist forces in the Spanish Civil War and, winning, became dictator for life.

TOM. I'm going out to smoke.

AMANDA. You smoke too much. A pack a day at fifteen cents a pack. How much would that amount to in a month? Thirty times fifteen is how much, Tom? Figure it out and you will be astounded at what you could save. Enough to give you a night-school course in accounting at Washington U.! Just think what a wonderful thing that would be for you, son! [TOM *is unmoved by the thought.*]

TOM. I'd rather smoke. [*He steps out on the landing, letting the screen door slam.*]

AMANDA [*sharply*]. I know! That's the tragedy of it. . . . [*Alone, she turns to look at her husband's picture.*] [*Dance music: "The World Is Waiting for the Sunrise!"*]

TOM [*to the audience*]. Across the alley from us was the Paradise Dance Hall. On evenings in spring the windows and doors were open and the music came outdoors. Sometimes the lights were turned out except for a large glass sphere that hung from the ceiling. It would turn slowly about and filter the dusk with delicate rainbow colors. Then the orchestra played a waltz or a tango, something that had a slow and sensuous rhythm. Couples would come outside, to the relative privacy of the alley. You could see them kissing behind ash pits and telephone poles. This was the compensation for lives that passed like mine, without any change or adventure. Adventure and change were imminent in this year. They were waiting around the corner for all these kids. Suspended in the mist over Berchtesgaden, caught in the folds of Chamberlain's[5] umbrella. In Spain there was Guernica! But here there was only hot swing music and liquor, dance halls, bars, and movies, and sex that hung in the gloom like a chandelier and flooded the world with brief, deceptive rainbows. . . . All the world was waiting for bombardments! [AMANDA *turns from the picture and comes outside.*]

AMANDA [*sighing*]. A fire escape landing's a poor excuse for a porch. [*She spreads a newspaper on a step and sits down, gracefully and demurely as if she were settling into a swing on a Mississippi veranda.*] What are you looking at?

TOM. The moon.

AMANDA. Is there a moon this evening?

TOM. It's rising over Garfinkel's Delicatessen.

AMANDA. So it is! A little silver slipper of a moon. Have you made a wish on it yet?

TOM. Um-hum.

AMANDA. What did you wish for?

TOM. That's a secret.

AMANDA. A secret, huh? Well, I won't tell mine either. I will be just as mysterious as you.

TOM. I bet I can guess what yours is.

AMANDA. Is my head so transparent?

TOM. You're not a sphinx.

AMANDA. No, I don't have secrets. I'll tell you what I wished for on the moon. Success and happiness for my precious children! I wish for that whenever there's a moon, and when there isn't a moon, I wish for it, too.

[5] Prime Minister of Great Britain from 1937 to 1940, Chamberlain met with Hitler at Berchtesgaden, Hitler's mountain retreat, in hopes of appeasing the German dictator and thereby averting World War Two.

TOM. I thought perhaps you wished for a gentleman caller.

AMANDA. Why do you say that?

TOM. Don't you remember asking me to fetch one?

AMANDA. I remember suggesting that it would be nice for your sister if you brought home some nice young man from the warehouse. I think that I've made that suggestion more than once.

TOM. Yes, you have made it repeatedly.

AMANDA. Well?

TOM. We are going to have one.

AMANDA. *What?*

TOM. A gentleman caller! [*The annunciation is celebrated with music.*] [AMANDA *rises.*] [*Image on screen:* A caller with a bouquet.]

AMANDA. You mean you have asked some nice young man to come over?

TOM. Yep. I've asked him to dinner.

AMANDA. You really did?

TOM. I did!

AMANDA. You did, and did he—*accept?*

TOM. He did!

AMANDA. Well, well—well, well! That's—lovely!

TOM. I thought that you would be pleased.

AMANDA. It's definite then?

TOM. Very definite.

AMANDA. Soon?

TOM. Very soon.

AMANDA. For heaven's sake, stop putting on and tell me some things, will you?

TOM. What things do you want me to tell you?

AMANDA. *Naturally* I would like to how when he's *coming!*

TOM. He's coming tomorrow.

AMANDA. *Tomorrow?*

TOM. Yep. Tomorrow.

AMANDA. But, Tom!

TOM. Yes, Mother?

AMANDA. Tomorrow gives me no time!

TOM. Time for what?

AMANDA. Preparations! Why didn't you phone me at once, as soon as you asked him, the minute that he accepted? Then, don't you see, I could have been getting ready!

TOM. You don't have to make any fuss.

AMANDA. Oh, Tom, Tom, Tom, of course I have to make a fuss! I want things nice, not sloppy! Not thrown together, I'll certainly have to do some fast thinking, won't I?

TOM. I don't see why you have to think at all.

AMANDA. You just don't know. We can't have a gentleman caller in a pigsty! All my wedding silver has to be polished, the monogrammed table linen ought to be laundered! The windows have to be washed and fresh curtains put up. And how about clothes? We have to *wear* something, don't we?

TOM. Mother, this boy is no one to make a fuss over!

AMANDA. Do you realize he's the first young man we've introduced to your sister? It's terrible, dreadful, disgraceful that poor little sister has never received a single gentleman caller! Tom, come inside! [*She opens the screen door.*]

TOM. What for?

AMANDA. I want to ask you some things.

TOM. If you're going to make such a fuss, I'll call it off, I'll tell him not to come!

AMANDA. You certainly won't do anything of the kind. Nothing offends people worse than broken engagements. It simply means I'll have to work like a Turk! We won't be brilliant, but we will pass inspection. Come on inside. [TOM *follows her inside, groaning.*] Sit down.

TOM. Any particular place you would like me to sit?

AMANDA. Thank heavens I've got that new sofa! I'm also making payments on a floor lamp I'll have sent out! And put the chintz covers on, they'll brighten things up! Of course I'd hoped to have these walls re-papered. . . . What is the young man's name?

TOM. His name is O'Connor.

AMANDA. That, of course, means fish—tomorrow is Friday! I'll have that salmon loaf— with Durkee's dressing! What does he do? He works at the warehouse?

TOM. Of course! How else would I—

AMANDA. Tom, he—doesn't drink?

TOM. Why do you ask me that?

AMANDA. Your father *did!*

TOM. Don't get started on that!

AMANDA. He *does* drink, then?

TOM. Not that I know of!

AMANDA. Make sure, be certain! The last thing I want for my daughter's a boy who drinks!

TOM. Aren't you being a little bit premature? Mr. O'Connor has not yet appeared on the scene!

AMANDA. But will tomorrow. To meet your sister, and what do I know about his character? Nothing! Old maids are better off than wives of drunkards!

TOM. Oh, my God!

AMANDA. Be still!

TOM [*leaning forward to whisper*]. Lots of fellows meet girls whom they don't marry!

AMANDA. Oh, talk sensibly, Tom—and don't be sarcastic! [*She has gotten a hairbrush.*]

TOM. What are you doing?

AMANDA. I'm brushing that cowlick down! [*She attacks his hair with the brush.*] What is this young man's position at the warehouse?

TOM [*submitting grimly to the brush and the interrogation*]. This young man's position is that of a shipping clerk, Mother.

AMANDA. Sounds to me like a fairly responsible job, the sort of a job *you* would be in if you just had more *get-up.* What is his salary? Have you any idea?

TOM. I would judge it to be approximately eighty-five dollars a month.

AMANDA. Well—not princely, but—

TOM. Twenty more than I make.

AMANDA. Yes, how well I know! But for a family man, eighty-five dollars a month is not much more than you can just get by on. . . .

TOM. Yes, but Mr. O'Connor is not a family man.

AMANDA. He might be, mightn't he? Some time in the future?

TOM. I see. Plans and provisions.

AMANDA. You are the only young man that I know of who ignores the fact that the future becomes the present, the present the past, and the past turns into everlasting regret if you don't plan for it!

TOM. I will think that over and see what I can make of it.

AMANDA. Don't be supercilious with your mother! Tell me some more about this— what do you call him?

TOM. James D. O'Connor. The D. is for Delaney.

AMANDA. Irish on *both* sides! *Gracious!* And doesn't drink?

TOM. Shall I call him up and ask him right this minute?

AMANDA. The only way to find out about those things is to make discreet inquiries at the proper moment. When I was a girl in Blue Mountain and it was suspected that a young man drank, the girl whose attentions he had been receiving, if any girl *was,* would sometimes speak to the minister of his church, or rather her father would if her father was living, and sort of feel him out on the young man's character. That is the way such things are discreetly handled to keep a young woman from making a tragic mistake!

TOM. Then how did you happen to make a tragic mistake?

AMANDA. That innocent look of your father's had everyone fooled! He *smiled*—the world was *enchanted!* No girl can do worse than put herself at the mercy of a handsome appearance! I hope that Mr. O'Connor is not too good-looking.

TOM. No, he's not too good-looking. He's covered with freckles and hasn't too much of a nose.

AMANDA. He's not right-down homely, though?

TOM. Not right-down homely. Just medium homely, I'd say.

AMANDA. Character's what to look for in a man.

TOM. That's what I've always said, Mother.

AMANDA. You've never said anything of the kind and I suspect you would never give it a thought.

TOM. Don't be so suspicious of me.

AMANDA. At least I hope he's the type that's up and coming.

TOM. I think he really goes in for self-improvement.

AMANDA. What reason have you to think so?

TOM. He goes to night school.

AMANDA [*beaming*]. Splendid! What does he do, I mean study?

TOM. Radio engineering and public speaking!

AMANDA. Then he has visions of being advanced in the world! Any young man who studies public speaking is aiming to have an executive job some day! And radio engineering? A thing for the future! Both of these facts are very illuminating. Those are the sort of things that a mother should know concerning any young man who comes to call on her daughter. Seriously or—not.

TOM. One little warning. He doesn't know about Laura. I didn't let on that we had dark ulterior motives. I just said, why don't you come and have dinner with us? He said okay and that was the whole conversation.

AMANDA. I bet it was! You're eloquent as an oyster. However, he'll know about Laura when he gets here. When he sees how lovely and sweet and pretty she is, he'll thank his lucky stars he was asked to dinner.

TOM. Mother, you mustn't expect too much of Laura.

AMANDA. What do you mean?

TOM. Laura seems all those things to you and me because she's ours and we love her. We don't even notice she's crippled any more.

AMANDA. Don't say crippled! You know that I never allow that word to be used!

TOM. But face facts, Mother. She is and—that's not all—

AMANDA. What do you mean "not all"?

TOM. Laura is very different from other girls.

AMANDA. I think the difference is all to her advantage.

TOM. Not quite all—in the eyes of others—strangers—she's terribly shy and lives in a world of her own and those things make her seem a little peculiar to people outside the house.

AMANDA. Don't say peculiar.

TOM. Face the facts. She is. [*The dance hall music changes to a tango that has a minor and somewhat ominous tone.*]

AMANDA. In what way is she peculiar—may I ask?

TOM [*gently*]. She lives in a world of her own—a world of little glass ornaments, Mother. . . . [*He gets up.* AMANDA *remains holding the brush, looking at him, troubled.*] She plays old phonograph records and—that's about all— [*He glances at himself in the mirror and crosses to the door.*]

AMANDA [*sharply*]. Where are you going?

TOM. I'm going to the movies. [*He goes out the screen door.*]

AMANDA. Not to the movies, every night to the movies! [*She follows quickly to the screen door.*] I don't believe you always go to the movies! [*He is gone.* AMANDA *looks worriedly after him for a moment. Then vitality and optimism return and she turns from the door, crossing to the portieres.*] Laura! Laura! [LAURA *answers from the kitchenette.*]

LAURA. Yes, Mother.

AMANDA. Let those dishes go and come in front! [LAURA *appears with a dish towel.* AMANDA *speaks to her gaily.*] Laura, come here and make a wish on the moon! [*Screen image:* The Moon.]

LAURA [*entering*]. Moon—moon?

AMANDA. A little silver slipper of a moon. Look over your left shoulder, Laura, and make a wish! [LAURA *looks faintly puzzled as if called out of sleep.* AMANDA *seizes her shoulders and turns her at an angle by the door.*] Now! Now, darling, wish!

LAURA. What shall I wish for, Mother?

AMANDA [*her voice trembling and her eyes suddenly filling with tears*]. Happiness! Good fortune! [*The sound of the violin rises and the stage dims out.*]

SCENE VI

The light comes up on the fire escape landing. TOM *is leaning against the grill, smoking.* [*Screen image:* The high school hero.]

TOM. And so the following evening I brought Jim home to dinner. I had known Jim slightly in high school. In high school Jim was a hero. He had tremendous Irish good nature and vitality with the scrubbed and polished look of white chinaware. He seemed to move in a continual spotlight. He was a star in basketball, captain of the debating club, president of the senior class and the glee club and he sang the male lead in the annual light operas. He was always running or bounding, never just walking. He seemed always at the point of defeating the law of gravity. He was shooting with such velocity through his adolescence that you would logically expect him to arrive at nothing short of the White House by the time he was thirty. But Jim apparently ran into more interference after his graduation from Soldan. His speed had definitely slowed. Six years after he left high school he was holding a job that wasn't much better than mine. [*Screen image:* The Clerk.] He was the only one at the warehouse with whom I was on friendly terms. I was valuable to him as someone who could remember his former glory, who had seen him win basketball games and the silver cup in debating. He knew of my secret practice of retiring to a cabinet of the washroom to work on poems when business was slack in the warehouse. He called me Shakespeare. And while the other boys in the warehouse regarded me with suspicious hostility, Jim took a humorous attitude toward me. Gradually his attitude affected the others, their hostility wore off and they also began to smile at me as people smile at an oddly fashioned dog who trots across their path at some distance. I knew that Jim and Laura had known each other at Soldan, and I had heard Laura speak admiringly of his voice. I didn't know if Jim remembered her or not. In high school Laura had been as unobtrusive as Jim had been astonishing. If he did remember Laura, it was not as my sister, for when I asked him to dinner, he grinned and said, "You know, Shakespeare, I never thought of you as having folks!" He was about to discover that I did. . . . [*Legend on screen:* "The accent of a coming foot."] [*The light dims out on* TOM *and comes up in the Wingfield living room—a delicate lemony light. It is about five on a Friday evening of late spring which comes "scattering poems in the sky."*] [AMANDA *has worked like a turk in preparation for the gentleman caller. The results are astonishing. The new floor lamp with its rose silk shade is in place, a colored paper lantern conceals the broken light fixture in the ceiling, new billowing white curtains are at the windows, chintz covers are on the chairs and sofa, a pair of new sofa pillows make their initial appearance. Open boxes and tissue paper are scattered on the floor.*] [LAURA *stands in the middle of the room with lifted arms while* AMANDA *crouches before her adjusting the hem of a new dress, devout and ritualistic. The dress is colored and designed by memory. The arrangement of* LAURA'S *hair is changed; it is softer and more becoming. A fragile, unearthly prettiness has come out in* LAURA: *she is like a piece of translucent glass touched by light, given a momentary radiance, not actual, not lasting.*]

AMANDA [*impatiently*]. Why are you trembling?

LAURA. Mother, you've made me so nervous!

AMANDA. How have I made you nervous?

LAURA. By all the fuss! You make it seem so important!

AMANDA. I don't understand you, Laura. You couldn't be satisfied with just sitting home, and yet whenever I try to arrange something for you, you seem to resist it. [*She gets up.*] Now take a look at yourself. No, wait! Wait just a moment—I have an idea!

LAURA. What is it now? [AMANDA *produces two powder puffs which she wraps in handkerchiefs and stuffs in* Laura's *bosom.*]

LAURA. Mother, what are you doing?

AMANDA. They call them "Gay Deceivers"!

LAURA. I won't wear them!

AMANDA. You will!

LAURA. Why should I?

AMANDA. Because, to be painfully honest, your chest is flat.

LAURA. You make it seem like we were setting a trap.

AMANDA. All pretty girls are a trap, a pretty trap, and men expect them to be. [*Legend on screen:* "A pretty trap."] Now look at yourself, young lady. This is the prettiest you will ever be! [*She stands back to admire* LAURA.] I've got to fix myself now! You're going to be surprised by your mother's appearance! [AMANDA *crosses through the portieres, humming gaily.* LAURA *moves slowly to the long mirror and stares solemnly at herself. A wind blows the white curtains inward in a slow, graceful motion and with a faint, sorrowful sighing.*]

AMANDA [*from somewhere behind the portieres*]. It isn't dark enough yet. [LAURA *turns slowly before the mirror with a troubled look.*] [*Legend on screen:* "This is my sister: Celebrate her with strings!" *Music plays.*]

AMANDA [*laughing, still not visible*]. I'm going to show you something. I'm going to make a spectacular appearance!

LAURA. What is it, Mother?

AMANDA. Possess your soul in patience—you will see! Something I've resurrected from that old trunk! Styles haven't changed so terribly much after all. . . . [*She parts the portieres.*] Now just look at your mother! [*She wears a girlish frock of yellowed voile with a blue silk sash. She carries a bunch of jonquils—the legend of her youth is nearly revived. Now she speaks feverishly:*] This is the dress in which I led the cotillion. Won the cakewalk twice at Sunset Hill, wore one Spring to the Governor's Ball in Jackson! See how I sashayed around the ballroom, Laura? [*She raises her skirt and does a mincing step around the room.*] I wore it on Sundays for my gentlemen callers! I had it on the day I met your father. . . . I had malaria fever all that Spring. The change of climate from East Tennessee to the Delta—weakened resistance. I had a little temperature all the time—not enough to be serious—just enough to make me restless and giddy! Invitations poured in—parties all over the Delta! "Stay in bed," said Mother, "you have a fever!"—but I just wouldn't. I took quinine but kept on going, going! Evenings, dances! Afternoons, long, long rides! Picnics—lovely! So lovely, that country in May—all lacy with dogwood, literally flooded with jonquils! That was the spring I had the craze for jonquils. Jonquils became an absolute obsession. Mother said, "Honey, there's no more room for jonquils." And still I kept on bringing in more jonquils. Whenever, wherever I saw them, I'd say, "Stop! Stop! I see jonquils!" I made the young men help me gather the jonquils! It was a joke, Amanda and her jonquils. Finally there were no more vases to hold them, every available space was filled with jonquils. No vases to hold them? All right, I'll hold them myself! And then I—[*She stops in front of the picture. Music plays.*] met your father! Malaria fever and jonquils and then—this—boy. . . . [*She switches on the rose-colored lamp.*] I hope they get here before it starts to rain. [*She crosses the room and places the jonquils in a bowl on the table.*] I gave your brother a little extra change so he and Mr. O'Connor could take the service car home.

LAURA [*with an altered look*]. What did you say his name was?

AMANDA. O'Connor.

LAURA. What is his first name?

AMANDA. I don't remember. Oh, yes, I do. It was—Jim! [LAURA *sways slightly and catches hold of a chair.*] [*Legend on screen:* "Not Jim!"]

LAURA [*faintly*]. Not—Jim!

AMANDA. Yes, that was it, it was Jim! I've never known a Jim that wasn't nice! [*The music becomes ominous.*]

LAURA. Are you sure his name is Jim O'Connor?

AMANDA. Yes. Why?

LAURA. Is he the one that Tom used to know in high school?

AMANDA. He didn't say so. I think he just got to know him at the warehouse.

LAURA. There was a Jim O'Connor we both knew in high school—[*then, with effort*] If that is the one that Tom is bringing to dinner—you'll have to excuse me, I won't come to the table.

AMANDA. What sort of nonsense is this?

LAURA. You asked me once if I'd ever liked a boy. Don't you remember I showed you this boy's picture?

AMANDA. You mean the boy you showed me in the yearbook?

LAURA. Yes, that boy.

AMANDA. Laura, Laura, were you in love with that boy?

LAURA. I don't know, Mother. All I know is I couldn't sit at the table if it was him!

AMANDA. It won't be him! It isn't the least bit likely. But whether it is or not, you will come to the table. You will not be excused.

LAURA. I'll have to be, Mother.

AMANDA. I don't intend to humor your silliness, Laura. I've had too much from you and your brother, both! So just sit down and compose yourself till they come. Tom has forgotten his key so you'll have to let them in, when they arrive.

LAURA [*panicky*]. Oh, Mother—*you* answer the door!

AMANDA [*lightly*]. I'll be in the kitchen—busy!

LAURA. Oh, Mother, please answer the door, don't make me do it.!

AMANDA [*crossing into the kitchenette*]. I've got to fix the dressing for the salmon. Fuss, fuss—silliness!—over a gentleman caller! [*The door swings shut.* LAURA *is left alone.*] [*Legend on screen:* "Terror!"] [*She utters a low moan and turns off the lamp—sits stiffly on the edge of the sofa, knotting her fingers together.*] [*Legend on screen: "The Opening of a Door!"*] [TOM *and* JIM *appear on the fire escape steps and climb to the landing. Hearing their approach,* LAURA *rises with a panicky gesture. She retreats to the portieres. The doorbell.* LAURA *catches her breath and touches her throat. Low drums sound.*]

AMANDA [*calling*]. Laura, sweetheart! The door! [LAURA *stares at it without moving.*]

JIM. I think we just beat the rain.

TOM. Uh-huh. [*He rings again, nervously.* JIM *whistles and fishes for a cigarette.*]

AMANDA [*very, very gaily*]. Laura, that is your brother and Mr. O'Connor! Will you let them in, darling? [LAURA *crosses toward the kitchenette door.*]

LAURA [*breathlessly*]. Mother—you go to the door! [AMANDA *steps out of the kitchenette and stares furiously at* LAURA. *She points imperiously at the door.*]

LAURA. Please, please!

AMANDA [*in a fierce whisper*]. What is the matter with you, you silly thing?

LAURA [*desperately*]. Please, you answer it, *please!*

AMANDA. I told you I wasn't going to humor you, Laura. Why have you chosen this moment to lose your mind?

LAURA. Please, please, you go!

AMANDA. You'll have to go to the door because I can't!

LAURA [*despairingly*]. I can't either!

AMANDA. *Why?*

LAURA. I'm *sick!*

AMANDA. I'm sick, too—of your nonsense! Why can't you and your brother be normal people? Fantastic whims and behavior! [TOM *gives a long ring.*] Preposterous goings on! Can you give me one reason—[*She calls out lyrically.*] Coming! *Just one second!*—why you should be afraid to open a door? Now you answer it, Laura!

LAURA. Oh, oh, oh . . . [*She returns through the portieres, darts to the Victrola, winds it frantically and turns it on.*]

AMANDA. Laura Wingfield, you march right to that door!

LAURA. *Yes*—yes, Mother! [*A faraway, scratchy rendition of "Dardanella" softens the air and gives her strength to move through it. She slips to the door and draws it cautiously open.* TOM *enters with the caller,* JIM O'CONNOR.]

TOM. Laura, this is Jim. Jim, this is my sister, Laura.

JIM [*stepping inside*]. I didn't know that Shakespeare had a sister!

LAURA [*retreating, stiff and trembling, from the door*]. How—how do you do?

JIM [*heartily, extending his hand*]. Okay! [LAURA *touches it hesitantly with hers.*] Your hand's *cold,* Laura!

LAURA. Yes, well—I've been playing the Victrola. . . .

JIM. Must have been playing classical music on it! You ought to play a little hot swing music to warm you up!

LAURA. Excuse me—I haven't finished playing the Victrola. . . . [*She turns awkwardly and hurries into the front room. She pauses a second by the Victrola. Then she catches her breath and darts through the portieres like a frightened deer.*]

JIM [*grinning*]. What was the matter?

TOM. Oh—with Laura? Laura is—terribly shy.

JIM. Shy, huh? It's unusual to meet a shy girl nowadays. I don't believe you ever mentioned you had a sister.

TOM. Well, now you know. I have one. Here is the *Post Dispatch*. You want a piece of it?

JIM. Uh-huh.

TOM. What piece? The comics?

JIM. Sports! [*He glances at it.*] Ole Dizzy Dean is on his bad behavior.

TOM [*uninterested*]. Yeah? [*He lights a cigarette and goes over to the fire-escape door.*]

JIM. Where are *you* going?

TOM. I'm going out on the terrace.

JIM [*going after him*]. You know, Shakespeare—I'm going to sell you a bill of goods!

TOM. What goods?

JIM. A course I'm taking.

TOM. Huh?

JIM. In public speaking? You and me, we're not the warehouse type.

TOM. Thanks—that's good news. But what has public speaking got to do with it?

JIM. It fits you for—executive positions!

TOM. Awww.

JIM. I tell you it's done a helluva lot for me. [*Image on screen:* Executive at his desk.]

TOM. In what respect?

JIM. In every! Ask yourself what is the difference between you an' me and men in the office down front? Brains?—No!—Ability?—No! Then what? Just one little thing—

TOM. What is that one little thing?

JIM. Primarily it amounts to—social poise! Being able to square up to people and hold your own on any social level!

AMANDA [*from the kitchenette*]. Tom?

TOM. Yes, Mother?

AMANDA. Is that you and Mr. O'Connor?

TOM. Yes, Mother.

AMANDA. Well, you just make yourselves comfortable in there.

TOM. Yes, Mother.

AMANDA. Ask Mr. O'Connor if he would like to wash his hands.

JIM. Aw, no—no—thank you—I took care of that at the warehouse. Tom—

TOM. Yes?

JIM. Mr. Mendoza was speaking to me about you.

TOM. Favorably?

JIM. What do you think?

TOM. Well—

JIM. You're going to be out of a job if you don't wake up.

TOM. I am waking up—

JIM. You show no signs.

TOM. The signs are interior. [*Image on screen:* The sailing vessel with the Jolly Roger again.*]

TOM. I'm planning to change. [*He leans over the fire-escape rail, speaking with quiet exhilaration. The incandescent marquees and signs of the first-run movie houses light his face from across the alley. He looks like a voyager.*] I'm right at the point of commiting myself to a future that doesn't include the warehouse and Mr. Mendoza or even a night-school course in public speaking.

JIM. What are you gassing about?

TOM. I'm tired of the movies.

JIM. Movies!

TOM. Yes, movies! Look at them—[*a wave toward the marvels of Grand Avenue*] All of those glamorous people—having adventures—hogging it all, gobbling the whole thing up! You know what happens? People go to the *movies* instead of *moving!* Hollywood characters are supposed to have all the adventures for everybody in America, while everybody in America sits in a dark room and watches them have them! Yes, until there's a war. That's when adventure becomes available to the masses! *Everyone's* dish, not only Gable's! Then the people in the dark room come out of the dark room to have some adventures themselves—goody, goody! It's our turn now, to go to the South Sea Island—to make a safari—to be exotic, far-off! But I'm not patient. I don't want to wait till then. I'm tired of the *movies* and I am *about* to *move!*

JIM [*incredulously*]. Move?

TOM. Yes.

JIM. When?

TOM. Soon!

JIM. Where? Where? [*The music seems to answer the question, while* TOM *thinks it over. He searches in his pockets.*]

TOM. I'm starting to boil inside. I know I seem dreamy, but inside—well, I'm boiling! Whenever I pick up a shoe, I shudder a little thinking how short life is and what I am doing! Whatever that means, I know it doesn't mean shoes—except as something to wear on a traveler's feet! [*He finds what he has been searching for in his pockets and holds out a paper to Jim.*] Look—

JIM. What?

TOM. I'm a member.

JIM [*reading*]. The Union of Merchant Seamen.

TOM. I paid my dues this month, instead of the light bill.

JIM. You will regret it when they turn the lights off.

TOM. I won't be here.

JIM. How about your mother?

TOM. I'm like my father. The bastard son of a bastard! Did you notice how he's grinning in his picture in there? And he's been absent going on sixteen years!

JIM. You're just talking, you drip. How does your mother feel about it?

TOM. Shhh! Here comes Mother! Mother is not acquainted with my plans!

AMANDA [*coming through the portieres*]. Where are you all?

TOM. On the terrace, Mother. [*They start inside. She advances to them.* TOM *is distinctly shocked at her appearance. Even* JIM *blinks a little. He is making his first contact with girlish Southern vivacity and in spite of the night-school course in public speaking is somewhat thrown off the beam by the unexpected outlay of social charm. Certain responses are attempted by* JIM *but are swept aside by* AMANDA'S *gay laughter and chatter.* TOM *is embarrassed but after the first shock* JIM *reacts very warmly. He grins and chuckles, is altogether won over.*] [*Image on screen: Amanda as a girl.*]

AMANDA [*coyly smiling, shaking her girlish ringlets*]. Well, well, well, so this is Mr. O'Connor. Introductions entirely unnecessary. I've heard so much about you from my boy. I finally said to him, Tom—good gracious!—why don't you bring this paragon to supper? I'd like to meet this nice young man at the warehouse!—instead of just hearing him sing your praises so much! I don't know why my son is so stand-offish—that's not Southern behavior! Let's sit down and—I think we could stand a little more air in here! Tom, leave the door open. I felt a nice fresh breeze a moment ago. Where has it gone to? Mmm, so warm already! And not quite summer, even. We're going to burn up when summer really gets started. However, we're having—we're having a very light supper. I think light things are better fo' this time of year. The same as light clothes are. Light clothes an' light food are what warm weather calls fo'. You know our blood gets so thick during th' winter—it takes a while fo' us to *adjust* ou'selves—when the season changes. . . . It's come so quick this year. I wasn't prepared. All of a sudden—heavens! Already summer! I ran to the trunk an' pulled out this light dress—terribly old! Historical almost! But feels so good—so good an' co-ol, y' know. . . .

TOM. Mother—

AMANDA. Yes, honey?

TOM. How about—supper?

AMANDA. Honey, you go ask Sister if supper is ready! You know that Sister is in full charge of supper! Tell her you hungry boys are waiting for it. [*to* JIM] Have you met Laura?

JIM. She—

AMANDA. Let you in? Oh, good, you've met already! It's rare for a girl as sweet an' pretty as Laura to be domestic! But Laura is, thank heavens, not only pretty but also very domestic. I'm not at all. I never was a bit. I never could make a thing but angel-food cake. Well, in the South we had so many servants. Gone, gone, gone. All vestiges of gracious living! Gone completely! I wasn't prepared for what the future brought me. All of my gentlemen callers were sons of planters and so of course I assumed that I would be married to one and raise my family on a large piece of land with plenty of servants. But man proposes—and woman accepts the proposal! To vary that old, old saying a little bit—I married no planter! I married a man who worked for the telephone company! That gallantly smiling gentleman over there! [*She points to the picture.*] A telephone man who—fell in love with long-distance! Now he travels and I don't even know where! But what am I going on for about my—tribulations? Tell me yours—I hope you don't have any! Tom?

TOM [*returning*]. Yes, Mother?

AMANDA. Is supper nearly ready?

TOM. It looks to me like supper is on the table.

AMANDA. Let me look—[*She rises prettily and looks through the portieres.*] Oh, lovely! But where is Sister?

TOM. Laura is not feeling well and she says that she thinks she'd better not come to the table.

AMANDA. What? Nonsense! Laura? Oh, Laura!

LAURA [*from the kitchenette, faintly*]. Yes, Mother.

AMANDA. You really must come to the table. We won't be seated until you come to the table! Come in, Mr. O'Connor. You sit over there, and I'll. . . . Laura? Laura Wingfield! You're keeping us waiting, honey! We can't say grace until you come to the table! [*The kitchenette door is pushed weakly open and* LAURA *comes in. She is obviously quite faint, her lips trembling, her eyes wide and staring. She moves unsteadily toward the table.*] [*Screen legend:* "Terror!"] [*Outside a summer storm is coming on abruptly. The white curtains billow inward at the windows and there is a sorrowful murmur from the deep blue dusk.*] [LAURA *suddenly stumbles; she catches at a chair with a faint moan.*]

TOM. Laura!

AMANDA. Laura! [*There is a clap of thunder.*] [*Screen legend:* "Ah!"] [*despairingly*] Why, Laura, you *are* ill, darling! Tom, help your sister into the living room, dear! Sit in the living room, Laura—rest on the sofa. Well! [*to* JIM *as* TOM *helps his sister to the sofa in the living room*] Standing over the hot stove made her ill! I told her it was just too warm this evening, but—[TOM *comes back to the table.*] Is Laura all right now?

TOM. Yes.

AMANDA. What *is* that? Rain? A cool rain has come up! [*She gives* JIM *a frightened look.*] I think we may—have grace—now . . . [TOM *looks at her stupidly.*] Tom, honey—you say grace!

TOM. Oh . . . "For these and all thy mercies—" [*They bow their heads,* AMANDA *stealing a nervous glance at* JIM. *In the living room* LAURA, *stretched on the sofa, clenches her hand to her lips, to hold back a shuddering sob.*] "God's Holy Name be praised—" [*The scene dims out.*]

SCENE VII

It is half an hour later. Dinner is just being finished in the dining room, LAURA *is still huddled upon the sofa, her feet drawn under her, her head resting on a pale blue pillow, her eyes wide and mysteriously watchful. The new floor lamp with its shade of rose-colored silk gives a soft, becoming light to her face, bringing out the fragile, unearthly prettiness which usually escapes attention. From outside there is a steady murmur of rain, but it is slackening and soon stops; the air outside becomes pale and luminous as the moon breaks through the clouds. A moment after the curtain rises, the lights in both rooms flicker and go out.*

JIM. Hey, there, Mr. Light Bulb! [AMANDA *laughs nervously.*] [*Legend on screen:* "Suspension of public service."]

AMANDA. Where was Moses when the lights went out? Ha-ha. Do you know the answer to that one, Mr. O'Connor?

JIM. No, Ma'am, what's the answer?

AMANDA. In the dark! [JIM *laughs appreciatively.*] Everybody sit still. I'll light the candles.

Isn't it lucky we have them on the table? Where's a match? Which of you gentlemen can provide a match?

JIM. Here.

AMANDA. Thank you, Sir.

JIM. Not at all, Ma'am!

AMANDA [*as she lights the candles*]. I guess the fuse has burnt out. Mr. O'Connor, can you tell a burnt-out fuse? I know I can't and Tom is a total loss when it comes to mechanics. [*They rise from the table and go into the kitchenette, from where their voices are heard.*] Oh, be careful you don't bump into something. We don't want our gentleman caller to break his neck. Now wouldn't that be a fine howdy-do?

JIM. Ha-ha! Where is the fuse-box?

AMANDA. Right here next to the stove. Can you see anything?

JIM. Just a minute.

AMANDA. Isn't electricity a mysterious thing? Wasn't it Benjamin Franklin who tied a key to a kite? We live in such a mysterious universe, don't we? Some people say that science clears up all the mysteries for us. In my opinion it only creates more! Have you found it yet?

JIM. No, Ma'am. All these fuses look okay to me.

AMANDA. Tom!

TOM. Yes, Mother?

AMANDA. That light bill I gave you several days ago. The one I told you we got the notices about? [*Legend on screen:* "Ha!"]

TOM. Oh—yeah.

AMANDA. You didn't neglect to pay it by any chance?

TOM. Why I—

AMANDA. Didn't! I might have known it!

JIM. Shakespeare probably wrote a poem on that light bill, Mrs. Wingfield.

AMANDA. I might have known better than to trust him with it! There's such a high price for negligence in this world!

JIM. Maybe the poem will win a ten-dollar prize.

AMANDA. We'll just have to spend the remainder of the evening in the nineteenth century, before Mr. Edison made the Mazda lamp!

JIM. Candlelight is my favorite kind of light.

AMANDA. That shows you're romantic! But that's no excuse for Tom. Well, we got through dinner. Very considerate of them to let us get through dinner before they plunged us into everlasting darkness, wasn't it, Mr. O'Connor?

JIM. Ha-ha!

AMANDA. Tom, as a penalty for your carelessness you can help me with the dishes.

JIM. Let me give you a hand.

AMANDA. Indeed you will not!

JIM. I ought to be good for something.

AMANDA. Good for something? [*Her tone is rhapsodic.*] *You?* Why, Mr. O'Connor, nobody, *nobody's* given me this much entertainment in years—as you have!

JIM. Aw, now, Mrs. Wingfield!

AMANDA. I'm not exaggerating, not one bit! But Sister is all by her lonesome. You go keep her company in the parlor! I'll give you this lovely old candelabrum that used to be on the altar at the church of the Heavenly Rest. It was melted a little out of shape when the church burnt down. Lightning struck it one spring. Gypsy Jones was holding a revival at the time and he intimated that the church was destroyed because the Episcopalians gave card parties.

JIM. Ha-ha.

AMANDA. And how about you coaxing Sister to drink a little wine? I think it would be good for her! Can you carry both at once?

JIM. Sure. I'm Superman!

AMANDA. Now, Thomas, get into this apron! [JIM *comes into the dining room, carrying the candelabrum, its candles lighted, in one hand and a glass of wine in the other. The door of the kitchenette swings closed on* AMANDA'S *gay laughter; the flickering light approaches the portieres.* LAURA *sits up nervously as* JIM *enters. She can hardly speak from the almost intolerable strain of being alone with a stranger.*] [*Screen legend:* "I don't suppose you remember me at all!"] [*At first, before* JIM'S *warmth overcomes her paralyzing shyness,* LAURA'S *voice is thin and breathless, as though she had just run up a steep flight of stairs.* JIM'S *attitude is gently humorous. While the incident is apparently unimportant, it is to* LAURA *the climax of her secret life.*]

JIM. Hello there, Laura.

LAURA [*faintly*]. Hello. [*She clears her throat.*]

JIM. How are you feeling now? Better?

LAURA. Yes. Yes, thank you.

JIM. This is for you. A little dandelion wine. [*He extends the glass toward her with extravagant gallantry.*]

LAURA. Thank you.

JIM. Drink it—but don't get drunk! [*He laughs heartily.* LAURA *takes the glass uncertainly; she laughs shyly.*] Where shall I set the candles?

LAURA. Oh—oh, anywhere . . .

JIM. How about here on the floor? Any objections?

LAURA. No.

JIM. I'll spread a newspaper under to catch the drippings. I like to sit on the floor. Mind if I do?

LAURA. Oh, no.

JIM. Give me a pillow?

LAURA. What?

JIM. A pillow?

LAURA. Oh . . . [*She hands him one quickly.*]

JIM. How about you? Don't you like to sit on the floor?

LAURA. Oh—yes.

JIM. Why don't you, then?

LAURA. I—will.

JIM. Take a pillow! [LAURA *does. She sits on the floor on the other side of the candelabrum.* JIM *crosses his legs and smiles engagingly at her.*] I can't hardly see you sitting way over there.

LAURA. I can—see you.

JIM. I know, but that's not fair, I'm in the limelight. [LAURA *moves her pillow closer.*] Good! Now I can see you! Comfortable?

LAURA. Yes.

JIM. So am I. Comfortable as a cow! Will you have some gum?

LAURA. No, thank you.

JIM. I think that I will indulge, with your permission. [*He musingly unwraps a stick of gum and holds it up.*] Think of the fortune made by the guy that invented the first piece of chewing gum. Amazing, huh? The Wrigley Building is one of the sights of Chicago—I saw it when I went up to the Century of Progress. Did you take in the Century of Progress?

LAURA. No, I didn't.

JIM. Well, it was quite a wonderful exposition. What impressed me most was the Hall of Science. Gives you an idea of what the future will be in America, even more wonderful than the present time is! [*There is a pause.* JIM *smiles at her.*] Your brother tells me you're shy. Is that right, Laura?

LAURA. I—don't know.

JIM. I judge you to be an old-fashioned type of girl. Well, I think that's a pretty good type to be. Hope you don't think I'm being too personal—do you?

LAURA [*hastily, out of embarrassment*]. I believe I *will* take a piece of gum, if you—don't mind. [*clearing her throat*] Mr. O'Connor, have you—kept up with your singing?

JIM. Singing? Me?

LAURA. Yes. I remember what a beautiful voice you had.

JIM. When did you hear me sing? [LAURA *does not answer, and in the long pause which follows a man's voice is heard singing offstage.*]

> VOICE:
> O blow, ye winds, heigh-ho,
> A-roving I will go!
>   I'm off to my love
>   With a boxing glove—
> Ten thousand miles away!

JIM. You say you've heard me sing?

LAURA. Oh, yes! Yes, very often . . . I—don't suppose—you remember me—at all?

JIM [*smiling doubtfully*]. You know I have an idea I've seen you before. I had that idea as soon as you opened the door. It seemed almost like I was about to remember your name. But the name that I started to call you—wasn't a name! And so I stopped myself before I said it.

LAURA. Wasn't it—Blue Roses?

JIM [*springing up, grinning*]. Blue Roses! My gosh, yes—Blue Roses! That's what I had on my tongue when you opened the door! Isn't it funny what tricks your memory plays? I didn't connect you with high school somehow or other. But that's where it was; it was high school. I didn't even know you were Shakespeare's sister! Gosh, I'm sorry.

LAURA. I didn't expect you to. You—barely knew me!

JIM. But we did have a speaking acquaintance, huh?

LAURA. Yes, we—spoke to each other.

JIM. When did you recognize me?

LAURA. Oh, right away!

JIM. Soon as I came in the door?

LAURA. When I heard your name I thought it was probably you. I knew that Tom used to know you a little in high school. So when you came in the door—well, then I was—sure.

JIM. Why didn't you *say* something, then?

LAURA [*breathlessly*]. I didn't know what to say, I was—too surprised!

JIM. For goodness sakes! You know, this sure is funny!

LAURA. Yes! Yes, isn't it, though . . .

JIM. Didn't we have a class in something together?

LAURA. Yes, we did.

JIM. What class was that?

LAURA. It was—singing—chorus!

JIM. Aw!

LAURA. I sat across the aisle from you in the Aud.

JIM. Aw.

LAURA. Mondays, Wednesdays, and Fridays.

JIM. Now I remember—you always came in late.

LAURA. Yes, it was so hard for me, getting upstairs. I had that brace on my leg—it clumped so loud!

JIM. I never heard any clumping.

LAURA [*wincing at the recollection*]. To me it sounded like—thunder!

JIM. Well, well, well, I never even noticed.

LAURA. And everybody was seated before I came in. I had to walk in front of all those people. My seat was in the back row. I had to go clumping all the way up the aisle with everyone watching!

JIM. You shouldn't have been self-conscious.

LAURA. I know, but I was. It was always such a relief when the singing started.

JIM. Aw, yes, I've placed you now! I used to call you Blue Roses. How was it that I got started calling you that?

LAURA. I was out of school a little while with pleurosis. When I came back you asked me what was the matter. I said I had pleurosis—you thought I said *Blue Roses*. That's what you always called me after that.

JIM. I hope you didn't mind.

LAURA. Oh, no—I liked it. You see, I wasn't acquainted with many—people. . . .

JIM. As I remember you sort of stuck by yourself.

LAURA. I—I—never have had much luck at—making friends.

JIM. I don't see why you wouldn't.

LAURA. Well, I—started out badly.

JIM. You mean being—

LAURA. Yes, it sort of—stood between me—

JIM. You shouldn't have let it!

LAURA. I know, but it did, and—

JIM. You were shy with people!

LAURA. I tried not to be but never could—

JIM. Overcome it?

LAURA. No, I—I never could!

JIM. I guess being shy is something you have to work out of kind of gradually.

LAURA [*sorrowfully*]. Yes—I guess it—

JIM. Takes time!

LAURA. Yes—

JIM. People are not so dreadful when you know them. That's what you have to remember! And everybody has problems, not just you, but practically everybody has got some problems. You think of yourself as having the only problems, as being the only one who is disappointed. But just look around you and you will see lots of people as disappointed as you are. For instance, I hoped when I was going to high school that I would be further along at this time, six years later, than I am now. You remember that wonderful write-up I had in *The Torch?*

LAURA. Yes! [*She rises and crosses to the table.*]

JIM. It said I was bound to succeed in anything I went into! [LAURA *returns with the high school yearbook.*] Holy Jeez, *The Torch!* [*He accepts it reverently. They smile across the book with mutual wonder.* LAURA *crouches beside him and they begin to turn the pages.* LAURA'*s shyness is dissolving in his warmth.*]

LAURA. Here you are in *The Pirates of Penzance!*

JIM [*wistfully*]. I sang the baritone lead in that operetta.

LAURA [*raptly*]. So—*beautifully!*

JIM [*protesting*]. Aw—

LAURA. Yes, yes—beautifully—beautifully!

JIM. You heard me?

LAURA. All three times!

JIM. No!

LAURA. Yes!

JIM. All three performances?

LAURA [*looking down*]. Yes.

JIM. Why?

LAURA. I—wanted to ask you to—autograph my program. [*She takes the program from the back of the yearbook and shows it to him.*]

JIM. Why didn't you ask me to?

LAURA. You were always surrounded by your own friends so much that I never had a chance to.

JIM. You should have just—

LAURA. Well, I—thought you might think I was—

JIM. Thought I might think you was—what?

LAURA. Oh—

JIM [*with reflective relish*]. I was beleaguered by females in those days.

LAURA. You were terribly popular!

JIM. Yeah—

LAURA. You had such a friendly way—

JIM. I was spoiled in high school.

LAURA. Everybody—liked you!

JIM. Including you?

LAURA. I—yes, I—did, too—[*She gently closes the book in her lap.*]

JIM. Well, well, well! Give me that program, Laura. [*She hands it to him. He signs it with a flourish.*] There you are—better late than never!

LAURA. Oh, I—what a—surprise!

JIM. My signature isn't worth very much right now. But some day—maybe—it will increase in value! Being disappointed is one thing and being discouraged is something else. I am disappointed but I am not discouraged. I'm twenty-three years old. How old are you?

LAURA. I'll be twenty-four in June.

JIM. That's not old age!

LAURA. No, but—

JIM. You finished high school?

LAURA [*with difficulty*]. I didn't go back.

JIM. You mean you dropped out?

LAURA. I made bad grades in my final examinations. [*She rises and replaces the book and the program on the table. Her voice is strained.*] How is—Emily Meisenbach getting along?

JIM. Oh, that kraut-head!

LAURA. Why do you call her that?

JIM. That's what she was.

LAURA. You're not still—going with her?

JIM. I never see her.

LAURA. It said in the "Personal" section that you were—engaged!

JIM. I know, but I wasn't impressed by that—propaganda!

LAURA. It wasn't—the truth?

JIM. Only in Emily's optimistic opinion!

LAURA. Oh— [*Legend: "What have you done since high school?"*] [JIM *lights a cigarette and leans indolently back on his elbows smiling at* LAURA *with a warmth and charm which lights her inwardly with altar candles. She remains by the table, picks up a piece from the glass menagerie collection, and turns it in her hands to cover her tumult.*]

JIM [*after several reflective puffs on his cigarette*]. What have you done since high school? [*She seems not to hear him.*] Huh? [LAURA *looks up.*] I said what have you done since high school, Laura?

LAURA. Nothing much.

JIM. You must have been doing something these six long years.

LAURA. Yes.

JIM. Well, then, such as what?

LAURA. I took a business course at business college—

JIM. How did that work out?

LAURA. Well, not very—well—I had to drop out, it gave me—indigestion—[JIM *laughs gently.*]

JIM. What are you doing now?

LAURA. I don't do anything—much. Oh, please don't think I sit around doing nothing! My glass collection takes up a good deal of time. Glass is something you have to take good care of.

JIM. What did you say—about glass?

LAURA. Collection I said—I have one—[*She clears her throat and turns away again, acutely shy.*]

JIM [*abruptly*]. You know what I judge to be the trouble with you? Inferiority complex! Know what that is? That's what they call it when someone low-rates himself! I understand it because I had it, too. Although my case was not so aggravated as yours seems to be. I had it until I took up public speaking, developed my voice, and learned that I had an aptitude for science. Before that time I never thought of myself as being outstanding in any way whatsoever! Now I've never made a regular study of it, but I have a friend who says I can analyze people better than doctors that make a profession of it. I don't claim that to be necessarily true, but I can sure guess a person's psychology, Laura! [*He takes out his gum.*] Excuse me, Laura. I always take it out when the flavor is gone. I'll use this scrap of paper to wrap it in. I know how it is to get it stuck on a shoe. [*He wraps the gum in paper and puts it in his pocket.*] Yep—that's what I judge to be your principal trouble. A lack of confidence in yourself as a person. You don't have the proper amount of faith in yourself. I'm basing that fact on a number of your remarks and also on certain observations I've made. For instance that clumping you thought was so awful in high school. You say that you even dreaded to walk into class. You see what you did? You dropped out of school, you gave up an education because of a clump, which as far as I know was practically nonexistent! A little physical defect is what you have. Hardly noticeable even! Magnified thousands of times by imagination! You know what my strong advice to you is? Think of yourself as *superior* in some way!

LAURA. In what way would I think?

JIM. Why, man alive, Laura! Just look about you a little. What do you see? A world full of common people! All of 'em born and all of 'em going to die! Which of them has one-tenth of your good points! Or mine! Or anyone else's, as far as that goes—gosh! Everybody excels in some one thing. Some in many! [*He unconsciously glances at himself in the mirror.*] All you've got to do is discover in *what*! Take me, for instance. [*He adjusts his tie at the mirror.*] My interest happens to lie in electrodynamics. I'm taking a course in radio engineering at night school, Laura, on top of a fairly responsible job at the warehouse. I'm taking that course and studying public speaking.

LAURA. Ohhhh.

JIM. Because I believe in the future of television! [*turning his back to her*] I wish to be ready to go up right along with it. Therefore I'm planning to get in on the ground floor. In fact I've already made the right connections and all that remains is for the industry itself to get under way! Full steam—[*His eyes are starry.*] Knowledge—Zzzzzp! *Money*—Zzzzzp!—*Power!* That's the cycle democracy is built on! [*His attitude is convincingly dynamic.* LAURA *stares at him, even her shyness eclipsed in her absolute wonder. He suddenly grins.*] I guess you think I think a lot of myself!

LAURA. No—o-o-o, I—

JIM. Now how about you? Isn't there something you take more interest in than anything else?

LAURA. Well, I do—as I said—have my—glass collection— [*A peal of girlish laughter rings from the kitchenette.*]

JIM. I'm not right sure I know what you're talking about. What kind of glass is it?

LAURA. Little articles of it, they're ornaments mostly! Most of them are little animals made out of glass, the tiniest little animals in the world. Mother calls them a glass menagerie! Here's an example of one, if you'd like to see it! This one is one of the oldest. It's nearly thirteen. [*Music: "The Glass Menagerie."*] [*He stretches out his hand.*] Oh, be careful—if you breathe, it breaks!

JIM. I'd better not take it. I'm pretty clumsy with things.

LAURA. Go on, I trust you with him! [*She places the piece in his palm.*] There now— you're holding him gently! Hold him over the light, he loves the light! You see how the light shines through him!

JIM. It sure does shine!

LAURA. I shouldn't be partial, but he is my favorite one.

JIM. What kind of a thing is this one supposed to be?

LAURA. Haven't you noticed the single horn on his forehead?

JIM. A unicorn, huh?

LAURA. Mmmm-hmmm!

JIM. Unicorns—aren't they extinct in the modern world?

LAURA. I know!

JIM. Poor little fellow, he must feel sort of lonesome.

LAURA [*smiling*]. Well, if he does, he doesn't complain about it. He stays on a shelf with some horses that don't have horns and all of them seem to get along nicely together.

JIM. How do you know?

LAURA [*lightly*]. I haven't heard any arguments among them!

JIM [*grinning*]. No arguments, huh? Well, that's a pretty good sign! Where shall I set him?

LAURA. Put him on the table. They all like a change of scenery once in a while!

JIM. Well, well, well, well—[*He places the glass piece on the table, then raises his arms and stretches.*] Look how big my shadow is when I stretch!

LAURA. Oh, oh, yes—it stretches across the ceiling!

JIM [*crossing to the door*]. I think it's stopped raining. [*He opens the fire-escape door and the background music changes to a dance tune.*] Where does the music come from?

LAURA. From the Paradise Dance Hall across the alley.

JIM. How about cutting the rug a little, Miss Wingfield?

LAURA. Oh, I—

JIM. Or is your program filled up? Let me have a look at it. [*He grasps an imaginary card.*] Why, every dance is taken! I'll just have to scratch some out. [*Waltz music:*

"La Golondrina."] Ahhh, a waltz! [*He executes some sweeping turns by himself, then holds his arms toward* LAURA.]

LAURA [*breathlessly*]. I—can't dance!

JIM. There you go, that inferiority stuff!

LAURA. I've never danced in my life!

JIM. Come on, try!

LAURA. Oh, but I'd step on you!

JIM. I'm not made out of glass.

LAURA. How—how—how do we start?

JIM. Just leave it to me. You hold your arms out a little.

LAURA. Like this?

JIM [*taking her in her arms*]. A little bit higher. Right. Now don't tighten up, that's the main thing about it—relax.

LAURA [*laughing breathlessly*]. It's hard not to.

JIM. Okay.

LAURA. I'm afraid you can't budge me.

JIM. What do you bet I can't? [*He swings her into motion.*]

LAURA. Goodness, yes, you can!

JIM. Let yourself go, now, Laura, just let yourself go.

LAURA. I'm—

JIM. Come on!

LAURA. —trying!

JIM. Not so stiff—easy does it!

LAURA. I know but I'm—

JIM. Loosen th' backbone! There now, that's a lot better.

LAURA. Am I?

JIM. Lots, lots better! [*He moves her about the room in a clumsy waltz.*]

LAURA. Oh, my!

JIM. Ha-ha!

LAURA. Oh, my goodness!

JIM. Ha-ha-ha! [*They suddenly bump into the table, and the glass piece on it falls to the floor.* JIM *stops the dance.*] What did we hit on?

LAURA. Table.

JIM. Did something fall off it? I think—

LAURA. Yes.

JIM. I hope that it wasn't the little glass horse with the horn!

LAURA. Yes. [*She stoops to pick it up.*]

JIM. Aw, aw, aw. Is it broken?

LAURA. Now it is just like all the other horses.

JIM. It's lost its—

LAURA. Horn! It doesn't matter. Maybe it's a blessing in disguise.

JIM. You'll never forgive me. I bet that that was your favorite piece of glass.

LAURA. I don't have favorites much. It's no tragedy, Freckles. Glass breaks so easily. No matter how careful you are. The traffic jars the shelves and things fall off them.

JIM. Still I'm awfully sorry that I was the cause.

LAURA [*smiling*]. I'll just imagine he had an operation. The horn was removed to make him feel less—freakish! [*They both laugh.*] Now he will feel more at home with the other horses, the ones that don't have horns. . . .

JIM. Ha-ha, that's very funny! [*Suddenly he is serious.*] I'm glad to see that you have a sense of humor. You know—you're—well—very different! Surprisingly different from anyone else I know! [*His voice becomes soft and hesitant with a genuine feeling.*] Do you mind me telling you that? [LAURA *is abashed beyond speech.*] I mean it in a nice way— [LAURA *nods shyly, looking away.*] You make me feel sort of—I don't know how to put it! I'm usually pretty good at expressing things, but—this is something that I don't know how to say! [LAURA *touches her throat and clears it—turns the broken unicorn in her hands. His voice becomes softer.*] Has anyone ever told you that you were pretty? [*There is a pause, and the music rises slightly.* LAURA *looks up slowly, with wonder, and shakes her head.*] Well, you are! In a very different way from anyone else. And all the nicer because of the difference, too. [*His voice becomes low and husky.* LAURA *turns away, nearly faint with the novelty of her emotions.*] I wish that you were my sister. I'd teach you to have some confidence in yourself. The different people are not like other people, but being different is nothing to be ashamed of. Because other people are not such wonderful people. They're one hundred times one thousand. You're one times one! They walk all over the earth. You just stay here. They're common as—weeds, but—you—well, you're—*Blue Roses!* [*Image on screen:* Blue Roses.] [*The music changes.*]

LAURA. But blue is wrong for—roses. . . .

JIM. It's right for you! You're—pretty!

LAURA. In what respect am I pretty?

JIM. In all respects—believe me! Your eyes—your hair—are pretty! Your hands are pretty! [*He catches hold of her hand.*] You think I'm making this up because I'm invited to dinner and have to be nice. Oh, I could do that! I could put on an act for you, Laura, and say lots of things without being very sincere. But this time I am. I'm talking to you sincerely. I happened to notice you had this inferiority complex that keeps you from feeling comfortable with people. Somebody needs to build your confidence up and make you proud instead of shy and turning away and—blushing. Somebody—ought to—*kiss* you, Laura! [*His hand slips slowly up her arm to her shoulder as the music swells tumultuously. He suddenly turns her about and kisses her on the lips. When he releases her,* LAURA *sinks on the sofa with a bright, dazed look.* JIM *backs away and fishes in his pocket for a cigarette.*] [*Legend on screen:* "A souvenir."] Stumblejohn! [*He lights the cigarette, avoiding her look. There is a peal of girlish laughter from* AMANDA *in the kitchenette.* LAURA *slowly raises and opens her hand. It still contains the little broken glass animal. She looks at it with a tender, bewildered expression.*] Stumblejohn! I shouldn't have done that—that was way off the beam. You don't smoke, do you? [*She looks up, smiling, not hearing the question. He sits beside her rather gingerly. She looks at him speechlessly—waiting. He coughs decorously and moves a little farther aside as he considers the situation and senses her feelings, dimly, with perturbation.*]

He speaks gently.] Would you—care for a—mint? [*She doesn't seem to hear him but her look grows brighter even.*] Peppermint? Life Saver? My pocket's a regular drugstore—wherever I go. . . . [*He pops a mint in his mouth. Then he gulps and decides to make a clean breast of it. He speaks slowly and gingerly.*] Laura, you know, if I had a sister like you, I'd do the same thing as Tom. I'd bring out fellows and—introduce her to them. The right type of boys—of a type to—appreciate her. Only—well—he made a mistake about me. Maybe I've got no call to be saying this. That may not have been the idea in having me over. But what if it was? There's nothing wrong about that. The only trouble is that in my case—I'm not in a situation to—do the right thing. I can't take down your number and say I'll phone. I can't call up next week and—ask for a date. I thought I had better explain the situation in case you—misunderstood it and—I hurt your feelings. . . . [*There is a pause. Slowly, very slowly,* LAURA'S *look changes, her eyes returning slowly from his to the glass figure in her palm.* AMANDA *utters another gay laugh in the kitchenette.*]

LAURA [*faintly*]. You—won't—call again?

JIM. No, Laura, I can't. [*He rises from the sofa.*] As I was just explaining, I've—got strings on me. Laura, I've—been going steady! I go out all the time with a girl named Betty. She's a home-girl like you, and Catholic, and Irish, and in a great many ways we—get along fine. I met her last summer on a moonlight boat trip up the river to Alton, on the *Majestic*. Well—right away from the start it was— love! [*Legend:* Love!] [LAURA *sways slightly forward and grips the arm of the sofa. He fails to notice, now enrapt in his own comfortable being.*] Being in love has made a new man of me! [*Leaning stiffly forward, clutching the arm of the sofa,* LAURA *struggles visibly with her storm. But* JIM *is oblivious; she is a long way off.*] The power of love is really pretty tremendous! Love is something that—changes the whole world, Laura! [*The storm abates a little and* LAURA *leans back. He notices her again.*] It happened that Betty's aunt took sick, she got a wire and had to go to Centralia. So Tom—when he asked me to dinner—I naturally just accepted the invitation, not knowing that you—that he—that I—[*He stops awkwardly.*] Huh— I'm a stumblejohn! [*He flops back on the sofa. The holy candles on the altar of* LAURA'S *face have been snuffed out. There is a look of almost infinite desolation.* JIM *glances at her uneasily.*] I wish that you would—say something. [*She bites her lip which was trembling and then bravely smiles. She opens her hand again on the broken glass figure. Then she gently takes his hand and raises it level with her own. She carefully places the unicorn in the palm of his hand, then pushes his fingers closed upon it.*] What are you—doing that for? You want me to have him? Laura? [*She nods.*]

LAURA. A—souvenir. . . . [*She rises unsteadily and crouches beside the Victrola to wind it up.*] [*Legend on screen:* "Things have a way of turning out so badly!" *Or image:* "Gentleman caller waving goodbye—gaily."] [*At this moment* AMANDA *rushes brightly back into the living room. She bears a pitcher of fruit punch in an old-fashioned cut-glass pitcher, and a plate of macaroons. The plate has a gold border and poppies painted on it.*]

AMANDA. Well, well, well! Isn't the air delightful after the shower? I've made you children a little liquid refreshment. [*She turns gaily to* JIM.] Jim, do you know that song about lemonade?

"Lemonade, lemonade
Made in the shade and stirred with a spade—
Good enough for any old maid!"

JIM [*uneasily*]. Ha-ha! No—I never heard it.

AMANDA. Why, Laura! You look so serious!

JIM. We were having a serious conversation.

AMANDA. Good! Now you're better acquainted!

JIM [*uncertainly*]. Ha-ha! Yes.

AMANDA. You modern young people are much more serious-minded than my generation. I was so gay as a girl!

JIM. You haven't changed, Mrs. Wingfield.

AMANDA. Tonight I'm rejuvenated! The gaiety of the occasion, Mr. O'Connor! [*She tosses her head with a peal of laughter, spilling some lemonade.*] Oooo! I'm baptizing myself!

JIM. Here—let me—

AMANDA [*setting the pitcher down*]. There now. I discovered we had some maraschino cherries. I dumped them in, juice and all!

JIM. You shouldn't have gone to that trouble, Mrs. Wingfield.

AMANDA. Trouble, trouble? Why, it was loads of fun! Didn't you hear me cutting up in the kitchen? I bet your ears were burning! I told Tom how outdone with him I was for keeping you to himself so long a time! He should have brought you over much, much sooner! Well, now that you've found your way, I want you to be a very frequent caller! Not just occasional but all the time. Oh, we're going to have a lot of gay times together! I see them coming! Mmm, just breathe that air! So fresh, and the moon's so pretty! I'll skip back out—I know where my place is when young folks are having a—serious conversation!

JIM. Oh, don't go out, Mrs. Wingfield. The fact of the matter is I've got to be going.

AMANDA. Going, now? You're joking! Why, it's only the shank of the evening, Mr. O'Connor!

JIM. Well, you know how it is.

AMANDA: You mean you're a young workingman and have to keep workingmen's hours. We'll let you off early tonight. But only on the condition that next time you stay later. What's the best night for you? Isn't Saturday night the best night for you workingmen?

JIM. I have a couple of time-clocks to punch, Mrs. Wingfield. One at morning, another one at night!

AMANDA. My, but you *are* ambitious! You work at night, too?

JIM. No, Ma'am, not work but—Betty! [*He crosses deliberately to pick up his hat. The band at the Paradise Dance Hall goes into a tender waltz.*]

AMANDA. Betty? Betty? Who's—Betty! [*There is an ominous cracking sound in the sky.*]

JIM. Oh, just a girl. The girl I go steady with! [*He smiles charmingly. The sky falls.*] [*Legend:* "The Sky Falls."]

AMANDA [*a long-drawn exhalation*]. Ohhhh . . . Is it a serious romance, Mr. O'Connor?

JIM. We're going to be married the second Sunday in June.

AMANDA. Ohhhh—how nice! Tom didn't mention that you were engaged to be married.

JIM. The cat's not out of the bag at the warehouse yet. You know how they are. They call you Romeo and stuff like that. [*He stops at the oval mirror to put on his hat. He carefully shapes the brim and the crown to give a discreetly dashing effect.*] It's been a wonderful evening, Mrs. Wingfield. I guess this is what they mean by Southern hospitality.

AMANDA. It really wasn't anything at all.

JIM. I hope it don't seem like I'm rushing off. But I promised Betty I'd pick her up at the Wabash depot, an' by the time I get my jalopy down there her train'll be in. Some women are pretty upset if you keep 'em waitin.

AMANDA. Yes, I know— The tyranny of women! [*Extends her hand.*] Good-bye, Mr. O'Connor. I wish you luck—and happiness—and success! All three of them, and so does Laura!—Don't you, Laura?

LAURA. Yes!

JIM [*taking her hand*]. Good-bye, Laura. I'm certainly going to treasure that souvenir. And don't you forget the good advice I gave you. [*Raises his voice to a cheery shout.*] So long, Shakespeare! Thanks again, ladies—Good night! [*He grins and ducks jauntily out.*]

[*Still bravely grimacing,* AMANDA *closes the door on the gentleman caller. Then she turns back to the room with a puzzled expression. She and* LAURA *don't dare to face each other.* LAURA *crouches beside the victrola to wind it.*]

AMANDA [*faintly*]. Things have a way of turning out so badly. I don't believe that I would play the victrola. Well, well—well— Our gentleman caller was engaged to be married! Tom!

TOM [*from back*]. Yes, Mother?

AMANDA. Come in here a minute. I want to tell you something awfully funny.

TOM [*enters with macaroon and a glass of the lemonade*]. Has the gentleman caller gotten away already?

AMANDA. The gentleman caller has made an early departure. What a wonderful joke you played on us!

TOM. How do you mean?

AMANDA. You didn't mention that he was engaged to be married.

TOM. Jim? Engaged?

AMANDA. That's what he just informed us.

TOM. I'll be jiggered! I didn't know about that.

AMANDA. That seems very peculiar.

TOM. What's peculiar about it?

AMANDA. Didn't you call him your best friend down at the warehouse?

TOM. He is, but how did I know?

AMANDA. It seems extremely peculiar that you wouldn't know your best friend was going to be married!

TOM. The warehouse is where I work, not where I know things about people!

AMANDA. You don't know things anywhere! You live in a dream; you manufacture illusions! [*He crosses to door.*] Where are you going?

TOM. I'm going to the movies.

AMANDA. That's right, now that you've had us make such fools of ourselves. The effort, the preparations, all the expense! The new floor lamp, the rug, the clothes for Laura! All for what? To entertain some other girl's fiancé! Go to the movies, go! Don't think about us, a mother deserted, an unmarried sister who's crippled and has no job! Don't let anything interfere with your selfish pleasure! Just go, go, go—to the movies!

TOM. All right, I will! The more you shout about my selfishness to me the quicker I'll go, and I won't go to the movies!

AMANDA. Go, then! Then go to the moon—you selfish dreamer!

[TOM *smashes his glass on the floor. He plunges out on the fire escape, slamming the door.* LAURA *screams—cut by door.*]

[*Dance-hall music up.* TOM *goes to the rail and grips it desperately, lifting his face in the chill white moonlight penetrating the narrow abyss of the alley. Legend on screen: "And So Good-bye . . ."*]

[TOM's *closing speech is timed with the interior pantomime. The interior scene is played as though viewed through sound-proof glass.* AMANDA *appears to be making a comforting speech to* LAURA *who is huddled upon the sofa. Now that we cannot hear the mother's speech, her silliness is gone and she has dignity and tragic beauty.* LAURA's *dark hair hides her face until at the end of the speech she lifts it to smile at her mother.* AMANDA's *gestures are slow and graceful, almost dancelike, as she comforts the daughter. At the end of her speech she glances a moment at the father's picture— then withdraws through the Portieres. At close of* TOM's *speech,* LAURA *blows out the candles, ending the play.*]

TOM. I didn't go to the moon, I went much further—for time is the longest distance between two places— Not long after that I was fired for writing a poem on the lid of a shoe-box. I left Saint Louis. I descended the steps of the fire escape for a last time and followed, from then on, in my father's footsteps, attempting to find in motion what was lost in space— I traveled around a great deal. The cities swept about me like dead leaves, leaves that were brightly colored but torn away from the branches. I would have stopped, but I was pursued by something. It always came upon me unawares, taking me altogether by surprise. Perhaps it was a familiar bit of music. Perhaps it was only a piece of transparent glass. Perhaps I am walking along a street at night, in some strange city, before I have found companions. I pass the lighted window of a shop where perfume is sold. The window is filled with pieces of colored glass, tiny transparent bottles in delicate colors, like bits of a shattered rainbow. Then all at once my sister touches my shoulder. I turn around and look into her eyes. Oh, Laura, Laura, I tried to leave you behind me, but I am more faithful than I intended to be! I reach for a cigarette, I cross the street, I run into the movies or a bar, I buy a drink, I speak to the nearest stranger—anything that can blow your candles out! [LAURA *bends over the candles.*] For nowadays the world is lit by lightning! Blow out your candles, Laura— and so goodbye. . . . [*She blows the candles out.*]

[1944—U.S.A.]

Questions

1. Though in part realistic, *The Glass Menagerie* has many nonrealistic elements. What are the main such elements? How do they tie in with the play's basic premise—that it is a memory?
2. There are a good many stage symbols in this play—physical objects, sounds, actions, lightning, music, and so forth. For instance, consider Tom's motion in putting on his scarf (p. 829): "He snatches it angrily from the closet, tosses it around his neck and pulls both ends tight." What does this suggest symbolically about Tom's feelings about his mother's protective-ness? What does Laura's blowing out the candles at the end of the play suggest? What other stage symbols do you find? What do they mean in the context in which they occur? Are they intrusive or do they seem inevitable?
3. Coincidence in *A Doll's House* might seem a bit too convenient and somewhat forced. Would you say the same of Jim's having been Laura's secret high-school crush? Why or why not?
4. Some critics hold that narration has no place in drama because everything in a play (or movie) should be dramatized. What of *The Glass Menagerie* on this score? Is the narrative integral to the play, or does the narration seem merely a device of exposition and intrusive at that? Explain.
5. How are American men portrayed in this play? How women? In what way are these portrayals cultural stereotypes? Do the stereotypes persist today or does the play seem dated in this regard? If the stereotypes do persist, what does the play have to tell us as to our images of ourselves? If they don't, the play nevertheless has something to tell us about our cultural past. What, exactly?
6. "There is a fifth character in the play," Tom tells us in his opening monologue (p. 816). In what way is the father indeed a character in the play even though he doesn't appear on stage? From one way of reading the play, he might even be called its "presiding spirit." How so?
7. A central aspect of characterization, as we have seen, involves change—by way of either growth or disintegration. What of Tom and Laura in this regard? How does each change as we see them through Tom's memory, and what brings each to do so?
8. In part, Williams's play concerns the relation of the past and the present, or how in the present we tend to fictionalize the past in the rose-colored atmosphere of memory. Discuss how each of the play's characters, either immediately or ultimately, falls into illusion in the present with respect to the past as remembered. What, then, is the play's master theme? What does the play say about illusion as opposed to reality?
9. *The Glass Menagerie* is usually classified as a "tragicomedy." What are its comic elements? In what way if any is the play tragic? Close to the end of the play we find the following stage direction: *"Legend on screen:* 'Things have a way of turning out so badly!' *Or image:* Gentleman caller waving goodbye—gaily' " (p. 854). How would a director's choosing

one over the other of these alternatives affect interpretation of the play? Which one would you choose and why?

Writing Assignments

1. What are the most effective nonrealistic aspects of *The Glass Menagerie?* In a short paper, enumerate several such aspects and discuss what they mean in context and why they are effective.

2. Pretend that you have just seen *The Glass Menagerie* on opening night. Now write a review of the play, pointing out the strengths you find it to have and any weaknesses you perceive. Be sure to tell your projected readers why they should or should not see the play.

3. Most productions of this play omit the device of the screen (which in his "Production Notes" Williams indicates is to be one of the back walls). Write an essay considering the effect of the screen device and what the play would gain or lose by its omission.

4. Because of various references to poverty, the masses, war, and so forth, there is a sense here that reality is harsh and basically grim. Write an essay detailing this background and suggesting how each of the Wingfields escapes the harshness of reality in his or her own way. Are they peculiar in this regard, or are they typical of people in general? Conclude your essay by considering this question.

5. In a short paper, consider the main symbols of the play. What are they, how are they established, and what do they mean in context? Which are conventional and which created? How do we come to know what they mean? Is the play enriched by them or might at least some be so blatant as to detract from its final effect?

6. Can we help but fictionalize the past? Can we ever escape illusion? These are questions that the play raises. Write an essay suggesting what Williams's answers are. Be sure to consider all four characters in terms of their outlook on the past and their illusions (if any) in the present.

7. Does *The Glass Menagerie* strike you as a comedy, a tragedy, or—as I have suggested it is usually thought of—a "tragicomedy." Each position has been held by critics. Write an essay arguing that it is one or another of these possible modes. Follow your own response to the play, but try to demonstrate what in the play validates that response.

SECTION V

THE ESSAY

LITERARINESS AND THE PROVINCE OF THE ESSAY

Every piece of writing is literary in a sense, or at least has literary aspects and/ or potential, even the most practical, matter-of-fact term paper or report—your writing included. For, to some extent, all writing reveals the mind and sensibility of the writer, and, to one degree or another, all writers use language not just with the intention of communicating ideas but also in hopes of expressing themselves and pleasing their readers by, for instance, an apt turn of phrase here and a well-chosen word there. The difference between straight news reports or even cookbook recipes and poems, say, is not so much a matter of kind as of degree. Even a recipe can contain a pleasing phrase that communicates something more than cooking information—the verve and charm of the writer-cook, for instance—and there are news reports that have outlived their occasion because of the force of their writing.

A piece of writing is literary, then, to the extent that it communicates a sense of a personal perspective through its construction and language and takes a certain delight in itself as verbal structure, yielding pleasure through how it is put together and what its language does. In that some works meet these criteria more fully than others, some are more literary than others. That is, there is a gradation with respect to literariness from the purely literary—a poem, for instance—to the almost purely discursive—a set of instructions, say—with many degrees of more or less literary in between. The essay—a generally short, generally nonfictional piece of prose aimed at informing, analyzing, or persuading—occupies this middle ground. Some essays seem almost to be short stories; others are more like impersonal reports. Though most essays fall between these extremes, there is a fine line, certainly, between many essays and short stories on the one hand and many other essays and simple reports on the other. For instance, I recently found James Thurber's "The Night the Bed Fell" in my daughter's seventh-grade reader in the essay section, whereas I have placed it in this text with fiction (pp. 88–91); and one could make a good case that Langston Hughes's "Salvation" is a story and not an essay, though it is in with the essays here (pp. 929–30). At the other extreme, William Zinsser's "Simplicity" (pp. 964–66), which expounds a clear-cut thesis—that "Clutter is the disease of American writing"—is much more discursive. Indeed, it is close to the dividing line, where all categories are tested and proved.

The juxtaposition of "Salvation" and "Simplicity" suggests an important point about essays. Every report, dissertation, and so forth has a thesis, whereas every story, poem, and play has a theme or themes. The essay may go in either direction: it may have a thesis, stated overtly and argued logically, or it may have a theme, implied and supported by example. What makes the latter sort of essay an essay is difficult to say: perhaps it is that whatever form they take, essays ask us to focus on ideas in themselves to a much greater degree than do the other literary genres. What makes an essay something other than a straight report—what makes it literary— is easier to discern. Whether factual or imagined (and essays do not have to be factual, though they usually are), an essay is literary to the extent that it exhibits the two qualities I have already mentioned in defining the word "literary": (1) a personal perspective—that is, all arguments and interpretations in the essay have the effect, because of the essay's construction and language, of funneling through an individual sensibility—and (2) an attention to language and its effects found elsewhere mainly in poems, stories, and plays. With regard to this second quality, along with other works of literature, essays such as those gathered in this section are like stained-glass windows: while letting the light shine through, they ask to be looked at for themselves.

TYPES OF ESSAY

That an essay may center on a thesis or a theme allows us to categorize essays accordingly. What a thesis is, you already know from your reading of Section I of this book. In sum, a thesis is what an essay that argues a thesis argues, what its support material supports, what gives such an essay point and focus. Everything said in connection with your writing in Section I about stating and arguing a thesis applies equally to professional essays in which a thesis is argued—and *most* do present and argue a thesis. This is one type of essay. Like stories and poems, a second type, broadly speaking, entails a theme as you have come to understand the word (pp. 43–45) rather than a thesis. The main difference between the two is overtness: themes are implied; theses are stated in so many words. Barbara Tuchman's "The Historian as Artist" (pp. 949–53), for instance, argues a thesis clearly stated at the beginning of the essay: "I want to talk about a particular kind of writer—the Historian—not just as historian but as artist." Langston Hughes's "Salvation," in contrast, contains a theme—that in the adult world saying is often more important than believing. This theme is nowhere stated but everywhere implied by the narrative that composes the essay. Russell Baker's "Little Red Riding Hood Revisited" (pp. 896–97) provides another example. The theme of this essay ("theme" because it is not stated) is that the characteristic prose style of our day is marked by abstract diction and involuted syntax, and that this style is laughable. That is what the dialogue of Little Red Riding Hood and the wolf establishes and supports.

Though they are both thematic, these last two essays are quite different in feel and the direction of their concerns: Hughes delves into the inner world of memory and childhood; Baker tackles the external world of public language and its misuse. This difference suggests another way of classifying or thinking about essays. I like to think of essays as being either centrifugal or centripetal, their energies moving either outward or inward, their sights focused either on the world external to the self or on the self. Accordingly, the centrifugal essay—whether it presents a thesis or conveys a theme—can be argued with or against: it could be argued, for instance, that the historian is not an artist or that the characteristic prose style of our time is not laughable. Because personal, the centripetal essay, in contrast, is not open to refutation. "This is what happened to me when I was a boy," Hughes's essay implicitly declares, "and this is what it meant to me." One can hardly argue with that. Naturally, these two directions of energy and focus are sometimes mixed together in a single essay.

But to return to the primary distinction: in reading an essay, judge early on whether it has a thesis or a theme. If you find no statement of thesis, then the essay must have a theme, which you should try to articulate as you read on. If the essay has a thesis—and whether or not it does will almost always be immediately apparent—underscore its thesis statement and watch how the rest of the essay relates to its thesis point by point. In either case, try always to come to an understanding of how an essay is constructed and what its language does stylistically, or what elements go into its making and how they are used with respect to embodying a theme or supporting a thesis. Then consciously carry over what you learn to your own writing.

THE ELEMENTS OF THE ESSAY

Every piece of writing is composed of various elements, so to understand a given work fully one must come to understand the elements of which it is composed. As to the essay, you are already familiar with all of its elements from your study of exposition in Section I and of the elements of stories, poems, and plays in Sections II, III, and IV, elements that by and large overlap with those of the essay. But let us consider these elements again, now with an eye to how they function in specific essays and how you might make use of them in your writing.

The Sense of an Audience

More than any other literary genre, the essay is tailored to a specific audience. What this means to you as a reader of a given essay—a reader not probably a member of the audience addressed in the essay—is that you must determine the audience intended as you read (by inference if not direct reference) and then read accordingly. And any judgments that you make must be made in light of that audience. The question of whether an essay succeeds or fails, for instance, cannot be answered without such a consideration.

Take Alice Walker's book review, "Nuclear Madness: What You Can Do" (pp. 954–56). Her essay begins and ends as follows:

> *Nuclear Madness* is a book you should read immediately. Before brushing your teeth. Before making love. Before lunch. . . .

> But first, read Caldicott's book [*Nuclear Madness*], and remember: the good news may be that Nature is phasing out the white man, but the bad news is that's who She thinks we all are.

Walker's targeted audience is educated (the essay is a book review) American blacks, whom she addresses directly in hopes of having a personal impact (an intent suggested, too, by her title). It is this audience that accounts for Walker's diction and tone—that of an insider talking as only an insider can to other insiders. The essay's warm, chummy tone is established by the informality of its beginning and maintained by such sentences as: "Write letters to . . . senators and congressmen . . . : tell them if they don't change, 'cullud' are going to invade their fallout shelters." To understand the essay fully, then, and to account for its diction, tone, and phrasing as well as to judge the efficacy of Walker's approach to her subject, you as reader must determine Walker's intended audience and take it into account as you read. The writer's sense of audience is a pervasive element of exposition and so an attribute of essays that the reader should never lose sight of.

To you as writer, the sense of audience that you will pick up as you read essays in this book—if, that is, you keep an eye out for that sense—should help sharpen your own sense of audience. Again, as I suggested in connection with your writing in Section I, good expository prose is shaped with the reader in mind. Seeing how this is so in the essays you read subsequently should help you apply the principle in the compositions you write for your courses now and later in what you write in connection with whatever occupation you pursue.

Narration

Many essays contain narrative passages (passages in which the author tells a story) used to exemplify a point or flesh out an argument. For, carrying the authority of direct experience, narrative can be a powerful tool of exposition. Let me tell you the story of how I learned the power of narration: A teenager at the time, I was alone in a huge old house in a foreign city; it was midnight; unable to sleep, I went into the library and pulled a book from a shelf—Poe's *Murders in the Rue Morgue;* I read it through and was literally scared stiff; I couldn't move for terror; next morning I awoke in the chair in which I had read Poe's tale. Now, there was a little narrative passage, whose purpose is to exemplify, in an otherwise nonnarrative context. This kind of passage is to be found in all types of essays.

Some essays, of course, are entirely narrative. Telling stories from the past of people moving through time, biographical, autobiographical, and historical essays are usually of this sort. (Note: narrative passages like mine in the last paragraph and narrative essays alike are almost always structured chronologically.) A typical historical essay, for instance, proceeds to tell the story of historical personages and events as they occurred, as does the following excerpt from Barry Lopez's "Buffalo" (pp. 933–36).

> In January 1845, after a week of cold but brilliantly clear weather, it began to snow in southern Wyoming. Snow accumulated on the flat in a dead calm to a depth of four feet in only a few days. The day following the storm was breezy and warm—chinook weather. A party of Cheyenne camped in a river bottom spent the day tramping the snow down, felling cottonwood trees for their horses, and securing game, in response to a dream by one of them, a thirty-year-old man called Blue Feather on the Side of His Head, that they would be trapped by a sudden freeze.
>
> That evening the temperature fell fifty degrees and an ice crust as rigid, as easily broken, as sharp as window glass formed over the snow. The crust held for weeks.

Lopez here speaks of other people of another time. Third-person narration like his is apt for this kind of recounting.

An autobiographical reminiscence, Langston Hughes's "Salvation" exemplifies a more personal kind of narration, one that concerns the narrator directly and is, thus, related in the first person. "Salvation" begins:

> I was saved from sin when I was going on thirteen. But not really saved. It happened like this. There was a big revival at my Auntie Reed's church. Every night for weeks there had been much preaching, singing, praying, and shouting, and some very hardened sinners had been brought to Christ, and the membership of the church had grown by leaps and bounds. Then just before the revival ended, they held a special meeting for children, "to bring the young lambs to the fold." My aunt spoke of it for days ahead. That night I was escorted to the front row and placed on the mourner's bench with all the other young sinners, who had not yet been brought to Jesus.

"It happened like this"—and we're off. Following the chronology of the events as they occurred, Hughes goes on to tell the story of "that night." The point of the story—its theme, in this case—has to do with what Hughes as a boy discovered: that in the adult world saying can be more important than believing, and that people can be easily fooled because of their own beliefs and desires. This is what the story told exemplifies, its narrative being a means, finally, of definition.

Now see what you can do with narration. You have a world of experiences stored up in you. Tap them as you write, using incidents in your life to exemplify and argue your point. Beginning writers, I find, rarely make use of the wealth they possess—their experiences in the world and the knowledge that comes with experience. As a result, their writing, even if coherent, tends to be pallid, lacking a sense of immediacy and the vibrance that comes thereof. When you read essays in this book, see how professional writers draw on their experience and to what effect. Then, when you turn to write, incorporate relevant incidents from your own life to make your discussion come alive and help move it forward. By doing so, you will find that your writing is more interesting and has much greater impact.

Tone and Voice

All essays convey a sense of voice—a sense of a particular person expressing a particular attitude especially through the kinds of words used (diction) and the way they are put together (syntax), or through the tone of voice established thereby. Instructive in this regard is the essay whose speaker is a character to whom we are *not* meant to assent, as opposed to the author speaking in all earnestness. To create such a speaker, the essayist must carefully manipulate diction and syntax, for instance (see "Style" later in Section V), creating, thus, the appropriate tone and voice for the ends at hand—stuffy, perhaps, or naive, or malevolent, or insane. Consider, for instance, two paragraphs from Jonathan Swift's "A Modest Proposal," a classic example of an essay with an imaginary speaker.

> I have been assured by a very knowing American of my acquaintance in London, that a young healthy child well nursed is at a year old a most delicious, nourishing and wholesome food, whether stewed, roasted, baked, or boiled, and I make no doubt that it will equally serve in a fricassee, or a ragout.
>
> I do therefore humbly offer it to public consideration, that of the hundred and twenty thousand children already computed, twenty thousand may be reserved for breed, whereof only one fourth part to be males, which is more than we allow to sheep, black-cattle, or swine, and my reason is that these children are seldom the fruits of marriage,

a circumstance not much regarded by our savages, therefore one male will be sufficient to serve four females. That the remaining hundred thousand may at a year old be offered in sale to the persons of quality, and fortune, through the kingdom, always advising the mother to let them suck plentifully in the last month, so as to render them plump, and fat for a good table. A child will make two dishes at an entertainment for friends, and when the family dines alone, the fore or hind quarter will make a reasonable dish, and seasoned with a little pepper or salt will be very good boiled on the fourth day, especially in winter.

[1729—Great Britain]

This passage is not meant to be taken as spoken by Swift. Rather, we are to hear the voice of an imaginary bureaucrat who has lost sight of human values in his abstract musings about governmental problems and solutions (bureaucrats in the eighteenth century were not unlike those of today). The point of the essay, thus, is ironic, opposite from the point its speaker makes. But my point is that the tone and voice of "A Modest Proposal" were crafted by Swift for a purpose. The everyday diction of the passage and its simple (for the eighteenth century) phrasing help to produce a casual tone, a tone reinforced by the lack of emotion in and understatement of the passage. But the tone is entirely wrong for the subject matter. Is the speaker insane? Yes, he is, and that is the point: Swift carefully crafted the tone and voice of the essay to suggest dramatically the insanity that so often governs our lawmakers, whose laws so often arise out of expediency rather than rectitude.

What I have said about "A Modest Proposal"—that its tone and voice were crafted for a purpose—is no less true of any essay, though it is easy to lose sight of this fact. An accomplished writer chooses words, sentence patterns, and so forth with the aim of creating a tonal posture right for the subject matter and the purpose at hand. With this principle in mind, read the following paragraph from E. M. Forster's "Tolerance" (pp. 921–23) and determine what its tone is and the qualities of its voice. Determine, too, whether or not the paragraph's tone and voice are appropriate and effective with respect to what is being said. Then read the second paragraph— my rewrite—and contrast it with Forster's as to effect. Why did Forster *choose* the style he did rather than the style of my rewrite?

The world is very full of people—appallingly full; it has never been so full before— and they are all tumbling over each other. Most of these people one doesn't know and some of them one doesn't like; doesn't like the colour of their skins, say, or the shapes of their noses, or the way they blow them or don't blow them, or the way they talk, or their smell, or their clothes, or their fondness for jazz or their dislike of jazz, and so on. Well, what is one to do? There are two solutions. One of them is the Nazi solution. If you don't like people, kill them, banish them, segregate them, and then strut up and down proclaiming that you are the salt of the earth. The other way is much less thrilling, but it is on the whole the way of the democracies, and I prefer it. If you don't like people, put up with them as well as you can. Don't try to love them; you can't, you'll only strain yourself. But try to tolerate them. On the basis of that tolerance a civilized future may be built. Certainly I can see no other foundation for the post-war world.

The world is vastly overpopulated—appallingly so; grotesquely overburdened with multitudes of homo sapiens as never before—and they interfere with each other in

their diurnal endeavors. One is acquainted with only a miniscule fraction of these homi-
noids, and some of those of whom one is cognizant, one does not care for; does not
care for the hue of their skin-tones, perhaps, or the dimensions of their proboscises, or
how they expel or do not expel air through their nostrils to clear them, or the way they
expostulate, or their odors, or their garments, or their liking or disliking music of a
popular cast, et cetera. What, one may well ponder, is one's response to this situation to
be, this situation in which one finds oneself helplessly enmeshed, hopelessly mired,
and, though one tries to keep one's sense of perspective, in which that sense seems
impossible to maintain, eroding, as it does, in proportion to one's proximity to one or
another population center? Having perused the problem carefully and for some duration,
I find there to be—and believe the reader will assent to my conclusion—two possible
resolutions to the situation with which we are confronted, nay, two and only two practicable
solutions: we must either endure these hordes in patience or, in Conrad's memorable
phrase, "Exterminate the brutes." [Which do you think the speaker of this passage would
be for?]

Established by diction and syntax—the diction and syntax of ordinary good English—as well as a gently wry kind of humor (for example, "you'll only strain yourself"), the voice of Forster's passage is that of an open, friendly, engaging person
speaking to the reader as a friend, a voice that itself seems tolerant and so one that
lends Forster's argument credence and authority. In contrast, the voice of the rewrite
is persnickety, aloof, frigid to the core. Content, note, has been held constant; the
difference is a matter of diction throughout and syntax toward the end. Just compare
Forster's "they are all tumbling over each other" and "they interfere with each other"
of the rewrite. The latter abstraction sounds disengaged and official; because of the
charming concretion "tumbling," the original seems warm and loving.

Differences like these are not accidental; they result from deliberation and choice
on the part of authors, who shape our feelings in large measure by way of tone
and voice. To read an essay well, therefore, is to be aware of the various qualities
of its voice and how they are created.

Such an awareness is equally valuable to you as a writer: when writing, try to
be alert to the voice you are creating (anything you write will exhibit voice, whether
or not under your control) and try to control those aspects of writing that shape
voice (diction and syntax especially) in order to create the voice you want. To gain
control takes time and practice. But if you keep questioning essays as to voice, you
will come to grasp how voice is established and how it functions in essays; then,
perhaps, you will get the element of voice under control in your writing. With this
end in mind, you might try your hand at forging a speaker other than yourself.
Writing an essay with a fictional speaker will help distance you and so help you
see more clearly what you must do to fashion the voice you want.

People (the Character Sketch)

Because more often than not what essays concern entails people, the character
sketch is a common element of the essay, one frequently used to provide an example
or to flesh out an idea by giving us a sense of the person whose idea it is (or was).

Indeed, because people are fascinating in themselves, an entire essay may be given over to a character sketch of a specific person (real or imagined) or, perhaps, of a type of person in general. Isak Dinesen's "Pooran Singh" (pp. 911–12), for instance, is a character sketch of an Indian blacksmith who had been in Dinesen's employ in Africa. The essay proceeds to paint a portrait of him in words, a portrait as full and immediate as any found in fiction.

> Pooran Singh's little blacksmith's shop down by the mill was a miniature Hell on the farm, with all the orthodox attributes of that place. It was built of corrugated iron, and when the sun shone down upon the roof of it, and the flames of the furnace rose inside it, the air itself, in and around the hut, was white-hot. All day long, the place resounded with the deafening noise of the forge,—iron on iron, on iron once more,— and the hut was filled with axes, and broken wheels, that made it look like some ancient gruesome picture of a place of execution.
>
> All the same the blacksmith's shop had a great power of attraction, and when I went down to watch Pooran Singh at work I always found people in it and round it. Pooran Singh worked at a superhuman pace, as if his life depended upon getting the particular job of work finished within the next five minutes, he jumped straight up in the air over the forge, he shrieked out his orders to his two young Kikuyu assistants in a high bird's voice and behaved altogether like a man who is himself being burnt at the stake, or like some chafed over-devil at work. But Pooran Singh was no devil, but a person of the meekest disposition; out of working hours he had a little maidenly affectation of manner. He was our Fundee of the farm, which means an artisan of all work, carpenter, saddler and cabinet-maker, as well as blacksmith; he constructed and built more than one waggon for the farm, all on his own. But he liked the work of the forge best, and it was a very fine, proud sight, to watch him tiring a wheel.

When reading an essay like this, pay special attention to details and how they are used. Just like the characters in fiction, the people (or characters) in essays are brought to life by the details. That is, it is not enough for a writer to describe a person abstractly: "Ever cheerful, Pooran Singh was a blacksmith and so did all of the metal work around the ranch." We as readers demand more: we want to see Pooran Singh at his forge and to feel the white-hot flames and air, to hear the hammer pounding on the anvil and the rhythms of "iron on iron, on iron once more." We want to know him as he knew himself, not just to be told things about him. What animates a character sketch is the details. By paying attention to detail when reading "Pooran Singh," say, you will see this for yourself; by paying attention to detail generally, you will develop a habit of mind that will serve you well by keeping your writing concrete and thus vivid and immediate.

Setting

Though an essay need not indicate a setting, many essays are located in time and place. Narrative essays, for instance (see "Narration") almost always entail setting, for stories concern people, and people exist only in a given place at a given time. In many such essays, setting functions only as a necessary backdrop, though the specific time and place described often help to create a mood as well. In some essays, however, setting is integral to the meaning: in this type of essay, setting or some aspect thereof becomes symbolic. Consider the following from Joan Didion's "Bureaucrats" (pp. 905–08) in this regard.

> The closed door upstairs at 120 South Spring Street in downtown Los Angeles is marked OPERATIONS CENTER. In the windowless room beyond the closed door a reverential hush prevails. From six A.M. until seven P.M. in this windowless room men sit at consoles watching a huge board flash colored lights. "There's the heart attack," someone will murmur, or "we're getting the gawk effect." 120 South Spring is the Los Angeles office of Caltrans, or the California Department of Transportation, and the Operations Center is where Caltrans engineers monitor what they call "the 42-Mile Loop." . . . The windowless room at 120 South Spring is where incidents get "verified." "Incident verification" is turning on the closed-circuit TV on the console and watching the traffic slow down to see (this is "the gawk effect") where the Camaro tore out the fence.

Caltrans is a closed system having nothing to do with the real world (and so, too, bureaucracy in general, according to Didion): this is what the "closed door" and especially the "windowless room" come to symbolize. Here, that is, the setting indicated provides a backdrop and much more: it also provides mute commentary on Caltrans and all like bureaucracies.

When considering setting in an essay, ask what the setting is doing or what is being done with it. Does the setting create mood?—What mood and why? Does the setting seem symbolic?—How so and of what? Questions like these will lead you to the heart of an essay in which setting is a prominent element. And remember to look for and at details. The "habit of mind" I refer to at the end of the last subsection will develop by your attending to all the details of an essay—those of setting if a setting is indicated no less than those used to sketch a character or create a certain kind of voice—and should be exercised with respect to all its concretions.

Examples and Other Concretions

Right in the middle of Bertrand Russell's essay "How I Write" (pp. 943–45) comes the following:

> . . . Having, by a time of very intense concentration, planted the problem in my subconsciousness, it would germinate underground until, suddenly, the solution emerged with blinding clarity, so that it only remained to write down what had appeared as if in a revelation.
>
> The most curious example of this process, and the one which led me subsequently to rely upon it, occurred at the beginning of 1914. I had undertaken to give the Lowell Lectures at Boston, and had chosen as my subject "Our Knowledge of the External World." Throughout 1913 I thought about this topic. In term time in my rooms at Cambridge, in vacations in a quiet inn on the upper reaches of the Thames, I concentrated with such intensity that I sometimes forgot to breathe and emerged panting as from a trance. But all to no avail. To every theory that I could think of I could perceive fatal objections. At last, in despair, I went off to Rome for Christmas, hoping that a holiday would revive my flagging energy. I got back to Cambridge on the last day of 1913, and although my difficulties were still completely unresolved I arranged, because the remaining time was

short, to dictate as best as I could to a stenographer. Next morning, as she came in at the door, I suddenly saw exactly what I had to say, and proceeded to dictate the whole book without a moment's hesitation.

The process referred to is an abstraction; the example is a concretion. This movement from the abstract to the concrete, or from what is formless (ideas, feelings) to what can be visualized or otherwise sensed in the imagination (like Russell's narrative example), is characteristic of well-written essays. Why? The answer is that, having form and dimension, we are concrete beings in a concrete world who understand best when given concretions to relate to. Thus, "for example," "for instance," "to take an example," and other such phrases are frequent in essays. The example makes tangible what otherwise would be formless, whether idea or feeling. Among the many concretions found in essays are stories, character sketches, sounds and prose rhythms, and figures of speech of all kinds (for instance, Didion's symbolic "windowless room" in "Bureaucrats"). With respect to concretion, essayists are much like poets: both understand that genuine communication takes place only when the whole being of the reader is engaged and not just his or her intellect alone.

As a reader, observe how the writers you read concretize their thought, never straying too far or staying away too long from concretions. Good essayists, at least, always come back and back again to examples, or incorporate stories along the way, or use metaphors and symbols to give shape to their ideas. Once you have observed as much through your reading, apply the principle to your own writing: be as concrete as possible; never keep your reader in the thin air of abstraction for more than four or five sentences running. Note my metaphor and how it makes my thought about abstraction palpable and thus immediate. Such is the power of full-blooded concretions, which sustain the life of the intellect.

Figurative Language

The topic of concretion leads easily to that of figuration, for all figures of speech are concrete in that they all figure, or give shape to, otherwise formless ideas and feelings by tying them to sensory experience (visual, olfactory, auditory, gustatory, tactile, or kinesthetic). Though we tend to associate figures of speech with poetry, all can be found in essays. Personification, for instance, is used by Virginia Woolf in her well-known essay "The Death of the Moth" (pp. 961–63). Here Woolf conveys her feeling about the moth she describes through the image of its "dancing." Of course, only people literally dance. To speak of the moth as dancing, thus, is to personify it and thereby express feelings about it on the part of the human observer.

Symbols, too, are found in essays, as we saw when looking at Joan Didion's "Bureaucrats." But take another essay by Didion, this one entitled "On Morality" (pp. 901–04), which begins:

As it happens I am in Death Valley, in a room at the Enterprise Motel and Trailer Park, and it is July, and it is hot. In fact it is 119°. I cannot seem to make the air conditioner work, but there is a small refrigerator, and I can wrap ice cubes in a towel and hold them against the small of my back. With the help of the ice cubes I have been trying to think, because *The American Scholar* asked me to, in some abstract way about "morality," a word I distrust more every day, but my mind veers inflexibly toward the particular.

Here, as throughout the essay, Didion makes us feel miserably hot and sticky, prickly, nervous, like a two-legged lizard dashing across steaming pavement. Arguing against abstract moral codes, Didion herself stays to concretions—the concretion of rhythm, for instance (see "Sound and Rhythm," the next subsection), and especially of symbolic images. Everything we are made to feel in connection with the concrete desert imagery as described in the essay (hot, sticky, prickly, nervous) we are to carry over to "nature" in general. Here the desert comes to symbolize Didion's central theme: the hostility of nature, which necessitates the kind of morality—concrete and practical—that Didion believes in. Her symbolism works to communicate and support both contentions.

But the most pervasive figure in essays, just as in language however used, is metaphor—explicit or implicit, discrete or extended (pp. 284–94). Indeed, so pervasive is metaphor that I feel safe in saying, though I haven't taken even a statistical sampling, that no essay in this book, however straightforward and informational, does not contain metaphors of some sort; and a great many contain centrally important metaphors, and some are structured on metaphor by way of metaphorical extension. But I need not go outside my own text to exemplify, for there are discrete and extended metaphors, both explicit and implicit, throughout. For instance, at the end of the last subsection I speak of "the thin air of abstraction" and extend the metaphor slightly by saying that concretions, like oxygen vis-à-vis the brain, "sustain the life of the intellect." Earlier, I use a metaphor in likening essays to "stained-glass windows." An example of full-fledged (itself a metaphor) metaphorical extension occurs in Section II, where I first say, "an interpretation is like a map, always simpler than the region it is meant to guide the traveler through" (p. 30), and subsequently extend the metaphor thus:

> Think of a map: a map is a guide to a region but no substitute for traveling in it. Missing are the specific features of the region the map defines generally—the rocks and crags, paths and bypaths, springs and rivulets, not to mention sounds, odors, the variety of coloration; in a word, all that makes the place unique. So, too, theme or its articulation is no substitute for the experience of a story itself. (pp. 43–44)

Even earlier, at the very outset of this book, I extend a metaphor to bring home the fact that practice in writing is necessary for ultimate mastery:

> . . . the more one writes, the less difficult writing becomes, just as the more time one puts in practicing a sport, the less difficult the sport becomes and the greater one's facility. One must know the ground rules to begin with, of course, as well as the purposes of and ways of handling whatever equipment the sport entails. The same is true of writing. To continue the analogy, this whole chapter is aimed at acquainting you with the ground rules of exposition. As to equipment, we have the types of exposition, each type being a different piece of equipment that you need to learn how to handle. (p. 9)

In each case, metaphor helps me to concretize my thought; to express it in terms that my intended audience (you) will probably grasp easily—for I assume that you don't know what I'm getting at but that you do know something about breathing, stained-glass windows, maps, and sports; and, especially with the fully extended metaphors, to give structure to my ideas and, thus, to my writing.

In sum, figurative language is as important to the essayist as to the poet. It is one of the main tools (figuratively speaking) of any writer who hopes to reach an audience and truly communicate ideas and feelings. For, once more, ideas and feelings are shapeless; but we only feel that we truly understand when we have, either physically or mentally, seen, smelled, heard, tasted, touched, or felt kinesthetically. So part of the writer's job is to tie thoughts and feelings to sensation, thereby making them palpable and real. This is your job as a writer, too. As a writer, you must try to convince your audience—teachers, fellow students—of the validity of whatever position you take. You will stand a good chance of doing so if you can come to wield (metaphorically) a metaphor and with it strike home. For there is nothing like a well-tempered metaphor to capture the attention of readers and make them yield to the justice of your cause. (For a further consideration, see "Using Metaphors," pp. 301–03.)

Sound and Rhythm

Sound and rhythm are no less concrete than figures of speech (for sounds we hear directly and rhythms we feel kinesthetically); and both should be considerations of every writer. To be sure, the essayist cannot pay the kind of attention to them that the poet pays. Nevertheless, the essayist is concerned with the way words move and how they sound together and, in particular, is careful to expunge sounds that call attention to themselves unduly and sounds as well as rhythms that are harsh or halting for no specific reason. Then, most essayists now and again use special kinds of sound for special purposes—to gain emphasis, perhaps, or to help convey a mood. Take these two sentences from Langston Hughes's "Salvation": "Suddenly the whole room broke into a sea of shouting, as they saw me rise. Waves of rejoicing swept the place." There is much gleeful excitement in these sentences, excitement underpinned by their sound: by the *s* alliteration (that is, the repetition of the *s* sound) in combination with the concentration of the high-pitched vowels *e* (*-ly*, *sea, me, re-*), *a* (*they, waves, place*), and *i* (*rise*). Up in feeling (because of their wavelengths, high-pitched vowels in concentration often create a sense of glee), Hughes's sound as much as his denotative meaning communicates the thrill of the moment.

Essayists also use rhythm for special effect. Listen again to the opening of Joan Didion's "On Morality."

> As it happens I am in Death Valley, in a room at the Enterprise Motel and Trailer Park, and it is July, and it is hot. In fact it is 119°. I cannot seem to make the air conditioner work.

Because of their length and syntax, these sentences are rhythmically panting; and through their panting rhythm they communicate the feel of what they describe. Listen again, too, to a sentence quoted earlier from Isak Dinesen's "Pooran Singh":

"All day long, the place resounded with the deafening noise of the forge,—iron on iron, on iron once more." That last phrase beautifully captures in its rhythm the rhythm of the forge itself.

When reading essays, pay some attention to sounds and to rhythms like Didion's and to their effects, if, that is, the sound and/or rhythm of a sentence or passage seems to have some special function. You might also pay attention when both reading and writing to how paragraphs move and to rhythm overall. Granted, prose rhythms are difficult to analyze, for we just don't have the tools to do so. Still, different essays and passages within essays move in different ways and have different rhythmic feels. Some move rapidly, some ponderously, some evenly, some erratically. Syntax (see "Style," which follows) has much to do with such differences in movement: a passage or an essay composed mainly of short, syntactically simple sentences, say, will move much more rapidly than and so have a different effect from a passage or an essay composed mainly of long, syntactically complex sentences. For instance, contrast the next two excerpts as to syntax and rhythmic effect.

> As individuals we must join others. No time to quibble about survival being "a white issue." No time to claim you don't live here, too. Massive demonstrations are vital. Massive civil disobedience. And, in fact, massive anything that's necessary to save our lives.
>
> Talk with your family; organize your friends. Educate anybody you can get your mouth on. Raise money. Support those who go to jail.
>
> —Alice Walker, "Nuclear Madness: What You Can Do"

> Moths that fly by day are not properly to be called moths; they do not excite that pleasant sense of dark autumn nights and ivy-blossom which the commonest yellow-underwing asleep in the shadow of the curtain never fails to rouse in us. They are hybrid creatures, neither gay like butterflies nor sombre like their own species. Nevertheless the present specimen, with his narrow hay-coloured wings, fringed with a tassel of the same colour, seemed to be content with life.
>
> —Virginia Woolf, "The Death of the Moth"

Composed entirely of very short, syntactically simple sentences, the first passage has a sense of urgency about it—a sense apt for the subject matter—produced by its sharp, insistent rhythm. In contrast, the second passage is slow and graceful in its forward motion. The mind here is at ease, peaceful and in a state of self-reflexive meditation. Take note of such general differences as you read and try to relate the way an essay moves to its meaning.

Look also at your own writing in this regard. Are most of your sentences short? Why? To what effect? Or are they mainly long and complex? Again, why and to what effect? (Remember, of course, that normally sentences should be varied in length and syntactical construction.) You might wish to rewrite a passage just for the sake of rhythm (or for sound if the sound is unpleasant) if its rhythm—which you should be able to hear if you read your writing aloud—seems somehow out of keeping with your meaning: for example, your sentences are mainly short and so rhythmically quick, but you are discussing a tragic killing and a funeral. Consider as well what I call the "rhythm of closure," which can help make the end of an essay particularly satisfying. I can't define this rhythm for you, I'm afraid, but maybe I can exemplify it. Take the last paragraph of Annette Dula's "No Home in Africa" (pp. 914–16).

> I am not patriotic, but I am a product of America. I believe in freedom of speech, even if it is only token. I take education for granted though we may not receive it equally. I believe in the working of democracy even though it never seems to work. I am forced to accept that I am an American and that here in America lie my cultural roots—whether I like it or not.

Now read the paragraph again, but this time stop before the dash in the last sentence. To my ear, the paragraph and thus the essay would seem truncated if it ended, "here in America lie my cultural roots." The paragraph needs the phrase that follows the dash not so much for sense as for rhythm: the last phrase is needed to bring the paragraph to a halt rhythmically, to give the ending the sense of an ending. You can develop this sense yourself by paying special attention to the endings of the essays you read (which you should do for rhetorical reasons as well)—for instance, by reading closing paragraphs aloud and observing what syntactical configurations lead to a strong stop at the end. Once you have developed this sense of closure, it will serve you well thereafter by helping you attain something that is always difficult to attain but always of value in terms of an essay's effect on its readers—an ending that feels like an ending. (This last phrase, I think, has the feel I mean.)

Style (Diction and Syntax)

Generally speaking, style entails all the choices made by a writer and their effects. One writer writes a narrative essay full of metaphors and descriptions of place (setting); another presents a thesis and supports it with examples, using sound for special effect. These are all matters of style or stylistic choice. Specifically, style refers to **diction** and **syntax**—that is, to the kinds of words chosen by a writer and the sentence patterns they are used to form—along with their effects. Diction and syntax are of particular significance because both are instrumental in shaping tone and thence voice, and syntax is also by far the most important operative in the creation of prose rhythm. These effects are beautifully demonstrated by Lincoln's "Gettysburg Address," perhaps his best-remembered piece of writing.

> Four score and seven years ago our fathers brought forth on this continent, a new nation, conceived in Liberty, and dedicated to the proposition that all men are created equal. Now we are engaged in a great civil war, testing whether that nation or any nation so conceived and so dedicated, can long endure. We are met on a great battlefield of that war. We have come to dedicate a portion of that field, as a final resting place for those who here gave their lives that that nation might live. It is altogether fitting and proper that we should do this. But, in a larger sense, we can not dedicate—we can not consecrate—we can not hallow—this ground. The brave men, living and dead, who struggled here, have consecrated it, far above our poor power to add or detract. The world will little note, nor long remember what we say here, but it can

never forget what they did here. It is for us the living, rather, to be dedicated here to the unfinished work which they who fought here have thus far so nobly advanced. It is rather for us to be here dedicated to the great task remaining before us—that from these honored dead we take increased devotion to that cause for which they gave the last full measure of devotion—that we here highly resolve that these dead shall not have died in vain—that this nation, under God, shall have a new birth of freedom—and that government of the people, by the people, for the people, shall not perish from the earth.

Lincoln might have begun his short address "Eighty-seven years ago" or even "A while back." But the diction of the second phrase is too informal for the occasion, too relaxed, and therefore out of keeping with what is being spoken of. And the first phrase, though unobjectionable, is bland, whereas "Four score and seven" has the ring of the Old Testament prophets, which perhaps explains why it is such an arresting beginning. At any rate, the religious tone of the phrase is right for someone speaking of the hallowed dead and wishing to impress upon his audience with all the authority he can muster the necessity of giving themselves over entirely to the cause of the war so that those commemorated should not have died in vain. The standard diction (that is, the speech is mainly in standard English) and straightforward syntax of the rest of the address create a tone of earnestness and engagement and the voice of sincerity. Pomposity and self-aggrandizement are precluded by Lincoln's diction and phrasing. Further, their very simplicity lends a stateliness to the utterance as it moves quietly but emphatically from point to point. In sum, the voice of Lincoln's speech is that of a simple man roused to passionate conviction by the gravity of the moment.

We would be wrong, of course, to think that Lincoln's address is indeed the spontaneous outpouring of a simple man speaking from the heart, with no thought of matters of rhetoric and style. Clearly, the diction of the opening sentence was carefully calculated. And so was that of the rest of the speech: Lincoln created the voice of his address consciously and with deliberation in light of the effect he desired it to have on his audience. It is only the artist who can sound truly sincere, and Lincoln was a great artist as well as, to be sure, a sincere man (though in no way a simple one). One aspect in particular of Lincoln's syntax demonstrates his artistry— parallelism (the grouping of like thoughts into identical syntactical constructions), which might put one in mind of the Old Testament again in that parallelism is its most prominent syntactical feature. The address contains a number of instances of parallel construction, two of which are especially striking: "we can not dedicate— we can not consecrate—we can not hallow" and "of the people, by the people, for the people." Stylistically, parallelism tends to lend emphasis and a sense of sureness to the voice of an essay. It also creates a rhythm of balance and suggests, thereby, a balanced, reasoning mind at work. Then, too, parallel phrases and sentences (and sometimes paragraphs) are often memorable, as Lincoln's "government of the people, by the people, for the people" has proved to be.

Clearly, Lincoln was a master of words and verbal patterns. Indeed, he possessed the highest artistry—that which conceals itself. For this reason alone he is widely considered a great prose stylist, one who could control the element of style and make it serve his purpose. There is no way of putting words together that will not exhibit style of some sort—whether mature or childish, arresting or vapid, lively or dull. The trick is to control style, to choose words (a matter of diction) and to put them together (a matter of syntax) in such a way as to get the point across effectively: by, for instance, creating a voice and a tone of voice best suited to one's purposes as well as the right pace and overall movement. Granted, as I suggest in Section II, style is elusive and difficult to master. But the more you read, the better the chance that you will grasp what constitutes various styles and what differentiates them from each other. Then, perhaps, you will begin to look at your own writing from a stylistic point of view.

The two paragraphs that follow should help you toward this end. (You might also look back at the contrasting paragraphs on pp. 867–68.) Contrast them as to diction and syntax, and judge them as to the effectiveness of their respective styles overall. I'm not revealing too much, I think, when I say that the second paragraph is much the better of the two. But why? This is for you to ponder.

In the next few minutes, it is my intention to do three things. First will be a description of the features of greatest salience of what is popularly called medicalese. Second will be a description of two consequences of that style. And third will be the presentation of one rule of great simplicity which if followed about 75% of the time would result in the transformation of medicalese into a prose of greater clarity that merely happened to be about medicine. A further intention in the presentation of the following is the illustration of that greater clarity of style. You have in your hands another version of what I will read, a version expressly written for the illustration of the differences between the style in use in this speech and in a prose style of utter straightforwardness.

In the next few minutes, I intend to do three things. First, I will describe the most salient feature of what is popularly called medicalese. Second, I will describe two consequences of that style. And third, I will present one very simple rule which if followed about 75% of the time would almost entirely transform medicalese into clear prose that merely happened to be about medicine. Furthermore, I intend to illustrate what I consider to be that clearer style in the way I present what follows. You have in your hands another version of what I will read, a version expressly written to differ from the style I am using now in the same way that medicalese differs from utterly straightforward prose.

Means of Support

Of the possible ways of supporting an argument, the most common are exemplification (which includes narration), definition, appeal to authority, and analogy. We will look at each in turn.

Exemplification.   Although we have already considered the use of examples (see "Examples and Other Concretions" as well as "Narration" earlier in Section V), we will take up the subject again here because exemplification is so important as to merit further discussion. Indeed, examples are the lifeblood of essays. Illustration by way of concrete instances (examples) serves to animate the abstract statement an essay makes overall and to support that statement by showing how (and that) it relates to the everyday world we rightly take as our measuring rod. Isak Dinesen's "The Iguana" (pp. 909–10), for instance, consists of three examples serving to support her concluding statement: " 'I have conquered them all, but I am standing amongst graves.' " Here is the first of her examples:

> Once I shot an Iguana. I thought that I should be able to make some pretty things from his skin. A strange thing happened then, that I have never afterwards forgotten. As I went up to him, where he was lying dead upon his stone, and actually while I was walking the few steps, he faded and grew pale, all colour died out of him as in one long sigh, and by the time that I touched him he was grey and dull like a lump of concrete. It was the live impetuous blood pulsating within the animal, which had radiated out all that glow and splendour. Now that the flame was put out, and the soul had flown, the Iguana was as dead as a sandbag.

"Possession is one with loss"—Dante's fine phrase sums up Dinesen's point, the truth of which she drives home by giving us concrete instances, which help validate and support the essay's abstract idea.

Definition.   Definition, which can give rise to a thesis (that such and such is so and so), is also a way of supporting a point. Take E. M. Forster's "Tolerance." Forster argues in this essay that what most is needed if Europe is to rise from the ashes after World War Two is simply tolerance, which he defines as follows:

> Tolerance is a very dull virtue. It is boring. Unlike love, it has always had a bad press. It is negative. It merely means putting up with people, being able to stand things.

The very modesty of Forster's definition suggests that tolerance may well be the virtue needed for Europe to recover. And that, of course, is his thesis, which his definition of tolerance therefore supports.

Appeal to Authority.   Appeal to authority is just that—the supporting of a point by way of what experts or revered personages have said or by the authority of immediate experience. Statistics, too, are commonly used as authoritative support. As to experts and revered personages, William Zinsser supplies a fine example in his essay "Simplicity," in which he argues that prose should be simple and straightforward. He enlists Thoreau, one of America's greatest writers, to help support his (Zinsser's) contention thus:

> Simplify, simplify. Thoreau said it, as we are so often reminded, and no American writer more consistently practiced what he preached. Open _Walden_ to any page and you will find a man saying in a plain and orderly way what is on his mind:
>
> > I love to be alone. I never found the companion that was so companionable as solitude. We are for the most part more lonely when we go abroad among men than when we stay in our chambers. A man thinking or working is always alone, let him be where he will. Solitude is not measured by the miles of space that intervene between a man and his fellows. The really diligent student in one of the crowded hives of Cambridge College is as solitary as a dervish in the desert.

As to experience as authority, the paragraph from Dinesen's "The Iguana" quoted in the subsection on exemplification is an excellent example. Her appeal to her immediate experience carries a weight of authority, for it is not to be denied. Because one can hardly argue with such support if it is credible, the appeal to actual experience is always effective in arguing a general contention.

Analogy.   Analogy is a type of inference based on the assumption that if things are alike in some significant way, they are probably alike in other ways as well. It is a means of support in that, by invoking the similarities of A to B, one means to back up some thesis about A. For example, consider the thesis of the following paragraph and how the validity of that thesis is suggested:

> The R/B Railway Co. is like the Ford Motor Corporation of recent years: like Ford before it came up with Taurus, R/B tries and tries and tries, always believing that, despite hard times at present, it will succeed in the end. Given its stubborn perseverance, the chances are good that R/B will indeed be like Ford and make it over the top at last.

The point here is that the R/B line will probably succeed; the support offered is that, like Ford in its perseverance, it will also be like Ford in its ultimate success. In sum, analogy is a way of making a point and suggesting, if not proving, its validity.

Structural Elements

There are a number of ways in which paragraphs in an essay and an essay as a whole can be structured. But the five we looked at in Section I are by far the most frequent: chronology, spatial sequence, comparison and contrast, enumeration, and order of climax. Because we have considered these elements already (pp. 14–16), I shall here simply exemplify each in turn with excerpts from the essays (arranged alphabetically by author) that follow this introduction.

Chronology

> In January 1845, after a week of cold but brilliantly clear weather, it began to snow in southern Wyoming. Snow accumulated on the flat in a dead calm to a depth of four feet in only a few days. The day following the storm was breezy and warm—chinook weather. A party of Cheyenne camped in a river bottom spent the day tramping the snow down, felling cottonwood trees for their horses, and securing game, in response to a dream by one of them, a thirty-year-old man called Blue Feather on the Side of His Head, that they would be trapped by a sudden freeze.
>
> That evening the temperature fell fifty degrees and an ice crust as rigid, as easily broken, as sharp as a window glass formed over the snow. The crust held for weeks.
>
> —Barry Lopez, "Buffalo"

Spatial Sequence

> . . . [O]n the outskirts of Kassel . . . there stands a palace large and splendid enough to house a full-blown emperor. And from the main façade of this palace there rises to the very top of the neighbouring mountain one of the most magnificent architectural gardens in the world. This garden, which is like a straight wide corridor of formal stone-work driven through the hillside forest, climbs up to a nondescript building in the grandest Roman manner, almost as large as a cathedral and surmounted by a colossal bronze

statue of Hercules. Between Hercules at the top and the palace at the bottom lies an immense series of terraces, with fountains and cascades, pools, grottos, spouting tritons, dolphins, nereids and all the other mythological fauna of an eighteenth-century water-garden.

—Aldous Huxley, "Waterworks and Kings"

Comparison and Contrast

The artist writes compulsively, as a way of knowing himself, or of clarifying what he does not know about himself. He writes, let us say, for those glimpses of order that form can make momentarily visible. But add that he writes in about the way a drunkard drinks. His passion springs not from reason, but from thirst.

The artist-writer and the drunkard are both aware—if only in moments of painful sobriety—that there are consequences to what they do, but for both of them the doing itself is the real consequence. The happy difference between the writer's compulsion and the drunkard's is that the drunkard hopes to lose himself in his bottle, whereas the writer hopes to find himself on his page.

—John Ciardi, "Of Writing and Writers"

Enumeration

I liked Pooran Singh's forge, and it was popular with the Kikuyus, for two reasons.

First, because of the iron itself, which is the most fascinating of all raw materials, and sets people's imagination travelling on long tracks. The plough, the sword and cannon and the wheel,—the civilization of man—man's conquest of Nature in a nut, plain enough to be understood or guessed by the primitive people,—and Pooran Singh hammered the iron.

Secondly, the Native world was drawn to the forge by its song. The treble, sprightly, monotonous, and surprising rhythm of the blacksmith's work has a mythical force. It is so virile that it appals and melts the women's hearts, it is straight and unaffected and tells the truth and nothing but the truth.

—Isak Dinesen, "Pooran Singh"

Note: Classification, which entails the breaking of something into its classes or types, always proceeds by enumeration. For example, I classify titles into six types in the next subsection and then go on to enumerate each in turn. Any thesis that specifies a given number of types—for example, "There are five primary structural elements"— springs from classification and calls for enumeration (first, second, and so on) as to essay structure.

Order of Climax

. . . Of course we would all like to "believe" in something, like to assuage our private guilts in public causes, like to lose our tiresome selves; like, perhaps, to transform the white flag of defeat at home into the brave white banner of battle away from home. And of course it is all right to do that; that is how, immemorially, things have gotten done. But I think it is all right only so long as we do not delude ourselves about what we are doing, and why. It is all right only so long as we remember that all the *ad hoc* committees, all the picket lines, all the brave signatures in *The New York Times,* all the tools of agitprop straight across the spectrum, do not confer upon anyone any *ipso facto* virtue. It is all right only so long as we recognize that the end may or may not be expedient, may or may not be a good idea, but in any case has nothing to do with "morality." Because when we start deceiving ourselves into thinking not that we want something or need something, not that it is a pragmatic necessity for us to have it, but that it is a *moral imperative* that we have it, then is when we join the fashionable madmen, and then is when the thin whine of hysteria is heard in the land, and then is when we are in bad trouble. And I suspect we are already there.

—Joan Didion, "On Morality"

Most of the essays grouped after this introduction exhibit one or another of these structural elements or several at once. When reading the essays, you can gain a good deal if you are alert to matters of structure: to enumeration when points are enumerated; to comparison and contrast and how each is carried out; to order of climax and its effect. By seeing these basic structures used well, you should be in a good position to use them well yourself. To further this end, you may wish to do some of the essay writing assignments that involve the imitation of the structure of a given essay. (I shall elaborate on this possibility of imitation shortly.)

Titles

The title of an essay is the first thing that a reader sees, the element that first focuses the reader's attention and thinking. Therefore, as I noted in Section I, titles are important and should not be neglected by you as reader or writer. As you might suspect, there are a number of categories of title—six by my reckoning, some of which overlap. In thinking about the titles of essays you read and in forging titles of your own, consider the following types of title with respect to how each is formed and what each does.

1. A title may indicate—and the majority of titles do—the topic area of an essay: "On Morality," "On Writing and Writers," "Tolerance." This type of title leads the reader gently into an essay so titled and to its thesis statement. (For further discussion, see p. 7).

2. It is possible, however, for a title to point directly to a thesis (without exactly stating it) or to the conclusion drawn from arguing the thesis: Stephen Jay Gould's title "The Nonscience of Human Nature," for instance, points us to the essay's thesis that there is no such thing as a "science" of human nature; Katherine Anne Porter's title "The Necessary Enemy" sums up her conclusion that hate is as necessary to human life as love is. In each case, the title serves to clarify what the author deems central to the essay at hand.

3. Titles may also be used for emphasis (the second and third categories overlap). Forster's title "My Wood" (pp. 884–86) provides a good example. Of the four ill effects of owning property that Forster enumerates, the fourth—selfishness—is regarded by him as the most damnable: thus, Forster emphasizes this fourth effect by

way of order of climax and his title (which should be heard with the stress on the first word).

4. Then, some titles are "grabbers," grabbing our attention and piquing our curiosity: for example, "Nuclear Madness: What You Can Do," "A Sweet Devouring," "The Necessary Enemy." Titles that prove to be ironic with respect to the essays they head are also grabbers of sorts, albeit in retrospect.

5. Further, a title may be figurative—metaphorical or symbolic. This kind of title may establish a metaphor to be developed in the essay proper or, perhaps, distill its meaning into a single image: Eudora Welty's fine title "A Sweet Devouring," for instance, sets going a metaphor (to the author as a child, reading was like eating candy) that helps to structure her essay; and Barry Lopez's title "Buffalo" comes to have symbolic significance in context, distilling all that the essay suggests has been lost with the triumph of Western modes of thought.

6. Finally, there is the type of title that serves as a thesis statement and, by so serving, allows the writer to bypass the beginning and plunge right into the middle. This possibility is exemplified by Alice Walker's title "Nuclear Madness: What You Can Do." Walker's title says it all; therefore, she can begin directly with her argument, the resultant feeling of abruptness serving in this case to communicate a sense of urgency. You might try out this last type of title and its resultant essay structure, as you should try all the other types enumerated here; but be aware that the title-as-thesis will work only in certain circumstances and should not be used simply to avoid the work of a sound beginning. Only an accomplished writer can use (I'm tempted to say "get away with") this sixth class of title well; and if you are to become accomplished, you must master thesis presentation, which means that you must master beginnings.

WRITING ON AND AFTER ESSAYS

Before even thinking of writing, read the essay you are going to focus on carefully and well. Read first for enjoyment, letting yourself respond emotionally as well as intellectually to the essay's concerns and presentation. Also, try to take a sounding of its overall shape and import by the time you finish your first reading. Then decide, if you have not already, whether the essay in question embodies a theme or argues a thesis. Now read the essay again, articulating its theme to yourself and noting how it is gotten across or observing where the thesis is stated and how it is supported (for instance, by examples, analogy, appeals to authority). At this stage, you should also analyze the essay's various elements by asking such questions as: What is the intended audience? What kind of diction marks the essay? Why? What effect does the diction have on tone and thence voice? What best describes the essay's voice? What is its effect? How is the essay structured? What concretions does it incorporate? What is the effect of its style? Once you have read an essay carefully and well—which means that you have asked of it questions like those here enumerated and have answered them to your satisfaction—you should be ready to write.

But write what? That depends on whether you wish or have been asked to write on or after a given essay. Let me explain each possibility. Writing *on* an essay generally involves a discussion of its theme or thesis and how the one is established and supported or the other supported and argued. If the essay you are going to write on is thematic, you could, for instance, state what its theme is (your statement of theme being *your* thesis); then, by analyzing the essay's elements, show how that theme is made manifest and supported; and conclude with a consideration of the essay's significance in general. For example, take one last passage from Hughes's "Salvation":

> I heard the songs and the minister saying: "Why don't you come? My dear child, why don't you come to Jesus? Jesus is waiting for you. He wants you. Why don't you come? Sister Reed, what is this child's name?"
>
> "Langston," my aunt sobbed.
>
> "Langston, why don't you come? Why don't you come and be saved? Oh, Lamb of God! Why don't you come?"
>
> Now it was really getting late. I began to be ashamed of myself, holding everything up so long. . . . So I decided that maybe to save further trouble, I'd better lie . . . and say that Jesus had come, and get up and be saved.
>
> So I got up.
>
> Suddenly the whole room broke into a sea of shouting, as they saw me rise. Waves of rejoicing swept the place. Women leaped in the air. My aunt threw her arms around me. The minister took me by the hand and led me to the platform.

Hughes's theme, again, is that in the adult world saying is sometimes as important as believing. That this *is* Hughes's theme could be *your* thesis. But how do we know that this is the theme? How is it established and how supported in the passage just quoted and elsewhere in the essay? Such would be the concern of the middle of your paper: here you would want to talk especially about why the boy's calculated lie was not caught by the adults, blinded by their own enthusiasm (which is reflected in the sound and rhythm of the last paragraph of the passage quoted, both of which you could use as evidence); with regard to the essay's support, you could, for instance, define its kind of narration (first person) and discuss the authority of experience. In closing, you might bear witness to the validity of Hughes's theme with a relevant incident from your life, suggesting, thus, that the essay is of wide significance and of relevance to each life in its journey to adulthood.

As to the essay that expounds a thesis, you could analyze, for instance, how the essay gets its point across and why the essay is persuasive (if it is). To do so, you would need to consider the essay's main elements and how they work together toward convincing the reader of the merit of the position taken. You would want to look at style, tone and voice, and means of support especially, and secondarily, perhaps, at rhythm, figures of speech, and the like. Or you could analyze a single element, such as an extended metaphor, if used extensively, or the structure of the essay and how it holds together. Or you could evaluate the essay, both its thesis and its effectiveness. Or you could write on the general significance of the essay if it has wider implications. That is the approach of the first sample essay that follows, which concerns the social ramifications of E. M. Forster's "My Wood" (also to follow) while touching on the essay's voice, structure, and style as well.

What I have said so far about writing on essays is analogous to what I said about writing on stories, poems, and plays. But because essays—unlike stories, poems, and plays—are similar to what you are usually called upon to write, they offer a further possibility with respect to writing: that of imitation, or of writing *after* as well as on. I mentioned this possibility when considering "Structural Elements" because structure is particularly valuable to imitate. But you could also imitate voice, style, rhythm, or any other element prominent in an essay. Or you could imitate an essay in toto, which is what the second sample essay following shortly does: in imitation of "My Wood," the sample has the same thesis and, like Forster's essay, proceeds via a developed example and is structured enumeratively, incorporating the same transitions as are used in the essay it imitates. When you read this sample essay, be sure to compare it with the original essay point by point. By so doing, I think you will see the purpose and value of imitation: while making clear the craft of the writer imitated, it helps one acquire craft oneself. But first, read carefully the primary essay—"My Wood"—from which the two samples take off.

MY WOOD

―――――――――― ❊ E. M. FORSTER ❊ ――――――――――

A few years ago I wrote a book which dealt in part with the difficulties of 1
the English in India. Feeling that they would have had no difficulties in India
themselves, the Americans read the book freely. The more they read it the
better it made them feel, and a cheque to the author was the result. I bought
a wood with the cheque. It is not a large wood—it contains scarcely any trees,
and it is intersected, blast it, by a public footpath. Still, it is the first property
that I have owned, so it is right that other people should participate in my
shame, and should ask themselves, in accents that will vary in horror, this
very important question: What is the effect of property upon the character?
Don't let's touch economics: the effect of private ownership upon the community
as a whole is another question—a more important question, perhaps, but another
one. Let's keep to psychology. If you own things, what's their effect on you?
What's the effect on me of my wood?

In the first place, it makes me feel heavy. Property does have this effect. 2
Property produces men of weight, and it was a man of weight who failed to
get into the Kingdom of Heaven. He was not wicked, that unfortunate millionaire
in the parable, he was only stout; he stuck out in front, not to mention behind,
and as he wedged himself this way and that in the crystalline entrance and
bruised his well-fed flanks, he saw beneath him a comparatively slim camel
passing through the eye of a needle and being woven into the robe of God.
The Gospels all through couple stoutness and slowness. They point out what
is perfectly obvious, yet seldom realized: that if you have a lot of things you
cannot move about a lot, that furniture requires dusting, dusters require servants,
servants require insurance stamps, and the whole tangle of them makes you
think twice before you accept an invitation to dinner or go for a bathe in the
Jordan. Sometimes the Gospels proceed further and say with Tolstoy that prop-

erty is sinful; they approach the difficult ground of asceticism here, where I cannot follow them. But as to the immediate effects of property on people, they just show straightforward logic. It produces men of weight. Men of weight cannot, by definition, move like the lightning from the East unto the West, and the ascent of a fourteen-stone bishop into a pulpit is thus the exact antithesis of the coming of the Son of Man. My wood makes me feel heavy.

In the second place, it makes me feel it ought to be larger.   3

The other day I heard a twig snap in it. I was annoyed at first, for I thought   4
that someone was blackberrying, and depreciating the value of the undergrowth. On coming nearer, I saw it was not a man who had trodden on the twig and snapped it, but a bird, and I felt pleased. My bird. The bird was not equally pleased. Ignoring the relation between us, it took fright as soon as it saw the shape of my face, and flew straight over the boundary hedge into a field, the property of Mrs. Henessy, where it sat down with a loud squawk. It had become Mrs. Henessy's bird. Something seemed grossly amiss here, something that would not have occurred had the wood been larger. I could not afford to buy Mrs. Henessy out, I dared not murder her, and limitations of this sort beset me on every side. Ahab did not want that vineyard—he only needed it to round off his property, preparatory to plotting a new curve—and all the land around my wood has become necessary to me in order to round off the wood. A boundary protects. But—poor little thing—the boundary ought in its turn to be protected. Noises on the edge of it. Children throw stones. A little more, and then a little more, until we reach the sea. Happy Canute! Happier Alexander! And after all, why should even the world be the limit of possession? A rocket containing a Union Jack, will, it is hoped, be shortly fired at the moon. Mars. Sirius. Beyond which . . . But these immensities ended by saddening me. I could not suppose that my wood was the destined nucleus of universal dominion—it is so very small and contains no mineral wealth beyond the blackberries. Nor was I comforted when Mrs. Henessy's bird took alarm for the second time and flew clean away from us all, under the belief that it belonged to itself.

In the third place, property makes its owner feel that he ought to do   5
something to it. Yet he isn't sure what. A restlessness comes over him, a vague sense that he has a personality to express—the same sense which, without any vagueness, leads the artist to an act of creation. Sometimes I think I will cut down such trees as remain in the wood, at other times I want to fill up the gaps between them with new trees. Both impulses are pretentious and empty. They are not honest movements towards money-making or beauty. They spring from a foolish desire to express myself and from an inability to enjoy what I have got. Creation, property, enjoyment form a sinister trinity in the human mind. Creation and enjoyment are both very, very good, yet they are often unattainable without a material basis, and at such moments property pushes itself in as a substitute, saying, "Accept me instead—I'm good enough for all three." It is not enough. It is, as Shakespeare said of lust, "The expense of spirit in a waste of shame": it is "Before, a joy proposed; behind, a dream." Yet we don't know how to shun it. It is forced on us by our economic system

as the alternative to starvation. It is also forced on us by an internal defect in the soul, by the feeling that in property may lie the germs of self-development and of exquisite or heroic deeds. Our life on earth is, and ought to be, material and carnal. But we have not yet learned to manage our materialism and carnality properly; they are still entangled with the desire for ownership, where (in the words of Dante) "Possession is one with loss."

And this brings us to our fourth and final point: the blackberries.   6

Blackberries are not plentiful in this meagre grove, but they are easily   7
seen from the public footpath which traverses it, and all too easily gathered. Foxgloves, too—people will pull up the foxgloves, and ladies of an educational tendency even grub for toadstools to show them on the Monday in class. Other ladies, less educated, roll down the bracken in the arms of their gentlemen friends. There is paper, there are tins. Pray, does my wood belong to me or doesn't it? And, if it does, should I not own it best by allowing no one else to walk there? There is a wood near Lyme Regis, also cursed by a public footpath, where the owner has not hesitated on this point. He had built high stone walls each side of the path, and has spanned it by bridges, so that the public circulate like termites while he gorges on the blackberries unseen. He really does own his wood, this able chap. Dives in Hell did pretty well, but the gulf dividing him from Lazarus could be traversed by vision, and nothing traverses it here. And perhaps I shall come to this in time. I shall wall in and fence out until I really taste the sweets of property. Enormously stout, endlessly avaricious, pseudo-creative, intensely selfish, I shall weave upon my forehead the quadruple crown of possession until those nasty Bolshies come and take it off again and thrust me aside into the outer darkness.

[1936—Great Britain]

Big Game or Small?

Funnel
beginning
If you're out for big game, E. M. Forster's "My Wood" might not seem like much. It's a little, cuddly thing, not the sort that anyone would track for maximum payoff. Or is our sense of distance off, making us misjudge the extent and weight of this creature? In fact, the more steadily one looks at Forster's "little" essay, the more it seems to concern large, weighty issues, however miniature its example and seemingly slight its scope. That is, the
Thesis   effects of ownership enumerated by Forster

are analogous to and examples of the more elusive effects of a far more insidious (or so Forster would move the reader to feel) type of ownership on the British public.

Topic sentence

The date of the essay and a knowledge of its intended audience are key to an understanding of its full range. Dating

Support

from the 1930s (when the British Empire was still intact) and aimed at literate Britishers, the essay assumes that its targeted readers would be concerned with the issue of Empire (a pressing political concern in the '30s) and would grasp that Forster's novel A Passage to India is the book alluded to in the first paragraph. The intended audience would also have known that this novel—Forster's most widely celebrated single work—depicts British imperialism and its adverse effects on the

Support

British themselves. Once understood, this allusion alone suggests that "My Wood" concerns something rather more embracing than the ownership of a small patch of woods in some byway in Great Britain. It suggests that the wood and the effects on the speaker of his ownership as described in the essay should be taken as part of an unstated analogy: that his wood is to Forster what the Empire is to the British. So the essay concerns "the effect of property upon the character" not only of the individual but of the nation at large.

Transition and topic sentence

The effects enumerated by Forster of his owning a piece of property, therefore,

Support

are also to be understood as the effects he sees in the British of their possession of colonies. Like him, they have become heavy ——heavy by being weighted down by an empire ("if you have a lot of things you cannot move about a lot") and heavy by having become like the rich man in Christ's parable ("It is easier for a camel to go through the eye of a needle, than for a rich man to enter into the kingdom of God"). Physical heaviness here is symbolic of spiritual heaviness, of a pompous and self-satisfied state of soul. It is this that Forster sees in his fellow Britishers——a spiritual heaviness stemming from their colonial power and rule.

Topic sentence

    As indirectly depicted by Forster, the British are also seen as expansionist and all but damnably acquisitive. Such is what

Support

his analogy suggests with respect to the second effect of owning property enumerated: just as Forster would extend the boundaries of his wood, acquiring property without end, so the British actually did extend the boundaries of the Empire in their avariciousness. The

Support

reference to Ahab, the infidel Old Testament king who married Jezebel, suggests that the desire to expand——whether on the part of an individual or a nation——is as treacherous and immoral as Ahab and Jezebel themselves (the reference is to 1 Kings 21:1-7).

Topic
sentence

The third charge against colonization is exemplified by Forster's desire to "express" his personality through doing something to his piece of property. Most

Support

suburbs bear witness to this expressive fallacy in their proliferating lawn ornaments, not to mention the lawns themselves and the enormous energy wasted in a vain attempt at self-expression through lawn maintenance. Property surely does "push . . . itself in as a substitute" for true "creation and enjoyment." The

Support

implication of this expressive fallacy when extended to the Empire is that the energies of the British have been misdirected into and sapped by their colonial expansion. "Possession is one with loss" for mighty nations no less than for private individuals.

Topic
sentence

Finally, there is selfishness—whether with regard to blackberries or colonies.

Support

Put in climactic order, this evil in particular redounds against the property owner and colonist alike by making both mean-spirited and petty. This is what Forster's last example declares, as subtly does his title if we put the stress on its first word. The "sweets of property," whether a wood or an empire, are the sweets of sin.

Transitional paragraph
Summation
and transition

To be sure, Forster does not refer to the British Empire directly (except for the pointed comment about "a rocket containing a

Union Jack" attaining "universal dominion");
he tells us only about himself and his
wood. But his various references--to the
Bible, for instance, and to Dante--intimate
that he has something bigger in mind,
something of the scope of those references,
and that the effects detailed of the
ownership of a small piece of property
exemplify something more far-reaching. To
grasp the essay in full, then, we must grasp

Restatement of second part of thesis and topic statement of next paragraph

its implied analogy. Whether or not we
assent to the analogy or even to the essay's
basic premise (that " 'Possession is one with
loss' ") is another matter. But that Forster
wished us to assent, as authors usually do,
to his thesis (both limited and extended)
can be seen in his use of various rhetorical
means aimed at achieving that end--namely,
diction, tone, and voice as well as
structuring and style.

Support

One of the charms of the essay is its
warm and congenial voice, the voice of a man
who does not take himself too seriously but
who has great respect for his audience.
Created in large part by diction--that of
good conversational English, neither
condescendingly pompous nor self-
ingratiatingly chummy--the voice of "My
Wood" makes me for one want to agree with
its argument. I like the speaker, I like
his tone (for instance, that of his very
human and very British aside "blast it"),
and liking both, I am inclined to give my

Support

assent. I also find the essay's structure

appealing and a little miraculous. For here, one
of the most mundane and expository of
structures——enumeration, unabashedly
emphasized by the paragraphing——is turned
into a vehicle for something like poetic
insight. Yet the structure of "My Wood" is
always immediately clear, which also helps
to win me over, as does, finally, Forster's

Support

general style. Marked by a straightforward
syntax and sentences of average length and
grammatical complexity as well as a diction
I have already characterized as that of
"good conversational English," the style of
"My Wood" is lucid and elegant in its
simplicity. It is a style well suited to
persuasion.

**Transition
and summary
leading
to . . .**

   But what is most elegant about "My
Wood" is how its little world comes to stand
for the big world and how the essay's little
example of the effects of ownership
objectifies, makes concrete, and thus brings
home ideas and feelings that in the big
world get lost in abstractions. In other
words, the essay's techniques are aimed at
getting us to see what is impossible to see
full size. No, Forster does not take us

Conclusion

after small game. It is big game he is
after and big game he would have us pursue.
Acting as a guide, he helps by providing a
lucid structure and style. But we are left
to track ourselves the essay's implicit
analogy, thereby coming to appreciate the
full range and scope of Forster's
undertaking.

My Brownstone
(After E. M. Forster)

Funnel
beginning

Some time ago, I had the luck, or so it seemed at the time, to acquire a typical brownstone in the West Side of Manhattan. Like Peter Minuit when he bought the island itself, I got my small apartment building for a song. And when I was informed that mine was the best bid, I literally danced a jig for joy. Little did I know what owning a building with four apartments entails. Innocent and heedless, I plunged into ownership, thinking that I would live in one of the apartments and rent the other three,

Thesis

thereby reducing my cost to zero. Now, however, I have come to feel that such ownership is not only unprofitable and dreadful for the digestion but downright bad for the soul.

Topic
sentences

In the first place, it makes you lose weight. A lean and hungry look is the only result of trying to reduce your costs to

Support

zero. For first the furnace goes, then the taxes fall due, and to top things off, the tenants decide to go on a rent strike until the furnace is repaired. With nothing coming in and everything draining out, what else is there to do but pull your hair out fistful by fistful. I became bald from this folly and dangerously underweight. Weight Watchers has nothing on me. If you really want to lose weight, buy your own brownstone and manage it for a year or two.

Topic sentence

In the second place, owning one brownstone gives you--at least it did me-- delusions of grandeur, making it seem desirable and possible to own the whole block. And after that, what? I could feel

Support

what Alexander must have felt when he cried about having conquered the whole world. My desire was to own more and more, my secret passion being to wind up, like Peter Minuit, owning the whole Big Apple. This was a daydream, of course, and absurd.

Support

Nevertheless, I entertained the delusion and even planned out how I could parlay the equity from the one building (once there was any equity) into borrowing power to buy the next, and the equity from that building to buy the next, and so on and on. After all, there are a good number of books that prove that this is the way to become rich. But my

Support

point is that desires and calculations of this sort can drive you mad! And, by leading to a sense of constant frustration, they also further the thinning process that owning property in the first place gives rise to.

Topic sentence

In the third place, property makes its owner feel that it ought to be improved in some self-expressive way. When I first

Support

acquired my brownstone, I savored ownership, like Midas with his gold. Here was something that I owned--though actually it owned me. But I didn't know this right away. The I was in possession, wanting to express itself through improvements, like

the way I changed the facade. I thought of
painting my building green out of some
pastoral fantasy or putting in colonial
windows to express my interest in American
history. That's why, when the furnace broke
down, I had no money for repairs. I had
spent every extra cent on New Orleans—
style wrought—iron railings and window
guards to express my sympathies with the
South.

Transition
and topic
sentence
(isolated for
emphasis)

"Sympathies" brings me to my fourth
and final point: my tenants and my feelings
for them.

Support

My tenants were my children, my people,
my possessions. I listened to their
complaints endlessly and sympathized with
them all. I also felt fiercely protective
of—how shall I say—my wards and their

Support

interests. And how did they pay me back?
They called various city authorities; they
withheld their rent; they moved out. I
caught one, a Joan le Beau, sneaking her
stuff out in the middle of the night.
"Why?" I asked her. "Just look around," she
replied. "Look at the pushers and
prostitutes! They do business on the stoop;
they even get into the lobby and harass us

Transition
and
summation
leading
to . . .

day and night." Well, I should have had the
lock fixed, but what with one thing and
another, I just never found the time. But
that's the point. Between worry and weight
loss, my planning to acquire more and more
property, my improving my building's facade,

Conclusion
(of sorts)

and my listening to my tenants' gripes,
there was no time to do anything else. I'm
glad the city finally confiscated my
brownstone. Now, maybe, I can be free, be
myself again. I'm thinking of a warehouse
downtown. That sounds like me. And it
won't have any tenants!

ESSAYS FOR STUDY AND WRITING ASSIGNMENTS

LITTLE RED RIDING HOOD REVISITED

❖ RUSSELL BAKER ❖

In an effort to make the classics accessible to contemporary readers, I am translating them into the modern American language. Here is the translation of "Little Red Riding Hood": 1

Once upon a point in time, a small person named Little Red Riding Hood initiated plans for the preparation, delivery and transportation of foodstuffs to her grandmother, a senior citizen residing at a place of residence in a forest of indeterminate dimension. 2

In the process of implementing this program, her incursion into the forest was in mid-transportation process when it attained interface with an alleged perpetrator. This individual, a wolf, made inquiry as to the whereabouts of Little Red Riding Hood's goal as well as inferring that he was desirous of ascertaining the contents of Little Red Riding Hood's foodstuffs basket, and all that. 3

"It would be inappropriate to lie to me," the wolf said, displaying his huge jaw capability. Sensing that he was a mass of repressed hostility intertwined with acute alienation, she indicated. 4

"I see you indicating," the wolf said, "but what I don't see is whatever it is you're indicating at, you dig?" 5

Little Red Riding Hood indicated more fully, making one thing perfectly clear—to wit, that it was to her grandmother's residence and with a consignment of foodstuffs that her mission consisted of taking her to and with. 6

At this point in time the wolf moderated his rhetoric and proceeded to grandmother's residence. The elderly person was then subjected to the disadvantages of total consumption and transferred to residence in the perpetrator's stomach. 7

"That will raise the old woman's consciousness," the wolf said to himself. He was not a bad wolf, but only a victim of an oppressive society, a society that not only denied wolves' rights, but actually boasted of its capacity for keeping the wolf from the door. An interior malaise made itself manifest inside the wolf. 8

"Is that the national malaise I sense within my digestive tract?" wondered the wolf. "Or is it the old person seeking to retaliate for her consumption by telling wolf jokes to my duodenum?" It was time to make a judgment. The time was now, the hour had struck, the body lupine cried out for decision. The wolf was up to the challenge. He took two stomach powders right away and got into bed. 9

The wolf had adopted the abdominal-distress recovery posture when Little   10
Red Riding Hood achieved his presence.

"Grandmother," she said, "your ocular implements are of an extraordinary   11
order of magnitude."

"The purpose of this enlarged viewing capability," said the wolf, "is to   12
enable your image to register a more precise impression upon my sight systems."

"In reference to your ears," said Little Red Riding Hood, "it is noted with   13
the deepest respect that far from being underprivileged, their elongation and
enlargement appear to qualify you for unparalleled distinction."

"I hear you loud and clear, kid," said the wolf, "but what about these   14
new choppers?"

"If it is not inappropriate," said Little Red Riding Hood, "it might be observed   15
that with your new miracle masticating products you may even be able to
chew taffy again."

This observation was followed by the adoption of an aggressive posture   16
on the part of the wolf and the assertion that it was also possible for him,
due to the high efficiency ratio of his jaw, to consume little persons, plus, as
he stated, his firm determination to do so at once without delay and with all
due process and propriety, notwithstanding the fact that the ingestion of one
entire grandmother had already provided twice his daily recommended choles-
terol intake.

There ensued flight by Little Red Riding Hood accompanied by pursuit in   17
respect to the wolf and a subsequent intervention on the part of a third party,
heretofore unnoted in the record.

Due to the firmness of the intervention, the wolf's stomach underwent   18
ax-assisted aperture with the result that Red Riding Hood's grandmother was
enabled to be removed with only minor discomfort.

The wolf's indigestion was immediately alleviated with such effectiveness   19
that he signed a contract with the intervening third party to perform with
grandmother in a television commercial demonstrating the swiftness of this
dramatic relief for stomach discontent.

"I'm going to be on television," cried grandmother.   20

And they all joined her happily in crying, "What a phenomena!"   21

[1979—U.S.A.]

Questions

1. Why should the classics need to be translated "into the modern American language"?
2. Comment on the overall diction of the present "translation." With respect to diction, what
   does the essay satirize?
3. What else is satirized here? For instance, what is the satiric point of paragraph 8? What is
   the satiric point of the error in the last three words of the essay?
4. What kind of voice does the diction here produce? Is the voice that of the author or of an
   imagined speaker? How do you know?
5. What contrasting type of diction is found in the essay? Where? Why?

6. What theme underlies this essay? Formulate it in a sentence or two and tell what leads you to this conclusion.

Writing Assignments

1. In brief, translate a fairy tale of your own choosing into language like Baker's. Then translate it again into slang. Finally, write a paragraph on the difference in effect between your two translations.
2. Rewrite the second to fifth paragraphs of "Little Red Riding Hood Revisited" in plain English. Then write a paragraph commenting on the difference between the two versions.
3. This essay is a satire. Write a paragraph or more on what it satirizes and how it does so.
4. Is Baker's piece an essay? Write a paper arguing that it is. In doing so, consider its intent along with the reader's final focus and interest.

OF WRITING AND WRITERS

JOHN CIARDI

There is no formula by which a man can become a writer, and there is no end to the number of ways in which a man can be one. Writing can be an art, a trade, a craft, or a hobby. The artist writes compulsively, as a way of knowing himself or of clarifying what he does not know about himself. He writes, let us say, for those glimpses of order that form can make momentarily visible. But add that he writes in about the way a drunkard drinks. His passion springs not from reason, but from thirst. 1

The artist-writer and the drunkard are both aware—if only in moments of painful sobriety—that there are consequences to what they do, but for both of them the doing itself is the real consequence. The happy difference between the writer's compulsion and the drunkard's is that the drunkard hopes to lose himself in his bottle, whereas the writer hopes to find himself on his page. In his act of writing, the writer finds himself wiser, more sentient, more pertinent to his own life, perhaps more confused by it, but more meaningfully confused. He is a language-haunted man and a cadence-haunted man and a form-haunted man and an image-haunted man, and he knows that whatever ghosts he gathers about him in the writing are, finally, his best sense of himself. And he knows that those ghosts are the shadowy tribesmen of every man's first-and-last identity. The writer as artist does say things, but he does not write for the sake of saying. The saying is inevitable but secondary. He writes to be in the company of his necessary ghosts, much as a man will trek halfway round the world to get back home to the company of what names him. 2

The man who writes as a trade is simply an employed person, a wage-earner. He may be more or less serious about his trade. He may be good or bad at it. He may, at times, confuse his own motives and try to write as an 3 artist does. He may even refuse easy assignments that could produce fat checks. Still, as a man practicing a trade, he must write, finally, to make a living. That is to say he must write not for himself (compelled) but for the check his writing will bring.

The difference between the craftsman and the hobbyist is, as I see it, a matter of intensity. Or perhaps there is no real difference except that the word "craft" implies at root an agonizing exertion, whereas the word "hobby" carries no feeling with it but the sense of idle play. The craftsman works at his writing harder than does the hobbyist, whether for pay or not, and is likely to be more self-demanding without ever quite achieving the passion and the compulsion of the artist. I am tempted to think of Dr. Samuel Johnson,[1] lexicographer, as practicing the craft of writing without quite managing to make a trade of it. But who would dare call him a hobbyist? The hobbyist simply amuses himself. The center of what he does with his life is somewhere else. The writing, like a stamp collection, is a way of passing a quiet evening in a room somewhere off the center of the house.

In writing, trade blurs into craft, and craft blurs into hobby, but there can be no blurring of the line between the artist-writer and every other kind of writer. Except, perhaps, that it is possible to write well on any of these four levels. Even the hobbyist might turn out an enduring if slight fragment—say, a memorable piece of light verse. Even a craftsman or a man plying a trade— say, a Daniel Defoe[2]—might turn out a piece of real or imagined journalism so firmly marshaled upon itself that it stays memorable and firm. But only the writer-as-artist, I believe, can write in a way that burns forever.

Combustion is, of course, the heart of it. And combustion in art can be produced only by the passion of compulsive men. The artist is once more like the drunkard in that he cannot stop to count the cost of his compulsion. The writer may write himself (as the drunkard may drink himself) out of employment, family, social acceptance, and out of health and life itself. There is no help for it: the man *must* do what he does. There is no mercy in it: no page cares what it has cost the writer.

All writing is measured, in the long run, by its memorableness. A man either writes in forms that cling to human memory, and so become unforgettable; or he writes forgettably and is soon forgotten—with, perhaps, the temporary exception that the American school system often seems to be a conspiracy to keep some unflaggingly forgettable writing in student memory by forced feeding.

The fact is that language supremely used will survive the death of its own mother tongue. Latin and Greek are both dead languages, but the high moments of Greek and Latin writing are still alive in men's minds. Man needs language because he lives by it and knows himself by it, and because he lives in it and knows himself in it without recourse to logic, but as an act of identity he can never hope to reason out or do without. He will store great acts of language for the simple reason that he lives by them.

[1] *Dr. Johnson* (1709–1784): British critic, essayist, and poet who compiled the first English dictionary.
[2] *Daniel Defoe* (1660?–1731): British novelist, author of *Robinson Crusoe*.

The combustion of the artist-writer springs from the passion with which   9
he engages that mysterious act of identity, losing himself in it as his only
hope of finding himself. The writer may be wrong, of course. And there is no
mercy for the wrong. If a man ruins himself in his compulsion to write a dull
book, I am left with no compulsion to read it. Another man may write, no,
not easily, but joyously, thriving on his difficulties because he has an appetite
for them, and that man may come in a glow of well-being to write a good
book. The page has treated him kindly.

But the reader does not care what it costs the man. Why should he? The   10
library is full of books, and he owes no duty to any but those that please him.
He reads joyously through the happy man's good book without a thought for
the self-ruined failure whose volume continues to gather dust until it becomes
itself dust. Or, finished with the happy man's good book, the reader may lose
himself next in the good book another man killed himself to write. What should
the reader care? He does not so much as see the corpse. There is no corpse
in good writing: the writing is always a life. It is the writer who becomes the
corpse, but never in his writing—not if it is of the memorable and burning.

And add one thing more about the writing—on whatever level, the success   11
of the writing is measured by the most democratic process in human experience.
Whoever you are as a person, whoever you were, the writing lives or dies
outside of you and apart from you. Whether you write from a throne or a
dungeon, and whether or not you deserve to be on the one or in the other,
the reader does not know you and does not care and has no reason to care.
Take a piece of paper, put a life on it or a piece of a life, make that life burn
to reality (that is to say, to the illusion of a reality) in the act of language in
which you summon it—and the reader (always the unknown reader) is yours
without a thought of who you are in yourself on the other side of that page.

[1964—U.S.A.]

Questions

1. What is Ciardi's primary concern here? How does the focus of the first paragraph signal
   that concern?
2. How does Ciardi extend the artist/drunkard analogy—that is, what similarities does he
   note between them? What key point of contrast does the comparison lead to?
3. What is the thesis of this essay? How is it established and where is it stated? Why there?
4. In what way is the essay's thesis definitional? How does classification serve definition here?

Writing Assignments

1. At the end of the seventh paragraph, Ciardi charges our school system with perpetuating
   "forgettable writing." In a paragraph or more, discuss your own primary and secondary
   education in this regard and the merit or lack of merit of the charge.
2. Pick a topic area and get a thesis that lends itself to development like that of "Of Writing
   and Writers"—that is, by definition entailing classification. Now write a paper in which

you proceed to define by way of classification, establishing what defines what you wish to define by contrast with other things in the same class. For instance, you could define one type of music or musician by classifying the various types of either (classical, jazz, pop) and holding the type you are interested in against the others.

ON MORALITY

✻ JOAN DIDION ✻

As it happens I am in Death Valley, in a room at the Enterprise Motel and Trailer Park, and it is July, and it is hot. In fact it is 119°. I cannot seem to make the air conditioner work, but there is a small refrigerator, and I can wrap ice cubes in a towel and hold them against the small of my back. With the help of the ice cubes I have been trying to think, because *The American Scholar* asked me to, in some abstract way about "morality," a word I distrust more every day, but my mind veers inflexibly toward the particular.

Here are some particulars. At midnight last night, on the road in from Las Vegas to Death Valley Junction, a car hit a shoulder and turned over. The driver, very young and apparently drunk, was killed instantly. His girl was found alive but bleeding internally, deep in shock. I talked this afternoon to the nurse who had driven the girl to the nearest doctor, 185 miles across the floor of the Valley and three ranges of lethal mountain road. The nurse explained that her husband, a talc miner, had stayed on the highway with the boy's body until the coroner could get over the mountains from Bishop, at dawn today. "You can't just leave a body on the highway," she said. "It's immoral."

It was one instance in which I did not distrust the word, because she meant something quite specific. She meant that if a body is left alone for even a few minutes on the desert, the coyotes close in and eat the flesh. Whether or not a corpse is torn apart by coyotes may seem only a sentimental consideration, but of course it is more: one of the promises we make to one another is that we will try to retrieve our casualties, try not to abandon our dead to the coyotes. If we have been taught to keep our promises—if, in the simplest terms, our upbringing is good enough—we stay with the body, or have bad dreams.

I am talking, of course, about the kind of social code that is sometimes called, usually pejoratively, "wagon-train morality." In fact that is precisely what it is. For better or worse, we are what we learned as children: my own childhood was illuminated by graphic litanies of the grief awaiting those who failed in their loyalties to each other. The Donner-Reed Party, starving in the Sierra snows, all the ephemera of civilization gone save that one vestigial taboo, the provision that no one should eat his own blood kin. The Jayhawkers, who quarreled and separated not far from where I am tonight. Some of them died in the Funerals and some of them died down near Badwater and most of the rest of them died in the Panamints. A woman who got through gave the Valley its name. Some might say that the Jayhawkers were killed by the desert summer, and the Donner Party by the mountain winter, by circumstances beyond control; we were taught instead that they had somewhere abdicated their responsibilities, somehow breached their primary loyalties, or they would not have found themselves helpless in the mountain winter or the desert summer, would not have given way to acrimony, would not have deserted one another, would not have *failed.* In brief, we heard such stories as cautionary tales, and they still suggest the only kind of "morality" that seems to me to have any but the most potentially mendacious meaning.

You are quite possibly impatient with me by now; I am talking, you want   5
to say, about a "morality" so primitive that it scarcely deserves the name, a code that has as its point only survival, not the attainment of the ideal good. Exactly. Particularly out here tonight, in this country so ominous and terrible that to live in it is to live with antimatter, it is difficult to believe that "the good" is a knowable quantity. Let me tell you what it is like out here tonight. Stories travel at night on the desert. Someone gets in his pickup and drives a couple of hundred miles for a beer, and he carries news of what is happening, back wherever he came from. Then he drives another hundred miles for another beer, and passes along stories from the last place as well as from the one before; it is a network kept alive by people whose instincts tell them that if they do not keep moving at night on the desert they will lose all reason. Here is a story that is going around the desert tonight: over across the Nevada line, sheriff's deputies are diving in some underground pools, trying to retrieve a couple of bodies known to be in the hole. The widow of one of the drowned boys is over there; she is eighteen, and pregnant, and is said not to leave the hole. The divers go down and come up, and she just stands there and stares into the water. They have been diving for ten days but have found no bottom to the caves, no bodies and no trace of them, only the black 90° water going down and down and down, and a single translucent fish, not classified. The story tonight is that one of the divers has been hauled up incoherent, out of his head, shouting—until they got him out of there so that the widow could not hear—about water that got hotter instead of cooler as he went down, about light flickering through the water, about magma, about underground nuclear testing.

That is the tone stories take out here, and there are quite a few of them   6
tonight. And it is more than the stories alone. Across the road at the Faith Community Church a couple of dozen old people, come here to live in trailers and die in the sun, are holding a prayer sing. I cannot hear them and do not want to. What I can hear are occasional coyotes and a constant chorus of "Baby the Rain Must Fall" from the jukebox in the Snake Room next door, and if I were also to hear those dying voices, those Midwestern voices drawn to this lunar country for some unimaginable atavistic rites, *rock of ages cleft for me,* I think I would lose my own reason. Every now and then I imagine I

hear a rattlesnake, but my husband says that it is a faucet, a paper rustling, the wind. Then he stands by a window, and plays a flashlight over the dry wash outside.

What does it mean? It means nothing manageable. There is some sinister 7
hysteria in the air out here tonight, some hint of the monstrous perversion to which any human idea can come. "I followed my own conscience." "I did what I thought was right." How many madmen have said it and meant it? How many murderers? Klaus Fuchs said it, and the men who committed the Mountain Meadows Massacre said it, and Alfred Rosenberg said it. And, as we are rotely and rather presumptuously reminded by those who would say it now, Jesus said it. Maybe we have all said it, and maybe we have been wrong. Except on that most primitive level—our loyalties to those we love—what could be more arrogant than to claim the primacy of personal conscience? ("Tell me," a rabbi asked Daniel Bell when he said, as a child, that he did not believe in God. "Do you think God cares?") At least some of the time, the world appears to me as a painting by Hieronymous Bosch;[1] were I to follow my conscience then, it would lead me out onto the desert with Marion Faye, out to where he stood in *The Deer Park*[2] looking east to Los Alamos and praying, as if for rain, that it would happen: ". . . *let it come and clear the rot and the stench and the stink, let it come for all of everywhere, just so it comes and the world stands clear in the white dead dawn.*"

Of course you will say that I do not have the right, even if I had the 8
power, to inflict that unreasonable conscience upon you; nor do I want you to inflict your conscience, however reasonable, however enlightened, upon me. ("We must be aware of the dangers which lie in our most generous wishes," Lionel Trilling once wrote. "Some paradox of our nature leads us, when once we have made our fellow men the objects of our enlightened interest, to go on to make them the objects of our pity, then of our wisdom, ultimately of our coercion.") That the ethic of conscience is intrinsically insidious seems scarcely a revelatory point, but it is one raised with increasing infrequency; even those who do raise it tend to *segue* with troubling readiness into the quite contradictory position that the ethic of conscience is dangerous when it is "wrong," and admirable when it is "right."

You see I want to be quite obstinate about insisting that we have no way 9
of knowing—beyond that fundamental loyalty to the social code—what is "right" and what is "wrong," what is "good" and what "evil." I dwell so upon this because the most disturbing aspect of "morality" seems to me to be the frequency with which the word now appears; in the press, on television, in the most perfunctory kinds of conversation. Questions of straightforward power (or survival) politics, questions of quite indifferent public policy, questions of almost anything: they are all assigned these factitious moral burdens. There is something facile going on, some self-indulgence at work. Of course we would all like to

[1] *Bosch* (1450?–1516): Dutch painter of weird, hellish scenes, which we would call "surrealistic."
[2] *The Deer Park:* a novel by Norman Mailer, in which Marion Faye is a prominent character.

"believe" in something, like to assuage our private guilts in public causes, like to lose our tiresome selves; like, perhaps, to transform the white flag of defeat at home into the brave white banner of battle away from home. And of course it is all right to do that; that is how, immemorially, things have gotten done. But I think it is all right only so long as we do not delude ourselves about what we are doing, and why. It is all right only so long as we remember that all the *ad hoc* committees, all the picket lines, all the brave signatures in *The New York Times,* all the tools of agitprop straight across the spectrum, do not confer upon anyone any *ipso facto* virtue. It is all right only so long as we recognize that the end may or may not be expedient, may or may not be a good idea, but in any case has nothing to do with "morality." Because when we start deceiving ourselves into thinking not that we want something or need something, not that it is a pragmatic necessity for us to have it, but that it is a *moral imperative* that we have it, then is when we join the fashionable madmen, and then is when the thin whine of hysteria is heard in the land, and then is when we are in bad trouble. And I suspect we are already there.

[1965—U.S.A.]

Questions

1. Analyze the sentences of the first paragraph syntactically. What kind of rhythm does the syntax here produce? Why this rhythm?
2. The essay's thesis, which entails definition, is suggested at the end of the first paragraph. How? What is that thesis? Where in the essay is it stated overtly?
3. What audience was this essay written for? What does the reference to *The American Scholar* suggest? What in the essay is accounted for by its intended audience?
4. Why the emphasis on setting here? How does this emphasis tie in with the essay's thesis? How does the particularity of the setting contrast with the "ethic of conscience," which we are told "is intrinsically insidious" (paragraph 8)?
5. Much disparate material is brought together here coherently. How does Didion achieve coherence? For instance, how does she make the transition between paragraphs?
6. The image of the deputies diving to recover the two bodies is an emblem of Didion's understanding of morality. How so? What does the image say about the relation of humans and the natural world? How else is the nature of this relationship intimated in the essay? How does Didion's view of the relationship account for her sense of morality?

Writing Assignments

1. (a) In a paragraph, write a critique of "On Morality." State its thesis; then consider the validity of the thesis as well as how it is argued and how well the case is made.
   (b) In a separate paragraph, state your response to the essay and why you so respond.
2. In two or more paragraphs, compare "On Morality" with Frost's "Stopping By Woods on a Snowy Evening" (p. 216) as to the idea that morality means "to keep our promises" (paragraph 3). Both poem and essay subscribe to this view. How so?
3. Write an essay like "On Morality." For topic, choose an abstraction about which you feel you have something to say—democracy, duty, salvation, good, evil, or whatever. Then

develop a thesis and argue it entirely by way of particulars—for instance, the particulars of concrete examples, of the details of a specified setting, of imagery. You may draw on disparate areas as long as you are coherent and provide whatever transitions are necessary.

BUREAUCRATS

JOAN DIDION

The closed door upstairs at 120 South Spring Street in downtown Los Angeles is marked OPERATIONS CENTER. In the windowless room beyond the closed door a reverential hush prevails. From six A.M. until seven P.M. in this windowless room men sit at consoles watching a huge board flash colored lights. "There's the heart attack," someone will murmur, or "we're getting the gawk effect." 120 South Spring is the Los Angeles office of Caltrans, or the California Department of Transportation, and the Operations Center is where Caltrans engineers monitor what they call "the 42-Mile Loop." The 42-Mile Loop is simply the rough triangle formed by the intersections of the Santa Monica, the San Diego and the Harbor freeways, and 42 miles represents less than ten per cent of freeway mileage in Los Angeles County alone, but these particular 42 miles are regarded around 120 South Spring with a special veneration. The Loop is a "demonstration system," a phrase much favored by everyone at Caltrans, and is part of a "pilot project," another two words carrying totemic weight on South Spring. 1

The Loop has electronic sensors embedded every half-mile out there in the pavement itself, each sensor counting the crossing cars every twenty seconds. The Loop has its own mind, a Xerox Sigma V computer which prints out, all day and night, twenty-second readings on what is and is not moving in each of the Loop's eight lanes. It is the Xerox Sigma V that makes the big board flash red when traffic out there drops below fifteen miles an hour. It is the Xerox Sigma V that tells the Operations crew when they have an "incident" out there. An "incident" is the heart attack on the San Diego, the jackknifed truck on the Harbor, the Camaro just now tearing out the Cyclone fence on the Santa Monica. "Out there" is where incidents happen. The windowless room at 120 South Spring is where incidents get "verified." "Incident verification" is turning on the closed-circuit TV on the console and watching the traffic slow down to see (this is "the gawk effect") where the Camaro tore out the fence. 2

As a matter of fact there is a certain closed-circuit aspect to the entire mood of the Operations Center. "Verifying" the incident does not after all "prevent" the incident, which lends the enterprise a kind of tranced distance, and on the day recently when I visited 120 South Spring it took considerable effort to remember what I had come to talk about, which was that particular part of the Loop called the Santa Monica Freeway. The Santa Monica Freeway 3 is 16.2 miles long, runs from the Pacific Ocean to downtown Los Angeles through what is referred to at Caltrans as "the East-West Corridor," carries more traffic every day than any other freeway in California, has what connoisseurs of freeways concede to be the most beautiful access ramps in the world, and appeared to have been transformed by Caltrans, during the several weeks before I went downtown to talk about it, into a 16.2-mile parking lot.

The problem seemed to be another Caltrans "demonstration," or "pilot," a foray into bureaucratic terrorism they were calling "The Diamond Lane" in their promotional literature and "The Project" among themselves. That the promotional literature consisted largely of schedules for buses (or "Diamond Lane Expresses") and invitations to join a car pool via computer ("Commuter Computer") made clear not only the putative point of The Project, which was to encourage travel by car pool and bus, but also the actual point, which was to eradicate a central Southern California illusion, that of individual mobility, without anyone really noticing. This had not exactly worked out. "FREEWAY FIASCO," the *Los Angeles Times* was headlining page-one stories. "THE DIAMOND LANE: ANOTHER BUST BY CALTRANS." "CALTRANS PILOT EFFORT ANOTHER IN LONG LIST OF FAILURES." "OFFICIAL DIAMOND LANE STANCE: LET THEM HOWL."

All "The Diamond Lane" theoretically involved was reserving the fast inside lanes on the Santa Monica for vehicles carrying three or more people, but in practice this meant that 25 per cent of the freeway was reserved for 3 per cent of the cars, and there were other odd wrinkles here and there suggesting that Caltrans had dedicated itself to making all movement around Los Angeles as arduous as possible. There was for example the matter of surface streets. A "surface street" is anything around Los Angeles that is not a freeway ("going surface" from one part of town to another is generally regarded as idiosyncratic), and surface streets do not fall directly within the Caltrans domain, but now the engineer in charge of surface streets was accusing Caltrans of threatening and intimidating him. It appeared that Caltrans wanted him to create a "confused and congested situation" on his surface streets, so as to force drivers back to the freeway, where they would meet a still more confused and congested situation and decide to stay home, or take a bus. "We are beginning a process of deliberately making it harder for drivers to use freeways," a Caltrans director had in fact said at a transit conference some months before. "We are prepared to endure considerable public outcry in order to pry John Q. Public out of his car. . . . I would emphasize that this is a political decision, and one that can be reversed if the public gets sufficiently enraged to throw us rascals out."

Of course this political decision was in the name of the greater good, was in the interests of "environmental improvement" and "conservation of resources," but even there the figures had about them a certain Caltrans opacity. The Santa Monica normally carried 240,000 cars and trucks every day. These 240,000 cars and trucks normally carried 260,000 people. What Caltrans described as its ultimate goal on the Santa Monica was to carry the same 260,000 people, "but in 7,800 fewer, or 232,200 vehicles." The figure "232,200" had a visionary precision to it that did not automatically create confidence, especially since the only effect so far had been to disrupt traffic throughout the Los Angeles basin, triple the number of daily accidents on the Santa Monica, prompt the initiation of two lawsuits against Caltrans, and cause large numbers of Los Angeles County residents to behave, most uncharacteristically, as an ignited and conscious proletariat. Citizen guerrillas splashed paint and scattered nails in the Diamond Lanes. Diamond Lane maintenance crews expressed fear of hurled objects. Down at 120 South Spring the architects of the Diamond Lane had taken to regarding "the media" as the architects of their embarrassment, and Caltrans statements in the press had been cryptic and contradictory, reminiscent only of old communiqués out of Vietnam.

To understand what was going on it is perhaps necessary to have participated   7
in the freeway experience, which is the only secular communion Los Angeles has. Mere driving on the freeway is in no way the same as participating in it. Anyone can "drive" on the freeway, and many people with no vocation for it do, hesitating here and resisting there, losing the rhythm of the lane change, thinking about where they came from and where they are going. Actual participants think only about where they are. Actual participation requires a total surrender, a concentration so intense as to seem a kind of narcosis, a rapture-of-the-freeway. The mind goes clean. The rhythm takes over. A distortion of time occurs, the same distortion that characterizes the instant before an accident. It takes only a few seconds to get off the Santa Monica Freeway at National-Overland, which is a difficult exit requiring the driver to cross two new lanes of traffic streamed in from the San Diego Freeway, but those few seconds always seem to me the longest part of the trip. The moment is dangerous. The exhilaration is in doing it. "As you acquire the special skills involved," Reyner Banham observed in an extraordinary chapter about the freeways in his 1971 *Los Angeles: The Architecture of Four Ecologies,* "the freeways become a special way of being alive . . . the extreme concentration required in Los Angeles seems to bring on a state of heightened awareness that some locals find mystical."

Indeed some locals do, and some nonlocals too. Reducing the number of   8
lone souls careering around the East-West Corridor in a state of mechanized rapture may or may not have seemed socially desirable, but what it was definitely not going to seem was easy. "We're only seeing an initial period of unfamiliarity," I was assured the day I visited Caltrans. I was talking to a woman named Eleanor Wood and she was thoroughly and professionally grounded in the diction of "planning" and it did not seem likely that I could interest her in considering the freeway as regional mystery. "Any time you try to rearrange people's daily habits, they're apt to react impetuously. All this project requires is a certain rearrangement of people's daily planning. That's really all we want."

It occurred to me that a certain rearrangement of people's daily planning   9
might seem, in less rarefied air than is breathed at 120 South Spring, rather a

great deal to want, but so impenetrable was the sense of higher social purpose there in the Operations Center that I did not express this reservation. Instead I changed the subject, mentioned an earlier "pilot project" on the Santa Monica: the big electronic message boards that Caltrans had installed a year or two before. The idea was that traffic information transmitted from the Santa Monica to the Xerox Sigma V could be translated, here in the Operations Center, into suggestions to the driver, and flashed right back out to the Santa Monica. This operation, in that it involved telling drivers electronically what they already knew empirically, had the rather spectral circularity that seemed to mark a great many Caltrans schemes, and I was interested in how Caltrans thought it worked.

"Actually the message boards were part of a larger pilot project," Mrs.   10
Wood said. "An ongoing project in incident management. With the message boards we hoped to learn if motorists would modify their behavior according to what we told them on the boards."

I asked if the motorists had.   11

"Actually no," Mrs. Wood said finally. "They didn't react to the signs exactly   12
as we'd hypothesized they would, no. *But.* If we'd *known* what the motorist would do . . . then we wouldn't have needed a pilot project in the first place, would we."

The circle seemed intact. Mrs. Wood and I smiled, and shook hands. I   13
watched the big board until all lights turned green on the Santa Monica and then I left and drove home on it, all 16.2 miles of it. All the way I remembered that I was watched by the Xerox Sigma V. All the way the message boards gave me the number to call for CAR POOL INFO. As I left the freeway it occurred to me that they might have their own rapture down at 120 South Spring, and it could be called Perpetuating the Department. Today the California Highway Patrol reported that, during the first six weeks of the Diamond Lane, accidents on the Santa Monica, which normally range between 49 and 72 during a six-week period, totaled 204. Yesterday plans were announced to extend the Diamond Lane to other freeways at a cost of $42,500,000.

[1979—U.S.A.]

Questions

1. In the first two paragraphs, the phrases "the closed door" and "the windowless room" repeat several times. Why? What might the two images symbolize?
2. There are many references to and images of circularity here. Pick out three or four. What does circularity come to symbolize in "Bureaucrats"? How does it tie in with the images of "closed door" and "windowless room"?
3. There is much repetition in "Bureaucrats." Why? What does Didion achieve through repetition?
4. Throughout the essay, words associated with religion are used in connection with Caltrans and the freeway (the oft-repeated "rapture," for example). What is the point of such diction? In what way is the analogy implied by the diction ironic?

5. Didion makes few direct comments about Caltrans. How, then, is her attitude conveyed? What is the tone of the essay? How is tone established and maintained here?
6. What is the theme of this essay? In what way is it about diction?

Writing Assignments

1. Have you ever been caught in a bureaucratic tangle? If so, describe and discuss it in a paragraph or more. You might end with a consideration of the general significance of the incident if you feel it says something about, for instance, the educational establishment, or the military, or society at large.
2. In a paper, discuss some group with which you are familiar that has its own special jargon. Establish what that jargon is and then discuss why it is used by the group and why plain English is eschewed.
3. Didion lets the facts speak for themselves, though she loads her language to communicate an ironic perspective on those facts. Choose something that interests you and write an essay in which you report on what you have chosen *without direct comment*. Imply your attitude (and thus your thesis), as does Didion, through strategic repetition, diction, tone, and so on.

THE IGUANA

❖ ISAK DINESEN ❖

In the Reserve I have sometimes come upon the Iguana, the big lizards, as they were sunning themselves upon a flat stone in a riverbed. They are not pretty in shape, but nothing can be imagined more beautiful than their colouring. They shine like a heap of precious stones or like a pane cut out of an old church window. When, as you approach, they swish away, there is a flash of azure, green and purple over the stones, the colour seems to be standing behind them in the air, like a comet's luminous tail.

Once I shot an Iguana. I thought that I should be able to make some pretty things from his skin. A strange thing happened then, that I have never afterwards forgotten. As I went up to him, where he was lying dead upon his stone, and actually while I was walking the few steps, he faded and grew pale, all colour died out of him as in one long sigh, and by the time that I touched him he was grey and dull like a lump of concrete. It was the live impetuous blood pulsating within the animal, which had radiated out all that glow and splendour. Now that the flame was put out, and the soul had flown, the Iguana was as dead as a sandbag.

Often since I have, in some sort, shot an Iguana, and I have remembered the one of the Reserve. Up at Meru I saw a young Native girl with a bracelet on, a leather strap two inches wide, and embroidered all over with very small turquoise-coloured beads which varied a little in colour and played in green, light blue and ultramarine. It was an extraordinarily live thing; it seemed to draw breath on her arm, so that I wanted it for myself, and made Farah buy it from her. No sooner had it come upon my own arm than it gave up the ghost. It was nothing now, a small, cheap, purchased article of finery. It had been the play of colours, the duet between the turquoise and the "nègre",— that quick, sweet, brownish black, like peat and black pottery, of the Native's skin,—that had created the life of the bracelet.

In the Zoological Museum of Pietermaritzburg, I have seen, in a stuffed   4
deep-water fish in a showcase, the same combination of colouring, which there had survived death; it made me wonder what life can well be like, on the bottom of the sea, to send up something so live and airy. I stood in Meru and looked at my pale hand and at the dead bracelet, it was as if an injustice had been done to a noble thing, as if truth had been suppressed. So sad did it seem that I remembered the saying of the hero in a book that I had read as a child: "I have conquered them all, but I am standing amongst graves."

In a foreign country and with foreign species of life one should take measures   5
to find out whether things will be keeping their value when dead. To the settlers of East Africa I give the advice: "For the sake of your own eyes and heart, shoot not the Iguana."

[1937—Denmark]

Questions

1. The voice of this essay has the ring of authority. What gives it this quality? Why is it necessary for Dinesen to establish an authoritative voice?
2. Why is the beginning of paragraph 2 startling? How are paragraphs 2 and 3 related? What accounts for the tight coherence of the essay?
3. What is Dinesen's thesis? Where is it stated? Why there? Is the statement necessary?
4. What audience is the essay directed toward? How is its statement of thesis (which is not to say its thesis statement) accounted for by its intended audience together with Dinesen's evident intent vis-à-vis that audience?
5. E. M. Forster's quotation from Dante—"Possession is one with loss" (p. 886)—could serve as a statement of the larger meaning of "The Iguana," of its theme as distinguished from its belatedly articulated thesis. How so?

Writing Assignments

1. The richness of its detail gives "The Iguana" weight and authority. Pick some creature or object that you have lived with and really know. Then, in a paragraph or more, describe it in detail so that your reader will see it imaginatively, as one can see Dinesen's iguana and bracelet.
2. Do what is suggested in the first assignment, only now set your descriptive paragraphs in a framework that will make them something more than simply descriptive. You could provide a thesis, for instance, that would make an example out of the creature or object presented; or you could frame your description in such a way that a theme emerges; or perhaps you could do both at once, as Dinesen does. In any case, let the details of your paper say most of what you have to say.

POORAN SINGH

⁑ ISAK DINESEN ⁑

Pooran Singh's little blacksmith's shop down by the mill was a miniature   1
Hell on the farm, with all the orthodox attributes of that place. It was built of
corrugated iron, and when the sun shone down upon the roof of it, and the
flames of the furnace rose inside it, the air itself, in and around the hut, was
white-hot. All day long, the place resounded with the deafening noise of the
forge,—iron on iron, on iron once more,—and the hut was filled with axes,
and broken wheels, that made it look like some ancient gruesome picture of
a place of execution.

All the same the blacksmith's shop had a great power of attraction, and   2
when I went down to watch Pooran Singh at work I always found people in it
and round it. Pooran Singh worked at a superhuman pace, as if his life depended
upon getting the particular job of work finished within the next five minutes,
he jumped straight up in the air over the forge, he shrieked out his orders to
his two young Kikuyu assistants in a high bird's voice and behaved altogether
like a man who is himself being burnt at the stake, or like some chafed over-
devil at work. But Pooran Singh was no devil, but a person of the meekest
disposition; out of working hours he had a little maidenly affectation of manner.
He was our Fundee of the farm, which means an artisan of all work, carpenter,
saddler and cabinet-maker, as well as blacksmith; he constructed and built
more than one waggon for the farm, all on his own. But he liked the work of
the forge best, and it was a very fine, proud sight, to watch him tiring a wheel.

Pooran Singh, in his appearance, was something of a fraud. When fully   3
dressed, in his coat and large folded white turban, he managed, with his big
black beard, to look a portly, ponderous man. But by the forge, bared
to the waist, he was incredibly slight and nimble, with the Indian hour-glass
torso.

I liked Pooran Singh's forge, and it was popular with the Kikuyus, for two   4
reasons.

First, because of the iron itself, which is the most fascinating of all raw   5
materials, and sets people's imagination travelling on long tracks. The plough,
the sword and cannon and the wheel,—the civilization of man—man's conquest
of Nature in a nut, plain enough to be understood or guessed by the primitive
people,—and Pooran Singh hammered the iron.

Secondly, the Native world was drawn to the forge by its song. The treble,   6
sprightly, monotonous, and surprising rhythm of the blacksmith's work has a
mythical force. It is so virile that it appals and melts the women's hearts, it is
straight and unaffected and tells the truth and nothing but the truth. Sometimes
it is very outspoken. It has an excess of strength and is gay as well as strong,
it is obliging to you and does great things for you, willingly, as in play. The
Natives, who love rhythm, collected by Pooran Singh's hut and felt at their
ease. According to an ancient Nordic law a man was not held responsible for

what he had said in a forge. The tongues were loosened in Africa as well, in the blacksmith's shop, and the talk flowed freely; audacious fancies were set forth to the inspiring hammer-song.

Pooran Singh was with me for many years and was a well-paid functionary   7
of the farm. There was no proportion between his wages and his needs, for he was an ascetic of the first water. He did not eat meat, he did not drink, or smoke, or gamble, his old clothes were worn to the thread. He sent his money over to India for the education of his children. A small silent son of his, Delip Singh, once came over from Bombay on a visit to his father. He had lost touch with the iron, the only metal that I saw about him was a fountain pen in his pocket. The mythical qualities were not carried on in the second generation.

But Pooran Singh himself, raging above the forge, kept his halo as long   8
as he was on the farm, and I hope as long as he lived. He was the servant of the gods, heated through, white-hot, an elemental spirit. In Pooran Singh's blacksmith's shop the hammer sang to you what you wanted to hear, as if it was giving voice to your own heart. To me myself the hammer was singing an ancient Greek verse, which a friend had translated:

> "Eros struck out, like a smith with his hammer,
> So that the sparks flew from my defiance.
> He cooled my heart in tears and lamentations,
> Like red-hot iron in a stream."

[1937—Denmark]

Questions

1. Read the first paragraph aloud. Can you spot where Dinesen forges a rhythm to match her subject? Where does it come? How do her words match the rhythm of the forge?

2. What other concretions—for instance, visual, aural, tactile, or gustatory images—does Dinesen use? To what effect? What purpose is served by the repetition of the epithet "white-hot," used in both paragraph 1 and paragraph 8?

3. "Pooran Singh" is basically a character sketch, though somewhat more indirect than most such sketches. Nevertheless, we learn a good deal about Pooran Singh. What exactly do we learn? People, we have reason to believe, are many-faceted and therefore usually inconsistent in one way or another. What inconsistency does Dinesen's portrait of the blacksmith underscore?

4. What kinds of organization do paragraphs 5 and 6 follow? Why is the material of the sixth paragraph put second?

5. "Pooran Singh" is a character sketch and more. How does the mythic element here extend the meaning of the essay? How does the mythic element tie in with the erotic element? How does Pooran's Singh's son with his "fountain pen" stand against everything else in the essay? What might we take as its theme with respect to Delip Singh's pen?

Writing Assignments

1. Choose someone you know fairly well, someone whose occupation or life history or eccentricities make him or her particularly interesting, and write a character sketch of the person.

Try to capture the person's contradictions no less than the surface that he or she presents. Try, too, to make your portrait vivid by using concrete details all along the way. Study Dinesen's essay in this regard and model your essay after hers with regard to imagistic detail and specificity.

2. Dinesen refers or alludes to various mythologies and mythological figures: the Christian heaven and hell, the Norse god Vulcan, the Greek gods Hephaistos and Prometheus. Research these concepts and figures; then write a paper using your research to explicate (that is, to make clear) their function and meaning in the essay at hand.

THE GUIDETTE

❖ LISA DONOFRIO ❖

There she goes, my favorite guidette on campus. She must be a Gina, Maria, Luisa, Theresa—one of those names that end in *i-a* and sound natural when their boyfriends preface them with "Yo." Definitely not a Harriet or an Anne. She's a HOT BABE. At least, that's what her T-shirt says. Oh, here it comes, the true test of the perfect guidette: can she walk up the quad steps while chewing gum and simultaneously applying purple eyeshadow without tripping on her three-inch white pumps or splitting her jeans? Whew, she made it! Oh, and look. . . . The back of her T-shirt says "BRONX GIRLS, BEST IN THE WORLD." The T-shirt is nice. But what will she do in the winter? I don't think they make sweaters in neon pink.

She is in my history class. I saw her there yesterday. I turned round because there was a deafening explosion in my left ear. I came face to face with fuchsia lipstick, foundation makeup lines, and a big pink bubble that popped in my face. I lost all sense of reality for a moment (at least my reality). She leaned back to admire her matching fuchsia nails. My hearing returned and I looked back at the professor once more.

Later I saw her in a Bon Jovi T-shirt. She was telling her friend, named something *i-a,* about the concert the night before. According to her, it was a "pissa," the height of pop entertainment. But how could you expect anything but a great night from music idols who are the paragons of masculinity, stuffing socks down the crotch of their leather pants and looking prettier than half the girls on campus?

She was quite pleased with herself. She managed to push her way to the front row, she told her friend, and get onstage and into the backstage party. From the hundreds of Ginas, Marias, Luisas, and Theresas, she was picked to go to bed with the lead singer's head bodyguard. "I was smart, though. I made him use protection. He said he would get me backstage for the Madison Square Garden concert. Do you think he'll call? God! I hope Tony doesn't find out. He's so possessive. When he picked me up in his Trans-Am today, he wouldn't even kiss me because I wore these jeans. He would have made me go home and change except that we didn't have enough time because he had to drive back to his house because he forgot his brush and gold chain." I turned around and asked if she had heard about the red-alert hair spray shortage. A wave of terror overtook her. The bell rang for the next class—religion, for me, which I strolled to contemplating a vision of Jesus saving the world and bringing everyone to heaven in yellow Camaros.

I wonder what guidettes major in. I can't see them writing a research   5 paper; I can't see them reading anything besides Cosmopolitan; I can't even imagine them driving a car, much less designing an engine. But they graduate somehow. Some enter the corporate world. Some even go on to medical or law school. I can see it now, guidette lawyers suing their fathers for depriving them of a sweet-sixteen party with alcohol at Leonard's or Vinny's Clam Bar. And oh, my goodness, these guidettes will marry guidos and have little guidos and guidettes who will go to school with my children. I'm seized by panic when I think of a possible future: my eight-year-old son coming home from school saying, "Yo, ma, be a good broad and get me a brew."

[1988—U.S.A.]

Questions

1. What does Donofrio set out to do in "The Guidette" (*gwē-dĕt,* derived from "Guido")? In what way could this essay be thought of as a definition? What does it define? Why did the author not give her focal character a specific name?
2. Contrast "The Guidette," which is a character sketch of sorts, with "Pooran Singh" (pp. 911–12). How do they differ in mood and aim?
3. "The Guidette" is a satire. What makes it satirical? Why is it funny?

Writing Assignments

1. In two or more paragraphs, contrast "The Guidette" and "Pooran Singh." Focus especially on the difference in aim between the two essays, a difference that can be gotten at by a consideration of the fact that Donofrio does not give her character a name.
2. Write an essay in which you define a given type of character by drawing a satirical portrait of that character. Try to make your portrait as specific and detailed as Donofrio's, and see if you can't make it funny as well.

NO HOME IN AFRICA

———————————— ✜ ANNETTE DULA ✜ ————————————

I have no cultural roots in Africa nor do I want any. I have discovered   1 that Egypt is not black Africa. The skin isn't black enough and the hair isn't kinky enough. An Egyptian merchant put his light brown arm next to my black arm and said, "My skin isn't black but I'm African, too." Sincerity was not in his voice.

In Khartoum, the Sudan, a near-riot developed when I appeared to be an African woman walking down the street in a leather miniskirt. I liked melting into the anonymity of hundreds of black faces, but I also wanted the freedom that tourists enjoy.

I went to Ethiopia with Kay, who is white. The people were hostile. They pelted me with rotten tomatoes. They did not bother Kay. Didn't they realize that I was black like them?

In East Africa, the Africans were too servile toward whites. I got extremely angry when a gnarled little old man would bow down and call my friend "Mensaab." An African woman would not become angry.

I hated the mercenary Indians of East Africa more than the Africans hated them. Two years after the incident, I can still taste the bitterness. I wanted to buy material for a blouse. At the time, most shopkeepers in East Africa were Indians. I had walked in ahead of Kay. The shopkeeper continued talking to another Indian. Kay walked in. The shopkeeper rushed up to her.

"Can I help you, madam?" he asked, with the proper servility.

"My friend wants to buy material," she said.

"How much does she want to pay for it?" he asked.

"Perhaps you'd better talk to her, sir."

Completely ignoring her suggestion, he continued explaining to Kay the virtues of expensive imported materials over cheaper native ones. "You know, these Africans are lazy. They just aren't capable of the superior quality you get in Western work!"

I walked out. I knew what prejudice was—but not this kind. This was the type my parents had known in North Carolina 25 years ago. I rejoiced when the Indians were kicked out of Uganda.

I do have the appearance of a black African. I have even been asked by Africans, "To what tribe do you belong?" And, "From what part of Africa do you come?" When it was to my advantage to be considered African, it pleased me. At other times, embarrassing situations could develop.

Once when I was walking from a restaurant at around 9:30 P.M., four or five policemen jumped out of a squad car, surrounded me, and pointed their loaded guns at me. Though they were speaking in Swahili, I soon gathered that I was being arrested on prostitution charges. The more I protested in English, the more incensed they became. I reacted as any American woman would. "Who do you think you are? Get those guns out of my face. I am an American. I want to call the Ambassador." (Later, I learned that Kenya had a new law making it illegal for unescorted African women to be on the street after 9:30 P.M.).

More often than not, I resented being treated as an African by Africans. I was truly galled at the customs station between Zaire and the Central African

Republic. Tourists usually pass customs by merely showing their passports. Africans are subjected to a thorough search. As I was about to move along with other tourists, I was roughly grabbed from behind and thrust back into the crowd. I had to be freed by other tourists. The mob attitude was: "Who do you think you are? You're not a tourist! You're one of us." Why didn't I protest the preferential treatment that tourists receive? Because I felt as the American tourists do: "We are entitled to these considerations."

When I understood that the average African male has little respect for the   15
female intellect, I was surprised. Ngimbus, a close friend of mine, decided that I was a militant feminist when I lectured him on male-female equality!

"She looks like an African, but she talks nonsense," he said later.   16

Often, I found myself defending black Americans to nationalist West-Africans.   17
A favorite question was "Why do you call yourselves *Afro*-American?" I usually answered in terms of cultural heritage, identity oppression, and other nebulous words that explain nothing. The conversation would continue: "You have for-feited the right to call yourselves *Afro*-Americans. If you were worthy of the name *Afro-*, your people would never have taken all those years of such treatment. We sympathize with you, but you're too docile for us."

"What about South Africa and Mozambique?" I would always ask.   18

The question was usually ignored or if answered, the time factor was brought   19
in: "We have accomplished more in eighty years than you have accomplished in 400 years." The conversation always left me with a need to explain our differences. But there never were acceptable explanations.

My experiences in Africa typify the reciprocal misunderstandings between   20
black Americans and Africans. Our common color is not enough. Too much time has passed.

I am not patriotic, but I am a product of America. I believe in freedom of   21
speech, even if it is only token. I take education for granted though we may not receive it equally. I believe in the working of democracy even though it never seems to work. I am forced to accept that I am an American and that here in America lie my cultural roots—whether I like it or not.

[1975—U.S.A.]

Questions

1. The first sentence of this essay might be printed as a separate paragraph. What might be gained by printing it thus?
2. Dula reports some incidents and uses dialogue to re-create others. In what way(s) is each technique appropriate to the nature of the event that the technique is used to unfold?
3. What means of support does Dula use? Does she do so effectively? Is hers a good way to argue in general? Why or why not?
4. What generalization does the title here point to? What is the theme of this essay? Is the generalization well supported? Does it seem like a just conclusion drawn from the facts given? Why or why not?

Writing Assignments

1. Did you ever feel the odd man out? Were you ever in a strange place where you felt misunderstood by people who reacted only to your race, sex, style of dress or hair, or something else equally superficial? If so, write a paragraph or more on the incident. Describe it, using dialogue if you like, and move to a reflection on its meaning.
2. What experiences of your own could be used to support a thesis or embody a theme? Write an essay incorporating these experiences as examples. If you have a thesis in mind, state it and then marshal your examples behind it. But if you think that the material speaks for itself, then let it, making sure, however, that your theme clearly binds together the incidents you report.

HOW TO TALK ABOUT THE WORLD

✳ PETER FARB ✳

If human beings paid attention to all the sights, sounds, and smells that besiege them, their ability to codify and recall information would be swamped. Instead, they simplify the information by grouping it into broad verbal categories. For example, human eyes have the extraordinary power to discriminate some ten million colors, but the English language reduces these to no more than four thousand color words, of which only eleven basic terms are commonly used. That is why a driver stops at all traffic lights whose color he categorizes as *red,* even though the lights vary slightly from one to another in their hues of redness. Categorization allows people to respond to their environment in a way that has great survival value. If they hear a high-pitched sound, they do not enumerate the long list of possible causes of such sounds: a human cry of fear, a scream for help, a policeman's whistle, and so on. Instead they become alert because they have categorized high-pitched sounds as indicators of possible danger.

Words, therefore, are more than simply labels for specific objects; they are also parts of sets of related principles. To a very young child, the word *chair* may at first refer only to his highchair. Soon afterward, he learns that the four-legged object on which his parents sit at mealtimes is also called a *chair.* So is the thing with only three legs, referred to by his parents as a *broken chair,* and so is the upholstered piece of furniture in the living room. These objects form a category, *chair,* which is set apart from all other categories by a unique combination of features. A *chair* must possess a seat, legs, and back; it may also, but not necessarily, have arms; it must accommodate only one person. An object that possesses these features with but a single exception— it accommodates three people—does not belong to the category *chair* but rather to the category *couch,* and that category in turn is described by a set of unique features.

Furthermore, Americans think of *chairs* and *couches* as being related to   3
each other because they both belong to a category known in English as *household
furniture*. But such a relationship between the category *chair* and the category
couch is entirely arbitrary on the part of English and some other speech communities. Nothing in the external world decrees that a language must place these
two caregories together. In some African speech communities, for example,
the category *chair* would most likely be thought of in relation to the category
spear, since both are emblems of ruler's authority.

The analysis of words by their categories for the purpose of determining   4
what they mean to speakers of a particular language—that is, what the native
speaker, and not some visiting linguist, feels are the distinguishing features or
components of that word—is known as "componential analysis" or "formal
semantic analysis." The aim, in brief, is to determine the components or features
that native speakers use to distinguish similar terms from one another so that
more exact meanings can be achieved.

Anyone who visits an exotic culture quickly learns that the people are   5
linguistically deaf to categories he considers obvious, yet they are extraordinarily
perceptive in talking about things he has no easy way to describe. An English-
speaking anthropologist studying the Koyas of India, for example, soon discovers
that their language does not distinguish between dew, fog, and snow. When
questioned about these natural phenomena, the Koyas can find a way to describe
them, but normally their language attaches no significance to making such
distinctions and provides no highly codable words for the purpose. On the
other hand, a Koya has the linguistic resources to speak easily about seven
different kinds of bamboo—resources that the visiting anthropologist utterly
lacks in his own language. More important than the significance, or the lack
of it, that a language places on objects and ideas is the way that language
categorizes the information it does find significant. A *pig,* for example, can be
categorized in several ways: a mammal with cloven hoofs and bristly hairs
and adapted for digging with its snout; a mold in which metal is cast; a British
sixpence coin. The Koyas categorize the pig in none of these ways; they simply
place it in the category of animals that are edible. Their neighbors, Muslims,
think of it in a different way by placing it in the category of defiled animals.

Everyone, whether he realizes it or not, classifies the items he finds in   6
his environment. Most speakers of English recognize a category that they call
livestock, which is made up of other categories known as *cattle, horses, sheep,*
and *swine* of different ages and sexes. An English speaker who is knowledgeable
about farm life categorizes a barnyardful of these animals in a way that establishes
relationships based on distinguishing features. For example, he feels that a
cow and a *mare,* even though they belong to different species, are somehow
in a relationship to each other. And of course they are, because they both
belong to the category of Female Animal under the general category of Livestock.
The speaker of English unconsciously groups certain animals into various sub-
categories that exclude other animals:

	Cattle	Horses	Sheep	Swine
LIVESTOCK				
Female	cow	mare	ewe	sow
Intact Male	bull	stallion	ram	boar
Castrated Male	steer	gelding	wether	barrow
Immature	heifer	colt/filly	lamb	shoat/gilt
Newborn	calf	foal	yearling	piglet

A table such as this shows that speakers of English are intuitively aware of certain contrasts. They regard a *bull* and a *steer* as different—which they are, because one belongs to a category of Intact Males and the other to a category of Castrated Males. In addition to discriminations made on the basis of livestock's sex, speakers of English also contrast mature and immature animals. A *foal* is a newborn horse and a *stallion* is a mature male horse.

The conceptual labels by which English-speaking peoples talk about barnyard animals can now be understood. The animal is defined by the point at which two distinctive features intersect: sex (male, female, or castrated) and maturity (mature, immature, or newborn). A *stallion* belongs to a category of horse that is both intact male and mature; a *filly* belongs to a category of horse that is both female and immature. Nothing in external reality dictates that barnyard animals should be talked about in this way; it is strictly a convention of English and some other languages.

In contrast, imagine that an Amazonian Indian is brought to the United States so that linguists can intensively study his language. When the Indian returns to his native forests, his friends and relatives listen in disbelief as he tells about all the fantastic things he saw. He summarizes his impressions of America in terms of the familiar categories his language has accustomed him to. He relates that at first he was bewildered by the strange animals he saw on an American farm because each animal not only looked different but also seemed to represent a unique concept to the natives of the North American tribe. But after considerable observation of the curious folkways of these peculiar people, at last he understood American barnyard animals. He figured out that some animals are good for work and that some are good for food. Using these two components—rather than the Americans' features of sex and maturity—his classification of livestock is considerably different. He categorized *stallion, mare,* and *gelding* as belonging to both the Inedible and Work (Riding) categories. The *bull* also belonged to the Inedible category but it was used for a different kind of Work as a draught animal. He further placed a large number of animals—*cow, ewe, lamb, sow,* and so on—in the category of Edible but Useless for Work. Since his method of categorizing the barnyard failed to take into account the breeding process, which depends upon the categories of sex and maturity, he no doubt found it inexplicable that some animals—

ram, colt, boar, and so on—were raised even though they could not be eaten or used for work.

To an American, the Amazonian Indian's classification of barnyard animals appears quite foolish, yet it is no more foolish than the American's system of classification by the features of sex and maturity. Speakers of each language have the right to recognize whatever features they care to. And they have a similar right to then organize these features according to the rules of their own speech communities. No one system is better than another in making sense out of the world in terms that can be talked about; the systems are simply different. A speaker of English who defines a *stallion* as a mature, male horse is no wiser than the Amazonian who claims it is inedible and used for riding. Both the speaker of English and the speaker of the Amazonian language have brought order out of the multitudes of things in the environment—and, in the process, both have shown something about how their languages and their minds work.

[1973—U.S.A.]

Questions

1. What is Farb's purpose in this essay? What is its thesis? The thesis here is unfolded step by step in paragraphs 6, 8, and 10. What specific sentences when taken together form the thesis statement?
2. Why did Farb not state his thesis all at once at the beginning? Is his method effective? How so?
3. Farb moves from colors to furniture to livestock. What accounts for this order of his enumerated items? Why colors first and livestock last?
4. The material of paragraph 4 is somewhat extraneous. How does Farb make the paragraph coherent—that is, how does it relate to paragraphs 3 and 5?
5. At the end of the essay, Farb states as a conclusion the final part of his thesis. Does his evidence support his statement? Is it indeed drawn from the evidence, or is it simply a prejudice slipped in in such a way as to seem logical?

Writing Assignments

1. Make a chart like Farb's classifying some group of people, animals, or things: teachers, dogs, clothing. Then, in a paragraph or more, explain your criteria for so classifying and justify your categories on some basis (for instance, their usefulness).
2. Look over the titles of the essays you have read in this book. Classify them according to some system appropriate to the material: prosaic versus poetic, elaborate versus simple, to-the-point versus tangential, descriptive versus intriguing, or any combination of these or other categories. Now write a paper on what makes for a good title. Does your classification shed light on why some titles are more effective than others? How? Or do good titles cut across categories? If so, what can be concluded from that?
3. Farb would have us believe that all systems of classification are equal. But couldn't it be argued on some basis or other that this is not so? Write an essay specifying why one system might be preferable to another. To do so convincingly, you will have to find cogent reasons and to exemplify them clearly and well.

TOLERANCE

──────────── ✳ E. M. FORSTER ✳ ────────────

Everybody is talking about reconstruction. Our enemies have their schemes   1
for a new order in Europe, maintained by their secret police, and we on our
side talk of rebuilding London or England, or western civilization, and we
make plans how this is to be done. Which is all very well, but when I hear
such talk, and see the architects sharpening their pencils and the contractors
getting out their estimates, and the statesmen marking out their spheres of
influence, and everyone getting down to the job, a very famous text occurs to
me: "Except the Lord build the house, they labour in vain that build it." Beneath
the poetic imagery of these words lies a hard scientific truth, namely, unless
you have a sound attitude of mind, a right psychology, you cannot construct
or reconstruct anything that will endure. The text is true, not only for religious
people, but for workers whatever their outlook, and it is significant that one
of our historians, Dr. Arnold Toynbee, should have chosen it to preface his
great study of the growth and decay of civilizations. Surely the only sound
foundation for a civilization is a sound state of mind. Architects, contractors,
international commissioners, marketing boards, broadcasting corporations will
never, by themselves, build a new world. They must be inspired by the proper
spirit, and there must be the proper spirit in the people for whom they are
working. For instance, we shall never have a beautiful new London until people
refuse to live in ugly houses. At present, they don't mind; they demand more
comfort, but are indifferent to civic beauty; indeed they have no taste. I live
myself in a hideous block of flats, but I can't say it worries me, and until we
are worried all schemes for reconstructing London beautifully must automatically
fail.

What, though, is the proper spirit? We agree that the basic problem is   2
psychological, that the Lord must build if the work is to stand, that there must
be a sound state of mind before diplomacy or economics or trade conferences
can function. But what state of mind is sound? Here we may differ. Most people,
when asked what spiritual quality is needed to rebuild civilization, will reply
"Love." Men must love one another, they say; nations must do likewise, and
then the series of cataclysms which is threatening to destroy us will be checked.

Respectfully but firmly, I disagree. Love is a great force in private life; it is   3
indeed the greatest of all things; but love in public affairs does not work. It
has been tried again and again: by the Christian civilizations of the Middle
Ages, and also by the French Revolution, a secular movement which reasserted
the Brotherhood of Man. And it has always failed. The idea that nations should
love one another, or that business concerns or marketing boards should love
one another, or that a man in Portugal should love a man in Peru of whom
he has never heard—it is absurd, unreal, dangerous. It leads us into perilous
and vague sentimentalism. "Love is what is needed," we chant, and then sit

back and the world goes on as before. The fact is, we can only love what we know personally. And we cannot know much. In public affairs, in the rebuilding of civilization, something much less dramatic and emotional is needed, namely tolerance. Tolerance is a very dull virtue. It is boring. Unlike love, it has always had a bad press. It is negative. It merely means putting up with people, being able to stand things. No one has ever written an ode to tolerance, or raised a statue to her. Yet this is the quality which will be most needed after the war. This is the sound state of mind which we are looking for. This is the only force which will enable different races and classes and interests to settle down together to the work of reconstruction.

The world is very full of people—appallingly full; it has never been so   4
full before—and they are all tumbling over each other. Most of these people one doesn't know and some of them one doesn't like; doesn't like the colour of their skins, say, or the shapes of their noses, or the way they blow them or don't blow them, or the way they talk, or their smell, or their clothes, or their fondness for jazz or their dislike of jazz, and so on. Well, what is one to do? There are two solutions. One of them is the Nazi solution. If you don't like people, kill them, banish them, segregate them, and then strut up and down proclaiming that you are the salt of the earth. The other way is much less thrilling, but it is on the whole the way of the democracies, and I prefer it. If you don't like people, put up with them as well as you can. Don't try to love them; you can't, you'll only strain yourself. But try to tolerate them. On the basis of that tolerance a civilized future may be built. Certainly I can see no other foundation for the post-war world.

For what it will most need is the negative virtues: not being huffy, touchy,   5
irritable, revengeful. I have lost all faith in positive militant ideals; they can so seldom be carried out without thousands of human beings getting maimed or imprisoned. Phrases like "I will purge this nation," "I will clean up this city," terrify and disgust me. They might not have mattered when the world was emptier; they are horrifying now, when one nation is mixed up with another, when one city cannot be organically separated from its neighbours. And another point: reconstruction is unlikely to be rapid. I do not believe that we are psychologically fit for it, plan the architects never so wisely. In the long run, yes, perhaps; the history of our race justifies that hope. But civilization has its mysterious regressions, and it seems to me that we are fated now to be in one of them, and must recognize this and behave accordingly. Tolerance, I believe, will be imperative after the establishment of peace. It's always useful to take a concrete instance; and I have been asking myself how I should behave if, after peace was signed, I met Germans who had been fighting against us. I shouldn't try to love them; I shouldn't feel inclined. They have broken a window in my little ugly flat for one thing. But I shall try to tolerate them, because it is common sense, because in the post-war world we shall have to live with Germans. We can't exterminate them, any more than they have succeeded in exterminating the Jews. We shall have to put up with them, not for any lofty reason, but because it is the next thing that will have to be done.

I don't then, regard tolerance as a great eternally established divine principle, though I might perhaps quote "In my Father's house are many mansions" in support of such a view. It is just a makeshift, suitable for an overcrowded and overheated planet. It carries on when love gives out, and love generally gives out as soon as we move away from our home and our friends, and stand among strangers in a queue for potatoes. Tolerance is wanted in the queue; otherwise we think, "Why will people be so slow?"; it is wanted in the tube, or "Why will people be so fat?"; it is wanted at the telephone, or "Why are they so deaf?" or, conversely, "Why do they mumble?" It is wanted in the street, in the office, at the factory, and it is wanted above all between classes, races and nations. It's dull. And yet it entails imagination. For you have all the time to be putting yourself in someone else's place. Which is a desirable spiritual exercise.   6

This ceaseless effort to put up with other people seems tame, almost ignoble, so that it sometimes repels generous natures, and I don't recall many great men who have recommended tolerance. St. Paul certainly did not. Nor did Dante. However, a few names occur. Going back over two thousand years, and to India, there is the great Buddhist Emperor Asoka, who set up inscriptions recording not his own exploits but the need for mercy and mutual understanding and peace. Going back about four hundred years, to Holland, there is the Dutch scholar Erasmus, who stood apart from the religious fanaticism of the Reformation and was abused by both parties in consequence. In the same century there was the Frenchman Montaigne, subtle, intelligent, witty, who lived in his quiet country house and wrote essays which still delight and confirm the civilized. And England: there was John Locke, the philosopher; there was Sydney Smith, the Liberal and liberalizing divine; there was Lowes Dickinson, writer of *A Modern Symposium,* which might be called the Bible of Tolerance. And Germany—yes, Germany: there was Goethe. All these men testify to the creed which I have been trying to express: a negative creed, but necessary for the salvation of this crowded jostling modern world.   7

Two more remarks. First, it is very easy to see fanaticism in other people, but difficult to spot in oneself. Take the evil of racial prejudice. We can easily detect it in the Nazis; their conduct has been infamous ever since they rose to power. But we ourselves—are we guiltless? We are far less guilty than they are. Yet is there no racial prejudice in the British Empire? Is there no colour question? I ask you to consider that, those of you to whom tolerance is more than a pious word. My other remark is to forestall a criticism. Tolerance is not the same as weakness. Putting up with people does not mean giving in to them. This complicates the problem. But the rebuilding of civilization is bound to be complicated. I only feel certain that unless the Lord builds the house they will labour in vain who build it. Perhaps, when the house is completed, love will enter it, and the greatest force in our private lives will also rule in public life.   8

[1942—Great Britain]

Questions

1. What is Forster's thesis? How do you know? Where is it stated?
2. "Tolerance" was written as a speech. How does Forster's style reflect this?
3. Look at the sentences in the second and third paragraphs with respect to length and syntax. Forster adeptly varies both. How? Why?
4. What means of support does Forster use in paragraph 7? Is this type of support effective here? Why or why not?
5. What kind of a voice do you hear when reading "Tolerance"? What is the essay's tone? How are tone and the sense of voice created here? In what way is the essay's tone (a matter of form) at one with its content?

Writing Assignments

1. Choose a thesis and, in a paragraph or more, argue it by referring to authorities who have held the same view (as Forster does in paragraph 7). Be sure to have a reason for the arrangement of the authorities you enumerate.
2. Forster presents tolerance as a "state of mind" and then argues for it in a tone that is his best example. Pick another state of mind—serenity, say, or joy—and, in an essay focused on the virtues of the attitude you choose, discuss it in a tone (created by diction and syntax as well as the epithets you use and other aspects of your verbal structure) that itself conveys the attitude you name.

THE NONSCIENCE OF HUMAN NATURE
❊ STEPHEN JAY GOULD ❊

When a group of girls suffered simultaneous seizures in the presence of an accused witch, the justices of seventeenth century Salem could offer no explanation other than true demonic possession. When the followers of Charlie Manson attributed occult powers to their leader, no judge took them seriously. In nearly three hundred years separating the two incidents, we have learned quite a bit about social, economic, and psychological determinants of group behavior. A crudely literal interpretation of such events now seems ridiculous.

An equally crude literalism used to prevail in interpreting human nature and the differences among human groups. Human behavior was attributed to innate biology; we do what we do because we are made that way. The first lesson of an eighteenth-century primer stated the position succinctly: In Adam's fall, we sinned all. A movement away from this biological determinism has been a major trend in twentieth-century science and culture. We have come to see ourselves as a learning animal; we have come to believe that the influences of class and culture far outweigh the weaker predispositions of our genetic constitution.

Nonetheless, we have been deluged during the past decade by a resurgent biological determinism, ranging from "pop ethology" to outright racism.

With Konrad Lorenz[1] as godfather; Robert Ardrey as dramatist, and Desmond Morris as raconteur, we are presented with man, "the naked ape," descended from an African carnivore, innately aggressive and inherently territorial.   4

Lionel Tiger and Robin Fox try to find a biological basis for outmoded Western ideals of aggressive, outreaching men and docile, restricted women. In discussing cross-cultural differences between men and women, they propose a hormonal chemistry inherited from the requirements of our supposed primal roles as group hunters and child rearers.   5

Carleton Coon offered a prelude of events to come with his claim (*The Origin of Races,* 1962) that five major human races evolved independently from *Homo erectus* ("Java" and "Peking" man) to *Homo sapiens,* with black people making the transition last. More recently, the IQ test has been (mis) used to infer genetic differences in intelligence among races (Arthur Jensen and William Shockley) and classes (Richard Herrnstein)—always, I must note, to the benefit of the particular group to which the author happens to belong. . . .   6

All these views have been ably criticized on an individual basis; yet they have rarely been treated together as expressions of a common philosophy—a crude biological determinism. One can, of course, accept a specific claim and reject the others. A belief in the innate nature of human violence does not brand anyone a racist. Yet all these claims have a common underpinning in postulating a direct genetic basis for our most fundamental traits. If we are programmed to be what we are, then these traits are ineluctable. We may, at best, channel them, but we cannot change them, either by will, education, or culture.   7

If we accept the usual platitudes about "scientific method" at face value, then the coordinated resurgence of biological determinism must be attributed to new information that refutes the earlier findings of twentieth-century science. Science, we are told, progresses by accumulating new information and using it to improve or replace old theories. But the new biological determinism rests upon no recent fund of information and can cite in its behalf not a single unambiguous fact. Its renewed support must have some other basis, most likely social or political in nature.   8

Science is always influenced by society, but it operates under a strong constraint of fact as well. The Church eventually made its peace with Galileo because, after all, the earth does go around the sun. In studying the genetic components of such complex human traits as intelligence and aggressiveness, however, we are freed from the constraint of fact, for we know practically nothing. In these questions, "science" follows (and exposes) the social and political influences acting upon it.   9

What then, are the nonscientific reasons that have fostered the resurgence of biological determinism? They range, I believe, from pedestrian pursuits of high royalties for best sellers to pernicious attempts to reintroduce racism as   10

---

[1] *Lorenz et al.:* Scientists and popular writers who have argued for biological determinism, or for the idea that biology and biological history are a kind of fate determining human character and destiny. Some of the people and ideas referred to here are discussed at greater length later in the essay.

respectable science. Their common denominator must lie in our current malaise. How satisfying it is to fob off the responsibility for war and violence upon our presumably carnivorous ancestors. How convenient to blame the poor and the hungry for their own condition—lest we be forced to blame our economic system or our government for an abject failure to secure a decent life for all people. And how convenient an argument for those who control government and, by the way, provide the money that science requires for its very existence.

Deterministic arguments divide neatly into two groups—those based on the supposed nature of our species in general and those that invoke presumed differences among "racial groups" of *Homo sapiens*. I discuss the first subject here and treat the second in [another] essay.   11

Summarized briefly, mainstream pop ethology contends that two lineages of hominids inhabited Pleistocene Africa. One, a small, territorial carnivore, evolved into us; the other, a larger, presumably gentle herbivore, became extinct. Some carry the analogy of Cain and Abel to its full conclusion and accuse our ancestors of fratricide. The "predatory transition" to hunting established a pattern of innate violence and engendered our territorial urges: "With the coming of the hunting life to the emerging hominid came the dedication to territory" (Ardrey, *The Territorial Imperative*). We may be clothed, citified, and civilized, but we carry deep within us the genetic patterns of behavior that served our ancestor, the "killer ape." In *Africa Genesis* Ardrey champions Raymond Dart's contention that "the predatory transition and the weapons fixation explained man's bloody history, his eternal aggression, his irrational, self-destroying, inexorable pursuit of death for death's sake."   12

Tiger and Fox extend the theme of group hunting to proclaim a biological basis for the differences between men and women that Western cultures have traditionally valued. Men did the hunting; women stayed home with the kids. Men are aggressive and combative, but they also form strong bonds among themselves that reflect the ancient need for cooperation in the killing of big game and now find expression in touch football and rotary clubs. Women are docile and devoted to their own children. They do not form intense bonds among themselves because their ancestors needed none to tend their homes and their men: sisterhood is an illusion. "We are wired for hunting. . . . We remain Upper Paleolithic hunters, fine-honed machines designed for the efficient pursuit of game" (Tiger and Fox, *The Imperial Animal*).   13

The story of pop ethology has been built on two lines of supposed evidence, both highly disputable: 14

1. Analogies with the behavior of other animals (abundant but imperfect data). No one doubts that many animals (including some, but not all, primates) display innate patterns of aggression and territorial behavior. Since we exhibit similar behavior, can we not infer a similar cause? The fallacy of this assumption reflects a basic issue in evolutionary theory. Evolutionists divide the similarities between two species into *homologous* features shared by common descent and a common genetic constitution, and *analogous* traits evolved separately.   15

Comparisons between humans and other animals lead to causal assertions   16
about the genetics of our behavior only if they are based on homologous
traits. But how can we know whether similarities are homologous or analogous?
It is hard to differentiate even when we deal with concrete structures, such as
muscles and bones. In fact, most classical arguments in the study of phylogeny
involve the confusion of homology and analogy, for analogous structures can
be strikingly similar (we call this phenomenon evolutionary convergence). How
much harder it is to tell when similar features are only the outward motions
of behavior! Baboons may be territorial; their males may be organized into a
dominance hierarchy—but is our quest for Lebensraum[2] and the hierarchy of
our armies an expression of the same genetic makeup or merely an analogous
pattern that might be purely cultural in origin? And when Lorenz compares
us with geese and fish, we stray even further into pure conjecture; baboons,
at least, are second cousins.

2. Evidence from hominid fossils (scrappy but direct data). Ardrey's claims   17
for territoriality rest upon the assumption that our African ancestor *Australopithe-*
cus africanus, was a carnivore. He derives his "evidence" from accumulations
of bones and tools at the South African cave sites and the size and shape of
teeth. The bone piles are no longer seriously considered; they are more likely
the work of hyenas than of hominids.

Teeth are granted more prominence, but I believe that the evidence is   18
equally poor if not absolutely contradictory. The argument rests upon relative
size of grinding teeth (premolars and molars). Herbivores need more surface
area to grind their gritty and abundant food. *A. robustus,* the supposed gentle
herbivore, possessed grinding teeth relatively larger than those of its carnivorous
relative, our ancestor *A. africanus.*

But *A. robustus* was a larger creature than *A. africanus.* As size increases,   19
an animal must feed a body growing as the cube of length by chewing with
tooth areas that increase only as the square of length if they maintain the
same relative size. . . . This will not do, and larger mammals must have differen-
tially larger teeth than smaller relatives. I have tested this assertion by measuring
tooth areas and body sizes for species in several groups of mammals (rodents,
piglike herbivores, deer, and several groups of primates). Invariably, I find
that larger animals have relatively larger teeth—not because they eat different
foods, but simply because they are larger.

Moreover, the "small" teeth of *A. africanus* are not at all diminutive. They   20
are *absolutely larger* than ours (although we are three times as heavy), and
they are about as big as those of gorillas weighing nearly ten times as much!
The evidence of tooth size indicates to me that *A. africanus* was primarily
herbivorous.

The issue of biological determinism is not an abstract matter to be debated   21
within academic cloisters. These ideas have important consequences, and they
have already permeated our mass media. Ardrey's dubious theory is a prominent

---

[2] *Lebensraum:* "living space"; additional territory felt necessary by a nation for its economic well-being.

theme in Stanley Kubrick's film *2001*. The bone tool of our apelike ancestor first smashes a tapir's skull and then twirls about to transform into a space station of our next evolutionary stage—as the superman theme of Richard Strauss' *Zarathustra* yields to Johann's *Blue Danube.* Kubrick's next film, *Clockwork Orange,* continues the theme and explores the dilemma inspired by claims of innate human violence. (Shall we accept totalitarian controls for mass deprogramming or remain nasty and vicious within a democracy?) But the most immediate impact will be felt as male privilege girds its loins to battle a growing women's movement. As Kate Millett remarks in *Sexual Politics:* "Patriarchy has a tenacious or powerful hold through its successful habit of passing itself off as nature."

[1977—U.S.A.]

Questions

1. Clear thinking produces clear writing. Nowhere is this maxim better exemplified than in the work of Stephen Jay Gould. To see how splendidly coherent the essay at hand is, outline its progression of ideas and how they are brought together coherently, noting all transitional material from paragraph 2 on; indicate the topic sentence of each paragraph or paragraph cluster; and write a sentence or so summarizing the point of each paragraph or cluster of paragraphs. Also, note where the thesis is presented and what it is, and indicate what paragraphs are transitional in nature (the point of these paragraphs is transition). Finally, note any familiar structures you find in the essay—for example, order of climax or enumeration.
2. Gould's title does a good deal of work. How so? How, for instance, does his title allow Gould to delay his thesis statement?
3. Why does the thesis statement come where it comes?
4. "The Nonscience of Human Nature" begins with a contrast that leads to an analogy in paragraph 2. What rhetorical function does this beginning have? How might it predispose the reader to accept Gould's argument against the new determinists? Is Gould's an effective way to begin? Why?
5. The last paragraph here is a reverse funnel. How so? What Gould says in the last two sentences could have been said in the second half of paragraph 10. Why did Gould save this material for last? Is the end of the essay effective in its appeal to authority? Why or why not?

Writing Assignments

1. Write a paragraph or more in imitation of "The Nonscience of Human Nature." Find a topic that lends itself to enumeration. Then begin with some striking contrast or analogy or both in sequence (as does Gould), enumerate your points according to some plan, and conclude with a quotation from someone of note that backs you up.
2. Much of Gould's essay entails the drawing of a clear distinction—specifically, between science and masquerade science. Write a paper yourself involving distinction. For instance, there are different types of laughter, though we usually do not distinguish among them. To do so could make an excellent paper, as could a discussion of the different types of tears or of smiles. In this paper you will be categorizing first and then enumerating as

you draw your distinction(s). Be sure to provide transitions between all major blocks of material.

3. Write an essay like Gould's in general structure. Begin by summarizing in a few paragraphs a position opposed to your own on the given topic (which you must somehow specify); then, in a paragraph, state your thesis (which basically will be that the position you sum up in the beginning of your paper is in error); and then argue your case, bringing as much evidence to bear as is necessary. In your conclusion you might suggest various ramifications of your hypothetical opponent's position and indicate why, in light of these ramifications, that position not only is in error but is potentially downright harmful.

SALVATION

———————— ✳ LANGSTON HUGHES ✳ ————————

I was saved from sin when I was going on thirteen. But not really saved. It happened like this. There was a big revival at my Auntie Reed's church. Every night for weeks there had been much preaching, singing, praying, and shouting, and some very hardened sinners had been brought to Christ, and the membership of the church had grown by leaps and bounds. Then just before the revival ended, they held a special meeting for children, "to bring the young lambs to the fold." My aunt spoke of it for days ahead. That night I was escorted to the front row and placed on the mourners' bench with all the other young sinners, who had not yet been brought to Jesus.   1

My aunt told me that when you were saved you saw a light, and something happened to you inside! And Jesus came into your life! And God was with you from then on! She said you could see and hear and feel Jesus in your soul. I believed her. I had heard a great many old people say the same thing and it seemed to me they ought to know. So I sat there calmly in the hot, crowded church, waiting for Jesus to come to me.   2

The preacher preached a wonderful rhythmical sermon, all moans and shouts and lonely cries and dire pictures of hell, and then he sang a song about the ninety and nine safe in the fold, but one little lamb was left out in the cold. Then he said: "Won't you come? Won't you come to Jesus? Young lambs, won't you come?" And he held out his arms to all us young sinners there on the mourners' bench. And the little girls cried. And some of them jumped up and went to Jesus right away. But most of us just sat there.   3

A great many old people came and knelt around us and prayed, old women with jet-black faces and braided hair, old men with work-gnarled hands. And the church sang a song about the lower lights are burning, some poor sinners to be saved. And the whole building rocked with prayer and song.   4

Still I kept waiting to *see* Jesus.   5

Finally all the young people had gone to the altar and were saved, but one boy and me. He was a rounder's[1] son named Westley. Westley and I were   6

[1] *rounder:* a dissolute and/or dishonest person.

surrounded by sisters and deacons praying. It was very hot in the church, and getting late now. Finally Westley said to me in a whisper: "God damn! I'm tired o' sitting here. Let's get up and be saved." So he got up and was saved.

Then I was left all alone on the mourners' bench. My aunt came and   7
knelt at my knees and cried, while prayers and songs swirled all around me in the little church. The whole congregation prayed for me alone, in a mighty wail of moans and voices. And I kept waiting serenely for Jesus, waiting, waiting— but he didn't come. I wanted to see him, but nothing happened to me. Nothing! I wanted something to happen to me, but nothing happened.

I heard the songs and the minister saying: "Why don't you come? My dear   8
child, why don't you come to Jesus? Jesus is waiting for you. He wants you. Why don't you come? Sister Reed, what is this child's name?"

"Langston," my aunt sobbed.   9

"Langston, why don't you come? Why don't you come and be saved? Oh,   10
Lamb of God! Why don't you come?"

Now it was really getting late. I began to be ashamed of myself, holding   11
everything up so long. I began to wonder what God thought about Westley, who certainly hadn't seen Jesus either, but who was now sitting proudly on the platform, swinging his knickerbockered legs and grinning down at me, surrounded by deacons and old women on their knees praying. God had not struck Westley dead for taking his name in vain or for lying in the temple. So I decided that maybe to save further trouble, I'd better lie, too, and say that Jesus had come, and get up and be saved.

So I got up.   12

Suddenly the whole room broke into a sea of shouting, as they saw me   13
rise. Waves of rejoicing swept the place. Women leaped in the air. My aunt threw her arms around me. The minister took me by the hand and led me to the platform.

When things quieted down, in a hushed silence, punctuated by a few ecstatic   14
"Amens," all the new young lambs were blessed in the name of God. Then joyous singing filled the room.

That night, for the last time in my life but one—for I was a big boy twelve   15
years old—I cried. I cried, in bed alone, and couldn't stop. I buried my head under the quilts, but my aunt heard me. She woke up and told my uncle I was crying because the Holy Ghost had come into my life, and because I had seen Jesus. But I was really crying because I couldn't bear to tell her that I had lied, that I had deceived everybody in the church, that I hadn't seen Jesus, and that now I didn't believe there was a Jesus any more, since he didn't come to help me.

[1940—U.S.A.]

Questions

1. The title of this essay is ironic. How so? How does the irony, underscored by the second sentence of the first paragraph, lend dramatic tension to the essay overall?

2. Aside from the reasons given at the end, why did the boy remembered here cry the night he lied? What is the theme of the essay?
3. There are many details involving setting in "Salvation." Why? What purpose do they serve?
4. Varying between the poetic and the mundane, Hughes's diction is worth looking at. Find examples of each kind of diction. What effects does the diction here have? How does the diction tie in with the essay's theme?
5. How would you describe the style in general of "Salvation"? Why is it appropriate to the subject matter? What is the effect on pace of the one-sentence paragraphs? There are other fine rhythmic effects here. Locate two or three and describe them.
6. From Hughes's autobiography, *The Big Sea,* "Salvation" is close to being a story. What makes it an essay? Consider intent and reader psychology.

Writing Assignments

1. Write two paragraphs on the same subject but opposite in diction (poetic versus mundane, for instance, or technical versus slangy) and/or syntax (sentence length and sentence type). Then sum up the difference in effect between your two paragraphs.
2. Were you ever pressured into doing something as a child that you believed wrong? If so, write an essay on the incident. Try to make your narration immediate by your descriptive details and dramatic by the way you pace it and build to a climax.
3. In a paper, compare and contrast Russell Baker's "Little Red Riding Hood Revisited" (pp. 896–97) and "Salvation." Both are narratives of sorts and both can be considered essays, yet they are quite different, and they are essays for different reasons. Focus especially on the differences as to why each is an essay.

WATERWORKS AND KINGS

❖ ALDOUS HUXLEY ❖

In the chancelleries of eighteenth-century Europe nobody bothered very   1
much about Hesse. Its hostility was not a menace, its friendship brought no positive advantages. Hesse was only one of the lesser German states—a tenth-rate Power.

Tenth-rate: and yet, on the outskirts of Kassel, which was the capital of   2
this absurdly unimportant principality, there stands a palace large and splendid enough to house a full-blown emperor. And from the main façade of this palace there rises to the very top of the neighbouring mountain one of the most magnificent architectural gardens in the world. This garden, which is like a straight wide corridor of formal stone-work driven through the hillside forest, climbs up to a nondescript building in the grandest Roman manner, almost as large as a cathedral and surmounted by a colossal bronze statue of Hercules. Between Hercules at the top and the palace at the bottom lies an immense series of terraces, with fountains and cascades, pools, grottos, spouting tritons, dolphins, nereids and all the other mythological fauna of an eighteenth-

century water-garden. The spectacle, when the waters are flowing, is magnificent. There must be the best part of two miles of neo-classic cataract and elegantly canalized foam. The waterworks at Versailles are tame and trivial in comparison.

It was Whit Sunday when I was at Kassel. With almost the entire population of the town I had climbed up to the shrine of Hercules on the hilltop. Standing there in the shadow of the god, with the waters in full splash below me and the sunshine brilliant on the green dome of the palace at the long cataract's foot, I found myself prosaically speculating about ways and means and motives. How could a mere prince of Hesse run to such imperial splendours? And why, having somehow raised the money, should he elect to spend it in so fantastically wasteful a fashion? And, finally, why did the Hessians ever put up with his extravagance? The money, after all, was theirs; seeing it all squandered on a house and garden, why didn't they rise up against their silly, irresponsible tyrant? 3

The answer to these last questions was being provided, even as I asked them, by the good citizens of Kassel around me. *Schön, herrlich, prachtvoll* [roughly: beautiful, magnificent, splendid]—their admiration exploded emphatically on every side. Without any doubt, they were thoroughly enjoying themselves. In six generations, humanity cannot undergo any fundamental change. There is no reason to suppose that the Hessians of 1750 were greatly different from those of 1932. Whenever the prince allowed his subjects to visit his waterworks, they came and, I have no doubt, admired and enjoyed their admiration just as much as their descendants do today. The psychology of revolutionaries is apt to be a trifle crude. The magnificent display of wealth does not necessarily, as they imagine, excite a passion of envy in the hearts of the poor. Given a reasonable amount of prosperity, it excites, more often, nothing but pleasure. The Hessians did not rise up and kill their prince for having wasted so much money on his house and garden; on the contrary, there were probably grateful to him for having realized in solid stone and rainbow-flashing water their own vague day-dreams of a fairy-tale magnificence. One of the functions of royalty is to provide people with a vicarious, but none the less real, fulfilment of their wishes. Kings who make a fine show are popular; and the people not only forgive, but actually commend, extravagances which, to the good Marxian, must seem merely criminal. Wise kings always ear-marked a certain percentage of their income for display. Palaces and waterworks were good publicity for kingship, just as an impressive office building is good publicity for a business corporation. Business, indeed, has inherited many of the responsibilities of royalty. It shares with the State and the municipality the important duty of providing the common people with vicarious wish-fulfilments. Kings no longer build palaces; but newspapers and insurance companies do. Popular restaurants are as richly marbled as the mausoleum of the Escorial; hotels are more splendid than Versailles. In every society there must always be some person or some organization whose task it is to realize the day-dreams of the masses. Life in a perfectly sensible, utilitarian community would be intolerably dreary. Occasional explosions of magnificent folly are as essential to human well-being as a sewage 4 system. More so, probably. Sanitary plumbing, it is significant to note, is a very recent invention; the splendours of kingship are as old as civilization itself.

[1937—Great Britain]

Questions

1. There is a certain playfulness in Huxley's title if one recalls Lewis Carroll. What is the allusion here? What light does it shed on Huxley's attitude?
2. What is the topic sentence of paragraph 4? How does this sentence give the paragraph and the essay as a whole unity?
3. What is the essay's theme? Where is it implied?
4. What examples does Huxley make use of? What is the main example and what are the subsidiary examples?

Writing Assignments

1. If you had to choose between a sewer system and "occasional explosions of magnificent folly," which would it be? Write a paragraph or more stating your reasoning.
2. Write a paper based on one solid example of whatever your thesis is. State your thesis, and then proceed in your argument by developing your example point by point.

BUFFALO

❋ BARRY LOPEZ ❋

In January 1845, after a week of cold but brilliantly clear weather, it began to snow in southern Wyoming. Snow accumulated on the flat in a dead calm to a depth of four feet in only a few days. The day following the storm was breezy and warm—chinook weather. A party of Cheyenne camped in a river bottom spent the day tramping the snow down, felling cottonwood trees for their horses, and securing game, in response to a dream by one of them, a thirty-year-old man called Blue Feather on the Side of His Head, that they would be trapped by a sudden freeze.

That evening the temperature fell fifty degrees and an ice crust as rigid, as easily broken, as sharp as window glass formed over the snow. The crust held for weeks.

Access across the pane of ice to game and pasturage on the clear, wind-blown slopes of the adjacent Medicine Bow Mountains was impossible for both Indian hunters and a buffalo herd trapped nearby. The buffalo, exhausted from digging in the deep snow, went to their knees by the thousands, their legs slashed by the razor ice, glistening red in the bright sunlight. Their woolly carcasses lay scattered like black boulders over the blinding white of the prairie, connected by a thin crosshatching of bloody red trails.

Winds moaned for days in the thick fur of the dead and dying buffalo,   4
broken by the agonized bellows of the animals themselves. Coyotes would
not draw near. The Cheyenne camped in the river bottom were terrified. As
soon as they were able to move they departed. No Cheyenne ever camped
there again.

The following summer the storm and the death of the herd were depicted   5
on a buffalo robe by one of the Cheyenne, a man called Raven on His Back.
Above the scene, in the sky, he drew a white buffalo. The day they had left
camp a man was supposed to have seen a small herd of buffalo, fewer than
twenty, leaving the plains and lumbering up the Medicine Bow River into the
mountains. He said they were all white, and each seemed to him larger than
any bull he had ever seen. There is no record of this man's name, but another
Cheyenne in the party, a medicine man called Walks Toward the Two Rivers,
carried the story of the surviving white buffalo to Crow and Teton Sioux in
an effort to learn its meaning. In spite of the enmity among these tribes their
leaders agreed that the incident was a common and disturbing augury. They
gathered on the Box Elder River in southeastern Montana in the spring of
1846 to decipher its meaning. No one was able to plumb it, though many had
fasted and bathed in preparation.

Buffalo were never seen again on the Laramie Plains after 1845, in spite   6
of the richness of the grasses there and the size of the buffalo herds nearby
in those days. The belief that there were still buffalo in the Medicine Bow
Mountains, however, survivors of the storm, persisted for years, long after the
disappearance of buffalo (some 60 million animals) from Wyoming and neighboring territories by the 1880s.

In the closing years of the nineteenth century, Arapaho and Shoshoni war-   7
riors who went into the Medicine Bow to dream say they did, indeed, see
buffalo up there then. The animals lived among the barren rocks above timberline, far from any vegetation. They stood more than eight feet at the shoulder;
their coats were white as winter ermine and their huge eyes were light blue.
At the approach of men they would perch motionless on the granite boulders,
like mountain goats. Since fogs are common in these high valleys in spring
and summer it was impossible, they say, to tell how many buffalo there
were.

In May 1887 a Shoshoni called Long Otter came on two of these buffalo   8
in the Snowy Range. As he watched they watched him. They began raising
and lowering their hooves, started drumming softly on the rocks. They began
singing a death song, way back in the throat like the sound of wind moaning
in a canyon. The man, Long Otter, later lost his mind and was killed in a
buckboard accident the following year. As far as I know this is the last report
of living buffalo in the Medicine Bow.

It is curious to me that in view of the value of the hides no white man   9
ever tried to find and kill one of these buffalo. But that is the case. No detail

of the terrible storm of that winter, or of the presence of a herd of enormous white buffalo in the Medicine Bow, has ever been found among the papers of whites who lived in the area or who might have passed through in the years following.

It should be noted, however, by way of verification, that a geology student 10
from Illinois called Fritiof Fryxell came upon two buffalo skeletons in the Snowy Range in the summer of 1925. Thinking these barren heights an extraordinary elevation at which to find buffalo, he carefully marked the location on a topographic map. He measured the largest of the skeletons, found the size staggering, and later wrote up the incident in the May 1926 issue of the *Journal of Mammalogy*.

In 1955, a related incident came to light. In the fall of 1911, at the request 11
of the Colorado Mountain Club, a party of Arapaho Indians were brought into the Rocky Mountains in the northern part of the state to relate to white residents the history of the area prior to 1859. The settlers were concerned that during the years when the white man was moving into the area, and the Indian was being extirpated, a conflict in historical records arose such that the white record was incomplete and possibly in error.

The Arapaho were at first reluctant to speak; they made up stories of the 12
sort they believed the whites would like to hear. But the interest and persistence of the white listeners made an impression upon them and they began to tell what had really happened.

Among the incidents the Arapaho revealed was that in the winter of 1845 13
(when news of white settlers coming in covered wagons first reached them) there was a terrible storm. A herd of buffalo wintering in Brainard Valley (called then Bear in the Hole Valley) began singing a death song. At first it was barely audible, and it was believed the wind was making the sound until it got louder and more distinct. As the snow got deeper the buffalo left the valley and began to climb into the mountains. For four days they climbed, still singing the moaning death song, followed by Arapaho warriors, until they reached the top of the mountain. This was the highest place but it had no name. Now it is called Thatchtop Mountain.

During the time the buffalo climbed they did not stop singing. They turned 14
red all over; their eyes became smooth white. The singing became louder. It sounded like thunder that would not stop. Everyone who heard it, even people four or five days' journey away, was terrified.

At the top of the mountain the buffalo stopped singing. They stood motionless 15
in the snow, the wind blowing clouds around them. The Arapaho men who had followed had not eaten for four days. One, wandering into the clouds with his hands outstretched and a rawhide string connecting him to the others, grabbed hold of one of the buffalo and killed it. The remaining buffalo disappeared into the clouds; the death song began again, very softly, and remained behind them. The wind was like the singing of the buffalo. When the clouds cleared the men went down the mountain.

The white people at the 1911 meeting said they did not understand the 16 purpose of telling such a story. The Arapaho said this was the first time the buffalo tried to show them how to climb out through the sky.

The notes of this meeting in 1911 have been lost, but what happened there remained clear in the mind of the son of one of the Indians who was present. It was brought to my attention by accident one evening in the library of the university where I teach. I was reading an article on the introduction of fallow deer in Nebraska in the August 1955 issue of the *Journal of Mammalogy* when this man, who was apparently just walking by, stopped and, pointing at the opposite page, said, "This is not what this is about." The article he indicated was called "An Altitudinal Record for Bison in Northern Colorado." He spoke briefly of it, as if to himself, and then departed.   17

Excited by this encounter I began to research the incident. I have been able to verify what I have written here. In view of the similarity between the events in the Medicine Bow and those in Colorado, I suspect that there were others in the winter of 1845 who began, as the Arapaho believe, trying to get away from what was coming, and that subsequent attention to this phenomenon is of some importance.   18

I recently slept among weathered cottonwoods on the Laramie Plains in the vicinity of the Medicine Bow Mountains. I awoke in the morning to find my legs broken.   19

[1981—U.S.A.]

Questions

1. Combining fiction and nonfiction, scholarly research and imagination, "Buffalo" is both a story and an essay. In what way is it a story? In what way is it an essay?
2. The narrator here should be taken as fictional and not Lopez himself. Considering the narrator's diction, the way he approaches things, and his general cast of mind, characterize him. Why this narrator? What is his function? What dramatic irony is there here arising out of the narrator's approach to the Indian stories and the stories themselves?
3. History is history and myth is myth. But in "Buffalo" they merge. What is the point of this blurring of distinction between fact and fiction?
4. "Buffalo" involves implicitly a criticism of our world view, that of the modern West. How so? What is that criticism? What is Lopez's theme? In light of this theme, what is the meaning of the broken legs referred to in the last paragraph?

Writing Assignments

1. In a few paragraphs, contrast the Indian view of animals as portrayed in "Buffalo" with ours, especially with regard to our pets. Which view is more wholesome, finally?
2. We cannot be sure what is fact and what fiction in "Buffalo." Does it matter? Write a paper defending Lopez's blurring of the two and showing how it serves his purposes or, on some rational ground, condemning the mixture and showing why it fails to persuade the reader. In either case, you will need to articulate the theme of "Buffalo" and consider the meaning of the narrator's broken legs mentioned at the end.

THE NECESSARY ENEMY

✳ KATHERINE ANNE PORTER ✳

She is a frank, charming, fresh-hearted young woman who married for love. She and her husband are one of those gay, good-looking young pairs who ornament this modern scene rather more in profusion perhaps than ever before in our history. They are handsome, with a talent for finding their way in their world, they work at things that interest them, their tastes agree and their hopes. They intend in all good faith to spend their lives together, to have children and do well by them and each other—to be happy, in fact, which for them is the whole point of their marriage. And all in stride, keeping their wits about them. Nothing romantic, mind you; their feet are on the ground.

Unless they were this sort of person, there would be not much point to what I wish to say; for they would seem to be an example of the high-spirited, right-minded young whom the critics are always invoking to come forth and do their duty and practice all those sterling old-fashioned virtues which in every generation seem to be falling into disrepair. As for virtues, these young people are more or less on their own, like most of their kind; they get very little moral or other aid from their society; but after three years of marriage this very contemporary young woman finds herself facing the oldest and ugliest dilemma of marriage.

She is dismayed, horrified, full of guilt and forebodings because she is finding out little by little that she is capable of hating her husband, whom she loves faithfully. She can hate him at times as fiercely and mysteriously, indeed in terribly much the same way, as often she hated her parents, her brothers and sisters, whom she loves, when she was a child. Even then it had seemed to her a kind of black treacherousness in her, her private wickedness that, just the same, gave her her only private life. That was one thing her parents never knew about her, never seemed to suspect. For it was never given a name. They did and said hateful things to her and to each other as if by right, as if in them it was a kind of virtue. But when they said to her, "Control your feelings," it was never when she was amiable and obedient, only in the black times of her hate. So it was her secret, a shameful one. When they punished her, sometimes for the strangest reasons, it was, they said, only because they loved her—it was for her good. She did not believe this, but she thought herself guilty of something worse than ever they had punished her for. None of this really frightened her: the real fright came when she discovered that at times her father and mother hated each other; this was like standing on the doorsill of a familiar room and seeing in a lightning flash that the floor was gone, you were on the edge of a bottomless pit. Sometimes she felt that both of them hated her, but that passed, it was simply not a thing to be thought of, much less believed. She thought she had outgrown all this, but here it was again, an element in her own nature she could not control, or feared she could not. She would have to hide from her husband, if she could, the same spot in her feelings she had hidden from her parents, and for the same no doubt disreputable, selfish reason: she wants to keep his love.

Above all, she wants him to be absolutely confident that she loves him, for that is the real truth, no matter how unreasonable it sounds, and no matter how her own feelings betray them both at times. She depends recklessly on his love; yet while she is hating him, he might very well be hating her as much or even more, and it would serve her right. But she does not want to be served right, she wants to be loved and forgiven—that is, to be sure he would forgive her anything, if he had any notion of what she had done. But best of all she would like not to have anything in her love that should ask for forgiveness. She doesn't mean about their quarrels—they are not so bad. Her feelings are out of proportion, perhaps. She knows it is perfectly natural for people to disagree, have fits of temper, fight it out; they learn quite a lot about each other that way, and not all of it disappointing either. When it passes, her hatred seems quite unreal. It always did.   4

Love. We are early taught to say it. I love you. We are trained to the thought of it as if there were nothing else, or nothing else worth having without it, or nothing worth having which it could not bring with it. Love is taught, always by precept, sometimes by example. Then hate, which no one meant to teach us, comes of itself. It is true that if we say I love you, it may be received with doubt, for there are times when it is hard to believe. Say I hate you, and the one spoken to believes it instantly, once for all.   5

Say I love you a thousand times to that person afterward and mean it every time, and still it does not change the fact that once we said I hate you, and meant that too. It leaves a mark on that surface love had worn so smooth with its eternal caresses. Love must be learned, and learned again and again; there is no end to it. Hate needs no instruction, but waits only to be provoked . . . hate, the unspoken word, the unacknowledged presence in the house, that faint smell of brimstone among the roses, that invisible tongue-tripper, that unkempt finger in every pie, that sudden oh-so-curiously *chilling* look— could it be boredom?—on your dear one's features, making them quite ugly. Be careful: love, perfect love, is in danger.   6

If it is not perfect, it is not love, and if it is not love, it is bound to be hate sooner or later. This is perhaps a not too exaggerated statement of the extreme position of Romantic Love, more especially in America, where we are all brought up on it, whether we know it or not. Romantic Love is changeless, faithful, passionate, and its sole end is to render the two lovers happy. It has no obstacles save those provided by the hazards of fate (that is to say, society), and such sufferings as the lovers may cause each other are only another word for delight: exciting jealousies, thrilling uncertainties, the ritual dance of court-ship within the charmed closed circle of their secret alliance; all *real* troubles come from without, they face them unitedly in perfect confidence. Marriage is not the end but only the beginning of true happiness, cloudless, changeless   7 to the end. That the candidates for this blissful condition have never seen an example of it, nor ever knew anyone who had, makes no difference. That is the ideal and they will achieve it.

How did Romantic Love manage to get into marriage at last, where it was most certainly never intended to be? At its highest it was tragic; the love of Héloïse and Abélard. At its most graceful, it was the homage of the trouvère for his lady. In its most popular form, the adulterous strayings of solidly married couples who meant to stray for their own good reasons, but at the same time do nothing to upset the property settlements or the line of legitimacy; at its most trivial, the pretty trifling of shepherd and shepherdess.

This was generally condemned by church and state and a word of fear to honest wives whose mortal enemy it was. Love within the sober, sacred realities of marriage was a matter of personal luck, but in any case, private feelings were strictly a private affair having, at least in theory, no bearing whatever on the fixed practice of the rules of an institution never intended as a recreation ground for either sex. If the couple discharged their religious and social obligations, furnished forth a copious progeny, kept their troubles to themselves, maintained public civility and died under the same roof, even if not always on speaking terms, it was rightly regarded as a successful marriage. Apparently this testing ground was too severe for all but the stoutest spirits; it too was based on an ideal, as impossible in its way as the ideal Romantic Love. One good thing to be said for it is that society took responsibility for the conditions of marriage, and the sufferers within its bonds could always blame the system, not themselves. But Romantic Love crept into the marriage bed, very stealthily, by centuries, bringing its absurd notions about love as eternal springtime and marriage as a personal adventure meant to provide personal happiness. To a Western romantic such as I, though my views have been much modified by painful experience, it still seems to me a charming work of the human imagination, and it is a pity its central notion has been taken too literally and has hardened into a convention as cramping and enslaving as the older one. The refusal to acknowledge the evils in ourselves which therefore are implicit in any human situation is as extreme and unworkable a proposition as the doctrine of total depravity; but somewhere between them, or maybe beyond them, there does exist a possibility for reconciliation between our desires for impossible satisfactions and the simple unalterable fact that we also desire to be unhappy and that we create our own sufferings; and out of these sufferings we salvage our fragments of happiness.

Our young woman who has been taught that an important part of her human nature is not real because it makes trouble and interferes with her peace of mind and shakes her self-love, has been very badly taught; but she has arrived at a most important stage of her re-education. She is afraid her marriage is going to fail because she has not love enough to face its difficulties; and this because at times she feels a painful hostility toward her husband, and cannot admit its reality because such an admission would damage in her own eyes her view of what love should be, an absurd view, based on her vanity of power. Her hatred is real as her love is real, but her hatred has the advantage at present because it works on a blind instinctual level, it is lawless; and her love is subjected to a code of ideal conditions, impossible by their very nature of fulfillment, which prevents its free growth and deprives it of its right to recognize its human limitations and come to grips with them. Hatred is natural in a sense that love, as she conceives it, a young person brought up in the tradition of Romantic Love, is not natural at all. Yet it did not come by hazard, it is the very imperfect expression of the need of the human imagination to create beauty and harmony out of chaos, no matter how mistaken its notion of these things may be, nor how clumsy its methods. It has conjured love out of the air, and seeks to preserve it by incantations; when she spoke a vow to love and honor her husband until death, she did a very reckless thing, for it is not possible by an act of the will to fulfill such an engagement. But it was the necessary act of faith performed in defense of a mode of feeling, the statement of honorable intention to practice as well as she is able the noble, acquired faculty of love, that very mysterious overtone to sex which is the best thing in it. Her hatred is part of it, the necessary enemy and ally.

[1948—U.S.A.]

Questions

1. What is the effect of the first paragraph of this essay? Why, do you think, would an essayist find such an effect desirable?
2. "The Necessary Enemy" divides itself into three parts. Describe each in a sentence or two. How do the first and second parts differ? Why did Porter put the first first and the second second? What is gained by Porter's beginning as she does (that is, with paragraphs 1–4)?
3. What metaphors are found in paragraphs 3 and 6? What is their effect?
4. What kind of structural element does Porter make use of in paragraph 5 and thereafter? How is this type of structuring related to her thesis?
5. What is that thesis? Where is it stated? What is the inherent paradox that it entails? Why is the "enemy" "necessary"? What does the essay teach about the nature of reality?

Writing Assignments

1. Why, according to Porter, is hate "necessary"? Write a paragraph addressed to this matter, bringing your own experience to bear.
2. Porter holds that "we are all brought up on" romantic love, "especially in America." Is this true according to your experience? If so, then write a paper in which you first define this amorphous concept and then discuss how you came by it. For example, how has your conception been influenced by the media, TV and the movies in particular? Conclude by stating whether you still believe in romantic love or have cast off the idea and why.
3. Write an essay in which you begin with and spend the first several paragraphs on a concrete example of something. Then, having established what that something is, analyze the example to make your point. Use "The Necessary Enemy" as your model.

WORDSWORTH COUNTRY

(A Review of David B. Pirie's *William Wordsworth: The Poetry of Grandeur and of Tenderness*)

❊ EDWARD PROFFITT ❊

Despite all of the work done in Wordsworth[1] studies over the last two decades, Wordsworth has remained largely uncharted. Taking much of that work to task, David B. Pirie provides us with an adequate map at last. No more shall we get lost on the byways of debate over the two Wordsworths, or Wordsworth and apocalypse, or Wordsworth and mortality. With Pirie in hand, every reader should find ready passage to Wordsworth in all his topological complexity.

Pirie takes his bearings from two lines from a manuscript fragment of *The Prelude*:[2] "Two feelings have we also from the first / Of grandeur and of tenderness." The grandeur is the grandeur of the natural world, where "woods decay . . . , never to be decay'd," where, that is, one cannot distinguish the trees from the forest, where each being is a cell in the one body of life. Here we must live, and here we would feel at home. The sense of grandeur, then, is a sense of being at home, of feeling oneself part of the process of life. "But there's a Tree, of many, one," says Wordsworth in the "Immortality Ode." It is also human to separate out, to see the trees rather than the forest, to become attached to particular things and especially to particular human beings. Such is the nature of human tenderness. Are grandeur and tenderness then at strife?

"My own view," Pirie writes, "is that the unease of their incompatibilities is what stirs [Wordsworth's] best verse to greatness." I would put the matter somewhat differently. In the Great Decade, Wordsworth had faith that he could marry mind and world in a "spousal verse," as he puts it in the "Prospectus" to *The Recluse,* and could do so by speaking of "nothing more than what we are." In full, this is his vision: of the possibility of the human mind to find the earth a home and yet remain human—in other words, to synthesize the dual impulses of grandeur and of tenderness. Much the same could be said of other Romantic poets (e.g., Coleridge and Keats), in whose work is a probing of the same ontological problem: how to be human in a non-reflecting, undifferentiating world, yet feel oneself to be part of that world. At any rate, having faith that a "unity of being," in Yeats's phrase, could be achieved, Wordsworth could explore the divisions and tensions of our beings "before the blissful hour arrives, . . . / Of this great consummation."

This difference is one of emphasis. I agree entirely with Pirie that it is only after the Great Decade that Wordsworth fell into a comfortable union, or

---

[1] [*William*] *Wordsworth* (1770–1850): the great romantic landscape poet.
[2] *The Prelude:* Wordsworth's longest poem, an autobiography of the growth of his mind.

into assertion that the goal had been achieved. But Pirie's emphasis does lead him to misread, I think, at least one moment of joint grandeur and tenderness, "A Slumber Did My Spirit Seal."[3] Taking the poem's "She" as alternately the poet's spirit and the dead loved one, Pirie forces the poem rather mechanically to yield what it must to support his thesis. He all but allegorizes the poem and thereby misses the rich complexity of its closure. "Rolled round in earth's diurnal course, / With rocks, and stones, and trees"—here, surely, grandeur and tenderness, nature's calm and human passion, are held together inextricably. The lines speak both consolation and grief simultaneously, attaining a kind of synthesis.

But quibbles aside, *yes:* "Wordsworth's best verse speaks to both instincts.   5 It insists that the strength of feeling which accompanies them proves that neither can be dismissed in favour of the other. At the most instinctual level, we recognize both the magnificence of the integrated universe *and* the preciousness of the few people that we set apart from it." And yes, Wordsworth's greatness lies in the singular honesty of his best work, in his refusal to manipulate his people toward the desired end, in his tenacious exploration of the tensions between our needs. With these bearings of grandeur and tenderness, Pirie achieves the miraculous: intricate, delicate, and thoroughly convincing readings of nearly every major poem in the canon, readings that together give a detailed picture of the Wordsworthian terrain.

Most of Pirie's readings, full of fresh insights in and of themselves, cumulate   6 to impart the range of Wordsworth's endeavor—both psychological and linguistic. No one before has found such fullness of meaning in the language of this poet who so mistrusted language. To be sure, Wordsworth's diction and syntax have been treated well by earlier critics (e.g., William Empson, Donald Davie, Josephine Miles), but Pirie has a special touch. At every turn he reveals nuances in Wordsworth's language that have hitherto passed by the rest of us. Page by page, Pirie teaches us how careless we have been with Wordsworth and how careful Wordsworth was himself with words.

Thereby Pirie engenders a trust in this poet who of all great poets has   7 been the least trusted, even by his admirers. Also, as readable as many a recent book has been unreadable, Pirie's book—and especially his last chapter—dispels forever any notion that Wordsworth is in some vague way mystical or just soft-headed. Pirie details conclusively that at his best Wordsworth is a hard realist, exploring our existential dilemmas without allowing himself any easy outs. Oh, how bewildered (and sloppy) we have been! But no more. We now know the place—for the first time.

[1984—U.S.A.]

Questions

1. An implicit metaphor is suggested by the title here and extended in paragraph 1 and further in paragraphs 2, 5, and 7. What is that metaphor? What words and phrases in

---

[3] *"A Slumber Did My Spirit Seal":* for the poem in full, see page 229.

paragraph 1 accomplish the extension? What words extend the metaphor in paragraphs 2, 5, and 7? What functions does the metaphor have?

2. The one negative thing said about Pirie's book is said in paragraph 4. Why here and not at the beginning or the end? Why is what is said in paragraph 4 called a "quibble" in 5?

3. Look at the end of each paragraph and the beginning of the next and point out what makes the movement from one to the next coherent in each case.

Writing Assignments

1. In a paragraph or more, analyze the metaphor extended in this book review. What is it? How is it established? Where and how is it extended? What functions does it have? In what way is it apt in a discussion of Wordsworth?

2. Take a nonfiction book you have recently read—perhaps in connection with a course you have had—and write a book review. First state your reaction to the book; then try to convince your reader of the rightness of that reaction by an examination of the book's ideas and appropriate quotations from it.

HOW I WRITE

❊ BERTRAND RUSSELL ❊

I cannot pretend to know how writing ought to be done, or what a wise critic would advise me to do with a view to improving my own writing. The most that I can do is to relate some things about my own attempts. 1

Until I was twenty-one, I wished to write more or less in the style of John Stuart Mill.[1] I liked the structure of his sentences and his manner of developing a subject. I had, however, already a different ideal, derived, I suppose, from mathematics. I wished to say everything in the smallest number of words in which it could be said clearly. Perhaps, I thought, one should imitate Baedeker[2] rather than any more literary model. I would spend hours trying to find the shortest way of saying something without ambiguity, and to this aim I was willing to sacrifice all attempts at aesthetic excellence. 2

At the age of twenty-one, however, I came under a new influence, that of my future brother-in-law, Logan Pearsall Smith.[3] He was at that time exclusively interested in style as opposed to matter. His gods were Flaubert[4] and Walter Pater,[5] and I was quite ready to believe that the way to learn how to write was to copy their technique. He gave me various simple rules, of which I remember only two: "Put a comma every four words," and "never use 'and' except at the beginning of a sentence." His most emphatic advice was that 3

---

[1] *John Stuart Mill* (1806–1873): British economist and philosopher, whose style is rather cut-and-dry.
[2] *[Karl] Baedeker* (1801–1859): publisher of a series of European guidebooks, now called "Baedekers" after him.
[3] *Logan Pearsall Smith* (1865–1946): American essayist and prose stylist.
[4] *[Gustave] Flaubert* (1821–1880): the great French stylist, author of *Madame Bovary*.
[5] *Walter Pater* (1839–1894): British essayist noted for the clarity of his style.

one must always rewrite. I conscientiously tried this, but found that my first draft was almost always better than my second. This discovery has saved me an immense amount of time. I do not, of course, apply it to the substance, but only to the form. When I discover an error of an important kind, I rewrite the whole. What I do not find is that I can improve a sentence when I am satisfied with what it means.

Very gradually I have discovered ways of writing with a minimum of worry   4
and anxiety. When I was young each fresh piece of serious work used to seem to me for a time—perhaps a long time—to be beyond my powers. I would fret myself into a nervous state from fear that it was never going to come right. I would make one unsatisfying attempt after another, and in the end have to discard them all. At last I found that such fumbling attempts were a waste of time. It appeared that after first contemplating a book on some subject, and after giving serious preliminary attention to it, I needed a period of subconscious incubation which could not be hurried and was if anything impeded by deliberate thinking. Sometimes I would find, after a time, that I had made a mistake, and that I could not write the book I had had in mind. But often I was more fortunate. Having, by a time of very intense concentration, planted the problem in my subconsciousness, it would germinate underground until, suddenly, the solution emerged with blinding clarity, so that it only remained to write down what had appeared as if in a revelation.

The most curious example of this process, and the one which led me   5
subsequently to rely upon it, occurred at the beginning of 1914. I had undertaken to give the Lowell Lectures at Boston, and had chosen as my subject "Our Knowledge of the External World." Throughout 1913 I thought about this topic. In term time in my rooms at Cambridge, in vacations in a quiet inn on the upper reaches of the Thames, I concentrated with such intensity that I sometimes forgot to breathe and emerged panting as from a trance. But all to no avail. To every theory that I could think of I could perceive fatal objections. At last, in despair, I went off to Rome for Christmas, hoping that a holiday would revive my flagging energy. I got back to Cambridge on the last day of 1913, and although my difficulties were still completely unresolved I arranged, because the remaining time was short, to dictate as best as I could to a stenographer. Next morning, as she came in at the door, I suddenly saw exactly what I had to say, and proceeded to dictate the whole book without a moment's hesitation.

I do not want to convey an exaggerated impression. The book was very   6
imperfect, and I now think that it contains serious errors. But it was the best that I could have done at that time, and a more leisurely method (within the time at my disposal) would almost certainly have produced something worse. Whatever may be true of other people, this is the right method for me. Flaubert and Pater, I have found, are best forgotten so far as I am concerned.

Although what I now think about how to write is not so very different   7
from what I thought at the age of eighteen, my development has not been by any means rectilinear. There was a time, in the first years of this century, when I had more florid and rhetorical ambitions. This was the time when I

wrote *A Free Man's Worship,* a work of which I do not now think well. At that time I was steeped in Milton's prose, and his rolling periods reverberated through the caverns of my mind. I cannot say that I no longer admire them, but for me to imitate them involves a certain insincerity. In fact, all imitation is dangerous. Nothing could be better in style than the Prayer Book and the Authorized Version of the Bible, but they express a way of thinking and feeling which is different from that of our time. A style is not good unless it is an intimate and almost involuntary expression of the personality of the writer, and then only if the writer's personality is worth expressing. But although direct imitation is always to be deprecated, there is much to be gained by familiarity with good prose, especially in cultivating a sense for prose rhythm.

There are some simple maxims—not perhaps quite so simple as those   8
which my brother-in-law Logan Pearsall Smith offered me—which I think might be commended to writers of expository prose. First: never use a long word if a short word will do. Second: if you want to make a statement with a great many qualifications, put some of the qualifications in separate sentences. Third: do not let the beginning of your sentence lead the reader to an expectation which is contradicted by the end. Take, say, such a sentence as the following, which might occur in a work on sociology: "Human beings are completely exempt from undesirable behavior patterns only when certain prerequisites, not satisfied except in a small percentage of actual cases, have, through some fortuitous concourse of favorable circumstances, whether congenital or environmental, chanced to combine in producing an individual in whom many factors deviate from the norm in a socially advantageous manner." Let us see if we can translate this sentence into English. I suggest the following: "All men are scoundrels, or at any rate almost all. The men who are not must have had unusual luck, both in their birth and in their upbringing." This is shorter and more intelligible, and says just the same thing. But I am afraid any professor who used the second sentence instead of the first would get the sack.

This suggests a word of advice to such of my readers as may happen to   9
be professors. I am allowed to use plain English because everybody knows that I could use mathematical logic if I chose. Take the statement: "Some people marry their deceased wives' sisters." I can express this in language which only becomes intelligible after years of study, and this gives me freedom. I suggest to young professors that their first work should be written in a jargon only to be understood by the erudite few. With that behind them, they can ever after say what they have to say in a language "understanded of the people." In these days, when our very lives are at the mercy of the professors, I cannot but think that they would deserve our gratitude if they adopted my advice.

[1935—Great Britain]

Questions

1. The statement of purpose here (the second sentence of the first paragraph) suggests a way of structuring. What is that way? Is this the way of the essay at hand? How so?

2. Russell speaks of "the shortest way of saying something without ambiguity." This is the golden rule of good writing, at least writing directed toward an audience and aimed at communication. Why? But does this mean that all sentences should be short? What does the amendment "without ambiguity" suggest in this regard?
3. "I can[not] improve a sentence when I am satisfied with what it means," Russell states. What, then, is his criterion of judgment? Is this criterion good and worth adopting? Why or why not?
4. Russell uses as an example of bad writing a fifty-five-word sentence (paragraph 8) whose diction and syntax are the same as Joan Didion (pp. 905–08) derides. What are the damnable qualities of such diction and syntax? Russell restates the sentence in twenty-eight words and concludes that the "shorter and more intelligible [statement] . . . says just the same thing." But this is not exactly the case, for the two sentences differ in pace, tone, voice, and ultimate stance. How so?
5. How does Russell's "advice" to "young professors" at the end of "How I Write" serve to summarize his main point about good writing?

Writing Assignments

1. What Russell says about writing is much like what William Zinsser holds in his essay "Simplicity" (pp. 964–66). In a paragraph or more, compare the views of these two essayists, concluding with a statement summarizing what both writers hold good writing to be.
2. Different writers write in different ways, and we each must find the way best suited at any given time to our own temperament and needs. Russell's title tacitly acknowledges this—"How I Write" and not "How to Write." Now, how do you write? Write an essay detailing how you go about writing an essay at this stage in your life, how you came to write in this manner, and how you hope to write in the future.

FITTING IN

JOHN TARKOV

Not quite two miles and 30 years from the church where these thoughts came to me, is a small, graveled parking lot cut out of the New Jersey pines, behind a restaurant and a dance hall. On road signs, the town is called Cassville. But to the several generations of Russian-Americans whose center of gravity tipped to the Old World, it was known as Roova Farms. I think the acronym stands for Russian Orthodox Outing and Vacation Association. In the summers, the place might as well have been on the Black Sea. 1

One day during one of those summers, my old man showed up from a job, just off a cargo ship. He made his living that way, in the merchant marine. With him, he had a brittle new baseball glove and a baseball as yet unmarked by human error. We went out to that parking lot and started tossing the ball back and forth; me even at the age of 8 at ease with the motions of this American game, him grabbing at the ball with his bare hands then sending it 2 back with an unpolished stiff-armed heave. It was a very hot day. I remember that clearly. What I can't remember is who put the first scuff mark on the ball. Either I missed it, or he tossed it out of my reach.

I chased it down, I'm sure with American-kid peevishness. I wonder if I said anything. Probably I mouthed off about it.   3

Last winter, the phone call comes on a Saturday morning. The old man's heart had stopped. They had started it beating again. When I get to the hospital, he's not conscious. They let me in to see him briefly. Then comes an afternoon of drinking coffee and leaning on walls. Around 4 o'clock, two doctors come out of coronary care. One of them puts his hand on my arm and tells me. A nurse takes me behind the closed door.   4

Two fragments of thought surface. One is primitive and it resonates from somewhere deep: *This all began in Russia long ago.* The other is sentimental: *He died near the sea.*   5

I join the tips of the first three fingers of my right hand and touch them to his forehead, then his stomach, then one side of his chest, then the other. It's what I believe. I pause just briefly, then give him a couple of quick cuffs on the side of his face, the way men do when they want to express affection but something stops them from embracing. The nurse takes me downstairs to sign some forms.   6

He never did quite get the hang of this country. He never went to the movies. Didn't watch television on his own. Didn't listen to the radio. Ate a lot of kielbasa. Read a lot. Read the paper almost cover to cover every day. He read English well, but when he talked about what he'd read, he'd mispronounce some words and put a heavy accent on them all. The paper was the window through which he examined a landscape and a people that were nearly as impenetrable to him as they were known and manageable to me. For a touch of home, he'd pick up *Soviet Life*. "I'm not a Communist," he used to tell me. "I'm a Russian." Then he'd catch me up about some new hydroelectric project on the Dnieper.   7

And so he vaguely embarrassed me. Who knows how many times, over the years, this story has repeated itself: the immigrant father and the uneasy son. This Melting Pot of ours absorbs the second generation over a flame so high that the first is left encrusted on the rim. In college, I read the literature—Lenski on the three-generation hypothesis, stuff like that—but I read it to make my grades, not particularly to understand that I was living it.   8

When he finally retired from the ocean, he took his first real apartment, on the Lower East Side, and we saw each other more regularly. We'd sit there on Saturday or Sunday afternoons, drinking beer and eating Chinese food. He bought a television set for our diversion, and, depending on the season, the voices of Keith Jackson and Ara Parseghian or Ralph Kiner and Lindsey Nelson would overlap with, and sometimes submerge, our own.   9

After the game, he'd get us a couple more beers, and we would become emissaries: from land and sea, America and ports of destination. We were never strangers—never that—but we dealt, for the most part, in small talk. It   10 was a son trying—or maybe trying to try—to share what little he knew with his father, and flinching privately at his father's foreignness. And it was a father outspokenly proud of his son, beyond basis in reason, yet at times openly frustrated that the kid had grown up unlike himself.

Every father has a vision of what he'd like his son to be. Every son has a vision in kind of his father. Eventually, one of them goes, and the one remaining has little choice but to extinguish the ideal and confront the man of flesh and blood who was. Time and again it happens: The vision shed, the son, once vaguely embarrassed by the father, begins to wear the old man's name and story with pride.

Though he read it daily, the old man hated this newspaper. Sometimes I think he bought it just to make himself angry. He felt the sports editor was trying to suppress the growth of soccer in America. So naturally, I would egg him on. I'd say things like: "Yeah, you're right. It's a conspiracy. The sports editor plus 200 million other Americans." Then we'd start yelling.

But when it came time to put the obituary announcements in the press, after I phoned one in to the Russian-language paper, I started to dial *The Times*. And I remembered. And I put the phone down. And started laughing. "O.K.," I said. "O.K. They won't get any of our business."

So he went out Russian, like he came in. Up on the hill, the church is topped by weathered gold onion domes—sort of like back in the Old Country, but in fact just down the road from his attempt to sneak us both into America through a side door in New Jersey, by tossing a baseball back and forth on a hot, still, bake-in-the-bleachers kind of summer day.

I believe he threw the thing over my head, actually. It *was* a throwing error, the more I think about it. No way I could have caught it. But it was only a baseball, and he was my father, so it's no big deal. I bounced a few off his shins that day myself. Next time, the baseball doesn't touch the ground.

[1985—U.S.A.]

Questions

1. Describe the event mentioned in and the setting of the opening paragraphs. What do both intimate about father and son?
2. Tarkov uses colloquial language and even slang here and there. What are some examples of the latter? What does the diction of this essay say about father and son?
3. The theme of this essay is intimated in paragraph 8. What is it? What metaphor embodies this theme?

Writing Assignments

1. Write an essay in which you describe some aspect of your own heritage and how you have stayed true to it or departed from it. In either case, what are your feelings on this matter?
2. Write an essay on your relationship to your father. Find some point of focus (like baseball

in Tarkov's essay) and, keeping your focus constant, try to convey the various feelings, some perhaps contradictory, that the thought of your father raises in you.

THE HISTORIAN AS ARTIST

✦ BARBARA TUCHMAN ✦

I would like to share some good news with you. I recently came back from skiing at Aspen, where on one occasion I shared the double-chair ski-lift with an advertising man from Chicago. He told me he was in charge of all copy for his firm in all media: TV, radio, *and* the printed word. On the strength of this he assured me—and I quote—that "Writing is coming back. *Books* are coming back." I cannot tell you how pleased I was, and I knew you would be too.

Now that we know that the future is safe for writing, I want to talk about a particular kind of writer—the Historian—not just as historian but as artist; that is, as a creative writer on the same level as the poet or novelist. What follows will sound less immodest if you will take the word "artist" in the way I think of it, not as a form of praise but as a category, like clerk or laborer or actor.

Why is it generally assumed that in writing, the creative process is the exclusive property of poets and novelists? I would like to suggest that the thought applied by the historian to his subject matter can be no less creative than the imagination applied by the novelist to his. And when it comes to writing as an art, is Gibbon[1] necessarily less of an artist in words than, let us say, Dickens? Or Winston Churchill less so than William Faulkner or Sinclair Lewis?

George Macaulay Trevelyan, the late professor of modern history at Cambridge and the great champion of literary as opposed to scientific history, said in a famous essay on his muse that ideally history should be the exposition of facts about the past, "in their full emotional and intellectual value to a wide public by the difficult art of literature." Notice "wide public." Trevelyan always stressed writing for the general reader as opposed to writing just for fellow scholars because he knew that when you write for the public you have to be *clear* and you have to be *interesting* and these are the two criteria which make for good writing. He had no patience with the idea that only imaginative writing is literature. Novels, he pointed out, if they are bad enough, are *not* literature, while even pamphlets, if they are good enough, and he cites those of Milton, Swift, and Burke,[2] are.

The "difficult art of literature" is well said. Trevelyan was a dirt farmer in

1

2

3

4

5

---

[1] [*Edward*] *Gibbon* (1737–1794): British historian, author of *The Decline and Fall of the Roman Empire.*
[2] [*Edmund*] *Burke:* British statesman and philosopher (1729–1797) who, like Milton and Swift before him, wrote eloquent political tracts (pamphlets).

that field and he knew. I may as well admit now that I have always *felt* like an artist when I work on a book but I did not think I ought to say so until someone else said it first (it's like waiting to be proposed to). Now that an occasional reviewer here and there has made the observation, I feel I can talk about it. I see no reason why the word should always be confined to writers of fiction and poetry while the rest of us are lumped together under that despicable term "Nonfiction"—as if we were some sort of remainder. I do not feel like a Non-something; I feel quite specific. I wish I could think of a name in place of "Nonfiction." In the hope of finding an antonym I looked up "Fiction" in Webster and found it defined as opposed to "Fact, Truth and Reality." I thought for a while of adopting FTR, standing for Fact, Truth, and Reality, as my new term, but it is awkward to use. "Writers of Reality" is the nearest I can come to what I want, but I cannot very well call us "Realtors" because that has been pre-empted—although as a matter of fact I would like to. "Real Estate," when you come to think of it, is a very fine phrase and it is exactly the sphere that writers of nonfiction deal in: the real estate of man, of human conduct. I wish we could get it back from the dealers in land. Then the categories could be poets, novelists, and realtors.

I should add that I do not entirely go along with Webster's statement that   6
fiction is what is distinct from fact, truth, and reality because good fiction (as opposed to junk), even if it has nothing to do with fact, is usually *founded* on reality and *perceives* truth—often more truly than some historians. It is exactly this quality of perceiving truth, extracting it from irrelevant surroundings and conveying it to the reader or the viewer of a picture, which distinguishes the artist. What the artist has is an *extra* vision and an *inner* vision plus the ability to express it. He supplies a view or an understanding that the viewer or reader would not have gained without the aid of the artist's creative vision. This is what Monet does in one of those shimmering rivers reflecting poplars, or El Greco in the stormy sky over Toledo, or Jane Austen compressing a whole society into Mr. and Mrs. Bennet, Lady Catherine, and Mr. Darcy. We realtors, at least those of us who aspire to write literature, do the same thing. Lytton Strachey perceived a truth about Queen Victoria and the Eminent Victorians, and the style and form which he created to portray what he saw have changed the whole approach to biography since his time. Rachel Carson perceived truth about the seashore or the silent spring, Thoreau about Walden Pond, De Tocqueville and James Bryce about America, Gibbon about Rome, Karl Marx about Capital, Carlyle about the French Revolution.[3] Their work is based on study, observation, and accumulation of fact, but does anyone suppose that these realtors did not make use of their imagination? Certainly they did; that is what gave them their extra vision.

Trevelyan wrote that the best historian was he who combined knowledge   7
of the evidence with "the largest intellect, the warmest human sympathy and the highest imaginative powers." The last two qualities are no different than

---

[3] Among the people referred to in this paragraph are two painters (Monet, El Greco), a novelist (Jane Austen, with reference to her novel *Pride and Prejudice*), two essayists (Carson, Thoreau), a political and economic theorist (Marx), and four historians (De Tocqueville, Bryce, Gibbon, and Carlyle).

those necessary to a great novelist. They are a necessary part of the historian's equipment because they are what enable him to *understand* the evidence he has accumulated. Imagination stretches the available facts—extrapolates from them, so to speak, thus often supplying an otherwise missing answer to the "Why" of what happened. Sympathy is essential to the understanding of motive. Without sympathy and imagination the historian can copy figures from a tax roll forever—or count them by computer as they do nowadays—but he will never know or be able to portray the people who paid the taxes.

When I say that I felt like an artist, I mean that I constantly found myself perceiving a historical truth (at least, what *I* believe to be truth) by seizing upon a suggestion; then, after careful gathering of the evidence, conveying it in turn to the reader, not by piling up a list of all the facts I have collected, which is the way of the Ph.D., but by exercising the artist's privilege of selection.

Actually the idea for *The Proud Tower* evolved in that way from a number of such perceptions. The initial impulse was a line I quoted in *The Guns of August* from Belgian Socialist poet Emile Verhaeren. After a lifetime as a pacifist dedicated to the social and humanitarian ideas which were then believed to erase national lines, he found himself filled with hatred of the German invader and disillusioned in all he had formerly believed in. And yet, as he wrote, "Since it seems to me that in this state of hatred my conscience becomes diminished, I dedicate these pages, with emotion, to the man I used to be."

I was deeply moved by this. His confession seemed to me so poignant, so evocative of a time and mood, that it decided me to try to retrieve that vanished era. It led to the last chapter in *The Proud Tower* on the Socialists, to Jaurès the authentic Socialist, to his prophetic lines, "I summon the living, I mourn the dead," and to his assassination as the perfect and dramatically right ending for the book, both chronologically and symbolically.

Then there was Lord Ribblesdale. I owe this to *American Heritage,* which back in October 1961 published a piece on Sargent and Whistler[4] with a handsome reproduction of the Ribblesdale portrait. In Sargent's painting Ribblesdale stared out upon the world, as I later wrote in *The Proud Tower,* "in an attitude of such natural arrogance, elegance and self-confidence as no man of a later day would ever achieve." Here too was a vanished era which came together in my mind with Verhaeren's line, "the man I used to be"—like two globules of mercury making a single mass. From that came the idea for the book. Ribblesdale, of course, was the suggestion that ultimately became the opening chapter on the Patricians. This is the reward of the artist's eye: It always leads you to the right thing.

As I see it, there are three parts to the creative process: first, the extra vision with which the artist perceives a truth and conveys it by suggestion. Second, medium of expression: language for writers, paint for painters, clay or stone for sculptors, sound expressed in musical notes for composers. Third, design or structure.

8

9

10

11

12

---

[4] *Sargent and Whistler:* John Singer Sargent (1856–1925) and James Whistler (1834–1903), both well-known American painters.

When it comes to language, nothing is more satisfying than to write a   13
good sentence. It is no fun to write lumpishly, dully, in prose the reader
must plod through like wet sand. But it is a pleasure to achieve, if one can, a
clear running prose that is simple yet full of surprises. This does not just
happen. It requires skill, hard work, a good ear, and continued practice, as
much as it takes Heifetz to play the violin. The goals, as I have said, are clarity,
interest, and aesthetic pleasure. On the first of these I would like to quote
Macaulay, a great historian and great writer, who once wrote to a friend, "How
little the all important art of making meaning pellucid is studied now! Hardly
any popular writer except myself thinks of it."

As to structure, my own form is narrative, which is not every historian's, I   14
may say—indeed, it is rather looked down on now by the advanced academics,
but I don't mind because no one could possibly persuade me that telling a
story is not the most desirable thing a writer can do. Narrative history is neither
as simple nor as straightforward as it might seem. It requires arrangement,
composition, planning just like a painting—Rembrandt's "Night Watch," for
example. He did not fit in all those figures with certain ones in the foreground
and others in back and the light falling on them just so, without much trial
and error and innumerable preliminary sketches. It is the same with writing
history. Although the finished result may look to the reader natural and inevitable,
as if the author had only to follow the sequence of events, it is not that easy.
Sometimes, to catch attention, the crucial event and the causative circumstance
have to be reversed in order—the event first and the cause afterwards, as in
The Zimmermann Telegram. One must juggle with time.

In *The Proud Tower,* for instance, the two English chapters were originally   15
conceived as one. I divided them and placed them well apart in order to give
a feeling of progression, of forward chronological movement to the book.
The story of the Anarchists with their ideas and deeds set in counterpoint to
each other was a problem in arrangement. The middle section of the Hague
chapter on the Paris Exposition of 1900 was originally planned as a separate
short centerpiece, marking the turn of the century, until I saw it as a bridge
linking the two Hague Conferences, where it now seems to belong.

Structure is chiefly a problem of selection, an agonizing business because   16
there is always more material than one can use or fit into a story. The problem
is how and what to select out of all that happened without, by the very process
of selection, giving an over- or under-emphasis which violates truth. One cannot
put in everything: The result would be a shapeless mass. The job is to achieve
a narrative line without straying from the essential facts or leaving out any
essential facts and without twisting the material to suit one's convenience. To
do so is a temptation, but if you do it with history you invariably get tripped
up by later events. I have been tempted once or twice and I know.

The most difficult task of selection I had was in the Dreyfus[5] chapter. To   17
try to skip over the facts about the *bordereau* and the handwriting and the

---

[5] [*Alfred*] *Dreyfus* (1859–1935): a French army officer wrongly convicted of treason and subsequently
(1906) acquitted. The case became notorious and had wide political repercussions.

forgeries—all the elements of the Case as distinct from the Affair—in order to focus instead on what happened to France and yet at the same time give the reader enough background information to enable him to understand what was going on, nearly drove me to despair. My writing slowed down to a trickle until one dreadful day when I went to my study at nine and stayed there all day in a blank coma until five, when I emerged without having written a single word. Anyone who is a writer will know how frightening that was. You feel you have come to the end of your powers; you will not finish the book; you may never write again.

There are other problems of structure peculiar to writing history: how to explain background and yet keep the story moving; how to create suspense and sustain interest in a narrative of which the outcome (like who won the war) is, to put it mildly, known. If anyone thinks this does not take creative writing, I can only say, try it.   18

Mr. Capote's *In Cold Blood,*[6] for example, which deals with real life as does mine, is notable for conscious design. One can see him planning, arranging, composing his material until he achieves his perfectly balanced structure. That is art, although the hand is too obtrusive and the design too contrived to qualify as history. His method of investigation, moreover, is hardly so new as he thinks. He is merely applying to contemporary material what historians have been doing for years. Herodotus[7] started it more than two thousand years ago, walking all over Asia Minor asking questions. Francis Parkman went to live among the Indians: hunted, traveled, and ate with them so that his pages would be steeped in understanding; E. A. Freeman, before he wrote *The Norman Conquest,* visited every spot the Conqueror had set foot on. New to these techniques, Mr. Capote is perhaps naïvely impressed by them. He uses them in a deliberate effort to raise what might be called "creative" journalism to the level of literature. A great company from Herodotus to Trevelyan have been doing the same with history for quite some time.   19

[1966—U.S.A.]

Questions

1. In the first paragraph, Tuchman three times refers to "you," meaning her audience. At whom do you think Tuchman aimed her essay? How does the intended audience account for the essay's diction? What else does this audience account for?
2. There are many arresting metaphors in this essay. Pick out two or three. What is the function of each in its context? Why does each work well in communicating the idea it was intended to communicate?
3. What is Tuchman's thesis and where is it stated? Why is it not stated in the first paragraph? What is the function of paragraph 1?
4. The present essay is finely coherent, in part because of the transitions supplied by Tuchman. Look through the essay and bracket all transitional words, phrases, sentences, and paragraphs.

[6] *In Cold Blood:* a novel that is based on an actual murder case and that stays close to the facts of that case.
[7] *Herodotus* (5th cen. B.C.): Greek historian often called the "father of history."

Sometimes transitions are not needed because the material coheres of its own accord. Where is this true in the essay at hand? Explain why.

5. Tuchman makes use of all four means of support we have looked at (exemplification, definition, appeal to authority, and analogy) and at least three of the five structural elements we have considered (chronology, enumeration, and comparison and contrast). Locate an instance of each kind of support and each kind of element. In what way do these various types of support and structure serve Tuchman with respect to her final goal (to communicate to her audience and to persuade us of the validity of her thesis)?

6. "The Historian as Artist" contains many good ideas about writing and gives insight into the writing process. What are some of those ideas? What have you learned from the essay about the writing process?

7. According to Tuchman, good writing must be *"clear* and . . . *interesting."* Does Tuchman's essay fulfill these criteria? How so? Is her essay thereby persuasive? Why or why not?

Writing Assignments

1. In a paragraph or two, enumerate the ideas about writing that you find in "The Historian as Artist" and evaluate their worth to you.

2. This essay contains many diverse parts, yet it is thoroughly coherent. Write a short paper analyzing how Tuchman made the parts cohere into a comprehensible whole. Be specific and use examples throughout.

3. Go to the library and read an essay by Oscar Wilde entitled "The Critic as Artist," which Tuchman almost assuredly had in mind in titling her work. Then write an essay comparing the two as to point, focus, and overall design.

NUCLEAR MADNESS: WHAT YOU CAN DO

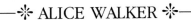
ALICE WALKER

Nuclear Madness is a book you should read immediately. Before brushing your teeth. Before making love. Before lunch. Its author is Helen Caldicott (with the assistance of Nancy Herrington and Nahum Stiskin), a native Australian, pediatrician, and mother of three children. It is a short, serious book about the probability of nuclear catastrophe in our lifetime, eminently thoughtful, readable, and chilling, as a book written for nuclear nonexperts, as almost all Americans are, would have to be.   1

Caldicott was six years old when the atomic bomb was dropped on Hiroshima, and calls herself a child of the atomic age. She grew up, as many of us did, under the threat of nuclear war. She recalls the fifties, when students were taught to dive under their desks at the sound of the air-raid siren and Americans by the thousands built underground fallout shelters.   2

During the sixties, political assassinations, the Civil Rights Movement, and the Vietnam War turned many people away from concern about atomic weapons and toward problems they felt they could do something about. However, as   3

Caldicott states, the Pentagon continued resolutely on its former course, making bigger and "better" bombs every year.

Sometime during the sixties Robert McNamara, then Secretary of Defense, said that between the United States and the Soviet Union there already existed some four hundred nuclear bombs, enough to kill millions of people on both sides, a viable "deterrent," in his opinion, to nuclear war. The Pentagon and the Kremlin, however, apparently assumed this was not enough, and so today between the two "superpowers" there are some *fifty thousand* bombs.

What this means is that the U.S. and the U.S.S.R. literally have more bombs than they know what to do with: so they have targeted every city in the Northern Hemisphere with a population of at least twenty-five thousand with the number of bombs formerly set aside to wipe out whole countries. So even as you squeeze out your toothpaste, kiss your lover's face, or bite into a turkey sandwich, you are on the superpowers' nuclear hit list, a hit list made up by people who have historically been unable to refrain from showing off every new and shameful horror that they make.

For several years Caldicott has been on leave from her work at the Harvard Medical Center, and spends all her time practicing what she calls "preventative medicine," traveling across the Earth attempting to make people aware of the dangers we face. Like most medicine, hers is bitter, but less bitter, she believes, than watching helplessly while her child patients suffer and die from cancer and genetic diseases that are directly caused by the chemical pollutants inevitably created in the production of nuclear energy.

The nuclear industry, powerful, profit-oriented, totally unconcerned about our health, aided and abetted by a government that is its twin, is murdering us and our children every day. And it is up to us, each one of us, to stop it. In the event of a nuclear war all life on the planet will face extinction, certainly human beings. But even if there is no war we will face the same end—unless we put an end to the nuclear-power industry itself—only it will be somewhat slower in coming, as the air, the water, and the soil become too poisoned from nuclear waste (for which there is no known safe disposal) to support life.

What can we do? Like Caldicott, but even more so, I do not believe we should waste any time looking for help from our legal system. Nor do I have faith in politicians, scientists, or "experts." I have great faith, however, in individual people: you with the toothbrush, you in the sack, and you there not letting any of this shit get between you and that turkey sandwich. If it comes down to it, I know one of us *individuals* (just think of Watergate)[1] may have to tackle the killer who's running to push the catastrophe button, and I even hope said tackle will explain why so many of us are excellent football players.

4

5

6

7

8

---

[1] *Watergate:* refers to the break-in of Democratic headquarters (located in a building complex known as "Watergate") ordered by Republican higher-ups and the subsequent attempt by Richard Nixon, the thirty-seventh President of the United States, to cover up the truth. Brought to light by two crusading individuals (Woodward and Bernstein, both reporters on *The Washington Post*), the scandal resulted in the resignation of Nixon, the only President ever to resign.

(Just as I hope *something* will soon illustrate for us what our brothers learned of protecting life in Vietnam.)

As individuals we must join others. No time to quibble about survival   9
being "a white issue." No time to claim you don't live here, too. Massive demonstrations are vital. Massive civil disobedience. And, in fact, massive anything that's necessary to save our lives.

Talk with your family; organize your friends. Educate anybody you can   10
get your mouth on. Raise money. Support those who go to jail. Write letters to those senators and congressmen who are making it easy for the nuclear-power industry to kill us: tell them if they don't change, "cullud" are going to invade their fallout shelters. In any case, this is the big one. We must save Earth, and relieve those who would destroy it of the power to do so. Join up with folks you don't even like, if you have to, so that we may all live to fight each other again.

But first, read Caldicott's book, and remember: the good news may be   11
that Nature is phasing out the white man, but the bad news is that's who She thinks we all are.

[1982—U.S.A.]

Questions

1. Who is the "you" of the first sentence here? That is, who comprises Walker's intended audience (see the end of paragraph 8 and the beginning of paragraph 9)? Why does Walker address her audience as personally as she does?
2. As this essay moves on, the personal mode of address seems almost symbolic, symbolizing the need for . . . what?
3. The very sentence structure of paragraphs 9 and 10 suggests the sense of urgency that Walker would impart. How so? What is the rhythmic feel of these paragraphs?
4. What is Walker's thesis? Where is it stated? What effect does its positioning have?

Writing Assignments

1. Write a short essay in which you "target" an audience—young people, say, or college students—and try to persuade your targeted audience to do something that you think they should be doing at this point in history.
2. Taking a book you have recently read, write a review of it in which you try to persuade your reader not only to read the book but to take it to heart and act on its main thesis. You might try using your title as your thesis statement.

A SWEET DEVOURING

❈ EUDORA WELTY ❈

When I used to ask my mother which we were, rich or poor, she refused   1
to tell me. I was then nine years old and of course what I was dying to hear

was that we were poor. I was reading a book called *Five Little Peppers* and my heart was set on baking a cake for my mother in a stove with a hole in it. Some version of rich, crusty old Mr. King—up till that time not living on our street—was sure to come down the hill in his wheelchair and rescue me if anything went wrong. But before I could start a cake at all I had to find out if we were poor, and poor *enough;* and my mother wouldn't tell me, she said she was too busy. I couldn't wait too long; I had to go on reading and soon Polly Pepper got into more trouble, some that was a little harder on her and easier on me.

Trouble, the backbone of literature, was still to me the original property of the fairy tale, and as long as there was plenty of trouble for everybody and the rewards for it were falling in the right spots, reading was all smooth sailing. At that age a child reads with higher appetite and gratification, and with those two stars sailing closer together, than ever again in his growing up. The home shelves had been providing me all along with the usual books, and I read them with love—but snap, I finished them. I read everything just alike—snap. I even came to the *Tales from Maria Edgeworth* and went right ahead, without feeling the bump—then. It *was* noticeable that when her characters suffered she punished them for it, instead of rewarding them as a reader had rather been led to hope. In her stories, the children had to make their choice between being unhappy and good about it and being unhappy and bad about it, and then she helped them to choose wrong. In *The Purple Jar,* it will be remembered, there was the little girl being taken through the shops by her mother and her downfall coming when she chooses to buy something beautiful instead of something necessary. The purple jar, when the shop sends it out, proves to have been purple only so long as it was filled with purple water, and her mother knew it all the time. They don't deliver the water. That's only the cue for stones to start coming through the hole in the victim's worn-out shoe. She bravely agrees she must keep walking on stones until such time as she is offered another choice between the beautiful and the useful. Her father tells her as far as he is concerned she can stay in the house. If I had been at all easy to disappoint, that story would have disappointed me. Of course, I did feel, what is the good of walking on rocks if they are going to let the water out of the jar too? And it seemed to me that even the illustrator fell down on the characters in that book, not alone Maria Edgeworth, for when a rich, crusty old gentleman gave Simple Susan a guinea for some kind deed she'd done him, there was a picture of the transaction and where was the guinea? I couldn't make out a feather. But I liked *reading* the book all right—except that I finished it.

My mother took me to the Public Library and introduced me: "Let her have any book she wants, except *Elsie Dinsmore.*" I looked for the book I couldn't have and it was a row. That was how I learned about the Series Books. The *Five Little Peppers* belonged, so did *The Wizard of Oz,* so did *The Little Colonel,* so did *The Green Fairy Book.* There were many of everything, generations of everybody, instead of one. I wasn't coming to the end of reading, after all—I was saved.

2

3

Our library in those days was a big rotunda lined with shelves. A copy of   4
V. V.'s Eyes seemed to follow you wherever you went, even after you'd read
it. I didn't know what I liked, I just knew what there was a lot of. After *Randy's*
Spring there came *Randy's Summer, Randy's Fall* and *Randy's Winter*. True, I
didn't care very much myself for her spring, but it didn't occur to me that I
might not care for her summer, and then her summer didn't prejudice me
against her fall, and I still had hopes as I moved on to her winter. I was
disappointed in her whole year, as it turned out, but a thing like that didn't
keep me from wanting to read every word of it. The pleasures of reading
itself—who doesn't remember?—were like those of a Christmas cake, a sweet
devouring. The "Randy Books" failed chiefly in being so soon over. Four seasons
doesn't make a series.

All that summer I used to put on a second petticoat (our librarian wouldn't   5
let you past the front door if she could see through you), ride my bicycle up
the hill and "through the Capitol" (shortcut) to the library with my two read
books in the basket (two was the limit you could take out at one time when
you were a child and also as long as you lived), and tiptoe in ("Silence") and
exchange them for two more in two minutes. Selection was no object. I coasted
the two new books home, jumped out of my petticoat, read (I suppose I ate
and bathed and answered questions put to me), then in all hope put my petticoat
back on and rode those two books back to the library to get my next two.

The librarian was the lady in town who wanted to be it. She called me by   6
my full name and said, "Does your mother know where you are? You know
good and well the fixed rule of this library: *Nobody is going to come running*
back here with any book on the same day they took it out. Get both those
things out of here and don't come back till tomorrow. And I can practically
see through you."

My great-aunt in Virginia, who understood better about needing more to   7
read than you *could* read, sent me a book so big it had to be read on the
floor—a bound volume of six or eight issues of *St. Nicholas* from a previous
year. In the very first pages a serial began: *The Lucky Stone* by Abbie Farwell
Brown. The illustrations were right down my alley: a heroine so poor she
was ragged, a witch with an extremely pointed hat, a rich, crusty old gentleman
in—better than a wheelchair—a runaway carriage; and I set to. I gobbled up
installment after installment through the whole luxurious book, through the
last one, and then came the words, turning me to *un*lucky stone: "To be concluded." The book had come to an end and *The Lucky Stone* wasn't finished!
The witch had it! I couldn't believe this infidelity from my aunt. I still had my
secret childhood feeling that if you hunted long enough in a book's pages,
you could find what you were looking for, and long after I knew books better
than that, I used to hunt again for the end of *The Lucky Stone*. It never occurred
to me that the story had an existence anywhere else outside the pages of that
single green-bound book. The last chapter was just something I would have
to do without. Polly Pepper could do it. And then suddenly I tried something—
I read it again, as much as I had of it. I was in love with books at least partly
for what they looked like; I loved the printed page.

In my little circle books were almost never given for Christmas, they cost too much. But the year before, I'd been given a book and got a shock. It was from the same classmate who had told me there was no Santa Claus. She gave me a book, all right—*Poems by Another Little Girl*. It looked like a real book, was printed like a real book—but it was *by her. Homemade* poems? Illusion-dispelling was her favorite game. She was in such a hurry, she had such a pile to get rid of—her mother's electric runabout was stacked to the bud vases with copies—that she hadn't even time to say, "Merry Christmas!" With only the same raucous laugh with which she had told me, "Been filling my own stocking for years!" she shot me her book, received my Japanese pencil box with a moonlight scene on the lid and a sharpened pencil inside, jumped back into the car and was sped away by her mother. I stood right where they had left me, on the curb in my Little Nurse's uniform, and read that book, and I had no better way to prove when I got through than I had when I started that this was not a real book. But of course it wasn't. The printed page is not absolutely everything.

Then this Christmas was coming, and my grandfather in Ohio sent along in his box of presents an envelope with money in it for me to buy myself the book I wanted.

I went to Kress's.[1] Not everybody knew Kress's sold books, but children just before Christmas know everything Kress's ever sold or will sell. My father had showed us the mirror he was giving my mother to hang above her desk, and Kress's is where my brother and I went to reproduce that by buying a mirror together to give her ourselves, and where our little brother then made us take him and he bought her one his size for fifteen cents. Kress's had also its version of the Series Books, called, exactly like another series, "The Camp Fire Girls," beginning with *The Camp Fire Girls in the Woods*.

I believe they were ten cents each and I had a dollar. But they weren't all that easy to buy, because the series stuck, and to buy some of it was like breaking into a loaf of French bread. Then after you got home, each single book was as hard to open as a box stuck in its varnish, and when it gave way it popped like a firecracker. The covers once prized apart would never close; those books once open stayed open and lay on their backs helplessly fluttering their leaves like a turned-over June bug. They were as light as a matchbox. They were printed on yellowed paper with corners that crumbled, if you pinched on them too hard, like old graham crackers, and they smelled like attic trunks, caramelized glue, their own confinement with one another and, over all, the Kress's smell—bandannas, peanuts and sandalwood from the incense counter. Even without reading them I loved them. It was hard, that year, that Christmas is a day you can't read.

What could have happened to those books?—but I can tell you about the leading character. His name was Mr. Holmes. He was not a Camp Fire Girl: he wanted to catch one. Through every book of the series he gave chase. He pursued Bessie and Zara—those were the Camp Fire Girls—and kept scooping

8

9

10

11

12

---

[1] *Kress's:* a five-and-dime that rivaled Woolworth's.

them up in his touring car, while they just as regularly got away from him. Once Bessie escaped from the second floor of a strange inn by climbing down a gutter pipe. Once she escaped by driving away from Mr. Holmes in his own automobile, which she had learned to drive by watching him. What Mr. Holmes wanted with them—either Bessie or Zara would do—didn't give me pause; I was too young to be a Camp Fire Girl; I was just keeping up. I wasn't alarmed by Mr. Holmes—when I cared for a chill, I knew to go to Dr. Fu Manchu, who had his own series in the library. I wasn't fascinated either. There was one thing I wanted from those books, and that was for me to have ten to read at one blow.

Who in the world wrote those books? I knew all the time they were the false "Camp Fire Girls" and the ones in the library were the authorized. But book reviewers sometimes say of a book that if anyone else had written it, it might not have been this good, and I found it out as a child—their warning is justified. This was a proven case, although a case of the true not being as good as the false. In the true series the characters were either totally different or missing (Mr. Holmes was missing), and there was too much time given to teamwork. The Kress's Campers, besides getting into a more reliable kind of trouble than the Carnegie Campers, had adventures that even they themselves weren't aware of: the pages were in wrong. There were transposed pages, repeated pages, and whole sections in upside down. There was no way of telling if there was anything missing. But if you knew your way in the woods at all, you could enjoy yourself tracking it down. I read the library "Camp Fire Girls," since that's what they were there for, but though they could be read by poorer light they were not as good.

And yet, in a way, the false Campers were no better either. I wonder whether I felt some flaw at the heart of things or whether I was just tired of not having any taste; but it seemed to me when I had finished that the last nine of those books weren't as good as the first one. And the same went for all Series Books. As long as they are keeping a series going, I was afraid, nothing can really happen. The whole thing is one grand prevention. For my greed, I might have unwittingly dealt with myself in the same way Maria Edgeworth dealt with the one who put her all into the purple jar—I had received word it was just colored water.

And then I went again to the home shelves and my lucky hand reached and found Mark Twain—twenty-four volumes, not a series, and good all the way through.

[1957—U.S.A.]

Questions

1. "A Sweet Devouring" is a narrative. What is its structural type? There are some fine, organic transitions here. What, for instance, supplies transition between paragraphs 1 and 2?
2. What is the significance of Welty's reference to Mark Twain at the end of the essay? What is her theme? How does her theme account for the organizational mode of the essay?

3. With what does Welty begin the essay? That is, what are we given in paragraph 1? Why is this a good way for her to begin? How does the essay proceed after the first paragraph? Why does it proceed thus?

4. The title, "A Sweet Devouring," provides a metaphor that is extended over the course of the essay. What is the metaphor? In what ways is it appropriate here? Where is it extended?

5. Their drama heightened by the paragraphing, paragraphs 9 and 15 are dramatic in terms of content. How so? Paragraph 15 points to the future as it brings the essay to a close. Why is such an ending satisfying?

Writing Assignments

1. Titles can do a good deal of work. A title can even state the thesis of an essay, as is the case with the essay before this—"Nuclear Madness: What You Can Do." As to Welty's essay, its title establishes its dominant metaphor. Write a paragraph or more on that metaphor: what it is, how it is extended, and how it bears on the meaning of the essay.

2. Find a point of focus in your own childhood, as reading is Welty's, and discuss your childhood in relation to this event, sequence of events, or whatever. Try to end with a suggestion of the future (that is, from the perspective of you as child).

3. Choose whatever topic and thesis (or theme) you will and write an essay "after" "A Sweet Devouring" with respect to metaphor. Establish a metaphor—perhaps in your title—and then extend it by bringing it back and back again in one way or another. Use Welty's essay as your model. To do so, you must answer question 4 above with care.

THE DEATH OF THE MOTH

❊ VIRGINIA WOOLF ❊

Moths that fly by day are not properly to be called moths; they do not excite that pleasant sense of dark autumn nights and ivy-blossom which the commonest yellow-underwing asleep in the shadow of the curtain never fails to rouse in us. They are hybrid creatures, neither gay like butterflies nor sombre like their own species. Nevertheless the present specimen, with his narrow hay-coloured wings, fringed with a tassel of the same colour, seemed to be content with life. It was a pleasant morning, mid-September, mild, benignant, yet with a keener breath than that of the summer months. The plough was already scoring the field opposite the window, and where the share had been, the earth was pressed flat and gleamed with moisture. Such vigour came rolling in from the fields and the down beyond that it was difficult to keep the eyes strictly turned upon the book. The rooks too were keeping one of their annual festivities; soaring round the tree tops until it looked as if a vast net with thousands of black knots in it had been cast up into the air; which, after a few moments sank slowly down upon the trees until every twig seemed to have a knot at the end of it. Then, suddenly, the net would be thrown into the air again in a wider circle this time, with the utmost clamour and vociferation, as though to be thrown into the air and settle slowly down upon the tree tops were a tremendously exciting experience.

The same energy which inspired the rooks, the ploughmen, the horses,   2 and even, it seemed, the lean bare-backed downs, sent the moth fluttering from side to side of his square of the window-pane. One could not help watching him. One was, indeed, conscious of a queer feeling of pity for him. The possibilities of pleasure seemed that morning so enormous and so various that to have only a moth's part in life, and a day moth's at that, appeared a hard fate, and his zest in enjoying his meagre opportunities to the full, pathetic. He flew vigorously to one corner of his compartment, and, after waiting there a second, flew across to the other. What remained for him but to fly to a third corner and then to a fourth? That was all he could do, in spite of the size of the downs, the width of the sky, the far-off smoke of houses, and the romantic voice, now and then, of a steamer out at sea. What he could do he did. Watching him, it seemed as if a fibre, very thin but pure, of the enormous energy of the world had been thrust into his frail and diminutive body. As often as he crossed the pane, I could fancy that a thread of vital light became visible. He was little or nothing but life.

Yet, because he was so small, and so simple a form of the energy that   3 was rolling in at the open window and driving its way through so many narrow and intricate corridors in my own brain and in those of other human beings, there was something marvellous as well as pathetic about him. It was as if someone had taken a tiny bead of pure life and decking it as lightly as possible with down and feathers, had set it dancing and zigzagging to show us the true nature of life. Thus displayed one could not get over the strangeness of it. One is apt to forget all about life, seeing it humped and bossed and garnished and cumbered so that it has to move with the greatest circumspection and dignity. Again, the thought of all that life might have been had he been born in any other shape caused one to view his simple activities with a kind of pity.

After a time, tired by his dancing apparently, he settled on the window   4 ledge in the sun, and, the queer spectacle being at an end, I forgot about him. Then, looking up, my eye was caught by him. He was trying to resume his dancing, but seemed either so stiff or so awkward that he could only flutter to the bottom of the window-pane; and when he tried to fly across it he failed. Being intent on other matters I watched these futile attempts for a time without thinking, unconsciously waiting for him to resume his flight, as one waits for a machine, that has stopped momentarily, to start again without considering the reason of its failure. After perhaps a seventh attempt he slipped from the wooden ledge and fell, fluttering his wings, on to his back on the window sill. The helplessness of his attitude roused me. It flashed upon me that he was in difficulties; he could no longer raise himself; his legs struggled vainly. But, as I stretched out a pencil, meaning to help him to right himself, it came over me that the failure and awkwardness were the approach of death. I laid the pencil down again.

The legs agitated themselves once more. I looked as if for the enemy   5
against which he struggled. I looked out of doors. What had happened there?
Presumably it was mid-day, and work in the fields had stopped. Stillness and
quiet had replaced the previous animation. The birds had taken themselves
off to feed in the brooks. The horses stood still. Yet the power was there all
the same, massed outside indifferent, impersonal, not attending to anything in
particular. Somehow it was opposed to the little hay-coloured moth. It was
useless to try to do anything. One could only watch the extraordinary efforts
made by those tiny legs against an oncoming doom which could, had it chosen,
have submerged an entire city, not merely a city, but masses of human beings;
nothing, I knew, had any chance against death. Nevertheless after a pause of
exhaustion the legs fluttered again. It was superb this last protest, and so frantic
that he succeeded at last in righting himself. One's sympathies, of course, were
all on the side of life. Also, when there was nobody to care or to know, this
gigantic effort on the part of an insignificant little moth, against a power of
such magnitude, to retain what no one else valued or desired to keep, moved
one strangely. Again, somehow, one saw life, a pure bead. I lifted the pencil
again, useless though I knew it to be. But even as I did so, the unmistakable
tokens of death showed themselves. The body relaxed, and instantly grew stiff.
The struggle was over. The insignificant little creature now knew death. As I
looked at the dead moth, this minute wayside triumph of so great a force
over so mean an antagonist filled me with wonder. Just as life had been strange
a few minutes before, so death was now as strange. The moth having righted
himself now lay most decently and uncomplainingly composed. O yes, he seemed
to say, death is stronger than I am.

[1942—Great Britain]

Questions

1. What is the primary figurative mode of this essay? In what way is this mode appropriate
   to the essay?
2. A meditation, "The Death of the Moth" achieves a kind of definition of . . . of what? What
   is the essay's theme?
3. What is the purpose of the description in paragraph 2 of what the speaker can see through
   the window? How does the description relate to the essay's theme?
4. What unifies "The Death of the Moth" and gives it focus?

Writing Assignments

1. There are many little happenings in nature that one could focus on in a paper—for example,
   a bee banging on a window to get out, even though the window is open. Take this or
   some other phenomenon and write a short paper, beginning with a description of the
   phenomenon and seeking definition.
2. Choose something—event, person, natural phenomenon—as a point of focus for meditation.
   Then, having let your mind play around this focal point, write a coherent essay in which
   you attempt to capture the essence and texture of your meditation.

SIMPLICITY

-·⁖· WILLIAM ZINSSER ·⁖·-

Clutter is the disease of American writing. We are a society strangling in   1
unnecessary words, circular constructions, pompous frills and meaningless
jargon.

Who really knows what the average businessman is trying to say in the   2
average business letter? What member of an insurance or medical plan can
decipher the brochure that tells him what his costs and benefits are? What
father or mother can put together a child's toy—on Christmas Eve or any
other eve—from the instructions on the box? Our national tendency is to inflate
and thereby sound important. The airline pilot who wakes us to announce
that he is presently anticipating experiencing considerable weather wouldn't
dream of saying that there's a storm ahead and it may get bumpy. The sentence
is too simple—there must be something wrong with it.

But the secret of good writing is to strip every sentence to its cleanest   3
components. Every word that serves no function, every long word that could
be a short word, every adverb that carries the same meaning that is already
in the verb, every passive construction that leaves the reader unsure of who
is doing what—these are the thousand and one adulterants that weaken the
strength of a sentence. And they usually occur, ironically, in proportion to
education and rank.

During the late 1960's the president of Princeton University wrote a letter   4
to mollify the alumni after a spell of campus unrest. "You are probably aware,"
he began, "that we have been experiencing very considerable potentially explosive expressions of dissatisfaction on issues only partially related." He meant
that the students had been hassling them about different things. As an alumnus
I was far more upset by the president's syntax than by the students' potentially
explosive expressions of dissatisfaction. I would have preferred the presidential
approach taken by Franklin D. Roosevelt when he tried to convert into English
his own government's memos, such as this blackout order of 1942:

> Such preparations shall be made as will completely obscure all Federal buildings
> and non-Federal buildings occupied by the Federal government during an air raid
> for any period of time from visibility by reason of internal or external illumination.

"Tell them," Roosevelt said, "that in buildings where they have to keep   5
the work going to put something across the windows."

Simplify, simplify. Thoreau said it, as we are so often reminded, and no   6
American writer more consistently practiced what he preached. Open *Walden*
to any page and you will find a man saying in a plain and orderly way what is
on his mind:

> I love to be alone. I never found the companion that was so companionable as
> solitude. We are for the most part more lonely when we go abroad among men
> than when we stay in our chambers. A man thinking or working is always alone, let

him be where he will. Solitude is not measured by the miles of space that intervene between a man and his fellows. The really diligent student in one of the crowded hives of Cambridge College is as solitary as a dervish in the desert.

How can the rest of us achieve such enviable freedom from clutter? The answer is to clear our heads of clutter. Clear thinking becomes clear writing: one can't exist without the other. It is impossible for a muddy thinker to write good English. He may get away with it for a paragraph or two, but soon the reader will be lost, and there is no sin so grave, for he will not easily be lured back.

7

Who is this elusive creature, the reader? He is a person with an attention span of about twenty seconds. He is assailed on every side by forces competing for his time: by newspapers and magazines, by television and radio and stereo, by his wife and children and pets, by his house and his yard and all the gadgets that he has bought to keep them spruce, and by that most potent of competitors, sleep. The man snoozing in his chair with an unfinished magazine open on his lap is a man who was being given too much unnecessary trouble by the writer.

8

It won't do to say that the snoozing reader is too dumb or too lazy to keep pace with the train of thought. My sympathies are with him. If a reader is lost, it is generally because the writer has not been careful enough to keep him on the path.

9

This carelessness can take any number of forms. Perhaps a sentence is so excessively cluttered that the reader, hacking his way through the verbiage, simply doesn't know what it means. Perhaps a sentence has been so shoddily constructed that the reader could read it in any of several ways. Perhaps the writer has switched pronouns in mid-sentence, or has switched tenses, so the reader loses track of who is talking or when the action took place. Perhaps Sentence B is not a logical sequel to Sentence A—the writer, in whose head the connection is clear, has not bothered to provide the missing link. Perhaps the writer has used an important word incorrectly by not taking the trouble to look it up. He may think that "sanguine" and "sanguinary" mean the same thing, but the difference is a bloody big one. The reader can only infer (speaking of big differences) what the writer is trying to imply.

10

Faced with these obstacles, the reader is at first a remarkably tenacious bird. He blames himself—he obviously missed something, and he goes back over the mystifying sentence, or over the whole paragraph, piecing it out like an ancient rune, making guesses and moving on. But he won't do this for long. The writer is making him work too hard, and the reader will look for one who is better at his craft.

11

The writer must therefore constantly ask himself: What am I trying to say? Surprisingly often, he doesn't know. Then he must look at what he has written and ask: Have I said it? Is it clear to someone encountering the subject for the first time? If it's not, it is because some fuzz has worked its way into the machinery. The clear writer is a person clear-headed enough to see this stuff for what it is: fuzz.

12

I don't mean that some people are born clear-headed and are therefore   13
natural writers, whereas others are naturally fuzzy and will never write well.
Thinking clearly is a conscious act that the writer must force upon himself,
just as if he were embarking on any other project that requires logic: adding
up a laundry list or doing an algebra problem. Good writing doesn't come
naturally, though most people obviously think it does. The professional writer
is forever being bearded by strangers who say that they'd like to "try a little
writing some time" when they retire from their real profession. Good writing
takes self-discipline and, very often, self-knowledge.

Many writers, for instance, can't stand to throw anything away. Their sen-   14
tences are littered with words that mean essentially the same thing and with
phrases which make a point that is implicit in what they have already said.
When students give me these littered sentences I beg them to select from the
surfeit of words the few that most precisely fit what they want to say. Choose
one, I plead, from among the three almost identical adjectives. Get rid of the
unnecessary adverbs. Eliminate "in a funny sort of way" and other such qualifi-
ers—they do no useful work.

The students look stricken—I am taking all their wonderful words away. I   15
am only taking their superfluous words away, leaving what is organic and
strong.

"But," one of my worst offenders confessed, "I never can get rid of anything—   16
you should see my room." (I didn't take him up on the offer.) "I have two
lamps where I only need one, but I can't decide which one I like better, so I
keep them both." He went on to enumerate his duplicated or unnecessary
objects, and over the weeks ahead I went on throwing away his duplicated
and unnecessary words. By the end of the term—a term that he found acutely
painful—his sentences were clean.

"I've had to change my whole approach to writing," he told me. "Now I   17
have to *think* before I start every sentence and I have to *think* about every
word." The very idea amazed him. Whether his room also looked better I
never found out. I suspect that it did.

[1976—U.S.A.]

Questions

1. The two sentences that compose paragraph 1 could be reversed. Why did Zinsser put his
   thesis sentence first? What is gained thereby? And why did he state the thesis as it is
   stated in the first sentence?
2. What is the function of paragraph 2? What does it serve to do?
3. Contrast the quote at the end of paragraph 4 with paragraph 5 as to diction and syntax.
   Why did Zinsser make Roosevelt's sentence a separate paragraph?
4. What is the function of the quotation from Thoreau in paragraph 6? How does the quotation
   help Zinsser exemplify his point?
5. At the beginning of paragraph 10, there is an implicit metaphor. What is it? What does it
   imply? The word "bloody" at the end of the same paragraph is particularly apt. How so?
   (Look up "sanguine" and "sanguinary" before answering.)

6. In "How I Write," Bertrand Russell states: "What I do not find is that I can improve a sentence when I am satisfied with what it means" (p. 944, paragraph 3). In what way(s) is this statement analogous to Zinsser's central tenet that "clear thinking becomes clear writing" (paragraph 7)?

Writing Assignments

1. "Our national tendency is to inflate," says Zinsser (paragraph 2). Find an example of inflated, cluttered prose—in an editorial, perhaps, or a political speech, or possibly even in this book—and then, in a paragraph or more, analyze your example, pointing out why it is cluttered and how it could be pared down.
2. Take a paragraph of your own that you now feel is cluttered, pare it down, and then write a paper contrasting the original and the rewrite.
3. Write a paper comparing Zinsser and Didion (pp. 905–08) or Russell (pp. 943–45) as to what Zinsser and the writer you choose say about using the English language. Or you might take the essays of all three authors, abstract the principles of good writing found therein, and, after your introduction, devote a paragraph or two to a discussion of each principle.
4. Write an essay "after" Zinsser. Begin immediately with your thesis sentence, then draw your reader in by relating what you have to say to common experience, and then argue your thesis by examples and apt quotations. For topic, you might take some other area of human endeavor (other than writing) in which simplicity should be the rule but clutter actually is. Or you could choose some other aspect of writing (other than clutter) that could be addressed as Zinsser addresses clutter in his essay.

A BRIEF GUIDE TO THE USE AND DOCUMENTATION OF SOURCES AND RELATED MATTERS

USING SOURCES

Plagiarism

Plagiarism is the unacknowledged use—whether intentional or not—of another person's words or ideas. What you should know first about the use of source material is that anything not your own in a paper will be considered plagiarized if it is not attributed properly. Every direct quotation must be either put within quotation marks or blocked and indented, and a citation must be given referring to a Works Cited list at the end of your paper. Summaries and paraphrases also call for citations. If you cite your sources appropriately, there will be no problem. If you don't, your theft—for that is what it will be—will most likely be caught. Plagiarism usually shouts its presence, especially if the student has lifted something from a published text. Even if the instructor does not know the source, plagiarism can be recognized on stylistic or ideational grounds alone. And how silly plagiarism is. It insults the intelligence of the reader and shows that the student has completely misunderstood the purpose of research. When you do research, proudly show the work you've done by your citations. What is impressive is how you use your sources to buttress *your* ideas.

Referring to Titles

The way titles are quoted is simple: as a general rule, the title of something published in a longer work with a title of its own is put within quotation marks; the title of anything published as an independent unit is italicized (underlined in a typed text). For instance, the title of any short work in this book should be put in quotation marks: "Just Lather, That's All" or "Mending Wall" or "My Wood." Should you refer to the book as a whole, underline its title: <u>Reading and Writing About</u>

Literature. Titles of books, newspapers, and magazines are underlined; the titles of chapters within books, articles in magazines, short stories and lyric poems, and so forth are put in quotation marks. Incidentally, just as quotation marks and italics (underlining) are not used in titles of the works themselves, you should use neither when you place your own title at the head of your paper. However, if your paper title *includes* a story or book title, these should be put in quotation marks or underlined, as appropriate. Here are two examples of paper titles containing titles of published works:

```
The Humor of Plot in James Thurber's "The Night the Bed Fell"
The Use of the Elements of Drama as Defined in Reading and
     Writing About Literature
```

Remember that your *whole* title should not have quotation marks around it or be underlined (unless, of course, your title consists of nothing but the title of the work you are writing about—a practice almost always to be discouraged).

Continuous vs. Blocked Quotations

When quoting from a source, you must make a decision depending upon what is being quoted and how much of it. That is, one or two lines of verse and up to four lines of prose should be put in quotation marks and typed so as to be continuous with your text. (Note: When two lines of poetry are quoted continuously, they are separated by a slash thus: "Had we but world enough and time, / This coyness, lady, were no crime.") The following exemplifies this mode of quotation and the way it looks: I began this paragraph by saying, "When quoting from a source, you must make a decision depending upon what is being quoted and how much of it." However, more than four lines of prose or two lines of verse should be blocked and indented—that is, separated from the lines of your own writing by being indented from the left ten spaces. Such quotations are often introduced by a clause ending in a colon, though other punctuation, or even none, may sometimes serve, depending on how the beginning of the quoted text flows grammatically from your own text. The following blocked quotation illustrates these points.

```
Dylan Thomas's haunting story "After the Fair" is illuminated
by a sentence from William James:
          Or if the hypothesis were offered us of a world in
          which . . . utopias should all be outdone, and
          millions kept permanently happy on the one simple
          condition that a certain lost soul on the far-off
          edge of things should lead a life of lonely torment,
          what except a specific and independent sort of
```

```
emotion can it be which would make us immediately
feel, even though an impulse arose within us to
clutch at the happiness so offered, how hideous a
thing would be its enjoyment when deliberately
accepted as the fruit of such a bargain?
```

This is the look of a blocked quotation. (It would be followed by a parenthetical citation, but we will consider such documentation later in this appendix.) Note that there are no quotation marks around the material blocked; the blocking itself signals quotation. Another note of caution: do not use long quotations to excess. Summarize or paraphrase whenever possible. Use your sources for evidence, not padding.

A quotation within a blocked quotation—that is, something being quoted by the author of your source—is put within normal (double) quotation marks (" "). In continuous quotations, such an interior quotation goes within single quotation marks, as in the following sentences quoted from Thurber's "The Owl Who Was God": " 'Aren't you afraid?' he asked. 'Who?' said the owl calmly, for he could not see the truck." Observe the punctuation here. In American English, periods and commas always go *inside* the closing quotation marks thus: "for he could not see the truck." Semicolons and colons go outside. Exclamation points and questions marks go inside if they are part of the quotation and outside if they are your own.

Changing Punctuation

There are, then, two minor changes of punctuation that you can and often must make with respect to continuous quotations: (1) if quotation marks are found *within* the material you are quoting, change those quotation marks from double (" ") to single (' ') ones; (2) if necessary to make the quotation fit smoothly into your sentence, use a comma (or ellipsis dots—see the next subsection) within the closing quotation mark even though the original may have had no mark of punctuation there or some other mark, such as a period, that you will be replacing with the comma. Consider, for instance, the punctuation changes we must make if we wish to incorporate Thurber's sentence just quoted as part of the following sentence of our own:

```
When Thurber writes, "'Who?' said the owl calmly, for he could
not see the truck," we can almost feel the truck bearing
inexorably down upon the complacent bird and his disciples.
```

Here Thurber's double quotation marks around the first word, *Who,* have been changed to single ones. And the period at the end of Thurber's original sentence (after *truck*) has been changed to a comma to make Thurber's sentence fit into the new structure. (You may wish to look at Thurber's original sentence on page 49.)

Ellipsis and Square Brackets

Quotations must be exact, except for the two minor changes of punctuation we have just mentioned in connection with continuing quotations. However, quotations need not be complete. You can quote anything you like, from a paragraph or more down to a phrase or even a word. You can also leave words out of a quotation or add words of your own. The first is accomplished by ellipsis. Consider this sentence from Bertrand Russell's "How I Write" (p. 945) and then the version of it shortened by ellipsis:

```
"There are some simple maxims--not perhaps quite so simple as
those which my brother-in-law Logan Pearsall Smith offered
me--which I think might be commended to writers of expository
prose."
```

```
"There are some simple maxims . . . which I think might be
commended to writers of expository prose."
```

Seldom used at the beginning of a quotation (for the reader knows that your quotation is an excerpt), ellipsis entails the use of three spaced dots to show that something from the source has been left out (only three dots, note, except when the ellipsis comes at the end of a sentence, in which case the period is also required).

If you wish to insert words of your own into a quotation for some reason—to make the quotation fit smoothly with the structure of your sentence as a whole, perhaps, or to comment on something within the quotation—you can do so by the use of square brackets. Here, for example, is how you might add a comment of your own in brackets if you were quoting the sentence by Bertrand Russell that we used to illustrate ellipsis above:

```
"There are some simple maxims [Russell goes on to name three]
. . . which I think might be commended to writers. . . ."
```

Fitting Quotations with Contexts

A quotation must be exact, yet—as we have noted—it must also fit smoothly into the context in which you are putting it. Often the context, the quotation, or both must be adjusted to make the necessary accommodation. A quotation can be adjusted by ellipsis, by additions in brackets, and by paraphrase (that is, what does not grammatically fit your context can be restated in your own words and the rest quoted). Your own context can also be adjusted. For instance, if you were quoting from my discussion of "The Shawl" in Section II, you would not want to write:

```
In reconsidering "The Shawl," Proffitt stated that he "find no
reason to alter my initial feelings."
```

The quotation is exact but, in its new context, ungrammatical and confusing. The problem might be solved in various ways. One way would be to change your own sentence by adding the word *could* (which fits grammatically with the quotation's first word, *find*) and by making a bracketed insertion in the quotation itself to change *my* to *his* (the brackets alert the reader that the word is yours, not in the original source):

```
In reconsidering "The Shawl," Proffitt stated that he could
"find no reason to alter [his] initial feelings."
```

Introducing Quotations

In your remarks introducing a quotation, you will usually want to incorporate the name of the person being quoted, and in any case you will want to make sure that the reason for your quotation is immediately clear. If the reason may not be clear, introduce the quotation by briefly suggesting why you are using it in the present context. For instance, let's say that in a paper on William Carlos Williams's story "The Use of Force" (pp. 167–69) you write:

```
The opening of the girl's mouth in the story is described in
exceptionally concrete terms.  We are made aware, however, of
a symbolic meaning to the opening of the mouth.  "No ideas but
in things."
```

You would need to revise this statement to introduce the quotation "No ideas but in things" (a line from a poem by Williams), for here it just sits, a puzzlement to the reader and so an obstacle to achieving your purpose. Note how, in the following version, the quotation is introduced in a way that clarifies its purpose:

```
The opening of the girl's mouth in the story is described in
exceptionally concrete terms.  We are made aware, however, of
a symbolic meaning to the opening of the mouth.  Something
Williams wrote in a poem captures the dual nature of this
image:  "No ideas but in things."
```

In both versions, of course, you would need to add a citation to the specific source of the line being quoted—a procedure we will consider shortly.

Quotation, Summary, and Paraphrase

Quotation is not the only way, or always the best way, to present the ideas of another. Often a summary or a paraphrase will prove more effective. A summary is a condensation of someone else's thinking down to the core of that person's idea. For instance, the paragraph headed "Fitting Quotations with Contexts" could be summarized as follows:

> Proffitt emphasizes that quotations must fit smoothly into
> their new contexts (971).

A paraphrase is more elaborate but is still a condensation in that it restates someone else's thought in brief. A paraphrase of the paragraph on context that we just summarized would be something like this:

> As Proffitt emphasizes, in order to make a quotation fit
> smoothly into its new context—and it is important for the
> writer to do so—the context itself can be adjusted by, for
> instance, the use of paraphrase, and the quotation adjusted by
> ellipsis or by addition in square brackets (971–72).

Observe that the paraphrase, like the summary, is restricted to the ideas in the source and that the paraphrase follows its sequence of ideas. Be sure to be alert and recognize that you are summarizing or paraphrasing if you are. Then provide the proper citations.

SOURCES: PRIMARY AND SECONDARY

Sources can be divided into *primary* and *secondary*. A primary source is just that: it is a work that comes *first*. In a paper on "The Road Not Taken," for instance, "The Road Not Taken" would be a primary source. So would any document by Frost—a letter, say, or a journal in which he wrote about the poem. Secondary sources include works of commentary, criticism, history, and so forth. What you need to remember is that primary sources are direct evidence and secondary sources are not. One uses secondary sources to bolster an argument and to lend authority to one's views. But just because so and so said such and such in a published book or periodical does not make it so. Finally, the only valid evidence is the primary source, and secondary sources should not be used to substitute for the grappling with a primary text that alone can give rise to a worthwhile paper.

CITING SOURCES

Whether you are quoting directly, summarizing, or paraphrasing, you must provide an appropriate citation in your text. The dual purpose of any citation is to acknowledge your borrowing as smoothly and concisely as possible within the text and to enable your reader to locate full information about your source in a list called Works Cited, which is arranged alphabetically by authors' last names and placed at the end of a paper. Thus the key element of a citation within your paper is the author's last name, together with the specific page number(s) on which the cited material appears in the source.

Put the author's last name and the page reference (the page or pages on which the material you are quoting, summarizing, or paraphrasing can be found) in parentheses at the end of the quotation, summary, or paraphrase:

> "Whether you are quoting directly, summarizing, or
> paraphrasing, you must provide an appropriate citation in your
> text" (Proffitt 973).

> Quotations must fit smoothly into their new context (Proffitt
> 971).

Often it is smoother, however, to mention the author's name in introducing the summary, paraphrase, or quotation, in which case you need not repeat the name in the parenthetical citation; the page reference alone is then enough:

> As Proffitt says, "Whether you are quoting directly,
> summarizing, or paraphrasing, you must provide an appropriate
> citation in your text" (973).

> Proffitt stresses that quotations must fit smoothly in their
> new context (971).

Parenthetical citation is used for books, stories, articles, and newspapers alike, with more detailed information left for the Works Cited list put at the end of a paper (we shall take up this matter shortly).

Citing Continuous vs. Blocked Quotations

There is one small difference between citations coming after continuous quotations and those coming after blocked quotations. When citations for continuous quotations come at the ends of sentences (as they most often do), the sentence period comes *after* the citation, as in the following example:

> The story reaches its most surreal moment with the image of "a
> butterfly touching a silver vine" (Ozick 37).

With blocked quotations, on the other hand, the period comes at the end of the quotation, and the citation stands alone two spaces to the right of the period. Here, for instance, are the first sentences of the previous subsection as they would appear and be cited in a blocked quotation:

> Whether you are quoting directly, summarizing, or paraphrasing, you must provide an appropriate citation in your text. The dual purpose of any citation is to acknowledge your borrowing as smoothly and concisely as possible within the text and to enable your reader to locate full information about your source in a list called Works Cited, which is arranged alphabetically by authors' last names and placed at the end of a paper. (Proffitt 973–74)

Three Problem Spots

There are a few other matters concerning citation that you will need to know when doing a properly documented paper. If you have parenthetical citations for two or more works by the same author, then each citation must include not only the author's last name but also a short form of the title of the work (followed, of course, by the page reference). For instance, in a paper that contained the following sentences referring to two different stories by William Carlos Williams in this book, "The Use of Force" and "The Buffalos," here is how the citations would be handled:

> The most startling moment comes when the doctor says that he had "fallen in love with the savage brat" (Williams, "Use" 168).

> Williams's narrator tells us that "once I had a beautiful friend" (Williams, "Buffalos" 137).

Without the short-title designations in the citations, the reader would not be able to tell which of the two works by Williams is being quoted in each case. Of course, if the author or the work or both are identified in the sentence itself, neither the one nor the other nor both need appear in the citation.

A somewhat similar problem is that of two or more authors having the same last name. In this case, each citation must include a first name or initial, as follows: (Marianne Moore 490), (Elizabeth Moore 490).

Further, in citing an anonymous work, such as a news report, use instead of the author's name the first word or phrase (omitting initial articles "A," "An," or "The") of the title of the piece, followed by the page reference: ("Myth" 112) for a citation to page 112 of an article entitled "Myth and the Mythic Mind" in *The Book of All Mythologies*. The reader will be able to locate the full reference in the Works Cited list because anonymous works are alphabetized by the first word of their titles. Finally, a special case of the anonymous work is an article in an encyclopedia or other reference volume in which the articles are arranged alphabetically. When you cite these articles, no page reference is required because the reader can quickly look up the article in its alphabetical location. In sum, use common sense. The main purpose of parenthetical citation is to allow the reader to use the appended Works Cited list with ease. Everything done should serve this purpose.

THE WORKS CITED LIST

At the end of your paper, on its own page, should be a list called Works Cited containing an entry for each of the sources you have used. As we have seen, the information in the citations within your paper is abbreviated. In Works Cited you list your sources alphabetically by the last name of each author (or the title if there is no author indicated) and give your reader complete information for each source so that the reader can go to the source to confirm the validity of your citation or to study the subject further. There are a great many possible kinds of entries and so, naturally, a great many possible complications in getting a Works Cited list into shape. However, for our purposes—and, in fact, for the purposes of most people most of the time—only a few types of entry need be considered. We will examine here the most common types, especially those that will be valuable to you in using this book. A Works Cited list including the main examples discussed in this appendix appears at the conclusion (pp. 981–82). The style followed here, as throughout this appendix, is the one most commonly used in literature and composition courses, that of the Modern Language Association of America. (Some other styles are used in other disciplines.) Should you happen to need information beyond what is presented here, consult the most recent edition of Joseph Gibaldi and Walter S. Achtert, *MLA Handbook for Writers of Research Papers,* New York: MLA, which is sure to be in your college library.

Books and Journal Articles

The works most frequently cited are books and articles. An entry for a book should include the name of the author, last name first (if a work has two or more authors, names of authors after the first are straightforward); the full title of the work, including subtitle (separated from the title by a colon), underlined; the edition, if other than the first edition; and finally the city of publication followed by a colon, a shortened form of the publisher's name, and the date of publication. Here are two examples:

Brooks, Cleanth, R. W. B. Lewis, and Robert Penn Warren.

    American Literature: The Makers and the Making.

    Shorter ed. New York: St. Martin's, 1974.

Forster, E. M. Aspects of the Novel. New York: Harcourt,

    1954.

When a work has more than three authors, give only the first author's name, followed by a comma and the phrase "et al." (except not in quotation marks), which is Latin for "and others." For instance, had the first book listed above had four authors rather than three, the author would have been given as follows: Brooks, Cleanth, et al.

For articles, treat the author's name exactly as for a book. Then comes the title of the article in quotation marks; next, the name of the journal, underlined; and finally the volume number, issue number, date of publication, and the inclusive page numbers of the article (not the page reference for your specific citation, which appears in parentheses in the text of your paper). For a daily, weekly, or monthly periodical, however, omit volume and issue numbers and give the specific date instead. Following are two typical entries:

Funey, Sean. "The Aroma of Paterson in Williams's Stories."

    Journal of Short Fiction Studies 18.2 (1984): 23–41.

Staggs, Sam. "James Dickey." Publishers Weekly 29 May 1987:

    62–63.

In the entry for the Funey article, the volume number of the journal is 18, and the issue number is 2 (with this information, only the year of publication, 1984, is given); the article runs from page 23 to page 41. Because the Staggs entry is for a weekly publication, the specific date replaces the volume and issue number.

Observe the spacing in all four entries above: two spaces are used after each discrete item of information, which is followed by a period—after the author's name, for example, and again after the title of the book or article, and still again after the edition, as in the entry for Brooks, Lewis, and Warren. The same would be true of other discrete items of information, such as the name of an editor or translator (as other examples in this appendix will show). Note, too, that the first line of an entry is not indented and the rest of the lines are indented five spaces.

Anthologies

For an anthology, give the editor's name, last name first (as for an author), followed by a comma, a space, and the abbreviation "ed." Then give the title and the rest of the information as for any other book. Such an entry looks like this:

```
Proffitt,  Edward,  ed.   Reading and Writing About Literature.
     San Diego: Harcourt, 1990.
```

In a paper in which, for instance, you compare two stories found in the present text, this would be your main entry. How the individual stories would be entered in the list is covered in the next subsection.

A Work in an Anthology

For a story or other selection found in an anthology for which you have provided a main entry as shown just above, begin with the author of the selection (in the usual way). Next give the selection title, followed by a period, in quotation marks (exception: titles of plays are underlined); if the selection is a translation, next give the translator's name preceded by "Trans."; and finally give the last name of the anthology's editor and the inclusive page numbers of the story or other selection as it appears in the anthology. Here are two examples:

```
Chekhov,  Anton.   "The Lottery Ticket."  Trans. Constance
     Garnett.  Proffitt 72–75.
Williams,  William Carlos.  "The Buffalos."  Proffitt 137–40.
```

This kind of entry, referring to a main entry for the anthology itself (in this case the main entry for Proffitt shown in the preceding subsection), is convenient if you cite more than one selection from the same anthology; it saves you the trouble of repeating all the information about the anthology in the entry for each selection. However, if you refer to only one selection from the anthology, you will find it more efficient simply to use one full entry as follows:

```
Williams,  William Carlos.  "The Use of Force."  Reading and
     Writing About Literature.  Ed. Edward Proffitt.  San
     Diego: Harcourt, 1990, 167–69.
```

Reference Books and Anonymous Material

Treat a *signed* article in an encyclopedia or other reference book as you would an article or story in a collection, except do not include the name of the editor of the reference work:

```
Edel,  Leon.   "Henry James and His Followers."  Encyclopaedia
     Britannica: Macropaedia.  1974 ed.
```

If the article is not signed or if you are listing a book with no author given, the name of the book or article should appear alphabetically thus:

<pre>
The Times Atlas of the World. 5th ed. New York: New York
     Times, 1975.
"Williams, William Carlos." The Columbia Encyclopaedia. 1950
     ed.
</pre>

Titles beginning with "A," "An," or "The" are alphabetized according to the second word of the title. Note, too, how an edition is indicated, and observe that if the materials within the source volume are arranged alphabetically you may omit volume and page numbers.

Newspaper Articles

To list an article from a newspaper, begin with the writer's name if specified (if not, begin with the title of the article), followed by the title of the article (the major headline) in quotation marks, the name of the paper (excluding initial "A," "An," or "The") underlined, the complete date, the edition if an edition, and the section letter, if the paper is divided into sections, along with the inclusive page numbers if the article is continuous (see first example to follow) or the first page number followed by a plus sign if the article is continued after skipping pages (see second example).

<pre>
Crane, Stephen. "Captain Murphy's Shipwrecked Crew." Florida
     Times Union 5 Jan. 1897: 1-2.
"The Literate and the Damned." Bar Harbour Post Dispatch 12
     July 1953, late ed.: B17+.
</pre>

In the second entry, the article begins on page 17 of section B and then skips to a page farther back, as often happens in magazines and newspapers. Note, incidentally, that the names of all months except May, June, and July (in other words, all months with names more than four letters long) are abbreviated in Works Cited entries ("*Jan.*" in the first entry above but "*July*" in the second).

Two or More Works by the Same Author

For two or more works by the same author, give the author's name for the first work and then, for the other works, use three typed hypens in place of the author's name (the hyphens are followed by a period, as is the author's name). Arrange the works alphabetically by title.

Williams, William Carlos. "The Buffalos." Proffitt 137–40.

———. <u>Paterson</u>. New York: New Directions, 1946.

———. "The Use of Force." Proffitt 167–69.

When different books are involved, a full citation for each is necessary, though the author's name is still indicated by the three typed hyphens for the second and subsequent works in the list.

Sample Works Cited List and Sample Manuscript

On the next page is a typewritten Works Cited list in the proper MLA format, listing many of the works referred to in the preceding discussions. Study it carefully and be sure that you understand the entries individually and also the reasons for the order in which they are presented. Following this sample list is the sample essay on Ozick's "The Shawl" from pages 40–42 of this book, now revised (for the purpose of illustration) to incorporate documented sources and typewritten in MLA format so that you can see how margins, spacing, page numbering, and other matters are handled.

1" ½" Proffitt 00

Double space.
First author
listed last
name first.

Indent five
spaces.

Works Cited

Brooks, Cleanth, R. W. B. Lewis, and Robert ← 1"
 Penn Warren. American Literature: The   Punctuation
within titles
  Makers and the Making. Shorter ed.   always
underlined.
  New York: St. Martin's, 1974.

← 1" → Crane, Stephen. "Captain Murphy's Shipwrecked Crew." Florida Times
  Union 5 Jan. 1897: 1–2.

Edel, Leon. "Henry James and His Followers." Encyclopaedia Britannica:
  Macropaedia. 1974 ed.

Forster, E. M. Aspects of the Novel. New
  York: Harcourt, 1954.

Funey, Sean. "The Aroma of Paterson in
  Williams's Stories." Journal of Short
  Fiction Studies 18.2 (1984): 23–41.

Gibaldi, Joseph, and Walter S. Achert.
  MLA Handbook for Writers of Research   Major elements
separated by a
Anonymous   Papers. 2nd ed. New York: MLA, 1984.   period plus two
spaces.
article
alphabetized by
title (ignoring "The Literate and the Damned." Bar Harbor
"The").
  Post Dispatch 12 July 1953, late ed.:   Article skips
pages after
  B17+.   beginning on
page B17.

Proffitt, Edward, ed. Reading and Writing
  About Literature. San Diego: Harcourt,
  1990.

Staggs, Sam. "James Dickey." Publishers
  Weekly 29 May 1987: 62–63.

1"

½ " {

Proffitt 00

Entry for
selection, refers
to main entry
for anthology.

The Times Atlas of the World. 5th ed. New

York: New York Times, 1975.

Williams, William Carlos. "The Buffalos."

Proffitt 137—40.

Works by
same author
(Williams).

———. Paterson. New York: New Directions,

1946.

———. "The Use of Force." Proffitt 167—69.

"Williams, William Carlos." The Columbia

Encyclopedia. 1950 ed.

No page numbers
required for
article in
alphabetized
reference work.

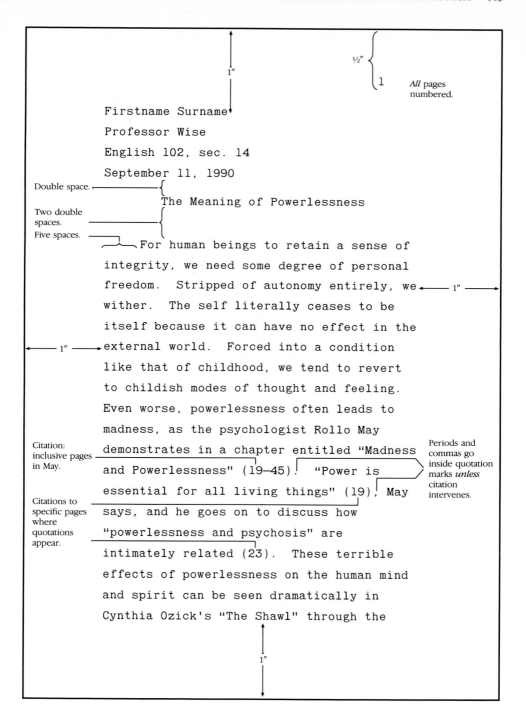

½"

1   *All* pages numbered.

Firstname Surname
Professor Wise
English 102, sec. 14
September 11, 1990

1"

Double space.

The Meaning of Powerlessness

Two double spaces.

Five spaces.

For human beings to retain a sense of
integrity, we need some degree of personal
freedom. Stripped of autonomy entirely, we
wither. The self literally ceases to be
itself because it can have no effect in the
external world. Forced into a condition
like that of childhood, we tend to revert
to childish modes of thought and feeling.
Even worse, powerlessness often leads to
madness, as the psychologist Rollo May
demonstrates in a chapter entitled "Madness
and Powerlessness" (19–45). "Power is
essential for all living things" (19), May
says, and he goes on to discuss how
"powerlessness and psychosis" are
intimately related (23). These terrible
effects of powerlessness on the human mind
and spirit can be seen dramatically in
Cynthia Ozick's "The Shawl" through the

1"

Citation: inclusive pages in May.

Citations to specific pages where quotations appear.

Periods and commas go inside quotation marks *unless* citation intervenes.

1"

Last name precedes page number on pages after the first.

deterioration of Rosa, its central character.

When we first meet Rosa, on the march, she has become physically decrepit, but her mind is still intact. Despite the dislocating effect of the march itself and the foul treatment received on it, she is still capable of logical thought and rational choice. Thus, she conceives a plan to give Magda away to someone at the side of the road; thinking the plan through, however, she realizes its impossibility and so rejects it. Here we have the operation of a rational mind. How different from this Rosa is the Rosa we leave at the end of the story. Her deterioration proceeds subtly but inevitably.

The first mark of that deterioration occurs soon after the incident just outlined. Suddenly we are told that "It was a magic shawl" (Ozick 34), and this idea is pursued. Because Ozick's narrator makes us see through Rosa's eyes, we know that it is Rosa who has started to believe in magic. That the shawl is not magical,

Author's name included here because not mentioned in text leading to this first citation.

Surname 3

of course, is suggested by the story's
title: the shawl is merely a shawl. Even
more, the fact that it doesn't finally
protect Magda but instead is the cause of
her being discovered evidences its lack of
magic properties. But that Rosa should
come to feel the shawl to be magical
quietly reveals her deterioration, or the
start thereof. A belief in magic, we might
recall, was associated by Freud both with
schizophrenic hallucinations and with
childhood (83—84).

Author's name
(Freud) not
needed here
because given in
text leading to
the reference.

    Rosa's way of seeing as communicated
by some of the story's images, especially
at the end, is further evidence of her
deterioration. In the context of the
prison camp as described, images like
"jolly light" (35), "a clown out of Magda's
shawl" (36), "light tapped the helmet and
sparkled it into a goblet" (36), and, most
pointedly, "a butterfly touching a silver
vine" (37) suggest a mind projecting
itself onto the world in order thus to
change reality. P. J. Miller rightly
summarizes the effect of the
story's imagery as having "a surreal

Only page
references
necessary
because author
(Ozick) is clear
in the context.

Surname 4

Ellipsis signals an intentional omission.

Square brackets show that word not in original source has been added.

quality . . . in [the] context, a quality
that imparts a growing sense of madness"
(152).

And Rosa does go mad. At the end of
the story her deterioration is complete:
she has herself become an infant sucking on
and trying to devour Magda's blanket. With
no choice possible as to external action,
she retreats into herself entirely. But
nothing I can say could communicate the
final stage of her deterioration
as well as the last lines of the story

Blocked quotation indented ten spaces.

itself:

Regular double space before (and after) blocked quotation.

so she took Magda's shawl and filled
her own mouth with it, stuffed it in
and stuffed it in, until she was
swallowing up the wolf's screech and
tasting the cinnamon and almond depth

Citation after blocked quotation *follows* the final period.

of Magda's saliva; and Rosa drank
Magda's shawl until it dried. (37)

Two spaces.

Rosa's steady deterioration to this
point, portrayed subtly and in depth,
communicates vividly the effects of
powerlessness on the mind and spirit.
Every human being needs a sense of control,
however minimal, over his or her own life.
Robbed of this sense, the mind and spirit
wither. Stripped of autonomy, what can the

Surname 5

self do but, like Rosa, fall into fantasy
and then madness? How truly terrible
powerlessness is, but especially in a world
in which power and not pity is the dominant
force.

½"

1"

Surname 6

Works Cited page(s) numbered consecutively with others.

Works Cited

Double space.

Book. —

Freud, Sigmund. <u>Totem and Taboo</u>. Trans.

Translator's name comes after title.

Five spaces. —

James Strachey. New York: Norton,

1950.

← 1" → May, Rollo. <u>Power and Innocence</u>. New   ← 1" →

York: Norton, 1972.

Article in journal.

Miller, P. J. "Patterns of Imagery in the

Stories of Cynthia Ozick." <u>American</u>

<u>Literature Review</u> 12.2 (1987): 147–61.   — Volume.

— Issue.

Author of selection.
Selection in anthology.

Ozick, Cynthia. "The Shawl." <u>Reading and</u>

<u>Writing About Literature</u>. Ed. Edward

Editor of anthology.

Proffitt. San Diego: Harcourt, 1990.

34–37.

1"

GLOSSARY

Note: Terms printed in **bold type** within an entry have entries of their own, to which the reader may wish to refer. The numbers in parentheses refer to the pages in the text where the terms are discussed.

abstraction   Any word that denotes a concept, a quality, a feeling, a classification, or whatever, without stimulating in the mind a particular sensation—for example, "refraction" as opposed to "green, red, and blue." Contrast **concretion.** (241, 870–71)

accentuation   The **stress** placed on one syllable as opposed to another in pronunciation. (317)

alexandrine   A line composed of six iambic feet—for example, the last line of the **Spenserian stanza.**

allegory   A kind of symbolic work in which humans, animals, events, or whatever stand for and enact ideas in a consistent manner. (183)

alliteration   The repetition of a consonantal sound (placed conspicuously at the beginning of adjacent words or internally stressed syllables) in a sequence of words—for example, "When to the *s*essions of *s*weet *s*ilent thought." (354)

allusion   An *indirect* reference to something assumed to be known by the listener or reader—for instance, the phrase "a mighty white whale, large enough to swallow a boat" alludes to both Melville's *Moby Dick* and the biblical story of Jonah. Compare **reference.**

ambiguity   Anything that has two or more possible meanings simultaneously may be said to exhibit ambiguity. Purposeful ambiguity can enrich a text by its addition of another level of meaning. Unintentional ambiguity, however, interferes with clarity.

analogy   The exemplifying, explaining, or interpreting of something by way of its similarities to something else. There are two broad types of analogy, literal and figurative. Involving comparison between things that are essentially alike—American men and Arab men, for instance—literal analogy is a means of **support** (though not a proof). Involving comparison between things that are essentially unalike—for example, American men and lions—figurative analogy is the basis of **metaphor.** (285, 879)

analytic prose   Prose in which a subject is divided into its component parts and examined accordingly. (9–10)

anapest/anapestic   A **beat** or **foot** consisting of two unstressed syllables followed by a stressed syllable—for example, "Ĭn thĕ héat / ŏf thĕ níght." (323)

assonance   The repetition of similar vowel sounds in a sequence of nearby words—for example, "Thou still unravished br*i*de of qu*i*etness, / Thou foster ch*i*ld of s*i*lence and slow t*i*me." (352)

audience   An element particularly of expository prose, many features of which are conditioned by the nature of the audience addressed. (8–9, 864–65)

authorial attitude   The attitude or viewpoint expressed by a work *as a whole* rather than through any single element or feature.

authority, appeal to   A means of **support** that entails the use of what authorities in a given field have said or statistics or personal experience as evidence backing up a contention or point. (878–79)

beat   The basic rhythmic unit (also called a **foot**) of which a metrical line is composed. The common beats of English verse are: **iamb, trochee, anapest,** and **dactyl.** Every beat consists of a stressed syllable (the beat itself, indicated thus: ´) and one or two unstressed or slack syllables (indicated thus: ˘) coming either before or after the beat. If a given beat recurs a set number of times per line, then we have a **meter.** We describe meters by the kind of beat that recurs and the number of recurrences per line—for example, **iambic pentameter.** (322)

blank verse   Lines in **iambic pentameter** that are *unrhymed* (*blank* means "unrhymed"). (325–26)

caesura   Any marked pause *within* a line—for example, "That time of year thou mayest in me behold / When yellow leaves, ∧ or none, ∧ or few, ∧ do hang." (318)

centrifugal exposition   A kind of exposition, usually having an overtly stated thesis, in which the focus is outward, on ideas, events, or whatever in the external world. Contrast **centripetal exposition.** (863)

centripetal exposition   A kind of exposition, usually entailing an unstated theme, in which the focus is inward, on the self and its history, musings, and so forth. Contrast **centrifugal exposition.** (863)

character/characterization   Character refers to either a personage in a work or the psychological makeup of that personage. Our sense of character in a work of literature depends on characterization, which refers to any technique whereby a work communicates the nature of its characters. Broadly, there are three types of literary character: **flat, round,** and **stock.** (99–101, 234–37, 536–37, 868–69)

character sketch   A type of essay that paints a detailed portrait of an individual. (868–69)

chronological organization   The organization of a piece of writing according to some time sequence. For instance, a paragraph or paper that moves from "at first" to "later" to "still later" to "at the last" is organized chronologically. (14, 879)

circumstantial irony   Refers to a discrepancy felt by the reader between what seems (or is expected) to be and what actually is, or between what is expected (or intended) to happen and what does happen. (152)

classification   The breaking of something into its classes or types—for example, the six types of title, the two broad classes of the essay—for the purposes of definition. Classification always proceeds by the **enumeration** of types one by one. (880)

closed couplet   Two rhymed lines that form a self-contained (closed) grammatical unit and express a complete thought. For example, "Had we but world enough and time, / This coyness, lady, were no crime." (390)

coherence   The sense that the relationship of parts in a piece of writing is logical and clear. (25–28)

comedy   A literary **genre** that makes us laugh in one way or another. The laughter of comedy may be scornful—as is that of much satire—or, conversely, warm and accepting—the kind of laughter evoked by **situation comedy,** which almost always ends happily. Though comedies often include material that is ridiculous, they may be serious in underlying intent. (530–32)

comparison and contrast   A prime way of understanding, comparison and contrast is also a tool of analysis and a mode of organization. It entails the focusing on the likenesses or differences or both between two or more things in order to see at least one of them with heightened clarity. (14–15, 880)

conceit   A metaphor whose comparison is particularly unexpected, even shocking at first—for instance, Donne's comparison of his love to a flea. Because the so-called "metaphysical poets" (Donne, Herbert, Marvell) were especially fond of this kind of metaphor, it is often called a *metaphysical conceit.*

concretion   Any word, phrase, or aspect of a text that has immediate sensory effect—for example, "a juicy steak." Contrast **abstraction.** (241, 259, 870–71)

conflict   Any struggle, internal or external, on the part of literary characters. If the struggle is external, it usually gives rise to **plot.** (69–70, 536)

connotation/denotation   Denotation is the literal meaning of a word—simply what it refers to. Connotation is what the word suggests or implies through the associations it evokes over and above its denotative meaning. For instance, though denoting only the place where one resides, the word "home" has a wealth of connotative meaning. (241)

consonance   The repetition of a sequence of consonants in nearby words with a change in the intervening vowels—for example, "tick/tock," "life/loaf," "breed/bread." (353)

context   The whole passage or work in which a given detail is found and from which it gains its meaning. The *cultural context*—the whole set of culturally shared meanings, associations, and understandings out of which a work grows—also helps to shape the work's meaning and guide interpretation.

controlling element   Any element in a given text that is of particular importance in guiding the response of the reader. In comedy, for instance, characterization is often a controlling element.

conventional symbol   Any **symbol** that means what it means by virtue of its cultural **context.** "Mom and apple pie," for instance, is a conventional symbol in the context of American culture: over and above its literal meaning, it suggests old-fashioned values, the good life, the American dream. (181–82, 538)

couplet   Two contiguous lines that rhyme. See **closed couplet, heroic couplet, open couplet.** (389)

created symbol   Anything that is symbolic primarily by virtue of its literary **context,** which signals **symbolic** intent and, in turn, guides and validates interpretation. (182, 538)

dactyl/dactylic   A **beat** or **foot** consisting of a stressed syllable followed by two unstressed syllables—for example, "fámǐly̌/elěphǎnt." (323)

dead metaphor   Any metaphor that, through overuse, no longer has metaphorical effect: "sly as a fox," "feed the computer." (302)

definition   A means of **support,** often entailing **classification** and **exemplification,** that involves the delineation of the meaning of a word or concept, the traits of a person, or whatever. (878)

denotation   See **connotation/denotation.**

denouement   The final outcome of the **conflict** and/or **plot** of a story or play. Etymologically, denouement means "unraveling." (535)

dialogue   Any part of a literary work spoken by individuals directly to each other rather than reported by a narrator or speaker. (122)

diction   The choice of words, or the kind of words chosen, in a given passage or utterance. A few possible distinctions as to diction are: abstract/concrete; denotative/connotative; formal/colloquial; general/specific; technical/common. Diction is a prime element of **style.** (153, 240–41, 538, 875–77)

discourse/discursive   Discourse refers to verbal expression in speech or writing. Discursive refers specifically to that type of verbal expression that proceeds according to the principles and goals of **expository prose.**

discrete paragraph   A paragraph that is self-contained, that stands alone as a short composition in itself. (11–13)

dissonance   The effect of sounds that are harsh and grating. Dissonance is often produced in poetry by **consonance, off-rhyme,** and the use of such hard consonants as *k* or *x*. (353–54, 359)

drama   One play, a group of related plays (as in "classical drama"), or the totality of works written to be acted (that is, the name of a **genre,** distinguished from such genres as poetry and fiction).

dramatic   Said of anything that communicates directly (that is, without comment) by virtue of what it is.

dramatic irony   Refers to a discrepancy between what a character believes and what the reader knows to be true. (152, 537)

dramatic monologue   A kind of poem clearly spoken by a character, the object of which is character revelation. See, for example, Robert Browning's "My Last Duchess," pp. 235–37.

end-rhyme   The rhyme that occurs at the end of lines in rhymed poetry, as distinguished from **internal rhyme. (357)**

end-stopped   Said of a line of poetry that comes to a marked pause at its end—for example, "Whose woods these are I think I know. ⌃ / His house is in the village, though; ⌃ / He will not. . . ." Contrast **enjambed.** (318)

enjambed   Said of a line of poetry that does not come to a marked pause at its end, but forces the reader (because of grammar and syntax) to read on into the next line—for example, "Its loveliness increases; it will never / Pass into nothingness. . . ." Enjambments can be graceful (as is the example here) or awkward, depending on the kind of grammatical and syntactical unit broken by the line division. Contrast **end-stopped.** (318)

enumeration   A way of organizing material that falls into distinct parts, stages, or whatever. If, for instance, there are three reasons for believing something, then one can proceed by enumeration—first, second, and third. (15–16, 880)

epigram/epigrammatic   A short concise statement that makes a single point. **Heroic couplets** are often epigrammatic. Epigrams are most often witty. (389)

etymology   The origins and historical development of a word. Etymology also refers to the study of word origins and development in general.

exemplification   A prime means of **support** that entails the illustration of theoretical statements, abstractions, and so forth with concrete instances. (870–71, 877–78)

explicit metaphor   A kind of metaphor in which the **tenor** (subject) and **vehicle** (defining word) are both expressed—for instance, "*deserts* [vehicle] of vast *eternity* [tenor]." Compare **metaphor.** (284–85, 286–87)

exposition/expository   Any portion of a work given over to explanation—whether story, play, or poem—is called its exposition. **Expository prose** (as distinguished from prose fiction) is called "expository" because its main task is to explain.

expository prose   Writing designed to explain something in a clear, concise manner. With regard to literature, the essay is the chief form of expository prose. Essays, which may support a **theme** or argue a **thesis,** are aimed at communicating thoughts with clarity and, ideally, with pleasure. (9–10, 862–63)

extended metaphor   See **metaphorical extension.**

fable   A tale designed to illustrate some "moral" regarding human behavior. (44–45)

falling meter Any meter with **trochees** or **dactyls** as dominant beats, for these beats begin with a stressed syllable and then, as to the movement of the voice, fall off—for example, "Fálling, fálling, downward tŏ dárknĕss." Contrast **rising meter.** (323)

fiction A literary **genre** including such prose works as stories and novels—works that, though they may be based on fact, take their shape in the imagination. (30–32)

figurative language Any use of words not meant to be taken literally. Any expression involving **metaphor,** for instance, or **hyperbole** or **personification** is figurative: "Harold the ox" (if said of a human being rather than an ox), "I won by a mile" (when literally the win was by a few feet), "the long arm of the law." Often, whether something is literal or figurative depends on the **context.** Contrast **literal language.** (281–82, 871–73)

figure of speech Any expression that is **figurative** as opposed to **literal.** Common figures of speech are: **hyperbole, understatement, synesthesia, metonymy, synecdoche, personification,** and **metaphor.**

first-person narration **Narration** in which the teller of the story is a character who refers to himself or herself as "I." First-person narrators can be either credible or unreliable. Narrative essays can also be in the first person. (122–24, 865–66)

fixed forms A stanza or poem written in accordance with some traditional rhyme scheme and/or metrical pattern—for example, see **Spenserian stanza** and **sonnet.**

flashback A passage or episode that breaks the chronology of a work by taking us back to some moment in time earlier than the passage or episode we have been following. (68)

flat character Any character governed by a few traits alone, which remain constant over the course of a work. (100)

foot The basic rhythmic unit of which a metrical line is composed. See **beat.**

foreshadowing Said of anything in a text that prepares the reader for something later in that text.

free verse Any poem deliberately divided into lines (unlike prose) but that does not conform to a regular metrical pattern. Most poems in free verse have irregular line lengths and do not rhyme. (319–20)

genre The category into which a literary work falls by virtue of its style, form, and purpose. Drama, for example, is a distinct genre, as are poetry and prose fiction.

haiku A Japanese poetic form composed of three lines of five, seven, and five syllables exactly. Haikus usually convey the impression of a natural object or scene. (325, footnote)

heroic couplet A **closed couplet** in **iambic pentameter.** Heroic couplets are found in longer poems composed all of such units. (391)

hexameter A meter that consists of six **beats** per line (*hex-* means "six"). (323)

hyperbole A **figure of speech** entailing exaggeration—for example, "I won by a mile" or "by a nose" when in fact the win was by a few feet in both cases. Contrast **understatement.** (282)

iamb/iambic A **beat** or **foot** consisting of an unstressed syllable followed by a stressed syllable—for example, "Ĕnóugh, Ĭ've hád ĕnóugh tŏdáy." (323)

iambic pentameter A line composed of five **iambs** (˘ ´) or ten syllables alternating between unstressed and stressed—for example, "Thĕ wórld ĭs tóo múch wĭth ŭs, láte ănd sóon." This is the meter of **blank verse** specifically and the fundamental meter of English verse generally.

image/imagery Images are verbal **concretions** (words that call sensations to mind) used to convey feelings and states of mind through sense impression. Often, imagery is used to form metaphors and symbols, thus reinforcing or determining the meaning of a work. (267, 872)

implicit metaphor   A kind of metaphor in which the **tenor** or **vehicle** or both are not overtly expressed but somehow immediately implied—for instance, "biting words," which implies that the "words" (tenor) are teeth (implicit vehicle). Compare **metaphor.** (289–90)

inflection   The degree of **stress** thrown on a syllable or monosyllabic word.

informational prose   Prose the purpose of which is to convey information. For example, the consequences of anti-Semitism in Nazi Germany could be the subject of an informational essay. (9)

In-Memoriam stanza   A **quatrain** rhyming *abba* and used as a **stanzaic** unit. It is also called the "envelope" stanza. (387)

interior monologue   Any passage or work focused solely on a character's thoughts and feelings as revealed by that character in silent introspection.

internal rhyme   Any rhyme that occurs within (as opposed to at the end) of a line of poetry.

inversion (syntactical)   Refers to deviations from normal word order. For instance, "My money, I earn" is an inversion of "I earn my money." See **syntax.**

inverted foot   A metrically deviant **beat,** the mirror image of the dominant beat. In an **iambic** context, for instance, a **trochee** would be an inverted foot.

irony   Refers to a discrepancy or incongruity between what is said and what is meant **(verbal irony),** between what seems to be and what actually is **(circumstantial irony),** or between what a person or character believes and what we know to be true **(dramatic irony).** The virtue of irony as a literary device lies in its ability to direct attitude without discursive comment. (151–53)

juxtaposition   The placing of two or more images, scenes, or whatever next to each other so as to produce a specific effect or meaning thereby. Metaphors are often created by juxtaposition. (291)

lexical stress   The **stress** normally placed on one syllable as opposed to another in polysyllabic words as indicated by the dictionary (thus, "lexical"). (317)

limerick   A fixed form that rhymes *aabba* and is usually **anapestic** in **meter.** The first, second, and fifth lines are usually anapestic **trimeters** (or some variant), and the third and fourth lines are usually anapestic dimeters (that is, consisting of two anapestic beats each). Limericks are almost always comic. (374–75)

listener   The person designated in a poem (if someone is designated) as the one to whom its speaker is speaking. (234)

literal language   Any use of words meant to be taken strictly at face value, or language so taken—for instance, "It's time to get to work" as opposed to "It's time to get hopping." Contrast **figurative language.**

lyric/lyrical   The term "lyric" originally meant a poem sung to the accompaniment of the lyre. Now, however, it refers to any short poem that gives voice to the mental and emotional state of a speaker. Closer to its etymological root, lyrical refers to any aspect of a poem that is songlike.

medial sounds   The consonant or vowel sounds at the end of one word and the beginning of the next. These sounds determine whether words ellide or whether they must be said discretely and thus help to mold the rhythm of a line as to relative speed or slowness. (354)

metaphor   Any **figurative** expression entailing an analogy—whether explicit or implicit—between essentially unlike things (it is the essential unlikeness of its terms that makes the expression figurative in the first place). The object of metaphor is definition: definition of one term of the verbal construction (the **tenor**) by way of the other (the **vehicle**)—

for example, "He [tenor] is an ox [vehicle]." See **analogy, explicit metaphor, implicit metaphor,** and **simile.** (284–95, 301–03, 872–73)

metaphorical extension The sustaining of some prime metaphor over a passage or even over the length of an entire work. Metaphors are extended by a writer's staying to the same **vehicle** throughout a given passage or at least drawing all vehicles in the passage from the same general area. For instance, "You *light* up my life: you are a *candle* in my darkness, the *rays* of my hope, the *sun* of all my days." (292–93, 872–73)

metaphysical conceit See **conceit.**

meter The regular recurrence of some rhythmic configuration or pulse, called a **beat** or **foot.** The meter characteristic of English verse is called "accentual-syllabic," for our sense of recurrence springs from our perception of a set number of syllables per line and a set pattern of accentuation (that is, a set pattern of stressed and unstressed syllables). Such patterns are analyzed by the kind of beat that recurs and the number of beats per line. The basic beats of English verse are: the **iamb,** the **trochee,** the **anapest,** and the **dactyl;** the usual number of recurrences is: **trimeter** (three), **tetrameter** (four), **pentameter** (five), or **hexameter** (six). Thus, a metrical composition (a piece of writing that exhibits rhythmic recurrence) containing five iambs per line (or ten syllables alternating between **slack** and **stress**) would be analyzed as iambic pentameter; a piece containing three trochees per line (or six syllables alternating between stress and slack) would be trochaic trimeter. (322–24)

metonymy A **figure of speech** in which something is called by the name of something else with which it is closely associated—for example, "jock" for a male athlete. Compare **synecdoche.** (283)

metrical deviation Any beat in a metered poem that does not conform to the metrical norm. (328)

metrical stress The **stress** established in a poem in **meter** by the metrical norm. (328)

mixed metaphor Metaphors that in combination or extension do not work together—for example, "It's time to take a stand in the public eye." (302)

monosyllable/monosyllabic A word of one syllable only—for example, *a, word, of, one.* Contrast **polysyllable.**

mood Describable by such adjectives as "lighthearted," "nostalgic," "humorous," "sad," or "tragic," mood is the feeling(s) that a work of literature has been designed to arouse in the reader. (150–51, 537)

motivation An aspect of characterization involving a character's reasons for thinking or doing what is thought or done.

narrator/narration/narrative Narrator refers to the teller of a tale, be it fictional or factual. Narration points to how tales are told: in the **first person,** for instance, with the tellers speaking of themselves as well as others; or in the **third person,** with the tellers speaking only of others. Narrative refers to the tale itself, or to the fact that a given piece is a tale: for instance, to say that an essay is a narrative is to say that it tells a story. The most important point to understand about narrators is that they do not necessarily speak for authors, whether of stories or of essays; the **authorial attitude** is expressed through a work as a whole, not through just one or another of its elements. (121–25, 237, 537, 865–66)

nonrealistic drama Drama, usually symbolic, that calls attention to itself as theater, or to its own theatricality, and that makes no pretense at imitating the ordinary, everyday world. (533–35)

octave The first eight lines of a **Petrarchan sonnet,** which rhyme *abbaabba* and form an integral thematic unit.

off-rhyme   Words that are close in sound but that do not in fact **rhyme**—for example, "down/noon." (359)

onomatopoeia/onomatopoetic   Specifically, words whose sounds are like the sounds of what they name (*buzz, splash, moo*); generally, any language that sounds like what it names.

open couplet   Two rhymed lines that do not form a self-contained grammatical unit. For example, "Now therefore, while the youthful hue / Sits on thy skin like morning dew, // And while thy willing soul transpires / At every pore with instant fires, // Now. . . ." (390)

order of climax   The movement of a sentence, paragraph, or paper from less important details or support to more important. Order of climax is so important psychologically that whatever other type of order a paragraph or paper may follow, order of climax should be respected and violated only for special purpose. (16, 880–81)

ottava rima   An eight-line **stanza** that rhymes *abababcc*. (386)

overstatement   See **hyperbole.**

oxymoron   A **figure of speech** consisting of terms that in ordinary usage are contraries—for example, "a heavy lightness," "a frugal plenty," "the living dead." Compare **paradox.** (282)

pace   The rapidity or slowness of an utterance.

paradox   Any statement that seems to be self-contradictory but that, upon analysis, turns out to have validity—for example, "And death once dead, there's no more dying then."

parallelism   The grouping of like thoughts into identical syntactical patterns: "of the people, by the people, and for the people." Parallelism is a matter of both grammar and **syntax.** As regards syntax, parallelism is also an aspect of **style.** (876)

paraphrase   A restatement of the gist of a passage or work—poem, story, essay, or whatever—in one's own words, or the act of so restating. (973)

pause   The points in an utterance at which the voice rests. Poetic analysis entails a distinction between two types of pause: caesural pause, or any pause within a line (see **caesura**); end-line pause, or a pause at the end of a line resulting from the line's being **end-stopped.**

pentameter   A **meter** that consists of five beats per line (*pent-* means "five"). (323)

persona   Meaning "mask" etymologically, the word persona is sometimes used to refer to a literary speaker, emphasizing the distinction between speaker and author. (237–38)

personification   A **figure of speech** in which some human quality is attributed to an abstraction, an inanimate object, an animal, or whatever—for example, "Let justice *decide*"; "the *fury* of the gale"; "the *hopeful* robin's song." (284)

persuasive prose   Prose designed chiefly to persuade the reader of the rightness of the writer's judgment. (10)

Petrarchan sonnet   A type of **sonnet** that rhymes *abbaabba/cdecde* (or some variant thereof in the last six lines). Clearly, the Petrarchan sonnet divides itself into an **octave** (the first *eight* lines) and a **sestet** (the closing six lines); further, it divides itself into two **quatrains** (four-line units) and two **tercets** (three-line units). Usually, there is some sort of a dramatic shift (called a "volta") between octave and sestet. (375–76, 377–78)

pitch   The property of a tone determined by the frequency of its sound waves. Some tones—of vowels and of voice—are high-pitched, some are low-pitched, and some are in between—for example, *e* as in "beet" versus *oo* as in "boot." In poetry and sometimes in prose, concentrations of vowel sounds as to pitch have specific effects and are an aspect of the meaning. (350–51)

player Anyone in a poem other than its **speaker** and **listener** (if it has one). Players are people whom speakers interact with or react to, thereby revealing much about themselves. (234)

plot The sequence of events that constitutes the story line of a **narrative** work. Plot always entails causality. (68–69, 535–36)

point of view The perspective devised by an author through which characters, actions, settings, and so forth are presented to the reader. The basic **narrative** points of view are **first person** and **third person.** (121–25)

polysyllabic rhyme **Rhymes** of two or more syllables in succession—for example, "bending/ending," "anticipate/dissipate."

polysyllable/polysyllabic A word of two or more syllables—for example, *syl·la·ble*. Contrast **monosyllable.**

production element Any aspect of a play that comes to life and imparts meaning mainly in actual performance. Music, for instance, would be a production element, as would a **stage symbol.** (539)

proofreading Reading over a piece of writing in order to correct errors in spelling, agreement, punctuation, and so forth. The final proofreading is for typographical errors. (28)

protagonist The central character in a literary work.

pyrrhic foot A deviant (nonrecurring) metrical **foot** consisting of two unstressed metrical syllables—for example, the first beat of "Ĭn thĕ/bĕgín/nĭng Gód" is pyrrhic. (323)

quatrain Any four-line **stanzaic** unit: for example, the ballad stanza (*abcb*) and the **In-Memoriam stanza** (*abba*). The four line units that compose the **octave** of the **Petrarchan sonnet** and the first twelve lines of the **Shakespearean sonnet** are also called quatrains.

realistic drama Drama that fosters the illusion of everyday reality and that sets out to explore matters of everyday concern. (532–33)

reference *Overt* mention of someone or something in our cultural past or present to evoke a certain meaning or set of associations in the mind of the reader. For instance, to say "He is the Babe Ruth of songwriters" would suggest a writer with so many big "hits" as to be legendary. Compare **allusion.**

rhetorical stress The **stress** thrown by the voice for the purpose of special emphasis. (317, 329–31)

rhyme Words that end in the same vowel and consonant sounds but that are otherwise different: "rhyme/chime," "vowel/towel," "otherwise/not my size." Rhymes define traditional **stanzas** and **fixed forms,** and are used by poets for purposes ranging from lyrical to comic. (356)

rhyme scheme The pattern of end-rhymes that characterizes traditional **stanzas** and **fixed forms.** Rhyme schemes are signified with letters: like letters indicate what lines, by virtue of the words with which they end, rhyme with what other lines. For example, *abab* indicates that the first and third lines rhyme and the second and fourth; *abab/cdcd/efef* indicates a likeness in the pattern of rhyme of each **quatrain** but a difference in the particular rhyme sounds of each (if they remained the same, the notation would be: *abab/abab/abab*). Capital letters are used to signify the repetition of an entire line. (374)

rhythm The way words move (*rhythm* comes from a Greek word meaning "to flow") as determined by **accentuation, inflection, pace,** and **pause.** In that these variables affect how an utterance is interpreted, rhythm is a prime determinant of meaning. (154, 316, 873–75)

rising meter Any meter with **iambs** or **anapests** as dominant beats, for these beats begin with unstressed syllables and then, as to the movement of the voice, rise to stressed syllables—for example, "Ărĭse ănd shĭne, fŏr tŏdáy ĭs thĭne." Contrast **falling meter.** (323)

round character   Any character treated in some depth and developed so as to impart a sense of the actual complexity of human beings. (100)

sarcasm   A type of **verbal irony** used to show scorn.

satire   Writing, usually comic, that holds a subject up to ridicule.

scansion   The name of metrical notation and analysis. We scan a metrical composition by dividing its lines into syllables and then indicating which syllables receive **stress** and which do not (that is, which are **slack**). The purpose of scansion is to determine what kind of beat recurs in a given poem, how many beats there are per line, and, thus, what the basic meter is. For example: "Whăt óft/wăs thóught/bŭt né'er/sŏ wéll/ĕxpréssed" (iambic pentameter). By scanning a poem thus, one can then see where deviant beats occur and where special emphasis **(rhetorical stress)** is thrown. Scanned well, the **meter** of a poem is a guide to rhythm and thence meaning. (331–32)

sestet   The last six lines of the **Petrarchan sonnet,** which rhyme *cdecde* (or some variant thereof).

setting   The location of a literary work as to time and place. Setting often allows a reader to infer a good deal about characters and speakers, and often a setting or a detail of a setting is used symbolically. (179–80, 261, 537–38, 869–70)

Shakespearean sonnet   A type of **sonnet** that rhymes *abab/cdcd/efef/gg.* By virtue of its rhyme scheme, the Shakespearean sonnet divides itself into three **quatrains** (four-line units) and a concluding **couplet.** This is the norm, though some Shakespearean sonnets are divided (like the **Petrarchan sonnet**) into an **octave** (eight-line unit) and a **sestet** (six-line unit). (375–77)

simile   A type of **explicit metaphor** in which the comparison is made logical by the use of *as* or *like* or sometimes the suffix -*y.* For instance: "My love is *like* a red, red rose." (284–86)

situation   Literary works with little in the way of action or events are said to present a situation rather than a **plot.** Such works (especially stories and **lyric** poems) concern the inner lives of their characters or speaker rather than their lives in the external world of action. (69, 265–66, 535–36)

situation comedy   Strictly speaking, a play whose **comedy** arises out of the right people being thrown together in the right situation, one that brings out all their quirkiness. The focus of such a play is entirely on character. More generally, any comedy that takes off from a given situation (for instance, the living arrangement of one male and two female roommates) and involves us in a comic way in their lives. (531)

slack   A syllable that is not stressed in pronunciation. For example, the first, third, and last syllables of *prŏ·nún·cĭ·a·tĭon* are slack. Contrast **stress.**

sonnet   Normally a fourteen-line poem in **iambic pentameter** that conforms to one or another traditional rhyme scheme. The dominant types in English are: **Shakespearean** and **Petrarchan.** (375–76)

spatial sequence   The organization of a paragraph or an essay according to the spatial relationship of the parts of the subject being considered. For instance, one might describe the motor of a car from top to bottom. If a subject lends itself to spatial treatment, what one must do is to let the reader know how one is going to proceed and then follow through. (14, 879–80)

speaker   Every story, poem, and essay has a speaker. But we usually refer to the speaker of a narrative essay or story as the **narrator;** of the self-reflective essay or poem as "the writer" or "the poet" (or by the author's name directly); and of a story, poem, or essay clearly spoken by a character by the name of that character or of some attribute if no name is given ("the doctor," "the Duke"). Though any of these (story, narrative essay, poem) could be and sometimes has to be assigned to a "speaker," the word is most often used as a synonym of **persona,** suggesting thus a difference between the speaker and the author. (237–38, 866–67)

Spenserian stanza   A nine-line **stanza** that rhymes *ababbcbcc,* with the first eight lines in **iambic pentameter** and the last in iambic **hexameter** (such a line being called an **alexandrine**). (384–85)

spondee/spondaic   A deviant (nonrecurring) metrical **foot** consisting of two stressed sylla- bles—for example, the second beat of Tennyson's line "Thĕ lóng/ líght shákes/ ăcróss/ thĕ lákes" is a spondee. (323)

stage symbol   Any prop or visual or aural occurrence in a play that has symbolic meaning. It is called a stage symbol because it comes into being primarily when the play is acted. (539)

stanza/stanzaic   A grouping of lines demarked by spacing always and, with respect to tradi- tional forms, by a recurrent rhyme scheme and a repeating pattern of lines as per number and length. Many unrhymed and free-verse poems are divided into stanzas demarked by the number of lines and by space between groups of lines. Poems divided into stanzas are called stanzaic.

stock character   Any character that exhibits but one dominant trait or that is based on a stereotype. For instance, whether in white or black hats, cowboys in older westerns are uniformly stock. (100–01)

stream of consciousness   A narrative technique that renders the thoughts of a character, with all the jumps and inconsistencies that mark actual thought, as the character thinks them.

stress   The emphasis placed on one syllable as opposed to another in pronunciation. For instance, the word "pronunciation" has the following pattern of stress: *prŏ· nún·cĭ·á·tiŏn.* The first, third, and last syllables are **slack** (unstressed); the second and fourth are stressed, the fourth being more heavily stressed (a matter of **inflection**) than the second. (317)

strong ending   Said of a line of poetry that ends with a stressed syllable. For example, each of the following lines has a strong ending: "Hăd wé bŭt wórld ĕnoúgh ănd *tíme,* / Thĭs cóyness, lády, wére nŏ *críme.*" Contrast **weak ending.**

style   The sum of the choices a writer makes as to the selection of words **(diction)** and type of sentence structure **(syntax).** Style tends to be characteristic of a writer, though every writer adjusts style to fit characters and circumstance. (153–54, 537, 875–77)

subordination   The combining of ideas so that one is made grammatically dependent on the other by being cast into a phrase or a subordinate clause. The purpose of subordination is to gain **coherence** as well as to reinforce a sense of **unity** by making prime information stand out. (25–27)

summary   A brief condensation of someone else's ideas. (973)

support   The material used to demonstrate the validity of a **thesis.** One can subdivide support material into *major* and *minor,* minor support serving to back up major sup- port, which in turn backs up the governing thesis of paragraph or essay. The prime *means of support* are: **analogy, authority, definition,** and **exemplification.** (11–13, 877–79)

surreal/surrealistic   Adjectives used in connection with any work that is dreamlike and that seems to tap the workings of the unconscious.

symbol/symbolism   Anything in a text that, because of the literary and/or cultural **context,** conveys meaning different from (though usually related to) its literal meaning. Two broad types of symbol are **conventional** and **created.** Most texts contain *reinforcing* symbols (symbols that reflect and enhance the meaning established by plot, characterization, and so forth); in some texts, meaning is conveyed primarily by symbols, in which case the symbolism is *controlling.* (181–84, 295–96, 537–39, 871–72)

synecdoche   A **figure of speech** in which a part or an attribute of something gives its name to the whole—for example, "hands" for sailors and laborers, "bow-wow" for a dog, "wheels" for a car. Compare **metonymy.** (283)

synesthesia   A **figure of speech** that involves speaking of one sensation in terms of another, or of speaking of something in terms of a sensory mode not actually appropriate to it— for example, "a *cool* green," "a *loud* tie," "a *dry* martini." (282)

syntax   The relationship of the position of words in sentences to meaning, as well as the way in which words are put together to form various sentence patterns. In English, meaning is primarily determined by syntax: for instance, "Dog bites man" versus "Man bites dog." As to sentence patterns, the two main types are *loose* (with the main information coming at the head) and *periodic* (with the main information coming last in the sentence). Along with **diction,** syntax is a prime constituent of **style.** (153–54, 349–50, 875–77)

tenor   The subject of a **metaphor,** or the term being defined by way of the transference (from **vehicle** to tenor) that metaphor entails. In the metaphor "Deserts of vast eternity," for instance, "eternity" is the tenor, which the image of "deserts" serves to define. (285)

tercet   Any three-line poetic unit, such as the **terza rima** stanza or the tercets that compose the **sestet** of the **Petrarchan sonnet.**

terza rima   A **stanzaic** form composed of **tercets** (three-line units) marked by interlinking rhymes: *aba/bcb/cdc/ded* and so on. (383)

tetrameter   A meter that consists of four beats per line (*tetr-* means "four"). (323)

theme   The controlling attitude, insight, or point *implied* in a story, poem, play, or thematic essay. Theme should not be confused with a "moral" or a "message" or even a simple idea. Rather, a theme is what any of the aforementioned is about in its fullness. Note, shorter works usually present a single theme; longer works, however, often develop more than one theme, though most often all themes in a longer work are subsumed under a *master theme.* (43–45, 540, 863–64)

thesis   The main point of a piece of **expository prose,** that point usually being stated *overtly* (with the exception of the thematic essay, which develops a **theme** that is implied): that which is demonstrated, exemplified, and argued in the body of the piece. A thesis, it should be noted, is not the same as a topic. A topic is what a thesis makes a statement about. "Cats" is a topic; "Cats are man's best friend" is a thesis—conceivably, something that someone could argue against. Compare **theme.** (7–8, 863–64)

third-person narration   **Narration** in which the teller speaks of others exclusively and therefore stands entirely outside of the narration. With regard to fiction, third-person narrators can be omniscient, subjective, or objective. Narrative essays can also be in the third person. (124–25, 865)

tone   The way something is said as that way reveals the feelings or attitude of a narrator or speaker, other characters, or—taking the work as a whole—the author. Tone is often communicated in literature by **diction.** Compare **authorial attitude.** (153, 239, 538, 866–68)

topic   See **thesis.**

tragedy   A **genre** that, according to Aristotle, begins in prosperity and ends in adversity for the tragic hero, always of noble origins. This *sense* of tragedy was altered in the Renaissance by the addition of the death of the tragic **protagonist.** In more recent times, though the Renaissance sense that the tragic protagonist must die has been adhered to, the tragic protagonist has been allowed to be of "low" origins and position (for example, Willy Loman [low-man] in Arthur Miller's benchmark play *Death of a Salesman*). (529–30)

transition   Anything in a piece of writing that facilitates the movement from one segment to another. (26–27)

trimeter   A meter that consists of three beats per line (*tri-* means "three"). (323)

trochee/trochaic   A **beat** or **foot** consisting of a stressed syllable followed by an unstressed syllable—for example, "Móthĕr, fáthĕr, lístĕn pléase tŏ whát Ĭ háve tŏ téll yŏu." (323)

understatement   A **figure of speech** in which emphasis is gained by a deliberate underplaying of the magnitude or effect of what is being described. For instance, "Last week I saw a woman flayed, and you will hardly believe how much it altered her person for the worse" (Swift). Contrast **hyperbole.** (282)

unity   The sense that everything in a piece of writing works to one end, or relates to one central idea. A lack of unity results from the presence of extraneous material or material that seems unrelated to the central idea because the writer has failed to make the relationship clear. (25–27)

vehicle   The figurative word of a **metaphor,** or the term used to define a **tenor** by way of the transference (from vehicle to tenor) that metaphor always entails. In the metaphor "Deserts of vast eternity," for example, "deserts" is the vehicle defining the abstraction "eternity" (the tenor). (285)

verbal irony   Refers to any statement in which there is a discrepancy felt between what is said and what is meant. For example, on a rotten day someone might say, "Oh, what a beautiful day it is today." We would judge the speaker either mad or ironic, depending on the circumstance. **Sarcasm** is a form of verbal irony. (151–52)

verisimilitude   Meaning "trueness to life," verisimilitude is a criterion of judgment of any text that is meant to be judged directly against life. Many texts, of course, are not realistic and so not to be judged on this ground.

verse   Any composition that is deliberately divided into lines. The word "verse" comes from the Latin meaning "to turn" (that is, at the end of the *line*). This suggests a defining difference between poetry and prose: in prose, line breaks are arbitrary; in poetry, they are deliberate and meaningful. However different, both **free verse** and verse in **meter** share this deliberate division into lines.

verse paragraph   The unit of division of nonstanzaic poems. For instance, the formal divisions of poems both in **blank verse** and **heroic couplets** are called verse paragraphs.

villanelle   A fixed form consisting of five **tercets** (three-line units) and a **quatrain** (four-line unit) on two rhymes. The first line is repeated as the sixth, twelfth, and eighteenth lines, and the third line is repeated as the ninth, fifteenth, and nineteenth lines thus: AbA′/abA/abA′/abA/abA′/abAA′. (382)

voice   The quality or flavor of spoken utterance in writing, especially poems and essays. (239, 538, 866–68)

volume   The degree of loudness or softness of, in particular, a poetic utterance.

vowel gradation   The step-by-step shifting of vowels from high-pitched to low or low to high. In the following line, for instance, there is a clear gradated movement from high-pitched to low-pitched vowel sounds: *"I hate to see that evenin' sun go down."* (352)

vowel length   The length of time it takes to say a vowel, short vowels taking less time to say than long vowels—for example, compare the *e* in "bet" with the *ee* in "beet." (Also called vowel *quantity*.)

weak ending   Said of a line of poetry that ends with an unstressed syllable. For example, each of the first two lines that follow has a weak ending: "A thing of beauty is a joy forever: / Its loveliness increases; it will never / Pass into nothingness . . ." (Keats). Contrast **strong ending**.

ALTERNATE GROUPINGS
BY ELEMENT, THEME, AND MODE

Death

Emptiness

Experiments in Technique

Fable

The Family

Fantasy/The Surreal

THE ESSAY (SECTION V)

Enumeration

Exemplification

Note: Exemplification is to be found in all of the essays in the text. The essays that follow were selected simply because examples are a prominent means in each.

Metaphor (Discrete and Extended)

Narration/Narrator

Order of Climax/Climax and Anticlimax

Paragraphing

WORKS CITED

I Reading and Writing

    Mill, John Stuart. "The Subjugation of Women." *Essays on Sexual Equality.* Ed. A. S. Rossi. Chicago: Chicago U., 1970. 143–68.

II Fiction

Chapter 3

    Forster, E. M. *Aspects of the Novel.* New York: Harcourt, 1954.

Chapter 5

    Maugham, Somerset. "Preface" to *Collected Stories.* Vol. 2. London: Penguin, 1963. 2 vols.

III Poetry

Chapter 1

    Smith, Barbara Herrnstein. *On the Margins of Discourse.* Chicago: Chicago U., 1978.
    Stevens, Wallace. "Stevens's 'The Emperor of Ice-Cream.' " *Explicator.* 7.2 (1948): Item 18.

Chapter 7

    Hopkins, G. M. *The Correspondence of G. M. Hopkins and R. W. Dixon.* 2nd ed. Ed. C. C. Abbott. London: Oxford, 1955.

IV Drama

    Aristotle. *The Poetics.* Trans. S. H. Butcher. 4th ed. New York: Dover, 1951.

COPYRIGHTS AND ACKNOWLEDGMENTS

IV Drama

V The Essay

INDEX OF AUTHORS, TITLES, AND FIRST LINES OF POEMS